# Child
# Development

Canadian Edition

John W. Santrock
University of Texas at Dallas

Nicole J. Conrad
Saint Mary's University

Leanna M. Closson
Saint Mary's University

## Child Development
## Canadian Edition

The Internet addresses listed in the text were accurate at the time of publication. The inclusion of a website does not indicate an endorsement by the authors or McGraw-Hill Ryerson, and McGraw-Hill Ryerson does not guarantee the accuracy of information presented at these sites.

ISBN-13: 978-1-25-902474-0
ISBN-10: 1-25-902474-1

7 8 9 10 11   WEB   20 19 18

Printed and bound in Canada

Care has been taken to trace ownership of copyright material contained in this text; however, the publisher will welcome any information that enables it to rectify any reference or credit for subsequent editions.

Director of Product Management: *Rhondda McNabb*
Product Managers: *Marcia Siekowski, Jason Chih*
Senior Marketing Manager: *Margaret Greenfield*
Product Developers: *Catherine Gillespie-Lopes, Jennifer Cressman*
Senior Product Team Associate: *Marina Seguin*
Supervising Editor: *Cathy Biribauer*
Photo/Permissions Researcher: *Derek Capitaine, www.mrmassociates.ca*
Copy Editor: *Judy Sturrup*
Plant Production Coordinator: *Scott Morrison*
Manufacturing Production Coordinator: *Emily Hickey*
Cover and Inside Design: *Peter Papayanakis*
Composition: *Laserwords Private Limited*
Cover Photo: *Rolfo/Getty Images*
Printer: *Webcom*

### Library and Archives Canada Cataloguing in Publication Data

Santrock, John W., author
      Child development / John W. Santrock, Nicole Conrad, Leanna Closson. — Canadian edition.
Includes bibliographical references and index.
ISBN 978-1-25-902474-0 (bound)
      1. Child development—Textbooks. I. Conrad, Nicole, 1972-, author II.
Closson, Leanna, author III. Title.

RJ131.S25 2015          618.92          C2014-905174-3

With special appreciation to my wife, Mary Jo; my children, Tracy and Jennifer; and my grandchildren, Jordan, Alex, and Luke, J. W. S.

To Michael, for your love and support, and Robert, for making the words come alive, N.C.

To my nephew and niece—James and Claire, L.C.

# about the authors

John Santrock (centre) teaching an undergraduate psychology course.

## John W. Santrock

John Santrock received his Ph.D. from the University of Minnesota in 1973. He taught at the University of Charleston and the University of Georgia before joining the program in Psychology and Human Development at the University of Texas at Dallas, where he currently teaches a number of undergraduate courses.

John has been a member of the editorial boards of *Child Development* and *Developmental Psychology*. His research on father custody is widely cited and used in expert witness testimony to promote flexibility and alternative considerations in custody disputes. John also has authored these exceptional McGraw-Hill texts: *Psychology* (7th edition), *Children* (11th edition), *Adolescence* (13th edition), *Lifespan Development* (13th edition), and *Educational Psychology* (5th edition).

For many years John was involved in tennis as a player, a teaching professional, and a coach of professional tennis players. He has been married for more than 35 years to his wife, Mary Jo, who is a Realtor. He has two daughters—Tracy, who also is a Realtor, and Jennifer, who is a medical sales specialist. He has one granddaughter, Jordan, age 19, and two grandsons, Alex, age 6, and Luke, age 4. In the last decade, John also has spent time painting expressionist art.

## Nicole J. Conrad

Nicole J. Conrad received her B.A. (Honours) from Saint Mary's University and her Ph.D. in psychology from McMaster University. For her doctoral research, she examined how children acquire, store, and retrieve the various types of cognitive and linguistic knowledge needed to develop fluent reading. During a post-doctoral position at McMaster University, Dr. Conrad studied reading development of children in French Immersion programs. She is currently an Associate Professor at Saint Mary's University.

Dr. Conrad has been continuously teaching Developmental Psychology since graduate school and believes that "perfecting" course material and learning strategies is an ongoing process. She is passionate about teaching and developing new methods to enhance student learning. She has received research funding from Saint Mary's University to study the effect of Web-based supplemental resources on student learning and has published on incorporating writing into large classrooms.

Dr. Conrad currently lives in Halifax with her brand new baby son and fiancé. She is an avid squash player, kayaker, and regularly practices Pilates.

## Leanna M. Closson

Leanna M. Closson received her B.A. (Honours) in Psychology from the University of Saskatchewan, her M.A. in Psychology from Carleton University, and her Ph.D. in Human Development, Learning, and Culture from the University of British Columbia. As a post-doctoral researcher at Carleton University, she studied the effects of parents' maladaptive behaviours on children's socioemotional development. Dr. Closson's current research explores the role of peer relationships in the development of social competence, with a particular focus on social status, aggression, and prosocial behaviour.

Dr. Closson's university teaching career began at the University of British Columbia where she participated in a community of practice, co-teaching courses in child development for pre-service teachers. She subsequently taught introductory psychology at the University of British Columbia Okanagan. Dr. Closson is presently an Assistant Professor at Saint Mary's University where she teaches courses in developmental psychology.

Dr. Closson currently resides in Halifax. Since childhood, she has had a love for travel. Having lived coast-to-coast across Canada, she now enjoys exploring Canada's Atlantic Provinces.

brief contents

# contents

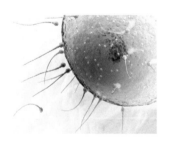

## SECTION 3   COGNITION AND LANGUAGE   159

# SECTION 4    SOCIOEMOTIONAL DEVELOPMENT    278

# SECTION 5 SOCIAL CONTEXTS OF DEVELOPMENT 390

## Canadian Edition

Faced with the challenge of creating a Canadian textbook from the well-established and highly respected 14th edition of an American textbook was very daunting! But having the opportunity to develop a textbook that actually includes the many (Canadian) topics, (Canadian) issues, and (Canadian) research studies we regularly incorporate into our classrooms was too wonderful to pass up. As we both continually strive to create engaging and interactive classrooms, we saw this as an opportunity to respond to informal feedback provided over the years by hundreds of students. It was important to us to create a textbook incorporating Canadian content—Canadian statistics and laws, educational practices, social policies, and cultural references—to engage and inspire today's students. Equally important was to include coverage of topics that reflect the cultural diversity that exists in Canada, as well as topics that are uniquely relevant to Canadian students.

Our second goal with this textbook was to highlight the richness of the landscape within Canada in Developmental Psychology. Much pioneering research has occurred in Canada, from Janet Werker's speech perception studies to the research into parenting effects on children's socialization from the lab of Joan Grusec. We have attempted to balance these and other classic studies with contemporary Canadian research. As is evidenced by the over 400 new Canadian citations included in this textbook, the tradition of research excellence is alive and well in Canada.

With this new Canadian edition, we have attempted to maintain the accessible writing, depth of coverage, and excellent scholarship established by John Santrock. We have retained the *Connections* theme from the original textbook, as well as many of the pedagogical features, all of which are outlined below. However, we have also made some changes to provide a perspective that is unique and engaging for Canadian students. These changes are also summarized below.

## Changes to the Canadian Edition

As indicated above, we have made some changes to the Canadian edition to provide a perspective that is unique and engaging for Canadian students. Throughout each chapter, we have:

- Added numerous new studies to highlight Canadian research
- Added new *Connecting to Current Controversy* boxes to increase focus on topics that are contemporary and relevant within a Canadian context
- Added application questions in the new *Case Study Connections* feature
- Added a new critical thinking question to each *Connecting Through Research* box
- Incorporated Canadian statistics
- Included Canadian examples to illustrate applications of developmental theory

In addition to these changes, we have made the following chapter-by-chapter changes.

### Chapter 1: Introduction

- New opening vignette contrasts the development of two well-known Canadians, Karla Homolka and Lincoln Alexander
- Included description of Canadian children's rights advocate, Cindy Blackstock
- New section on age and cohort effects
- New *Connecting to Current Controversy* box on nature-nurture, continuity-discontinuity, and early-later experience

- Highlighted Albert Bandura's Canadian roots
- Expanded discussion of physiological methods of data collection
- New section on sequential research designs to complement new section on cohort effects
- Updated and Canadianized the ethics section to include the Canadian *Tri-Council Policy Statement* (TCPS-2) guidelines for conducting ethical research in Canada
- Removed the section "Child Development: Yesterday and Today" on the basis of feedback from a number of instructors
- Updated information on leading journals publishing child development research

## Chapter 2: Biological Beginnings

- Inserted Canadian statistics on various chromosomal and genetic disorders
- New *Connecting to Current Controversy* box highlights Canadian stem cell research
- Updated section on prenatal diagnostic tests to reflect Canadian practices
- Updated section on infertility and reproductive technologies to reflect Canadian statistics and practices
- Incorporated new Canadian research into section on adoption
- Extended discussion of the increasingly popular epigenetic view of gene-environment interactions and incorporation of Canadian research
- New coverage of the Thousand Genomes Project, the most detailed study of human genetic variation to date

## Chapter 3: Prenatal Development and Birth

- Updated research indicating that high amounts of caffeine consumption by pregnant women does not increase the risk of miscarriage, congenital malformations, or growth retardation (Brent, Christian, & Diener, 2011)
- Extended coverage of Fetal Alcohol Spectrum Disorder within a Canadian context
- New Canadian research on the effects of marijuana use during pregnancy
- New Canadian research on the effects of maternal stress following the Quebec ice storms on prenatal development
- New coverage of Canadian prenatal programs, including the Canadian Prenatal Nutrition Program
- New discussion of the increasing inclusion of exercise in prenatal care programs
- Extended coverage of the role of midwives and doulas in a Canadian context
- New *Connecting to Current Controversy* box highlights paternal postpartum depression
- New discussion on the risk of HIV infection in Canadian newborns
- New research by Canadian Ann Bigelow on skin-to-skin contact highlighted in the *Connecting with Research* box

## Chapter 4: Physical Development and Health

- New opening vignette describing a healthy living program implemented in elementary schools in British Columbia, Alberta, and Manitoba (Healthy Buddies)
- New discussion of diabetes among Canadians of Aboriginal heritage

- Updated and extended discussion of how "screen time" affects exercise and obesity in childhood and adolescence
- Updated research studies on Sudden Infant Death syndrome (SIDS) and increased coverage of proposed causes of SIDS
- New section on the increasingly popular neuroconstructivist view to introduce the material on the development of the brain
- New research on using EEG to explore brain development by Canadian Laurel Trainor highlighted in the *Connecting with Research* box
- New *Connecting to Current Controversy* box highlights childhood sleep disorders and the research of Canadian Penny Corkum
- New discussion of the genetic and environmental contributions to puberty
- New research from the Canadian Longitudinal Survey of Children and Youth on the effects of early sexual maturation in girls
- New research on the eating behaviour of Canadian youths

## Chapter 5: Motor, Sensory, and Perceptual Development

- Incorporated Canadian content and Canadian research
- New *Connecting to Current Controversy* box discusses the role of playing sports in children's development
- Revised, updated coverage of high-amplitude sucking as a measure of infant perceptual development
- Much expanded and updated coverage of the dramatic increase in the use of sophisticated eye-tracking equipment in the study of infant perception
- New coverage of the longitudinal research of Canadian researcher Daphne Maurer and her colleagues on infants whose cataracts were removed at different points in development that illustrates how deprivation and experience influence visual development
- Added commentary suggesting that most perception is intermodal perception

## Chapter 6: Cognitive Developmental Approaches

- New *Connecting to Current Controversy* box highlights the role of pretend play in children's development
- Expanded conclusions about the themes of the current field of infant cognitive development to emphasize the substantial increase in interest in cognitive developmental neuroscience and links between brain processes and cognitive processes
- New coverage of neo-Piagetians, with an emphasis on Canadian researchers
- Expanded discussion of object permanence

## Chapter 7: Information Processing

- New opening vignette that is more relevant to a Canadian context
- Expanded discussion on theories of childhood amnesia and incorporation of Canadian research
- Extensive editing to update and clarify sections on executive function, critical thinking, metacognition, and mindfulness
- New *Connecting to Current Controversy* box discusses the effects of watching television during infancy
- Updated description of working memory to include the episodic buffer component
- Revised *Connecting with Diversity* box to include Canadian content and to focus more specifically on autobiographical memory

- New material on using computer exercises to improve children's attention, including a website (www.teach-the-brain.org/learn/attention/index.htm) about how to use the games with children
- Expanded coverage of attention in adolescence including new material on the importance of controlling attention and being able to reduce distractions that can interfere with learning
- Expanded coverage of cognitive factors other than theory of mind that might be involved in autism, including eye gaze, face processing, memory, and language impairment
- Expanded coverage of the dual process model of decision making to include material on the importance of adolescents quickly getting the gist of a dangerous situation, which can cue personal values that will reduce the likelihood that adolescents engage in risky decision making
- Inclusion of information about how adolescents who have a higher trait level of inhibition (self-control) and find themselves in risky situations are less likely to engage in risky decision making
- Expanded description of what metacognition involves
- New Canadian research on joint attention
- New Canadian research on the links between early attention and later academic outcomes
- New Canadian commentary on factors that contribute to inaccuracies in children's memory

## Chapter 8: Intelligence

- New opening vignette describes the extremes of intelligence
- Updated and expanded coverage of emotional intelligence as it relates specifically to children and within a Canadian context
- Revised *Connecting Through Research* box to incorporate Canadian early intervention programs for disadvantaged youths
- New and updated coverage of male-female differences in intelligence
- Updated coverage of the Stanford-Binet and Wechsler Intelligence Tests to reflect the latest editions of each
- Replaced the term "mental retardation" with "intellectual disability" to be consistent with terminology used in the recently released *Diagnostic and Statistical Manual—5th Edition*
- New *Connecting to Current Controversy* box discusses the research of Canadian researcher Glen Schellenberg on the role of music education on intelligence
- Revised section on gifted children to reflect Canadian educational practices
- Revised section on intellectual disability to incorporate new criteria used within the DSM-5 to classify severity of intellectual disability

## Chapter 9: Language Development

- New *Connecting to Current Controversy* box highlights the issues surrounding French Immersion in Canada, and the work of Canadian researchers studying these issues
- New coverage of Canadian researcher Janet Werker in the section on recognizing speech sounds
- New material on principles related to vocabulary development
- Updated section on bilingualism and second language learning to make it relevant to a Canadian audience and highlight new Canadian research
- New material related to Aboriginal language learning incorporated into *Connecting with Diversity* box
- New Canadian research on factors related to literacy skills

## Chapter 10: Emotional Development

- Included Canadian research on the factors that shape children's emotional competence
- Added description of a Canadian study on the MindUp program
- Included Canadian research on how children's effortful control can be increased
- New *Connecting Through Research* box highlights a Canadian study on helping inhibited children through play
- Added description of cross-cultural research on behavioural inhibition in children
- Added Canadian research on the similarities of the Strange Situation conducted in the laboratory and at home
- Added Canadian research on infant attachment styles, including their stability and the behaviours of mothers of babies with a disorganized attachment style
- Added Canadian statistics on caregiver roles of mothers and fathers
- New discussion of parental leave in Canada
- New discussion on child care in Canada
- Expanded description of cross-cultural research on parental leave practices
- New *Connecting to Current Controversy* box on the prospect of a nation-wide child care system in Canada

## Chapter 11: The Self and Identity

- New opening vignette describes a classic study on the development of self-conceptions by Montemayor and Eisen (1977)
- New *Connecting Through Research* box describes a recent Canadian study on infant self- and other-awareness
- Added cross-cultural research on the association between global self-esteem and self-evaluations of physical appearance
- New description of Canadian study on the effects of mothers' behaviour on children's subsequent self-esteem
- Included Canadian research on self-esteem and sport participation
- New *Connecting to Current Controversy* box on the development of self-esteem
- New definitions of sexual identity and gender identity
- New coverage of outcomes associated with ethnic identity among Canadian Aboriginal children and adolescents
- New *Connecting with Diversity* box describes research on ethnic and national identity among Canadian youth

## Chapter 12: Gender

- New opening vignette on the life of Canadian Bruce Reimer
- New description of gender dysphoria in children
- Added Canadian research on peer relationships and gender inappropriate behaviour
- Added Canadian research on gender differences in children's drawings
- New description of Canadian research on the development of gender stereotyping
- Added research on reading achievement among Canadian boys and girls
- New coverage of gender differences in math aptitude among Canadian children

- Added description of gender differences in academic engagement and achievement among Canadian youth
- Included Statistics Canada (2013) data on post-secondary program enrolment among males and females
- Added Canadian research on gender differences in expressing emotions
- New *Connecting to Current Controversy* box on the differences and similarities between males and females

## Chapter 13: Moral Development

- New opening vignette describing the achievements of Canadian Craig Kielburger
- Added research on gender and age differences in empathy among Canadian children
- New coverage of the Roots of Empathy program
- New *Connecting Through Research* box on the development of lying, highlighting cultural differences between Canadian and Chinese children
- New commentary on character education in Canada by Sue Winton
- Included research on the cardiovascular benefits of volunteering for Canadian youth
- Added discussion of Canadian research on children's understanding of equality
- Added prevalence rates for conduct disorder in Canadian boys and girls and violent delinquency among Canadian youth
- Added description of how youth criminal acts are treated under the Criminal Code of Canada and the Youth Criminal Justice Act
- Included Canadian research on the risk factors for delinquency
- New *Connecting to Current Controversy* box on whether young people should be tried based on the severity of the crime, regardless of age
- New section on intervention and prevention of criminal involvement in Canada
- Included Canadian moral exemplars Doug Wilson and The Famous Five, who respectively played important roles in the gay rights movement and the women's movement

## Chapter 14: Families

- Included Canadian study on the effect of parental scaffolding on the development of children's executive functioning
- Added description of the effect of parental depression on children's emotional problems from the Canadian National Longitudinal Survey of Children and Youth
- Added the adolescent pregnancy rate in Canada and the pregnancy rate for Canadian women over the age of thirty
- Added description of parenting behaviours and their associated outcomes for Canadian children from various ethnic backgrounds
- Included description of corporal punishment in Canada
- New *Connecting to Current Controversy* box on the consequences of corporal punishment for children's development
- Included Canadian study on the prevalence of child maltreatment
- New *Connecting Through Research* box describes a Canadian study on the importance of family dinners for the well-being of youth
- Added Canadian prevalence rates for working parents, same-sex parents, stepfamilies, and divorce

- Expanded discussion of the parenting style of Chinese parents
- New *Connecting with Diversity* box on acculturation and ethnic minority parenting, highlighting research on Canadian immigrant families

## Chapter 15: Peers

- New coverage of hostile attribution bias
- Updated section on peer group social status to reflect current methodological approaches
- New discussion of the characteristics of popular children, highlighting Canadian research
- New *Connecting to Current Controversy* box on the risks associated with popularity
- Added a definition of bullying
- Added prevalence rates of bullying and victimization in Canada
- Included description of a Canadian study on what youth are bullied about
- Added coverage of cyberbullying, highlighting current legislation in Canada and two Canadian adolescents (Rehtaeh Parsons and Amanda Todd) who, after being victims of cyberbullying, committed suicide
- New *Connecting Through Research* box on the role of peer bystanders in bullying, with a focus on describing Canadian studies
- New coverage of the WITS Canadian anti-bullying program
- New section on trends in play
- Updated research on intimacy in friendships for boys and girls
- New section on other-sex friendships
- Expanded discussion of adolescent romantic relationships

## Chapter 16: Schools and Technology

- New *Connecting to Current Controversy* box on early childhood education
- Included coverage of Head Start programs in Canada
- Added prevalence rates of early school leaving in Canada
- Updated research on children with ADHD
- New section on sustained attention, effort, and task persistence
- Expanded and updated coverage of self-regulation
- Included prevalence rates for screen time, video game play, and Internet use among Canadian children
- Updated discussion of the impact of technology use on children's cognitive development
- Added Canadian research on the effects of video game play on physical violence
- New commentary by Lucia O'Sullivan about Canadian adolescents' perceptions of their online activities as public versus private
- New *Connecting Through Research* box on computer and Internet use and friendship quality, highlighting Canadian research

## Connections

The *connections* theme provides a systematic, integrative approach to identifying the goals of this textbook, which are as follows:

1. **Connecting with today's students**—To help students *learn* about child development more effectively

2. **Connecting research to what we know about children's development**—To provide students with the best and most recent *theory and research* in the world today about each of the periods of child development

3. **Connecting development processes**—To guide students in making *developmental connections* across different points in child development

4. **Connecting development to real life**—To help students understand ways to *apply* content about child development to the real world and improve people's lives, and to motivate students to think deeply about *their own personal journey through life* and better understand who they were, are, and will be

## *Connecting* with Today's Students

Students often report development courses to be challenging due to the amount of material covered. To help today's students focus on the key ideas, the Learning Objectives system developed for *Child Development* provides extensive learning connections throughout the chapters. The learning system connects the chapter-opening outline, learning objectives for the chapter, mini chapter maps that open each main section of the chapter, *Review, Connect, and Reflect* at the end of each main section, and the chapter summary at the end of each chapter.

The learning system keeps the key ideas in front of the student from the beginning to the end of the chapter. The main headings of each chapter correspond to the learning objectives, which are presented in the chapter-opening spread. Mini chapter maps that link up with the learning goals are presented at the beginning of each major section in the chapter.

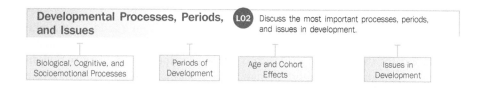

Then, at the end of each main section of a chapter, the learning objective is repeated in *Review, Connect, and Reflect*, which prompts students to review the key topics in the section, connect these topics to existing knowledge, and relate what they learned to their own personal journey through life. *Reach Your Learning Goals*, at the end of the chapter, guides students through the bulleted chapter review, connecting with the chapter outline/learning objectives at the beginning of the chapter and the *Review, Connect, and Reflect* material at the end of major chapter sections.

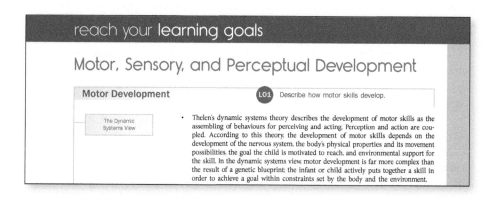

## Connecting Research to What We Know About Children's Development

Over the years, it has been important to include the most up-to-date research available. The Canadian edition continues this tradition by looking closely at specific areas of research involving experts in related fields and updating research throughout. *Connecting Through Research* describes both individual studies as well as up-to-date research summaries to illustrate both how research studies are conducted and how research findings are synthesized to inform our understanding of the discipline. Topics range from "Do Children Conceived Through In Vitro Fertilization Show Significantly Different Outcomes in Adolescence?" (Chapter 2) to "How Can We Study Newborns' Perception?" (Chapter 5) to "How Does Theory of Mind Differ in Children with Autism?" (Chapter 7).

### connecting through research

**Using EEGs to Explore Brain Development in Infancy**

One study by Laurel Trainor and her colleagues at McMaster University illustrates how an electroencephalograph (EEG) can be used to explore the role of early

FIGURE **4.8**
**MEASURING THE ACTIVITY OF AN INFANT'S BRAIN.** By attaching electrodes to a baby's scalp to measure the brain's activity, Laurel Trainor (Trainor, Lee, & Bosnyak, 2011) has found that infants produce distinctive brain waves that reveal they can distinguish between different auditory stimuli. *Why is it so difficult to measure infants' brain activity?*

The tradition of obtaining detailed, extensive input from a number of leading experts in different areas of child development also continues in this Canadian edition. Finally, the research discussions have been updated in every period and topic. We expended every effort to make this Canadian edition of *Child Development* as contemporary and up-to-date as possible. To that end, there are more than 1,500 citations from 2012, 2013, and 2014 in the text.

### Connecting Development Processes

Too often we forget or fail to notice the many connections between one point in child development and another. We have substantially increased the connections made in the text narrative. Two features help students connect topics across the stages of child development. *Developmental Connection*, which appears multiple times in each chapter, points readers to where the topic is discussed in a previous, current, or subsequent chapter. This feature highlights links across topics of development *and* connections among biological, cognitive, and socioemotional processes. The key developmental processes are typically discussed in isolation from each other, and so students often fail to see their connections. Included in each *Developmental Connection* is a brief description of the backward or forward connection. For example, consider the rapidly increasing interest in the field of developmental cognitive neuroscience that focuses on connections among development, cognitive processes, and the brain. This topic is initially presented in Chapter 1, "Introduction," and then highlighted again in various chapters, especially Chapter 4, "Physical Development and Health."

Furthermore, a *Connect* question is included in the section of self-reviews—*Review, Connect, and Reflect*—so students can practise making connections among topics. For example, in Chapter 8, students are asked to connect what they learned in Chapter 5 about the effect of culture on motor development to what they just read about how different cultures have different concepts of intelligence.

---

### developmental **connection**

**Conditions, Diseases, and Disorders.** Intellectual disability can be classified in several ways. Chapter 8, LO 3

### developmental **connection**

**Education.** Applications of Vygotsky's theory to children's education have been made in recent years. Chapter 6, LO 3

## Review *Connect* Reflect

**LO1** Explain the concept of intelligence.

### Review

- What is intelligence?
- What are the main individual tests of intelligence?
- What theories of multiple intelligences have been developed? Do people have one intelligence or many intelligences?
- What are some links between the brain and intelligence?
- What evidence indicates that heredity influences IQ scores? What evidence indicates that environment influences IQ scores?
- What is known about the intelligence of people from different cultures and ethnic groups?

### *Connect*

- In this section you learned that different cultures have different concepts of intelligence, and in Chapter 5 you learned about culture's effect on motor development. What do these findings have in common?

**Reflect** *Your Own Personal Journey of Life*

- A CD-ROM is being sold to parents for testing their child's IQ. Several parents tell you that they purchased the CD-ROM and assessed their children's IQs. Why might you be skeptical about giving your children an IQ test and interpreting the results yourself?

## *Connecting* Development to Real Life

In addition to helping students make research and developmental connections, *Child Development* shows the important connections among the concepts discussed and the real world. In this edition, real-life connections are explicitly made in the chapter-opening vignette, the coverage of diversity, and the newly created *Case Study Connections* and *Connecting to Current Controversy*. Each chapter begins with a story designed to increase students' interest and motivation to read the chapter. *Case Study Connections* include questions that ask

### connecting to current controversy

#### Sleep Disturbances During Infancy and Childhood

Good sleep is important for optimal growth and development. However, there are a variety of sleep disorders and disturbances that infants and children can experience that affect sleep quality. During infancy, babies under 6 months of age will sleep for 14 to 18 hours a day in many short episodes of sleep and wakefulness. Around 6 months of age, most infants will sleep for more than 6 consecutive hours, which is often considered "sleeping through the night." Infants who do not achieve this sleep pattern may be considered to have sleep problems (Weiss & Corkum, 2012).

The type of sleep problems experienced during toddlerhood and childhood can be different than those experienced during early infancy. In one recent study, parents reported that night wakings and short sleep durations were the main problems experienced during infancy and early toddlerhood (6 to 24 months of age), while nightmares, night terrors, and restless sleep were the main problems reported for older toddlers (aged 24 to 36 months) (Byars & others, 2012). Over all of childhood, the most common sleep disorder, affecting approximately 25 percent of typically developing children, is behavioural insomnia (Weiss & Corkum, 2012). Behavioural insomnia is characterized by difficulties in settling in to sleep, falling asleep, and staying asleep during the night.

There are immediate negative outcomes associated with sleep problems in children. Research has revealed that behavioural insomnia results in daytime difficulties with school performance, learning, and mood and/or behaviour for the child, as well as increased daytime fatigue and loss of work productivity for parents (Vriend & others, 2013). The long-term outcomes of sleep disturbances during childhood are less well understood. In a recent research review, Gregory and Sadeh (2012) revealed that long-term outcomes may include depression, early use of drugs and alcohol, and attention problems. Due to the scarcity of research in this area, however, it is difficult to determine whether these effects are a result of sleep problems experienced during infancy and/or childhood, or a result of currently experienced sleep disturbances.

Despite the negative outcomes associated with childhood sleep disturbances, only about 1 percent of children with behavioural insomnia are effectively treated (Weiss & Corkum, 2012). Often parents are unaware of what actually constitutes a sleep problem, and as a result do not discuss these issues with the child's health care provider.

Other barriers to effective treatment include a lack of regular screening for sleep disturbances by health care providers, as well as a lack of knowledge of effective treatments when the problems are identified. Medications, including melatonin, are not recommended for the treatment of behavioural insomnia in children (Cummings, 2012; Health Canada, 2006). Rather, behavioural interventions are the most effective means to treat behavioural insomnia in children (Weiss & Corkum, 2012). Not only do these programs generally improve sleep quality for the child, they also increase the daytime functioning of both the child and parent.

One such intervention program is the Better Nights, Better Days program initiated by Researcher Penny Corkum at Dalhousie University (http://betternightsbetterdays.weebly.com/). This program to treat behavioural insomnia in children between the ages of 1 and 10 years is a web-based program that instructs parents about various behaviours that will create healthy sleep habits including age-appropriate and consistent bedtimes and wake times, establishment of daily routines, regular exercise, relaxing routines at bedtime (e.g., no electronics) and a quiet, dark, and comfortable room. This program addresses some of the barriers to effective treatment of behavioural insomnia in children. However, more research is needed to determine the long-term effects of infant and childhood sleep disturbances, the factors that mediate the negative outcomes of sleep problems, and how sleep problems should best be addressed to increase the overall health of Canadian children.

*What effects might behavioural sleep insomnia have on cognitive development and academic performance?*

students to connect what they have read in the chapter with the chapter-opening vignette. *Connecting to Current Controversy* provides a discussion of how new research is having an impact on social policy, educational practices, and parenting in a Canadian context. Topics range from "Sleep Disturbances During Infancy and Childhood" (Chapter 4) to "Does Music Make You Smarter?" (Chapter 8) to "Is Striving for Popularity Something Parents and Teachers Should Discourage?" (Chapter 15).

*Child Development*, Canadian edition, puts a strong emphasis on diversity. Leading experts on diversity have ensured that the content provides students with current, accurate, sensitive information related to diversity in children's development.

Diversity is discussed in every chapter. Further, *Connecting with Diversity* appears throughout the text, focusing on a diversity topic from a Canadian perspective. Topics range from "The Increased Diversity of Adopted Children and Adoptive Parents" (Chapter 2) to "Aboriginal Language Learning" (Chapter 9) to "Ethnic Identity and Canadian Identity" (Chapter 11).

## connecting with diversity

### Cross-Cultural Variations in the Incidence and Causes of Low Birth Weight

In 2010 almost 15 million babies worldwide were born preterm (Chang & others, 2013). In some countries, such as India and Sudan, where poverty is rampant and the health and nutrition of mothers are poor, the number of low birth weight babies reaches as high as 31 percent. In Canada, there has been an increase in low birth weight infants in the last two decades. The Canadian low birth weight rate of 7.8 percent in 2010 is below the global average of 11.1 percent (see Figure 3.8; Blencowe & others, 2012), but still higher than that of many other developed countries (Chang & others, 2013). For example, only 5–6 percent of the infants born in Sweden, Finland, Norway, and France are low birth weight.

In both developed and developing countries, adolescents who give birth when their bodies have not fully matured are at risk for having low birth weight babies (Malamitsi-Puchner & Boutsikou, 2006). Further, the increase in the number of low birth weight infants has been attributed to drug use, poor nutrition, multiple births, reproductive technologies, and improved technology and prenatal care that result in more high-risk babies surviving (Chang & others, 2013). Nonetheless, poverty continues to be a major factor in preterm birth. Women living in poverty are more likely to be obese, have diabetes and hypertension, smoke cigarettes, and use illicit drugs, and they are less likely to receive regular prenatal care (Goldenberg & Nagahawatte, 2008).

FIGURE **3.8**

**PERCENTAGE OF INFANTS BORN WITH LOW BIRTH WEIGHT IN SELECTED COUNTRIES.**

In the preceding sentence, we learned that women living in poverty are less likely to receive regular prenatal care. *What did you learn earlier in the chapter about the benefits of regular prenatal care? Aside from women living in poverty, which other demographic group is not likely to receive adequate prenatal care?*

Finally, part of applying knowledge of child development to the real world is understanding how it impacts oneself. Accordingly, one of the goals of this text is to motivate students to think deeply about their own journey of life. In reflecting about ways to encourage students to make personal connections to content in the text, a *Reflect: Your Own Personal Journey of Life* prompt was added in the end-of-section reviews. This question asks students to reflect on some aspect of the discussion in the section they have just read and connect it to their own life. For example, in Chapter 1, related to a discussion of the early-later experience issue in development in the section, students are asked,

> *Can you identify an early experience that you believe contributed in important ways to your development?*
> *Can you identify a recent or current (later) experience that you think had (is having) a strong influence on your development?*

# Resources

**McGraw-Hill Connect®**

*Child Development*, Canadian edition, is supported by a highly collaborative and integrated program of supplements for instructors and students of developmental psychology.

McGraw-Hill Connect™ is a web-based assignment and assessment platform that gives students the means to better connect with their coursework, with their instructors, and with the important concepts that they will need to know for success now and in the future.

With Connect, instructors can deliver assignments, quizzes, and tests online. Instructors can edit existing questions and author entirely new problems. Track individual student performance—by question, assignment or in relation to the class overall—with detailed grade reports. Integrate grade reports easily with Learning Management Systems (LMS).

By choosing Connect, instructors are providing their students with a powerful tool for improving academic performance and truly mastering course material. Connect allows students to practice important skills at their own pace and on their own schedule. Importantly, students' assessment results and instructors' feedback are all saved online, so students can continually review their progress and plot their course to success.

Connect also provides 24/7 online access to an eBook—an online edition of the text—to aid them in successfully completing their work, wherever and whenever they choose.

## Key Features

### Simple Assignment Management

With Connect, creating assignments is easier than ever, so you can spend more time teaching and less time managing.

- Create and deliver assignments easily with selectable end-of-chapter questions and testbank material to assign online.
- Streamline lesson planning, student progress reporting, and assignment grading to make classroom management more efficient than ever.
- Go paperless with the eBook, and online submission and grading of student assignments.

### Smart Grading

When it comes to studying, time is precious. Connect helps students learn more efficiently by providing feedback and practice material when they need it, where they need it.

- Automatically score assignments, giving students immediate feedback on their work and side-by-side comparisons with correct answers.
- Access and review each response; manually change grades or leave comments for students to review.
- Reinforce classroom concepts with practice tests and instant quizzes.

### Instructor Library

The Connect Instructor Library is your course creation hub. It provides all the critical resources you'll need to build your course, just how you want to teach it.

- Assign eBook readings and draw from a rich collection of textbook-specific assignments.
- Access instructor resources, including ready-made PowerPoint presentations and media to use in your lectures.

- View assignments and resources created for past sections.
- Post your own resources for students to use.

## eBook

Connect reinvents the textbook learning experience for the modern student. Every Connect subject area is seamlessly integrated with Connect eBooks, which are designed to keep students focused on the concepts key to their success.

- Provide students with a Connect eBook, allowing for anytime, anywhere access to the textbook.
- Merge media, animation and assessments with the text's narrative to engage students and improve learning and retention.
- Pinpoint and connect key concepts in a snap using the powerful eBook search engine.
- Manage notes, highlights and bookmarks in one place for simple, comprehensive review.

# LEARNSMART

No two students are alike. Why should their learning paths be? LearnSmart uses revolutionary adaptive technology to build a learning experience unique to each student's individual needs. It starts by identifying the topics a student knows and does not know. As the student progresses, LearnSmart adapts and adjusts the content based on his or her individual strengths, weaknesses and confidence, ensuring that every minute spent studying with LearnSmart is the most efficient and productive study time possible.

# SMARTBOOK

As the first and only adaptive reading experience, SmartBook is changing the way students read and learn. SmartBook creates a personalized reading experience by highlighting the most important concepts a student needs to learn at that moment in time. As a student engages with SmartBook, the reading experience continuously adapts by highlighting content based on what each student knows and doesn't know. This ensures that he or she is focused on the content needed to close specific knowledge gaps, while it simultaneously promotes long-term learning.

## Instructor Resources

**Instructor's Manual**—This fully integrated tool helps instructors more easily locate and choose among the many resources available for the course by linking each element of the Instructor's Manual to a particular teaching topic within the chapter. These elements include lecture suggestions, classroom activities, personal applications, research project ideas, video suggestions, and handouts.

**Computerized Test Bank**—By increasing the rigor of the Test Bank development process, McGraw-Hill Ryerson aims to raise the bar for student assessment. Multiple choice, essay, and short-answer questions were prepared to test factual, applied, and conceptual understanding and are keyed to Bloom's taxonomy, difficulty level, and learning objective.

**Microsoft® PowerPoint® Lecture Slides**—These presentations cover the key points of each chapter and include charts and graphs from the text. They can be used as-is, or you may modify them to meet your specific needs.

# Superior Learning Solutions and Support

The McGraw-Hill Ryerson team is ready to help you assess and integrate any of our products, technology, and services into your course for optimal teaching and learning performance. Whether it's helping your students improve their grades, or putting your entire course online, the McGraw-Hill Ryerson team is here to help you do it. Contact your Learning Solutions Consultant today to learn how to maximize all of McGraw-Hill Ryerson's resources!

For more information on the latest technology and Learning Solutions offered by McGraw-Hill Ryerson and its partners, please visit us online: **www.mheducation.ca/he/solutions**.

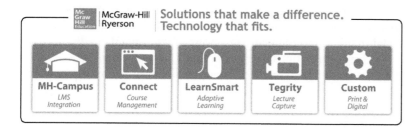

## acknowledgments

We very much appreciate the support and guidance provided to us by many people at McGraw-Hill Ryerson. Special thanks are due to Catherine Gillespie-Lopes, Product Developer; Jennifer Cressman, Senior Product Developer; Marcia Siekowski, Senior Product Manager; Jason Chih, Product Manager; and Cathy Biribauer, Supervising Editor, who all did a wonderful job directing and monitoring the development and publication of this text. Other members of the McGraw-Hill Ryerson team each played a pivotal role in putting this textbook together, including Judy Sturrup, Derek Capitaine, and Joanne Barnett, and deserve thanks for helping us achieve our goals.

We also want to thank our families, friends and colleagues, who provided invaluable support and input during the development of this Canadian edition. In particular, I, Nicole, want to thank Michael, for his incredible support that enabled me to complete this book while also enjoying our newborn son, Robert. Writing about child development, particularly prenatal development and development in infancy, as it occurred in front of me, was a wondrous experience. And I, Leanna, want to thank Jeff for being an inspiration to me as a father and the best big brother a sister could ask for.

Special thanks go to the many reviewers of the Canadian edition of this text. Their extensive contributions have made this a far better book.

Finally, we would like to thank our students, who continue to inspire us every day.

## Reviewers

Child development has become an enormous, complex field and no single author can possibly be an expert in all areas of the field. To solve this problem, beginning with the sixth edition, John Santrock sought the input of leading experts in many different areas of child development. This tradition continues in this Canadian edition. We owe a special gratitude to the reviewers who provided detailed feedback about the book:

Ajit Bedi, *Memorial University of Newfoundland*

Georgette Bigelow, *Seneca College*

Wendy Bourque, *St. Thomas University*

Elizabeth Bowering, *Mount Saint Vincent University*

Christine Cadieux, *Centennial College*

Jason Daniels, *University of Alberta*

Faizal Junus, *Dalhousie University*

Elizabeth Levin, *Laurentian University*

David Lockwood, *Humber College*

Michael Mueller, *Ryerson University*

Melanie Soderstrom, *University of Manitoba*

Natalie Stelmach, *George Brown College*

Colleen Thomas, *George Brown College*

Susan Thompson, *Kwantlen Polytechnic University*

Anthony Volk, *Brock University*

Greg Wells, *Red Deer College*

*In every child who is born, under no matter what circumstances, and of no matter what parents, the potentiality of the human race is born again.*

—JAMES AGEE
*American Writer, 20th Century*

# The Nature of Child Development

Examining the shape of childhood allows us to understand it better. Every childhood is distinct, the first chapter of a new biography in the world. This book is about children's development, its universal features, its individual variations, its nature at the beginning of the twenty-first century. *Child Development* is about the rhythm and meaning of children's lives, about turning mystery into understanding, and about weaving together a portrait of who each of us was, is, and will be. In Section 1, you will read one chapter: "Introduction" (Chapter 1).

# chapter 1 | Introduction

K arla Homolka was born in Port Credit, Ontario, in 1970. Along with her two younger sisters, Lori and Tammy, she was raised in St. Catharines. Homolka was a bright young girl. Her elementary school teachers described her as "eager" and "a good student." As a child, Homolka dreamed of one day becoming a police officer or a veterinarian. During her teenage years, Homolka worked part-time at a pet store and eventually was hired to work full-time at a veterinary clinic. In 1987, while in Scarborough at a convention for her job, Homolka met Paul Bernardo. At the time, Homolka was 17 and Bernardo was 23. The two were married four years later.

At the time of their first meeting, Bernardo had already committed a series of sexual assaults against women, and shortly thereafter became known as the Scarborough Rapist. During the early 1990s, Homolka helped Bernardo kidnap, rape, and murder young women, including Homolka's 15-year-old sister, Tammy. Although Tammy's death was ruled an accident, Homolka was convicted of manslaughter for the deaths of two teenage girls and sentenced to 12 years in prison. She was released in 2005 and is currently living in the Caribbean with her new husband and their three children. Bernardo, on the other hand, is currently serving a life sentence at Millhaven Institution, a maximum security prison in Ontario.

Paul Bernardo and Karla Homolka

Long before Homolka and Bernardo met, Lincoln Alexander was facing significant challenges in his life. Alexander had grown up knowing the brutal effects of poverty and racism. Born in Toronto in 1922 to parents who were recent immigrants, he was determined not to spend his life as a railway porter, as his father had. When Alexander was a teenager, he moved to Harlem, in New York City, with his mother after a violent altercation with his father. Returning to Canada in 1939, Alexander finished high school, went to university to study history and economics, and graduated from law school in 1953. Despite the odds against him, Alexander not only became a lawyer, but a sergeant in the Royal Canadian Air Force, Canada's first Black Member of Parliament, the federal Minister of Labour, and the 24th Lieutenant Governor of Ontario.

What leads some individuals to commit brutal acts of violence while others overcome poverty and trauma to achieve success? If you have ever wondered why people turn out the way they do, you have asked yourself the central question we will explore in this book.

Lincoln Alexander overcame many obstacles to become Canada's first Black MP and federal Cabinet minister. His lifelong career of public service culminated in his appointment as 24th Lieutenant Governor of Ontario.

# preview

Why study children? Perhaps you are or will be a parent or teacher, and responsibility for children is or will be a part of your everyday life. The more you learn about children and the way researchers study them, the better you can guide them. Perhaps you hope to gain an understanding of your own history—as an infant, as a child, and as an adolescent. Perhaps you accidentally came across the course description and found it intriguing. Whatever your reasons, you will discover that the study of child development is provocative, intriguing, and informative. In this first chapter, we will explore historical views and the modern study of child development, consider why caring for children is so important, examine the nature of development, and outline how science helps us to understand it.

## Caring for Children    **L01**    Identify five areas in which children's lives need to be improved, and explain the role of resilience in children's development.

Improving the Lives of Children

---

*Children are the legacy we leave for the time we will not live to see.*

**—ARISTOTLE**
*Greek Philosopher, 4th Century BC*

What do we mean when we speak of an individual's development? **Development** is the pattern of change that begins at conception and continues through the life span. Most development involves growth, although it also includes decline. Anywhere you turn today, the development of children captures public attention. Caring for children is an important theme of this text. To understand why caring for children is so important, we will explore why it is beneficial to study children's development and identify some areas in which children's lives need to be improved.

*We reach backward to our parents and forward to our children to a future we will never see, but about which we need to care.*

**—CARL JUNG**
*Swiss Psychoanalyst, 20th Century*

## IMPROVING THE LIVES OF CHILDREN

If you were to pick up a newspaper or magazine in any Canadian town or city, you might see headlines like these: "Political Leanings May Be Written in the Genes," "Mother Drives Drunk with Children in Vehicle," "Cyberbullied Teen Commits Suicide," and "Health Canada Warns About ADHD Drug." Researchers are examining these and many other topics of contemporary concern. The roles that health and well-being, parenting, education, sociocultural contexts, and resilience play in child development are a particular focus of this textbook.

**development** The pattern of movement or change that begins at conception and continues through the life span.

**context** The settings, influenced by historical, economic, social, and cultural factors, in which development occurs.

**culture** The behaviour patterns, beliefs, and all other products of a group that are passed on from generation to generation.

**Health and Well-Being** Does a pregnant woman endanger her fetus if she has a few beers a week? How does a poor diet affect a child's ability to learn? Are children exercising less today than in the past? What roles do parents and peers play in whether adolescents abuse drugs? Throughout this text, we will discuss many questions like these regarding health and well-being.

Health professionals today recognize the roles played by lifestyles and psychological states in determining health and well-being (Hahn, Payne, & Lucas, 2011; Sparling & Redican, 2011). In every chapter of this book, issues of health and well-being are integrated into our discussion.

**Parenting**   Can two gay men raise a healthy family? Are children harmed if both parents work outside the home? Does spanking have negative consequences for a child's development? How damaging is divorce to children's development? Controversial answers to questions like these reflect pressures on the contemporary family (Patterson, 2009). We'll examine these questions and others that provide a context for understanding factors that influence parents' lives and their effectiveness in raising their children. How parents, as well as other adults, can make a positive difference in children's lives is another major theme of this book.

You might be a parent someday or might already be one. You should take seriously the importance of rearing your children, because they are the future of our society. Good parenting takes considerable time. If you plan to become a parent, commit yourself day after day, week after week, month after month, and year after year to providing your children with a warm, supportive, safe, and stimulating environment that will make them feel secure and allow them to reach their full potential as human beings. The poster on this page that states "Children learn to love when they are loved" reflects this theme.

Understanding the nature of children's development can help you become a better parent. Many parents learn parenting practices from their parents. Unfortunately, when parenting practices and child-care strategies are passed from one generation to the next, both the desirable and undesirable practices are usually perpetuated. This book and your instructor's lectures in this course can help you become more knowledgeable about children's development and sort through the practices in your own upbringing to identify which ones you should continue with your own children and which ones you should abandon.

**Education**   There is widespread agreement that something needs to be done to improve the education of children (Johnson & others, 2011; McCombs, 2010). Among the questions involved in improving schools are: Are schools teaching children to be immoral? Are schools failing to teach students how to read and write and calculate adequately? Should there be more accountability in schools? Should schools challenge students more? Should schools focus only on developing children's knowledge and cognitive skills, or should they pay more attention to the whole child and consider the child's socioemotional and physical development, as well? In this text, we will examine such questions and consider recent research on solutions to educational problems (Nieto, 2010; Suarez-Orosco & Suarez-Orosco, 2010).

**Sociocultural Contexts and Diversity**   Health and well-being, parenting, and education—like development itself—are all shaped by their sociocultural context (Cole & Cagigas, 2010; Shiraev & Levy, 2010). The term **context** refers to the settings in which development occurs. These settings are influenced by historical, economic, social, and cultural factors. Four contexts to which we will pay special attention are culture, ethnicity, socioeconomic status, and gender.

**Culture** encompasses the behaviour patterns, beliefs, and all other products of a particular group of people that are passed on from generation to generation. Culture results from the interaction of people over many years. A cultural group can be as large as Canada or as small as an isolated northern town. Whatever its size, the group's culture influences the behaviour of its members (Goodnow, 2010; Hall, 2010; Kitayama, 2011). **Cross-cultural studies** compare aspects of two or more cultures. The comparison provides information about the degree to which development is similar, or universal, across cultures, or is culture-specific (Larson, Wilson, & Rickman, 2009; Shiraev & Levy, 2010).

*Ah! What would the world be to us If the children were no more? We should dread the desert behind us Worse than the dark before.*

—HENRY WADSWORTH LONGFELLOW
*American Poet, 19th Century*

**cross-cultural studies** Comparisons of one culture with one or more other cultures. These provide information about the degree to which children's development is similar, or universal, across cultures, and the degree to which it is culture specific.

Cindy Blackstock, executive director of the First Nations and Family Caring Society, has been a tireless advocate of aboriginal children's rights and has been instrumental in calling attention to the needs of children. *What are some of these needs?*

### developmental **connection**

**Peers.** Peers especially play an important role in gender development during childhood. Chapter 15, LO 1

**Ethnicity** (the word *ethnic* comes from the Greek word for nation) is rooted in cultural heritage, nationality, race, religion, and language. Black Canadians, Asian Canadians, First Nations peoples, Polish Canadians, and Italian Canadians are a few examples of ethnic groups. Diversity exists within each ethnic group (Banks, 2010; Spring, 2010). Contrary to stereotypes, not all Aboriginal people live in low-income circumstances; not all Asian Canadians are high school math whizzes (Florence, 2010).

**Socioeconomic status (SES)** refers to a person's position within society based on occupational, educational, and economic characteristics. Socioeconomic status implies certain inequalities. Generally, members of a society have (1) occupations that vary in prestige, and some individuals have more access than others to higher-status occupations; (2) different levels of educational attainment, and some individuals have more access than others to better education; (3) different economic resources; and (4) different levels of power to influence a community's institutions. These differences in the ability to control resources and to participate in society's rewards produce unequal opportunities (Huston & Bentley, 2010; McLoyd & others, 2009).

Gender is another key dimension of children's development (Best, 2010; Martin & Ruble, 2010). **Gender** refers to the characteristics of people as males and females. The ways in which you view yourself, your relationships with other people, your life, and your goals are shaped to a great extent by whether you are male or female and how your culture defines what is appropriate behaviour for males and females.

In North America the sociocultural context has become increasingly diverse in recent years (Banks, 2010; Tamis-LeMonda & Fadden, 2010). Canada's population includes a greater variety of cultures and ethnic groups than ever before. This changing demographic contributes to the richness that diversity produces (Huston & Bentley, 2010; McLoyd & others, 2009). We will discuss sociocultural contexts and diversity in each chapter. In addition, *Connecting with Diversity,* which highlights an issue related to diversity, appears in every chapter. The *Connecting with Diversity* feature in this chapter focuses on gender, families, and children's development around the world.

| Source | Characteristic |
|---|---|
| **Individual** | Good intellectual functioning |
| | Appealing, sociable, easygoing disposition |
| | Self-confidence, high self-esteem |
| | Talents |
| | Faith |
| **Family** | Close relationship to caring parent figure |
| | Authoritative parenting: warmth, structure, high expectations |
| | Socioeconomic advantages |
| | Connections to extended supportive family networks |
| **Extrafamilial Context** | Bonds to caring adults outside the family |
| | Connections to positive organizations |
| | Attending effective schools |

## FIGURE **1.1**

**CHARACTERISTICS OF RESILIENT CHILDREN AND THEIR CONTEXTS.**

**Resilience** Some children develop confidence in their abilities despite negative stereotypes about their gender or their ethnic group, and some children triumph over poverty or other adversities. They show *resilience* (Gutman, 2008). Think back to the chapter-opening story about Lincoln Alexander. In spite of racism and poverty, he went on to become Canada's first Black Member of Parliament.

Are there certain characteristics that make children like Lincoln Alexander resilient? Are there other characteristics that make children lash out against society, like Karla Homolka, who became one of Canada's most notorious criminals? After analyzing research on this topic, Ann Masten and her colleagues (2006, 2009a, b; Masten, Burt, & Coatsworth, 2006; Masten & others, 2009a, b) concluded that a number of individual factors influence resiliency, such as good intellectual functioning. In addition, as Figure 1.1 shows, their families and resources outside the children's families tend to show certain features. For example, resilient children are likely to have a close relationship to a caring parent figure and bonds to caring adults outside the family.

# Gender, Families, and Children's Development

Around the world, the experiences of male and female children and adolescents continue to be quite different (Best, 2010; UNICEF, 2009, 2010). One analysis found that a higher percentage of girls than boys around the world have never had any education (UNICEF, 2004) (see Figure 1.2). The countries with the fewest females being educated are in Africa, where in some areas girls and women are receiving no education at all. Canada, the United States, and Russia have the highest percentages of educated women. In developing countries, 67 percent of women over the age of 25 (compared with 50 percent of men) have never been to school. At the beginning of the twenty-first century, 80 million more boys than girls were in primary and secondary educational settings around the world (United Nations, 2002).

Of special cross-cultural concern are the educational and psychological conditions of women around the world (UNICEF, 2009, 2010). Inadequate educational opportunities, violence, and mental health issues are just some of the problems faced by many women.

In many countries, adolescent females have less freedom to pursue a variety of careers and engage in various leisure acts than males (Helgeson, 2009). Gender differences in sexual expression are widespread, especially in India, Southeast Asia, Latin America, and Middle Eastern countries, where there are far more restrictions on the sexual activity of adolescent females than males. In certain areas around the world, these gender differences do appear to be narrowing over time. In some countries, educational and career opportunities for women are expanding, and in some parts of the world control over adolescent girls' romantic and sexual relationships is weakening. However, in many countries females still experience considerable discrimination, and much work is needed to bridge the gap between the rights of males and females.

Consider Dhaka, Bangladesh, where sewers overflow, garbage rots in the streets, and children are undernourished. Nearly two-thirds of the young women in Bangladesh get married before they are 18. Doly Akter, age 17, who lives in a slum in Dhaka, recently created an organization supported by UNICEF in which girls go door-to-door to monitor the hygiene habits of households in their neighborhood. The girls' monitoring has led to improved hygiene and health in the families. Also, the organization Doly formed has managed to stop several child marriages by meeting with parents and convincing them that early marriage is not in their daughters' best interests. When talking with parents in their neighbourhoods, the girls in the organization emphasize that staying in school will improve their daughters' futures. Doly says the girls in her organization are far more aware of their rights than their mothers were (UNICEF, 2007).

*What health and well-being, parenting, and educational problems and interventions have affected the development of females worldwide?*

## FIGURE 1.2

**PERCENTAGE OF CHILDREN 7 TO 18 YEARS OF AGE AROUND THE WORLD WHO HAVE NEVER BEEN TO SCHOOL OF ANY KIND.**
When UNICEF (2004) surveyed the education that children around the world are receiving, it found that far more girls than boys receive no formal schooling at all.

Doly Akter

## Review Connect Reflect

**LO1** Identify five areas in which children's lives need to be improved, and explain the role of resilience in children's development.

### Review

- What are several aspects of children's development that need to be improved?
- What characterizes resilience in children's development?

### Connect

- How is the concept of resilience related to the story you read at the beginning of this chapter?

### Reflect *Your Own Personal Journey of Life*

- Imagine what your development as a child would have been like in a culture that offered choices that were fewer or distinctively different from your own. How might your development have been different if your family had been significantly richer or poorer than it was as you were growing up?

---

## Developmental Processes, Periods, and Issues

 **LO2** Discuss the most important processes, periods, and issues in development.

| Biological, Cognitive, and Socioemotional Processes | Periods of Development | Age and Cohort Effects | Issues in Development |

Each of us develops in certain ways like *all* other individuals, like *some* other individuals, and like *no* other individuals. Most of the time, our attention is directed to a person's uniqueness, but psychologists who study development are drawn to both our shared characteristics and those that make us unique. As humans, we all have travelled some common paths. Each of us—Leonardo da Vinci, Joan of Arc, Albert Einstein, Nelson Mandela, and you—walked at about the age of one, engaged in fantasy play as a young child, and became more independent as a youth. What shapes this common path of human development, and what are its milestones?

## BIOLOGICAL, COGNITIVE, AND SOCIOEMOTIONAL PROCESSES

The pattern of human development is created by the interplay of three key processes. They are biological, cognitive, and socioemotional in nature.

**biological processes** Changes in an individual's body.

**Biological Processes**   Biological processes produce changes in an individual's body. Genes inherited from parents, the development of the brain, height and weight gains, development of motor skills, and the hormonal changes of puberty all reflect the role of biological processes in development.

**cognitive processes** Changes in an individual's thinking, intelligence, and language.

**Cognitive Processes**   Cognitive processes refer to changes in an individual's thinking, intelligence, and language. Watching a mobile swinging above a crib, putting together a two-word sentence, memorizing a poem, solving a math problem, and imagining what it would be like to be a movie star all involve cognitive processes.

**socioemotional processes** Changes in an individual's relationships with other people, emotions, and personality.

**Socioemotional Processes**   Socioemotional processes involve changes in an individual's relationships with other people, changes in emotions, and changes in personality. An infant's smile in response to her mother's touch, a child's attack on a playmate, another's development of assertiveness, and an adolescent's joy at the senior prom all reflect socioemotional development.

### Connecting Biological, Cognitive, and Socioemotional Processes

According to Adele Diamond, one of Canada's leading experts in child development, biological, cognitive, and socioemotional processes are inextricably intertwined (Diamond, 2009; Diamond, Casey, & Munakata, 2011). Consider a baby smiling in response to a parent's touch. This response depends on biological processes (the physical nature of touch and responsiveness to it), cognitive processes (the ability to understand intentional acts), and socioemotional processes (the act

of smiling often reflects a positive emotional feeling, and smiling helps to connect us in positive ways with other human beings).

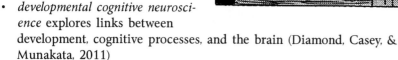

PEANUTS © United Features Syndicate, Inc.

Nowhere is the connection across biological, cognitive, and socioemotional processes more obvious than in two rapidly emerging fields:

- *developmental cognitive neuroscience* explores links between development, cognitive processes, and the brain (Diamond, Casey, & Munakata, 2011)

- *developmental social neuroscience* examines connections between development, socioemotional processes, and the brain (Calkins & Bell, 2010; de Haan & Gunnar, 2009; Johnson & others, 2009)

In many instances, biological, cognitive, and socioemotional processes are bidirectional. For example, biological processes can influence cognitive processes and vice versa. Thus, although usually we will study the different processes of development (biological, cognitive, and socioemotional) in separate locations, keep in mind that we are talking about the development of an integrated individual with a mind and body that are interdependent (see Figure 1.3).

In many places throughout the book we will call attention to connections between biological, cognitive, and socioemotional processes. A feature titled *Developmental Connections* appears multiple times in each chapter to highlight these as well as other content connections earlier or later in the text.

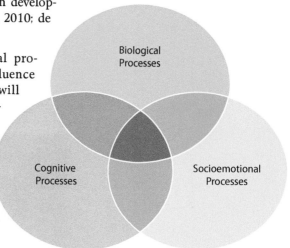

FIGURE **1.3**

**CHANGES IN DEVELOPMENT ARE THE RESULT OF BIOLOGICAL, COGNITIVE, AND SOCIOEMOTIONAL PROCESSES.** The processes interact as individuals develop.

## PERIODS OF DEVELOPMENT

For purposes of organization and understanding, a child's development is commonly described in terms of periods that correspond to approximate age ranges. The most widely used classification of developmental periods describes a child's development in terms of the following sequence: the prenatal period, infancy, early childhood, middle and late childhood, and adolescence.

The **prenatal period** is the time from conception to birth, roughly a nine-month period. During this amazing time, a single cell grows into an organism, complete with a brain and behavioural capabilities.

**Infancy** is the developmental period that extends from birth to about 18 to 24 months of age. Infancy is a time of extreme dependence on adults. Many psychological activities are just beginning—the abilities to speak, to coordinate sensations and physical actions, to think with symbols, and to imitate and learn from others.

**Early childhood** is the developmental period that extends from the end of infancy to about 5 or 6 years of age; sometimes this period is called the

**prenatal period** The time from conception to birth.

**infancy** The developmental period that extends from birth to about 18 to 24 months.

**early childhood** The developmental period that extends from the end of infancy to about 5 or 6 years of age, sometimes called the preschool years.

*"This is the path to adulthood. You're here."*

**middle and late childhood** The developmental period that extends from about 6 to 11 years of age, sometimes called the elementary school years.

**adolescence** The developmental period of transition from childhood to early adulthood, entered at approximately 10 to 12 years of age and ending at 18 or 19 years of age.

preschool years. During this time, young children learn to become more self-sufficient and to care for themselves, they develop school readiness skills (following instructions, identifying letters), and they spend many hours in play and with peers. First grade typically marks the end of this period.

**Middle and late childhood** is the developmental period that extends between about 6 and 11 years of age; sometimes this period is referred to as the elementary school years. Children master the fundamental skills of reading, writing, and arithmetic, and they are formally exposed to the larger world and its culture. Achievement becomes a more central theme of the child's world, and self-control increases.

**Adolescence** is the developmental period of transition from childhood to early adulthood, entered at approximately 10 to 12 years of age and ending at about 18 to 19 years of age. Adolescence begins with rapid physical changes—dramatic gains in height and weight, changes in body contour, and the development of sexual characteristics such as enlargement of the breasts, growth of pubic and facial hair, and deepening of the voice. The pursuit of independence and an identity are prominent features of this period of development. More and more time is spent outside the family. Thought becomes more abstract, idealistic, and logical.

Today, developmentalists do not believe that change ends with adolescence (Depp, Vahia, & Jeste, 2010; Schaie, 2010, 2011). They describe development as a lifelong process. However, the purpose of this text is to describe the changes in development that take place from conception through adolescence. All of these periods of development are produced by the interplay of biological, cognitive, and socioemotional processes (see Figure 1.4).

**Periods of Development**

Prenatal period   Infancy   Early childhood   Middle and late childhood   Adolescence

Biological Processes

Cognitive Processes          Socioemotional Processes

**Processes of Development**

FIGURE **1.4**

**PROCESSES AND PERIODS OF DEVELOPMENT.** Development moves through the prenatal, infancy, early childhood, middle and late childhood, and adolescence periods. These periods of development are the result of biological, cognitive, and socioemotional processes.

# AGE AND COHORT EFFECTS

A cohort is a group of people who are born at a similar point in history and share similar experiences as a result, such as living through the Vietnam War or growing up in the same city around the same time. These shared experiences may produce a range of differences between cohorts (Schaie, 2012). For example, adults who grew up during the Great Depression and World War II are likely to differ from their counterparts who grew up during the booming 1990s in their educational opportunities and economic status, in how they were raised, their attitudes and experiences related to gender, and their exposure to technology. In research on development, **cohort effects** are due to a person's time of birth, era, or generation but not to actual age.

In recent years, generations have been given labels by the popular culture. The most recent label is **Millennials**, referring to the generation born after 1980—the first to come of age and enter emerging adulthood in the new millennium. Thus, today's children and many of their parents are Millennials. Two characteristics of Millennials stand out: (1) their ethnic diversity, and (2) their connection to technology (Pew Research Center, 2010).

As their ethnic diversity has increased over prior generations, many Millennial adolescents and emerging adults are more tolerant and open-minded than their counterparts in previous generations. One survey indicated that 60 percent of today's adolescents say their friends include a diversity of ethnic groups (Teenage Research Unlimited, 2004).

Another major cohort change involving Millenials is the dramatic increase in their use of technology and media (Gross, 2013; Roblyer & Doering, 2013). According to one analysis

> They are history's first "always connected" generation. Steeped in digital technology and social media, they treat their multi-tasking hand-held gadgets almost like a body-part—for better or worse. More than 8 in 10 say they sleep with a cell phone glowing by the bed, poised to disgorge texts, phone calls, emails, songs, news, videos, games, and wake-up jingles. But sometimes convenience yields to temptation. Nearly two-thirds admit to texting while driving (Pew Research Center, 2010, p. 1).

**cohort effects** Effects due to a person's time of birth, era, or generation, but not to actual age.

**Millennials** The generation born after 1980, the first to come of age and enter emerging adulthood in the new millenium.

# ISSUES IN DEVELOPMENT

Was Karla Homolka born a criminal or did her life turn her into one? Did her early experiences determine her later life? Is your own journey through life marked out ahead of time, or can your experiences change your path? Are experiences that occur early in your journey more important than later ones? Is your journey like taking an elevator up a skyscraper with distinct stops along the way, or more like a cruise down a river with smoother ebbs and flows? These questions point to three issues about the nature of development: the roles played by nature and nurture, stability and change, and continuity and discontinuity.

**Nature and Nurture**   The **nature-nurture issue** involves the debate about whether development is primarily influenced by nature or by nurture (Goodnow, 2010; Kagan, 2010). *Nature* refers to an organism's biological inheritance, *nurture* to its environmental experiences. Almost no one today argues that development can be explained by nature alone or by nurture alone. But some (nature proponents) claim that the most important influence on development is biological inheritance, and others (nurture proponents) claim that environmental experiences are the most important influence.

According to the nature proponents, just as a sunflower grows in an orderly way—unless it is defeated by an unfriendly environment—so does a person. The range of environments can be vast, but evolutionary and genetic foundations produce commonalities in growth and development (Cosmides, 2011; Goldsmith, 2011; Mader, 2011). We walk before we talk, speak one word before two words,

**nature-nurture issue** Debate about whether development is primarily influenced by nature or nurture. The nature proponents claim biological inheritance is the most important influence on development; the nurture proponents claim that environmental experiences are the most important.

developmental **connection**

**Biological Processes.** Can specific genes be linked to specific environmental experience? Chapter 2, LO 4

grow rapidly in infancy and less so in early childhood, and experience a rush of sexual hormones in puberty. Extreme environments—those that are psychologically barren or hostile—can stunt development, but nature proponents emphasize the influence of tendencies that are genetically wired into humans (Brooker, 2011; Raven, 2011).

By contrast, other psychologists emphasize the importance of nurture, or environmental experiences, to development (Gauvain & Parke, 2010; Grusec, 2011; Kopp, 2011). Experiences run the gamut from the individual's biological environment (nutrition, medical care, drugs, and physical accidents) to the social environment (family, peers, schools, community, media, and culture). For example, a child's diet can affect how tall the child grows and even how effectively the child can think and solve problems. Despite their genetic wiring, a child born and raised in a poor village in Bangladesh and a child in the suburbs of Calgary are likely to have different skills, different ways of thinking about the world, and different ways of relating to people.

**Continuity and Discontinuity**  Think about your own development for a moment. Did you become the person you are gradually, like the seedling that slowly, cumulatively grows into a giant oak? Or did you experience sudden, distinct changes, like the caterpillar that changes into a butterfly? (See Figure 1.5.)

The **continuity-discontinuity issue** focuses on the extent to which development involves gradual, cumulative change (continuity) or distinct stages (discontinuity). For the most part, developmentalists who emphasize nurture usually describe development as a gradual, continuous process, like the seedling's growth into an oak. Those who emphasize nature often describe development as a series of distinct stages, like the change from caterpillar to butterfly.

Consider continuity first. As the oak grows from seedling to giant oak, it becomes more oak—its development is continuous. Similarly, a child's first word, though seemingly an abrupt, discontinuous event, is actually the result of weeks and months of growth and practice. Puberty, another seemingly abrupt, discontinuous occurrence, is actually a gradual process occurring over several years.

Viewed in terms of discontinuity, each person is described as passing through a sequence of stages in which change is qualitatively rather than quantitatively different. As the caterpillar changes to a butterfly, it does not become more caterpillar but a different kind of organism—its development is discontinuous. Similarly, at some point a child moves from not being able to think abstractly about the world to being able to do so. This change is a qualitative, discontinuous change in development, not a quantitative, continuous change.

**Early and Later Experience**  The **early-later experience issue** focuses on the degree to which early experiences (especially in infancy) or later experiences are the key determinants of the child's development. That is, if infants experience harmful circumstances, can those experiences be overcome by later, positive ones? Or are the early experiences so crucial—possibly because they are the infant's first, prototypical experiences—that they cannot be overridden by a later, better environment? To those who emphasize early experiences, life is an unbroken trail on which a psychological quality can be traced back to its origin (Kagan, 1992, 2000). In contrast, to those who emphasize later experiences, development is like a river, continually ebbing and flowing.

The early-later experience issue has a long history and continues to be hotly debated among developmentalists (Kagan, 2010; McElwain, 2009). Plato was sure that infants who were rocked frequently became better athletes. Nineteenth-century ministers told parents in Sunday afternoon sermons that the way they handled their infants would determine their children's later character. Some developmentalists argue that unless infants and young children experience warm, nurturing care, their development will never quite be optimal (Finger & others, 2009).

**continuity-discontinuity issue** Debate about whether development involves gradual, cumulative change (continuity) or distinct stages (discontinuity).

Continuity

Discontinuity

FIGURE **1.5**

**CONTINUITY AND DISCONTINUITY IN DEVELOPMENT.** Is human development more like that of a seedling gradually growing into a giant oak or more like that of a caterpillar suddenly becoming a butterfly?

**early-later experience issue** Controversy regarding the degree to which early experiences (especially during infancy) or later experiences are the key determinants of children's development.

In contrast, later-experience advocates argue that children are malleable throughout development and that later sensitive caregiving is just as important as earlier sensitive caregiving. A number of developmentalists stress that too little attention has been given to later experiences in development (Baltes & Smith, 2008; Schaie, 2010, 2011; Scheibe & Carstensen, 2010; Staudinger & Gluck, 2011). They accept that early experiences are important contributors to development, but assert that they are no more important than later experiences. Jerome Kagan (2000, 2010) points out that even children who show the qualities of an inhibited temperament, which is linked to heredity, have the capacity to change their behaviour. In his research, almost one third of a group of children who had an inhibited temperament at 2 years of age were not unusually shy or fearful when they were 4 years of age (Kagan & Snidman, 1991).

People in Western cultures, especially those influenced by Freudian theory, have tended to support the idea that early experiences are more important than later experiences (Lamb & Sternberg, 1992). The majority of people in the world do not share this belief. For example, people in many Asian countries believe that experiences occurring after about 6 or 7 years of age are more important to development than are earlier experiences. This stance stems from the long-standing belief in Eastern cultures that children's reasoning skills begin to develop in important ways during middle childhood.

*What is the nature of the early and later experience issue?*

Where do most developmentalists stand with respect to the issues of nature-nurture, continuity-discontinuity, and early-later experience? To find out see *Connecting to Current Controversy.*

## connecting to current controversy

### Evaluating the Developmental Issues

Most developmentalists recognize that it is unwise to take an extreme position on the issues of nature and nurture, continuity and discontinuity, and early and later experiences. Development is not all nature or all nurture, not all continuity or all discontinuity, and not all early or later experiences. Nature and nurture, continuity and discontinuity, and early and later experiences all play a part in development through the human life span. Along with this consensus, there is still spirited debate about how strongly development is influenced by each of these factors

(Blakemore, Berenbaum, & Liben, 2009; Kagan, 2010). Are girls less likely to do well in math mostly because of inherited characteristics or because of society's expectations and because of how girls are raised? Can enriched experiences during adolescence remove deficits resulting from poverty, neglect, and poor schooling during childhood? The answers also have a bearing on social policy decisions about children and adolescents, and consequently on each of our lives.

*How strongly is development influenced by nature and nurture, continuity and discontinuity, or early and later experiences?*

### Review Connect Reflect

 Discuss the most important processes, periods, and issues in development.

### Review
- What are biological, cognitive, and socioemotional processes?
- What are the main periods of development?
- What are three important issues in development?

### Connect
- Based on what you read earlier in this chapter, what do you think Lincoln Alexander would have to say about the early-later experience issue?

### Reflect Your Own Personal Journey of Life
- Can you identify an early experience that you believe contributed in important ways to your development? Can you identify a recent or current (later) experience that you think had (or is having) a strong influence on your development?

## The Science of Child Development

 **LO3** Summarize why research is important in child development, the main theories in child development, and research methods, designs, and challenges.

| The Importance of Research | Research Methods for Collecting Data | Challenges in Child Development Research |
| --- | --- | --- |

| Theories of Child Development | Research Designs |
| --- | --- |

*Science refines everyday thinking.*

—ALBERT EINSTEIN
*German-born Theoretical Physicist, 20th Century*

Some people have difficulty thinking of child development as a science like physics, chemistry, and biology. Can a discipline that studies how parents nurture children, how peers interact, the ways in which children's thinking develops over time, and whether watching TV hour after hour is linked with being overweight be equated with disciplines that study the molecular structure of a compound and how gravity works? Is child development really a science?

A grade 12 student mentors a kindergarten child as part of a Book Buddy mentoring program. *If a researcher wanted to study the effects of the mentoring program on children's academic achievement by following the scientific method, what steps would the researcher take in setting up the study?*

**scientific method** An approach that can be used to obtain accurate information by carrying out four steps: (1) conceptualize the problem, (2) collect data, (3) analyze data and draw conclusions, and (4) revise research conclusions and theory.

**theory** An interrelated, coherent set of ideas that helps to explain and make predictions.

**hypothesis** Specific assumption and prediction that can be tested to determine its accuracy.

## THE IMPORTANCE OF RESEARCH

The answer to the last question is yes. Science is defined not by *what* it investigates, but by *how* it investigates. Whether you're studying photosynthesis, butterflies, Saturn's moons, or children's development, it is the way you study that makes the approach scientific or not. How can we determine, for example, whether special care can repair the harm inflicted by child neglect or whether mentoring can improve children's achievement in school?

Scientific research provides the best answers to such questions. *Scientific research* is objective, systematic, and testable. It reduces the likelihood that information will be based on personal beliefs, opinions, and feelings (Graziano & Raulin, 2010; Smith & Davis, 2010; Stangor, 2011). In conducting research, child development researchers use the **scientific method**, a four-step process: (1) conceptualize a process or problem to be studied, (2) collect research information (data), (3) analyze data and draw conclusions, and (4) revise research conclusions and theory.

## THEORIES OF CHILD DEVELOPMENT

Theorizing is part of the scientific study of children's development. In the scientific method just described, theories often guide the conceptualization of a process or problem to be studied. A **theory** is an interrelated, coherent set of ideas that helps to explain and to make predictions. For example, a theory on mentoring might attempt to explain and predict why sustained support, guidance, and concrete experience make a difference in the lives of children from impoverished backgrounds. The theory might focus on children's opportunities to model the behaviour and strategies of mentors, or it might focus on the effects of individual attention, which might be missing in the children's lives. A **hypothesis** is a specific, testable assumption or prediction. A hypothesis is often written as an *if-then* statement. In our example, a sample hypothesis might be: *If children from impoverished backgrounds are given individual attention by mentors, then the children will spend more time studying and earn higher grades.* Testing a hypothesis can inform researchers whether a theory is likely to be accurate.

| Oral Stage | Anal Stage | Phallic Stage | Latency Stage | Genital Stage |
|---|---|---|---|---|
| Infant's pleasure centers on the mouth. | Child's pleasure focuses on the anus. | Child's pleasure focuses on the genitals. | Child represses sexual interest and develops social and intellectual skills. | A time of sexual reawakening; source of sexual pleasure becomes someone outside the family. |
| Birth to 1½ Years | 1½ to 3 Years | 3 to 6 Years | 6 Years to Puberty | Puberty Onward |

## FIGURE 1.6
**FREUDIAN STAGES.**

Wide-ranging theories make understanding children's development a challenging undertaking. This section outlines key aspects of five theoretical orientations to development: psychoanalytic, cognitive, behavioural and social cognitive, ethological, and ecological. Each contributes an important piece to the puzzle of understanding children's development. Although the theories disagree about certain aspects of development, many of their ideas are complementary rather than contradictory. Together they let us see the total landscape of children's development in all its richness.

**Psychoanalytic Theories**   Psychoanalytic theories describe development as primarily unconscious (beyond awareness) and heavily colored by emotion. Psychoanalytic theorists emphasize that behaviour is merely a surface characteristic and that a true understanding of development requires analyzing the symbolic meanings of behaviour and the deep inner workings of the mind. Psychoanalytic theorists also stress that early experiences with parents extensively shape development. These characteristics are highlighted in the psychoanalytic theory of Sigmund Freud (1856–1939).

*Freud's Theory*   As Freud listened to, probed, and analyzed his patients, he became convinced that their problems were the result of experiences early in life. He thought that as children grow up their focus of pleasure and sexual impulses shifts from the mouth to the anus and eventually to the genitals. As a result, we go through five stages of psychosexual development: oral, anal, phallic, latency, and genital (see Figure 1.6). Our adult personality, Freud (1917) claimed, is determined by the way we resolve conflicts between sources of pleasure at each stage and the demands of reality.

Freud's theory has been significantly revised by a number of psychoanalytic theorists. Many of today's psychoanalytic theorists maintain that Freud overemphasized sexual instincts; they place more emphasis on cultural experiences as determinants of an individual's development. Unconscious thought remains a central theme, but thought plays a greater role than Freud envisioned. Next, we will outline the ideas of an important revisionist of Freud's ideas—Erik Erikson.

*Erikson's Psychosocial Theory*   Erik Erikson (1902–1994) recognized Freud's contributions but believed that Freud misjudged some important dimensions of human development. For one thing, Erikson (1950, 1968) said we develop in psychosocial stages, rather than in psychosexual stages, as Freud maintained. According to Freud, the primary motivation for human behaviour is sexual in nature; according to Erikson it is social and reflects a desire to affiliate with other people. According to Freud, our basic personality is shaped in the first five years of life; according to Erikson, developmental change occurs throughout the life span. Thus, in terms of the early-versus-later-experience issue described earlier in the chapter, Freud viewed early experience as far more important than later experiences, whereas Erikson emphasized the importance of both early and later experiences.

In **Erikson's theory**, eight stages of development unfold as we go through life (see Figure 1.7). At each stage, a unique developmental task confronts

**psychoanalytic theories** Theories that describe development as primarily unconscious and heavily coloured by emotion. Behaviour is merely a surface characteristic, and the symbolic workings of the mind have to be analyzed to understand behaviour. Early experiences with parents are emphasized.

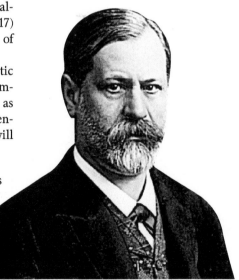

Sigmund Freud, the pioneering architect of psychoanalytic theory. *What are some characteristics of Freud's theory?*

**Erikson's theory** Description of eight stages of human development. Each stage consists of a unique developmental task that confronts individuals with a crisis that must be resolved.

| Erikson's Stages | Developmental Period |
|---|---|
| Integrity versus despair | Late adulthood (60s onward) |
| Generativity versus stagnation | Middle adulthood (40s, 50s) |
| Intimacy versus isolation | Early adulthood (20s, 30s) |
| Identity versus identity confusion | Adolescence (10 to 20 years) |
| Industry versus inferiority | Middle and late childhood (elementary school years, 6 years to puberty) |
| Initiative versus guilt | Early childhood (preschool years, 3 to 5 years) |
| Autonomy versus shame and doubt | Infancy (1 to 3 years) |
| Trust versus mistrust | Infancy (first year) |

## FIGURE **1.7**
**ERIKSON'S EIGHT LIFE-SPAN STAGES.**

### developmental **connection**

**Culture and Ethnicity.** What characterizes an adolescent's ethnic identity? Chapter 11, LO 3

Erik Erikson with his wife, Joan, an artist. Erikson generated one of the most important developmental theories of the twentieth century. *Which stage of Erikson's theory are you in? Does Erikson's description of this stage characterize you?*

individuals with a crisis that must be resolved. According to Erikson, this crisis is not a catastrophe but a turning point marked by both increased vulnerability and enhanced potential. The more successfully an individual resolves the crises, the healthier development will be.

*Trust versus mistrust* is Erikson's first psychosocial stage, which is experienced in the first year of life. Trust in infancy sets the stage for a lifelong expectation that the world will be a good and pleasant place to live.

*Autonomy versus shame and doubt* is Erikson's second stage. This stage occurs in late infancy and toddlerhood (1 to 3 years). After gaining trust in their caregivers, infants begin to discover that their behaviour is their own. They start to assert their sense of independence or autonomy. They realize their will. If infants and toddlers are restrained too much or punished too harshly, they are likely to develop a sense of shame and doubt.

*Initiative versus guilt,* Erikson's third stage of development, occurs during the preschool years. As preschool children encounter a widening social world, they face new challenges that require active, purposeful, responsible behaviour. Feelings of guilt may arise, though, if the child is irresponsible and is made to feel too anxious.

*Industry versus inferiority* is Erikson's fourth developmental stage, occurring approximately in the elementary school years. Children now need to direct their energy toward mastering knowledge and intellectual skills. The negative outcome is that the child may develop a sense of inferiority—feeling incompetent and unproductive.

During the adolescent years, individuals face finding out who they are, what they are all about, and where they are going in life. This is Erikson's fifth developmental stage, *identity versus identity confusion.* If adolescents explore roles in a healthy manner and arrive at a positive path to follow in life, then they achieve a positive identity; if not, identity confusion reigns.

*Intimacy versus isolation* is Erikson's sixth developmental stage, which individuals experience during the early adulthood years. At this time, individuals face the developmental task of forming intimate relationships. If young adults form healthy friendships and an intimate relationship with another, intimacy will be achieved; if not, isolation will result.

*Generativity versus stagnation,* Erikson's seventh developmental stage, occurs during middle adulthood. By generativity Erikson means primarily a concern for helping the younger generation to develop and lead useful lives. The feeling of having done nothing to help the next generation is stagnation.

*Integrity versus despair* is Erikson's eighth and final stage of development, which individuals experience in late adulthood. During this stage, a person reflects on the past. If the person's life review reveals a life well spent, integrity will be achieved; if not, the retrospective glances likely will yield doubt or gloom—the despair Erikson described.

We will discuss Erikson's theory again in the chapters on socioemotional development.

*Evaluating Psychoanalytic Theories*   Contributions of psychoanalytic theories include an emphasis on a developmental framework, family relationships, and unconscious aspects of the mind. Criticisms include a lack of scientific support, too much emphasis on sexual underpinnings (Freud's theory), too much credit given to the unconscious mind, and an image of children that is too negative (Freud's theory).

**Cognitive Theories**   Whereas psychoanalytic theories stress the importance of the unconscious, cognitive theories emphasize conscious thoughts. Three important cognitive theories are Piaget's cognitive developmental theory, Vygotsky's sociocultural cognitive theory, and information-processing theory.

*Piaget's Cognitive Developmental Theory*   **Piaget's theory** states that children actively construct their understanding of the world and go through four stages of cognitive development. Two processes underlie the four stages of development in Piaget's theory: organization and adaptation. To make sense of our world, we organize our experiences. For example, we separate important ideas from less important ideas, and we connect one idea to another. In addition to organizing our observations and experiences, we *adapt*, adjusting to new environmental demands (Byrnes, 2008).

Piaget (1954) also held that we go through four stages in understanding the world (see Figure 1.8). Each stage is age related and consists of a distinct way of thinking, a *different* way of understanding the world. Thus, according to Piaget, the child's cognition is *qualitatively* different in one stage compared with another. What are Piaget's four stages of cognitive development like?

The *sensorimotor stage*, which lasts from birth to about 2 years of age, is the first Piagetian stage. In this stage, infants construct an understanding of the world by coordinating sensory experiences (such as seeing and hearing) with physical, motoric actions—hence the term *sensorimotor*.

The *preoperational stage*, which lasts from approximately 2 to 7 years of age, is Piaget's second stage. In this stage, children begin to go beyond simply connecting

*One's children's children's children. Look back to us as we look to you; we are related by our imaginations. If we are able to touch, it is because we have imagined each other's existence, our dreams running back and forth along a cable from age to age.*

—Roger Rosenblatt
*American Writer, 20th Century*

**Piaget's theory** Theory stating that children actively construct their understanding of the world and go through four stages of cognitive development.

| **Sensorimotor Stage** | **Preoperational Stage** | **Concrete Operational Stage** | **Formal Operational Stage** |
|---|---|---|---|
| The infant constructs an understanding of the world by coordinating sensory experiences with physical actions. An infant progresses from reflexive, instinctual action at birth to the beginning of symbolic thought toward the end of the stage. | The child begins to represent the world with words and images. These words and images reflect increased symbolic thinking and go beyond the connection of sensory information and physical action. | The child can now reason logically about concrete events and classify objects into different sets. | The adolescent reasons in more abstract, idealistic, and logical ways. |
| **Birth to 2 Years of Age** | **2 to 7 Years of Age** | **7 to 11 Years of Age** | **11 Years of Age Through Adulthood** |

FIGURE **1.8**

**PIAGET'S FOUR STAGES OF COGNITIVE DEVELOPMENT.**

sensory information with physical action and represent the world with words, images, and drawings. However, according to Piaget, preschool children still lack the ability to perform what he calls *operations*, which are internalized mental actions that allow children to do mentally what they previously could only do physically. For example, if you imagine putting two sticks together to see whether they would be as long as another stick, without actually moving the sticks, you are performing a concrete operation.

The *concrete operational stage*, which lasts from approximately 7 to 11 years of age, is the third Piagetian stage. In this stage, children can perform operations that involve objects, and they can reason logically as long as reasoning can be applied to specific or concrete examples. For instance, concrete operational thinkers cannot imagine the steps necessary to complete an algebraic equation, which is too abstract for thinking at this stage of development.

The *formal operational stage*, which appears between the ages of 11 and 15 and continues through adulthood, is Piaget's fourth and final stage. In this stage, individuals move beyond concrete experiences and think in abstract and more logical terms. As part of thinking more abstractly, adolescents develop images of ideal circumstances. They might think about what an ideal parent is like and compare their parents to this ideal standard. They begin to entertain possibilities for the future and are fascinated with what they can be. In solving problems, they become more systematic, developing hypotheses about why something is happening the way it is and then testing these hypotheses.

The preceding discussion is a brief introduction to Piaget's theory. It is provided here, along with other theories, to give you a broad understanding. In Chapter 6, "Cognitive Developmental Approaches," we will return to Piaget and examine his theory in more depth.

**developmental** **connection**

**Cognitive Theory.** We owe to Piaget the entire field of children's cognitive development, but a number of criticisms of his theory have been made. Chapter 6, LO 2

Jean Piaget (1896–1980), the famous Swiss developmental psychologist, changed the way we think about the development of children's minds. *What are some key ideas in Piaget's theory?*

There is considerable interest today in Lev Vygotsky's sociocultural cognitive theory of child development. *What were Vygotsky's basic ideas about children's development?*

**Vygotsky's theory** A sociocultural cognitive theory that emphasizes how culture and social interaction guide cognitive development.

*Vygotsky's Sociocultural Cognitive Theory* Like Piaget, the Russian developmentalist Lev Vygotsky (1896–1934) argued that children actively construct their knowledge. However, Vygotsky (1962) gave social interaction and culture far more important roles in cognitive development than Piaget did. **Vygotsky's theory** is a socio-cultural cognitive theory that emphasizes how culture and social interaction guide cognitive development.

Vygotsky portrayed the child's development as inseparable from social and cultural activities (Gauvain & Parke, 2010; Holzman, 2009). He argued that development of memory, attention, and reasoning involves learning to use the inventions of society, such as language, mathematical systems, and memory strategies. Thus, in one culture, children might learn to count with the help of a computer; in another, they might learn by using beads. According to Vygotsky, children's social interaction with more-skilled adults and peers is indispensable to their cognitive development. Through this interaction, they learn to use the tools that will help them adapt and be successful in their culture. For example, if you regularly help children learn how to read, you not only advance their reading skills but also communicate to them that reading is an important activity in their culture.

Vygotsky's theory has stimulated considerable interest in the view that knowledge is *situated* and *collaborative* (Gauvain & Parke, 2010). In this view, knowledge is not generated from within the individual but rather is constructed through interaction with other people and objects in the culture, such as books. This suggests that knowledge can best be advanced through interaction with others in cooperative activities.

Vygotsky's theory, like Piaget's, remained virtually unknown to North American psychologists until the 1960s, but eventually both became influential among educators as well as psychologists. We will further examine Vygotsky's theory in Chapter 6.

*The Information-Processing Theory*   Early computers may be the best candidates for the title of "founding fathers" of information-processing theory. Although many factors stimulated the growth of this theory, none was more important than the computer. Psychologists began to wonder if the logical operations carried out by computers might tell us something about how the human mind works. They drew analogies between a computer's hardware and the brain and between computer software and cognition.

This line of thinking helped to generate **information-processing theory,** which emphasizes that individuals manipulate information, monitor it, and strategize about it. Unlike Piaget's theory but like Vygotsky's theory, information-processing theory does not describe development as happening in stages. Instead, according to this theory, individuals develop a gradually increasing capacity for processing information, which allows them to acquire increasingly complex knowledge and skills (Sternberg, 2010a, b).

Robert Siegler (2006), a leading expert on children's information processing, states that thinking is information processing. In other words, when individuals perceive, encode, represent, store, and retrieve information, they are thinking. Siegler emphasizes that an important aspect of development is learning good strategies for processing information. For example, becoming a better reader might involve learning to monitor the key themes of the material being read.

*Evaluating the Cognitive Theories*   Contributions of cognitive theories include a positive view of development and an emphasis on the active construction of understanding. Criticisms include skepticism about the pureness of Piaget's stages and assertions that too little attention is paid to individual variations.

**Behavioural and Social Cognitive Theories**   At about the same time that Freud was interpreting patients' unconscious minds through their early childhood experiences, Ivan Pavlov and John B. Watson were conducting detailed observations of behaviour in controlled laboratory settings. Their work provided the foundations of *behaviourism,* which essentially holds that we can study scientifically only what can be directly observed and measured. Out of the behavioural tradition grew the belief that development is observable behaviour that can be learned through experience with the environment (Chance, 2009). In terms of the continuity-discontinuity issue discussed earlier in this chapter, the behavioural and social cognitive theories emphasize continuity in development and argue that development does not occur in stages. The three versions of the behavioural approach that we will explore are Pavlov's classical conditioning, Skinner's operant conditioning, and Bandura's social cognitive theory.

*Pavlov's Classical Conditioning*   In the early 1900s, the Russian physiologist Ivan Pavlov (1927) knew that dogs salivate when they taste food. He became curious when he observed that dogs also salivate at various sights and sounds before eating their food. For example, when an individual paired the ringing of a bell with the food, the bell ringing subsequently elicited salivation from the dogs when it was presented by itself. With this experiment, Pavlov discovered the principle of *classical conditioning,* in which a neutral stimulus (in our example, hearing a bell ring) acquires the ability to produce a response originally produced by another stimulus (in our example, tasting food).

*developmental* **connection**

**Education.** Applications of Vygotsky's theory to children's education have been made in recent years. Chapter 6, LO 3

**information-processing theory** Emphasizes that individuals manipulate information, monitor it, and strategize about it. Central to this theory are the processes of memory and thinking.

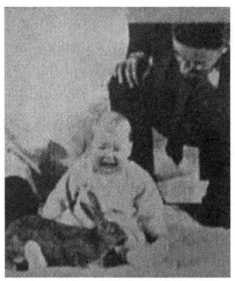

In 1920, Watson and Rayner conditioned 11-month-old Albert to fear a white rat by pairing the rat with a loud noise. When little Albert was subsequently presented with other stimuli similar to the white rat, such as the rabbit shown here with little Albert, he was afraid of them, too. This illustrates the principle of stimulus generalization in classical conditioning.

B. F. Skinner was a tinkerer who liked to make new gadgets. The younger of his two daughters, Deborah, was raised in Skinner's enclosed Air-Crib, which he invented because he wanted to control her environment completely. The Air-Crib was soundproofed and temperature controlled. Debbie, shown here as a child with her parents, is currently a successful artist, is married, and lives in London, England. *What do you think about Skinner's Air-Crib?*

In the early twentieth century, John Watson and Rosalie Rayner (1920) demonstrated that classical conditioning occurs in human beings. He showed an infant named Albert a white rat to see if he was afraid of it. He was not. As Albert played with the rat, a loud noise was sounded behind his head. As you might imagine, the noise caused little Albert to cry. After several pairings of the loud noise and the white rat, Albert began to cry at the sight of the rat even when the noise was not sounded. Albert had been classically conditioned to fear the rat. Similarly, many of our fears may result from classical conditioning: fear of the dentist may be learned from a painful experience, fear of driving from being in an automobile accident, fear of heights from falling off a highchair when we were infants, and fear of dogs from being bitten.

*Skinner's Operant Conditioning*   Classical conditioning may explain how we develop many involuntary responses such as fears, but B. F. Skinner argued that a second type of conditioning accounts for the development of other types of behaviour. According to Skinner (1938), through *operant conditioning* the consequences of a behaviour produce changes in the probability of the behaviour's occurrence. A behaviour followed by a rewarding stimulus is more likely to recur, whereas a behaviour followed by a punishing stimulus is less likely to recur. For example, when a person smiles at a child after the child has done something, the child is more likely to engage in the activity than if the person gives the child a nasty look.

According to Skinner, such rewards and punishments shape development. For example, Skinner's approach argues that shy people learned to be shy as a result of experiences they had while growing up. It follows that modifications in an environment can help a shy person become more socially oriented. Also, for Skinner the key aspect of development is behaviour, not thoughts and feelings. He emphasized that development consists of the pattern of behavioural changes that are brought about by rewards and punishments.

*Bandura's Social Cognitive Theory*   Some psychologists agree with the behaviourists' notion that development is learned and is influenced strongly by environmental interactions. However, unlike Skinner, they argue that cognition is also

Albert Bandura has been one of the leading architects of social cognitive theory. *How does Bandura's theory differ from Skinner's?*

important in understanding development. **Social cognitive theory** holds that behaviour, environment, and cognition are the key factors in development.

Canadian-born psychologist Albert Bandura (1925– ) is the leading architect of social cognitive theory. Bandura (2001, 2007, 2009, 2010a, b) emphasizes that cognitive processes have important links with the environment and behaviour. His early research program focused heavily on *observational learning* (also called *imitation* or *modeling*), which is learning that occurs through observing what others do. For example, a young boy might observe his father yelling in anger and treating other people with hostility; with his peers, the young boy later acts very aggressively, showing the same characteristics his father displayed. A girl might adopt the dominant and sarcastic style of her teacher, saying to her younger brother, "You are so slow. How can you do this work so slowly?" Social cognitive theorists stress that people acquire a wide range of behaviours, thoughts, and feelings through observing others' behaviour and that these observations form an important part of children's development.

What is *cognitive* about observational learning, in Bandura's view? He proposes that people cognitively represent the behaviour of others and then sometimes adopt this behaviour themselves.

Bandura's (2001, 2007, 2009, 2010a, b) most recent model of learning and development includes three elements: behaviour, the person/cognition, and the environment. An individual's confidence that he or she can control his or her success is an example of a person factor; strategies are an example of a cognitive factor. As shown in Figure 1.9, behaviour, person/cognition, and environmental factors operate interactively. Behaviour can influence person factors and vice versa. Cognitive activities can influence the environment. The environment can change the person's cognition, and so on.

*Evaluating the Behavioural and Social Cognitive Theories*   Contributions of the behavioural and social cognitive theories include an emphasis on scientific research and environmental determinants of behaviour, and in Bandura's social cognitive theory reciprocal links between the environment, behaviour, and person/cognitive factors. Criticisms include too little emphasis on cognition in Skinner's view and giving inadequate attention to developmental changes and biological foundations.

Behavioural and social cognitive theories emphasize the importance of environmental experiences in human development. Next we turn our attention to a theory that underscores the importance of the biological foundations of development—ethological theory.

**Ethological Theory**   Developmental psychologists began to pay attention to the biological bases of development during the mid-twentieth century thanks to the work of European zoologists who pioneered the field of ethology. **Ethology** stresses that behaviour is strongly influenced by biology, is tied to evolution, and is characterized by critical or sensitive periods. These are specific time frames during which, according to ethologists, the presence or absence of certain experiences has a long-lasting influence on individuals.

European zoologist Konrad Lorenz (1903–1989) helped bring ethology to prominence. In his best-known experiment, Lorenz (1965) studied the behaviour of greylag geese, which will follow their mothers as soon as they hatch.

In a remarkable set of experiments, Lorenz separated the eggs laid by one goose into two groups. One group he returned to the goose to be hatched by her. The other group was hatched in an incubator. The goslings in the first group performed as predicted. They followed their mother as soon as they hatched. However, those in the second group, which saw Lorenz when they first hatched, followed him everywhere, as though he were their mother. Lorenz marked the goslings and then placed both groups under a box. Mother goose and "mother" Lorenz stood aside as the box lifted. Each group of goslings went directly to its "mother." Lorenz called this process *imprinting*—rapid, innate learning within a limited, critical period of time that involves attachment to the first moving object seen.

**social cognitive theory** The view of psychologists who emphasize behaviour, environment, and cognition as the key factors in development.

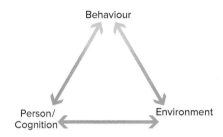

**FIGURE 1.9**
**BANDURA'S SOCIAL COGNITIVE MODEL.** The arrows illustrate how relations between behaviour, person/cognition, and environment are reciprocal rather than unidirectional.

*developmental* **connection**

**Attachment.** Human babies go through a series of phases in developing an attachment to a caregiver. Chapter 10, LO 4

**ethology** Stresses that behaviour is strongly influenced by biology, is tied to evolution, and is characterized by critical or sensitive periods.

Konrad Lorenz, a pioneering student of animal behaviour, is followed through the water by three imprinted greylag geese. *Do you think his experiment would have the same results with human babies? Why or why not?*

At first, ethological research and theory had little or nothing to say about the nature of social relationships across the *human* life span, and the theory stimulated few studies involving people. Ethologists' viewpoint that normal development requires that certain behaviours emerge during a *critical period,* a fixed time period very early in development, seemed to be overstated. However, John Bowlby's work (1969, 1989) illustrated an important application of ethological theory to human development. Bowlby argued that attachment to a caregiver over the first year of life has important consequences throughout the life span. In his view, if this attachment is positive and secure, the infant will likely develop positively in childhood and adulthood. If the attachment is negative and insecure, children's development will likely not be optimal. Thus, in this view the first year of life is a *sensitive period* for the development of social relationships. In Chapter 10, "Emotional Development," we will explore the concept of infant attachment in greater detail.

*Evaluating Ethological Theory*   Contributions of ethological theory include a focus on the biological and evolutionary basis of development, and the use of careful observations in naturalistic settings. Critics assert that too much emphasis is placed on biological foundations and that the critical and sensitive period concepts might be too rigid.

Another theory that emphasizes the biological aspects of human development— evolutionary psychology—will be presented in Chapter 2, "Biological Beginnings," along with views on the role of heredity in development.

**Ecological Theory**   Whereas ethological theory stresses biological factors, ecological theory emphasizes environmental factors. One ecological theory that has important implications for understanding children's development was created by Urie Bronfenbrenner (1917–2005).

**Bronfenbrenner's ecological theory** (1986, 2000, 2004; Bronfenbrenner & Morris, 1998, 2006) holds that development reflects the influence of several environmental systems. The theory identifies five environmental systems (see Figure 1.10):

- *Microsystem:* The setting in which the individual lives. These contexts include the person's family, peers, school, neighbourhood, and work. It is within the microsystem that the most direct interactions with social agents take place—with parents, peers, and teachers, for example.
- *Mesosystem:* Relations between microsystems or connections between contexts. Examples are the relationships between family experiences and school experiences, school experiences and experiences within a religious organization, and family experiences and peer experiences. For example, children whose parents have rejected them may have difficulty developing positive relationships with teachers.

**Bronfenbrenner's ecological theory** An environmental systems theory that focuses on five environmental systems: microsystem, mesosystem, exosystem, macrosystem, and chronosystem.

- *Exosystem:* Links between a social setting in which the individual does not have an active role and the individual's immediate context. For example, a child's experience at home may be influenced by a mother's experiences at work. The mother might receive a promotion that requires more travel, which might increase conflict with her spouse and change patterns of interaction with the child.

- *Macrosystem:* The culture in which individuals live. Remember from earlier in this chapter that *culture* refers to the behaviour patterns, beliefs, and all other products of a group of people that are passed on from generation to generation. Remember also that cross-cultural studies—comparisons of one culture with one or more other cultures—provide information about the generality of development (Kitayama, 2011; Shiraev & Levy, 2010).

- *Chronosystem:* The patterning of environmental events and transitions over the life course,

as well as sociohistorical circumstances (Schaie, 2009, 2010, 2011). For example, divorce is one transition. Researchers have found that the negative effects of divorce on children often peak in the first year after the divorce (Hetherington, 1993, 2006). By two years after the divorce, family interaction is less chaotic and more stable. As an example of sociohistorical circumstances, consider how career opportunities for women have increased during the last 30 years.

Bronfenbrenner (2000, 2004; Bronfenbrenner & Morris, 1998, 2006) has added biological influences to his theory and now describes it as a *bioecological* theory. Nonetheless, ecological, environmental contexts still predominate in Bronfenbrenner's theory (Gauvain & Parke, 2010).

*Evaluating Ecological Theory* Contributions of ecological theory include a systematic examination of macro and micro dimensions of environmental systems, and attention to connections between environmental systems. A further contribution of Bronfenbrenner's theory is its emphasis on a range of social contexts beyond the family, such as neighbourhood, religious organization, school, and workplace, as influential in children's development (Gauvain & Parke, 2010). Criticisms include giving inadequate attention to biological factors as well as placing too little emphasis on cognitive factors.

**An Eclectic Theoretical Orientation** No single theory described in this chapter can explain entirely the rich complexity of children's development, but each has contributed to our understanding of development. Psychoanalytic theory

**FIGURE 1.10**

**BRONFENBRENNER'S ECOLOGICAL THEORY OF DEVELOPMENT.** Bronfenbrenner's ecological theory consists of five environmental systems: microsystem, mesosystem, exosystem, macrosystem, and chronosystem.

**Macrosystem**
Attitudes and ideologies of the culture

**Exosystem**

**Mesosystem**

**Microsystem**

Friends of family

Neighbours

Family

School

Health services

The individual
Sex
Age
Health
etc.

Peers

Religious group

Neighbourhood play area

Mass media

Legal services

Social welfare services

**Chronosystem**
Patterning of environmental events and transitions over the life course; sociohistorical conditions

**Time**
(sociohistorical conditions and time since life events)

Urie Bronfenbrenner developed ecological theory, a perspective that is receiving increased attention. *What is the nature of ecological theory?*

best explains the unconscious mind. Erikson's theory best describes the changes that occur in adult development. Piaget's, Vygotsky's, and the information-processing views provide the most complete description of cognitive development. The behavioural and social cognitive and ecological theories have been the most adept at examining the environmental determinants of development. The ethological theories have highlighted biology's role and the importance of sensitive periods in development.

In short, although theories are helpful guides, relying on a single theory to explain development is probably a mistake. This book instead has an **eclectic theoretical orientation**, which does not follow any one theoretical approach but rather selects from each theory whatever is considered its best features. In this way, you can view the study of development as it actually exists—with different theorists making different assumptions, stressing different empirical problems, and using different strategies to discover information. Figure 1.11 compares the main theoretical perspectives in terms of how they view important issues in children's development.

**eclectic theoretical orientation** An orientation that does not follow any one theoretical approach but rather selects from each theory whatever is considered its best aspects.

## RESEARCH METHODS FOR COLLECTING DATA

If they follow an eclectic orientation, how do scholars and researchers determine that one feature of a theory is somehow better than another? The scientific method discussed earlier in this chapter provides the guide. Recall that the steps in the scientific method involve conceptualizing the problem, collecting data, drawing conclusions, and revising research conclusions and theories. Through scientific research, the features of theories can be tested and refined.

Whether we are interested in studying attachment in infants, the cognitive skills of children, or peer relations among adolescents, we can choose from several ways of collecting data. Here we outline the measures most often used, looking at the advantages and disadvantages of each.

**Observation**   Scientific observation requires an important set of skills (Christensen, Johnson, & Turner, 2011). Unless we are trained observers and practice our skills regularly, we might not know what to look for, we might not remember what we

| THEORY | ISSUES | | |
| --- | --- | --- | --- |
| | **Nature and nurture** | **Early and later experience** | **Continuity and discontinuity** |
| **Psychoanalytic** | Freud's biological determinism interacting with early family experiences; Erikson's more balanced biological/cultural interaction perspective | Early experiences in the family very important influences | Emphasis on discontinuity between stages |
| **Cognitive** | Piaget's emphasis on interaction and adaptation; environment provides the setting for cognitive structures to develop. Vygotsky's theory involves interaction of nature and nurture with strong emphasis on culture. The information-processing approach has not addressed this issue extensively; mainly emphasizes biological/environment interaction. | Childhood experiences important influences | Discontinuity between stages in Piaget's theory; no stages in Vygotsky's theory or the information-processing approach |
| **Behavioural and Social Cognitive** | Environment viewed as the main influence on development | Experiences important at all points in development | Continuity with no stages |
| **Ethological** | Strong biological view | Early experience very important, which can contribute to change early in development; after early critical or sensitive period has passed, stability likely to occur | Discontinuity because of early critical or sensitive period; no stages |
| **Ecological** | Strong environmental view | Experiences involving the five environmental systems important at all points in development | No stages but little attention to the issue |

FIGURE **1.11**

**A COMPARISON OF THEORIES AND ISSUES IN CHILD DEVELOPMENT.**

*What are some important strategies in conducting observational research with children?*

saw, we might not realize that what we are looking for is changing from one moment to the next, and we might not communicate our observations effectively.

For observations to be effective, they have to be systematic. We have to have some idea of what we are looking for. We have to know who we are observing, when and where we will observe, how the observations will be made, and how they will be recorded.

Where should we make our observations? We have two choices: the laboratory and the everyday world.

When we observe scientifically, we often need to control certain factors that determine behaviour but are not the focus of our inquiry (Babble, 2011). For this reason, some research in life-span development is conducted in a **laboratory**, a controlled setting from which many of the complex factors of the "real world" have been removed. For example, suppose you want to observe how children react when they see other people behave aggressively. If you observe children in their homes or schools you have no control over how much aggression the children observe, what kind of aggression they see, which people they see acting aggressively, or how other people treat the children. In contrast, if you observe the children in a laboratory, you can control these and other factors and therefore have more confidence about how to interpret your observations.

> **laboratory** A controlled setting from which many of the complex factors of the "real world" have been removed.

Laboratory research does have some drawbacks, however, including the following:

- It is almost impossible to conduct research without letting participants know they are being studied.
- The laboratory setting is unnatural and therefore can cause the participants to behave unnaturally.
- People who are willing to come to a university laboratory may not fairly represent groups from diverse cultural backgrounds.
- People who are unfamiliar with university settings and with the idea of "helping science" may be intimidated by the laboratory setting.
- Some aspects of children's development are difficult, if not impossible, to examine in the laboratory.
- Laboratory studies of certain types of stress may even be unethical.

Naturalistic observation provides insights that we sometimes cannot achieve in the laboratory. **Naturalistic observation** means observing behaviour in real-world settings, making no effort to manipulate or control the situation. Child

> **naturalistic observation** Behavioural observation that takes place in real-world settings.

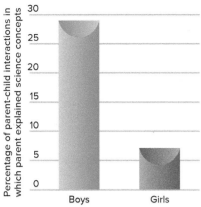

## FIGURE 1.12

**PARENTS' EXPLANATIONS OF SCIENCE TO SONS AND DAUGHTERS AT A SCIENCE MUSEUM.** In a naturalistic observation study at a children's science museum, parents were more than three times more likely to explain science to boys than to girls (Crowley & others, 2001). The gender difference occurred regardless of whether the father, the mother, or both parents were with the child, although the gender difference was greatest for fathers' science explanations to sons and daughters.

**standardized test** A test with uniform procedures for administration and scoring. Many standardized tests allow a person's performance to be compared with the performance of other individuals.

**case study** An in-depth look at a single individual.

Mahatma Gandhi was the spiritual leader of India in the middle of the twentieth century. Erik Erikson conducted an extensive case study of his life to determine what contributed to his identity development. *What are some limitations of the case study approach?*

development researchers conduct naturalistic observations in homes, child-care centres, schools, neighbourhoods, malls, and other contexts.

Naturalistic observation was used in one study that focused on conversations in a children's science museum (Crowley & others, 2001). Parents were more than three times as likely to engage boys than girls in explanatory talk while visiting exhibits at the science museum, suggesting a gender bias that encourages boys more than girls to be interested in science (see Figure 1.12). In another study, parents who had completed high school used more explanations with their children when visiting a science museum than parents who had not completed high school (Tenenbaum & others, 2002).

**Survey and Interview**   Sometimes the best and quickest way to get information about people is to ask them for it. One technique is to interview them directly. A related method is the survey (sometimes referred to as a questionnaire), which is especially useful when information from many people is needed (Nardi, 2006). A standard set of questions is used to obtain people's self-reported attitudes or beliefs about a particular topic. In a good survey, the questions are clear and unbiased, allowing respondents to answer unambiguously.

Surveys and interviews can be used to study a wide range of topics, from religious beliefs to sexual habits to attitudes about technology to beliefs about how to improve schools. Surveys and interviews today are conducted in person, over the telephone, and over the Internet.

One problem with surveys and interviews is the tendency for participants to answer questions in a way that they think is socially acceptable or desirable rather than telling what they truly think or feel (Creswell, 2008). For example, on a survey or in an interview some individuals might say that they do not take drugs even though they do.

**Standardized Test**   A **standardized test** has uniform procedures for administration and scoring. Many standardized tests allow a person's performance to be compared with the performance of other individuals, thus providing information about individual differences among people (Drummond & Jones, 2010). One example is the Stanford-Binet intelligence test, which is described in Chapter 8, "Intelligence." Your score on the Stanford-Binet test shows how your performance compares with that of thousands of other people who have taken the test.

Standardized tests have three key weaknesses. First, they do not always predict behaviour in non-test situations. Second, standardized tests are based on the belief that a person's behaviour is consistent and stable, yet personality and intelligence—two primary targets of standardized testing—can vary with the situation. For example, individuals may perform poorly on a standardized intelligence test in an office setting but score much higher at home, where they are less anxious. This criticism is especially relevant for members of minority groups, some of whom have been inaccurately classified as intellectually disabled on the basis of their scores on intelligence tests. A third weakness of standardized tests is that many psychological tests developed in Western cultures might not be appropriate in other cultures (Hall, 2010). The experiences of people in differing cultures may lead them to interpret and respond to questions differently.

**Case Study**   A **case study** is an in-depth look at a single individual. Case studies are performed mainly by mental health professionals when, for either practical or ethical reasons, the unique aspects of an individual's life cannot be duplicated and tested in other ways. A case study provides information about one person's fears, hopes, fantasies, traumatic experiences, upbringing, family relationships, health, or anything that helps the psychologist understand the person's mind and behaviour. In later chapters, we discuss vivid case studies, such as that of Michael Rehbein, who had much of the left side of his brain removed at 7 years of age to end severe epileptic seizures.

Case histories provide dramatic, in-depth portrayals of people's lives, but remember that we must be cautious when generalizing from this information (McMillan & Wergin, 2010). The subject of a case study is unique, with a genetic makeup and personal history that no one else shares. In addition, case studies involve judgments of unknown reliability. Psychologists who conduct case studies rarely check to see if other psychologists agree with their observations.

**Physiological Measures**   Researchers are increasingly using physiological measures when they study children's development (Nelson, 2011). These techniques are used to measure the relationship between physiological responses and behaviour; that is, to explore the biological underpinnings of behaviour. For example, as puberty unfolds, the blood levels of certain hormones increase. To determine the nature of these hormonal changes, researchers take blood samples from willing adolescents (Susman & Dorn, 2009). Other physiological measures could include heart rate, galvanic skin response, and measures of brain functioning, including electroencephalogram (EEG) recording of the brain's electrical activity.

Another physiological measure that is increasingly being used is neuroimaging, especially functional magnetic resonance imaging (fMRI), in which electromagnetic waves are used to construct images of a person's brain tissue and biochemical activity (see Figure 1.13). We will have much more to say about neuroimaging and other physiological measures at various points in this book.

## RESEARCH DESIGNS

Suppose you want to find out whether the children of permissive parents are more likely than other children to be rude and unruly. The data-collection method that researchers choose often depends on the goal of their research. The goal may be simply to describe a phenomenon, or it may be to describe relationships between phenomena or to determine the causes or effects of a phenomenon.

Perhaps you decide that you need to observe both permissive and strict parents with their children and compare them. How would you do that? In addition to choosing a method for collecting data, you would need to select a

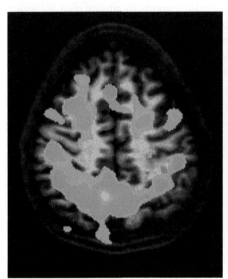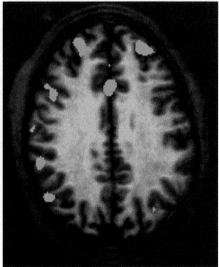

FIGURE **1.13**

**BRAIN IMAGING OF 15-YEAR-OLD ADOLESCENTS.** The two brain images indicate how alcohol can influence the functioning of an adolescent's brain. Notice the pink and red colouring (which indicates effective brain functioning involving memory) in the brain of the 15-year-old non-drinker (*left*) while engaging in a memory task and the lack of those colours in the brain of the 15-year-old under the influence of alcohol (*right*).

research design. There are three main types of research designs: descriptive, correlational, and experimental.

**Descriptive Research**   All of the data-collection methods that we have discussed can be used in **descriptive research**, which aims to observe and record behaviour. For example, a researcher might observe the extent to which people behave altruistically or aggressively toward each other. By itself, descriptive research cannot prove what causes a specific phenomenon, but it can yield important information about people's behaviour (Leedy & Ormrod, 2010).

**Correlational Research**   In contrast with descriptive research, correlational research goes beyond describing phenomena and provides information that helps predict how people will behave. In **correlational research**, the goal is to describe the strength of the relationship between two or more events or characteristics. The more strongly the two events are correlated (or related or associated), the more effectively we can predict one event from the other (McMillan & Wergin, 2010).

For example, to determine whether children of permissive parents have less self-control than other children, you would need to carefully record observations of parents' permissiveness and their children's self-control. The data could then be analyzed statistically to yield a numerical measure, called a **correlation coefficient**, a number based on a statistical analysis that is used to describe the degree of association between two variables. The correlation coefficient ranges from −1.00 to +1.00. A negative number means an inverse relation. For example, researchers often find a negative correlation between permissive parenting and children's self-control. By contrast, they often find a positive correlation between parental monitoring of children and children's self-control.

The higher the correlation coefficient (whether positive or negative), the stronger the association between the two variables. A correlation of 0 means that there is no association between the variables. A correlation of −.40 is stronger than a correlation of +.20 because we disregard whether the correlation is positive or negative in determining the strength of the correlation.

A caution is in order, however. Correlation does not equal causation (Heiman, 2011; Kiess & Green, 2010). The correlational finding just mentioned does not mean that permissive parenting necessarily causes low self-control in children. It might mean that a child's lack of self-control caused the parents to simply give up trying to control the child. It might also mean that other factors, such as heredity or poverty, caused the correlation between permissive parenting and low self-control in children. Figure 1.14 illustrates these possible interpretations of correlational data.

Throughout this book you will read about numerous correlational research studies. Keep in mind how easy (and misleading) it can be to assume causality when two events or characteristics merely are correlated (Howell, 2010).

**descriptive research** Research that involves observing and recording behaviour.

**correlational research** Research in which the goal is to describe the strength of the relationship between two or more events or characteristics.

**correlation coefficient** A number based on statistical analysis that is used to describe the degree of association between two variables.

**Observed Correlation:**  As permissive parenting increases, children's self-control decreases.

**Possible explanations for this observed correlation**

Permissive parenting  causes → Children's lack of self-control

Children's lack of self-control  causes → Permissive parenting

A third factor such as genetic tendencies or poverty  causes both → Permissive parenting and children's lack of self-control

An observed correlation between two events cannot be used to conclude that one event causes the second event. Other possibilities are that the second event causes the first event or that a third event causes the correlation between the first two events.

FIGURE **1.14**

**POSSIBLE EXPLANATIONS OF CORRELATIONAL DATA.**

**Experimental Research** To study causality, researchers turn to experimental research. An **experiment** is a carefully regulated procedure in which one or more factors believed to influence the behaviour being studied are manipulated while all other factors are held constant. If the behaviour under study changes when a factor is manipulated, we say that the manipulated factor has caused the behaviour to change. In other words, the experiment has demonstrated cause and effect. The cause is the factor that was manipulated. The effect is the behaviour that changed because of the manipulation. Non-experimental research methods (descriptive and correlational research) cannot establish cause and effect because they do not involve manipulating factors in a controlled way (Mitchell & Jolley, 2010).

**experiment** A carefully regulated procedure in which one or more of the factors believed to influence the behaviour being studied are manipulated while all other factors are held constant.

*Independent and Dependent Variables* Experiments include two types of changeable factors, or variables: independent and dependent. An independent variable is a manipulated, influential, experimental factor. It is a potential cause. The label *independent* is used because this variable can be manipulated independently of other factors to determine its effect. One experiment may include several independent variables.

A dependent variable is a factor that can change in an experiment in response to changes in the independent variable. As researchers manipulate the independent variable, they measure the dependent variable for any resulting effect.

For example, suppose that you conducted a study to determine whether aerobic exercise by pregnant women changes the breathing and sleeping patterns of their newborn babies. You might require one group of pregnant women to engage in a certain amount of exercise each week; the amount of exercise is thus the independent variable. When the infants are born, you would observe and measure their breathing and sleeping patterns. These patterns are the dependent variable, the factor that changes as the result of your manipulation.

*Experimental and Control Groups* Experiments can involve one or more experimental groups and one or more control groups. An experimental group is a group whose experience is manipulated. A control group is a comparison group that is as much like the experimental group as possible and that is treated in every way like the experimental group except for the manipulated factor (independent variable). The control group serves as a baseline against which the effects of the manipulated condition can be compared.

Random assignment is an important principle for deciding whether each participant will be placed in the experimental group or in the control group. Random assignment means that researchers assign participants to experimental and control groups by chance. It reduces the likelihood that the experiment's results will be due to any pre-existing differences between groups (Graziano & Raulin, 2010). In the example of the effects of aerobic exercise by pregnant women on the breathing and sleeping patterns of their newborns, you would randomly assign half of the pregnant women to engage in aerobic exercise over a period of weeks (the experimental group) and the other half to not exercise over the same number of weeks (the control group). Figure 1.15 illustrates the nature of experimental research.

**Time Span of Research** Researchers in child development have a special concern with studies that focus on the relationship between age and some other variable. To do this, they study different individuals of different ages and compare them, or they study the same individuals as they age over time.

*Cross-Sectional Approach* The **cross-sectional approach** is a research strategy in which individuals of different ages are

**cross-sectional approach** A research strategy in which individuals of different ages are compared at the same point in time.

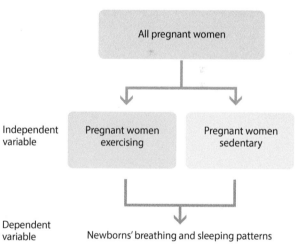

FIGURE **1.15**

**PRINCIPLES OF EXPERIMENTAL RESEARCH.** Imagine that you decide to conduct an experimental study of the effects of aerobic exercise by pregnant women on their newborns' breathing and sleeping patterns. You would randomly assign pregnant women to experimental and control groups. The experimental-group women would engage in aerobic exercise over a specified number of sessions and weeks. The control group would not. Then, when the infants are born, you would assess their breathing and sleeping patterns. If the breathing and sleeping patterns of newborns whose mothers were in the experimental group are more positive than those of the control group, you would conclude that aerobic exercise caused the positive effects.

compared at one time. A typical cross-sectional study might include a group of 5-year-olds, 8-year-olds, and 11-year-olds. The groups can be compared with respect to a variety of dependent variables: IQ, memory, peer relations, attachment to parents, hormonal changes, and so on. All of this can be accomplished in a short time. In some studies, data are collected in a single day. Even in large-scale cross-sectional studies with hundreds of participants, data collection does not usually take longer than several months to complete.

The main advantage of the cross-sectional study is that researchers don't have to wait for children to grow older. Despite its efficiency, the cross-sectional approach has its drawbacks. It gives no information about how individual children change or about the stability of their characteristics. It can obscure the increases and decreases of development—the hills and valleys of growth and development.

**longitudinal approach** A research strategy in which the same individuals are studied over a period of time, usually several years.

*Longitudinal Approach*  The **longitudinal approach** is a research strategy in which the same individuals are studied over a period of time, usually several years or more. For example, if a study of self-esteem were conducted longitudinally, the same children might be assessed three times—at 5, 8, and 11 years of age. Some longitudinal studies take place over shorter time frames, even just a year or so.

Longitudinal studies provide a wealth of information about important issues such as stability and change in development and the influence of early experience on later development, but they are not without problems (Gibbons, Hedeker, & DuToit, 2010). They are expensive and time-consuming. Also, the longer the study lasts, the greater the number of participants who drop out. For example, children's families may move, get sick, lose interest, and so forth. Those who remain in the study may be dissimilar to those who drop out, biasing the results. Those individuals who remain in a longitudinal study over a number of years may be more compulsive and conformity-oriented than average, for example, or they might lead more stable lives.

Theories are often linked with a particular research method or methods. Therefore, methods that researchers use are associated with their particular theoretical approaches. Figure 1.16 illustrates connections between research methods and theories.

| Research Method | Theory |
|---|---|
| Observation | • All theories emphasize some form of observation.<br>• Behavioural and social cognitive theories place the strongest emphasis on laboratory observation.<br>• Ethological theory places the strongest emphasis on naturalistic observation. |
| Interview/survey | • Psychoanalytic and cognitive studies (Piaget, Vygotsky) often use interviews.<br>• Behavioural social cognitive, and ethological theories are the least likely to use surveys or interviews. |
| Standardized test | • None of the theories discussed emphasize the use of this method. |
| Correlational research | • All of the theories use this research method, although psychoanalytic theories are the least likely to use it. |
| Experimental research | • The behavioural and social cognitive theories and the information-processing theories are the most likely to use the experimental method.<br>• Psychoanalytic theories are the least likely to use it. |
| Cross-sectional/longitudinal/sequential methods | • No theory described uses these methods more than any other. |

**FIGURE 1.16**

**CONNECTIONS OF RESEARCH METHODS TO THEORIES.**

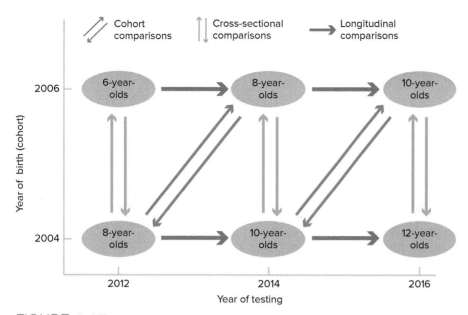

FIGURE **1.17**
**THE SEQUENTIAL APPROACH.**

*The Sequential Approach* The **sequential approach** is a combination of a longitudinal design and a cross-sectional design. Figure 1.17 illustrates the basic design of the sequential approach. The advantage of a sequential approach is that it enables a separation of age-related changes from changes caused by the unique experiences of a particular age cohort. Thus by following different cohorts for a period of time, researchers are able to isolate cohort effects. For example, if researchers wanted to measure the development of expressive vocabulary over time, they could start by selecting samples of different aged children, much like a cross-sectional design. This might include a group of 6-year-olds and a group of 8-year-olds. Next, the researchers would follow up with each group at various time points, perhaps every two years. Thus the 6-year-olds are now 8-year-olds and the 8-year-olds are now 10-year-olds. Following each age group over a period of time is the longitudinal component of this approach. Thus, the sequential approach enables developmentalists to explore age-related changes in expressive vocabulary, just like a longitudinal design, but is more time and cost effective. In addition, the sequential approach also isolates the potential cohort effect that is often a confounding variable in cross-sectional designs. By comparing the different cohorts, researchers can determine whether the changes seen in expressive vocabulary are age-related changes or a result of the unique experiences of each cohort; perhaps one group of 8-year-olds started school using a different literacy curriculum than the other, and this influenced the development of expressive vocabulary. Such a finding would be considered a cohort effect.

So far we have discussed many aspects of scientific research in child development, but where can you read about this research firsthand? Read *Connecting Through Research* to find out.

**sequential approach** A research strategy in which two or more groups of individuals are studied over a period of time, usually several years, thus combining the cross-sectional and longitudinal approaches.

## CHALLENGES IN CHILD DEVELOPMENT RESEARCH

The scientific foundation of research in child development helps to minimize the effect of research bias and maximize the objectivity of the results. Still, subtle challenges remain for each researcher to resolve. One is to ensure that research is conducted in an ethical way; another is to recognize, and try to overcome, deeply buried personal biases.

## Where Is Child Development Research Published?

Regardless of whether you pursue a career in child development, psychology, or some related scientific field, you can benefit from learning about the journal process. As a student you might be required to look up original research in journals. As a parent, teacher, or nurse you might want to consult journals to obtain information that will help you understand and work more effectively with people. And, as an inquiring person, you might look up information in journals after you have heard or read something that piqued your curiosity.

A journal publishes scholarly and academic information, usually in a specific domain such as physics, math, sociology, or our current interest, child development. Scholars in these fields publish most of their research in journals, which are the source of core information in virtually every academic discipline.

An increasing number of journals publish information about child development. Among the leading journals in child development are *Developmental Psychology, Child Development, Journal of Abnormal Child Psychology, Developmental Review, Infant Behavior and Development, Journal of Experimental Child Psychology, Journal of Research on Adolescence, Developmental Science,* and many others. Also, a number of journals that do not focus solely on development include articles on various aspects of human development. These journals include *Journal of Educational Psychology, Sex Roles, Journal of Cross-Cultural Research, Journal of Marriage and the Family, Exceptional Children,* and *Aggressive Behavior.*

Every journal has a board of experts who evaluate articles submitted for publication. Each submitted paper is accepted or rejected on the basis of factors such as its contribution to the field, methodological excellence, and clarity of writing. Some of the most prestigious journals, such as *Child Development,* reject as many as 80 to 90 percent of the articles submitted.

Journal articles are usually written for other professionals in the specialized field of the journal's focus; therefore, they often contain technical language and terms specific to the discipline that are difficult for non-professionals to understand. They usually consist of the following elements: abstract, introduction, method, results, discussion, and references.

Research journals are the core of information in virtually every academic discipline. Those shown here are among the increasing number of research journals that publish information about child development. *What are the main parts of a research article that presents findings from original research?*

The *abstract* is a brief summary that appears at the beginning of the article. The abstract lets readers quickly determine whether the article is relevant to their interests. The *introduction* introduces the problem or issue that is being studied. It includes a concise review of research relevant to the topic, theoretical ties, and one or more hypotheses to be tested. The *method* section consists of a clear description of the subjects evaluated in the study, the measures used, and the procedures that were followed. The method section should be sufficiently clear and detailed so that reading it could allow another researcher to repeat or replicate the study. The *results* section reports the analysis of the data collected. In most cases, the results section includes statistical analyses that are difficult for non-professionals to understand. The *discussion* section describes the author's conclusions, inferences, and interpretation of what was found. Statements are usually made about whether the hypotheses presented in the introduction were supported, limitations of the study, and suggestions for future research. The last part of the journal article, called *references,* includes bibliographic information for each source cited in the article. The references section is often a good resource for finding other articles relevant to a topic that interests you.

Where do you find journals such as those we have described? Your college or university library likely has some of them, and some public libraries also carry journals. Online databases such as PsycINFO or Google Scholar, which can facilitate the search for journal articles, are available to students on many campuses.

The research published in the journals mentioned above shapes our lives. It not only informs the work of other child development researchers, but it also informs the practices of law and policy makers, physicians, educators, parents, and many others. In fact, much of what is new in this edition of this textbook comes directly from research that can be found in the journals mentioned above.

*How might the research methods described in this chapter be written up for publication in a journal devoted to child development?*

**Conducting Ethical Research**   The explosion in technology has forced society to grapple with looming ethical questions that were unimaginable only a few decades ago. The same line of research that enables previously sterile couples to have children might someday let prospective parents "call up and order" the characteristics they prefer in their children or tip the balance of males and females in the world. For example, should embryos left over from procedures for increasing fertility be saved or discarded? Should people with inheritable fatal diseases (such as Huntington's disease) be discouraged from having their own biological children?

Researchers also face ethical questions both new and old. They have a responsibility to anticipate the personal problems their research might cause and to at least inform the participants of the possible fallout. Safeguarding the rights of research participants is a challenge because the potential harm is not always obvious (Fisher, 2009).

Ethics in research may affect you personally if you ever serve as a participant in a study. In that event, you need to know your rights as a participant and the responsibilities of researchers to assure that these rights are safeguarded.

If you ever become a researcher in child development yourself, you will need an even deeper understanding of ethics. Even if you only carry out research projects in psychology courses, you must consider the rights of the participants in those projects.

Today, proposed research at colleges and universities must pass the scrutiny of a research ethics committee before the research can be initiated. The research ethics committees follow the ethical principles laid out in the *Tri-Council Policy Statement: Ethical Conduct for Research Involving Humans* (2010), a collaborative statement produced by three government agencies: the Canadian Institutes of Health Research, the Natural Sciences and Engineering Research Council of Canada, and the Social Sciences and Humanities Research Council of Canada. Respect for human dignity is the underlying value upon which this ethics statement is built. This document instructs researchers to protect their participants from mental and physical harm, and addresses four important issues: informed consent, confidentiality, debriefing, and deception.

- *Informed consent.* All participants must know what their participation will involve and what risks might develop. For example, participants in a study on dating should be told beforehand that a questionnaire might stimulate thoughts about issues in their relationship that they had not considered. Participants also should be informed that in some instances a discussion of the issues might improve their relationship, but in others it might worsen the relationship and even end it. Even after informed consent is given, participants must retain the right to withdraw from the study at any time and for any reason.

- *Confidentiality.* Researchers are responsible for keeping all of the data they gather on individuals completely confidential and, when possible, completely anonymous.

- *Debriefing.* After the study has been completed, participants should be informed of its purpose and the methods that were used. In most cases, the experimenter also can inform participants in a general manner beforehand about the purpose of the research without leading participants to behave in a way they think that the experimenter is expecting. When preliminary information about the study is likely to affect the results, participants can at least be debriefed after the study has been completed.

- *Deception.* This is an ethical issue that researchers debate extensively. In some circumstances, telling the participants beforehand what the research study is about substantially alters the participants' behaviour and invalidates the researcher's data. In all cases of deception, however, the psychologist must ensure that the deception will not harm the participants and that the participants will be told the complete nature of the study (debriefed) as soon as possible after the study is completed.

**Minimizing Bias**   Studies of children's development are most useful when they are conducted without bias or prejudice toward any particular group of people. Of special concern is bias based on gender and bias based on culture or ethnicity.

*Gender Bias*   For most of its existence, our society has had a strong gender bias, a preconceived notion about the abilities of males and females that prevented individuals from pursuing their own interests and achieving their full potential (Etaugh & Bridges, 2010). Gender bias also has had a less obvious effect within the field of child development. For example, it is not unusual for conclusions to be drawn about females' attitudes and behaviours from research conducted with males as the only participants.

Furthermore, when researchers find gender differences, their reports sometimes magnify those differences (Denmark & others, 1988). For example, a researcher might report that 74 percent of the boys in a study had high achievement expectations versus only 67 percent of the girls and go on to talk about the differences in some detail. In reality, this might be a rather small difference. It also might disappear if the study was repeated, or the study might have methodological problems that don't allow such strong interpretations.

*Cultural and Ethnic Bias*   The realization that research on children's development needs to include more children from diverse ethnic groups has also been building (Ceballo, Huerta, & Ngo, 2010; Rowley, Kurtz-Costes, & Cooper, 2010). Historically, children from ethnic minority groups were excluded from most research in North America and simply thought of as variations from the norm or average. If minority children were included in samples and their scores didn't fit the norm, they were viewed as confounds or "noise" in data and discounted. Given the fact that children from diverse ethnic groups were excluded from research on child development for so long, we might reasonably conclude that children's real lives are perhaps more varied than research data have indicated in the past.

**ethnic gloss** Use of an ethnic label such as *Asian* or *Middle Eastern* in a superficial way that portrays an ethnic group as being more homogeneous than it really is.

Researchers also have tended to overgeneralize about ethnic groups (Banks, 2010; Liu & others, 2009). **Ethnic gloss** is using an ethnic label such as *Asian*

Look at these two photographs, one of all Caucasian male children, the other of a diverse group of girls and boys from different ethnic groups. Consider a topic in child development, such as parenting, cultural values, or independence seeking. *If you were conducting research on this topic, might the results of the study be different depending on whether the participants in your study were the children in the left or right photograph?*

or *Middle Eastern* in a superficial way that portrays an ethnic group as being more homogeneous than it really is (Trimble, 1988). For example, a researcher might describe a research sample like this: "The participants were 60 Asians." A more complete description of the Asian group might be something like this: "The 60 Asian participants were of Chinese descent from low-income neighbourhoods in Vancouver. Thirty-six were from homes in which Mandarin is the dominant language spoken, 24 from homes in which English is the main language spoken. Thirty were born in Canada, 30 in China. Thirty described themselves as Chinese Canadian, 15 as Chinese, and 15 as Canadian." Ethnic gloss can cause researchers to obtain samples of ethnic groups that are not representative of the group's diversity, which can lead to overgeneralization and stereotyping.

Research on ethnic minority children and their families has not been given adequate attention, especially in light of their significant rate of growth within the North American population (Tamis-Lemonda & McFadden, 2010). Until recently, ethnic minority families were combined in the category "minority," which masks important differences among ethnic groups as well as diversity within an ethnic group. At present and in the foreseeable future, the growth of minority families in Canada will be mainly due to the immigration of Asian families. Researchers need to take into account their acculturation level and generational status of parents and children, and how both factors influence family processes and child outcomes (Bornstein & Cote, 2010). More attention also needs to be given to biculturalism because the complexity of diversity means that some children identify with two or more ethnic groups (Levine & McClosky, 2009).

## Review Connect Reflect

 **LO3** Summarize why research is important in child development, the main theories of child development, and research methods, designs, and challenges.

### Review

- What is scientific research, what is it based on, and why is scientific research on child development important?
- What are the main theories of child development?
- What are the main research methods for collecting data about children's development?
- What types of research designs do child development researchers use?
- What are some research challenges in studying children's development?

### Connect

- Which of the research methods for collecting data would be appropriate or inappropriate for studying Erikson's stage of trust versus mistrust? Why?

### Reflect *Your Own Personal Journey of Life*

- Which of the theories of child development do you think best explains your own development? Why?

# case study connections

1. How might each theoretical perspective presented in Chapter 1 explain the different developmental outcomes described for Karla Homolka and Lincoln Alexander?

2. How does the theme of early-late experiences relate to the two individuals described in the opening vignette? How much and which of their early experiences account for the development outcomes, and how much and which of their later experiences may have played a role?

3. What factors contribute to the differences in resiliency seen in the two individuals described in the opening vignette?

4. If we wanted to further study the factors that contributed to the different developmental outcomes described in the opening vignette, which research methods might be best suited for this research question?

# reach your learning goals

# Introduction

## Caring for Children

Improving the Lives of Children

 **L01** Identify five areas in which children's lives need to be improved, and explain the role of resilience in children's development.

- Health and well-being is an important area in which children's lives can be improved. Today, many children in Canada and around the world need improved health care. We now recognize the importance of lifestyles and psychological states in promoting health and well-being. Parenting is an important influence on children's development. One-parent families, working parents, and child care are among the family issues that influence children's well-being. Education can also contribute to children's health and well-being. There is widespread concern that the education of children needs to be more effective, and there are many views in contemporary education about ways to improve schools. Sociocultural contexts are the contexts in which development occurs. Lastly, factors related to diversity, including ethnicity, gender, and socioeconomic status can all influence the path of development. Some children triumph over adversity—they are resilient. Researchers have found that resilient children are likely to have a close relationship with a parent figure and bonds with caring people outside the family.

## Developmental Processes, Periods, and Issues

Biological, Cognitive, and Socioemotional Processes

Periods of Development

Age and Cohort Effects

**L02** Discuss the most important processes, periods, and issues in development.

- Three key processes of development are biological, cognitive, and socioemotional. Biological processes (such as genes inherited from parents) involve changes in an individual's body. Cognitive processes (such as thinking) consist of changes in an individual's thought, intelligence, and language. Socioemotional processes (such as smiling) include changes in an individual's relationships with others, in emotions, and in personality.

- Childhood's five main developmental periods are (1) prenatal, from conception to birth, (2) infancy, from birth to 18 to 24 months, (3) early childhood, from the end of infancy to about 5 or 6 years of age, (4) middle and late childhood, from about 6 to 11 years of age, and (5) adolescence, which begins at about 10 or 12 and ends at about 18 or 19 years of age.

- Development can be affected by an individual's time of birth, era, or generation, rather than simply age. For example, individuals growing up in the booming 1990s may have different experiences than individuals growing up during the 1970s, and these experiences, rather than age, can influence development.

- The nature-nurture issue focuses on the extent to which development is mainly influenced by nature (biological inheritance) or nurture (environmental experience). Some developmentalists describe development as continuous (gradual, cumulative change), while others describe it as discontinuous (a sequence of distinct stages). The early-later experience issue focuses on whether early experiences (especially in infancy) are more important in development than later experiences. Most developmentalists recognize that extreme positions on the nature-nurture, continuity-discontinuity, and early-later experience issues are not supported by research. Despite this consensus, they continue to debate the degree to which each position influences children's development.

# The Science of Child Development

 **L03** Summarize why research is important in child development, the main theories of child development, and research methods, designs, and challenges.

The Importance
of Research

- Scientific research is objective, systematic, and testable. Scientific research is based on the scientific method, which includes these steps: conceptualize the problem, collect data, draw conclusions, and revise theory. Scientific research on child development reduces the likelihood that the information gathered is based on personal beliefs, opinions, and feelings.

Theories of Child
Development

- Psychoanalytic theories describe development as primarily unconscious and as heavily coloured by emotion. The two main psychoanalytic theories in developmental psychology are Freud's and Erikson's. Freud also proposed that individuals go through five psychosexual stages—oral, anal, phallic, latency, and genital. Erikson's theory emphasizes eight psychosocial stages of development. The three main cognitive theories are Piaget's cognitive developmental theory, Vygotsky's sociocultural theory, and information-processing theory. Cognitive theories emphasize conscious thoughts. In Piaget's theory, children go through four cognitive stages: sensorimotor, preoperational, concrete operational, and formal operational. Vygotsky's sociocultural cognitive theory emphasizes how culture and social interaction guide cognitive development. The information-processing theory emphasizes that individuals manipulate information, monitor it, and strategize about it. Three versions of the behavioural and social cognitive theories are Pavlov's classical conditioning, Skinner's operant conditioning, and Bandura's social cognitive theory. Ethology stresses that behaviour is strongly influenced by biology, is tied to evolution, and is characterized by critical or sensitive periods. Ecological theory is Bronfenbrenner's environmental systems view of development. It consists of five environmental systems: microsystem, mesosystem, exosystem, macrosystem, and chronosystem. An eclectic theoretical orientation does not follow any one theoretical approach, but rather selects from each theory whatever is considered the best in it.

Research Methods
for Collecting Data

- Research methods for collecting data about child development include observation (in a laboratory or a naturalistic setting), survey (questionnaire) or interview, standardized test, case study, and physiological measures.

Research Designs

- Descriptive research aims to observe and record behaviour. In correlational research, the goal is to describe the strength of the relationship between two or more events or characteristics. Experimental research involves conducting an experiment, which can determine cause and effect. An independent variable is the manipulated, influential, experimental factor. A dependent variable is a factor that can change in an experiment, in response to changes in the independent variable. Experiments can involve one or more experimental groups and control groups. In random assignment, researchers assign participants to experimental and control groups by chance. When researchers decide about the time span of their research, they can conduct cross-sectional, longitudinal, or sequential studies.

- Researchers' ethical responsibilities include seeking participants' informed consent, ensuring their confidentiality, debriefing them about the purpose and potential personal consequences of participating, and avoiding unnecessary deception of participants. Researchers need to guard against gender, cultural, and ethnic bias in research. Every effort should be made to make research equitable for both females and males. Individuals from varied ethnic backgrounds need to be included as participants in child research, and overgeneralization about diverse members within a group must be avoided.

Mc Graw Hill Education **connect**    Mc Graw Hill Education **|LEARNSMART**    Mc Graw Hill Education **|SMARTBOOK**

# section two

# Biological Processes, Physical Development, and Perceptual Development

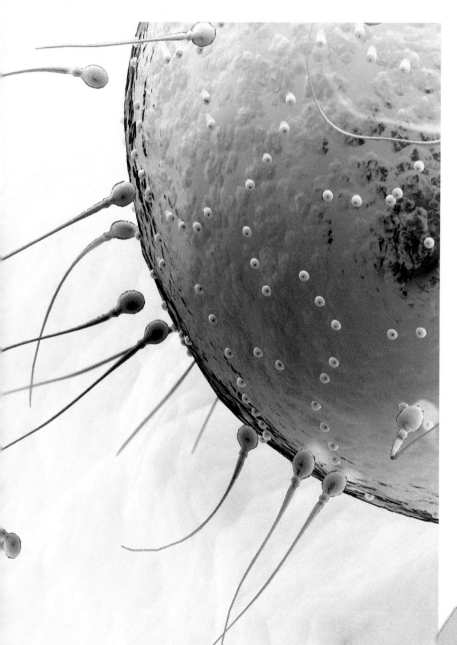

The rhythm and meaning of life involve beginnings, with questions raised about how, from so simple a beginning, complex forms develop, grow, and mature. What was this organism, what is this organism, and what will this organism be? In Section 2, you will read four chapters: "Biological Beginnings" (Chapter 2), "Prenatal Development and Birth" (Chapter 3), "Physical Development and Health" (Chapter 4), and "Motor, Sensory, and Perceptual Development" (Chapter 5).

# chapter 2 | Biological Beginnings

Jim Springer and Jim Lewis are identical twins. They were separated at four weeks of age and did not see each other again until they were 39 years old. Both worked as part-time deputy sheriffs, vacationed in Florida, drove Chevrolets, had dogs named Toy, and married and divorced women named Betty. One twin named his son James Allan, and the other named his son James Alan. Both liked math but not spelling, enjoyed carpentry and mechanical drawing, chewed their fingernails down to the nubs, had almost identical drinking and smoking habits, had hemorrhoids, put on ten pounds at about the same point in development, first suffered headaches at the age of 18, and had similar sleep patterns.

Jim and Jim do have some differences. One wears his hair over his forehead; the other slicks it back and has sideburns. One expresses himself best orally; the other is more proficient in writing. But, for the most part, their profiles are remarkably similar.

Jim Lewis (*left*) and Jim Springer (*right*)

Jim and Jim were part of the Minnesota Study of Twins Reared Apart, one of the largest twin registries in the world. The study brings identical twins (identical genetically because they come from the same fertilized egg) and fraternal twins (who come from different fertilized eggs) from all over the world to Minneapolis to investigate their lives. There the twins complete personality and intelligence tests, and they provide detailed medical histories, including information about diet and smoking, exercise habits, chest X-rays, heart stress tests, and EEGs. The twins are asked more than 15,000 questions about their family and childhood, personal interests, vocational orientation, values, and aesthetic judgments (Bouchard & others, 1990).

When genetically identical twins who were separated as infants show such striking similarities in their tastes and habits and choices, can we conclude that their genes must have caused the development of those tastes and habits and choices? Other possible causes need to be considered. The twins shared not only the same genes but also some experiences. Some of the separated twins lived together for several months prior to their adoption, some of the twins had been reunited prior to testing (in some cases, many years earlier), adoption agencies often place twins in similar homes, and even strangers who spend several hours together and start comparing their lives are likely to come up with some coincidental similarities (Joseph, 2006). The Minnesota study of identical twins points to both the importance of the genetic basis of human development and the need for further research on genetic and environmental factors (Lykken, 2001).

# preview

The example of Jim and Jim stimulates us to think about our genetic heritage and the biological foundations of our existence. However, organisms are not like billiard balls, moved by simple external forces to predictable positions on life's table. Environmental experiences and biological foundations work together to make us who we are. Our coverage of life's biological beginnings focuses on evolution, genetic foundations, challenges and choices regarding reproduction, and the interaction of heredity and environment.

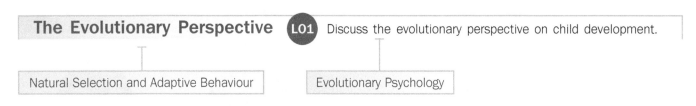

The Evolutionary Perspective **L01** Discuss the evolutionary perspective on child development.

Natural Selection and Adaptive Behaviour    Evolutionary Psychology

In evolutionary time, humans are relative newcomers to Earth. As our earliest ancestors left the forest to forage on the savannahs, and then to form hunting societies on the open plains, their minds and behaviours changed, and they eventually established humans as the dominant species on Earth. How did this evolution come about?

## NATURAL SELECTION AND ADAPTIVE BEHAVIOUR

*There are one hundred and ninety-three living species of monkeys and apes. One hundred and ninety-two of them are covered with hair. The exception is the naked ape, self-named Homo sapiens.*

—DESMOND MORRIS
*British Zoologist, 20th Century*

*Natural selection* is the evolutionary process by which those individuals of a species that are best adapted are the ones that survive and reproduce. To understand what this means, let's return to the middle of the nineteenth century, when the British naturalist Charles Darwin was travelling around the world, observing many different species of animals in their natural surroundings. Darwin, who published his observations and thoughts in *On the Origin of Species* (1859), noted that most organisms reproduce at rates that would cause enormous increases in the population of most species and yet populations remain nearly constant. He reasoned that an intense, constant struggle for food, water, and resources must occur among the many young born each generation, because many of the young do not survive. Those that do survive and reproduce pass on their characteristics to the next generation. Darwin argued that these survivors are better *adapted* to their world than are the nonsurvivors (Brooker, 2011; Raven, 2011). The best-adapted individuals survive to leave the most offspring. Over the course of many generations, organisms with the characteristics needed for survival make up an increasing percentage of the population. Over many, many generations, this could produce a gradual modification of the whole population. If environmental conditions change, however, other characteristics might become favoured by natural selection, moving the species in a different direction (Mader, 2010).

All organisms must adapt to particular places, climates, food sources, and ways of life (Audesirk, Audesirk, & Byers, 2011). An eagle's claws are a physical adaptation that facilitates predation. *Adaptive behaviour* is behaviour that promotes an organism's survival in the natural habitat (Johnson & Losos, 2010). For example, attachment between a caregiver and a baby ensures the infant's closeness to a caregiver for feeding and protection from danger, thus increasing the infant's chances of survival.

## EVOLUTIONARY PSYCHOLOGY

Although Darwin introduced the theory of evolution by natural selection in 1859, his ideas only recently have become a popular framework for explaining behaviour. Psychology's newest approach, **evolutionary psychology**, emphasizes the importance of adaptation, reproduction, and "survival of the fittest" in shaping behaviour. "Fit" in this sense refers to the ability to bear offspring that survive long enough to bear offspring of their own. In this view, natural selection favours behaviours that increase reproductive success—the ability to pass genes to the next generation (Confer & others, 2010; Cosmides, 2011).

**evolutionary psychology** Branch of psychology that emphasizes the importance of adaptation, reproduction, and "survival of the fittest" in shaping behaviour.

David Buss (1995, 2004, 2008) has been especially influential in stimulating new interest in how evolution can explain human behaviour. He reasons that just as evolution shapes our physical features, such as body shape and height, it also pervasively influences how we make decisions, how aggressive we are, our fears, and our mating patterns. For example, assume that our ancestors were hunters and gatherers on the plains, that men did most of the hunting, and women stayed close to home gathering seeds and plants for food. If you have to travel some distance from your home in an effort to find and slay a fleeing animal, you need not only certain physical traits but also the ability to do certain types of spatial thinking. Men born with these traits would be more likely than men without them to survive, to bring home lots of food, and to be considered attractive mates—and thus to reproduce and pass on these characteristics to their children. In other words, these traits would provide a reproductive advantage for males. Over many generations, men with good spatial thinking skills might become more numerous in the population. Critics point out that this scenario might or might not have actually happened.

### Evolutionary Developmental Psychology

Recently, interest has grown in using the concepts of evolutionary psychology to understand human development (Bjorklund, 2007; Greve & Bjorklund, 2009). Here we discuss some ideas proposed by evolutionary developmental psychologists (Bjorklund & Pellegrini, 2002).

*How does the attachment of this Vietnamese baby to its mother reflect the evolutionary process of adaptive behaviour?*

An extended childhood period evolved because humans require time to develop a large brain and learn the complexity of human societies. Humans take longer to become reproductively mature than any other mammal. During this extended childhood period, they develop a large brain and the experiences needed to become competent adults in a complex society (see Figure 2.1).

Many evolved psychological mechanisms are domain-specific—that is, the mechanisms apply only to a specific aspect of a person's makeup. Information processing is one example. According to evolutionary psychology, the mind is not a general-purpose device that can be applied equally to a vast array of problems. Instead, as our ancestors dealt with certain recurring problems, such as hunting and finding shelter, specialized modules evolved that process information related to those problems—for example, a module for physical knowledge for tracking animals, a module for mathematical knowledge for trading, and a module for language.

Evolved mechanisms are not always adaptive in contemporary society. Some behaviours that were adaptive for our prehistoric ancestors may not serve us well today. For example, the scarcity of food in the environment of our ancestors likely led to humans' propensity to gorge when food is available and to crave high-calorie foods, a trait that might lead to an epidemic of obesity when food is plentiful.

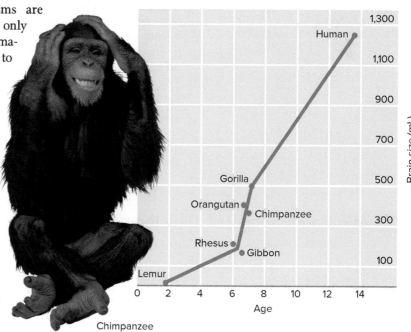

Chimpanzee

## FIGURE 2.1

**THE BRAIN SIZES OF VARIOUS PRIMATES AND HUMANS IN RELATION TO THE LENGTH OF THE CHILDHOOD PERIOD.** Compared with other primates, humans have both a larger brain and a longer childhood period. *What conclusions can you draw from the relationship indicated by this graph?*

Children in all cultures are interested in the tools that adults in their cultures use. For example, this 11-month-old boy from the Efe culture in the Democratic Republic of the Congo in Africa is trying to cut a papaya with an *apopau* (a smaller version of a machete). *Might the infant's behaviour be evolutionary-based or be due to both biological and environmental conditions?*

**Evaluating Evolutionary Psychology**   Although the popular press gives a lot of attention to the ideas of evolutionary psychology, it remains just one theoretical approach. Like the theories described in Chapter 1, it has limitations, weaknesses, and critics. Albert Bandura (1998), whose social cognitive theory was described in Chapter 1, acknowledges the important influence of evolution on human adaptation. However, he rejects what he calls "one-sided evolutionism," which sees social behaviour as the product of evolved biology. An alternative is a bidirectional view, in which environmental and biological conditions influence each other. In this view, evolutionary pressures created changes in biological structures that allowed the use of tools, which enabled our ancestors to manipulate the environment, constructing new environmental conditions. In turn, environmental innovations produced new selection pressures that led to the evolution of specialized biological systems for consciousness, thought, and language.

In other words, evolution gave us bodily structures and biological potentialities; it does not dictate behaviour. People have used their biological capacities to produce diverse cultures—aggressive and pacific, egalitarian and autocratic. As American scientist Stephen Jay Gould (1981) concluded, in most domains of human functioning, biology allows a broad range of cultural possibilities.

The "big picture" idea of natural selection leading to the development of human traits and behaviours is difficult to refute or test because it is on a time scale that does not lend itself to empirical study. Thus, studying specific genes in humans and other species—and their links to traits and behaviours—may be the best approach for testing ideas coming out of the evolutionary psychology perspective.

## Review *Connect* Reflect

 **LO1** Discuss the evolutionary perspective on child development.

### Review

- How can natural selection and adaptive behaviour be defined?
- What is evolutionary psychology? What are some basic ideas about human development proposed by evolutionary psychologists? How might evolutionary influences have different effects at different points in the life span? How can evolutionary psychology be evaluated?

### *Connect*

- In Chapter 1, you learned about how different developmental processes interact. How was that principle reinforced by the information in this section?

### **Reflect** *Your Own Personal Journey of Life*

- Which do you think is more persuasive in explaining your development: the views of evolutionary psychologists or those of their critics? Why?

## Genetic Foundations of Development

**LO2** Describe what genes are and how they influence children's development.

- The Collaborative Gene
- Genes and Chromosomes
- Genetic Principles
- Chromosomal and Gene-Linked Abnormalities

Genetic influences on behaviour evolved over time and across many species. The many traits and characteristics that are genetically influenced have a long evolutionary history that is retained in our DNA. Our DNA is not just inherited from our parents; it's also what we as a species have inherited from other species that came before our own.

How are characteristics that suit a species for survival transmitted from one generation to the next? Darwin could not answer this question because genes and the principles of genetics had not yet been discovered. Each of us carries a human *genetic code* that we inherited from our parents. Because a fertilized egg carries this human code, a fertilized human egg cannot grow into an egret, eagle, or elephant.

## THE COLLABORATIVE GENE

Each of us began life as a single cell weighing about one twenty-millionth of an ounce! This tiny piece of matter housed our entire genetic code—instructions that orchestrated growth from that single cell to a person made of trillions of cells, each containing a replica of the original code. That code is carried by our genes (Mader, 2010). What are genes and what do they do? For the answer, we need to look into our cells.

The nucleus of each human cell contains **chromosomes**, which are thread-like structures made up of deoxyribonucleic acid, or DNA. **DNA** is a complex molecule with a double helix shape (like a spiral staircase) that is made of four chemical building blocks called nucleotides: guanine (G), adenine (A), thymine (T), and cytosine (C). The sequence of these bases determines the biological instructions, or "genetic code" for building an organism, much like letters are put together to form different words. **Genes**, the units of hereditary information, are short segments of DNA, as you can see in Figure 2.2. They direct cells to reproduce themselves and to assemble proteins. Proteins, in turn, are the building blocks of cells as well as the regulators that direct the body's processes (Freeman, 2011).

Each gene has its own location, its own designated place on a particular chromosome. Today, there is a great deal of enthusiasm about efforts to discover the specific locations of genes that are linked to certain functions (Lewis, 2010). An important step in this direction is the Human Genome Project's efforts to map the human genome—the complete set of developmental instructions for creating proteins that initiate the making of a human organism (Willey, Sherwood, & Woolverton, 2011).

One of the big surprises of the Human Genome Project was an early report indicating that humans have only about 30,000 genes (U.S. Department of Energy, 2001). More recently, the number of human genes has been revised further downward to approximately 20,500 (*Science Daily,* 2008). Scientists had thought that humans had as many as 100,000 or more genes. They had also maintained that each gene programmed just one protein. In fact, humans have far more proteins than they have genes, so there cannot be a one-to-one correspondence

**chromosomes** Threadlike structures that come in 23 pairs, with one member of each pair coming from each parent. Chromosomes contain the genetic substance DNA.

**DNA** A complex molecule that contains genetic information.

**genes** Units of hereditary information composed of DNA. Genes direct cells to reproduce themselves and manufacture the proteins that maintain life.

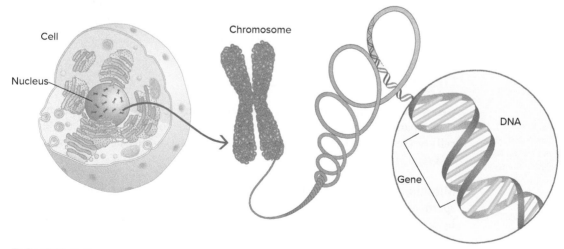

## FIGURE **2.2**

**CELLS, CHROMOSOMES, DNA, AND GENES.** (*Left*) The body contains trillions of cells. Each cell contains a central structure, the nucleus. (*Middle*) Chromosomes are threadlike structures located in the nucleus of the cell. Chromosomes are composed of DNA. (*Right*) DNA has the structure of a spiral staircase. A gene is a segment of DNA.

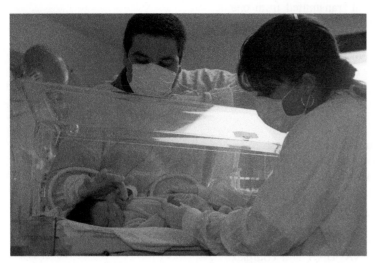

A positive result from the Human Genome Project. Shortly after Andrew Gobea was born, his cells were genetically altered to prevent his immune system from failing.

between genes and proteins (Commoner, 2002). Each gene is not translated, in automaton-like fashion, into one and only one protein. A gene does not act independently, as developmental psychologist David Moore (2001) emphasized by titling his book *The Dependent Gene.*

Rather than being a group of independent genes, the human genome consists of many genes that collaborate both with each other and with non-genetic factors inside and outside the body. The collaboration operates at many points. For example, the cellular machinery mixes, matches, and links small pieces of DNA to reproduce the genes—and that machinery is influenced by what is going on around it.

Whether a gene is turned "on," working to assemble proteins, is also a matter of collaboration. The activity of genes (genetic expression) is affected by their environment (Gottlieb, 2007). For example, hormones that circulate in the blood make their way into the cell where they can turn genes "on" and "off." And the flow of hormones can be affected by environmental conditions, such as light, day length, nutrition, and behaviour. Numerous studies have shown that external events outside of the original cell and the person, as well as events inside the cell, can excite or inhibit gene expression (Gottlieb, Wahlsten, & Lickliter, 2006). For example, one recent study revealed that an increase in the concentration of stress hormones such as cortisol produced a fivefold increase in DNA damage (Flint & others, 2007). Other research has shown that experiences early in development can alter gene expression and this expression is related to later behaviour (Francis & others, 2003).

In short, a single gene is rarely the source of a protein's genetic information, much less of an inherited trait (Gottlieb, 2007).

## GENES AND CHROMOSOMES

Genes are not only collaborative, they are enduring. How do the genes manage to get passed from generation to generation and end up in all of the trillion cells in the body? Three processes explain the heart of the story: mitosis, meiosis, and fertilization.

**Mitosis, Meiosis, and Fertilization**   Every cell in your body, except the sperm and egg, has 46 chromosomes arranged in 23 pairs. These cells reproduce by a process called **mitosis** (see Figure 2.3a). During mitosis, the cell's nucleus—including the chromosomes—duplicates itself and the cell divides. Two new cells are formed, each containing the same DNA as the original cell, arranged in the same 23 pairs of chromosomes.

However, a different type of cell division—**meiosis** (see Figure 2.3b)—forms eggs and sperm (or gametes). During meiosis, a cell of the testes (in men) or ovaries

**mitosis** Cellular reproduction in which the cell's nucleus duplicates itself with two new cells being formed, each containing the same DNA as the parent cell, arranged in the same 23 pairs of chromosomes.

**meiosis** A specialized form of cell division that forms eggs and sperm (or gametes).

**fertilization** A stage in reproduction whereby an egg and a sperm fuse to create a single cell, called a zygote.

**zygote** A single cell formed through fertilization.

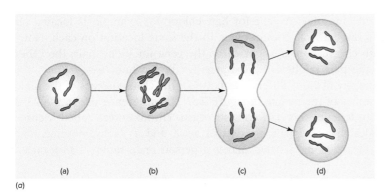

(a)

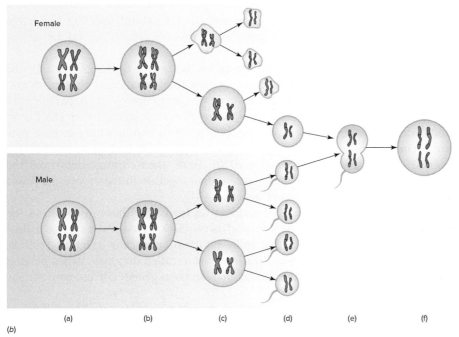

(b)

## FIGURE 2.3

**MITOSIS AND MEIOSIS.** *(a)* Mitosis: The zygote divides and keeps dividing to produce a multi-cellular organism. In (a) is a zygote with only four chromosomes, rather than the 46 each cell normally contains. In (b) each chromosome splits in half (length-wise) to produce a duplicate of itself. In (c) the duplicates move away from each other as the cell begins to divide. In (d) the cell has divided in two, and each new cell has the same set of chromosomes as the other and as the original parent cell (a).
*(b)* Meiosis: The reproductive cells divide to produce new germ cells with half the normal complement of chromosomes. As meiosis (a type of cell division that produces male and female reproductive cells) begins in both sexes, all the chromosomes in the cell replicate themselves as if they were about to undergo mitosis, or normal cell division. In (a) are the results of this replication (shows cells with only two pairs, rather than the full complement of 23 pairs). In (b) crossing over between chromosomes ensures the zygote's unique genetic inheritance. In (c) the male chromosome pairs separate to form two cells, each with 23 chromosomes. In the female, two cells are also formed, but one is non-functional and may or may not produce two more non-functional cells. In (d) the chromosomes separate once again, forming four sperm cells in the male and, in the female, a single ovum and a fourth non-functional cell. (The genetic material in the female's four non-functional cells degenerates.) When a sperm cell fertilizes an ovum, (e) a zygote is formed (f) with 23 chromosome pairs, or 46 in all.

(in women) duplicates its chromosomes but then divides twice, thus forming four cells, each of which has only half of the genetic material of the parent cell (Klug & others, 2010; Mader, 2010). By the end of meiosis, each egg or sperm has 23 unpaired chromosomes.

During **fertilization**, an egg and a sperm fuse to create a single cell, called a **zygote** (see Figure 2.4). In the zygote, the 23 unpaired chromosomes from the egg and the 23 unpaired chromosomes from the sperm combine to form one set of 23 paired chromosomes—one chromosome of each pair from the mother's egg and the other from the father's sperm. In this manner, each parent contributes half of the offspring's genetic material.

Figure 2.5 shows 23 paired chromosomes of a male and a female. The members of each pair of chromosomes are both similar and different: Each chromosome in the pair contains varying forms of the same genes, at the same

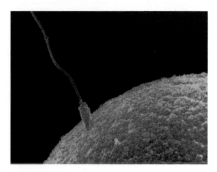

## FIGURE 2.4

**A SINGLE SPERM PENETRATING AN EGG AT THE POINT OF FERTILIZATION.**

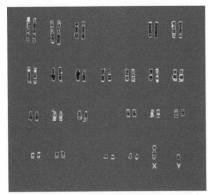

(a)

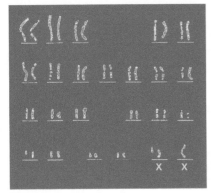

(b)

## FIGURE 2.5

**THE GENETIC DIFFERENCE BETWEEN MALES AND FEMALES.** Set (*a*) shows the chromosome structure of a male, and set (*b*) shows the chromosome structure of a female. The last pair of 23 pairs of chromosomes is in the bottom right box of each set. Notice that the Y chromosome of the male is smaller than the X chromosome of the female. To obtain this kind of chromosomal picture, a cell is removed from a person's body, usually from the inside of the mouth. The chromosomes are stained by chemical treatment, magnified extensively, and then photographed.

**genotype** A person's genetic heritage; the actual genetic material.

**phenotype** The way an individual's genotype is expressed in observable and measurable characteristics.

location on the chromosome. A gene for hair colour, for example, is located on both members of one pair of chromosomes, in the same location on each. However, one of those chromosomes might carry the gene for blond hair; the other chromosome in the pair might carry the gene for brown hair.

Do you notice any obvious differences between the chromosomes of the male and the chromosomes of the female in Figure 2.5? The difference lies in the 23rd pair. Ordinarily in females this pair consists of two chromosomes called X chromosomes; in males the 23rd pair consists of an X and a Y chromosome. The presence of a Y chromosome is what makes a person male rather than female.

**Sources of Variability** Combining the genes of two parents in their offspring increases genetic variability in the population, which is valuable for a species because it provides more characteristics for natural selection to operate on (Starr, 2011). In fact, the human genetic process creates several important sources of variability.

First, the chromosomes in the zygote are not exact copies of those in the mother's ovaries and the father's testes. During the formation of the sperm and egg in meiosis, the members of each pair of chromosomes are separated, but which chromosome in the pair goes to the gamete is a matter of chance. In addition, before the pairs separate, pieces of the two chromosomes in each pair are exchanged, creating a new combination of genes on each chromosome in a process called crossing-over (Mader, 2010). Thus, when chromosomes from the mother's egg and the father's sperm are brought together in the zygote, the result is a truly unique combination of genes.

If each zygote is unique, how do identical twins like those discussed in the opening of the chapter exist? *Identical twins* (also called monozygotic twins) develop from a single zygote that splits into two genetically identical replicas, each of which becomes a person. *Fraternal twins* (called dizygotic twins) develop from separate eggs and separate sperm, making them genetically no more similar than ordinary siblings.

Even when their genes are identical, however, people vary. The difference between genotypes and phenotypes helps us to understand this source of variability. All of a person's genetic material makes up his or her **genotype.** However, not all of the genetic material is apparent in our observed and measurable characteristics. A **phenotype** consists of observable characteristics. Phenotypes include physical characteristics (such as height, weight, and hair colour) and psychological characteristics (such as personality and intelligence).

Another source of variability comes from DNA (Brooker, 2011). Chance, a mistake by cellular machinery, or damage from an environmental agent such as radiation may produce a mutated gene, which is a permanently altered segment of DNA. These mutations may or may not produce observable changes in the phenotype.

For each genotype, a range of phenotypes can be expressed, providing another source of variability (Gottlieb, 2007). An individual can inherit the genetic potential to grow very large, for example, but good nutrition, among other things, will be essential to achieving that potential.

## GENETIC PRINCIPLES

What determines how a genotype is expressed to create a particular phenotype? Much is unknown about the answer to this question (Starr, 2011). However, a number of genetic principles have been discovered, among them those of dominant-recessive genes, sex-linked genes, genetic imprinting, and polygenically determined characteristics.

**Dominant-Recessive Genes Principle** In some cases, one gene of a pair always exerts its effects; it is *dominant,* overriding the potential influence of the other gene, called the recessive gene. This is the *dominant-recessive genes* *principle*. As illustrated in Figure 2.6, a recessive gene exerts its influence only if the two genes of a pair are both recessive. If you inherit a recessive gene for a trait from each of your parents, you will show the trait. If you inherit a recessive gene from only one parent, you may never know you carry the gene. Brown hair, farsightedness, and dimples rule over blond hair, nearsightedness, and freckles in the world of dominant-recessive genes.

Can two brown-haired parents have a blond-haired child? Yes, they can. Suppose that each parent has a dominant gene for brown hair and a recessive gene for blond hair. Since dominant genes override recessive genes, the parents have brown hair, but both are carriers of blondness and pass on their recessive genes for blond hair. With no dominant gene to override them, the recessive genes can make the child's hair blond.

**Sex-Linked Genes**   Most mutated genes are recessive. When a mutated gene is carried on the X chromosome, the result is called *X-linked inheritance*. The implications for males may be very different from those for females (Petersen, Wang, & Willems, 2008). Remember that males have only one X chromosome. Thus, if there is an altered, disease-creating gene on the X chromosome, males have no backup copy to counter the harmful gene and therefore may carry an X-linked disease (see Figure 2.7). However, females have a second X chromosome, which is likely to be unchanged. As a result, they are not likely to have the X-linked disease. Thus, most individuals who have X-linked diseases are males. Females who have one changed copy of the X gene are known as *carriers*, and they usually do not show any signs of the X-linked disease. Hemophilia, a disorder in which the blood fails to clot, colour blindness, and Fragile-X syndrome, which we will discuss later in the chapter, are all examples of X-linked inheritance diseases (Rogaev & others, 2009).

**Genetic Imprinting**   Genetic imprinting occurs when the expression of a gene has different effects depending on whether the mother or the father passed on the gene (Zaitoun & others, 2010). A chemical process "silences" one member of the gene pair. For example, as a result of imprinting, only the maternally derived copy of the expressed gene might be active, while the paternally derived copy of the same expressed gene is silenced—or vice versa. Only a small percentage of human genes appear to undergo imprinting, but it is a normal and important aspect of development (Koerner & Barlow, 2010). When imprinting goes awry, development is disturbed, as in the case of Beckwith-Wiedemann syndrome, a growth disorder, and Wilms tumor, a type of cancer (Hartwig & others, 2010).

**Polygenic Inheritance**   Genetic transmission is usually more complex than the simple examples we have examined thus far (Fry, 2009). Few characteristics reflect the influence of only a single gene or pair of genes. Most are determined by the interaction of many different genes; they are said to be polygenically determined. Even a simple characteristic such as height, for example, reflects the interaction of many genes, as well as the influence of the environment. Most diseases, such as cancer and diabetes, develop as a consequence of complex gene interactions and environmental factors (Ekeblad, 2010; Vimaleswaran & Loos, 2010).

The term *gene-gene interaction* is increasingly used to describe studies that focus on the interdependence of two or more genes in influencing characteristics, behaviour, diseases, and development (Costanzo & others, 2010). For example, recent studies have documented gene-gene interaction in cancer (Chen & others, 2009) and cardiovascular disease (Jylhava & others, 2009).

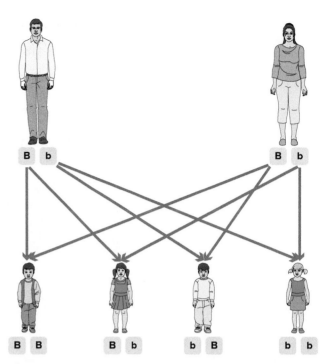

FIGURE **2.6**

**GENETIC TRANSMISSION OF A TRAIT CARRIED ON RECESSIVE GENES.** When both brown-haired parents have the dominant gene for brown hair (B) and the recessive gene for blond hair (b), they have a 1 in 4 chance of having a child with blond hair.

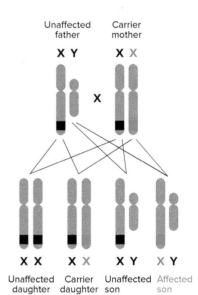

FIGURE **2.7**

**X-LINKED INHERITANCE.** An example of genetic transmission for an X-linked condition, like hemophilia.

**developmental connection**

**Conditions, Diseases, and Disorders.**
Intellectual disability can be classified in
several ways. Chapter 8, LO 3

# CHROMOSOMAL AND GENE-LINKED ABNORMALITIES

Sometimes abnormalities characterize the genetic process. Some of these abnormalities involve whole chromosomes that do not separate properly during meiosis. Other abnormalities are produced by harmful genes.

**Chromosomal Abnormalities**   When a gamete is formed, sometimes the male's sperm and/or the female's ovum do not have their normal set of 23 chromosomes. The most notable examples involve Down syndrome and abnormalities of the sex chromosomes (see Figure 2.8).

*Down Syndrome*   An individual with **Down syndrome** usually has distinctive physical features including a round face, a flattened skull, an extra fold of skin over the eyelids, a protruding tongue, and short limbs, as well as intellectual disabilities (Fidler, 2008). The syndrome, also named trisomy 21, is caused by the presence of an extra copy of chromosome 21. It is not known why the extra chromosome is present, but the health of the male sperm or female ovum may be involved.

In Canada, Down syndrome appears approximately once in every 900 live births (Wyatt, 2000). Women between the ages of 16 and 34 are less likely to give birth to a child with Down syndrome than are younger or older women.

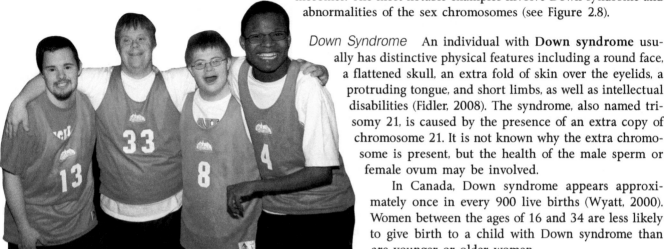

These athletes, some of whom have Down syndrome, are participating in a Special Olympics competition. *What causes Down syndrome?*

**Down syndrome** A chromosomally transmitted form of intellectual disability, caused by the presence of an extra copy of chromosome 21.

**Klinefelter syndrome** A chromosomal disorder in which males have an extra X chromosome, making them XXY instead of XY.

*Sex-Linked Chromosomal Abnormalities*   Recall that a newborn normally has either an X and a Y chromosome, or two X chromosomes. Human embryos must possess at least one X chromosome to be viable. The most common sex-linked chromosomal abnormalities involve the presence of an extra chromosome (either an X or Y) or the absence of one X chromosome in females.

**Klinefelter syndrome** is a genetic disorder in which males have an extra X chromosome, making them XXY instead of XY. Males with this disorder have undeveloped testes, and they usually have enlarged breasts and become tall (Ross & others, 2008). Approximately 20 to 30 percent of individuals with

| Name | Description | Treatment | Incidence |
|---|---|---|---|
| Down syndrome | An extra chromosome causes mild to severe intellectual disability and physical abnormalities. | Surgery, early intervention, infant stimulation, and special learning programs | 1 in 1,900 births at age 20<br>1 in 300 births at age 35<br>1 in 30 births at age 45 |
| Klinefelter syndrome (XXY) | An extra X chromosome causes physical abnormalities. | Hormone therapy can be effective | 1 in 600 male births |
| Fragile X syndrome | An abnormality in the X chromosome can cause intellectual disability, learning disabilities, or short attention span. | Special education, speech and language therapy | More common in males than in females |
| Turner syndrome (XO) | A missing X chromosome in females can cause intellectual disability and sexual underdevelopment. | Hormone therapy in childhood and puberty | 1 in 2,500 female births |
| XYY syndrome | An extra Y chromosome can cause above-average height. | No special treatment required | 1 in 1,000 male births |

## FIGURE **2.8**

**SOME CHROMOSOMAL ABNORMALITIES.** The treatments for these abnormalities do not necessarily erase the problem but may improve the individual's adaptive behaviour and quality of life.

Klinefelter syndrome show deficiencies in verbal intelligence and the degree of deficiency is related to the number of extra X chromosomes present. Klinefelter syndrome occurs approximately once in every 600 live male births.

**Fragile X syndrome** is a genetic disorder that results from an abnormality in the X chromosome, which becomes constricted and often breaks (Penagari-kano, Mulle, & Warren, 2007). Fragile X syndrome is the most common inherited form of intellectual disability, affecting 1 in 4,000 males and 1 in 6,000 females from all ethnic and socio-economic backgrounds (www.fragilexcanada.ca). It is a spectrum disorder, with intellectual disability ranging from a learning disability, a short attention span or severe intellectual disability. A recent study revealed that boys with fragile X syndrome were characterized by cognitive deficits in inhibition, memory, and planning (Hooper & others, 2008). This disorder occurs more frequently in males than in females, possibly because the second X chromosome in females negates the effects of the other abnormal X chromosome (Gomez-Raposo & others, 2010).

**Turner syndrome** is a chromosomal disorder in females in which either an X chromosome is missing, making the person XO instead of XX, or part of one X chromosome is deleted. Females with Turner syndrome are short in stature and have a webbed neck. They might be infertile and have difficulty in mathematics, but their verbal ability is often quite good (Murphy & Mazzocco, 2008). Turner syndrome occurs in approximately 1 of every 2,500 live female births.

The **XYY syndrome** is a chromosomal disorder in which the male has an extra Y chromosome and occurs in approximately 1 in 1,000 male births (Isen & Baker, 2008). There are no distinct physical characteristics associated with XYY syndrome, sexual development is typically normal, and there appears to be no distinct effect on intelligence (Milunsky, 2010). Early interest in this syndrome focused on the belief that the extra Y chromosome found in some males contributed to aggression and violence. However, researchers subsequently found that XYY males are no more likely to commit crimes than are XY males (Witkin & others, 1976).

**Gene-Linked Abnormalities** Abnormalities can be produced not only by an uneven number of chromosomes, but also by harmful genes (Presson & Jenner, 2008). More than 7,000 such genetic disorders have been identified, although most of them are rare.

**Phenylketonuria (PKU)** is a genetic disorder in which the individual cannot properly metabolize phenylalanine, an amino acid. It results from a recessive gene and occurs about once in every 10,000 to 20,000 live births. Today, phenylketonuria is easily detected, and it is treated by a diet that prevents an excess accumulation of phenylalanine. If phenylketonuria is left untreated, however, excess phenylalanine builds up in the child, producing intellectual disability and hyperactivity. Phenylketonuria accounts for approximately 1 percent of institutionalized individuals who have intellectual disabilities, and it occurs primarily in Caucasians.

The story of phenylketonuria has important implications for the nature-nurture issue. Although phenylketonuria is a genetic disorder (nature), how or whether a gene's influence in phenylketonuria is played out depends on environmental influences since the disorder can be treated (nurture) (van Spronsen & Enns, 2010). That is, the presence of a genetic defect does not inevitably lead to the development of the disorder if the individual develops in the right environment (one free of phenylalanine) (Grosse, 2010). This is one example of the important principle of heredity-environment interaction. Under one environmental condition (phenylalanine in the diet), intellectual disability results, but when other nutrients replace phenylalanine, intelligence develops in the normal range. The same genotype has different outcomes depending on the environment (in this case, the nutritional environment).

**Sickle-cell anemia,** which is common among individuals of African descent, is a genetic disorder that impairs the body's red blood cells. Red blood cells

**fragile X syndrome** A genetic disorder involving an abnormality in the X chromosome, which becomes constricted and often breaks.

**Turner syndrome** A chromosome disorder in females in which either an X chromosome is missing, making the person XO instead of XX, or the second X chromosome is partially deleted.

**XYY syndrome** A chromosomal disorder in which males have an extra Y chromosome.

**phenylketonuria (PKU)** A genetic disorder in which an individual cannot properly metabolize an amino acid. PKU is now easily detected but, if left untreated, results in intellectual disability and hyperactivity.

**sickle-cell anemia** A genetic disorder that affects the red blood cells and occurs most often in people of African descent.

| Name | Description | Treatment | Incidence |
|---|---|---|---|
| Cystic fibrosis | Glandular dysfunction that interferes with mucus production; breathing and digestion are hampered, resulting in a shortened life span. | Physical and oxygen therapy, synthetic enzymes, and antibiotics; most individuals live to middle age. | 1 in 2,000 births |
| Diabetes | Body does not produce enough insulin, which causes abnormal metabolism of sugar. | Early onset can be fatal unless treated with insulin. | 1 in 2,500 births |
| Hemophilia | Delayed blood clotting causes internal and external bleeding. | Blood transfusions/injections can reduce or prevent damage due to internal bleeding. | 1 in 10,000 males |
| Huntington disease | Central nervous system deteriorates, producing problems in muscle coordination and mental deterioration. | Does not usually appear until age 35 or older; death likely 10 to 20 years after symptoms appear. | 1 in 20,000 births |
| Tay-Sachs disease | Deceleration of mental and physical development caused by an accumulation of lipids in the nervous system. | Medication and special diet are used, but death is likely by 5 years of age. | 1 in 30 of European Jewish descent and French Canadians are carriers. |
| Wilson disease | Neuropsychiatric symptoms and liver disease caused by an accumulation of copper in the body. | Medication, diet low in copper, liver transplant. | 1–4 in 100,000 births |
| Muscular dystrophy | A group of diseases that weaken the muscles of the body. | No cure, but physiotherapy, occupational therapy, and speech therapy can help. | Rates differ depending on type. |

## FIGURE 2.9
**SOME GENE-LINKED ABNORMALITIES.**

carry oxygen to the body's cells and are usually shaped like disks. In sickle-cell anemia, a recessive gene causes the red blood cell to become a hook-shaped "sickle" that cannot carry oxygen properly and dies quickly. As a result, the body's cells do not receive adequate oxygen, causing anemia and early death (Benson & Therrell, 2010). An exact prevalence of sickle-cell anemia among Canadians of African descent is not known, but Health Canada estimates that within this population, approximately 1 in 400 babies are born with the disease and 1 in 10 are carriers of the trait (Health Canada, 2000). Recently, the Ontario and Nova Scotia provincial governments implemented newborn screening for sickle-cell anemia, recognizing that early detection and intervention can reduce mortality rates (Nova Scotia Government, 2013).

Other diseases that result from genetic abnormalities include cystic fibrosis, diabetes, hemophilia, Huntington disease, muscular dystrophy, Wilson disease, and Tay-Sachs disease (Velagaleti & O'Donnell, 2010; Viet & Schmidt, 2010). Figure 2.9 provides further information about these diseases. Canadian scientists are actively involved in identifying the genes and mutations involved in several genetic diseases, including muscular dystrophy (Wiltshire, Hegeleb, Innesc, & Brownella, (2013) and Wilson disease (Pon, Davies, Macintrye, & Cox, 2011). Once the specific changes or mutations are identified, scientists may be able to identify why these and other genetic abnormalities occur and discover how to cure them.

**Dealing with Genetic Abnormalities** Every individual carries DNA variations that might predispose the person to serious physical disease or mental disorder. But not all individuals who carry a genetic disorder display the disorder. Other genes or developmental events sometimes compensate for genetic abnormalities (Gottlieb, Wahlsten, & Lickliter, 2006). For example, recall the earlier example of phenylketonuria: Even though individuals might carry the genetic disorder of phenylketonuria, it is not expressed when phenylalanine is replaced by other nutrients in their diet.

During a physical examination for a college football tryout, Jerry Hubbard, 32, learned that he carried the gene for sickle-cell anemia. Daughter Sara is healthy, but daughter Avery (in the print dress) has sickle-cell anemia. *If you were a genetic counselor, would you recommend that this family have more children? Explain.*

## Stem Cell Research

Stem cells are undifferentiated cells that retain the ability to become any type of cell. Because of this property, stem cells have the potential to treat a variety of diseases.

Canadian scientists have been at the forefront of stem cell research since James Till and Ernest McCulloch, researchers at the University of Toronto, first identified and named stem cells in 1963 (Becker, McCulloch, & Ernest, 1963). Stem cells are undifferentiated cells that retain the potential to differentiate into other cell types. Because of this property, stems cells have the potential to treat a variety of diseases, such as spinal cord injury, diabetes, Parkinson's disease, and Alzheimer's disease.

There are three basic forms of stem cells, embryonic stem cells, embryonic germ cells, and adult cells. Embryonic stem cells come from the inner cell mass of the blastocyst during the embryonic period of prenatal development. These cells are pluripotent, which means they are capable of generating any cell in the body. Adult stem cells are also undifferentiated cells and are found in various tissues within the body. Like embryonic stem cells, adult stem cells have the ability to renew themselves; however, unlike embryonic stem cells, adult stem cells can only generate cells and tissue that match the ones they came from—that is, skin stem cells can only become skin cells. Because of this property, embryonic stem cells are more desirable for research.

Opposition to stem cell research is generally based on ethical issues. Opponents argue that the use of embryonic stem cells in research, either from embryos created for research purposes, or donated after in vitro fertilization, destroys a potential human life. Others cite concerns about the procurement of embryonic stem cells, suggesting that women will be induced to sell their stem cells or to have more embryos created than needed during in vitro fertilization.

In response to some of these ethical concerns, the Canadian Parliament passed Bill C-6, the *Assisted Human Reproductive Act,* S.C., 2004, C.2 in 2004, to regulate assisted human reproduction and related research. This act prohibits the creation of embryos for research purposes, as well as the purchase of reproductive tissue, including embryos. Consequently, embryonic stem cell research in Canada depends on the donation of surplus embryos created for reproductive purposes. Donors also must provide free and informed consent, fully understanding the purpose of their donations. Although this act establishes guidelines for embryonic stem cell research, it does not fully address the ethical concern related to the destruction of potential life.

However, in 2009 a Canadian-Scottish research team lead by Dr. Andras Nagy at Mount Sinai Hospital in Toronto developed a new method to create embryonic-like stem cells from adult cells (Wolten & Others, 2009). In this ground-breaking research, ordinary adult skin cells were reprogrammed into stem cells. These stem cells could potentially become any other type of cell, just like embryonic stem cells. Not only does this research into adult stem cells have the potential to eliminate ethical concerns about using embryonic stem cells in experiments, but it is also a step forward scientifically. This new approach to the generation of stem cells means they can potentially be created from any adult tissue, including a patient's own skin, thereby reducing the risk of rejection of the new cells by the patient's body. Continued study of all types of stem cells will lead to new discoveries in therapeutic treatments for a range of degenerative diseases.

*How might the use of stem cells for research influence decisions women make about the use of reproductive technologies?*

Thus, genes are not destiny, but genes that are missing, nonfunctional, or mutated can be associated with disorders (Zaghloul & Katsanis, 2010). Identifying such genetic flaws could enable doctors to predict an individual's risks, recommend healthy practices, and prescribe the safest and most effective drugs (Wider, Foroud, & Wszolek, 2010). Genetic counselors, usually physicians or biologists who are well versed in the field of medical genetics, help prospective parents assess the likelihood that their children will be free of hereditary diseases through analyses of family histories, blood tests, and DNA analyses (Boks & others, 2010; Sivell & others, 2008). A decade or two from now, parents of a newborn baby may be able to leave the hospital with a full genome analysis of their offspring that reveals disease risks.

**Review** *Connect* **Reflect**

**L02** Describe what genes are and how they influence children's development.

**Review**

- What are genes?
- How are genes passed on?
- What basic principles describe how genes interact?
- What are some chromosome and gene-linked abnormalities?

*Connect*

- Explain how environment interacts with genes in gene-linked abnormalities.

**Reflect** *Your Own Personal Journey of Life*

- Would you want to be able to access a full genome analysis of yourself or your offspring? Why or why not?

## Reproductive Challenges and Choices  Identify some important reproductive challenges and choices.

Prenatal Diagnostic Tests | Infertility and Reproductive Technology | Adoption

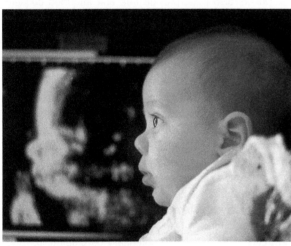

A 6-month-old infant with the ultrasound sonography record taken four months into the baby's prenatal development. *What are some of the ethical issues associated with the non-medical use of ultrasound sonography?*

The facts and principles we have discussed regarding meiosis, genetics, and genetic abnormalities are a small part of the recent explosion of knowledge about human biology. This knowledge not only helps us understand human development but also opens up many new choices to prospective parents—choices that can also raise ethical questions.

## PRENATAL DIAGNOSTIC TESTS

One choice open to prospective mothers is the option to undergo prenatal testing. A number of tests can indicate whether a fetus is developing normally, including ultrasound sonography, maternal serum testing, chorionic villus sampling, amniocentesis, fetal MRI, and non-invasive prenatal diagnosis (Lenzi & Johnson, 2008).

Most women in Canada have at least one ultrasound test between 18–21 weeks of pregnancy. *Ultrasound sonography* is a prenatal medical procedure in which high-frequency sound waves are directed into the pregnant woman's abdomen. The echo from the sounds is transformed into a visual representation of the fetus's inner structures. This technique can detect many structural abnormalities in the fetus, including microencephaly, a form of intellectual disability involving an abnormally small brain. Although there is virtually no risk to the woman or the fetus with an ultrasound, there are ethical concerns regarding the non-medical use of this technology. Because ultrasound can provide clues to the baby's sex (Gerards & others, 2008), some physicians advocate that sex not be revealed until after 30 weeks of pregnancy to prevent abortion of female fetuses, a practice that occurs, albeit infrequently, in Canada (Kale, 2012). In addition, the Society of Obstetricians and Gynaecologists of Canada recently released a policy statement advising that a fetus should not be exposed to ultrasound for commercial or entertainment purposes. These professionals cite concerns that fetal exposure to energy may not be properly monitored, that unsafe levels of abdominal pressure and fetal manoeuvring may be used to secure a commercial product, and that the individuals operating ultrasound machines may be poorly trained to identify abnormalities (Salem, Kim, & Van den Hof, 2014).

Also available to all pregnant women in Canada is integrated maternal serum testing. This blood test measures naturally occurring pregnancy hormones and screens for various genetic conditions. The blood test is conducted twice during pregnancy, usually between 9–13 weeks and again during the second trimester between 16–18 weeks. There is no risk to the woman or fetus with this screening test.

Women considered at risk because of their age or history of miscarriage usually have an earlier ultrasound test as well, between 11 and 13 weeks. Results of this ultrasound test, in conjunction with the results of the integrated maternal serum testing are used to calculate the risk that a baby may have specific chromosomal problems, such as Down syndrome. When the risk is assessed as high, pregnant women have the option of further diagnostic tests, including chorionic villus sampling and amniocentesis. Both of these tests can definitively determine whether or not certain chromosomal abnormalities or genetic conditions are present.

At some point between the 11th and 13th weeks of pregnancy, chorionic villus sampling may be used to detect genetic defects and chromosomal abnormalities such as those discussed in the previous section. *Chorionic villus sampling (CVS)* is a prenatal medical procedure in which a small sample of the placenta (the vascular organ that links the fetus to the mother's uterus) is removed. Diagnosis takes about 10 days. There is a 1 percent greater risk of miscarriage when CVS is used.

Between the 16th and 20th weeks of pregnancy, amniocentesis may be performed. *Amniocentesis* is a prenatal medical procedure in which a sample of amniotic fluid is withdrawn by syringe and tested for chromosomal or metabolic disorders (Nagel & others, 2007). The amnionic fluid is found within the amnion, a thin sac in which the embryo is suspended. Ultrasound sonography is often used during amniocentesis so that the syringe can be placed precisely. The later in the pregnancy amniocentesis is performed, the better its diagnostic potential. The earlier it is performed, the more useful it is in deciding how to handle a pregnancy. It may take two weeks for enough cells to grow and amniocentesis test results to be obtained. Amniocentesis brings a small risk of miscarriage: about 1 woman in every 400 miscarries after the procedure.

Both amniocentesis and chorionic villus sampling provide valuable information about the presence of birth defects, but they also raise difficult issues for parents about whether an abortion should be obtained if birth defects are present (Quadrelli & others, 2007; Zhang & others, 2010). Chorionic villus sampling allows parents to make a decision sooner, near the end of the first 13 weeks of pregnancy, when abortion is safer and less traumatic than later. Although earlier reports indicated that chorionic villus sampling brings a slightly higher risk of pregnancy loss than amniocentesis, a recent study of more than 40,000 pregnancies found that loss rates for CVS decreased over the period from 1998 to 2003 and that there is no longer a difference in pregnancy loss risk between CVS and amniocentesis (Caughey, Hopkins, & Norton, 2006).

The development of brain-imaging techniques has led to increasing use of *fetal MRI* to diagnose fetal malformations (Daltro & others, 2010; Duczkowska & others, 2010) (see Figure 2.10). MRI stands for *magnetic resonance imaging* and uses a powerful magnet and radio images to generate detailed images of the body's organs and structures. Currently, ultrasound is still the first choice in fetal screening, but fetal MRI can provide more detailed images than ultrasound. In many instances, ultrasound will indicate a possible abnormality and then fetal MRI will be used to obtain a clearer, more detailed image (Obenauer & Maestre, 2008). Among the fetal malformations that fetal MRI may be able to detect better than ultrasound sonography are certain abnormalities of the central nervous system, chest, gastrointestinal tract, genital/urinary system, and placenta (Baysinger, 2010; Panigrahy, Borzaga, & Blumi, 2010; Weston, 2010).

*Noninvasive prenatal diagnosis (NIPD)* is increasingly being explored as an alternative to procedures such as chorionic villus sampling and amniocentesis because it has a reduced risk of miscarriage (Susman & others, 2010). At this point, NIPD has mainly focused on the isolation and examination of fetal cells circulating in the mother's blood and analysis of cell-free fetal DNA in maternal plasma (Prakash, Powell, & Geva, 2010).

Researchers already have used NIPD to successfully test for genes inherited from a father that cause cystic fibrosis and Huntington disease. They also are

*developmental* **connection**

**Biological Processes.** Discover what the development of the fetus is like at the time chorionic villus sampling and amniocentesis can be used. Chapter 3, LO 1

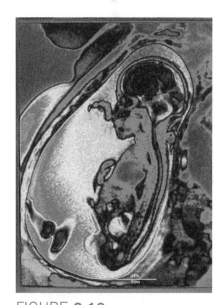

FIGURE **2.10**

**A FETAL MRI, WHICH IS INCREASINGLY BEING USED IN PRENATAL DIAGNOSIS OF FETAL MALFORMATIONS.**

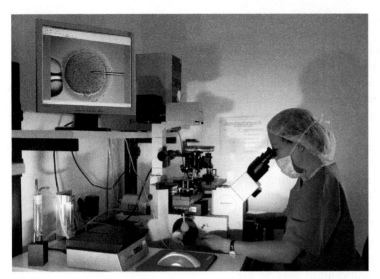

A technician uses a micro-needle to inject human sperm into a human egg cell as part of an in vitro fertilization procedure. The injected sperm fertilizes the egg, and the resulting zygote is then grown in the laboratory until it reaches an early stage of embryonic development. Then it is implanted in the uterus.

exploring the potential for using NIPD to identify a baby's sex as early as five weeks after conception and to diagnose Down syndrome (Avent & others, 2008). As previously discussed, however, being able to detect an offspring's sex and various diseases and defects so early raises ethical concerns about a couple's motivation to terminate a pregnancy (Benn & Chapman, 2010).

## INFERTILITY AND REPRODUCTIVE TECHNOLOGY

Recent advances in biological knowledge have also opened up many choices for infertile people. Approximately 11 to 16 percent of couples in Canada experience infertility, which is defined as the inability to conceive a child after 12 months of regular intercourse without contraception (Bushnik, 2012). The cause of infertility can rest with the woman or the man (Verhaak & others, 2010; Walsh, Pera, & Turek, 2010). The woman may not be ovulating (releasing eggs to be fertilized), she may be producing abnormal ova, her fallopian tubes—by which ova normally reach the womb—may be blocked, or she may have a disease that prevents implantation of the embryo into the uterus. The man may produce too few sperm, the sperm may lack motility (the ability to move adequately), or he may have a blocked passageway (Kini & others, 2010).

In Canada, approximately 380,000 couples seek help for infertility every year. In some cases of infertility, surgery may correct the cause; in others, hormone-based drugs may improve the probability of having a child. Of those couples who seek help for infertility every year, about 20 percent try high-tech assisted reproduction. By far the most common technique used is *in vitro fertilization* (IVF), in which eggs and sperm are combined in a laboratory dish. If any eggs are successfully fertilized, one or more of the resulting fertilized eggs is transferred into the woman's uterus. A national study in Canada conducted by the Canadian Fertility and Andrology Society (Gunby & others, 2010) found the success rate of IVF depends on the mother's age (see Figure 2.11).

As with any new reproductive technology, regulations need to be in place to ensure their ethical use. In Canada, the *Assisted Human Reproductive Act*, S.C., 2004, C.2, governs the use of IVF. For example, it is prohibited in Canada to buy sperm or eggs from a donor, although donors may be reimbursed for their expenses. In addition, the Act prohibits any act that increases the probability that an embryo will be a particular sex, unless this act will prevent, diagnose, or treat a sex-linked disorder or disease. Not covered under the Act are regulations regarding pre-implantation diagnostic testing. New technologies now enable certain genetic conditions to be identified before the fertilized egg is implanted into the woman's uterus. This new technology enables prospective parents to avoid severe genetic conditions that would result in stillbirth or miscarriage. However, opponents raise concerns about this technology being used for sex selection and the creation of "designer babies." In addition, IVF is an expensive option for families, with costs for the procedure estimated to be between $7,750 and $12,250. In 2015, Ontario will become the third province in Canada to partially fund IVF, joining Quebec and Manitoba as leaders in making treatment for infertility more accessible for all Canadians (CBC News, April 10, 2014).

The creation of families by means of the new reproductive technologies also raises important questions about the physical

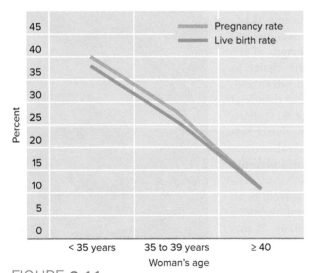

## FIGURE 2.11

**SUCCESS RATES OF IN VITRO FERTILIZATION VARY ACCORDING TO THE WOMAN'S AGE.**

and psychological consequences for children (Steel & Sutcliff, 2010; Wisborg, Ingerslev, & Henriksen, 2010). One result of fertility treatments is an increase in multiple births (Jones, 2007). Twenty-five to 30 percent of pregnancies achieved by fertility treatments—including in vitro fertilization—now result in multiple births. A recent *meta-analysis* (a statistical technique that combines the results of multiple studies to determine the strength of the effect) revealed that twins conceived through IVF have a slightly increased risk of low birth weight (McDonald & others, 2010), and another meta-analysis found that IVF singletons have a significant risk of low birth weight (McDonald & others, 2009). To read about a study that addresses longer-term consequences of IVF, see *Connecting Through Research.*

## ADOPTION

Although surgery and fertility drugs can sometimes solve the infertility problem, another choice is to adopt a child (Bernard & Dozier, 2008; Cohen & others, 2008). Adoption is the social and legal process by which a parent-child relationship is established between persons unrelated at birth. As discussed in *Connecting with Diversity,* an increase in diversity has characterized the adoption of children in Canada in recent years.

How do adopted children fare after they are adopted? Children who are adopted very early in their lives are more likely to have positive outcomes than children adopted later in life. In one study, the later adoption occurred, the more problems the adoptees had. Infant adoptees had the fewest adjustment difficulties; those adopted after they were 10 years of age had the most problems (Sharma, McGue, & Benson, 1996). In general, adopted children and adolescents are more

## connecting through research

### Do Children Conceived Through In Vitro Fertilization Show Significantly Different Developmental Outcomes in Adolescence?

A longitudinal study examined 34 in vitro fertilization families, 49 adoptive families, and 38 families with a naturally conceived child (Golombok, MacCallum, & Goodman, 2001). Each type of family included a similar portion of boys and girls. Also, the age of the young adolescents did not differ according to family type (mean age of 11 years, 11 months).

Children's socioemotional development was assessed by (1) interviewing the mother and obtaining detailed descriptions of any problems the child might have, (2) administering a Strengths and Difficulties questionnaire to the child's mother and teacher, and (3) administering the Social Adjustment Inventory for Children and Adolescents, which examines functioning in school, peer relationships, and self-esteem.

No significant differences between the children from the in vitro fertilization, adoptive, and naturally conceiving families were found. The results from the Social Adjustment Inventory for Children and Adolescents are shown in Figure 2.12. Another study also revealed no psychological differences between IVF babies and those not conceived by IVF, but more research is needed to reach firm conclusions in this area (Goldbeck & others, 2008).

*What role do nature and nurture play in the developmental outcomes associated with children conceived through in vitro fertilization?*

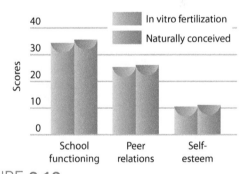

### FIGURE 2.12

**SOCIOEMOTIONAL FUNCTIONING OF CHILDREN CONCEIVED THROUGH IN VITRO FERTILIZATION OR NATURALLY CONCEIVED.** This graph shows the results of a study that compared the socioemotional functioning of young adolescents who had either been conceived through in vitro fertilization (IVF) or naturally conceived (Golombok, MacCallum, & Goodman, 2001). For each type of family, the study included a similar portion of boys and girls and children of similar age (mean age of 11 years, 11 months). Although the means for the naturally conceived group were slightly higher, this is likely due to chance: there were no significant differences between the groups.

## The Increased Diversity of Adopted Children and Adoptive Parents

A number of changes have characterized adoptive children and adoptive parents in the last three to four decades (Brodzinsky & Pinderhughes, 2002). In the first half of the twentieth century, most adopted children were healthy, White infants who were adopted at birth or soon after; however, in recent decades, as abortion became legal and contraception increased, fewer of these infants became available for adoption. Increasingly, couples adopted a much wider diversity of children. In Canada, children are increasingly adopted from other countries, including China, Ethiopia, and Haiti, as well as from other ethnic groups within Canada. Most provincial and territorial adoption agencies in Canada now have policies in place to ensure that the unique heritage and cultural ties of Aboriginal and Black Canadian children are preserved when placed with an adoptive family.

Changes also have characterized adoptive parents in the last three to four decades (Brodzinsky & Pinderhughes, 2002). In the first half of the twentieth century, most adoptive parents were from highly educated middle or upper socioeconomic status backgrounds who were married and did not have any type of disability. However, in recent decades, increased diversity has characterized adoptive parents. Throughout Canada, adults from a wide range of backgrounds are allowed to adopt children, including single adults, older adults, and same-sex couples.

*What are some of the challenges to the development of social and cultural identity that may be experienced by both adoptive parents and adoptive children as a result of the increased diversity in adoption practices?*

likely than non-adopted children to experience psychological and school-related problems (Keyes & others, 2008), to use mental health services (Juffer & van Ijzendoorn, 2005), to show more behaviour problems, and to have a learning disability (Altarac & Saroha, 2007). However, adopted adolescents are also less likely to be withdrawn and more likely to engage in prosocial behaviour, such as being altruistic, caring, and supportive of others, than their non-adopted peers (Sharma, McGue, & Benson, 1996). Further, a recent research review of 88 studies revealed no difference in the self-esteem of adopted and non-adopted children (Juffer & van Ijzendoorn, 2007). Most studies of adopted and non-adopted children compare different families (adoptive and non-adoptive). In a recent study, a different strategy was followed: families were studied who had a biological child of their own as well as a child they had adopted (Glover & others, 2010). Findings similar to studies of between-family comparisons occurred with only a slight (but non-significant) trend for adopted children to show more internalized (such as depression) and externalized problems (such as antisocial behaviour).

In other comparisons, adopted children fare much better than children raised in long-term foster care or in an institutional environment (Bernard & Dozier, 2008). Several Canadian longitudinal studies of infants adopted from orphanages in China, Russia, and East Asia revealed that their cognitive development improved two to six months following their adoption into Canadian families (Cohen & others, 2008; Pomerleau & others, 2005). Overall, the majority of adopted children (including those adopted at older ages, transracially, and across national borders) adjust effectively, and their parents report considerable satisfaction with their decision to adopt (Brodzinsky & Pinderhughes, 2002; Castle & others, 2010).

## Review Connect Reflect

 Identify some important reproductive challenges and choices.

### Review

- What are some common prenatal diagnostic tests?
- What are some techniques that help infertile people to have children?
- How does adoption affect children's development?

### Connect

- In Chapter 1, you learned about different methods for collecting data. How would you characterize the methods used in prenatal diagnostic testing?

### Reflect *Your Own Personal Journey of Life*

- If you were an adult who could not have children, would you want to adopt a child? Why or why not?

# Heredity and Environment Interaction: The Nature-Nurture Debate

Explain some of the ways that heredity and environment interact to produce individual differences in development.

Behaviour Genetics

Shared and Non-shared Environmental Experiences

Conclusions About Heredity-Environment Interaction

Heredity-Environment Correlations

The Epigenetic View and Heredity × Environment (H × E) Interaction

Is it possible to untangle the influence of heredity from that of environment and discover the role of each in producing individual differences in development? When heredity and environment interact, how does heredity influence the environment and vice versa?

## BEHAVIOUR GENETICS

**Behaviour genetics** is the field that seeks to discover the influence of heredity and environment on individual differences in human traits and development (Kandler, Riemann, & Kampfe, 2009). Note that behaviour genetics does not determine the extent to which genetics or the environment affects an individual's traits. Instead, behaviour geneticists try to figure out what is responsible for the differences among people—that is, to what extent people differ because of differences in genes, environment, or a combination of these (Silberg, Maes, & Eaves, 2010). To study the influence of heredity on behaviour, behaviour geneticists often use either twins or adoption situations (Mustelin & others, 2009).

In the most common **twin study**, the behavioural similarity of identical twins (who are genetically identical) is compared with the behavioural similarity of fraternal twins. Recall that although fraternal twins share the same womb, they are no more genetically alike than any other brothers or sisters. Thus, by comparing groups of identical and fraternal twins, behaviour geneticists capitalize on the basic knowledge that identical twins are more similar genetically than are fraternal twins (Isen & others, 2009; Loehlin, 2010). For example, one study found that conduct problems were more prevalent in identical twins than fraternal twins; the researchers concluded that the study demonstrated an important role for heredity in conduct problems (Scourfield & others, 2004).

However, several issues complicate interpretation of twin studies. For example, perhaps the environments of identical twins are more similar than the environments of fraternal twins. Adults might stress the similarities of identical twins more than those of fraternal twins, and identical twins might perceive themselves as a "set" and play together more than fraternal twins do. If so, the influence of the environment on the observed similarities between identical and fraternal twins might be very significant.

In an **adoption study**, investigators seek to discover whether the behaviour and psychological characteristics of adopted children are more like those of their adoptive parents, who have provided a home environment, or more like those of their biological parents, who have contributed their heredity (Loehlin, Horn, & Ernst, 2007). Another form of the adoption study compares adoptive and biological siblings.

## HEREDITY-ENVIRONMENT CORRELATIONS

The difficulties that researchers encounter when they interpret the results of twin studies and adoption studies reflect the complexities of heredity-environment interaction. Some of these interactions are *heredity-environment correlations*, which

**behaviour genetics** The field that seeks to discover the influence of heredity and environment on individuals' differences in human traits and development.

**twin study** A study in which the behavioural similarity of identical twins is compared with the behavioural similarity of fraternal twins.

Twin studies compare identical twins with fraternal twins. Identical twins develop from a single fertilized egg that splits into two genetically identical organisms. Fraternal twins develop from separate eggs, making them genetically no more similar than non-twin siblings. *What is the nature of the twin study method?*

**adoption study** A study in which investigators seek to discover whether, in behaviour and psychological characteristics, adopted children are more like their adoptive parents, who provided a home environment, or more like their biological parents, who contributed their heredity. Another form of the adoption study is one that compares adoptive and biological siblings.

| Heredity-Environment Correlation | Description | Examples |
|---|---|---|
| Passive | Children inherit genetic tendencies from their parents, and parents also provide an environment that matches their own genetic tendencies. | Musically inclined parents usually have musically inclined children and are likely to provide an environment rich in music for their children. |
| Evocative | The child's genetic tendencies elicit stimulation from the environment that supports a particular trait. Thus, genes evoke environmental support. | A happy, outgoing child elicits smiles and friendly responses from others. |
| Active (niche-picking) | Children actively seek out "niches" in their environment that reflect their own interests and talents and are thus in accord with their genotype. | Libraries, sports fields, and a store with musical instruments are examples of environmental niches children might seek out if they have an intellectual interest in books, talent in sports, or musical talents, respectively. |

FIGURE **2.13**

**EXPLORING HEREDITY-ENVIRONMENT CORRELATIONS.**

**passive genotype-environment correlations** Correlations that exist when the natural parents, who are genetically related to the child, provide a rearing environment for the child.

**evocative genotype-environment correlations** Correlations that exist when the child's genotype elicits certain types of physical and social environments.

**active (niche-picking) genotype-environment correlations** Correlations that exist when children seek out environments they find compatible and stimulating.

means that individuals' genes may influence the types of environments to which they are exposed. In a sense, individuals "inherit" environments that may be related or linked to genetic propensities. Behaviour geneticist Sandra Scarr (1993) described three ways that heredity and environment are correlated (see Figure 2.13):

- **Passive genotype-environment correlations** occur because biological parents, who are genetically related to the child, provide a rearing environment for the child. For example, the parents might have a genetic predisposition to be intelligent and read skillfully. Because they read well and enjoy reading, they provide their children with books to read. The likely outcome is that their children, given their own inherited predispositions from their parents and their book-filled environment, will become skilled readers.

- **Evocative genotype-environment correlations** occur because a child's characteristics elicit certain types of environments. For example, active, smiling children receive more social stimulation than passive, quiet children do. Co-operative, attentive children evoke more pleasant and instructional responses from the adults around them than uncooperative, distractible children do.

- **Active (niche-picking) genotype-environment correlations** occur when children seek out environments that they find compatible and stimulating. *Niche-picking* refers to finding a setting that is suited to one's abilities. Children select from their surrounding environment some aspect that they respond to, learn about, or ignore. Their active selections of environments are related to their particular genotype. For example, outgoing children tend to seek out social contexts in which to interact with people, whereas shy children don't. Children who are musically inclined are likely to select musical environments in which they can successfully perform their skills.

Scarr observes that there is a change in the relative importance of the three genotype-environment correlations as children develop from infancy through adolescence. In infancy, much of the environment that children experience is provided by adults. Thus, passive genotype-environment correlations are more common in the lives of infants and young children than they are for older children and adolescents who can extend their experiences beyond the family's influence and create their environments to a greater degree.

## SHARED AND NON-SHARED ENVIRONMENTAL EXPERIENCES

Behaviour geneticists have argued that to understand the environment's role in differences between people, we should distinguish between shared and non-shared environments. That is, we should consider experiences that children have in common with other children living in the same home and experiences that are not shared (Burt, McGue, & Iacono, 2010; Cerda & others, 2010).

**Shared environmental experiences** are siblings' common experiences, such as their parents' personalities or intellectual orientation, the family's socioeconomic status, and the neighbourhood in which they live. By contrast, **non-shared environmental experiences** are a child's unique experiences, both within the family and outside the family, that are not shared with a sibling. Even experiences occurring within the family can be part of the non-shared environment. For example, parents often interact differently with each sibling, and siblings interact differently with parents. Siblings often have different peer groups, different friends, and different teachers at school.

Behaviour geneticist Robert Plomin (2004) has found that shared environment accounts for little of the variation in children's personality or interests. In other words, even though two children live under the same roof with the same parents, their personalities are often very different. Further, Plomin argues that heredity influences the non-shared environments of siblings through the heredity-environment correlations we described earlier. For example, a child who has inherited a genetic tendency to be athletic is likely to spend more time in environments related to sports, and a child who has inherited a tendency to be musically inclined is more likely to spend time in environments related to music.

What are the implications of Plomin's interpretation of the role of shared and non-shared environments in development? In *The Nurture Assumption*, Judith Harris (1998, 2009) argued that what parents do does not make a difference in their children's and adolescents' behaviour. Yell at them. Hug them. Read to them. Ignore them. Harris says it won't influence how they turn out. She argues that genes and peers are far more important than parents in children's and adolescents' development.

Genes and peers do matter, but Harris' descriptions of peer influences do not take into account the complexity of peer contexts and developmental trajectories (Hartup, 2009). In addition, Harris is wrong in saying that parents don't matter. For example, in the early childhood years parents play an important role in selecting children's peers and indirectly influencing children's development (Baumrind, 1999). A large volume of parenting literature with many research studies documents the important and direct role of parents in children's development (Meaney, 2010; Schultz & others, 2009). We will discuss parents' important roles throughout this book.

## THE EPIGENETIC VIEW AND GENE ×
## ENVIRONMENT (G × E) INTERACTION

Critics argue that the concept of heredity-environment correlation gives heredity too much one-sided influence in determining development because it does not consider the role of prior environmental influences in shaping the correlation itself (Gottlieb, 2007). However, earlier in the chapter we discussed how genes are collaborative, not determining an individual's traits in an independent manner but rather interacting with the environment.

**The Epigenetic View** In line with the concept of a collaborative gene, Gilbert Gottlieb (2007) emphasizes the epigenetic view, which is a branch of biology used by developmental psychologists to explain how the environment can play a role in gene expression. In this view, early life experiences such as housing and child-rearing practices, and environmental factors such as maternal stress and smoking, can produce heritable changes in gene expression (the phenotype) that are not coded in the DNA itself. Rather, it is the proteins that regulate

**shared environmental experiences**
Siblings' common environmental experiences, such as their parents' personalities and intellectual orientation, the family's socioeconomic status, and the neighbourhood in which they live.

**non-shared environmental experiences**
The child's own unique experiences, both within the family and outside the family, that are not shared by another sibling. Thus, experiences occurring within the family can be part of the non-shared environment.

**epigenetic view** Emphasizes that development is a result of a bidirectional interchange between heredity and environment, in which environmental factors can influence how genes are expressed.

Canadian siblings Michael and Lauren Wilkinson both competed in the 2012 Summer Olympics as rowers. *What might be some shared and non-shared environmental experiences they had while they were growing up that contributed to their athletic success?*

genetic activity that are modified by experience, altering the way our genes function or are expressed.

Let's look at an example that reflects the epigenetic view. A baby inherits genes from both parents at conception. During prenatal development, toxins, nutrition, and stress can influence some genes to stop functioning while others become stronger or weaker. For example, Dr. Timothy Oberlander and his team at the University of British Columbia are exploring how maternal depression might alter the way genes are expressed to produce individual differences in the health, development, and behaviour of offspring (Weikum, Mayes, Grunau, Brain, & Oberlander, 2013; Oberlander, 2012). During infancy, the same environmental experiences such as toxins, nutrition, stress, learning, and encouragement continue to modify genetic activity and the activity of the nervous system that directly underlies behaviour. Heredity and environment operate together—or collaborate—to produce a person's intelligence, temperament, height, weight, ability to pitch a baseball, ability to read, and so on (Gottlieb, 2007; Meaney, 2010).

**Gene × Environment (G × E) Interaction**  An increasing number of studies are exploring how the interaction of heredity and environment influence development, including interactions that involve specific DNA sequences (Caspi, 2010; Keers & others, 2010; Pauli-Pott & others, 2009; Shen, 2009; Wright & Christiani, 2010). One research study found that individuals who have a short version of a genotype labeled 5-HTTLPR (a gene involving the neurotransmitter serotonin) have an elevated risk of developing depression only if they also have stressful lives (Caspi, 2003). Thus, the specific gene did not link directly to the development of depression, but rather interacted with environmental exposure to stress to predict whether individuals would develop depression; however, some studies have not replicated this finding (Goldman & others, 2010; Risch & others, 2009). In a recent study, adults who experienced parental loss as young children were more likely to have unresolved attachment as adults only when they had the short version of the 5-HTTLPR gene (Caspers & others, 2009). The long version of the serotonin transporter gene apparently provided some protection and ability to cope better with parental loss.

The research just described is referred to as **gene × environment (G × E) interaction**—the interaction of a specific, measured variation in the DNA and a specific, measured aspect of the environment (Caspi & others, 2010; Seabrook & Avison, 2010). The field of *pharmacogenetics* is the study of gene-environment interaction involving the individual's genotype and drug treatment (the environment factor) (Cheok & others, 2009; Keers & others, 2010). The goal of many pharmacogenetic studies is to discover whether certain drugs are safer or more dangerous to use if the individual's genotype is known (Berlin, Paul, & Vesell, 2009; Lima & others, 2009).

## CONCLUSIONS ABOUT HEREDITY-ENVIRONMENT INTERACTION

If an attractive, popular, intelligent girl is elected president of her senior class in high school, is her success due to heredity or to environment? Of course the answer is both.

The relative contributions of heredity and environment are not additive. That is, we can't say that such-and-such a percentage of nature and such-and-such a percentage of experience make us who we are. Neither is it accurate to say that full genetic expression happens once, around conception or birth, after which we carry our genetic legacy into the world to see how far it takes us. Genes produce proteins throughout the life span, in many different

**gene × environment (G × E) interaction**
The interaction of a specific measured variation in the DNA and a specific measured aspect of the environment.

*developmental* **connection**

**Biological Processes.** A recent study revealed links between infant attachment, responsive parenting, and the short/long version of the 5-HTTLPR gene. Chapter 10, LO 4

environments. Or they don't produce these proteins, depending in part on how harsh or nourishing those environments are.

The emerging view is that complex behaviours have some genetic loading that gives people a propensity for a particular developmental trajectory (Guo & Tillman, 2009). However, the actual development requires more: an environment. And that environment is complex, just like the mixture of genes we inherit (Duncan, Ziol-Guest, & Kalil, 2010; Gauvain & Parke, 2010). Environmental influences range from the things we lump together under "nurture" (such as parenting, family dynamics, schooling, and neighbourhood quality) to biological encounters (such as viruses, birth complications, and even biological events in cells).

Imagine for a moment that there is a cluster of genes somehow associated with youth violence (this example is hypothetical because we don't know of any such combination). The adolescent who carries this genetic mixture might experience a world of loving parents, regular nutritious meals, lots of books, and a series of masterful teachers. Or the adolescent's world might include parental neglect, a neighbourhood in which gunshots and crime are everyday occurrences, and inadequate schooling. In which of these environments are the adolescent's genes likely to manufacture the biological underpinnings of criminality?

If heredity and environment interact to determine the course of development, is that all there is to answering the question of what causes development? Are children completely at the mercy of their genes and environment as they develop? Genetic heritage and environmental experiences are pervasive influences on development (Sameroff, 2010; Wermter & others, 2010). But children's development is not solely the outcome of their heredity and environment; children also can author a unique developmental path by changing their environment. As one psychologist recently concluded

> In reality, we are both the creatures and creators of our worlds. We are . . . the products of our genes and environments. Nevertheless . . . the stream of causation that shapes the future runs through our present choices . . . Mind matters . . . Our hopes, goals, and expectations influence our future. (Myers, 2010, p.168)

*developmental* **connection**

**Nature vs. Nurture.** The nature-nurture issue is one of the main issues in the study of lifespan development. Chapter 1, LO 2

## Review *Connect* Reflect

 **LO4** Explain some of the ways that heredity and environment interact to produce individual differences in development.

### Review

- What is behaviour genetics?
- What are three types of heredity-environment correlations?
- What is meant by the concepts of shared and non-shared environmental experiences?
- What is the epigenetic view of development? What characterizes gene × environment (G × E) interaction?
- What conclusions can be reached about heredity-environment interaction?

### Connect

- Of passive, evocative, and active genotype-environment correlations, which is the best explanation for the similarities discovered between the twins discussed in the story that opened this chapter?

### Reflect *Your Own Personal Journey of Life*

- Imagine that someone tells you that he or she has analyzed your genetic background and environmental experiences and reached the conclusion that the environment you grew up in as a child definitely had little influence on your intelligence. What would you say about this analysis?

# Case Study Connections

1. What are some examples from the twins' stories that opened this chapter that illustrate how hereditary and environmental factors interact in development?

2. The twins discussed in the story that opened this chapter were adopted. What influence might adoption have on the developmental outcomes of twins?

3. What are some examples of shared and non-shared environments from the story of the twins that opened this chapter?

# reach your learning goals

# Biological Beginnings

## The Evolutionary Perspective

 **LO1** Discuss the evolutionary perspective on child development.

- Natural Selection and Adaptive Behaviour

- Evolutionary Psychology

- Natural selection is the process by which those individuals of a species that are best adapted to the environment survive and reproduce. Darwin proposed that natural selection fuels evolution. In evolutionary theory, adaptive behaviour is behaviour that promotes the organism's survival in a natural habitat.

- Evolutionary psychology holds that adaptation, reproduction, and "survival of the fittest" are important in shaping behaviour. Ideas proposed by evolutionary developmental psychology include the view that an extended childhood period is needed to develop a large brain and learn the complexity of human social communities. Like other theoretical approaches to development, evolutionary psychology has limitations. Bandura rejects "one-sided evolutionism" and argues for a bidirectional link between biology and environment. Biology allows for a broad range of cultural possibilities.

## Genetic Foundations of Development

 **LO2** Describe what genes are and how they influence children's development.

- The Collaborative Gene

- Genes and Chromosomes

- Genetic Principles

- Chromosome and Gene-Linked Abnormalities

- Short segments of DNA constitute genes, the units of hereditary information that direct cells to reproduce and manufacture proteins. Genes act collaboratively, not independently.

- Genes are passed on to new cells when chromosomes are duplicated during the process of mitosis and meiosis, which are two ways in which new cells are formed. When an egg and a sperm unite in the fertilization process, the resulting zygote contains the genes from the chromosomes in the father's sperm and the mother's egg. Despite this transmission of genes from generation to generation, variability is created in several ways, including the exchange of chromosomal segments during meiosis, mutations, and environmental influences.

- Genetic principles include those involving dominant-recessive genes, sex-linked genes, genetic imprinting, and polygenic inheritance.

- Chromosome abnormalities produce Down syndrome, which is caused by the presence of an extra copy of chromosome 21, as well as sex-linked chromosomal abnormalities such as Klinefelter syndrome, fragile X syndrome, Turner syndrome, and XYY syndrome. Gene-linked abnormalities involve harmful genes. Gene-linked disorders include phenylketonuria (PKU) and sickle-cell anemia. Genetic counseling offers couples information about their risk of having a child with inherited abnormalities.

## Reproductive Challenges and Choices  Identify some important reproductive challenges and choices.

Prenatal Diagnostic Tests

Infertility and Reproductive Technology

Adoption

- Ultrasound sonography, fetal MRI, chorionic villus sampling, amniocentesis, and maternal serum testing are used to determine whether a fetus is developing normally. Non-invasive prenatal diagnosis is increasingly being explored.

- Approximately 11 to 16 percent of Canadian couples have infertility problems, some of which can be corrected through surgery or fertility drugs. An additional option is in vitro fertilization.

- Although adopted children and adolescents have more problems than their non-adopted counterparts, the vast majority of adopted children adapt effectively. When adoption occurs very early in development, the outcomes for the child are improved. Because of the dramatic changes that occurred in adoption in recent decades, it is difficult to generalize about the average adopted child or average adoptive family.

## Heredity and Environment Interaction: The Nature-Nurture Debate  Explain some of the ways that heredity and environment interact to produce individual differences in development.

Behaviour Genetics

Heredity-Environment Correlations

Shared and Non-shared Environmental Experiences

The Epigenetic View and Gene × Environment (G × E) Interaction

Conclusions About Heredity-Environment Interaction

- Behaviour genetics is the field concerned with the influence of heredity and environment on individual differences in human traits and development. Methods used by behaviour geneticists include twin studies and adoption studies.

- In Scarr's heredity-environment correlations view, heredity directs the types of environments that children experience. She describes three genotype-environment correlations: passive, evocative, and active (niche-picking). Scarr argues that the relative importance of these three genotype-environment correlations changes as children develop.

- Shared environmental experiences refer to siblings' common experiences, such as their parents' personalities and intellectual orientation, the family's socioeconomic status, and the neighbourhood in which they live. Non-shared environmental experiences involve the child's unique experiences, both within a family and outside a family, that are not shared with a sibling. Many behaviour geneticists argue that differences in the development of siblings are due to non-shared environmental experiences (and heredity) rather than shared environmental experiences.

- The epigenetic view emphasizes that development is the result of a bidirectional interchange between heredity and environment, in which environmental factors can influence how genes are expressed. Gene × environment interaction involves the interaction of a specific, measured variation in the DNA and a specific, measured aspect of the environment. An increasing number of G × E studies are being conducted.

- Complex behaviours have some genetic loading that gives people a propensity for a particular developmental trajectory. However, actual development also requires an environment, and that environment is complex. The interaction of heredity and environment is extensive. Much remains to be discovered about the specific ways that heredity and environment interact to influence development. Although heredity and environment are pervasive influences on development, humans can author a unique developmental path by changing their environment.

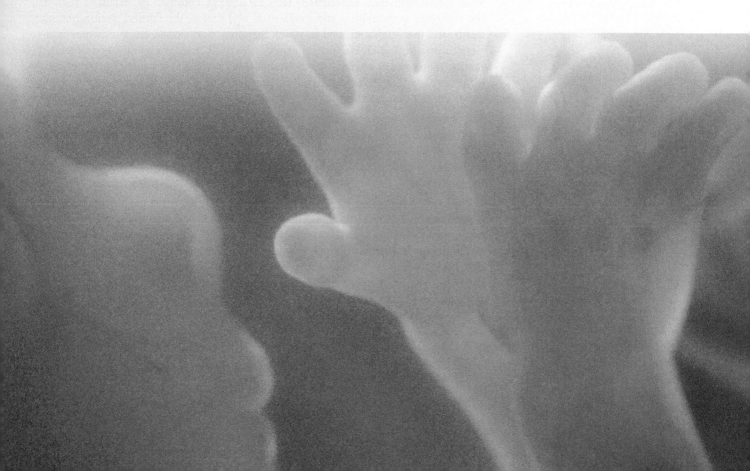

# chapter 3 | Prenatal Development and Birth

Diana and Roger married when he was 38 and she was 34. Both worked full time and were excited when Diana became pregnant. Two months later Diana began to have some unusual pains and bleeding. Just two months into her pregnancy she had lost the baby. Diana thought deeply about why she was unable to carry the baby to full term. It was about the time she became pregnant that the federal government began to warn that eating certain types of fish with a high mercury content on a regular basis during pregnancy can cause a miscarriage. Now she eliminated these fish from her diet.

Six months later, Diana became pregnant again. She and Roger read about pregnancy and signed up for birth preparation classes. Each Friday night for eight weeks they practised simulated contractions. They talked about what kind of parents they wanted to be and discussed how their lives would change after the baby was born. When they found out that their offspring was going to be a boy, they gave him a nickname: Mr. Littles.

This time, Diana's pregnancy went well, and Alex was born. During the birth, however, Diana's heart rate dropped precipitously and she was given a stimulant to raise it. Apparently the stimulant also increased Alex's heart rate and breathing to a dangerous point, and he had to be placed in a neonatal intensive care unit (NICU).

Alex, also known as Mr. Littles.

Several times a day, Diana and Roger visited Alex in the NICU. A number of babies in the NICU who had a very low birth weight had been in intensive care for weeks, and some of these babies were not doing well. Fortunately, Alex was in better health. After several days in the NICU, his parents were permitted to take home a very healthy Alex.

preview

This chapter chronicles the truly remarkable developments from conception through birth. We will look at normal development as well as hazards to normal development (such as mercury, mentioned in the preceding story). We will outline the birth process and the tests used to assess the newborn. We will examine the physical, emotional, and psychological adjustments that a mother goes through during the time following birth—the postpartum period.

Prenatal Development  **L01**  Describe prenatal development.

| The Course of Prenatal Development | Teratology and Hazards of Prenatal Development | Prenatal Care | Normal Prenatal Development |

Imagine how Alex (Mr. Littles) came to be. Out of thousands of eggs and millions of sperm, one egg and one sperm united to produce him. Had the union of sperm and egg come a day or even an hour earlier or later, he might have been very different—maybe even of the opposite sex. *Conception* occurs when a single sperm cell from the male unites with an ovum (egg) in the female's fallopian tube in a process called fertilization. Over the next few months, the genetic code discussed in Chapter 2 directs a series of changes in the fertilized egg, but many events and hazards will influence how that egg develops and becomes tiny Alex.

## THE COURSE OF PRENATAL DEVELOPMENT

Typical prenatal development begins with fertilization and ends with birth, lasting between 266 and 280 days (from 38 to 40 weeks). It can be divided into three periods: germinal, embryonic, and fetal.

**germinal period** The period of prenatal development that takes place in the first two weeks after conception. It includes the creation of the zygote, continued cell division, and the attachment of the zygote to the uterine wall.

**The Germinal Period**   The **germinal period** is the period of prenatal development that takes place in the first two weeks after conception. It includes the creation of the fertilized egg, called a zygote, followed by cell division and attachment of the zygote to the uterine wall.

Rapid cell division by the zygote continues throughout the germinal period (recall from Chapter 2 that this cell division occurs through a process called *mitosis*). By approximately one week after conception, the differentiation of these cells—their specialization for different tasks—has already begun. At this stage, the group of cells, now called the **blastocyst**, consists of an inner mass of cells that will eventually develop into the embryo, and the **trophoblast**, an outer layer of cells that later provides nutrition and support for the embryo. *Implantation*, the attachment of the zygote to the uterine wall, takes place about 11 to 15 days after conception. Figure 3.1 illustrates some of the most significant developments during the germinal period.

**blastocyst** The inner layer of cells that develops during the germinal period. These cells later develop into the embryo.

**trophoblast** The outer layer of cells that develops in the germinal period. These cells provide nutrition and support for the embryo.

**embryonic period** The period of prenatal development that occurs from two to eight weeks after conception. During the embryonic period, the rate of cell differentiation intensifies, support systems for the cells form, and organs appear.

**The Embryonic Period**   The **embryonic period** is the period of prenatal development that occurs from two to eight weeks after conception. During the embryonic period, the rate of cell differentiation intensifies, support systems for cells form, and organs appear.

This period begins as the blastocyst attaches to the uterine wall. The mass of cells is now called an *embryo*, and three layers of cells form. The embryo's *endoderm* is the inner layer of cells, which will develop into the digestive and respiratory

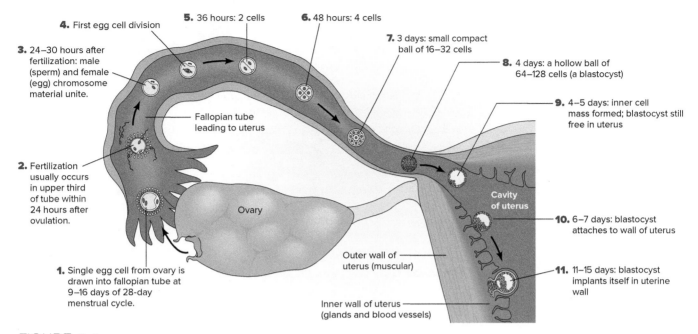

**FIGURE 3.1**

**SIGNIFICANT DEVELOPMENTS IN THE GERMINAL PERIOD.** Just one week after conception, cells of the blastocyst have already begun specializing. The germination period ends when the blastocyst attaches to the uterine wall. *Which of the steps shown in the drawing occur in the laboratory when IVF (described in Chapter 2) is used?*

systems. The *mesoderm* is the middle layer, which will become the circulatory system, bones, muscles, excretory system, and reproductive system. The *ectoderm* is the outermost layer, which will become the nervous system and brain, sensory receptors (ears, nose, and eyes, for example), and skin parts (hair and nails, for example). Every body part eventually develops from these three layers. The endoderm primarily produces internal body parts, the mesoderm primarily produces parts that surround the internal areas, and the ectoderm primarily produces surface parts.

As the embryo's three layers form, life-support systems for the embryo develop rapidly. These life-support systems include the amnion, the umbilical cord (both of which develop from the fertilized egg, not the mother's body), and the placenta. The **amnion** is like a bag or an envelope and contains a clear fluid in which the developing embryo floats. The amniotic fluid provides an environment that is temperature and humidity controlled, as well as shockproof. The **umbilical cord** contains two arteries and one vein, and connects the baby to the placenta. The **placenta** consists of a disk-shaped group of tissues in which small blood vessels from the mother and the offspring intertwine but do not join.

Figure 3.2 illustrates the placenta, the umbilical cord, and the blood flow in the expectant mother and developing organism. Very small molecules—oxygen, water, salt, food from the mother's blood, as well as carbon dioxide and digestive wastes from the offspring's blood—pass back and forth between the mother and embryo or fetus (Woolett, 2011). Virtually any drug or chemical substance the pregnant woman ingests can cross the placenta to some degree, unless it is metabolized or altered during passage, or it is too large (Hutson & others, 2013; Iqbal & others, 2012). A recent study revealed that cigarette smoke weakens and increases the oxidative stress of fetal membranes, from which the placenta develops (Menon & others, 2011). Large molecules that cannot pass through the placental wall include red blood cells and harmful substances, such as most bacteria, maternal wastes, and hormones. The mechanisms that govern the transfer of substances across the placental barrier are complex and are still not entirely understood (Matlow & others, 2013; Saunders, Liddelow, & Dziegielewska, 2012; Yuen & others, 2013).

By the time most women know they are pregnant, the embryo's major organs have begun to form. **Organogenesis** is the name given to the process of organ

**amnion** Prenatal life-support system that is a bag or envelope that contains a clear fluid in which the developing embryo floats.

**umbilical cord** A life-support system that contains two arteries and one vein, and connects the baby to the placenta.

**placenta** A life-support system that consists of a disk-shaped group of tissues in which small blood vessels from the mother and offspring intertwine.

**organogenesis** Organ formation that takes place during the first two months of prenatal development.

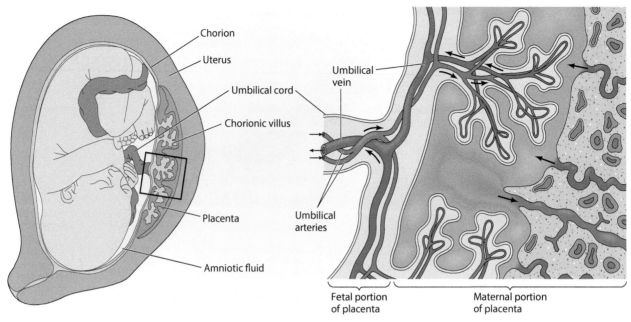

**FIGURE 3.2**

**THE PLACENTA AND THE UMBILICAL CORD.** The area bound by the square in the right half of the illustration is enlarged. Arrows indicate the direction of blood flow. Maternal blood flows through the uterine arteries to the spaces housing the placenta, and it returns through the uterine veins to the maternal circulation. Fetal blood flows through the umbilical arteries into the capillaries of the placenta and returns through the umbilical vein to the fetal circulation. The exchange of materials takes place across the layer separating the maternal and fetal blood supplies, so the bloods never come into contact. *What is known about how the placental barrier works and its importance?*

formation during the first two months of prenatal development. While they are being formed, the organs are especially vulnerable to environmental changes (Wei & others, 2013). In the third week after conception, the neural tube that eventually becomes the spinal cord forms. At about 21 days eyes begin to appear, and at 24 days the cells for the heart begin to differentiate. During the fourth week, the urogenital system becomes apparent, and arm and leg buds emerge. Four chambers of the heart take shape and blood vessels appear. From the fifth to the eighth week, arms and legs differentiate further; at this time, the face starts to form but still is not very recognizable. The intestinal tract develops and the facial structures fuse. At eight weeks, the developing organism weighs about 1 gram and is just over 2.5 cm long.

**The Fetal Period**  The **fetal period**, lasting about seven months, is the prenatal period between two months after conception and birth in typical pregnancies. Growth and development continue their dramatic course during this time.

Three months after conception, the fetus is about 7.5 cm long and weighs about 85 grams. It has become active, moving its arms and legs, opening and closing its mouth, and moving its head. The face, forehead, eyelids, nose, and chin are distinguishable, as are the upper arms, lower arms, hands, and lower limbs. In most cases, the genitals can be identified as male or female. By the end of the fourth month of pregnancy, the fetus has grown to just over 15 cm in length and weighs 113 to 200 grams. At this time, a growth spurt occurs in the body's lower parts. For the first time, the mother can feel arm and leg movements.

By the end of the fifth month, the fetus is about 30.5 cm long and weighs close to half a kilogram. Structures of the skin have formed—toenails and fingernails, for example. The fetus is more active, showing a preference for a particular position in the womb. By the end of the sixth month the fetus is about 35.5 cm long and has gained another quarter to half kilogram. The eyes and eyelids are completely formed, and a fine layer of hair covers the head. A grasping reflex is present and irregular breathing movements occur.

As early as six months of pregnancy (about 24 to 25 weeks after conception), the fetus for the first time has a chance of surviving outside of the womb—that is, it is *viable*. Infants who are born early, or between 24 and 37 weeks of

**fetal period** The period from two months after conception until birth, lasting about seven months in typical pregnancies.

> The history of man for nine months preceding his birth would, probably, be far more interesting, and contain events of greater moment than all three score and ten years that follow it.
>
> —SAMUEL TAYLOR COLERIDGE
> *English Poet, Essayist, 19th Century*

pregnancy, usually need help breathing because their lungs are not yet fully mature. By the end of the seventh month the fetus is about 40.5 cm long and weighs about 1.3 kilograms.

During the last two months of prenatal development, fatty tissues develop, and the functioning of various organ systems—heart and kidneys, for example—steps up. During the eighth and ninth months, the fetus grows longer and gains substantial weight—almost another 2 kilograms. At birth, the average North American baby weighs about 3.17 kilograms (7 pounds) and is about 50.8 cm (20 inches) long.

Figure 3.3 gives an overview of the main events during prenatal development. Notice that instead of describing development in terms of germinal, embryonic, and fetal periods, Figure 3.3 divides prenatal development into equal periods of three months, called *trimesters*. Remember that the three trimesters are not the same as the three prenatal periods we

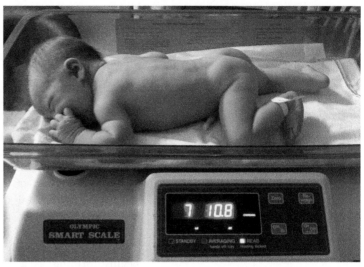

This one-hour-old baby was born at term weighing 7 pounds and 10.8 ounces (3.45 kilograms). *What are some of the developmental changes that have occurred prior to this baby's birth?*

## Prenatal Growth

### First trimester (first 3 months)

**Conception to 4 weeks**
- Is less than 0.25cm long
- Beginning development of spinal cord, nervous system, gastrointestinal system, heart, and lungs
- Amniotic sac envelops the preliminary tissues of entire body
- Is called a "zygote"

**8 weeks**
- Is just over 25mm long
- Face is forming with rudimentary eyes, ears, mouth, and tooth buds
- Arms and legs are moving
- Brain is forming
- Fetal heartbeat is detectable with ultrasound
- Is called an "embryo"

**12 weeks**
- Is about 76mm long and weighs about 28g
- Can move arms, legs, fingers, and toes
- Fingerprints are present
- Can smile, frown, suck, and swallow
- Sex is distinguishable
- Can urinate
- Is called a "fetus"

### Second trimester (middle 3 months)

**16 weeks**
- Is about 15cm long and weighs about 113 to 198g
- Heartbeat is strong
- Skin is thin, transparent
- Downy hair (lanugo) covers body
- Fingernails and toenails are forming
- Has coordinated movements; is able to roll over in amniotic fluid

**20 weeks**
- Is about 31cm long and weighs close to 454g
- Heartbeat is audible with ordinary stethoscope
- Sucks thumb
- Hiccups
- Hair, eyelashes, eyebrows are present

**24 weeks**
- Is about 36cm long and weighs 454 to 680g
- Skin is wrinkled and covered with protective coating (vernix caseosa)
- Eyes are open
- Waste matter is collected in bowel
- Has strong grip

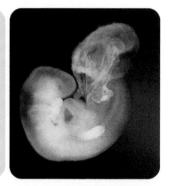

### Third trimester (last 3 months)

**28 weeks**
- Is about 41cm long and weighs about 1.4kg
- Is adding body fat
- Is very active
- Rudimentary breathing movements are present

**32 weeks**
- Is 42 to 46cm long and weighs 4 to 5 pounds
- Has periods of sleep and wakefulness
- Responds to sounds
- May assume the birth position
- Bones of head are soft and flexible
- Iron is being stored in liver

**36 to 38 weeks**
- Is 48 to 51cm long and weighs 2.7 to 3.4kg
- Skin is less wrinkled
- Vernix caseosa is thick
- Lanugo is mostly gone
- Is less active
- Is gaining immunities from mother

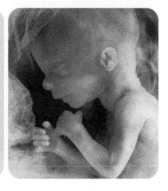

## FIGURE 3.3

**THE THREE TRIMESTERS OF PRENATAL DEVELOPMENT.** Both the germinal and embryonic periods occur during the first trimester. The end of the first trimester as well as the second and third trimesters are part of the fetal period.

have discussed. The germinal and embryonic periods occur in the first trimester. The fetal period begins toward the end of the first trimester and continues through the second and third trimesters. Viability (the possibility of surviving outside the womb) occurs at the very end of the second trimester.

**The Brain** One of the most remarkable aspects of the prenatal period is the development of the brain (Nelson, 2011). By the time babies are born, they have approximately 100 billion **neurons**, or nerve cells, that handle information processing at the cellular level in the brain. During prenatal development neurons spend time moving to the right locations and are starting to become connected. The basic architecture of the human brain is assembled during the first two trimesters of prenatal development. In typical development, the third trimester of prenatal development and the first two years of postnatal life are characterized by connectivity and functioning of neurons (Moulson & Nelson, 2008).

As the human embryo develops inside its mother's womb, the nervous system begins forming as a long, hollow tube located on the embryo's back. This pear-shaped *neural tube,* which forms at about 18 to 24 days after conception, develops out of the ectoderm. The tube closes at the top and bottom at about 24 days after conception. Figure 3.4 shows that the nervous system still has a tubular appearance six weeks after conception.

Two birth defects related to a failure of the neural tube to close are anencephaly and spina bifida. The highest regions of the brain fail to develop when fetuses have anencephaly or when the head end of the neural tube fails to close. Such infants die in the womb, during childbirth, or shortly after birth (Levene & Chervenak, 2009). Spina bifida results in varying degrees of paralysis of the lower limbs. Individuals with spina bifida usually need assistive devices such as crutches, braces, or wheelchairs. Research has revealed that maternal diabetes and maternal obesity place the fetus at risk for developing neural tube defects (McGuire, Dyson, & Renfrew, 2010). However, a strategy that can help to prevent neural tube defects is for women to take adequate amounts of the B vitamin folic acid, a topic we will discuss later in the chapter (Collins & others, 2011).

In a normal pregnancy, once the neural tube has closed, a massive proliferation of new immature neurons begins to takes place at about the fifth prenatal week and continues throughout the remainder of the prenatal period. The generation of new neurons is called *neurogenesis* (Kronenberg & others, 2010). At the peak of neurogenesis, it is estimated that as many as 200,000 neurons are being generated every minute.

At approximately 6 to 24 weeks after conception, *neuronal migration* occurs (Nelson, 2011). This involves cells moving outward from their point of origin to their appropriate locations and creating the different levels, structures, and regions of the brain (Cozzi & others, 2010). Once a cell has migrated to its target destination, it must mature and develop a more complex structure.

At about the 23rd prenatal week, connections between neurons begin to occur, a process called *synaptogenesis,* that continues postnatally (Kostovic, Judas, & Sedmak, 2011). We will have much more to say about the structure of neurons, their connectivity, and the development of the infant brain in Chapter 4.

# TERATOLOGY AND HAZARDS OF PRENATAL DEVELOPMENT

For Alex, the baby discussed at the opening of this chapter, the course of prenatal development went smoothly. His mother's womb protected him as he developed. Despite this protection, the environment can affect the embryo or fetus in many well-documented ways.

**neurons** Nerve cells that handle information processing at the cellular level in the brain.

developmental **connection**

**Brain Development.** At birth, the brain's weight is approximately 25 percent of its adult weight. Chapter 4, LO 2

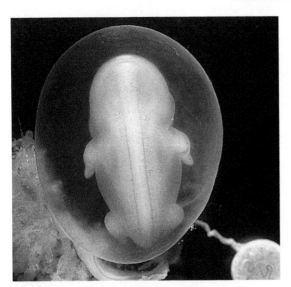

FIGURE **3.4**

**EARLY FORMATION OF THE NERVOUS SYSTEM.** The photograph shows the primitive, tubular appearance of the nervous system at six weeks in the human embryo.

**General Principles** A **teratogen** is any agent that can potentially cause a birth defect or negatively alter cognitive and behavioural outcomes. (The word comes from the Greek word *teras*, meaning "monster."). So many teratogens exist that practically every fetus is exposed to at least some teratogens. For this reason, it is difficult to determine which teratogen causes which problem. In addition, it may take a long time for the effects of a teratogen to show up. Only about half of all potential effects appear at birth.

The field of study that investigates the causes of birth defects is called *teratology*. Some exposures to teratogens do not cause physical birth defects but can alter the developing brain and influence cognitive and behavioural functioning, in which case the field of study is called *behavioural teratology*.

The dose, genetic susceptibility, and the time of exposure to a particular teratogen influence both the severity of the damage to an embryo or fetus and the type of defect:

- *Dose*. The dose effect is rather obvious—the greater the dose of an agent, such as a drug, the greater the effect.
- *Genetic susceptibility*. The type or severity of abnormalities caused by a teratogen is linked to the genotype of the pregnant woman and the genotype of the embryo or fetus (Charlet & others, 2012). For example, how a mother metabolizes a particular drug can influence the degree to which the drug effects are transmitted to the embryo or fetus. The extent to which an embryo or fetus is vulnerable to a teratogen may also depend on its genotype (Dufour-Rainfray & others, 2011). Also, for unknown reasons, male fetuses are far more likely to be affected by teratogens than female fetuses.
- *Time of exposure*. Teratogens do more damage when they occur at some points in development than at others (Weiner & Buhimschi, 2009). Damage during the germinal period may even prevent implantation. In general, the embryonic period is more vulnerable than the fetal period (Levine & O'Connor, 2012).

Figure 3.5 summarizes additional information about the effects of time of exposure to a teratogen. The probability of a structural defect is greatest early in the embryonic period, when organs are being formed (Holmes, 2012). Each body structure has its own critical period of formation. Recall from Chapter 1 that a *critical period* is a fixed time period very early in development during which certain experiences or events can have a long-lasting effect on development. The critical period for the nervous system (week 3) is earlier than for arms and legs (weeks 4 and 5).

After organogenesis is complete, teratogens are less likely to cause anatomical defects. Instead, exposure during the fetal period is more likely to stunt growth or to create problems in the way organs function. To examine some key teratogens and their effects, let's begin with drugs.

**Prescription and Non-prescription Drugs** Many women are given prescriptions for drugs while they are pregnant—especially antibiotics, analgesics, and asthma medications. Prescription as well as non-prescription drugs, however, may have effects on the embryo or fetus that the women never imagine.

Prescription drugs that can function as teratogens include antibiotics, such as streptomycin and tetracycline; some antidepressants; certain hormones, such as progestin and synthetic estrogen; and Accutane (which often is prescribed for acne) (Koren & Nordeng, 2012).

Non-prescription drugs that can be harmful include diet pills and high dosages of aspirin (Norgard & others, 2006). However, recent research indicated that low doses of aspirin pose no harm for the fetus but that high doses can contribute to maternal and fetal bleeding (Bennett, Bagot, & Arya, 2012).

**teratogen** From the Greek word *teras*, meaning "monster." Any agent that causes a birth defect. The field of study that investigates the causes of birth defects is called teratology.

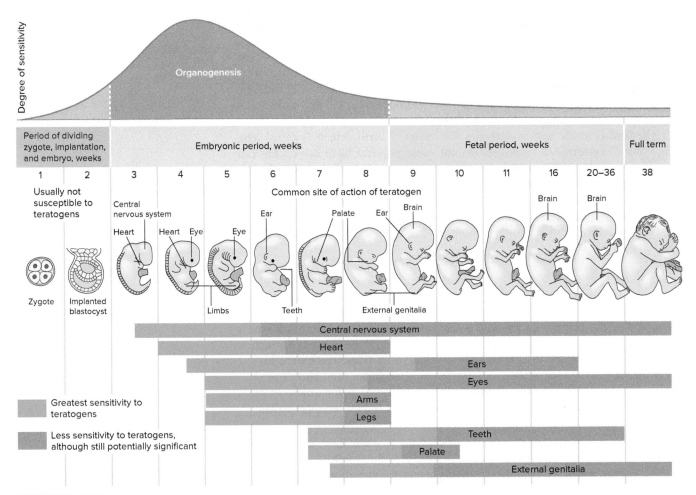

## FIGURE **3.5**

**TERATOGENS AND THE TIMING OF THEIR EFFECTS ON PRENATAL DEVELOPMENT.** The danger of structural defects caused by teratogens is greatest early in embryonic development. The period of organogenesis (red colour) lasts for about six weeks. Later assaults by teratogens (blue colour) mainly occur in the fetal period and instead of causing structural damage are more likely to stunt growth or cause problems of organ function.

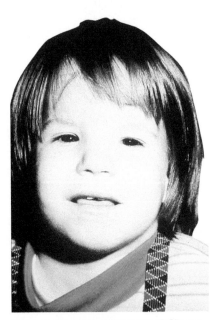

Fetal alcohol spectrum disorders (FASD) are characterized by a number of physical abnormalities and learning problems. Notice the wide-set eyes, flat cheekbones, and thin upper lip in this child with FASD.

**Psychoactive Drugs** *Psychoactive drugs* are drugs that act on the nervous system to alter states of consciousness, modify perceptions, and change moods. Examples include caffeine, alcohol, and nicotine, as well as illicit drugs such as cocaine, methamphetamine, marijuana, and heroin.

*Caffeine*   People often consume caffeine by drinking coffee, tea, or colas, or by eating chocolate. Although many health organizations recommend that pregnant women either not consume caffeine or consume it only sparingly, a recent research review found that high amounts of caffeine consumption by pregnant women does not increase the risk of miscarriage, congenital malformations, or growth retardation (Brent, Christian, & Diener, 2011).

*Alcohol*   Heavy drinking by pregnant women can be devastating to their off-spring (Brocardo, Gil-Mohapel, & Christie, 2011; Frost, Gist, & Adriano, 2011). **Fetal alcohol spectrum disorder (FASD)** is an umbrella term that describes a range of neuropsychological and behavioural deficits that can appear in the offspring of mothers who drink alcohol heavily during pregnancy. Children with FASD often, but not always, have physical abnormalities as well, including facial deformities and defective limbs, face, and heart (Klingenberg & others, 2010). Most children with FASD have learning problems, and many have an intellectual disability (Paintner, Williams, & Burd, 2012). Although FASD is considered the leading non-genetic cause of intellectual disability in North America, prevalence rates in Canada are not available (Davis, Desrocher, & Moore, 2011). A few small studies suggest that FASD may occur at higher rates among Aboriginal populations in Canada (Davis & others, 2011; Muckle & others, 2011; Robinson & others, 1987) and different patterns of strengths and weaknesses may be evident in Aboriginal children with FASD compared to non-Aboriginal children with FASD. For example, Aboriginal children score higher on measures of visual memory, while non-Aboriginal children score higher on measures of verbal memory (Rasmussen & others, 2006). These differences have implications for intervention and treatment.

Although women who drink heavily during pregnancy are at a higher risk of having a child with FASD, not all pregnant heavy drinkers have children with FASD. Other risk factors associated with FASD include lower socioeconomic status, lower maternal education, and frequent maternal binge drinking (Sood & others, 2001). A lack of access to comprehensive health care in Northern communities in Canada may be a contributing factor to the higher prevalence of FASD among Aboriginal peoples (Davis & others, 2011).

Prevention is the best way to treat FASD and programs are designed to educate pregnant women about the harms of prenatal drinking. What are some guidelines for alcohol use during pregnancy? Even drinking just one or two servings of beer or wine or one serving of hard liquor a few days a week can have negative effects on the fetus, although it is generally agreed that this level of alcohol use will not cause FASDs (Valenzuela & others, 2012). Health Canada states that there is no determined safe level of alcohol consumption during pregnancy. And research suggests that it may not be wise to consume alcohol at the time of conception. One study revealed that alcohol intake by both men and women during the weeks of conception increased the risk of early pregnancy loss (Henriksen & others, 2004).

*Nicotine* Cigarette smoking by pregnant women can also adversely influence prenatal development, birth, and postnatal development. Preterm births and low birth weights, fetal and neonatal deaths, respiratory problems, childhood non-Hodgkin lymphoma, attention deficit hyperactivity disorder, and sudden infant death syndrome (SIDS, also known as crib death), are all more common among the offspring of mothers who smoked during pregnancy (Abbott & Winzer-Serhan, 2012; Antonopoulos & others, 2011; Brown & Graves, 2013; Burstyn & others, 2012; Sagiv & others, 2013). Researchers have also documented that environmental tobacco smoke is linked to increased risk of low birth weight in offspring (Leonardi-Bee & others, 2008) and to diminished ovarian functioning in female offspring (Kilic & others, 2012). Further, a recent study revealed that environmental tobacco smoke was associated with 114 deregulations in the fetal cells of offspring, especially those involving immune functioning (Votavova & others, 2012). Clearly, there is a range of negative outcomes associated with maternal smoking during pregnancy.

*Cocaine* Does cocaine use during pregnancy harm the developing embryo and fetus? A recent research review concluded that cocaine quickly crosses the placenta to reach the fetus (De Giovanni & Marchetti, 2012) and is associated with a range of negative outcomes. The most consistent finding is that cocaine exposure during prenatal development is associated with reduced birth weight, length, and head circumference (Gouin & others, 2011). In other studies, prenatal cocaine exposure has been linked to lower arousal, less effective self-regulation, higher excitability, and lower quality of reflexes at 1 month of age (Ackerman, Riggins, & Black, 2010; Lester & others, 2002); to impaired motor development at 2 years of age and a slower rate

**fetal alcohol spectrum disorder (FASD)** An umbrella term that describes a range of neuropsychological and behavioural deficits that appear in the offspring of mothers who drink alcohol heavily during pregnancy.

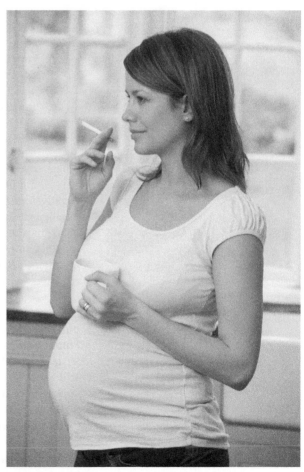

*What are some links between expectant mothers' drinking and cigarette smoking, and outcomes for their offspring?*

of growth through 10 years of age (Richardson, Goldschmidt, & Willford, 2008); to elevated blood pressure at 9 years of age (Shankaran & others, 2010); to deficits in behavioural self-regulation (Ackerman, Riggins, & Black, 2010); to impaired language development and information processing (Beeghly & others, 2006), including attention deficits—especially impulsivity (Accornero & others, 2006; Richardson & others, 2011); to learning disabilities at age 7 (Morrow & others, 2006); to increased likelihood of being in a special education program that involves support services (Levine & others, 2008); and to increased behavioural problems, especially externalizing problems such as high rates of aggression and delinquency (Minnes & others, 2010; Richardson & others, 2011).

Some researchers argue that these findings should be interpreted cautiously (Accornero & others, 2006). Why? Because other factors in the lives of pregnant women who use cocaine (such as poverty, malnutrition, and other substance abuse) often cannot be ruled out as possible contributors to the problems found in their children (Hurt & others, 2005; Messiah & others, 2011). For example, cocaine users are more likely than non-users to smoke cigarettes, use marijuana, drink alcohol, and take amphetamines.

Despite these cautions, the weight of research evidence indicates that children born to mothers who use cocaine are likely to have neurological, medical, and cognitive deficits (Cain, Bornick, & Whiteman, 2013; Field, 2007; Mayer & Zhang, 2009; Richardson & others, 2011). Cocaine use by pregnant women is never recommended.

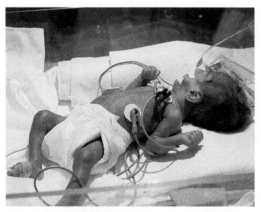

This baby was exposed to cocaine prenatally. *What are some of the possible effects on development of being exposed to cocaine prenatally?*

*Methamphetamine* Methamphetamine, like cocaine, is a stimulant, speeding up an individual's nervous system. Babies born to mothers who use methamphetamine, or "meth," during pregnancy are at risk for a number of problems, including higher rates of infant mortality, low birth weight, and developmental and behavioural problems (Piper & others, 2011). A recent study revealed that prenatal meth exposure was associated with smaller head circumference, increased rates of neonatal intensive care unit (NICU) admission, and referral to child protective services (Shah & others, 2012). And another study found that prenatal exposure to meth was linked to less brain activation in a number of areas, especially the frontal lobes, in 7- to 15-year-olds (Roussotte, 2011).

*Marijuana* Canadian researcher Peter Fried and his team at Carleton University have been studying the effects of prenatal marijuana use for over three decades through the Ottawa Prenatal Prospective Study. Overall, findings have indicated that marijuana use by pregnant women has negative outcomes for the offspring, which include poor visual memory and lower intelligence in children (Fried, 2011). And more recent research found that prenatal marijuana exposure interferes with the formation of connections between neurons in the cerebral cortex of the fetus (Cristino & Di Marzo, 2014; Tortoriello & others, 2014), which could result in the neurocognitive deficits previously reported. In sum, marijuana use is not recommended for pregnant women.

*Heroin* It is well documented that infants whose mothers are addicted to heroin show several behavioural difficulties at birth (Steinhausen, Blattmann, & Pfund, 2007). The difficulties include withdrawal symptoms, such as tremors, irritability, abnormal crying, disturbed sleep, and impaired motor control. Many still show behavioural problems at their first birthday, and attention deficits may appear later in development. The most common treatment for heroin addiction, methadone, is associated with very severe withdrawal symptoms in newborns (Binder & Vavrinkova, 2008).

**Incompatible Blood Types** Incompatibility between the mother's and father's blood types poses another risk to prenatal development. Blood types are created by differences in the surface structure of red blood cells. One type of difference in the surface of red blood cells creates the familiar blood groups—A, B, O, and AB. A second difference creates what is called Rh-positive and Rh-negative blood. If a surface marker, called the *Rh-factor*, is present in an individual's red blood cells, the person is said to be Rh-positive; if the Rh-marker is not present, the person is said to be Rh-negative. If a pregnant woman is Rh-negative and her partner is Rh-positive, the fetus may be Rh-positive. If the fetus's blood is Rh-positive and the mother's is Rh-negative, the mother's immune system may produce antibodies that will attack the fetus. This can result in any number of problems, including miscarriage or stillbirth, anemia, jaundice, heart defects, brain damage, or death soon after birth (Li & others, 2010).

Generally, the first Rh-positive baby of an Rh-negative mother is not at risk, but with each subsequent pregnancy the risk increases. A vaccine (RhoGAM) may be given to the mother within three days of the first child's birth to prevent her body from making antibodies that will attack any future Rh-positive fetuses in subsequent pregnancies. Also, babies affected by Rh incompatibility can be given blood transfusions before or right after birth (Flegal, 2007).

**Environmental Hazards**  Many aspects of our modern industrial world can endanger the embryo or fetus. Some specific hazards to the embryo or fetus include radiation, toxic wastes, and other chemical pollutants (Wiesel & others, 2011).

X-ray radiation can affect the developing embryo or fetus, especially in the first several weeks after conception, when women do not yet know they are pregnant (Urbano & Tait, 2004). Women and their physicians should weigh the risk of an X-ray when an actual or potential pregnancy is involved (Rajaraman & others, 2011). However, a routine diagnostic X-ray of a body area other than the abdomen, with the woman's abdomen protected by a lead apron, is generally considered safe (Brent, 2009, 2011).

Environmental pollutants and toxic wastes are also sources of danger to unborn children. Among the dangerous pollutants are carbon monoxide, mercury, and lead, as well as certain fertilizers and pesticides.

**Maternal Diseases**  Maternal diseases and infections can produce defects in offspring by crossing the placental barrier, or they can cause damage during birth. Rubella (German measles) is one disease that can cause prenatal defects. Women who plan to have children should have a blood test before they become pregnant to determine whether they are immune to the disease (Rasmussen, 2012).

Syphilis (a sexually transmitted infection) is more damaging later in prenatal development—four months or more after conception. Damage includes eye lesions, which can cause blindness, and skin lesions.

Another infection that has received widespread attention is genital herpes. Newborns contract this virus when they are delivered through the birth canal of a mother with genital herpes (Hollier & Wendel, 2008). About one-third of babies delivered through an infected birth canal die; another one-fourth become brain damaged. If an active case of genital herpes is detected in a pregnant woman close to her delivery date, a Caesarean section can be performed (in which the infant is delivered through an incision in the mother's abdomen) to keep the virus from infecting the newborn (Sellner & others, 2009).

*AIDS* is a sexually transmitted infection that is caused by the human immunodeficiency virus (HIV), which destroys the body's immune system. A mother can infect her offspring with HIV/AIDS in three ways: (1) during gestation across the placenta, (2) during delivery through contact with maternal blood or fluids, and (3) postpartum (after birth) through breastfeeding. Babies born to HIV-infected mothers can be (1) infected and symptomatic (show HIV symptoms), (2) infected but asymptomatic (not show HIV symptoms), or (3) not infected at all. Since maternal antiretroviral therapy was introduced in Canada in 1994, HIV infection in newborn babies is uncommon. Prospective mothers receiving this treatment

An explosion at the Chernobyl nuclear power plant in Ukraine produced radioactive contamination that spread to surrounding areas. Thousands of infants were born with health problems and deformities as a result of the nuclear contamination, including this boy whose arm did not form. *Other than radioactive contamination, what are some other types of environmental hazards to prenatal development?*

Because the fetus depends entirely on its mother for nutrition, it is important for the pregnant woman to have good nutritional habits. In Kenya, this government clinic provides pregnant women with information about how their diet can influence the health of their fetus and offspring. *What might the information about diet be like?*

will not transmit the virus to their unborn child, and estimates indicate less than 2 percent of babies are born with HIV in Canada (Public Health Agency of Canada, 2012). However, the transmission of AIDS through breastfeeding is especially a problem in many developing countries (UNICEF, 2010).

The more widespread disease of diabetes, characterized by high levels of sugar in the blood, also affects offspring (Desai, Beall, & Ross, 2013). The prevalence of diabetes among pregnant women is increasing. A large-scale study revealed that twice as many women and five times as many adolescents giving birth had diabetes in 2005 as in 1999 (Lawrence & others, 2008). In addition, Aboriginal women in Canada experience higher rates of gestational diabetes than do non-Aboriginal women (Public Health Agency of Canada, 2011),

Women who have gestational diabetes are at risk of delivering a preterm baby and may deliver very large infants (weighing 4.5 kilograms or more). In addition, these infants are at risk for diabetes themselves (Gluck & others, 2009).

**Other Parental Factors**   So far we have discussed a number of drugs, environmental hazards, maternal diseases, and incompatible blood types that can harm the embryo or fetus. Here we will explore other characteristics of the mother and father that can affect prenatal and child development, including nutrition, age, and emotional states and stress.

*Maternal Diet and Nutrition*   A developing embryo or fetus depends completely on its mother for nutrition, which comes from the mother's blood (Shapira, 2008). The nutritional status of the embryo or fetus is determined by the mother's total caloric intake and by her intake of proteins, vitamins, and minerals. Children born to malnourished mothers are more likely than other children to be malformed.

Being overweight before and during pregnancy can also put the embryo or fetus at risk, and an increasing number of pregnant women in North America are overweight (Marengo, Farag, & Canfield, 2013). Maternal obesity adversely affects pregnancy outcomes through elevated rates of hypertension, diabetes, respiratory complications, and infection in the mother (Nodine & Hastings-Tolsma, 2012). Management of obesity that includes weight loss and increased exercise prior to pregnancy is likely to benefit the mother and the baby (Vesco & others, 2012).

One aspect of maternal nutrition that is important for normal prenatal development is consumption of folic acid, a B-complex vitamin (Waddell, 2012). A study of more than 34,000 women indicated that taking folic acid either alone or as part of a multivitamin for at least one year prior to conceiving was linked with a 70 percent lower risk of delivering from 20 to 28 weeks and a 50 percent lower risk of delivering between 28 and 32 weeks (Bukowski & others, 2008). Another recent study revealed that toddlers of mothers who did not use folic acid supplements in the first trimester of pregnancy had more behaviour problems (Roza & others, 2010). Also, as indicated earlier in the chapter, a lack of folic acid is related to neural tube defects in offspring, such as spina bifida (a defect in the spinal cord) (Stern & others, 2011). Health Canada recommends that pregnant women consume a minimum of 400 micrograms of folic acid per day (about twice the amount the average woman gets in one day). Orange juice and dark leafy greens such as spinach are examples of foods rich in folic acid.

*developmental* **connection**

**Nutrition and Weight.** What are some key factors that influence whether children become obese? Chapter 4, LO 4

Eating fish is often recommended as part of a healthy diet, but pollution has made many fish a risky choice for pregnant women. Some fish contain high levels of mercury, which is released into the air both naturally and by industrial pollution (Wells & others, 2011). When mercury falls into the water it can accumulate in large fish, such as shark, swordfish, king mackerel, and some species of large tuna (Mayo Clinic, 2013). Mercury is easily transferred across the placenta, and the embryo's developing brain and nervous system are highly sensitive to the metal. Researchers have found that prenatal mercury exposure is linked to adverse outcomes, including miscarriage, preterm birth, and lower intelligence (Triche & Hossain, 2007; Xue & others, 2007).

*Maternal Age* When possible harmful effects on the fetus and infant are considered, two maternal ages are of special interest: adolescence and 35 years and older (Malizia, Hacker, & Penzias, 2009; Rudang & others, 2012). The mortality rate of infants born to adolescent mothers is double that of infants born to mothers in their twenties. Adequate prenatal care decreases the probability that a child born to an adolescent girl will have physical problems. However, among women in all age groups adolescents are the least likely to obtain prenatal assistance from clinics and health services.

Maternal age is also linked to the risk that a child will have Down syndrome (Allen & others, 2009; Ghosh & others, 2010). As discussed in Chapter 2, an individual with Down syndrome has distinctive facial characteristics, short limbs, and deficits in motor and mental abilities. A baby with Down syndrome rarely is born to a mother 16 to 34 years of age. However, when the mother reaches 40 years of age, the probability is slightly over 1 in 100 that a baby born to her will have Down syndrome, and by age 50 it is almost 1 in 10. When mothers are 35 years and older, risks also increase for low birth weight, for preterm delivery, and for fetal death (Koo & others, 2012).

*What are some of the risks for infants born to adolescent mothers?*

We still have much to learn about the role of the mother's age in pregnancy and childbirth. As women remain active, exercise regularly, and are careful about their nutrition, their reproductive systems may remain healthier at older ages than was thought possible in the past.

*Emotional States and Stress* When a pregnant woman experiences intense fears, anxieties, and other emotions or negative mood states, physiological changes occur that may affect her fetus (Breedlove & Fryzelka, 2011). For example, research conducted after the 1998 ice storms in Quebec suggested that prenatal stress may trigger the release of certain hormones associated with altered immune functioning and asthma (Turcotte-Tremblay & others, 2014). High maternal anxiety and stress during pregnancy can also have long-term cognitive consequences for the offspring. Further studies conducted following Quebec's 1998 natural disaster revealed that maternal stress resulting from factors such as power outages and dislocation was associated with lower cognitive and linguistic abilities in 2-year-olds (Laplante & others, 2004) and 5-year-olds (Laplante & others, 2008). A mother's stress may also influence the fetus indirectly by increasing the likelihood that the mother will engage in unhealthy behaviours, such as taking drugs and engaging in poor prenatal care.

*Paternal Factors* So far, we have discussed how characteristics of the mother—such as drug use, disease, diet and nutrition, age, and emotional states—can influence prenatal development and the development of the child. Might there also be some paternal risk factors? Indeed, there are several. Men's exposure to lead, radiation, certain pesticides, and petrochemicals may cause abnormalities

In one study, in China, the longer fathers smoked the greater the risk that their children would develop cancer (Ji & others, 1997). *What are some other paternal factors that can influence the development of the fetus and the child?*

in sperm that lead to miscarriage or diseases, such as childhood cancer (Cordier, 2008). The father's smoking during the mother's pregnancy also can cause problems for the offspring. In one study, heavy paternal smoking during pregnancy was associated with the risk of early pregnancy loss (Venners & others, 2004). This negative outcome may be related to secondhand smoke. And a recent study revealed that paternal smoking around the time of the child's conception was linked to an increased risk of the child developing leukemia (Milne & others, 2012). Paternal age is also a risk factor. There is an increased risk of spontaneous abortion, autism, and schizophrenic disorders when the father is 40 years of age or older (Reproductive Endocrinology and Infertility Committee & others, 2011). In one study, children born to fathers who were 40 years of age or older had increased risk of developing autism because of an increase in random gene mutation in the older fathers (Kong & others, 2012).

## PRENATAL CARE

Although prenatal care varies enormously, it usually involves a defined schedule of visits for medical care, which typically includes screening for manageable conditions and treatable diseases that can affect the baby or the mother (London & others, 2011). The majority of prenatal care in Canada is provided by physicians or midwives in one-on-one visits. However, some prenatal programs include comprehensive educational, social, and nutritional services in addition to medical care.

The Canadian Prenatal Nutrition Program (CPNP) is a federally funded program run through community organizations to provide support for soon-to-be mothers and their babies who are facing challenging life circumstances. These challenges might include poverty, teen pregnancy, social and geographic isolation, substance use and family violence. The CPNP program also increases the availability of culturally sensitive prenatal support for Aboriginal women and recent immigrants. This comprehensive program includes nutrition counselling, prenatal vitamins, food and food coupons, food preparation training, counselling in prenatal care and child development, breastfeeding education and support, and referrals to other agencies if needed.

Other prenatal care programs also exist in Canada. For example, CenteringPregnancy (Steming, 2008) has recently been introduced in Canada with some success (Benediktsson & others, 2013). This program is relationship-centred and provides complete prenatal care in a group setting. CenteringPregnancy replaces traditional 15-minute physician visits with 90-minute peer group support settings and self-examination led by a physician or certified nurse-midwife.

A CenteringPregnancy program. This rapidly expanding program alters routine prenatal care by bringing women out of exam rooms and into relationship-oriented groups.

Groups of up to 10 women (and often their partners) meet regularly beginning at 12 to 16 weeks of pregnancy. The sessions emphasize empowering women to play an active role in experiencing a positive pregnancy.

Exercise increasingly is recommended as part of a comprehensive prenatal care program (Field, 2012; Field & others, 2013). Exercise during pregnancy conditions the body and is associated with a more positive mental state (Robledo-Colonia & others, 2012). A recent experimental study found that pregnant women who completed a three-month supervised aerobic exercise program showed improved health-related quality of life, including better physical functioning and reduced bodily pain, than their counterparts who did not participate in the program (Montoya Arizabaleta & others, 2010). However, it is important to remember not to overdo it. Pregnant women should always consult their physician before starting any exercise program (Olson & others, 2009).

**Normal Prenatal Development**   Much of our discussion so far in this chapter has focused on what can go wrong with prenatal development. Prospective parents should take steps to avoid the vulnerabilities to fetal development that we have described. But it is important to keep in mind that most of the time, prenatal development does not go awry, and development occurs along the positive path that we described at the beginning of the chapter.

## Review Connect Reflect

**L01** Describe prenatal development.

### Review

- What is the course of prenatal development?
- What is teratology, and what are some of the main hazards to prenatal development?
- What are some good prenatal care strategies?
- Why is it important to take a positive approach to prenatal development?

### Connect

- In Chapter 2, we discussed chromosomal and gene-linked abnormalities that can affect prenatal development.
- How are the symptoms of the related conditions or risks similar or different from those caused by teratogens or other hazards?

### Reflect Your Own Personal Journey of Life

- If you are a woman, imagine that you have just found out that you are pregnant. What health-enhancing strategies will you follow during the prenatal period? For men, imagine that you are the partner of a woman who has just found out she is pregnant. What will be your role in increasing the likelihood that the prenatal period will go smoothly?

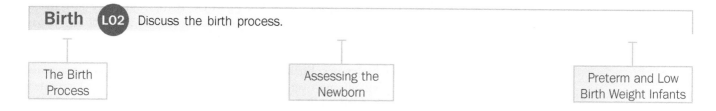

## Birth   **L02**   Discuss the birth process.

| The Birth Process | Assessing the Newborn | Preterm and Low Birth Weight Infants |

Nature writes the basic script for how birth occurs, but parents make important choices about conditions surrounding birth. We look first at the sequence of physical steps that take place when a child is born.

# THE BIRTH PROCESS

The birth process occurs in stages, occurs in different contexts, and in most cases involves one or more attendants.

**Stages of Birth**   The birth process occurs in three stages. The first stage is the longest of the three. Uterine contractions are 15 to 20 minutes apart at the beginning and last up to a minute each. These contractions cause the woman's cervix to stretch and open. As the first stage progresses, the contractions come closer together, appearing every two to five minutes. Their intensity increases. By the end of the first birth stage, contractions dilate the cervix to an opening of about 10 centimetres (4 inches), so that the baby can move from the uterus into the birth canal. For a woman having her first child, the first stage lasts an average of 6 to 12 hours; for subsequent children, this stage typically is much shorter.

The second birth stage begins when the baby's head starts to move through the cervix and the birth canal. It terminates when the baby emerges completely from the mother's body. With each contraction, the mother bears down hard to push the baby out of her body. By the time the baby's head is out of the mother's body, the contractions come almost every minute and last for about a minute each. This stage typically lasts 45 minutes to an hour.

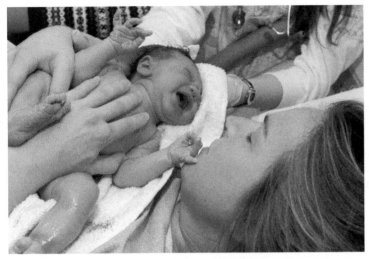

After the long journey of prenatal development, birth takes place. During birth the baby is on a threshold between two worlds. *What is the fetus/newborn transition like?*

**afterbirth** The third stage of birth, when the placenta, umbilical cord, and other membranes are detached and expelled.

**Afterbirth** is the third stage, at which time the placenta, umbilical cord, and other membranes are detached and expelled. This final stage is the shortest of the three birth stages, lasting only minutes.

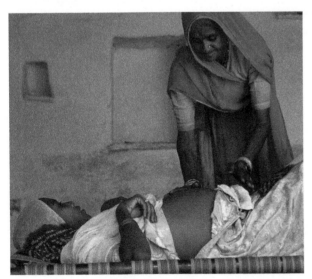

In India, a midwife checks on the size, position, and heartbeat of a fetus. Midwives deliver babies in many cultures around the world. *What are some cultural variations in prenatal care?*

**Childbirth Setting and Attendants**   In Canada, 99 percent of births take place in hospitals, although births also occur at home and in birthing centres. The people who help a mother during birth vary across cultures. In Canadian hospitals, it has become the norm for fathers or birth coaches to be with the mother throughout labour and delivery. In the East African Nigoni culture, men are completely excluded from the childbirth process. When a woman is ready to give birth, female relatives move into the woman's hut and the husband leaves, taking his belongings (clothes, tools, weapons, and so on) with him. He is not permitted to return until after the baby is born. In some cultures, childbirth is an open, community affair. For example, in the Pukapukan culture in the Pacific Islands, women give birth in a shelter that is open for villagers to observe.

*Midwives*   Midwifery is practised in most countries throughout the world (Jesse & Kilpatrick, 2013). Midwifery in Canada is a legal and regulated profession in most (but not all) Canadian provinces. Midwives attend births in hospitals, at home, and in birthing centres, and can prescribe and administer medications used in pregnancy, birth, and the postpartum period. One large-scale Canadian study examining over 12,000 births in a four year period revealed that planned home births with midwives were as safe as planned hospital births with either midwives or physicians attending, and resulted in lower rates of obstetric interventions (Janssen & others, 2009). Recent research also reveals increased satisfaction with midwife-led care during the birthing process (Sutcliffe & others, 2012).

*Doulas* In some countries, a doula attends a childbearing woman. *Doula* is a Greek word that means "a woman who helps." A **doula** is a caregiver who provides non-clinical physical, emotional, and educational support for the mother before, during, and after childbirth. Doulas remain with the parents throughout labour, assessing and responding to the mother's needs. Researchers have found positive effects when a doula is present at the birth of a child (Akhavan & Lundgren, 2012; Torres, 2013).

In Canada, most doulas work as independent providers hired by the expectant parents. Although doulas are not regulated in Canada, certification is possible in some provinces. Doulas typically function as part of a "birthing team," serving as an adjunct to the midwife or the hospital's obstetric staff.

## Methods of Childbirth

Hospitals offer a range of options regarding the method of delivery for expectant parents. Key choices involve the use of medication, whether to use any of a number of non-medicated techniques to reduce pain, and when to have a Caesarean delivery.

*Medication* The Canadian national guidelines for family-centred maternity and newborn care (Health Canada, 2001) suggest that Canadian women who are expected to have a low-risk delivery require little to no drug intervention during their delivery. However, in many cases, drugs are still often used to make the birth process easier for the mother or to save the baby's life during complicated deliveries. Three basic kinds of drugs that are used for labour are analgesia, anaesthesia, and oxytocin/pitocin.

*Analgesia* is used to relieve pain. Analgesics include tranquilizers, barbiturates, and narcotics (such as Demerol).

*Anaesthesia* is used in late first-stage labour and during delivery to block sensation in an area of the body or to block consciousness. There is a trend toward not using general anaesthesia, which blocks consciousness, in normal births because general anaesthesia can be transmitted through the placenta to the fetus (Lieberman & others, 2005). An *epidural block* is regional anaesthesia that numbs the woman's body from the waist down. Researchers are continuing to explore safer drug mixtures for use at lower doses to improve the effectiveness and safety of epidural anaesthesia (Samhan & others, 2013).

*Oxytocin* is a synthetic hormone that is used to stimulate contractions; pitocin is the most widely used oxytocin. Physicians tend to use oxytocin to augment or help along labour. The benefits and risks of oxytocin as a part of childbirth continue to be debated (Vasdev, 2008).

Predicting how a drug will affect an individual woman and her fetus is difficult (Lowdermilk, Perry, & Cashion, 2010; Smith, 2009). A particular drug might have only a minimal effect on one fetus yet have a much stronger effect on another. The drug's dosage also is a factor. Stronger doses of tranquilizers and narcotics given to decrease the mother's pain potentially have a more negative effect on the fetus than mild doses. It is important for the mother to assess her level of pain and have a voice in the decision of whether she should receive medication.

*Natural and Prepared Childbirth* For a brief time not long ago, the idea of avoiding all medication during childbirth gained favour in North America. Instead, many women chose to reduce the pain of childbirth through techniques known as natural childbirth and prepared childbirth. Today, at least some medication is used in the typical childbirth, but elements of natural childbirth and prepared childbirth remain popular (Oates & Abraham, 2010).

**Natural childbirth** is the method that aims to reduce the mother's pain by decreasing her fear through education about childbirth and by teaching her

**doula** A caregiver who provides non-clinical physical, emotional, and educational support for the mother before, during, and after childbirth.

A doula assisting a birth. *What types of support do doulas provide?*

**natural childbirth** This method attempts to reduce the mother's pain by decreasing her fear through education about childbirth and relaxation techniques during delivery.

and her partner to use breathing methods and relaxation techniques during delivery.

French obstetrician Ferdinand Lamaze developed a method similar to natural childbirth that is known as **prepared childbirth**, or the Lamaze method. It includes a special breathing technique to control pushing in the final stages of labour, as well as more detailed education about anatomy and physiology. The pregnant woman's partner usually serves as a coach who attends childbirth classes with her and helps her with her breathing and relaxation during delivery.

In sum, proponents of current prepared childbirth methods conclude that when information and support are provided, women *know* how to give birth.

*Caesarean Delivery*   Normally, the baby's head comes through the vagina first. But if the baby is in a **breech position**, the baby's buttocks are the first part to emerge from the vagina. In 1 of every 25 deliveries, the baby's head is still in the uterus when the rest of the body is out. Breech births can cause respiratory problems. As a result, if the baby is in a breech position, a surgical procedure known as a Caesarean section, or a Caesarean delivery, is usually performed. In a **Caesarean delivery**, the baby is removed from the mother's uterus through an incision made in her abdomen (Lee, El-Sayed, & Gould, 2008). The benefits and risks of Caesarean sections continue to be debated (Gibbons & others, 2013; O'Neill & others, 2013). Caesarean section rates have been increasing worldwide over the past few decades, with most countries exceeding the World Health Organization recommended rate of 15 percent of all deliveries (Sherrie & others, 2013). In Canada, approximately 27 percent of deliveries are by Caesarean section (Canadian Institute for Health Information, 2012), which causes concern as Caesarean deliveries are associated with immediate and long term complications, as well as increased health costs (Henderson & others, 2001; Villar & others, 2007).

## ASSESSING THE NEWBORN

Almost immediately after birth, after the baby and its parents have been introduced, a newborn is taken to be weighed, cleaned up, and tested for signs of developmental problems that might require urgent attention (Miyakoshi & others, 2013; Therrell & others, 2010). The **Apgar Scale** is widely used to assess the health of newborns at one and five minutes after birth. The Apgar Scale evaluates an infant's heart rate, respiratory effort, muscle tone, body colour, and reflex irritability. An obstetrician or a nurse does the evaluation and gives the newborn a score, or reading, of 0, 1, or 2 on each of these five health signs (see Figure 3.6). A total score of 7 to 10 indicates that the newborn's condition is good. A score of 5 indicates there may be developmental difficulties. A score of 3 or below signals an emergency and indicates that the baby might not survive.

The Apgar Scale is especially good at assessing the newborn's ability to cope with the stress of delivery and the new environment (Reynolds, 2010; Shehata & others, 2010). It also identifies high-risk infants who need resuscitation.

A recent study revealed that compared to children with a high Apgar score (9 to 10), the risk of developing attention deficit hyperactivity disorder (ADHD) in childhood was 75 percent higher for newborns with a low Apgar score (1 to 4) and 63 percent higher for those with an Apgar score of 5 to 6 (Li & others, 2011). For a more thorough assessment of the newborn, the Brazelton Neonatal Behavioral Assessment Scale or the Neonatal Intensive Care Unit Network Neurobehavioral Scale may be used.

The **Brazelton Neonatal Behavioral Assessment Scale (NBAS)** is typically performed within 24 to 36 hours after birth. It is also used as a sensitive index of neurological competence up to one month after birth for typical infants and as a measure in many studies of infant development (Costa & Figueiredo,

**prepared childbirth** Developed by French obstetrician Ferdinand Lamaze, this childbirth strategy is similar to natural childbirth but includes a special breathing technique to control pushing in the final stages of labour and a more detailed anatomy and physiology course.

**breech position** The baby's position in the uterus that causes the buttocks to be the first part to emerge from the vagina.

**Caesarean delivery** Removal of the baby from the mother's uterus through an incision made in her abdomen.

*What characteristics are used to assess the health of a newborn?*

**Apgar Scale** A widely used method to assess the health of newborns at one and five minutes after birth. The Apgar Scale evaluates an infant's heart rate, respiratory effort, muscle tone, body colour, and reflex irritability.

**Brazelton Neonatal Behavioral Assessment Scale (NBAS)** A measure that is used in the first month of life to assess the newborn's neurological development, reflexes, and reactions to people and objects.

| Score | 0 | 1 | 2 |
|---|---|---|---|
| **Heart rate** | Absent | Slow—less than 100 beats per minute | Fast—100–140 beats per minute |
| **Respiratory effort** | No breathing for more than one minute | Irregular and slow | Good breathing with normal crying |
| **Muscle tone** | Limp and flaccid | Weak, inactive, but some flexion of extremities | Strong, active motion |
| **Body colour** | Blue and pale | Body pink, but extremities blue | Entire body pink |
| **Reflex irritability** | No response | Grimace | Coughing, sneezing and crying |

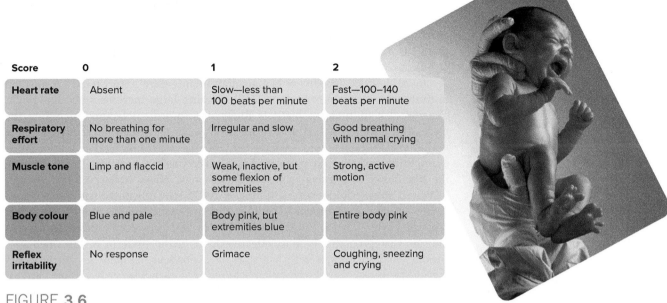

FIGURE **3.6**

**THE APGAR SCALE.** A newborn's score on the Apgar Scale indicates whether the baby has urgent medical problems.

2011; Hernandez-Martinez & others, 2011). The NBAS assesses the newborn's neurological development, reflexes, and reactions to people and objects. Sixteen reflexes, such as sneezing, blinking, and rooting are assessed, along with reactions to animate stimuli (such as a face and voice) and inanimate stimuli (such as a rattle). (We will have more to say about reflexes in Chapter 4, when we discuss motor development in infancy.)

An offspring of the NBAS, the **Neonatal Intensive Care Unit Network Neurobehavioral Scale (NNNS)** provides another assessment of the newborn's behaviour, neurological and stress responses, and regulatory capacities (Brazelton, 2004; Lester, Tronick, & Brazelton, 2004). Whereas the NBAS was developed to assess normal, healthy, full-term infants, T. Berry Brazelton, along with Barry Lester and Edward Tronick, developed the NNNS to assess the at-risk infant. It is especially useful for evaluating preterm infants (although it may not be appropriate for those of less than 30 weeks' gestational age) and substance-exposed infants (Boukydis & Lester, 2008). A recent NNNS assessment (at one month of age) of preterm infants who were exposed to substance abuse prenatally revealed that the NNNS predicted certain developmental outcomes, such as neurological difficulties, IQ, and school readiness at 4.5 years of age (Liu & others, 2010).

**Neonatal Intensive Care Unit Network Neurobehavioral Scale (NNNS)** An offspring of the NBAS, the NNNS provides an assessment of the at-risk newborn's behaviour, neurological and stress responses, and regulatory capacities.

**low birth weight infant** Infant that weighs less than 2.4 kilograms at birth.

**preterm infants** Those born before the completion of 37 weeks of gestation (the time between fertilization and birth).

## PRETERM AND LOW BIRTH WEIGHT INFANTS

Different conditions that pose threats for newborns have been given different labels. We will examine these conditions and discuss interventions for improving outcomes of preterm infants.

**Preterm and Small for Date Infants** Three related conditions pose threats to many newborns: low birth weight, preterm delivery, and being small for date. **Low birth weight infants** weigh less than 2.5 kilograms at birth. *Very low birth weight* newborns weigh under 1.5 kilograms, and *extremely low birth weight* newborns weigh under 1 kilogram. **Preterm infants** are those born three weeks or more before the pregnancy has reached its full term—in other words, before the

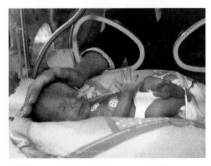

A "kilogram kid," weighing about 1 kilogram at birth. *What are some long-term outcomes for weighing so little at birth?*

completion of 37 weeks of gestation (the time between fertilization and birth). **Small for date infants** (also called *small for gestational age infants*) are those whose birth weights are below normal when the length of the pregnancy is considered. They weigh less than 90 percent of all babies of the same gestational age. Small for date infants may be preterm or full term. One study found that small for date infants had a more than fourfold increased risk of death (Regev & others, 2003).

In 2011–2012, 7.8 percent of Canadian infants were born preterm (Canadian Institute for Health Information, 2012), a rather large increase since the 1980s. The increase in preterm birth is likely due to several factors, including the increasing number of births to women 35 years and older, increasing rates of multiple births, increased management of maternal and fetal conditions (for example, inducing labour preterm if medical technology indicates it will increase the likelihood of survival), increased substance abuse (tobacco, alcohol), and increased stress (Goldenberg & Culhane, 2007). Recently, there has been considerable interest in exploring the role that progestin might play in reducing preterm births (Likis & others, 2013; O'Brien & Lewis, 2009). Research reviews indicate that progestin is most effective in reducing preterm births when it is administered to women with a history of a previous spontaneous birth at less than 37 weeks (da Fonseca & others, 2009), to women who have a short cervical length of 15 mm or less (da Fonseca & others, 2009), and to women pregnant with a singleton rather than twins (Norman & others, 2009; Rode & others, 2009).

Might exercise during pregnancy reduce the likelihood of preterm birth? A recent study found that compared to sedentary pregnant women, women who engaged in light leisure time physical activity had a 24 percent reduced likelihood of preterm delivery, and those who participated in moderate to heavy leisure time physical activity had a 66 percent reduced risk of preterm delivery (Hegaard & others, 2008). Researchers also have found that yoga is positively linked to pregnancy outcomes (Narendran & others, 2005).

The incidence of low birth weight varies considerably from country to country. To read about cross-cultural variations in low birth weight, see *Connecting with Diversity.*

### Consequences of Preterm Birth and Low Birth Weight

Although most preterm and low birth weight infants are healthy, as a group they experience more health and developmental problems than infants of normal birth weight (Minde & Zelkowitz, 2008). For preterm birth, the terms *extremely preterm* and *very preterm* are increasingly used. *Extremely preterm infants* are those born before the 28th week of pregnancy, and *very preterm infants* are those born before 33 weeks of gestational age. Figure 3.7 shows the results of a recent Norwegian study indicating that the earlier preterm infants are born, the more likely they are to drop out of school (Swamy, Ostbye, & Skjaerven, 2008).

The number and severity of these problems increase when infants are born very early and as their birth weight decreases. Survival rates for infants who are born very early and very small have risen, but with this improved survival rate have come increases in rates of severe brain damage (Casey, 2008). Children born at low birth weights are more likely than their normal birth weight counterparts to develop a learning disability, attention deficit hyperactivity disorder, or a breathing problem such as asthma (Anderson & others, 2011). Approximately 50 percent of all low birth weight children are enrolled in special education programs.

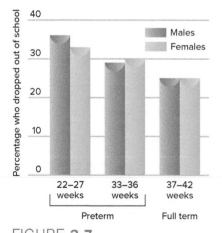

### Nurturing Low Birth Weight and Preterm Infants

Two increasingly used interventions in the neonatal intensive care unit (NICU) are kangaroo care and massage therapy. The interest in **kangaroo care** grew in 1979, when neotatologists Edgar Rey and Hector Martinez, in Bogotá, Colombia, found themselves without enough incubators to care for all the premature babies in their hospital. Instead, they put the tiny babies, wearing only a diaper, upright against the mothers' bodies, thus providing skin-to-skin contact. Babies and mothers were

---

## Cross-Cultural Variations in the Incidence and Causes of Low Birth Weight

In 2010 almost 15 million babies worldwide were born preterm (Chang & others, 2013). In some countries, such as India and Sudan, where poverty is rampant and the health and nutrition of mothers are poor, the number of low birth weight babies reaches as high as 31 percent. In Canada, there has been an increase in low birth weight infants in the last two decades. The Canadian low birth weight rate of 7.8 percent in 2010 is below the global average of 11.1 percent (see Figure 3.8; Blencowe & others, 2012), but still higher than that of many other developed countries (Chang & others, 2013). For example, only 5–6 percent of the infants born in Sweden, Finland, Norway, and France are low birth weight.

In both developed and developing countries, adolescents who give birth when their bodies have not fully matured are at risk for having low birth weight babies (Malamitsi-Puchner & Boutsikou, 2006). Further, the increase in the number of low birth weight infants has been attributed to drug use, poor nutrition, multiple births, reproductive technologies, and improved technology and prenatal care that result in more high-risk babies surviving (Chang & others, 2013). Nonetheless, poverty continues to be a major factor in preterm birth. Women living in poverty are more likely to be obese, have diabetes and hypertension, smoke cigarettes, and use illicit drugs, and they are less likely to receive regular prenatal care (Goldenberg & Nagahawatte, 2008).

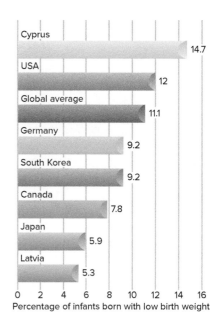

### FIGURE 3.8
**PERCENTAGE OF INFANTS BORN WITH LOW BIRTH WEIGHT IN SELECTED COUNTRIES.**

In the preceding sentence, we learned that women living in poverty are less likely to receive regular prenatal care. *What did you learn earlier in the chapter about the benefits of regular prenatal care? Aside from women living in poverty, which other demographic group is not likely to receive adequate prenatal care?*

then wrapped in cloth carriers to keep the baby warm, much as a baby kangaroo is carried inside its mother's pouch. The babies thrived. Kangaroo care is typically practiced for two to three hours per day, skin-to-skin, over an extended time in early infancy (see Figure 3.9).

Why use kangaroo care with preterm infants? Preterm infants often have difficulty coordinating their breathing and heart rate, and the close physical contact with the parent provided by kangaroo care can help to stabilize the preterm infant's heartbeat, temperature, and breathing (Cong, Ludington-Hoe, & Walsh, 2011; Kaffashi & others, 2013). Preterm infants who experience kangaroo care also gain more weight than their counterparts who are not given this care (Gathwala, Singh, & Balhara, 2008). And a recent

A new mother practicing kangaroo care. *What are the benefits of kangaroo care for preterm and term infants?*

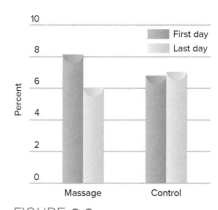

### FIGURE 3.9
**PRETERM INFANTS SHOW REDUCED STRESS BEHAVIOURS AND ACTIVITY AFTER FIVE DAYS OF MASSAGE THERAPY.**
(Hernandez-Reif, Diego, & Field, 2007)

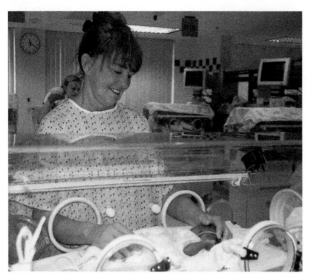

Shown here is Tiffany Field massaging a newborn infant. *What types of infants has massage therapy been shown to help?*

research review concluded that kangaroo care decreased the risk of infant mortality in low birth weight infants (Conde-Aguedelo, Belizan, & Diaz-Rossello, 2011). To learn about the benefits of kangaroo care and skin-to-skin contact for all babies, not just preterm infants, see *Connecting Through Research*.

Many adults will attest to the therapeutic effects of receiving a massage. In fact, many will pay a premium to receive one at a spa on a regular basis. But can massage play a role in improving developmental outcomes for preterm infants? Research has revealed that massage therapy can reduce stress behaviours, such as crying and grimacing, in preterm infants (Hernandez-Reif, Diego, & Field, 2007). Stress reduction is especially important because preterm infants encounter numerous stressors while they are hospitalized. Mothers can be taught to massage their infants to produce benefits. For example, babies who were massaged with moderate pressure by their mothers once a day for the first month of life gained more weight, performed better on the orientation scale of the Brazelton, were less excitable and less depressed, and were less agitated during sleep (Field & others, 2010). Massage therapy is also beneficial for preterm infants exposed to cocaine in utero (Wheeden & others, 1993) and depressed adolescent mothers (Field & others, 1996). A review of massage therapy with preterm infants revealed that the most consistent benefits of massage therapy were increased weight gain and earlier discharge from the hospital (Field & others, 2004).

## connecting through research

## How Does Skin-to-Skin Contact Affect the Social Cognitive Development of Babies?

Skin-to-skin contact or kangaroo care is increasingly recommended in Canadian hospitals and birthing centres for all newborn babies and their mothers. There are a range of neurophysiological benefits associated with skin-to-skin contact during the first few hours and days of life for both preterm and term infants, including more stable temperatures, heart rates and respiratory rates, more restful sleep, less crying, longer breastfeeding, less pain experienced from routine procedures, and earlier discharge from the hospital (Bigelow & others, 2014; Charpak & others, 2001; Feldman & Eidelman, 2003; Gray & others, 2000; Moore & others, 2012; Mori & others, 2010).

Dr. Ann Bigelow at Saint Francis Xavier University in Nova Scotia studies the social cognitive benefits of skin-to-skin contact. In one recent study, the effect of skin-to-skin contact on infants' responses to maternal behaviour in the Still Face Task was assessed over the first three months of life (see Figure 3.10). The Still Face Task (Tronick, Als, Adamson, Wise, & Brazelton, 1978) has three phases. During the first phase, mothers engage infants in normal face-to-face interaction. Mothers then become suddenly still and expressionless during the second phase, followed by resumed interaction in the third phase. Infants between 2 and 9 months of age typically show decreased visual attention and decreased positive affect (non-distressed vocalizations and decreased smiling), during the still phase compared to interactive phases. This behaviour, known as the Still Face Effect, illustrates the babies' attempts to re-engage the mother, and is used as a measure of infants' awareness of the effect of their behaviour on others' responses.

In this study, babies born at term were divided into a skin-to-skin contact (SSC) group and a no skin-to-skin contact or control group. Researchers went into the homes when babies were 1 week, 1 month, 2 months, and 3 months of age. Infants' responsiveness was scored by the duration of visual attention, smiles, and vocalizations during each of the three phases of the Still Face Task. Overall, SSC infants responded to the changes in their mothers' behaviour during the task at an earlier age than the control infants. Although no differences were found between groups for either smiling or visual attention at any age, differences between groups in non-distressed vocalizations were found. At 1 month of age only the SSC infants showed the Still Face Effect with their non-distressed vocalizations. By 3 months of age, infants in the SSC group, but not the control group, increased their non-distress vocalizations during the still face phase, suggesting they were actively attempting to re-engage their unresponsive mother. Thus, on the measure of non-distressed vocalizations, the SSC infants showed enhanced awareness of the effect of their behaviour on their mothers' responsiveness, suggesting that skin-to-skin contact may facilitate social cognitive development. The results of this study provide converging evidence of a range of positive outcomes associated with skin-to-skin contact.

*What other possible factors or variables might account for the increased responsiveness of the infants in the skin-to-skin contact group?*

**(continued)**

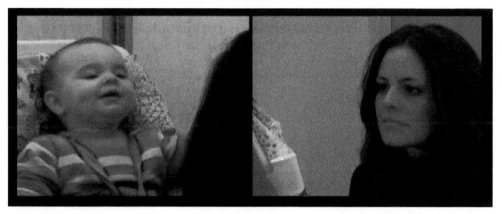

## FIGURE 3.10

The Still Face Task is used to measure infants' awareness of the effect their behaviour has on others' behaviour. In this task, a mother and infant interact for a period of time before the mother suddenly becomes still and expressionless. Following this "still face" phase, the mother resumes interaction. The duration of infants' smiling, non-distressed vocalizations and visual attention is measured and compared in all three phases.

## Review *Connect* Reflect

 Discuss the birth process.

### Review

- What are the three main stages of birth? What are some different birth strategies? What is the transition from fetus to newborn like for the infant?
- What are three measures of neonatal health and responsiveness?
- What are the outcomes for children if they are born preterm or with a low birth weight?

### *Connect*

- What correlations have been found between birth weight and country of birth, and what might the causes be?

### Reflect *Your Own Personal Journey of Life*

- If you are a female who would like to have a baby, which birth strategy do you prefer? Why? If you are a male, how involved would you want to be in helping your partner through the birth of your baby? Explain.

## The Postpartum Period  Explain the changes that take place in the postpartum period.

Physical Adjustments

Emotional and Psychological Adjustments

The weeks after childbirth present challenges for many new parents and their offspring. This is the **postpartum period**, the period after childbirth or delivery that lasts for about six weeks or until the mother's body has completed its adjustment and has returned to a nearly pre-pregnant state. It is a time when the woman adjusts physically, emotionally, and psychologically to the process of childbearing.

**postpartum period** The period after childbirth when the mother adjusts physically, emotionally, and psychologically to the process of childbirth. This period lasts about six weeks or until her body has completed its adjustment and returned to a near pre-pregnant state.

## PHYSICAL ADJUSTMENTS

A woman's body makes numerous physical adjustments in the first days and weeks after childbirth (Mattson & Smith, 2011). She may have a great deal of energy or feel exhausted and let down. Though these changes are normal, the fatigue can undermine the new mother's sense of well-being and confidence in her ability to cope with a new baby and a new family life (Runquist, 2007).

A concern is the loss of sleep that the primary caregiver experiences in the postpartum period (Gunderson & others, 2008). Numerous studies reveal that parental sleep is substantially reduced in the first six months after birth (e.g., Chang & others, 2010; Hunter, Rychnovsky, & Yount, 20097). The loss of sleep can contribute to stress, marital conflict, and impaired decision making (Meerlo, Sgoifo, & Suchecki, 2008).

After delivery, a mother's body undergoes sudden and dramatic changes in hormone production. When the placenta is delivered, estrogen and progesterone levels drop steeply and remain low until the ovaries start producing hormones again. These changes in hormone levels can result in a number of emotional and psychological adjustments, in addition to the physical adjustments a new mother experiences.

*Involution* is the process by which the uterus returns to its pre-pregnant size five or six weeks after birth. Immediately following birth, the uterus weighs 1 to 1.3 kilograms. By the end of five or six weeks, the uterus weighs 56 to 100 grams. Nursing the baby helps contract the uterus at a rapid rate.

## EMOTIONAL AND PSYCHOLOGICAL ADJUSTMENTS

Emotional fluctuations are common for mothers in the postpartum period. For some women, emotional fluctuations decrease within several weeks after the delivery, but other women experience more long-lasting mood swings.

Many new mothers have what are called the postpartum blues. About two to three days after birth, they begin to feel depressed, anxious, and upset. These feelings may come and go for several months after the birth, often peaking about three to five days after birth. Even without treatment, these feelings usually go away after one or two weeks.

## connecting to current controversy

### Developing Awareness of Paternal Postpartum Depression

The transition to parenthood can be a period of adjustment not only for the mother, but for the father, as well. However, we know far less about the challenges faced by fathers during the postnatal period. For example, postpartum depression is not limited to mothers, as fathers can also experience severe anxiety, sadness, and despair after the birth of a child (Paulson & Bazemore, 2010). Paternal postpartum depression has traditionally been a neglected topic in both research and public health agencies.

According to a recent meta-analysis, postpartum depression in the first year after the birth of a child affects 10.4 percent of new fathers worldwide (Paulson & Bazemore, 2010). The greatest incidence (25.6 percent) occurs 3 to 6 months after birth, but the onset can be earlier or later. In Canada, it is estimated that 11.2 percent of new fathers experience postpartum

depression within the first year after birth (Hall & Long, 2007). These rates are more than double that of depression in the general male population during a similar time period, illustrating the significance of this mental health concern. As with maternal postpartum depression, there are negative outcomes associated with paternal postpartum depression, as it can have a negative impact on the father's parenting (Wilson & Durbin, 2010) and is associated with future psychological problems in the child (Lewinson, Olino, & Klein, 2005; Ramchandani & others, 2008).

To date, identified risk factors associated with paternal postpartum depression include a history of depression, fathering at a young age, and the general psychological distress experienced during a first pregnancy (Habib, 2012). However, the greatest risk factor is whether or not the mother is experiencing postpartum depression. Studies report a significantly high correlation between maternal and paternal postpartum depression (Paulson & Bazemore, 2010), and some research has revealed that this relation

*(continued)*

# connecting to current controversy

The postpartum period is a time of considerable adjustment and adaptation for the father as well as the mother.

*(continued)*

may result from the associated lack of spousal support the father receives and his dissatisfaction with the relationship when the mother is experiencing depression (Don & Mickelson, 2012).

The controversy associated with paternal postpartum depression is the lack of awareness surrounding this mental health issue. Men tend to seek less help for health related purposes than do women and are less likely to disclose psychological or emotional difficulties to primary health care providers (Habib, 2012). In addition to this bias curtailing our understanding and effective treatment of postpartum depression, a number of other barriers preventing fathers from seeking help have been identified by a group of Canadian researchers (Letourneau & others, 2011). These barriers include a lack of knowledge (not realizing anything is wrong), minimal contact with health care providers during the postnatal period, fear of the stigma associated with depression, and being told that it's important to focus on the mother during this period (Letourneau & others, 2011). Given the relatively high rates of paternal postpartum depression and the effects it can have on children, it is crucial that we learn more about the risk factors, outcomes, and potential treatments for paternal postpartum depression. Canadian researchers are currently tackling the issue of support for fathers with postpartum depression (e.g., Letourneau & others, 2011) and will help bring greater awareness to this mental health issue.

*How might paternal postpartum depression affect developmental outcomes of the child?*

However, some women develop **postpartum depression**, which involves a major depressive episode that typically occurs about four weeks after delivery. In other words, women with postpartum depression have such strong feelings of sadness, anxiety, or despair that for at least a two-week period they have trouble coping with their daily tasks and often regard their new baby with ambivalence or uninterest. Without treatment, postpartum depression may become worse and last for many months (Nolen-Hoeksema, 2011). Unfortunately, many women with postpartum treatment don't seek help. For example, one study found that 15 percent of women reported postpartum depression symptoms but less than half sought help (McGarry & others, 2009). Estimates indicate that 3 to 20 percent of new mothers experience postpartum depression.

While it is unclear which mothers will experience postpartum depression, there are several known risk factors. Mothers who have experienced episodes of depression pre-pregnancy are more likely to experience postpartum depression. And a recent Canadian study revealed that mothers living in larger cities are more likely to experience postpartum depression than new mothers in rural settings (Vigod & others, 2013). This finding suggests that social support may be a key determinant for reducing incidences of postpartum depression.

Several antidepressant drugs are effective in treating postpartum depression and appear to be safe for women who are breastfeeding (Logsdon, Wisner, & Hanusa, 2009). Psychotherapy, especially cognitive therapy, also is an effective treatment of postpartum depression for many women (Miller & Larusso, 2011). Also, engaging in regular exercise may help in treating postpartum depression (Daley, Macarthur, & Winter, 2007).

**postpartum depression** Characteristic of women who have such strong feelings of sadness, anxiety, or despair that they have trouble coping with daily tasks during the postpartum period.

Can a mother's postpartum depression affect the way she interacts with her infant? A recent research review concluded that the interaction difficulties of depressed mothers and their infants occur across cultures and socioeconomic status groups, and encompass less sensitivity of the mothers and less responsiveness on the part of their infants (Field, 2010). Several caregiving activities also are compromised, including feeding (especially breastfeeding), sleep routines, and safety practices. Fathers also undergo considerable adjustment during the postpartum period, even when they work away from home all day. When the mother experiences postpartum depression, many fathers also develop depressed feelings (Letourneau & others, 2012; Ramchandani & others, 2011). Many fathers feel that the baby comes first and gets all of the mother's attention; some feel that they have been replaced by the baby. To learn more about the challenges fathers face during this transition period, read *Connecting to Current Controversy*.

The father's support and caring can play a role in whether the mother develops postpartum depression (Dietz & others, 2009; Persson & others, 2011). One study revealed that higher support by fathers was related to lower rates of postpartum depression in women (Smith & Howard, 2008).

## Review *Connect* Reflect

 **L03** Explain the changes that take place in the postpartum period.

### Review

- What does the postpartum period involve? What physical adjustments does the woman's body make during this period?
- What emotional and psychological adjustments characterize the postpartum period?

### *Connect*

- How can exercise help pregnant women before delivery and women with postpartum depression after giving birth?

### **Reflect** *Your Own Personal Journey of Life*

- If you are a female who plans to have children, what can you do to adjust effectively in the postpartum period? If you are the partner of a new mother, what can you do to help in the postpartum period?

# case study **connections**

1. What are some teratogens that may have contributed to the loss of the baby described in the opening case?

2. The opening story describes a case in which a baby was lost at two months into the pregnancy. Describe the characteristics of the fetus at this point of prenatal development.

3. What type of prenatal care might the parents in the opening vignette have engaged in prior to the birth of little Alex?

# Prenatal Development and Birth

## Prenatal Development

 **L01** **Describe prenatal development.**

**The Course of Prenatal Development**

- Prenatal development is divided into three periods: germinal (conception until 10 to 14 days later), which ends when the zygote (a fertilized egg) attaches to the uterine wall; embryonic (two to eight weeks after conception), during which the embryo differentiates into three layers, life-support systems develop, and organ systems form (organogenesis); and fetal (two months after conception until about nine months, or when the infant is born), a time when organ systems have matured to the point at which life can be sustained outside of the womb. The growth of the brain during prenatal development is nothing short of remarkable. By the time babies are born they have approximately 100 billion neurons, or nerve cells. Neurogenesis is the term that means the formation of new neurons. The nervous system begins with the formation of a neural tube at 18 to 24 days after conception. Proliferation and migration are two processes that characterize brain development in the prenatal period. The basic architecture of the brain is formed in the first two trimesters of prenatal development.

**Teratology and Hazards of Prenatal Development**

- Teratology is the field that investigates the causes of congenital (birth) defects. Any agent that causes birth defects is called a teratogen. The dose, genetic susceptibility, and time of exposure influence the severity of the damage to an unborn child and the type of defect that occurs. Prescription drugs that can be harmful include antibiotics, some antidepressants, certain hormones, and Accutane. Non-prescription drugs that can be harmful include diet pills and aspirin. Legal psychoactive drugs that are potentially harmful to prenatal development include caffeine, alcohol, and nicotine. Fetal alcohol spectrum disorders are a cluster of abnormalities that appear in offspring of mothers who drink heavily during pregnancy. Even when pregnant women drink moderately (one to two drinks a few days a week), negative effects on their offspring have been found. Cigarette smoking by pregnant women has serious adverse effects on prenatal and child development (such as low birth weight). Illegal psychoactive drugs that are potentially harmful to offspring include methamphetamine, marijuana, cocaine, and heroin. Incompatibility of the mother's and father's blood types can also be harmful to the fetus. Environmental hazards include radiation, environmental pollutants, and toxic wastes. Syphilis, rubella (German measles), genital herpes, and AIDS are infectious diseases that can harm the fetus. Other parental factors include maternal diet and nutrition, age, emotional states and stress, and paternal factors. A developing fetus depends entirely on its mother for nutrition. Maternal age can negatively affect the offspring's development if the mother is an adolescent or over 35. High stress in the mother is linked with less than optimal prenatal and birth outcomes. Paternal factors that can adversely affect prenatal development include exposure to lead, radiation, certain pesticides, and petrochemicals.

**Prenatal Care**

- Prenatal care varies extensively but usually involves medical care services with a defined schedule of visits.

**Normal Prenatal Development**

- It is important to remember that, although things can and do go wrong during pregnancy, most of the time pregnancy and prenatal development go well.

# Birth

**L02** Discuss the birth process.

The Birth Process

- Childbirth occurs in three stages. The first stage, which lasts about 6 to 12 hours for a woman having her first child, is the longest stage. The cervix dilates to about 10 centimetres (4 inches) at the end of the first stage. The second stage begins when the baby's head starts to move through the cervix and ends with the baby's complete emergence. The third stage involves the delivery of the placenta after birth. Childbirth strategies involve the childbirth setting and attendants. In many countries, a doula attends a childbearing woman. Methods of delivery include medicated, natural or prepared, and Caesarean. Being born involves considerable stress for the baby, but the baby is well prepared and adapted to handle the stress.

Assessing the Newborn

- For many years, the Apgar Scale has been used to assess the health of newborn babies. The Brazelton Neonatal Behavioral Assessment Scale (NBAS) examines the newborn's neurological development, reflexes, and reactions to people. Recently, the Neonatal Intensive Care Unit Network Neurobehavioral Scale (NNNS) was created to assess at-risk infants.

Preterm and Low Birth Weight Infants

- Low birth weight infants weigh less than 2.5 kilograms, and they may be preterm (born before the completion of 37 weeks of gestation) or small for date (also called small for gestational age), which refers to an infant whose birth weight is below normal when the length of pregnancy is considered. Small for date infants may be preterm or full term. Although most low birth weight and preterm infants are normal and healthy, as a group they experience more illness and developmental problems than normal birth weight infants. Kangaroo care and massage therapy have been shown to have benefits for preterm infants.

# The Postpartum Period

**L03** Explain the changes that take place in the postpartum period.

Physical Adjustments

- The postpartum period is the period after childbirth or delivery. The period lasts for about six weeks or until the woman's body has completed its adjustment. Physical adjustments in the postpartum period include fatigue, involution (the process by which the uterus returns to its pre-pregnant size five or six weeks after birth), and hormonal changes.

Emotional and Psychological Adjustments

- Emotional fluctuations on the part of the mother are common in this period, and they can vary greatly from one mother to the next. Postpartum depression characterizes women who have such strong feelings of sadness, anxiety, or despair that they have trouble coping with daily tasks in the postpartum period. Postpartum depression occurs in about 11.5 percent of new mothers. The father also goes through a postpartum adjustment.

connect ⁞LEARNSMART ⁞SMARTBOOK™

For more information on the resources available from McGraw-Hill Ryerson, go to www.mheducation.ca/he/solutions

# Physical Development and Health | chapter 4

On Thursday afternoons children from a grade 7 class in rural Manitoba meet with their assigned buddies from grade 2 to discuss the importance of healthy eating. In today's class, the older students are leading the young children through a game of Go Fuel Bingo to help the younger ones practise identifying foods within each of Health Canada's four food groups. This activity is designed to increase the children's awareness of healthy food and the leaders discuss with the younger children why it is important to make healthy food choices. On Friday the same buddies will meet in the gym to do a series of physical activities together. These children are participating in Healthy Buddies, a school-based peer mentoring program that pairs younger children with older children to learn about healthy eating habits, physical activity, and positive self-image.

Once a week students meet with their buddies in the classroom to discuss issues such as setting goals for a healthier life, the importance of sleep, how to respond to outside influences on body image, and why eating healthy is important. In addition, buddies meet twice a week in the gym to engage in the physical activity portion of the program. To date, the Healthy Buddies program has been implemented in British Columbia, Alberta, and Manitoba, in rural and urban as well as First Nations schools. The Healthy Buddies program is one of several school-based health promotion initiatives found in schools across Canada, and the goals of these healthy living programs are the focus of this chapter.

# preview

Think about how much you changed physically as you grew up. You came into this life as a small being but grew very rapidly in infancy, more slowly in childhood, and once again more rapidly during puberty. In this chapter, we will explore changes in physical development including body growth, the development of the brain, the role of sleep in physical growth, and aspects of children's health.

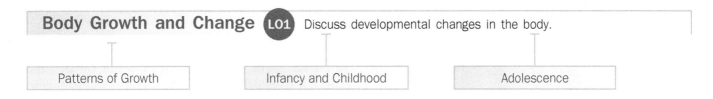

**Body Growth and Change** **L01** Discuss developmental changes in the body.

Patterns of Growth | Infancy and Childhood | Adolescence

In the journey of childhood, we go through many bodily changes. Let's begin by studying some basic patterns of growth and then turn to the bodily changes that occur from infancy through adolescence.

## PATTERNS OF GROWTH

During prenatal development and early infancy, the head constitutes an extraordinarily large portion of the total body (see Figure 4.1). Gradually, the body's proportions change. Why? Growth is not random. Instead, it generally follows two patterns: the cephalocaudal pattern and the proximodistal pattern.

The **cephalocaudal pattern** is the sequence in which the fastest growth always occurs at the top—the head. Physical growth in size, weight, and feature differentiation gradually works its way down from the top to the bottom—for example, from neck to shoulders, to middle trunk, and so on. This same pattern occurs in the head area: the top parts of the head—the eyes and brain—grow faster than the lower parts, such as the jaw.

**cephalocaudal pattern** The sequence in which the fastest growth occurs at the top of the body—the head—with physical growth in size, weight, and feature differentiation gradually working from top to bottom.

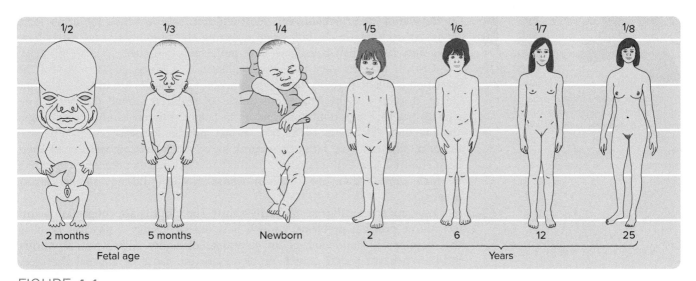

## FIGURE 4.1

**CHANGES IN PROPORTIONS OF THE HUMAN BODY DURING GROWTH.** As individuals develop from infancy through adulthood, one of the most noticeable physical changes is that the head becomes smaller in relation to the rest of the body. The fractions listed refer to head size as a proportion of total body length at different ages.

developmental **connection**

**Dynamic Systems Theory.** Sensory and motor development are intertwined in many aspects of children's acquisition of skills. Chapter 5, LO 1

**proximodistal pattern** The sequence in which growth starts at the centre of the body and moves toward the extremities.

The **proximodistal pattern** is the growth sequence that starts at the centre of the body and moves toward the extremities. For example, muscle control of the truck and arms matures before control of the hands and fingers. Further, infants use their whole hand as a unit before they can control several fingers. Sensory and motor development also generally proceed according to the cephalocaudal and proximodistal principles. For example, infants see objects before they can control their torso, and they can use their hands long before they can crawl or walk. We will have much more to say about sensory and motor development in Chapter 5.

## INFANCY AND CHILDHOOD

Height and weight increase rapidly in infancy (Lampl, 2008). Growth takes a slower course during the childhood years.

**Infancy** The average North American newborn is 50.8 cm long and weighs 3.2 kilograms (7 pounds). Ninety-five percent of full-term newborns are 45.7 to 55.9 cm long and weigh between 2.5 and 4.5 kilograms (5.5 and 10 pounds).

In the first several days of life, most newborns lose 5 to 7 percent of their body weight. Once infants adjust to sucking, swallowing, and digesting, they grow rapidly, gaining an average of 142 to 170 grams per week during the first month. They have doubled their birth weight by the age of 4 months and have nearly tripled it by their first birthday. Infants grow about 2.5 cm per month during the first year, reaching approximately one and a half times their birth length by their first birthday.

In the second year of life, an infant's rate of growth slows considerably (Burns & others, 2013). By 2 years of age, infants weigh approximately 11.8 to 14.5 kilograms, having gained 113 to 127 grams per month during the second year; at age 2 they have reached about one-fifth of their adult weight. The average 2-year-old is 81.3 to 88.9 cm, which is nearly one half of adult height.

**Early Childhood** As the preschool child grows older, the annual percentage of increase in height and weight decreases with each additional year (McMahon & Stryjewski, 2012). Girls are only slightly smaller and lighter than boys during these years. Both boys and girls slim down as the trunks of their bodies lengthen. Although their heads are still somewhat large for their bodies, by the end of the preschool years most children have lost their top-heavy look. Body fat declines slowly but steadily during the preschool years. Girls have more fatty tissue than boys; boys have more muscle tissue.

Growth patterns vary individually (Florin & Ludwig, 2011). Much of the variation is due to heredity, but environmental experiences are involved to some extent. A review of the height and weight of children around the world concluded that two important contributors to height differences are ethnic origin and nutrition (Meredith, 1978). Also, urban, middle socioeconomic status, and firstborn children were taller than rural, lower socioeconomic status, and later-born children. The children whose mothers smoked during pregnancy were half an inch shorter than the children whose mothers did not smoke during pregnancy.

Why are some children unusually short? The culprits are congenital factors (genetic or prenatal problems), growth hormone deficiency, a physical problem that develops in childhood, or an emotional difficulty (Wit, Kiess, & Mullis, 2011). When congenital growth problems are the cause of unusual shortness, often the child can be treated with hormones. Usually this treatment is directed at the pituitary gland, the body's master gland, located at the base of the brain. This gland secretes growth-related hormones. Physical problems during childhood that can stunt growth include malnutrition and chronic infections. However, if the problems are properly treated, normal growth usually is attained.

The bodies of 5-year-olds and 2-year-olds are different. Notice how the 5-year-old is not only taller and weighs more, but also has a longer trunk and legs than the 2-year-old. *What might be some other physical differences in 2- and 5-year-olds?*

**Middle and Late Childhood**   The period of middle and late childhood—from about 6 to 11 years of age—involves slow, consistent growth. This is a period of calm before the rapid growth spurt of adolescence.

During the elementary school years, children grow an average of 5 to 7.5 cm a year. At the age of 8 the average girl and the average boy are 142 cm tall. During the middle and late childhood years, children gain about 2.26 to 3.17 kilograms a year. The average 8-year-old girl and the average 8-year-old boy weigh 25.4 kilograms (National Center for Health Statistics, 2000). The weight increase is due mainly to increases in the size of the skeletal and muscular systems, as well as the size of some body organs. Muscle mass and strength gradually increase as "baby fat" decreases in middle and late childhood (Hockenberry & Wilson, 2009).

The loose movements of early childhood give way to improved muscle tone in middle and late childhood. Children also double their strength capacity during these years. The increase in muscular strength is due to heredity and to exercise. Because they have more muscle cells, boys tend to be stronger than girls.

Changes in proportion are among the most pronounced physical changes in middle and late childhood. Head circumference, waist circumference, and leg length decrease in relation to body height (Burns & others, 2013). A less noticeable physical change is that bones continue to harden during middle and late childhood; still, they yield to pressure and pull more than mature bones.

*What characterizes physical growth during middle and late childhood?*

## ADOLESCENCE

After slowing through childhood, growth surges during puberty. **Puberty** is a period of rapid physical maturation involving hormonal and bodily changes that occur primarily in early adolescence. The features and proportions of the body change as the individual becomes capable of reproducing. We will begin our exploration of puberty by describing its determinants and then examine important physical changes and psychological accompaniments of puberty.

**puberty** A period of rapid physical maturation involving hormonal and bodily changes that take place primarily in early adolescence.

**Determinants of Puberty**   Puberty is not the same as adolescence. For virtually everyone, puberty has ended long before adolescence is over. Puberty is often thought of as the most important marker for the beginning of adolescence.

From *Penguin Dreams and Stranger Things*, by Berke Breathed. Copyright © 1985 by The Washington Post Company. By permission of Little, Brown & Company, Inc. and International Creative Management.

There are wide variations in the onset and progression of puberty. Puberty might begin as early as 10 years of age or as late as 13½ for boys and as early as 9 years of age for girls. It might end as early as 13 years or as late as 17 years.

In fact, over the years the timing of puberty has changed. Imagine a 3-year-old girl with fully developed breasts or a boy just slightly older with a deep male voice. That is what toddlers would be like by the year 2250 if the age at which puberty arrives were to continue decreasing as it did for much of the twentieth century. For example, in Norway, **menarche**—a girl's first menstruation—now occurs at just over 13 years of age, compared with 17 years of age in the 1840s (Petersen, 1979). In Canada, where children mature up to a year earlier than in European countries, the average age of menarche has dropped to about 12½ years (Al-Sahab & others, 2010). Some researchers have found evidence that the age of puberty is still dropping for North American girls; others suggest that the evidence is inconclusive or that the decline in age is slowing (Herman-Giddens, 2007). A recent study also found that puberty is occurring earlier for boys, although critics say the study sample is skewed toward including more early maturing boys because parents likely brought their sons to see the participating physicians because of health concerns (Herman-Giddens, & others, 2012). The earlier onset of puberty is likely the result of improved health and nutrition, leading to rapid body growth (Herman-Giddens, 2007).

The normal range for the onset and progression of puberty is wide enough that, given two boys of the same chronological age, one might complete the pubertal sequence before the other one has begun it. For girls, the age range of menarche is even wider. It is considered within a normal range when it occurs between the ages of 9 and 15.

**Precocious puberty** is the term used to describe the very early onset and rapid progression of puberty. Precocious puberty is usually diagnosed when pubertal onset occurs before 8 years of age in girls and before 9 years of age in boys. Precocious puberty occurs approximately 10 times more often in girls than in boys. When precocious puberty occurs, it usually is treated by medically suppressing gonadotropic secretions, which temporarily stops pubertal change. The reasons for this treatment is that children who experience precocious puberty are ultimately likely to have short stature, early sexual capability, and the potential for engaging in age-inappropriate behaviour (Blakemore, Berenbaum, & Liben, 2009).

*Heredity and Environmental Influences*   Puberty is not an environmental accident. It does not take place at 2 or 3 years of age, and it does not occur in the twenties. Programmed into the genes of every human being is timing for the emergence of puberty. Recently, scientists have begun to conduct molecular genetic studies in an attempt to identify specific genes that are linked to the onset and progression of puberty (Dvornyk & Waqar-ul-Haq, 2012). Environmental factors, such as family influences and stress, can also influence its onset and duration (Arim & others, 2011). Experiences that are linked to earlier pubertal onset include adoption, father absences, low socioeconomic status, family conflict, maternal harshness, child maltreatment, and early substance use (Deardorff & others, 2011; Ellis & others, 2011). In many cases, puberty comes months earlier in these situations, and this earlier onset of puberty is likely explained by high rates of conflict and stress in these social contexts. One study revealed that early onset of menarche was associated with severe child abuse (Boynton-Jarrett & others, 2013).

*Hormones*   Behind the first whisker in boys and the widening of hips in girls is a flood of hormones. **Hormones** are powerful chemical substances secreted by the endocrine glands and carried through the body by the bloodstream. In the case of puberty, the secretion of key hormones is controlled by the interaction of the hypothalamus, the pituitary gland, and the gonads (sex glands). The *hypothalamus* is a structure in the brain best known for monitoring eating, drinking, and sex. The *pituitary gland* is an important endocrine gland that controls growth and regulates other glands. The *gonads* are the sex glands—the testes in males, the ovaries in females.

**menarche** A girl's first menstruation.

**precocious puberty** Very early onset and rapid progression of puberty.

**hormones** Powerful chemical substances secreted by the endocrine glands and carried through the body by the bloodstream.

The key hormonal changes involve two classes of hormones that have significantly different concentrations in males and females (Susman & Dorn, 2013). **Androgens** are the main class of male sex hormones. **Estrogens** are the main class of female hormones.

**Testosterone** is an androgen that is a key hormone in the development of puberty in boys. As the testosterone level rises during puberty, external genitals enlarge, height increases, and the voice changes. **Estradiol** is an estrogen that plays an important role in female pubertal development. As the estradiol level rises, breast development, uterine development, and skeletal changes occur. In one study, testosterone levels increased eighteenfold in boys but only twofold in girls across puberty; estradiol levels increased eightfold in girls but only twofold in boys across puberty (Nottleman & others, 1987) (see Figure 4.2).

Are there links between concentrations of hormones and adolescent behaviour? Findings are inconsistent (Vermeersch & others, 2008). In any event, hormonal factors alone are not responsible for adolescent behaviour (Graber, 2008). For example, one study found that social factors accounted for two to four times as much variance as hormonal factors in young adolescent girls' depression and anger (Brooks-Gunn & Warren, 1989). Hormones do not act independently; hormonal activity is influenced by many environmental factors, including parent-adolescent relationships. Stress, eating patterns, sexual activity, and depression can also activate or suppress various aspects of the hormone system (Susman & Dorn, 2013).

**Growth Spurt**   Puberty ushers in the most rapid increases in growth since infancy. As indicated in Figure 4.3, the growth spurt associated with puberty occurs approximately two years earlier for girls than for boys. The mean beginning of the growth spurt in North America today is 9 years of age for girls and 11 years of age for boys. Pubertal change peaks at an average of 11.5 years for girls and 13.5 years for boys. During their growth spurt, girls increase in height about 8.9 cm per year, boys about 10 cm.

Boys and girls who are shorter or taller than their peers before adolescence are likely to remain so during adolescence. At the beginning of adolescence, girls tend to be as tall as or taller than boys their age, but by the end of the middle school years most boys have caught up, or in many cases even surpassed girls in height. And although height in elementary school is a good predictor of height later in adolescence, as much as 30 percent of the height of individuals in late adolescence is unexplained by height in the elementary school years.

**Sexual Maturation**   Think back to the onset of your puberty. Of the striking changes that were taking place in your body, what was the first change that occurred? Researchers have found that male pubertal characteristics develop in this order: increase in penis and testicle size, appearance of straight pubic hair, minor voice change, first ejaculation (which usually occurs through masturbation or a wet dream), appearance of pubic hair, onset of maximum body growth, growth of hair in armpits, more detectable voice changes, and growth of facial hair. Three of the most noticeable areas of sexual maturation in boys are penis elongation, testes development, and growth of facial hair.

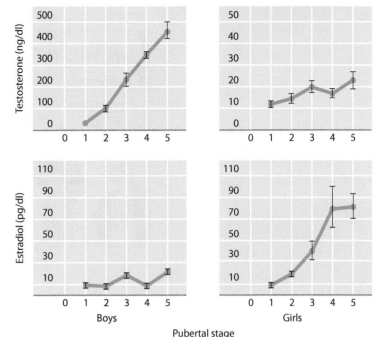

FIGURE **4.2**

**HORMONE LEVELS BY SEX AND PUBERTAL STAGE FOR TESTOSTERONE AND ESTRADIOL.** The five stages range from the early beginning of puberty (stage 1) to the most advanced stage of puberty (stage 5). Notice the significant increase in testosterone in boys and the significant increase in estradiol in girls.

**androgens** The main class of male sex hormones.

**estrogens** The main class of female sex hormones.

**testosterone** An androgen that is a key hormone in boys' pubertal development.

**estradiol** An estrogen that is a key hormone in girls' pubertal development.

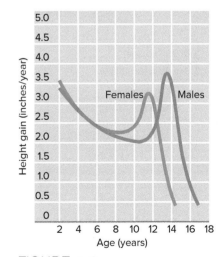

FIGURE **4.3**

**PUBERTAL GROWTH SPURT.** On the average, the peak of the growth spurt that characterizes pubertal change occurs two years earlier for girls (11½) than for boys (13½).

**ZITS** By Jerry Scott and Jim Borgman

© ZITS Partnership. King Features Syndicate.

What is the order of appearance of physical changes in females? First, on average the breasts enlarge and then pubic hair appears. These are two of the most noticeable aspects of female pubertal development. A recent longitudinal study revealed that on average girls' breast development preceded their pubic hair development by about two months (Susman & others, 2010). Later hair appears in the armpits. As these changes occur, the female grows in height, and her hips become wider than her shoulders. Her first menstruation (menarche) occurs rather late in the pubertal cycle; it is considered normal if it occurs between the ages of 9 and 15. Initially, her menstrual cycles may be highly irregular. For the first several years, she might not ovulate during every menstrual cycle. Some girls do not become fertile until two years after their periods begin. Pubertal females do not experience voice changes comparable to those in pubertal males. By the end of puberty, the female's breasts have become more fully rounded. The normal range and average age of development in boys and girls for these sexual characteristics, along with height spurt, is shown in Figure 4.4.

## Psychological Dimensions of Puberty

*Body Image* One psychological aspect of physical change in puberty is certain: Adolescents are preoccupied with their bodies and develop images of what their bodies are like (Park & Epstein, 2013; Williams, Wyatt, & Winters, 2013). Preoccupation with body image is strong throughout adolescence, but a recent study found that both boys' and girls' body images became more positive as they moved from the beginning to the end of adolescence (Holsen, Carlson Jones, & Skogbrott Birkeland, 2012).

Gender differences characterize adolescents' perceptions of their bodies. In general, girls are less happy with their bodies and have more negative body images than boys throughout puberty (Benowitz-Fredericks & others, 2012). As pubertal change proceeds, girls often become more dissatisfied with their bodies, probably because their body fat increases. In contrast, boys become more satisfied as they move through puberty, probably because their muscle mass increases.

Although we have described gender differences in the body images of adolescents, emphasizing that girls tend to have more negative body images than boys, keep in mind that there is considerable variation, with many adolescent girls having positive body images and many adolescent boys having negative body images.

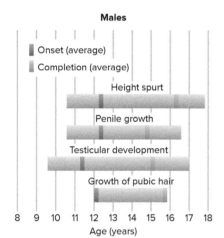

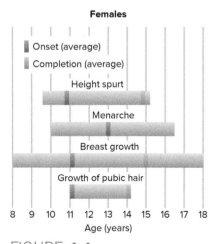

## FIGURE **4.4**

**NORMAL RANGE AND AVERAGE DEVELOPMENT OF SEXUAL CHARACTERISTICS IN MALES AND FEMALES.**

**Early and Late Maturation** Did you enter puberty early, late, or on time? When adolescents mature earlier or later than their peers, they often perceive themselves differently and their maturational timing is linked to their socioemotional development and whether they develop problems (Negriff, Susman, & Trickett, 2011). In one longitudinal study conducted some years ago, early-maturing boys perceived themselves more positively and had more successful peer relations than did late-maturing boys (Jones, 1965). The findings for early-maturing girls were similar but not as strong as for boys. When the late-maturing boys were in their thirties, however, they had developed a more positive identity than the early-maturing boys had (Peskin, 1967). Perhaps the late-maturing boys had more time to explore life's options, or perhaps the early-maturing boys continued to focus on their physical status instead of paying attention to career development and achievement.

*What gender differences characterize body image in adolescents? What might explain the differences?*

An increasing number of researchers have found that early maturation increases girls' vulnerability to a number of problems (Cavanagh, 2009; Negriff, Susman & Trickett, 2011; Susman & Dorn, 2013). Data from the Canadian Longitudinal Survey of Children and Youth revealed that early-maturing girls are more likely to smoke and drink than their peers (Arim & others, 2011). Other studies have found links between early maturation and depression, eating disorders, and struggles for earlier independence from parents. In addition, their bodies are likely to elicit responses from males that lead to earlier dating and earlier sexual experiences (de Rose & others, 2011; Negriff, Susman, & Trickett, 2011). And early maturing girls are more likely to drop out of high school and cohabit and marry earlier (Cavanagh, 2009). Apparently as a result of their social and cognitive immaturity, combined with early physical development, early-maturing girls are easily lured into problem behaviours, not recognizing the possible long-term effects of these on their development. Two recent studies document the negative outcomes of early pubertal timing in girls:

- Early maturing girls were more likely to engage in substance abuse and early sexual intercourse (Gaudineau & others, 2010).
- A study of 9- to 13-year old girls revealed that early pubertal timing was linked to a later higher level of sexual activity, which in turn was linked to a later higher rate of delinquency (Negriff, Susman, & Trickett, 2011).

*developmental* **connection**

**Self-esteem and self-concept.** Self-esteem incorporates the evaluative dimension of the self, including self-image. Chapter 11, LO 2

## Review *Connect* Reflect

 Discuss developmental changes in the body.

### Review

- What are cephalocaudal and proximodistal patterns?
- How do height and weight change in infancy and childhood?
- What changes characterize puberty?

### *Connect*

- Describe the influence of nature and nurture on the relationship between hormones and puberty.

### Reflect *Your Own Personal Journey of Life*

- Did you experience puberty early, late, or on time? How do you think this affected your social relationships and development?

In every physical change we have described so far, the brain is involved in some way. Structures of the brain help to regulate not only behaviour but metabolism, the release of hormones, and other aspects of the body's physiology.

We described the amazing growth of the brain from conception to birth in Chapter 3. In this section, we initially explore the neuroconstructivist view, describe basic structures and function of the brain, and then examine developmental changes in the brain from infancy through adolescence.

## THE NEUROCONSTRUCTIVIST VIEW

Until recently, little was known for certain about how the brain changes as children develop. Not long ago, scientists thought that our genes determined how our brains were "wired" and that unlike most cells, the cells in the brain responsible for processing information just maturationally unfolded with little or no input from environmental experiences. People were essentially stuck with whatever brain heredity dealt them. This view, however, turned out to be wrong. Instead, the brain has plasticity, and its development depends on context (Diamond, 2013; Nelson, 2011).

According to the increasingly popular **neuroconstructivist view**, (a) biological processes (genes, for example) and environmental conditions (enriched or impoverished, for example) influence the brain's development, (b) the brain has plasticity and is context dependent, and (c) development of the brain is closely linked with the child's cognitive development. These factors constrain or advance the child's construction of cognitive skills (Diamond, 2013; Peltzer-Karpf, 2012; Westermann, Thomas, & Karmiloff-Smith, 2011). The neuroconstructivist view emphasizes the importance of considering interactions between experience and gene expression in the brain's development, much the same way the epigenetic view proposes (see Chapter 2).

## BRAIN PHYSIOLOGY

The brain includes a number of major structures. The key components of these structures are *neurons*, the nerve cells that handle information processing, which we initially described in Chapter 3.

**Structure and Function**  Observed from above, the brain has two halves, or hemispheres (see Figure 4.5). The top portion of the brain, farthest from the spinal cord, is known as the *forebrain*. Its outer layer of cells, the cerebral cortex, covers it like a cap. The *cerebral cortex* is responsible for about 80 percent of the brain's volume and is critical in perception, thinking, language, and other important functions.

Each hemisphere of the cortex has four major areas, called *lobes*. Although the lobes usually work together, each has a somewhat different primary function (see Figure 4.6):

- *Frontal lobes* are involved in voluntary movement, thinking, personality, and intentionality or purpose.
- *Occipital lobes* function in vision.
- *Temporal lobes* have an active role in hearing, language processing, and memory.
- *Parietal lobes* play important roles in registering spatial location, attention, and motor control.

### developmental **connection**

**Nature and Nurture.** In the epigenetic view, development is a result of a bidirectional interchange between heredity and the environment, in which environmental factors can influence how genes are expressed. Chapter 2, LO 4

**Neuroconstructivist view.** Theory of brain development emphasizing the following points: (a) biological processes and environmental conditions influence brain development, (b) the brain has plasticity and is context dependent, and (c) the development of the brain and the child's cognitive development are closely linked.

### developmental **connection**

**Intelligence.** Are some regions of the brain linked with children's development more than others? Chapter 8, LO 1

## FIGURE **4.5**

**THE HUMAN BRAIN'S HEMISPHERES.** The two halves (hemispheres) of the human brain are clearly seen in this photograph.

Deeper in the brain, beneath the cortex, lie other key structures. These include the hypothalamus and the pituitary gland as well as the *amygdala*, which plays an important role in emotions, and the *hippocampus*, which is especially active in memory and emotion.

**Neurons**   How do neurons work? As we indicated, the neurons process information. Figure 4.7 shows some important parts of the neuron, including the *axon* and *dendrites*. Basically, an axon sends electrical signals away from the central part of the neuron. At the end of the axon are terminal buttons, which release chemicals called *neurotransmitters* into *synapses*, which are tiny gaps between neurons' fibres. Chemical interactions in synapses connect axons and dendrites, allowing information to pass from neuron to neuron (Turrigiano, 2010). Think of the synapse as a river that blocks a road. A grocery truck arrives at one bank of the river, crosses by ferry, and continues its journey to market. Similarly, a message in the brain is "ferried" across the synapse by a neurotransmitter, which pours out information contained in chemicals when it reaches the other side of the river.

Most axons are covered by a myelin sheath, which is a layer of fat cells. The sheath helps impulses travel faster along the axon, increasing the speed with which information travels from neuron to neuron. The myelin sheath developed as the brain evolved. As brain size increased, it became necessary for information to travel faster over longer distances in the nervous system. We can compare the myelin sheath's development to the evolution of freeways as cities grew. A freeway is a shielded road, and it keeps fast-moving, long-distance traffic from getting snarled by slow local traffic.

Which neurons get which information? Clusters of neurons known as *neural circuits* work together to handle particular types of information (Homae & others, 2011). The brain is organized in many neural circuits (Rueda & Posner, 2013; Short & others, 2013). For example, one neural circuit is important in attention and working memory (the type of memory that holds information for a brief time and is like a "mental workbench" as we perform a task) (Krimer & Goldman-Rakic, 2001). This neural circuit uses the neurotransmitter dopamine and lies in the prefrontal cortex and midbrain areas of the brain (D'Ardenne & others, 2012).

To some extent, the type of information handled by neurons depends on whether they are in the left or right hemisphere of the cortex (Griffiths & others, 2013). Speech and grammar, for example, depend on activity in the left hemisphere in most people; humour and the use of metaphors depend on activity in the right hemisphere (McGettigan & others, 2012). This specialization of function in one hemisphere of the cerebral cortex or the other is called **lateralization**. However, most neuroscientists agree that complex functions such as reading or performing music involve both hemispheres (Ibrahim & Evitar, 2013). Labelling people as *left-brained* because they are logical thinkers and *right-brained* because they are creative thinkers does not correspond to the way the brain's hemispheres work. Complex thinking in normal people is the outcome of communication between both hemispheres of the brain (Liegeois & others, 2008). For example, a recent meta-analysis revealed no hemispheric specialization in creative thinking (Mihov, Denzler, & Forster, 2010).

## INFANCY

As we saw in Chapter 3, brain development occurs extensively during the prenatal period. The brain's development is also substantial during infancy and later (Diamond, 2013; Nelson, 2011; Zelazo, 2013).

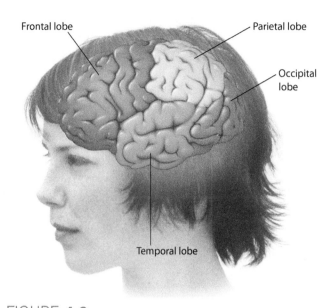

## FIGURE **4.6**

**THE BRAIN'S FOUR LOBES.** Shown here are the locations of the brain's four lobes: frontal, occipital, temporal, and parietal.

**lateralization** Specialization of function in one hemisphere of the cerebral cortex or the other.

developmental **connection**

**Brain development.** How does the brain change from conception to birth? Chapter 3, LO 1

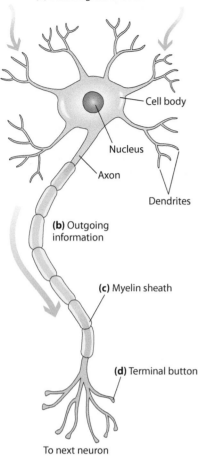

**(a)** Incoming information

Cell body

Nucleus

Axon

Dendrites

**(b)** Outgoing information

**(c)** Myelin sheath

**(d)** Terminal button

To next neuron

## FIGURE **4.7**

**THE NEURON.** (*a*) The dendrites receive information from other neurons, muscles, or glands. (*b*) Axons transmit information away from the cell body. (*c*) A myelin sheath covers most axons and speeds information transmission. (*d*) As the axon ends, it branches out into terminal buttons.

Because the brain is still developing so rapidly in infancy, the infant's head should be protected from falls or other injuries and the baby should never be shaken. *Shaken baby syndrome*, which includes brain swelling and haemorrhaging, is a leading cause of death in children under the age of 2 years. A recent analysis found that fathers were the most frequent perpetrators of shaken baby syndrome, followed by child care providers and by a boyfriend of the victim's mother (National Center on Shaken Baby Syndrome, 2010).

Studying the brain's development in infancy is not as easy as it might seem. Even the latest brain-imaging technologies (described in Chapter 1) cannot make out fine details in adult brains and cannot be used with babies (Nelson, 2011). Positron-emission tomography (PET) scans pose a radiation risk to babies, and infants wriggle too much to allow technicians to capture accurate images using magnetic resonance imaging (MRI). However, researchers have been successful in using the electroencephalogram (EEG), a measure of the brain's electrical activity, to learn about the brain's development in infancy (Bell & Cuevas, 2012; 2013).

Among the researchers who are making strides in finding out more about the brain's development in infancy are Laurel Trainor and her colleagues at McMaster University in Ontario (Butler & Trainor, 2013; Fujioka, Mourad, & Trainor, 2011; Trainor, Lee, & Bosnyak, 2011; Trainor & others, 2012). In her research, Trainor attaches up to 128 electrodes to a baby's scalp (see Figure 4.8) to explore how infants' brains respond to different sounds and musical tones. To learn more about how an EEG is used to study brain development in infancy, see *Connecting Through Research*.

As an infant walks, talks, runs, shakes a rattle, smiles, and frowns changes in its brain are occurring. Consider that the infant began life as a single cell and nine months later was born with a brain and nervous system that contained approximately 100 billion nerve cells, or neurons. What determines how those neurons communicate with each other?

**Early Experience and the Brain** Children who grow up in a deprived environment may also have depressed brain activity (Kolb, 2011; Zeanah, Fox, & Nelson, 2011). As shown in Figure 4.9, a child who grew up in the unresponsive and unstimulating environment of a Romanian orphanage showed considerably depressed brain activity compared with a normal child.

# connecting through research

## Using EEGs to Explore Brain Development in Infancy

One study by Laurel Trainor and her colleagues at McMaster University illustrates how an electroencephalograph (EEG) can be used to explore the role of early

## FIGURE **4.8**

**MEASURING THE ACTIVITY OF AN INFANT'S BRAIN.** By attaching electrodes to a baby's scalp to measure the brain's activity, Laurel Trainor (Trainor, Lee, & Bosnyak, 2011) has found that infants produce distinctive brain waves that reveal they can distinguish between different auditory stimuli. *Why is it so difficult to measure infants' brain activity?*

*(continued)*

# connecting through research

*(continued)*

auditory experiences on brain development (Trainor, Lee, & Bosnyak, 2011). The EEG is a measure of ongoing electrical activity in the brain, but when this electrical activity is time-locked to the presentation of a particular stimulus, like a sound, it can provide information about how the brain responds to that particular stimulus. This event-related potential (ERP) provides information about the time course of processing in response to that stimulus, through analyses of the various peaks and dips in the map of electrical activity that is produced from the EEG recording (DeBoer, Scott, & Nelson, 2007). One such peak, termed the *mis-match negativity* (MMN) component, occurs in response to a new sound that violates the expectations established from the preceding ongoing sequence of sounds. Thus, the MMN reflects a detection of change in auditory stimuli.

In this study, 4-month-old infants were exposed to melodies played on either a guitar or a marimba each day for one week. At the end of the week, infants were brought into the lab and an EEG was recorded while they listened to guitar and marimba tones at pitches not previously heard. Results found that the MMN component was larger in response to the guitar than marimba tones for infants exposed to the melodies in the guitar, but larger in response to the marimba than guitar tones for infants exposed to the melodies in the marimba. Trainor and her colleagues (2012) also found differences in EEG responses for 6-month-old infants enrolled in an active music program compared with infants in a program with passive listening to music in the background. These results suggest that auditory experiences can affect how the brain processes sounds, suggesting that environmental experiences play a role in brain development. In addition to sensory experiences, like what a baby hears or sees, other experiences can also influence brain development during infancy. Canadian researcher Bryan Kolb (2011) notes in a recent review that parent-child relationships, peer relationships, gonadal hormones, diet, stress, and psychoactive drugs can all alter how the brain develops.

*How do the results of this study support a neuroconstructivist view?*

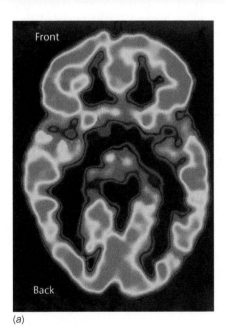 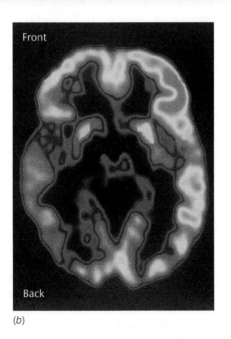

*(a)*        *(b)*

## FIGURE **4.9**

**EARLY DEPRIVATION AND BRAIN ACTIVITY.** These two photographs are PET (positron emission tomography) scans (which use radioactive tracers to image and analyze blood flow and metabolic activity in the body's organs) of the brains of (*a*) a normal child and (*b*) an institutionalized Romanian orphan who experienced substantial deprivation since birth. In PET scans, the highest to lowest brain activity is reflected in the colours of red, yellow, green, blue, and black, respectively. As can be seen, red and yellow show up to a much greater degree in the PET scan of the normal child than the deprived Romanian orphan.

Are the effects of deprived environments irreversible? There is reason to think the answer is no. The brain demonstrates both flexibility and resilience. Consider 14-year-old Michael Rehbein. At age 7, he began to experience uncontrollable seizures—as many as 400 a day. Doctors said the only solution was to remove the left hemisphere of his brain where the seizures were

(a)

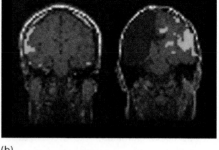

(b)

FIGURE **4.10**

**PLASTICITY IN THE BRAIN'S**

**HEMISPHERES.** (*a*) Michael Rehbein at 14 years of age. (*b*) Michael's right hemisphere (*right*) has reorganized to take over the language functions normally carried out by corresponding areas in the left hemisphere of an intact brain (*left*). However, the right hemisphere is not as efficient as the left at handling language, and more areas of the brain are recruited to process speech.

occurring. Recovery was slow, but his right hemisphere began to reorganize and take over functions that normally occur in the brain's left hemisphere, including speech (see Figure 4.10). One study of 10 children who had experienced an arterial stroke perinatally (during or around birth) revealed that in 8 of the 10 the right hemisphere was dominant in processing language (Guzzetta & others, 2008).

Neuroscientists believe that what wires the brain—or rewires it, in the case of Michael Rehbein—is repeated experience. Each time a baby tries to touch an attractive object or gazes intently at a face, tiny bursts of electricity shoot through the brain, knitting together neurons into circuits. The results are some of the behavioural milestones we discuss in this chapter.

In sum, the infant's brain is waiting for experiences to determine how connections are made (Dalton & Bergenn, 2007). Before birth, it appears that genes mainly direct basic wiring patterns. Neurons grow and travel to distant places awaiting further instructions (Nelson, 2011). After birth, the inflowing stream of sights, sounds, smells, touches, language, and eye contact help shape the brain's neural connections (Diamond, 2013; Lamb, 2013; Nelson, 2011).

**Changing Neurons**   At birth, the newborn's brain is about 25 percent of its adult weight. By the second birthday, the brain is about 75 percent of its adult weight. Two key developments during these first two years involve the myelin sheath (the layer of fat cells that speeds up the electrical impulse along the axon) and connections between dendrites.

**Myelination**, the process of encasing axons with a myelin sheath, begins prenatally and continues after birth (see Figure 4.11). The myelin sheath insulates axons and helps electrical signals travel faster down the axon, thereby increasing the speed of processing information (Markant & Thomas, 2013; Nelson, 2011). It is also involved in providing energy to neurons (Harris & Attwell, 2012). Myelination for visual pathways occurs rapidly after birth, being completed in the first six months. Auditory myelination is not completed until 4 or 5 years of age. Some aspects of myelination continue even into adolescence. Indeed, the most extensive changes in myelination in the frontal lobes occur during adolescence (Giedd, 2012).

Dramatic increases in dendrites and synapses (the tiny gaps between neurons across which neurotransmitters carry information) also characterize the development of the brain in the first two years of life (see Figure 4.11). Nearly twice as

**myelination** The process of encasing axons with a myelin sheath that increases the speed of processing information.

many of these connections are made as will ever be used (Huttenlocher & others, 1991; Huttenlocher & Dabholkar, 1997). The connections that are used become strengthened and survive; the unused ones are replaced by other pathways or disappear (Nelson, 2011). That is, connections are "pruned" (Faissner & others, 2010). Figure 4.12 vividly illustrates the growth and later pruning of synapses in the visual, auditory, and prefrontal cortex areas of the brain (Huttenlocher & Dabholkar, 1997).

As shown in Figure 4.13, "blooming and pruning" vary considerably by brain region in humans. For example, the peak synaptic overproduction in the area concerned with vision occurs about the fourth postnatal month, followed by a gradual pruning until the middle to end of the preschool years (Huttenlocher & Dabholkar, 1997). In areas of the brain involved in hearing and language, a similar, though somewhat later, course is detected. However, in the *prefrontal cortex* (the area of the brain where higher-level thinking and self-regulation occur), the peak of overproduction occurs at just after 3 years of age. Both heredity and environment are thought to influence synaptic overproduction and subsequent pruning.

**Changing Structures** At birth, the hemispheres already have started to specialize: Newborns show greater electrical activity in the left hemisphere than in the right hemisphere when they are making or listening to speech sounds (Imada & others, 2007).

In general, some areas of the brain, such as the primary motor areas, develop earlier than others, such as the primary sensory areas. The frontal lobes are immature in the newborn. However, as neurons in the frontal lobes become myelinated and interconnected during the first year of life, infants develop an ability to regulate their physiological states, such as sleep, and gain more control over their reflexes. Cognitive skills that require deliberate thinking do not emerge until later in the first year (Bell & Cuevas, 2013).

# CHILDHOOD

The brain and other parts of the nervous system continue developing through childhood and adolescence. These changes enable children to plan their actions, to attend to stimuli more effectively, and to make considerable strides in language development (Diamond, 2013).

During early childhood, the brain and head grow more rapidly than any other part of the body. Figure 4.14 shows how the growth curve for the head and brain advances more rapidly than the growth curve for height and weight. Some of the brain's increase in size is due to myelination and some is due to an increase in the number and size of dendrites. Some developmentalists

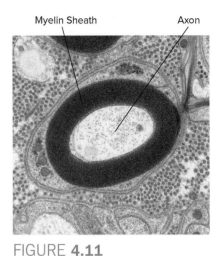

Myelin Sheath          Axon

FIGURE **4.11**

**A MYELINATED NERVE FIBRE.** The myelin sheath, shown in brown, encases the axon (white). This image was produced by an electron microscope that magnified the nerve fibre 12,000 times. *What role does myelination play in the brain's development?*

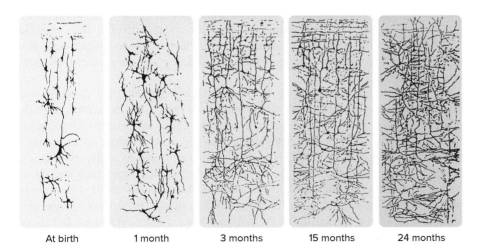

At birth    1 month    3 months    15 months    24 months

FIGURE **4.12**

**THE DEVELOPMENT OF DENDRITIC SPREADING.** Note the increase in connectedness between neurons over the course of the first two years of life.

Reprinted by permission of the publisher from *The Postnatal Development of the Human Cerebral Cortex, Volumes I-VIII* by Jesse LeRoy Conel, Cambridge, MA: Harvard University Press, Copyright © 1939, 1941, 1947, 1951, 1955, 1959, 1963, 1967 by the President and Fellows of Harvard College. Copyright © renewed 1967, 1969, 1975, 1983, 1991.

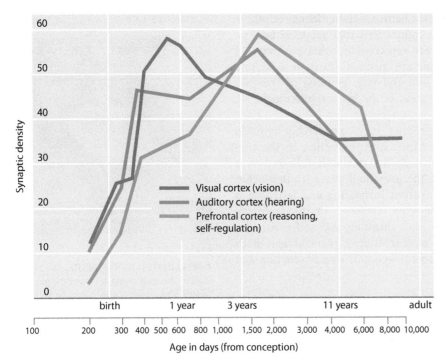

## FIGURE 4.13

**SYNAPTIC DENSITY IN THE HUMAN BRAIN FROM INFANCY TO ADULTHOOD.** The graph shows the dramatic increase and then pruning in synaptic density for three regions of the brain: visual cortex, auditory cortex, and prefrontal cortex. Synaptic density is believed to be an important indication of the extent of connectivity between neurons.

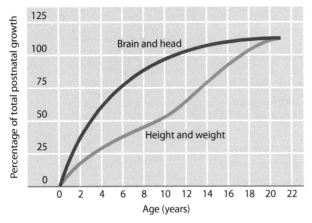

## FIGURE 4.14

**GROWTH CURVES FOR THE HEAD AND BRAIN AND FOR HEIGHT AND WEIGHT.** The more rapid growth of the brain and head can easily be seen. Height and weight advance more gradually over the first two decades of life.

conclude that myelination is important in the maturation of a number of abilities in children (Fair & Schlaggar, 2008). For example, myelination in the areas of the brain related to hand-eye coordination is not complete until about 4 years of age. A functional magnetic resonance imaging (fMRI) study of children (mean age, 4 years) found that those who were characterized by developmental delay of motor and cognitive milestones had significantly reduced levels of myelination (Pujol & others, 2004). Myelination in the areas of the brain related to focusing attention is not complete until middle or late childhood.

The brain in early childhood is not growing as rapidly as in infancy. However, the anatomical changes in the child's brain between the ages of 3 and 15 are dramatic. By repeatedly obtaining brain scans of the same children for up to four years, scientists have found that children's brains experience rapid, distinct bursts of growth (Gogtay & Thompson, 2010; Thompson & others, 2000). The amount of brain material in some areas can nearly double in as little as one year, followed by a drastic loss of tissue as unneeded cells are purged and the brain continues to reorganize itself. The overall size of the brain does not increase dramatically from 3 to 15. What does dramatically change are local patterns within the brain (Gogtay & Thompson, 2010; Thompson & others, 2000). From 3 to 6 years of age, the most rapid growth occurs in the frontal lobe areas involved in planning and organizing new actions and in maintaining attention to tasks (Diamond, 2013). From age 6 through puberty, the most dramatic growth takes place in the temporal and parietal lobes, especially in areas that play major roles in language and spatial relations.

Developmental neuroscientist Mark Johnson and his colleagues (2009) recently proposed that the prefrontal cortex likely orchestrates the functions of many other brain regions during development. As part of this neural leadership and organizational role, the prefrontal cortex may provide an advantage to neural connections and networks that include the prefrontal cortex. In the view of these researchers, the prefrontal cortex likely coordinates the best neural connections for solving a problem.

Links between the changing brain and children's cognitive development involve activation of brain areas, with some areas increasing in activation while others decrease. One shift in activation that occurs as children develop in middle and late childhood is from diffuse, larger areas to more focal, smaller areas (Durston & others, 2006). This shift is characterized by synaptic pruning in which areas of the brain not being used lose synaptic connections and those being used show an increase in connections. In a recent study, researchers found less diffusion and more focal activation in the prefrontal cortex (the highest level of the frontal lobes) from 7 to 30 years of age (Durston & others, 2006). The activation change was accompanied by increased efficiency in cognitive performance, especially in *cognitive control*, which involves flexible and effective control in a number of areas. These areas include controlling attention, reducing interfering thoughts, inhibiting motor actions, and being flexible in switching between competing choices (Carlson, Zelazo, & Faja, 2013; Diamond, 2013).

## ADOLESCENCE

Along with the rest of the body, the brain is changing during adolescence, but the study of adolescent brain development is in its infancy (Blakemore & Mills, 2014; Giedd & others, 2012). As advances in technology take place, significant strides will also likely be made in charting developmental changes in the adolescent brain. What do we know now?

Earlier we indicated that connections between neurons become pruned as children and adolescents develop. The pruning means that the connections that are used strengthen and survive, while the unused ones are replaced by other pathways or disappear. What results from this pruning is that by the end of adolescence individuals have "fewer, more selective, more effective neuronal connections than they did as children" (Kuhn, 2009, p. 153). And this pruning indicates that the activities adolescents choose to engage in and not to engage in influence which neural connections will be strengthened and which will disappear.

Using fMRI brain scans, scientists have recently discovered that adolescents' brains undergo significant structural changes (Chein & others, 2011; Lenroot & Giedd, 2011). The **corpus callosum**, where fibres connect the brain's left and right hemispheres, thickens in adolescence; this improves adolescents' ability to process information. We just described advances in the development of the **prefrontal cortex**—the highest level of the frontal lobes involved in reasoning, decision making, and self-control. The prefrontal cortex doesn't finish maturing until the emerging adult years (approximately 18 to 25 years of age) or later, but the **amygdala**—the seat of emotions—matures earlier than the prefrontal cortex (Casey, Duhoux, & Malter-Cohen, 2010). Figure 4.15 shows the locations of the corpus callosum, prefrontal cortex, and amygdala. A recent study of 137 early adolescents revealed a positive link between the volume of the amygdala and the duration of adolescents' aggressive behaviour during interactions with parents (Whittle & others, 2008).

Many of the changes in the adolescent brain that have been described involve the rapidly emerging field of *developmental social neuroscience*, which involves connections between development, the brain, and socioemotional processes (Blakemore & Mills, 2014; Salley, Miller, & Bell, 2013). For example, consider leading researcher Charles Nelson's (2003) view that although adolescents

**corpus callosum** Brain area where fibres connect the brain's left and right hemispheres.

**prefrontal cortex** The highest level of the frontal lobes that is involved in reasoning, decision making, and self-control.

**amygdala** The seat of emotions in the brain.

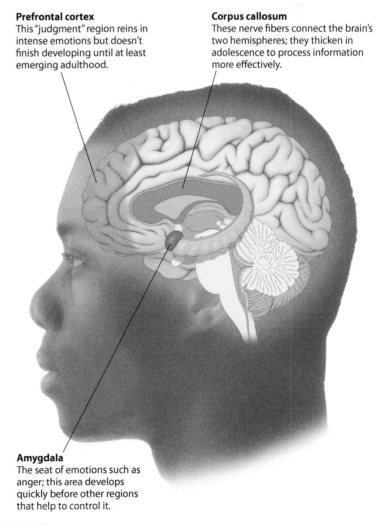

**Prefrontal cortex**
This "judgment" region reins in intense emotions but doesn't finish developing until at least emerging adulthood.

**Corpus callosum**
These nerve fibers connect the brain's two hemispheres; they thicken in adolescence to process information more effectively.

**Amygdala**
The seat of emotions such as anger; this area develops quickly before other regions that help to control it.

FIGURE **4.15**

**CHANGES IN THE ADOLESCENT BRAIN.**

*developmental* **connection**

**Brain Development.** Developmental social neuroscience is a recently developed field that focuses on connections between development, socioemotional factors, and neuroscience. Chapter 1, LO 3

*developmental* **connection**

**Brain Development.** How might developmental changes in the adolescent's brain be linked to adolescents' decision-making skills and risky behaviour? Chapter 7, LO 4

are capable of very strong emotions, their prefrontal cortex hasn't developed to the point at which they can control these passions. It is as if their brain doesn't have the brakes to slow down their emotions. Or consider this interpretation of the development of emotion and cognition in adolescents: "early activation of strong 'turbo-charged' feelings with a relatively unskilled set of 'driving skills' or cognitive abilities to modulate strong emotions and motivations" (Dahl, 2004, p. 18).

Of course, a major issue is which comes first: biological changes in the brain or experiences that stimulate these changes (Lerner, Boyd, & Du, 2009). Consider a study by Tomas Paus at the University of Toronto in which the prefrontal cortex thickened and more brain connections formed when adolescents resisted peer pressure (Paus & others, 2007). Scientists have yet to determine whether the brain changes come first or whether they result from experiences with peers, parents, and others. Once again, we encounter the nature/nurture issue that is so prominent in examining development.

## Review *Connect* Reflect

**LO2** Describe how the brain changes.

### Review

- What is the nature of brain physiology?
- How does the brain change in infancy?
- What characterizes the development of the brain in childhood?
- How does the brain change in adolescence, and how might this change be linked to adolescents' behaviour?

### *Connect*

- Both infancy and adolescence are times of significant change in the brain. Compare and contrast these changes.

### **Reflect** *Your Own Personal Journey of Life*

- A parent tells you that his or her child is left-brained and that this aspect of the brain explains why the child does well in school. Is the parent likely to be providing an accurate explanation or probably off base? Explain.

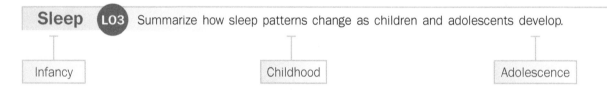

**Sleep** **LO3** Summarize how sleep patterns change as children and adolescents develop.

| Infancy | Childhood | Adolescence |

Sleep restores, replenishes, and rebuilds our brains and bodies. Some neuroscientists believe that sleep gives neurons that have been used while we are awake a chance to shut down and repair themselves (National Institute of Neurological Disorders and Stroke, 2009). How do sleeping patterns change during the childhood years?

## INFANCY

When we were infants, sleep consumed more of our time than it does now. Newborns sleep 16 to 17 hours a day, although some sleep more and others less. The range is from a low of about 10 hours to a high of about 21 hours per day. A recent research review concluded that infants 0 to 2 years of age slept an average of 12.8 hours out of the 24, within a range of 9.7 to 15.9 hours (Galland & others, 2012). A recent study also revealed that by 6 months of age the majority of infants slept through the night, awakening their mothers only once or twice a week (Weinraub & others, 2012).

Sleep that knits up the ravelled sleave of care . . . Balm of hurt minds, nature's second course. Chief nourisher in life's feast.

—WILLIAM SHAKESPEARE
*English Playwright, 17th Century*

Although total sleep remains somewhat consistent for young infants, their sleep during the day does not always follow a rhythmic pattern. An infant might change from sleeping several long bouts of 7 or 8 hours to three or four shorter sessions only several hours in duration. By about 1 month of age, most infants have begun to sleep longer at night. By 6 months of age, they usually have moved closer to adult-like sleep patterns, spending their longest span of sleep at night and their longest span of waking during the day (Sadeh, 2008).

The most common infant sleep-related problem reported by parents is night waking (The Hospital for Sick Children & others, 2010). Surveys indicate that 20 to 30 percent of infants have difficulty going to sleep at night and staying asleep all night (Sadeh, 2008). A recent study revealed that mothers' emotional availability at bedtime was linked to fewer infant sleep problems, supporting the premise that parents' emotional availability to infants in sleep contexts increases feelings of safety and security, and consequently promotes better-regulated infant sleep (Teti & others, 2010). Further, another study found that a higher involvement of fathers in overall infant care was related to fewer infant sleep problems (Tikotzky, Sadeh, & Glickman-Gavrieli, 2010). However, infant nighttime waking problems have consistently been linked to excessive parental involvement in sleep-related interactions with their infant (Sadeh, 2008). A recent review also revealed that maternal depression during pregnancy, early introduction of solid foods, infant TV viewing, and child care attendance were related to shorter duration of infant sleep (Nevarez & others, 2010). Infant sleep problems are associated with sleep problems later in childhood, as well. One longitudinal study revealed that nighttime wakings at 1 year of age predicted lower sleep efficiency at 4 years of age (Tikotzky & Shaashua, 2012).

**REM Sleep**    In *REM sleep*, the eyes flutter beneath closed lids; in *non-REM sleep*, this type of eye movement does not occur and sleep is quieter. Figure 4.16 shows developmental changes in the average number of total hours spent in REM and non-REM sleep. By the time they reach adulthood, individuals spend about one-fifth of their night in REM sleep, and REM sleep usually appears about one hour after non-REM sleep. However, about half of an infant's sleep is REM sleep, and infants often begin their sleep cycle with REM sleep rather than non-REM sleep (Sadeh, 2008). A much greater amount of time is taken up by REM sleep in infancy than at any other point in the life span. By the time infants reach 3 months of age, the percentage of time they spend in REM sleep falls to about 40 percent, and REM sleep no longer begins their sleep cycle.

Why do infants spend so much time in REM sleep? Researchers are not certain. The large amount of REM sleep may provide infants with added self-stimulation, since they spend less time awake than do older children. REM sleep also might promote the brain's development in infancy (Graven, 2006).

When adults are awakened during REM sleep, they frequently report that they have been dreaming—but when they are awakened during non-REM sleep, they are much less likely to report they have been dreaming (Cartwright & others, 2006). Since infants spend more time than adults in REM sleep, can we conclude that they dream a lot? We don't know whether infants dream or not, because they don't have any way of reporting dreams.

**Shared Sleeping**    Some child experts stress that there are benefits to shared sleeping (as when an infant sleeps in the same bed with its mother). They state it can promote breast-feeding, lets the mother respond more quickly to the baby's cries, and allows her to detect breathing pauses in the baby that might be dangerous (Pelayo & others, 2006). Sharing a

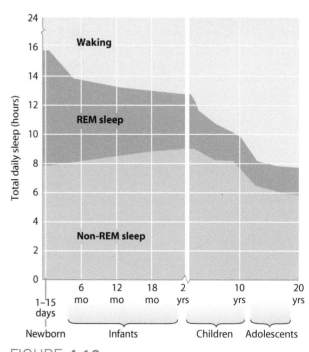

FIGURE **4.16**

**DEVELOPMENTAL CHANGES IN REM AND NON-REM SLEEP.**

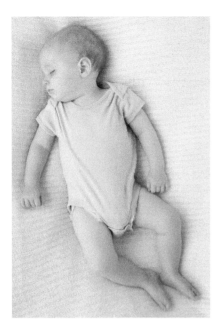

*Is this a good sleep position for infants? Why or why not?*

**sudden infant death syndrome (SIDS)**
A condition that occurs when an infant stops breathing, usually during the night, and suddenly dies without an apparent cause.

bed with a mother is a common practice in many cultures, such as Guatemala and China, whereas in others, such as Canada and Great Britain, most newborns sleep in a crib, either in the same room as the parents or in a separate room.

Shared sleeping remains a controversial issue, with some experts recommending it and others arguing against it, although most recent recommendations have been to avoid infant-parent bed sharing, especially until the infant is at least six months of age (Byard, 2012a, b; Weber & others, 2012). The Canadian Foundation for the Study of Infant Deaths and the Public Health Agency of Canada (2011) discourage shared sleeping. These organizations argue that in some instances bed sharing might lead to sudden infant death syndrome (SIDS) or a sleeping mother rolling over onto her baby. In support of this recommendation, a recent international study found that bed sharing was linked with a greater incidence of SIDS, even if the infant was breastfed and the parents do not smoke (Carpenter & others, 2012). In addition, a recent study of 2-month-old infants revealed that they had more sleep problems such as disordered breathing when they shared the bed with parents (Kelmanson, 2010).

**SIDS**  Sudden infant death syndrome (SIDS) is a condition that occurs when infants stop breathing, usually during the night, and die suddenly without an apparent cause. The exact cause of SIDS is unknown. However, many researchers believe that SIDS results from a combination of factors. For example, the triple-risk hypothesis states that SIDS occurs when an infant has an underlying vulnerability, such as abnormal or immature arousal functioning, combined with an external stressor, such as tummy sleeping on soft bedding, during a critical period of development (Ramirez & Malloy, 2013). The peak period of risk for SIDS is between 2 and 4 months of age. Although rates of SIDS have been steadily decreasing in Canada since the 1980s (Rusen & others, 2004), SIDS is still a major public health concern, accounting for 5 percent of all infant deaths in Canada (Public Health Agency of Canada, 2008).

The Public Health Agency of Canada and The Canadian Foundation for the Study of Infant Deaths (2011) have recommended that infants be placed to sleep on their backs to reduce the risk of SIDS. Researchers have found that SIDS does indeed decrease when infants sleep on their backs rather than their stomachs or sides (Darrah & Bartlett, 2013). Among the reasons given for prone (stomach) sleeping being a high risk factor for SIDS are that it impairs the infant's arousal from sleep and restricts the infant's ability to swallow effectively (Moon & Fu, 2012). In addition to sleeping in a prone position, researchers have found that the following are risk factors for SIDS:

- SIDS occurs more often in infants with abnormal brain stem functioning involving the neurotransmitter serotonin (Broadbent & others, 2012; Duncan & others, 2010).
- Heart arrhythmias are estimated to occur in as many as 15 percent of SIDS cases, and two recent studies found that gene mutations were linked to the occurrence of these arrhythmias (Brion & others, 2012; Van Norstrand & others, 2012).
- Low birth weight infants are five to ten times more likely to die of SIDS than are their normal-weight counterparts (Horne & others, 2002).
- Infants whose siblings have died of SIDS are two to four times as likely to die of it (Lenoir, Mallet, & Calenda, 2000).
- Six percent of infants with *sleep apnea,* a temporary cessation of breathing in which the airway is completely blocked, usually for ten seconds or longer, die of SIDS (McNamara & Sullivan, 2000).
- SIDS is the leading cause of infant death in the Inuit population, with rates significantly higher than Canadian rates (Collins & others, 2012).
- SIDS is more common in lower socioeconomic groups (Mitchell & others, 2000).

- SIDS is more common in infants who are passively exposed to cigarette smoke (Dietz & others, 2010).
- Breastfeeding is linked to a lower incidence of SIDS (Hauck & others, 2011; Zotter & Pichler, 2012).
- SIDS is more likely to occur in infants who do *not* use a pacifier when they go to sleep than in those who do use a pacifier (Jenik & Vain, 2010).
- SIDS is more common if infants sleep in soft bedding (Moon & Fu, 2012).
- SIDS is less common when infants sleep in a bedroom with a fan. A recent study revealed that sleeping in a bedroom with a fan lowers an infant's risk of SIDS by 70 percent (Coleman-Phox, Odouli, & Li, 2008).
- SIDS is more common when infants and parents share the same bed (Senter & others, 2010).

## CHILDHOOD

A good night's sleep is an important aspect of a child's development (El-Sheikh, 2013). Experts recommend that young children get 11 to 13 hours of sleep each night and that first- to fifth-graders get 10 to 11 hours of sleep each night (National Sleep Foundation, 2013). Most young children sleep through the night and have one daytime nap. Not only is the amount of sleep children get important, but so is uninterrupted sleep (Moore, 2012). To improve sleep, experts recommend ensuring that children have a bedroom that is cool, dark, and comfortable; consistent bed times and wake times; and positive family relationships (El-Sheikh, 2013). Also, helping the child slow down before bedtime often contributes to less resistance in going to bed. Reading the child a story, playing quietly with the child in the bath, and letting the child sit on the caregiver's lap while listening to music are quieting activities.

Children can experience a number of sleep problems (El-Sheikh, 2011). One estimate indicates that more than 40 percent of children experience a sleep problem at some point in their development (Boyle & Cropley, 2004). The following research studies indicate links between children's sleep problems and negative developmental outcomes:

- Children who had trouble sleeping in childhood were more likely to have alcohol use problems in adolescence and early adulthood (Wong & others, 2010).
- Sleep problems in early childhood were a subsequent indicator of attention problems that in some cases persisted into early adolescence (O'Callaghan & others, 2010).
- A recent analysis concluded that chronic sleep disorders that deprive children of adequate sleep may result in impaired brain development (Jan & others, 2010).
- Emotional security in parent and marital relationships when children were in the third grade predicted fewer sleep problems when they reached the fifth grade (Keller & El-Sheikh, 2010).

To learn more about sleep problems during infancy and childhood, read *Connecting to Current Controversy.*

## ADOLESCENCE

There has recently been a surge of interest in adolescent sleep patterns (Mak & others, 2012; Short & others, 2012). This interest focuses on the belief that many adolescents are not getting enough sleep, that there are physiological underpinnings to the desire of

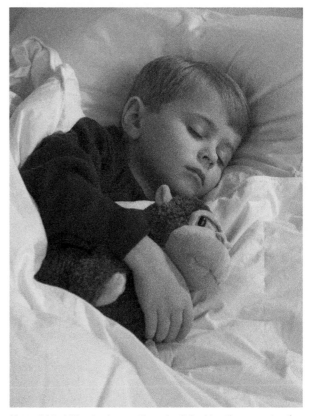

*How might children's sleep patterns be linked to other aspects of development?*

## Sleep Disturbances During Infancy and Childhood

Good sleep is important for optimal growth and development. However, there are a variety of sleep disorders and disturbances that infants and children can experience that affect sleep quality. During infancy, babies under 6 months of age will sleep for 14 to 18 hours a day in many short episodes of sleep and wakefulness. Around 6 months of age, most infants will sleep for more than 6 consecutive hours, which is often considered "sleeping through the night." Infants who do not achieve this sleep pattern may be considered to have sleep problems (Weiss & Corkum, 2012).

The type of sleep problems experienced during toddlerhood and childhood can be different than those experienced during early infancy. In one recent study, parents reported that night wakings and short sleep durations were the main problems experienced during infancy and early toddlerhood (6 to 24 months of age), while nightmares, night terrors, and restless sleep were the main problems reported for older toddlers (aged 24 to 36 months) (Byars & others, 2012). Over all of childhood, the most common sleep disorder, affecting approximately 25 percent of typically developing children, is behavioural insomnia (Weiss & Corkum, 2012). Behavioural insomnia is characterized by difficulties in settling in to sleep, falling asleep, and staying asleep during the night.

There are immediate negative outcomes associated with sleep problems in children. Research has revealed that behavioural insomnia results in daytime difficulties with school performance, learning, and mood and/or behaviour for the child, as well as increased daytime fatigue and loss of work productivity for parents (Vriend & others, 2013). The long-term outcomes of sleep disturbances during childhood are less well understood. In a recent research review, Gregory and Sadeh (2012) revealed that long-term outcomes may include depression, early use of drugs and alcohol, and attention problems. Due to the scarcity of research in this area, however, it is difficult to determine whether these effects are a result of sleep problems experienced during infancy and/or childhood, or a result of currently experienced sleep disturbances.

Despite the negative outcomes associated with childhood sleep disturbances, only about 1 percent of children with behavioural insomnia are effectively treated (Weiss & Corkum, 2012). Often parents are unaware of what actually constitutes a sleep problem, and as a result do not discuss these issues with the child's health care provider.

Other barriers to effective treatment include a lack of regular screening for sleep disturbances by health care providers, as well as a lack of knowledge of effective treatments when the problems are identified. Medications, including melatonin, are not recommended for the treatment of behavioural insomnia in children (Cummings, 2012; Health Canada, 2006). Rather, behavioural interventions are the most effective means to treat behavioural insomnia in children (Weiss & Corkum, 2012). Not only do these programs generally improve sleep quality for the child, they also increase the daytime functioning of both the child and parent.

One such intervention program is the Better Nights, Better Days program initiated by Researcher Penny Corkum at Dalhousie University (http://betternightsbetterdays.weebly.com/). This program to treat behavioural insomnia in children between the ages of 1 and 10 years is a web-based program that instructs parents about various behaviours that will create healthy sleep habits including age-appropriate and consistent bedtimes and wake times, establishment of daily routines, regular exercise, relaxing routines at bedtime (e.g., no electronics) and a quiet, dark, and comfortable room. This program addresses some of the barriers to effective treatment of behavioural insomnia in children. However, more research is needed to determine the long-term effects of infant and childhood sleep disturbances, the factors that mediate the negative outcomes of sleep problems, and how sleep problems should best be addressed to increase the overall health of Canadian children.

*What effects might behavioural sleep insomnia have on cognitive development and academic performance?*

adolescents, especially older ones, to stay up later at night and sleep longer in the morning, and that these findings have implications for understanding the times of day when adolescents learn most effectively in school (Hansen & others, 2005). For example, one survey found that 8 percent of middle school students and 14 percent of high school students are late for school or miss school because they oversleep (National Sleep Foundation, 2006). Also in this survey, 6 percent of middle school students and 28 percent of high school students fall asleep in school on any given day. Studies have recently confirmed that adolescents in other countries also are not getting adequate sleep (Leger & others, 2012; Short & others, 2012).

Getting too little sleep in adolescence is linked to a number of problems, including delinquency (Clinkinbeard & others, 2011), sleep disturbances in emerging and early adulthood (Dregan & Armstrong, 2010), and less effective attention (Beebe, Rose, & Amin, 2010). A longitudinal study in which adolescents completed daily diaries for 14-day periods in ninth, tenth, and twelfth grades found that regardless of how much students studied each day, when the students sacrificed sleep time to study more than usual, they had difficulty understanding what was taught in class and were more likely to struggle with class assignments the next day (Gillen-O'Neel, Huynh, & Fuligni, 2012).

Mary Carskadon (2002, 2004, 2005, 2006, 2011) has conducted a number of research studies on adolescent sleep patterns. She has found that adolescents sleep an average of 9 hours and 25 minutes when given the opportunity to sleep as long as they like. Most adolescents get considerably less sleep than this, especially during the week. This creates a sleep debt, which adolescents often try to make up on the weekend. Carskadon also found that older adolescents are often more sleepy during the day than are younger adolescents and concluded that this was not because of factors such as academic work and social pressures. Rather, her research suggests that adolescents' biological clocks undergo a hormonal phase shift as they get older. This pushes the time of wakefulness to an hour later than when they were young adolescents. Carskadon found that this shift was caused by a delay in the nightly presence of the hormone *melatonin*, which is produced by the brain's pineal gland in preparation for the body to sleep. Melatonin is secreted at about 9:30 p.m. in younger adolescents but is produced approximately an hour later in older adolescents, which delays the onset of sleep.

Carskadon determined that early school starting times can result in grogginess and lack of attention in class and poor performance on tests. Based on this research, some schools are now starting later. Discipline problems and the number of students who report an illness or depression have dropped with later start times, and one recent study found that just a 30-minute delay in school start time was linked to improvements in adolescents' sleep, alertness, mood, and health (Owens, Belon, & Moss, 2010).

In Mary Carskadon's sleep laboratory at Brown University, an adolescent girl's brain activity is being monitored. Carskadon (2005) says that in the morning, sleep-deprived adolescents' "brains are telling them it's night time . . . and the rest of the world is saying it's time to go to school" (p. 19).

## Review *Connect* Reflect

 **L03** Summarize how sleep patterns change as children and adolescents develop.

### Review

- How can sleep be characterized in infancy?
- What changes occur in sleep during childhood?
- How does adolescence affect sleep?

### *Connect*

- In this section, you learned that exposure to cigarette smoke can affect an infant's risk for SIDS. In Chapter 3, what did you learn about cigarette smoke's effect on fetal development?

### **Reflect** *Your Own Personal Journey of Life*

- Did your sleep patterns start to change when you became an adolescent? Have they changed since you went through puberty? If so, how?

What are the major threats to children's health today? We will look first at the major illnesses and injuries experienced by children and adolescents before turning to less obvious threats to healthy development: poor nutrition and eating habits, and lack of exercise. The formation of healthy habits in childhood, such as eating foods low in fat and cholesterol and engaging in regular exercise, not only has immediate benefits but also contributes to the delay or prevention of premature disability and mortality in adulthood from heart disease, stroke, diabetes, and cancer. Adolescence is a critical juncture in the adoption of many health-enhancing behaviours, such as regular exercise, and health-compromising behaviours, such as smoking (Catalano & others, 2012; Phillips & Edwards, 2013).

## ILLNESS AND INJURIES AMONG CHILDREN

In this section, we first examine broad patterns in the causes of illness and death among children and adolescents. Then, we turn to the difficulties faced by poor children in Canada and around the world.

**Early Childhood** Young children's active and exploratory nature, coupled with being unaware of danger in many situations, often puts them at risk for injuries. Most of the cuts, bumps, and bruises sustained by young children are minor, but some accidental injuries can produce serious impairment or even death. In Canada unintentional injuries are the leading cause of death for youths, followed by cancer, congenital abnormalities, flu and pneumonia, and cardiovascular disease (Statistics Canada, 2012) (see Figure 4.17). In addition to motor vehicle accidents, other accidental deaths in children involve drowning, falls, burns, and poisoning (Conde, 2012).

Parental smoking is another danger to children's health. An increasing number of studies reach the conclusion that children are at risk for health problems when they live in homes in which a parent smokes (Been & others, 2013; Chang, 2009). Children exposed to tobacco smoke in the home are more likely to develop wheezing symptoms and asthma than children in non-smoking homes (Yi & others, 2012). A recent study revealed that parental smoking was a risk factor for higher blood pressure in children (Simonetti & others, 2011). And another study revealed that exposure to second-hand smoke was related to young children's sleep problems, including sleep-disordered breathing (Yolton & others, 2010).

**Middle and Late Childhood** For the most part, middle and late childhood is a time of excellent health (Van Dyck, 2007). Disease and death are less prevalent in this period than in early childhood and adolescence.

The most common cause of severe injury and death in middle and late childhood is motor vehicle accidents, either as a pedestrian or as a passenger (Frisbie, Hummer, & McKinnon, 2009). Using seatbelts is important in reducing the severity of motor vehicle injuries.

Most accidents occur in or near the child's home or school. The most effective prevention strategy is to educate

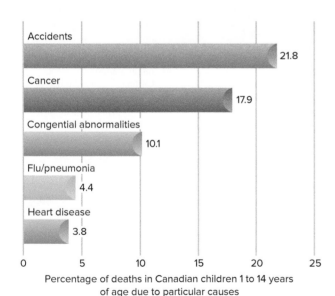

| | |
|---|---|
| Accidents | 21.8 |
| Cancer | 17.9 |
| Congential abnormalities | 10.1 |
| Flu/pneumonia | 4.4 |
| Heart disease | 3.8 |

Percentage of deaths in Canadian children 1 to 14 years of age due to particular causes

## FIGURE 4.17

**MAIN CAUSES OF DEATH IN CHILDREN 1 THROUGH 14 YEARS OF AGE.** These figures show the percentage of deaths in Canadian children 1 to 14 years of age due to particular causes in 2009 (Statistics Canada, 2012).

the child about the hazards of risk taking and improper use of equipment (Snowdon & others, 2008). Appropriate safety helmets, protective eye and mouth shields, and protective padding are recommended for children who engage in active sports.

*Cancer* Children not only are vulnerable to injuries, they also may develop life-threatening diseases. Cancer is the second leading cause of death in children 1 to 14 years of age. Almost 18 percent of all children's deaths in this age period are due to cancer.

Childhood cancers have a different profile from adult cancers. Cancers in adults attack mainly the lungs, colon, breast, prostate, and pancreas. In children, cancers mainly attack the white blood cells (leukemia), brain, bone, lymphatic system, muscles, kidneys, and nervous system. Researchers are intensely searching for possible genetic links to childhood cancers (Crespi, 2011; Spector & others, 2013).

The most common cancer in children is leukemia, a cancer of the tissues that make blood cells (Kelly & others, 2013). In leukemia, the bone marrow makes an abundance of white blood cells that don't function properly. They crowd out normal cells, making the child susceptible to bruising and infection.

Because of advancements in cancer treatment, children with cancer are surviving longer (Sung & others, 2013). Approximately 80 percent of children with acute lymphoblastic leukaemia are cured with current chemotherapy treatment (Wayne, 2011).

*Cardiovascular Disease* Cardiovascular disease is uncommon in children. Nonetheless, environmental experiences and behaviour in the childhood years can sow the seeds for cardiovascular disease in adulthood. Many elementary-school-aged children already possess one or more of the risk factors for cardiovascular disease, such as hypertension and obesity (Malatesta-Muncher & Mitsnefes, 2012; Peters & others, 2012). One study found that an increasing percentage of North American children and adolescents had elevated blood pressure from 1988 to 2006 (Ostchega & others, 2009). In this study, children who were obese were more likely to have elevated blood pressure. Further, one study revealed that high blood pressure goes undiagnosed in 75 percent of children with the disease (Hansen, Gunn, & Kaelber, 2007).

*Type 2 Diabetes* Although traditionally considered an adult disease, childhood Type 2 diabetes is an emerging disease in Canada, particularly among our Aboriginal population (Amed & others, 2010; Sellers, Moore, & Dean, 2009). Type 2 diabetes is a metabolic disorder in which the body does not produce enough insulin, resulting in an inability to convert glucose (sugar) into energy. In addition to a decreased quality of life, diabetes can lead to kidney disease and cardiovascular disease. According to the Canadian Diabetes Association, approximately 44 percent of children diagnosed with Type 2 diabetes are of Aboriginal heritage. In fact, the Aboriginal youth of Manitoba have one of the highest incidence rates of Type 2 diabetes in the world (Sellers & others, 2009). Although there are genetic factors believed to be related to this disease (Millar & Dean, 2012), Type 2 diabetes is associated with obesity in both Aboriginal and non-Aboriginal populations (Pulgaron, 2013; Wilson & others, 2007; Young & others, 2000).

**Health, Illness, and Poverty Among the World's Children** Approximately 8 percent of Canadian children live in poverty (Statistics Canada, 2012b). Children living in poverty are at a higher risk for health related problems. One approach to children's health aims to treat not only medical problems of the individual child but also the conditions of the entire family. In fact, some programs seek to identify children who are at risk for problems and then try to alter the risk factors in an effort to prevent illness and disease.

*What are some of the main causes of death in young children around the world?*

Poverty in Canada is dwarfed by poverty in developing countries around the world. Devastating effects on the health of young children occur in countries where poverty rates are high (UNICEF, 2012). The poor are the majority in nearly one of every five nations in the world (UNICEF, 2012). Each year UNICEF produces a report entitled *The State of the World's Children*. In recent years, the following factors that are especially influenced by poverty are linked to the under-5 mortality rate: the nutritional health and health knowledge of mothers, the level of immunization, dehydration, availability of maternal and child health services, income, food availability in the family, availability of clean water and safe sanitation, and the overall safety of the child's environment.

In the last decade, there has been a dramatic increase in the number of young children worldwide who have died because HIV/AIDS was transmitted to them by their parents (UNICEF, 2012). Deaths in young children due to HIV/AIDS occur most frequently in countries with high rates of poverty and low levels of education. For example, uneducated people are four times more likely to believe that there is no way to avoid AIDS and three times more likely to be unaware that the virus can be transmitted from mother to child (UNICEF, 2006).

Many of the deaths of young children around the world can be prevented by a reduction in poverty and improvements in nutrition, sanitation, education, and health services (UNICEF, 2012).

## NUTRITION AND EATING BEHAVIOUR

Poverty influences health in part through its effects on nutrition. However, it is not just children living in low-income families who have health-related nutrition problems; across the spectrum of income levels, recent decades have seen a dramatic increase in the percentage of North American children who are overweight.

**Infancy**   From birth to 1 year of age, human infants nearly triple their weight and increase their length by 50 percent. What do they need to sustain this growth?

*Nutritional Needs*   Individual differences among infants in terms of their nutrient reserves, body composition, growth rates, and activity patterns make it difficult to define actual nutrient needs (Schiff, 2013). However, because parents need guidelines, nutritionists recommend that infants consume approximately 50 calories per day for each pound they weigh—more than twice an adult's requirement per pound. While many of these calories come from breast milk or formula, Health Canada (2014) recently recommended that iron-rich foods such as meats, meat alternatives, and iron-fortified cereals be introduced at 6 months of age, followed by fruits and vegetables. To ensure all nutritional needs are being met, Health Canada also recommends that all breast fed infants receive a daily vitamin D supplement.

*Breast Versus Bottle Feeding*   For years, debate has focused on whether breastfeeding is better for the infant than bottle feeding. The growing consensus is that breastfeeding is better for the baby's health. Health Canada and the World Health Organization recommend that babies are exclusively fed breast milk for the first six months of life to maximize health benefits, with solid foods being gradually introduced at six months. Increasingly, Canadian mothers are breastfeeding their infants. An annual national health survey recently reported that 26 percent of Canadian mothers exclusively breastfeed their infants for the first six months of life in 2012, up from 17 percent in 2003. Those mothers that do exclusively breastfeed tend to be in their 30s or older and have advanced degrees (Health Canada, 2013).

What are some of the benefits of breastfeeding? The following conclusions are based on the current status of research:

Human milk or an alternative formula is a baby's source of nutrients for the first six months. The growing consensus is that breastfeeding is better for the baby's health, although controversy still swirls about the issue of breastfeeding versus bottle feeding. *Why is breastfeeding strongly recommended by pediatricians?*

**Evaluation of Outcomes for Child**

- *Gastrointestinal infections.* Breastfed infants have fewer gastrointestinal infections (Garofalo, 2010).
- *Lower respiratory tract infections.* Breastfed infants have fewer infections of the lower respiratory tract (Prameela, 2012).
- *Allergies.* A research review indicated that there is no evidence that breastfeeding reduces the risk of allergies in children (Greer & others, 2008). The research review also concluded that modest evidence exists for feeding hyperallergenic formulas to susceptible babies if they are not solely breastfed.
- *Asthma.* Research suggests that exclusive breastfeeding for three months protects against wheezing in babies, but whether it prevents asthma in older children is unclear (Greer & others, 2008).
- *Otitis media.* Breastfed infants are less likely to develop this middle ear infection (Rovers, de Kok, & Schilder, 2006).
- *Atopic dermatitis.* Breastfed babies are less likely to have this chronic inflammation of the skin (Snijders & others, 2007). In addition, for infants with a family history of allergies, breastfeeding exclusively for at least four months is linked to a lower risk of skin rashes (Greer & others, 2008).
- *Overweight and obesity.* Consistent evidence indicates that breastfed infants are less likely to become overweight or obese in childhood, adolescence, and adulthood (Li & others, 2007; Khuc & others, 2013).
- *Diabetes.* Breastfed infants are less likely to develop Type 1 diabetes in childhood (Ping & Hagopian, 2006) and Type 2 diabetes in adulthood (Villegas & others, 2008).
- *SIDS.* Breast fed infants are less likely to experience SIDS (Zotter & Pichler, 2012).

In recent large-scale research reviews, no conclusive evidence for the benefits of breastfeeding was found for children's cognitive development and cardiovascular system (Agency for Healthcare Research and Quality, 2007; Ip & others, 2009).

## Evaluation of Outcomes for Mother

- *Breast cancer.* Consistent evidence indicates a lower incidence of breast cancer in women who breastfeed their infants (Akbari & others, 2010; Shema & others, 2007).
- *Ovarian cancer.* Evidence also reveals a reduction in ovarian cancer in women who breastfeed their infants (Jordan & others, 2008; Stuebe & Schwartz, 2010).
- *Type 2 diabetes.* Some evidence suggests a small reduction in Type 2 diabetes in women who breastfeed their infants (Ip & others, 2009; Stuebe & Schwartz, 2010).

In recent large-scale research reviews, no conclusive evidence could be found for maternal benefits of breastfeeding with regard to return to pre-pregnancy weight, osteoporosis, and postpartum depression (Agency for Healthcare Research and Quality, 2007; Ip & others, 2009). However, a recent study revealed that women who breastfed their infants had a lower incidence of metabolic syndrome (a disorder characterized by obesity, hypertension, and insulin resistance) in midlife (Ram & others, 2008).

Many health professionals have argued that breastfeeding facilitates the development of an attachment bond between the mother and infant (Britton, Britton, & Gronwaldt, 2006; Wittig & Spatz, 2008). However, a recent research review found that the positive role of breastfeeding on the mother-infant relationship is not supported by research (Jansen, de Weerth, & Riksen-Walraven, 2008). The review concluded that recommending breastfeeding should not be based on its role in improving the mother-infant relationship but rather on its positive effects on infant and maternal health.

Are there circumstances when mothers should not breastfeed? Yes, a mother should not breastfeed (1) when she is infected with HIV or some other infectious disease that can be transmitted through her milk, (2) if she has active tuberculosis, or (3) if she is taking any drug that may not be safe for the infant (Goga & others, 2012).

Some women cannot breastfeed their infants because of physical difficulties; others feel guilty if they terminate breastfeeding early. Mothers may also worry that they are depriving their infants of important emotional and psychological benefits if they bottle feed rather than breastfeed. Some researchers have found, however, that there are no psychological differences between breastfed and bottle fed infants (Ferguson, Harwood, & Shannon, 1987; Young, 1990).

A further issue in interpreting the benefits of breastfeeding was underscored in recent large-scale research reviews (Agency for Healthcare Research and Quality, 2007; Ip & others, 2009). While highlighting a number of breastfeeding benefits for children and mothers, the report issued a caution about breastfeeding research: None of the findings imply causality. Breast versus bottle feeding studies are correlational rather than experimental, and women who breastfeed are wealthier, older, more educated, and likely more health conscious than their bottle feeding counterparts, which could explain why breastfed children are healthier.

*developmental* **connection**

**Research Methods.** How does a correlational study differ from an experimental study? Chapter 1, LO 3

**Malnutrition in Infancy** Early weaning of infants from breast milk to inadequate sources of nutrients, such as unsuitable and unsanitary cow's milk formula, can cause protein deficiency and malnutrition in infants (Kramer, 2003). Something that looks like milk but is not, usually a form of tapioca or rice, is also often substituted for breast milk. In many of the world's developing countries, mothers used to breastfeed their infants for at least two years. To become more modern, they stopped breastfeeding much earlier and replaced it with bottle feeding. Comparisons of breastfed and bottle-fed infants in countries such as Afghanistan, Haiti, Ghana, and Chile document that the mortality rate of bottle-fed infants is as much as five times that of breastfed infants (Grant, 1997). However, in the *Connecting with Diversity* interlude below, you can read about a recent concern regarding breastfeeding.

## The Stories of Latonya and Ramona: Breast and Bottle Feeding in Africa

Latonya is a newborn baby in Ghana. During her first days of life, she has been kept apart from her mother and bottle fed. Manufacturers of infant formula provide free or subsidized milk powder to the hospital where she was born. Her mother has been persuaded to bottle feed rather than breastfeed Latonya. When her mother bottle feeds Latonya, she overdilutes the milk formula with unclean water. Latonya's feeding bottles have not been sterilized. Latonya becomes very sick, and she dies before her first birthday.

Ramona was born in Nigeria, where her family takes part in a "baby-friendly" program. In this program, babies are not separated from their mothers when they are born, and the mothers are encouraged to breastfeed them. The mothers are told of the perils that bottle feeding can bring because of unsafe water and unsterilized bottles. They also are informed about the advantages of breast milk, which include its nutritious and hygienic qualities, its ability to immunize babies against common illnesses, and its role in reducing the mother's risk of breast and ovarian cancer. Ramona's mother is breastfeeding her. At 1 year of age, Ramona is very healthy.

For many years, maternity units in hospitals encouraged bottle feeding and did not give mothers adequate information about the benefits of breastfeeding. In recent years, the World Health Organization and UNICEF have tried to reverse the trend toward bottle feeding of infants in many impoverished countries. They instituted the baby-friendly program in many countries (Grant, 1993). They also persuaded the International Association of Infant Formula Manufacturers to stop marketing their baby formulas to hospitals in countries where the governments support the baby-friendly initiatives (Grant, 1997). For the hospitals themselves, costs actually were reduced as infant formula, feeding bottles, and separate nurseries become unnecessary. For example, baby-friendly Jose Fabella Memorial Hospital in the Philippines reported saving 8 percent of its annual budget.

The advantages of breastfeeding in impoverished countries are substantial. However, these advantages must be balanced against the risk of passing HIV to the babies through breast milk if the mothers have the virus; the majority of mothers don't know that they are infected (Goga & others, 2012). In some areas of Africa, more than 30 percent of mothers have the human immunodeficiency virus (HIV).

(*Left*) An HIV-infected mother breastfeeding her baby in Nairobi, Africa. (*Right*) A Rwandan mother bottle feeding her baby. *What are some concerns about breast versus bottle feeding in impoverished African countries? In what ways does education play a role in the health decisions discussed in this interlude?*

Two life-threatening conditions that can result from malnutrition are marasmus and kwashiorkor. **Marasmus** is caused by a severe protein–calorie deficiency and results in a wasting away of body tissues in the infant's first year. The infant becomes grossly underweight and his or her muscles atrophy. **Kwashiorkor**, caused by severe protein deficiency, usually appears between 1 and 3 years of age. Children with kwashiorkor sometimes appear to be well fed even though they are not because the disease can cause the child's abdomen and feet to swell with water.

**marasmus** Severe malnutrition caused by an insufficient protein–calorie intake, resulting in a shrunken, elderly appearance.

**kwashiorkor** Severe malnutrition caused by a protein-deficient diet, causing the feet and abdomen to swell with water.

This Honduran child has kwashiorkor. Notice the telltale sign of kwashiorkor—a greatly expanded abdomen. *What are some other characteristics of kwashiorkor?*

Kwashiorkor causes a child's vital organs to collect the nutrients that are present and deprive other parts of the body of them. The child's hair becomes thin, brittle, and colourless, and the child's behaviour often becomes listless.

Even if it is not fatal, severe and lengthy malnutrition is detrimental to physical, cognitive, and social development (Schiff, 2013). A study of Indian children documented the negative influence of chronic malnutrition on children's cognitive development. Children who had a history of chronic malnutrition performed more poorly on tests of attention and memory than their counterparts who were not malnourished (Kar, Rao, & Chandramouli, 2008).

Another study linked the diets of rural Guatemalan infants with their social development at the time they entered elementary school (Barrett, Radke-Yarrow, & Klein, 1982). Children whose mothers had been given nutritious supplements during pregnancy, and who themselves had been given more nutritious, high-calorie foods in their first two years of life, were more active, more involved, more helpful with their peers, less anxious, and happier than their counterparts who had not been given nutritional supplements. Also, a recent study found that two food-assisted maternal and child health nutrition programs (both emphasizing food provision, communication about behaviour change, and preventive health services) helped to reduce the negative impact of economic hardship on children's growth in Haiti (Donegan & others, 2010). Adequate early nutrition is an important aspect of healthy development (Schiff, 2013). In addition to sound nutrition, children need a nurturing, supportive environment (Lumeng & others, 2012). Caregivers who are not sensitive to developmental changes in infants' nutritional needs, neglectful caregivers, and conditions of poverty can contribute to the development of eating problems in infants (Black & Lozoff, 2008). A recent study revealed that low maternal sensitivity when infants were 15 and 24 months of age was linked to a higher risk of obesity in adolescence (Anderson & others, 2012).

**Childhood** Poor nutrition in childhood can lead to a number of problems and occurs more frequently in low-income than in higher-income families (Ruel & others, 2008). A special concern is the increasing epidemic of overweight children.

*Eating Behaviour and Parental Feeding Styles* For most children in North America, insufficient food is not the key problem. Instead, unhealthy eating habits and being overweight threaten their present and future health (Bolling & Daniels, 2008). Children's eating behaviour is strongly influenced by their caregivers' behaviour (Black & Hurley, 2007; Liu & others, 2013). Children's eating behaviour improves when caregivers eat with children on a predictable schedule, model eating healthy food, make meal times pleasant occasions, and engage in certain feeding styles. Distractions from television, family arguments, and competing activities should be minimized so children can focus on eating. A sensitive/responsive caregiver feeding style is recommended, in which the caregiver is nurturant, provides clear information about what is expected, and responds appropriately to children's cues (Black & Hurley, 2007). Forceful and restrictive caregiver behaviours are not recommended. For example, a restrictive feeding style is linked to children being overweight (Black & Lozoff, 2008).

*Overweight Children* Being overweight has become a serious health problem in early childhood (Blake, 2011; Marcdante, Kliegman, & Behrman, 2011). A recent national study revealed that nearly a third of 5- to 17-year-olds were overweight or obese in Canada (Roberts & others, 2012). Recent studies have revealed that poor eating habits are contributing to this public health concern. For example, one study revealed that 85.8 percent of children failed to meet minimum Canadian guidelines for fruit and vegetable intake (Attorp & others, 2014). In addition, Canadian children consume more than 41 percent of their daily snack calories from foods such as potato chips, chocolate bars, soft drinks, and fruit drinks (Roblin, 2007), while one fifth of children reported eating from a fast food restaurant the day before being interviewed for the Canadian Community Health survey (2004). There are concerns about unhealthy choices and high caloric intake with fast food, although healthier options are becoming increasingly available.

The percentages of young children who are overweight or at risk for being overweight in Canada have increased dramatically in recent decades (Roberts & others, 2012). and these percentages are likely to grow unless changes are made in children's lifestyles (Sorte, Daeschel, & Amador, 2011; Thompson, Manore, & Vaughn, 2011). The good news is that the percentages of overweight/obese children have been levelling off rather than increasing over the last decade (Roberts, 2012).

Still, the number of children who are overweight or at risk for being overweight remains far too high (Donatelle, 2011; Frisco, 2009). Note that in Canada, boys are more likely to be overweight than girls (Roberts & others, 2012), and obesity rates are greater among Canada's Aboriginal populations (Bruce & others, 2011). But it is not just in North America that children are becoming more overweight. Recent surveys and policy prescriptions in Australia, mainland China, Hong Kong, and other countries indicate that children in many countries around the world are becoming more overweight (Chan, 2008; Li & others, 2009).

The risk that overweight children will continue to be overweight when they become older was documented in one study in which children's weight at 5 years of age was significantly linked to their weight at 9 years of age (Gardner & others, 2009). And another study revealed that preschool children who were overweight were at a significant risk for being overweight at age 12 (Shankaran & others, 2012). Being overweight in childhood is also linked to being overweight in adulthood. One study revealed that girls who were overweight in childhood were 11 to 30 times more likely to be obese in adulthood than girls who were not overweight in childhood (Thompson & others, 2007).

The increase in overweight children in recent decades is cause for great concern because being overweight raises the risk of developing many medical and psychological problems (Anspaugh & Ezell, 2013). Diabetes, hypertension (high blood pressure), and elevated blood cholesterol levels are common in children who are overweight (Pulgaron, 2013; Riley & Bluhm, 2012). Once considered rare, childhood hypertension has become increasingly common in overweight children (Amed & others, 2010). Social and psychological consequences of being overweight in childhood include low self-esteem, depression, and exclusion of obese children from peer groups (Gibson & others, 2008). In one study, obese children were perceived as less attractive, more tired, and more socially withdrawn than non-obese peers (Zeller, Reiter-Purtill, & Ramey, 2008). In another study, overweight children reported being teased more by their peers and family members than did normal-weight children (McCormack & others, 2011).

Both heredity and environment influence whether children will become overweight. Genetic analysis indicates that heredity is an important factor in children becoming overweight (Morandi & others, 2012; Xia & Grant, 2013). Overweight parents tend to have overweight children, even if they are not living in the same household (Schiff, 2013). One study found that the greatest risk factor for being overweight at 9 years of age was having a parent who was overweight (Agras & others, 2004).

Environmental factors that influence whether children become overweight include availability of food (especially food high in fat content), use of energy-saving devices, lack of declining physical

*What are some concerns about overweight children?*

activity, lack of parental monitoring of children's eating habits, the context in which a child eats, and heavy screen time (watching TV, playing video games, texting) (Costigan & others, 2013; Mitchell & others, 2013). A recent behaviour modification study of overweight and obese children made watching TV contingent on their engagement in exercise (Goldfield, 2011). The intervention markedly increased their exercise and reduced their TV viewing time.

Parents play an important role in preventing children from becoming overweight (Barr-Anderson & others, 2013; Rodenburg & others, 2012). Recent research studies indicate intervention programs that emphasize getting parents to engage in healthier lifestyles themselves, as well as feeding their children healthier food and getting them to exercise more, can produce weight reduction in overweight and obese children (Brotman & others, 2012). In sum, healthy eating and an active rather than a sedentary lifestyle play important roles in children's development (Kotte, Winkler, & Takken, 2013; Wang & others, 2013).

## EXERCISE

Exercise can make significant contributions to not only children's physical development, but also their cognitive development (Wuest & Fisette, 2012; Davis & others, 2011). We explore developmental aspects of children's exercise and the role of parents, schools, and screen-based activity.

**Childhood**   Routine physical activity should be a daily occurrence for young children. The Canadian Society for Exercise Physiology (2011) recommends that children and youth engage in 60 minutes of moderate to vigorous physical activity daily in addition to unstructured play/physical activity. However, research suggests that children are not getting enough exercise (Fahey, Insel, & Roth, 2011; Lumpkin, 2011).

Observations of 3- to 5-year-old children during outdoor play at preschools revealed that the preschool children were mainly sedentary even when participating in outdoor play (Brown & others, 2009). In this study, throughout the day the preschoolers were sedentary 89 percent of the time, engaged in light activity 8 percent of the time, and participated in moderate to vigorous physical activity only 3 percent of the time. What factors contribute to the less than adequate amounts of physical activity? One recent research review concluded that a higher level of screen time (watching TV or using a computer) at 4 to 6 years of age was linked to a lower activity level as well as being overweight from preschool through adolescence (Velde & others, 2012). However, children's physical activity can be enhanced by family members engaging in sports together

*What are some positive outcomes when young children exercise regularly?*

and by parents' perception that it is safe for their children to play outside (Beets & Foley, 2008).

An increasing number of studies document the importance of exercise in children's physical and cognitive development (Best, 2010; Morano & others, 2012). One study found that 45 minutes of moderate physical activity and 15 minutes of vigorous physical activity daily were related to decreased odds that the children were overweight (Wittmeier, Mollard, & Kriellaars, 2008). Another study of 9-year-olds revealed that a higher level of physical activity was linked to a lower level of metabolic disease risk based on measures such as cholesterol, waist circumference, and insulin (Parrett & others, 2011). Studies have also documented that aerobic exercise had significant benefits for insulin resistance and body fat levels of overweight/obese elementary school children, regardless of ethnicity or gender (Davis & others, 2012) and is increasingly linked to children's cognitive skills (Best, 2010). Aerobic exercise has been found to benefit children's attention, memory, effortful and goal-directed thinking and behaviour, and creativity (Davis & Cooper, 2011; Davis & others, 2007; 2011; Monti, Hillman, & Cohen, 2012).

**Adolescence**   Exercise is linked to a number of positive outcomes in adolescence as well, including weight regulation and lower levels of blood pressure and Type 2 diabetes (Goldfield & others, 2012; So & others, 2013). Consider also these recent studies that found positive effects of exercise on a range of adolescent outcomes:

- Adolescents who engaged in higher levels of exercise had lower levels of alcohol, cigarette, and marijuana use (Teery-McElrath, O'Malley, & Johnston, 2011).
- A daily running program for three weeks improved the sleep quality, mood, and concentration of adolescents (Kalak & others, 2012).
- Engaging in a 12-week exercise intervention lowered the depression of adolescents who were depressed and not regular exercisers (Dopp & others, 2012).
- Participating in regular exercise was associated with higher academic achievement in young adolescents (Hashim, Freddy, & Rosmatunisah, 2012).

**Parents, Peers, Schools, and the Media**   Parents play important roles in children's and adolescents' exercise habits (Davis & others, 2013; Loprinzi & others, 2012). Growing up with parents who regularly exercise provides positive models of exercise for children and adolescents. Peers also play an important role in children and adolescents' physical activity (Fitzgerald, Fitzgerald, & Aherne, 2012). In one research review, peer support of exercise, better friendship quality and acceptance, and not having experienced peer victimization were linked to adolescents' physical activity.

One of the biggest factors associated with low levels of physical activity are screen-based activities, such as watching television, using computers, talking on the phone, texting, and instant messaging (Mitchell, Pate, & Blair, 2012). One recent study revealed that children and adolescents who engaged in the highest amount of daily screen-based activity (TV/video/video games in this study) were less likely to exercise daily (Sisson & others, 2010). In this study, children and adolescents who engaged in low physical activity and high screen-based activity were almost twice as likely to be overweight as their more active, less sedentary counterparts. A recent review of the research literature concluded that screen-based activity is linked to a number of adolescent health problems, such as being overweight, sleep problems, lower levels of physical activity/fitness and well-being, and higher levels of depression (Costigan & others, 2013).

## Review *Connect* Reflect

**LO4** Characterize health in children.

### Review

- What are the key health problems facing children?
- What are some important aspects of children's nutrition and eating behaviour?
- What role does exercise play in children's development?

### Connect

- Nutrition was discussed earlier in the chapter as well. What did you learn about nutrition's effect on growth?

### Reflect *Your Own Personal Journey of Life*

- What were your eating habits like as a child? In what ways are they similar to or different from your current eating habits? Do you think your early eating habits predicted whether you would have weight problems in adulthood?

# case study **connections**

1. How does the health promotion program described in the chapter opening incorporate physical activity and nutrition to enhance children's physical development and health?

2. After reading this chapter, what are some other components that would be valuable in a health promotion program like that described in the chapter opening?

3. How might a health promotion program such as that described in the chapter opening be tailored to specific ages? Or to specific populations, such as Canada's Aboriginal youths or low-income youths?

# reach your **learning goals**

# Physical Development and Health

## chapter 4

## Body Growth and Change

 Discuss developmental changes in the body.

Patterns of Growth

- Human growth follows cephalocaudal and proximodistal patterns. In a cephalocaudal pattern, the fastest growth occurs at the top—the head. Physical growth in size, weight, and feature differentiation occurs gradually and moves from the top of the body to the bottom. In a proximodistal pattern, growth begins at the centre of the body and then moves toward the extremities.

Infancy and Childhood

- Height and weight increase rapidly in infancy and then take a slower course during childhood. The average North American newborn is about 51 cm long and weighs 3.17 kilograms (7 pounds). Infants grow about 2.5 cm per month during their first year. In early childhood, girls are only slightly smaller and lighter than boys. Growth is slow and consistent in middle and late childhood, and head circumference, waist circumference, and leg length decrease in relation to body height.

Adolescence

- Puberty is a rapid maturation involving hormonal and body changes that occur primarily in early adolescence. Puberty began to occur at younger ages during the twentieth century. There are wide individual variations in the age at which puberty begins. Heredity plays an important role in determining the onset of puberty. Key hormones involved in puberty are testosterone and estradiol. Rising testosterone levels in boys cause voice changes, enlargement of external genitals, and increased height. In girls, increased levels of estradiol influence breast and uterine development and skeletal change. Key physical changes of puberty include a growth spurt as well as sexual maturation. The growth spurt occurs an average of two years earlier for girls than for boys. Adolescents are preoccupied with their bodies and develop images of their bodies. Adolescent girls have more negative body images than adolescent boys. Early maturation favours boys during adolescence, but in adulthood late-maturing boys have a more successful identity. Early-maturing girls are vulnerable to a number of problems including eating disorders, smoking, and depression.

# The Brain

 Describe how the brain changes.

The Neuroconstructivist View

Brain Physiology

Infancy

Childhood

Adolescence

- The old view was that genes determined how a child's brain is wired and that environmental experiences play little or no role in the brain's development. However, in the neuroconstructivist view, (a) biological processes and environmental conditions influence the brain's development, (b) the brain has plasticity and is context dependent, and (c) the development of the brain and the child's cognitive development are closely linked.

- Each hemisphere of the brain's cerebral cortex has four lobes (frontal, occipital, temporal, and parietal) with somewhat different primary functions. Neurons are nerve cells in the brain that process information. Communication between neurons occurs through the release of neurotransmitters at gaps called synapses. Communication is speeded by the myelin sheath that covers most axons. Clusters of neurons, known as neural circuits, work together to handle particular types of information. Specialization of functioning occurs in the brain's hemispheres, as in speech and grammar, but for the most part both hemispheres are involved in most complex functions, such as reading or performing music.

- Researchers have found that experience influences the brain's development. Early experiences are very important in brain development, and growing up in deprived environments can harm the brain. Myelination continues throughout the childhood years and even into adolescence for some brain areas such as the frontal lobes. Dramatic increases in dendritic and synaptic connections occur in infancy. These connections are overproduced and later pruned.

- During early childhood, the brain and head grow more rapidly than any other part of the body. Rapid, distinct bursts of growth occur in different areas of the brain between 3 and 15 years of age. One shift in brain activation in middle and late childhood is from diffuse, larger areas to more focal, smaller areas, especially in cognitive control.

- In adolescence, the corpus callosum thickens, and this improves information processing. Also, the amygdala, which is involved in emotions such as anger, develops earlier than the prefrontal cortex, which functions in reasoning and self-regulation. This gap in development may help to explain the increase in risk-taking behaviour that characterizes adolescence.

## Sleep

 **L03** Summarize how sleep patterns change as children and adolescents develop.

Infancy

Childhood

Adolescence

- The typical newborn sleeps 16 to 17 hours a day. By 6 months of age, most infants have sleep patterns similar to those of adults. REM sleep occurs more in infancy than in childhood and adulthood. Sleeping arrangements vary across cultures, and there is controversy about shared sleeping. SIDS is a special concern in early infancy.

- Most young children sleep through the night and have one daytime nap. It is recommended that preschool children sleep 11 to 13 hours each night and 5- to 12-year-old children 10 to 12 hours each night. Sleep problems in childhood are linked to negative outcomes in other areas of children's development.

- Many adolescents stay up later than when they were children and are getting less sleep than they need. Research suggests that as adolescents get older, the hormone melatonin is released later at night, shifting the adolescent's biological clock. Inadequate sleep is linked to an unhealthy diet, low exercise level, depression, and ineffective stress management.

## Health

 **L04** Characterize health in children.

Illness and Injuries Among Children

Nutrition and Eating Behaviour

Exercise

- Unintentional injuries are the number one cause of death in childhood. For the most part, middle and late childhood is a time of excellent health. Caregivers play an important role in preventing childhood injuries. Three diseases of special concern are cancer, cardiovascular disease, and Type 2 diabetes. A special concern also is the health of children living in poverty here and abroad. Improvements are needed in sanitation, nutrition, education, and health services in addition to a reduction in poverty. In low-income countries, there has been a dramatic increase in the number of children who have died from HIV/AIDS that was transmitted to them by their parents.

- The importance of adequate energy intake consumed in a loving and supportive environment during infancy cannot be overstated. Breastfeeding is increasingly recommended over bottle feeding. Marasmus and kwashiorkor are diseases caused by severe malnutrition. Concerns about nutrition in childhood focus on malnutrition, fat content in diet, and overweight/obese children. The percentage of overweight children has increased dramatically in recent years. Being overweight increases a child's risk of developing many medical and psychological problems. Parents play an important role in helping children avoid weight problems.

- Most children and adolescents are not getting nearly enough exercise. Boys and girls become less active as they reach and progress through adolescence. Parents, schools, peers, and screen-based activities play important roles in whether children and adolescents are physically fit or unfit.

For more information on the resources available from McGraw-Hill Ryerson, go to www.mheducation.ca/he/solutions

# Motor, Sensory, and Perceptual Development

## chapter 5

chapter outline

### Motor Development

 **LO1** Describe how motor skills develop.

The Dynamic Systems View
Reflexes
Gross Motor Skills
Fine Motor Skills

### Sensory and Perceptual Development

 **LO2** Outline the course of sensory and perceptual development.

What Are Sensation and Perception?
The Ecological View
Visual Perception
Other Senses
Intermodal Perception
Nature, Nurture, and Perceptual Development

### Perceptual-Motor Coupling

 **LO3** Discuss the connections between perception and action.

I n 1950, the newly born Steveland Morris was placed in an incubator in which he was given too much oxygen. The result was permanent blindness.

In 1962, as 12-year-old singer and musician Stevie Wonder, he began a career that has included such hits as "My Cherie Amour" and "Signed, Sealed, Delivered." At the beginning of the twenty-first century, his music is still perceived by some as "wondrous."

At age 12, Andrea Bocelli lost his sight in a soccer mishap. Today, now in his forties and after a brief career as a lawyer, Andrea has taken the music world by storm with his magnificent, classically trained voice.

Although Bocelli's and Stevie Wonder's accomplishments are great, imagine how very difficult it must have been for them as children to do many of the things we take for granted in sighted children. Yet children who lose one channel of sensation—such as vision—often compensate for the loss by enhancing their sensory skills in another area, such as hearing or touch. For example, researchers have found that blind individuals are more accurate at locating a sound source and have greater sensitivity to touch than sighted individuals (Lewald, 2012; Proulx & others, 2013). In one study, blind children were more skillful than blindfolded sighted children at using hearing to detect walls (Ashmead & others, 1998). In this study, acoustic information was most useful when the blind children were within one meter of a wall—at which point, sound pressure increases.

Two singing sensations: Andrea Bocelli (*left*) and Stevie Wonder (*right*). *How have they adapted to life without sight?*

# preview

Think about what is required for children to find their way around their environment, to play sports, or to create art. These activities require both active perception and precisely timed motor actions. Neither innate, automatic movements nor simple sensations are enough to let children do the things they do every day. How do children develop perceptual and motor abilities? In this chapter, we will focus first on the development of motor skills, then on sensory and perceptual development, and finally on the coupling of perceptual and motor skills.

> A baby is the most complicated object made by unskilled labour.
>
> —ANONYMOUS

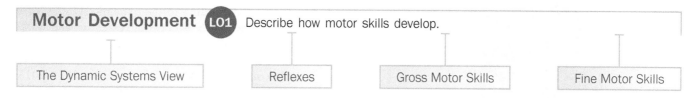

| **Motor Development** **L01** Describe how motor skills develop. | | | |
|---|---|---|---|
| The Dynamic Systems View | Reflexes | Gross Motor Skills | Fine Motor Skills |

Most adults are capable of coordinated, purposive actions of considerable skill, including driving a car, playing golf, and typing effectively on a computer keyboard. Some adults have extraordinary motor skills, such as those involved in winning an Olympic pole vault competition, performing heart surgery, painting a masterpiece or, in the case of Stevie Wonder, being extraordinarily talented at playing the piano. Look all you want at a newborn infant, but you will observe nothing even remotely approaching these skilled actions. How, then, do the motor behaviours of adults come about?

## THE DYNAMIC SYSTEMS VIEW

Arnold Gesell (1934) thought his painstaking observations revealed how people develop their motor skills. He had discovered that infants and children develop rolling, sitting, standing, and other motor skills in a fixed order and within specific time frames. These observations, said Gesell, show that motor development comes about through the unfolding of a genetic plan, or *maturation*.

Later studies, however, demonstrated that the sequence of developmental milestones is not as fixed as Gesell indicated and not due as much to heredity as Gesell argued (Adolph & Berger, 2013; Adolph & Robinson, 2013). In the last two decades, the study of motor development experienced a renaissance as psychologists developed new insights about *how* motor skills develop (Thelen & Smith, 1998, 2006). One increasingly influential theory is dynamic systems theory, proposed by Esther Thelen.

According to **dynamic systems theory**, infants assemble motor skills for perceiving and acting. Notice that perception and action are coupled, according to this theory (Thelen & Smith, 2006). To develop motor skills, infants must perceive something in the environment that motivates them to act and then use their perceptions to fine-tune their movements. Motor skills represent solutions to the infant's goals (Clearfield & others, 2009).

How is a motor skill developed, according to this theory? When infants are motivated to do something, they might create a new motor behaviour. The new behaviour is the result of many converging factors: the development of the nervous system, the body's physical properties and its possibilities for movement, the goal the child is motivated to reach, and the environmental support for the skill (von Hofsten, 2008).

**dynamic systems theory** A theory, proposed by Esther Thelen, that seeks to explain how motor behaviours are assembled for perceiving and acting.

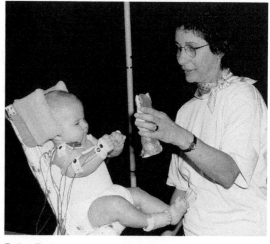

Esther Thelen is shown conducting an experiment to discover how infants learn to control their arms to reach and grasp for objects. A computer device is used to monitor the infant's arm movements and to track muscle patterns. Thelen's research is conducted from a dynamic systems perspective. *What is the nature of this perspective?*

How might dynamic systems theory explain the development of learning to walk?

developmental **connection**

**Nature–Nurture.** The epigenetic view states that development is a result of a bidirectional interchange between heredity and environment, in which environmental factors can influence how genes are expressed. Chapter 2, LO 4

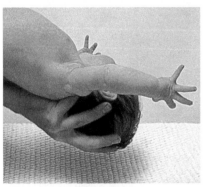
Moro reflex

The Moro reflex usually disappears around three months.

For example, babies learn to walk only when maturation of the nervous system allows them to control certain leg muscles, when their legs have grown enough to support their weight, and when they want to move.

Mastering a motor skill requires the infant's active efforts to coordinate several components of the skill. Infants explore and select possible solutions to the demands of a new task; they assemble adaptive patterns by modifying their current movement patterns. The first step occurs when the infant is motivated by a new challenge—such as the desire to cross a room—and gets into the "ballpark" of the task demands by taking a couple of stumbling steps. Then, the infant refines these movements to make them smoother and more effective. The refining is achieved through repeated cycles of action and perception of the consequences of that action. According to the dynamic systems view, even universal milestones, such as crawling, reaching, and walking, are learned through this process of adaptation: infants modulate their movement patterns to fit a new task by exploring and selecting possible configurations (Adolph & Berger, 2011, 2013; Spencer & others, 2009; Thelen & Smith, 2006).

To see how dynamic systems theory explains motor behaviour, imagine that you offer a new toy to a baby named Gabriel (Thelen & others, 1993). There is no exact program that can tell Gabriel ahead of time how to move his arm and hand and fingers to grasp the toy. Gabriel must adapt to his goal—grasping the toy—and the context. From his sitting position, he must make split-second adjustments to extend his arm, holding his body steady so that his arm and torso don't plow into the toy. Muscles in his arm and shoulder contract and stretch in a host of combinations, exerting a variety of forces. He improvises a way to reach out with one arm and wrap his fingers around the toy.

Thus, according to dynamic systems theory, motor development is not a passive process in which genes dictate the unfolding of a sequence of skills over time. Rather, the infant actively puts together a skill to achieve a goal within the constraints set by the infant's body and environment. Nature and nurture, the infant and the environment, are all working together as part of an ever-changing system.

As we examine the course of motor development, we will describe how dynamic systems theory applies to some specific skills. First, though, let's examine how the story of motor development begins with reflexes.

## REFLEXES

The newborn is not completely helpless. Among other things, it has some basic reflexes. For example, the newborn automatically holds its breath and contracts its throat to keep water out. **Reflexes** are built-in reactions to stimuli; they govern the newborn's movements, which are automatic and beyond the newborn's control. Reflexes are genetically carried survival mechanisms. They allow infants to respond adaptively to their environment before they have had an opportunity to learn.

The rooting and sucking reflexes are important examples. Both have survival value for newborn mammals, who must find a mother's breast to obtain nourishment. The **rooting reflex** occurs when the infant's cheek is stroked or the side of the mouth is touched. In response, the infant turns its head toward the side that was touched in an apparent effort to find something to suck. The **sucking reflex** occurs when newborns automatically suck an object placed in their mouths. This reflex enables newborns to get nourishment before they have associated a nipple with food; sucking also serves as a self-soothing or self-regulating mechanism.

| Reflex | Stimulation | Infant's Response | Developmental Pattern |
|---|---|---|---|
| Blinking | Flash of light, puff of air | Closes both eyes | Permanent |
| Babinski | Sole of foot stroked | Fans out toes, twists foot in | Disappears after 9 months to 1 year |
| Grasping | Palms touched | Grasps tightly | Weakens after 3 months, disappears after 1 year |
| Moro (startle) | Sudden stimulation, such as hearing loud noise or being dropped | Startles, arches back, throws head back, flings out arms and legs and then rapidly closes them to center of body | Disappears after 3 to 4 months |
| Rooting | Cheek stroked or side of mouth touched | Turns head, opens mouth, begins sucking | Disappears after 3 to 4 months |
| Stepping | Infant held above surface and feet lowered to touch surface | Moves feet as if to walk | Disappears after 3 to 4 months |
| Sucking | Object touching mouth | Sucks automatically | Disappears after 3 to 4 months |
| Swimming | Infant put face down in water | Makes coordinated swimming movements | Disappears after 6 to 7 months |
| Tonic neck | Infant placed on back | Forms fists with both hands and usually turns head to the right (sometimes called the "fencer's pose" because the infant looks like it is assuming a fencer's position) | Disappears after 2 months |

## FIGURE 5.1

**INFANT REFLEXES.** This chart describes some of the infant's reflexes.

Another example is the **Moro reflex**, which occurs in response to a sudden, intense noise or movement. When startled, the newborn arches its back, throws back its head, and flings out its arms and legs. Then the newborn rapidly closes its arms and legs. The Moro reflex is believed to be a way of grabbing for support while falling; it would have had survival value for our primate ancestors.

Some reflexes—coughing, sneezing, blinking, shivering, and yawning, for example—persist throughout life. They are as important for the adult as they are for the infant. Other reflexes, though, disappear several months following birth, as the infant's brain matures and voluntary control over many behaviours develops (Pedroso, 2008). The rooting and Moro reflexes, for example, tend to disappear when the infant is three to four months old.

The movements of some reflexes eventually become incorporated into more complex, voluntary actions. One important example is the **grasping reflex**, which occurs when something touches the infant's palms. The infant responds by grasping tightly. By the end of the third month, the grasping reflex diminishes, and the infant shows a more voluntary grasp. As its motor development becomes smoother, the infant will grasp objects, carefully manipulate them, and explore their qualities. An overview of the reflexes we have discussed, along with others, is given in Figure 5.1.

Although reflexes are automatic and inborn, differences in reflexive behaviour are soon apparent. For example, the sucking capabilities of newborns vary considerably. Some newborns are efficient at forcefully sucking and obtaining milk; others are not as adept and get tired before they are full. Most infants take several weeks to establish a sucking style that is coordinated with the way the mother is holding the infant, the way milk is coming out of the bottle or breast, and the infant's temperament (Blass, 2008).

The old view of reflexes is that they were exclusively genetic, built-in mechanisms that govern the infant's movements. The new perspective on infant reflexes is that they are not automatic or completely beyond the infant's control. For example, infants can control such movements as alternating their legs to make a mobile jiggle or change their sucking rate to listen to a recording (Adolph & Berger, 2013).

**reflexes** Built-in reactions to stimuli.

**rooting reflex** A built-in reaction that occurs when a newborn's cheek is stroked or the side of the mouth is touched. In response, the infant turns its head toward the side that was touched, in an apparent effort to find something to suck.

**sucking reflex** A newborn's built-in reaction to automatically suck an object placed in its mouth. The sucking reflex enables the infant to get nourishment before it has associated a nipple with food.

**Moro reflex** A neonatal startle response that occurs in reaction to a sudden, intense noise or movement. When startled, the newborn arches its back, throws its head back, and flings out its arms and legs. Then the newborn rapidly closes its arms and legs to the centre of the body.

**grasping reflex** A neonatal reflex that occurs when something touches the infant's palms. The infant responds by grasping tightly.

Pediatrician T. Berry Brazelton (1956) observed how infants' sucking changed as they grew older. Over 85 percent of the infants engaged in considerable sucking behaviour unrelated to feeding. They sucked their fingers, their fists, and pacifiers. By the age of 1 year, most had stopped the sucking behaviour, but as many as 40 percent of children continued to suck their thumbs after starting school (Kessen, Haith, & Salapatek, 1970).

Physicians will test the newborn for specific reflexes to evaluate the soundness of the baby's central nervous system. Over the first few months of development, reflexes that are weak, not present, or do not disappear when they should often indicate problems with the developing nervous system and can provide a sign that further testing should be done.

## GROSS MOTOR SKILLS

Ask any parents about their baby, and sooner or later you are likely to hear about motor milestones, such as "Cassandra just learned to crawl," "Jesse is finally sitting alone," or "Angela took her first step last week." Parents proudly announce such milestones as their children transform themselves from babies unable to lift their heads to toddlers who grab things off the grocery store shelf, chase a cat, and participate actively in the family's social life (Thelen, 2000). These milestones are examples of **gross motor skills**, which are skills that involve large-muscle activities, such as arm movements and walking.

**gross motor skills** Actions that involve large-muscle activities, such as arm movements and walking.

**The Development of Posture**  How do gross motor skills develop? As a foundation, these skills require postural control (Adolph & Robinson, 2013). For example, to track moving objects, you must be able to control your head in order to stabilize your gaze; before you can walk, you must be able to balance on one leg.

Posture is more than just holding still and straight. Posture is a dynamic process that is linked with sensory information in the skin, joints, and muscles that tell us where we are in space, in vestibular organs in the inner ear that regulate balance and equilibrium, and in vision and hearing (Thelen & Smith, 2006).

Newborn infants cannot voluntarily control posture. Within a few weeks, though, they can hold their heads erect, and soon they can lift their heads while prone. By 2 months of age, babies can sit while supported on a lap or an infant seat, but they cannot sit independently until they are 6 or 7 months of age. Standing also develops gradually during the first year of life. By about 8 to 9 months of age, infants usually learn to pull themselves up and hold on to a chair, and they often can stand alone by about 10 to 12 months of age.

**Learning to Walk**  Locomotion and postural control are closely linked, especially in walking upright (Adolph & Berger, 2011; Adolph & Robinson, 2013). To walk upright, the baby must be able both to balance on one leg as the other is swung forward and to shift the weight from one leg to the other.

Even young infants can make the alternating leg movements that are needed for walking. The neural pathways that control leg alternation are in place from a very early age, even at birth or before. Indeed researchers have found that alternating leg movements occur during the fetal period and at birth (Adolph & Robinson, 2013).

When infants learn to walk, they typically take small steps because of their limited balance control and strength. However, a recent study revealed that infants occasionally take a few large steps that even exceed their leg length, and these large steps indicate increased balance and strength (Badaly & Adolph, 2008).

In learning to locomote, infants learn what kinds of places and surfaces are safe for locomotion (Adolph & Berger, 2011, 2013; Gill, Adolph, & Vereijken, 2009). Karen Adolph (1997) investigated how experienced and inexperienced crawling infants and walking infants go down steep slopes (see Figure 5.2).

What are some developmental changes in posture during infancy?

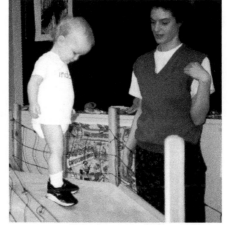

Newly crawling infant                         Experienced walker

FIGURE 5.2

**THE ROLE OF EXPERIENCE IN CRAWLING AND WALKING INFANTS' JUDGMENTS OF WHETHER TO GO DOWN A SLOPE.** Karen Adolph (1997) found that locomotor experience rather than age was the primary predictor of adaptive responding on slopes of varying steepness. Newly crawling and walking infants could not judge the safety of the various slopes. With experience, they learned to avoid slopes where they would fall. When expert crawlers began to walk, they again made mistakes and fell, even though they had judged the same slope accurately when crawling. Adolph referred to this as the *specificity of learning* because it does not transfer across crawling and walking.

Newly crawling infants, who averaged about 8½ months in age, rather indiscriminately went down the steep slopes, often falling in the process (with their mothers next to the slope to catch them). After weeks of practice, the crawling babies became more adept at judging which slopes were too steep to crawl down and which ones they could navigate safely. New walkers also could not judge the safety of the slopes, but experienced walkers accurately matched their skills with the steepness of the slopes. They rarely fell downhill, either refusing to go down the steep slopes or going down backward in a cautious manner. Experienced walkers perceptually assessed the situation—looking, swaying, touching, and thinking before they moved down the slope. With experience, both the crawlers and the walkers learned to avoid the risky slopes where they would fall, integrating perceptual information with the development of a new motor behaviour.

An important conclusion from Karen Adolph's (1997) study involves the *specificity of learning*—the idea that infants who have experience with one mode of locomotion (crawling, for example) don't seem to appreciate the dangers inherent in another mode of locomotion—risky walkways when they are making the transition to walking. Also in Adolph's (1997) research, we again see the importance of perceptual–motor coupling in the development of motor skills.

Practice is especially important in learning to walk (Adolph & others, 2012). However, practise does not involve exact repetition. Infants and toddlers accumulate an immense number of experiences with balance and locomotion. For example, the average toddler traverses almost 40 football fields a day and has 15 falls per hour (Adolph & others, 2012). From the perspective of Karen Adolph and her colleagues (2003, p. 495)

> Thousands of daily walking steps, each step slightly different from the last because of variations in the terrain and the continually varying bio-mechanical constraints on the body, may help infants to identify the relevant combination of strength and balance required to improve their walking skills.

**The First Year: Motor Development Milestones and Variations**   Figure 5.3 summarizes important accomplishments in gross motor skills during the first year, culminating in the ability to walk easily. The timing of these milestones, especially the later ones, may vary by as much as two to four months, and experiences can modify the onset of these accomplishments (Eaton, 2008). For example,

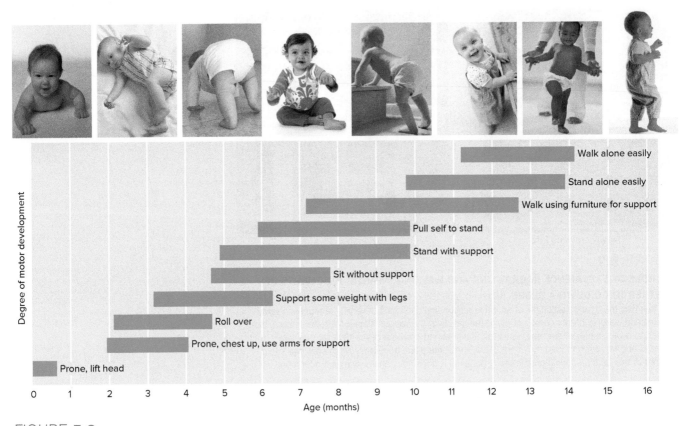

FIGURE **5.3**

**MILESTONES IN GROSS MOTOR DEVELOPMENT.**

since 1992, when pediatricians began recommending that parents place their babies on their backs when they sleep (see Chapter 4 for discussion of SIDS), fewer babies crawled (Davis & others, 1998). However, Canadian data revealed that motor milestones emerge at approximately the same age today as they did 20 years ago, when the back-to-sleep campaign was just beginning (Darrah & others, 2014). Also, some infants do not follow the standard sequence of motor accomplishments. For example, many North American infants never crawl on their bellies or on their hands and knees. They may discover an idiosyncratic form of locomotion before walking, such as rolling, or they might never locomote until they get upright (Adolph & Joh, 2009). There is a wide range of normal in motor development and for healthy infants the age of attainment for motor skills is *not* related to later cognitive ability (Hamadani & others, 2011; Jenni & others, 2013). According to Karen Adolph and Sarah Berger (2005; p. 273), "The old-fashioned view that growth and motor development reflect merely the age-related output of maturation is, at best, incomplete. Rather, infants acquire new skills with the help of their caregivers in a real-world environment of objects, surfaces, and planes."

**Development in the Second Year** The motor accomplishments of the first year bring increasing independence, allowing infants to explore their environment more extensively and to initiate interaction with others more readily. In the second year of life, toddlers become more motorically skilled and mobile. Motor activity during the second year is vital to the child's competent development, and few restrictions, except for safety, should be placed on their adventures.

By 13 to 18 months, toddlers can pull a toy attached to a string and use their hands and legs to climb up a number of steps. By 18 to 24 months, toddlers can walk quickly or run stiffly for a short distance, balance on their feet in a squatting position while playing with objects on the floor, walk backward without losing their balance, stand and kick a ball without falling, stand and throw a ball, and jump in place.

> The experiences of the first three years of life are almost entirely lost to us, and when we attempt to enter into a small child's world, we come as foreigners who have forgotten the landscape and no longer speak the native tongue.
>
> —SELMA FRAIBERG
> *Developmentalist and Child Advocate,*
> *20th Century*

Can parents give their babies a head start on becoming physically fit and physically talented through structured exercise classes? Most infancy experts recommend against structured exercise classes for babies. But there are other ways of guiding infants' motor development. Caregivers in some cultures do handle babies vigorously, and this might advance motor development, as we discuss in *Connecting with Diversity*.

**Childhood**  Our exploration of motor development in childhood begins with a focus on developmental changes in gross motor skills.

*Developmental Changes*  The preschool child no longer has to make an effort to stay upright and to move around. As children move their legs with more confidence and carry themselves more purposefully, moving around in the environment becomes more automatic.

At 3 years of age, children enjoy simple movements, such as hopping, jumping, and running back and forth, just for the sheer delight of performing these

## Cultural Variations in Guiding Infants' Motor Development

Mothers in developing countries tend to stimulate their infants' motor skills more than mothers in more modern countries (Hopkins, 1991). In many African, Indian, and Caribbean cultures, mothers massage and stretch their infants during daily baths (Adolph, Karasik, & Tamis-LeMonda, 2010). Jamaican and Mali mothers regularly massage their infants and stretch their arms and legs (Adolph, Karasik, & Tamis-LeMonda, 2010). Mothers in the Gusii culture of Kenya also encourage vigorous movement in their babies (Hopkins & Westra, 1988).

(*Left*) In the Algonquin culture in Quebec, Canada, babies are strapped to a cradleboard for much of their infancy. (*Right*) In Jamaica, mothers massage and stretch their infants' arms and legs. *To what extent do cultural variations in infants' activities influence the time at which they reach motor milestones?*

Do these cultural variations make a difference in the development of motor skills? When caregivers provide babies with physical guidance by physically handling them in special ways (such as stroking, massaging, or stretching) or by giving them opportunities for exercise, the infants often reach motor milestones earlier than infants whose caregivers have not provided these activities (Adolph, Karasik, & Tamis-LeMonda, 2010). For example, Jamaican mothers expect their infants to sit and walk alone two to three months earlier than English mothers do (Hopkins & Westra, 1990). And in sub-Saharan Africa, traditional practices in many villages involve mothers and siblings engaging babies in exercises, such as frequent exercise for trunk and pelvic muscles (Super & Harkness, 2010).

Many forms of movement restrictions—such as Chinese sandbags, orphanage constraints, and failure of caregivers to encourage movement—have been found to produce substantial delays in motor development (Adolph, Karasik, & Tamis-LeMonda, 2010). In some rural Chinese provinces, babies are placed in a

bag of fine sand, which acts as a diaper and is changed once a day. The baby is left alone, face up, and is visited only when being fed by the mother (Xie & Young, 1999). Some studies of swaddling show slight delays in motor development, but other studies show no delays. Cultures that do swaddle infants usually do so early in the infant's development when the infant is not mobile; when the infant becomes more mobile, swaddling decreases.

Nonetheless, even when infants' motor activity is restricted, many still reach the milestones of motor development at a normal age. For example, Algonquin infants in Quebec, Canada, spend much of their first year strapped to a cradleboard. Despite their inactivity, these infants still sit up, crawl, and walk within an age range similar to that of infants in cultures where they have had much greater opportunity for activity.

*To help babies with their motor development, is stroking, massaging, or stretching their arms and legs a better or worse strategy than engaging them in a structured exercise class?*

## Participating in Sports

Organized sports are one way of encouraging children to be active and to develop their motor skills. Seventy-five percent of Canadian children between the ages of 5 and 17 years participate in team and individual sports (Canadian Heritage, 2013). Schools and community agencies offer programs for children that involve soccer, hockey, swimming, basketball, baseball, gymnastics, and other sports. For children who participate in them, these programs may play a central role in their lives.

Participation in sports can have positive and negative outcomes for children (Coatsworth & Conroy, 2009; Myer & others, 2011). Participation can provide exercise, opportunities to develop a skill and learn how to compete, and a setting for developing peer relations and friendships (Morano, Colella, & Capranica, 2011; Theokas, 2009).

Further, participating in sports is associated with enhanced self-esteem and persistence, reduced body dissatisfaction for boys, and less likelihood that children will become depressed (Babiss & Gangwisch, 2009; Miller & Hoffman, 2009). Sports participation can also provide a mediating influence on the negative outcomes associated with bullying. For example, a team of Canadian researchers found that victimized children who participated in team sports at 8 years old were less likely to be depressed and exhibit externalizing behaviours at the age of 10 (Perron & others, 2012). Clearly, children who participate in team and individual sports activities are at an advantage for many positive developmental outcomes.

However, sports also can bring pressure to achieve and win, physical injuries, a distraction from academic work, and unrealistic expectations for success as an athlete (Lerch, Cordes, & Baumeister, 2011; Pakzad-Vaezi & Singhal, 2012). Participation in sports has also been linked to risky behaviours, such as alcohol overuse (Fauth, Roth, & Brooks-Gunn, 2007). The act of playing sports does not in itself cause these negative behaviours, rather the context in which sports occur becomes an important factor. High-pressure sports that involve championship play under the media spotlight cause special concern. Some psychologists argue that such activities put undue stress on children and teach them the wrong values—namely, a win-at-all-costs philosophy. Thus, in addition to personal characteristics, overly ambitious parents and the coaching relationship become important determinants of outcomes for children participating in sports (Coatsworth & Conroy, 2009; McCambridge, & Stricker, 2008). To help

overcome some of these barriers that prevent children from remaining active in sports throughout their lives, the Canadian Sport for Life organization has developed the Long-term Athletic Development program. This program provides guidelines for all sports that are based on research in child development and attaining long-term outcomes. To learn more about this program, visit www.canadiansportforlife.ca.

Another concern regarding sports activity is related to which children are, or rather are not, participating. Children and adolescents who participate in sports tend to come from higher income homes, while children from lower income homes are less likely to participate in organized sports (Canadian Heritage, 2013). This inequality of access to sporting activities likely occurs due to the rising cost of organized sports, as well as time constraints on parents from lower income backgrounds to support their children's participation in organized sports (Spinney & Millward, 2010). Recognizing the importance of sports for the social, motor, physical, and cognitive development of all children, non-profit organizations such as Kidsport Canada have emerged, that are devoted to helping children and their families overcome the financial barriers to participating in organized sport.

It is clear that there are positive and negative outcomes associated with sports participation. To maximize the benefits to developing children, research must continue beyond identifying associations to better understanding youth experiences in sports activities.

*How might participating in an organized sport such as hockey contribute to motor development?*

activities. They take considerable pride in showing how they can run across a room and jump all of 6 inches. The run-and-jump will win no Olympic gold medals, but for the 3-year-old the activity is a source of pride.

At 4 years of age, children are still enjoying the same kinds of activities, but they have become more adventurous. They scramble over low jungle gyms as they display their athletic prowess. Although they have been able to climb stairs with one foot on each step for some time, they are just beginning to be able to come down the same way.

At 5 years of age, children are even more adventuresome than they were at 4. It is not unusual for self-assured 5-year-olds to perform hair-raising stunts on practically any climbing object. They run hard and enjoy races with each other and their parents.

During middle and late childhood, children's motor development becomes much smoother and more coordinated than it was in early childhood. For example, only one child in a thousand can hit a tennis ball over the net at the age of 3, yet by the age of 10 or 11 most children can learn to play the sport. Running, climbing, skipping rope, swimming, bicycle riding, and skating are just a few of the many physical skills elementary school children can master. And, when mastered, these physical skills are a source of great pleasure and a sense of accomplishment. A recent study of 9-year-olds revealed that those who were more physically fit had a better mastery of motor skills (Haga, 2008). In gross motor skills involving large-muscle activity, boys usually outperform girls.

As children move through the elementary school years, they gain greater control over their bodies and can sit and pay attention for longer periods of time. However, elementary school children are far from being physically mature, and they need to be active. Elementary school children become more fatigued by long periods of sitting than by running, jumping, or bicycling (Wuest & Fisette, 2012). Physical action is essential for these children to refine their developing skills, such as batting a ball, skipping rope, or balancing on a beam. Children benefit from exercise breaks periodically during the school day on the order of 15 minutes every two hours (Keen, 2005). In sum, elementary school children should be engaged in active, rather than passive, activities. *Connecting to Current Controversy* discusses the pros and cons of organized sport as one type of active activity in which children can engage.

*What are some developmental changes in children's motor development in early childhood and middle and late childhood?*

## FINE MOTOR SKILLS

While gross motor skills involve large-muscle activity, **fine motor skills** involve finely tuned movements. Grasping a toy, using a spoon, buttoning a shirt, or doing anything that requires finger dexterity demonstrates fine motor skills.

**Infancy** Infants have hardly any control over fine motor skills at birth, but they do have many components of what will become finely coordinated arm, hand, and finger movements. The onset of reaching and grasping marks a significant achievement in an infant's ability to interact with its surroundings (Greif & Needham, 2012; Savelsbergh, van der Kamp, & van Wersmerskerken, 2013). During the first two years of life, infants refine how they reach and grasp (Libertus & Needham, 2011). Initially, infants reach by moving their shoulders and elbows crudely, swinging toward an object. Later, when infants reach for an object they move their wrists, rotate their hands, and coordinate their thumb and forefinger. Infants do not have to see their own hands in order to reach for an object (Clifton & others, 1993). Cues from muscles, tendons, and joints, not sight of the limb, guide reaching by 4-month-old infants.

Infants refine their ability to grasp objects by developing two types of grasps. Initially, infants grip with the whole hand, which is called the *palmer grasp*. Later, toward the end of the first year, infants also grasp small objects with their thumb and forefinger, which is called the *pincer grip*. Their grasping system is very flexible. They vary their grip on an object depending on its size, shape, and texture, as well as the size of their own hands relative to the object's size. Infants grip small objects with their thumb and forefinger (and sometimes their middle finger, too), whereas they grip large objects with all of the fingers of one hand or both hands.

Perceptual–motor coupling is necessary for the infant to coordinate grasping (Needham, 2011). Which perceptual system the infant is most likely to use to

**fine motor skills** Actions that involve more finely tuned movements, such as finger dexterity.

A young girl using a pincer grip to pick up puzzle pieces.

**developmental connection**

**Cognitive Development.** The ability to manipulate objects enables more to be learned about the surrounding world, contributing to cognitive and intellectual development. Chapter 6, LO 1; Chapter 7, LO 1; Chapter 8, LO 2

coordinate grasping varies with age. Four-month-old infants rely greatly on touch to determine how they will grip an object; 8-month-olds are more likely to use vision as a guide (Newell & others, 1989). This developmental change is efficient because vision lets infants pre-shape their hands as they reach for an object.

Experience plays a role in reaching and grasping. In one study, 3-month-old infants participated in play sessions wearing *sticky mittens*—"mittens with palms that stuck to the edges of toys and allowed the infants to pick up the toys" (Needham, Barrett, & Peterman, 2002, p. 279) (see Figure 5.4). Infants who participated in sessions with the mittens grasped and manipulated objects earlier in their development than a control group of infants who did not receive the mitten experience. The experienced infants looked at the objects longer, swatted at them more during visual contact, and were more likely to mouth the objects. In a recent study, 5-month-old infants whose parents trained them to use the sticky mittens for ten minutes a day over a two-week period showed advances in their reaching behaviour at the end of the two weeks (Libertus & Needham, 2011).

Just as infants need to exercise their gross motor skills, they also need to exercise their fine motor skills (Needham & Libertus, 2011). Especially when they can manage a pincer grip, infants delight in picking up small objects. Many develop the pincer grip and begin to crawl at about the same time, and infants at this time pick up virtually everything in sight, especially on the floor, and put the objects in their mouths. Thus, parents need to be vigilant in regularly monitoring what objects are within an infant's reach (Keen, 2005).

Around 18 to 24 months of age, toddlers begin to build towers with blocks (see Figure 5.5). Initially, they can only balance two- to three-block towers, but soon the tower increases to four, five, and even more blocks. To build a tower, toddlers must engage in the cognitive activity of planning, in this case a plan that involves a number of sequential movements in picking up and stacking blocks in a precise way (Keen, 2011). Also, they need to have developed the motor skill to release blocks smoothly so the tower won't topple. In a recent study, substantial individual differences in the tower building of 18- to 24-month-olds occurred (Chen & others, 2010). In this study, toddlers who built higher towers at this age continued to be more advanced in tower building at 3 years of age.

Rachel Keen (2011) emphasizes that tool use is an excellent context for studying problem solving in infants because tool use provides information about how infants plan to reach a goal. Researchers in this area have studied infants' intentional actions ranging from picking up a spoon in different orientations to retrieving rakes placed inside tubes.

**Childhood**   As children get older, their fine motor skills improve (Keen, 2011). At 3 years of age, children have had the ability to pick up the tiniest objects between their thumb and forefinger for some time, but they are still somewhat clumsy at it. Three-year-olds can build surprisingly high block towers, each block placed with intense concentration but often not in a completely straight line. When 3-year-olds play with a form board or a simple puzzle, they are rather rough in placing the pieces. When they try to position a piece in a hole, they often try to force the piece or pat it vigorously.

By 4 years of age, children's fine motor coordination is much more precise. Sometimes 4-year-old children have trouble building high towers with blocks because, in their desire to place each of the blocks perfectly, they upset those already stacked. By age 5, children's fine motor coordination has improved further. Hand, arm, and fingers all move together under better

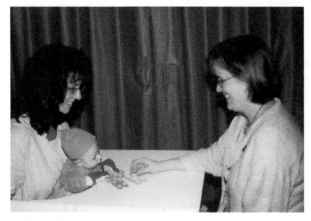

FIGURE **5.4**

**INFANTS' USE OF "STICKY MITTENS" TO EXPLORE OBJECTS.**
Amy Needham and her colleagues (2002) found that "sticky mittens" enhanced young infants' object exploration skills.

command of the eye. Mere towers no longer interest the 5-year-old, who now wants to build a house or a church, complete with steeple. (Adults may still need to be told what each finished project is meant to be.)

Increased myelination of the central nervous system is reflected in the improvement of fine motor skills during middle and late childhood. Recall from Chapter 4 that myelination involves the covering of the axon with a myelin sheath, a process that increases the speed with which information travels from neuron to neuron. By middle childhood, children can use their hands adroitly as tools. Six-year-olds can hammer, paste, tie shoes, and fasten clothes. By 7 years of age, children's hands have become steadier. At this age, children prefer a pencil to a crayon for printing, and reversal of letters is less common. Printing becomes smaller. At 8 to 10 years of age, children can use their hands independently with more ease and precision; children can now write rather than print words. Letter size becomes smaller and more even. At 10 to 12 years of age, children begin to show manipulative skills similar to the abilities of adults. The complex, intricate, and rapid movements needed to produce fine-quality crafts or to play a difficult piece on a musical instrument can be mastered. Girls usually outperform boys in fine motor skills.

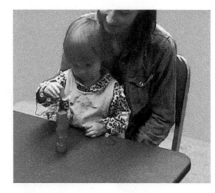

FIGURE **5.5**

**TOWER-BUILDING TODDLERS.** This 18-month-old is building a block tower in the study by Chen & others (2010). Note the kinematic sensors on the toddler's wrists for obtaining data on speed, location, and timing of movement.

## Review Connect Reflect

 Describe how motor skills develop.

### Review

- What is the dynamic systems view of motor development?
- What are some reflexes of infants?
- How do gross motor skills develop?
- How do fine motor skills develop?

### Connect

- In this section, you learned how infants explore their environment as they develop gross and fine motor skills.

How does this experience affect infants' neural connections (discussed in Chapter 4)?

### Reflect *Your Own Personal Journey of Life*

- If and when you become a parent, how would you evaluate the benefits and drawbacks of allowing your 7-year-old to play for a soccer team in a competitive league in your town or city?

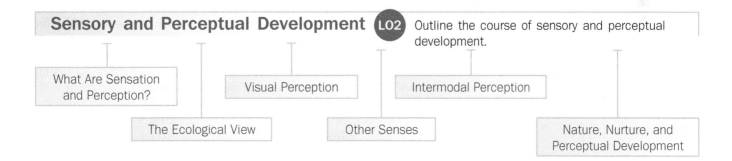

## Sensory and Perceptual Development **L02** Outline the course of sensory and perceptual development.

- What Are Sensation and Perception?
- The Ecological View
- Visual Perception
- Other Senses
- Intermodal Perception
- Nature, Nurture, and Perceptual Development

How do sensations and perceptions develop? Can a newborn see? If so, what can it perceive? What about the other senses—hearing, smell, taste, and touch? What are they like in the newborn, and how do they develop? Can an infant put together information from two modalities, such as sight and sound? What roles do nature and nurture play in perceptual development? These are among the intriguing questions that we will explore in this section.

## WHAT ARE SENSATION AND PERCEPTION?

How does a newborn know that her mother's skin is soft rather than rough? How does a 5-year-old know what colour his hair is? Infants and children know these things as a result of information that comes through the senses. Without vision,

How would you use the Gibsons' ecological theory of perception and the concept of affordance to explain the role that perception is playing in this toddler's activity?

hearing, touch, taste, and smell, we would be isolated from the world; we would live in dark silence, a tasteless, colourless, feelingless void.

**Sensation** occurs when information interacts with sensory *receptors*—the eyes, ears, tongue, nostrils, and skin. The sensation of hearing occurs when waves of pulsating air are collected by the outer ear and transmitted through the bones of the inner ear to the auditory nerve. The sensation of vision occurs as rays of light contact the eyes, become focused on the retina, and are transmitted by the optic nerve to the visual centres of the brain.

**Perception** is the interpretation of what is sensed. The air waves that contact the ears might be interpreted as noise or as musical sounds, for example. The physical energy transmitted to the retina of the eye might be interpreted as a particular colour, pattern, or shape, depending on how it is perceived.

## THE ECOLOGICAL VIEW

**sensation** Reaction that occurs when information contacts sensory receptors—the eyes, ears, tongue, nostrils, and skin.

**perception** The interpretation of sensation.

**ecological view** The view, proposed by the Gibsons, that people directly perceive information in the world around them. Perception brings people in contact with the environment in order to interact with it and adapt to it.

**affordances** Opportunities for interaction offered by objects that are necessary to perform activities.

**visual preference method** Developed by Fantz to determine whether infants can distinguish one stimulus from another by measuring the length of time they attend to different stimuli.

In recent decades, much of the research on perceptual development in infancy has been guided by the ecological view of Eleanor and James J. Gibson (E. Gibson, 1969, 1989, 2001; J. Gibson, 1966, 1979). They argue that we do not have to take bits and pieces of data from sensations and build up representations of the world in our minds. Instead, our perceptual system can select from the rich information that the environment itself provides.

According to the Gibsons' **ecological view**, we directly perceive information that exists in the world around us. The view is called *ecological* "because it connects perceptual capabilities to information available in the world of the perceiver" (Kellman & Arterberry, 2006, p. 112). Thus, perception brings us into contact with the environment in order to interact with and adapt to it. Perception is designed for action. Perception gives people such information as when to duck, when to turn their bodies to get through a narrow passageway, and when to put their hands up to catch something.

In the Gibsons' view, objects have **affordances**, which are opportunities for interaction offered by objects that fit within our capabilities to perform activities. A pot may afford you something to cook with, and it may afford a toddler something to bang. Adults typically know when a chair is appropriate for sitting, when a surface is safe for walking, or when an object is within reach. We directly and accurately perceive these affordances by sensing information from the environment—the light or sound reflecting from the surfaces of the world—and from our own bodies through muscle receptors, joint receptors, and skin receptors, for example (Ziemer, Plumert, & Pick, 2012).

As we described earlier in the section on motor development, infants who were just learning to crawl or just learning to walk were less cautious than experienced walkers or crawlers when confronted with a steep slope (Adolph, 1997). The more experienced crawlers and walkers perceived that a slope *affords* the possibility for not only faster locomotion but also for falling. Again, infants coupled perception and action to make a decision about what do in their environment. Through perceptual development, children become more efficient at discovering and using affordances.

Studying the infant's perception has not been an easy task. For instance, if newborns have limited communication abilities and are unable to tell us what they are seeing, hearing, smelling, and so on, how can we study their perception? *Connecting Through Research* describes some of the ingenious ways researchers study infants' perception.

## How Can We Study Newborns' Perception?

The creature has poor motor coordination and can move itself only with great difficulty. Although it cries when uncomfortable, it uses few other vocalizations. In fact, it sleeps most of the time, about 16 to 17 hours a day. You are curious about this creature and want to know more about what it can do. You think to yourself, "I wonder if it can see. How could I find out?"

You obviously have a communication problem with the creature. You must devise a way that will allow the creature to "tell" you that it can see. While examining the creature one day, you make an interesting discovery. When you move an object horizontally in front of the creature, its eyes follow the object's movement.

The creature's head movement suggests that it has at least some vision. In case you haven't already guessed, the creature you have been reading about is the human infant, and the role you played is that of a researcher interested in devising techniques to learn about the infant's visual perception. After years of work, scientists have developed research methods and tools sophisticated enough to examine the subtle abilities of infants and to interpret their complex actions (Bendersky & Sullivan, 2007).

### Visual Preference Method

Robert Fantz (1963) was a pioneer in the study of infants' perception. Fantz made an important discovery that advanced the ability of researchers to investigate infants' visual perception: Infants look at different things for different lengths of time. Fantz placed infants in a *looking chamber*, which had two visual displays on the ceiling above the infant's head. An experimenter viewed the infant's eyes by looking through a peephole. If the infant was fixating on one of the displays, the experimenter could see the display's reflection in the infant's eyes. This allowed the experimenter to determine how long the infant looked at each display. Fantz (1963) found that infants only 2 days old look longer at patterned stimuli, such as faces and concentric circles, than at red, white, or yellow discs. Infants 2 to 3 weeks old preferred to look at patterns—a face, a piece of printed matter, or a bull's eye—longer than at red, yellow, or white discs (see Figure 5.6). Fantz's research method—studying whether infants can distinguish one stimulus from another by measuring the length of time they attend to different stimuli—is referred to as the **visual preference method.**

### Habituation and Dishabituation

Another way that researchers have studied infants' perception is to present a stimulus (such as a sight or a sound) a number of times. If the infant decreases its response to the stimulus after several presentations, this indicates that the infant is no longer

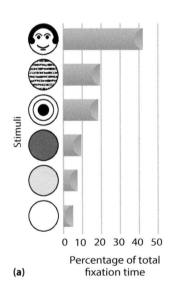

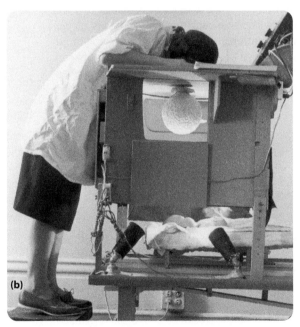

## FIGURE 5.6

**FANTZ'S EXPERIMENT ON INFANTS' VISUAL PERCEPTION.** (*a*) Infants 2 to 3 weeks old preferred to look at some stimuli more than others. In Fantz's experiment, infants preferred to look at patterns rather than at colour or brightness. For example, they looked longer at a face, a piece of printed matter, or a bull's eye than at red, yellow, or white discs. (*b*) Fantz used a "looking chamber" to study infants' perception of stimuli.

*(continued)*

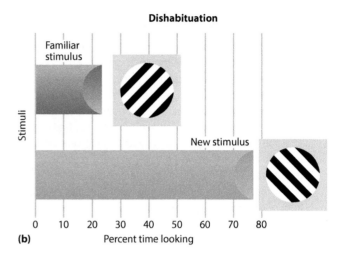

(a)

(b)

## FIGURE 5.7

**HABITUATION AND DISHABITUATION.** In the first part of one study, 7-hour-old newborns were shown the stimulus in (a). As indicated, the newborns looked at it an average of 41 seconds when it was first presented to them (Slater, Morison, & Somers, 1988). Over seven more presentations of the stimulus, they looked at it less and less. In the second part of the study, infants were presented with both the familiar stimulus to which they had just become habituated (a) and a new stimulus (shown in b, which was rotated 90 degrees). The newborns looked at the new stimulus three times as much as the familiar stimulus.

interested in looking at the stimulus. If the researcher now presents a new stimulus, the infant's response will recover, indicating that the infant could discriminate between the old and new stimuli (Colombo & others, 2010; Colombo, Brez, & Curtindale, 2013).

**Habituation** is the name given to decreased responsiveness to a stimulus after repeated presentations of the stimulus. **Dishabituation** is the recovery of a habituated response after a change in stimulation. Newborn infants can habituate to repeated sights, sounds, smells, or touches (Rovee-Collier, 2004). Among the measures researchers use in habituation studies are sucking behaviour (sucking stops when the young infant attends to a novel object), heart and respiration rates, and the length of time the infant looks at an object. Figure 5.7 shows the results of one study of habituation and dishabituation with newborns (Slater, Morison, & Somers, 1988).

### High-Amplitude Sucking

To assess an infant's attention to sound, researchers often use a method called *high-amplitude sucking*. In this method, infants are given a non-nutritive nipple to suck, and the nipple is connected to a sound generating system. The researcher computes a baseline high-amplitude sucking rate in a one-minute silent period. Following the baseline, presentation of a sound is made contingent on the rate of amplitude sucking. Initially babies suck frequently, so the noise occurs often. Gradually, they lose interest in hearing repetitions of the same noise and begin to suck less often. Then the researcher changes the sound that is being presented. If the babies renew vigorous sucking, we infer that they have discriminated the sound change and are sucking

more because they want to hear the interesting new sound (Menn & Stoel-Gammon, 2009).

### The Orienting Response

A technique that can be used to determine whether an infant can see or hear is the *orienting response*, in which they turn their head toward a sight or sound. Also, a startle response can be used as an indicator of an infant's reaction to a noise (Bendersky & Sullivan, 2007).

### Equipment

Technology can facilitate the use of most methods for investigating the infant's perceptual abilities. Videotape equipment allows researchers to investigate elusive behaviours. High-speed computers make it possible to perform complex data analysis in minutes. Other equipment records respiration, heart rate, body movement, visual fixation, and sucking behaviour, which provide clues to what the infant is perceiving. For example, some researchers use equipment that detects whether a change in infants' respiration follows a change in the pitch of a sound. If so, it suggests that the infants heard the pitch change.

### Eye-tracking

The most important recent advance in measuring infant perception is the development of sophisticated eye-tracking equipment (Franchak & others, 2011; Morgante, Zolfaghari, & Johnson, 2012; Navab & others, 2012). Figure 5.8 shows an infant wearing an eye-tracking headgear in a recent study on visually guided motor behaviour and social interaction.

*(continued)*

FIGURE **5.8**

**AN INFANT WEARING EYE-TRACKING HEADGEAR**
Using the ultra-light, wireless, head-mounted eye-tracking equipment shown here, researchers can record where infants are looking while they freely locomote (Source: Karen Adolph's laboratory at New York University).

One of the main reasons that infant perception researchers are so enthusiastic about the recent availability of sophisticated eye-tracking equipment is that looking time is among the most important measures of infant perceptual and cognitive development (Aslin, 2012). The new eye-tracking equipment allows for much greater precision than human observation in assessing various aspects of infant looking and gaze (Oakes, 2012). Among the areas of infant perception in which eye-tracking equipment is being used are memory, joint attention, and face processing (Falck-Ytter & others, 2012). Further, eye-tracking equipment is improving our understanding of atypically developing infants, such as those with autism (Sasson & Elison, 2013) and infants at risk for atypical developmental outcomes, including preterm infants (Bedford & others, 2012).

One recent eye-tracking study shed light on the effectiveness of TV programs and DVDs that claim to educate infants (Kirkorian, Anderson, & Keen, 2012). In this study, 1-year-olds, 4-year-olds, and adults watched *Sesame Street* and the eye-tracking equipment recorded precisely what they looked at on the screen. The 1-year-olds were far less likely to consistently look at the same part of the screen than their counterparts, suggesting that 1-year-olds showed little understanding of the *Sesame Street* video but instead were more likely to be attracted by what was salient than by what was relevant.

*How might a researcher use the visual preference procedure to measure infant auditory preferences?*

## VISUAL PERCEPTION

What do newborns see? How does visual perception develop in infancy? How does visual perception develop in childhood?

**Infancy**   Some important changes in visual perception can be traced to differences in how the eye itself functions over time as the child ages. These changes in the eye's functioning influence, for example, how clearly we can see an object, whether we can differentiate its colours, at what distance, and in what light (see Figure 5.9).

*Visual Acuity*   Psychologist William James (1890–1950) called the newborn's perceptual world a "blooming, buzzing confusion." More than a century later, we

**habituation** Decreased responsiveness to a stimulus after repeated presentations of the stimulus.

**dishabituation** The recovery of a habituated response after a change in stimulation.

As soon as 12 hours after birth, can discriminate mother's face from stranger's face.

By 8 weeks, can discriminate between some colours.

Can see at 20 feet what an adult can see at 240 feet.

Preference for patterned over non-patterned displays.

FIGURE **5.9**

**WHAT CAN AN INFANT SEE?**

can safely say that he was wrong (Atkinson & Braddick, 2013; Schmuckler, 2013). Even the newborn perceives a world with some order. That world, however, is far different from the one perceived by the toddler or the adult.

Just how well can infants see? At birth, the nerves and muscles and lens of the eye are still developing. As a result, newborns cannot see small things that are far away. The newborn's vision is estimated to be 20/240 on the well-known Snellen chart used for eye examinations, which means that a newborn can see at 20 feet what a normal adult can see at 240 feet (Aslin & Lathrop, 2008). In other words, an object 20 feet away is only as clear to the newborn as it would be if it were 240 feet away from an adult with normal vision (20/20). By 6 months of age, though, on *average* vision is 20/40 (Aslin & Lathrop, 2008).

*Face Perception*    Infants show an interest in human faces soon after birth (Lee & others, 2013). Figure 5.10 shows a computer estimation of what a picture of a face looks like to an infant at different ages from a distance of about 6 inches. Infants spend more time looking at their mother's face than a stranger's face as early as 12 hours after being born (Bushnell, 2003). By 3 months of age, infants match voices to faces, distinguish between male and female faces, and discriminate between faces of their own ethnic group and those of other ethnic groups (Kelly & others, 2007, 2009; Liu & others, 2011).

As infants develop, they change the way they gather information from the visual world, including human faces (Lee & others, 2013). A recent study recorded eye movements of 3-, 6-, and 9-month old infants as they viewed clips from an animated film—*A Charlie Brown Christmas* (Frank, Vul, & Johnson, 2009). From 3 to 9 months of age, infants gradually began focusing their attention more on the faces of the characters in the animated film and less on salient background stimuli.

*Pattern Perception*    As we discussed in *Connecting Through Research*, young infants can perceive certain patterns. With the help of his looking chamber, Robert Fantz (1963) revealed that even 2- to 3-week-old infants prefer to look at patterned displays rather than non-patterned displays. For example, they prefer to look at a normal human face rather than one with scrambled features, and they prefer to look at a bull's eye target or black-and-white stripes rather than a plain circle.

*Colour Vision*    The infant's colour vision also improves (Kellman & Arterberry, 2006). By 8 weeks, and possibly as early as 4 weeks, infants can discriminate between some colours (Kelly, Borchert, & Teller, 1997). By 4 months of age, they have colour preferences that mirror those of adults in some cases, preferring saturated colours such as royal blue over pale blue, for example (Bornstein, 1975). A recent study of 4- to 5-month-olds found that they looked longest at reddish hues and shortest at greenish hues (Franklin & others, 2010). In part, these changes in vision reflect maturation. Experience, however, is also necessary for

**developmental connection**

**Research Methods.** The still-face paradigm has been used to study face-to-face interaction between infants and caregivers. Chapter 10, LO 4

FIGURE **5.10**

**VISUAL ACUITY DURING THE FIRST MONTHS OF LIFE.** The four photographs represent a computer estimation of what a picture of a face looks like to a 1-month-old, 2-month-old, 3-month-old, and 1-year-old (which approximates the visual acuity of an adult).

vision to develop normally. For example, one study found that experience is necessary for normal colour vision to develop (Sugita, 2004).

*Perceptual Constancy*   Some perceptual accomplishments are especially intriguing because they indicate that the infant's perception goes beyond the information provided by the senses (Johnson, 2012, 2013; Slater & others, 2010, 2011). This is the case in *perceptual constancy*, in which sensory stimulation is changing but perception of the physical world remains constant. If infants did not develop perceptual constancy, each time they saw an object at a different distance or in a different orientation they would perceive it as a different object. Thus, the development of perceptual constancy allows infants to perceive their world as stable. Two types of perceptual constancy are size constancy and shape constancy.

**Size constancy** is the recognition that an object remains the same even though the retinal image of the object changes as you move toward or away from the object. The farther away from us an object is, the smaller is its image on our eyes. Thus, the size of an object on the retina is not sufficient to tell us its actual size. For example, you perceive a bicycle standing right in front of you as smaller than the car parked across the street, even though the bicycle casts a larger image on your eyes than the car does. When you move away from the bicycle, you do not perceive it to be shrinking even though its image on your retinas shrinks; you perceive its size as constant.

But what about babies? Do they have size constancy? Researchers have found that babies as young as 3 months of age show size constancy (Bower, 1966; Day & McKenzie, 1973). However, at 3 months of age, this ability is not full-blown. It continues to develop until 10 or 11 years of age (Kellman & Banks, 1998).

**Shape constancy** is the recognition that an object remains the same shape even though its orientation to us changes. Look around the room you are in right now. You likely see objects of varying shapes, such as tables and chairs. If you get up and walk around the room, you will see these objects from different sides and angles. Even though your retinal image of the objects changes as you walk and look, you will still perceive the objects as the same shape.

Do babies have shape constancy? As with size constancy, researchers have found that babies as young as 3 months of age have shape constancy (Bower, 1966; Day & McKenzie, 1973). Three-month-old infants, however, do not have shape constancy for irregularly shaped objects, such as tilted planes (Cook & Birch, 1984).

*Perception of Occluded Objects*   Look around the context where you are now. You likely see that some objects are partly occluded by other objects that are in front of them—possibly a desk behind a chair, some books behind a computer, or a car parked behind a tree. Do infants perceive an object as complete when it is occluded by an object in front of it?

In the first two months of postnatal development, infants don't perceive occluded objects as complete, instead only perceiving what is visible (Johnson, 2012, 2013). Beginning at about 2 months of age, infants develop the ability to perceive that occluded objects are whole (Slater, Field, & Hernandez-Reif, 2007). How does perceptual completion develop? In Scott Johnson's research (2004, 2009, 2010a, b; Johnson & others, 2000), learning, experience, and self-directed exploration via eye movements play key roles in the development of perceptual completion in young infants.

Many objects that are occluded appear and disappear behind closer objects, as when you are walking down the street and see cars appear and disappear behind buildings as they move or you move. Can infants predictively track briefly occluded moving objects? They develop the ability to track briefly occluded moving objects at about 3 to 5 months of age (Bertenthal, 2008). One study explored 5- to 9-month-old infants' ability to track moving objects that disappeared gradually behind an occluded partition, disappeared abruptly, or imploded (shrank quickly in size) (Bertenthal, Longo, & Kenny, 2007) (see Figure 5.11). In this study, the infants were more likely to accurately predict the

**size constancy** Recognition that an object remains the same even though the retinal image of the object changes.

**shape constancy** Recognition that an object remains the same even though its orientation to the viewer changes.

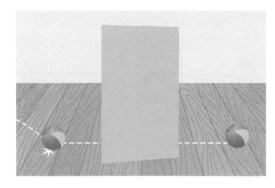

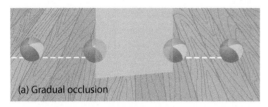

(a) Gradual occlusion

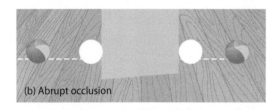

(b) Abrupt occlusion

(c) Implosion

## FIGURE 5.11

**INFANTS' PREDICTIVE TRACKING OF A BRIEFLY OCCLUDED MOVING BALL.** The top drawing shows a visual scene that infants experienced. At the beginning of each event, a multicoloured ball bounced up and down with an accompanying bouncing sound, and then rolled across the floor until it disappeared behind the partition. The bottom drawing shows the three stimulus events the 5- to 9-month-old infants experienced: occlusion, disappearance, and implosion. (a) *Gradual Occlusion:* The ball gradually disappears behind the right side of the occluding partition located in the centre of the display. (b) *Abrupt Disappearance:* The ball abruptly disappears when it reaches the location of the white circle and then abruptly reappears 2 seconds later at the location of the second white circle on the other side of the occluding partition. (c) *Implosion:* The rolling ball quickly decreases in size as it approaches the occluding partition and rapidly increases in size as it reappears on the other side of the occluding partition.

## FIGURE 5.12

**EXAMINING INFANTS' DEPTH PERCEPTION ON THE VISUAL CLIFF.** Eleanor Gibson and Richard Walk (1960) found that most infants would not crawl out on the glass, which, according to Gibson and Walk, indicated that they had depth perception. However, critics point out that the visual cliff is a better indication of the infant's social referencing and fear of heights than the infant's perception of depth.

path of the moving object when it disappeared gradually rather than when it disappeared abruptly or imploded.

*Depth Perception*    Might infants be able to perceive depth? In a classic study designed to investigate this question, Eleanor Gibson and Richard Walk (1960) constructed in their laboratory a miniature cliff with a dropoff covered by glass. They placed infants on the edge of this visual cliff and had their mothers coax them to crawl onto the glass (see Figure 5.12). Most infants would not crawl out on the glass, choosing instead to remain on the shallow side, an indication that they could perceive depth, according to Gibson and Walk. However, critics point out that the visual cliff likely is a better test of social referencing and fear of heights than depth perception.

The 6- to 12-month-old infants in the visual cliff experiment had extensive visual experience. Do younger infants without this experience still perceive depth? Since younger infants do not crawl, this question is difficult to answer. Two- to 4-month-old infants show differences in heart rate when they are placed directly on the deep side of the visual cliff instead of on the shallow side (Campos, Langer, & Krowitz, 1970). However, these differences might mean that young infants respond to differences in some visual characteristics of the deep and shallow cliffs, with no actual knowledge of depth.

Although researchers do not know exactly how early in life infants can perceive depth, more recent research using preferential-reaching procedures, preferential-looking procedures, and habituation paradigms, suggests that infants develop the ability to use binocular cues to discern depth by about 3 to 4 months of age and monocular cues by about 7 months of age (Arterberry, 2008).

**Childhood**    Perceptual development continues in childhood (Lee & others, 2013, Vida & Maurer, 2012). Children become increasingly efficient at detecting the boundaries between colours (such as red and orange) at 3 to 4 years of age (Gibson, 1969). When they are about 4 or 5 years old, most children's eye muscles are developed enough for them to move their eyes efficiently across a series of letters. Many preschool children are farsighted, unable to see close up as well as they can see far away. By the time they enter first grade, though, most children can focus their eyes and sustain their attention effectively on close-up objects.

After infancy, children's visual expectations about the physical world continue to develop (Keen, 2011). In one study, 2- to 4½-year-old children were given a task in which the goal was to find a toy ball that had been dropped through an opaque tube (Hood, 1995). As shown in

Figure 5.13, if the ball is dropped into the tube at the top right, it will land in the box at the bottom left. However, in this task, most of the 2-year-olds, and even some of the 4-year-olds, persisted in searching in the box immediately beneath the dropping point. For them, gravity ruled, and they had failed to perceive the end location of the curved tube.

In a recent study, 3-year-olds were presented with the same task shown in Figure 5.13 (Joh, Jaswal, & Keen, 2011). In the group that was told to imagine the various paths the ball might take, the young children were more accurate in predicting where the ball would land. In another recent study, 3-year-olds improved their performance on the ball dropping task show in Figure 5.13 when they were instructed to follow the tube with their eyes to the botton (Bascandziev & Harris, 2011). Thus, in these two studies, 3-year-olds were able to overcome the gravity bias and their impulsive tendencies when they were given verbal instructions from a knowledgeable adult (Keen, 2011).

How do children learn to deal with situations like that in Figure 5.13, and how do they come to understand other laws of the physical world? These questions are addressed by studies of cognitive development, which we will discuss in Chapters 6 and 7.

## OTHER SENSES

Other sensory systems besides vision also develop during infancy. We will explore development in hearing, touch and pain, smell, and taste.

**Hearing**    During the last two months of pregnancy, as the fetus nestles in its mother's womb, it can hear sounds such as the mother's voice, music, and so on (Kisilevsky & Hains, 2011; Kisilevsky & others, 2009). Two psychologists wanted to find out if a fetus that heard Dr. Seuss' classic story *The Cat in the Hat* while still in the mother's womb would prefer hearing the story after birth (DeCasper & Spence, 1986). During the last months of pregnancy, sixteen women read *The Cat in the Hat* to their fetuses. Then shortly after they were born, the mothers read either *The Cat in the Hat* or a story with a different rhyme and pace, *The King, the Mice and the Cheese* (which was not read to them during prenatal development). The infants sucked on a nipple in a different way when the mothers read the two stories, suggesting that the infants recognized the pattern and tone of *The Cat in the Hat* (see Figure 5.14). This study illustrates not only that a fetus can hear but also that it has a remarkable ability to learn even before birth.

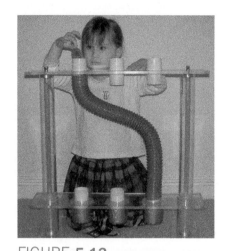

FIGURE **5.13**

**VISUAL EXPECTATIONS ABOUT THE PHYSICAL WORLD.** When young children see a ball dropped into the tube, many of them will search for it immediately below the dropping point. *How might verbal instructions from a knowledgeable adult help younger children overcome a gravity bias?*

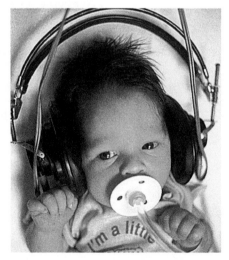

FIGURE **5.14**

**HEARING IN THE WOMB.** (a) Pregnant mothers read *The Cat in the Hat* to their fetuses during the last few months of pregnancy. (b) When they were born, the babies preferred listening to a recording of their mothers reading *The Cat in the Hat*—as evidenced by their sucking on a nipple—rather than another story, *The King, the Mice and the Cheese.*

A recent fMRI study assessed fetal brain response to auditory stimuli, confirming that the fetus can hear at 33 to 34 weeks gestation (Jardri & others, 2012).

The fetus can also recognize the mother's voice, as one study demonstrated (Kisilevsky & others, 2004). Sixty third-trimester fetuses (mean gestational age, 38.4 weeks) were exposed to a tape recording either of their mother or of a female stranger reading a passage. The sounds of the tape were delivered through a loudspeaker held just above the mother's abdomen. Fetal heart rate increased in response to the mother's voice but decreased in response to the stranger's voice.

Although the human ear is functionally mature shortly after birth, the underlying neural pathways in the brain continue to develop after birth. Auditory input to help fine-tune neural pathways is required for the continuing development of the auditory system (Moore, 2002). What kind of changes in hearing take place during infancy? They involve perception of a sound's loudness, pitch, and localization (see Figure 5.15):

developmental **connection**

**Biological Processes.** Prenatal development is divided into three periods: germinal (first 2 weeks after conception), embryonic (2 to 8 weeks after conception), and fetal (begins at 2 months after conception and lasts for 7 months on average). Chapter 3, LO 1

- *Loudness.* Immediately after birth, infants cannot hear soft sounds quite as well as adults can; a stimulus must be louder to be heard by a newborn than by an adult (Trehub & others, 1991). For example, an adult can hear a whisper from about four to five feet away, but a newborn requires that sounds be closer to a normal conversational level to be heard at that distance.

- *Pitch.* Infants are also less sensitive to the pitch of a sound than adults are. *Pitch* is the perception of the frequency of a sound. A soprano voice sounds high-pitched, a bass voice low-pitched. Infants are less sensitive to low-pitched sounds and are more likely to hear high-pitched sounds (Aslin, Jusczyk, & Pisoni, 1998). By 2 years of age, infants have considerably improved their ability to distinguish sounds with different pitches. And one study revealed that pitch preferences in 6- to 7-month-old infants may be context dependent. In this study, infants preferred to listen to high-pitched over low-pitched playsongs and low-pitched over high-pitched lullabies (Tsang & Conrad, 2010).

- *Localization.* Even newborns can determine the general location from which a sound is coming, but by 6 months of age, they are more proficient at *localizing* sounds or detecting their origins. Their ability to localize sounds continues to improve during the second year (Burnham & Mattock, 2010).

**Touch and Pain** Do newborns respond to touch? Can they feel pain?

Newborns do respond to touch. A touch to the cheek produces a turning of the head; a touch to the lips produces sucking movements.

Newborns can also feel pain (Gunnar & Quevado, 2007). If and when you have a son and consider whether he should be circumcised, the issue of an infant's pain perception probably will become important to you. Circumcision is usually performed on young boys about the third day after birth. Will your young son experience pain if he is circumcised when he is 3 days old? An investigation by Megan Gunnar and her colleagues (1987) found that newborn infant males cried

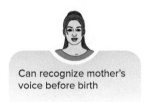

Can recognize mother's voice before birth

Cannot hear soft sounds as well as an adult

Prefer high-pitched over low-pitched sounds

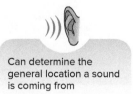

Can determine the general location a sound is coming from

FIGURE **5.15**

**WHAT CAN AN INFANT HEAR?**

intensely during circumcision. The circumcised infant also displays amazing resiliency. Within several minutes after the surgery, they can nurse and interact in a normal manner with their mothers. And, if allowed to, the newly circumcised newborn drifts into a deep sleep, which seems to serve as a coping mechanism.

For many years, doctors performed operations on newborns without anesthesia. This practice was accepted because of the dangers of anesthesia and because of the supposition that newborns do not feel pain. As researchers demonstrated that newborns can feel pain, the practise of operating on newborns without anesthesia is being challenged. Anesthesia now is used in some circumcisions (Taddio, 2008).

**Smell** Newborns can differentiate odours (Doty & Shah, 2008). The expressions on their faces seem to indicate that they like the way vanilla and strawberry smell but do not like the way rotten eggs and fish smell (Steiner, 1979). In one investigation, 6-day-old infants who were breastfed showed a clear preference for smelling their mother's breast pad rather than a clean breast pad (MacFarlane, 1975) (see Figure 5.16). However, when they were 2 days old, they did not show this preference, indicating that they require several days of experience to recognize this odour.

**Taste** Sensitivity to taste might be present even before birth (Doty & Shah, 2008). Human newborns learn tastes prenatally through the amniotic fluid and in breast milk after birth (Beauchamp & Mennella, 2009; Mennella, 2009). In one study, even at only 2 hours of age, babies made different facial expressions when they tasted sweet, sour, and bitter solutions (Rosenstein & Oster, 1988) (see Figure 5.17). At about 4 months of age, infants begin to prefer salty tastes, which as newborns they had found to be aversive (Harris, Thomas, & Booth, 1990).

## INTERMODAL PERCEPTION

Imagine yourself playing basketball or tennis. You are experiencing many visual inputs: the ball coming and going, other players moving around, and so on. However, you are experiencing many auditory inputs as well: the sound of the ball bouncing or being hit, the grunts and groans of the players, and so on. There is a good correspondence between much of the visual and auditory information. When you see the ball bounce, you hear a bouncing sound; when a player

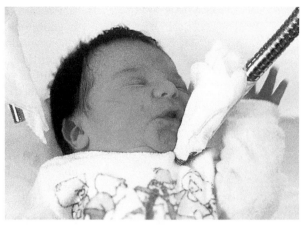

FIGURE **5.16**

**NEWBORNS' PREFERENCE FOR THE SMELL OF THEIR MOTHER'S BREAST PAD.** In the experiment by MacFarlane (1975), 6-day-old infants preferred to smell their mother's breast pad rather than a clean one that had never been used, but 2-day-old infants did not show this preference, indicating that this odour preference requires several days of experience to develop.

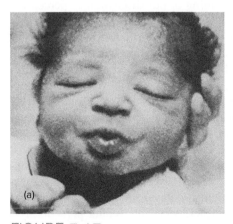
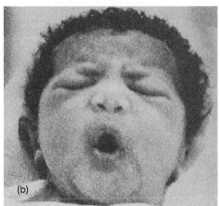
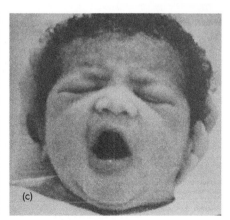

FIGURE **5.17**

**NEWBORNS' FACIAL RESPONSES TO BASIC TASTES.** Facial expression elicited by (a) a sweet solution, (b) a sour solution, and (c) a bitter solution.

**intermodal perception** The ability to relate and integrate information about two or more sensory modalities, such as vision and hearing.

*What are the senses this infant is using to integrate information about the jack-in-the-box?*

**developmental connection**

**Cognitive Development.** Piaget's theory states that children construct their understanding of the world and go through four stages of cognitive development. Chapter 1, LO 3; Chapter 6, LO 1

stretches to hit a ball, you hear a groan. When you look at and listen to what is going on, you do not experience just the sounds or just the sights—you put all these things together. You experience a unitary episode. This is **intermodal perception**, which involves integrating information from two or more sensory modalities, such as vision and hearing (Bremner & others, 2011). Most perception is intermodal (Bahrick, 2010).

Early, exploratory forms of intermodal perception exist even in newborns (Bahrick & Hollich, 2008). For example, newborns turn their eyes and heads toward the sound of a voice or rattle when the sound is maintained for several seconds (Clifton & others, 1981), but the newborn can localize a sound and look at an object only in a crude way (Bechtold, Bushnell, & Salapatek, 1979). These early forms of intermodal perception become sharpened with experience in the first year of life (Hollich, Newman, & Jusczyk, 2005). In one study, infants as young as 3 months old looked more at their mother when they also heard her voice and longer at their father when they also heard his voice (Spelke & Owsley, 1979). Thus, even young infants can coordinate visual–auditory information involving people.

Can young infants put vision and sound together as precisely as adults do? In the first six months, infants have difficulty connecting sensory input from different modes, but in the second half of the first year they show an increased ability to make this connection mentally.

The important ability to connect information about vision with information about touch also is evident early in infancy (Corbetta & Snapp-Childs, 2009). Coordination of vision and touch has been demonstrated in 2- to 3-month-olds (Streri, 1993).

Thus, babies are born into the world with some innate abilities to perceive relations among sensory modalities, but their intermodal abilities improve considerably through experience (Bahrick, 2010). As with all aspects of development, in perceptual development, nature and nurture interact and cooperate (Johnson, 2012, 2013; Maurer & Lewis, 2013).

## NATURE, NURTURE, AND PERCEPTUAL DEVELOPMENT

Now that we have discussed many aspects of perceptual development, let's explore one of developmental psychology's key issues as it relates to perceptual development: the nature–nurture issue. There has been a long-standing interest in how strongly infants' perception is influenced by nature and nurture (Aslin, 2009; Johnson, 2012, 2013; Slater & others, 2011). In the field of perceptual development, nature proponents are referred to as *nativists* and those who emphasize learning and experience are called *empiricists*.

In the nativist view, the ability to perceive the world in a competent, organized way is inborn or innate. At the beginning of our discussion of perceptual development, we examined the ecological view of the Gibsons because it has played such a pivotal role in guiding research in perceptual development. The Gibsons' ecological view leans toward a nativist explanation of perceptual development because it holds that perception is direct and evolved over time to allow the detection of size and shape constancy, a three-dimensional world, intermodal perception, and so on early in infancy. However, the Gibsons' view is not entirely nativist because they emphasized that "perceptual development involves distinctive features that are detected at different ages" (Slater & others, 2011).

The Gibsons' ecological view is quite different from Piaget's constructivist view, which reflects an empirical approach to explaining perceptual development. According to Piaget, much of perceptual development in infancy must await the development of a sequence of cognitive stages for infants to construct more complex perceptual tasks. Thus, in Piaget's view, intermodal perception as well as the ability to perceive size and shape constancy and a three-dimensional world and so on develops later in infancy than the Gibsons envision.

Today, it is clear that an extreme empirical position on perceptual development is unwarranted. Much of early perception develops from innate (nature) foundations and the basic foundation of many perceptual abilities can be detected in newborns, whereas other abilities unfold maturationally (Arterberry, 2008). However, as infants develop, environmental experiences (nurture) refine or calibrate many perceptual functions and may be the driving force behind some functions (Amos & Johnson, 2010).

The longitudinal research of Daphne Maurer and her colleagues at McMaster University in Ontario (Lewis & Maurer, 2005; 2009; Maurer & Lewis, 2013; Maurer & others, 1999) has focused on infants born with cataracts—a thickening of the lens of the eye that causes vision to become cloudy, opaque, and distorted, severely restricting infants' ability to experience their visual world. Studying infants whose cataracts were removed at different points in development, they discovered that those whose cataracts were removed and new lenses placed in their eyes in the first several months after birth showed a normal pattern of visual development. However, the longer the delay in removing the cataracts, the more their visual development was impaired. In their research, Maurer and her colleagues (2007) have found that experiencing patterned visual input early in infancy is important for holistic and detailed face processing after infancy. Maurer's research program illustrates

*What roles do nature and nurture play in the infant's perceptual development?*

how deprivation and experience influence visual development, particularly during an early sensitive period in which visual input is necessary for normal visual development (Maurer & Lewis, 2013).

Thus, the accumulation of experience with and knowledge about their perceptual world contributes to infants' ability to form coherent perceptions of people and things (Johnson, 2012, 2013). A full portrait of perceptual development includes the influence of nature, nurture, and a developing sensitivity to information (Arterberry, 2008; Maurer & Lewis, 2013).

## Review *Connect* Reflect

 **LO2** Outline the course of sensory and perceptual development.

### Review

- What are sensation and perception?
- What is the ecological view of perception? What are some research methods used to study infant perception?
- How does vision develop?
- How do the senses other than vision develop?
- What is intermodal perception, and how does it develop?
- What roles do nature and nurture play in perceptual development?

### *Connect*

- One of the topics we discussed in this section was vision. What did you learn about development, vision loss, and the other senses in the story that opened the chapter?

### **Reflect** *Your Own Personal Journey of Life*

- Imagine that you are the parent of a 1-year-old infant. What would you do to effectively stimulate the sensory development of your very young child?

## Perceptual–Motor Coupling   **LO3** Discuss the connections of perception and action.

As we come to the end of this chapter, we return to the important theme of perceptual–motor coupling. The distinction between perceiving and doing has been a time-honoured tradition in psychology. However, a number of experts on perceptual and motor development question whether this distinction makes sense (Adolph & Berger, 2013; Keen, 2011; Thelen & Smith, 2006). The main

*How are perception and action coupled in children's development?*

thrust of research in Esther Thelen's dynamic systems approach is to explore how people assemble motor behaviours for perceiving and acting. The main theme of the ecological approach of Eleanor and James J. Gibson is to discover how perception guides action. Action can guide perception, and perception can guide action. Only by moving one's eyes, head, hands, and arms and by moving from one location to another can an individual fully experience his or her environment and learn how to adapt to it. Perception and action are coupled (Keen, 2011).

Babies, for example, continually coordinate their movements with perceptual information to learn how to maintain balance, reach for objects in space, and move across various surfaces and terrains (Adolph & Robinson, 2013; Thelen & Smith, 2006). They are motivated to move by what they perceive. Consider the sight of an attractive toy across the room. In this situation, infants must perceive the current state of their bodies and learn how to use their limbs to reach the toy. Although their movements at first are awkward and uncoordinated, babies soon learn to select patterns that are appropriate for reaching their goals.

Equally important is the other part of the perception-action coupling. That is, action educates perception (Alolph & Berger, 2013; Thelen & Smith, 2006). For example, watching an object while exploring it manually helps infants to discriminate its texture, size, and hardness. Locomoting in the environment teaches babies about how objects and people look from different perspectives and whether surfaces will support their weight.

How do infants develop new perceptual–motor couplings? Recall from our discussion earlier in this chapter that in the traditional view of Gesell, infants' perceptual–motor development is prescribed by a genetic plan to follow a fixed and sequential progression of stages in development. The genetic determination view has been replaced by the dynamic systems view that infants learn new perceptual–motor couplings by assembling skills for perceiving and acting. New perceptual–motor coupling is not passively accomplished; rather, the infant actively develops a skill to achieve a goal within the constraints set by the infant's body and the environment.

Children perceive in order to move and move in order to perceive. Perceptual and motor development do not occur in isolation from each other but instead are coupled.

## Review Connect Reflect

**L03** Discuss the connection of perception and action.

### Review

- How are perception and motor actions coupled in development?

### Connect

- In this section, you learned that perceptual and motor development do not occur in isolation from each other but instead are coupled. How is this distinction similar to the distinction psychologists make when speaking of nature and nurture when describing development?

### Reflect *Your Own Personal Journey of Life*

- Think about your development as a child. Describe two examples, not given in the text, in which your perception guided your action. Then describe two examples, not given in the text, in which your action guided your perception.

1. How might the problems with sensation and perception described in the opening vignette affect motor development?

2. How would perceptual–motor coupling work for individuals who have no vision or are deaf?

3. Explain how the dynamic systems theory of motor development supports an active view of child development.

## reach your **learning goals**

# Motor, Sensory, and Perceptual Development

## Motor Development  Describe how motor skills develop.

The Dynamic Systems View

- Thelen's dynamic systems theory describes the development of motor skills as the assembling of behaviours for perceiving and acting. Perception and action are coupled. According to this theory, the development of motor skills depends on the development of the nervous system, the body's physical properties and its movement possibilities, the goal the child is motivated to reach, and environmental support for the skill. In the dynamic systems view, motor development is far more complex than the result of a genetic blueprint; the infant or child actively puts together a skill in order to achieve a goal within constraints set by the body and the environment.

Reflexes

- Reflexes—built-in reactions to stimuli—govern the newborn's movements. They include the sucking, rooting, and Moro reflexes, all of which typically disappear after three to four months. Some reflexes, such as blinking and yawning, persist throughout life; components of other reflexes are incorporated into voluntary actions.

Gross Motor Skills

- Gross motor skills involve large-muscle activities. Key skills developed during infancy include control of posture and walking. Gross motor skills improve dramatically during the childhood years. Boys usually outperform girls in gross motor skills involving large-muscle activity.

Fine Motor Skills

- Fine motor skills involve finely tuned movements. The onset of reaching and grasping marks a significant accomplishment. Fine motor skills continue to develop through the childhood years and by 4 years of age are much more precise. Children can use their hands as tools by middle childhood, and at 10 to 12 years of age start to show manipulative fine motor skills similar to those of adults.

## Sensory and Perceptual Development  Outline the course of sensory and perceptual development.

What Are Sensation and Perception?

- Sensation occurs when information interacts with sensory receptors. Perception is the interpretation of sensation.

The Ecological View

- The Gibsons' ecological view states that people directly perceive information that exists in the world. Perception brings people into contact with the environment in order to interact and adapt to it. Affordances are opportunities for interaction offered by objects that are necessary to perform activities. Researchers have developed a number of methods to assess infants' perceptions, including the visual preference method (which Fantz used to determine young infants' interest in looking at patterned over non-patterned displays), habituation and dishabituation, high-amplitude sucking, and eye tracking.

**Visual Perception**

- The infant's visual acuity increases dramatically in the first year of life. Infants show an interest in human faces soon after birth, and young infants systematically scan faces. Possibly by 4 weeks of age, infants can discriminate some colours. By 3 months of age, infants show size and shape constancy. At approximately 2 months of age, infants develop the ability to perceive that occluded objects are complete. In Gibson and Walk's classic study, infants as young as 6 months of age had depth perception. After infancy, children's visual expectations continue to develop, and further colour differentiation occurs from 3 to 4 years of age. A number of children experience vision problems.

**Other Senses**

- The fetus can hear several weeks prior to birth. Developmental changes in the perception of loudness, pitch, and localization of sound occur during infancy. Newborns can respond to touch and feel pain. Newborns can differentiate odors, and sensitivity to taste may be present before birth.

**Intermodal Perception**

- Intermodal perception is the ability to relate and integrate information from two or more sensory modalities. Crude, exploratory forms of intermodal perception are present in newborns and become sharpened over the first year of life.

**Nature, Nurture, and Perceptual Development**

- With regard to the study of perception, nature advocates are referred to as nativists and nurture proponents are called empiricists. The Gibsons' ecological view that has guided much of perceptual development research leans toward a nativist approach but still allows for developmental changes in distinctive features. Piaget's constructivist view leans toward an empiricist approach, emphasizing that many perceptual accomplishments must await the development of cognitive stages in infancy. A strong empiricist approach is unwarranted. A full account of perceptual development includes the roles of nature, nurture, and increasing sensitivity to information.

## Perceptual-Motor Coupling

 Discuss the connections of perception and action.

- Perception and action are coupled—individuals perceive in order to move and move in order to perceive. New perceptual-motor couplings do not occur as the result of genetic predetermination but rather because the infant actively assembles skills for perceiving and acting.

For more information on the resources available from McGraw-Hill Ryerson,
go to www.mheducation.ca/he/solutions

*Learning is an ornament in prosperity, a refuge in adversity.*

—ARISTOTLE
*Greek Philosopher, 4th Century BC*

# section three

# Cognition and Language

Children thirst to know and understand. In their effort to know and understand, they construct their own ideas about the world around them. They are remarkable for their curiosity and their intelligence. In Section 3, you will read four chapters: "Cognitive Developmental Approaches" (Chapter 6), "Information Processing" (Chapter 7), "Intelligence" (Chapter 8), and "Language Development" (Chapter 9).

# chapter 6 | Cognitive Developmental Approaches

Jean Piaget, the famous Swiss psychologist, was a meticulous observer of his three children— Laurent, Lucienne, and Jacqueline. His books on cognitive development are filled with these observations. Here are a few of Piaget's observations of his children in infancy (Piaget, 1952):

- At 21 days of age, "Laurent found his thumb after three attempts: prolonged sucking begins each time. But, once he has been placed on his back, he does not know how to coordinate the movement of the arms with that of the mouth and his hands draw back even when his lips are seeking them" (p. 27).

- During the third month, thumb sucking becomes less important to Laurent because of new visual and auditory interests. But, when he cries, his thumb goes to the rescue.

- Toward the end of Lucienne's fourth month, while she is lying in her crib, Piaget hangs a doll above her feet. Lucienne thrusts her feet at the doll and makes it move. "Afterward, she looks at her motionless foot for a second, then recommences. There is no visual control of her foot, for the movements are the same when Lucienne only looks at the doll or when I place the doll over her head. On the other hand, the tactile control of the foot is apparent: after the first shakes, Lucienne makes slow foot movements as though to grasp and explore" (p. 159).

- At 11 months, "Jacqueline is seated and shakes a little bell. She then pauses abruptly in order to delicately place the bell in front of her right foot; then she kicks hard. Unable to recapture it, she grasps a ball which she then places at the same spot in order to give it another kick" (p. 225).

- At 1 year, 2 months, "Jacqueline holds in her hands an object which is new to her: a round, flat box which she turns all over, shakes, (and) rubs against the bassinet. . . . She lets it go and tries to pick it up. But she only succeeds in touching it with her index finger, without grasping it. She nevertheless makes an attempt and presses on the edge. The box then tilts up and falls again" (p. 273). Jacqueline shows an interest in this result and studies the fallen box.

- At 1 year, 8 months, "Jacqueline arrives at a closed door with a blade of grass in each hand. She stretches out her right hand toward the [door] knob but sees that she cannot turn it without letting go of the grass. She puts the grass on the floor, opens the door, picks up the grass again, and enters. But when she wants to leave the room, things become complicated. She puts the grass on the floor and grasps the doorknob. But then she perceives that in pulling the door toward her she will simultaneously chase away the grass which she placed between the door and the threshold. She therefore picks it up in order to put it outside the door's zone of movement" (p. 339).

For Piaget, these observations reflect important changes in the infant's cognitive development. Later in the chapter, you will learn that Piaget argued that infants go through six substages of development and that the behaviours you have just read about characterize those substages.

# preview

Cognitive developmental approaches place a special emphasis on how children actively construct their thinking. They also focus heavily on how thinking changes from one point in development to another. In this chapter, we will highlight the cognitive developmental approaches of Jean Piaget and Lev Vygotsky.

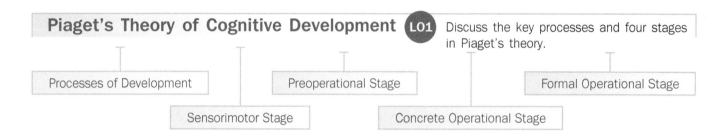

**Piaget's Theory of Cognitive Development** **L01** Discuss the key processes and four stages in Piaget's theory.

Processes of Development

Sensorimotor Stage

Preoperational Stage

Concrete Operational Stage

Formal Operational Stage

> We are born capable of learning.
>
> —JEAN-JACQUES ROUSSEAU
> *Swiss-Born French Philosopher, 18th Century*

**schemes** In Piaget's theory, actions or mental representations that organize knowledge.

Poet Nora Perry asked, "Who knows the thoughts of a child?" As much as anyone, Piaget knew. Through careful observations of his own three children—Laurent, Lucienne, and Jacqueline—and observations and interviews with other children, Piaget changed perceptions of the way children think about the world.

Piaget's theory is a general, unifying story of how biology and experience sculpt cognitive development. Piaget thought that, just as our physical bodies have structures that enable us to adapt to the world, we build mental structures that help us to adapt to the world. *Adaptation* involves adjusting to new environmental demands. Piaget stressed that children actively construct their own cognitive worlds; information is not just poured into their minds from the environment. He sought to discover how children at different points in their development think about the world and how systematic changes in their thinking occur.

## PROCESSES OF DEVELOPMENT

What processes do children use as they construct their knowledge of the world? Piaget stressed that the following processes are especially important in this regard: schemes, assimilation, accommodation, organization, and equilibration.

**Schemes**  Piaget (1954) said that as the child seeks to construct an understanding of the world, the developing brain creates **schemes**. These are actions or mental representations that organize knowledge. In Piaget's theory, behavioural schemes (physical activities) characterize infancy, and mental schemes (cognitive activities) develop in childhood (Lamb, Bornstein, & Teti, 2002). A baby's schemes are structured by simple actions that can be performed on objects, such as sucking, looking, and grasping. Older children have schemes that include strategies and plans for solving problems. For example, a 5-year-old might have a scheme that involves the strategy of classifying objects by size, shape, or colour. By the time we have reached adulthood, we have constructed an enormous number of diverse schemes, ranging from driving a car to balancing a budget to achieving fairness.

*In Piaget's view, what is a scheme? What schemes might this young infant be displaying?*

**Assimilation and Accommodation**  To explain how children use and adapt their schemes, Piaget proposed two concepts:

assimilation and accommodation. **Assimilation** occurs when children incorporate new information into their existing schemes. **Accommodation** occurs when children adjust their schemes to fit new information and experiences.

Think about a toddler who has learned the word *car* to identify the family's car. The toddler might call all moving vehicles on roads "cars," including motorcycles and trucks; the child has assimilated these objects into his or her existing scheme. But the child soon learns that motorcycles and trucks are not cars and then fine-tunes the category to exclude motorcycles and trucks, accommodating the scheme.

Assimilation and accommodation operate even in very young infants. Newborns reflexively suck everything that touches their lips; they assimilate all sorts of objects into their sucking scheme. By sucking different objects, they learn about their taste, texture, shape, and so on. After several months of experience, though, they construct their understanding of the world differently. Some objects, such as fingers and the mother's breast, can be sucked, and others, such as fuzzy blankets, should not be sucked. In other words, babies accommodate their sucking scheme.

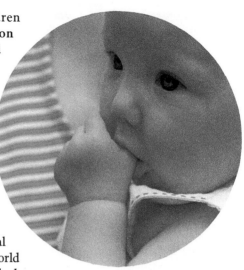

*How might assimilation and accommodation be involved in infants' sucking?*

**Organization**   To make sense out of their world, said Piaget, children cognitively organize their experiences. **Organization** in Piaget's theory is the grouping of isolated behaviours and thoughts into a higher-order system. Continual refinement of this organization is an inherent part of development. A boy who has only a vague idea about how to use a hammer may also have a vague idea about how to use other tools. After learning how to use each one, he relates these uses, grouping items into categories and organizing his knowledge.

**Equilibration and Stages of Development**   **Equilibration** is a mechanism that Piaget proposed to explain how children shift from one stage of thought to the next. The shift occurs as children experience cognitive conflict, or disequilibrium, in trying to understand the world. Eventually, they resolve the conflict and reach a balance, or equilibrium, of thought. Piaget argued that there is considerable movement between states of cognitive equilibrium and disequilibrium as assimilation and accommodation work in concert to produce cognitive change. For example, if a child believes that the amount of a liquid changes simply because the liquid is poured into a container with a different shape—for instance, from a container that is short and wide into a container that is tall and narrow—she might be puzzled by such issues as where the "extra" liquid came from and whether there is actually more liquid to drink. The child will eventually solve these puzzles as her thought becomes more advanced. In the everyday world, the child is constantly faced with such counterexamples and inconsistencies.

Assimilation and accommodation always take the child to a higher ground. For Piaget, the motivation for change is an internal search for equilibrium. As old schemes are adjusted and new schemes are developed, the child organizes and reorganizes the old and new schemes. Eventually, the new organization is fundamentally different from the old organization; it is a new way of thinking, a new stage. The result of these processes, according to Piaget, is that individuals go through four stages of development. A different way of understanding the world makes one stage more advanced than another. Cognition is *qualitatively* different in one stage compared with another. In other words, the way children reason at one stage is different from the way they reason at another stage.

Each of Piaget's stages is age related and consists of distinct ways of thinking. Piaget identified four stages of cognitive development: sensorimotor, preoperational, concrete operational, and formal operational (see Figure 6.1).

**assimilation** Piagetian concept of the incorporation of new information into existing knowledge.

**accommodation** Piagetian concept of adjusting schemes to fit new information and experiences.

**organization** Piaget's concept of grouping isolated behaviours into a higher-order, more smoothly functioning cognitive system; the grouping or arranging of items into categories.

**equilibration** A mechanism that Piaget proposed to explain how children shift from one stage of thought to the next. The shift occurs as children experience cognitive conflict, or disequilibrium, in trying to understand the world. Eventually, they resolve the conflict and reach a balance, or equilibrium, of thought.

*developmental* **connection**

**Continuous–discontinuous.** The nature of development can be viewed as continuous, reflecting gradual changes, or discontinuous, reflecting qualitative changes; Piaget's theory is an example of discontinuous development. Chapter 1, LO 2.

**Sensorimotor Stage**

Infants gain knowledge of the world from the physical actions they perform on it. Infants coordinate sensory experiences with these physical actions. An infant progresses from reflexive, instinctual action at birth to the beginning of symbolic thought toward the end of the stage.

**Birth to 2 Years of Age**

**Preoperational Stage**

The child begins to use mental representations to understand the world. Symbolic thinking, reflected in the use of words and images, is used in this mental representation, which goes beyond the connection of sensory information with physical action. However, there are some constraints on the child's thinking at this stage, such as egocentrism and centration.

**2 to 7 Years of Age**

**Concrete Operational Stage**

The child can now reason logically about concrete events, understands the concept of conservation, organizes objects into hierarchical classes (classification), and places objects in ordered series (seriation).

**7 to 11 Years of Age**

**Formal Operational Stage**

The adolescent reasons in more abstract, idealistic, and logical (hypothetical-deductive) ways.

**11 Years of Age Through Adulthood**

FIGURE **6.1**
PIAGET'S FOUR STAGES OF COGNITIVE DEVELOPMENT.

## SENSORIMOTOR STAGE

**sensorimotor stage** The first of Piaget's stages, which lasts from birth to about 2 years of age; infants construct an understanding of the world by coordinating sensory experiences (such as seeing and hearing) with motoric actions.

The **sensorimotor stage** lasts from birth to about 2 years of age. In this stage, infants construct an understanding of the world by coordinating sensory experiences (such as seeing and hearing) with physical, motoric actions—hence the term *sensorimotor*. At the beginning of this stage, newborns have little more than reflexive patterns with which to work. At the end of the sensorimotor stage, 2-year-olds can produce complex sensorimotor patterns and use primitive symbols. We first will summarize Piaget's descriptions of how infants develop. Later we will consider criticisms of his views.

**Substages**   Piaget divided the sensorimotor stage into six substages: (1) simple reflexes; (2) first habits and primary circular reactions; (3) secondary circular reactions; (4) coordination of secondary circular reactions; (5) tertiary circular reactions, novelty, and curiosity; and (6) internalization of schemes (see Figure 6.2).

1.  *Simple reflexes*, the first sensorimotor substage, corresponds to the first month after birth. In this substage, sensation and action are coordinated primarily through reflexive behaviours, such as the rooting and sucking reflexes. Soon the infant produces behaviours that resemble reflexes in the absence of the usual stimulus for the reflex. For example, a newborn will suck a nipple or bottle only when it is placed directly in the baby's mouth or touched to the lips. But soon the infant might suck when a bottle or nipple is only nearby. The infant is initiating action and is actively structuring experiences in the first month of life.

2.  *First habits and primary circular reactions* is the second sensorimotor substage, which develops between 1 and 4 months of age. In this substage, the infant coordinates sensation and two types of schemes: habits and primary circular reactions.

    •  A *habit* is a scheme based on a reflex that has become completely separated from its eliciting stimulus. For example, infants in substage 1

| Substage | Age | Description | Example |
|---|---|---|---|
| 1 Simple reflexes | Birth to 1 month | Coordination of sensation and action through reflexive behaviors. | Rooting, sucking, and grasping reflexes; newborns suck reflexively when their lips are touched. |
| 2 First habits and primary circular reactions | 1 to 4 months | Coordination of sensation and two types of schemes: habits (reflex) and primary circular reactions (reproduction of an event that initially occurred by chance). Main focus is still on the infant's body. | Repeating a body sensation first experienced by chance (sucking thumb, for example); then infants might accommodate actions by sucking their thumb differently from how they suck on a nipple. |
| 3 Secondary circular reactions | 4 to 8 months | Infants become more object-oriented, moving beyond self-preoccupation; repeat actions that bring interesting or pleasurable results. | An infant coos to make a person stay near; as the person starts to leave, the infant coos again. |
| 4 Coordination of secondary circular reactions | 8 to 12 months | Coordination of vision and touch—hand-eye coordination; coordination of schemes and intentionality. | Infant manipulates a stick in order to bring an attractive toy within reach. |
| 5 Tertiary circular reactions, novelty, and curiosity | 12 to 18 months | Infants become intrigued by the many properties of objects and by the many things they can make happen to objects; they experiment with new behaviour. | A block can be made to fall, spin, hit another object, and slide across the ground. |
| 6 Internalization of schemes | 18 to 24 months | Infants develop the ability to use primitive symbols and form enduring mental representations. | An infant who has never thrown a temper tantrum before sees a playmate throw a tantrum; the infant retains a memory of the event, then throws one himself the next day. |

## FIGURE 6.2
**PIAGET'S SIX SUBSTAGES OF SENSORIMOTOR DEVELOPMENT.**

suck when bottles are put to their lips or when they see a bottle. Infants in substage 2 might suck even when no bottle is present. A *circular reaction* is a repetitive action.

- A *primary circular reaction* is a scheme based on the attempt to reproduce an event that initially occurred by chance. For example, suppose an infant accidentally sucks his fingers when they are placed near his mouth. Later, he searches for his fingers to suck them again, but the fingers do not cooperate because the infant cannot coordinate visual and manual actions.

  Habits and circular reactions are stereotyped—that is, the infant repeats them the same way each time. During this substage, the infant's own body remains his or her centre of attention. There is no outward pull by environmental events.

3. *Secondary circular reactions* is the third sensorimotor substage, which develops between 4 and 8 months of age. In this substage, the infant becomes more object oriented, moving beyond preoccupation with the self. By chance, an infant might shake a rattle. The infant repeats this action for the sake of its fascination.

   The infant also imitates some simple actions, such as the baby talk or burbling of adults, and some physical gestures. However, the baby imitates only actions that he or she is already able to produce. Although directed toward objects in the world, the infant's schemes are not intentional or goal-directed.

4. *Coordination of secondary circular reactions* is Piaget's fourth sensorimotor substage, which develops between 8 and 12 months of age. To progress into this substage, the infant must coordinate vision and touch, eye and hand. Actions become more outwardly directed. Significant changes during this substage involve the coordination of schemes and intentionality. Infants readily combine and recombine previously learned schemes in a coordinated way. They might look at an object and grasp it simultaneously, or they might visually inspect a toy, such as a rattle, and finger it simultaneously, exploring it tactilely. Actions are even more outwardly directed than before. Related to this coordination is the second

This 17-month-old is in Piaget's stage of tertiary circular reactions. *What might the infant do that suggests she is in this stage?*

achievement—the presence of intentionality. For example, infants might manipulate a stick in order to bring a desired toy within reach, or they might knock over one block to reach and play with another one.

5. *Tertiary circular reactions, novelty, and curiosity* is Piaget's fifth sensorimotor substage, which develops between 12 and 18 months of age. In this substage, infants become intrigued by the many properties of objects and by the many things that they can make happen to objects. A block can be made to fall, spin, hit another object, and slide across the ground. *Tertiary circular reactions* are schemes in which the infant purposely explores new possibilities with objects, continually doing new things to them and exploring the results. Piaget says that this stage marks the starting point for human curiosity and interest in novelty.

6. *Internalization of schemes* is Piaget's sixth and final sensorimotor substage, which develops between 18 and 24 months of age. In this substage, the infant develops the ability to use primitive symbols. For Piaget, a *symbol* is an internalized sensory image or word that represents an event. Primitive symbols permit the infant to think about concrete events without directly acting them out or perceiving them. Moreover, symbols allow the infant to manipulate and transform the represented events in simple ways. In a favourite Piagetian example, Piaget's young daughter saw a matchbox being opened and closed. Later, she mimicked the event by opening and closing her mouth. This was an obvious expression of her image of the event.

**object permanence** The Piagetian term for one of an infant's most important accomplishments: understanding that objects and events continue to exist even when they cannot directly be seen, heard, or touched.

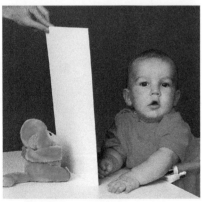

## FIGURE 6.3

**OBJECT PERMANENCE.** Piaget argued that object permanence is one of infancy's landmark cognitive accomplishments. For this 5-month-old boy, out of sight is literally out of mind. The infant looks at the toy monkey (*top*), but when his view of the toy is blocked (*bottom*), he does not search for it. Several months later, he will search for the hidden toy monkey, reflecting the presence of object permanence.

**Object Permanence** Imagine how chaotic and unpredictable your life would be if you could not distinguish between yourself and your world. This is what the life of a newborn must be like, according to Piaget. There is no differentiation between the self and world; objects have no separate, permanent existence.

By the end of the sensorimotor period, children understand that objects are both separate from the self and permanent. **Object permanence** is the understanding that objects and events continue to exist even when they cannot be seen, heard, or touched. Acquiring the sense of object permanence is one of the infant's most important accomplishments.

How can anyone know whether an infant has developed a sense of object permanence? The principal way that object permanence is studied is by watching an infant's reaction when an interesting object disappears (see Figure 6.3). If infants search for the object, it is assumed that they believe it continues to exist.

Object permanence is just one of the basic concepts about the physical world developed by babies. To Piaget, children—even infants—are much like little scientists, examining the world to see how it works, and they develop object permanence in a series of substages that correspond to the six substages of sensorimotor development (see Figure 6.4 ). But how can adult scientists determine what these "baby scientists" are finding out about the world and at what age they're finding it out? To answer this question, read the *Connecting Through Research* interlude that follows.

**Evaluating Piaget's Sensorimotor Stage** Piaget opened up a new way of looking at infants with his view that their main task is to coordinate their sensory impressions with their motor activity. However, the infant's cognitive world is not as neatly packaged as Piaget portrayed it, and some of Piaget's explanations for the cause of cognitive changes in development are debated. In the past several decades, sophisticated experimental techniques have been devised to study infants, and there have been a large number of research studies on infant development. Much of the new research suggests that Piaget's view of sensorimotor development needs to be modified (Baillargeon & others, 2012; 2011; de Hevia & Spelke, 2010; Diamond, 2013; Johnson, 2012; 2013; Meltzoff, 2011; Meltzoff & Williamson, 2013).

| Sensorimotor Stage | Age | Object permanence |
| --- | --- | --- |
| 2 First habits and primary circular reactions | 1–4 months | Infant will not search for object that is hidden from view |
| 3 Secondary circular reactions | 4–8 months | Infant will retrieve a partially concealed object |
| 4 Coordination of secondary circular reactions | 8–12 months | Infant will search for completely concealed object; A-not-B error occurs |
| 5 Tertiary circular reactions, novelty, and curiosity | 12–18 months | Infant will search for object where it was last seen; no invisible displacement |
| 6 Internalization of schemes | 18–24 months | Infant will search for concealed object, even if displaced out of sight; object permanence is complete, objects are mentally represented |

## FIGURE 6.4

**PIAGET'S STAGES OF OBJECT PERMANENCE WITH CORRESPONDING SUBSTAGES OF SENSORIMOTOR DEVELOPMENT,** Adapted from Piaget, J. (1970). "Piaget's theory." In P. H. Mussen (Ed.), *Carmichaels' Manual of Child Development,* (3rd edition, volume 1, pp. 703–732. New York: Wiley).

*The A-not-B Error*   One modification concerns Piaget's claim that certain processes are crucial in transitions from one stage to the next. The data do not always support his explanations. For example, in Piaget's theory, an important feature in the progression into substage 4, *coordination of secondary circular reactions,* is an infant's inclination to search for a hidden object in a familiar location rather than to look for the object in a new location. For example, if a toy is hidden twice, initially at location A and subsequently at location B, 8- to 12-month-old infants search correctly at location A initially. But when the toy is subsequently hidden at location B, they make the mistake of continuing to search for it at location A. **A-not-B error** (also called A-B error) is the term used to describe this common mistake. Older infants are less likely to make the A-not-B error because their concept of object permanence is more complete.

*Perceptual Development and Expectations*   A number of theorists, such as Eleanor Gibson (2001) and Elizabeth Spelke (2011), argue that infants' perceptual abilities are highly developed very early in life. Spelke concludes that young infants interpret the world as having predictable occurrences. For example, in Chapter 4 we discussed research that demonstrated the presence of intermodal perception—the ability to coordinate information from two or more sensory modalities, such as vision and hearing—by 3½ months of age, much earlier than Piaget would have predicted (Spelke & Owsley, 1979).

Research also suggests that infants develop the ability to understand how the world works at a very early age (Scott & Baillargeon, 2013). For example, by the time they are 3 to 4 months of age, infants develop expectations about future events. What kinds of expectations do infants form? Experiments by Spelke (1991, 2000; Spelke & Hespos, 2001) have addressed these questions. She placed babies before a puppet stage and showed them a series of actions that are unexpected if you know how the physical world works—for example, one ball seemed to roll through a solid barrier, another seemed to leap between two platforms, and a third appeared to hang in midair (Spelke, 1979). Spelke measured and compared the babies' looking times for unexpected and expected actions. She concluded that, by 4 months of age, even though infants do not yet have the ability to talk about objects, move and manipulate objects, or even see objects with high resolution, they expect objects to be solid and continuous. However, at 4 months of age, infants do not expect an object to obey gravitational constraints (Spelke & others, 1992). Similarly, research by Renée Baillargeon and her

**A-not-B error** Also called A-B error, this occurs when infants make the mistake of selecting the familiar hiding place (A) rather than the new hiding place (B) as they progress into substage 4 of Piaget's sensorimotor stage.

*developmental* **connection**

**Theories.** Eleanor Gibson was a pioneer in crafting the ecological perception view of development. Chapter 5, LO 2

## How Do Researchers Determine Infants' Understanding of Object Permanence and Causality?

Two accomplishments of infants that Piaget examined were the development of object permanence and the child's understanding of causality. Let's examine two research studies that address these topics.

In both studies, Canadian-born researcher Renée Baillargeon and her colleagues used a research method that involves *violation of expectations*. In this method, infants see an event happen as it normally would. Then, the event is changed in a way that violates what the infant expects to see. When infants look longer at the event that violates their expectations, it indicates they are surprised by it.

In one study focused on object permanence, researchers showed infants a toy car that moved down an inclined track, disappeared behind a screen, and then re-emerged at the other end, still on the track (Baillargeon & DeVoe, 1991) (see Figure 6.5a). After this sequence was repeated several times, something different occurred: A toy mouse was placed *behind* the tracks but was hidden by the screen while the car rolled by (b). This was the possible event. Then, the researchers created an impossible event: The toy mouse was placed *on* the tracks but was secretly removed after the screen was lowered so that the car seemed to go through the mouse (c). In this study, infants as young as 3½ months of age looked longer at the impossible event than at the possible event, indicating that they were surprised by it. Their surprise suggested that they remembered not only that the toy mouse still existed (object permanence) but its location.

Another study focused on infants' understanding of causality (Kotovsky & Baillargeon, 1994). In this research, a cylinder

rolls down a ramp and hits a toy bug at the bottom of the ramp. By 5½ and 6½ months of age, after infants have seen how far the bug will be pushed by a medium-sized cylinder, their reactions indicate that they understand that the bug will roll farther if it is hit by a large cylinder than if it is hit by a small cylinder. Thus, by the middle of the first year of life infants understand that the size of a moving object determines how far it will move a stationary object that it collides with.

In Baillargeon's (2008; Baillargeon & others, 2009; 2012; Luo & Baillargeon, 2010) view, infants have a pre-adapted, innate bias called the *principle of persistence* that explains their assumption that objects don't change their properties—including how solid they are, their location, their colour, and their form—unless some external factor (a person who moves the object, for example) obviously intervenes. Shortly, we will revisit the extent to which nature and nurture are at work in the changes that take place in the infant's cognitive development.

The research findings discussed in this interlude and other research indicate that infants develop object permanence and causal reasoning much earlier than Piaget proposed (Baillargeon, 2014; Baillargeon & others, 2009; 2012; Luo, Kaufman, & Baillargeon, 2009). Indeed, as you will see in the next section, a major theme of infant cognitive development today is that infants are more cognitively competent than Piaget envisioned.

*How do the methods described here to measure object permanence differ from the methods used by Piaget? Are both measures measuring the same construct?*

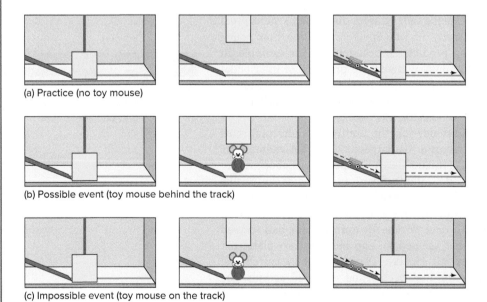

(a) Practice (no toy mouse)

(b) Possible event (toy mouse behind the track)

(c) Impossible event (toy mouse on the track)

## FIGURE 6.5

**USING THE VIOLATION OF EXPECTATIONS METHOD TO STUDY OBJECT PERMANENCE IN**

**INFANTS.** If infants looked longer at (c) than at (b), researchers reasoned that the impossible event in (c) violated the infants' expectations and that they remembered that the toy mouse existed. Researchers have found, however, that the A-not-B error does not show up consistently (Sophian, 1985). The evidence indicates that A-not-B errors are sensitive to the delay between hiding the object at B and the infant's attempt to find it (Diamond, 1985). Thus, the A-not-B error might be due to a failure in memory. Another explanation is that infants tend to repeat a previous motor behaviour (Clearfield & others, 2006).

colleagues (Baillargeon, 2008, 2014; Baillargeon & others, 2012) documents that infants as young as 3 to 4 months expect objects to be *substantial* (other objects cannot move through them) and *permanent* (objects continue to exist when they are hidden).

However, some critics, such as Andrew Meltzoff (2008; Moore & Meltzoff, 2008), argue that Spelke's and Baillargeon's research relies on how long infants look at unexpected events and thus assesses infants' *perceptual expectations* about where and when objects will reappear rather than tapping their *knowledge* about where the objects are when they are out of sight. Meltzoff points out that whether infants act on their perception is an important aspect of assessing object permanence and states that it does not appear that young infants can act on the information. Thus, Meltzoff (2008) concludes, it is still unclear whether longer looking time is a valid measure of object permanence and how early infants develop object permanence.

By 6 to 8 months, infants have learned to perceive gravity and support—that an object hanging on the end of a table should fall, that ball bearings will travel farther when rolled down a longer rather than a shorter ramp, and that cup handles will not fall when attached to a cup (Slater, Field, & Hernandez-Reif, 2007). As infants develop, their experiences with and actions on objects help them to understand physical laws (Bremner, 2007).

*The Nature–Nurture Issue*  In considering the big issue of whether nature or nurture plays the more important role in infant development, Elizabeth Spelke (Hyde & Spelke, 2012; Spelke, Bernier, & Snedeker, 2013; Spelke & Kinzler, 2009) comes down clearly on the side of nature. Spelke endorses a **core knowledge approach**, which states that infants are born with domain-specific innate knowledge systems. Among these domain-specific knowledge systems are those involving space, number sense, object permanence, and language (which we will discuss later in this chapter). Strongly influenced by evolution, the core knowledge domains are theorized to be prewired to allow infants to make sense of their world. After all, Spelke asks, how could infants possibly grasp the complex world in which they live if they didn't come into the world equipped with core sets of knowledge? In this approach, the innate core knowledge domains form a foundation around which more mature cognitive functioning and learning develop. The core knowledge approach argues that Piaget greatly underestimated the cognitive abilities of infants, especially young infants.

An intriguing domain of core knowledge that has been investigated in young infants is whether they have a sense of number. Spelke concludes that they do. Using the violations of expectations method discussed in the *Connecting Through Research* interlude, Karen Wynn (1992) conducted an early experiment on infants' sense of number (see Figure 6.6). Five-month-old infants were shown one or two Mickey Mouse dolls on a puppet stage. Then the experimenter hid the doll(s) behind a screen and visibly removed or added one. Next, when the screen was lifted, the infants looked longer when they saw the incorrect number of dolls. Spelke and her colleagues (de Hevia & Spelke, 2010; Hyde & Spelke, 2009, 2011; Izard & Spelke, 2010; Lipton & Spelke, 2004; Spelke & Kinsler, 2007; Xu, Spelke, & Goddard, 2005) have found that infants can distinguish between different numbers of objects, actions, and sounds. Not everyone agrees with Spelke's conclusions about young infants' math skills (Cohen, 2002). One criticism is that infants in the number experiments are merely responding to changes in the display that violated their expectations.

In criticizing the core knowledge approach, British developmental psychologist Mark Johnston (2008) says that the infants Spelke assesses in her research already have accumulated hundreds, and in some cases even thousands, of hours

A 4-month-old in Elizabeth Spelke's infant perception laboratory is tested to determine if she knows that an object in motion will not stop in midair. Spelke concluded that at 4 months babies don't expect objects like these balls to obey gravitational constraints, but that they do expect objects to be solid and continuous. Research by Spelke, Renée Baillargeon, and others suggest that infants develop an ability to understand how the world works earlier than Piaget envisioned. However, critics such as Andrew Meltzoff fault their research and conclude there is still controversy about how early some infant cognitive accomplishments occur.

**core knowledge approach** States that infants are born with domain-specific innate knowledge systems, such as those involving space, number sense, object permanence, and language.

*developmental* **connection**

**Nature–Nurture.** The nature–nurture issue involves the debate about whether development is primarily influenced by nature (biological inheritance) or nurture (environmental experiences). Chapter 1, LO 2; Chapter 2, LO 4

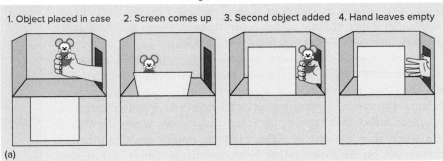

Original event

1. Object placed in case    2. Screen comes up    3. Second object added    4. Hand leaves empty

(a)

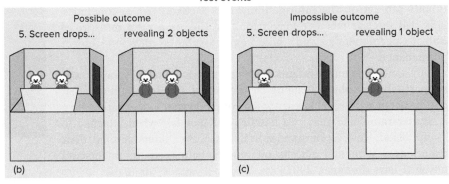

Test events

Possible outcome

5. Screen drops...    revealing 2 objects

(b)

Impossible outcome

5. Screen drops...    revealing 1 object

(c)

## FIGURE 6.6

**INFANTS' NUMBER SENSE.** Shown here is one of the sequences in Karen Wynn's (1992) study of 5-month-old infants' number sense. The experimenter was hidden behind the display and manipulated the objects through a trap door in the wall of the display. Five-month-old infants who saw the impossible event (only one Mickey Mouse doll) looked longer at the event than their 5-month-old counterparts who saw the possible event (two dolls). Reprinted by permission from Macmillan Publishers Ltd: *Nature,* 358, pp. 749–750, "Addition and subtraction by human infants" by Karen Wynn. Copyright © 1992.

*What revisions in Piaget's theory of sensorimotor development do contemporary researchers conclude need to be made?*

of experience in grasping what the world is about, which gives considerable room for the environment's role in the development of infant cognition (Highfield, 2008). According to Johnston (2008), infants likely come into the world with "soft biases to perceive and attend to different aspects of the environment, and to learn about the world in particular ways." Although debate about the cause and course of infant cognitive development continues, most developmentalists today agree that Piaget underestimated the early cognitive accomplishments of infants and that both nature and nurture are involved in infants' cognitive development.

*Conclusions* In sum, many researchers conclude that Piaget wasn't specific enough about how infants learn about their world and that infants, especially young infants, are more competent than Piaget thought (Bauer, 2013; Johnson, 2013; Rakison & Lawson, 2013). As they have examined the specific ways that infants learn, the field of infant cognition has become very specialized. Many researchers are at work on different questions, with no general theory emerging that can connect all of the different findings (Nelson, 1999). Their theories often are local theories, focused on specific research questions, rather than grand theories like Piaget's (Kuhn, 1998). If there is a unifying theme, it is that investigators in infant development seek to understand more precisely how developmental changes in cognition take place and to explore the big issue of nature and nurture (Aslin, 2009; Woodward & Needham, 2009). As they seek to identify more precisely the contributions of nature and nurture to infant development, researchers face the difficult task of determining whether the course of acquiring information, which is very rapid in some domains, is best accounted for by an innate set of biases (that is, core knowledge) or by the extensive input of environmental experiences to which the infant is exposed (Aslin, 2009, 2012). Recall from Chapter 1 that exploring connections between brain, cognition, and development involves the recently emerging field of developmental cognitive neuroscience (Bauer, 2013; Diamond, 2013; Morasch & others, 2013).

# PREOPERATIONAL STAGE

The cognitive world of the preschool child is creative, free, and fanciful. The imaginations of preschool children work overtime, and their mental grasp of the world improves. Piaget described the preschool child's cognition as *preoperational*. What did he mean?

Because Piaget called this stage preoperational, it might sound unimportant. Not so. Preoperational thought is anything but a convenient waiting period for the next stage, concrete operational thought. However, the label *preoperational* emphasizes that the child does not yet perform **operations**, which are internalized actions that allow children to do mentally what they could formerly do only physically. Operations are reversible mental actions. Mentally adding and subtracting numbers are examples of operations. *Preoperational thought* is the beginning of the ability to reconstruct in thought what has been established in behaviour.

The **preoperational stage**, which lasts from approximately 2 to 7 years of age, is the second Piagetian stage. In this stage, children begin to represent the world with words, images, and drawings. Symbolic thought goes beyond simple connections of sensory information and physical action. Stable concepts are formed, mental reasoning emerges, egocentrism is present, and magical beliefs are constructed. Preoperational thought can be divided into substages: the symbolic function substage and the intuitive thought substage.

**The Symbolic Function Substage** The **symbolic function substage** is the first substage of preoperational thought, occurring roughly between the ages of 2 and 4. In this substage, the young child gains the ability to mentally represent an object that is not actually present. This ability vastly expands the child's mental world (Carlson & Zelazo, 2008; Deloache, 2011). Young children use scribble designs to represent people, houses, cars, clouds, and so on; they begin to use language and engage in pretend play. However, although young children make distinct progress during this substage, their thought still has several important limitations, two of which are egocentrism and animism.

**Egocentrism** is the inability to distinguish between one's own perspective and someone else's perspective. The following telephone conversation between 4-year-old Mary, who is at home, and her father, who is at work, typifies Mary's egocentric thought:

> *Father:* Mary, is Mommy there?
> *Mary:* (Silently nods)
> *Father:* Mary, may I speak to Mommy?
> *Mary:* (Nods again silently)

Mary's response is egocentric in that she fails to consider her father's perspective before replying. A non-egocentric thinker would have responded verbally.

Piaget and Barbel Inhelder (1969) initially studied young children's egocentrism by devising the three-mountains task (see Figure 6.7). The child walks around the model of the mountains and becomes familiar with what the mountains look like from different perspectives, and she can see that there are different objects on the mountains. The child is then seated on one side of the table on which the mountains are placed. The experimenter moves a doll to different locations around the table, at each location asking the child to select

**operations** Internalized actions that allow children to do mentally what before they had done only physically. Operations also are reversible mental actions.

**preoperational stage** The second Piagetian developmental stage, which lasts from about 2 to 7 years of age, when children begin to represent the world with words, images, and drawings.

**symbolic function substage** The first substage of preoperational thought, occurring roughly between the ages of 2 and 4. In this substage, the young child gains the ability to represent mentally an object that is not present.

**egocentrism** An important feature of preoperational thought: the inability to distinguish between one's own and someone else's perspective.

**Model of Mountains**

Photo 1
(View from A)

Photo 2
(View from B)

Photo 3
(View from C)

Photo 4
(View from D)

## FIGURE 6.7

**THE THREE-MOUNTAINS TASK.** The mountain model on the far left shows the child's perspective from view A, where he or she is sitting. The four squares represent photos showing the mountains from four different viewpoints of the model—A, B, C, and D. The experimenter asks the child to identify the photo in which the mountains look as they would from position B. To identify the photo correctly, the child has to take the perspective of a person sitting at spot B. Invariably, a child who thinks in a preoperational way cannot perform this task. When asked what a view of the mountains looks like from position B, the child selects photo 1, taken from location A (the child's own view at the time) instead of photo 2, the correct view.

**animism** A facet of preoperational thought: the belief that inanimate objects have lifelike qualities and are capable of action.

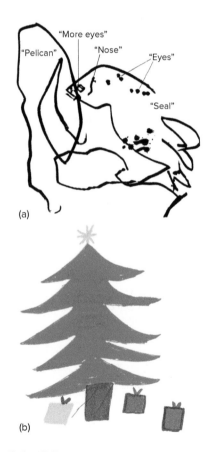

(a)

(b)

## FIGURE 6.8

**THE SYMBOLIC DRAWINGS OF YOUNG CHILDREN.** (*a*) A 3½-year-old's symbolic drawing. Halfway into this drawing, the 3½-year-old artist said it was "a pelican kissing a seal." (*b*) This 11-year-old's drawing is neater and more realistic but also less inventive.

from a series of photos the one photo that most accurately reflects the view the doll is seeing. Children in the preoperational stage often pick their own view rather than the doll's view. Preschool children frequently show perspective skills on some tasks but not others.

**Animism**, another limitation of preoperational thought, is the belief that inanimate objects have lifelike qualities and are capable of action (Gelman & Opfer, 2004; Opfer & Gelman, 2011). A young child might show animism by saying, "That tree pushed the leaf off, and it fell down" or "The sidewalk made me mad; it made me fall down." A young child who uses animism fails to distinguish the appropriate occasions for using human and nonhuman perspectives.

Possibly because young children are not very concerned about reality, their drawings are fanciful and inventive. Suns are blue, skies are yellow, and cars float on clouds in their symbolic, imaginative world. One 3½-year-old looked at a scribble he had just drawn and described it as a pelican kissing a seal (see Figure 6.8a). The symbolism is simple but strong, like abstractions found in some modern art. Twentieth-century Spanish artist Pablo Picasso commented, "I used to draw like Raphael but it has taken me a lifetime to draw like young children." In the elementary school years, a child's drawings become more realistic, neat, and precise (see Figure 6.8b). Suns are yellow, skies are blue, and cars travel on roads (Winner, 1986). To learn about the role of symbolic thought in children's play, see *Connecting to Current Controversy*.

**The Intuitive Thought Substage** The **intuitive thought substage** is the second substage of preoperational thought, occurring between approximately 4 and 7 years of age. In this substage, children begin to use primitive reasoning and want to know the answers to all sorts of questions. Consider 4-year-old Tommy, who is at the beginning of the intuitive thought substage. Although he is starting to develop his own ideas about the world he lives in, his ideas are still simple, and he is not very good at thinking things out. He has difficulty understanding events that he knows are taking place but that he cannot see. His fantasized thoughts bear little resemblance to reality. He cannot yet answer the question "What if?" in any reliable way. For example, he has only a vague idea of what would happen if a car were to hit him. He also has difficulty negotiating traffic because he cannot do the mental calculations necessary to estimate whether an approaching car will hit him when he crosses the road.

By the age of 5, children have just about exhausted the adults around them with "why" questions. The child's questions signal the emergence of interest in reasoning and in figuring out why things are the way they are. Following are some samples of the questions children ask during the questioning period of 4 to 6 years of age (Elkind, 1976):

"What makes you grow up?"

"What makes you stop growing?"

"Why does a lady have to be married to have a baby?"

"Who was the mother when everybody was a baby?"

"Why do leaves fall?"

"Why does the sun shine?"

Piaget called this substage *intuitive* because young children seem so sure about their knowledge and understanding yet are unaware of how they know what they know. That is, they know something but know it without the use of rational thinking.

### Centration and the Limitations of Preoperational Thought

One limitation of preoperational thought is **centration**, a centring of attention on one characteristic to the exclusion of all others. Centration is most clearly evidenced in young children's lack of **conservation**, the awareness that altering an object's or a substance's appearance does not change its basic properties. For example, to adults, it is obvious that a certain amount of liquid stays the same, regardless of a container's shape. But this is not at all obvious to young children. Instead, they are struck by the height of the liquid in the container; they focus on that characteristic to the exclusion of others.

The situation that Piaget devised to study conservation is his most famous task. In the conservation task, a child is presented with two identical beakers, each filled to the same level with liquid (see Figure 6.9). The child is asked if these beakers have the same amount of liquid, and she usually says "yes." Then the liquid from one beaker is poured into a third beaker, which is taller and thinner than the first two. The child is then asked if the amount of liquid in the tall, thin beaker is equal to that which remains in one of the original beakers. Children who are less than 7 or 8 years old usually say "no" and justify their answers in terms of the differing height or width of the beakers. Older

**intuitive thought substage** The second substage of preoperational thought, occurring between approximately 4 and 7 years of age, when children begin to use primitive reasoning.

**centration** Focusing attention on one characteristic to the exclusion of all others.

**conservation** The idea that altering an object's or substance's appearance does not change its basic properties.

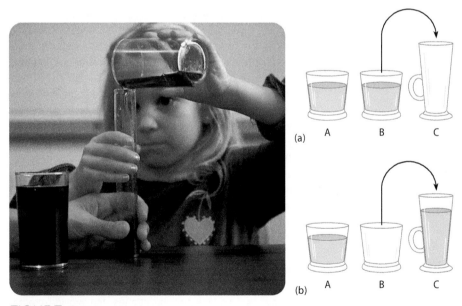

## FIGURE 6.9

**PIAGET'S CONSERVATION TASK.** The beaker test is a well-known Piagetian task to determine whether a child can think operationally—that is, can mentally reverse actions and show conservation of the substance. (*a*) Two identical beakers are presented to the child. Then, the experimenter pours the liquid from B into C, which is taller and thinner than A or B. (*b*) The child is asked if these beakers (A and C) have the same amount of liquid. The preoperational child says "no." When asked to point to the beaker that has more liquid, the preoperational child points to the tall, thin beaker.

children usually answer "yes" and justify their answers appropriately ("If you poured the water back, the amount would still be the same").

In Piaget's theory, failing the conservation-of-liquid task is a sign that children are at the preoperational stage of cognitive development. The preoperational child fails to show conservation not only of liquid but also of number, matter, length, volume, and area. Figure 6.10 portrays several of these dimensions of conservation.

Children often vary in their performance on different conservation tasks. Thus, a child might be able to conserve volume but not number. Recently, researchers have discovered links between children's number conservation and the brain's development (Poirel & others, 2012). A recent fMRI brain imaging study of conservation of number revealed that advances in a network in the parietal and frontal lobes were linked to 9- and 10-year-olds' conservation success when compared to non-conserving 5- and 6-year-olds (Houde & others, 2011).

Some developmentalists do not believe Piaget was entirely correct in his estimate of when children's conservation skills emerge. For example, Rochel Gelman (1969) showed that when the child's attention to relevant aspects of the conservation task is improved, the child is more likely to conserve. Gelman has also demonstrated that attentional training on one dimension, such as number, improves the preschool child's performance on another dimension, such as mass. Thus, Gelman suggests that conservation appears earlier than Piaget thought and that attention is especially important in explaining conservation.

> "Play is the answer to how anything new comes about."
>
> —JEAN PIAGET

## connecting to current controversy

### The Declining Rates of Unstructured Free Play and the Importance of Pretend Play

Media reports frequently question the wisdom of filling children's schedules with too many structured after-school and weekend activities, thereby reducing children's amount of unstructured free play. It is well documented that children have less time to engage in free play (Elkind, 2007; Hirsh-Pasek, Golonkoff, Berk, & Singer, 2009; Hofferth & Sandberg, 2010). For example, Hofferth and Sandberg (2010) found that over the last two decades, free time declined by 12 hours per week for North American children aged 3 to 12 years old. Further, general playtime decreased by 3 hours per week and unstructured outdoor activities declined by 50 percent. Unstructured free play has decreased in educational settings as well (Russ & Dillon, 2011) as educators are pressured to meet academic outcomes. Thus, statistics support media reports that today's children have less unstructured free play than previous generations. This decrease in unstructured free play may reduce the amount of pretend, or symbolic play in which children engage.

Pretend play is defined as "a symbolic behaviour in which one thing is playfully treated as if it were something else" (Fein, 1987, p. 282). Pretend play begins to occur around the later part of Piaget's sensorimotor stage of development, but really hits a peak during the second year of life, with the increased emergence of symbolic thought. During the preoperational stage of development, toddlers begin to represent their world with words, images, and drawings, and we see this emerging ability through make-believe tea parties, and the use of one object, such as a banana, to symbolize another object, such as a telephone. According to Piaget (1967), pretend play provides insight into children's developing cognitive schemes, and illustrates the process of assimilation. For example, children assimilate a banana into what they know about the function of telephones.

There is an abundance of evidence illustrating that pretend play is linked with positive outcomes in cognitive, social, and emotional development (Copple & Bredekamp, 2009). For example, pretend play is related to the development of theory of mind (Goldstein & Winner, 2012), executive function (Kelly, Hammond, Dissanayake, & Ihsen, 2011) and social competence (Lindsay & Colwell, 2013). However, not all researchers agree that these relations are causal. Smith (2010) suggests three possible theoretical explanations for these relations: pretend play is crucial to optimal development; pretend play contributes to some development, but is only one route to optimal development; or pretend play is simply a by-product of other developing skills and makes no real contribution to development. In a recent review of over 50 years of research, Lillard and colleagues (2013) concluded that the evidence across domains does not conclusively support the conclusion that pretend play is crucial to optimal development. However, Walker and Gopnik (2013) suggest a fourth possible theoretical explanation, suggesting that pretend play may emerge as a result of other developing skills, but then contributes to the optimal development of those skills. It is also possible that the nature of the relation between pretend play and development differs depending on which aspect of development is being examined. Further research with longitudinal designs and training studies can provide greater insight into these causal relations.

*How would pretend play look in each of Piaget's stages of cognitive development? How would pretend play differ in each stage?*

# CONCRETE OPERATIONAL STAGE

The **concrete operational stage**, which lasts from approximately 7 to 11 years of age, is the third Piagetian stage. In this stage, logical reasoning replaces intuitive reasoning as long as the reasoning can be applied to specific or concrete examples. For instance, concrete operational thinkers cannot imagine the steps necessary to complete an algebraic equation, which is too abstract for thinking at this stage of development. Children at this stage can perform *concrete operations*, which are reversible mental actions on real, concrete objects.

**concrete operational stage** Piaget's third stage, which lasts from approximately 7 to 11 years of age, when children can perform concrete operations, and logical reasoning replaces intuitive reasoning as long as the reasoning can be applied to specific or concrete examples.

**Conservation**    The conservation tasks demonstrate a child's ability to perform concrete operations. In the test of reversibility of thought involving conservation of matter (shown in Figure 6.10), a child is presented with two identical balls of clay. An experimenter rolls one ball into a long, thin shape; the other remains in its original ball shape. The child is then asked if there is more clay in the ball or in the long, thin piece of clay. By the time children reach the age 7 or 8, most answer that the amount of clay is the same. To answer this problem correctly, children have to imagine the clay ball rolling back into a ball after it has been changed into a long, thin shape; they have mentally reversed the action on the ball.

Concrete operations allow children to coordinate several characteristics rather than focus on a single property of an object. In the clay example, a preoperational child is likely to focus on height or width; a concrete operational child coordinates information about both dimensions. Conservation involves recognition that the length, number, mass, quantity, area, weight, and volume of objects and substances are not changed by transformations that merely alter their appearance.

Children do not conserve all quantities or conserve on all tasks simultaneously. The order of their mastery is number, length, liquid quantity, mass, weight, and volume. **Horizontal décalage** is Piaget's concept that similar abilities do not appear at the same time within a stage of development. During the concrete operational stage, conservation of number usually appears first and conservation of volume last. Also, an 8-year-old child may know that a long stick of clay can be rolled back into a ball but not understand that the ball and the stick weigh the same. At about 9 years of age, the child recognizes that they weigh the same, and eventually, at about 11 to 12 years of age, the child understands that the clay's volume is unchanged by rearranging it. Children initially master tasks in which the dimensions are more salient and visible, only later mastering those not as visually apparent, such as volume.

**horizontal décalage** Piaget's concept that similar abilities do not appear at the same time within a stage of development.

| Type of Conservation | Initial Presentation | Manipulation | Preoperational Child's Answer |
|---|---|---|---|
| Number | Two identical rows of objects are shown to the child, who agrees they have the same number. | One row is lengthened and the child is asked whether one row now has more objects. | Yes, the longer row. |
| Matter | Two identical balls of clay are shown to the child. The child agrees that they are equal. | The experimenter changes the shape of one of the balls and asks the child whether they still contain equal amounts of clay. | No, the longer one has more. |
| Length | Two sticks are aligned in front of the child. The child agrees that they are the same length. | The experimenter moves one stick to the right, then asks the child if they are equal in length. | No, the one on the top is longer. |

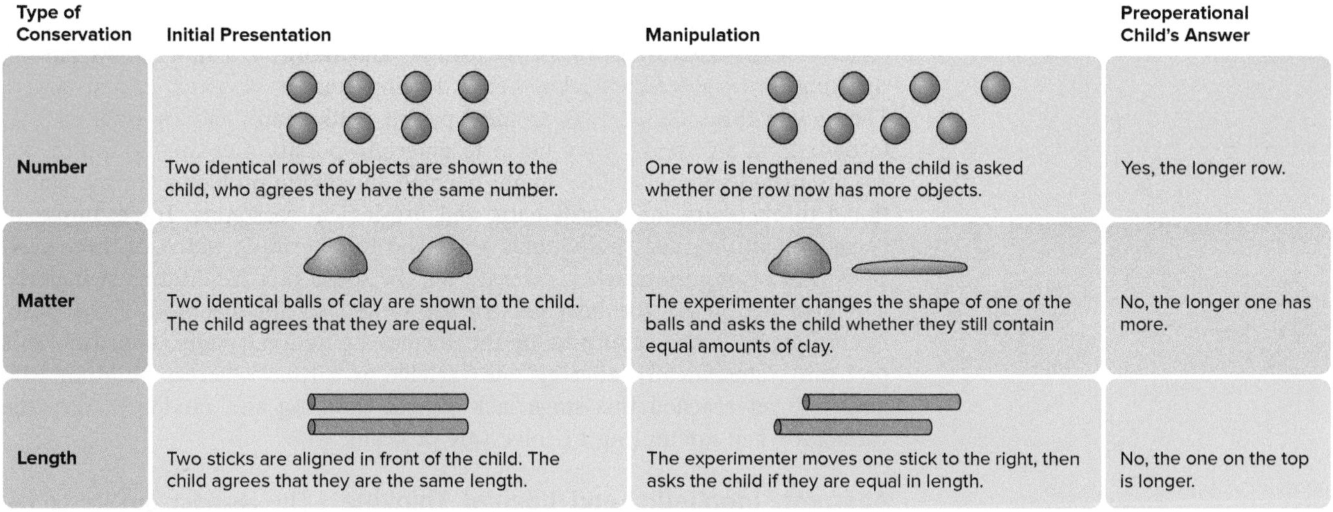

## FIGURE 6.10

**SOME DIMENSIONS OF CONSERVATION: NUMBER, MATTER, AND LENGTH.** *What characteristics of preoperational thought do children demonstrate when they fail these conservation tasks?*

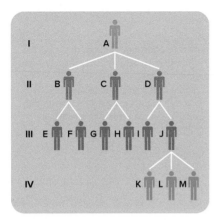

FIGURE **6.11**

**CLASSIFICATION: AN IMPORTANT ABILITY IN CONCRETE OPERATIONAL THOUGHT.** A family tree of four generations (I to IV): The preoperational child has trouble classifying the members of the four generations; the concrete operational child can classify the members vertically, horizontally, and obliquely (up and down and across). For example, the concrete operational child understands that a family member can be a son, a brother, and a father, all at the same time.

**seriation** The concrete operation that involves ordering stimuli along a quantitative dimension (such as length).

**transitivity** Principle that if a relation holds between a first object and a second object, and holds between the second object and a third object, then it holds between the first object and the third object. Piaget argued that an understanding of transitivity is characteristic of concrete operational thought.

**formal operational stage** Piaget's fourth and final stage, which occurs between the ages of 11 and 15, when individuals move beyond concrete experiences and think in more abstract and logical ways.

**Classification**   Many of the concrete operations identified by Piaget involve the ways children reason about the properties of objects. One important skill that characterizes children in the concrete operational stage is the ability to classify things and to consider their relationships. Specifically, concrete operational children can understand (1) the interrelationships among sets and subsets, (2) seriation, and (3) transitivity.

The ability of the concrete operational child to divide things into sets and subsets and understand their relationships is illustrated by a family tree of four generations (Furth & Wachs, 1975) (see Figure 6.11). This family tree suggests that the grandfather (A) has three children (B, C, and D), each of whom has two children (E through J), and that one of these children (J) has three children (K, L, and M). The concrete operational child understands that person J can, at the same time, be father, brother, and grandson. A child who comprehends this classification system can move up and down a level (vertically), across a level (horizontally), and up and down and across (obliquely) within the system.

**Seriation** is the ordering of stimuli along a quantitative dimension (such as length). To see if children can serialize, a teacher might haphazardly place eight sticks of varying lengths on a table. The teacher then asks the children to order the sticks by length. Many young children put the sticks into two or three small groups of "big" sticks or "little" sticks, rather than a correct ordering of all eight sticks. Or they line up the tops of the sticks but ignore the bottoms. The concrete operational thinker simultaneously understands that each stick must be longer than the one that precedes it and shorter than the one that follows it.

**Transitivity** involves the ability to reason about and logically combine relationships. If a relation holds between a first object and a second object, and also holds between the second object and a third object, then it also holds between the first and third objects. For example, consider three sticks (A, B, and C) of differing lengths. A is the longest, B is intermediate in length, and C is the shortest. Does the child understand that if A is longer than B, and B is longer than C, then A is longer than C? In Piaget's theory, concrete operational thinkers do and preoperational thinkers do not.

## FORMAL OPERATIONAL STAGE

So far we have studied the first three of Piaget's stages of cognitive development: sensorimotor, preoperational, and concrete operational. What are the characteristics of the fourth stage?

The **formal operational stage**, which appears between 11 and 15 years of age, is the fourth and final Piagetian stage. In this stage, individuals move beyond concrete experiences and think in abstract and more logical ways. As part of thinking more abstractly, adolescents develop images of ideal circumstances. They might think about what an ideal parent is like and compare their parents to their ideal standards. They begin to entertain possibilities for the future and are fascinated with what they might become. In solving problems, formal operational thinkers are more systematic and use logical reasoning. For example, in Piaget's pendulum task, individuals are asked to determine which of three variables is most important when determining the speed of a pendulum's swing—the length of the string, the heaviness of the weight, or the strength of the push. According to Piaget, children in the formal operational stage approach this problem systematically, altering one variable at a time, whereas children who have not yet reached this stage lack logical thinking and randomly vary the variables when attempting to solve this problem.

**Abstract, Idealistic, and Logical Thinking**   The abstract quality of the adolescent's thought at the formal operational level is evident in the adolescent's verbal problem-solving ability. The concrete operational thinker needs to see the concrete elements A, B, and C to be able to make the logical inference that if

A = B and B = C, then A = C. The formal operational thinker can solve this problem merely through verbal presentation.

Another indication of the abstract quality of adolescents' thought is their increased tendency to think about thought itself. One adolescent commented, "I began thinking about why I was thinking about what I was. Then I began thinking about why I was thinking about what I was thinking about what I was." If this sounds abstract, it is, and it characterizes the adolescent's enhanced focus on thought and its abstract qualities.

Accompanying the abstract thought of adolescence is thought full of idealism and possibilities. While children frequently think in concrete ways, or in terms of what is real and limited, adolescents begin to engage in extended speculation about ideal characteristics—qualities they desire in themselves and in others. Such thoughts often lead adolescents to compare themselves with others in regard to ideal standards. And the thoughts of adolescents are often fantasy flights into future possibilities. It is not unusual for the adolescent to become impatient with these newfound ideal standards and to become perplexed over which of many ideal standards to adopt.

*Might adolescents' ability to reason hypothetically and to evaluate what is ideal versus what is real lead them to engage in demonstrations, such as this protest related to improving education? What other causes might be attractive to adolescents' newfound cognitive abilities of hypothetical-deductive reasoning and idealistic thinking?*

As adolescents are learning to think more abstractly and idealistically, they are also learning to think more logically. Children are likely to solve problems in a trial-and-error fashion. Adolescents begin to think more as a scientist thinks, devising plans to solve problems and systematically testing solutions. They use **hypothetical-deductive reasoning**, which means that they develop hypotheses, or best guesses, and systematically deduce, or conclude, which is the best path to follow in solving the problem.

Assimilation (incorporating new information into existing knowledge) dominates the initial development of formal operational thought, and these thinkers perceive the world subjectively and idealistically. Later in adolescence, as intellectual balance is restored, these individuals accommodate to the cognitive upheaval that has occurred (they adjust to the new information).

Some of Piaget's ideas on formal operational thought are being challenged (Blakemore & Mills, 2014; Diamond, Casey, & Munakata, 2011; Kuhn, 2009; 2011). There is much more individual variation in formal operational thought than Piaget envisioned. Only about one in three young adolescents is a formal operational thinker. Many adults never become formal operational thinkers.

**hypothetical-deductive reasoning** Piaget's formal operational concept that adolescents have the cognitive ability to develop hypotheses about ways to solve problems and can systematically deduce which is the best path to follow in solving the problem.

**Adolescent Egocentrism**  In addition to thinking more logically, abstractly, and idealistically—characteristics of Piaget's formal operational thought stage—in what other ways do adolescents change cognitively? David Elkind (1978) has described how adolescent egocentrism governs the way that adolescents think about social matters. **Adolescent egocentrism** is the heightened self-consciousness of adolescents, which is reflected in their belief that others are as interested in them as they are in themselves, and in their sense of personal uniqueness and invincibility. Elkind proposes that adolescent egocentrism can be dissected into two types of social thinking—imaginary audience and personal fable.

The **imaginary audience** refers to the aspect of adolescent egocentrism that involves attention-getting behaviour—the attempt to be noticed, visible, and "onstage." An adolescent boy might think that others are as aware of a few hairs that are out of place as he is. An adolescent girl walks into her classroom and thinks that all eyes are riveted on her complexion. Adolescents especially sense that they are onstage in early adolescence, believing they are the main actors and all others are the audience.

**adolescent egocentrism** The heightened self-consciousness of adolescents, which is reflected in adolescents' beliefs that others are as interested in them as they are in themselves, and in adolescents' sense of personal uniqueness and invulnerability.

**imaginary audience** The aspect of adolescent egocentrism that involves attention-getting behaviour motivated by a desire to be noticed, visible, and "onstage."

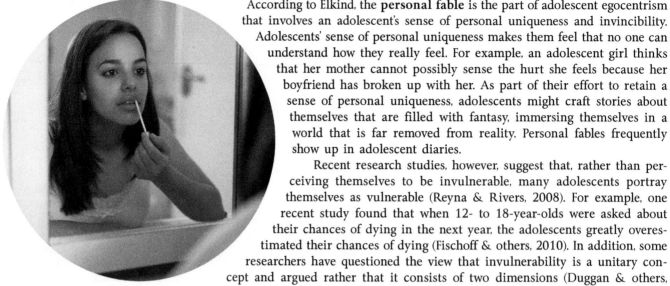

Many adolescent girls spend long hours in front of the mirror, depleting cans of hairspray, tubes of lipstick, and jars of cosmetics. *How might this behaviour be related to changes in adolescent cognitive and physical development?*

**personal fable** The part of adolescent egocentrism that involves an adolescent's sense of uniqueness and invincibility.

According to Elkind, the **personal fable** is the part of adolescent egocentrism that involves an adolescent's sense of personal uniqueness and invincibility. Adolescents' sense of personal uniqueness makes them feel that no one can understand how they really feel. For example, an adolescent girl thinks that her mother cannot possibly sense the hurt she feels because her boyfriend has broken up with her. As part of their effort to retain a sense of personal uniqueness, adolescents might craft stories about themselves that are filled with fantasy, immersing themselves in a world that is far removed from reality. Personal fables frequently show up in adolescent diaries.

Recent research studies, however, suggest that, rather than perceiving themselves to be invulnerable, many adolescents portray themselves as vulnerable (Reyna & Rivers, 2008). For example, one recent study found that when 12- to 18-year-olds were asked about their chances of dying in the next year, the adolescents greatly overestimated their chances of dying (Fischoff & others, 2010). In addition, some researchers have questioned the view that invulnerability is a unitary concept and argued rather that it consists of two dimensions (Duggan & others, 2000; Lapsley & Hill, 2010):

- *Danger invulnerability,* which involves adolescents' sense of indestructibility and tendency to take on physical risks (driving recklessly at high speeds, for example)
- *Psychological invulnerability,* which captures an adolescent's felt invulnerability related to personal or psychological distress (getting one's feelings hurt, for example).

A recent study revealed that adolescents who scored high on a danger invulnerability scale were more likely to engage in juvenile delinquency, substance abuse, or be depressed (Lapsley & Hill, 2010). In this study, adolescents who scored high on psychological invulnerability were less likely to be depressed, had higher self-esteem, and engaged in better interpersonal relationships. In terms of psychological invulnerability, adolescents often benefit from the normal developmental challenges of exploring identity options, making new friends, asking someone to go out on a date, and learning a new skill. All of these important adolescent tasks involve risk and failure as an option, but if successful result in enhanced self-image.

In the view of Daniel Lapsley and his colleagues (Hill, Duggan, & Lapsley, 2012; Lapsley & Stey, 2012), the separation-individuation process—which involves adolescents separating from their parents and developing independence and identity—is responsible for the findings just discussed, rather than cognitive developmental changes. With respect to personal fables, they argue that invulnerability and personal uniqueness are forms of adolescent narcissism.

## Review *Connect* Reflect

 **L01** Discuss the key processes and four stages in Piaget's theory.

### Review

- What are the key processes in Piaget's theory of cognitive development?
- What are the main characteristics of the sensorimotor stage? What revisions of Piaget's sensorimotor stage have been proposed?
- What are the main characteristics of the preoperational stage?
- What are the main characteristics of the concrete operational stage?
- What are the main characteristics of the formal operational stage? How has Piaget's formal operational stage been criticized?

### *Connect*

- How does Piaget's sensorimotor stage relate to what you learned about perceptual–motor coupling in Chapter 5?

### **Reflect** *Your Own Personal Journey of Life*

- Do you consider yourself to be a formal operational thinker? Do you still sometimes feel like a concrete operational thinker? Give examples.

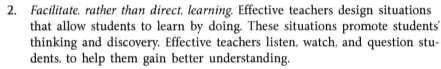

| Piaget and Education | Evaluating Piaget's Theory |

What are some applications of Piaget's theory to education? What are the main contributions and criticisms of Piaget's theory?

## PIAGET AND EDUCATION

Piaget was not an educator, but he provided a sound conceptual framework for viewing learning and education. Following are some ideas in Piaget's theory that can be applied to teaching children (Elkind, 1976; Heuwinkel, 1996):

*What are some educational strategies that can be derived from Piaget's theory?*

1. *Take a constructivist approach.* Piaget emphasized that children learn best when they are active and seek solutions for themselves. Piaget opposed teaching methods that treat children as passive receptacles. The educational implication of Piaget's view is that, in all subjects, students learn best by making discoveries, reflecting on them, and discussing them, rather than blindly imitating the teacher or doing things by rote.

2. *Facilitate, rather than direct, learning.* Effective teachers design situations that allow students to learn by doing. These situations promote students' thinking and discovery. Effective teachers listen, watch, and question students, to help them gain better understanding.

3. *Consider the child's knowledge and level of thinking.* Students do not come to class with empty minds. They have many ideas about the physical and natural world. They have concepts of space, time, quantity, and causality. These ideas differ from the ideas of adults. Teachers need to interpret what a student is saying and respond in a way that is not too far from the student's level. Also, Piaget suggested that it is important to examine children's mistakes in thinking, not just what they get correct, to help guide them to a higher level of understanding.

4. *Promote the student's intellectual health.* For Piaget, children's learning should occur naturally. Children should not be pushed and pressured into achieving too much too early in their development, before they are maturationally ready. Some parents spend long hours every day holding up large flash cards with words on them to improve their baby's vocabulary. In the Piagetian view, this is not the best way for infants to learn. It places too much emphasis on speeding up intellectual development, involves passive learning, and will not lead to positive outcomes.

5. *Turn the classroom into a setting of exploration and discovery.* What do actual classrooms look like when the teachers adopt Piaget's views? Several first- and second-grade math classrooms provide some examples (Kamii, 1985, 1989). The teachers emphasize students' own exploration and discovery. The classrooms are less structured than what we think of as a typical classroom. Workbooks and predetermined assignments are not used. Rather, the teachers observe the students' interests and natural participation in activities to determine the course of learning. For example, a math lesson might be constructed around counting the day's lunch money or dividing supplies among students. Often, games are used to stimulate

mathematical thinking. Teachers encourage peer interaction during the lessons and games because students' different viewpoints can contribute to advances in thinking.

## EVALUATING PIAGET'S THEORY

What were Piaget's main contributions? Has his theory withstood the test of time?

**Contributions**   Piaget was a giant in the field of developmental psychology, the founder of the present field of children's cognitive development. Psychologists owe him for a long list of masterful concepts of enduring power and fascination: assimilation, accommodation, object permanence, egocentrism, conservation, and others (Miller, 2011). Psychologists also owe him for the current vision of children as active, constructive thinkers. And they are indebted to him for creating a theory that generated a huge volume of research on children's cognitive development.

Piaget also was a genius when it came to observing children. His careful observations demonstrated inventive ways to discover how children act on and adapt to the world. Piaget showed us some important things to look for in cognitive development, such as the shift from preoperational to concrete operational thinking. He also showed us how children need to make their experiences fit their schemes (cognitive frameworks) yet simultaneously adapt their schemes to experience. Piaget also revealed how cognitive change is likely to occur if the context is structured to allow gradual movement to the next higher level. Concepts do not emerge suddenly, full-blown, but instead develop through a series of partial accomplishments that lead to increasingly comprehensive understanding (Rakison & Lawson, 2013; Diamond, Casey, & Munakata, 2011; Quinn, 2011).

**Criticisms**   Although Piaget's theory greatly advanced the field of developmental psychology, it has not gone unchallenged. Questions are raised about estimates of children's competence at different developmental levels, stages, the training of children to reason at higher levels, and culture and education. These challenges to Piaget's theory lead to the development of new theories by a group of researchers known as neo-Piagetians.

*Estimates of Children's Competence*   Some cognitive abilities emerge earlier than Piaget thought (Baillargeon, 2014; Carpenter, 2011; Miller, 2011). For example, as previously noted, some aspects of object permanence emerge earlier than he proposed. Even 2-year-olds are non-egocentric in some contexts. When they realize that another person will not see an object, they investigate whether the person is blindfolded or looking in a different direction. Some understanding of the conservation of number has been demonstrated as early as age 3, although Piaget did not think it emerged until 7. Young children are not as uniformly "pre" this and "pre" that (precausal, preoperational) as Piaget thought.

Cognitive abilities also can emerge later than Piaget thought (Brynes, 2012; Kuhn, 2009). Many adolescents still think in concrete operational ways or are just beginning to master formal operations. Even many adults are not formal operational thinkers. In sum, recent theoretical revisions highlight more cognitive competencies of infants and young children and more cognitive shortcomings of adolescents and adults.

*Stages*   Piaget conceived of stages as unitary structures of thought. Thus, his theory assumes developmental synchrony—that is, various aspects of a stage should emerge at the same time. However, some concrete operational concepts do not appear in synchrony. For example, children do not learn to conserve at the same time that they learn to cross-classify. Thus, most contemporary developmentalists agree that children's cognitive development is not as stage-like as Piaget thought (Kuhn, 2009).

Jean Piaget, the main architect of the field of cognitive development, at age 27.

*Effects of Training*   Children at one cognitive stage (such as preoperational) can sometimes be trained to reason at a higher cognitive stage (such as concrete operational). This poses a problem for Piaget's theory. He argued that such training is only superficial and ineffective, unless the child is at a maturational transition point between the stages (Gelman & Williams, 1998).

*Culture and Education*   Culture and education exert stronger influences on children's development than Piaget reasoned (Gauvain, 2013; Holzman, 2009). For example, the age at which children acquire conservation skills and an understanding of horizontality is related to how much practice their culture provides with these skills. Among Inuit children in Canada's Northwest Territories, 90 percent understood the concept of horizontality by 8 years of age, but only 60 percent had mastered conservation of liquids by 15 years of age. In contrast, 100 percent of Baoulé children of Africa's Ivory Coast had mastered conservation of liquids by the age of 10, but only 50 percent had an understanding of horizontality by 15 years of age (Dasen, 1984). The Inuit are hunter-gatherers, who rely on spatial skills and gain an understanding of spatial concepts like horizontality early, whereas the Baoulé are an agricultural society, relying on an understanding of quantity to produce, store, and market food.

*The Neo-Piagetian Approach*   To overcome some of the inconsistencies and perceived problems with Piaget's theory, several theorists have attempted to integrate Piagetian concepts with the fundamental assumptions of information processing theory. This group of **neo-Piagetians** includes two prominent Canadian researchers, Juan Pascual-Leone at York University and Robbie Case (1944–2000) at the University of Toronto. In both their theories, the basic sequence of stages proposed by Piaget was maintained, but the description of thought at each stage and the means through which children transition from one stage to the next differs from Piaget's work. For example, Pascual-Leone proposed that increases in information processing capacity lead to cognitive development. Information processing capacity consists of two components: mental power and mental concepts. Mental power is generally considered to be working memory. Mental concepts include concepts and schemes about the physical, biological, and social world, and the operations that can be performed on these concepts and schemes. In this theory, it is increases in mental power that enable the

**neo-Piagetians** Developmentalists who have elaborated on Piaget's theory, incorporating aspects of information processing theory to explain cognitive development.

development and functioning of mental concepts, and thus transition to the next stage of development (Demetriou, 2006). As we will read about in Chapter 7, increases in mental power result from automatization of mental processes and brain maturation.

Robbie Case's (1987; 1999) theory, much like that of Pascual-Leone, incorporated both processing capacity and mental structures, as well as proposing that advancement to the next stage of development resulted from increasingly complex mental structures developed through increases in processing capacity. However, Case (1987; 1999) proposed that children's conceptual knowledge was contained within mental structures called *central processing structures*, which are less domain-general than the schemes

An outstanding teacher and education in the logic of science and mathematics are important cultural experiences that promote the development of operational thought. *Might Piaget have underestimated the roles of culture and schooling in children's cognitive development?*

and operations proposed by Piaget. In addition, the transition from one stage to the next is much more complex in Case's theory than Pascual-Leone's, which proposed a simple linear progression. In both cases, these neo-Piagetians attempted to describe cognitive development, as well as cultural and individual differences in cognitive development, which Piaget largely ignored.

## Review *Connect* Reflect

**LO2** Apply Piaget's theory to education and evaluate his theory.

### Review

- How can Piaget's theory be applied to educating children?
- What are some key contributions and criticisms of Piaget's theory?

### *Connect*

- In this section, you learned that culture exerts a strong influence on cognitive development. In Chapter 5, what did we learn about the influence of different cultural practices on infants' motor skills?

### **Reflect** *Your Own Personal Journey of Life*

- How might thinking in formal operational ways rather than concrete operational ways help you to develop better study skills?

## Vygotsky's Theory of Cognitive Development

**LO3** Identify the main concepts in Vygotsky's theory and compare it with Piaget's theory.

- The Zone of Proximal Development
- Scaffolding
- Language and Thought
- Teaching Strategies
- Evaluating Vygotsky's Theory

Piaget's theory is a major developmental theory. Another developmental theory that focuses on children's cognition is Vygotsky's theory. Like Piaget, Vygotsky (1962) emphasized that children actively construct their knowledge and understanding. In Piaget's theory, children develop ways of thinking and understanding by their actions and interactions with the physical world. In Vygotsky's theory, children are more often described as social creatures than in Piaget's theory. They develop their ways of thinking and understanding primarily through social interaction (Mahn & John-Steiner, 2013). Their cognitive development depends on the tools provided by society, and their minds are shaped by the cultural context in which they live (Goncu & Gauvain, 2012).

We briefly described Vygotsky's theory in Chapter 1. Here we take a closer look at his ideas about how children learn and his view of the role of language in cognitive development.

## THE ZONE OF PROXIMAL DEVELOPMENT

Vygotsky's belief in the importance of social influences, especially instruction, on children's cognitive development is reflected in his concept of the zone of proximal development. **Zone of proximal development (ZPD)** is Vygotsky's term for the range of tasks that are too difficult for the child to master alone but that can be learned with guidance and assistance of adults or more-skilled children. Thus, the lower limit of the ZPD is the level of skill reached by the child working independently. The upper limit is the level of additional responsibility the child can accept with the assistance of an able instructor (see Figure 6.12). The ZPD captures the child's cognitive skills that are in the process of maturing and can be accomplished only with the assistance of a more-skilled person (Daniels, 2011; Petrick-Steward, 2012). Vygotsky (1962) called these the "buds" or "flowers" of development, to distinguish them from the "fruits" of development, which the child already can accomplish independently.

**zone of proximal development (ZPD)** Vygotsky's term for tasks that are too difficult for children to master alone but can be mastered with assistance from adults or more-skilled children.

Vygotsky's concept of the zone of proximal development—that children learn by interacting with more experienced adults and peers, who help them think beyond the "zone" in which they would be able to perform without assistance—has been applied primarily to academic learning. Barbara Rogoff (1990, 2003; Rogoff, Correa-Chavez, & Silva, 2011; Rogoff, Morelli, & Chavajay, 2010; Rogoff & others, 2007) argues that many of Vygotsky's ideas, including the zone of proximal development, are important in understanding children's development beyond the classroom in everyday interactions with adults and peers. To read further about Rogoff's ideas, see *Connecting with Diversity.*

## SCAFFOLDING

Closely linked to the idea of the ZPD is the concept of scaffolding. **Scaffolding** means changing the level of support. Over the course of a teaching session, a more-skilled person (a teacher or advanced peer) adjusts the amount of guidance to fit the child's current performance (Mahn & John-Steiner, 2013). When the student is learning a new task, the skilled person may use direct instruction. As the student's competence increases, less guidance is given.

*Dialogue* is an important tool of scaffolding in the zone of proximal development (Tappan, 1998). Vygotsky viewed children as having rich but unsystematic, disorganized, and spontaneous concepts. In a dialogue, these concepts meet with the skilled helper's more systematic, logical, and rational concepts. As a result, the child's concepts become more systematic, logical, and rational. For example, a dialogue might take place between a teacher and a child when the teacher uses scaffolding to help a child understand a concept like "transportation."

## LANGUAGE AND THOUGHT

The use of dialogue as a tool for scaffolding is only one example of the important role of language in a child's development. According to Vygotsky, children use speech not only for social communication, but also to help them solve tasks. Vygotsky (1962) further concluded that young children use language to plan, guide, and monitor their behaviour. This use of language for self-regulation is called *private speech.* For Piaget private speech is egocentric and immature, but for Vygotsky it is an important tool of thought during the early childhood years (John-Steiner, 2007; Wertsch, 2007).

Vygotsky said that language and thought initially develop independently of each other and then merge. He emphasized that all mental functions have external, or social, origins. Children must use language to communicate with others before they can focus inward on their own thoughts. Children also must communicate externally and use language for a long period of time before they can make the transition from external to internal speech. This transition period occurs between 3 and 7 years of age and involves talking to oneself. After a while, the self-talk becomes second nature to children, and they can act without verbalizing. When this occurs, children have internalized their egocentric speech in the form of *inner speech,* which becomes their thoughts.

Vygotsky reasoned that children who use a lot of private speech are more socially competent than those who don't. He argued that private speech represents an early transition in becoming more socially communicative. For Vygotsky, when young children talk to themselves, they are using language to govern their behaviour and guide themselves. For example, a child working on a puzzle might say to herself, "Which pieces should I put together first? I'll try those green ones first. Now I need some blue ones. No, that blue one doesn't fit there. I'll try it over here."

Piaget stressed that self-talk is egocentric and reflects immaturity. However, researchers have found support for Vygotsky's view that private speech plays a positive role in children's development (Winsler, Carlton, & Barry, 2000). Researchers have found that children use private speech more when tasks are

**Upper limit**
Level of additional responsibility child can accept with assistance of an able instructor

**Zone of proximal development (ZPD)**

**Lower limit**
Level of problem solving reached on these tasks by child working alone

## FIGURE 6.12

**VYGOTSKY'S ZONE OF PROXIMAL DEVELOPMENT.** Vygotsky's zone of proximal development has a lower limit and an upper limit. Tasks in the ZPD are too difficult for the child to perform alone. They require assistance from an adult or a more-skilled child. As children experience the verbal instruction or demonstration, they organize the information in their existing mental structures so that they can eventually perform the skill or task alone.

**scaffolding** In cognitive development, Vygotsky used this term to describe the practice of changing the level of support provided over the course of a teaching session, with the more-skilled person adjusting guidance to fit the child's current performance level.

*developmental* **connection**

**Parenting.** Scaffolding can also be an effective strategy for parents to adopt in interacting with their infants. Chapter 14, LO 2

*developmental* **connection**

**Language.** In thinking about links between language and cognition, we might ask: (1) Is language necessary for cognition? and (2) Is cognition necessary for language? Chapter 9, LO 4

## Guided Participation and Cultural Contexts

According to Rogoff (2003), children serve a sort of apprenticeship in thinking through *guided participation* in social and cultural activities. Guided participation may occur, for example, when adults and children share activities.

Parents can broaden or limit children's opportunities through their decisions about how much and when to expose children to books, television, and child care. They may give children opportunities to learn about cultural traditions and practices through their routines and play. For example, in the Zambian culture of Chewa, children play numerous games, such as "hide-and-seek, guessing games, complex sand drawing games, imaginative games representing local work and family routines, skill games like jacks and a rule game requiring considerable strategic planning and numerical calculations, and constructing models of wire or clay" (Rogoff, 2003, p. 297). In addition, through observational learning, or as Rogoff calls it, learning by "osmosis," children adopt values, skills, and mannerisms by simply watching and listening to peers and adults.

Guided participation is widely used around the world, but cultures may differ in the goals of development—what content is to be learned—and the means for providing guided participation (Rogoff & others, 2007). Around the world, caregivers and children arrange children's activities and revise children's responsibilities as they gain skill and knowledge. With guidance, children participate in cultural activities that socialize them into skilled activities. For example, Mayan mothers in Guatemala help their daughters learn to weave through guided participation. Throughout the world, learning occurs, not just by studying or by attending classes, but also through interaction with knowledgeable people.

In recent work, Rogoff and her colleagues (2011; Rogoff, Correa-Chavez, & Silva, 2011) have studied cultural variations in children's attention and learning. They highlight two contrasting approaches: (1) participation of children in a wide

At about 7 years of age, Mayan girls in Guatemala are assisted in beginning to learn to weave a simple belt, with the loom already set up for them. The young girl shown here is developmental psychologist Barbara Rogoff's daughter, being taught to weave by a Mayan woman. *What are some other ways that children learn through guided participation?*

variety of family and community activities, which characterizes many indigenous-heritage communities in North and South America, and (2) separation of children from a variety of family and community events and creating activities for them in specialized settings, such as school, which is prevalent in middle socioeconomic-status European-heritage communities. Rogoff and her colleagues conclude that in North America children's out-of-school time provides limited opportunities to learn by observing and participating in a variety of valued family and community activities. In their view, including children in meaningful family and community activities would help them to better understand valued work and other activities in their culture.

*How does Rogoff's concept of guided participation relate to Vygotsky's concept of the zone of proximal development?*

difficult, when they have made a mistake, and when they are not sure how to proceed (Berk, 1994). They also have revealed that children who use private speech are more attentive and improve their performance more than children who do not use private speech (Berk & Spuhl, 1995).

## TEACHING STRATEGIES

Vygotsky's theory has been embraced by many teachers and has been successfully applied to education (Costley, 2012; Daniels, 2011; Gauvain, 2013; Shayer & Adhami, 2010). Here are some ways Vygotsky's theory can be incorporated in classrooms:

1. *Assess the child's ZPD.* Like Piaget, Vygotsky did not think that formal, standardized tests are the best way to assess children's learning. Rather, Vygotsky

argued that assessment should focus on determining the child's zone of proximal development. The skilled helper presents the child with tasks of varying difficulty to determine the best level at which to begin instruction.

2. *Use the child's ZPD in teaching.* Teaching should begin toward the zone's upper limit, so that the child can reach the goal with help and move to a higher level of skill and knowledge. Offer just enough assistance. You might ask, "What can I do to help you?" Or simply observe the child's intentions and attempts and provide support when needed. When the child hesitates, offer encouragement. And encourage the child to practice the skill. You may watch and appreciate the child's practice or offer support when the child forgets what to do.

3. *Use more-skilled peers as teachers.* Remember that it is not just adults who are important in helping children learn. Children also benefit from the support and guidance of more-skilled children (Mahn & John-Steiner, 2013).

4. *Monitor and encourage children's use of private speech.* Be aware of the developmental change from externally talking to oneself when solving a problem during the preschool years to privately talking to oneself in the early elementary school years. In the elementary school years, encourage children to internalize and self-regulate their talk to themselves.

5. *Place instruction in a meaningful context.* Educators today are moving away from abstract presentations of material, instead providing students with opportunities to experience learning in real-world settings. For example, instead of just memorizing math formulas, students work on math problems with real-world implications.

6. *Transform the classroom with Vygotskian ideas.* What does a Vygotskian classroom look like? The Kamehameha Elementary Education Program (KEEP) is based on Vygotsky's theory (Tharp, 1994). The ZPD is the key element of instruction in this program and many of the learning activities take place in small groups. All children spend at least 20 minutes each morning in a setting called Center One. In this context, scaffolding is used to improve children's literary skills. The instructor asks questions, responds to students' queries, and builds on the ideas that students generate. Thousands of children from low-income families have attended KEEP public schools—in Hawaii, on an Arizona Navajo Indian reservation, and in Los Angeles. Compared with a control group of non-KEEP children, the KEEP children participated more actively in classroom discussion, were more attentive in class, and had higher levels of reading achievement (Tharp & Gallimore, 1988).

Lev Vygotsky (1896–1934), shown here with his daughter, believed that children's cognitive development is advanced through social interaction with skilled individuals embedded in a sociocultural backdrop.

## EVALUATING VYGOTSKY'S THEORY

Even though their theories were proposed at about the same time, most of the world learned about Vygotsky's theory later than they learned about Piaget's theory. As a result Vygotsky's theory has not yet been evaluated as thoroughly. Vygotsky's view of the importance of sociocultural influences on children's development fits with the current belief that it is important to evaluate the contextual factors in learning (Deater-Deckard, 2013; Gauvain, 2013).

We already have mentioned several distinctions between Vygotsky's and Piaget's theories, such as Vygotsky's emphasis on the importance of inner speech in development and Piaget's view

*How can Vygotsky's ideas be applied to educating children?*

|  | **Vygotsky** | **Piaget** |
|---|---|---|
| **Sociocultural Context** | Strong emphasis | Little emphasis |
| **Constructivism** | Social constructivist | Cognitive constructivist |
| **Stages** | No general stages of development proposed | Strong emphasis on stages (sensorimotor, preoperational, concrete operational, and formal operational) |
| **Key Processes** | Zone of proximal development, language, dialogue, tools of the culture | Schema, assimilation, accommodation, operations, conservation, classification |
| **Role of Language** | A major role; language plays a powerful role in shaping thought | Language has a minimal role; cognition primarily directs language |
| **View on Education** | Education plays a central role, helping children learn the tools of the culture | Education merely refines the child's cognitive skills that have already emerged |
| **Teaching Implications** | Teacher is a facilitator and guide, not a director; establish many opportunities for children to learn with the teacher and more-skilled peers | Also views teacher as a facilitator and guide, not a director; provide support for children to explore their world and discover knowledge |

## FIGURE **6.13**

**COMPARISON OF VYGOTSKY'S AND PIAGET'S THEORIES.**

**social constructivist approach** An emphasis on the social contexts of learning and the construction of knowledge through social interaction. Vygotsky's theory reflects this approach.

*developmental* **connection**

**Education.** Whether to follow a constructivist or direct instruction approach is a major issue for teachers. Chapter 16, LO 1

that such speech is immature. Although both theories are constructivist, Vygotsky's is a **social constructivist approach**, which emphasizes the social contexts of learning and the construction of knowledge through social interaction.

In moving from Piaget to Vygotsky, the conceptual shift is from the individual to collaboration, social interaction, and sociocultural activity (Mahn & John-Steiner, 2013). The end point of cognitive development for Piaget is formal operational thought. For Vygotsky, the endpoint can differ, depending on which skills are considered to be the most important in a particular culture. For Piaget, children construct knowledge by transforming, organizing, and reorganizing previous knowledge. For Vygotsky, children construct knowledge through social interaction (Rogoff & others, 2007). The implication of Piaget's theory for teaching is that children need support to explore their world and discover knowledge. The main implication of Vygotsky's theory for teaching is that students need many opportunities to learn with their teachers and more-skilled peers. In both Piaget's and Vygotsky's theories, teachers serve as facilitators and guides, rather than as directors and molders of learning. Figure 6.13 compares Vygotsky's and Piaget's theories.

Criticisms of Vygotsky's theory also have surfaced (Karpov, 2006). Some critics point out that Vygotsky was not specific enough about age-related changes (Gauvain, 2008). Another criticism asserts that Vygotsky does not adequately describe how changes in socioemotional capabilities contribute to cognitive development (Gauvain, 2008). Yet another criticism is that he overemphasized the role of language in thinking. Also, his emphasis on collaboration and guidance has potential pitfalls. Might facilitators be too helpful in some cases, as when a parent becomes too overbearing and controlling? Further, some children might become lazy and expect help when they might have learned more by doing something on their own.

**Review**

- What is the zone of proximal development?
- What is scaffolding?
- How did Vygotsky view language and thought?
- How can Vygotsky's theory be applied to education?
- What are some similarities and differences between Vygotsky's and Piaget's theories?
- What are some criticisms of Vygotsky's theory?

*Connect*

- Compare the strategies that were laid out in the section for using Piaget's theories in teaching to those for applying Vygotsky's theories in teaching. What are the similarities? Differences?

**Reflect** *Your Own Personal Journey of Life*

- Which theory—Piaget's or Vygotsky's—do you think is more effective in explaining your own cognitive development as a child?

# case study **connections**

1. How do the descriptions of Piaget's children in the opening case study reflect different types of schemes?

2. Identify an example of assimilation and accommodation from the description of Piaget's children at the beginning of the chapter.

3. In which stage of Piaget's theory of cognitive development would the descriptions of children's behaviour at the beginning of the chapter fall within, and why?

4. How do the descriptions provided at the beginning of the chapter illustrate Piaget's concept of equilibrium?

5. Compare and contrast the educational implications of the theories of Piaget and Vygotsky.

# reach your **learning goals**

# Cognitive Developmental Approaches

## Piaget's Theory of Cognitive Development

**L01** Discuss the key processes and four stages in Piaget's theory.

Processes of Development

- According to Piaget's theory, children construct their own cognitive worlds, building mental structures to adapt to their world. Schemes are actions or mental representations that organize knowledge. Behavioural schemes (physical activities) characterize infancy, and mental schemes (cognitive activities) develop in childhood. Adaptation involves assimilation and accommodation. Assimilation occurs when children incorporate new information into their existing schemes.

Accommodation refers to children's adjustment of their schemes to fit new information and experiences. Through organization, children group isolated behaviours into a higher-order, more smoothly functioning cognitive system. Equilibration is a mechanism Piaget proposed to explain how children shift from one cognitive stage to the next. As children experience cognitive conflict in trying to understand the world, they seek equilibrium. The result is equilibration, which brings the child to a new stage of thought. According to Piaget, there are four qualitatively different stages of thought: sensorimotor, preoperational, concrete operational, and formal operational.

Sensorimotor Stage

- In sensorimotor thought, the first of Piaget's four stages, the infant organizes and coordinates sensory experiences (such as seeing and hearing) with physical movements. This stage lasts from birth to about 2 years of age and is non-symbolic throughout, according to Piaget. Sensorimotor thought has six substages: simple reflexes; first habits and primary circular reactions; secondary circular reactions; coordination of secondary circular reactions; tertiary circular reactions, novelty, and curiosity; and internalization of schemes. One key aspect of this stage is object permanence, the ability to understand that objects continue to exist even though the infant is no longer observing them. Another aspect involves infants' understanding of cause and effect. In the past two decades, revisions of Piaget's view have been proposed based on research. For example, researchers have found that a stable and differentiated perceptual world is established earlier than Piaget envisioned. However, controversy surrounds the question of when object permanence emerges. The nature–nurture issue is a key aspect of infant cognitive development. Spelke's core knowledge approach is a strong naturist view. Most developmentalists conclude that nature and nurture are both important in infant cognitive development.

Preoperational Stage

- Preoperational thought is the beginning of the ability to reconstruct at the level of thought what has been established in behaviour. It involves a transition from a primitive to a more sophisticated use of symbols. In preoperational thought, the child does not yet think in an operational way. The symbolic function substage occurs roughly from 2 to 4 years of age and is characterized by symbolic thought, egocentrism, and animism. The intuitive thought substage stretches from about 4 to 7 years of age. It is called intuitive because children seem sure about their knowledge yet are unaware of how they know what they know. The preoperational child lacks conservation and asks a barrage of questions.

Concrete Operational Stage

- Concrete operational thought occurs roughly from 7 to 11 years of age. During this stage, children can perform concrete operations, think logically about concrete objects, classify things, and reason about relationships among classes of things. Concrete thought is not as abstract as formal operational thought.

Formal Operational Stage

- Formal operational thought appears between 11 and 15 years of age. Formal operational thought is more abstract, idealistic, and logical than concrete operational thought. Piaget maintains that adolescents become capable of engaging in hypothetical-deductive reasoning. But Piaget did not give adequate attention to individual variation in adolescent thinking. Many young adolescents do not think in hypothetical-deductive ways but rather are consolidating their concrete operational thinking. In addition, according to Elkind, adolescents develop a special kind of egocentrism that involves an imaginary audience and a personal fable about being unique and invulnerable. However, recent research questions the accuracy of the invulnerability aspect of the personal fable.

## Applying and Evaluating Piaget's Theory

 **L02** Apply Piaget's theory to education and evaluate his theory.

Piaget and Education

- Piaget was not an educator, but his constructivist views have been applied to teaching. These applications include an emphasis on facilitating rather than directing learning, considering the child's level of knowledge, promoting the student's intellectual health, and turning the classroom into a setting of exploration and discovery.

Evaluating Piaget's Theory

- We owe to Piaget the field of cognitive development. He was a genius at observing children, and he gave us a number of masterful concepts such as assimilation, accommodation, object permanence, and egocentrism. Critics question his estimates of competence at different developmental levels, his stage concept, and other ideas. Neo-Piagetians, who emphasize the importance of information processing, stress that children's cognition is more specific than Piaget thought.

## Vygotsky's Theory of Cognitive Development

 **L03** Identify the main concepts in Vygotsky's theory and compare it with Piaget's theory.

The Zone of Proximal Development

- Zone of proximal development (ZPD) is Vygotsky's term for the range of tasks that are too difficult for children to master alone but can be learned with the guidance and assistance of adults or more-skilled peers.

Scaffolding

- Scaffolding is a teaching technique in which a more-skilled person adjusts the level of guidance to fit the child's current performance level. Dialogue is an important aspect of scaffolding.

Language and Thought

- Vygotsky stressed that language plays a key role in cognition. Language and thought initially develop independently, but then children internalize their egocentric speech in the form of inner speech, which becomes their thoughts. This transition to inner speech occurs between 3 and 7 years of age.

Teaching Strategies

- Applications of Vygotsky's ideas to education include using the child's ZPD and scaffolding, using more-skilled peers as teachers, monitoring and encouraging children's use of private speech, and accurately assessing the ZPD. These practices can transform the classroom and establish a meaningful context for instruction.

Evaluating Vygotsky's Theory

- Like Piaget, Vygotsky emphasized that children actively construct their understanding of the world. Unlike Piaget, he did not propose stages of cognitive development, and he emphasized that children construct knowledge through social interaction. According to Vygotsky's theory, children depend on tools provided by the culture, which determines which skills they will develop. Vygotsky's view contrasts with Piaget's view that young children's speech is immature and egocentric. Critics of Vygotsky's theory assert that it lacks specificity about age-related changes and overemphasizes the role of language in thinking.

For more information on the resources available from McGraw-Hill Ryerson, go to www.mheducation.ca/he/solutions

# chapter 7 | Information Processing

Natalie Anderson is a seventh grade student at Northside Junior High. During a typical day, Natalie attends classes in many different subjects and interacts socially with many of her friends. Today, Natalie begins her day in Language Arts class, where she is to select a work of fiction to read and then prepare a report on the protagonist. Natalie selects a book called *The Hunger Games* and settles in to start reading. Next period Natalie has a math test, which probes her knowledge of algebra. After an hour of hard work, Natalie feels good about her performance.

During lunch Natalie and her friends discuss the latest antics of the newest celebrity, where Natalie is able to express her personal opinions with clarity and conviction while evaluating the arguments of her friends. After lunch Natalie has gym class, where the teacher introduces the class to the rules of lacrosse. A natural athlete, Natalie listens intently to understand what is being said and asks questions for clarification and elaboration when needed.

Finally, in the last period of the day, Natalie and a group of her peers are working hard to design an experiment to test the effects of rainwater on the erosion rates of cliffs covered with different types of grass. Together, her group is working on generating the hypothesis. The group members are evaluating different approaches and strategies to conduct their research as the final bell rings. Later this evening, Natalie will work on her oral report on monarch butterflies. She has already completed her research on this topic and is now working to integrate information from various sources into a coherent presentation for her peers. All of the activities Natalie has engaged in on this typical day involve a range of cognitive skills, including memory, attention, problem solving, critical thinking, and decision making, among others.

# preview

What do children notice in the environment? What do they remember? And how do they think about it? These questions illustrate the information-processing approach. Using this approach, researchers usually do not describe children as being in one stage of cognitive development or another. But they do describe and analyze how the speed of processing information, attention, memory, thinking, and metacognition change over time.

## The Information-Processing Approach  **L01**  Explain the information-processing approach.

| The Information-Processing Approach to Development | Cognitive Resources: Capacity and Speed of Processing Information | Mechanisms of Change | Comparisons with Piaget's Theory |

What are some of the basic ideas in the information-processing approach? How is it similar to and different from the cognitive developmental approaches we described in Chapter 6?

### developmental connection

**Theories.** In Skinner's behavioural view, it is external rewards and punishment that determine behaviour, not thoughts. Chapter 1, LO 3

**information-processing approach** An approach that focuses on the ways children process information about their world—how they manipulate information, monitor it, and create strategies to deal with it.

> You might be poor, your shoes might be broken, but your mind is a palace.
>
> —FRANK McCOURT
> *Author of* Angela's Ashes, *20th Century*

## THE INFORMATION-PROCESSING APPROACH TO DEVELOPMENT

The information-processing approach shares a basic characteristic with the theories of cognitive development that were discussed in Chapter 6. Like those theories, the information-processing approach rejected the behavioural approach that dominated psychology during the first half of the twentieth century. As we discussed in Chapter 1, the behaviourists argued that to explain behaviour it is important to examine associations between stimuli and behaviour. In contrast, the theories of Piaget and Vygotsky (described in Chapter 6) and the information-processing approach focus on how children think.

The **information-processing approach** analyzes how children manipulate information, monitor it, and create strategies for handling it (Halford & Andrews, 2011; Siegler, 2006, 2012, 2013). A computer metaphor can illustrate how the information-processing approach can be applied to development. A computer's information processing is *limited* by its hardware and software. The hardware limitations include the amount of data the computer can process—its capacity—and speed. The software limits the kind of data that can be used as input and the ways that data can be manipulated; word processing doesn't handle music, for example. Similarly, children's information processing may be limited by capacity and speed as well as by their ability to manipulate information—in other words, their ability to apply appropriate strategies to acquire and use knowledge. In the information-processing approach, children's cognitive development results from their ability to overcome processing limitations by increasingly executing basic operations, expanding information-processing capacity, and acquiring new knowledge and strategies.

## COGNITIVE RESOURCES: CAPACITY AND SPEED OF PROCESSING INFORMATION

Developmental changes in information processing are likely influenced by increases in both capacity and speed of processing (Frye, 2004). These two characteristics are often referred to as *cognitive resources*, which are proposed to have an important influence on memory and problem solving.

Both biology and experience contribute to growth in cognitive resources (Bjorklund, 2013; Goldstein, 2011; Reed, 2010). The changes in the brain we described in Chapter 4 provide a biological foundation for increased cognitive resources (Zelazo, 2013). Important biological developments occur both in brain structures, such as changes in the frontal lobes, and at the level of neurons, such as the blooming and pruning of connections between neurons. Also, as we discussed in Chapter 4, myelination (the process in which the axon is covered with a myelin sheath) increases the speed of electrical impulses in the brain. Myelination continues through childhood and adolescence (Steinberg, 2013).

Most information-processing psychologists argue that an increase in capacity also improves processing of information (Halford & Andrews, 2011; Kuhn, 2013). For example, as children's information-processing capacity increases, they likely can hold in mind several dimensions of a topic or problem simultaneously, whereas younger children are more prone to focus on only one dimension.

How does speed of processing information change during the childhood and adolescent years?

What is the role of processing speed? How quickly children can process information often influences what they can do with that information (Robinson-Riegler & Robinson-Riegler, 2012). If an adolescent is trying to add up mentally the cost of items he or she is buying at the grocery store, the adolescent needs to be able to compute the sum before he or she has forgotten the price of the individual items. Children's speed in processing information is linked with their competence in thinking (Bjorklund, 2005). Generally, fast processing is linked with good performance on cognitive tasks. However, some compensation for slower processing speed can be achieved by creating effective strategies.

Researchers have devised a number of ways to assess processing speed. For example, it can be assessed through a *reaction-time task* in which individuals are asked to push a button as soon as they see a stimulus such as a light. Or individuals might be asked to match letters or match numbers with symbols on a computer screen.

There is abundant evidence that the speed with which such tasks are completed improves dramatically across the childhood years (Hommel, Li, & Li, 2004; Kail, 2007; Kuhn, 2013). For example, one study of 8- to 13-year-old children revealed that processing speed increased with age, and furthermore, that the developmental change in processing speed preceded an increase in working memory capacity (Kail, 2007).

**developmental connection**

**Brain Development.** Developmental changes in brain and neuronal structure contribute to cognitive development. Chapter 4, LO 2

## MECHANISMS OF CHANGE

Robert Siegler (1998, 2012, 2013) argues that mechanisms of change are especially important in the advances children make in cognitive development. According to Siegler, three mechanisms work together to create changes in children's cognitive skills: encoding, automaticity, and strategy construction.

**Encoding** is the process by which information gets into memory. Changes in children's cognitive skills depend on increased skill at encoding relevant information and ignoring irrelevant information. For example, to a 4-year-old, an *s* in cursive writing is a shape very different from an *s* that is printed. But a 10-year-old has learned to encode the relevant fact that both are the letter *s* and to ignore the irrelevant differences in their shape.

**encoding** The mechanism by which information gets into memory.

*What are some important mechanisms of change in the development of children's information processing?*

**automaticity** The ability to process information with little or no effort.

**strategy construction** Creation of new procedures for processing information.

**metacognition** Cognition about cognition, or "knowing about knowing."

**Automaticity** refers to the ability to process information with little or no effort. Practice allows children to encode increasing amounts of information automatically. For example, once children have learned to read well, they do not think about each letter in a word as a letter; instead, they encode whole words. Once a task is automatic, it does not require conscious effort. As a result, as information processing becomes more automatic, we can complete tasks more quickly and handle more than one task at a time. If you did not encode words automatically but instead read this page by focusing your attention on each letter in each word, imagine how long it would take you to read it.

**Strategy construction** is the creation of new procedures for processing information. For example, children's reading benefits when they develop the strategy of stopping periodically to take stock of what they have read so far (Dimmitt & McCormick, 2012).

In addition, Siegler (2006, 2012, 2013) argues that children's information processing is characterized by *self-modification*. That is, children learn to use what they have learned in previous circumstances to adapt their responses to a new situation. Part of this self-modification draws on **metacognition**, which means knowing about knowing (Flavell, 2004). One example of metacognition is what children know about the best ways to remember what they have read. Do they know that they will remember what they have read better if they can relate it to their own lives in some way? Thus, in Siegler's application of the information-processing approach to development, children play an active role in their cognitive development.

## COMPARISONS WITH PIAGET'S THEORY

*developmental* **connection**

**Cognitive Theory.** Piaget theorized that cognitive development occurs in four stages: sensorimotor, preoperational, concrete operational, and formal operational. Chapter 6, LO 1

How does the information-processing approach compare with Piaget's theory? According to Piaget (as discussed in Chapter 6), children actively construct their knowledge and understanding of the world. Their thinking develops in distinct stages. At each stage, children develop qualitatively different types of mental structures (or schemes) that allow them to think about the world in new ways.

Like Piaget's theory, some versions of the information-processing approach are constructivist; they see children as directing their own cognitive development. And like Piaget, information-processing psychologists identify cognitive capabilities and limitations at various points in development (Siegler, 2013; Zelazo, 2013). They describe ways in which individuals do and do not understand important concepts at different points in life and try to explain how more advanced understanding grows out of a less advanced version. They emphasize the impact that existing understanding has on the ability to acquire a new understanding of something.

Unlike Piaget, however, developmentalists who take an information-processing approach do not see development as occurring abruptly in distinct stages with a brief transition period from one stage to the next. Instead, according to the information-processing approach, individuals develop a gradually increasing capacity to process information, which allows them to acquire increasingly complex knowledge and skills (Halford & Andrews, 2011; Kuhn, 2013; Sternberg, 2009). Compared with Piaget, the information-processing approach also focuses on more precise analysis of change and on the contributions made by ongoing cognitive activity—such as encoding and strategies—to that change.

### Review

- What is the information-processing approach to development?
- How do capacity and processing speed change developmentally?
- What are three important mechanisms of change involved in information processing?
- How can the information-processing approach be compared to Piaget's theory?

### Connect

- In this section, we learned that changes in the brain are linked to advances in information processing.

What did you learn about changes in brain structure and the cognitive abilities of infants, 5-year-olds, and 20-year-olds in Chapter 4?

### Reflect *Your Own Personal Journey of Life*

- In terms of your ability to learn, think about your early childhood, elementary, and middle-school years. Describe a task at which you were faster in processing information in elementary school than in preschool, and then describe a task at which you were faster in processing information in middle school than in elementary school.

## Attention (LO2) Define *attention* and outline its developmental changes.

| What Is Attention? | Infancy | Childhood | Adolescence |

The world holds a lot of information to perceive. Right now, you are perceiving the letters and words that make up this sentence. Now look around you and pick out something to look at other than this book. After that, curl up the toes on your right foot. In each of these circumstances, you engaged in the process of paying attention. What is attention, and what effect does it have on processing information? How does attention change with age?

## WHAT IS ATTENTION?

**Attention** is the focusing of mental resources. Attention improves cognitive processing for many tasks, from grabbing a toy to hitting a baseball or adding numbers. Children, like adults, can pay attention to only a limited amount of information at any one time. Children allocate their attention in different ways (Colombo, Brez, & Curtindale, 2013; Fisher & others, 2013; Rueda & Posner, 2013). Psychologists have labelled these types of allocation as selective attention, divided attention, sustained attention, and executive attention.

- **Selective attention** is focusing on a specific aspect of experience that is relevant while ignoring others that are irrelevant. Focusing on one voice among many in a crowded room or a noisy restaurant is an example of selective attention. When you switched your attention to the toes on your right foot, you were engaging in selective attention.

- **Divided attention** involves concentrating on more than one activity at the same time. If you are listening to music or the television while you are reading this, you are engaging in divided attention.

*What are some different ways that children allocate their attention?*

**attention** Concentrating and focusing mental resources.

**selective attention** Focusing on a specific aspect of experience that is relevant while ignoring others that are irrelevant.

**divided attention** Concentrating on more than one activity at the same time.

**sustained attention** The ability to maintain attention to a selected stimulus for a prolonged period of time. Sustained attention is also called *focused attention* and *vigilance*.

**executive attention** Involves action planning, allocating attention to goals, error detection and compensation, monitoring progress on tasks, and dealing with novel or difficult circumstances.

- **Sustained attention** is the ability to maintain attention to a selected stimulus for a prolonged period of time. Sustained attention is also called *focused attention* and *vigilance.*
- **Executive attention** involves action planning, allocating attention to goals, error detection and compensation, monitoring progress on tasks, and dealing with novel or difficult circumstances.

## INFANCY

How effectively can infants attend to something? Even newborns can detect a contour and fixate on it. Older infants scan patterns more thoroughly. By 4 months, infants can selectively attend to an object.

**Orienting/Investigative Process**    Attention in the first year of life is dominated by an *orienting/investigative process* (Posner & Rothbart, 2007). This process involves directing attention to potentially important locations in the environment (that is, *where*), and recognizing objects and their features, such as colour and form (that is, *what*) (Richards, 2011). From 3 to 9 months of age, infants begin to deploy their attention more flexibly and quickly. Another important type of attention is *sustained attention,* also referred to as *focused attention* (Martin, Razza, & Brooks-Dunn, 2012). New stimuli typically elicit an orienting response followed by sustained attention. It is sustained attention that allows infants to learn about and remember characteristics of a stimulus as it becomes familiar. Researchers have found that infants as young as 3 months of age can engage in 5 to 10 seconds of sustained attention. From this age through the second year, the length of sustained attention increases (Courage & Richards, 2008).

*developmental* **connection**

**Research Methods.** Among the measures researchers use in habituation studies are sucking behaviour, heart and respiration rates, and how long an infant looks at an object. Chapter 5, LO 2

This infant's attention is riveted on the red block that has just been placed in front of her. Her attention to the block will be strongly regulated by the processes of habituation and dishabituation. *What characterizes these processes?*

**joint attention** Individuals focusing on the same object or event; requires the ability to track another's behaviour, one person directing another's attention, and reciprocal interaction.

**Habituation and Dishabituation**    Closely linked with attention are the processes of habituation and dishabituation that we discussed in Chapter 5 (Kavsek, 2009, 2013). Recall that if a stimulus—a sight or sound—is presented to infants several times in a row, they usually pay less attention to it each time. This suggests they are bored with it. This is the process of *habituation*—decreased responsiveness to a stimulus after repeated presentations of the stimulus. *Dishabituation* is the recovery of a habituated response after a change in stimulation.

Infants' attention is so strongly governed by novelty and habituation that when an object becomes familiar, attention becomes shorter, making infants more vulnerable to distraction (Colombo, Brez, & Curtindale, 2013). Researchers study habituation to determine the extent to which infants can see, hear, smell, taste, and experience touch (Slater, Field, & Hernandez-Reif, 2007).

Parents can use knowledge of habituation and dishabituation to improve interaction with their infant. If parents keep repeating the same form of stimulation, the infant will stop responding. It is important for parents to do novel things and to repeat them often until the infant stops responding. Wise parents sense when the infant shows interest and know that many repetitions of the stimulus may be necessary for the infant to process the information. The parents stop or change their behaviour when the infant redirects attention (Rosenblith, 1992).

**Joint Attention**    Another aspect of attention that is an important aspect of infant development is **joint attention**, in which individuals focus on the same object or event. Joint attention requires (1) an ability to track another's behaviour, such as following someone's gaze; (2) one person directing another's attention; and (3) reciprocal interaction. Early in infancy, joint attention usually involves a caregiver pointing or using words to direct an infant's attention (Rossano,

Carpenter, & Tomasello, 2012). Emerging forms of joint attention occur at about 7 to 8 months, but it is not until toward the end of the first year that joint attention skills are frequently observed (Liszkowski, 2007). One study revealed that at 10 to 11 months of age infants first began engaging in *gaze following*, looking where another person has just looked (Brooks & Meltzoff, 2005; see Figure 7.1). And by their first birthday, infants have begun to direct adults to objects that capture the child's interest (Heimann & others, 2006).

Joint attention plays important roles in many aspects of infant development and considerably increases infants' ability to learn from other people (Carpenter, 2011; Mateus & others, 2013). Nowhere is this more apparent than in observations of interchanges between caregivers and infants as infants are learning language (Tomasello, 2011). When caregivers and infants frequently engage in joint attention, infants say their first word earlier and develop a larger vocabulary (Flom & Pick, 2003). Later in the textbook, in our discussion of language, we further discuss joint attention as an early predictor of language development in older infants and toddlers (Tomasello, 2011). Other studies illustrate that joint attention in infancy is linked to a greater range of cognitive abilities, including long-term memory and play behaviours during infancy, as well as self-regulation later in childhood (Bigelow, MacLean, & Proctor, 2004; Kopp & Lindenberger, 2012; Van Hecke & others, 2012). For example, one study by Ann Bigelow and colleagues at Saint Francis Xavier University in Nova Scotia revealed that joint attention was associated with more advanced types of play for 12-month-old infants (Bigelow, MacLean, & Proctor, 2004). Infants whose mothers directed their attention to toys were more likely to play with toys in an interactive and functional way rather than simply banging or mouthing the toys.

A mother and her infant daughter engaging in joint attention. *What about this photograph tells you that joint attention is occurring? Why is joint attention an important aspect of infant development?*

Further, joint attention emerges at roughly the same age across cultures. In a study comparing Canadian infants to infants in Peru and India, no differences were found in how frequently joint attention occurred (Callaghan & others, 2011). Results such as these illustrate the important role joint attention plays in infant learning and development.

## CHILDHOOD

The child's ability to pay attention improves significantly during the preschool years (Bell & Cuevas, 2013; Rueda & Posner, 2013). The toddler wanders around, shifts attention from one activity to another, and seems to spend little time focused on any one object or event. In contrast, the preschool child might watch television for a half-hour at a time. One study that observed 99 families in their

(a)

(b)

## FIGURE **7.1**

**GAZE FOLLOWING IN INFANCY.** Researcher Rechele Brooks shifts her eyes from the infant to a toy in the foreground (*a*). The infant then follows her eye movement to the toy (*b*). Brooks and colleague Andrew Meltzoff (2005) found that infants begin to engage in this kind of behaviour, called *gaze following*, at 10 to 11 months of age. *Why might gaze following be an important accomplishment for an infant?*

*What are some advances in children's attention as they go through early childhood and middle and late childhood?*

homes for 4,672 hours found that visual attention to television dramatically increased during the preschool years (Anderson & others, 1985). However, a recent research study revealed that television watching and video game playing were both linked to attention problems in children (Swing & others, 2010). To learn more about television watching and attention, see *Connecting to Current Controversy.*

Young children especially make advances in two aspects of attention—executive attention and sustained attention. Mary Rothbart and Maria Gartstein (2008, p. 332) described why advances in executive and sustained attention are so important in early childhood:

> The development of the . . . executive attention system supports the rapid increases in effortful control in the toddler and preschool years. Increases in attention are due, in part, to advances in comprehension and language development. As children are better able to understand their environment, this increased appreciation of their surroundings helps them to sustain attention for longer periods of time.

Control over attention shows important changes during middle and late childhood (Posner & Rothbart, 2007). External stimuli are likely to determine the target of the preschooler's attention; what is salient, or obvious, grabs the preschooler's attention. For example, suppose a flashy, attractive clown presents the directions for solving a problem. Preschool children are likely to pay attention to the clown and ignore the directions, because they are influenced strongly by the salient features of the environment. After the age of 6 or 7, children pay more attention to features relevant to performing a task or solving a problem, such as the directions. Thus, instead of being controlled by the most striking stimuli in their environment, older children can direct their attention to more important stimuli. This change reflects a shift to *cognitive control* of attention, so that children act less impulsively and reflect more. Sometimes children develop deficits in attention or attentional skills develop differently. Chapter 16 will discuss the learning disability known as Attention Deficit Hyperactivity Disorder.

*developmental* **connection**

**Attention Deficit Hyperactivity Disorder.** Attention deficit hyperactivity disorder (ADHD) is a disability in which children consistently show one or more of the following characteristics over a period of time: (1) inattention, (2) hyperactivity, and (3) impulsivity. Chapter 16, LO 2

## connecting to current controversy

### What Happens When Babies Watch Television?

The increasing availability of infant-directed videos and DVDs, as well as the increasing amount of time infants spend in front of the television (Rideout, 2007) have prompted debate on the effects of television viewing on infants' cognitive development. Supporters argue that age-appropriate and educational material for infants may provide many cognitive benefits as it does for preschool-aged children (e.g., Schmidt & Anderson, 2007). Others cite concerns that television viewing can impede cognitive development, regardless of the content. A recent research review by Mary Courage and Alissa Setliff (2010) at Memorial University in Newfoundland evaluated these concerns:

*Exposure to television might contribute to problems in the development of attention,* including increased distractibility, reduced attention span, and Attention Deficit Hyperactivity Disorder (ADHD). Although one widely reported study found that greater amounts of television viewing by children under the age of 3 was associated with later attention problems (Zimmerman & Christakis, 2007), other studies have failed to replicated this finding. As Zimmerman and Christakis themselves point out, the observed relation may not be causal. For example, Courage and Setliff suggest that children with ADHD may be encouraged to watch more television by their parents as a break from the high level of engagement required by these children. They conclude that there is little evidence to support a link between television viewing and later attention problems.

*(continued)*

*(continued)*

*Television viewing is a passive activity that might take away from time spent in more active and creative pursuits,* including toy play and exploration, reducing the amount of social and language interaction the infant has with caregivers and other children. One controversial American study widely reported in the media suggested that greater amounts of television viewing in infancy and toddlerhood were related to lower language abilities (Zimmerman, Christakis, & Meltzoff, 2007). More recently, however, researchers at the University of Ottawa reported that the *amount* of television viewing was not related to vocabulary, rather, the *quality* of television viewing is important. Viewing material not intended for children, background television, an earlier age of viewing and solitary viewing were all associated with lower vocabulary scores for both English- and French-speaking children, as well as bilingual children (Hudon, Fennell, & Hoftyzer, 2013).

*The presence of television in the background might distract infants from play and other activities that encourage cognitive development.* A recent Canadian study revealed that a television playing in the background might grab infants' attention, but it does not hold it (Setliff & Courage, 2011). In this study, the mean looking time to toys was shorter when the television was on compared to off, but the 6- and 12-month-old infants looked longer at their toys than the television when the television was playing. At this age, the authors argue, the television cannot hold infants' attention because they cannot comprehend the material, but the repeated orienting of attention to the television may interfere with sustained attention to toys or other activities that is required for learning to occur.

In sum, Courage and Setliff (2010) conclude that the evidence on the effects of television viewing during infancy is mixed. They state, however, that contrary to many marketing claims, it is unlikely that viewing any material will enhance cognitive development, as least during the first year of life.

*Why might a preschooler or school-aged child benefit more from age-appropriate video material than an infant?*

---

Preschool children's ability to control and sustain their attention is related to school readiness and achievement (Romano & others, 2010; Rothbart, 2011). For example, a study of more than 1,000 Canadian children from the National Longitudinal Survey of Children and Youth revealed that children's ability to sustain their attention at school entry was linked to academic outcomes in third grade (Romano & others, 2010). This result was replicated in a study with 1,145 French-speaking children in Quebec—that is, measures of attention in kindergarten were related to teacher-rated academic achievement in math and reading at the end of Grade 2 (Pagani & others, 2010).

## ADOLESCENCE

Adolescents typically have better attentional skills than children do, although there are wide individual differences in how effectively adolescents deploy their attention. Sustained and executive attention are very important aspects of adolescent cognitive development. As adolescents are required to engage in larger, increasingly complex tasks that require longer time frames to complete, their ability to sustain attention is critical for succeeding on the tasks. An increase in executive attention supports the rapid increase in effortful control required to effectively engage in these complex academic tasks (Rothbart & Gartstein, 2008).

One trend involving divided attention is adolescents' multi-tasking, which in some cases involves dividing attention not just between two activities, but even among three or more (Bauerlein, 2008). A major influence on the increase in multi-tasking is availability of multiple electronic media. Many adolescents have a range of electronic media at their disposal. It is not unusual for adolescents to simultaneously divide their attention among

*Is multi-tasking beneficial or distracting for adolescents?*

working on homework, engaging in an instant messaging conversation, surfing the Web, and listening to music on an iPod.

Is this multi-tasking beneficial or distracting? Multi-tasking expands the information adolescents attend to and forces the brain to share processing resources, which can distract the adolescent's attention from what might be most important at the moment (Begley & Interlandi, 2008). And, if the key task is at all complex and challenging, such as trying to figure out how to solve a homework problem, multi-tasking considerably reduces attention to the key task (Myers, 2008).

Controlling attention is a key aspect of learning and thinking in adolescence and emerging adulthood (Bjorklund, 2012; Rueda & Posner, 2013). Distractions that can interfere with attention in adolescence and emerging adulthood come from the external environment (other students talking while the student is trying to listen to a lecture or when the student switches on a computer screen to Facebook during a lecture and looks at a new friend request, for example) or intrusive distractions from competing thoughts in the individual's mind. Self-oriented thoughts, such as worrying, self-doubt, and intense emotions may especially interfere with focusing attention on thinking tasks (Gillig & Sanders, 2011; Walsh, 2011).

**developmental connection**

**Media.** A recent study revealed that when media multi-tasking is taken into account, 11- to 14-year-olds spent nearly 12 hours a day using media (Rideout, Foehr, & Roberts, 2010). Chapter 16, LO 4

## Review Connect Reflect

**LO2** Define *attention* and outline its developmental changes.

### Review

- What is attention? What are four ways in which children can allocate attention?
- How does attention develop in infancy?
- How does attention develop in childhood?
- What are some characteristics of attention in adolescence?

### Connect

- In this section, you learned about joint attention. How might a child's ability to engage in joint attention be important in the successful implementation of a zone of proximal development teaching strategy?

### Reflect *Your Own Personal Journey of Life*

- Imagine that you are an elementary school teacher. Devise some strategies to help children pay attention in class.

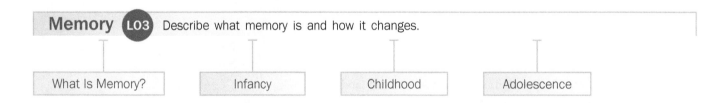

**Memory** **LO3** Describe what memory is and how it changes.

| What Is Memory? | Infancy | Childhood | Adolescence |

Twentieth-century American playwright Tennessee Williams once commented that life is all memory except for that one present moment that goes by so quickly that you can hardly catch it going. But just what do we do when we remember something, and how does our ability to remember develop?

## WHAT IS MEMORY?

**memory** Retention of information over time.

**Memory** is the retention of information over time. Without memory you would not be able to connect what happened to you yesterday with what is going on in your life today. Human memory is truly remarkable when you consider how much information we put into our memories and how much we must retrieve to perform all of life's activities.

**Processes and Types of Memory**   Researchers study how information is initially placed or encoded into memory, how it is retained or stored after being encoded, and how it is found or retrieved for a certain purpose later (see Figure 7.2). Encoding, storage, and retrieval are the basic processes required for memory. Failures can occur in any of these processes. Some part of an event might not be encoded, the mental representation of the event might not be stored, or even if the memory exists, you might not be able to retrieve it.

Examining the storage process led psychologists to classify memories based on their permanence. **Short-term memory** is a memory system with a limited capacity in which information is usually retained for up to 15 to 30 seconds unless strategies are used to retain it longer. **Long-term memory** is a relatively permanent and unlimited type of memory. People are usually referring to long-term memory when they talk about memory. When you remember the type of games you enjoyed playing as a child or the details of your first date, you are drawing on your long-term memory. But when you remember the word you just read a few seconds ago, you are using short-term memory.

When psychologists first analyzed short-term memory, they described it as if it were a passive storehouse with shelves to store information until it is moved to long-term memory. But we do many things with the information stored in short-term memory. For example, the words in this sentence are part of your short-term memory, and you are manipulating them to form a meaningful whole.

The concept of working memory acknowledges the importance of our manipulations of the information in short-term memory. **Working memory** is a kind of mental workbench where individuals manipulate and assemble information when they make decisions, solve problems, and comprehend written and spoken language (Baddeley, 1990, 2010, 2012). Many psychologists prefer the term *working memory* over *short-term memory* to describe how memory works.

Figure 7.3 shows Alan Baddeley's model of working memory. Notice that it includes two short-term stores—one for speech and one for visual and spatial information—as well as a *central executive* and an *episodic buffer*. It is the job of the central executive to monitor and control the system—determining what information is stored, relating information from long-term memory to the information in the short-term stores, and moving information into long-term memory. The episodic buffer acts as a store of information, in a multidimensional code, linking working memory to perception and long-term memory.

Working memory is linked to many aspects of children's development (Ang & Lee, 2010; Alloway, Gathercole, & Elliott, 2010; Baddeley, 2012). For example, children who have better working memory are more advanced in reading comprehension, math skills, and problem solving than their counterparts with less effective working memory (Dyck & Piek, 2010; Locascio & others, 2010; Nevo & Breznitz, 2013).

**short-term memory** Limited-capacity memory system in which information is usually retained for up to 30 seconds, assuming there is no rehearsal of the information. Using rehearsal, individuals can keep the information in short-term memory longer.

**long-term memory** A relatively permanent and unlimited type of memory.

**working memory** A mental "workbench" where individuals manipulate and assemble information when making decisions, solving problems, and comprehending written and spoken language.

*"Can we hurry up and get to the test? My short-term memory is better than my long-term memory."*
© Wm Hoest Enterprises, Inc. Reprinted courtesy of Bunny Hoest.

| Encoding | Storage | Retrieval |
|---|---|---|
| Getting information into memory | Retaining information over time | Taking information out of storage |

## FIGURE 7.2

**PROCESSING INFORMATION IN MEMORY.** As you read about the many aspects of memory in this chapter, think about the organization of memory in terms of these three main activities.

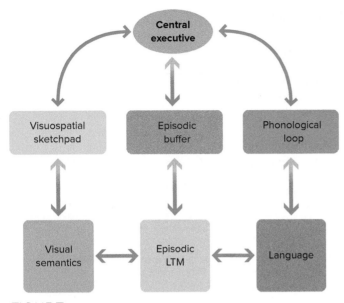

FIGURE **7.3**

**WORKING MEMORY.** In Baddeley's working memory model, working memory is like a mental workbench where a great deal of information processing is carried out. Working memory consists of four main components: the phonological loop and visuospatial working memory serve as assistants, helping the central executive do its work, while the episodic buffer combines information from the two assistants with information from long-term memory. Input from sensory memory goes to the phonological loop, where information about speech is stored and rehearsal takes place, and visuospatial working memory, where visual and spatial information, including imagery, are stored. Working memory is a limited-capacity system, and information is stored there for only a brief time. Working memory interacts with long-term memory, using information from long-term memory in its work and transmitting information to long-term memory for longer storage.

*developmental* **connection**

**Gender.** Gender schema theory emphasizes children's gender schemas that organize the world in terms of male and female. Chapter 12, LO 2

**schema theory** States that when people reconstruct information, they fit it into information that already exists in their minds.

**schemas** Mental frameworks that organize concepts and information.

**fuzzy trace theory** States that memory is best understood by considering two types of memory representations: (1) verbatim memory trace, and (2) fuzzy trace, or gist. In this theory, older children's better memory is attributed to the fuzzy traces created by extracting the gist of information.

Recent research with both English- and French-speaking children in Canada illustrates the importance of working memory in young children's cognitive development. One longitudinal study with French-speaking children revealed that working memory capacity in toddlerhood predicted number knowledge and receptive vocabulary in kindergarten (Fitzpatrick & Pagani, 2012). In turn, assessment of working memory in kindergarten predicated math achievement at the end of first grade (Monette, Bigras, & Guay, 2011). Working memory capacity is also related to literacy growth. Children at risk for reading problems in kindergarten scored lower on working memory tasks than children not at risk (Partanen & Siegel, 2014). And finally, bilingual children outperformed monolingual children on visuospatial working memory tasks, particularly when those tasks required greater use of executive functions (Morales, Calvo, & Bialystok, 2013). All these results speak to the importance of working memory to a variety of children's cognitive functions.

**Constructing Memories**   Memory is not like a tape recorder, or a camera, or even like computer memory; we don't store and retrieve bits of data in computer-like fashion. Children and adults construct and reconstruct their memories (Bauer, 2013; De Brigard, Szpunar, & Schacter, 2013).

*Schema Theory*   According to **schema theory**, people mould memories to fit information that already exists in their minds. This process is guided by **schemas**, which are mental frameworks that organize concepts and information. Suppose a football fan and a visitor from a country where the sport isn't played are eating at a restaurant and overhear a conversation about last night's game. Because the visitor doesn't have a schema for information about football, he or she is more likely than the fan to mishear what is said. Perhaps the visitor will interpret the conversation in terms of a schema for another sport, constructing a false memory of the conversation.

Schemas influence the way we encode, make inferences about, and retrieve information. We reconstruct the past rather than take an exact photograph of it, and the mind can distort an event as it encodes and stores impressions of it. Often when we retrieve information, we fill in the gaps with fragmented memories.

*Fuzzy Trace Theory*   Another variation of how individuals reconstruct their memories has been proposed by Charles Brainerd and Valerie Reyna (Halliday, Brainerd, & Reyna, 2011; Reyna & Brainerd, 1995). **Fuzzy trace theory** states that when individuals encode information, they create two types of memory representations: (1) a *verbatim memory trace*, which consists of precise details, and (2) a *fuzzy trace*, or *gist*, which is the central idea of the information. For example, consider a child who is presented with information about a pet store that has ten birds, six cats, eight dogs, and seven rabbits. Then the child is asked two types of questions: (1) verbatim questions, such as "How many cats are in the pet store, six or eight?" and (2) gist questions, such as "Are there more cats or more dogs in the pet store?" Researchers have found that preschool children tend to remember verbatim information more than gist information, but elementary-school-aged children are more likely to remember gist information (Brainerd & Gordon, 1994). The increased use of gist by elementary-school-aged children accounts for their improved memory because fuzzy traces are less likely to be forgotten than verbatim traces (Reyna & Rivers, 2008).

**Content Knowledge and Expertise** Our ability to remember new information about a subject depends considerably on what we already know about it (Staszewski, 2013). Much of the research on the role of knowledge in memory has compared experts and novices (Ericsson & others, 2006). *Experts* have acquired extensive knowledge about a particular content area; this knowledge influences what they notice and how they organize, represent, and interpret information. This in turn affects their ability to remember, reason, and solve problems. When individuals have expertise about a particular subject, their memory also tends to be good regarding material related to that subject (Gobet & Charness, 2006).

For example, one study found that 10- and 11-year-olds who were experienced chess players ("experts") were able to remember more information about chess pieces than college students who were not chess players ("novices") (Chi, 1978) (see Figure 7.4). In contrast, when the college students were presented with other stimuli, they were able to remember them better than the children were. Thus, the children's expertise in chess gave them superior memories, but only in chess.

There are developmental changes in expertise. Older children usually have more expertise about a subject than younger children do, which can contribute to their better memory for the subject. Thus, as children gain more knowledge about the world around them, memory will improve.

## INFANCY

Popular child-rearing expert Penelope Leach (1990) told parents that 6- to 8-month-old babies cannot hold in their mind a picture of their mother or father. Piaget argued that it was not until children acquired symbolic thought, between 18 and 24 months of age, that memory was possible. Child development researchers, however, have revealed that infants as young as 3 months of age show a limited type of memory (Courage, Howe, & Squires, 2004).

**First Memories** Carolyn Rovee-Collier (1987, 2007; Rovee-Collier & Bar, 2010) has conducted research demonstrating that infants can remember perceptual-motor information. In a characteristic experiment, she places a baby in a crib underneath an elaborate mobile and ties one end of a ribbon to the baby's ankle and the other end to the mobile. The baby kicks and makes the mobile move (see Figure 7.5). Weeks later, the baby is returned to the crib, but its foot is not tied to the mobile. The baby kicks, apparently trying to make the mobile move. However, if the mobile's makeup is changed even slightly, the baby doesn't kick. If the mobile is then restored to being exactly as it was when the baby's ankle was originally tied to it, the baby will begin kicking again. According to Rovee-Collier, even by 2½ months the baby's memory is incredibly detailed.

How well can infants remember? Some researchers such as Rovee-Collier have concluded that infants as young as 2 to 6 months of age can remember some experiences through 1½ to 2 years of age (Rovee-Collier & Barr, 2010). However, critics such as Jean Mandler (2000), a leading expert on infant cognition, argue that the infants in Rovee-Collier's experiments are displaying only implicit memory. **Implicit memory** refers to memory without conscious recollection—memories of skills and routine procedures that are performed

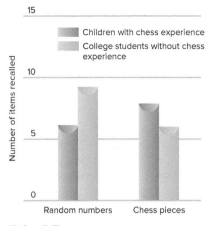

## FIGURE **7.4**

**MEMORY FOR NUMBERS AND CHESS PIECES.** Notice that when 10- and 11-year-old children and college students were asked to remember a string of random numbers that had been presented to them, the college students fared better. However, the 10- and 11-year-olds who had experience playing chess ("experts") had better memory for the location of chess pieces on a chess board than college students with no chess experience (Chi, 1978).

## FIGURE **7.5**

**THE TECHNIQUE USED IN ROVEE-COLLIER'S INVESTIGATION OF INFANT MEMORY.** In Rovee-Collier's experiment, operant conditioning was used to demonstrate that infants as young as 2½ months of age can retain information from the experience of being conditioned. *What did infants remember in Rovee-Collier's experiment?*

**implicit memory** Memory without conscious recollection; memory of skills and routine procedures that are performed automatically.

explicit memory Conscious memory of facts and experiences.

automatically, such as riding a bicycle. In contrast, **explicit memory** refers to the conscious memory of facts and experiences.

When people think about memory, they are usually referring to explicit memory. Most researchers find that babies do not show explicit memory until the second half of the first year (Bauer, 2013). Then explicit memory improves substantially during the second year of life (Ghetti & Bauer, 2012). In one longitudinal study, infants were assessed several times during their second year (Bauer & others, 2000). Older infants showed more accurate memory and required fewer prompts to demonstrate their memory than younger infants. Figure 7.6 summarizes how long researchers have found infants of different ages can remember information (Bauer, 2009). As indicated in Figure 7.6, researchers have documented that 6-month-olds can remember information for 24 hours, but by 20 months of age infants can remember information they encountered 12 months earlier.

What changes in the brain are linked to infants' memory development? From about 6 to 12 months of age, the maturation of the hippocampus and the surrounding cerebral cortex, especially the frontal lobes, makes the emergence of explicit memory possible (Bauer, 2013; Nelson, 2011) (see Figure 7.7). Explicit memory continues to improve in the second year, as these brain structures further mature and connections between them increase. Less is known about the areas of the brain involved in implicit memory in infancy.

**Childhood Amnesia**    Let's examine another aspect of memory. Do you remember your third birthday party? Probably not. Most adults can remember little, if anything, from the first three years of their life. This is called *infantile* or *childhood amnesia*. The few reported adult memories of life at age 2 or 3 are at best very sketchy (Howe, Courage, & Rooksby, 2009; Newcombe, 2007; Riggins, 2012). Elementary school children also do not remember much of their early childhood years (Lie & Newcombe, 1999).

What is the cause of childhood amnesia? Some researchers propose that memories from the first few years of life cannot be fully encoded in a manner that enables later retrieval until language, theory of mind, and/or a cognitive self emerges (Howe, 2011; Nelson, 1993; Perner & Ruffman, 1995). A sense of self, for example, would make organization and encoding of personal memories possible. However, childhood amnesia has also been found in non-humans (see Josselyn & Franklund, 2012), suggesting a biological component may be involved. Researchers have suggested that the immaturity of key brain regions, such as the prefrontal cortex, interferes with encoding and storage of long-lasting personal memories (Boyer & Diamond, 1992). More recently, Canadian researchers Sheena Josselyn and Paul Frankland (2012) proposed that the ongoing addition of new neural connections that occurs in the hippocampus for several years after birth interferes with the ability to form enduring memories. Recall from Chapter 4 that the hippocampus is heavily involved in memory formation. These new neural connections continually replace the pre-existing neural connections in the hippocampus, making the earlier stored memories inaccessible.

In sum, childhood amnesia likely results from the interaction of both cognitive and biological factors. Most of young infants' conscious memories appear to be rather fragile and short-lived, although their implicit memory of perceptual-motor actions can be substantial (Bauer, 2013; Mandler, 2004). By the end of the second year, long-term memory is more substantial and reliable (Ghetti & Bauer, 2012). In *Connecting with Diversity,* we will explore culture's role in children's memory for personally experienced events.

| Age Group | Length of Delay |
|---|---|
| 6-month-olds | 24 hours |
| 9-month-olds | 1 month |
| 10–11-month-olds | 3 months |
| 13–14-month-olds | 4–6 months |
| 20-month-olds | 12 months |

FIGURE **7.6**

AGE-RELATED CHANGES IN THE LENGTH OF TIME OVER WHICH MEMORY OCCURS (Bauer, 2009).

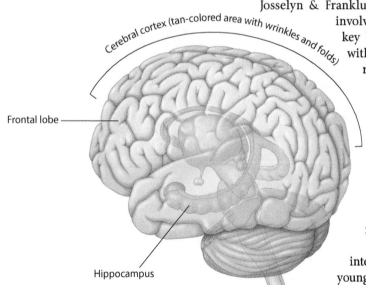

Cerebral cortex (tan-colored area with wrinkles and folds)

Frontal lobe

Hippocampus

FIGURE **7.7**

KEY BRAIN STRUCTURES INVOLVED IN MEMORY DEVELOPMENT IN INFANCY.

## Culture and Children's Memory

The emergence of autobiographical memory, our memory for personally experienced events, coincides with the waning of childhood amnesia, and there appear to be cultural differences in these memory phenomena. For example, when asked to recall their earliest memories, European and North American adults report events dating earlier than do Asian adults (Wang, 2001a), are able to access a greater number of earlier childhood memories than Chinese adults (Wang et al., 2004), and are more likely than Asian adults to recall specific one-time events focusing on their own roles and perspectives (Wang & Conway, 2004). Peterson and colleagues (2009) found similar results with children across different cultures. When asked to recall events from their earlier lives, Canadian children provided more memories than did Chinese children and had earlier first memories, by almost a year. What might account for these differences?

Research has explored parent-child memory sharing as one factor that may contribute to cross-cultural differences in the development of autobiographic memory (Nelson & Fivush, 2004). Parent-child conversations about events in children's lives play a role in the emergence of autobiographical memory, and cultural differences exist in the nature of these conversations. North American mothers tend to engage in high-elaborative memory conversations with their children in which parents supplement and embellish the children's contribution, scaffolding children's construction of elaborate and coherent narrative of past events.

How might a child's language skill contribute to memory sharing and the emergence of autobiographical memory?

In contrast, Asian mothers tend to initiate low-elaborative conversations that resemble memory tests in which parents tend to ask and repeat questions to elicit specific answers (Fivush & Wang, 2005; Fivush, Haden, & Reese, 2006). Over the long term, the more elaborative forms of memory sharing facilitate the consolidation of memories, helping children to retain them for longer periods of time, as well as contributing to an earlier offset of childhood amnesia (Nelson & Fivush, 2004; Peterson & McCabe, 2004).

## CHILDHOOD

Children's memory improves considerably after infancy (Bauer & Fivush, 2013; Bjorklund, 2013). Sometimes the long-term memories of preschoolers seem erratic, but young children can remember a great deal of information if they are given appropriate cues and prompts.

One reason children remember less than adults is that they are far less expert in most areas, but their growing knowledge is one likely source of their memory improvement. For example, a child's ability to recount what she has seen on a trip to the library depends greatly on what she already knows about libraries, such as where books on certain topics are located, how to check out books, and so on. If a child knows little about libraries, she will have a much more difficult time recounting what she saw there.

Fuzzy trace theory suggests another way in which memory develops during childhood. Recall from our earlier discussion that young children tend to encode, store, and retrieve verbatim traces, whereas elementary-school-aged children begin to use gist more. The increased use of gist likely produces more enduring memory traces of information. Other sources of improvement in children's memory include changes in memory span and their use of strategies.

**Memory Span**   Unlike long-term memory, short-term memory has a very limited capacity. One method of assessing that capacity is the *memory-span task*. You simply hear a short list of stimuli—usually digits—presented at a rapid pace (one per second, for example). Then you are asked to repeat the digits.

**developmental connection**

**Culture and Ethnicity.** Culture encompasses the behaviour patterns, beliefs, and all other products of a particular group of people that are passed on from generation to generation. Chapter 14, LO 1

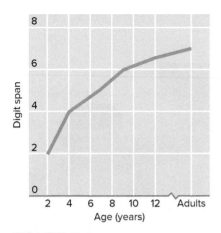

## FIGURE 7.8

**DEVELOPMENTAL CHANGES IN MEMORY SPAN.** In one study, memory span increased by about three digits from 2 years of age to 7 years of age (Dempster, 1981). By 12 years of age, memory span had increased, on average, another one and a half digits.

Research with the memory-span task suggests that short-term memory increases during childhood (Schneider, 2011). For example, in one investigation, memory span increased from about two digits in 2-year-old children to about five digits in 7-year-old children. Between 7 and 12 years of age, memory span increased by only one and a half digits (Dempster, 1981) (see Figure 7.8). Keep in mind, though, that individuals have different memory spans.

Why does memory span change with age? Speed of processing information is important, especially the speed with which memory items can be identified. For example, one study tested children on their speed at repeating words presented orally (Case, Kurland, & Goldberg, 1982). Speed of repetition was a powerful predictor of memory span. Indeed, when the speed of repetition was controlled, the 6-year-olds' memory spans were equal to those of young adults. Rehearsal of information is also important; older children rehearse the digits more than younger children.

**Strategies**   Learning to use effective strategies is a key aspect of improving memory (MacArthur, 2012; McCormick, Dimmitt, & Sullivan, 2013). According to Robert Siegler (2005; 1996), the development of strategies occurs in a gradual and continuous manner. Children do not abandon one strategy when they learn a new strategy to solve a particular problem. According to Siegler's *adaptive strategy choice model* (see Figure 7.9), children have multiple strategies available at any point in time and the strategy selected for use is dependent on the problem. When presented with new or less familiar problems, children tend to use less sophisticated but previously successful strategies. With increasing age, experience, and improved information processing, more sophisticated strategies become more common.

Increasingly sophisticated strategy use is evident in children's memory abilities. Rehearsal is just one of the strategies that can sometimes aid memory, although rehearsal is a better strategy for short-term memory than long-term memory. Following are some strategies that benefit children's long-term retention of information.

*Organization*   If children organize information when they encode it, their memory benefits. Consider this demonstration: Recall the 12 months of the year as quickly as you can. How long did it take you? What was the order of your recall? You probably answered something like "a few seconds" and "in chronological order." Now try to remember the months of the year in alphabetical order. Did you make any errors? How long did it take you? It should be obvious that your memory for the months of the year is organized in a particular way.

Organizing is a strategy that older children (and adults) typically use, and it helps them to remember information. Preschool children usually don't use strategies like organization; in middle and late childhood they are more likely to use organization when they need to remember something (Flavell, Miller, & Miller, 2002).

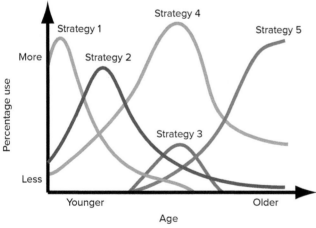

## FIGURE 7.9

**SIEGLER'S ADAPTIVE STRATEGY CHOICE MODEL.** Children have multiple strategies available at any point in time, with different strategies used more frequently at different ages. The use of more sophisticated strategies becomes increasingly more common with greater experience.

*Elaboration*   Another important strategy is elaboration, which involves engaging in more extensive processing of information. When individuals engage in elaboration, their memory benefits (Kellogg, 2007). Thinking of examples is a good way to elaborate information. For example, self-reference is an effective way to elaborate information. Thinking about personal associations with information makes the information more meaningful and helps children to remember it.

The use of elaboration changes developmentally (Pressley, 2003; Schneider, 2011). Adolescents are more likely than children to use elaboration spontaneously. Elementary-school-aged children can be taught to use elaboration strategies on a learning task, but they will be less likely than adolescents to use the strategies on other learning tasks in the future. Nonetheless, verbal elaboration can be an effective strategy even for young elementary-school-aged children.

*Imagery*  Creating mental images is another strategy for improving memory. However, using imagery to remember verbal information works better for older children than for younger children (Schneider, 2004, 2011). In one study, 20 sentences were presented to first- through sixth-grade children to remember—such as "The angry bird shouted at the white dog" and "The policeman painted the circus tent on a windy day" (Pressley & others, 1987). Children were randomly assigned to an imagery condition (in which they were told to make a picture in their head for each sentence) and a control condition (in which they were told just to try hard). Figure 7.10 shows that the imagery instructions helped older elementary-school-aged children (grades 4 through 6) but was not nearly as helpful to the younger elementary-school-aged children (grades 1 through 3). However, mental imagery can help young schoolchildren to remember pictures (Schneider, 2004, 2011; Schneider & Pressley, 1997).

*Teaching Strategies*  So far we have described several important strategies adults can adopt when guiding children to remember information more effectively over the long term. These strategies include guiding children to organize information, elaborate the information, and develop images of the information. Another good strategy is to encourage children to understand the material that needs to be remembered rather than memorizing it by rote. Two other strategies adults can use to guide children's retention of memory were recently proposed:

- *Repeat with variation on the instructional information, and link early and often.* These are memory development research expert Patricia Bauer's (2009) recommendations to improve children's consolidation and reconsolidation of the information they are learning. Variations on a lesson theme increase the number of associations in memory storage, and linking expands the network of associations in memory storage; both strategies expand the routes for retrieving information from storage.

- *Embed memory-relevant language when instructing children.* Teachers vary considerably in how much they use memory-relevant language that encourages students to remember information. In recent research that involved extensive observations of a number of first-grade teachers in the classroom, Peter Ornstein and his colleagues (Ornstein, Coffman, & Grammer, 2007, 2009; Ornstein & others, 2010) found that in the time segments observed, the teachers rarely used strategy suggestions or metacognitive (thinking about thinking) questions. In this research, when lower-achieving students were placed in classrooms in which teachers were categorized as

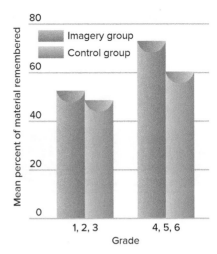

FIGURE **7.10**

**IMAGERY AND MEMORY OF VERBAL INFORMATION.** Imagery improved older elementary-school-aged children's memory for sentences more than younger elementary-school-aged children's memory for sentences.

Frank and Ernest

FRANK & ERNEST © Thaves/Dist. by United Features Syndicate, Inc.

"high-mnemonic teachers" who frequently embedded memory-relevant information in their teaching, their achievement increased (Ornstein, Coffman, & Grammer, 2007).

**Reconstructive Memory and Children as Eyewitnesses**  Children's memories, like those of adults, are constructive and reconstructive. Children have schemas for all sorts of information, and these schemas affect how they encode, store, and retrieve memories. If a teacher tells her class a story about two men and two women who were involved in a train crash in France, students won't remember every detail of the story and will reconstruct the story, putting their own individual stamp on it. One student might reconstruct the story by saying the characters died in a plane crash, another might describe three men and three women, another might say the crash was in Germany, and so on.

Reconstruction and distortion are nowhere more apparent than in clashing testimony given by eyewitnesses at trials. A special concern is susceptibility to suggestion and how this can alter memory (Bruck & Ceci, 2012; Lamb & Malloy, 2013). Consider a study of individuals who had visited Disneyland (Pickrell & Loftus, 2001). Four groups of participants read ads and answered questionnaires about a trip to Disneyland. One group saw an ad that mentioned no cartoon characters, the second read the same ad and saw a four-foot-tall cardboard figure of Bugs Bunny, the third read a fake ad for Disneyland with Bugs Bunny on it, and the fourth saw the same fake ad along with cardboard Bugs. Participants were asked whether they had ever met Bugs Bunny at Disneyland. Less than 10 percent of those in the first two groups reported having met Bugs Bunny at Disneyland, but approximately 30 to 40 percent of the third and fourth groups remembered meeting Bugs there. People were persuaded they had met Bugs Bunny at Disneyland, even though Bugs is a Warner Brothers character who would never appear at a Disney theme park.

Canadian researcher Carole Peterson (2012) suggested that certain questioning techniques may increase children's susceptibility to suggestion. For example, Peterson and Grant (2001) found that children tended to have poorer recall for events when yes/no questions were used, compared to wh- questions, as young children tend to have a "yes bias" to appear cooperative during interviews. Multiple choice questions, such as "did it happen in the living room or the dining room" can also lead to inaccurate recall of past events. Rocha, Marche, and Briere (2013) found that when young children were questioned about a personally experienced distressful event, such as a dental procedure, children were more likely to incorrectly accept one of the suggested options even if it was not true. This added element of suggestibility is problematic, given that children are generally more susceptible to suggestion than adults (Howe, 2011). The following conclusions about children as eyewitnesses indicate that a number of other factors can influence the accuracy of a young child's memory:

- *There are age differences in children's susceptibility to suggestion.* Preschoolers are the most suggestible age group in comparison with older children and adults (Ceci, Papierno, & Kulkofsky, 2007). For example, preschool children are more susceptible to believing misleading or incorrect information given after an event (Ghetti & Alexander, 2004). Despite these age differences, there is still concern about the reaction of older children when they are subjected to suggestive interviews (La Rooy, Brown, & Lamb, 2013; Poole & Lindsay, 1996).
- *There are individual differences in susceptibility.* Some preschoolers are highly resistant to interviewers' suggestions, whereas others immediately succumb to the slightest suggestion (Bruck & Ceci, 2012; Kuehnle & Connell, 2013).

In sum, whether a young child's eyewitness testimony is accurate may depend on a number of factors such as the type, number, and intensity of the suggestive

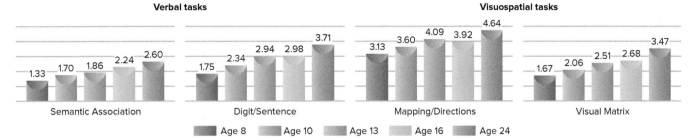

Verbal tasks | Visuospatial tasks

| Semantic Association | Digit/Sentence | Mapping/Directions | Visual Matrix |
|---|---|---|---|
| 1.33, 1.70, 1.86, 2.24, 2.60 | 1.75, 2.34, 2.94, 2.98, 3.71 | 3.13, 3.60, 4.09, 3.92, 4.64 | 1.67, 2.06, 2.51, 2.68, 3.47 |

■ Age 8   ■ Age 10   ■ Age 13   ■ Age 16   ■ Age 24

## FIGURE **7.11**

**DEVELOPMENTAL CHANGES IN WORKING MEMORY.** Note that the scores shown here are the means for each age group, and the age also represents a mean age. Higher scores reflect superior working memory performance.

techniques the child has experienced (Bruck & Ceci, 2012; Spencer & Lamb, 2013). To counter some of the difficulties associated with questioning methods and suggestibility, researchers are evaluating the Cognitive Interview for use with children. This interviewing technique involves the use of multiple retrieval cues to elicit an accurate narrative of a witnessed or experience event, cues that include reinstatement of the environment and describing the event in different sequences and from various perspectives. This technique has been shown to increase accurate recall of past events for adults (Memon, Meissner, & Fraser, 2010) and looks promising for use with children (e.g., Gentle & others, 2013; Verkampt & Ginet, 2010).

## ADOLESCENCE

There has been little research on memory changes in adolescence. As you saw in Figure 7.8, memory span (which is a measure of short-term memory) increases during adolescence. There also is evidence that working memory increases during adolescence. In one study, the performances of individuals from 6 to 57 years of age were examined on both verbal and visuospatial working memory tasks (Swanson, 1999). As shown in Figure 7.11, working memory increased substantially from 8 through 24 years of age no matter what the task. Thus, the adolescent years are likely to be an important developmental period for improvement in working memory. Note that working memory continues to improve through the transition to adulthood and beyond.

Four-year-old Jennifer Royal was the only eyewitness when one of her playmates was shot to death. She was allowed to testify in open court, and the clarity of her statements helped to convict the gunman. *What are some issues involved in whether young children should be allowed to testify in court?*

**Review** *Connect* **Reflect**

**L03** Describe what memory is and how it changes.

### Review

- What is memory? What are some important processes and types of memory?
- How does memory develop in infancy?
- How does memory change in childhood?
- How does memory change in adolescence?

### *Connect*

- In this section, we learned about *schemas* as they relate to memory. How is this concept similar to or different from the concept of *schemes*, as related to Piaget's theory of development discussed in Chapter 6?

### **Reflect** *Your Own Personal Journey of Life*

- What is your earliest memory? Why do you think you can remember this particular situation?

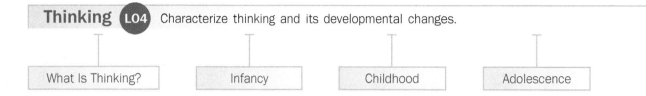

**thinking** Manipulating and transforming information in memory, usually to form concepts, reason, think critically, and solve problems.

**concepts** Cognitive groupings of similar objects, events, people, or ideas.

Attention and memory are often steps toward another level of information processing—thinking. What is thinking? How does it change developmentally? What is children's scientific thinking like, and how do they solve problems? Let's explore these questions.

## WHAT IS THINKING?

**Thinking** involves manipulating and transforming information in memory; it is the job of the central executive in Baddeley's model of working memory shown in Figure 7.3. We think in order to reason, reflect, evaluate ideas, solve problems, and make decisions. Let's explore how thinking changes developmentally, beginning with infancy.

## INFANCY

Interest in thinking during infancy has especially focused on concept formation and categorization (Gelman, 2013; Rakison & Lawson, 2013). **Concepts** are cognitive groupings of similar objects, events, people, or ideas. Without concepts, you would see each object and event as unique; you would not be able to make any generalizations.

Do infants form concepts? Yes, they do, although we do not know just how early concept formation begins (Quinn & others, 2013). Using habituation experiments like those described in Chapter 5, some researchers have found that infants as young as 3 months of age can group together objects with similar appearances (Quinn & others, 2013). This research capitalizes on the knowledge that infants are more likely to look at a novel object than a familiar object.

Jean Mandler (2004, 2010) argues that these early categorizations are best described as *perceptual categorization*. That is, the categorizations are based on similar perceptual features of objects, such as size, colour, and movement, as well as parts of objects, such as legs for animals. Mandler (2004) concludes that it is not until about 7 to 9 months of age that infants form *conceptual* categories rather than just making perceptual discriminations between different categories. In one study of 9- to 11-month-olds, infants classified birds as animals and airplanes as vehicles even though the objects were perceptually similar—airplanes and birds with their wings spread (Mandler & McDonough, 1993) (see Figure 7.12).

Further advances in categorization occur in the second year of life (Booth & Ware, 2010). Many infants' "first concepts are broad and global in nature, such as 'animal' or 'indoor thing.' Gradually, over the first two years these broad concepts become more differentiated into concepts such as 'land animal,' then 'dog,' or to 'furniture,' then 'chair'" (Mandler, 2009, p. 1). Also in the second year, infants often categorize objects on the basis of their shape (Landau, Smith, & Jones, 1998).

Do some very young children develop an intense, passionate interest in a particular category of objects or activities? One study confirmed that they do (DeLoache, Simcock, & Macari, 2007). A striking finding was the large gender difference in categories, with an intense interest in particular categories stronger for boys than girls. Categorization of boys' intense interests focused on vehicles, trains, machines, dinosaurs, and balls; girls' intense interests were more likely

## FIGURE 7.12

**CATEGORIZATION IN 9- TO 11-MONTH-OLDS.** These are the stimuli used in the study that indicated 9- to 11-month-old infants categorized birds as animals and airplanes as vehicles even though the objects are perceptually similar (Mandler & McDonough, 1993).

to involve dressing up and books/reading. When one author's grandson Alex was 18 to 24 months old, he already had developed an intense, passionate interest in the category of vehicles. For example, at this age, he categorized vehicles into such subcategories as cars, trucks, earth-moving equipment, and buses. In addition to common classifications of cars into police cars, jeeps, taxis, and such, and trucks into firetrucks, dump trucks, and the like, his categorical knowledge of earth-moving equipment included bulldozers and excavators, and he categorized buses into school buses, London buses, and funky Malta buses (retro buses on the island of Malta). Later, at 2 to 3 years of age, Alex developed an intense, passionate interest in categorizing dinosaurs.

In sum, the infant's advances in processing information—through attention, memory, imitation, and concept formation—is much richer, more gradual and less stage-like, and occurs earlier than was envisioned by earlier theorists, such as Piaget (Bauer, 2013; Diamond, 2013; Meltzoff & Williamson, 2013; Quinn & others, 2013). As leading infant researcher Jean Mandler (2004) concluded, "The human infant shows a remarkable degree of learning power and complexity in what is being learned and in the way it is represented" (p. 304).

## CHILDHOOD

To explore thinking in childhood, we will examine four important types of thinking: executive function, critical thinking, scientific thinking, and problem solving.

**Executive Function**   Recently, interest has increased regarding the development of children's **executive function**, an umbrella-like concept that encompasses several higher-level cognitive processes that are linked to the development of the prefrontal cortex, such as inhibition, working memory, and cognitive flexibility (Miyake & Friedman, 2012). Executive function involves managing one's thoughts to engage in goal-directed behaviour and to exercise self-control (Carlson, Zelazo, & Faja, 2013; Diamond, 2013). Earlier in this chapter, we described the recent interest in executive attention, which comes under the umbrella of executive function.

A recent research review revealed that the three dimensions of executive function may not be fully differentiated in preschool children (Lee, Bull & Ringo, 2013). The shift to two dimensions, working memory, and inhibition gradually occurs around the age of 5, with the third component, cognitive flexibility emerging around the age of 7 or later. Developmental advances in cognitive inhibition (such as inhibiting a strong tendency that is incorrect), cognitive flexibility (such as shifting attention to another object or topic), goal setting (such as sharing a toy or mastering a skill like catching a ball), and delay of gratification (the ability to forego an immediate pleasure or award for a more desirable one later) transform the relatively stimulus-driven toddler into a child capable of flexible, goal-directed problem solving that characterizes executive function (Zelazo & Muller, 2011). Piaget also described this transformation, but the information-processing perspective suggests a mechanism responsible for this shift—executive function.

How might executive function change during middle and late childhood years and be linked to children's success in school? Canadian researchers Adele Diamond and Kathleen Lee (2011) recently highlighted the following dimensions of executive function that they conclude are the most important for 4- to 11-year-old children's cognitive development and school success:

- *Self-control/inhibition.* Children need to develop self-control that will allow them to concentrate and persist on learning tasks, to inhibit their tendencies to repeat incorrect responses, and to resist the impulse to do something now that they would regret later.

**executive function** An umbrella-like concept that consists of a number of higher-level cognitive processes linked to the development of the brain's prefrontal cortex. Executive function involves managing one's thoughts to engage in goal-directed behaviour and to exercise self-control.

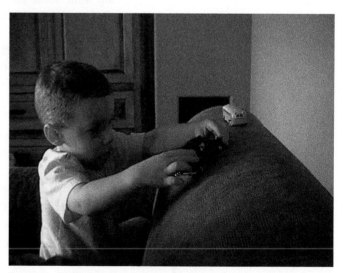

One author's grandson Alex at 2 years of age showing his intense, passionate interest in the category of vehicles while playing with a London taxi and a funky Malta bus.

- *Working memory.* Children need an effective working memory to process the masses of information they will encounter as they go through school and beyond.
- *Flexibility.* Children need to be flexible in their thinking to consider different strategies and perspectives.

Executive function is associated with a range of developmental outcomes. Longitudinal studies with both English-speaking (LeFevre & others, 2013) and French-speaking (Monette, Bigras, & Guay, 2011) children in Canada revealed that executive function is associated with later academic achievement, particularly math ability. Some researchers have found that executive function is a better predictor of school readiness than general IQ (Blair & Razza, 2007). Further, a longitudinal study of an important dimension of executive function—inhibitory control—found that 3- to 11-year-old children who had better inhibitory control (able to wait their turn, not easily distracted, more persistent, and less impulsive) were more likely to still be in school, less likely to engage in risk-taking behaviour, and less likely to be taking drugs in adolescence (Moffitt & others, 2011). Thirty years after they were initially assessed, the children with better inhibitory control had better physical and mental health (they were less likely to be overweight, for example), had better earnings in their career, were more law-abiding, and were happier (Moffitt, 2012; Moffitt & others, 2011).

Given that executive functions are so important for developmental outcomes, it is not surprising that recent research has focused on training programs to enhance these cognitive abilities. In a recent review paper, Canadian cognitive neuroscientist Adele Diamond (2013) noted several programs that increase executive function in children aged 4 to 12 years. These programs include computer-training of specific executive functions (e.g., working memory, interactive games) as well as programs that focus on the whole self, including traditional tae kwon do, martial arts, aerobics, and yoga. However, we still know relatively little about how long the benefits of executive function training last, to which domains the benefits may extend, and what other types of activities (e.g., music training, sports) may also improve executive function (Diamond, 2012; Diamond & Lee, 2011).

Some critics argue that not much benefit is derived from placing various cognitive processes under the broader concept of executive function. Although we have described a number of components of executive function here—working memory, cognitive inhibition, cognitive flexibility, for example—a consensus has not been reached on what the components are, how they are connected, and how they develop. That said, the concept of executive function is not likely to go away any time soon, and further research, especially meta-analyses, should provide a clearer picture of executive function and how it develops (Luszcz, 2013).

**Critical Thinking** Executive function also involves the ability to think critically in effective ways. Currently, there is considerable interest among psychologists and educators in critical thinking (Sternberg & Sternberg, 2013). **Critical thinking** involves thinking reflectively and productively, and evaluating evidence. If you think critically, you will do the following:

- Ask not only what happened but how and why.
- Examine supposed "facts" to determine whether there is evidence to support them.
- Argue in a reasoned way rather than through emotions.
- Recognize that there is sometimes more than one good answer or explanation.
- Compare various answers and judge which is the best answer.
- Evaluate what other people say rather than immediately accepting it as the truth.
- Ask questions and speculate beyond what is known to create new ideas and new information.

*developmental* **connection**

**The Brain.** The prefrontal cortex is the location in the brain where much of executive function occurs, Chapter 4, LO 2

**critical thinking** Thinking reflectively and productively, and evaluating the evidence.

In the view of critics such as Jacqueline and Martin Brooks (1993, 2001), few schools teach students to think critically. Schools push students to give a single correct answer rather than encouraging them to come up with new ideas and rethink conclusions. Too often teachers ask students to recite, define, describe, state, and list rather than to analyze, infer, connect, synthesize, criticize, create, evaluate, think, and rethink. As a result, many schools graduate students who think superficially, staying on the surface of problems rather than becoming deeply engaged in meaningful thinking.

One way to encourage students to think critically is to present them with controversial topics or both sides of an issue to discuss (Osborne, 2010). Some teachers shy away from having students debate issues because arguments supposedly are not "polite" or "nice" (Winn, 2004). But debates can motivate students to delve more deeply into a topic and examine issues, especially if teachers refrain from stating their own views so that students feel free to explore multiple perspectives.

According to Ellen Langer (2005), **mindfulness**—being alert, mentally present, and cognitively flexible while going through life's everyday activities and tasks—is an important aspect of thinking critically. Mindful children and adults maintain an active awareness of the circumstances in their lives and are motivated to find the best solutions to tasks. Mindful individuals create new ideas, are open to new information, and can operate from more than one perspective. By contrast, mindless individuals are entrapped in old ideas, engage in automatic behaviour, and operate from a single perspective.

Recently, Robert Roeser and Philip Zelazo have emphasized that mindfulness is an important mental process that children can engage in to improve a number of cognitive and socioemotional skills, such as executive function, focused attention, emotion regulation, and empathy (Roeser & Zelazo, 2012). It has been proposed that mindfulness training could be implemented in schools, using age appropriate activities that increase children's reflection on moment-to-moment experiences to improve self-regulation (Zelazo & Lyons, 2012). One such program implemented in elementary schools in Vancouver, British Columbia, has had some success with increasing optimism, socially competent behaviours, and self-concept for children in Grades 4 and 5 (Schonert-Reichl & Stewart-Lawlor, 2010).

*developmental* **connection**

**Exercise.** Recent research indicates that more physically fit children have better thinking skills, including those involving executive function, than less physically fit children. Chapter 4, LO 4

**Scientific Thinking** Some aspects of thinking are specific to a particular domain, such as mathematics, science, or reading. We will explore reading in Chapter 9, "Language Development." Here we will examine scientific thinking by children.

Like scientists, children ask fundamental questions about reality and seek answers to problems that seem utterly trivial or unanswerable to other people (e.g., Why is the sky blue?). Do children generate hypotheses, perform experiments, and reach conclusions about their data in ways resembling those of scientists?

Scientific reasoning often is aimed at identifying causal relationships. Like scientists, children place a great deal of emphasis on causal mechanisms (Martin & others, 2005). Their understanding of how events are caused weighs more heavily in their causal inferences than even such strong influences as whether the cause happened immediately before the effect.

There also are important differences between the reasoning of children and the reasoning of scientists (Kuhn, 2011, 2013). Children are more influenced by happenstance events than by an overall pattern, and children tend to maintain their old theories regardless of the evidence (Kuhn, Schauble, & Garcia-Mila, 1992). Children might go through mental gymnastics trying to reconcile seemingly contradictory new information with their existing beliefs. For example, after learning about the solar system, children sometimes conclude that there are two Earths, the seemingly flat world in which they live and the round ball floating in space that their teacher described.

Children also have difficulty designing experiments that can distinguish among alternative causes (Kuhn, 2011). Instead, they tend to bias the experiments in favour of whatever hypothesis they began with. Sometimes they see the results as supporting their original hypothesis even when the results directly contradict it. Thus, although there are important similarities between children and scientists, in their basic curiosity and in the kinds of questions they ask, there are also important differences in the degree to which they can separate theory and evidence and in their ability to design conclusive experiments (Lehrer & Schauble, 2006).

Too often, the skills scientists use, such as careful observation, graphing, self-regulatory thinking, and knowing when and how to apply one's knowledge to solve problems, are not routinely taught in schools (Zembal-Saul, McNeill, & Hershberger, 2013). Children have many concepts that are incompatible with science and reality. Good teachers perceive and understand a child's underlying scientific concepts, then use the concepts as a scaffold for learning. Effective science teaching helps children distinguish between fruitful errors and misconceptions, and detect plainly wrong ideas that need to be replaced by more accurate conceptions (Herrell, Jordan, & Eby, 2013). It is important for teachers to initially scaffold students' science learning, extensively monitor their progress, and ensure that they are learning science content (McNeill & Krajcik, 2013). Thus, in pursuing science investigations, students need to learn both inquiry skills and science content (Lehrer & Schauble, 2006).

**Solving Problems**   Children face many problems, both in school and out of school. *Problem solving* involves finding an appropriate way to attain a goal. Let's examine two ways children solve problems—by applying rules and by using analogies—and then consider some ways to help children learn effective strategies for solving problems.

*Using Rules to Solve Problems*   During early childhood, the relatively stimulus-driven toddler is transformed into a child capable of flexible, goal-directed problem solving (Zelazo & Muller, 2011). One element in this change is children's developing ability to form representations of reality.

For example, because they lack a concept of perspectives, 3- to 4-year-olds cannot understand that a single stimulus can be redescribed in a different, incompatible way (Perner & others, 2002). Consider a problem in which children must sort stimuli using the rule of *colour*. In the course of the colour sorting, a child may describe a red rabbit as a *red one* to solve the problem. However, in a subsequent task, the child may need to discover a rule that describes the rabbit as just a *rabbit* to solve the problem. If 3- to 4-year-olds fail to understand that it is possible to provide multiple descriptions of the same stimulus, they persist in describing the stimulus as a red rabbit. In other words, the 3- to 4-year-olds show representational inflexibility. Researchers have found that at about 4 years of age, children acquire the concept of perspectives, which allows them to appreciate that a single thing can be described in different ways (Frye, 1999).

With age, children also learn better rules to apply to problems (Williamson, Jaswal, & Meltzoff, 2010). Figure 7.13 provides an example; it shows the balance scale problem that has been used to examine children's use of rules in solving problems. The scale includes a fulcrum and an arm that can rotate around it. The arm can tip left or right or remain level, depending on how weights (metal disks with holes in the centre) are arranged on the pegs in each side of the fulcrum. The child's task is to look at the configuration of weights on the pegs in each problem and then predict whether the left side will go down, the right side will go down, or the arm will balance.

Robert Siegler (1976) hypothesized that children would use one of the four rules listed in Figure 7.13. He reasoned that presenting problems on which different rules would generate different outcomes would allow assessment of each child's rules. Through a child's pattern of correct answers and errors on a set of such problems, that child's underlying rule could be inferred.

What were the results? Almost all 5-year-olds used Rule I, in which the child considers only the weight on the scales. Almost all 9-year-olds used either Rule II, taking both weight and distance into account, or Rule III, which calls for guessing when the weight and distance dimensions would give conflicting information. Both 13-year-olds and 17-year-olds generally used Rule III.

In other words, the older children performed better at solving the problems because they used a better rule. But even 5-year-old children can be trained to use Rule III if they are taught to pay attention to differences in distance. As children learn more about what is relevant to a problem, and learn to encode the relevant information, their ability to use rules in problem solving improves.

Interestingly, despite the 17-year-olds having studied balance scales in physics, almost none of them used the only rule that generated consistently correct answers, Rule IV.

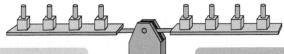

**Rule I.** If the weight is the same on both sides, predict that the scale will balance. If the weight differs, predict that the side with more weight will go down.

**Rule II.** If the weight is greater on one side, say that that side will go down. If the weights on the two sides are equal, choose the side on which the weight is farther from the fulcrum.

Balance scale apparatus

**Rule III.** Act as in Rule II, except that if one side has more weight and the weight on the other side is farther from the fulcrum, then guess.

**Rule IV.** Proceed as in Rule III, unless one side has more weight and the other more distance. In that case, calculate torques by multiplying weight times distance on each side. Then predict that the side with the greater torque will go down.

## FIGURE 7.13

**THE TYPE OF BALANCE SCALE USED BY SIEGLER (1976).** Weights could be placed on pegs on each side of the fulcrum; the torque (the weight on each side times the distance of that weight from the fulcrum) determined which side would go down.

Discussions with their teachers revealed why: The balance scale the students had studied was a pan balance, on which small pans could be hung from various locations along the arm, rather than an arm balance, with pegs extending upward. Retesting the children showed that most could consistently solve the problems when the familiar pan balance was used. This example illustrates a set of lessons that frequently emerge from studies of problem solving—learning is often quite narrow, generalization beyond one's existing knowledge is difficult, and even analogies that seem straightforward are often missed.

*Using Analogies to Solve Problems* An *analogy* involves correspondence in some respects between things that are dissimilar. Even very young children can draw reasonable analogies under some circumstances and use them to solve problems (Morrison, Doumas, & Richland, 2011). Under other circumstances, even college students fail to draw seemingly obvious analogies (as in the high school students' difficulty in extrapolating from the familiar pan balance to the unfamiliar arm balance).

In one effort to discover developmental changes in young children's analogical problem solving, Judy DeLoache (1989) created a situation in which 2½- and 3-year-olds were shown a small toy hidden within a scale model of a room. The child was then asked to find the toy in a real room that was a bigger version of the scale model. If the toy was hidden under the armchair in the scale model, it was also hidden under the armchair in the real room. Considerable development occurred between 2½ and 3 years of age on this task. Thirty-month-old children rarely could solve the problem, but most 36-month-old children could.

Why was the task so difficult for the 2½-year-olds? Their problem was not an inability to understand that a symbol can represent another situation. Shown line drawings or photographs of the larger room, 2½-year-olds had no difficulty finding the object. Instead, the difficulty seemed to come from the toddlers' simultaneously viewing the scale model as a symbol of the larger room and as an object in itself. When children were allowed to play with the scale model before using it as a symbol, their performance worsened, presumably because playing with it made them think of it more as an object in itself. Conversely, when the scale model was placed in a glass case, where the children could not handle it at all, more children used it successfully to find the object hidden in the larger room. The general lesson is that young children can use a variety of tools to draw analogies, but they easily can forget that an object is being used as a symbol of something else and instead treat it as an object in its own right (DeLoache, 2011).

Judy DeLoache (*left*) has conducted research that focuses on young children's developing cognitive abilities. She has demonstrated that children's symbolic representation between 2½ and 3 years of age enables them to find a toy in a real room that is a much bigger version of the scale model.

*Using Strategies to Solve Problems*   Good thinkers routinely use strategies and effective planning to solve problems (Bjorklund, 2013; McCormick, Dimmitt, & Sullivan, 2013). Children's selection of effective strategies in solving problems improves across childhood and into adolescence as children learn more about the world around them and gain more experience (Lemaire & Lecacheur, 2011). As discussed earlier in this chapter, children often use more than one strategy when solving a problem (Pressley, 2007). Most children benefit from generating a variety of alternative strategies and experimenting with different approaches to a problem, discovering what works well, when, and where. This is especially true for children from the middle elementary school grades on, although some cognitive psychologists stress that even young children should be encouraged to practice varying strategies (Siegler, 2012; 2013).

## ADOLESCENCE

In Deanna Kuhn's (2009) view, during the later years of childhood and continuing in adolescence, individuals approach cognitive levels that may or may not be achieved, in contrast with the largely universal cognitive levels that young children attain. By adolescence, considerable variation in cognitive functioning is present across individuals. This variability supports the argument that adolescents are producers of their own development to a greater extent than children.

Kuhn (2009) further argues that the most important cognitive change in adolescence is improvement in executive function, which we discussed earlier in this chapter. Our coverage of executive function in adolescence focuses on critical thinking and decision making.

**Critical Thinking**   Adolescence is an important transitional period in the development of critical thinking (Keating, 1990). Among the cognitive changes that allow improved critical thinking during this period are the following:

- Increased speed, automaticity, and capacity of information processing, which free cognitive resources for other purposes
- Greater breadth of content knowledge in a variety of domains
- Increased ability to construct new combinations of knowledge
- A greater range and more spontaneous use of strategies and procedures for obtaining and applying knowledge, such as planning, considering the alternatives, and cognitive monitoring

Although adolescence is an important period in the development of critical-thinking skills, if a solid basis of fundamental skills (such as literacy and math skills) was not developed during childhood, critical-thinking skills are unlikely to develop adequately in adolescence. In one study of fifth-, eighth-, and eleventh-graders, critical thinking increased with age but still occurred only in 43 percent of eleventh-graders (Keating, 1990).

**Decision Making**   Adolescence is a time of increased decision making: which friends to choose; which person to date; whether to have sex, buy a car, go to college, and so on (Stanovich, West, & Toplak, 2012; Steinberg, 2012, 2013). How competent are adolescents at making decisions? Older adolescents are described as more competent than younger adolescents, who in turn are more competent than children (Keating, 1990). Compared with children, young adolescents are more likely to generate different options, examine a situation from a variety of perspectives, anticipate the consequences of decisions, and consider the credibility of sources.

However, older adolescents' (as well as adults') decision-making skills are far from perfect, and having the capacity to make competent decisions does not guarantee they will be made in everyday life, where breadth of experience often

How do emotions and social contexts influence adolescents' decision making?

comes into play (Kuhn, 2009). As an example, driver-training courses improve adolescents' cognitive and motor skills to levels equal to, or sometimes superior to, those of adults. However, driver training has not been effective in reducing adolescents' high rate of traffic accidents, although researchers have found that implementing a graduated driver licensing (GDR) program can reduce crash and fatality rates for adolescent drivers (Keating, 2007). GDR components include a learner's holding period, practise-driving certification, night-driving restriction, and passenger restriction.

Most people make better decisions when they are calm rather than emotionally aroused, which often is especially true for adolescents (Steinberg, 2012, 2013). Recall from our discussion of brain development in Chapter 4 that adolescents have a tendency to be emotionally intense (Giedd & others, 2012). Thus, the same adolescent who makes a wise decision when calm may make an unwise decision when emotionally aroused. In the heat of the moment, then, adolescents' emotions may overwhelm their decision-making ability.

The social context plays a key role in adolescent decision making. For example, adolescents' willingness to make risky decisions is more likely to occur in contexts where alcohol, drugs, and other temptations are readily available (Reyna & Rivers, 2008). Recent research reveals that the presence of peers in risk-taking situations increases the likelihood that adolescents will make risky decisions (Albert & Steinberg, 2011a, b). In one study of risk taking involving a simulated driving task, the presence of peers increased an adolescent's decision to engage in risky driving by 50 percent but had no effect on adults (Gardner & Steinberg, 2005). One view is that the presence of peers activates the brain's reward system, especially its dopamine pathways (Albert & Steinberg, 2011a, b).

It is also important to consider how the stress level of situations and individual differences in risk taking can influence adolescents' decisions. Few research studies have examined how trait-like tendencies might influence the types of decisions adolescents make when faced with stressful and risky situations. A recent study found that adolescents took more risks in stressful than in non-stressful situations (Johnson, Dariotis, & Wang, 2012). However, risk taking in the stressful conditions was associated with the type of risk taker the adolescent was. In the stressful condition, impulsive risk takers were less accurate and planful, calculated risk takers took fewer risks, and conservative risk takers engaged in low risk taking in both the non-stressful and stressful conditions.

Adolescents need more opportunities to practice and discuss realistic decision making. Many real-world decisions on matters such as sex, drugs, and daredevil driving occur in an atmosphere of stress that includes time constraints and emotional involvement. One strategy for improving adolescent decision making is to provide more opportunities for them to engage in role playing and peer group problem solving. Another strategy is for parents to involve adolescents in appropriate decision-making activities.

To better understand adolescent decision making, Valerie Reyna and her colleagues (Reyna & Brainerd, 2011; Reyna & Farley, 2006; Reyna & others, 2010, 2011) have proposed the **dual-process model**, which states that decision making is influenced by two cognitive systems, one analytical and one experiential, which compete with each other. The dual-process model emphasizes that it is the experiential system—monitoring and managing actual experiences—that benefits adolescents' decision making, not the analytical system. In this view, adolescents don't benefit from engaging in reflective, detailed, higher-level cognitive analysis about a decision, especially in high-risk, real-world contexts. In such contexts, adolescents need to know that some circumstances are so dangerous that they must be avoided at all costs.

In the experiential system, in risky situations it is important for an adolescent to quickly get the gist, or meaning, of what is happening and glean that the situation is a dangerous context, which can cue personal values that will protect the adolescent from making a risky decision (Chick & Reyna, 2012). Further, adolescents have a higher level of trait inhibition (self-control that helps them to manage their impulses effectively) and find themselves in risky contexts are less likely to engage in risk-taking behaviour than their adolescent counterparts with a lower level of trait-inhibition (Chick & Reyna, 2012).

However, some experts on adolescent cognition argue that in many cases adolescents benefit from both analytical and experiential systems (Kuhn, 2009).

**dual-process model** States that decision making is influenced by two systems, one analytical and one experiential, that compete with each other. In this model, it is the experiential system—monitoring and managing actual experiences—that benefits adolescent decision making.

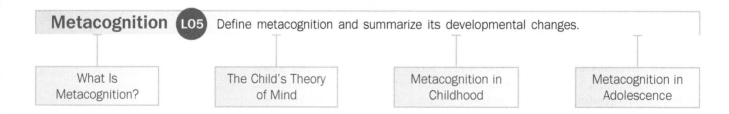

## Review *Connect* Reflect

**L04** Characterize thinking and its developmental changes.

### Review

- What is thinking?
- How does thinking develop in infancy?
- Can children engage in critical and scientific thinking? What are some ways that children solve problems?
- What are some important aspects of thinking in adolescence?

### *Connect*

- In this section, you learned about a study that found a difference between boys' and girls' interests in particular categories of objects or activities. Why do researchers need to be careful about making conclusions regarding gender based on their findings?

### **Reflect** *Your Own Personal Journey of Life*

- How good was your decision making in adolescence? What factors do you think contributed to whether you made good decisions during adolescence?

## Metacognition **L05** Define metacognition and summarize its developmental changes.

| What Is Metacognition? | The Child's Theory of Mind | Metacognition in Childhood | Metacognition in Adolescence |

As discussed earlier in this chapter, *metacognition* is cognition about cognition, or "knowing about knowing" (Flavell, 2004). It is a function of the central executive in Baddeley's model (see Figure 7.3).

# WHAT IS METACOGNITION?

Metacognition can take many forms. It includes thinking about and knowing when and where to use particular strategies for learning or for solving problems. Conceptualization of metacognition includes several dimensions such as planning (deciding on how much time to focus on the task, for example), evaluation (monitoring progress toward task completion, for example), and self-regulation (modifying strategies as work on the task progresses, for example) (Dimmitt & McCormick, 2012).

Metacognition helps children to perform many cognitive tasks more effectively (Flavell, 2004). In one study, students were taught metacognitive skills to help them solve math problems (Cardelle-Elawar, 1992). In each of 30 daily lessons involving math story problems, a teacher guided low-achieving students to recognize when they did not know the meaning of a word, did not have all of the information necessary to solve a problem, did not know how to subdivide the problem into specific steps, or did not know how to carry out a computation. After the 30 daily lessons, the students who were given this metacognitive training had better math achievement and attitudes toward math.

Metacognition can take many forms. It includes knowledge about when and where to use particular strategies for learning or for solving problems. **Metamemory**, individuals' knowledge about memory, is an especially important form of metacognition. Metamemory includes general knowledge about memory, such as knowing that recognition tests (such as multiple-choice questions) are easier than recall tests (such as essay questions). It also encompasses knowledge about one's own memory, such as knowing whether you have studied enough for an upcoming test.

Cognitive developmentalist John Flavell is a pioneer in providing insights about children's thinking. Among his many contributions are establishing the field of metacognition and conducting numerous studies in this area, including metamemory and theory of mind studies.

**metamemory** Knowledge about memory.

# THE CHILD'S THEORY OF MIND

Even young children are curious about the nature of the human mind (Apperly, 2012; Gelman, 2013). They have a **theory of mind**, which refers to awareness of one's own mental processes and the mental processes of others. Studies of theory of mind view the child as "a thinker who is trying to explain, predict, and understand people's thoughts, feelings, and utterances" (Harris, 2006, p. 847).

**theory of mind** Awareness of one's own mental processes and the mental processes of others.

*Developmental Changes*  Although whether infants have a theory of mind continues to be questioned by some (Rakoczy, 2012), the consensus is that some changes occur quite early in development, as we see next. From 18 months to 3 years of age, children begin to understand three mental states:

- *Perceptions*. By 2 years of age, children recognize that another person will see what's in front of their own eyes instead of what's in front of the child's eyes (Lempers, Flavell, & Flavell, 1977), and by 3 years of age, they realize that looking leads to knowing what's inside a container (Pratt & Bryant, 1990).
- *Emotions*. The child can distinguish between positive (for example, happy) and negative (sad, for example) emotions. A child might say, "Tommy feels bad."
- *Desires*. All humans have some sort of desires. But when do children begin to recognize that someone else's desires may differ from their own? Toddlers recognize that if people want something, they will try to get it. For instance, a child might say, "I want my mommy."

Two- to 3-year-olds understand the way that desires are related to actions and to simple emotions. For example, they understand that people will search for what they want and that if they obtain it, they are likely to feel happy, but if they don't they will keep searching for it and are likely to feel sad or angry (Wellman & Woolley, 1990). Children also refer to desires earlier and more

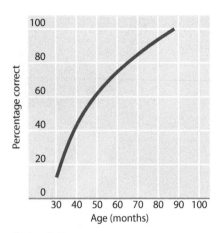

FIGURE **7.14**

**DEVELOPMENTAL CHANGES IN FALSE-BELIEF PERFORMANCE.** False-belief performance dramatically increases from 2½ years of age through the middle of the elementary school years. In a summary of the results of many studies, 2½-year-olds gave incorrect responses about 80 percent of the time (Wellman, Cross, & Watson, 2001). At 3 years, 8 months, they were correct about 50 percent of the time, and after that gave increasingly correct responses.

frequently than they refer to cognitive states such as thinking and knowing (Bartsch & Wellman, 1995).

One of the landmark developments in understanding others' desires is recognizing that someone else may have different desires from one's own (Doherty, 2009; Wellman, 2011). Eighteen-month-olds understand that their own food preferences may not match the preferences of others—they will give an adult the food to which she says "Yummy!" even if the food is something that the infants detest (Repacholi & Gopnik, 1997). As they get older, they can verbalize that they themselves do not like something but an adult might (Flavell & others, 1992).

Between the ages of 3 and 5, children come to understand that the mind can represent objects and events accurately or inaccurately (Low & Simpson, 2012). The realization that people can have *false beliefs*—beliefs that are not true—develops in a majority of children by the time they are 5 years old (Wellman, Cross, & Watson, 2001) (see Figure 7.14). This point is often described as a pivotal one in understanding the mind—recognizing that beliefs are not just mapped directly into the mind from the surrounding world, but also that different people can have different, and sometimes incorrect, beliefs (Gelman, 2009). In a classic false-belief task, young children were shown a Band-Aids box and asked what was inside (Jenkins & Astington, 1996). To the children's surprise, the box actually contained pencils. When asked what a child who had never seen the box would think was inside, 3-year-olds typically responded, "Pencils." However, the 4- and 5-year-olds, grinning at the anticipation of the false beliefs of other children who had not seen what was inside the box, were more likely to say "Band-Aids."

In a similar task, children are told a story about Sally and Anne: Sally places a toy in a basket and then leaves the room (see Figure 7.15). In her absence, Anne takes the toy from the basket and places it in a box. Children are asked where Sally will look for the toy when she returns. The major finding is that 3-year-olds tend to fail false-belief tasks, saying that Sally will look in the box (even though Sally could not know that the toy has moved to this new location). Four-year-olds and older children tend to pass the task, correctly saying that Sally will have a false belief—she will think the object is in the basket, even though that belief is now false. The conclusion from these studies is that children younger than 4 years old do not understand that it is possible to have a false belief.

It is only beyond the preschool years—at approximately 5 to 7 years of age—that children have a deepening appreciation of the mind itself rather than just an understanding of mental states (Wellman, 2011). For example, they begin to recognize that people's behaviours do not necessarily reflect their thoughts and feelings (Flavell, Green, & Flavell, 1993). Not until middle and late childhood do children see the mind as an active constructor of knowledge or a processing centre (Flavell, Green, & Flavell, 1998) and move from understanding that beliefs can be false to realizing that the same event can be open to multiple interpretations (Carpendale & Chandler, 1996). For example, in one study, children saw an ambiguous line drawing (for example, a drawing that could be seen as either a duck or a rabbit); one puppet told the child she believed the drawing was a duck while another puppet told the child he believed the drawing was a rabbit (see Figure 7.16). Before the age of 7, children said that there was one right answer, and it was not okay for the puppets to have different opinions.

While most research on children's theory of mind focuses on children around or before their preschool years, at 7 years of age and beyond there are important developments in the ability to understand the beliefs and thoughts of others. Although understanding that people

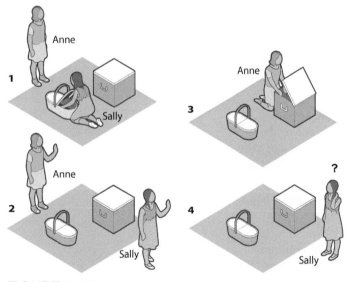

FIGURE **7.15**

**THE SALLY AND ANN FALSE-BELIEF TASK.** In the false-belief task, the skit above in which Sally has a basket and Anne has a box is shown to children. Sally places a toy in her basket and then leaves. While Sally is gone and can't watch, Anne removes the toy from Sally's basket and places it in her box. Sally then comes back and the children are asked where they think Sally will look for her toy. Children are said to "pass" the false-belief task if they understand that Sally looks in her basket first before realizing the toy isn't there.

may have different interpretations is important, it is also necessary to recognize that some interpretations and beliefs may still be evaluated on the basis of the merits of arguments and evidence (Kuhn, Cheney, & Weinstock, 2000). In early adolescence, children begin to understand that people can have ambivalent feelings (Flavell & Miller, 1998). They start to recognize that the same person can feel both happy and sad about the same event. They also engage in more recursive thinking: thinking about what other people are thinking about.

*Individual Differences*  As in other developmental research, there are individual differences in the ages when children reach certain milestones in their theory of mind. For example, children who talk with their parents about feelings frequently as 2-year-olds show better performance on theory of mind tasks (Ruffman, Slade, & Crowe, 2002), as do children who frequently engage in pretend play (Harris, 2000). Another individual difference in understanding the mind involves autism (Doherty, 2009). To learn how theory of mind differs in children with autism, see *Connecting Through Research*.

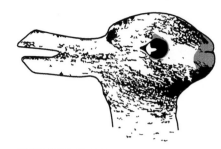

FIGURE **7.16**
**AMBIGUOUS LINE DRAWING.**

connecting through research

## How Does Theory of Mind Differ in Children with Autism?

Approximately 1 in 100 Canadian children is estimated to have some sort of autism spectrum disorder (Ouellette-Kuntz & others, 2012). Autism is usually diagnosed by the age of 5 years, and sometimes earlier. Children with autism show a number of behaviours different from children their age, including deficits in social interaction and communication as well as repetitive behaviours or interests. They often show indifference toward others, in many instances preferring to be alone and showing more interest in objects than people. It now is accepted that autism is linked to genetic and brain abnormalities (Deeley & Murphy, 2009; Glessner & others, 2009).

Children and adults with autism have difficulty in social interactions. These deficits are generally greater than deficits in children the same mental age with intellectual disability (Baron-Cohen, 2009, 2011). Researchers have found that children with autism have difficulty in developing a theory of mind, especially in understanding others' beliefs and emotions (Bertoglio & Hendren, 2009; Peterson & others, 2009). Although children with autism tend to do poorly reasoning in false-belief tasks (Peterson, 2005), they can perform much better on reasoning tasks requiring an understanding of physical causality.

In relation to theory of mind, however, it is important to consider the effects of individual variations in the abilities of children with autism (Harris, 2006). Children with autism are not a homogeneous group, and some have less severe social and communication problems than others. Thus, it is not surprising that children who have less severe forms of autism do better than those who have more severe forms of the disorder on some theory-of-mind tasks. For example, higher-functioning children with autism show reasonable progress in understanding others' desires (Harris, 2006). Recently it has been emphasized that

A young boy with autism. *What are some characteristics of children who have autism? What are some deficits in their theory of mind?*

children with autism might have difficulty in understanding others' beliefs and emotions not only because of theory-of-mind deficits but also due to other aspects of cognition such as problems in focusing attention, eye gaze, face recognition, memory, language impairment, or some general intellectual impairment (Boucher, 2012a, b; Boucher, Mayes, & Bigham, 2012).

Some recent theories of autism suggest that weaknesses in executive functioning may be related to the problems experienced by those with autism in performing theory-of-mind tasks. Other theories have pointed out that typically developing individuals process information by extracting the big picture, whereas those with autism process information in a very detailed, almost obsessive way. It may be that in autism a number of different but related deficits lead to social cognitive deficits (Rajendran & Mitchell, 2007).

## METACOGNITION IN CHILDHOOD

By 5 or 6 years of age, children usually know that familiar items are easier to remember than unfamiliar ones, that short lists are easier than long ones, that recognition is easier than recall, and that forgetting becomes more likely over time (Lyon & Flavell, 1993). However, the metamemory of young children is limited. They don't understand that related items are easier to remember than unrelated ones or that remembering the gist of a story is easier than remembering information verbatim (Kreutzer & Flavell, 1975). By fifth grade students understand that gist recall is easier than verbatim recall.

Preschool children also have an inflated opinion of their memory abilities. For example, in one study, a majority of preschool children predicted that they would be able to recall all 10 items of a list of 10 items. When tested, none of the young children managed this feat (Flavell, Friedrichs, & Hoyt, 1970). As they move through the elementary school years, children give more realistic evaluations of their memory skills (Schneider & Pressley, 1997).

Preschool children also have little appreciation for the importance of cues to memory, such as "It helps when you can think of an example of it." By 7 or 8 years of age, children better appreciate the importance of cueing for memory. In general, children's understanding of their memory abilities and their skill in evaluating their performance on memory tasks is relatively poor at the beginning of the elementary school years but improves considerably by 11 to 12 years of age (Bjorklund, 2012).

## METACOGNITION IN ADOLESCENCE

Important changes in metacognition take place during adolescence (Kuhn, 2008, 2009). Compared with when they were children, adolescents have an increased capacity to monitor and manage cognitive resources to effectively meet the demands of a learning task. This increased metacognitive ability results in cognitive functioning and learning becoming more effective.

A recent longitudinal study revealed that from 12 to 14 years of age, young adolescents increasingly used metacognitive skills and used them more effectively in math and history classes (van der Stel & Veenman, 2010). For example, 14-year-olds monitored their own text comprehension more frequently and did so more effectively than their younger counterparts. Another recent study documented the importance of metacognitive skills, such as planning, strategizing, and monitoring, in college students' ability to think critically (Magno, 2010).

An important aspect of cognitive functioning and learning is determining how much attention will be allocated to an available resource. Evidence is accumulating that adolescents have a better understanding of how to effectively deploy their attention to different aspects of a task than children do (Kuhn, 2009). Further, adolescents have a better meta-level understanding of strategies—that is, knowing the best strategy to use and when to use it in performing a learning task.

Keep in mind, though, that there is considerable individual variation in adolescents' metacognition. Indeed, some experts argue that individual variation in metacognition becomes much more pronounced in adolescence than in childhood (Kuhn, 2009). Thus, some adolescents are quite good at using metacognition to improve their learning, while others are far less so.

**L05** Define metacognition and summarize its developmental changes.

**Review**

- What is metacognition?
- What is theory of mind? How does children's theory of mind change developmentally?
- How does metacognition change during childhood?

*Connect*

- Compare the classic false-belief task study you learned about in this section with what you learned about A-not-B error studies in Chapter 6. What is similar and what is different about these studies and what they are assessing?

**Reflect** *Your Own Personal Journey of Life*

- Do you remember your teachers ever instructing you in ways to improve your use of metacognition—that is, your "knowing about knowing" and "thinking about thinking," when you were in elementary and secondary school? To help you to think further about this question, connect the discussion of metacognition that you just read with the discussion of strategies earlier in the chapter.

# case study **connections**

1. How is memory involved in the various academic activities described in the opening vignette?

2. How is executive function involved in the various academic activities described in the opening vignette?

3. How might language development contribute to cognitive development, and vice versa?

4. How might deficits in attention interfere with the academic activities described in the opening vignette?

# reach your **learning goals**

# Information Processing

## The Information-Processing Approach  **L01** Explain the information-processing approach.

The Information-Processing Approach to Development

- The information-processing approach analyzes how individuals manipulate information, monitor it, and create strategies for handling it. Attention, memory, and thinking are involved in effective information processing. The computer has served as a model for how humans process information. In the information-processing approach, children's cognitive development results from their ability to overcome processing limitations by increasingly executing basic operations, expanding information-processing capacity, and acquiring new knowledge and strategies.

Cognitive Resources: Capacity and Speed of Processing Information

- Capacity and speed of processing information, often referred to as cognitive resources, increase across childhood and adolescence. Changes in the brain serve as biological foundations for developmental changes in cognitive resources. In terms of capacity, the increase is reflected in older children being able to hold in mind several dimensions of a topic simultaneously. A reaction-time task has often been used to assess speed of processing. Processing speed continues to improve in early adolescence.

| Mechanisms of Change |

- According to Siegler, three important mechanisms of change are encoding (how information gets into memory), automaticity (ability to process information with little or no effort), and strategy construction (creation of new procedures for processing information). Children's information processing is characterized by self-modification, and an important aspect of this self-modification involves metacognition—that is, knowing about knowing.

| Comparisons with Piaget's Theory |

- Unlike Piaget, the information-processing approach does not see development as occurring in distinct stages. Instead, this approach holds that individuals develop a gradually increasing capacity for processing information, which allows them to develop increasingly complex knowledge and skills. Like Piaget's theory, some versions of the information-processing approach are constructivist—they see children directing their own cognitive development.

## Attention

 Define attention and outline its developmental changes.

| What Is Attention? |

- Attention is the focusing of mental resources. Four ways that children can allocate their attention are selective attention (focusing on a specific aspect of experience that is relevant while ignoring others that are irrelevant); divided attention (concentrating on more than one activity at the same time); sustained attention (maintaining attention to a selected stimulus for a prolonged period of time, also referred to as focused attention and vigilance); and executive attention (planning actions, allocating attention to goals, detecting errors and compensating for them, monitoring progress on tasks, and dealing with novel or difficult tasks).

| Infancy |

- Even newborns can fixate on a contour, but as infants get older they can scan a pattern more thoroughly. Attention in the first year of life is dominated by the orienting/investigative process. Attention in infancy is often studied through habituation and dishabituation. Habituation can provide a measure of an infant's maturity and well-being. Joint attention increases an infant's ability to learn from others.

| Childhood |

- Salient stimuli tend to capture the attention of the preschooler. After 6 or 7 years of age, there is a shift to more cognitive control of attention. Young children especially make advances in executive and sustained attention. Selective attention also improves through childhood. Children's attentional skills are increasingly being found to predict later cognitive competencies, such as school readiness.

| Adolescence |

- Adolescents typically have better attentional skills than children do, although there are wide individual differences in how effectively adolescents deploy their attention. Sustained attention and executive attention are especially important as adolescents are required to work on increasingly complex tasks that take longer to complete. Multi-tasking is an example of divided attention, and it can harm adolescents' attention when they are engaging in a challenging task.

## Memory

L03 Describe what memory is and how it changes.

| What Is Memory? |

- Memory is the retention of information over time. Psychologists study the processes of memory: how information is initially placed or encoded into memory, how it is retained or stored, and how it is found or retrieved for a certain purpose later. Short-term memory involves retaining information for up to 30 seconds, assuming there is no rehearsal of the information. Long-term memory is a relatively permanent and unlimited type of memory. Working memory is a kind of "mental workbench" where individuals manipulate and assemble information when they make decisions, solve problems, and comprehend written and spoken language. Many contemporary psychologists prefer the term *working memory* over *short-term memory*. Working memory is linked to children's reading comprehension and problem solving. People construct and reconstruct their memories. Schema theory states that people mould memories to fit the information that already exists in their minds. Fuzzy trace theory states that memory is best understood by considering two types of memory representation: (1) verbatim memory trace, and (2) fuzzy trace, or gist. According to this theory, older children's better memory is attributed to the fuzzy traces created by extracting the gist of information. Children's ability to remember new information about a subject depends extensively on what they already know about it. The contribution of content knowledge is especially relevant in the memory of experts. Experts have a number of characteristics that can explain why they solve problems better than novices do.

Infancy

- Infants as young as 2 to 3 months of age display implicit memory, which is memory without conscious recollection, as in memory of perceptual-motor skills. However, many experts stress that explicit memory, which is the conscious memory of facts and experiences, does not emerge until the second half of the first year of life. Older children and adults remember little if anything from the first three years of their lives.

Childhood

- Young children can remember a great deal of information if they are given appropriate cues and prompts. One method of assessing short-term memory is with a memory-span task, on which there are substantial developmental changes through the childhood years. Children's memory improves in the elementary school years as they begin to use gist more, acquire more content knowledge and expertise, develop large memory spans, and use more effective strategies. Organization, elaboration, and imagery are important memory strategies. Current research focuses on how accurate children's long-term memories are and the implications of this accuracy for children as eyewitnesses.

Adolescence

- Short-term memory, as assessed in memory span, increases during adolescence. Working memory also increases in adolescence.

# Thinking

LO4 Characterize thinking and its developmental changes.

What Is Thinking?

- Thinking involves manipulating and transforming information in memory. We can think about the past, reality, and fantasy. Thinking helps us reason, reflect, evaluate, solve problems, and make decisions.

Infancy

- Studies of thinking in infancy focus on concept formation and categorization. Concepts are categories that group objects, events, and characteristics on the basis of common properties. Infants form concepts early in their development, with perceptual categorization appearing as early as 3 months of age. Mandler argues that it is not until about 7 to 9 months of age that infants form conceptual categories. Infants' first concepts are broad. Over the first two years of life, these broad concepts gradually become more differentiated.

Childhood

- Advances in executive function, an umbrella-like concept that consists of a number of higher-level cognitive processes linked to the development of the prefrontal cortex, occur in childhood. Executive function involves managing one's thoughts to engage in goal-directed behaviour and to exercise self-control. Contemporary research reveals that executive functions may be enhanced through training programs or extra-curricular activities. Critical thinking involves thinking reflectively and productively, and evaluating the evidence. Mindfulness is an important aspect of critical thinking. Children and scientists think alike in some ways, but not alike in others. Problem solving relies on the use of strategies, rules, and analogies. Even young children can use analogies to solve problems in some circumstances.

Adolescence

- Two important aspects of adolescent thinking are critical thinking and decision making. Adolescence is an important transitional period in critical thinking because of cognitive changes such as increased speed, automaticity, and capacity of information processing; broadening of content knowledge; increased ability to construct new combinations of knowledge; and a greater range and spontaneous use of strategies. Older adolescents make better decisions than younger adolescents, who in turn are better at this than children are. Being able to make competent decisions, however, does not mean actually making them in everyday life, where breadth of experience comes into play. Adolescents often make better decisions when they are calm than when they are emotionally aroused. Social contexts, especially the presence of peers, influence adolescent decision making. The dual-process model has been advanced to explain the nature of adolescent decision making.

# Metacognition

**L05** Define metacognition and summarize its developmental changes.

What Is Metacognition?

The Child's Theory of Mind

- Metacognition is cognition about cognition, or knowing about knowing.

- Theory of mind refers to a child's awareness of his or her own mental processes and the mental processes of others. Young children are curious about the human mind, and this has been studied under the topic of theory of mind. A number of developmental changes characterize children's theory of mind. For example, by 5 years of age most children realize that people can have false beliefs—beliefs that are untrue. Individual variations also are involved in theory of mind. For example, children with autism have difficulty in developing a theory of mind.

Metacognition in Childhood

- Metamemory improves in middle and late childhood. As children progress through the elementary school years, they make more realistic judgments about their memory skills and increasingly understand the importance of memory cues.

Metacognition in Adolescence

- Adolescents have an increased capacity to monitor and manage resources to effectively meet the demands of a learning task, although there is considerable individual variation in metacognition during adolescence.

For more information on the resources available from McGraw-Hill Ryerson, go to www.mheducation.ca/he/solutions

# Intelligence | chapter 8

Michael is a healthy, happy, and energetic boy in grade 3. His parents first became concerned about his development when he didn't talk or walk on time. At 15 months he was far behind other children in many areas, particularly his speech and his lack of curiosity about the world around him. When he was 18 months, he started speech therapy. Now in grade 3, he has a significant delay in expressive language, speaking only in one- to four-word utterances. He knows ten letters in the alphabet but cannot print the letters of his name in sequence. He is able to dress and groom himself. The major emphasis of his education is on the development of self-help skills and functional academics, although he is integrated into a regular classroom. He has many friends at school, but he does have a short attention span and sometimes uses aggressive behaviour to meet his needs.

Ian taught himself to read, write, and count before he was 2. At 4 he assisted his kindergarten teacher by reading stories to other children. By the time he entered school, at 5, he was reading, with great enjoyment, E. B. White's *Charlotte's Web*. He took an equal delight in mathematical problem solving, having taught himself to add, subtract, multiply, and divide. The teacher's response to Ian's remarkable abilities was to place him, along with the other 5-year-olds, in a reading-readiness program and a math program that involved recognizing the numbers one through ten. Six months into Ian's first school year, his parents were called for an emergency conference with the school vice-principal, who informed them that the school wished to have Ian tested as a preliminary to referring him to a special school for behaviourally disturbed children. According to the vice-principal, Ian had become uncontrollable in class and was displaying frightening bouts of physical violence toward other children. The school psychologist assessed Ian on the Wechsler Intelligence Scale for Children as having an IQ of 170. On a standardized test of reading achievement, he had reading accuracy and comprehension ages of 12. He was just over 5 years old. The school psychologist recommended that Ian required an educational program adapted to his specific needs.

# preview

The two children described in the chapter opening illustrate the extremes of intelligence. In this chapter, you will see that there is spirited debate about whether people have a general intelligence or a number of specific intelligences. The concept of intelligence has also generated other controversies, including whether intelligence is more strongly influenced by heredity or by environment, whether there is cultural bias in intelligence testing, and whether intelligence tests are misused. We explore these controversies in this chapter, and trace the development of intelligence from infancy through adolescence. Finally, we will look at the extremes of intelligence and creativity.

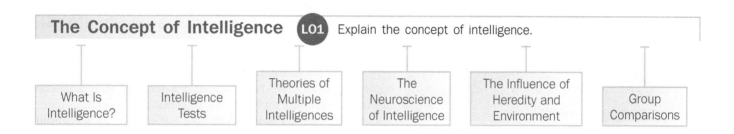

The Concept of Intelligence — **LO1** Explain the concept of intelligence.

What Is Intelligence? | Intelligence Tests | Theories of Multiple Intelligences | The Neuroscience of Intelligence | The Influence of Heredity and Environment | Group Comparisons

Intelligence is one of our most prized attributes. However, even the most intelligent people do not agree on how to define it and how to measure it.

## WHAT IS INTELLIGENCE?

What does the term *intelligence* mean to psychologists? Some experts describe intelligence as the ability to solve problems. Others describe it as the capacity to adapt and learn from experience. Still others argue that intelligence includes characteristics such as creativity and interpersonal skills.

The problem with intelligence is that, unlike height, weight, and age, intelligence cannot be directly measured. We can't peel back a person's scalp and see how much intelligence he or she has. We can evaluate intelligence only *indirectly,* by studying and comparing the intelligent acts that people perform.

The primary components of intelligence are similar to the cognitive processes of memory and thinking that we discussed in Chapter 7. The differences in how these cognitive processes are described, and how we will discuss intelligence, lie in the concepts of individual differences and assessment. *Individual differences* are the stable, consistent ways in which people differ from one another. Individual differences in intelligence generally have been measured by intelligence tests designed to tell us whether a person can reason better than others who have taken the test.

We will use as our definition of **intelligence** *the ability to solve problems and to adapt and learn from experiences.* But even this broad definition doesn't satisfy everyone. As you will see shortly, Howard Gardner proposes that musical skills should be considered part of intelligence. Also, a definition of intelligence based on a theory such as Vygotsky's, which we discussed in Chapter 6, would have to include the ability to use the tools of the culture with help from more-skilled individuals. Because intelligence is such an abstract, broad concept, it is not surprising that there are different ways to define it.

## INTELLIGENCE TESTS

The two main intelligence tests that are administered to children on an individual basis today are the Stanford-Binet test and the Wechsler scales. As you

As many people, as many minds, each in his own way.

—TERENCE
*Roman Playwright, 2nd Century BC*

**intelligence** The ability to solve problems and to adapt to and learn from experiences.

### developmental connection

**Information Processing.** The information processing approach emphasizes how children manipulate, monitor, and create strategies for handling information. Chapter 7, LO 1

Alfred Binet constructed the first intelligence test after being asked to create a measure to determine which children could benefit from instruction in France's schools and which could not.

**mental age (MA)** An individual's level of mental development relative to others.

**intelligence quotient (IQ)** An individual's mental age divided by chronological age and multiplied by 100; devised in 1912 by William Stern.

**normal distribution** A symmetrical distribution with a majority of the cases falling in the middle of the possible range of scores and few scores appearing toward the extremes of the range.

will see next, an early version of the Binet was the first intelligence test to be devised.

**The Binet Tests** In 1904, the French Ministry of Education asked psychologist Alfred Binet to devise a method of identifying children who were unable to learn in school. School officials wanted to reduce crowding by placing students who did not benefit from regular classroom teaching in special schools. Binet and his student Theophile Simon developed an intelligence test to meet this request. The test is called the 1905 Scale. It consisted of 30 questions, ranging from the ability to touch one's ear to the abilities to draw designs from memory and define abstract concepts.

Binet developed the concept of **mental age (MA)**, an individual's level of mental development relative to others. In 1912, William Stern created the concept of **intelligence quotient (IQ)**, which refers to a person's mental age divided by chronological age (CA), multiplied by 100. That is, $IQ = MA/CA \times 100$.

If mental age is the same as chronological age, then the person's IQ is 100. If mental age is above chronological age, then IQ is more than 100. For example, a 6-year-old with a mental age of 8 would have an IQ of 133. If mental age is below chronological age, then IQ is less than 100. For example, a 6-year-old with a mental age of 5 would have an IQ of 83.

The Binet test has been revised many times to incorporate advances in the understanding of intelligence and intelligence testing. These revisions are called the *Stanford-Binet tests* (because the revisions were made at Stanford University). By administering the test to large numbers of people of different ages from different backgrounds, researchers have found that scores on a Stanford-Binet test approximate a normal distribution (see Figure 8.1). A **normal distribution** is symmetrical, with a majority of the scores falling in the middle of the possible range of scores and few scores appearing toward the extremes of the range.

The current Stanford-Binet test is administered individually to people aged 2 through adult. It includes a variety of items, some of which require verbal responses, others non-verbal responses. For example, items that reflect a typical 6-year-old's level of performance on the test include the verbal ability to define at least six words, such as *orange* and *envelope*, as well as the non-verbal ability

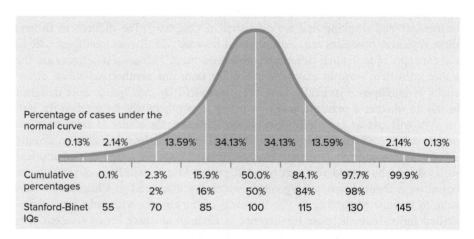

| Percentage of cases under the normal curve | | | | | | | | |
|---|---|---|---|---|---|---|---|---|
| 0.13% | 2.14% | | 13.59% | 34.13% | 34.13% | 13.59% | 2.14% | 0.13% |
| **Cumulative percentages** | 0.1% | 2.3% | 15.9% | 50.0% | 84.1% | 97.7% | 99.9% | |
| | | 2% | 16% | 50% | 84% | 98% | | |
| **Stanford-Binet IQs** | 55 | 70 | 85 | 100 | 115 | 130 | 145 | |

## FIGURE 8.1

**THE NORMAL CURVE AND STANFORD-BINET IQ SCORES.** The distribution of IQ scores approximates a normal curve. Most of the population falls in the middle range of scores. Notice that extremely high and extremely low scores are very rare. Slightly more than two-thirds of the scores fall between 84 and 116. Only about 1 in 50 individuals has an IQ of more than 132, and only about 1 in 50 individuals has an IQ of less than 68.

to trace a path through a maze. Items that reflect an average adult's level of performance include defining such words as *disproportionate* and *regard*, explaining a proverb, and comparing idleness and laziness.

The fifth edition of the Stanford-Binet was published in 2003. This version provides comprehensive coverage of five factors of cognitive ability: fluid reasoning, knowledge, quantitative reasoning, visual-spatial reasoning, and short-term memory. A general composite score is still obtained to reflect overall intelligence.

**The Wechsler Scales** Another set of tests more widely used in Canada to assess students' intelligence is called the *Wechsler Scales*, developed by psychologist David Wechsler. They include the Wechsler Preschool and Primary Scale of Intelligence, Fourth Edition (WPPSI-IV) to test children from 2 years, 6 months to 7 years, 3 months of age; the Wechsler Intelligence Scale for Children, Fifth Edition (WISC-V) for children and adolescents 6 to 16 years of age; and the Wechsler Adult Intelligence Scale, Fourth Edition (WAIS-IV).

The fifth edition of the WISC provides a full-scale IQ score and five composite scores of specific cognitive processing domains: verbal comprehension, fluid reasoning, working memory, visual-spatial, and processing speed. The subtest and composite scores allow the examiner to quickly determine the areas in which the child is strong or weak, while several extra subtests allow the examiner to probe for learning disabilities. It is important to note that the Wechsler scales have Canadian norms. These norms ensure that an individual child's performance is compared to a representative group of Canadian children, making the application and interpretation of these tests within a Canadian context more valid. Three of the Wechsler subscales are shown in Figure 8.2.

Intelligence tests such as the Stanford-Binet and Wechsler are given on an individual basis. A psychologist approaches an individual assessment of intelligence as a structured interaction between the examiner and the child. This provides the psychologist with an opportunity to sample the child's behaviour. During the testing, the examiner observes the ease with which rapport is established, the child's enthusiasm and interest, whether anxiety interferes with the child's performance, and the child's degree of tolerance for frustration.

**The Use and Misuse of Intelligence Tests** Intelligence tests have real-world applications as predictors of longevity, school success, and job success (Brody, 2007; Deary, 2012; Reynolds & Livingston, 2012). Researchers have found that lower intelligence in childhood is linked to illness, chronic disease, and how long people will live (Deary & Batty, 2011). Also, scores on tests of general intelligence are substantially correlated with school grades and achievement test performance, both at the time of the test and years later (Brody, 2007). IQ in the sixth grade correlates about .60 with the number of years of education the individual will eventually obtain (Jencks, 1979). Intelligence tests also are moderately correlated with work performance (Lubinski, 2000).

Despite the links between IQ and academic achievement and occupational success, it is important to keep in mind that many other factors contribute to success in school and work. These include the motivation to succeed, physical and mental health, and social skills (Sternberg, 2009a).

The single number provided by many IQ tests can easily lead to false expectations about an individual (Rosnow & Rosenthal, 1996). Sweeping generalizations are too often made

**Verbal Subscales**

**Similarities**

A child must think logically and abstractly to answer a number of questions about how things might be similar.

Example: "In what way are a lion and a tiger alike?"

**Comprehension**

This subscale is designed to measure an individual's judgment and common sense.

Example: "What is the advantage of keeping money in a bank?"

**Non-verbal Subscales**

**Block Design**

A child must assemble a set of multicolored blocks to match designs that the examiner shows.
Visual-motor coordination, perceptual organization, and the ability to visualize spatially are assessed.

Example: "Use the four blocks on the left to make the pattern on the right."

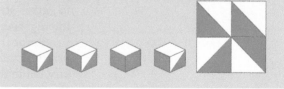

FIGURE **8.2**

**SAMPLE SUBSCALES OF THE WECHSLER INTELLIGENCE SCALE FOR CHILDREN–FIFTH EDITION (WISC-V).** Simulated items similar to those in the Wechsler Intelligence Scale for Children–Fifth Edition (WISC-V). Copyright © 2003 by NCS Pearson, Inc. Reproduced with permission. All rights reserved. *"Wechsler Intelligence Scale for Children"* and *"WISC"* are trademarks, in the US and/or other countries, of Pearson Education, Inc. or its affiliates.

*"How are her scores?"*
© Edward Koren/The New Yorker
Collection/www.cartoonbank.com

**triarchic theory of intelligence** Sternberg's theory that intelligence comes in three forms: analytical, creative, and practical.

Robert J. Sternberg, who developed the triarchic theory of intelligence

on the basis of an IQ score. IQ scores are misused and can become self-fulfilling prophecies (Weinstein, 2004).

To be effective, information about a child's performance on an intelligence test should be used in conjunction with other information about the child. For example, an intelligence test alone should not determine whether a child is placed in a special education or gifted class. The child's developmental history, medical background, performance in school, social competencies, and family experiences should be taken into account, too.

## THEORIES OF MULTIPLE INTELLIGENCES

Is it more appropriate to think of a child's intelligence as a general ability or as a number of specific abilities? Psychologists have thought about this question since early in the twentieth century and continue to debate the issue.

**Sternberg's Triarchic Theory**   According to Robert J. Sternberg's (1986, 2004, 2008, 2009b, d; 2010, c, d) **triarchic theory of intelligence**, intelligence comes in three forms: analytical, creative, and practical. *Analytical intelligence* involves the ability to analyze, judge, evaluate, compare, and contrast. *Creative intelligence* consists of the ability to create, design, invent, originate, and imagine. *Practical intelligence* focuses on the ability to use, apply, implement, and put into practice.

Sternberg (2009b, d; 2010c, d) says that students with different triarchic patterns look different in school. Students with high analytic ability tend to be favoured in conventional schools. They often do well in classes in which the teacher lectures and gives objective tests. These students typically get good grades, do well on traditional IQ tests and later gain admission to competitive universities.

Students high in creative intelligence often are not at the top of the class. Creatively intelligent students might not conform to teachers' expectations about how assignments should be done. They give unique answers, for which they might be reprimanded or marked down.

Like students high in creative intelligence, students who are practically intelligent often do not relate well to the demands of school. However, these students frequently do well outside the classroom's walls. Their social skills and common sense may allow them to become successful managers or entrepreneurs, despite undistinguished school records.

Sternberg (2004, 2010c, d) stresses that few tasks are purely analytic, creative, or practical. Most tasks require some combination of these skills. For example, when students write a book report, they might analyze the book's main themes, generate new ideas about how the book could have been written better, and think about how the book's themes can be applied to people's lives. Sternberg argues that it is important for classroom instruction to give students opportunities to learn through all three types of intelligence.

Sternberg (1998, 2009e, f) argues that wisdom is linked to both practical and academic intelligence. In his view, academic intelligence is a necessary but in many cases insufficient requirement for wisdom. Practical knowledge about the realities of life also is needed for wisdom. For Sternberg, balance between self-interest, the interests of others, and contexts produces a common good. Thus, wise individuals don't just look out for themselves—they also consider others' needs and perspectives as well as the particular context involved. Sternberg assesses wisdom by presenting problems that require solutions highlighting various intrapersonal, interpersonal, and contextual interests. He also emphasizes that such aspects of wisdom should be taught in schools (Sternberg, 2009f; Sternberg, Jarvin, & Reznitskaya, 2009).

**Gardner's Eight Frames of Mind** Howard Gardner (1983, 1993, 2002) says there are many specific types of intelligence or frames of mind. They are described here along with examples of the occupations in which they are reflected as strengths (Campbell, Campbell, & Dickinson, 2004):

*"You're wise, but you lack tree smarts."*
© Donald Reilly/The New Yorker Collection/
www.cartoonbank.com

- *Verbal skills:* The ability to think in words and to use language to express meaning.
  Occupations: Authors, journalists, speakers
- *Mathematical skills:* The ability to carry out mathematical operations
  Occupations: Scientists, engineers, accountants
- *Spatial skills:* The ability to think three-dimensionally
  Occupations: Architects, artists, sailors
- *Bodily-kinesthetic skills:* The ability to manipulate objects and be physically adept
  Occupations: Surgeons, craftspeople, dancers, athletes
- *Musical skills:* A sensitivity to pitch, melody, rhythm, and tone
  Occupations: Composers, musicians, and music therapists
- *Intrapersonal skills:* The ability to understand oneself and effectively direct one's life
  Occupations: Theologians, psychologists
- *Interpersonal skills:* The ability to understand and effectively interact with others
  Occupations: Teachers, mental health professionals
- *Naturalist skills:* The ability to observe patterns in nature and understand natural and human-made systems
  Occupations: Farmers, botanists, ecologists, landscapers

Recently, Gardner has considered adding a ninth type of intelligence to his list of multiple intelligences—*existentialist,* which involves exploring and finding meaning in life, especially regarding questions about life, death, and existence.

Gardner argues that each form of intelligence can be destroyed by a different pattern of brain damage, that each involves unique cognitive skills, and that each shows up in unique ways in both the gifted and idiot savants (individuals who have an intellectual disability but have an exceptional talent in a particular domain, such as drawing, music, or numerical computation).

**Emotional Intelligence** Both Gardner's and Sternberg's theories include one or more categories related to the ability to understand oneself and others and to get along in the world. In Gardner's theory, the categories are called interpersonal intelligence and intrapersonal intelligence; in Sternberg's theory, practical intelligence. Other theorists who emphasize interpersonal, intrapersonal, and practical aspects of intelligence focus on what is called *emotional intelligence,* which was popularized by Daniel Goleman (1995) in his book *Emotional Intelligence.*

The concept of emotional intelligence was initially developed by Peter Salovey and John Mayer (1990). They conceptualize **emotional intelligence** as the ability to perceive and express emotion accurately and adaptively (such as taking the perspective of others), to understand emotion and emotional knowledge (such as understanding the roles that emotions play in friendship and other relationships), to use feelings to facilitate thought (such as being in a positive mood, which is linked to creative thinking), and to manage emotions in oneself and others (such as being able to control one's anger).

There continues to be considerable interest in the concept of emotional intelligence (Gorgens-Eckermans & Brand, 2012; Rode & others, 2008). Recent research studies revealed that high emotional intelligence is generally associated with resiliency (Armstrong, Galligan, & Critchley, 2011), and other positive

**emotional intelligence** The ability to perceive and express emotion accurately and adaptively, to understand emotion and emotional knowledge, to use feelings to facilitate thought, and to manage emotions in oneself and others.

*developmental* **connection**

**Resiliency.** Differences in individual characteristics, including emotional intelligence, contribute to resiliency in childhood. Chapter 1, LO 1

developmental outcomes for school-aged children and adolescents, including higher academic performance (Galla & Wood, 2012; Hogan & others, 2010) and a better ability to get along with peers (Frederickson, Petrides, & Simmonds, 2012; Windingstad, McCallum, Bell, & Dunn, 2011). Critics, however, question whether these relations hold in other cultural groups. Given that culture influences how emotion is experienced and expressed, it is possible that emotional intelligence, as currently understood, is a reflection of European and North American socialization. For example, one study found that First Nations children and adolescents in Canada had lower emotional intelligence scores than non-Aboriginal children (Parker & others, 2005). Aboriginal youth are known to be at risk for a number of mental and physical outcomes that are associated with emotional intelligence in non-Aboriginal populations (Johnson & Cameron, 2001), but these relations have not yet been investigated within this population. Overall, the construct of emotional intelligence needs to be further researched.

### Do Children Have One Intelligence or Many Intelligences?

Figure 8.3 compares the views of Gardner, Sternberg, and Salovey/Mayer. Notice that Gardner includes a number of types of intelligence not addressed by the other views, and that Sternberg is unique in emphasizing creative intelligence. These theories of multiple intelligences have much to offer. They have stimulated us to think more broadly about what makes up people's intelligence and competence (Moran & Gardner, 2006). And they have motivated educators to develop programs that instruct students in different domains (Winner, 2006).

Theories of multiple intelligences have critics who conclude that the research base to support these theories has not yet developed (Jensen, 2008). In particular, some argue that Gardner's classification seems arbitrary. For example, if musical skills represent a type of intelligence, why don't we also refer to chess intelligence, prizefighter intelligence, and so on?

A number of psychologists still support the concept of *g* (general intelligence) (Jensen, 2008; Johnson, te Nijenhuis, & Bouchard, 2008). For example, one expert on intelligence, Nathan Brody (2007), argues that people who excel at one type of intellectual task are likely to excel at other intellectual tasks. Thus, individuals who do well at memorizing lists of digits are also likely to be good at solving verbal problems and spatial layout problems. This general intelligence includes abstract reasoning or thinking, the capacity to acquire knowledge, and problem-solving ability (Carroll, 1993).

Advocates of the concept of general intelligence point to its success in predicting school and job performance (Deary & others, 2007). For example, scores on tests of general intelligence are substantially correlated with school grades and achievement test performance, both at the time of the test and years later (Strenze, 2007). And intelligence tests are moderately correlated with job performance (Lubinski, 2000). Individuals with higher scores on tests designed to measure general intelligence tend to get higher-paying, more prestigious jobs (Strenze, 2007). However, general IQ tests predict only about one fourth of the variation in job success, with most variation being attributable to other factors such as motivation and education (Wagner & Sternberg, 1986).

Some experts who argue for the existence of general intelligence conclude that individuals also have specific intellectual abilities (Brody, 2007). In sum, controversy still characterizes whether it is more accurate to conceptualize intelligence as a general ability, specific abilities, or both (Brody, 2007; Horn, 2007; Sternberg, 2009a, b; 2010c, d).

Sternberg (2009a, b; 2010c, d) actually accepts that there is a *g* for the kinds of analytical tasks that traditional IQ tests assess but thinks that the range of tasks those tests measure is far too narrow.

| Gardner | Sternberg | Salovey/Mayer |
|---|---|---|
| Verbal<br>Mathematical | Analytical | |
| Spatial<br>Movement<br>Musical | Creative | |
| Interpersonal<br>Intrapersonal | Practical | Emotional |
| Naturalistic | | |

## FIGURE 8.3

**COMPARING STERNBERG'S, GARDNER'S, AND SALOVEY/ MAYER'S INTELLIGENCES.**

# THE NEUROSCIENCE OF INTELLIGENCE

In the current era of extensive research on the brain, interest in the neuroscientific underpinnings of intelligence has increased (Brans & others, 2010; Deary, 2012; Glascher & others, 2010; Haier, 2011; Neubauer & Fink, 2009). Among the questions asked about the brain's role in intelligence are the following: Is having a big brain linked to higher intelligence? Is intelligence located in certain brain regions? Is intelligence related to how fast the brain processes information?

Are individuals with a big brain more intelligent than those with a smaller brain? Recent studies using MRI scans to assess total brain volume indicate a moderate correlation (about +.3 to +.4) between brain size and intelligence (Carey, 2007; Luders & others, 2009).

Might intelligence be linked to specific regions of the brain? Early consensus was that the frontal lobes are the likely location of intelligence. However, researchers recently have found that intelligence is distributed more widely across brain regions (Lee & others, 2012; Karama & others, 2009; Luders & others, 2009). The most prominent finding from brain imaging studies is that a distributed neural network involving the frontal and parietal lobes is related to higher intelligence (Colom, Jung, & Haier, 2007; Colom & others, 2009; Deary, Penke, & Johnson, 2010; Glascher & others, 2010) (see Figure 8.4). A recent study revealed that the frontal/parietal network is responsible for cognitive control and connectivity to brain regions outside the network (Cole & others, 2012). Albert Einstein's total brain size was average, but a region of his brain's parietal lobe that is very active in processing math and spatial information was 15 percent larger than average (Witelson, Kigar, & Harvey, 1999). Other brain regions that have been linked to higher intelligence (although at a lower level of significance than the frontal/parietal lobe network) include the temporal and occipital lobes, as well as the cerebellum (Luders & others, 2009).

Examining the neuroscience of intelligence has also led to study of the role that neurological speed might play in intelligence (Waiter & others, 2009). Research results have not been consistent for this possible link, although one recent study did find that speed of neurological functioning was faster for intellectually gifted children than for children with average intelligence (Liu & others, 2007).

As the technology to study the brain's functioning continues to advance in coming decades, we are likely to see more specific conclusions about the brain's role in intelligence. As this research proceeds, keep in mind that both heredity and environment likely contribute to links between the brain and intelligence, including the connections we discussed between brain size and intelligence.

# THE INFLUENCE OF HEREDITY AND ENVIRONMENT

We have seen that intelligence is a slippery concept with competing definitions, tests, and theories. It is not surprising, therefore, that attempts to understand the concept of intelligence are filled with controversy. One of the most controversial areas in the study of intelligence centres on the extent to which intelligence is influenced by genetics and the extent to which it is influenced by environment (Davis, Arden, & Plomin, 2008; Ruano & others, 2010; Sternberg, 2009a). In Chapter 2, we indicated how difficult it is to tease apart these influences, but that has not kept psychologists from trying to unravel them.

*developmental* **connection**

**Brain Development.** The frontal lobes continue to develop through the adolescent and emerging adult years. Chapter 4, LO 2

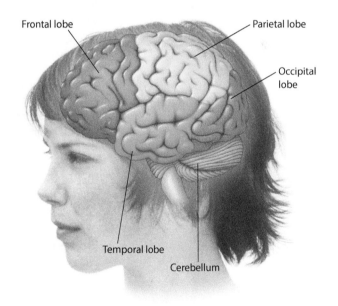

Frontal lobe

Parietal lobe

Occipital lobe

Temporal lobe

Cerebellum

## FIGURE **8.4**

**INTELLIGENCE AND THE BRAIN.** Researchers have found that a higher level of intelligence is linked to a distributed neural network in the frontal and parietal lobes. To a lesser extent than the frontal/parietal network, the temporal and occipital lobes, as well as the cerebellum, have also been found to have links to intelligence. The current consensus is that intelligence is likely to be distributed across brain regions rather than being localized in a specific region, such as the frontal lobes.

**Nature-Nurture.** The epigenetic view emphasizes that development is a result of a bidirectional interchange between heredity and environment, in which environmental factors can influence how genes are expressed. Chapter 2, LO 4

**heritability** The fraction of the variance in a population that is attributed to genetics.

**Genetic Influences**   To what degree do our genes make us smart? Etiological studies have revealed that the more genetically similar individuals are, the greater the intellectual resemblance; that is, monozygotic twins, who share all genetic material, have a higher IQ correlation than do dizygotic twins, who share only half their genes (Brant & others, 2009). However, scientists have not yet been able to identify the specific genes that contribute to intelligence (Nisbett & others, 2012). A recent research review concluded that there may be more than 1,000 genes that affect intelligence, each possibly having a small influence on an individual's intelligence, making the search for specific genes and gene combinations very difficult (Davies & others, 2011).

Adoption studies are often used in attempts to analyze the relative importance of heredity in intelligence (Plomin, DeFries, & Fulker, 2007). In most adoption studies, researchers determine whether the behaviour of adopted children is more like that of their biological parents or their adoptive parents. In two studies, the educational levels attained by biological parents were better predictors of children's IQ scores than were the IQs of the children's adoptive parents (Petrill & Deater-Deckard, 2004; Scarr & Weinberg, 1983). But studies of adoption also document the influence of environments. One recent study revealed a 12 to 18 point increase in IQ when children were adopted from low-income into middle- and upper-income homes (Nisbett & others, 2012).

How strong is the effect of heredity on intelligence? The concept of heritability attempts to separate the effects of heredity and environment in a population. **Heritability** is the fraction of the variance within a population that is attributed to genetics. The heritability index is computed using correlational techniques. Thus, the highest degree of heritabilty is 1.00, and correlations of .70 and above suggest a strong genetic influence. A committee of respected researchers convened by the American Psychological Association concluded that by late adolescence, the heritability of intelligence is about .75, which reflects a strong genetic influence (Neisser & others, 1996).

A key point to keep in mind about heritability is that it refers to a specific group (population), *not* to individuals. Researchers use the concept of heritability to try to describe why people differ. Heritability says nothing about why a single individual, like yourself, has a certain intelligence. Neither does heritability say anything about differences *between* groups.

Most research on heredity and environment does not include environments that differ radically. Thus, it is not surprising that many genetic studies show environment to be a fairly weak influence on intelligence.

The heritability index has several flaws. It is only as good as the data that are entered into its analysis and the interpretations made from it. The data are virtually all from traditional IQ tests, which some experts believe are not always the best indicator of intelligence (Gardner, 2002; Sternberg, 2009a). Also, the heritability index assumes that we can treat genetic and environmental influences as factors that can be separated, with each part contributing a distinct amount of influence. As we discussed in Chapter 2, genes and the environment always work together. Genes always exist in an environment, and the environment shapes their activity.

**Environmental Influences**   Most experts today agree that the environment also plays an important role in intelligence (Campbell, 2007; Sternberg, 2010c, d; Zhang & Sternberg, 2011). This means that improving children's environments can raise their intelligence (Barnett & others, 2011; Irvine & Berry, 2010). One argument for the importance of environment in intelligence involves the increasing scores on IQ tests around the world. Scores on these tests have been increasing so fast that a high percentage of people regarded as having average intelligence in the early 1900s would be considered below average in intelligence today (Flynn, 1999, 2007, 2013) (see Figure 8.5). If a representative sample of today's children took the Stanford-Binet test used in 1932, about one-fourth would be defined as very superior, a label usually accorded to less than 3 percent of the population. Because the increase has taken place in a relatively short period of time, it can't be due to heredity (Flynn

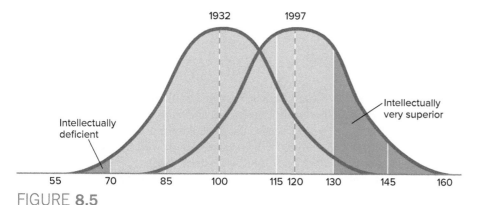

FIGURE **8.5**

**THE INCREASE IN IQ SCORES FROM 1932 TO 1997.** As measured by the Stanford-Binet intelligence test, North American children seem to be getting smarter. Scores of a group tested in 1932 fell along a bell-shaped curve with half below 100 and half above. Studies show that if children took that same test today, half would score above 120 on the 1932 scale. Very few of them would score in the "intellectually deficient" end, on the left side, and about one-fourth would rank in the "very superior" range.

& Rossi-Case, 2012). Rather, it might result from environmental factors such as increased exposure to information and education. One analysis indicated that the substantial increase in intelligence scores in recent years may be due to prenatal and early postnatal nutrition (Lynn, 2009). This worldwide increase in intelligence test scores over a short time frame is called the *Flynn effect,* after the researcher who discovered it, James Flynn (1999, 2007).

Studies of schooling also reveal effects on intelligence (Ceci & Gilstrap, 2000; Gustafsson, 2007). The biggest effects occurred when large groups of children were deprived of formal education for an extended period, resulting in lower intelligence. In one study, the intellectual functioning of ethnic Indian children in South Africa, whose schooling was delayed by four years because of the unavailability of teachers, was investigated (Ramphal, 1962). Compared with children in nearby villages who had teachers, the Indian children whose entry into school was delayed by four years experienced a drop of five IQ points for each year of delay.

Students in an elementary school in South Africa. *How might schooling influence the development of children's intelligence?*

Researchers increasingly are interested in manipulating the early environment of children who are at risk for impoverished intelligence (Campbell, 2007; Sternberg, 2009a). The emphasis is on prevention rather than remediation. Research has indicated that income level is associated with children's intellectual development (Duncan & Brooks-Gunn, 2000). Many low-income parents have difficulty providing an intellectually stimulating environment for their children. Early intervention programs, that educate parents and provide support services such as quality childcare programs, can enhance a child's intellectual development.

One such program is the Aboriginal Head Start Program implemented by the Canadian government in the mid-1990s to improve the education of Aboriginal children. This program targets preschool children in both on-reserve and off-reserve communities. The goals of the program are to provide Aboriginal children with "a positive sense of themselves, a desire for learning, and opportunities to develop fully as successful people" (Public Health Agency of Canada, 2004). The locally implemented and designed programs focus on six core domains: culture and language, education and school readiness, health promotion, nutrition, social support, and parental/family involvement.

The Public Health Agency of Canada (2011) reports that the Aboriginal Head Start program has had a positive effect on school readiness, including children's language, social and academic skills, and health promoting behaviours, such as exposure to daily physical activity. In addition, the program has enhanced

The highest-risk children often benefit the most cognitively when they experience early interventions.

—CRAIG RAMEY
*Contemporary Psychologist,*
*Georgetown University*

## Better Beginnings, Better Futures

In the Better Beginnings, Better Futures intervention project conducted by Queen's University professor Ray Peters and his colleagues, (Peters & others, 2010a; Peters & others, 2010b), 601 young children and their families from socioeconomically disadvantaged neighbourhoods in Ontario participated in a comprehensive early preventative intervention program. This program targeted a variety of development outcomes, including school readiness, children's socio-emotional, cognitive, and physical development, as well as children's mental health.

Compared with children from similar neighbourhoods, improvements in socio-emotional functioning and physical health were noted by Grade 3, but improvements in cognitive functioning and intelligence were not evident at this time. However, differences were found on measures of academic achievement at Grades 6 and 9. Although long-term data on improvements in IQ for children in this program are not available, evaluation of other preventative interventions, such as the Abecedarian Project in the United States does show both short and long-term benefits to intelligence. The success of the Abecedarian Project in improving IQ was evident by the time the children were 3 years of age. At that age, the experimental group showed normal IQs averaging 101, a 17-point advantage over the control group. Recent follow-up results suggest that the effects are long-lasting. More than a

decade later at the age of 15, children from the intervention group maintained an IQ advantage of 5 points over the control-group children (Campbell & others, 2001; Ramey, Ramey, & Lanzi, 2001), and continued to show educational advantages into adulthood (Campbell & others, 2012).

Positive developmental outcomes associated with preventative intervention programs are common. A review of the research on early interventions reached the following conclusions (Brooks-Gunn, 2003):

- High-quality centre-based (rather than home-based) interventions are associated with increases in children's intelligence and school achievement.
- Early interventions are most successful with children from low socioeconomic status homes.
- The positive benefits continue through adolescence but are stronger in early childhood and at the beginning of elementary school.
- The programs that are continued into middle and late childhood have the best long-term results.

*What implications do results of intervention studies have in the debate regarding the relative contribution of nature and nurture to intelligence?*

exposure to Aboriginal languages and cultures, which is associated with greater mental health. To learn more about other successful early intervention programs, see *Connecting Through Research*.

**Revisiting the Nature/Nurture Issue**   In sum, there is a consensus among psychologists that both heredity and environment influence intelligence (Grigorenko & Takanishi, 2010). This consensus reflects the nature/nurture issue that was highlighted in Chapter 1. Recall that the nature/nurture issue focuses on the extent to which development is influenced by nature (heredity) and nurture (environment). Although psychologists agree that intelligence is the product of both nature and nurture, there is still disagreement about how strongly each factor influences intelligence (Deary, Penke, & Johnson, 2010; Sternberg, 2009a; Wadsworth, Olson, & Defries, 2010).

## GROUP COMPARISONS

For decades, many controversies surrounding intelligence tests have grown from the tendency to compare one group with another. Two types of group comparisons have been extensively explored. These are differences between males and females and differences between different cultural and ethnic groups (Nisbett & others, 2012).

**Male-Female Comparisons**   Several research studies have concluded that there is no overall sex difference in general intelligence, or *g* but there are some specific cognitive areas that do show sex differences (Jensen, 1998; Johnson & Bouchard, 2007). In one large scale study, no overall sex difference in intelligence was found when assessed using 42 different mental ability tests, but results revealed a slight advantage for females on verbal tasks, such as word fluency and memory tasks, and for males on visual-spatial tasks like mental rotation (Johnson & Bouchard, 2007). Although some of these sex differences appear to be present from early infancy, many of these sex differences are reduced or eliminated when training on the task or positive stereotypes are provided (Nisbett & others, 2012). Thus, sex differences in cognitive abilities are likely a result of both biological and psychosocial factors (Nisbett & others, 2012).

**Cross-Cultural Comparisons**  Cultures vary in the way they describe what it means to be intelligent (Ang, Dyne, & Tan, 2011; Zhang & Sternberg, 2013). People in Western cultures tend to view intelligence in terms of reasoning and thinking skills, whereas people in Eastern cultures see intelligence as a way for members of a community to successfully engage in social roles (Nisbett, 2003). One study found that Taiwanese-Chinese conceptions of intelligence emphasize understanding and relating to others, including knowing when to show and when not to show one's intelligence (Yang & Sternberg, 1997). The different perceptions of what it means to be intelligent across cultures suggests that the tests traditionally used to measure intelligence may be measuring different things in different cultures.

**Cultural Bias in Testing**  Many of the early intelligence tests were culturally biased, favouring people who were from urban rather than rural environments, of middle socioeconomic status rather than lower socioeconomic status, and Caucasian rather than Black or Aboriginal (Miller-Jones, 1989; Provenzo, 2002). For example, one question on an early test asked what you should do if you find a 3-year-old child in the street. The correct answer was "call the police." But children from inner-city families who perceive the police as adversaries are unlikely to choose this answer. Similarly, children from rural areas might not choose this answer if there is no police force nearby. Such questions clearly do not measure the knowledge necessary to adapt to one's environment or to be "intelligent" in an inner-city neighbourhood or in rural areas (Scarr, 1984). Also, members of minority groups who do not speak English or who speak nonstandard English are at a disadvantage in trying to understand questions framed in standard English (Gibbs & Huang, 1989).

Psychologists have developed **culture-fair tests**, which are intelligence tests that aim to avoid cultural bias. Two types of culture-fair tests have been developed. The first includes questions that are familiar to people from all socioeconomic and ethnic backgrounds. For example, a child might be asked how a bird and a dog are different, on the assumption that virtually all children are familiar with birds and dogs. The second type of culture-fair test contains no verbal questions. Figure 8.6 shows a sample question from Raven's Progressive Matrices tests. Even though tests such as Raven's Progressive Matrices are

The intelligence of the Iatmul people of Papua New Guinea involves the ability to remember the names of many clans.

On the 680 Caroline Islands in the Pacific Ocean east of the Philippines, the intelligence of their inhabitants includes the ability to navigate by the stars. *Why might it be difficult to create one culture-fair intelligence test for the Iatmul children, Caroline Islands children, and U.S. children?*

**culture-fair tests** Intelligence tests that aim to avoid cultural bias.

## FIGURE **8.6**

**SAMPLE ITEM FROM RAVEN'S PROGRESSIVE MATRICES TESTS.** Individuals are presented with a matrix arrangement of symbols, such as the one at the top of this figure, and must then complete the matrix by selecting the appropriate missing symbol from a group of symbols, such as the ones at the bottom. Simulated items similar to those in *Raven's Progressive Matrices.* Copyright © 1998 by NCS Pearson, Inc. Reproduced by permission. All rights reserved. "Raven's Progressive Matrices" is a trademark, in the U.S. and/or other countries, of Pearson Education, Inc. or its affiliates.

## Why Is It So Hard to Create Culture-Fair Tests?

Most tests tend to reflect what the dominant culture thinks is important (Zhang & Sternberg, 2013). If tests have time limits, that will bias the test against groups that are not concerned with time. If languages differ, the same words might have different meanings for different language groups. Even pictures can produce bias because some cultures have less experience with drawings and photographs (Anastasi & Urbina, 1997). Within the same culture, different groups could have different attitudes, values, and motivations, and this could affect their performance on intelligence tests. Items that ask why buildings should be made of brick are biased against children with little or no experience with brick houses. Questions about railroads, furnaces, seasons of the year, distances between cities, and so on can be biased against groups who have less experience than others with these contexts. Because of such difficulties in creating culture-fair tests, Robert Sternberg and his colleagues (Sternberg, 2009e; Sternberg & Grigorenko, 2008; Zhang & Sternberg, 2011) conclude that there are no culture-fair tests, but only culture-reduced tests.

*What are some other solutions that might work to make intelligence testing less culturally biased?*

---

designed to be culture-fair, people with more education still score higher than those with less education (Greenfield, 2003). To read further about culture-fair tests, see *Connecting with Diversity*.

**Ethnic Comparisons**   Comparisons between different ethnic groups can tell us much about how the environment influences intelligence. For example, in the United States, children from African-American families score below children from Caucasian families on standardized intelligence tests. On average, African-American schoolchildren score 10 to 15 points lower on standardized intelligence tests than Caucasian-American schoolchildren (Brody, 2000; Lynn, 1996). These are *average scores*, however. About 15 to 25 percent of African-American schoolchildren score higher than half of Caucasian schoolchildren, and many Caucasians score lower than most African Americans. This is true because the distribution of scores for African Americans and Caucasians overlap.

As African Americans have gained social, economic, and educational opportunities, the gap between scores of African Americans and Caucasians on standardized intelligence tests has begun to narrow (Ogbu & Stern, 2001). This narrowing is especially apparent at the college level, where African-American and Caucasian students often experience more similar environments than they did during the elementary and high school years (Myerson & others, 1998). Also, when children from disadvantaged African-American families are adopted into more-advantaged middle-socioeconomic-status families, their scores on intelligence tests more closely resemble national averages for middle-socioeconomic-status children than those for lower-socioeconomic-status children (Scarr & Weinberg, 1983).

**stereotype threat** Anxiety that one's behaviour might confirm a stereotype about one's group.

*How might stereotype threat be involved in ethnic minority students' performance on standardized tests?*

One potential influence on intelligence test performance is **stereotype threat**, the anxiety that one's behaviour might confirm a negative stereotype about one's group (Hollis-Sawyer & Sawyer, 2008; Steele & Aronson, 2004). For example, when ethnic minority children take an intelligence test, they may experience anxiety about confirming old stereotypes that certain ethnic minorities are intellectually inferior. Some studies have confirmed the existence of stereotype threat (Beilock, Rydell, & McConnell, 2007; Kellow & Jones, 2008). For example, in the United States, African-American students do more poorly on standardized tests if they perceive that they are being evaluated. If they think the test doesn't count, they perform as well as Caucasian students (Aronson, 2002). However, critics argue that the extent to which stereotype threat explains the testing gap has been exaggerated (Sackett, Hardison, & Cullen, 2005).

## Review *Connect* Reflect

**L01** Explain the concept of intelligence.

### Review

- What is intelligence?
- What are the main individual tests of intelligence?
- What theories of multiple intelligences have been developed? Do people have one intelligence or many intelligences?
- What are some links between the brain and intelligence?
- What evidence indicates that heredity influences IQ scores? What evidence indicates that environment influences IQ scores?
- What is known about the intelligence of people from different cultures and ethnic groups?

### Connect

- In this section you learned that different cultures have different concepts of intelligence, and in Chapter 5 you learned about culture's effect on motor development. What do these findings have in common?

### Reflect *Your Own Personal Journey of Life*

- A CD-ROM is being sold to parents for testing their child's IQ. Several parents tell you that they purchased the CD-ROM and assessed their children's IQs. Why might you be skeptical about giving your children an IQ test and interpreting the results yourself?

---

## The Development of Intelligence    **L02** Discuss the development of intelligence.

| Tests of Infant Intelligence | Stability and Change in Intelligence Through Adolescence |

How can the intelligence of infants be assessed? Is intelligence stable through childhood? These are some of the questions we will explore as we examine the development of intelligence.

## TESTS OF INFANT INTELLIGENCE

The infant-testing movement grew out of the tradition of IQ testing. However, tests that assess infants are necessarily less verbal than IQ tests for older children. Tests for infants contain far more items related to perceptual-motor development. They also include measures of social interaction.

The most important early contributor to the testing of infants was Arnold Gesell (1934). He developed a measure that helped sort out potentially normal babies from abnormal ones. This was especially useful to adoption agencies, which had large numbers of babies awaiting placement. Gesell's examination was used widely for many years and still is frequently employed by pediatricians to distinguish between typically and non-typically developing infants. The current version of the Gesell test has four categories of behaviour: motor, language, adaptive, and personal-social. The **developmental quotient (DQ)** combines subscores in these categories to provide an overall score.

The widely used **Bayley Scales of Infant Development** were developed by Nancy Bayley (1969) to assess infant behaviour and predict later development. The current version, Bayley-III, has five scales: cognitive, language, motor, socio-emotional, and adaptive (Bayley, 2006). The first three scales are administered directly to the infant; the latter two are questionnaires given to the caregiver. The Bayley-III also is more appropriate for use in clinical settings than the two previous editions (Lennon & others, 2008).

**developmental quotient (DQ)** An overall developmental score that combines subscores on motor, language, adaptive, and personal-social domains in the Gesell assessment of infants.

**Bayley Scales of Infant Development** Initially created by Nancy Bayley, these scales are widely used in assessing infant development. The current version has five scales: cognitive, language, motor, socioemotional, and adaptive.

## Does Music Make You Smarter?

Throughout the 1990s, there was widespread interest in the effects of listening to music on cognitive performance. This reported phenomenon, labelled the Mozart Effect, led to a popularized reconceptualization of earlier research (Rauscher, Shaw, & Ky, 1993) suggesting that early childhood exposure to classical music had a beneficial effect on intellectual development. Several recent reviews of the research literature have concluded that the increase in cognitive performance following listening to music is actually a result of arousal and mood, and similar short-term improvements in performance also occur as a result of exposure to non-musical stimuli (Chabris, 1999; Schellenberg, 2012). However, these findings do not mean that music does not play a role in the developing cognitive abilities of children.

Using a variety of different research designs, Dr. Glenn Schellenberg at the University of Toronto has revealed a strong association between music lessons and IQ. For example, musically trained individuals outperform non-trained individuals on a variety of verbal and non-verbal tasks associated with general intelligence (Schellenberg, 2011). Duration of music lessons is also associated with IQ for both children and adults; that is, the longer one participates in music lessons, the higher one's IQ (Schellenberg, 2006). These relations remain even after controlling for other factors known to contribute to IQ, including parental education levels, family income, and participation in non-musical activities. However, many questions remain regarding the nature of the relation between music lessons and IQ (Schellenberg, 2011; Schellenberg & Peretz, 2008).

First, the direction of causation is unclear. It is possible that music lessons do increase a child's IQ, but it is also possible that children with higher IQs tend to take music lessons. To explore this issue, Schellenberg (2004) conducted an experimental study in which 144 6-year-old children were randomly assigned to either one of two music training groups (keyboard or vocal) or one of two control groups (drama lessons or no lessons). After one year of lessons, the musically trained children showed higher increases in IQ than the non-musically trained children (7.0 vs. 4.3 IQ points, respectively). This is one of the only empirical studies to date to clearly demonstrate that music lessons cause increases in cognitive ability. However, in a review

of the literature, Schellenberg (2011) concludes that the relation likely goes in both directions; children with higher IQs are more likely to take music lessons, which then further enhance their intellectual advantage.

A second unresolved issue is whether or not the association between music lessons and intelligence is mediated through a third skill, such as executive function (Hannon & Trainor, 2007; Schellenberg & Peretz, 2008). Executive function is a broadly defined construct, related to "conscious, goal-directed problem solving" (Zelazo, Carlson, & Kesek, 2008, p. 553) and benefits all cognitive tasks. Thus, it seems reasonable that music lessons may enhance executive function, which in turn, may improve intelligence. Although research has revealed an association between executive function and intelligence (e.g., Salthouse, 2005; Salthouse, Atkinson, & Berish, 2003), empirical support for a mediating role of executive function in the relation between music lessons and intelligence is inconclusive at this time (Schellenberg, 2011; Bialystok & DePape, 2009). Thus, the underlying reasons that music lessons are related to IQ remain unclear. Research exploring the potential benefits of music lessons as well as other curricular activities greatly contributes to our understanding of child development.

*What are the limits to the conclusions that can be made using the various research designs identified in this research? What are the benefits of using multiple different designs, as done by this researcher?*

How should a 6-month-old perform on the Bayley cognitive scale? The 6-month-old infant should be able to vocalize pleasure and displeasure, persistently search for objects that are just out of immediate reach, and approach a mirror that is placed in front of the infant by the examiner. By 12 months of age, the infant should be able to inhibit behaviour when commanded to do so, imitate words the examiner says (such as *mama*), and respond to simple requests (such as "take a drink").

The explosion of interest in infant development has produced many new measures, especially tasks that evaluate the ways infants process information

(Fagan, 2011). The Fagan Test of Infant Intelligence is increasingly being used (Fagan, 1992). This test focuses on the infant's ability to process information by encoding the attributes of objects, detecting similarities and differences between objects, forming mental representations, and retrieving these representations. For example, it estimates intelligence by comparing the amount of time babies look at a new object with the amount of time they spend looking at a familiar object.

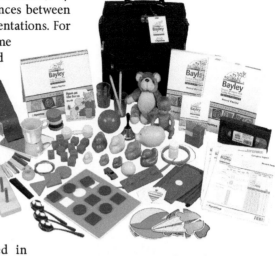

Items used in the Bayley Scales of Infant Development

Unlike the Gesell and Bayley scales, the Fagan test is correlated with measures of intelligence in older children. In fact, evidence is accumulating that measures of habituation and dishabituation are linked to intelligence in childhood, adolescence, and even adulthood. For example, one study revealed that selective attention to novelty at 6 to 12 months correlated positively with intelligence at 21 years of age (Fagan, Holland, & Wheeler, 2007). And a longitudinal study revealed that four information processing domains (attention, processing speed, memory and representational competence) assessed in infancy and early childhood were linked to general intelligence scores on the Wechsler Intelligence Scale for Children-III assessed at 11 years of age (Rose & others, 2012).

It is important, however, not to go too far and think that connections between cognitive development in early infancy and later cognitive development are so strong that no discontinuity takes place. As we discussed in Chapters 6 and 7, some important changes in cognitive development occur after infancy.

*developmental* **connection**

**Information Processing.** Habituation and dishabituation are important aspects of attention in infancy. Chapter 7, LO 2

## STABILITY AND CHANGE IN INTELLIGENCE THROUGH ADOLESCENCE

Several longitudinal studies reveal great stability in intelligence through preschool to childhood to adolescence. For example, one study examined the intelligence of 200 children from 12 months (using the Bayley scales) to 4 years of age using the Stanford-Binet test (Blaga & others, 2009). The results indicated considerable stability from late infancy through the preschool years.

Another study examined correlations between IQ at a number of different ages (Honzik, MacFarlane, & Allen, 1948). There was a strong relation between IQ scores obtained at the ages of 6, 8, and 9 and IQ scores obtained at the age of 10. For example, the correlation between IQ at the age of 8 and IQ at the age of 10 was .88. The correlation between IQ at the age of 9 and IQ at the age of 10 was .90. These figures show a very close relationship between IQ scores obtained in these years. The correlation between IQ in the preadolescent years and IQ at the age of 18 was slightly lower but was still statistically significant. For example, the correlation between IQ at the age of 10 and IQ at the age of 18 was .70.

What has been said so far about the stability of intelligence has been based on measures of groups of individuals. The stability of intelligence also can be evaluated through studies of individuals. Robert McCall and his associates (McCall, Appelbaum, & Hogarty, 1973) studied 140 children between the ages of 2½ and 17. They found that the average range of IQ scores was more than 28 points. The scores of one out of three children changed by as much as 40 points.

What can we conclude about stability and changes in intelligence during childhood? Intelligence test scores can fluctuate dramatically across the childhood years. Intelligence is not as stable as the original intelligence theorists envisioned. Children are adaptive beings. They have the capacity for intellectual change, but they do not become entirely new intelligent beings. In a sense, children's intelligence changes but remains connected with early points in development.

**Review**

- How is intelligence assessed during infancy?
- How much does intelligence change through childhood and adolescence?

*Connect*

- In this section, you learned about research on the development of intelligence. Referring back to Chapter 1,

identify which research methods and designs were used in these research studies and describe their pros and cons relative to their subject matter.

**Reflect** *Your Own Personal Journey of Life*

- As a parent, would you want to have your infant's intelligence tested? Why or why not?

# The Extremes of Intelligence and Creativity

 **L03** Describe the characteristics of intellectual disability, giftedness, and creativity.

Intellectual Disability — Giftedness — Creativity

Intellectual disability and intellectual giftedness are the extremes of intelligence. Often intelligence tests are used to identify exceptional individuals. After discussing intellectual disability and giftedness, we'll explore how creativity differs from intelligence.

## INTELLECTUAL DISABILITY

The most distinctive feature of intellectual disability (formerly called mental retardation) is inadequate intellectual functioning. Long before formal tests were developed to assess intelligence, individuals with an intellectual disability were identified by a lack of age-appropriate skills in learning and caring for themselves. Once intelligence tests were developed, they were used to identify degrees of intellectual disability. But of two individuals with an intellectual disability who have the same low IQ, one might be married, employed, and involved in the community while the other requires constant supervision in an institution. Such differences in social competence led psychologists to include deficits in adaptive behaviour in their definition of intellectual disability.

**Intellectual disability** is a condition of limited mental ability in which the individual (1) has a low IQ, usually below 70 on a traditional intelligence test, (2) has difficulty adapting to everyday life, and (3) first exhibits these characteristics during the developmental period. The age limit is included in the definition of intellectual disability because, for example, we don't usually think of a college student who suffers massive brain damage in a car accident, resulting in an IQ of 60, as having an intellectual disability. The low IQ and low adaptiveness should be evident in childhood, not after normal functioning is interrupted by damage of some form. About 1–3 percent of the Canadian population fits this definition of intellectual ability.

In the past, severity of intellectual disability has typically been classified using IQ scores. Most school systems use the classifications shown in Figure 8.7, which uses IQ scores to categorize disability as mild, moderate, severe, or profound. However, the recent release of the fifth edition of the *Diagnostic and Statistical Manual of Mental Disorders* by the American Psychiatric Association (2013) removes classification based on IQ scores alone and refers to levels of adaptive functioning as determining severity of intellectual disability.

**intellectual disability** A condition of limited mental ability in which the individual (1) has a low IQ, usually below 70 on a traditional intelligence test, (2) has difficulty adapting to everyday life, and (3) has an onset of these characteristics during the developmental period.

| Type of Intellectual Disability | IQ Range | Percentage |
|---|---|---|
| Mild | 55–70 | 85 |
| Moderate | 40–54 | 10 |
| Severe | 25–39 | 4 |
| Profound | Below 25 | 1 |

**FIGURE 8.7**

**CLASSIFICATION OF INTELLECTUAL DISABILITY BASED ON IQ (Langlois & others, 2011).**

Some cases of intellectual disability have an organic cause. *Organic intellectual disability* describes a genetic disorder or a lower level of intellectual functioning caused by brain damage. Down syndrome is one form of organic intellectual disability, and it occurs when an extra chromosome is present.

Other causes of organic intellectual disability include fragile X syndrome, an abnormality in the X chromosome that was discussed in Chapter 2; prenatal malformation; metabolic disorders; and diseases that affect the brain. Most people who suffer from organic retardation have IQs between 0 and 50.

When no evidence of organic brain damage can be found, cases of intellectual disability are labelled *cultural-familial intellectual disability.* Individuals with this type of disability have IQs between 55 and 70. Psychologists suspect that these types of disabilities often result from growing up in a below-average intellectual environment. Children with this type of disability can be identified in schools, where they often fail, need tangible rewards (candy rather than praise), and are highly sensitive to what others expect of them. However, as adults, they are usually unnoticed, perhaps because adult settings don't tax their cognitive skills as sorely. It may also be that they increase their intelligence as they move toward adulthood.

## GIFTEDNESS

There have always been people whose abilities and accomplishments have outshined others'—the whiz kid in class, the star athlete, the natural musician. People who are **gifted** have above-average intelligence (an IQ of 130 or higher) and/or superior talent for something such as music, arts, literature or science (Grigorenko & others, 2012). Estimates vary but indicate that approximately 3 to 5 percent of children are gifted (National Association for Gifted Children, 2009). This percentage is likely conservative, because it focuses more on children who are gifted intellectually and academically, often failing to include those who are gifted in creative thinking as well as the visual or performing arts (Ford, 2012). Non-cognitive contributors to giftedness have received increasing attention in recent years (Reis & Renzulli, 2011). Creativity, motivation, optimism, and physical and mental energy are examples of non-cognitive factors that influence whether children display giftedness.

What are the characteristics of children who are gifted? Despite speculation that giftedness is linked with having a mental disorder, no connection between giftedness and mental disorder has been found. Similarly, the idea that gifted children are maladjusted is a myth, as Lewis Terman (1925) found when he conducted an extensive study of 1,500 children whose Stanford-Binet IQs averaged 150. The children in Terman's study were socially well adjusted, and many went on to become successful doctors, lawyers, professors, and scientists. Studies support the conclusion that gifted people tend to be more mature than others, have fewer emotional problems than average, and grow up in a positive family climate (Davidson, 2000; Feldman, 2001).

Ellen Winner (1996) described three criteria that characterize gifted children, whether in art, music, or academic domains:

1. *Precocity.* Gifted children are precocious. They begin to master an area earlier than their peers. Learning in their domain is more effortless for them than for ordinary children. In most instances, these gifted children are precocious because they have an inborn high ability in a particular domain or domains.

2. *Marching to their own drummer.* Gifted children learn in a qualitatively different way from ordinary children. One way that they march to a different drummer is that they need minimal help, or scaffolding, from adults to learn. In many instances, they resist any kind of explicit instruction. They often make discoveries on their own and solve problems in unique ways.

This young boy has Down syndrome. *What causes a child to develop Down syndrome? In what major classification of intellectual disability does the condition fall?*

*developmental* **connection**

**Genetic Foundations of Development.** Many genetic and chromosomal abnormalities result in conditions with associated intellectual disabilities. Chapter 2, LO 2

At 2 years of age, art prodigy Alexandra Nechita coloured in colouring books for hours and also took up pen and ink. She had no interest in dolls or friends. By age 5 she was using watercolours. Once she started school, she would start painting as soon as she got home. At the age of 8, in 1994, she saw the first public exhibit of her work. In succeeding years, working quickly and impulsively on canvases as large as 5 feet by 9 feet, she has completed hundreds of paintings, some of which sell for close to $100,000 apiece. As a teenager, she continues to paint—relentlessly and passionately. It is, she says, what she loves to do. *What are some characteristics of children who are gifted?*

**giftedness** Possession of above-average intelligence (an IQ of 130 or higher) and/or superior talent for something.

3. *A passion to master.* Gifted children are driven to understand the domain in which they have high ability. They display an intense, obsessive interest and an ability to focus. They motivate themselves, says Winner, and do not need to be "pushed" by their parents.

**Nature–Nurture** Is giftedness a product of heredity or environment? Likely both (Sternberg, 2009b). Individuals who are gifted recall that they had signs of high ability in a particular area at a very young age, prior to or at the beginning of formal training (Howe & others, 1995). This suggests the importance of innate ability in giftedness. However, researchers have also found that individuals with world-class status in the arts, mathematics, science, and sports all report strong family support and years of training and practice (Bloom, 1985). Deliberate practice is an important characteristic of individuals who become experts in a particular domain. For example, in one study, the best musicians engaged in twice as much deliberate practice over their lives as did the least successful ones (Ericsson, Krampe, & Tesch-Romer, 1993).

**Developmental Changes and Domain-Specific Giftedness** Individuals who are highly gifted are typically not gifted in many domains, and research on giftedness is increasingly focused on domain-specific developmental trajectories (Feldman & Morelock, 2011). During the childhood years, the domains in which individuals are gifted usually emerge. Thus, at some point in the childhood years, the child who will become a gifted artist or the child who will become a gifted mathematician begins to show expertise in that domain.

Identifying an individual's domain-specific talent and providing the individual with individually appropriate and optional educational opportunities needs to be accomplished by adolescence at the latest (Keating, 2009). During adolescence, individuals who are talented become less reliant on parental support and increasingly pursue their own interests.

Some children who are gifted become gifted adults, but many gifted children do not become gifted and highly creative adults. In Terman's research on children with superior IQs, the children typically became experts in a well-established domain, such as medicine, law, or business. However, they did not become major creators (Winner, 2000). That is, they did not create a new domain or revolutionize an old domain.

**Education of Children Who Are Gifted** Students with exceptional talents or learning potential require specific knowledge and attention from educators. Underchallenged gifted children can become disruptive, skip classes, and lose interest in achieving. Sometimes these children just disappear into the woodwork, becoming passive and apathetic toward school. In Canada, the education of children who are gifted falls under provincial jurisdiction. Between and within provinces there are diverse educational programs that range from special schools and/or classes for children who are gifted, accelerated learning (i.e., skipping a grade), independent projects, and in-class enrichment activities that require students to probe deeper into a topic than required by the regular curriculum. It is extremely important for teachers to challenge gifted children to reach high expectations (Webb & others, 2007; Winner, 2009).

Ellen Winner (1996, 2006) argues that too often children who are gifted are socially isolated and underchallenged in the classroom. It is not unusual for them to be ostracized and labelled "nerds" or "geeks." A child who is truly gifted often is the only child in the classroom who does not have the opportunity to learn with students of like ability. Many eminent adults report that school was a negative experience for them, that they were bored and sometimes knew more than their teachers (Bloom, 1985). When some children are underchallenged, Winner recommends that they be allowed to attend advanced classes in their domain of exceptional ability. For example, some especially precocious middle school students should be allowed to take college classes in their area of expertise. For example, Bill Gates, founder of Microsoft, took college math classes and hacked a computer security system at 13; Yo-Yo Ma, famous cellist, graduated from high school at 15 and attended the Juilliard School of Music in New York City.

## CREATIVITY

We brought up the term "creative" on several occasions in our discussion of intelligence and giftedness. What does it mean to be creative? **Creativity** is the ability to think about something in novel and unusual ways and come up with unique solutions to problems.

**creativity** The ability to think in novel and unusual ways and come up with unique solutions to problems.

Intelligence and creativity are not the same thing (Kaufman & Sternberg, 2010). Most creative people are quite intelligent, but the reverse is not necessarily true. Many highly intelligent people (as measured by high scores on conventional tests of intelligence) are not very creative (Sternberg, 2009f). Many highly intelligent people produce large numbers of products that are not necessarily novel.

Why don't IQ scores predict creativity? Creativity requires divergent thinking (Guilford, 1967). **Divergent thinking** produces many answers to the same question. In contrast, conventional intelligence tests require **convergent thinking.** For example, a typical question on a conventional intelligence test is, "How many quarters will you get in return for 60 dimes?" There is only one correct answer to this question. In contrast, a question such as "What image comes to mind when you hear the phrase 'sitting alone in a dark room'?" has many possible answers; it calls for divergent thinking.

**divergent thinking** Thinking that produces many answers to the same question; characteristic of creativity.

**convergent thinking** Thinking that produces one correct answer; characteristic of the kind of thinking required on conventional intelligence tests.

Just as in being gifted, children show creativity in some domains more than others (Rickards, Moger, & Runco, 2009; Sternberg, 2010b, e). For example, a child who shows creativity in mathematics might not be as creative in art. A special concern is that children's creative thinking appears to be declining. A study of approximately 300,000 children and adults found that creativity scores rose until 1990, but since then have been steadily declining (Kim, 2010). Among the likely causes of the creativity decline are the number of hours North American children watch TV and play video games instead of engaging in creative activities, as well as the lack of emphasis on creative thinking in schools (Gregorson, Kaufman, & Snyder, 2013). Some countries, though, are placing increasing emphasis on creative thinking in schools. For example, creative thinking was historically discouraged in Chinese schools. However, Chinese educators are now encouraging teachers to spend more classroom time on creative activities (Plucker, 2010). Strategies to encourage creative thinking in the classroom include providing environments that stimulate creativity, **brainstorming,** encouraging internal motivation, and encouraging children to take intellectual risks (Hennessey, 2011).

**brainstorming** A technique in which children are encouraged to come up with creative ideas in a group, play off one another's ideas, and say practically whatever comes to mind.

### Review Connect Reflect

 **LO3** Describe the characteristics of intellectual disability, giftedness, and creativity.

### Review
- What is intellectual disability, and what are its causes?
- What makes individuals gifted?
- What makes individuals creative?

### Connect
- In this section you learned how intellectual disability is assessed and classified. What did you learn in Chapter 2 about the prevalence of Down syndrome in the population and the factors that might cause an infant to be born with Down syndrome?

### Reflect Your Own Personal Journey of Life
- If you were an elementary school teacher, what would you do to encourage students' creativity?

# case study **connections**

1. What role might nurture play in explaining the differences between the two children described in the chapter opening? What role might nature play?

2. How does the first child described in the chapter opening fit with the current definition of intellectual disability?

3. Would both children described in the chapter opening be classified as an extreme of intelligence using the various different measures of intelligence described in this chapter?

4. What evidence is present in the descriptions in the chapter opening to support the various different theoretical models of intelligence?

5. Explain the role that both nurture and nature have had in shaping your own intelligence.

# reach your **learning goals**

# Intelligence

## The Concept of Intelligence

**LO1** Explain the concept of intelligence.

> What Is Intelligence?

- Intelligence consists of the ability to solve problems and to adapt and learn from experiences. A key aspect of intelligence focuses on its individual variations. Traditionally, intelligence has been measured by tests designed to compare people's performance on cognitive tasks.

> Intelligence Tests

- Alfred Binet developed the first intelligence test and created the concept of mental age. William Stern developed the concept of IQ for use with the Binet test. Revisions of the Binet test are called the Stanford-Binet. The test scores on the Stanford-Binet approximate a normal distribution. The Wechsler scales, created by David Wechsler, are the other main intelligence assessment tools. These tests provide an overall IQ scores on a number of subtests, and several composite indexes. When used by a judicious examiner, tests can be valuable tools for determining individual differences in intelligence. Test scores should be only one type of information used to evaluate an individual. IQ scores can produce unfortunate stereotypes and false expectations.

> Theories of Multiple Intelligences

- Sternberg's triarchic theory states that there are three main types of intelligence: analytical, creative, and practical. Gardner maintains that there are eight types of intelligence, or frames of mind: verbal skills, mathematical skills, spatial skills, bodily-kinesthetic skills, musical skills, interpersonal skills, intrapersonal skills, and naturalist skills. Emotional intelligence is the ability to perceive and express emotion accurately and adaptively, to understand emotion and emotional knowledge, to use feelings to facilitate thought, and to manage emotions in oneself and others. The multiple-intelligences approaches have broadened the definition of intelligence and motivated educators to develop programs that instruct students in different domains. Critics maintain that Gardner's multiple-intelligence classification seems arbitrary. Critics also say that there is insufficient research to support the concept of multiple intelligences.

| The Neuroscience of Intelligence | • Interest in discovering links between the brain and intelligence has been stimulated by advances in brain imaging. A moderate correlation has been found between overall brain size and intelligence. Recent research has revealed a link between a distributed neural network in the frontal and parietal lobes and intelligence. Research on a connection between neural processing speed and intelligence has produced inconsistent findings. |
| --- | --- |
| The Influence of Heredity and Environment | • Some studies indicate that the IQs of adopted children are more similar to the IQs of their biological parents than to those of their adoptive parents. Many studies show that intelligence has a reasonably strong heritability component, but environmental influences are also important. Intelligence test scores have risen considerably around the world in recent decades—called the Flynn effect—and this supports the role of environment in intelligence. Researchers have found that being deprived of formal education lowers IQ scores. |
| Group Comparisons | • Cultures vary in the way they define intelligence. Early intelligence tests favoured Caucasian, middle-socioeconomic-status, urban individuals. Tests may be biased against certain groups that are not familiar with a standard form of English, with the content tested, or with the testing situation. Tests are likely to reflect the values and experience of the dominant culture. |

## The Development of Intelligence  Discuss the development of intelligence.

| Tests of Infant Intelligence | • A test developed by Gesell was an important early contributor to the developmental testing of infants. Tests designed to assess infant intelligence include the widely used Bayley scales. The Fagan Test of Infant Intelligence, which assesses how effectively infants process information, is increasingly being used. Infant information-processing tasks that involve attention—especially habituation and dishabituation—are related to standardized scores of intelligence in childhood. |
| --- | --- |
| Stability and Change in Intelligence Through Adolescence | • Intelligence is not as stable across childhood and adolescence as the original theorists believed. Many children's scores on intelligence tests fluctuate considerably. |

## The Extremes of Intelligence and Creativity  Describe the characteristics of intellectual disability, giftedness, and creativity.

| Intellectual Disability | • Intellectual disability is a condition of limited mental ability in which the individual (1) has a low IQ, usually below 70; (2) has difficulty adapting to everyday life; and (3) has an onset of these characteristics during the developmental period. Most affected individuals have an IQ in the 55 to 70 range (mild disability). Intellectual disability can have an organic cause (called organic intellectual disability) or be social and cultural in origin (called cultural-familial intellectual disability). |
| --- | --- |
| Giftedness | • Individuals who are gifted have above-average intelligence (an IQ of 130 or higher) and/or superior talent for something. Three characteristics of gifted children are precocity, marching to their own drummer, and a passion to master their domain. Giftedness is likely a consequence of both heredity and environment. Developmental changes characterize giftedness, and increasingly the domain-specific aspect of giftedness is emphasized. Concerns exist about the education of children who are gifted. |
| Creativity | • Creativity is the ability to think about something in novel and unusual ways and come up with unique solutions to problems. Although most creative people are intelligent, individuals with high IQs are not necessarily creative. Creative people tend to be divergent thinkers; traditional intelligence tests measure convergent thinking. Parents and teachers can use a number of strategies to increase children's creative thinking. |

# chapter 9 | Language Development

Astunning portrayal of a child isolated from the mainstream of language is the case of Helen Keller (1880–1968). At 18 months of age, Helen was an intelligent toddler in the process of learning to say her first words. Then she developed an illness that left her both deaf and blind, suffering the double affliction of sudden darkness and silence. For the next five years, she lived in a world she learned to fear because she could not see or hear.

Helen Keller

Even with her fears, Helen spontaneously invented a number of gestures to reflect her wants and needs. For example, when she wanted ice cream, she turned toward the freezer and shivered. When she wanted bread and butter, she imitated the motions of cutting and spreading. But this homemade language system severely limited her ability to communicate with the surrounding community, which did not understand her idiosyncratic gestures.

Alexander Graham Bell, the famous inventor of the telephone, suggested to her parents that they seek a teacher for Helen at the Perkins Institution, and Anne Sullivan was chosen to help Helen overcome her isolation. By using a form of tactile sign language, Anne was able to teach Helen to communicate. Anne realized that language learning needs to occur naturally, so she did not force Helen to memorize words out of context as in the drill methods that were in vogue at the time. Sullivan's success depended not only on the child's natural ability to organize language according to form and meaning but also on introducing language in the context of communicating about objects, events, and feelings about others. Helen Keller eventually graduated from Radcliffe with honours, became a very successful educator, and wrote books about her life and experiences. She had this to say about language:

> Whatever the process, the result is wonderful. Gradually from naming an object we advance step by step until we have traversed the vast distance between our first stammered syllable and the sweep of thought in a line of Shakespeare.

In this chapter, we will tell the remarkable story of language and how it develops. The questions we will explore include: What is language? What is the developmental course of language? What does biology contribute to language? How does experience influence language? How are language and cognition linked?

## What Is Language? **L01** Define language and describe its rule systems.

Defining Language

Language's Rule Systems

In 1799, a nude boy was observed running through the woods in France. The boy was captured when he was 11 years old. He was called the Wild Boy of Aveyron and was believed to have lived in the woods alone for six years (Lane, 1976). When found, he made no effort to communicate. He never learned to communicate effectively. Sadly, a modern-day wild child, a girl named Genie, was discovered in Los Angeles in 1970. Despite intensive intervention, Genie has acquired only a limited form of spoken language. Both cases—the Wild Boy of Aveyron and Genie—raise questions about the biological and environmental determinants of language, topics that we will examine later in the chapter. First, though, we need to define language.

### DEFINING LANGUAGE

> Words not only affect us temporarily; they change us, they socialize us, and they unsocialize us.
>
> —David Riesman
> *American Social Scientist, 20th Century*

**language** A form of communication, whether spoken, written, or signed, that is based on a system of symbols.

**infinite generativity** The ability to produce an endless number of meaningful sentences using a finite set of words and rules.

**Language** is a form of communication—whether spoken, written, or signed—that is based on a system of symbols. Language consists of the words used by a community and the rules for varying and combining them.

Think how important language is in our everyday lives. It is difficult to imagine what Helen Keller's life would have been like if she had never learned language. We need language to communicate with others—to speak, listen, read, and write. Our language enables us to describe past events in detail and to plan for the future. Language lets us pass down information from one generation to the next and create a rich cultural heritage.

All human languages have some common characteristics (Berko Gleason, 2009). These include infinite generativity and organizational rules. **Infinite generativity** is the ability to produce an endless number of meaningful sentences using a finite set of words and rules. When we say *rules*, we mean that language is orderly and that rules describe the way language works. Let's further explore what these rules involve.

### LANGUAGE'S RULE SYSTEMS

When 19th-century American writer Ralph Waldo Emerson said, "The world was built in order and the atoms march in tune," he must have had language in mind. Language is highly ordered and organized (Berko Gleason, 2009; Colombo, McCardle, & Freund, 2009). The organization involves five systems of rules: phonology, morphology, syntax, semantics, and pragmatics.

**phonology** The sound system of a language, which includes the sounds used and rules about how they may be combined.

**Phonology** Every language is made up of basic sounds. **Phonology** is the sound system of a language, including the sounds that are used and how they may be combined (Kuhl & Damasio, 2012). For example, English has the sounds *sp, ba,* and *ar,* but the sound sequences *zx* and *qp* do not occur. A *phoneme* is the basic unit of sound in a language; it is the smallest unit of sound that affects meaning. A good example of a phoneme in English is /k/, the sound represented by the letter *k* in the word *ski* and the letter *c* in the word *cat.* The /k/ sound is slightly different in these two words, and in some languages such as Arabic these two sounds are separate phonemes. However, this variation is not distinguished in English, and the /k/ sound is therefore a single phoneme.

**Morphology** Morphology is the rule system that governs how words are formed in a language. A *morpheme* is a minimal unit of meaning; it is a word or a part of a word that cannot be broken into smaller meaningful parts. Every word in the English language is made up of one or more morphemes. Some words consist of a single morpheme (for example, *help*), whereas others are made up of more than one morpheme (for example, *helper,* which has two morphemes, *help* and *er,* with the morpheme *-er* meaning "one who"—in this case "one who helps"). Thus, not all morphemes are words by themselves; for example, *pre-, -tion,* and *-ing* are morphemes.

Just as the rules that govern phonology describe the sound sequences that can occur in a language, the rules of morphology describe the way meaningful units (morphemes) can be combined in words (Brown, 2013). Morphemes have many jobs in grammar, such as marking tense (for example, she *walks* versus she *walked*) and number (*she* walks versus *they* walk).

**Syntax** Syntax involves the way words are combined to form acceptable phrases and sentences. The term *syntax* is often used interchangeably with the term *grammar.* If someone says to you, "Bob slugged Tom," or "Bob was slugged by Tom," you know who did the slugging and who was slugged in each case because you have a syntactic understanding of these sentence structures. You also understand that the sentence, "You didn't stay, did you?" is a grammatical sentence but that "You didn't stay, didn't you?" is unacceptable and ambiguous.

If you learn another language, English syntax will not get you very far. For example, in English an adjective usually precedes a noun (as in *blue sky*), whereas in French the adjective usually follows the noun (*ciel bleu*). Despite the differences in their syntactic structures, however, the world's languages have much in common (de Villiers & de Villiers, 2013; Saffran, 2009). For example, consider the following short sentences:

The cat killed the mouse.
The farmer chased the cat.

In many languages, it is possible to combine these sentences into more complex sentences. For example:

The farmer chased the cat that killed the mouse.
The mouse the cat killed ate the cheese.

However, no language we know of permits sentences like the following:

The mouse the cat the farmer chased killed ate the cheese.

Can you make sense of this sentence? If you can, you probably can do it only after wrestling with it for several minutes. You likely could not understand it at all if someone uttered it during a conversation. It appears that language users cannot process subjects and objects arranged in too complex a fashion in a sentence. That is good news for language learners, because it means that all syntactic systems have some common ground. Such findings are also considered important by researchers who are interested in the universal properties of syntax (Culicover, 2013; Whaley, 2013).

**Semantics** Semantics refers to the meaning of words and sentences. Every word has a set of semantic features, or required attributes related to meaning.

Language allows us to communicate with others. *What are some important characteristics of language?*

**morphology** The rule system that governs how words are formed in a language.

**syntax** The ways words are combined to form acceptable phrases and sentences.

**semantics** The meaning of words and sentences.

FRANK & ERNEST © Thaves. Distr. by United Features Syndicate, Inc.

*Girl* and *woman,* for example, share many semantic features but differ semantically with regard to age.

Words have semantic restrictions on how they can be used in sentences (Li, 2009). The sentence *The bicycle talked the boy into buying a candy bar* is syntactically correct but semantically incorrect. The sentence violates our semantic knowledge that bicycles don't talk.

**pragmatics** The appropriate use of language in different contexts.

**Pragmatics**     A final set of language rules involves **pragmatics**, the appropriate use of language in different contexts. Pragmatics covers a lot of territory. When you take turns speaking in a discussion or use a question to convey a command ("Why is it so noisy in here?" "What is this, Grand Central Station?") you are demonstrating knowledge of pragmatics. You also apply the pragmatics of English when you use polite language in appropriate situations (for example, when talking to your teacher) or tell stories that are interesting, jokes that are funny, and lies that convince. In each of these cases, you are demonstrating that you understand the rules of your culture for adjusting language to suit the context.

Pragmatic rules can be complex and differ from one culture to another (Bryant, 2012; Siegal & Surian, 2010). If you were to study the Japanese language, you would come face-to-face with countless pragmatic rules about conversing with individuals of various social levels and with various relationships to you. Some of these pragmatic rules concern the ways of saying *thank you.* Indeed, the pragmatics of saying *thank you* are complex even in our own culture. Preschoolers' use of the phrase *thank you* varies with sex, socioeconomic status, and the age of the individual they are addressing.

At this point, we have discussed five important rule systems involved in language. An overview of these rule systems is presented in Figure 9.1.

| Rule System | Description | Examples |
|---|---|---|
| **Phonology** | The sound system of a language. A phoneme is the smallest sound unit in a language. | The word *chat* has three phonemes or sounds: /ch/ /ă/ /t/. An example of a phonological rule in the English language is while the phoneme /r/ can follow the phonemes /t/ or /d/ in an English consonant cluster (such as *track* or *drab*), the phoneme /l/ cannot follow these letters. |
| **Morphology** | The system of meaningful units involved in word formation. | The smallest sound units that have a meaning are called morphemes, or meaning units. The word *girl* is one morpheme, or meaning unit; it cannot be broken down any further and still have meaning. When the suffix *s* is added, the word becomes *girls* and has two morphemes because the *s* changed the meaning of the word, indicating that there is more than one girl. |
| **Syntax** | The system that involves the way words are combined to form acceptable phrases and sentences. | Word order is very important in determining meaning in the English language. For example, the sentence "Sebastian pushed the bike" has a different meaning than "The bike pushed Sebastian." |
| **Semantics** | The system that involves the meaning of words and sentences. | Knowing the meaning of individual words—that is, vocabulary. For example, semantics includes knowing the meaning of such words as *orange, transportation,* and *intelligent.* |
| **Pragmatics** | The system of using appropriate conversation and knowledge of how to effectively use language in context. | An example is using polite language in appropriate situations, such as being mannerly when talking with one's teacher. Taking turns in a conversation involves pragmatics. |

## FIGURE **9.1**

**THE RULE SYSTEMS OF LANGUAGE.**

## Review *Connect* Reflect

**LO1** Define language and describe its rule systems.

### Review

- What is language?
- What are language's five main rule systems?

### *Connect*

- Describe how the use of dialogue in scaffolding, discussed in Chapter 6, is reflected in the story about Helen Keller and Anne Sullivan at the beginning of this chapter.

### **Reflect** *Your Own Personal Journey of Life*

- How good are your family members and friends at the pragmatics of language? Describe an example in which someone showed pragmatic skills and another in which another person did not.

## How Language Develops **LO2** Describe how language develops.

Infancy • Early Childhood • Middle and Late Childhood • Adolescence

According to an ancient historian, a 13th-century emperor of Germany, Frederick II, had a cruel idea. He wanted to know what language children would speak if no one talked to them. He selected several newborns and threatened their caregivers with death if they ever talked to the infants. Frederick never found out what language the children would speak because they all died, presumably from neglect. As we move forward in the twenty-first century, we are still curious about infants' development of language, although our experiments and observations are, to say the least, far more humane than Frederick's.

## INFANCY

Whatever language they learn, infants all over the world follow a similar path in language development. What are some key milestones in this development?

**Babbling and Other Vocalizations**   Long before infants speak recognizable words, they produce a number of vocalizations (Parish-Morris, Golinkoff, & Hirsh-Pasek, 2013; Sachs, 2009). The functions of these early vocalizations are to practise making sounds, to communicate, and to attract attention. Babies' sounds go through the following sequence during the first year:

1. *Crying.* Babies cry even at birth. Crying can signal distress, but as we will discuss in Chapter 10, different types of cries signal different things.

2. *Cooing.* Babies first coo at about 1 to 2 months. These are gurgling sounds that are made in the back of the throat and usually express pleasure during interaction with the caregiver.

3. *Babbling.* In the middle of the first year babies babble—that is, they produce strings of consonant-vowel combinations, such as *ba, ba, ba, ba.*

*developmental* **connection**

**Emotional Development.** Three of the cries that infants display are the basic cry, anger cry, and pain cry. Chapter 10, LO 2

Long before infants speak recognizable words, they communicate by producing a number of vocalizations and gestures. *At approximately what ages do infants begin to produce different types of vocalization and gestures?*

When deaf infants are born to deaf parents who use sign language, they babble with their hands and fingers at about the same age that hearing children babble vocally (Bloom, 1998). Such similarities in timing and structure between manual and vocal babbling indicate that a unified language capacity underlies signed and spoken language.

**Gestures** Infants start using gestures, such as showing and pointing, at about 8 to 12 months of age. They may wave bye-bye, nod to mean yes, show an empty cup to want more milk, and point to a dog to draw attention to it. Some early gestures are symbolic, as when an infant smacks her lips to indicate food or drink. Pointing is considered by language experts to be an important index of the social aspects of language, and it follows this developmental sequence: from pointing without checking on the adult gaze to pointing while looking back and forth between an object and the adult (Goldin-Meadow & Alibali, 2013).

Lack of pointing is a significant indicator of problems in the infant's communication system (Goldin-Meadow & Alibali, 2013). Pointing is a key aspect of the development of joint attention and an important index of the social aspects of language (Begus & Southgate, 2012). Failure to engage in pointing also characterizes many children with autism. The ability to use the pointing gesture effectively improves in the second year of life as advances in other aspects of language communication occur (Colonnesi & others, 2010).

A recent study found that parents of high socioeconomic status (SES) were more likely to use gestures when communicating with their 14-month-old infants (Rowe & Goldin-Meadow, 2009). Further, the infants' use of gestures at 14 months of age in high-SES families was linked to a larger vocabulary at 54 months of age.

**Recognizing Language Sounds** Long before they begin to learn words, infants can make fine discriminations among the sounds of language. In one classic study 5- and 6-month-old infants listened to numerous trials of speech syllables (Moffitt, 1971). One group of infants heard repetitions of "gah" followed by "bah," while another group heard repetitions of "bah" followed by "gah." A third group of infants heard repetitions of "bah" only. The first two groups of infants showed an increase in heart rate upon the change of sound, indicating they were able to perceive the different sounds. Canadian researcher Janet Werker and her colleagues have continued this research on infants' discriminatory ability (see Figure 9.2). A series of research studies revealed that from birth to about 6–8 months of age, infants are "citizens of the world"; they recognize when sounds change most of the time, no matter what language the phonemes come from. But over the next six months, infants get even better at perceiving the changes in sounds from their "own" language, the one their parents speak, and gradually lose the ability to recognize differences that are not present in their own languages (Werker, 1989; Werker & Tees, 1983; 1984; Werker & others, 1981). These studies reveal the role of both nature and nurture in infants' early language abilities (see Curtin & Werker, 2007 for review).

Infants must also fish out individual words from the non-stop stream of sound that makes up ordinary speech (Harris, Golinkiff, & Hirsh-Pasek, 2012). To do so, they must find the boundaries between words, which is very difficult for infants because adults don't pause between words when they speak. Still, infants begin to detect word boundaries by 8 months of age. For example, in one study, 8-month-old infants listened to recorded stories that contained unusual words, such as hornbill and python (Jusczyk & Hohne, 1997). Two weeks later, the researchers tested the infants with two lists of words, one made up of words in the stories, the other of new, unusual words that did not appear in the stories. The infants listened to the familiar words for a second longer, on average, than the new words, illustrating they had previously been able to parse those words out of the speech stream.

*What characterizes the infant's early word learning?*

FIGURE **9.2**

**FROM UNIVERSAL LINGUIST TO LANGUAGE-SPECIFIC LISTENER.** Using research methodologies discussed in Chapter 5, Janet Werker's research at the University of British Columbia has demonstrated that babies are universal linguists until about 6–8 months of age, but in the next six months become language-specific listeners. *Does Werker's research give support to the view that either nature or nurture is the source of language acquisition?*

**First Words** Infants understand words before they can produce or speak them (Pan & Uccelli, 2009). For example, many infants recognize their name when someone says it as early as 5 months of age. However, the infant's first spoken word, a milestone eagerly anticipated by every parent, usually doesn't occur until 10 to 15 months of age and at an average of about 13 months. Yet long before babies say their first words, they have been communicating with their parents, often by gesturing and using their own special sounds. The appearance of first words is a continuation of this communication process (Berko Gleason, 2009).

A child's first words include those that name important people (dada), familiar animals (kitty), vehicles (car), toys (ball), food (milk), body parts (eye), clothes (hat), household items (clock), and greeting terms (bye). These were the first words of babies 50 years ago. They are the first words of babies today. Children often express various intentions with their single words, so that "cookie" might mean "That's a cookie" or "I want a cookie."

As indicated earlier, children understand their first words earlier than they speak them. On the average, infants understand about 50 words at about 13 months, but they can't say this many words until about 18 months (Menyuk, Liebergott, & Schultz, 1995). Thus, in infancy *receptive vocabulary* (words the child understands) considerably exceeds *spoken vocabulary* (words the child uses). For example, a recent study revealed that 6-month-olds recognize words that refer to body parts, such as "hand" and "feet," but they cannot yet speak these words (Tincoff & Jusczyk, 2012).

The infant's spoken vocabulary rapidly increases once the first word is spoken (Parish-Morris, Golinkoff, & Hirsh-Pasek, 2013; Wagner & Hoff, 2013; Pan & Uccelli, 2009; Waxman, 2009). The average 18-month-old can speak about 50 words, but by the age of 2 years a child can speak about 200 words. This rapid increase in vocabulary that begins at approximately 18 months is called the *vocabulary spurt* (Bloom, Lifter, & Broughton, 1985).

Like the timing of a child's first word, the timing of the vocabulary spurt varies. Figure 9.3 shows the range for these two language milestones in 14 children. On average, these children said their first word at 13 months and had a vocabulary spurt at 19 months. However, the ages for the first word of individual children varied from 10 to 17 months and for their vocabulary spurt from 13 to 25 months.

Cross-linguistic differences occur in word learning. Children learning Mandarin Chinese, Korean, and Japanese acquire more verbs earlier in their development than do children learning English. This cross-linguistic difference reflects the greater use of verbs in these Asian languages.

Children sometimes overextend or underextend the meanings of the words they use (Woodward & Markman, 1998). Overextension is the tendency to apply a word to objects that are inappropriate for the word's meaning. For example,

*developmental* **connection**

**Newborn Perception.** How does the habituation procedure described in the preceding section on recognizing language sounds enable researchers to learn about infant perceptual abilities? Chapter 5, LO 2

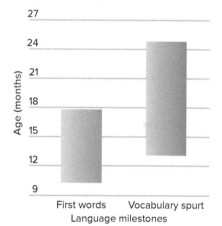

FIGURE **9.3**

**VARIATION IN LANGUAGE MILESTONES.**

*What is a difference in the way children learn Chinese Mandarin and English?*

Around the world, most young children learn to speak in two-word utterances at about 18 to 24 months of age. *What implications does this have for the biological basis of language?*

children at first may say "dada" not only for their own fathers but also for other men, strangers, or boys. Children may overextend word meanings because they don't know the appropriate word or can't recall it. With time, overextensions decrease and eventually disappear. Underextension is the tendency to apply a word too narrowly; it occurs when children fail to use a word to name a relevant event or object. For example, a child might use the word *boy* to describe a 5-year-old neighbour but not apply the word to a male infant or to a 9-year-old male. The most common explanation of underextension is that children have heard a name used in reference to a small, unrepresentative sample.

**Two-Word Utterances** By the time children are 18 to 24 months of age, they usually utter two-word messages. To convey meaning with just two words, the child relies heavily on gesture, tone, and context. The wealth of meaning children can communicate with a two-word utterance includes the following (Slobin, 1972):

- Identification: See doggie.
- Location: Book there.
- Repetition: More milk.
- Possession: My candy.
- Attribution: Big car.
- Agent-action: Mama walk.
- Question: Where ball?

Children use two-word utterances like these examples, whether their first language is English, German, Russian, Finnish, Turkish, or Samoan.

Notice that the two-word utterances omit many parts of speech and are remarkably succinct. In fact, in every language, a child's first combinations of words have this economical quality; they are telegraphic. **Telegraphic speech** is the use of short and precise words without grammatical markers such as articles, auxiliary verbs, and other connectives. Telegraphic speech is not limited to two words. "Mommy give ice cream" and "Mommy give Tommy ice cream" also are examples of telegraphic speech.

We have discussed a number of language milestones in infancy. Figure 9.4 summarizes the ages at which infants typically reach these milestones.

## EARLY CHILDHOOD

Toddlers move rather quickly from producing two-word utterances to creating three-, four-, and five-word combinations. Between 2 and 3 years of age they begin the transition from saying simple sentences that express a single proposition to saying complex sentences (Bloom, 1998).

Young children's understanding sometimes goes far beyond their speech. One 3-year-old, laughing with delight as an abrupt summer breeze stirred his hair and tickled his skin, commented, "I got breezed!" Many of the oddities of young children's language sound like mistakes to adult listeners. However, from the children's point of view, they are not mistakes. They represent the way young children perceive and understand their world. As children go through their early childhood years, their grasp of the rule systems that govern language increase.

As young children learn the special features of their own language, there are extensive regularities in how they acquire that particular language (Berko Gleason, 2009). For example, all children learn the prepositions *on* and *in* before other prepositions. Children learning other languages, such as Russian or Chinese, also acquire the particular features of those languages in a consistent order.

**telegraphic speech** The use of short, precise words without grammatical markers such as articles, auxiliary verbs, and other connectives.

| Typical Age | Language Milestones |
|---|---|
| Birth | Crying |
| 2 to 4 months | Cooing begins |
| 5 months | Understands first word |
| 6 months | Babbling begins |
| 7 to 11 months | Change from universal linguist to language-specific listener |
| 8 to 12 months | Uses gestures, such as showing and pointing<br>Comprehension of words appears |
| 13 months | First word spoken |
| 18 months | Vocabulary spurt starts |
| 18 to 24 months | Uses two-word utterances<br>Rapid expansion of understanding of words |

**FIGURE 9.4**

**SOME LANGUAGE MILESTONES IN INFANCY.** Despite great variations in the language input received by infants, around the world they follow a similar path in learning to speak.

**Understanding Phonology and Morphology** During the preschool years, most children gradually become more sensitive to the sounds of spoken words and become increasingly capable of producing all the sounds of their language. By the time, children are 3 years of age, they can produce all the vowel sounds and most of the consonant sounds (Menn & Stoel-Gammon, 2009).

Young children can even produce complex consonant clusters such as *str-* and *-mpt-*. They notice rhymes, enjoy poems, make up silly names for things by substituting one sound for another (such as bubblegum, bubblebum, bubbleyum), and clap along with each syllable in a phrase.

By the time children move beyond two-word utterances, they demonstrate a knowledge of morphology rules (Park & others, 2012). Children begin using the plural and possessive forms of nouns (such as *dogs* and *dog's*). They put appropriate endings on verbs (such as *-s* when the subject is third-person singular and *-ed* for the past tense). They use prepositions (such as *in* and *on*), articles (such as *a* and *the*), and various forms of the verb *to be* (such as "I was going to the store"). Some of the best evidence for changes in children's use of morphological rules occurs in their overgeneralization of the rules, as when a preschool child says "foots" instead of "feet," or "goed" instead of "went."

In a classic experiment that was designed to study children's knowledge of morphological rules, such as how to make a plural, Jean Berko (1958) presented preschool children and first-grade children with cards such as the one shown in Figure 9.5. Children were asked to look at the card while the experimenter read aloud the words on the card. Then the children were asked to supply the missing word. This might sound easy, but Berko was interested in the children's ability to apply the appropriate morphological rule—in this case, to say "wugs" with the *z* sound that indicates the plural.

Although the children's answers were not perfect, they were much better than they could have been by chance. What makes Berko's study impressive is that most of the words were made up for the experiment. Thus, the children could not base their responses on remembering past instances of hearing the words. Since they could make the plurals or past tenses of words they had never heard before, this was proof that they knew the morphological rules.

**Changes in Syntax and Semantics** Preschool children also learn and apply rules of syntax (Gertner & Fisher, 2012). They show a growing mastery of complex rules for how words should be ordered.

Consider *wh-* questions, such as "Where is Daddy going?" or "What is that boy doing?" To ask these questions properly, the child must know two important differences between *wh-* questions and affirmative statements (for instance, "Daddy is going to work" and "That boy is waiting for the school bus"). First, a *wh-* word must be added at the beginning of the sentence. Second, the auxiliary verb must be inverted—that is, exchanged with the subject of the sentence. Young children learn quite early where to put the *wh-* word, but they take much longer to learn the auxiliary-inversion rule. Thus, preschool children might ask, "Where Daddy is going?" and "What that boy is doing?"

Gains in semantics also characterize early childhood. Vocabulary development is dramatic (Crain & Zhou, 2012). Some experts have concluded that between 18 months and 6 years of age, young children learn approximately one new word every waking hour (Carey, 1977; Gelman & Kalish, 2006)! By the time they enter first grade, it is estimated that children know about 14,000 words (Clark, 1993).

Why can children learn so many new words so quickly? One possible explanation is **fast mapping**, which involves children's ability to make an initial connection between a word and its referent after only limited exposure to the word (Woodward, Markman, & Fitzimmons, 1994). Researchers have found that exposure to words on multiple occasions over several days results in more successful word learning than the same number of exposures in a single day (Childers & Tomasello, 2002).

This is a wug.

Now there is another one.
There are two of them.
There are two _____.

FIGURE **9.5**

**STIMULI IN BERKO'S STUDY OF YOUNG CHILDREN'S UNDERSTANDING OF MORPHOLOGICAL RULES.** In Jean Berko's (1958) study, young children were presented cards, such as this one with a "wug" on it. Then the children were asked to supply the missing word; in supplying the missing word, they had to say it correctly, too. "Wugs" is the correct response here.

**fast mapping** A process that helps to explain how young children learn the connection between a word and its referent so quickly.

Language researchers have proposed that young children may use a number of working hypotheses to accomplish their fast mapping (Pan & Uccelli, 2009). One working hypothesis children use is to give a novel label to a novel object. Parents can be especially helpful in aiding children's learning of novel labels for novel objects. As a mother looks at a picture book with her young child, she knows that the child understands the referent for *car* but not *bus,* so she says, "That's a bus, not a car. A bus is bigger than a car." Another working hypothesis children use is that a word refers to a whole object rather than parts of an object, such as labelling a tiger a tiger instead of a tail or paw. Sometimes children's initial mappings are incorrect. In such cases, they benefit from hearing the words mature speakers use to test and revise their word-referent connections (Gershkoff-Stowe & Hahn, 2007).

What are some important aspects of how word learning optimally occurs? Kathy Hirsh-Pasek and Roberta Golinkoff (Harris, Golinkoff, & Hirsh-Pasek, 2012; Hirsh-Pasek & Golinkoff, 2013) emphasize six key principles in young children's vocabulary development:

1. *Children learn the words they hear most often.* They learn the words that they encounter when interacting with parents, teachers, siblings, and peers, and also from books. They especially benefit from encountering words that they do not know.

2. *Children learn words for things and events that interest them.* Parents and teachers can direct young children to experience words in contexts that interest the children; playful peer interactions are especially helpful in this regard.

3. *Children learn words best in responsive and interactive contexts rather than in passive contexts.* Children who experience turn-taking opportunities, joint focusing experiences, and positive, sensitive socializing contexts with adults encounter the scaffolding necessary for optimal word learning.

4. *Children learn words best in contexts that are meaningful.* Young children learn new words more effectively when new words are encountered in integrated contexts rather than as isolated facts.

5. *Children learn words best when they access clear information about word meaning.* Children whose parents and teachers are sensitive to words the children might not understand and provide support and elaboration with hints about word meaning learn words better than children whose parents and teachers quickly state a new word and don't monitor whether children understand its meaning.

6. *Children learn words best when grammar and vocabulary are considered.* Children who experience a large number of words and diversity in verbal stimulation develop a richer vocabulary and better understanding of grammar. In many cases, vocabulary and grammar development are connected.

How parents talk to their children is linked with the children's vocabulary growth and the family's socioeconomic status. To read about how family environment affects children's language development, see *Connecting Through Research.*

**Advances in Pragmatics**   Changes in pragmatics also characterize young children's language development (Bryant, 2012). A 6-year-old is simply a much better conversationalist than a 2-year-old is. What are some of the improvements in pragmatics during the preschool years?

Young children begin to engage in extended discourse (Akhtar & Herold, 2008). For example, they learn culturally specific rules of conversation and

*How do children's language abilities develop during early childhood?*

# connecting through research

## How Does Family Environment Affect Young Children's Language Development?

What characteristics of families influence children's language development? Socioeconomic status has been linked with how much parents talk to their children and with young children's vocabulary. Betty Hart and Todd Risley (1995) observed the language environments of children whose parents were professionals and children whose parents were on welfare. Compared with the professional parents, the parents on welfare talked much less to their young children, talked less about past events, and provided less elaboration. As indicated in Figure 9.6, the children of the professional parents had a much larger vocabulary at 36 months of age than the children whose parents were on welfare.

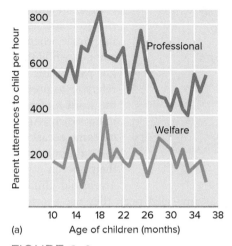 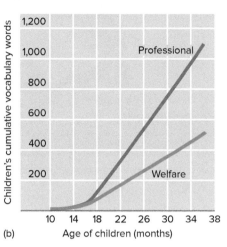

(a)         (b)

## FIGURE 9.6

**LANGUAGE INPUT IN PROFESSIONAL AND WELFARE FAMILIES, AND YOUNG CHILDREN'S VOCABULARY DEVELOPMENT.** (*a*) This American study (Hart & Risley, 1995) found that parents from professional families talked with their young children more than parents from welfare families. (*b*) All of the children learned to talk, but children from professional families developed vocabularies that were twice as large as those from welfare families. Thus, by the time children go to preschool they already have experienced considerable differences in language input in their families and developed different levels of vocabulary that are linked to their socioeconomic context. *Does this study indicate that poverty caused deficiencies in vocabulary development?*

Other research has explored the relationship between how much mothers speak to their infants and the infants' vocabularies. For example, in one study by Janellen Huttenlocher and her colleagues (1991), infants whose mothers spoke to them more often had markedly higher vocabularies. By age 2, vocabulary differences were substantial. However, a study of 1- to 3-year-old children living in low-income families found that the sheer amount of maternal talk was not the best predictor of a child's vocabulary growth (Pan & others, 2005). Rather, it was maternal language and literacy skills and mothers' use of diverse vocabulary that best predicted children's vocabulary development.

A recent study revealed that maternal sensitivity (warm response to the child's bids for attention and anticipation of her child's emotional needs, for example), regardless of socioeconomic status and ethnicity, was positively linked with growth in young children's receptive and expressive language development from 18 to 36 months of age (Pungello & others, 2009). In this study, negative intrusive parenting (physically restraining the child or dominating interaction with the child with unnecessary verbal direction, for example) was related to a slower rate of growth of receptive language.

These research studies demonstrate the important effect that early speech input and poverty can have on the development of a child's language skills. Children in low-income families are more likely to have less-educated parents, receive inadequate nutrition, live in low-income communities, and attend substandard schools than children in middle- and high-income families (Row, Burns, & Griffin, 1998). However, living in a low-income family should not be used as the sole identifier in predicting whether children will have difficulties in language development, such as a low vocabulary and reading problems. If children growing up in low-income families experience effective instruction and support, they can develop effective language skills (Barbarin & Aikens, 2009).

*What are some valuable components to include in a program to enhance language development for low-income families?*

politeness, and increasingly adapt their speech in different settings. Their developing linguistic skills and improving ability to understand the perspective of others contribute to their use of more competent narratives.

As children get older, they become increasingly able to talk about things that are not here (Grandma's house, for example) and not now (what happened to them yesterday or might happen tomorrow, for example). A preschool child can tell you what she wants for lunch tomorrow, something that would not have been possible at the two-word stage of language development.

*What characterizes advances in pragmatics during early childhood?*

At about 4 years of age, children develop a remarkable sensitivity to the needs of others in conversation. One way in which they show such sensitivity is through their use of the articles *the* and *an* (or *a*). When adults tell a story or describe an event, they generally use *an* (or *a*) when they first refer to an animal or an object, and then use *the* when referring to it later. (For example, "Two boys were walking through the jungle when *a* fierce lion appeared. *The* lion lunged at one boy while the other ran for cover.") Even 3-year-olds follow part of this rule; they consistently use the word *the* when referring to previously mentioned things. However, the use of the word *a* when something is initially mentioned develops more slowly. Although 5-year-old children follow this rule on some occasions, they fail to follow it on others.

At around 4 to 5 years of age, children learn to change their speech style to suit the situation. For example, even 4-year-old children speak differently to a 2-year-old than to a same-aged peer; they use shorter sentences with the 2-year-old. They also speak differently to an adult than to a same-aged peer, using more polite and formal language with the adult (Shatz & Gelman, 1973).

**Early Literacy**   Concern about children's reading and writing skills has led to a careful examination of preschool and kindergarten children's educational experiences, with the hope that a positive orientation toward reading and writing can be developed early in life (Jalongo, 2011; Otto, 2010; Wagner, 2010). What should a literacy program for preschool children be like? Instruction should be built

*What are some effective strategies for supporting young children's literacy skills?*

on what children already know about oral language, reading, and writing. Further, early precursors of literacy and academic success include language skills, phonological and syntactic knowledge, letter identification, and conceptual knowledge about print and its conventions and functions (Gunning, 2013). Parents and teachers need to provide a supportive environment to help children develop literacy skills (Beatty & Pratt, 2011). A recent meta-analysis (use of statistical techniques to combine the results of studies) revealed that parental involvement in reading activities in the home enhances reading acquisition (Sénéchal & Young, 2008). One study found that literacy experiences (such as how often the child was read to), the quality of the mother's engagement with her child (such as attempts to cognitively stimulate the child), and provision of learning materials (such as age-appropriate learning materials and books) were important home literacy experiences in low-income families that were linked to the children's language development in positive ways (Rodriguez & others, 2009).

The following longitudinal studies conducted with Canadian children indicate the importance of early language skills and experiences in developing literacy skills in both official languages:

- Phonological awareness, letter sound knowledge, grammatical ability, and naming speed in kindergarten were linked to third grade reading success in both English and French for children in French immersion programs (Jared & others, 2011).

- Literacy activities in the home while the children were in kindergarten predicted grade 4 reading fluency for French-speaking children (Sénéchal, 2006).

- Letter knowledge in kindergarten was linked to both spelling ability and reading fluency in grade 2 for English-speaking children (Georgiou & others, 2012).

So far, our discussion of early literacy has focused on children learning to read in Canada's two official languages, English and French. However, the extent to which phonological awareness is linked to learning to read effectively varies across language to some extent (McBride-Chang, 2004). One study of second-grade students from Beijing, Hong Kong, Korea, and the United States revealed that phonological awareness may be more important for early reading development in English and Korean than it is for Chinese (McBride-Chang & others, 2005). Further, rates of dyslexia differ across countries and are linked with the spelling and phonetic rules that characterize the language (McBride-Chang & others, 2008). English is one of the more difficult languages to learn because of its irregular spellings and pronunciations. In countries where English is spoken, the rate of dyslexia is higher than it is in countries where the alphabet script is more phonetically consistent.

**developmental connection**

**Conditions, Diseases, and Disorders.** Dyslexia is a severe impairment in the ability to read and spell; dysgraphia is a severe impairment in handwriting ability. Chapter 16, LO 2

## MIDDLE AND LATE CHILDHOOD

Children gain new skills as they enter school that make it possible for them to learn to read and write, or to advance the reading and writing skills they have developed in early childhood. These new skills include increasingly using language to talk about things that are not physically present, learning what a word is, and learning how to recognize and talk about sounds (Berko Gleason, 2005). They have to learn the alphabetic principle, that the letters of the alphabet represent sounds of the language. As children develop during middle and late childhood, changes in their vocabulary and grammar also take place (Vukelich, Christie, & Enz, 2008).

**Vocabulary, Grammar, and Metalinguistic Awareness** During middle and late childhood, changes occur in the way children's mental vocabulary is organized. When asked to say the first word that comes to mind when they hear a word, young children typically provide a word that often follows the word in a sentence. For example, when asked to respond to *dog* the young child may say "barks," or to the word *eat* say "lunch." At about 7 years of age, children begin to respond with a word that is the same part of speech as the stimulus word. For example, a child may now respond to the word *dog* with "cat" or "horse." To *eat*, they now might say "drink." This is evidence that at age 7 children have begun to categorize their vocabulary by parts of speech (Berko Gleason, 2003).

The process of categorizing becomes easier as children increase their vocabulary (Clark, 2012). Children's vocabulary increases from an average of about 14,000 words at 6 years of age to an average of about 40,000 words by 11 years of age.

Children make similar advances in grammar (Behrens, 2012). During the elementary school years, children's improvement in logical reasoning and analytical skills helps them to understand constructions such as the appropriate use of comparatives (shorter, deeper) and subjectives ("If you were president . . ."). During the elementary school years, children become increasingly able to understand and use complex grammar, such as the following sentence: "The boy who kissed his mother wore a hat." They also learn to use language to produce connected discourse. They become able to relate sentences to one another to produce descriptions, definitions, and narratives that make sense. Children must be able to do these things orally before they can be expected to deal with them in written assignments.

These advances in vocabulary and grammar during the elementary school years are accompanied by the development of **metalinguistic awareness**, which is knowledge about language, such as understanding what a preposition is or being able to discuss the sounds of a language. Metalinguistic awareness allows children "to think about their language, understand what words are, and even define them" (Berko Gleason, 2009, p. 4). This awareness improves considerably during the elementary school years (Pan & Uccelli, 2009). Defining words

> Children pick up words as pigeons peas.
>
> —JOHN RAY
> *English Naturalist, 17th Century*

**developmental connection**

**Information Processing.** Metacognition is cognition about cognition or knowing about knowing. Chapter 7, LO 5

**metalinguistic awareness** Knowledge about language.

This teacher is helping a student sound out words. Researchers have found that phonics instruction is a key aspect of teaching students to read, both for beginning readers and students with weak reading skills.

becomes a regular part of classroom discourse, and children increase their knowledge of syntax as they study and talk about the components of sentences such as subjects and verbs (Crain, 2012).

Children also make progress in understanding how to use language in culturally appropriate ways—pragmatics (Bryant, 2012). By the time they enter adolescence, most children know the rules for the use of language in everyday contexts—that is, what is appropriate to say and what is inappropriate to say.

**Reading** One classic model identifies five stages in the development of reading skills (Chall, 1979) (see Figure 9.7). The age boundaries are approximate and do not apply to every child—and researchers generally agree that reading acquisition no longer occurs in such abrupt stages—but the model conveys a sense of the developmental changes involved in learning to read.

Before learning to read, children learn to use language to talk about things that are not present, they learn what a word is, and they learn how to recognize sounds and talk about them (Berko Gleason, 2003). If they develop a large vocabulary, their path to reading is eased. Children who begin elementary school with a small vocabulary are at risk when it comes to learning to read (Berninger, 2006).

Vocabulary development plays an important role in reading comprehension (Cunningham, 2009). For example, one study revealed that a good vocabulary was linked with reading comprehension in second-grade students (Berninger & Abbott, 2005). Having a good vocabulary helps readers access word meaning effortlessly.

Analyses by Rich Mayer (2008) focused on the cognitive processes a child needs to go through in order to read a printed word. In his view, the three processes are (1) being aware of sound units in words, which consists of recognizing phonemes; (2) decoding words, which involves converting printed words into sounds; and (3) accessing word meaning, which consists of finding a mental representation of a word's meaning.

What are the most effective ways to teach children how to read? Education and language experts continue to debate how children should be taught to read. Currently debate focuses on the phonics approach versus the whole-language approach (Vacca & others, 2009).

The **phonics approach** emphasizes that reading instruction should focus on teaching basic rules for translating written symbols into sounds. Early reading instruction should involve simplified materials. Only after children have

| Phase | Age Range/Grade Level | Descripton |
|---|---|---|
| 0 | Birth to first grade | Children master several prerequisites for reading. Many learn the left-to-right progression and order of reading, how to identify letters of the alphabet, and how to write their names. Some learn to read words that appear on signs. As a result of TV shows like *Sesame Street* and attending preschool and kindergarten programs, many young children today develop greater knowledge about reading earlier than in the past. |
| 1 | First and second grades | Many children learn to read at this time. In doing so, they acquire the ability to sound out words (that is, translate letters into sounds and blend sounds into words). They also complete their learning of letter names and sounds. |
| 2 | Second and third grades | Children become more fluent at retrieving individual words and other reading skills. However, in this phase reading is still not used much for learning. The demands of reading are so taxing for children in this phase that they have few resources left over to process the content. |
| 3 | Fourth through eighth grades | In fourth through eighth grade, children become increasingly able to obtain new information from print. In other words, they read to learn. They still have difficulty understanding information presented from multiple perspectives within the same story. When children don't learn to read, a downward spiral unfolds that leads to serious difficulties in many academic subjects. |
| 4 | High school | Many students become fully competent readers. They develop the ability to understand material told from many perspectives. This allows them to engage in sometimes more sophisticated discussions of literature, history, economics, and politics. |

FIGURE **9.7**

**A MODEL OF DEVELOPMENTAL PHASES IN READING.**

learned the correspondence rules that relate spoken phonemes to the alphabet letters that represent them should they be given complex reading materials, such as books and poems (Cunningham & Hall, 2009).

By contrast, the **whole-language approach** stresses that reading instruction should parallel children's natural language learning. Reading materials should be whole and meaningful. That is, children should be given material in its complete form, such as stories and poems, so that they learn to understand language's communicative function. Reading should be connected with listening and writing skills. Although there are variations in whole-language programs, most share the premise that reading should be integrated with other skills and subjects, such as science and social studies, and that it should focus on real-world material. Thus, a class might read newspapers, magazines, or books, and then write about and discuss them. In some whole-language classes, beginning readers are taught to recognize whole words or even entire sentences, and to use the context of what they are reading to guess at unfamiliar words.

Which approach is better? Children can benefit from both approaches, but direct instruction in phonics needs to take place, especially in kindergarten and the first grade (Cunningham & Allington, 2010; Tompkins, 2011). An increasing number of experts in the field of reading now conclude that direct instruction in phonics is a key aspect of learning to read (Cunningham, 2013; Dow & Baer, 2013). Numerous studies reveal that phonics programs improve reading skill (e.g., Savage & others, 2009) and that awareness of phonemes is the single best predictor of reading success (Melby-Lervag, Lyster, & Hulme, 2012).

Beyond the phonics/whole-language issue in learning to read, becoming a good reader includes learning to read fluently (Gunning, 2013; Kamil, 2012). Many beginning or poor readers do not recognize words automatically. Their processing capacity is consumed by the demands of word recognition, so they have less capacity to devote to the comprehension of groupings of words as phrases or sentences. As their processing of words and passages becomes more automatic, it is said that their reading becomes more fluent (Fox, 2012). Metacognitive strategies, such as learning to monitor one's reading progress, getting the gist of what is being read, and summarizing also are important in becoming a good reader, as these strategies help with comprehension (Dimmitt & McCormick, 2012; McCormick, Dimmitt, & Sullivan, 2013).

Reading, like other important skills, takes time and effort. Children who read more become better readers, while children who read less become poorer readers, and this gap in ability increases over the elementary school years (Kempe & others, 2011; Stanovich, 1986). Thus, practice is important to the development of literacy skills, and children should be motivated to read by having an array of reading materials available to them.

**Writing** Children's writing emerges out of their early scribbles, which appear at around 2 to 3 years of age. In early childhood, children's motor skills usually develop to the point that they can begin printing letters. Most 4-year-olds can print their first name. Five-year-olds can reproduce letters and copy several short words. They gradually learn to distinguish the distinctive characteristics of letters, such as whether the lines are curved or straight, open or closed. Through the early elementary grades, many children continue to reverse letters such as *b* and *d* and *p* and *q* (Temple & others, 1993). At this age, if other aspects of the child's development are normal, letter reversals do not predict literacy problems.

As they begin to write, children often invent spellings. Canadian researcher Monique Sénéchal and her colleagues (Sénéchal & others, 2012) revealed that guiding children to use invented spellings enhanced reading acquisition. Sénéchal suggested that inventing spellings that are based on the sounds of words they hear may provide children with the opportunity to explore the relation between oral and written language. Parents and teachers should

**phonics approach** An approach that emphasizes that reading instruction should focus on phonics and its basic rules for translating written symbols into sounds.

**whole-language approach** An approach that stresses that reading instruction should parallel children's natural language learning. Reading materials should be whole and meaningful.

Children most at risk for reading difficulties in the first grade are those who began school with less verbal skill, less phonological awareness, less letter knowledge, and less familiarity with the basic purposes and mechanisms of reading.

—CATHERINE SNOW
*Professor of Education, Harvard University*

The devl and the babe goste

A DEVL NAPD iN THE
BRiTE SUN LiTE he SeD
iT iS HOLOWENE I HAV TO
GeT up AND GeT. ReDE TO ScEr
THE littL CHILJRiN WEN THAE GO
to CHRiCOR CHRETE FRST He
MADE A JACAL ETRN He PUT 2 CEDiS
iN iT TO RELE ScEr THEm THN He
MADE A COL JRiN TO CAST He
SPELS ON THE CHIL JRiN.

Anna Mudd is the 6-year-old author of "The Devl and the Babe Goste." Anna has been writing stories for at least two years. Her story includes poetic images, sophisticated syntax, and vocabulary that reflect advances in language development.

encourage children's early writing but not be overly concerned about letter formation or spelling.

Like becoming a good reader, becoming a good writer takes many years and lots of practice (Temple, Nathan, & Temple, 2013). Children should be given many writing opportunities in the elementary and secondary school years (Tompkins, 2013). As their language and cognitive skills improve with good instruction, so will their writing skills. For example, developing a more sophisticated understanding of syntax and grammar serves as an underpinning for better writing (Irvin, Buehl, & Klemp, 2007).

So do cognitive skills such as organization and logical reasoning (Perin, 2007). Through elementary, middle, and high school, students develop increasingly sophisticated methods of organizing their ideas. In early elementary school, they narrate and describe or write short poems. In late elementary and middle school, they move to projects such as book reports that combine narration with more reflection and analysis. In high school, they become more skilled at forms of exposition that do not depend on narrative structure (Conley, 2008). A recent meta-analysis revealed that the following interventions were the most effective in improving fourth- through twelfth-grade students' writing quality: (1) strategy instruction, (2) summarization, (3) peer assistance, and (4) setting goals (Graham & Perin, 2007).

As with reading, teachers play a critical role in students' development of writing skills (Rijlaarsdam & others, 2012). Classroom observations made by Michael Pressley and his colleagues (2007) indicate that students become good writers when teachers spend considerable time on writing instruction and are passionate about teaching students to write. Their observations also indicate that classrooms with students who receive high scores on writing assessments have walls that overflow with examples of effective writing, whereas it is much harder to find such examples on the walls of classrooms that have many students who receive low scores on writing assessments.

**Bilingualism and Second-Language Learning** Are there sensitive periods in learning a second language? That is, if individuals want to learn a second language, how important is the age at which they begin to learn it? For many years, it was claimed that if individuals did not learn a second language prior to puberty, they would never reach native-language-learners' proficiency in the second language (Johnson & Newport, 1991). However, recent research indicates a more complex conclusion: Sensitive periods likely vary across different language systems (Thomas & Johnson, 2008). Thus, for late language learners, such as adolescents and adults, new vocabulary is easier to learn than new sounds or new grammar (Neville, 2006). For example, children's ability to pronounce words with a native-like accent in a second language typically decreases with age, with

PEANUTS © United Features Syndicate, Inc.

an especially sharp drop occurring after the age of about 10 to 12. Also, adults tend to learn a second language faster than children, but their final level of second-language attainment is not as high as children's. And the way children and adults learn a second language differs somewhat. Compared with adults, children are less sensitive to feedback, less likely to use explicit strategies, and more likely to learn a second language from a large amount of input (Thomas & Johnson, 2008).

Some aspects of children's ability to learn a second language are transferred more easily to the second language than are others (Paradis, 2010; Pena & Bedore, 2009). A recent research review indicated that in learning to read, phonological awareness is rooted in general cognitive processes and thus transfers easily across languages; however, decoding is more language-specific and needs to be relearned with each language (Bialystok, 2007).

Although 5.8 million people in Canada report being bilingual, bilingualism rates have declined over the last 10 years, putting Canadian students at a disadvantage over their international peers (Lepage & Corbeil, 2013).

Bilingualism—the ability to speak two languages—has a positive effect on children's cognitive development (Gibbons & Ng, 2004). An extensive body of research conducted by Ellen Bialystok at York University in Toronto revealed that children who are fluent in two languages perform better than their single-language counterparts on tests of control of attention, concept formation, analytical reasoning, cognitive flexibility, executive control, and cognitive complexity (Bialystok, 2001, 2007, 2011; Barac & Bialystok, 2012). They also are more conscious of the structure of spoken and written language and better at noticing errors of grammar and meaning, skills that benefit their reading ability (Bialystok, 1997). Bilingualism may even contribute to a slowing down of cognitive decline in old age (Bialystok, Craik, & Luk, 2012). However, a research review concluded that bilingual children have lower formal language proficiency (smaller vocabulary, for example) in *each* language than monolingual children (Bialystok & Craik, 2010).

To learn more about bilingual education in Canada, read the *Connecting to Current Controversy* and *Connecting with Diversity* boxes.

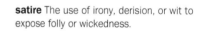

*developmental* **connection**

**Cognitive Theory.** According to Piaget, at 11 to 15 years of age a new stage—formal operational thought—emerges that is characterized by thought that is more abstract, idealistic, and logical. Chapter 6, LO 1

# ADOLESCENCE

Language development during adolescence includes increased sophistication in the use of words (Berman, 2010). With an increase in abstract thinking, adolescents are much better than children at analyzing the function a word performs in a sentence.

Adolescents also develop more subtle abilities with words. They make strides in understanding **metaphor**, which is an implied comparison between unlike things. For example, individuals "draw a line in the sand" to indicate a non-negotiable position; a political campaign is said to be "a marathon, not a sprint"; a person's faith is "shattered." And adolescents become better able to understand and to use **satire**, which is the use of irony, derision, or wit to expose folly or wickedness. Caricatures are an example of satire. More advanced logical thinking also allows adolescents, from about 15 to 20 years of age, to understand complex literary works.

Most adolescents are also much better readers and writers than children are. As indicated in Figure 9.7, many adolescents increase their understanding of material told from different

**metaphor** An implied comparison between two unlike things.

**satire** The use of irony, derision, or wit to expose folly or wickedness.

*What are some changes in language development in adolescence?*

## French Immersion Programs

French immersion is a type of bilingual education in which non-native French speakers receive a portion of their educational instruction in French. Immersion programs were introduced in Canada in 1965 to encourage bilingualism in Canada's two official languages and have proliferated across Canada in the ensuring 50 years (Genesee & Lindholm-Leary, 2007). Currently there are more than 300,000 students enrolled in French immersion programs across Canada (Lockyer & others, 2012).

According to Fred Genesee, at McGill University in Montreal, the goals of immersion programs are for students to achieve normal levels of first language proficiency, an advanced level of proficiency in written and oral forms of French, and grade appropriate levels of achievement in academic subjects (Genesee & Lindholm-Leary, 2007). Studies conducted by several Canadian researchers have found that these goals are being met: students in French immersion generally achieve the same level of reading, writing, listening and speaking proficiency in English as children attending English programs, as well as a level of proficiency in French that is superior to that of children receiving conventional language arts instruction in French. Grade appropriate levels in all academic subjects, such as mathematics and science, are also being met (Allen, 2004; Genesee, 1978; Genesee & Lindholm-Leary, 2007; Turnbull, Hart, & Lapkin, 2003).

Despite the advantages associated with French immersion programs, many children still withdraw from the program (Genessee & Jared, 2008). The attrition rate from early immersion programs may be a result of a short-term lag in academic achievement for children in immersion programs. However, research reveals that this lag is temporary, typically disappearing by Grade 6 (Genesee & Lindholm-Leary, 2007; Turnbull, Hart, & Lapkin, 2003). To better understand the reasons why children drop out of immersion programs, two issues emerge: what is the best time to begin immersion programs to reduce the difficulties children may have, and whether or not immersion programs are suitable for at-risk children.

*When to begin immersion?* There are three types of immersion programs, early immersion, beginning in kindergarten or grade 1, middle immersion, beginning in grade 4 or 5, and late immersion, beginning in grade 7 or during the first years of secondary education (Genesee & Lindholm-Leary, 2007). Currently, all Canadian provinces and territories, with the exception of New

Brunswick, offer early immersion programs beginning in kindergarten or grade 1. These education policies are consistent with research demonstrating that earlier learning of a second language is associated with better language outcomes (e.g., Bialystok, 1997; Pearson, Fernandez, & Oller, 1993). However, proponents of late immersion programs argue that it is better to build a strong foundation in English before a second language is introduced and that a later start enables parents to gain a better understanding of their child's abilities to help determine whether immersion is the right choice. On the basis of these arguments, in 2008, the Department of Education in New Brunswick proposed to replace early immersion programs, beginning in grade 1, with later immersion programs, beginning in grade 6. Before this change was set in place, the Department of Education responded to parental concern, and implemented a compromise, in which immersion would begin in grade 3. This decision is currently being re-evaluated (Lockyer & others, 2012). It is evident that the debate regarding when best to begin immersion is not yet over.

Are immersion programs suitable for at-risk children? The second issue is whether or not French immersion programs are suitable for children who are at risk for below-average academic achievement. At-risk children come from lower socio-economic backgrounds, have lower levels of intellectual ability and/or have impaired language learning. Parents of at-risk children are often advised against enrolling their children in immersion programs, or to remove their children from such programs if they experience difficulty for fear that their basic education will suffer (Genesee, 2007; Wise, 2012). According to Dr. Genesee (2007; 2012a), however, there is no empirical support to suggest that at-risk children are at any greater risk in an immersion program than an English-only program. Research indicates that at-risk children typically achieve the same level of reading and writing proficiency in English as disadvantaged children in English-only classrooms (Kruk & Reynolds, 2012), and greater levels of proficiency in French than similar children receiving traditional language arts instruction in French (see Genesee & Jared, 2008 for review). Research continues to focus on how best to support at-risk children in immersion programs, which type of immersion programs are best suited to meet the needs of at-risk children, and what proficiencies immersion teachers need to best support the diversity in their students.

*Would learning sign language, as you learned Helen Keller did in the chapter opening, be associated with the same cognitive benefits as learning a second spoken language?*

perspectives, which allows them to engage in more sophisticated discussions of various topics. When writing they are better at organizing ideas before they write, at distinguishing between general and specific points as they write, at stringing together sentences that make sense, and at organizing their writing into an introduction, body, and concluding remarks.

## Aboriginal Language Learning

English and French are not the only languages spoken in Canada. Over 60 Aboriginal languages were reported as being spoken by 17.2 percent of the Canadian population who reported an Aboriginal identity (First Nations, Inuit, or Métis) (Statistics Canada, 2011). The variety of Aboriginal languages spoken included Cree, Ojibway, Innu/Montagnais, Dene, Oji-Cree, and Mi'kmaq. The proportion of Aboriginal people who reported they were able to have a conversation in an Aboriginal language was larger than that which reported an Aboriginal language as their mother tongue, suggesting that many Aboriginal people acquire an Aboriginal language as a second language. However, the proportion of people speaking an Aboriginal language has been steadily declining, leading to concerns that these languages will be lost (Statistics Canada, 2011).

In response to these concerns, immersion programs are starting to emerge in Aboriginal communities across Canada. For example, a kindergarten to grade 6 Cree immersion program exists on the Onion Lake First Nation reserve in Alberta/Saskatchewan, and a similar Mi'kmaq immersion program exits in the Eskasoni First Nation reserve in Nova Scotia. Students enrolled in these immersion programs are following provincial educational curricula, but are being taught in their native language. Little research currently exists on the outcomes of Aboriginal language immersion programs, but what little does exist is generally positive. One recent study found that children enrolled in a Mi'kmaq immersion program had stronger Mi'kmaq language skills than children enrolled in Mi'kmaq as a second language program, and children in both programs had similar levels of English proficiency (Usborne, Peck, Smith, & Taylor, 2011).

Similarly, positive academic outcomes, such as higher graduation rates, have been associated with in-school learning of Aboriginal languages (Guevremont & Kohen, 2012). Academic achievement is not the only benefit associated with Aboriginal language immersion programs, as higher self-esteem for children enrolled in these programs has also been reported (Wright & Taylor, 1995). Although more research is needed to evaluate and refine Aboriginal language immersion programs, thus far the associated benefits are similar to those achieved by students enrolled in any type of immersion program

---

Everyday speech changes during adolescence, and "part of being a successful teenager is being able to talk like one" (Berko Gleason, 2005, p. 9). Young adolescents often speak a **dialect** with their peers that is characterized by jargon and slang (Cave, 2002). A dialect is a variety of language that is distinguished by its vocabulary, grammar, or pronunciation. For example, when meeting a friend, instead of saying hello, a young adolescent might say, "Hey, dude, 'sup?" Nicknames that are satirical and derisive ("Stilt," "Refrigerator," "Spaz") also characterize the dialect of young adolescents. Such labels might be used to show that one belongs to the group and to reduce the seriousness of a situation (Cave, 2002).

**dialect** A variety of language that is distinguished by its vocabulary, grammar, or pronunciation.

## Review Connect Reflect

 Describe how language develops.

### Review

- What are some key milestones of language development during infancy?
- How do language skills change during early childhood?
- How does language develop in middle and late childhood?
- How does language develop in adolescence?

### Connect

- Which of the teaching strategies inspired by Vygotsky's theory (discussed in Chapter 6) would you say is related to the whole-language approach to reading instruction discussed in this section?

### Reflect Your Own Personal Journey of Life

- How many languages can you speak and read? If and when you have children, do you want them to learn more than one language while they are young? Explain.

## Biological and Environmental Influences (L03) Discuss the biological and environmental contributions to language development.

| Biological Influences | Environmental Influences | An Interactionist View of Language |

We have described how language develops, but we have not explained what makes this amazing development possible. Everyone who uses language in some way "knows" its rules and has the ability to create an infinite number of words and sentences. Where does this knowledge come from? Is it the product of biology? Or is language learned and influenced by experiences?

## BIOLOGICAL INFLUENCES

Some language scholars view the remarkable similarities in how children acquire language all over the world, despite the vast variation in language input they receive, as strong evidence that language has a biological basis. What role did evolution play in the biological foundations of language?

In the wild, chimps communicate through calls, gestures, and expressions, which evolutionary psychologists believe might be the roots of true language.

### Evolution and the Brain's Role in Language

The ability to speak and understand language requires a certain vocal apparatus and a nervous system with certain capabilities. The nervous system and vocal apparatus of humanity's predecessors changed over hundreds of thousands or millions of years. With advances in the nervous system and vocal structures, Homo sapiens went beyond the grunting and shrieking of other animals to develop speech. Although estimates vary, many experts believe that humans acquired language about 100,000 years ago, which in evolutionary time represents a very recent acquisition. It gave humans an enormous edge over other animals and increased the chances of human survival (Pinker, 1994).

There is evidence that particular regions of the brain are predisposed to be used for language (Lee & others, 2012 Shafer & Garrido-Nag, 2010;). Two regions involved in language were first discovered in studies of individuals with brain damage: **Broca's area**, an area in the left frontal lobe of the brain involved in speech production and grammatical processing, and **Wernicke's area**, a region of the brain's left hemisphere involved in language comprehension (see Figure 9.8). Damage to either of these areas produces types of **aphasia**, which is a loss or impairment of language processing. Individuals with damage to Broca's area have difficulty producing words correctly; individuals with damage to Wernicke's area have poor comprehension and often produce fluent but incomprehensible speech.

### Chomsky's Language Acquisition Device (LAD)

Linguist Noam Chomsky (1957) proposed that humans are biologically prewired to learn language at a certain time and in a certain way. He said that children are born into the world with a **language acquisition device** (LAD), a biological endowment that enables the child to detect certain features and rules of language, including phonology, syntax, and semantics. Children are prepared by nature with the ability to detect the sounds of language, for example, and follow rules such as how to form plurals and ask questions.

Chomsky's LAD is a theoretical construct, not a physical part of the brain. Is there evidence for the existence of an LAD? Supporters of the LAD concept cite the uniformity of language milestones across languages and cultures, evidence that children create language even in the absence of well-formed input, and biological substrates of language. But as we will see, critics argue that even if infants have something like a LAD, it cannot explain the whole story of language acquisition.

## ENVIRONMENTAL INFLUENCES

Decades ago, behaviourists opposed Chomsky's hypothesis and argued that language represents nothing more than chains of responses acquired through reinforcement (Skinner, 1957). A baby happens to babble "ma-ma"; Mama rewards the baby with hugs and smiles; the baby says "mama" more and more. Bit by bit, said the behaviourists, the baby's language is built up. According to behaviourists, language is a complex, learned skill, much like playing the piano or dancing.

The behavioural view of language learning has several problems. First, it does not explain how people create novel sentences—sentences that people have never heard or spoken before. Second, children learn the syntax of their native language even if they are not reinforced for doing so. Social psychologist Roger Brown (1973) spent long hours observing parents and their young children. He found that parents did not directly or explicitly reward or correct the syntax of most children's utterances. That is, parents did not say "good," "correct," "right," "wrong," and so on. Also, parents did not offer direct corrections such as "You should say two shoes, not two shoe." However, as we will see shortly, many parents do expand on their young children's grammatically incorrect utterances and recast many of those that have grammatical errors (Clark, 2009).

The behavioural view is no longer considered a viable explanation of how children acquire language. But a great deal of research describes ways in which children's environmental experiences influence their language skills (Berko Gleason & Ratner, 2009). Many language experts argue that a child's experiences, the particular language to be learned, and the context in which learning takes place can strongly influence language acquisition (Goldfield & Snow, 2009).

Language is not learned in a social vacuum. Most children are bathed in language from a very early age (Sachs, 2009). The Wild Boy of Aveyron, who never learned to communicate effectively, had lived in social isolation for years. The support and involvement of caregivers and teachers greatly facilitate a child's language learning (Giorgis & Glazer, 2013; Hirsh-Pasek & Golinkoff, 2013; Tamis-LeMonda & Song, 2013). For example, one study found that when mothers immediately smiled and touched their 8-month-old infants after they babbled, the infants subsequently made more complex speechlike sounds than when mothers responded to their infants in a random manner (Goldstein, King, & West, 2003) (see Figure 9.9).

Michael Tomasello (2008, 2009, 2011; Tomasello & Hamann, 2012; Tomasello & Vaish, 2013) stresses that young children are intensely interested in their social world and that early in their development they can understand the intentions of other people. His interaction view of language emphasizes that children learn language in specific contexts. For example, when a toddler and a father are jointly focused on a book, the father might say, "See the birdie." In this case, even a toddler understands that the father intends to name something and knows to look in the direction of the pointing. Through this kind of joint attention, early in their development children are able to use their social skills to acquire language (Meltzoff, 2009; Tomasello, 2009).

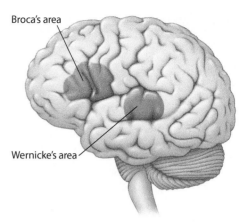

FIGURE **9.8**

**BROCA'S AREA AND WERNICKE'S AREA.** Broca's area is located in the frontal lobe of the brain's left hemisphere, and it is involved in the control of speech. Individuals with damage to Broca's area have problems saying words correctly. Also shown is Wernicke's area, a portion of the left hemisphere's temporal lobe that is involved in understanding language. Individuals with damage to this area cannot comprehend words; that is, they hear the words but don't know what they mean.

MIT linguist Noam Chomsky. *What is Chomsky's view of language?*

## FIGURE **9.9**

**SOCIAL INTERACTION AND BABBLING.**
One study focused on two groups of mothers and their 8-month-old infants (Goldstein, King, & West, 2003). One group of mothers was instructed to smile and touch their infants immediately after the babies cooed and babbled; the other group was also told to smile and touch their infants but in a random manner, unconnected to sounds the infants made. The infants whose mothers immediately responded in positive ways to their babbling subsequently made more complex, speechlike sounds, such as "da" and "gu." The research setting for this study, which underscores how important caregivers are in the early development of language, is shown here.

**child-directed speech** Language spoken in a higher pitch than normal, with simple words and sentences.

One intriguing component of the young child's linguistic environment is **child-directed speech**, language spoken in a higher pitch than normal with simple words and sentences (Clark, 2009). It is hard to use child-directed speech when not in the presence of a baby. As soon as you start talking to a baby, though, you shift into child-directed speech. Much of this is automatic and something most parents are not aware they are doing. As mentioned previously in this chapter, even 4-year-olds speak in simpler ways to 2-year-olds than to their 4-year-old friends. Child-directed speech has the important function of capturing the infant's attention and maintaining communication (Jaswal & Fernald, 2007).

Adults often use strategies other than child-directed speech to enhance the child's acquisition of language, including recasting, expanding, and labelling:

- **Recasting** is rephrasing something the child has said, perhaps turning it into a question or restating the child's immature utterance in the form of a fully grammatical sentence. For example, if the child says, "The dog was barking," the adult can respond by asking, "Was the dog barking?" Effective recasting lets the child indicate an interest and then elaborates on that interest.

- **Expanding** is restating, in a linguistically sophisticated form, what a child has said. For example, a child says, "Doggie eat," and the parent replies, "Yes, the doggie is eating."

- **Labelling** is identifying the names of objects. Young children are forever being asked to name objects. Roger Brown (1958) called this "the original word game" and claimed that much of a child's early vocabulary is motivated by this adult pressure to identify the words associated with objects.

Parents use these strategies naturally and in meaningful conversations. Parents do not (and should not) use any deliberate method to teach their children to talk, even for children who are slow in learning language. Children usually benefit when parents guide their children's discovery of language rather than overloading them with language; "following in order to lead" helps a child learn language. If children are not ready to take in some information, they are likely to tell you (perhaps by turning away). Thus, giving the child more information is not always better.

Infants, toddlers, and young children benefit when adults read books to and with them (shared reading) (Hirsh-Pasek & Golinkoff, 2013). A recent analysis found that the earlier children were read to and the more often they were read to, the better were their literacy and language skills (Dunst, Simkus, & Hamby, 2012). In this analysis, the average age of children when adults began reading to them was 22 months of age. Storybook reading especially benefits children when parents extend the meaning of the text by discussing the text with children and encouraging them to ask and answer questions (Barbarin & Miller, 2009; Whitehurst & Lonigan, 1998).

Our discussion of environmental influences on language development has mainly focused on parents. However, children interact with many other people who can influence their language development, including teachers and peers. A recent study of more than 1,800 4-year-olds focused on ways in which peers might influence children's language development (Mashburn & others, 2009). In this study, peers' expressive language abilities were positively linked with young children's receptive and expressive language development.

*How might peers' language skills influence a child's language development?*

# AN INTERACTIONIST VIEW OF LANGUAGE

If language acquisition depended only on biology, then Genie and the Wild Boy of Aveyron (discussed earlier in the chapter) should have talked without difficulty. A child's experiences influence language acquisition. But we have seen that language does have strong biological foundations (Shafer & Garrido-Nag, 2010). No matter how much you converse with a dog, it won't learn to talk. In contrast, children are biologically prepared to learn language. Children all over the world acquire language milestones at about the same time and in about the same order. However, there are cultural variations in the type of support given to children's language development. For example, caregivers in the Kaluli culture prompt young children to use a loud voice and particular morphemes that direct the speech act performed (calling out) and to refer to names, kinship relations, and places where there has been a shared past experience that indicates a closeness to the person being addressed (Ochs & Schieffelin, 2008; Schieffelin, 2005).

What is shared reading and how might it benefit infants and toddlers?

An interactionist view emphasizes that both biology and experience contribute to language development (Bohannon & Bonvillian, 2009; Mueller & Hoff, 2010; Wagner & Hoff, 2013). This interaction of biology and experience can be seen in the variations in the acquisition of language. Children vary in their ability to acquire language, and this variation cannot be readily explained by differences in environmental input alone. For children who are slow in developing language skills, however, opportunities to talk and be talked with are important. Children whose parents provide them with a rich verbal environment show many positive benefits. Parents who pay attention to what their children are trying to say, who expand their children's utterances, who read to them, and who label things in the environment are providing valuable, if unintentional, benefits (Berko Gleason, 2009).

Today, most language acquisition researchers maintain that children from a wide variety of cultural contexts acquire their native language without explicit teaching. In some cases, they do so even without encouragement. However, caregivers greatly facilitate a child's language learning (Berko Gleason, 2009; Goldfield & Snow, 2009).

**recasting** Rephrasing a statement that a child has said, perhaps turning it into a question, or restating a child's immature utterance in the form of a fully grammatical utterance.

**expanding** Restating, in a linguistically sophisticated form, what a child has said.

**labelling** Identifying the names of objects.

The linguistics problems children have to solve are always embedded in personal and interpersonal contexts.

—LOIS BLOOM
*Contemporary Psychologist, Columbia University*

---

## Review *Connect* Reflect

 Discuss the biological and environmental contributions to language development.

### Review

- What are the biological foundations of language?
- What are the behavioural and environmental aspects of language?

- How does an interactionist view describe language?

### *Connect*

- In this section, you learned about two areas in the left hemisphere of the brain that are involved in speech production and recognition. Related to this, what did you learn in Chapter 2 about hemisphere specialization in infants?

### Reflect *Your Own Personal Journey of Life*

- If and when you become a parent, how should you respond to your child's grammatical mistakes when conversing with the child? Will you allow the mistakes to continue and assume that your young child will grow out of them, or will you closely monitor your young child's grammar and correct mistakes whenever you hear them? Explain.

As a teenager, Wendy Verougstraete felt that she was on the road to becoming a professional author. "You are looking at a professional author," she said. "My books will be filled with drama, action, and excitement. And everyone will want to read them. I am going to write books, page after page, stack after stack."

Overhearing her remarks, you might have been impressed not only by Wendy's optimism and determination, but also by her expressive verbal skills. In fact, at a young age Wendy showed a flair for writing and telling stories. Wendy has a rich vocabulary, creates lyrics for love songs, and enjoys telling stories. You probably would not be able to immediately guess that she has an IQ of only 49 and cannot tie her shoes, cross the street by herself, read or print words beyond the first-grade level, or do even simple arithmetic.

Wendy Verougstraete has Williams syndrome, a genetic birth disorder that was first described in 1961 and affects about 1 in 20,000 births (Mervis & Becerra, 2007; Morris, 2010). Williams syndrome stems from a genetic deletion on chromosome 7 (Haas & others, 2009; Palomares, Landau, & Egeth, 2009). The most noticeable features of the syndrome include a unique combination of expressive verbal skills and extremely low IQ, and limited visuospatial skills and motor control (O'Hearn & Luna, 2009). Children with Williams syndrome are natural-born storytellers who provide highly expressive narratives (Martens & others, 2009; Mervis & John, 2010; Palomoares, Landau, & Egeth, 2009). Figure 9.10 shows the great disparity in the verbal and motor skills of one person with Williams syndrome.

Individuals with Williams syndrome often have good musical skills and interpersonal skills (Lincoln & others, 2007). One study indicated that children with Williams syndrome were more sociable than normally developing children, reflecting a genetic predisposition for sociability in children with Williams syndrome (Zitzer-Comfort & others, 2007). The syndrome also includes a number of physical characteristics as well, such as heart defects and a pixielike facial appearance. Despite having excellent verbal skills and competent interpersonal skills, most individuals with Williams syndrome cannot live independent lives (American Academy of Pediatrics, 2001). For example, Wendy Verougstraete lives in a group home for adults with intellectual disabilities.

The verbal abilities of individuals with Williams syndrome are very distinct from those shown by individuals with Down syndrome, a type of intellectual disability that we discussed in Chapters 2 and 8 (Brock, 2007). On vocabulary tests, children with Williams syndrome show a liking for unusual words. When asked to name as many animals as they can think of in one minute, Williams children come up with creatures like ibex, chihuahua, saber-toothed tiger, weasel, crane, and newt. Children with Down syndrome give simple examples like dog, cat, and mouse. When children with Williams syndrome tell stories, their voices come alive with drama and emotion, punctuating the dialogue with audience attention-grabbers like "gadzooks" or "lo and behold!" By contrast, children with Down syndrome tell very simple stories with little emotion.

Aside from being an interesting genetic disorder, Williams syndrome offers insights into the normal development of thinking and language (Carney, Brown, & Henry, 2013). In our society, verbal ability is generally associated with high intelligence. But Williams syndrome raises the possibility that thinking and language might not be so closely related. Williams disorder is due

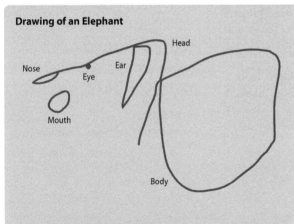

**Drawing of an Elephant**

**Verbal Description of an Elephant**

And what an elephant is, it is one of the animals. And what the elephant does, it lives in the jungle. It can also live in the zoo. And what it has, it has long gray ears, fan ears, ears that can blow in the wind. It has a long trunk that can pick up grass, or pick up hay.... If they're in a bad mood it can be terrible.... If the elephant gets mad it could stomp; it could charge. Sometimes elephants can charge. They have big long tusks. They can damage a car.... It could be dangerous. When they're in a pinch, when they're in a bad mood it can be terrible. You don't want an elephant as a pet. You want a cat or a dog or a bird....

FIGURE **9.10**
**DISPARITY IN THE VERBAL AND MOTOR SKILLS OF AN INDIVIDUAL WITH WILLIAMS SYNDROME.**

to a defective gene that seems to protect expressive verbal ability but not reading and many other cognitive skills (Haas & others, 2009). Thus, cases like Wendy Verougstraete's cast some doubt on the general categorization of intelligence as verbal ability and prompt the question, "What is the relationship between thinking and language?"

Two basic and separate issues characterize connections between language and cognition. The first is whether cognition is necessary for language. Although some researchers have noted that certain aspects of language development typically follow mastery of selected cognitive skills in both normally developing children and children with an intellectual disability, it is not clear that language development depends on any specific aspect of cognitive abilities (Lenneberg, 1967). Some experts argue that it is more likely that language and cognitive development occur in parallel but dissociated fashions (Cromer, 1987). Thus, according to research and experts' judgments, cognition is not necessary for language development.

The second issue is whether language is necessary for (or important to) cognition. This issue is addressed by studies of deaf children. On a variety of thinking and problem-solving skills, deaf children perform at the same level as children of the same age who have no hearing problems. Some of the deaf children in these studies do not even have command of written or sign language (Furth, 1973). Thus, based on studies of deaf children, language is not necessary for cognitive development.

There is, however, evidence of links between the cognitive and language worlds of children (Oates & Grayson, 2004). Piaget's concept of object permanence has been the focus of some research that connects cognitive and language development. Piaget emphasized that children come to learn about the world first and then they learn to label what they know. Infants may need a concept of object permanence before they start to use words for disappearance, such as "all gone" (Gopnik & Meltzoff, 1997).

One study examined whether four aspects of information processing skills—memory, representational competence, processing speed, and attention—were related to infants' and young children's language development (Rose, Feldman, & Jankowski, 2009). In this study, memory and representational competence assessed at 12 months of age predicted language at 36 months of age independently of birth status, 12-month language, and 12-month scores on the Bayley Developmental Scales. The dimensions of memory that best predicted language development were recognition and recall but not short-term memory; the dimensions of representation competence that best predicted language development were cross-modal transfer (matching touch to vision) and object permanence. Other research has found that joint attention in infancy is linked to vocabulary development in childhood (Colombo & others, 2009a, b).

---

## Review Connect Reflect

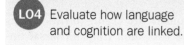 Evaluate how language and cognition are linked.

### Review

- What characterizes children with Williams syndrome? To what extent are language and cognition linked? Are they part of a single, automated cognitive system?

### Connect

- In Chapter 8, you learned how Down syndrome is classified as intellectual disability. In this section of Chapter 9, you learned that Williams syndrome is not classified as intellectual disability. Why not?

### Reflect Your Own Personal Journey of Life

- Did you always think in words when you were growing up? Explain.

1. The chapter opening describes the case of Helen Keller. Given that Helen was not able to hear any language, how did experience play a role in the development of her language abilities?

2. What does the case of Helen Keller tell us about the link between language and cognition?

3. How do infants' babbling and language perception abilities support the role of nature and nurture in language development?

4. Children must learn five rule systems (phonology, morphology, syntax, semantics, pragmatics) to master language usage. How might development in one of these rule systems contribute to development in another rule system?

reach your **learning goals**

# Language Development

## What Is Language?

 Define language and describe its rule systems.

Defining Language

- Language is a form of communication, whether spoken, written, or signed, that is based on a system of symbols. Language consists of all the words used by a community and the rules for varying and combining them. Infinite generativity is the ability to produce an endless number of meaningful sentences using a finite set of words and rules.

Language's Rule Systems

- The five main five rule systems of language are phonology, morphology, syntax, semantics, and pragmatics. Phonology is the sound system of a language, including the sounds used and the particular sound sequences that may occur in the language. Morphology refers to how words are formed. Syntax is the way words are combined to form acceptable phrases and sentences. Semantics involves the meaning of words and sentences. Pragmatics is the appropriate use of language in different contexts.

## How Language Develops

 Describe how language develops.

Infancy

- Among the milestones in infant language development are crying (birth), cooing (1 to 2 months), babbling (6 months), making the transition from universal linguist to language-specific listener (6 to 12 months), using gestures (8 to 12 months), recognition of their name (as early as 5 months), first word spoken (10 to 15 months), vocabulary spurt (18 months), rapid expansion of understanding words (18 to 24 months), and two-word utterances (18 to 24 months).

Early Childhood

- Advances in phonology, morphology, syntax, semantics, and pragmatics continue in early childhood. The transition to complex sentences begins at 2 or 3 years and continues through the elementary school years. Currently, there is considerable interest in the early literacy of children.

| Middle and Late Childhood | • In middle and late childhood, children become more analytical and logical in their approach to words and grammar. Chall's model proposes five phases in reading, ranging from birth/first grade to high school. Current debate involving how to teach children to read focuses on the phonics approach versus the whole-language approach. Researchers have found strong evidence that the phonics approach should be used in teaching children to read, especially in kindergarten and the first grade, and with struggling readers, but that children also benefit from the whole-language approach. Children's writing emerges out of scribbling. Advances in children's language and cognitive development provide the underpinnings for improved writing. Strategy instruction is especially effective in improving children's writing. Bilingual education aims to teach academic subjects to immigrant children in their native languages, while gradually adding English instruction. Researchers have found that bilingualism does not interfere with performance in either language. Success in learning a second language is greater in childhood than in adolescence. |
| --- | --- |
| Adolescence | • In adolescence, language changes include more effective use of words; improvements in the ability to understand metaphor, satire, and adult literary works; and improvements in writing. Young adolescents often speak a dialect with their peers, using jargon and slang. |

## Biological and Environmental Influences  Discuss the biological and environmental contributions to language development.

| Biological Influences | • In evolution, language clearly gave humans an enormous edge over other animals and increased their chance of survival. A substantial portion of language processing occurs in the brain's left hemisphere, with Broca's area and Wernicke's area being important left-hemisphere locations. Chomsky argues that children are born with the ability to detect basic features and rules of language. In other words, they are biologically equipped to learn language with a prewired language acquisition device (LAD). |
| --- | --- |
| Environmental Influences | • The behavioural view of language acquisition—that children acquire language as a result of reinforcement—is no longer supported. Adults help children acquire language through child-directed speech, recasting, expanding, and labelling. Environmental influences are demonstrated by differences in the language development of children as a consequence of being exposed to different language environments in the home. Parents should talk extensively with an infant, especially about what the baby is attending to. |
| An Interactionist View of Language | • An interactionist view emphasizes the contributions of both biology and experience in language. |

## Language and Cognition  Evaluate how language and cognition are linked.

• Children with Williams syndrome have a unique combination of expressive verbal skills and an extremely low IQ and limited visuospatial skills and motor control. Study of these children offers insights into the normal development of thinking and language. Two basic and separate issues are these: (1) Is cognition necessary for language? (2) Is language necessary for cognition? At an extreme, the answer to these questions is likely no, but there is evidence of linkages between language and cognition. A recent study revealed that infants' information-processing skills were linked to the growth of language development in early childhood.

For more information on the resources available from McGraw-Hill Ryerson, go to www.mheducation.ca/he/solutions

# section four

*I am what I hope and give.*

—ERIK ERIKSON
*European-Born American Psychotherapist, 20th Century*

# Socioemotional Development

As children develop, they form bonds with loved ones. They split the universe into two halves: "me" and "not me." They juggle the need to curb their own will with becoming what they can will freely. They also want to fly but discover that first they have to learn to stand and walk and climb and dance. As they become adolescents, they try on one face after another, looking for a face of their own. In Section 4, you will read four chapters: "Emotional Development" (Chapter 10), "The Self and Identity" (Chapter 11), "Gender" (Chapter 12), and "Moral Development" (Chapter 13).

# Emotional Development | chapter 10

Many fathers are spending more time with their infants today than in the past.

On weekdays, 17-month-old Matthieu's father, a writer, cares for him during the day while his mother works full-time as a landscape architect. Matthieu's father is doing a great job of caring for him. Matthieu's father keeps Matthieu nearby while he is writing and spends lots of time talking to him and playing with him. From their interactions, it is clear that they genuinely enjoy each other's company.

Last month, Matthieu began spending one day a week at a child-care centre. His parents carefully selected the centre after observing a number of centres and interviewing teachers and centre directors. His parents placed him in the centre one day a week because they wanted Matthieu to get some experience with peers and to give his father some time out from his caregiving.

Matthieu's father looks to the future and imagines the Little League games Matthieu will play in and the many other activities he can enjoy with Matthieu. Remembering how little time his own father spent with him, he is dedicated to making sure that Matthieu has an involved, nurturing experience with his father.

When Matthieu's mother comes home in the evening, she spends considerable time with him. Matthieu is an easygoing toddler with a sense of curiosity about the world and people around him. He has a secure attachment with both his mother and his father.

# preview

For many years, emotion was neglected in the study of children's development. Today, emotion is increasingly important in conceptualizations of development. Even infants show different emotional styles, display varying temperaments, and begin to form emotional bonds with their caregivers. In this chapter, we will study the roles of temperament and attachment in development. But first we will examine emotion itself, exploring the functions of emotions in children's lives and the development of emotion from infancy through middle and late childhood.

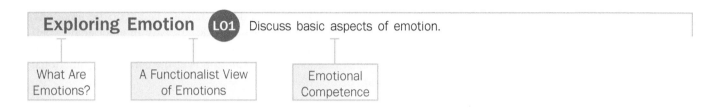

**Exploring Emotion** **LO1** Discuss basic aspects of emotion.

| What Are Emotions? | A Functionalist View of Emotions | Emotional Competence |

Imagine your life without emotion. Emotion is the colour and music of life, as well as the tie that binds people together. How do psychologists define and classify emotions, and why are they important to development?

## WHAT ARE EMOTIONS?

For our purposes, we will define **emotion** as the feeling, or affect, that occurs when people are in a state or an interaction that is important to them, especially one that influences their well-being. In many instances emotions involve people's communication with the world. Although emotion consists of more than communication, in infancy the communication aspect is at the forefront of emotion (Witherington & others, 2010).

Psychologists classify the broad range of emotions in many ways, but almost all classifications designate an emotion as either positive or negative (Christenfeld & Mandler, 2013; Izard, 2009). Positive emotions include enthusiasm, joy, and love. Negative emotions include anxiety, anger, guilt, and sadness.

Emotions are influenced by biological foundations and experience (Calkins, 2012; Kagan, 2013). In evolutionary theory, evolution endowed human beings with a biological foundation for emotion that involves the development of the nervous system. Emotions are linked with early-developing regions of the human nervous system, including structures of the limbic system and the brain stem (de Haan & Matheson, 2009; Easterbrooks & others, 2013). The capacity of infants to show distress, excitement, and rage reflects the early emergence of these biologically rooted emotional brain systems. Significant advances in emotional responding occur during infancy and childhood as a result of changes in neurobiological systems (including the frontal regions of the cerebral cortex) that can exert control over the more primitive limbic system (Cuevas & others, 2012). As children develop, maturation of the cerebral cortex allows a decrease in unpredictable mood swings and an increase in the self-regulation of emotion. However, such mood swings increase during adolescence, likely as a result of the earlier development of the amygdala (which is extensively involved in emotional processing) and the protracted development of the frontal cortex (which is heavily involved in reasoning and self-regulation) (Giedd & others, 2012; Steinberg, 2013).

Social relationships, including those with caregivers, provide the setting for the development of a rich variety of emotions (Duncombe & others, 2012; Thompson, 2013c, d). Caregivers play a role in the infant's neurobiological regulation of emotions (Thompson, 2013b, c, d; Ursache & others, 2013). For example, when toddlers hear their parents quarrelling, they often react with distress and

**emotion** Feeling, or affect, that occurs when people are engaged in an interaction that is important to them, especially one that influences their well-being.

Blossoms are scattered by
the wind
And the wind cares nothing, but
The Blossoms of the heart,
No wind can touch.

—YOUSHIDA KENKO
*Buddhist Monk, 14th Century*

**developmental connection**

**Brain Development.** The prefrontal cortex is not as well developed in adolescence as it is in adults. For adolescents, it is as if their brain doesn't have the brakes to slow down their emotions. Chapter 4, LO 2

inhibit their play. By soothing the infant when the infant cries and shows distress, caregivers help infants to modulate their emotion and reduce the level of stress hormones (Gunnar & Quevado, 2007).

Cultural variations reveal the role of experience in emotion (Tamis-Lemonda & Song, 2013). For example, display rules—when, where, and how emotions should be expressed—are not culturally universal. Researchers have found that East Asian infants display less frequent and less intense positive and negative emotions than Caucasian infants (Camras & others, 1998). Throughout childhood, East Asian parents encourage their children to show emotional reserve rather than emotional expressivity (Cole & Tan, 2007). Further, Japanese parents try to prevent their children from experiencing negative emotions, whereas Caucasian mothers are more likely to respond after their children become distressed and then help them cope (Cole & Tan, 2007).

In sum, biological evolution has endowed human beings to be emotional, but relationships with others and culture provide diversity in emotional experiences (Tamis-LeMonda & Song, 2013; Thompson, 2013c, d). As we see next, this emphasis on the role of relationships in emotion is at the core of the functionalist view of emotion.

## A FUNCTIONALIST VIEW OF EMOTIONS

Many developmentalists today view emotions as the result of individuals' attempts to adapt to specific contextual demands (Saarni & others, 2006). Thus, a child's emotional responses cannot be separated from the situations in which they are evoked. In many instances, emotions are elicited in interpersonal contexts. For example, emotional expressions serve the important functions of signalling to others how one feels, regulating one's own behaviour, and playing pivotal roles in social interaction.

One implication of the functionalist view is that emotions are *relational, rather than strictly internal, intra-psychic phenomena* (Thompson, 2013c, d). Consider just some of the roles of emotion in parent-child relationships. The beginnings of an emotional bond between parents and an infant are based on affectively toned interactions, as when an infant cries and the caregiver sensitively responds. By the end of the first year, a parent's facial expression—either smiling or fearful—influences whether an infant will explore an unfamiliar environment. Well-functioning families often include humour in their interactions, sometimes making each other laugh and creating a light mood state to defuse conflict. When a positive mood has been induced in a child, the child is more likely to comply with a parent's directions.

A second implication of the functionalist view is that emotions are *linked with an individual's goals in a variety of ways* (Saarni & others, 2006). Regardless of what the goal is, an individual who overcomes an obstacle to attain a goal experiences happiness. By contrast, a person who must abandon a goal as unattainable experiences sadness. And a person who faces difficult obstacles in pursuing a goal often experiences frustration, which can develop into anger when the obstacles are perceived as unfair or intentionally put in the way to hinder the individual's goal attainment.

Moreover, the specific nature of the goal can affect the experience of a given emotion. For example, the avoidance of threat is linked with fear, the desire to atone is related to guilt, and the wish to avoid the scrutiny of others is associated with shame.

## EMOTIONAL COMPETENCE

In Chapter 8, we briefly described the concept of emotional intelligence. Here we will examine a closely related concept, emotional competence, which focuses on the adaptive nature of emotional experience. Carolyn Saarni (1999; Saarni & others, 2006) argues that becoming emotionally competent involves developing a number of skills in social contexts. Figure 10.1 describes these skills and provides examples of each one. As children acquire these emotional competence skills in a variety of

How do Japanese mothers handle their infants' and children's emotional development differently from Caucasian mothers?

### developmental **connection**

**Intelligence.** Emotional intelligence involves perceiving and expressing emotions accurately, understanding emotion and emotional knowledge, using feelings to facilitate thought, and managing emotions effectively. Chapter 8, LO 1

contexts, they are more likely to effectively manage their emotions, become resilient in the face of stressful circumstances, and develop more positive relationships.

What shapes a child's emotional competence? According to Dale Stack and his colleagues at Concordia University, parenting behaviours affect children's emotional competence over time and even across generations (Stack & others, 2010). In addition, research from the National Longitudinal Study for Children and Youth (NLSCY) showed that parent-related adversity such as parental depression, marital dissatisfaction, and alcohol abuse in the family, led to increased emotional problems among Canadian children over time (MacMillan & Violato, 2008).

It is important to note that emotional competence skills can be learned outside the home. Recent research shows that school-based emotional skills programs have positive effects on children's emotional competence. For example, MindUP is one such program that has met with success. In MindUP, children are taught mindfulness techniques including quieting the mind by focusing on the chime of a bell or their own breath, using mindful attention to their sensations, thoughts, and feelings, managing negative thoughts and emotions, and acknowledging self and others. One study found that Canadian children who experienced the MindUP program showed significant increases in optimism and self-concept as well as socially competent behaviours in the classroom (Schonert-Reichl & Lawlor, 2010).

| Skill | Example |
|---|---|
| Awareness of one's emotional states | Being able to differentiate whether sad or anxious |
| Detecting others' emotions | Understanding when another person is sad rather than afraid |
| Using the vocabulary of emotion terms in socially and culturally appropriate ways | Appropriately describing a social situation in one's culture when a person is feeling distress |
| Empathic and sympathetic sensitivity to others' emotional experiences | Being sensitive to others when they are feeling distressed |
| Recognizing that inner emotional states do not have to correspond to outer expressions | Recognizing that one can feel very angry yet manage one's emotional expression so that it appears more neutral |
| Adaptively coping with negative emotions by using self-regulatory strategies that reduce the intensity or duration of such emotional states | Reducing anger by walking away from an aversive situation and engaging in an activity that takes one's mind off of the aversive situation |
| Awareness that the expression of emotions plays a major role in a relationship | Knowing that expressing anger toward a friend on a regular basis is likely to harm the friendship |
| Viewing oneself overall as feeling the way one wants to feel | Feeling like one can cope effectively with the stress in one's life and feeling that one is doing this successfully |

FIGURE **10.1**

**EMOTIONAL COMPETENCE SKILLS.**

## Review *Connect* Reflect

 **LO1** Discuss basic aspects of emotion.

### Review
- How is emotion defined?
- What characterizes functionalism in emotion?
- What constitutes emotional competence, according to Saarni?
- What are some ways emotional competence is shaped at home and school?

### *Connect*
- How are the competence skills listed in Figure 10.1 related to the four aspects of emotional intelligence described in Chapter 8?

### **Reflect** *Your Own Personal Journey of Life*
- Think back to your childhood and adolescent years. How would you describe your emotional competence as a child and adolescent, based on the descriptions in Figure 10.1?

| Infancy | Early Childhood | Middle and Late Childhood |

Does an older child's emotional life differ from a younger child's? Does a young child's emotional life differ from an infant's? Does an infant even have an emotional life? In this section, we will sketch an overview of the changes in emotion from infancy through middle childhood, looking not only at changes in emotional experience but also at the development of emotional competence.

## INFANCY

What are some early developmental changes in emotions? What functions do infants' cries serve? When do infants begin to smile?

**Early Emotions**    A leading expert on infant emotional development, Michael Lewis (2008, 2010) distinguishes between primary emotions and self-conscious emotions. **Primary emotions** are emotions that are present in humans and other animals; these emotions appear in the first six months of the human infant's development. Primary emotions include surprise, interest, joy, anger, sadness, fear, and disgust (see Figure 10.2 for infants' facial expressions of some of these early emotions). In Lewis's classification, **self-conscious emotions** require self-awareness that involves consciousness and a sense of "me." Self-conscious emotions include jealousy, empathy, embarrassment, pride, shame, and guilt. Lewis argues that these self-conscious emotions occur for the first time at some point in the second half of the first year through the second year. Some experts on emotion call self-conscious emotions such as embarrassment, shame, guilt, and pride *other-conscious emotions* because they involve the emotional reactions of others when they are generated (Saarni & others, 2006). For example, approval from parents is linked to toddlers beginning to show pride when they successfully complete a task.

**primary emotions** Emotions that are present in humans and other animals, and emerge early in life; examples are joy, anger, sadness, fear, and disgust.

**self-conscious emotions** Emotions that require self-awareness, especially consciousness and a sense of "me"; examples include jealousy, empathy, and embarrassment.

Leading researchers such as Joseph Campos (2009) and Michael Lewis (2008) debate how early in the infant and toddler years the emotions that we have described first appear and their sequence. As an indication of the controversy regarding when certain emotions are first displayed by infants, consider jealousy. Some researchers argue that jealousy does not emerge until approximately 18 months of age (Lewis, 2008), whereas others emphasize that it is displayed much earlier (Draghi-Lorenz, Reddy, & Costall, 2001). Consider a research study in which 6-month-old infants observed their mothers giving attention either to a life-like baby doll (hugging or gently rocking it, for example) or to a book (Hart & Carrington, 2002). When mothers directed their attention to the doll, the infants were more likely to display negative emotions, such as anger and sadness, which may have indicated their jealousy (see Figure 10.3). However, their expressions of anger and sadness may have reflected frustration in not being able to have the novel doll to play with.

Debate about the onset of an emotion such as jealousy illustrates the complexity and difficulty of indexing early emotions. That said, some experts on infant socioemotional development, such as Jerome Kagan (2010), conclude that the structural immaturity of the infant brain make it unlikely that emotions requiring

## FIGURE **10.2**
**EXPRESSION OF DIFFERENT EMOTIONS IN INFANTS.**

thought—such as guilt, pride, despair, shame, empathy, and jealousy—can be experienced in the first year. Thus, both Kagan (2010) and Campos (2009) argue that so-called "self-conscious" emotions don't occur until after the first year, which increasingly reflects the view of most developmental psychologists. Thus, in regard to the photograph in Figure 10.3, it is unlikely that the 6-month old infant is experiencing jealousy.

**Emotional Expression and Social Relationships** Emotional expressions are involved in infants' first relationships. The ability of infants to communicate emotions permits coordinated interactions with their caregivers and the beginning of an emotional bond between them (Thompson, 2013a, d). Not only do parents change their own emotional expressions in response to their infants' emotional expressions, but infants also modify their emotional expressions in response to their parents' emotional expressions. In other words, these interactions are mutually regulated (Bridgett & others, 2009). Because of this coordination, the interactions are described as *reciprocal*, or *synchronous*, when all is going well. Sensitive, responsive parents help their infants grow emotionally, whether the infants respond in distressed or happy ways (Brownell & others, 2012).

Crying and smiling are two emotional expressions that infants display when interacting with parents. These are babies' first forms of emotional communication.

*Crying* Crying is the most important mechanism newborns have for communicating with their world. The first cry verifies that the baby's lungs have filled with air. Cries also may provide information about the health of the newborn's central nervous system. Newborns even tend to respond with cries and negative facial expressions when they hear other newborns cry (Dondi, Simion, & Caltran, 1999). However, a recent study revealed that newborns of depressed mothers showed less vocal distress when another infant cried, reflecting emotional and physiological dysregulation (Jones, 2012).

Babies have at least three types of cries:

- **Basic cry:** A rhythmic pattern that usually consists of a cry, followed by a briefer silence, then a shorter whistle that is somewhat higher in pitch than the main cry, then another brief rest before the next cry. Some infancy experts argue that hunger is one of the conditions that incite the basic cry.
- **Anger cry:** A variation of the basic cry in which more excess air is forced through the vocal cords.
- **Pain cry:** A sudden long, initial loud cry followed by breath holding; no preliminary moaning is present. The pain cry is caused by a high-intensity stimulus.

Most adults can determine whether an infant's cries signify anger or pain (Zeskind, Klein, & Marshall, 1992). Parents, however, are especially attuned to their children and can distinguish the cries of their own baby better than those of another baby.

FIGURE **10.3**

**IS THIS THE EARLY EXPRESSION OF JEALOUSY?** In the study by Hart and Carrington (2002), the researchers concluded that the 6-month old infants who observed their mothers giving attention to a baby doll may indicate the early appearance of jealousy because of the negative emotions—such as anger and sadness—they displayed. However, experts on emotional development, such as Joseph Campos (2009) and Jerome Kagan (2010) argue that emotions such as jealousy don't appear during the first year. *Why do they conclude that jealousy does not occur in the first year?*

*What are some different types of cries?*

**basic cry** A rhythmic pattern usually consisting of a cry, a briefer silence, a shorter inspiratory whistle that is higher pitched than the main cry, and then a brief rest before the next cry.

**anger cry** A cry similar to the basic cry but with more excess air forced through the vocal cords.

**pain cry** A sudden appearance of loud crying without preliminary moaning, and a long initial cry followed by an extended period of breath holding.

## FIGURE 10.4

**A 6-MONTH-OLD'S STRONG SMILE.** This strong smile reflects the Duchenne marker (eye constriction) and mouth opening.

**reflexive smile** A smile that does not occur in response to external stimuli. It happens during the month after birth, usually during sleep.

**social smile** A smile in response to an external stimulus, which, early in development, typically is a face.

**stranger anxiety** An infant's fear of and wariness toward strangers; it tends to appear in the second half of the first year of life.

**separation protest** Occurs when infants experience a fear of being separated from a caregiver, which results in crying when the caregiver leaves.

*Smiling*   Smiling is critical as a means of developing a new social skill and is a key social signal (Campos, 2009). Two types of smiling can be distinguished in infants:

- **Reflexive smile:** A smile that does not occur in response to external stimuli and appears during the first month after birth, usually during sleep.
- **Social smile:** A smile that occurs in response to an external stimulus, typically a face in the case of the young infant. Social smiling occurs as early as 4 to 6 weeks of age in response to a caregiver's voice (Campos, 2005).

Daniel Messinger (2008) described the developmental course of infant smiling. From two to six months after birth, infants' social smiling increases considerably, both in self-initiated smiles and smiles in response to others' smiles. At 6 to 12 months of age, smiles that couple what is called the Duchenne marker (eye constriction) and mouth opening occur in the midst of highly enjoyable interactions and play with parents (see Figure 10.4). In the second year, smiling continues to occur in such positive circumstances with parents, and in many cases an increase in smiling occurs when interacting with peers. Also in the second year, toddlers become increasingly aware of the social meaning of smiles, especially in their relationship with parents.

Infants also engage in *anticipatory smiling,* in which they communicate pre-existing positive emotion by smiling at an object and then turning their smile toward an adult. One study revealed that anticipatory smiling at 9 months of age was linked to parents' rating of the child's social competence at 2½ years of age (Parlade & others, 2009).

*Fear*   One of a baby's earliest emotions is fear, which typically first appears at about 6 months of age and peaks at about 18 months. However, abused and neglected infants can show fear as early as 3 months (Witherington & others, 2010). Researchers have found that infant fear is linked to guilt, empathy, and low aggression at 6 to 7 years of age (Rothbart, 2011).

The most frequent expression of an infant's fear involves **stranger anxiety**, in which an infant shows a fear and wariness of strangers. Stranger anxiety usually emerges gradually. It first appears at about 6 months of age in the form of wary reactions. By age 9 months, the fear of strangers is often more intense, and it continues to escalate through the infant's first birthday (Scher & Harel, 2008).

Not all infants show distress when they encounter a stranger. Besides individual variations, whether an infant shows stranger anxiety also depends on the social context and the characteristics of the stranger (Kagan, 2008).

Infants show less stranger anxiety when they are in familiar settings. For example, in one study, 10-month-olds showed little stranger anxiety when they met a stranger in their own home but much greater fear when they encountered a stranger in a research laboratory (Sroufe, Waters, & Matas, 1974). Also, infants show less stranger anxiety when they are sitting on their mothers' laps than when they are placed in an infant seat several feet away from their mothers (Bohlin & Hagekull, 1993). Thus, it appears that when infants feel secure, they are less likely to show stranger anxiety.

Who the stranger is and how the stranger behaves also influence stranger anxiety in infants. Infants are less fearful of child strangers than adult strangers. They also are less fearful of friendly, outgoing, smiling strangers than of passive, unsmiling strangers (Bretherton, Stolberg, & Kreye, 1981).

In addition to stranger anxiety, infants experience fear of being separated from their caregivers (Scher & Harel, 2008). The result is **separation protest**—crying when the caregiver leaves. Separation protest tends to peak at about 15 months among North American infants (Kagan, 2008). In fact, one study found that separation protest peaked at about 13 to 15 months in four different cultures (Kagan, Kearsley, & Zelazo, 1978). As indicated in Figure 10.5, the percentage of infants who engaged in separation protest varied across cultures, but the infants reached a peak of protest at about the same age—just before the middle of the second year of life.

**Emotional Regulation and Coping**   During the first year of life, infants gradually develop an ability to inhibit, or minimize, the intensity and duration of emotional reactions (Calkins, 2012). From early in infancy, babies put their thumbs in their mouths to soothe themselves. But at first, infants mainly depend on caregivers to help them soothe their emotions, as when a caregiver rocks an infant to sleep, sings lullabies to the infant, gently strokes the infant, and so on.

The caregivers' actions influence the infant's neurobiological regulation of emotions (Thompson, 2013c, d). For example, a recent study found that emotionally reactive infants who also showed a high level of emotional regulation were more likely to have primary caregivers who engaged in positive parenting behaviour during a parent-child interaction task (Ursache & others, 2013). By soothing the infant, caregivers help infants to modulate their emotion and reduce the level of stress hormones (de Haan & Gunnar, 2009). Many developmentalists stress that it is a good strategy for a caregiver to soothe an infant before the infant gets into an intense, agitated, uncontrolled state (Thompson, 1994).

In the second year of life, when they become aroused, infants sometimes redirect their attention or distract themselves in order to reduce their arousal (Grolnick, Bridges, & Connell, 1996). By 2 years of age, toddlers can use language to define their feeling states and the context that is upsetting them (Kopp & Neufeld, 2002). A toddler might say, "Feel bad. Dog scare." This type of communication may help caregivers to assist the child in regulating emotion.

Contexts can influence emotional regulation (Easterbrooks & others, 2013). Infants are often affected by fatigue, hunger, time of day, which people are around them, and where they are. Infants must learn to adapt to different contexts that require emotional regulation. Further, new demands appear as the infant becomes older and parents modify their expectations. For example, a parent may take it in stride if a 6-month-old infant screams in a grocery store but may react very differently if a 2-year-old starts screaming.

To soothe or not to soothe—should a crying baby be given attention and soothed, or does this spoil the infant? Many years ago, the behaviourist John Watson (1928) argued that parents spend too much time responding to infant crying. As a consequence, he said, parents reward crying and increase its incidence. Some researchers have found that a caregiver's quick, soothing response to crying increased crying (Gewirtz, 1977). However, infancy experts Mary Ainsworth (1979) and John Bowlby (1989) stress that you can't respond too much to infant crying in the first year of life. They argue that a quick, comforting response to the infant's cries is an important ingredient in the development of a strong bond between the infant and caregiver. In one of Ainsworth's studies, infants whose mothers responded quickly when they cried at 3 months of age cried less later in the first year of life (Bell & Ainsworth, 1972).

Controversy still characterizes the question of whether or how parents should respond to an infant's cries. However, developmentalists increasingly argue that an infant cannot be spoiled in the first year of life, which suggests that parents should soothe a crying infant. This reaction should help infants develop a sense of trust and secure attachment to the caregiver.

## EARLY CHILDHOOD

The young child's growing awareness of self is linked to the ability to feel an expanding range of emotions. Young children, like adults, experience many emotions during the course of a day. At times, they also try to make sense of other

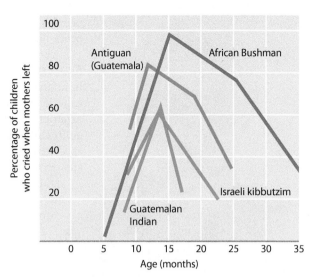

**FIGURE 10.5**

**SEPARATION PROTEST IN FOUR CULTURES.** Note that separation protest peaked at about the same time in all four cultures in this study (13 to 15 months of age) (Kagan, Kearsley, & Zelazo, 1978). However, a higher percentage (100 percent) of infants in an African Bushman culture engaged in separation protest compared to only about 60 percent of infants in Guatemalan Indian and Israeli kibbutzim cultures. *What might explain the fact that separation protest peaks at about the same time in these cultures?*

*Should a baby be given attention and soothed or does this spoil the infant? Should the infant's age, the type of cry, and the circumstances be considered?*

A child expressing the emotion of shame, which occurs when a child evaluates his or her actions as not living up to standards. A child experiencing shame wishes to hide or disappear. *Why is shame called a self-conscious emotion?*

people's emotional reactions and to control their own emotions. Parents and peers play important roles in children's emotional development.

**Expressing Emotions** Recall from our discussion of emotional development in infancy that there is controversy about how early in their development infants experience what Michael Lewis (2008, 2010) called *self-conscious emotions*. To experience self-conscious emotions such as pride, shame, embarrassment, and guilt, children must be able to refer to themselves and be aware of themselves as distinct from others (Lewis, 2008, 2010). Self-conscious emotions do not appear to develop until self-awareness appears at around 18 months of age.

During the early childhood years, emotions such as pride and guilt become more common. They are especially influenced by parents' responses to children's behaviour. For example, a young child may experience shame when a parent says, "You should feel bad about biting your sister."

**Understanding Emotions** According to Jeremy Carpendale at the University of Victoria, among the most important changes in emotional development in early childhood is an increased understanding of emotion (Carpendale & Lewis, 2011). During early childhood, young children increasingly understand that certain situations are likely to evoke particular emotions, that facial expressions indicate specific emotions, that emotions affect behaviour, and that emotions can be used to influence the emotions of others (Cole & others, 2009). One meta-analysis revealed that emotion knowledge (such as understanding emotional cues—for example, when a young child understands that a peer feels sad about being left out of a game) was positively related to 3- to 5-year-olds' social competence (such as offering an empathic response to the child left out of a game) and negatively related to their internalizing (high level of anxiety, for example) and externalizing problems (high level of aggressive behaviour, for example) (Trentacosta & Fine, 2009). Another study also found that young children's understanding of emotions was linked to their prosocial behaviour (Ensor, Spencer, & Hughes, 2010).

Between 2 and 4 years of age, children considerably increase the number of terms they use to describe emotions. During this time, they are also learning about the causes and consequences of feelings (Denham & others, 2012).

When they are 4 to 5 years of age, children show an increased ability to reflect on emotions. They also begin to understand that the same event can elicit different feelings in different people. Moreover, they show a growing awareness that they need to manage their emotions to meet social standards. And, by 5 years of age, most children can accurately identity emotions that are produced by challenging circumstances and describe strategies they might call on to cope with everyday stress (Cole & others, 2009).

**Regulating Emotions** Emotional regulation especially plays a key role in children's ability to manage the demands and conflicts they face in interacting with others (Eisenberg, 2010; Lewis, Todd, & Xu, 2011). Many researchers consider the growth of emotional regulation in children to be fundamental to the development of social competence (Perry & others, 2013; Thompson, 2013a, b). Emotional regulation can be conceptualized as an important component of self-regulation or of executive function. Recall from Chapter 5 that executive function is increasingly thought to be a key concept in describing the young child's higher-level cognitive functioning (Carlson & White, 2013). Let's explore the roles that parents and peers play in children's emotional regulation.

*Parenting and Children's Emotional Development* According to Joan Grusec at the University of Toronto, parents can play an important role in helping young children regulate their emotions (Grusec, 2011; Grusec & Davidor, 2010). Depending on how they talk with their children about emotion, parents can be described as taking an *emotion-coaching* or an *emotion-dismissing* approach

(Gottman, 2013). The distinction between these approaches is most evident in the way the parent deals with the child's negative emotions (anger, frustration, sadness, and so on). *Emotion-coaching parents* monitor their children's emotions, view their children's negative emotions as opportunities for teaching, assist them in labelling emotions, and coach them in how to deal effectively with emotions. In contrast, *emotion-dismissing parents* view their role as to deny, ignore, or change negative emotions. Emotion-coaching parents interact with their children in a less rejecting manner, use more scaffolding and praise, and are more nurturant than are emotion-dismissing parents (Gottman & DeClaire, 1997). Moreover, the children of emotion-coaching parents are better at soothing themselves when they get upset, more effective in regulating their negative affect, focus their attention better, and have fewer behaviour problems than the children of emotion-dismissing parents. Having emotion-dismissing parents is linked with children's poor emotional regulation (Lunkenheimer, Shields, & Cortina, 2007). And another recent study found that fathers' emotion coaching was related to children's social competence (Baker, Fenning, & Crnic, 2011).

Parents' knowledge of their children's emotional world can help them guide their children's emotional development and show them how to cope effectively with problems. For example, a recent study found that Canadian mothers' knowledge about what distresses and comforts their children predicts the children's coping, empathy, and prosocial behaviour (Vinik, Almas, & Grusec, 2011).

A problem that parents face is that young children typically don't want to talk about difficult emotional topics, such as being distressed or engaging in negative behaviours. Among the strategies young children use to avoid these conversations is to not talk at all, change the topic, push away, or run away. Ross Thompson and his colleagues (2009) found that young children were more likely to openly discuss difficult emotional circumstances when they were securely attached to their mother and when their mother conversed with them in a way that validated and accepted the child's views. And Cybelle Raver and her colleagues (McCoy & Raver, 2011; Raver & others, 2011, 2012; Zhai, Raver, & Jones, 2012) are using interventions, such as increasing caregiver emotional expressiveness, to improve young children's emotional regulation and reduce children's behaviour problems.

*Regulation of Emotion and Peer Relations*   Emotions play a strong role in determining the success of a child's peer relationships (Howes, 2009). Specifically, the ability to modulate one's emotions is an important skill that benefits children in their relationships with peers. Moody and emotionally negative children are more likely to experience rejection by their peers, whereas emotionally positive children are more accepted (Stocker & Dunn, 1990). Furthermore, emotional regulation typically increases as children mature. Compared to 3-year-olds, 4-year-olds better recognize and generate more strategies for controlling their anger (Cole & others, 2009).

## MIDDLE AND LATE CHILDHOOD

During middle and late childhood, many children show marked improvement in understanding and managing their emotions (Cunningham, Kliewer, & Garner, 2009). However, in some instances, as when they experience stressful circumstances, their coping abilities can be challenged.

**Developmental Changes in Emotion**   Here are some important developmental changes in emotions

*What are some developmental changes in emotion in middle and late childhood?*

during middle and late childhood (Denham, Bassett, & Wyatt, 2007; Denham & others, 2012; Kuebli, 1994; Thompson, 2013c, d):

- *Improved emotional understanding.* Children in elementary school develop an increased ability to understand complex emotions such as pride and shame. These emotions become less tied to the reactions of other people; they become more self-generated and integrated with a sense of personal responsibility.

- *Increased understanding that more than one emotion can be experienced in a particular situation.* A third-grader, for example, may realize that achieving something might involve both anxiety and joy.

- *Increased tendency to be aware of the events leading to emotional reactions.* A fourth-grader may become aware that her sadness today is influenced by her friend moving to another town last week.

- *Ability to suppress or conceal negative emotional reactions.* A fifth-grader has learned to tone down his anger better than he used to when one of his classmates irritates him.

- *The use of self-initiated strategies for redirecting feelings.* During the elementary school years, children become more reflective about their emotional lives and increasingly use strategies to control their emotions. They become more effective at cognitively managing their emotions, such as by soothing themselves after an upset.

- *A capacity for genuine empathy.* For example, a fourth-grader feels sympathy for a distressed person and experiences vicariously the sadness the distressed person is feeling.

**Coping with Stress**   An important aspect of children's lives is learning how to cope with stress (Findlay, Coplan, & Bowker, 2009; Mash & Wolfe, 2013; Morris & others, 2013). As children get older, they are able to more accurately appraise a stressful situation and determine how much control they have over it. Older children generate more coping alternatives to stressful conditions and use more cognitive coping strategies (Saarni & others, 2006). For example, older children are better than younger children at intentionally shifting their thoughts to a topic that is less stressful. Older children are also better at reframing, or changing their perceptions of a stressful situation. For example, younger children may be very disappointed that their teacher did not say hello to them when they arrived at school. Older children may reframe this type of situation and think, "She may have been busy with other things and just forgot to say hello."

By 10 years of age, most children are able to use cognitive strategies to cope with stress (Saarni & others, 2006). However, in families that have not been supportive and are characterized by turmoil or trauma, children may be so overwhelmed by stress that they do not use such strategies (Thabet & others, 2009).

Disasters can especially harm children's development and produce adjustment problems (McDermott & Cobham, 2012). Among the outcomes for children who experience disasters are acute stress reactions, depression, panic disorder, and post-traumatic stress disorder (Salloum & Overstreet, 2012). The likelihood that a child will face these problems following a disaster depends on factors such as the nature and severity of the disaster, as well as the support available to the child. The September 11, 2001 terrorist attacks on the World Trade Center in New York City, Hurricane Katrina in

*What are some strategies to help children cope with traumatic events such as the tsunami devastation of Japan in March 2011?*

2005, and the 2011 tsunami that devastated Japan raise special concerns about how to help children cope with such stressful events.

Following are descriptions of recent studies exploring how various aspects of traumatic events and disasters affect children:

- In a study of mothers and their children aged 5 years and younger who were directly exposed to the 9/11 attacks in New York City, the mothers who developed post-traumatic stress disorder (PTSD) and depression were less likely to help their children regulate their emotions and behaviour than mothers who were only depressed or only had PTSD (Chemtob & others, 2010). This outcome was linked to their children having anxiety, depression, aggression, and sleep problems.
- A study of the effects of the 2004 tsunami in Sri Lanka found that severe exposure to the tsunami combined with more exposure to other adversities, such as an ongoing war and family violence, was linked to poor adjustment after the tsunami disaster (Catani & others, 2010).
- A research review revealed that children with disabilities are more likely than children without disabilities to live in poverty conditions, which increases their exposure to hazards and disasters (Peek & Stough, 2010). When a disaster occurs, children with disabilities have more difficulty escaping from the disaster.

In research on disasters/trauma, the term *dose-response effects* is often used. A widely supported finding in this research area is that the more severe the disaster/trauma (dose), the worse the adaptation and adjustment (response) following the disaster/trauma (Masten, 2013).

Recommendations for parents, teachers, and other adults caring for children who are involved in disasters and terrorist attacks include the following (Gurwitch & others, 2001, pp. 4–11):

- Reassure children (numerous times, if necessary) of their safety and security.
- Allow children to retell events, and be patient in listening to them.
- Encourage children to talk about any disturbing or confusing feelings, reassuring them that such feelings are normal after a stressful event.
- Protect children from re-exposure to frightening situations and reminders of the trauma—for example, by limiting discussion of the event in front of the children.
- Help children make sense of what happened, keeping in mind that children may misunderstand what took place. For example, young children "may blame themselves, believe things happened that did not happen, believe that terrorists are in the school, etc. Gently help children develop a realistic understanding of the event" (p. 10).

## Review Connect Reflect

 **L02** Describe the development of emotion.

### Review
- How does emotion develop in infancy?
- What characterizes emotional development in early childhood?
- What changes take place in emotion during middle and late childhood?

### Connect
- In this section, you learned about how children develop the ability to recognize and react appropriately to the emotions of others. How is this ability related to children's theory of mind (discussed in Chapter 7)?

### Reflect *Your Own Personal Journey of Life*
- Imagine that you are the parent of an 8-month-old baby and you are having difficulty getting any sleep because the baby wakes up in the middle of the night crying. How would you deal with this situation?

Describing and Classifying Temperament

Biological Foundations and Experience

Goodness of Fit and Parenting

**temperament** Involves individual differences in behavioural styles, emotions, and characteristic ways of responding.

Do you get upset often? Does it take much to get you angry, or to make you laugh? Even at birth, babies seem to have different emotional styles. One infant is cheerful and happy much of the time; another baby seems to cry constantly. These tendencies reflect **temperament**, which involves individual differences in behavioural styles, emotions, and characteristic ways of responding. With regard to its link to emotion, temperament refers to individual differences in how quickly the emotion is shown, how strong it is, how long it lasts, and how quickly it fades away (Campos, 2009).

## DESCRIBING AND CLASSIFYING TEMPERAMENT

How would you describe your temperament or the temperament of a friend? Researchers have described and classified the temperament of individuals in different ways. Here we will examine three of those ways.

**Chess and Thomas's Classification**   Psychiatrists Alexander Chess and Stella Thomas (Chess & Thomas, 1977; Thomas & Chess, 1991) identified three basic types, or clusters, of temperament:

**easy child** A temperament style in which the child is generally in a positive mood, quickly establishes regular routines, and adapts easily to new experiences.

**difficult child** A temperament style in which the child tends to react negatively and cry frequently, engages in irregular daily routines, and is slow to accept new experiences.

**slow-to-warm-up child** A temperament style in which the child has a low activity level, is somewhat negative, and displays a low intensity of mood.

- An **easy child** is generally in a positive mood, quickly establishes regular routines in infancy, and adapts easily to new experiences.
- A **difficult child** reacts negatively and cries frequently, engages in irregular daily routines, and is slow to accept change.
- A **slow-to-warm-up child** has a low activity level, is somewhat negative, and displays a low intensity of mood.

In their longitudinal investigation, Chess and Thomas found that 40 percent of the children

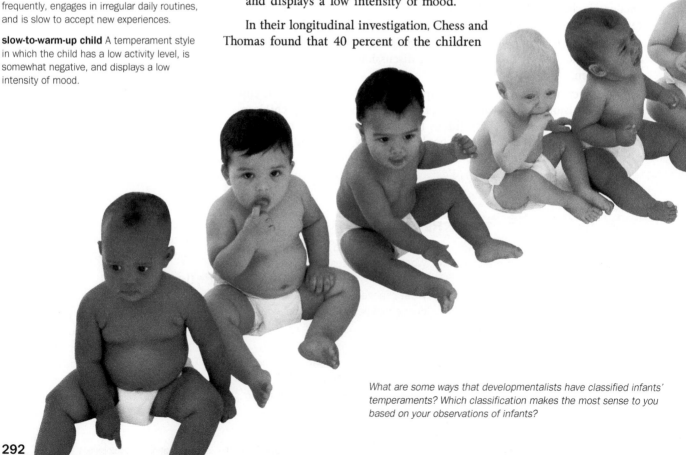

*What are some ways that developmentalists have classified infants' temperaments? Which classification makes the most sense to you based on your observations of infants?*

they studied could be classified as easy, 10 percent as difficult, and 15 percent as slow to warm up. Notice that 35 percent did not fit any of the three patterns. Researchers have found that these three basic clusters of temperament are moderately stable across the childhood years. And one study revealed that young children with a difficult temperament showed more problems when they experienced low-quality child care and fewer problems when they experienced high-quality child care than did young children with an easy temperament (Pluess & Belsky, 2009).

**Kagan's Behavioural Inhibition**   Another way of classifying temperament focuses on the differences between a shy, subdued, timid child and a sociable, extraverted, bold child (Asendorph, 2008; Clauss & Blackford, 2012). Jerome Kagan (2002, 2008, 2010, 2013) regards shyness with strangers (peers or adults) as one feature of a broad temperament category called *inhibition to the unfamiliar*. Inhibited children react to many aspects of unfamiliarity with initial avoidance, distress, or subdued affect, beginning at about 7 to 9 months of age.

Inhibition shows moderate stability from infancy through early adolescence (Karevold & others, 2012). In one study, toddlers were classified into extremely inhibited, extremely uninhibited, and intermediate groups (Pfeifer & others, 2002). Follow-up assessments occurred at 4 and 7 years of age. Continuity was demonstrated for both inhibition and lack of inhibition, although a substantial number of the inhibited children moved into the intermediate groups at 7 years of age.

**Rothbart and Bates' Classification**   New classifications of temperament continue to be forged. Mary Rothbart and John Bates (2006) argue that three broad dimensions best represent what researchers have found to characterize the structure of temperament: extraversion/surgency, negative affectivity, and effortful control (self-regulation):

- *Extraversion/surgency* includes "positive anticipation, impulsivity, activity level, and sensation seeking" (Rothbart, 2004, p. 495). Kagan's uninhibited children fit into this category.

- *Negative affectivity* includes "fear, frustration, sadness, and discomfort" (Rothbart, 2004, p. 495). These children are easily distressed; they may fret and cry often. Kagan's inhibited children fit this category. Negative emotional reactivity or irritability reflect the core of Chess and Thomas' category of the difficult child (Bates & Pettit, 2007).

- *Effortful control (self-regulation)* includes "attentional focusing and shifting, inhibitory control, perceptual sensitivity, and low-intensity pleasure"

(Rothbart, 2004, p. 495). Infants who are high on effortful control show an ability to keep their arousal from getting too high and have strategies for soothing themselves. By contrast, children low on effortful control are often unable to control their arousal; they become easily agitated and intensely emotional (Rothbart & Sheese, 2007). A study of school-age children in the United States and China revealed that in both cultures low effortful control was linked to externalizing problems, such as lying, cheating, being disobedient, and being overly aggressive (Zhou, Lengua, & Wang, 2009). Canadian researcher Adele Diamond (2012) notes that children lower in effortful control than their peers can "catch up" through regular participation in activities that improve these skills such as computer-based training and traditional martial arts.

In Rothbart's (2004, p. 497) view, "early theoretical models of temperament stressed the way we are moved by our positive and negative emotions or level of arousal, with our actions driven by these tendencies." The more recent emphasis on effortful control, however, advocates that individuals can engage in a more cognitive, flexible approach to stressful circumstances.

An important point about temperament classifications such as those devised by Chess and Thomas and by Rothbart and Bates is that children should not be pigeonholed as having only one temperament dimension, such as "difficult" or "negative affectivity." A good strategy when attempting to classify a child's temperament is to think of temperament as consisting of multiple dimensions (Bates, 2008, 2012a, b). For example, a child might be extraverted, show little emotional negativity, and have good self-regulation. Another child might be introverted, show little emotional negativity, and have a low level of self-regulation.

Rothbart and Maria Gartstein (2008, p. 323) described the following developmental changes in temperament during infancy. During early infancy, smiling and laughter are emerging as part of the positive affectivity dimension of temperament. Also, by 2 months of age, infants show anger and frustration when their actions don't produce an interesting outcome. During this time, infants often are susceptible to distress and overstimulation. From 4 to 12 months of age fear and irritability become more differentiated, with inhibition (fear) increasingly linked to new and unpredictable experiences. Not all temperament characteristics are in place by the first birthday. Positive emotionality becomes more stable later in infancy, and the characteristics of extraversion/surgency can be determined in the toddler period. Improved attention skills in the toddler and preschool years are related to an increase in effortful control, which serves as a foundation for improved self-regulation.

The developmental changes just described reflect normative capabilities of children, not individual differences in children. The development of these capabilities, such as effortful control, allows individual differences to emerge (Bates, 2008, 2012a, b). For example, although maturation of the brain's prefrontal lobes must occur for any child's attention to improve and the child to achieve effortful control, some children develop effortful control and others do not. And it is these individual differences in children that are at the heart of what temperament is (Bates, 2008, 2012a, b).

## BIOLOGICAL FOUNDATIONS AND EXPERIENCE

How does a child acquire a certain temperament? Kagan (2002, 2010) argues that children inherit a physiology that biases them to have a particular type of temperament. However, through experience they may learn to modify their temperament to some degree. For example, children may inherit a physiology that biases them to be fearful and inhibited, but, as described in *Connecting Through Research*, they can learn to reduce their fear and inhibition to some degree.

**Biological Influences** Physiological characteristics have been linked with different temperaments (Diaz & Bell, 2012; Mize & Jones, 2012). In particular, an

# connecting through research

## Helping Inhibited Children Through Play

Longitudinal studies show that extremely inhibited young children are at risk for developing anxiety disorders (Hudson & Rapee, 2000). Yet there has been very little research on early intervention and prevention (Rubin & others, 2011).

Researchers Robert Coplan at Carleton University and Barry Schneider at the University of Ottawa and their colleagues developed and evaluated an early intervention program, called Play Skills for Shy Children, which was designed to improve the social and emotional skills of extremely inhibited preschoolers (Coplan & others, 2010).

The study was conducted over a 6-month period. In September, each mother completed questionnaires about her child's behavioural inhibition and psychosocial adjustment. Extremely inhibited preschool-aged children were randomly assigned to one of two conditions: Social Skills Facilitated Play or Waitlist Control. In October and early November, teachers completed questionnaires about the children's adjustment with peers. Also at this time, research assistants visited the children's preschool to observe their behaviours during indoor free play. The intervention program took place from November to early January, with the same observations and teacher ratings completed immediately after.

Children assigned to the Play Skills for Shy Children program met in small groups with trained adult leaders for weekly sessions. Each session began with five minutes of unstructured free play to allow children to warm up to one another, while parents slowly made their way out of the room. Ten minutes of circle time followed, where adult leaders provided social skills training using songs, games, and puppets in addition to emotion-regulation

*What are some benefits of social skills training programs for inhibited children?*

strategies and relaxation techniques. Next was forty minutes of leader-facilitated free play that mirrored the free play time that occurs in preschools, with one exception: adult leaders actively encouraged and facilitated social interactions between children while modelling and reinforcing skills learned at circle time. Each session wrapped up with five minutes of playing parachute games as a fun activity for the entire group.

At the end of the program, the extremely inhibited children who received the training displayed significantly fewer socially anxious behaviours and significantly more socially competent behaviours at preschool as compared to extremely inhibited children who were in the waitlist group.

---

inhibited temperament is associated with a unique physiological pattern that includes high and stable heart rate, high level of the hormone cortisol, and high activity in the right frontal lobe of the brain (Kagan, 2003, 2010, 2013). This pattern may be tied to the excitability of the amygdala, a structure of the brain that plays an important role in fear and inhibition (Kagan, 2003, 2010, 2013). An inhibited temperament or negative affectivity may also be linked to low levels of the neurotransmitter serotonin, which may increase an individual's vulnerability to fear and frustration (Pauli-Pott & others, 2009).

What is heredity's role in the biological foundations of temperament? An inhibited temperament has been linked to carrying the short allele of the serotonin transporter (5-HTT) polymorphism gene (Fox & others, 2005). Twin and adoption studies suggest that heredity has a moderate influence on differences in temperament within a group of people (Plomin & others, 2009). The contemporary view is that temperament is a biologically based but evolving aspect of behaviour; it evolves as the child's experiences are incorporated into a network of self-perceptions and behavioural preferences that characterize the child's personality (Easterbrooks & others, 2013).

**Gender, Culture, and Temperament**  Gender may be an important factor shaping the context that influences the fate of temperament (Gaias & others, 2012).

### developmental connection

**Research Methods.** Twin and adoption studies have been used to sort out hereditary and environmental influences on development. Chapter 2, LO 4

Parents might react differently to an infant's temperament depending on whether the baby is a boy or a girl. For example, in one study, mothers were more responsive to the crying of irritable girls than to the crying of irritable boys (Crockenberg, 1986).

Similarly, the reaction to an infant's temperament may depend in part on culture (Chen & others, 2011; Fung, 2011). For example, an active temperament might be valued in individualistic cultures (such as Canada) but not in collectivistic cultures (such as China) (Chen & others, 1998). Indeed, children's temperaments can vary across cultures (Putnam, Sanson, & Rothbart, 2002). Behavioural inhibition is more common among Chinese and Korean children than Italian, Australian, and Canadian children (Chen & others, 1998; Rubin & others, 2006) Even within Canada, children of East Asian descent are more inhibited than children of European descent (Chen & Tse, 2008). However, recent research suggests inhibition is becoming less favourable among Chinese children, possibly due to an increasing Westernization of Chinese culture and economy (Chen, 2011).

**Developmental Connections** Do young adults show the same behavioural style and characteristic emotional responses as they did when they were infants or young children? Activity level is an important dimension of temperament. Are children's activity levels linked to their personality in early adulthood? In one longitudinal study, children who were highly active at age 4 were likely to be very outgoing at age 23, which reflects continuity (Franz, 1996). From adolescence into early adulthood, most individuals show fewer emotional mood swings, become more responsible, and engage in less risk-taking behaviour, which reflects discontinuity (Caspi, 1998).

Is temperament in childhood linked with adjustment in adulthood? Here is what we know based on the few longitudinal studies that have been conducted on this topic (Caspi, 1998). In one longitudinal study, children who had an easy temperament at 3 to 5 years of age were likely to be well adjusted as young adults (Chess & Thomas, 1977). In contrast, many children who had a difficult temperament at 3 to 5 years of age were not well adjusted as young adults. Also, other researchers have found that boys with a difficult temperament in childhood are less likely as adults to continue their formal education, whereas girls with a difficult temperament in childhood are more likely to experience marital conflict as adults (Wachs, 2000).

Inhibition, described earlier in *Connecting Through Research*, is another temperament characteristic that has been studied extensively (Kagan, 2008, 2010, 2013). Research shows that inhibition in childhood affects children's adjustment later in life. For example, one study revealed that behavioural inhibition at 3 years of age was linked to shyness four years later (Volbrecht & Goldsmith, 2010). Another study found that 24-month-olds who were fearful in situations relatively low in threat displayed higher anxiety levels in kindergarten (Buss, 2011). Also, research indicates that individuals with an inhibited temperament in childhood are less likely as adults to be assertive or to experience social support, and more likely to delay entering a stable job track (Asendorph, 2008). One study revealed that infants classified as highly reactive (vigorous motor activity and frequent crying) to unfamiliar stimuli were likely to avoid unfamiliar events in infancy and often were subdued, cautious, and wary of new situations in adolescence (Kagan & others, 2007). By contrast, low-reactive infants were likely to approach unfamiliar events in infancy and to be emotionally spontaneous and sociable in adolescence. Some, but not all, inhibited infants grow up to become withdrawn and socially anxious (Bohlin & Hagekull, 2009; Degnan & Fox, 2007).

Yet another aspect of temperament involves emotionality and the ability to control emotions. In one longitudinal study, when 3-year-old children showed good control of their emotions and were resilient in the face of stress, they were likely to continue to handle emotions effectively as adults (Block, 1993). By contrast, when 3-year-olds had low emotional control and were not very resilient, they were likely to show problems in these areas as young adults.

In sum, these studies reveal some continuity between certain aspects of temperament in childhood and adjustment in early adulthood. However, keep in mind that these connections between childhood temperament and adult adjustment are based on only a small number of studies; more research is needed to verify these linkages (Shiner & DeYoung, 2013; Wachs & Bates, 2010).

**Developmental Contexts**  What accounts for the continuities and discontinuities between a child's temperament and an adult's personality? Physiological and hereditary factors likely are involved in continuity (Kagan, 2008, 2010, 2013). Theodore Wachs (1994, 2000) proposed ways that linkages between temperament in childhood and personality in adulthood might vary depending on the contexts in individuals' experience. Figure 10.6 summarizes how one characteristic might develop in different ways, depending on the context.

In short, many aspects of a child's environment can encourage or discourage the persistence of temperament characteristics (Bates, 2012a, b; Rothbart, 2011). One useful way of thinking about these relationships applies the concept of goodness of fit, which we examine next.

*developmental* **connection**

**Culture and Ethnicity.**  Cross-cultural studies seek to determine culture-universal and culture-specific aspects of development. Chapter 1, LO 2

**goodness of fit** The match between a child's temperament and the environmental demands the child must cope with.

# GOODNESS OF FIT AND PARENTING

**Goodness of fit** refers to the match between a child's temperament and the environmental demands the child must cope with. Suppose John is an active toddler who is made to sit still for long periods of time and Jack is a slow-to-warm-up toddler who is abruptly pushed into new situations on a regular basis. Both John and Jack face a lack of fit between their temperament and environmental demands. Lack of fit can produce adjustment problems (Rothbart, 2011).

Some temperament characteristics pose more parenting challenges than others, at least in modern Western societies (Rothbart, 2011). When children

*How do biology and culture influence this Asian Canadian infant's temperament?*

**Initial Temperament Trait: Inhibition**

| | Child A | Child B |
|---|---|---|
| | **Intervening Context** | |
| **Caregivers** | Caregivers (parents) who are sensitive and accepting, and who let the child set his or her own pace. | Caregivers who use inappropriate "low-level control" and attempt to force the child into new situations. |
| **Physical Environment** | Presence of "stimulus shelters" or "defensible spaces" that the children can retreat to when there is too much stimulation. | Child continually encounters noisy, chaotic environments that allow no escape from stimulation. |
| **Peers** | Peer groups with other inhibited children with common interests, so the child feels accepted. | Peer groups consist of athletic extroverts, so the child feels rejected. |
| **Schools** | School is "undermanned," so inhibited children are more likely to be tolerated and feel they can make a contribution. | School is "overmanned," so inhibited children are less likely to be tolerated and more likely to feel undervalued. |
| | **Personality Outcomes** | |
| | As an adult, individual is closer to extraversion (outgoing, sociable) and is emotionally stable. | As an adult, individual is closer to introversion and has more emotional problems. |

## FIGURE **10.6**

**TEMPERAMENT IN CHILDHOOD, PERSONALITY IN ADULTHOOD, AND INTERVENING CONTEXTS.** Varying experiences with caregivers, the physical environment, peers, and schools may modify links between temperament in childhood and personality in adulthood. The example given here is for inhibition.

are prone to distress, as exhibited by frequent crying and irritability, their parents may eventually respond by ignoring the child's distress or trying to force the child to "behave." In one research study, though, extra support and training for mothers of distress-prone infants improved the quality of mother-infant interaction (van den Boom, 1989). The training led the mothers to alter their demands on the child, improving the fit between the child and the environment. Researchers have also found that decreases in infants' negative emotionality are linked to higher levels of parental sensitivity, involvement, and responsivity (Bates, 2012a, b; Penela & others, 2012).

Many parents don't become believers in temperament's importance until the birth of their second child. They viewed their first child's behaviour as a result of how they treated the child. But then they find that some strategies that worked with their first child are not as effective with the second child. Some problems experienced with the first child (such as those involved in feeding, sleeping, and coping with strangers) do not exist with the second child, but new problems arise. Such experiences strongly suggest that children differ from each other very early in life, and that these differences have important implications for parent-child interaction (Kwak & others, 1999; Rothbart, 2011).

## Review Connect Reflect

**L03** Characterize variations in temperament and their significance.

### Review

- How can temperament be described and classified?
- How is temperament influenced by biological foundations and experience?
- What is goodness of fit?

### Connect

- In this section, you learned that twin and adoption studies suggest that heredity has a moderate influence on differences in temperament. In Chapter 2, what did you learn were the issues that complicate the interpretation of twin studies?

### Reflect Your Own Personal Journey of Life

- Consider your own temperament. We described a number of temperament categories. Which one best describes your temperament? Has your temperament changed as you have gotten older? If your temperament has changed, what factors contributed to the changes?

## Social Orientation/Understanding, Attachment, and Child Care

**L04** Explain the early development of social orientation/understanding, attachment, and child care.

Social Orientation/Understanding     Attachment     Fathers and Mothers as Caregivers     Child Care

So far, we have discussed how emotions and emotional competence change as children develop. We have also examined the role of emotional style; in effect, we have seen how emotions set the tone of our experiences in life. But emotions also write the lyrics because they are at the core of our interest in the social world and our relationships with others.

## SOCIAL ORIENTATION/UNDERSTANDING

As socioemotional beings, infants show a strong interest in their social world and are motivated to orient to it and understand it (Thompson, 2013a). In earlier chapters, we described many of the biological and cognitive foundations that contribute to the infant's development of social orientation and understanding.

We will call attention to relevant biological and cognitive factors as we explore social orientation; locomotion; intention, goal-directed behaviour, and cooperation; and social referencing. We discuss biological, cognitive, and social processes together because, as University of British Columbia researcher Adele Diamond points out, these processes are intricately intertwined (Diamond, 2009, 2011).

**Social Orientation** From early in their development, infants are captivated by their social world. As we discussed in our coverage of infant perception in Chapter 5, young infants stare intently at faces and are attuned to the sounds of human voices, especially their caregiver's (Lowe & others, 2012). Later, they become adept at interpreting the meaning of facial expressions.

*Face-to-face play* often begins to characterize caregiver-infant interactions when the infant is about 2 to 3 months of age and decreases after 7 months of age as infants become more mobile (Thompson, 2006). The focused social interaction of face-to-face play may include vocalizations, touch, and gestures (Leppanen & others, 2007). Such play is part of many mothers' motivation to create a positive emotional state in their infants (Thompson, 2013a, d).

In part because of such positive social interchanges between caregivers and infants, by 2 to 3 months of age infants respond to people differently from the way they respond to objects, showing more positive emotion toward people than inanimate objects, such as puppets (Legerstee, 1997). At this age, most infants expect people to react positively when the infants initiate a behaviour, such as a smile or a vocalization. This finding has been discovered using a method called the *still-face paradigm*, in which the caregiver alternates between engaging in face-to-face interaction with the infant and remaining still and unresponsive (Bigelow & Power, 2012; Lee & others, 2013). As early as 2 to 3 months of age, infants show more withdrawal, negative emotions, and self-directed behaviour when their caregivers are still and unresponsive (Adamson & Frick, 2003). Researchers have found that infants' higher positive affect and lower negative affect, as displayed during the still-face paradigm, are linked to secure attachment at 1 year of age (Mesman, van IJzendoorn, & Bakersman-Kranenburg, 2009).

Infants also learn about their social world through contexts other than face-to-face play with a caregiver (Easterbrooks & others, 2013). Even though infants as young as 6 months of age show an interest in each other, their interaction with peers increases considerably in the last half of the second year. Between 18 and 24 months of age, children markedly increase their imitative and reciprocal play, such as imitating nonverbal actions like jumping and running (Eckerman & Whitehead, 1999). One study involved presenting 1- and 2-year-olds with a simple cooperative task that consisted of pulling a lever to get an attractive toy (Brownell, Ramani, & Zerwas, 2006) (see Figure 10.7). Any coordinated actions of the 1-year-olds appeared to be mostly coincidental rather than cooperative, whereas the 2-year-olds' behaviour was characterized more as active cooperation to reach a goal. As increasing numbers of North American infants experience child care outside the home, they are spending more time in social play with peers (Lamb & Lewis, 2013). Later in the chapter, we will further discuss child care.

**Locomotion** Recall from earlier in the chapter how important independence is for infants, especially in the second year of life. As infants develop the ability to crawl, walk, and run, they are able

A mother and her baby engaging in face-to-face play. *At what age does face-to-face play usually begin, and when does it typically start decreasing in frequency?*

*developmental* **connection**

**Dynamic Systems Theory.** Dynamic systems theory is increasingly recognized as an important theory in understanding children's development. Chapter 5, LO 1

### FIGURE **10.7**

**THE COOPERATION TASK.** The cooperation task consisted of two handles on a box, atop which was an animated musical toy, surreptitiously activated by remote control when both handles were pulled. The handles were placed far enough apart that one child could not pull both handles. The experimenter demonstrated the task, saying, "Watch! If you pull the handles, the doggie will sing" (Brownell, Ramani, & Zerwas, 2006).

to explore and expand their social world. These newly developed self-produced locomotor skills allow the infant to independently initiate social interchanges on a more frequent basis (Laible & Thompson, 2007). Remember from Chapter 5 that the development of these gross motor skills is the result of a number of factors including the development of the nervous system, the goal the infant is motivated to reach, and environmental support for the skill (Adolph & Berger, 2013; Adolph & Robinson, 2013).

The infant's and toddler's push for independence also is likely paced by the development of locomotor skills. Locomotion is also important for its motivational implications (Adolph & Berger, 2013). Once infants have the ability to move in goal-directed pursuits, the reward from these pursuits leads to further efforts to explore and develop skills.

**Intention, Goal-Directed Behaviour, and Cooperation**   Perceiving people as engaging in intentional and goal-directed behaviour is an important social cognitive accomplishment, and this initially occurs toward the end of the first year (Thompson, 2013a, d). Joint attention and gaze following help the infant to understand that other people have intentions (Mateus & others, 2013). Recall from Chapter 7 that *joint attention* occurs when the caregiver and infant focus on the same object or event. Emerging aspects of joint attention occur at about 7 to 8 months, but at about 10 to 11 months of age joint attention intensifies and infants begin to follow the caregiver's gaze. By their first birthday, infants have begun to direct the caregiver's attention to objects that capture their interest (Heimann & others, 2006). A recent Canadian study found that the pointing gesture initially emerges from an infant's own attention to and exploration of nearby objects. Infants gradually become aware of the meaning of pointing and begin using it as a social cue to adults (Carpendale & Carpendale, 2010).

**Social Referencing**   Another important social cognitive accomplishment in infancy is developing the ability to read the emotions of other people (Cornew & others, 2012). **Social referencing** is the term used to describe reading emotional cues in others to help determine how to act in a particular situation. The development of social referencing helps infants to interpret ambiguous situations more accurately, as when they encounter a stranger and need to know whether to fear the person (Pelaez, Virues-Ortega, & Gewirtz, 2012). By the end of the first year, a mother's facial expression—either smiling or fearful—influences whether an infant will explore an unfamiliar environment.

Infants become better at social referencing in the second year of life. At this age, they tend to check with their mother before they act; they look at her to see if she is happy, angry, or fearful. For example, in one study, 14- to 22-month-old infants were more likely to look at their mother's face as a source of information for how to act in a situation than were 6- to 9-month-old infants (Walden, 1991).

**Infants' Social Sophistication and Insight**   In sum, researchers are discovering that infants are more socially sophisticated and insightful at younger ages than was previously envisioned (Thompson, 2013a, d). This sophistication and insight is reflected in infants' perceptions of others' actions as intentionally motivated and goal-directed (Brune & Woodward, 2007) and their motivation to share and participate in that intentionality by their first birthday (Tomasello, Carpenter, & Liszkowski, 2007). The more advanced social cognitive skills of infants could be expected to influence their understanding and awareness of attachment to a caregiver.

## ATTACHMENT

What is attachment? **Attachment** is a close emotional bond between two people. Interest in attachment has especially focused on infants and their caregivers.

**social referencing** Reading emotional cues in others to help determine how to act in a particular situation.

**attachment** A close emotional bond between two people.

**Theories of Attachment** There is no shortage of theories about why infants become attached to a caregiver. Three theorists discussed in Chapter 1—Freud, Erikson, and Bowlby—proposed influential views.

Freud reasoned that infants become attached to the person or object that provides oral satisfaction. For most infants, this is the mother, since she is most likely to feed the infant. Is feeding as important as Freud thought? A classic study by Harry Harlow (1958) reveals that the answer is no (see Figure 10.8).

Harlow removed infant monkeys from their mothers at birth; for six months they were reared by surrogate (substitute) "mothers." One surrogate mother was made of wire, the other of cloth. Half of the infant monkeys were fed by the wire mother, half by the cloth mother. Periodically, the amount of time the infant monkeys spent with either the wire or the cloth mother was computed. Regardless of which mother fed them, the infant monkeys spent far more time with the cloth mother. Even if the wire mother but not the cloth mother provided nourishment, the infant monkeys spent more time with the cloth mother. And when Harlow frightened the monkeys, those "raised" by the cloth mother ran to the mother and clung to it; those raised by the wire mother did not. Whether the mother provided comfort seemed to determine whether the monkeys associated the mother with security. This study clearly demonstrated that feeding is not the crucial element in the attachment process, and that contact comfort is important.

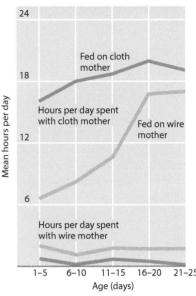

FIGURE **10.8**

**CONTACT TIME WITH WIRE AND CLOTH SURROGATE MOTHERS.** Regardless of whether the infant monkeys were fed by a wire or a cloth mother, they overwhelmingly preferred to spend contact time with the cloth mother. *How do these results compare with what Freud's theory and Erikson's theory would predict about human infants?*

Physical comfort also plays a role in Erik Erikson's (1968) view of the infant's development. Recall Erikson's proposal that the first year of life represents the stage of trust versus mistrust. Physical comfort and sensitive care, according to Erikson (1968), are key to establishing a basic trust in infants. The infant's sense of trust, in turn, is the foundation for attachment and sets the stage for a lifelong expectation that the world will be a good and pleasant place to be.

British psychiatrist John Bowlby (1969, 1989) also stresses the importance of attachment in the first year of life and the responsiveness of the caregiver. Bowlby points out that both infants and their primary caregivers are biologically predisposed to form attachments. He argues that the newborn is biologically equipped to elicit attachment behaviour. The baby cries, clings, coos, and smiles. Later, the infant crawls, walks, and follows the mother. The immediate result is to keep the primary caregiver nearby; the long-term effect is to increase the infant's chances of survival.

Attachment does not emerge suddenly but rather develops in a series of phases, moving from a baby's general preference for human beings to a partnership with primary caregivers. Following are four such phases based on Bowlby's conceptualization of attachment (Schaffer, 1996):

- *Phase 1: From birth to 2 months.* Infants instinctively orient to human figures. Strangers, siblings, and parents are equally likely to elicit smiling or crying from the infant.
- *Phase 2: From 2 to 7 months.* Attachment becomes focused on one figure, usually the primary caregiver, as the baby gradually learns to distinguish familiar from unfamiliar people.

*In Bowlby's model, what are the four phases of attachment?*

- *Phase 3: From 7 to 24 months.* Specific attachments develop. With increased locomotor skills, babies actively seek contact with regular caregivers, such as the mother or father.
- *Phase 4: From 24 months on.* Children become aware of others' feelings, goals, and plans and begin to take these into account in directing their own actions. Researchers' recent findings that infants are more socially sophisticated and insightful than previously envisioned suggests that some of the characteristics of Bowlby's phase 4, such as understanding the goals and intentions of the attachment figure, appear to be developing in phase 3 as attachment security is taking shape (Thompson, 2008).

Bowlby argued that infants develop an *internal working model* of attachment: a simple mental model of the caregiver, their relationship, and the self as deserving of nurturant care. The infant's internal working model of attachment with the caregiver influences the infant's and later the child's subsequent responses to other people (Bretherton, 2012; Roisman & Groh, 2011). The internal model of attachment also has played a pivotal role in the discovery of links between attachment and subsequent emotion understanding, conscience development, and self-concept (Thompson, 2013a).

In sum, attachment emerges from the social cognitive advances that allow infants to develop expectations for the caregiver's behaviour and to determine the affective quality of their relationship (Thompson, 2013a). These social cognitive advances include recognizing the caregiver's face, voice, and other features, as well as developing an internal working model of expecting the caregiver to provide pleasure in social interaction and relief from distress.

**Individual Differences in Attachment**    Although attachment to a caregiver intensifies midway through the first year, isn't it likely that the quality of babies' attachment experiences varies? Mary Ainsworth (1979) thought so. After completing her training in psychology at the University of Toronto, Ainsworth went on to create the **Strange Situation**, an observational measure of infant attachment in which the infant experiences a series of introductions, separations, and reunions with the caregiver (usually the child's mother) and an adult stranger in a prescribed order. In using the Strange Situation, researchers hope that their observations will provide information about the infant's motivation to be near the caregiver and the degree to which the caregiver's presence provides the infant with security and confidence.

Based on how babies respond in the Strange Situation, they are described as being securely attached or insecurely attached (in one of three ways) to the caregiver:

- **Securely attached babies** use the caregiver as a secure base from which to explore the environment. When they are in the presence of their caregiver, securely attached infants explore the room and examine toys that have been placed in it. When the caregiver departs, securely attached infants might protest mildly, and when the caregiver returns these infants re-establish positive interaction with her, perhaps by smiling or climbing onto her lap. Subsequently, they often resume playing with the toys in the room.
- **Insecure avoidant babies** show insecurity by avoiding the caregiver. In the Strange Situation, these babies engage in little interaction with the caregiver, are not distressed when she leaves the room, usually do not re-establish contact with her on her return, and may even turn their back on her. If contact is established, the infant usually leans away or looks away.
- **Insecure resistant babies** often cling to the caregiver and then resist her by fighting against the closeness, perhaps by kicking or pushing away. In the Strange Situation, these babies often cling anxiously to the caregiver and don't explore the playroom. When the caregiver leaves, they often cry loudly and push away if she tries to comfort them on her return.

**Strange Situation** Ainsworth's observational measure of infant attachment to a caregiver, which requires the infant to move through a series of introductions, separations, and reunions with the caregiver and an adult stranger in a prescribed order.

**securely attached babies** Babies who use the caregiver as a secure base from which to explore the environment.

**insecure avoidant babies** Babies who show insecurity by avoiding the caregiver.

**insecure resistant babies** Babies who might cling to the caregiver, then resist her by fighting against the closeness, perhaps by kicking or pushing away.

- **Insecure disorganized babies** are disorganized and disoriented. In the Strange Situation, these babies might appear dazed, confused, and fearful. To be classified as disorganized, babies must show strong patterns of avoidance and resistance or display certain specified behaviours, such as extreme fearfulness around the caregiver.

**insecure disorganized babies** Babies who show insecurity by being disorganized and disoriented.

*Evaluating the Strange Situation* Does the Strange Situation capture important differences among infants? As a measure of attachment, it may be culturally biased. For example, German and Japanese babies often show patterns of attachment different from those of American infants. As illustrated in Figure 10.9, German infants are more likely to show an avoidant attachment pattern and Japanese infants are less likely to display this pattern than U.S. infants (van IJzendoorn & Kroonenberg, 1988). The avoidant pattern in German babies likely occurs because their caregivers encourage them to be independent (Grossmann & others, 1985). Also as shown in Figure 10.9, Japanese babies are more likely than American babies to be categorized as resistant. This may have more to do with the Strange Situation as a measure of attachment than with attachment insecurity itself. Japanese mothers rarely let anyone unfamiliar with their babies care for them. Thus, the Strange Situation might create considerably more stress for Japanese infants than for American infants, who are more accustomed to separation from their mothers (Miyake, Chen, & Campos, 1985). Even though there are cultural variations in attachment classification, the most frequent classification in every culture studied so far is secure attachment (Thompson, 2006, 2012; van IJzendoorn & Kroonenberg, 1988).

Some critics stress that behaviour in the Strange Situation—like other laboratory assessments—might not indicate what infants would do in a natural environment. But researchers at the University of Western Ontario have found that infants' behaviours in the Strange Situation are closely related to how they behave at home in response to separation and reunion with their mothers (Pederson & Moran, 1996). Thus, many infant researchers conclude that the Strange Situation continues to show merit as a measure of infant attachment.

*Interpreting Differences in Attachment* Do individual differences in attachment matter? Ainsworth observes that secure attachment in the first year of life provides an important foundation for psychological development later in life. The securely attached infant moves freely away from the mother but keeps track of where she is through periodic glances. The securely attached infant responds positively to being picked up by others and, when put back down, freely moves away to play. An insecurely attached infant, by contrast, avoids the mother or is ambivalent toward her, fears strangers, and is upset by minor, everyday separations.

If early attachment to a caregiver is important, it should relate to a child's social behaviour later in development. For some children, early attachments seem to foreshadow later functioning (Bretherton, 2012). In the extensive longitudinal study conducted by Alan Sroufe and his colleagues (2005; Sroufe, Coffino, & Carlson, 2010), early secure attachment (assessed by the Strange Situation at 12 and 18 months) was linked with positive emotional health, high self-esteem, self-confidence, and socially competent interaction with peers, teachers, camp counselors, and romantic partners through adolescence. Another study found that attachment security at 24 and

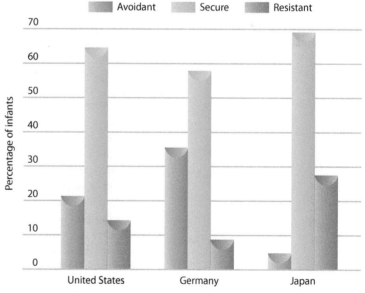

FIGURE **10.9**

**CROSS-CULTURAL COMPARISON OF ATTACHMENT.** In one study, infant attachment in three countries—the United States, Germany, and Japan—was measured in the Ainsworth Strange Situation (van IJzendoorn & Kroonenberg, 1988). The dominant attachment pattern in all three countries was secure attachment. However, German infants were more avoidant and Japanese infants were less avoidant and more resistant than U.S. infants. *What are some explanations for differences in how German, Japanese, and U.S. infants respond to the Strange Situation?*

36 months was linked to the child's enhanced social problem-solving skills at 54 months (Raikes & Thompson, 2009). And a meta-analysis found that disorganized attachment was more strongly linked to externalizing problems (aggression, hostility, opposition problems, for example) than were avoidant and resistant attachment (Fearon & others, 2010).

Few studies have assessed infants' attachment security to the mother and the father separately. However, a recent study revealed that infants who were insecurely attached to their mother and father (double-insecure) at 15 months of age had more externalizing problems (out-of-control behaviour, for example) in the elementary school years than their counterparts who were securely attached to at least one parent (Kochanska & Kim, 2013).

An important issue regarding attachment is whether infancy is a critical or sensitive period for development. Many, but not all, research studies reveal the power of infant attachment to predict subsequent development (Fraley, Roisman, & Haltigan, 2013; Roisman & Groh, 2011; Thompson, 2013a). In one longitudinal study, attachment classification in infancy did not predict attachment classification at 18 years of age (Lewis, Feiring, & Rosenthal, 2000). In this study, the best predictor of an insecure attachment classification at 18 was the occurrence of parental divorce in the intervening years.

Consistently positive caregiving over a number of years is likely an important factor in connecting early attachment with the child's functioning later in development. Indeed, researchers have found that early secure attachment *and* subsequent experiences, especially maternal care and life stresses, are linked with children's later behaviour and adjustment (Thompson, 2013a). For example, a longitudinal study revealed that changes in attachment security/insecurity from infancy to adulthood were linked to stresses and supports in socioemotional contexts (Van Ryzin, Carlson, & Sroufe, 2011). These results suggest that attachment continuity may reflect stable social contexts as much as early working models. The study just described (Van Ryzin, Carlson, & Sroufe, 2011) reflects an increasingly accepted view of the development of attachment and its influence on development. That is, it is important to recognize that attachment security in infancy does not always by itself produce long-term positive outcomes, but rather is linked to later outcomes through connections with the way children and adolescents subsequently experience various social contexts as they develop.

The Van Ryzin, Carlson, and Sroufe (2011) study reflects a **developmental cascade model**, which involves connections across domains over time that influence developmental pathways and outcomes (Cicchetti, 2013; Masten, 2013). Developmental cascades can include connections between a wide range of biological, cognitive, and socioemotional processes (attachment, for example), and also can involve social contexts such as families, peers, schools, and culture. Further, links can produce positive or negative outcomes at different points in development, such as infancy, early childhood, middle and late childhood, adolescence, and adulthood.

Some developmentalists conclude that too much emphasis has been placed on the attachment bond in infancy (Newcombe, 2007). Jerome Kagan (1987, 2002), for example, points out that infants are highly resilient and adaptive; he argues that they are evolutionarily equipped to stay on a positive developmental course, even in the face of wide variations in parenting. Kagan and others stress that genetic characteristics and temperament play more important roles in a child's social competence than the attachment theorists, such as Bowlby and Ainsworth, are willing to acknowledge (Bakermans-Kranenburg & others, 2007). For example, if some infants inherit a low tolerance for stress, this—rather than an insecure attachment bond—may be responsible for an inability to get along with peers. One study found that infants with the short version of the serotonin transporter gene—5-HTTLPR—developed a disorganized attachment style only when their mothers were low in responsiveness to them (Spangler & others, 2009). This is an example of a finding involving gene-environment interactions related to infant attachment (Luijk & others, 2011; Roisman & Fraley, 2012).

**developmental cascade model** Involves connections across domains over time that influence developmental pathways and outcomes.

*developmental* **connection**

**Nature-Nurture.** What is involved in gene-environment (G × E) interaction? Chapter 2, LO 4

Another criticism of attachment theory is that it ignores the diversity of socializing agents and contexts that exists in an infant's world. A culture's value system can influence the nature of attachment (Jin & others, 2012). Mothers' expectations for infants to be independent are high in northern Germany, whereas Japanese mothers are more strongly motivated to keep their infants close to them (Grossmann & others, 1985; Rothbaum & Trommsdorff, 2007). Not surprisingly, northern German infants tend to show less distress than Japanese infants when separated from their mothers. Also, in some cultures, infants show attachments to many people. Among the Hausa (who live in Nigeria), both grandmothers and siblings provide a significant amount of care for infants (Harkness & Super, 1995). Infants in agricultural societies tend to form attachments to older siblings, who are assigned a major responsibility for younger siblings' care. Researchers recognize the importance of competent, nurturant caregivers in an infant's development (Grusec & others, 2013). At issue, though, is whether or not secure attachment, especially to a single caregiver, is crucial (Fraley, Roisman, & Haltigan, 2013; Thompson, 2013c, d).

Despite such criticisms, there is ample evidence that security of attachment is important to development (Bretherton, 2012; Crugnola & others, 2013; Sroufe, Coffino, & Carlson, 2010; Thompson, 2013c, d). Secure attachment in infancy is important because it reflects a positive parent-infant relationship and provides a foundation that supports healthy socioemotional development in the years that follow.

In the Hausa culture, siblings and grandmothers provide a significant amount of care for infants. *How might this practice affect attachment?*

**Caregiving Styles and Attachment**   Is the style of caregiving linked with the quality of the infant's attachment? Securely attached babies have caregivers who are sensitive to their signals and are consistently available to respond to their infants' needs (Bigelow & others, 2010; Jin & others, 2012). These caregivers often let their babies have an active part in determining the onset and pacing of interaction in the first year of life. Maternal sensitivity in parenting is related to secure attachment in infants in Canada, the United States and Colombia (Carbonell & others, 2002; Moran & others, 2008). Although maternal sensitivity is positively linked to the development of secure attachment in infancy, it is important to note that the link is not especially strong (Campos, 2009).

How do the caregivers of insecurely attached babies interact with them? Caregivers of avoidant babies tend to be unavailable or rejecting (Posada & Kaloustian 2010). They often don't respond to their babies' signals and have little physical contact with them. When they do interact with their babies, they may behave in an angry and irritable way. Caregivers of resistant babies tend to be inconsistent; sometimes they respond to their babies' needs, and sometimes they don't. In general, they tend not to be very affectionate with their babies and show little synchrony when interacting with them. Using the Strange Situation, Canadian researcher Greg Moran and his colleagues observed that mothers of disorganized infants demonstrated atypical and fearful behaviour (Moran & others, 2008). Indeed, caregivers of disorganized babies often neglect or physically abuse them (Bohlin & others, 2012; Cicchetti, 2013). In some cases, these caregivers are depressed (Thompson, 2008). In sum, caregivers' interactions with infants influence whether the infants are securely or insecurely attached to them (Stroufe, Coffino, & Carlson, 2010).

Do changes in the caregiving relationship overtime affect the stability of attachment patterns? A study by Ellen Moss and her colleagues at the University of Quebec at Montreal found that 44 percent to 72 percent of children's attachment patterns remained stable over two years. However, some children shifted from secure to insecure attachment patterns following dramatic changes in the quality of the mother-child interaction, low marital satisfaction, and significant family events such as the death or hospitalization of a caregiver (Moss & others, 2005).

So far in our discussion of attachment, we have focused on the importance of secure attachment in infancy and the role of sensitive parenting in attachment (Berlin, 2012; Bretherton, 2012; Thompson, 2013a). The attachment process continues to be an important aspect of children's development in the childhood years. In middle and late childhood, attachment becomes more sophisticated and as children's social worlds expand to include peers, teachers, and others, they typically spend less time with parents.

Kathryn Kerns and her colleagues (Brumariu, Kerns, & Siebert, 2012; Kerns & Siebert, 2012; Kerns, Siener, & Brumariu, 2011; Siener & Kerns, 2012) have studied links between attachment to parents and various child outcomes in the middle and late childhood years. They have found that during this period of development, secure attachment is associated with a lower level of internalized symptoms, anxiety, and depression in children (Brumariu & Kerns, 2010). For example, a recent study revealed that children who were less securely attached to their mother reported having more anxiety (Brumariu, Kerns, & Seibert, 2012). Also in this study, secure attachment was linked to a higher level of children's emotional regulation and less difficulty in identifying emotions.

### Developmental Social Neuroscience and Attachment
In Chapter 1, we described the emerging field of developmental social neuroscience that examines connections between socioemotional processes, development, and the brain (Singer, 2012). Attachment is one of the main areas in which theory and research on developmental social neuroscience has focused. These connections of attachment and the brain involve the neuroanatomy of the brain, neurotransmitters, and hormones.

Theory and research on the role of the brain's regions in mother-infant attachment is just emerging (De Haan & Gunnar, 2009). One theoretical view proposed that the prefrontal cortex likely has an important role in maternal attachment behaviour, as do the subcortical (areas of the brain lower than the cortex) regions of the amygdala (which is strongly involved in emotion) and the hypothalamus (Gonzalez, Atkinson, & Fleming, 2009). An ongoing fMRI longitudinal study is exploring the possibility that different attachment patterns can be distinguished by different patterns of brain activity (Strathearn, 2007, 2011).

Research on the role of hormones and neurotransmitters in attachment has emphasized the importance of two neuropeptide hormones—oxytocin and vasopressin—in the formation of the maternal-infant bond (Strathearn & others, 2012). Oxytocin, a mammalian hormone that also acts as a neurotransmitter in the brain, is released during breastfeeding and by contact and warmth (Ebstein & others, 2012). Oxytocin is especially thought to be a likely candidate in the formation of infant-mother attachment (Feldman, 2012). A recent research review concluded that strong links exist between levels or patterns of oxytocin and mother-infant attachment (Galbally & others, 2011).

The influence of these neuropeptides on the neurotransmitter dopamine in the nucleus accumbens (a collection of neurons in the forebrain that are involved in pleasure) likely is important in motivating approach to the attachment object (de Haan & Gunnar, 2009). Figure 10.10 shows the regions of the brain we have described that are likely to be important in infant-mother attachment.

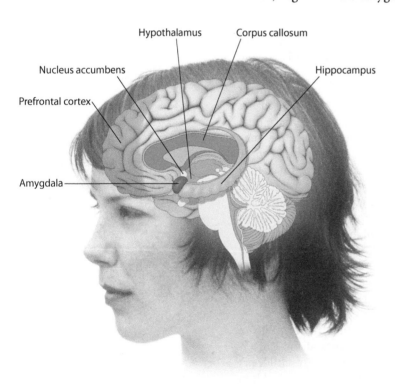

## FIGURE **10.10**

**REGIONS OF THE BRAIN PROPOSED AS LIKELY IMPORTANT IN INFANT-MOTHER ATTACHMENT.** This illustration shows the brain's left hemisphere. The corpus collosum is the large bundle of axons that connect the brain's two hemispheres.

# FATHERS AND MOTHERS AS CAREGIVERS

Much of our discussion of attachment has focused on mothers as caregivers. Do mothers and fathers differ in their caregiving roles?

On average, Canadian mothers spend considerably more time in caregiving with infants and children than do fathers. One recent study found that among Canadian families with a preschool child, one-third of parents shared caregiving responsibilities equally (Ornstein & Stalker, 2013). The study also found that mothers were the primary caregivers in three out of five families compared to only a few percent of families where fathers were the primary caregivers.

Can fathers take care of infants as competently as mothers can? Observations of fathers and their infants suggest that fathers have the ability to act as sensitively and responsively as mothers with their infants (Parke & Buriel, 2006; Parke & Clarke-Stewart, 2011; Shaw, 2013). Fathers play an important role in their children's lives. For example, a recent study found that infants who showed a higher level of externalizing, disruptive problems at 1 year of age had fathers who displayed a low level of engagement with their infants as early as the third month of life (Ramchandani & others, 2013). Another study revealed that fathers with a university-level education engaged in more stimulating physical activities with their infants and that fathers in a conflicting couple relationship participated in less caregiving and physical play with their infants (Cabrera, Hofferth, & Chae, 2011).

Consider the Aka pygmy culture in Africa where fathers spend as much time interacting with their infants as do their mothers (Hewlett, 1991, 2000; Hewlett & MacFarlan, 2010). Remember, however, that although fathers can be active, nurturant, involved caregivers with their infants as Aka pygmy fathers are, in many cultures men have not chosen to follow this pattern (Lamb & Lewis, 2013). Also, if fathers have mental health problems, they may not interact as effectively with their infants. For example, a recent study revealed that depressed fathers focused more on their own needs than their infants' needs and that they directed more negative and critical speech toward their infant (Sethna, Murray, & Ramchandani, 2012).

Do fathers behave differently from mothers with their infants? Maternal interactions usually centre on child-care activities—feeding, changing diapers, and bathing. Mothers especially are more likely to engage in the managerial role with their children, coordinating their activities, making sure their health care needs are fulfilled, and so on (Parke & Buriel, 2006). Paternal interactions are more likely to include play (Lamb & Lewis, 2013; Parke & Clarke-Stewart, 2011). Fathers engage in more rough-and-tumble play. They bounce infants, throw them up in the air, tickle them, and so on. Mothers do play with their infants, but their play is less physical and arousing than that of fathers.

In one study, fathers were interviewed about their caregiving responsibilities when their children were 6, 15, 24, and 36 months of age (NICHD Early Child Care Research Network, 2000). Some of the fathers were videotaped while playing with their children at 6 and 36 months. Fathers were more involved in caregiving—bathing, feeding, dressing the child, taking the child to child care, and so on—when they worked fewer hours and mothers worked more hours, when mothers and fathers were younger, when mothers reported greater marital intimacy, and when the children were boys.

Do children benefit when fathers are positively involved in their caregiving? One study of more than 7,000 children who were assessed from infancy to adulthood revealed that those whose fathers were extensively involved in their lives (such as engaging in various activities with them and showing a strong interest in their education) were more successful in school (Flouri & Buchanan, 2004).

An Aka pygmy father with his infant son. In the Aka culture, fathers were observed to be holding or near their infants 47 percent of the time (Hewlett, 1991).

**Parental Leave**   The Canadian federal and provincial/territorial governments have parental leave policies. According to the *Employment Insurance Act*, parents of a newborn or adopted child can divide 35 weeks of partially-paid parental leave, in addition to 15 weeks of maternity leave (Marshall, 2008). However, parents who are self-employed or have not worked for 600 hours in the past 52 weeks are not eligible for these provisions. Employment Insurance, a federal government program, can assist parents during their leave. In addition, some employers contribute to the government benefits when employees take maternity or parental leave. For the 20 percent of mothers who received top-up payments from their employers, the average length of parental leave was 48 weeks in 2008, compared to 46 weeks for mothers without top-up provisions, and 34 weeks for those with no benefits (Marshall, 2010). Under the Quebec provincial government Parental Insurance Plan introduced in 2006, mothers, including those who are self-employed, may take 18 weeks maternity leave at up to 70 percent wages. Parental leave is available, with 32 weeks for birth parents and 37 weeks for adoptive parents. In Canadian provinces and territories outside of Quebec, parental benefits only cover 55 percent of weekly earnings, so lower-income mothers tend to return to work earlier than higher-income mothers (Marshall, 2003). More fathers today are choosing to take parental leave than in the past. One in five fathers choose to take a portion or all of the parental leave benefits available to them. However, Canadian fathers residing in Quebec are nearly five times more likely to take advantage of the parental leave benefits than those residing in other provinces/territories (Marshall, 2008). As described in *Connecting with Diversity*, many countries provide extensive parental leave policies.

## Parental Leave Policies Around the World

Parental leave policies around the world vary (O'Brien & Moss, 2010; Tolani & Brooks-Gunn, 2008). Europe led the way in creating new standards of parental leave: The European Union (EU) mandated a paid 14-week maternity leave in 1992. In most European countries today, working parents on leave receive from 70 to 100 percent of their prior wage, and paid leave averages about 16 weeks (Tolani & Brooks-Gunn, 2008). The United States currently allows up to 12 weeks of unpaid leave for caring for a newborn.

Most countries restrict eligible benefits to women employed for a minimum time prior to childbirth. In Denmark, even unemployed mothers are eligible for extended parental leave related to childbirth. In Germany, child-rearing leave is available to almost all parents. The Nordic countries (Denmark, Norway, and Sweden) have extensive gender-equity family leave policies for childbirth that emphasize the contributions of both women and men (O'Brien & Moss, 2010; Tolani & Brooks-Gunn, 2008). For example, in Sweden, parents can take an 18-month job-protected parental leave with benefits allowed to be shared by parents and applied to full-time or part-time work.

Scandinavian fathers are much more likely to take parental leave than fathers in Canada. Around 90 percent of fathers from Norway and Sweden have used or plan to use parental leave benefits compared to 48 percent of fathers from Quebec and 10 percent of Canadian fathers from outside of Quebec (Marshall, 2008).

*Why might Canadian fathers be less likely to take time off of work to care for their young children than fathers in Scandinavian countries?*

*How are child care policies in many European countries, such as Sweden, different from those in Canada?*

# CHILD CARE

Many North American children today experience multiple caregivers. Most do not have a parent staying home to care for them; instead, the children have some type of care provided by others—"child care." Many parents worry that child care will reduce their infants' emotional attachment to them, delay infants' cognitive development, fail to teach them how to control anger, and allow them to be unduly influenced by their peers. How extensive is the use of child care? Are the worries of these parents justified?

**Child Care in Canada**   The options and requirements for non-parental child care vary in Canada. One option is child care provided in a regulated facility which must meet provincial standards. In 2007, there were 837,923 regulated child care facilities in Canada (Beach & others, 2009). This works out to less than one space for every four children under the age of twelve. The minimum educational requirements for full-time staff at these facilities vary across Canada from no training required in the Northwest Territories and Nunavut, to a one-year Early Childhood Education (ECE) certificate in Saskatchewan (for at least 30 percent of staff), Newfoundland, and Alberta, to a two-year ECE diploma in Ontario.

A high staff-child ratio and small group sizes for child care facilities are important to the quality of child care. Recommendations by Canadian researcher Beach and colleagues (1998) range from a staff-child ratio of 1:3 and maximum group size of 6 for children under the age of 1 year old, to a staff-child ratio of 1:9 and maximum group size of 18 for children between the ages of 4 through 6 years old. Although provincial and territorial requirements regarding adult-child ratios are similar to those suggested by Beach and colleagues, there are differences in the maximum group size allowed across Canada. For example, the maximum group size for infants in Nova Scotia is 10 compared to 6 for infants in Manitoba. Child care can also be provided in private homes by relatives or non-relatives. Requirements for child care providers in private homes varies by province and territory. Licencing is required for home-based child care providers with as few as 3 or more children under their care in British Columbia to as many as 9 or more children in Saskatchewan. Nearly 70 percent of Canadian children with two working parents or one working single parent were cared for by a relative, an in-home caregiver, or an unregulated child care provider (Beach & others, 2009).

In Canada, there is no single system of child care. Provinces and territories are primarily responsible for child care services. Each province and territory has its own child care program that falls under provincial and territorial Acts regulating staff-child ratios, maximum group size, staff educational requirements, and other conditions about the physical environment and program. Would Canadian families benefit from a single, coherent nationwide child care system? To explore this controversial question, see *Connecting to Current Controversy*.

**Effects of Child Care**   About 80 percent of Canadian children under the age of four years whose mother works out of the home or is completing post-secondary education are involved in some form of child care (Beach & others, 2009). Many factors influence the effects of child care, including the time spent in child care and the quality of the program.

The number of child care arrangements impact the well-being of children. For example, a study of 2- and 3-year-old children revealed that an increase in the number of child care arrangements the children experienced was linked to an increase in behavioural problems and a decrease in prosocial behaviour (Morrissey, 2009). The quantity of child care predicts some child outcomes. In a study by Ramey (2005), children who spent extensive amounts of time in child care beginning in infancy experienced less sensitive interactions with their

## Would Canadian Families Benefit from a Nation-wide Child Care System?

Clyde Hertzman of the Human Early Learning Partnership (HELP) at the University of British Columbia has demonstrated that social investment in early childhood services is linked to improved outcomes in health and well-being over the lifespan (Hertzman & others, 2010). Nevertheless, in 2005, Canada spent considerably less on child care and early educational services for children under the age of six years compared to other countries, including the United States and Denmark, and ranked second to last among the Organisation for Economic Cooperation and Development (OECD) nations in terms of public services for children under six (OECD, 2005). In OECD's 2007 assessment, Canada placed 21 out of 29 countries for "over-all child well-being." The United Nations Children's Fund placed Canada 26th out of 26 countries, given we had only reached one of ten "benchmarks" on early learning and care (Hertzman, 2009). According to Keon (2009), the Canadian Senate is exploring what countries are doing and making recommendations to Parliament to study and advance the provision of universal child development services in Canada. Some argue that Sweden may be a good role model for Canada, as Sweden met all ten of the OECD's benchmarks. Sweden's national child care system extends from prenatal care through the early school years (Hertzman, 2009). Is such a system possible in Canada?

In Quebec, families have universal access to public child care, which costs seven dollars per day. However, outside of Quebec, provision of child care services is not readily accessible to all families and tends to be inadequate and expensive. In 2010, the average cost for a year of full-time child care for a 2-year-old ranged from $1,820 in Quebec to $10,199.80 in British Columbia (Canadian Child Care Federation, 2013). Some Canadian politicians and child care advocates argue that child care is a women's rights issue and suggest that low-income mothers have government subsidized access to child care (Hallgrimsdottir & others, 2013). For the most part, parents outside of Quebec are responsible for the costs of child care, yet many families cannot afford regulated child care. Fee subsidies do exist for low-income parents, but there are not enough subsidies available for all low-income families. Subsidies cover some or all of the parent fee, but do not fund the child care program itself. Recognizing that a considerable number of Canadian families are in need of support for child care services, the federal government introduced the Universal Child Care Benefit in 2006, which pays every parent of a child under six years old one hundred dollars per month per child, regardless of whether parents are engaged in the labour market. Although helpful, this benefit covers only a fraction of the cost for full-time child care.

Is a universally accessible, affordable, and unified child care system possible (and necessary) for Canada? Such an initiative would likely cost taxpayers more money, but some believe the benefits to the Canadian population would outweigh the costs by resulting in a better-educated and healthier society (Hertzman & others, 2010).

What are some benefits and drawbacks of a nation-wide child care system with universal access for Canadians?

mother, showed more behaviour problems, and had higher rates of illness. Many of these comparisons involved children in child care for less than 30 hours a week versus those in child care for more than 45 hours a week. In general, though, when children spent 30 hours or more per week in child care, their development was less than optimal.

Child care quality also makes a difference. What constitutes a high-quality child care program for infants? In high-quality child care (Clarke-Stewart & Miner, 2008, p. 273),

> . . . caregivers encourage the children to be actively engaged in a variety of activities, have frequent, positive interactions that include smiling, touching, holding, and speaking at the child's eye level, respond properly to the child's questions or requests, and encourage children to talk about their experiences, feelings, and ideas.

High-quality child care also involves providing children with a safe environment, access to age-appropriate toys and participation in age-appropriate activities, and a low caregiver-to-child ratio that allows caregivers to spend considerable time with children on an individual basis.

According to an extensive longitudinal study of child care experiences in the United States, quality of child care has a significant impact on child development (NICHD Early Child Care Network, 2001, 2002, 2003, 2004, 2005, 2006, 2010). When quality of caregivers' care was high, children performed better on cognitive and language tasks, were more cooperative with their mothers during play, showed more positive and skilled interaction with peers, and had fewer behaviour problems. Caregiver training and good child-staff ratios were linked with higher cognitive and social competence when children were 54 months of age. Higher-quality child care was also related to higher-quality mother-child interaction among the families that used non-maternal care. However, positive caregiving by non-parents in child-care settings was infrequent—only 12 percent of the children studied experienced positive non-parental child care (such as positive talk, lack of detachment or flat affect, and language stimulation). Further, poor-quality care was related to an increase of insecure attachment to the mother among infants who were 15 months of age, but only when the mother was low in sensitivity and responsiveness. However, child care quality was not linked to attachment security at 36 months of age. A study by researchers at the Université de Montréal also examined links between child care quality and children's emotional development. The researchers found that children in low-quality child care had a heightened level of cortisol, indicating an increased level of stress (Geoffroy & others, 2006).

Children are more likely to experience poor-quality child care if they come from families with few resources (psychological, social, and economic) (Cabrera, Hutchens, & Peters, 2006). Many researchers have examined the role of poverty in quality of child care (Lucas & others, 2008). One study found that extensive child care was harmful to low-income children only when the care was of low quality (Votruba-Drzal, Coley, & Chase-Lansdale, 2004). Even if the child was in child care more than 45 hours a week, high-quality care was linked with fewer internalizing problems (anxiety, for example) and externalizing problems (aggressive and destructive behaviours, for example). Children from low-income families benefit in terms of school readiness and language development when their parents select higher-quality child care (McCartney & others, 2007).

Fortunately, the positive effects parents and families can have on children are not weakened by extensive child care. Results from the NICHD study consistently showed family factors are considerably stronger and more consistent predictors of a wide variety of child outcomes than are child-care experiences (quality, quantity, type). The worst outcomes for children occur when both home and child care settings are of poor quality. For example, a recent study revealed that worse socioemotional outcomes (more problem behaviour, low level of prosocial behaviour) for children occurred when they experienced both home and child care environments that conferred risk (Watamura & others, 2011).

**Review**

- What characterizes the early development of social orientation and social understanding?
- How does attachment develop in infancy?
- How do mothers and fathers interact with infants?
- What is the nature of child care?

*Connect*

- In this section, you learned that maternal sensitive responding was linked (if not strongly) to security of infant attachment. What did you learn about maternal sensitivity and children's language development in the *Connecting Through Research* interlude in Chapter 9?

**Reflect** *Your Own Personal Journey of Life*

- Imagine that a friend of yours is getting ready to put her baby in child care. What advice would you give to her? Do you think she should stay home with the baby? Why or why not? What type of child care would you recommend?

# case study **connections**

1. Consider the chapter-opening story about Matthieu and his father. How has his father influenced Matthieu's temperament?

2. In the chapter-opening vignette, you read about Matthieu and his father. How do you think Matthieu's attachment to his father may affect Matthieu's development?

3. Consider the chapter-opening story about Matthieu and his father. In what Canadian province or territory do you expect Matthieu and his family to reside? What information from this chapter supports your answer?

# reach your **learning goals**

# Emotional Development

## Exploring Emotion

**L01** Discuss basic aspects of emotion.

What Are Emotions?

- Emotion is feeling, or affect, that occurs when people are engaged in interactions that are important to them, especially those that influence their well-being. Emotions can be classified as positive or negative. Darwin described the evolutionary basis of emotions, and today psychologists stress that emotions, especially facial expressions of emotions, have a biological foundation. Facial expressions of emotion are similar across cultures, but display rules are not culturally universal. Biological evolution endowed humans to be emotional, but culture and relationships with others provide diversity in emotional experiences.

A Functionalist View of Emotions

- The functionalist view of emotion emphasizes the importance of contexts and relationships in emotion. For example, when parents induce a positive mood in their child, the child is more likely to follow the parents' directions. In this view, goals are involved in emotions in a variety of ways, and the goal's specific nature can affect the individual's experience of a given emotion.

| Emotional Competence |
| --- |

- Saarni argues that becoming emotionally competent involves developing a number of skills such as being aware of one's emotional states, discerning others' emotions, adaptively coping with negative emotions, and understanding the role of emotions in relationships. Emotional competence is shaped both in the home and at school.

## Development of Emotion

 Describe the development of emotion.

| Infancy |
| --- |

- Infants display a number of emotions early in their development, although researchers debate the onset and sequence of these emotions. Lewis distinguishes between primary emotions and self-conscious emotions. Primary emotions include joy, anger, and fear, while self-conscious emotions include pride, shame, and guilt. Crying is the most important mechanism newborns have for communicating with their world. Babies have at least three types of cries—basic, anger, and pain cries. Social smiling in response to a caregiver's voice occurs as early as 4 to 6 weeks of age. Two fears that infants develop are stranger anxiety and separation from a caregiver (which is reflected in separation protest). Controversy swirls about whether babies should be soothed when they cry, although increasingly experts recommend immediately responding in a caring way during the first year. Infants gradually develop an ability to inhibit the duration and intensity of their emotional reactions.

| Early Childhood |
| --- |

- Advances in young children's emotions involve expressing emotions, understanding emotions, and regulating emotions. Young children's range of emotions expands during early childhood as they increasingly experience self-conscious emotions such as pride, shame, and guilt. Between 2 and 4 years old, children use an increasing number of terms to describe emotion and learn more about the causes and consequences of feelings. At 4 to 5 years of age, children show an increased ability to reflect on emotions and understand that a single event can elicit different emotions in different people. They also show a growing awareness of the need to manage emotions to meet social standards. Emotion-coaching parents have children who engage in more effective self-regulation of their emotions than do emotion-dismissing parents. Young children in a secure attachment relationship with their mother are more willing to engage in conversation about difficult emotional circumstances. Emotional regulation plays an important role in successful peer relations.

| Middle and Late Childhood |
| --- |

- In middle and late childhood, children show a growing awareness about controlling and managing emotions to meet social standards. Also in this age period, they show improved emotional understanding, markedly improve their ability to suppress or conceal negative emotions, use self-initiated strategies for redirecting feelings, have an increased tendency to take into fuller account the events that lead to emotional reactions, and develop a capacity for genuine empathy.

## Temperament

 Characterize variations in temperament and their significance.

| Describing and Classifying Temperament |
| --- |

- Temperament involves individual differences in behavioural styles, emotions, and characteristic ways of responding. Developmentalists are especially interested in the temperament of infants. Chess and Thomas classified infants as (1) easy, (2) difficult, or (3) slow to warm up. Kagan argues that inhibition to the unfamiliar is an important temperament category. Rothbart and Bates' view of temperament emphasizes the following classification: (1) extraversion/surgency, (2) negative affectivity, and (3) effortful control (self-regulation).

| Biological Foundations and Experience |
| --- |

- Physiological characteristics are associated with different temperaments, and a moderate influence of heredity has been found in twin and adoption studies of the heritability of temperament. Children inherit a physiology that biases them to have a particular type of temperament, but through experience they learn to modify their temperament style to some degree. Very active young children are likely to become outgoing adults. In some cases, a difficult temperament is linked with adjustment problems in early adulthood. The link between childhood temperament and adult personality depends in part on context, which helps shape the reaction to a child and thus the child's experiences. For example, the reaction to a child's temperament depends in part on the child's gender and on the culture.

**Goodness of Fit and Parenting**

- Goodness of fit refers to the match between a child's temperament and the environmental demands the child must cope with. Goodness of fit can be an important aspect of a child's adjustment.

## Social Orientation/Understanding, Attachment, and Child Care

 **L04** Explain the early development of social orientation/ understanding, attachment, and child care.

**Social Orientation/ Understanding**

- Infants show a strong interest in their social world and are motivated to understand it. Infants orient to their social world early in their development. Face-to-face play with a caregiver begins to occur at 2 to 3 months of age. Newly developed self-produced locomotion skills significantly expand the infant's ability to initiate social interchanges and explore their social world more independently. Perceiving people as engaging in intentional and goal-directed behaviour is an important social cognitive accomplishment, and this occurs toward the end of the first year. Social referencing increases in the second year of life.

**Attachment**

- Attachment is a close emotional bond between two people. In infancy, contact comfort and trust are important in the development of attachment. Bowlby's ethological theory stresses that the caregiver and the infant are biologically predisposed to form an attachment. Attachment develops in four phases during infancy. Securely attached babies use the caregiver, usually the mother, as a secure base from which to explore the environment. Three types of insecure attachment are avoidant, resistant, and disorganized. Ainsworth created the Strange Situation, an observational measure of attachment. Ainsworth points out that secure attachment in the first year of life provides an important foundation for psychological development later in life. The strength of the link between early attachment and later development has varied somewhat across studies. Some critics argue that attachment theorists have not given adequate attention to genetics and temperament. Other critics stress that they have not adequately taken into account the diversity of social agents and contexts. Cultural variations in attachment have been found, but in all cultures studied to date, secure attachment is the most common classification. Caregivers of secure babies are sensitive to the babies' signals and are consistently available to meet their needs. Caregivers of avoidant babies tend to be unavailable or rejecting. Caregivers of resistant babies tend to be inconsistently available to their babies and usually are not very affectionate. Caregivers of disorganized babies often neglect or physically abuse their babies. Increased interest has been directed toward the role of the brain in the development of attachment. The hormone oxytocin is a key candidate for influencing the development of maternal-infant attachment.

**Fathers and Mothers as Caregivers**

- In recent years fathers have increased the amount of time they interact with infants, but mothers still spend considerably more time in caregiving with infants than do fathers. The mother's primary role when interacting with the infant is caregiving; the father's is playful interaction.

**Child Care**

- Increasingly more Canadian children are in non-parental child care. The quality and accessibility of child care is uneven, and child care remains a controversial topic. Spending excessive amount of time in child care that is of low quality can have adverse effects such as increased stress for children. Higher quality child care is linked with positive child outcomes including social and cognitive competence and higher-quality mother-child interaction.

# The Self and Identity | chapter 11

Raymond Montemayor and Marvin Eisen (1977) discovered a great deal about how children and adolescents understand the notions of self and identity. They asked students in grades 4 through 12 to write 20 different answers to the question "Who am I?" Some of their answers are below.

*9-year-old: My name is Bruce C. I have brown eyes. I have brown hair . . . I'm 9 years old . . . I have 7 people in my family . . . I have lots of friends! I live at 1923 Pinecrest Drive. I have an uncle who is almost 7 feet tall. My teacher is Mrs. V. I play hockey! I'm almost the smartest boy in the class. I LOVE food! , . . I LOVE school!*

*11½-year-old: My name is A. I'm a human being . . . a girl . . . a truthful person. I'm not pretty. I do so-so in my studies. I'm a very good cellist. I'm a little bit tall for my age. I like several boys . . . I am a very good swimmer . . . I try to be helpful . . . Mostly I'm good, but I lose my temper. I'm not well-liked by some girls and boys.*

*17-year-old: I am a human being . . . a girl . . . an individual . . . I don't know who I am. I am a Pisces. I am a moody person . . . an indecisive person . . . an ambitious person . . . a very curious person. I am not an individual. I am a loner. I am an atheist. I am not a classifiable person.* (Montemayor & Eisen, 1977; pp. 317–318)

The self-descriptions provided by children and adolescents in Montemayor and Eisen's (1977) classic study reflect important aspects of each of our lives as we grow up: our efforts to understand ourselves and to develop an identity. This chapter is about the self and identity. As we examine these topics, reflect on how well you understood yourself at different points in your life as you were growing up, and think about how you acquired the stamp of your identity.

## Self-Understanding and Understanding Others LO1 Discuss the development of self-understanding and understanding others.

Self-Understanding    Understanding Others

The **self** consists of all of the characteristics of a person. Theorists and researchers who focus on the self usually argue that the self is the central aspect of the individual's personality and that the self lends an integrative dimension to our understanding of different personality characteristics (Harter, 2012; Rochat, 2013). Several aspects of the self have been studied more than others. These include self-understanding, self-esteem, and self-concept.

Recent research studies have revealed that young children are more psychologically aware of themselves and others than previously thought (Thompson, 2013b, c). This awareness reflects young children's expanding psychological sophistication.

**self** All of the characteristics of a person.

## SELF-UNDERSTANDING

**Self-understanding** is a child's cognitive representation of the self—the substance and content of the child's self-conceptions. For example, an 11-year-old boy understands that he is a student, a boy, a golfer, a family member, a nature lover, and a rock music fan. A 13-year-old girl understands that she is a middle school student, in the midst of puberty, a girl, a hockey player, a student council member, and a movie fan. A child's self-understanding is based, in part, on the various roles and membership categories that define who children are (Harter, 2006, 2012). Though not the whole of personal identity, self-understanding provides its rational underpinnings.

**self-understanding** A child's cognitive representation of the self—the substance and content of a child's self-conceptions.

**Developmental Changes**    Children are not just given a self by their parents or culture; rather, they construct selves. As children develop, their self-understanding changes.

*Infancy*    According to Ross Thompson (2007), studying the self in infancy is difficult mainly because infants cannot tell us how they experience themselves. Infants cannot verbally express their views of the self. They also cannot understand complex instructions from researchers.

A rudimentary form of self-recognition—being attentive and positive toward one's image in a mirror—appears as early as 3 months of age (Mascolo & Fischer, 2007; Pipp, Fischer, & Jennings, 1987). However, a central, more complete index of self-recognition—the ability to recognize one's physical features—does not emerge until around the second year (Thompson, 2006).

One ingenious strategy to test infants' visual self-recognition is the use of a mirror technique, in which an infant's mother first plays with her child in

When I say "I," I mean something absolutely unique, not to be confused with any other.

—UGO BETTI
*Italian Playwright, 20th Century*

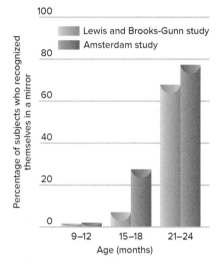

## FIGURE 11.1

**THE DEVELOPMENT OF SELF-RECOGNITION IN INFANCY.** The graph shows the findings of two studies in which infants less than 1 year of age did not recognize themselves in the mirror. A slight increase in the percentage of infant self-recognition occurred around 15 to 18 months of age. By 2 years of age, a majority of children recognized themselves. *Do you agree that the mirror self-recognition task is an accurate indicator of self-recognition? How else might researchers study self-recognition in infancy?*

front of a mirror. After the infant has looked at herself in the mirror several times, the mother pretends to wipe off the infant's nose and puts a dot of rouge on the infant's nose. Then an observer watches to see how often the infant touches her nose with the mirror out of sight. Next, the infant is placed in front of the mirror again, and observers detect whether nose touching increases. Why does this matter? The idea is that increased nose touching indicates that the infant recognizes herself in the mirror and is trying to touch or rub off the rouge because the rouge violates what the infant knows to be true about her own body.

Figure 11.1 displays the results of two investigations that used the mirror technique. The researchers found that before they were 1 year old, infants did not recognize themselves in the mirror (Amsterdam, 1968; Lewis & Brooks-Gunn, 1979). Signs of self-recognition began to appear among some infants when they were 15 to 18 months old. By the time they were 2 years old, most children recognized themselves in the mirror. In sum, infants begin to develop a self-understanding called *self-recognition* at approximately 18 months of age (Hart & Karmel, 1996; Lewis & others, 1989).

Researchers at Memorial University and Lakehead University have found that self-recognition gradually emerges from 15 to 23 months of age (Courage, Edison, & Howe, 2004). In their study, self-recognition first appeared in the form of mirror recognition, followed by saying their own name and then by recognizing a photo of themselves. These aspects of self-recognition are often referred to as the first indications of toddlers' understanding of the mental state of *me*, "that they are objects in their own mental representation of the world" (Lewis, 2005, p. 363).

Mirrors are not familiar to infants in all cultures (Rogoff, 2003). Thus, physical self-recognition may be a more important marker of self-recognition in Western than non-Western cultures (Thompson & Virmani, 2010). Supporting this cultural variation view, one study revealed that 18- to 20-month-old toddlers from urban middle socioceconomic status (SES) German families were more likely to recognize their mirror images than were toddlers from rural Cameroon farming families.

Late in the second year and early in the third year, toddlers show other emerging forms of self-awareness that reflect a sense of *me* (Laible & Thompson, 2007). For example, they refer to themselves by saying "Me big"; they label internal experiences such as emotions; they monitor themselves, as when a toddler says, "Do it myself"; and they say that things are theirs (Bullock & Lutkenhaus, 1990; Fasig, 2000). According to one study of Canadian infants, it is not until the second year that they develop an awareness of their own bodies (Moore & others, 2007). This developmental change in body awareness marks the beginning of children's representation of their own three-dimensional body shape and appearance, providing an early step in the development of their self-image and identity (Brownell, 2009). To learn more about the development of self-understanding in infancy, see *Connecting Through Research*.

*Early Childhood*   Because children can communicate verbally, research on self-understanding in childhood is not limited to visual self-recognition, as it is during infancy (Harter, 2012). Mainly through interviews, researchers have probed many aspects of children's self-understanding (Carpendale & Lewis, 2011; Thompson, 2013b, c). Here are five main characteristics of self-understanding in young children:

- *Confusion of self, mind, and body.* Young children generally confuse self, mind, and body. Most young children conceive of the self as part of the body, which usually means the head. For them, the self can be described along many material dimensions, such as size, shape, and colour.
- *Concrete descriptions.* Preschool children mainly think of themselves and define themselves in concrete terms. A young child might say, "I know my

## How Do Self- and Other-Awareness Help Infants Learn by Observing Adults?

Self-awareness and the awareness of others emerge together during the mid-to-latter part of the second year of life. An infant's understanding of self and others is a necessary first step in acquiring more complex skills, including third-party learning, where the infant is able to imitate another person's behaviour even if that person is not directly interacting with the infant (Moore, 2007). According to Chris Moore (2007) at Dalhousie University, imitative third-party learning is possible because self- and other-awareness enables an infant to imagine him/herself in the place of another person and successfully interpret information demonstrated by that person.

A recent study by Matheson, Moore, and Akhtar (2013, p. 166) explored self- and other-awareness using a mirror self-recognition task and an imitative third-party learning task. Infants observed a female experimenter while sitting on their caregiver's lap. As if talking to herself, the experimenter said, "I found a new toy I think I want to play with." The experimenter looked at a doorbell and said, "I think I am going to see how this works, I want to see how this works." Using her elbow, she rang the doorbell. She then said, "Oh, cool, that is how it works. I think I'm going to see one more time how this works."

Once again, the experimenter rang the doorbell with her elbow and repeated the reaction phrase. Next, the experimenter moved aside and the caregiver said, "[Infant's name], can you show me how that works?" The experimenter watched to see if the infant used his or her elbow to ring the doorbell. The procedure was repeated, but instead of ringing a doorbell, infants observed the experimenter illuminate a dome light with her forehead and were tested to see whether they imitated the experimenter's actions. After completing the doorbell and dome light task, infants completed a mirror self-recognition task. The experimenter pretended to wipe dirt from the infant's forehead and placed a round sticker on the forehead. The infant was immediately placed facing a mirror. Infants passed the test, indicating self-recognition, if they touched or removed the sticker. The results from the experiment revealed that only infants who successfully passed the mirror self-recognition task imitated the experimenter's actions and rang the doorbell with their elbow or illuminated the dome light with their forehead.

*How does this research relate to what you learned in Chapter 7 about children's theory of mind?*

---

ABCs," "I can count," and "I live in a big house" (Harter, 2006). Although young children mainly describe themselves in terms of concrete, observable features and action tendencies, at about 4 to 5 years of age, as they hear others use psychological trait and emotion terms, they begin to include these in their own self-descriptions (Thompson, 2006). Thus, in a self-description, a 4-year-old might say, "I'm not scared. I'm always happy."

- *Physical descriptions.* Young children also distinguish themselves from others through many physical and material attributes. Says 4-year-old Sandra, "I'm different from Jennifer because I have brown hair and she has blond hair." Says 4-year-old Ralph, "I am different from Hank because I am taller, and I am different from my sister because I have a bicycle."

- *Active descriptions.* The *active dimension* is a central component of the self in early childhood. For example, preschool children often describe themselves in terms of activities such as play.

- *Unrealistic positive overestimations.* Self-evaluations during early childhood are often unrealistically positive and represent an overestimation of personal attributes (Harter, 2012). These unrealistic positive overestimations of the self occur because young children (1) have difficulty in differentiating their desired and actual competence, (2) cannot yet generate an ideal self that is distinguished from a real self, and (3) rarely engage in *social comparison*—exploring how they compare with others. This overestimation of one's attributes helps to protect young children against negative self-evaluations.

However, as in virtually all areas of children's development, there are individual variations in young children's self-conceptions, and there is increasing evidence that some children are vulnerable to negative self-attributions

The living self has one purpose only: to come into its own fullness of being, as a tree comes into full blossom, or a bird into spring beauty, or a tiger into lustre.

— D. H. LAWRENCE
*English Author, 20th Century*

*What characterizes young children's self-understanding?*

(Thompson, 2011). For example, one study revealed that insecurely attached preschool children whose mothers reported a high level of parenting stress and depressive symptoms had a lower self-concept than other young children in more positive family circumstances (Goodwin & others, 2008). This research indicates that young children's generally optimistic self-ascriptions do not buffer them from adverse, stressful family conditions.

*Middle and Late Childhood* Children's self-evaluation becomes more complex during middle and late childhood. Five key changes characterize the increased complexity:

- *Psychological characteristics and traits.* In middle and late childhood, especially from 8 to 11 years of age, children increasingly describe themselves with psychological characteristics and traits in contrast to the more concrete self-descriptions of younger children. Older children are more likely to describe themselves as *popular, nice, helpful, mean, smart,* and *dumb* (Harter, 2006, 2012). Older children also are less likely than younger children to overestimate their abilities or to cite only virtuous aspects of the self. Rather, they now have the cognitive capabilities to realize that they can be both *nice* and *mean, smart* as well as *dumb.*

- *Social descriptions.* In middle and late childhood, children begin to include *social aspects* such as references to social groups in their self-descriptions (Harter, 2006, 2012; Lively & Bromley, 1973). For example, a child might describe herself as a Girl Guide, as a Catholic, or as someone who has two close friends.

- *Social comparison.* Children's self-understanding in middle and late childhood includes increasing reference to social comparison (Harter, 2006, 2012). At this point in development, children are more likely to distinguish themselves from others in comparative rather than in absolute terms. That is, elementary-school-age children are likely to think about what they can do in comparison with others. If they feel they fall short of others, they are likely to evaluate themselves negatively.

- *Real self and ideal self.* In middle and late childhood, children begin to distinguish between their real and ideal selves (Harter, 2006, 2012). This involves differentiating their actual competencies from those they aspire to have and think are the most important. This discrepancy also can lead to negative self-evaluations.

- *Realistic.* In middle and late childhood, children's self-evaluations become more realistic (Harter, 2006, 2012). This may occur because of increased social comparison and perspective taking.

**Adolescence** The development of self-understanding in adolescence is complex and involves a number of aspects of the self (Harter, 2006, 2012):

- *Abstract and idealistic.* Remember from our discussion of Piaget's theory of cognitive development in Chapter 6 that many adolescents begin to think in more *abstract* and *idealistic* ways. When asked to describe themselves, adolescents are more likely than children to use abstract and idealistic labels. Consider 14-year-old Laurie's abstract description of herself: "I am a human being. I am indecisive. I don't know who I am." Also consider her idealistic description of herself: "I am a naturally sensitive person who really cares about people's feelings. I think I'm pretty good-looking." Not

**developmental connection**

**Cognitive Theory.** In Piaget's fourth stage of cognitive development thought becomes more abstract, idealistic, and logical. Chapter 6, LO 1

all adolescents describe themselves in idealistic ways, but most adolescents distinguish between the real self and the ideal self.

- *Self-consciousness.* Adolescents are more likely than children to be *self-conscious* about and *preoccupied* with their self-understanding. This self-consciousness and self-preoccupation reflect adolescent egocentrism, which we discussed in Chapter 6.

- *Contradictions within the self.* As adolescents begin to differentiate their concept of the self into multiple roles in different relationship contexts, they sense potential contradictions between their differentiated selves (Harter, 2006, 2012). An adolescent might use this self-description: "I'm moody *and* understanding, ugly *and* attractive, bored *and* inquisitive, caring *and* uncaring, and introverted *and* fun-loving" (Harter, 1986). These contradictions characterize the self-descriptions of young adolescents more than older adolescents.

- *The fluctuating self.* The adolescent's self-understanding fluctuates across situations and across time (Harter, 2006, 2012). The adolescent's self continues to be characterized by instability until the adolescent constructs a more unified theory of self, usually not until late adolescence or emerging adulthood.

- *Real and ideal selves.* The adolescent's emerging ability to construct ideal selves in addition to actual ones can be perplexing and agonizing to the adolescent. In one view, an important aspect of the ideal or imagined self is the **possible self**—what individuals might become, what they would like to become, and what they are afraid of becoming (Markus & Kitayama, 2010, 2012). Thus, adolescents' possible selves include what adolescents hope to be as well as what they dread they will become. The attributes of future positive selves (getting into a good university, being admired, having a successful career) can direct future positive states. The attributes of future negative selves (being unemployed, being lonely, not getting into a good university) can identify what is to be avoided.

- *Social comparison.* The tendency to compare themselves with others continues to increase during the adolescent years. However, when asked whether they engage in social comparison, most adolescents deny it because they are aware that it is somewhat socially undesirable to do so. That is, they think that acknowledging their social comparison motives will endanger their popularity. An individual's beliefs about how he or she is viewed by others is referred to as the *looking glass* self.

- *Self-integration.* In late adolescence and emerging adulthood, self-understanding becomes more *integrative*, with the disparate parts of the self more systematically pieced together (Harter, 2006, 2012). Older adolescents are more likely to detect inconsistencies in their earlier self-descriptions as they attempt to construct a general theory of self and an integrated sense of identity.

*How does self-understanding change in adolescence?*

Know thyself, for once we know ourselves, we may learn how to care for ourselves, but otherwise we never shall.

—SOCRATES
*Greek Philosopher, 5th Century BC*

**possible self** What an individual might become, would like to become, and is afraid of becoming.

**social cognition** The processes involved in understanding the world around us, especially how we think and reason about other people.

## UNDERSTANDING OTHERS

According to Jeremy Carpendale at the University of Victoria, young children are more sophisticated than was previously thought at understanding not only themselves, but others (Carpendale & Lewis, 2011). The term **social cognition** refers to the processes involved in understanding the world around us, especially how we think and reason about other people. Developmental psychologists

*What characterizes adolescents' possible selves?*

are increasingly studying how children develop this understanding of others (Mills, 2013; Rubin & others, 2013).

In Chapter 10, "Emotional Development," we described the development of social understanding in infancy. Recall that perceiving people as engaging in intentional and goal-directed behaviour is an important social cognitive accomplishment, and this occurs toward the end of the first year. Social referencing, which involves reading emotional cues in others to help determine how to act in a particular situation, increases in the second year of life. Here we will describe further changes in social understanding that occur during the child and adolescent years.

**developmental connection**

**Attention.** Joint attention and gaze following help the infant to understand that other people have intentions. Chapter 10, LO 4

**Early Childhood**   Children also make advances in their understanding of others in early childhood (Mills, 2013). As we saw in Chapter 7, "Information Processing," young children's theory of mind includes understanding that other people have emotions and desires (Astington & Hughes, 2013; Wellman, 2011). And at about 4 to 5 years, children not only start describing themselves in terms of psychological traits but also begin to perceive others in terms of psychological traits. Thus, a 4-year-old might say, "My teacher is nice."

An important step in children's development is beginning to understand that people don't always give accurate reports of their beliefs (Gee & Heyman, 2007). Kang Lee at the University of Toronto and his colleagues have found that even 4-year-olds understand that people may make untrue statements to obtain what they want or to avoid trouble (Lee & others, 2002). One study also revealed that 4- and 5-year-olds were increasingly skeptical of another child's claim to be sick when the children were informed that the child was motivated to avoid having to go to camp (Gee & Heyman, 2007).

Both the extensive research into theory of mind and the recent research on young children's social understanding underscore that young children are not as egocentric as Piaget envisioned (Sokol, Snjezana, & Muller, 2010; Thompson, 2012). Piaget's concept of egocentrism has become so ingrained in people's thinking about young children that too often the current research on social awareness in infancy and early childhood has been overlooked. Research increasingly shows that young children are more socially sensitive and perceptive than previously envisioned, suggesting that parents and teachers can help them to better understand and interact in the social world by how they interact with them (Thompson, 2013b, c). If young children are seeking to better understand various mental and emotional states (intentions, goals, feelings, desires) that they know underlie people's actions, then talking with them about these internal states can improve young children's understanding of them (Thompson, 2013b, c).

However, debate continues about whether young children are socially sensitive or basically egocentric. Ross Thompson (2012, 2013b, c) comes down on the side of viewing young children as socially sensitive, while Susan Harter (2012) argues that there is still evidence to support the conclusion that young children are essentially egocentric.

Barry Schneider at the University of Ottawa and his colleagues note that another important aspect of understanding others involves understanding joint commitments (Schneider & others, 2011). For example, one study revealed that 3-year-olds, but not 2-year-olds, recognize when an adult is committed and when they themselves are committed to joint activity that involves obligation to a partner (Grafenhain & others, 2009).

Individual differences characterize young children's social understanding (Lewis & Carpendale, 2011). Some young children are better than others at understanding what people are feeling and what they desire, for example. To some degree, these individual differences are linked to conversations caregivers have with young children about other people's feelings and desires, and children's opportunities to observe others talking about people's feelings and desires. For example, a mother might say to a 3-year-old, "You should think about Raphael's feelings next time before you hit him."

To understand others, it is necessary to take their perspective. **Perspective taking** is the social cognitive process involved in assuming the perspective of others and understanding their thoughts and feelings. Executive functioning, discussed in Chapter 7, is at work in perspective taking (Galinsky, 2010). Among the executive functions called on when children engage in perspective taking are cognition inhibition (controlling one's own thoughts to consider the perspective of others) and cognitive flexibility (seeing situations in different ways).

### Middle and Late Childhood
In middle and late childhood, children show an increase in perspective taking. In Robert Selman's view (1980), at about 6 to 8 years of age children begin to understand that others may have differing perspectives because some people have more access to information. Then, he says, in the next several years, children become aware that each individual is aware of the other's perspective and that putting oneself in the other's place is a way of judging the other person's intentions, purposes, and actions.

Perspective taking is thought to be especially important in determining whether children develop prosocial or antisocial attitudes and behaviour. In terms of prosocial behaviour, taking another's perspective improves children's likelihood of understanding and sympathizing with others who are distressed or in need (Eisenberg, Fabes, & Spinrad, 2006). A recent study revealed that in children characterized as being emotionally reactive, perspective-taking skills were linked to being able to regain a neutral emotional state after being emotionally aroused (Bengtsson & Arvidsson, 2011). In this study, children who made gains in perspective-taking skills reduced their emotional reactivity over a two-year period. In terms of antisocial behaviour, children who have low levels of perspective-taking skills engage in more antisocial behaviour than children who have higher levels (Chandler, 1973).

Earlier we indicated that even 4-year-old children show some skepticism of others' claims (Mills, Elashi, & Archacki, 2011). In middle and late childhood, children become increasingly skeptical of some sources of information about psychological traits. For example, in one study, 10- to 11-year-olds were more likely to reject other children's self-reports that they were *smart* and *honest* than were 6- to 7-year-olds (Heyman & Legare, 2005). The more psychologically sophisticated 10- to 11-year-olds also showed a better understanding than the 6- to 7-year-olds that others' self-reports may involve socially desirable tendencies. Elementary-school-aged children also begin to understand other motivations. For example, they understand that a desire to win a prize may tarnish someone's judgment (Mills & Keil, 2005).

### Adolescence
Of course, becoming a competent adolescent involves not only understanding oneself but also understanding others. Among the aspects of understanding others that are important in adolescent development are perspective taking, perceiving others' traits, and social cognitive monitoring.

*Perspective Taking* In Robert Selman's (1980) developmental theory, perspective taking begins with having an egocentric viewpoint in early childhood and ends with using in-depth perspective taking in adolescence. Only recently has research on

Young children are more psychologically aware of themselves and others than previously thought. Some children are better than others at understanding people's feelings and desires—and, to some degree, these individual differences are influenced by conversations caregivers have with young children about feelings and desires.

**perspective taking** The social cognitive process involved in assuming the perspective of others and understanding their thoughts and feelings.

#### developmental connection

**Cognitive Theory.** *Theory of mind* refers to awareness of one's own mental processes and the mental processes of others. Chapter 7, LO 5

*What are some changes in children's understanding of others in middle and late childhood?*

perspective taking in adolescence taken hold. Following are the results of several recent research investigations on this topic:

- Among sixth to eighth graders, girls engaged in more social perspective taking than boys did (Smith & Rose, 2011), and girls also experienced more empathic distress, which involves taking on their friend's distress as their own, than did boys.
- Among ninth to twelfth graders, adolescents assumed a social perspective that was naïve to the disparities that exist between vulnerable and less vulnerable social groups in regard to racism and sexism (Rubenstein, 2012). In this study, twelfth-graders showed more sophisticated social justice understanding than ninth-graders did.
- A lower level of perspective taking was linked to increased relational aggression (such as harming someone by using strategies such as spreading rumours) one year later in middle school students (Batanova & Loukas, 2011).

*Perceiving Others' Traits*   One way to study how adolescents perceive others' traits is to ask them about the extent to which others' self-reports are accurate. In one comparison of 6- and 10-year-olds, the 10-year-olds were much more skeptical about others' self-reports of their intelligence and social skills than the 6-year-olds were (Heyman & Legare, 2005). In this study, the 10-year-olds understood that other people at times may distort the truth about their own traits to make a better impression on others.

As adolescence proceeds, teenagers develop a more sophisticated understanding of others. They come to understand that other people are complex and have public and private faces (Harter, 2006).

*Social Cognitive Monitoring*   In Chapter 7, you read that an important cognitive activity in metacognition is cognitive monitoring, which can also be very helpful in social situations (McCormick, Dimmitt, & Sullivan, 2013). As part of their increased awareness of themselves and others, adolescents monitor their social world more extensively than they did when they were children. Adolescents engage in a number of social cognitive monitoring activities on virtually a daily basis. An adolescent might think, "I would like to get to know this guy better, but he is not very open. Maybe I can talk to some other students about what he is like." Another adolescent might check incoming information about a club or a clique to determine whether it is consistent with her impressions of the club or clique. Yet another adolescent might question someone or paraphrase what the person has just said about her feelings to make sure that he has accurately understood them. Adolescents' ability to monitor their social cognition may be an important aspect of their social maturity (Flavell, 1979).

---

## Review *Connect* Reflect

 **LO1** Discuss the development of self-understanding and understanding others.

### Review

- What is self-understanding? How does self-understanding change from infancy through adolescence?
- How does the understanding of others develop?

### *Connect*

- In this section, you learned that in middle and late childhood, children show an increase in perspective

taking. Which disorder (discussed in Chapter 7) involves children who have difficulty understanding others' beliefs and emotions?

### **Reflect** *Your Own Personal Journey of Life*

- If a psychologist had interviewed you at 10 and at 16 years of age, how would your self-understanding have differed?

| What Are Self-Esteem and Self-Concept? | Assessment | Variations in Self-Esteem |
| --- | --- | --- |

Self-conception involves more than self-understanding. Not only do children try to define and describe attributes of the self (self-understanding), but they also evaluate these attributes. These evaluations create self-esteem and self-concept, and they have far-reaching implications for children's development.

## WHAT ARE SELF-ESTEEM AND SELF-CONCEPT?

Sometimes the terms *self-esteem* and *self-concept* are used interchangeably, or they are not precisely defined (Harter, 2006, 2012). Here we use **self-esteem** to refer to a person's self-worth or self-image, a global evaluation of the self. For example, a child might perceive that she is not merely a person but a good person. (To evaluate your self-esteem, see Figure 11.2.) We use the term **self-concept** to refer to domain-specific evaluations of the self. Children can make self-evaluations in many domains of their lives—academic, athletic, physical appearance, and so on. In sum, self-esteem refers to global self-evaluations, self-concept to more domain-specific evaluations. Having high self-esteem and a positive self-concept are important aspects of children's well-being (Baumeister, 2013; Campbell, 2012).

The foundations of self-esteem and self-concept emerge from the quality of parent-child interaction in infancy and early childhood. Thus, if children have low self-esteem in middle and late childhood, they may have experienced neglect or abuse in relationships with their parents earlier in development. Children with

**self-esteem** The global evaluative dimension of the self; also called self-worth or self-image.

**self-concept** Domain-specific self-evaluations.

---

These items are from a widely used measure of self-esteem, the Rosenberg Scale of Self-Esteem. The items deal with your general feelings about yourself. Place a check mark in the column that best describes your feelings about yourself:
1 = strongly agree, 2 = agree, 3 = disagree, 4 = strongly disagree.

| | 1 | 2 | 3 | 4 |
| --- | --- | --- | --- | --- |
| 1. I feel that I am a person of worth, at least on an equal plane with others. | | | | |
| 2. I feel that I have a number of good qualities. | | | | |
| 3. All in all, I am inclined to feel that I am a failure. | | | | |
| 4. I am able to do things as well as most other people. | | | | |
| 5. I feel I do not have much to be proud of. | | | | |
| 6. I take a positive attitude toward myself. | | | | |
| 7. On the whole, I am satisfied with myself. | | | | |
| 8. I wish I could have more respect for myself. | | | | |
| 9. I certainly feel useless at times. | | | | |
| 10. At times I think I am no good at all. | | | | |

To obtain your self-esteem score, reverse your scores for items 3, 5, 8, 9, and 10. (That is, on item 3 if you gave yourself a 1, instead give yourself a 4.) Add those scores to your scores for items 1, 2, 4, 6, and 7 for your overall self-esteem score. Scores can range from 10 to 40. If you scored below 20, consider contacting the counselling centre at your college or university for help in improving your self-esteem.

FIGURE **11.2**

**EVALUATING SELF-ESTEEM.**

high self-esteem are more likely to be securely attached to their parents and have parents who engage in sensitive caregiving (Thompson, 2011, 2013a, b, c, d).

For most children, high self-esteem and a positive self-concept are important aspects of their well-being (Campbell, 2012). However, for some children, self-esteem reflects perceptions that do not always match reality (Vohs & Baumeister, 2012). A child's self-esteem might reflect a belief about whether he or she is intelligent and attractive, for example, but that belief is not necessarily accurate. Thus, high self-esteem may refer to accurate, justified perceptions of one's worth as a person and one's successes and accomplishments, but it can also refer to an arrogant, grandiose, unwarranted sense of superiority over others. In the same manner, low self-esteem may reflect either an accurate perception of one's shortcomings or a distorted, even pathological insecurity and inferiority.

## ASSESSMENT

Measuring self-esteem and self-concept hasn't always been easy (Dusek & McIntyre, 2003). An example of a useful measure developed to assess self-evaluations by children is Susan Harter's (1985) Self-Perception Profile for Children. It taps general self-worth plus self-concept for five specific domains: scholastic competence, athletic competence, social acceptance, physical appearance, and behavioural conduct.

The Self-Perception Profile for Children is designed to be used with third-grade through sixth-grade children. Harter also developed a separate scale for adolescents, the Self-Perception Profile for Adolescents (Harter, 1989). It assesses global self-worth and the five domains tested for children plus three additional domains—close friendship, romantic appeal, and job competence.

Harter's measures can separate self-evaluations in different domains of one's life. How are these specific self-evaluations related to self-esteem in general? Even children have both a general level of self-esteem and varying levels of self-conceptions in particular domains of their lives (Harter, 1998; Ward, 2004). For example, a child might have a moderately high level of general self-esteem but have varying self-conceptions in specific areas: high in athletic competence, high in social acceptance, high in physical appearance, high in behavioural conduct, but low in scholastic competence.

Self-esteem appears to have an especially strong tie with self-perception in one domain in particular: physical appearance. This association between physical appearance and self-esteem is not confined to adolescence; it holds from early childhood through middle age (Harter, 1999, 2006). Several researchers have found that global self-esteem is correlated more strongly with perceived physical appearance than with scholastic competence, social acceptance, behavioural conduct, or athletic competence (Harter, 2012), but this is not true of all cultures. For example, among Taiwanese children, global self-esteem is correlated with self-perceived physical appearance, yet this correlation is just as strong as the correlations between global self-esteem and both scholastic competence and behavioural conduct (Wu & Smith, 1997). Figure 11.3 shows the correlation between global self-esteem and self-evaluations of physical appearance among children from Canada (Hymel & others, 1999), the United States (Harter, 2012), England (Fox & others, 2009), Portugal (Faria, 2001), and Taiwan (Wu & Smith, 1997). Although the values of the correlations differ across countries, the association between global self-esteem and physical appearance are all moderately high.

| Country | Correlation Coefficient |
|---|---|
| Canada | .67 |
| United States | .65 |
| England | .63 |
| Portugal | .55 |
| Taiwan | .46 |

## FIGURE 11.3

**CORRELATIONS BETWEEN GLOBAL SELF-ESTEEM AND SELF-EVALUATIONS OF PHYSICAL APPEARANCE.** Recall from Chapter 1 that correlation coefficients can range from −1.00 to +1.00. The positive values of these correlation coefficients indicate that as children's ratings of their global self-esteem increase, their ratings of their physical appearance also increase.

## VARIATIONS IN SELF-ESTEEM

Variations in self-esteem have been linked with many aspects of children's development. However, much of the research is *correlational* rather than *experimental*. Recall from Chapter 1 that correlation does not equal causation. Thus, if a correlational study finds an association between children's low self-esteem and low academic achievement, low academic achievement could cause the low self-esteem as much as low self-esteem might cause low academic achievement (Bowles, 1999). In fact, there are only moderate correlations between school performance and self-esteem, and these correlations do not suggest that high self-esteem produces better school performance (Baumeister & others, 2003). Efforts to increase students' self-esteem have not always led to improved school performance (Davies & Brember, 1999).

Children with high self-esteem show greater initiative, but this can produce positive or negative outcomes (Baumeister & others, 2003). High-self-esteem children are prone to both prosocial and antisocial actions (Bushman & others, 2009). For example, they are more likely than children with low self-esteem to defend victims against bullies, but they are also more likely to be bullies themselves.

Researchers have also found strong links between self-esteem and happiness (Baumeister & others, 2003). For example, the two were strongly related in an international study of 13,000 students from 49 universities in 31 countries (Diener & Diener, 1995). It seems likely that high self-esteem increases happiness (Baumeister & others, 2003). Many studies have found that individuals with low self-esteem report that they feel more depressed than individuals with high self-esteem (Orth & others, 2009). Low self-esteem has also been linked to suicide attempts and to anorexia nervosa (Brockmeyer & others, 2012; Kleiman & Riskand, 2013). One study found that low self-esteem in childhood was linked with depression in adolescence and early adulthood (Orth & others, 2008).

Are a parent's characteristics and behaviour linked to a child's self-esteem? In the most extensive investigation of parent-child relationships and self-esteem, the following attributes of parenting were associated with boys' high self-esteem (Coopersmith, 1967): expression of affection; concern about the child's problems; harmony in the home; participation in joint family activities; availability to give competent, organized help when needed; setting clear and fair rules; abiding by these rules; and allowing the children freedom within well-defined limits. Remember that these findings are correlational, and so we cannot say that these parenting attributes cause children's high self-esteem. And what about for girls? In a longitudinal study, Joan Grusec at the University of Toronto and her colleagues found that both male and female infants whose mothers were low in anger and high in respect-based control exhibited higher self-esteem at age 12 (Awong, Grusec, & Sorenson, 2008).

A current concern is that too many of today's children and adolescents grow up receiving empty praise and as a consequence develop inflated self-esteem (Graham, 2005; Stipek, 2005). Too often they are given praise for performance that is mediocre or even poor. They may have difficulty handling competition and criticism. Harter (1999) argues that intervention must occur at the level of the causes of self-esteem if the individual's self-esteem is to improve significantly. Children have the highest self-esteem when they perform competently in domains that are important to them. Therefore, children should be encouraged to identify and to value areas in which they are competent. For example, participation in sports is a commonly enjoyed activity among children, although athletic ability may play an important role in how sports participation relates to self-esteem. Indeed, research by Anne Bowker at Carleton University has shown that sport participation is related to elevated self-esteem, particularly for early adolescents who are competent athletes (Bowker 2006; Findlay & Bowker, 2009).

Self-esteem is often increased when children face a problem and try to cope with it rather than avoiding it (Compas, 2004). If coping rather than avoidance prevails, children often face problems realistically, honestly, and nondefensively. This produces favourable self-evaluative thoughts, which lead to the self-generated approval that raises self-esteem. The converse is true of

*What are some issues involved in understanding children's self-esteem in school?*

# connecting to current controversy

## Does Self-esteem Change Across the Lifespan?

Researchers disagree about the extent to which self-esteem varies with age. One study found that self-esteem is high in childhood, declines in adolescence, and increases in adulthood until late adulthood, when it declines again (Robins & others, 2002) (see Figure 11.4). Some researchers argue that although there may be a decrease in self-esteem during adolescence, the drop is actually very slight and not nearly as pronounced as it is presented in the media (Harter, 2002; Hyde & Else-Quest, 2013). Fluctuations in self-esteem are also associated with life events and transitions (Baldwin & Hoffmann, 2002). For example, a Canadian study revealed that self-esteem increased during the transition into adulthood (18 to 25 years of age) (Galambos, Barker, & Krahn, 2006).

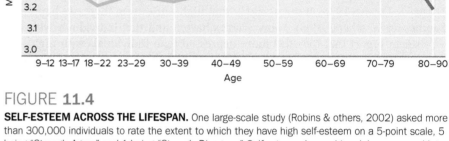

## FIGURE **11.4**

**SELF-ESTEEM ACROSS THE LIFESPAN.** One large-scale study (Robins & others, 2002) asked more than 300,000 individuals to rate the extent to which they have high self-esteem on a 5-point scale, 5 being "Strongly Agree" and 1 being "Strongly Disagree." Self-esteem dropped in adolescence and late adulthood. Self-esteem of females was lower than self-esteem of males through most of the life span.

Notice in Figure 11.4 that the self-esteem of males was higher than that of females through most of the life span. During adolescence, the self-esteem of girls declined more than that of boys. Another study revealed that male adolescents had higher self-esteem than did female adolescents (Bacchini & Magliulo, 2003). One explanation for this gender difference holds that the drop in self-esteem is driven by a negative body image and that girls have more negative body images during pubertal change than boys do. Another explanation emphasizes the greater interest that adolescent girls take in social relationships and society's failure to reward that interest (Impett, & others, 2008). But also note in Figure 11.4 that despite the drop in self-esteem among adolescent girls, their average self-esteem score (3.3) was still higher than the neutral point on the scale (3.0).

*What other factors could explain why gender differences in self-esteem emerge after childhood?*

low self-esteem: unfavourable self-evaluations trigger denial, deception, and avoidance, which lead to self-generated disapproval. Does self-esteem change across the lifespan? To find out, read *Connecting to Current Controversy.*

## Review *Connect* Reflect

 **LO2** Explain self-esteem and self-concept.

### Review

- What are self-esteem and self-concept?
- What are two measures for assessing self-esteem and self-concept?
- How is self-esteem linked with age?
- What are some variations in self-esteem, and how are they linked to children's development? What role do parent-child relationships play in self-esteem?

### *Connect*

- Discussed in the Parenting and Children's Emotional Development section of Chapter 10, which parenting approach might help increase children's self-esteem?

### **Reflect** *Your Own Personal Journey of Life*

- Review the characteristics of self-understanding in adolescence. Which of these characteristics do you associate most closely with your self-understanding as an adolescent?

Who am I? What am I all about? What am I going to do with my life? What is different about me? How can I make it on my own? These questions reflect the search for an identity. By far the most comprehensive and provocative theory of identity development is Erik Erikson's. In this section, we examine his views on identity. We also discuss contemporary research on how identity develops and how social contexts influence that development.

## WHAT IS IDENTITY?

Identity is who a person is, representing a synthesis and integration of self-understanding. Identity is a self-portrait composed of many pieces, including:

- The career and work path the person wants to follow (vocational/career identity)
- Whether the person is conservative, liberal, or middle-of-the-road (political identity)
- The person's spiritual beliefs (religious identity)
- Whether the person is single, married, divorced, and so on (relationship identity)
- The extent to which the person is motivated to achieve and is intellectually oriented (achievement, intellectual identity)
- The label(s) the person prefers to use in reference to their sexuality, such as gay, lesbian, straight, or bisexual (sexual identity)
- The label(s) the person prefers to use in reference to their gender, such as boy/man, girl/woman, or transgender (gender identity)
- Which part of the world or country a person is from and how intensely the person identifies with his or her cultural heritage (cultural/ethnic identity)
- The kind of things a person likes to do, which can include sports, music, hobbies, and so on (interests)
- The individual's personality characteristics, such as being introverted or extraverted, anxious or calm, friendly or hostile, and so on (personality)
- The individual's body image (physical identity)

We put these pieces together to form a sense of ourselves continuing through time within a social world. Synthesizing the identity components can be a long and drawn-out process, with many negations and affirmations of various roles and faces. Identity development takes place in bits and pieces. Decisions are not made once and for all, but have to be made again and again. Identity development does not happen neatly, nor does it happen cataclysmically (Coté, 2009, Moshman, 2011).

*What are some important dimensions of identity?*

## ERIKSON'S VIEW

Questions about identity surface as common, virtually universal, concerns during adolescence. It was Erik Erikson (1950, 1968) who first understood how central such questions are to understanding adolescent development. That identity is now believed to be a key aspect of adolescent development is a result of Erikson's masterful thinking and analysis. Recall that his fifth developmental stage, which individuals experience during adolescence, is **identity versus identity confusion**. During this time, said Erikson, adolescents are faced with deciding who they are, what they are all about, and where they are going in life.

**identity versus identity confusion** Erikson's fifth developmental stage, which individuals experience during the adolescent years. At this time, adolescents examine who they are, what they are all about, and where they are going in life.

**psychosocial moratorium** Erikson's term for the gap between childhood security and adult autonomy that adolescents experience as part of their identity exploration.

These questions about identity occur throughout life, but they become especially important for adolescents. Erikson points out that adolescents face an overwhelming number of choices. As they gradually come to realize that they will be responsible for themselves and their own lives, adolescents try to determine what those lives are going to be.

The search for an identity during adolescence is aided by a **psychosocial moratorium**, which is Erikson's term for the gap between childhood security and adult autonomy. During this period, society leaves adolescents relatively free of responsibilities and able to try out different identities. Adolescents in effect search their culture's identity files, experimenting with different roles and personalities. They may want to pursue one career one month (lawyer, for example) and another career the next month (doctor, actor, teacher, social worker, or astronaut, for example). They may dress neatly one day, sloppily the next. This experimentation is a deliberate effort on the part of adolescents to find out where they fit in the world.

Youth who successfully cope with these conflicting identities emerge with a new sense of self that is both refreshing and acceptable. Adolescents who do not successfully resolve this identity crisis suffer what Erikson calls *identity confusion*. The confusion takes one of two courses: individuals withdraw, isolating themselves from peers and family, or they immerse themselves in the world of peers and lose their identity in the crowd.

There are hundreds of roles for adolescents to try out, and probably just as many ways to pursue each role. Erikson stresses that, by late adolescence, vocational roles are central to identity development. This is especially the case in a highly technological society like Canada. Youth who have been well trained to enter a workforce that offers the potential of reasonably high self-esteem will experience the least stress during this phase of identity development.

A current concern about the development of identity in adolescence and emerging adulthood was voiced by William Damon (2008) in his book, *The Path to Purpose*. Damon acknowledges that successful identity development is a long-term process of extended exploration and reflection, and in some instances it can involve postponing decisions for a number of years. However, Damon feels that too many of today's youth aren't moving toward any identity resolution. In Damon's (2008, pp. 5, 7) words,

> Their delay is characterized more by indecision than by motivated reflection, more by confusion than by pursuit of clear goals, more by ambivalence than by determination. Directionless shift is not a constructive moratorium in either a developmental or a societal sense. Without a sense of direction, opportunities are lost, and doubt and self-absorption can set in. Maladaptive habits are established and adaptive ones not built . . . What is too often missing is . . . the kind of wholehearted dedication to an activity or interest that stems from serious purpose, a purpose that can give meaning and direction to life.

In Damon's (2008, p. 47) view, too many youth are left to their own devices in dealing with some of life's biggest questions: "What is my calling? What can I contribute to the world? What am I here for?" Damon acknowledges that adults can't make youths' decisions for them, but he emphasizes that it is very important for parents, teachers, mentors, and other adults to provide guidance, feedback, and contexts that will improve the likelihood that youth will develop a positive identity. Youth need a cultural climate that inspires rather than demoralizes them and supports their chances of reaching their aspirations.

## DEVELOPMENTAL CHANGES

Although questions about identity are particularly likely to emerge during adolescence, identity formation neither begins nor ends during these years (McLean & Syed, 2013; Schwartz & others, 2013; Syed, 2013). It begins with the appearance of attachment, the development of the sense of self, and the emergence of independence in infancy; the process reaches its final phase with a life review and integration in old age. What is important about identity development in adolescence, especially late adolescence, is that for the first time, physical development,

Erik Erikson

cognitive development, and socioemotional development advance to the point at which the individual can begin to sort through and synthesize childhood identities and identifications to construct a viable path toward adult maturity.

Some decisions made during adolescence might seem trivial: whom to date, whether or not to break up, which major to study, whether to study or play, whether or not to be politically active, and so on. Over the years of adolescence, however, such decisions begin to form the core of what the individual is all about as a human being—what is called his or her identity.

As individuals mature from early adolescence to emerging adulthood, they increasingly pursue in-depth exploration of their identity (Klimstra & others, 2010). Adolescents who are highly committed in their identity development are characterized by higher levels of conscientiousness and emotional stability (Meeus, 2011).

One way that researchers are examining identity changes in depth is to use a *narrative approach*, which involves asking individuals to tell their life stories and then evaluating the extent to which their stories are meaningful and integrated (McAdams, 2012; Syed, 2010, 2011, 2013). A recent study using the narrative identity approach revealed that from age 11 to 18, boys increasingly engaged in thinking about the meaningfulness of their lives, especially meaning related to the self as changing (McLean, Breen, & Fournier, 2010).

**Identity Statuses**  How do individual adolescents go about the process of forming an identity? Canadian researcher James Marcia (1980, 1994) proposes that Erikson's theory of identity development contains four statuses of identity, or ways of resolving the identity crisis: identity diffusion, identity foreclosure, identity moratorium, and identity achievement. What determines an individual's identity status? Marcia classifies individuals based on the existence or extent of their crisis or commitment (see Figure 11.5). **Crisis** is defined as a period of identity development during which the individual is exploring alternatives. Most researchers use the term *exploration* rather than crisis. **Commitment** is personal investment in identity.

The four statuses of identity are as follows:

- **Identity diffusion** is the status of individuals who have not yet experienced a crisis or made any commitments. Not only are they undecided about occupational and ideological choices, they are also likely to show little interest in such matters.
- **Identity foreclosure** is the status of individuals who have made a commitment but not experienced a crisis. This occurs most often when parents hand down commitments to their adolescents, usually in an authoritarian way, before adolescents have had a chance to explore different approaches, ideologies, and vocations on their own.
- **Identity moratorium** is the status of individuals who are in the midst of a crisis but whose commitments are either absent or are only vaguely defined.
- **Identity achievement** is the status of individuals who have undergone a crisis and made a commitment.

To evaluate your identity in different areas of development, see Figure 11.6. Let's explore some examples of Marcia's identity statuses. Thirteen-year-old Mia has neither begun to explore her identity in any meaningful way nor made an identity commitment; she is identity diffused. Eighteen-year-old Oliver's parents want him to be a medical doctor, so he is planning on majoring in pre-medicine at university and has not explored other options; he is identity foreclosed. Nineteen-year-old Sasha is not quite sure what life paths she wants to follow, but she recently went to the counselling centre at her community college to find out about different careers; she is in identity moratorium status. Twenty-one-year-old Marcelo extensively explored several career options in university, eventually getting his degree

FIGURE **11.5**
**MARCIA'S FOUR STATUSES OF IDENTITY.**

**crisis** A period of identity development during which the adolescent is choosing among meaningful alternatives.

**commitment** Personal investment in identity.

**identity diffusion** Marcia's term for the status of individuals who have not yet experienced a crisis (that is, they have not yet explored meaningful alternatives) or made any commitments.

**identity foreclosure** Marcia's term for the status of individuals who have made a commitment but have not experienced a crisis.

**identity moratorium** Marcia's term for the status of individuals who are in the midst of a crisis but whose commitments either are absent or are only vaguely defined.

**identity achievement** Marcia's term for the status of individuals who have undergone a crisis and made a commitment.

Think deeply about your exploration and commitment in the areas listed here. For each area, check whether your identity status is diffused, foreclosed, moratorium, or achieved.

| Identity Component | Identity Status | | | |
|---|---|---|---|---|
| | Diffused | Foreclosed | Moratorium | Achieved |
| Vocational (career) | | | | |
| Political | | | | |
| Religious | | | | |
| Relationships | | | | |
| Achievement | | | | |
| Sexual | | | | |
| Gender | | | | |
| Ethnic/Cultural | | | | |
| Interests | | | | |
| Personality | | | | |
| Physical | | | | |

FIGURE **11.6**

**EXPLORING YOUR IDENTITY.** If you checked diffused or foreclosed for any areas, take some time to think about what you need to do to move into a moratorium identity status in those areas.

in science education, and is looking forward to his first year of teaching high school students; his status is identity achieved. These examples focused on the career dimension, but remember that identity has a number of dimensions.

In Marcia's terms, young adolescents are primarily in the identity statuses of diffusion, foreclosure, or moratorium. To move to the status of identity achievement, young adolescents need three things (Marcia, 1987, 1996): (1) they must be confident that they have parental support, (2) they must have an established sense of industry, and (3) they must be able to adopt a self-reflective stance toward the future.

As James Coté at the University of Western Ontario points out, the identity status approach has been sharply criticized by some researchers and theoreticians (Coté, 2009). Critics maintain that the identity status approach distorts and trivializes Erikson's notions of crisis and commitment. For example, Erikson's idea of commitment loses the meaning of investing oneself in certain lifelong projects and is interpreted simply as having made a firm decision or not. Others argue that the identity status approach is a valuable contribution to understanding identity (Marcia, 2002; Waterman, 1992).

**Emerging Adulthood and Beyond** A consensus is developing that the key changes in identity are more likely to take place in emerging adulthood (18 to 25 years of age) or later, than in adolescence (Schwartz & others, 2013; Syed, 2013). For example, Alan Waterman (1985, 1992) has found that from the years preceding high school through the last few years of post-secondary education, the number of individuals who are identity achieved increases, whereas the number who are identity diffused decreases. University students who are in their final year of study are more likely to be identity achieved than first-year university students or high school students. Many young adolescents, on the other hand, are identity diffused. These developmental changes are especially true for vocational choice. In terms of religious beliefs and political ideology, fewer college or university students reach the identity-achieved status; a substantial number are characterized by foreclosure and diffusion. Thus, the timing of identity development may depend on the particular dimension involved.

Why might post-secondary education produce some key changes in identity? Increased complexity in the reasoning skills of university students combined

As long as one keeps searching, the answers come.

—JOAN BAEZ
*American Folk Singer, 20th Century*

*How does identity change in emerging adulthood?*

with a wide range of new experiences that highlight contrasts between home and university and between themselves and others stimulates them to reach a higher level of integrating various dimensions of their identity (Phinney, 2008).

A recent meta-analysis of 124 studies revealed that identity moratorium status rose steadily to 19 years of age and then declined, identity achievement rose across late adolescence and early adulthood, and foreclosure and diffusion statuses declined across the high school years but fluctuated in late adolescence and early adulthood (Kroger, Martinussen, & Marcia, 2010). A large portion of individuals were not identity achieved by early adulthood. This important finding—that significant numbers of older adolescents and emerging adults had not reached an identity achieved status—suggests that mastering identity development by the end of adolescence is more elusive for most individuals than Erikson (1968) envisioned.

A recent research review concluded that identity is more stable in adulthood than in adolescence (Meeus, 2011), but resolution of the identity issue during adolescence and emerging adulthood does not mean that identity will be stable through the remainder of life (McAdams, 2012). Many individuals who develop positive identities follow what are called MAMA cycles; that is, their identity status changes from *m*oratorium to *a*chievement to *m*oratorium to *a*chievement (Marcia, 1994). These cycles may be repeated throughout life. Marcia (2002) points out that the first identity is just that—it is not, and should not be expected to be, the final product.

## SOCIAL CONTEXTS

Social contexts play important roles in identity. Let's examine how family, culture, and ethnicity are linked to identity development.

**Family Influences** Parents are important figures in the adolescent's development of identity (Cooper, 2011). It is during adolescence that the search for balance between the need for autonomy and the need for connectedness becomes especially important to identity. Developmentalists Catherine Cooper and Harold Grotevant (Cooper, 2011; Cooper & Grotevant, 1989; Grotevant & Cooper, 1985, 1998) found that the presence of a family atmosphere that promotes both individuality and connectedness are important to the adolescent's identity development:

- **Individuality** consists of two dimensions: self-assertion—the ability to have and communicate a point of view—and separateness—the use of communication patterns to express how one is different from others.

*developmental* **connection**

**Attachment.** Even while adolescents seek autonomy, attachment to parents is important; secure attachment in adolescence is linked to a number of positive outcomes. Chapter 14, LO 2

**individuality** Consists of two dimensions: self-assertion—the ability to have and communicate a point of view—and separateness—the use of communication patterns to express how one is different from others.

**connectedness** Consists of two dimensions: mutuality, sensitivity to and respect for others' views, and permeability, openness to others' views.

- **Connectedness** also consists of two dimensions: mutuality, which involves sensitivity to and respect for others' views, and permeability, which involves openness to others' views.

In general, Cooper and Grotevant's research indicates that identity formation is enhanced by family relationships that are both individuated, which encourages adolescents to develop their own point of view, and connected, which provides a secure base from which to explore the widening social worlds of adolescence. When connectedness is strong and individuation weak, adolescents often have an identity-foreclosure status. When connectedness is weak, adolescents often reveal identity confusion.

Research interest also has increased regarding the role that attachment to parents might play in identity development. A meta-analysis found weak to moderate correlations between attachment to parents in adolescence and identity development (Arseth & others, 2009). In this study, though, securely attached adolescents were far more likely to be identity achieved than their counterparts who were identity diffused or identity foreclosed.

**Peer/Romantic Relationships**   Researchers have recently found that the capacity to explore one's identity during adolescence and emerging adulthood is linked to the quality of friendships and romantic relationships (Galliher & Kerpelman, 2012). For example, a recent study found that an open, active exploration of identity when adolescents are comfortable with close friends contributes to the positive quality of the friendship (Deamen & others, 2012). In another study, friends were often a safe context for exploring identity-related experiences, providing a means for testing how self-disclosing comments are viewed by others (McLean & Jennings, 2012).

In terms of links between identity and romantic relationships in adolescence and emerging adulthood, two individuals in a romantic relationship are both in the process of constructing their own identities and each person provides the other with a context for identity exploration (Pittman & others, 2012). The extent of their secure attachment with each other can influence how each partner constructs his or her own identity.

**Culture and Ethnicity**   Most research on identity development has been based on data obtained from adolescents and emerging adults in the United States and Canada, most of whom were from a European ethnic background (Schwartz & others, 2013). Many of these individuals have grown up with a cultural identity that emphasizes the individual. However, in many countries around the world, adolescents and emerging adults have grown up influenced by a collectivist emphasis on fitting in with the group and connecting with others. The collectivist emphasis is especially prevalent in East Asian countries such as China. Researchers have found that self-oriented identity exploration may not be the main process through which identity achievement is attained in East Asian countries (Schwartz & others, 2013). Rather, East Asian adolescents and emerging adults may develop their identity through identification with and imitation of others in the cultural group (Bosma & Kunnen, 2001). This emphasis on interdependence in East Asian cultures includes an expectation that adolescents and emerging adults will accept and embrace social and family roles (Berman & others, 2011). Thus, some patterns of identity development, such as the foreclosed status, may be more adaptive in East Asian countries than in North American countries (Cheng & Berman, 2013).

Seth Schwartz and his colleagues (2013) recently noted that while everyone identifies with a particular culture, many individuals in cultural majority groups take their cultural identity for granted. Thus, many adolescents and emerging adults who are part of the cultural majority of individuals with European heritage

*How is an adolescent's identity development influenced by parents?*

in Canada are unlikely to spend much time thinking of themselves as "European Canadian." However, for many adolescents and emerging adults who have grown up as members of an ethnic minority group in Canada or emigrated from another country, cultural dimensions likely are an important aspect of their identity.

**Ethnic identity** is an enduring aspect of the self that includes a sense of membership in an ethnic group, along with the attitudes and feelings related to that membership (Phinney, 2006).

Throughout the world, ethnic minority groups have struggled to maintain their ethnic identities while fitting in with the dominant culture (Erikson, 1968). Many adolescents develop a **bicultural identity**. That is, they identify in some ways with their ethnic group and in other ways with the majority culture (Cooper, 2011; Marks, Patton, & Garcia Coll, 2011; Phinney & Balderlomar, 2011). For example, a study of Mexican American and Asian American college students found that they identified both with the American mainstream culture and with their culture of origin (Devos, 2006). And another recent study exploring bicultural identity in 14- to 21-year-olds found that younger bicultural adolescents primarily responded to the label "White" with an inhibited response, suggesting hesitation in determining whether the label was "like me" or "not like me" (Marks, Patton, & Garcia Coll, 2011).

Many aspects of sociocultural contexts may influence ethnic identity (Phinney & Baldelomar, 2011; Syed & Azmitia, 2010). Ethnic identity tends to be stronger among members of minority groups than among members of mainstream groups. For example, in one study, the exploration of ethnic identity was higher among ethnic minority college students than among Caucasian college students (Phinney & Alipuria, 1990).

Time is another aspect of the sociocultural context that influences ethnic identity. The indicators of identity often differ for each succeeding generation of immigrants (Phinney, 2003; Phinney & Ong, 2007). First-generation immigrants are likely to be secure in their identities and unlikely to change much; they may or may not develop a new identity. The degree to which they begin to feel a sense of national identity appears to be related to whether or not they learn the language of their new country, develop social networks beyond their ethnic group, and become culturally competent in their new country. Second-generation immigrants are more likely to have a sense of national identity, possibly because citizenship is granted at birth. For second-generation immigrants, ethnic identity is likely to be linked to retention of their ethnic language and social networks. In the third and later generations, the issues become more complex. Broad social factors may affect the extent to which members of this generation retain their ethnic identities. For example, media images may encourage members of an ethnic group to identify with their group or retain parts of its culture. Discrimination against newcomers to Canada may force people to see themselves as cut off from the majority group and encourage them to seek support from their own ethnic culture (Li, 2009). To read further about ethnic and national identity, see *Connecting with Diversity.*

Researchers are also increasingly finding that a positive ethnic identity is related to positive outcomes for ethnic minority children and adolescents. For example, Canadian studies on the positive outcomes for Aboriginal children and adolescents have indicated that First Nation youth's positive ethnic identity was linked to higher self-esteem, positive attitudes toward ingroup members, less victimization by peers, and higher grades in school (Corenblum & Armstrong, 2012; Flanagan & others, 2011; Fryberg & others, 2013). A recent study by Gfellner and Armstrong (2011) at Brandon University also showed that First Nation adolescents with a strong sense of aboriginal identity are more likely to embody characteristics that are key to psychosocial development according to Erik Erikson, such as fidelity and wisdom, as compared to First Nation adolescents with a bicultural identity.

Jean Phinney (2006) described how ethnic identity may change in emerging adulthood, especially highlighting how certain experiences of ethnic minority individuals may shorten or lengthen emerging adulthood. For ethnic minority individuals who must take on family responsibilities and cannot pursue

**ethnic identity** An enduring aspect of the self that includes a sense of membership in an ethnic group, along with the attitudes and feelings related to that membership.

**bicultural identity** Identity formation that occurs when adolescents identify in some ways with their ethnic group and in other ways with the majority culture.

*How might this second-generation young Canadian's ethnic and national identity differ from that of his first-generation father?*

## Ethnic Identity and Canadian Identity

Studies of ethnic identity and national identity go hand in hand (Phinney & Ong, 2007). Whereas ethnic identity refers to one's sense of membership in an ethnic group, national identity refers to one's sense of membership and connection to an entire country.

Adolescents who are newcomers to Canada tend to feel a lower sense of belonging to Canada than those who have lived in the country since they were born (Darwich, 2013). Indeed, one study found that 15 percent of immigrant youth, compared to 40 percent of non-immigrant youth, felt a strong connection to Canada (Lee & Hebert, 2006).

Is there a link between one's ethnic identity and Canadian identity? John Berry at Queen's University and his colleagues (2006) studied ethnic and national identity among more than 5,000 immigrant youth from 13 countries, including Canada. For Canadian immigrant youth, ethnic, and Canadian identity were not correlated. However, in another study examining identity among Chinese youth born in Canada, Chinese identity and Canadian identity were positively correlated (Costigan & Su, 2004).

Although the research described above seems to suggest that only those born in Canada identify with *both* their ethnic group and Canada, this may not always be the case (Costigan, Su, & Hua,

2009). For example, Lina Darwich at the University of British Columbia (2013) studied an ethnically diverse sample of adolescents and found that a feeling of pride in one's ethnic group was positively correlated with a sense of belonging to Canada, regardless of how long they have lived in Canada. And another study revealed that 11 percent of immigrant youth said they felt confident about keeping their ethnic heritage while simultaneously developing a sense of belonging to Canada. As one girl in the study stated, "I've adapted to become Canadian, keeping my fundamental heritage roots but also welcoming the Canadian patriotic esteem and values close within me" (Lee & Hebert, 2006, p. 509).

Children and adolescents from ethnic minority backgrounds, particularly recent immigrant youth, face several challenges adjusting to life in Canada. Some of these challenges include learning the norms of a society that may be quite different from those they had previously been accustomed, as well as learning a new language. Amid these challenges, ethnic minority youth who recently immigrated to Canada have also reported experiencing ethnic discrimination (Closson & others, 2014; Darwich, 2013; Li, 2009; 2010). These experiences could potentially impact these youths' sense of belonging to both their ethnic group and Canada.

*What features of children's lives could have a positive impact on their ethnic identity and Canadian identity?*

---

post-secondary education, identity formation may occur earlier. By contrast, especially for ethnic minority individuals who go to college or university, identity formation may take longer because of the complexity of exploring and understanding a bicultural identity. The cognitive challenges of higher education likely stimulate ethnic minority individuals to reflect on their identity and examine changes in the way they want to identify themselves. This increased reflection may focus on integrating parts of one's ethnic minority culture with elements of the mainstream culture. For example, some emerging adults have to come to grips with resolving a conflict between the family loyalty and interdependence emphasized in their ethnic minority culture and the values of independence and self-assertion emphasized by the mainstream culture (Arnett, 2006).

## Review *Connect* Reflect

 **LO3** Describe identity and its development.

### Review

- What is identity?
- What is Erikson's view of identity?
- How do individuals develop their identity? What identity statuses can be used to classify individuals?
- How do the social contexts of family, peers/romantic relationships, culture, and ethnicity influence identity?

### *Connect*

- Identity vs. identity confusion is the fifth stage of Erikson's theory of development. What crisis should a

child have resolved in the fourth stage to be able to successfully move on to confront the identity vs. identity confusion crisis?

### **Reflect** *Your Own Personal Journey of Life*

- How did your identity change as you developed through adolescence? How does your current identity differ from your identity as an adolescent? To guide your self-evaluation of your identity changes, revisit Figure 11.6 and reflect on what are likely some of the key aspects of your identity.

1. How would you characterize developmental differences in self-understanding based on each child's description presented in the chapter opening vignette?

2. From the chapter opening vignette, which individual's self-descripton best reflects someone with high self-esteem? What evidence do you have for your choice?

3. From the chapter opening vignette, under which category of Marcia's identity statuses would you classify the 17-year-old? Why?

# reach your **learning goals**

# The Self and Identity

## Self-Understanding and Understanding Others  Discuss the development of self-understanding and understanding others.

Self-Understanding

- Self-understanding is a child's cognitive representation of the self—the substance and content of the child's self-conceptions. It provides the rational underpinnings for personal identity. Infants develop a rudimentary form of self-recognition as early as 3 months of age and a more complete form of self-understanding at approximately 18 months of age. Self-understanding in early childhood is characterized by confusion of self, mind, and body; concrete, physical, and active descriptions; and unrealistic positive overestimations. Self-understanding in middle and late childhood involves an increase in the use of psychological characteristics and traits, social descriptions, and social comparison; distinction between the real and ideal self; and an increase in realistic self-evaluations. Adolescents develop abstract and idealistic conceptions of themselves, become more self-conscious about their self-understanding, and engage in more social comparison than when they were children. Their self-understanding often fluctuates, and they construct multiple selves, including possible selves.

Understanding Others

- Young children display more sophisticated self-understanding and understanding of others than was previously thought. Even 4-year-olds understand that people make statements that aren't true to obtain what they want or to avoid trouble. Children increase their perspective taking in middle and late childhood, and they become even more skeptical of others' claims. Three important aspects of understanding others in adolescence are perspective taking, perceiving others' traits, and social cognitive monitoring.

## Self-Esteem and Self-Concept  Explain self-esteem and self-concept.

What Are Self-Esteem and Self-Concept?

- Self-esteem, also referred to as self-worth or self-image, is the global, evaluative dimension of the self. Self-concept refers to domain-specific evaluations of the self.

- Harter's Self-Perception Profile for Children is used with third-grade through sixth-grade children to assess general self-worth and self-concept in five skill domains. Harter's Self-Perception Profile for Adolescents assesses global self-worth in five skill domains, plus additional domains dealing with friendship, romance, and job competence.

- Researchers have found only moderate correlations between self-esteem and school performance. Individuals with high self-esteem have greater initiative than those with low self-esteem, and this can produce positive or negative outcomes. Self-esteem is related to perceived physical appearance and happiness. Low self-esteem is linked with depression, suicide attempts, and anorexia nervosa. In Coopersmith's study, children's self-esteem was associated with parental acceptance and allowing children freedom within well-defined limits.

- Some researchers have found that self-esteem drops in adolescence, more so for girls than boys, but there is controversy about how extensively self-esteem varies with age.

## Identity

**L03** Describe identity and its development.

| What Is Identity? |
| --- |

| Erikson's View |
| --- |

| Developmental Changes |
| --- |

| Social Contexts |
| --- |

- Identity development is complex and takes place in bits and pieces. At a bare minimum, identity involves commitment to a vocational direction, an ideological stance, and a sexual orientation. Synthesizing identity components can be a long, drawn-out process.

- Erikson argues that identity versus identity confusion is the fifth stage of the human life span, which individuals experience during adolescence. This stage involves entering a psychosocial moratorium between the security of childhood and the autonomy of adulthood. Personality and role experimentation are important aspects of identity development. In technological societies like those in North America, the vocational role is especially important.

- Identity development begins during infancy and continues through old age. James Marcia proposed four identity statuses—identity diffusion, foreclosure, moratorium, and achievement—that are based on crisis (exploration) and commitment. Some experts argue the main changes in identity occur in emerging adulthood rather than adolescence. Individuals often follow *moratorium–achievement–moratorium–achievement (MAMA)* cycles in their lives.

- Parents are important figures in adolescents' identity development. Both individuality and connectedness in family relations are related to identity development. Peer and romantic relationships also provide social contexts that influence adolescents' identity development. Throughout the world, ethnic minority groups have struggled to maintain their identities while fitting into the majority culture. A positive ethnic identity is linked to positive outcomes for ethnic minority adolescents.

# Gender | chapter 12

In 1967, Bruce and Brian Reimer, identical twin boys were born in Winnipeg, Manitoba. When the twins were 8 months old, Bruce lost his penis due to a severe injury during circumcision. His parents sought the advice of a leading sex researcher, Dr. John Money, who recommended their 21-month-old son be physically transformed into a female and that the child would not become aware she was born male. Bruce was castrated, renamed Brenda and raised as a girl. Brenda and Brian made regular visits to Money's office where he observed the twins and treated Brenda (Colapinto, 2000). As Brenda reached puberty, she was given female hormones to develop feminine physical characteristics.

David Reimer as an adult

Early indications were that the gender reassignment had positive outcomes, as Money was eager to prove gender was socialized. At age 5, Brenda was tomboyish, but compared to her twin brother she displayed more stereotypical female behaviours and interests (Money, 1975). As news of Brenda's story reached the scientific community and popular media, her case was viewed as evidence that gender develops as a result of socialization (Colapinto, 2000). However, the case was later shown to offer strong support of the influence of biology on gender development (Diamond & Sigmundson, 1997).

A follow-up study by Milton Diamond and Keith Sigmundson (1997) revealed Brenda had not adjusted well as a girl and was quite miserable growing up. Over time, Brenda preferred stereotypical male activities and around the age of 10 knew that she did not feel like a girl. In an effort to stop the bullying and ostracism by classmates as a result of her masculinity, Brenda tried to act more feminine. But after years of pressure to act like a girl and struggles with her gender identity, at age 13 Brenda was told about the sex reassignment and shortly after decided to live as a male and take the name David.

David underwent hormonal and surgical treatment, got married at age 25, and adopted his wife's children (Colapinto, 2000). In his 30s, David endured a number of difficult life events: his twin brother died, David lost his job, and his marriage was failing. In 2004, when David was 38 years old, he committed suicide. Whether his childhood experiences contributed to his suicide is unknown.

# preview

We begin this chapter by examining what gender involves, then turn our attention to various influences on gender development—biological, social, and cognitive. Next, we explore gender stereotypes, similarities, and differences. Our final discussion focuses on how gender roles are classified.

## What Is Gender? **L01** Summarize what gender involves.

Gender refers to the characteristics of people as males and females. **Gender identity** involves a sense of one's own gender, including knowledge, understanding, and acceptance of being male or female (Blakemore, Berenbaum, & Liben, 2009; Leaper, 2013; Perry, 2012). **Gender roles** are sets of expectations that prescribe how females or males should think, act, and feel. During the preschool years, most children increasingly act in ways that match their culture's gender roles. **Gender typing** refers to acquisition of a traditional masculine or feminine role. For example, fighting is more characteristic of a traditional masculine role and crying is more characteristic of a traditional feminine role.

One aspect of gender identity involves knowing whether you are a boy or a girl (Perry, 2012). Until recently, it was thought that this aspect of gender identity emerged at about 2½ years. However, a longitudinal study that explored the acquisition of gender labels in infancy and their implications for gender-typed play revealed that gender identity likely emerges before 2 years of age (Zosuls & others, 2009). In this study, infants began using gender labels on average at 19 months of age, with girls beginning to use gender labels earlier than boys. This gender difference became present at 17 months of age and increased at 21 months of age. Use of gender labels was linked to gender-typed play, indicating that knowledge of gender categories may affect gender typing earlier than 2 years of age.

Gender-stereotypical play preferences emerge early in childhood. According to a study by Lisa Serbin and her colleagues at Concordia University, preferences for gender-stereotyped toys begin to appear around 18 months of age (Serbin & others, 2001). And another study revealed that gender-typed behaviour (boys playing with cars and girls with jewellery, for example) increased during the preschool years and children that who engaged in the most gender-typed behaviour during the preschool years were still doing so at 8 years of age (Golombok & others, 2008).

Some children experience **gender dysphoria**. These children are extremely uncomfortable with the gender assigned to them at birth and express an intense desire to be the other gender. In many cases, such children do not continue to have gender dysphoria when they grow older (Zucker & Bradley, 1995). Nevertheless, most children and adolescents with gender dysphoria experience adjustment problems. For example, Canadian and Dutch researchers recently studied behavioural and emotional problems and peer relations of children and adolescents with gender dysphoria who had been referred to gender identity clinics (Steensma & others, 2014). The study results showed that behavioural and emotional problems were more severe among adolescents than children. In addition, males had more problematic peer relations compared to females and were also more likely to experience emotional difficulties than behavioural difficulties. Compared to Dutch children and adolescents, Canadians fared worse, partly due to having poorer quality peer relations.

> To be meek, patient, tactful, modest, honorable, brave, is not to be either manly or womanly; it is to be humane.
>
> —JANE HARRISON
> *English Writer, 20th Century*

**gender identity** The sense of being male or female, which most children acquire by the time they are 2 years old.

**gender role** A set of expectations that prescribes how females or males should think, act, and feel.

**gender typing** Acquisition of a traditional masculine or feminine role.

**gender dysphoria** The experience of extreme discomfort with one's gender assigned at birth.

*At what age do children know whether they are male or female?*

Fortunately, one of the world's major gender identity clinics is at the Centre for Addiction and Mental Health in Toronto and all provincial health insurance plans in Canada cover the cost of assessment at the clinic (CAMH, 2012).

## Review *Connect* Reflect

**LO1** Summarize what gender involves.

**Review**

- What is gender? What are some components of gender?

*Connect*

- In Chapter 1, what did you learn about gender and research that you should keep in mind as you read more about research in the area of gender and development in the following sections of this chapter?

**Reflect** *Your Own Personal Journey of Life*

- As you begin this chapter, think about the role of gender in your life as you were growing up. What are some examples of how your behaviour as a child reflected a masculine or feminine role?

## Influences on Gender Development

**LO2** Discuss the main biological, social, and cognitive influences on gender.

Biological Influences     Social Influences     Cognitive Influences

*developmental* **connection**

**Biological Processes.** Hormones are powerful chemical substances secreted by the endocrine glands and carried through the body by the bloodstream. Chapter 4, LO 1

How is gender influenced by biology? By children's social experiences? By cognitive factors?

## BIOLOGICAL INFLUENCES

It was not until the 1920s that researchers confirmed the existence of human sex chromosomes, the genetic material that determines our sex. Humans normally have 46 chromosomes, arranged in pairs. A 23rd pair with two X-shaped chromosomes produces a female. A 23rd pair with an X chromosome and a Y chromosome produces a male.

**Hormones**    In Chapter 4, we discussed the two classes of hormones that have the most influence on gender: estrogens and androgens. Estrogens and androgens occur in both females and males, but in very different concentrations.

Estrogens primarily influence the development of female physical sex characteristics and help regulate the menstrual cycle. Estrogens are a general class of hormones. An example of an important estrogen is estradiol. In females, estrogens are produced mainly by the ovaries.

Androgens primarily promote the development of male genitals and secondary sex characteristics. One important androgen is testosterone. Androgens are produced by the adrenal glands in males and females, and by the testes in males.

In the first few weeks of gestation, female and male embryos look alike. Male sex organs start to differ from female sex organs when a gene on the Y chromosome directs a small piece of tissue in the embryo to turn into testes. Once the tissue has turned into testes they begin to secrete testosterone. Because females have no Y chromosome, the tissue turns into ovaries. To explore biological influences on gender, researchers have studied individuals who are exposed to unusual levels of sex hormones early in development (Hines, 2013). Here are three examples of effects that may occur as a result (Lippa, 2005, pp. 122–124, 136–137):

- *Congenital adrenal hyperplasia (CAH).* Some girls have this condition, which is caused by a genetic defect. Their adrenal glands enlarge, resulting in abnormally high levels of androgens. Although CAH girls are XX females, they vary in how much their genitals look like male or female genitals. Their genitals may be surgically altered to look more like those of a typical female. Although CAH girls usually grow up to think of themselves as girls and women, they are less content with being a female and show a stronger interest in being a male than non-CAH girls (Berenbaum & Bailey, 2003; Ehrhardt & Baker, 1974; Hall & others, 2004). They like sports and enjoy playing with boys and boys' toys. CAH girls usually don't like typical girl activities such as playing with dolls and wearing makeup.
- *Androgen-insensitive males.* Because of a genetic error, a small number of XY males don't have androgen cells in their bodies. Their bodies look female, they develop a female gender identity, and they usually are sexually attracted to males.
- *Pelvic field defect.* A small number of newborns have a disorder called pelvic field defect, which in boys involves a missing penis. These XY boys have normal amounts of testosterone prenatally but usually have been castrated just after being born and raised as females. One study revealed that despite the efforts by parents to rear them as girls, most of the XY children insisted that they were boys (Reiner & Gearhart, 2004). Apparently, normal exposure to androgens prenatally had a stronger influence on their gender identity than being castrated and raised as girls.

Although sex hormones alone do not determine behaviour, researchers have found links between sex hormone levels and certain behaviours (Hines, 2013). The most established effects of testosterone on humans involve aggressive behaviour and sexual behaviour (Hyde & Else-Quest, 2013). Levels of testosterone are correlated with sexual behaviour in boys during puberty (Udry & others, 1985). And one study revealed that higher fetal testosterone levels measured from amniotic fluid were linked to increased male-typical play, such as increased aggression, in 6- to 10-year-old boys and girls (Auyeung & others, 2009).

**The Evolutionary Psychology View** In Chapter 2 we described the approach of evolutionary psychology, which emphasizes that adaptation during the evolution of humans produced psychological differences between males and females (Buss, 1995, 2008, 2012). Evolutionary psychologists argue that primarily because of their differing roles in reproduction, males and females faced different pressures in primeval environments when the human species was evolving. In particular, because having multiple sexual liaisons improves the likelihood that males will pass on their genes, natural selection favoured males who adopted short-term mating strategies. These males competed with other males to acquire more resources in order to access females. Therefore, say evolutionary psychologists, males evolved dispositions that favour violence, competition, and risk taking.

In contrast, according to evolutionary psychologists, females' contributions to the gene pool were enhanced by securing resources for their offspring, which was promoted by obtaining long-term mates who could support a family. As a consequence, natural selection favoured females who devoted effort to parenting and chose mates who could provide their offspring with resources and protection. Females developed preferences for successful, ambitious men who could provide these resources (Buss, 2012).

Critics of evolutionary psychology argue that its hypotheses are backed by speculations about prehistory, not evidence, and that in any event people are not locked into behaviour that was adaptive in the evolutionary past. Critics also claim that the evolutionary view pays little attention to cultural and individual variations in gender differences (Hyde & Else-Quest, 2013).

*developmental* **connection**

**Theories.** Evolutionary psychology emphasizes the importance of adaptation, reproduction, and "survival of the fittest" in shaping behaviour. Chapter 2, LO 1

# SOCIAL INFLUENCES

Many social scientists do not locate the cause of psychological gender differences in biological dispositions. Rather, they argue that these differences are due to social experiences. Three theories that reflect this view have been influential—social role theory, psychoanalytic theory, and social cognitive theory.

Alice Eagly (2001, 2010, 2013) proposed **social role theory**, which states that gender differences result from the contrasting roles of women and men. In most cultures around the world, women have less power and status than men do and they control fewer resources (UNICEF, 2011). Compared with men, women perform more domestic work, spend fewer hours in paid employment, receive lower pay, and are more thinly represented in the highest levels of organizations. In Eagly's view, as women adapted to roles with less power and less status in society, they showed more cooperative, less dominant profiles than men. Thus, the social hierarchy and division of labour are important causes of gender differences in power, assertiveness, and nurture (Eagly, 2010).

The **psychoanalytic theory of gender** stems from Sigmund Freud's view that the preschool child develops erotic feelings toward the opposite-sex parent. Eventually, these feelings arouse anxiety, so that at 5 or 6 years of age the child renounces these feelings and identifies with the same-sex parent, unconsciously adopting the same-sex parent's characteristics. However, developmentalists do not believe gender development proceeds as Freud proposed (Callan, 2001).

The social cognitive approach discussed in Chapter 1 provides an alternative explanation of how children develop gender-typed behaviour (see Figure 12.1). According to the **social cognitive theory of gender**, children's gender development occurs through observation and imitation, and through the rewards and punishments children experience for gender-appropriate and gender-inappropriate behaviour (Bussey & Bandura, 1999).

*Parental Influences*   Parents, by action and example, influence their children's and adolescents' gender development (Hilliard & Liben, 2012). As soon as the label *girl* or *boy* is assigned, virtually everyone, from parents to siblings to strangers, begins treating the infant in gender-specific ways (see Figure 12.2). Parents often use rewards and punishments to teach their daughters to be feminine ("Karen, you are such a good mommy with your dolls") and their sons to be masculine ("C'mon now, Keith, big boys don't cry").

As noted by Nancy Galambos at the University of Alberta and her colleagues, mothers and fathers often interact differently with their children and adolescents. Mothers are more involved with their children and adolescents than are fathers, although fathers increase the time they spend in parenting when they have sons and are less likely to become divorced when they have sons (Galambos, Berenbaum,

## developmental connection

**Social Cognitive Theory.** Social cognitive theory holds that behaviour, environment, and person/cognitive factors are the key aspects of development. Chapter 1, LO 3

**social role theory** A theory stating that gender differences result from the contrasting roles of women and men—social hierarchy and division of labour strongly influence gender differences in power, assertiveness, and nurture.

**psychoanalytic theory of gender** A theory that stems from Freud's view that preschool children develop erotic feelings toward the opposite-sex parent. Eventually these feelings cause anxiety, so that at 5 or 6 years of age children renounce these feelings and identify with the same-sex parent, unconsciously adopting the same-sex parent's characteristics.

**social cognitive theory of gender** This theory emphasizes that children's gender development occurs through observation and imitation of gender behaviour, and through rewards and punishments they experience for gender-appropriate and gender-inappropriate behaviour.

| Theory | Processes | Outcome |
|---|---|---|
| Psychoanalytic theory | Sexual attraction to opposite-sex parent at 3 to 5 years of age; anxiety about sexual attraction and subsequent identification with same-sex parent at 5 to 6 years of age | Gender behaviour similar to that of same-sex parent |
| Social cognitive theory | Rewards and punishments of gender-appropriate and -inappropriate behaviour by adults and peers; observation and imitation of models' masculine and feminine behaviour | Gender behaviour |

## FIGURE 12.1

**PARENTS INFLUENCE THEIR CHILDREN'S GENDER DEVELOPMENT BY ACTION AND EXAMPLE.**

## FIGURE 12.2

**EXPECTATIONS FOR BOYS AND GIRLS.**
First imagine that this is a photograph of a baby girl. *What expectations would you have for her?* Then imagine that this is a photograph of a baby boy. *What expectations would you have for him?*

& McHale, 2009). Mothers' interactions with their children and adolescents often centre on caregiving and teaching activities, while fathers' interactions often involve leisure activities (Galambos, Berenbaum, & McHale, 2009).

Mothers and fathers often interact differently with sons and daughters, and these gendered interactions that begin in infancy usually continue through childhood and adolescence. In reviewing research on this topic, Phyllis Bronstein (2006) recently provided these conclusions:

- *Mothers' socialization strategies.* In many cultures mothers socialize their daughters to be more obedient and responsible than their sons. They also place more restrictions on daughters' autonomy.

- *Fathers' socialization strategies.* Fathers show more attention to sons than daughters, engage in more activities with sons, and put forth more effort to promote sons' intellectual development.

Thus, according to Bronstein (2006), many parents promote behaviours and perceptions consistent with traditional gender role norms, despite Western societies' increased awareness of the detrimental effects of gender stereotyping.

*Peers*   As children get older, peers become increasingly important. Peers extensively reward and punish gender behaviour (Leaper, 2013). For example, when children play in ways that the culture says are sex-appropriate, they tend to be rewarded by their peers. According to a study by researchers at Carleton University, children who engage in activities that are considered sex-inappropriate tend to be criticized or abandoned by their peers (Coplan, Closson, & Arbeau, 2007). It is generally more accepted for girls to act more like boys than it is for boys to act more like girls; thus, use of the term *tomboy* to describe masculine girls is often thought of as less derogatory than the term *sissy* to describe feminine boys (Pasterski, Golombok, & Hines, 2011).

Children show a clear preference for being with and liking same-sex peers, and this tendency usually becomes stronger during the middle and late childhood years (Maccoby, 2002) (see Figure 12.3). What kind of socialization takes place in these same-sex play groups? In one study, researchers observed preschoolers over a period of six months (Martin & Fabes, 2001). The more time boys spent interacting with other boys, the more their activity level, rough-and-tumble play, and sex-typed choice of toys and games increased, and the less time boys spent near adults. By contrast, the more time preschool girls spent interacting with other girls, the more their activity level and aggression decreased, and the more their girl-type play activities and time spent near adults increased. After watching elementary school children repeatedly play in same-sex groups, two researchers characterized the playground as "gender school" (Luria & Herzog, 1985). In another study, Canadian researcher Sandra Bosacki at Brock University and her colleagues found that even children's drawings of themselves playing differ for boys and girls, where girls' drawings focus on the social and psychological aspects of play and boys' drawings focus on physical activities (Bosacki, Varnish, & Akseer, 2008).

In adolescence, peer approval or disapproval is a powerful influence on gender attitudes and behaviour (Mrug & McCay, 2013). Peer groups in adolescence are more likely to be a mix of boys and girls than they were in childhood. However, a recent study of 15- to 17-year-olds indicated that gender segregation characterizes some aspects of adolescents' social life (Mehta & Strough, 2010). In this study, 72 percent of peers said they were most likely to "hang out" with the same gender of adolescents as themselves.

*How do mothers and fathers interact differently with their children and adolescents?*

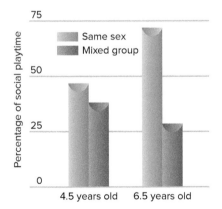

## FIGURE 12.3

**DEVELOPMENTAL CHANGES IN PERCENTAGE OF TIME SPENT IN SAME-SEX AND MIXED-GROUP SETTINGS.**
Observations of children show that they are more likely to play in same-sex than mixed-sex groups. This tendency increases between 4 and 6 years of age.

*Schools and Teachers*   Some observers have expressed concerns that schools and teachers have biases against both boys and girls (Mullola & others, 2012). What evidence might indicate that the classroom is biased against boys? Here are some factors to consider (DeZolt & Hull, 2001):

- Compliance, following rules, and being neat and orderly are valued and reinforced in many classrooms. These are behaviours that usually characterize girls more than boys.
- A large majority of teachers are female, especially in the elementary school. This trend may make it more difficult for boys than for girls to identify with their teachers and model their teachers' behaviour. A recent study revealed that male teachers perceived boys more positively and saw them as being more educationally competent than did female teachers (Mullola & others, 2012).
- Boys are more likely than girls to have a learning disability or ADHD and to drop out of school.
- Boys are more likely than girls to be criticized.
- School personnel tend to ignore the fact that many boys are clearly having academic problems, especially in the language arts.
- School personnel tend to stereotype boys' behaviour as problematic.

What evidence suggests that the classroom is biased against girls? Consider the following (Sadker & Sadker, 2005):

- In a typical classroom, girls are more compliant, boys more rambunctious. Boys demand more attention, girls are more likely to quietly wait their turn. Teachers are more likely to scold and reprimand boys, as well as send boys to school authorities for disciplinary action. Educators worry that girls' tendency to be compliant and quiet comes at a cost: diminished assertiveness.
- In many classrooms, teachers spend more time watching and interacting with boys, whereas girls work and play quietly on their own. Most teachers don't intentionally favour boys by spending more time with them, yet somehow the classroom frequently ends up with this type of gendered profile.
- Boys get more instruction than girls and more help when they have trouble with a question. Teachers often give boys more time to answer a question, provide more hints regarding the correct answer, and allow further tries if they give the wrong answer.
- Boys are more likely than girls to get lower grades and to be grade repeaters, yet girls are less likely to believe that they will be successful in college work.
- Girls and boys enter first grade with roughly equal levels of self-esteem. Yet by the middle school years, girls' self-esteem is lower than boys'.
- When elementary school children are asked to list what they want to do when they grow up, boys describe more career options than girls do.

Thus, there is evidence of gender bias against both males and females in schools. Many school personnel are not aware of their gender-biased attitudes. These attitudes are deeply entrenched in and supported by the general culture. Increasing awareness of gender bias in schools is clearly an important strategy for reducing such bias.

*Media Influences*   The messages about gender roles carried by the mass media also are important influences on children's and adolescents' gender development (Adams, 2012; Silverman, 2012). Often men are portrayed as more powerful than women on TV shows. In addition, a recent study of MTV videos indicated that the scenarios depicted in the videos reinforced stereotypical notions of women as sexual objects and females as subordinate to males (Wallis, 2011). The media also influence adolescents' body images, and some studies reveal gender differences in this area (Frechette, 2012; Hyde & Else-Quest, 2013; Pecot-Hebert, 2012). For example, one study of 10- to 17-year-olds found that girls were more likely than boys to perceive that the media influences their body images (Polce-Lynch & others, 2001). However, recent research has shown that boys are exposed to a highly muscular body ideal for males in media outlets, especially in advertisements that include professional athletes and in video games (Near, 2013). Another study revealed that the more time that adolescent girls and boys spent watching entertainment television, the more negative their body images were (Anderson & others, 2001). Thus, girls are more likely than boys to believe that the media affects their body images, but in reality, both genders are succeptible to media influences.

## COGNITIVE INFLUENCES

Observation, imitation, rewards, and punishment—these are the mechanisms by which gender develops according to social cognitive theory. Interactions between the child and the social environment are the main keys to gender development in this view. Some critics argue that this explanation pays too little attention to the child's own mind and understanding, and portrays the child as passively acquiring gender roles (Martin, Ruble, & Szkrybalo, 2002).

One influential cognitive theory is **gender schema theory**, which states that gender-typing emerges as children gradually develop gender schemas of what is gender-appropriate and gender-inappropriate in their culture (Blakemore, Berenbaum, & Liben, 2009; Miller & others, 2013). A *schema* is a cognitive structure, a network of associations that guide an individual's perceptions. A *gender schema* organizes the world in terms of female and male. Children are internally motivated to perceive the world and to act in accordance with their developing schemas. Bit by bit, children pick up what is gender-appropriate and gender-inappropriate in their culture, and develop gender schemas that shape how they perceive the world and what they remember (Conry-Murray, Kim, & Turiel, 2012). Children are motivated to act in ways that conform with these gender schemas. Thus, gender schemas fuel gender-typing.

How do young children use gender schemas to make judgments about occupations? To find out, see *Connecting Through Research*.

In sum, cognitive factors contribute to the way children think and act as males and females. Through biological, social, and cognitive processes, children develop their gender attitudes and behaviours (Leaper, 2013).

*What are some developmental changes that characterize the gender makeup of children's peer relations?*

**gender schema theory** According to this theory, gender typing emerges as children gradually develop schemas of what is gender-appropriate and gender-inappropriate in their culture.

# connecting through research

## How Do Young Children Use Gender Schemas to Make Judgments About Occupations?

In one study, researchers interviewed children 3 to 7 years old about 10 traditionally masculine occupations (e.g., airplane pilot, car mechanic) and feminine occupations (e.g., clothes designer, secretary), using questions such as the following (Levy, Sadovsky, & Troseth, 2000):

• *Example of a traditionally masculine occupation item:* An airplane pilot is a person who "flies airplanes for people." Who

do you think would do the best job as an airplane pilot, a man or a woman?

• *Example of a traditionally feminine occupation item:* A clothes designer is a person "who draws up and makes clothes for people." Who do you think would do the best job as a clothes designer, a man or a woman?

*(continued)*

# connecting through research

**(continued)**

|  | Boy | Girl |
|---|---|---|
| **"Masculine Occupations"** |  |  |
| Percentage who judged men more competent | 87 | 70 |
| Percentage who judged women more competent | 13 | 30 |
| **"Feminine Occupations"** |  |  |
| Percentage who judged men more competent | 35 | 8 |
| Percentage who judged women more competent | 64 | 92 |

## FIGURE 12.4

**CHILDREN'S JUDGMENTS ABOUT THE COMPETENCE OF MEN AND WOMEN IN GENDER-STEREOTYPED OCCUPATIONS** *How might children's judgments about gender-stereotyped occupations affect their own gender development?*

As indicated in Figure 12.4, the children had well-developed gender schemas, in this case reflected in stereotypes of occupations. They "viewed men as more competent than women in masculine occupations, and rated women as more competent than men in feminine occupations" (p. 993). Also, "girls' ratings of women's competence at feminine occupations were substantially higher than their ratings of men's competence at masculine occupations. Conversely, boys' ratings of men's competence at masculine occupations were considerably

greater than their ratings of women's competence at feminine occupations" (p. 1002). These findings demonstrate that most children as young as 3 to 4 years of age tend to have strong gender schemas regarding the perceived competencies of men and women in gender-typed occupations.

The researchers also asked the children to select from a list of emotions how they would feel if they grew up to have each of the 10 occupations. Girls said they would be happy with the feminine occupations and angry or disgusted with the masculine occupations. As expected, boys reversed their choices, saying they would be happy if they grew up to have the masculine occupations but angry and disgusted with the feminine occupations. However, the boys' emotions were more intense (more angry and disgusted) in desiring to avoid the feminine occupations than girls in wanting to avoid the masculine occupations. This finding supports other research that indicates gender roles tend to constrict boys more than girls (Hyde, 2007a; Matlin, 2012).

It is important to note that the children in this study were at the height of gender stereotyping, a topic that will be discussed shortly. Most older children, adolescents, and adults become more flexible about occupational roles (Hyde, 2007a; Leaper & Friedman, 2007).

---

## Review Connect Reflect

 **LO2** Discuss the main biological, social, and cognitive influences on gender.

### Review

- What are some ways that biology may influence gender?
- What are three social theories of gender and how might social contexts influence gender development?
- What are two cognitive views of gender?

### Connect

- In this section, you learned that in most cultures around the world,

women have less power and status than men do and they control fewer resources. How might this be related to what you read about gender and education in the *Connecting with Diversity* box in Chapter 1?

### Reflect *Your Own Personal Journey of Life*

- How do you think your parents influenced your gender development? How do you think your peers influenced your gender development?

---

## Gender Stereotypes, Similarities, and Differences  **LO3** Describe gender stereotypes, similarities, and differences.

| Gender Stereotyping | Gender Similarities and Differences |
|---|---|

How pervasive is gender stereotyping? What are the real differences between boys and girls?

# GENDER STEREOTYPING

**Gender stereotypes** are general impressions and beliefs about females and males. For example, men are powerful; women are weak. Men make good mechanics; women make good nurses. Men are good with numbers; women are good with words. Women are emotional; men are not. All of these are stereotypes. They are generalizations about a group that reflect widely held beliefs (Matlin, 2012).

**Traditional Masculinity and Femininity**  A classic study in the early 1970s assessed which traits and behaviours college students believed were characteristic of females and which they believed were characteristic of males (Broverman & others, 1972). The traits associated with males were labeled *instrumental:* They included characteristics such as being independent, aggressive, and power oriented. The traits associated with females were labeled *expressive:* They included characteristics such as being warm and sensitive.

Thus, the instrumental traits associated with males suited them for the traditional masculine role of going out into the world as the breadwinner. The expressive traits associated with females paralleled the traditional feminine role of being the sensitive, nurturing caregiver in the home. These roles and traits, however, are not just different; they also are unequal in terms of social status and power. The traditional feminine characteristics are childlike, suitable for someone who is dependent upon and subordinate to others. The traditional masculine characteristics equip a person to deal competently with the wider world and to wield authority.

**Stereotyping and Culture**  How widespread is gender stereotyping? In a far-ranging study of students attending post-secondary educational institutions in 30 countries, stereotyping of females and males was pervasive (Williams & Best, 1982). Males were widely believed to be dominant, independent, aggressive, achievement oriented, and enduring. Females were widely believed to be nurturant, affiliative, less esteemed, and more helpful in times of distress.

Of course, in the decades since this study was conducted, traditional gender stereotypes and gender roles have been challenged in many societies, and social inequalities between men and women have diminished. Do gender stereotypes change when the relationship between men and women changes? In a subsequent study, women and men who lived in relatively wealthy, industrialized countries perceived themselves as more similar than did women and men who lived in less-developed countries (Williams & Best, 1989). In the more-developed countries, the women were more likely to pursue post-secondary education and to be gainfully employed. Thus, as sexual equality increases, gender stereotypes may diminish.

However, recent research continues to find that gender stereotyping is pervasive (Leaper, 2013). For example, one study found extensive differences in the stereotyping of females' and males' emotions (Durik & others, 2006). Females were stereotyped as expressing more fear, guilt, love, sadness, shame, surprise, and sympathy than their male counterparts. Males were stereotyped as expressing more anger and pride than their female counterparts. Researchers also have found that boys' gender stereotypes are more rigid than girls' (Blakemore, Berenbaum, & Liben, 2009).

**Developmental Changes in Gender Stereotyping**  Earlier we described how young children stereotype occupations as being masculine or feminine. When do children begin to engage in gender stereotyping? According to Canadian researchers Diane Poulin-Dubois and Lisa Serbin, at around 2 years of age children begin to show some awareness of stereotypical male and female activities (Poulin-Dubois & Serbin, 2006; Poulin-Dubois & others, 2002). In one of their studies, the

**gender stereotypes** Broad categories that reflect impressions and widely held beliefs about what behaviour is appropriate for females and males.

> If you are going to generalize about women, you will find yourself up to here in exceptions.
>
> —DOLORES HITCHENS
> *American Mystery Writer, 20th Century*

researchers presented 2-year-olds with photos of a man and a woman performing the same activity and observed how long the toddlers spent looking at each photo (Serbin, Poulin-Dubois, & Eichstedt, 2002). Staring at the photo for a longer time indicated the toddler was shocked by the image. The activities depicted in the photos were either stereotypically masculine (such as hammering), stereotypically feminine (such as feeding a baby), or neutral (such as putting on shoes). The toddlers stared longer at photos of men performing the stereotypically feminine activities than when the same activities were performed by a woman. However, the toddlers *did not* stare longer at photos of women performing the stereotypically masculine activities than when the same activities were performed by a man. Based on the findings, the authors suggested that the infants might have witnessed more stereotyping of feminine activities in their homes.

Another study examined the extent to which children and their mothers engage in gender stereotyping (Gelman, Taylor, & Nguyen, 2004). The researchers videotaped mothers and their 2-, 4-, and 6-year-old sons and daughters as they discussed a picture book with stereotyped (a boy playing football, for example) and nonstereotyped (a female race car driver, for example) gender activities. Children engaged in more gender stereotyping than did their mothers. However, mothers expressed gender concepts to their children by referencing categories of gender ("Why do you think only *men* can be firefighters?" for example), labelling gender ("That looks like a daddy," for example), and contrasting males and females ("Is that a girl job or a boy job?" for

*What are some developmental changes in children's gender stereotyping?*

example). Gender stereotyping by children was present even in the 2-year-olds, but increased considerably by 4 years of age. This study demonstrated that even when adults don't explicitly engage in gender stereotyping when talking with children, they provide children with information about gender by categorizing gender, labelling gender, and contrasting males and females. Children use these cues to construct an understanding of gender and to guide their behaviour (Leaper & Bigler, 2004).

Gender stereotyping continues to change during middle and late childhood and adolescence (Blakemore, Berenbaum, & Liben, 2009; Miller & others, 2013). By the time children enter elementary school, they have considerable knowledge about which activities are linked with being male or female. Until about 7 to 8 years of age, gender stereotyping is extensive because young children don't recognize individual variations in masculinity and femininity. By 5 years of age, both boys and girls stereotype boys as powerful and in more negative terms, such as mean, and girls in more positive terms, such as nice (Miller & Ruble, 2005). Across the elementary school years, children become more flexible in their gender attitudes (Trautner & others, 2005).

Boys and girls differ in the extent to which they engage in gender stereotyping. One study of 3- to 10-year-old U.S. children revealed that girls and older children used a higher percentage of gender stereotypes (Miller & others, 2009). In this study, appearance stereotypes were more prevalent on the part of girls, while activity (sports, for example) and trait (aggressive, for example) stereotyping was more commonly engaged in by boys. Another study by Lisa Serbin and her colleagues at Concordia University showed that by 18 months of age, girls (but not boys) associated photos of dolls with girls' faces and photos of vehicles with boys' faces (Serbin & others, 2001).

## GENDER SIMILARITIES AND DIFFERENCES

What is the reality behind gender stereotypes? Let's examine some of the differences between the sexes, keeping in mind that (1) the differences are averages and do not apply to all females or all males; (2) even when gender differences occur, there often is considerable overlap between males and females; and (3) the differences may be due to biological factors, sociocultural factors, or both.

**Physical Similarities and Differences**   We could devote pages to describing physical differences between the average male and female. For example, women have about twice the body fat of men, with most of it concentrated around their breasts and hips. In males, fat is more likely to go to the abdomen. On the average, males grow to be 10 percent taller than females. Androgens (the male hormones) promote the growth of long bones; estrogens (the female hormones) stop such growth at puberty.

Many physical differences between men and women are tied to health. From conception on, females have a longer life expectancy than males, and females are less likely than males to develop physical or mental disorders. Females are more resistant to infection and their blood vessels are more elastic than males'. Males have higher levels of stress hormones, which cause faster clotting and higher blood pressure.

Does gender matter when it comes to brain structure and activity? Human brains are much more alike than different, whether the brain belongs to a male or a female (Hyde, 2007b). However, researchers have found some brain differences between females and males. Among the differences that have been discovered are the following:

- Female brains are smaller than male brains, but female brains have more folds; the larger folds (called *convolutions*) allow more surface brain tissue within the skulls of females than males (Luders & others, 2004).
- One part of the hypothalamus involved in sexual behaviour tends to be larger in men than in women (Swaab & others, 2001).
- Portions of the corpus callosum—the band of tissues through which the brain's two hemispheres communicate—may be larger in females than in males, although some studies have found this not to be the case (Bishop & Wahlsten, 1997; Driesen & Raz, 1995; LeVay, 1994).
- An area of the parietal lobe that functions in visuospatial skills tends to be larger in males than in females (Frederikse & others, 2000).
- The areas of the brain involved in emotional expression tend to show more metabolic activity in females than in males (Gur & others, 1995).

Although some differences in brain structure and function have been found, many of these differences are either small or inconsistently supported by research. Also, when sex differences in the brain have been revealed, in many cases they have not been directly linked to psychological differences (Blakemore, Berenbaum, & Liben, 2009). Although research on sex differences in the brain is still in its infancy, it is likely that there are far more similarities than differences in the brains of females and males. A further point is worth noting: Anatomical sex differences in the brain may be due to the biological origins of these differences, behavioural experiences (which underscores the brain's continuing plasticity), or a combination of these factors.

**Cognitive Similarities and Differences**   No gender differences in general intelligence have been revealed, but gender differences have been found in some cognitive areas (Blakemore, Berenbaum, & Liben, 2009; Halpern, 2012). Research has shown that girls and women generally have slightly better verbal skills than boys and men (Blakemore, Berenbaum, & Liben, 2009). For example, some Canadian research has shown that girls perform better than boys in reading achievement (Bussiere & others, 2007; Lynch, 2002). However, a longitudinal study by Linda Phillips at the University of Alberta and her colleagues revealed that in first through third grade, more boys than girls were below average in reading achievement, but this gender difference disappeared in fourth through sixth grade (Phillips & others, 2002).

*developmental* **connection**

**Brain Development.** The human brain has two hemispheres (left and right). To some extent the type of information processed by neurons depends on whether they are in the left or right hemisphere of the brain. Chapter 4, LO 2

"So according to the stereotype, you can put two and two together, but I can read the handwriting on the wall." © 1994 Joel Pett. All Rights Reserved.

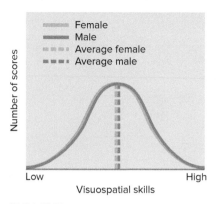

## FIGURE 12.5

**VISUOSPATIAL SKILLS OF MALES AND FEMALES.** Notice that, although an average male's visuospatial skills are higher than an average female's, scores for the two sexes almost entirely overlap. Not all males have better visuospatial skills than all females—the overlap indicates that, although the average male score is higher, many females outperform most males on such tasks.

Are there gender differences in math aptitude? Girls tend to receive higher grades than boys in math classes at school (Halpern & others, 2007; Priess & Hyde, 2010). However, according to results from standardized testing in the United States and Canada, adolescent boys achieve higher math scores than girls (Bussiere & others, 2007). Compared to Canadian adolescent boys, Canadian adolescent girls have lower perceptions of their competence and expected success in mathematics, which reduces the likelihood of pursuing further math education and career options (Watt & others, 2012).

One area of math that has been examined for possible gender differences is visuospatial skills, which include being able to rotate objects mentally and determine what they would look like when rotated. These types of skills are important in courses such as plane and solid geometry and geography. A recent research review revealed that boys have better visuospatial skills than girls (Halpern & others, 2007). Researchers at the Univeristy of New Brunswick found that gender differences in visuospatial abilities increase in adolescence (Voyer, Voyer, & Bryden, 1995). However, some experts argue that the gender difference in visuospatial skills is small (Hyde & Else-Quest, 2013) (see Figure 12.5).

Girls show greater overall academic interest and achievement than boys. For example, a recent study of boys and girls in seventh, eighth, and ninth grade from 12 countries (including Canada) revealed that girls reported higher levels of school engagement than boys and their teachers rated girls' academic performance higher than boys' (Lam & others, 2012). Boys are more likely than girls to be assigned to special/remedial education classes. Moreover, girls are more likely to be attentive in class, put forth more academic effort, and participate more in class than boys are (DeZolt & Hull, 2001).

During the high school years, Canadian girls perceive math and science as more difficult than boys and are less likely to plan to enter the fields of science, technology, engineering, and math (Lupart, Cannon, & Telfer, 2004). Compared to females, males are three times more likely to enrol in programs related to mathematics, computer, and information sciences, and are almost five times more likely to enrol in engineering programs (Statistics Canada, 2013). However, approximately equal numbers of males and females enrol in post-secondary education programs in the areas of physical and life sciences and technologies (Statistics Canada, 2013).

Might same-sex education be better for children than co-ed education? The research evidence related to this question is mixed (Blakemore, Berenbaum, & Liben, 2009). Some research indicates that same-sex education has positive outcomes for girls' achievement, whereas other research does not show any improvements in achievement for girls or boys in same-sex education (Mael, 1998; Warrington & Younger, 2003).

### Socioemotional Similarities and Differences

Four areas of socioemotional development in which gender similarities and differences have been studied extensively are aggression, relationship communication, emotion, and prosocial behaviour.

*Aggression* As noted by Canadian researchers Mara Brendgen and Richard Tremblay, one of the most consistent gender differences is that boys are more physically aggressive than girls (Brendgen, 2009; Tremblay, 2009). The difference occurs in all cultures and appears very early in children's development. The physical aggression difference is especially pronounced when children are provoked. Both biological and environmental factors have been proposed to account for gender differences in aggression. Biological factors include heredity and hormones. Environmental factors include cultural expectations,

*What are some gender differences in aggression?*

adult and peer models, and social agents that reward aggression in boys and punish aggression in girls.

Although boys are consistently more physically aggressive than girls, might girls show at least as much verbal aggression (such as yelling) as boys? When verbal aggression is examined, gender differences often disappear; sometimes, though, verbal aggression is more pronounced in girls than boys (Eagly & Steffen, 1986).

Recently, increased interest has been shown in *relational aggression*, which involves harming someone by manipulating a relationship (Crick & others, 2009; Salmivalli & Peets, 2009). Relational aggression includes such behaviours as trying to make others dislike a certain individual by spreading malicious rumors about the person. Mixed findings have characterized research on whether girls show more relational aggression than boys, but one consistency in findings is that relational aggression comprises a greater percentage of girls' overall aggression than is the case for boys (Putallaz & others, 2007). However, a research review revealed that girls engage in more relational aggression than boys in adolescence but not in childhood (Smith, Rose, & Schwartz-Mette, 2010).

*Relationship Communication*  Are males and females so dramatically different that "men are from Mars" and "women are from Venus," as was proposed in a popular book (Gray, 1992)? Perhaps the gender differences that fascinate people most involve how males and females communicate with each other.

In relationship communication, sociolinguist Deborah Tannen (1990) distinguishes between rapport talk and report talk:

- **Rapport talk** is the language of conversation and a way of establishing connections and negotiating relationships. Girls enjoy rapport talk and conversation that is relationship oriented more than boys do.
- **Report talk** is talk that gives information. Public speaking is an example of report talk. Males hold centre stage through report talk with verbal performances such as storytelling, joking, and lecturing with information.

Tannen says that boys and girls grow up in different worlds of talk—parents, siblings, peers, teachers, and others talk to boys and girls differently. The play of boys and girls is also different. Boys tend to play in large groups that are hierarchically structured, and their groups usually have a leader who tells the others what to do and how to do it. Boys' games have winners and losers and often are the subject of arguments. And boys often boast of their skill and argue about who is best at what. In contrast, girls are more likely to play in small groups or pairs, and at the centre of a girl's world is often a best friend. In girls' friendships and peer groups, intimacy is pervasive. Turn-taking is more characteristic of girls' games than of boys' games. And much of the time, girls simply like to sit and talk with each other, concerned more about being liked by others than jockeying for status in some obvious way.

In sum, Tannen concludes that females are more relationship oriented than males—and that this relationship orientation should be prized as a skill in our culture more than it currently is. Note, however, that some researchers criticize Tannen's ideas as being overly simplified and suggest that communication between males and females is more complex than Tannen indicates (Edwards & Hamilton, 2004). Further, some researchers have found similarities in males' and females' relationship communication strategies (Hyde, 2007a, b). In one study, in their talk men and women described and responded to relationship problems in ways that were more similar than different (MacGeorge, 2004).

Researchers have found that girls are more *people* oriented and boys are more *things* oriented (Galambos & others, 2009; Su, Rounds, & Armstrong, 2009). In a recent research review on gender and adolescent development, this conclusion was supported by findings that girls spend more time in relationships, while

## developmental **connection**

**Relational Aggression.** Behaviours that are intended to harm a peer by manipulating his or her relationships with others, such as spreading rumours or exclusion. Chapter 15, LO 1

**rapport talk** The language of conversation and a way of establishing connections and negotiating relationships; more characteristic of females than of males.

**report talk** Talk that conveys information; more characteristic of males than females.

*What conclusions can be reached about gender similarities/ differences in relationship communication?*

What gender differences characterize children's prosocial behaviour?

boys spend more time alone, playing video games, and playing sports; that girls work at part-time jobs that are people-oriented such as waitressing and babysitting, while boys are more likely to take part-time jobs that involve manual labour and using tools; and that girls are interested in careers that are more people-oriented, such as teaching and social work, while boys are more likely to be interested in object-oriented careers, such as mechanics and engineering (Perry & Pauletti, 2011). Also, in support of Tannen's view, researchers have found that adolescent girls engage in more self-disclosure (communication of intimate details about themselves) in close relationships and are better at actively listening in a conversation than are boys (Leaper & Friedman, 2007).

*Emotion and Its Regulation*   Are there gender differences in processing of emotions? Girls are more likely to express their emotions openly and intensely than are boys, especially in displaying sadness and fear (Blakemore, Berenbaum, & Liben, 2009). According to Melanie Perron of Laurentian University, boys are better at producing a facial expression of anger, whereas girls are better at producing both sad and happy facial expressions (Perron & Gosselin, 2004). Girls also are better at reading others' emotions and more likely to show empathy than boys are (Blakemore, Berenbaum, & Liben, 2009). A recent meta-analysis found that overall gender differences in children's emotional expression were small, with girls showing more positive emotion (sympathy, for example) and more internalized emotions (sadness and anxiety, for example) than boys (Chaplin & Aldao, 2013). In this analysis, the gender difference in positive emotions became more pronounced with age as girls more strongly expressed positive emotions than boys in middle and late childhood and in adolescence.

An important skill is to be able to regulate and control one's emotions and behaviour (Thompson, 2013c, d). Boys usually show less self-regulation of emotion than girls (Pascual & others, 2012). This lower level of self-control can translate into behavioural problems.

**developmental connection**

**Moral Development.** Prosocial behaviour involves behaviour intended to benefit other people. Chapter 13, LO3

*Prosocial Behaviour*   Are there gender differences in prosocial behaviour? Females view themselves as more prosocial and empathic than males (Eisenberg, Spinrad, & Morris, 2013). Across childhood and adolescence, females engage in more prosocial behaviour (Hastings, Utendale, & Sullivan, 2007). The biggest gender difference occurs for kind and considerate behaviour, with a smaller difference in sharing.

The extent to which males and females are different has long been debated. To read more about this controversy, see *Connecting to Current Controversy*.

## connecting to current controversy

### Are Males and Females Really that Different?

Controversy continues about the extent of gender differences and what might cause them (Blakemore, Berenbaum, & Liben, 2009; Leaper, 2013). As we saw earlier, evolutionary psychologists such as David Buss (2012) argue that gender differences are extensive and caused by the adaptive problems humans have faced across their evolutionary history. Alice Eagly (2010, 2013) also concludes that gender differences are substantial, but she reaches a very different conclusion about their cause. She emphasizes that gender differences are due to social conditions that have resulted in women having less power and controlling fewer resources than men.

By contrast, Janet Shibley Hyde (2007b; 2014; Hyde & Else-Quest, 2013) concludes that gender differences have

*(continued)*

*(continued)*

been greatly exaggerated, especially fueled by popular books such as John Gray's (1992) *Men Are from Mars, Women Are from Venus* and Deborah Tannen's (1990) *You Just Don't Understand.* She argues that the research indicates females and males are similar on most psychological factors. In a research review, Hyde (2005) summarized the results of 44 meta-analyses of gender differences and similarities. A *meta-analysis* is a statistical analysis that combines the results of many different studies. In most areas, gender differences either were nonexistent or small, including math ability and communication. Gender differences in physical aggression were moderate. The largest difference occurred on motor skills

(favouring males), followed by sexuality (males masturbate more and are more likely to endorse sex in a casual, uncommitted relationship) and physical aggression (males are more physically aggressive than are females). A research review also concluded that gender differences in adolescence are quite small (Perry & Pauletti, 2011).

Hyde's summary of meta-analyses is still not likely to quiet the controversy about gender differences and similarities, but further research should continue to provide a basis for more accurate judgments about this controversy.

*What possible factors contribute to differences and similarities between males and females?*

---

## Review *Connect* Reflect

 **LO3** Describe gender stereotypes, similarities, and differences.

### Review

- What are gender stereotypes? How extensive is gender stereotyping?
- What are some gender similarities and differences in the areas of biological, cognitive, and socioemotional development?

### *Connect*

- In this section, you learned about gender similarities and differences. How does what you learned in this

section relate to the research on gender and temperament described in Chapter 10?

**Reflect** *Your Own Personal Journey of Life*

- How is your gender behaviour and thinking similar to or different from your mother's and grandmothers' if you are a female? How is your gender behaviour and thinking different from your father's and grandfathers' if you are a male?

---

**Gender-Role Classification** **LO4** Identify how gender roles can be classified.

| What Is Gender-Role Classification? | Masculinity in Childhood and Adolescence | Gender Role Transcendence | Gender in Context |

Not long ago, it was accepted that boys should grow up to be masculine and girls to be feminine, that boys are made of "snips and snails and puppy dogs' tails" and girls are made of "sugar and spice and everything nice." Let's further explore gender classifications of boys and girls as "masculine" and "feminine."

## WHAT IS GENDER-ROLE CLASSIFICATION?

In the past, a well-adjusted boy was expected to be independent, aggressive, and powerful. A well-adjusted girl was expected to be dependent, non-aggressive, and uninterested in power. The masculine characteristics were valued more highly by society than the feminine ones.

In the 1970s, as both females and males became dissatisfied with the burdens imposed by their stereotypic roles, alternatives to femininity and masculinity were proposed. Instead of describing masculinity and femininity as a continuum

**androgyny** The presence of masculine and feminine characteristics in the same person.

in which more of one means less of the other, it was proposed that individuals could have both masculine and feminine traits. This thinking led to the development of the concept of **androgyny**, the presence of masculine and feminine characteristics in the same person (Bem, 1977; Spence & Helmreich, 1978). The androgynous boy might be assertive (masculine) and nurturant (feminine). The androgynous girl might be powerful (masculine) and sensitive to others' feelings (feminine). In one study, it was confirmed that societal changes are encouraging females to be more assertive (Spence & Buckner, 2000).

Measures have been developed to assess androgyny. One of the most widely used measures is the Bem Sex-Role Inventory. To find out whether your gender-role classification is masculine, feminine, or androgynous, see Figure 12.6.

Gender experts such as Sandra Bem argue that androgynous individuals are more flexible, competent, and mentally healthy than their masculine or feminine counterparts. To some degree, though, deciding which gender-role classification is best depends on the context involved (Woodhill & Samuels, 2004). For example, in close relationships, feminine and androgynous orientations might be more desirable because of the expressive nature of such relationships. However, masculine and androgynous orientations might be more desirable in traditional academic and work settings because of the achievement demands in these contexts. For example, one study found that masculine and androgynous individuals had higher expectations for being able to control the outcomes of their academic efforts than feminine or undifferentiated (neither masculine nor feminine) individuals (Choi, 2004).

## MASCULINITY IN CHILDHOOD AND ADOLESCENCE

Concern about the ways boys traditionally have been brought up to behave has been called a "national crisis of boyhood" by William Pollack (1999) in his book *Real Boys*. Pollack says that although there has been considerable talk about the "sensitive male," little has been done to change what he calls the "boy code." He says that this code tells boys they should show little if any emotion as they are growing up. Too often boys are socialized to not show their feelings and to act tough, says Pollack. Boys learn the boy code in many different contexts—sandboxes, playgrounds, schoolrooms, camps, hangouts—and are taught the code by parents, peers, coaches, teachers, and other adults. Pollack, as well as many others, argues that boys would benefit from being socialized to express their anxieties and concerns rather than keep them bottled up, as well as being guided in how to better regulate their aggression.

There also is a special concern about boys who adopt a strong masculine role in adolescence, because this is associated with problem behaviours. Joseph Pleck (1995) points out that what defines traditional masculinity in many Western cultures includes behaviours that do not have social approval but nonetheless validate the adolescent boy's masculinity. In the male adolescent culture, male adolescents perceive that they will be thought of as more masculine if they engage in premarital sex, drink alcohol, take drugs, and participate in illegal delinquent activities.

Recent research suggests that intensely adopting gender roles could potentially be problematic for males as well as females. For example, a recent study revealed that both boys and girls who engaged in extreme gender-typed (hypergender) behaviours had lower levels of school engagement and school attachment (Ueno & McWilliams, 2010).

## GENDER-ROLE TRANSCENDENCE

Some critics of androgyny say that there has been too much talk about gender and that androgyny is less of a solution than originally envisioned. An alternative is *gender-role transcendence*, the view that when an individual's

**Examples of masculine items**

Defends open beliefs
Forceful
Willing to take risks
Dominant
Aggressive

**Examples of feminine items**

Does not use harsh language
Affectionate
Loves children
Understanding
Gentle

*Scoring: The items are scored on independent dimensions of masculinity and femininity as well as androgyny and undifferentiate classifications.*

## FIGURE **12.6**

**THE BEM SEX-ROLE INVENTORY.** These items are from the Bem Sex-Role Inventory (BSRI). When taking the BSRI, an individual is asked to indicate on a 7-point scale how well each of the 60 characteristics describes herself or himself. The scale ranges from 1 (never or almost never true) to 7 (always or almost always true). The items are scored on independent dimensions of masculinity and femininity. Individuals who score high on the masculine items and low on the feminine items are categorized as masculine; those who score high on the feminine items and low on the masculine items are categorized as feminine; and those who score high on both the masculine and feminine items are categorized as androgynous.

competence is at issue, it should be conceptualized on a personal basis rather than on the basis of masculinity, femininity, or androgyny (Pleck, 1983). That is, we should think about ourselves as people first, not as being masculine, feminine, or androgynous. Parents should rear their children to be competent boys and girls, not masculine, feminine, or androgynous, say the gender-role critics. They stress that such gender-role classification leads to too much stereotyping.

## GENDER IN CONTEXT

The concept of gender-role classification involves categorization of a person in terms of personality traits. However, it may be helpful to think of personality in terms of person-situation interaction rather than traits alone (Cloninger, 2013). Thus, in our discussion of gender-role classification, we described how some gender roles might be more appropriate than others, depending on the context, or setting, involved.

To see the importance of considering gender in context, let's examine helping behaviour and emotion. The stereotype is that females are better than males at helping. However, the difference depends on the situation. Females are more likely than males to volunteer their time to help children with personal problems and to engage in caregiving behaviour (Taylor, 2002). However, in situations in which males feel a sense of competence, especially circumstances that involve danger, males are more likely than females to help (Eagly & Crowley, 1986). For example, a male is more likely than a female to stop and help a person who is stranded by the roadside with a flat tire.

"She is emotional; he is not"—that is the master emotional stereotype. However, like differences in helping behaviour, emotional differences in males and females depend on the particular emotion involved and the context in which it is displayed (Shields, 1998). Males are more likely to show anger toward strangers, especially male strangers, when they feel they have been challenged. Males also are more likely to turn their anger into aggressive action. Emotional differences between females and males often show up in contexts that highlight social roles and relationships. For example, females are more likely than males to discuss emotions in terms of relationships, and they are more likely to express fear and sadness.

The importance of considering gender in context is nowhere more apparent than when examining what is culturally prescribed behaviour for females and males in various countries around the world (Best, 2010; Matsumoto & Juang, 2013). To read further about cross-cultural variations in gender, see *Connecting with Diversity.*

*developmental* **connection**

**Theories.** Bronfenbrenner's ecological theory emphasizes the importance of contexts; in his theory, the macrosystem includes cross-cultural comparisons. Chapter 1, LO 3

## connecting with diversity

### Gender Roles Across Cultures

In recent decades, roles assumed by males and females in North America have become increasingly similar—that is, more androgynous. In many countries, though, gender roles have remained more gender specific (UNICEF, 2011). For example, in a number of Middle Eastern countries, the division of labour between males and females is dramatic: males are socialized to work in the public sphere, females in the private world of home and child rearing; a man's duty is to provide for his family, the woman's to care for her family and household. Any deviations from this traditional gender-role orientation receive severe disapproval.

Access to education for girls has improved somewhat around the world, but girls' education still lags behind boys' education. For example, according to a UNICEF (2003) analysis of education around the world, by age 18, girls have received, on average, 4.4 years less education than boys have. This lack of education reduces their chances of developing their potential. Noticeable

*(continued)*

Although access to education for girls has improved, boys still receive approximately 4.4 years more education around the world than girls do. Shown here is a private school for boys in Africa.

exceptions to lower participation and completion rates in education for girls occur in Western nations, Japan, and the Philippines (Brown & Larson, 2002). In most countries, more men than women gain advanced training or advanced degrees (Fussell & Greene, 2002).

Although most countries still have gender gaps that favour males, evidence of increasing gender equality is appearing (Brown & Larson, 2002). For example, among upper socioeconomic status families in India and Japan, fathers are assuming more child-rearing responsibilities (Stevenson & Zusho, 2002; Verma & Saraswathi, 2002). Rates of employment and career opportunities for women are expanding in many countries. Control over adolescent girls' social relationships, especially sexual and romantic relationships, is decreasing in some countries.

*How does gender equality differ between North America and other countries?*

## Review *Connect* Reflect

 **L04** Identify how gender roles can be classified.

### Review

- What is gender-role classification?
- What are some risks of masculinity in childhood and adolescence?
- What is gender-role transcendence?
- How can gender be conceptualized in terms of context?

### Connect

- In this section, you learned about risks related to masculinity in childhood and adolescence. How might early or late maturation (discussed in Chapter 4) affect these risks?

### Reflect *Your Own Personal Journey of Life*

- If and when you have a child, how sensitive will you likely be in rearing the child to be masculine, feminine, or androgynous? Explain.

# case study **connections**

1. How do gender identity, gender role, and gender typing apply to the Reimer twins' story from the chapter opening vignette?

2. In this chapter, you learned about the biological, social, and cognitive influences on gender. How might each of these influences have affected the gender development of Brenda/David Reimer as described in the chapter opening vignette?

3. In this chapter, you learned about gender stereotyping. Based on the story of the Reimer twins described in the chapter opening vignette, how did gender stereotyping affect the twins' gender development?

# reach your **learning goals**

# Gender

## What Is Gender?

 Summarize what gender involves.

- Gender refers to the characteristics of people as males and females. Among the components of gender are gender identity, gender roles, and gender stereotyping. Recent research indicates that knowing whether you are a boy or a girl emerges by 2 years of age. Some children experience gender dysphoria, but many outgrow it.

## Influences on Gender Development

**L02** Discuss the main biological, social, and cognitive influences on gender.

Biological Influences

- The 23rd pair of chromosomes determines our sex. Ordinarily, females have two X chromosomes, and males have one X and one Y. Males and females also produce different concentrations of the hormones known as androgens and estrogens. Early hormonal production is linked with later gender development. In the evolutionary psychology view, evolutionary adaptations produced psychological sex differences that are especially present in sexual behaviour and mating strategies. Chromosomes determine anatomical sex differences, but culture and society strongly influence gender.

Social Influences

- In social role theory, gender differences result from men's and women's contrasting roles; in most cultures, women have less power and status than men and control fewer resources. This gender hierarchy and sexual division of labour are important causes of sex-differentiated behaviour. Psychoanalytic theory of gender emphasizes sexual attraction to the same-sex parent, anxiety about this attraction, and subsequent adoption of the same-sex parent's gender characteristics. Social cognitive theory emphasizes rewards and punishments for gender-appropriate and gender-inappropriate behaviour. Parents and other adults also might assign gender roles to children and reward or punish behaviour along gender lines. Peers are especially adept at rewarding gender-appropriate behaviour. Schools and teachers, as well as the media, influence children's gender development.

Cognitive Influences

- Gender schema theories emphasize the role of cognition in gender development. In gender schema theory, gender typing emerges gradually as children develop gender schemas of what their culture considers to be gender-appropriate and gender-inappropriate.

## Gender Stereotypes, Similarities, and Differences

 Describe gender stereotypes, similarities, and differences.

Gender Stereotyping

- Gender stereotypes are general impressions and beliefs about males and females. Gender stereotypes are widespread. Gender stereotyping changes developmentally; it is present even at 2 years of age but increases considerably in early childhood. In middle and late childhood, children become more flexible in their gender attitudes, but gender stereotyping may increase again in early adolescence. By late adolescence, gender attitudes are often more flexible.

| Gender Similarities and Differences | • Physical and biological differences between males and females are substantial. Women have about twice the body fat of men, are less likely to develop physical or mental disorders, and have a longer life expectancy. Boys and girls show similar achievement in math, although boys have slightly better visuospatial skills. Girls perform better in writing and reading. Some experts, such as Hyde, argue that cognitive differences between males and females have been exaggerated. Males are more physically aggressive than females, while females are more likely to show stronger affiliative interests in adolescence, express their emotions openly and intensely, have better emotional control, and engage in more prosocial behaviour. There is considerable controversy about how similar or different females and males are in a number of areas. |
|---|---|

## Gender-Role Classification

 Identify how gender roles can be classified.

| What Is Gender-Role Classification? | • In the past, the well-adjusted male was supposed to show masculine traits, the well-adjusted female, feminine traits. During the 1970s, alternatives to traditional gender roles were introduced. It was proposed that competent individuals could show both masculine and feminine traits. This thinking led to the development of the concept of androgyny, the presence of masculine and feminine traits in one individual. Gender-role measures often categorize individuals as masculine, feminine, androgynous, or undifferentiated. Most androgynous individuals are flexible and mentally healthy, although the particular context and the individual's culture also determine the adaptiveness of a gender-role orientation. |
|---|---|
| Masculinity in Childhood and Adolescence | • A special concern is that boys raised in a traditional manner are socialized to conceal their emotions. Researchers have found that problem behaviours often characterize highly masculine adolescents. |
| Gender-Role Transcendence | • One alternative to androgyny is gender-role transcendence, a theory which states that there has been too much emphasis on gender and that a better strategy is to think about competence in terms of people rather than gender. |
| Gender in Context | • In thinking about gender, it is important to keep in mind the context in which gender behaviour is displayed. In many countries, traditional gender roles remain dominant. |

# Moral Development | chapter 13

Craig Kielburger was born in Thornhill, Ontario, in 1982. When Craig was 12 years old, he read a news story in the *Toronto Star* about another 12-year-old boy from Pakistan who was forced into bonded labour in a carpet factory when he was just four years old. The young Pakistani boy who spoke out against child labour had been murdered. The story motivated Craig to begin researching child labour and formulated a group with his classmates called the Twelve-Twelve-Year-Olds.

Eventually, this group became Free the Children, an international charitable organization dedicated to helping children across the world. When Craig was 13 years old, he travelled to South Asia to see the living conditions. Learning that the prime minister of Canada was also visiting India, Craig tried to arrange a meeting. When his meeting was denied, Craig held a press conference where he called for Prime Minister Jean Chrétien to take action against child labour because he was morally responsible to do so. Craig's strategy was successful in getting attention from both the media and the prime minister. Chrétien then met with Craig and also spoke to the president of Pakistan and the prime minister of India on the issue of child labour.

Craig Kielburger *(left)* and his brother Marc

Today, Free the Children has built over 650 schools and projects in 45 developing countries. Given the organization's approach of "children helping children," most of the charity's funds are raised by youth. Along with his brother Marc, Craig Kielburger is also the co-founder of Me to We. This social enterprise sells socially conscious products such as ethically made organic clothing and also focuses on youth empowerment by offering leadership camps and international volunteer trips for youth. Half of the annual profits of Me to We are donated to Free the Children.

Craig has been recognized with numerous awards for his charitable work, including the Nelson Mandela Award for Health and Human Rights. In 2007, he was named a Member of the Order of Canada.

# preview

Most people have strong opinions not only about moral and immoral behaviour but also about how moral behaviour should be fostered in children. We will begin our coverage of moral development by exploring its main domains. Next we examine some important contexts that influence moral development. The chapter concludes with an overview of children's prosocial and antisocial behaviour.

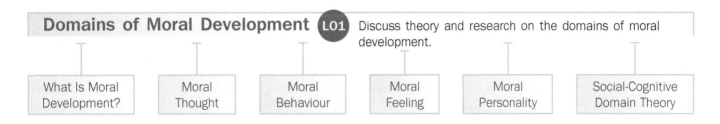

**Domains of Moral Development** (LO1) Discuss theory and research on the domains of moral development.

| What Is Moral Development? | Moral Thought | Moral Behaviour | Moral Feeling | Moral Personality | Social-Cognitive Domain Theory |

What is moral development? What are its main domains?

## WHAT IS MORAL DEVELOPMENT?

**Moral development** involves changes in thoughts, feelings, and behaviours regarding standards of right and wrong. Moral development has an *intrapersonal* dimension, which regulates a person's activities when she or he is not engaged in social interaction, and an *interpersonal* dimension, which regulates social interactions and arbitrates conflict (Walker, 2006). To understand moral development, we need to consider five basic questions:

*First, how do individuals* reason *or* think *about moral decisions?* For example, we might present them with a story in which someone has a conflict about whether or not to cheat in a specific situation, such as taking a test in school. Then they are asked to decide what is appropriate for the character to do and why. The focus is placed on the reasoning the children and adolescents use to justify their moral decisions.

*Second, how do individuals actually* behave *when they must make a moral decision?* For example, with regard to cheating, we might observe whether they resist the temptation to cheat and the environmental circumstances that produced the resistance or cheating. We could conduct our study through a one-way mirror as they are taking a test. We might note whether they take out "cheat" notes, look at another student's answers, and so on.

*Third, how do children and adolescents* feel *about moral matters?* In the example of cheating, do they feel enough guilt to resist temptation? If they do cheat, do feelings of guilt after the transgression keep them from cheating the next time they face temptation?

*Fourth, what comprises children's and adolescents' moral* personality? Continuing with the example of cheating, do they have a moral identity and moral character that is so strong they resist the temptation to cheat?

*Fifth, how is children's and adolescents'* moral domain *different from their social conventional and personal domains?* In domain theory (discussed later in this chapter), cheating resides in the moral domain, along with lying, stealing, and harming another person. Behaviours such as cutting in a line or speaking out of turn are in the social conventional rather than the moral domain, and choosing friends is in the personal domain.

Keep in mind that although we have separated moral development into different domains, the components often are interrelated. For example, if the focus is on the child or adolescent's behaviour, it is still important to evaluate

It is one of the beautiful compensations of this life that no one can sincerely try to help another without helping himself.

—CHARLES DUDLEY WARNER
*American Essayist, 19th Century*

**moral development** Changes in thoughts, feelings, and behaviours regarding standards of right and wrong.

his or her intentions (moral thought). Similarly, emotions accompany, and can distort, moral reasoning.

Let's now discuss the various domains of moral development. We begin with the cognitive domain.

## MORAL THOUGHT

developmental **connection**

**Cognitive Theory.** In which of Piaget's cognitive stages is a 5-year-old heteronomous thinker likely to be? Chapter 6, LO 1

How do individuals think about what is right and wrong? Are children able to evaluate moral questions in the same way that adults can? Piaget had some answers to these questions. So did Lawrence Kohlberg.

**Piaget's Theory**   Interest in how children think about moral issues was stimulated by Piaget (1932), who extensively observed and interviewed children from the ages of 4 through 12. Piaget watched children play marbles to learn how they used and thought about the game's rules. He also asked children about ethical issues—theft, lies, punishment, and justice, for example. Piaget concluded that children go through two distinct stages, separated by a transition period, in how they think about morality.

**heteronomous morality** The first stage of moral development in Piaget's theory, occurring from 4 to 7 years of age. Justice and rules are conceived of as unchangeable properties of the world, removed from the control of people.

- From 4 to 7 years of age, children display **heteronomous morality**, the first stage of moral development in Piaget's theory. Children think of justice and rules as unchangeable properties of the world, removed from the control of people.
- From 7 to 10 years of age, children are in a transition showing some features of the first stage of moral reasoning and some stages of the second stage, autonomous morality.
- From about 10 years of age and older, children show **autonomous morality**, Piaget's second stage of moral development. They become aware that rules and laws are created by people, and in judging an action they consider the actor's intentions as well as the consequences.

**autonomous morality** The second stage of moral development in Piaget's theory, displayed by older children (about 10 years of age and older). The child becomes aware that rules and laws are created by people and that, in judging an action, one should consider the actor's intentions as well as the consequences.

Because young children are heteronomous moralists, they judge the rightness or goodness of behaviour by considering its consequences, not the intentions of the actor. For example, to the heteronomous moralist, breaking twelve cups accidentally is worse than breaking one cup intentionally. As children develop into moral autonomists, intentions assume paramount importance.

The heteronomous thinker also believes that rules are unchangeable and are handed down by all-powerful authorities. When Piaget suggested to young children that they use new rules in a game of marbles, they resisted. By contrast, older children—moral autonomists—accept change and recognize that rules are merely convenient conventions, subject to change.

**immanent justice** Piaget's concept of the childhood expectation that if a rule is broken, punishment will be dealt out immediately.

The heteronomous thinker also believes in **immanent justice**, the concept that if a rule is broken, punishment will be dealt out immediately. The young child believes that a violation is connected automatically to its punishment. Thus, young children often look around worriedly after doing something wrong, expecting inevitable punishment. Immanent justice also implies that if something unfortunate happens to someone, the person must have transgressed earlier. Older children, who are moral autonomists, recognize that punishment occurs only if someone witnesses the wrongdoing and that, even then, punishment is not inevitable. They also realize that bad things can happen to innocent people.

How is this child's moral thinking likely to be different about stealing a cookie depending on whether he is in Piaget's heteronomous or autonomous stage?

How do these changes in moral reasoning occur? Piaget argued that, as children develop, they become more sophisticated in thinking about social matters, especially about the possibilities and conditions of cooperation. Piaget reasoned that this social understanding comes about through the mutual give-and-take of peer relations. In the peer group, plans are negotiated and coordinated, and disagreements are reasoned about and eventually settled. Canadian research by Lawrence Walker supports Piaget's belief that children can achieve advanced moral reasoning through peer discussion (Walker, Hennig, & Krettenauer, 2000). Parent-child relations, in which parents have the power and children do not, are less likely to advance moral reasoning, because rules are often handed down in an authoritarian way (Walker & Hennig, 1999; Walker & Taylor, 1991).

According to the contemporary view, young children are not as egocentric as Piaget envisioned. Thompson (2012) further elaborated on this view, arguing that recent research indicates that young children often show a non-egocentric awareness of others' goals, feelings, and desires and how such internal states are influenced by the actions of others. These ties between advances in moral understanding and theory of mind indicate that young children possess cognitive resources that allow them to be aware of others' intentions and to know when someone violates a moral prohibition. One study of 3-year-olds found that they were less likely to offer assistance to an adult they had previously observed being harmful to another person (Vaish, Carpenter, & Tomasello, 2010).

However, because of limitations in their self-control skills, social understanding, and cognitive flexibility, young children's moral advancements often are inconsistent and vary across situations. They still have a long way to go before they have the capacity for developing a consistent moral character and making ethical judgments.

**Kohlberg's Theory**  A second major perspective on moral development was proposed by Lawrence Kohlberg (1958, 1986). Piaget's cognitive stages of development serve as the underpinnings for Kohlberg's theory, but Kohlberg suggested that there are six stages of moral development. These stages, he argued, are universal. Development from one stage to another, said Kohlberg, is fostered by opportunities to take the perspective of others and to experience conflict between one's current stage of moral thinking and the reasoning of someone at a higher stage.

Kohlberg arrived at his view after 20 years of using a unique interview with children. In the interview, children are presented with a series of stories in which characters face moral dilemmas. The following is the most popular Kohlberg dilemma:

Lawrence Kohlberg

> In Europe a woman was near death from a special kind of cancer. There was one drug that the doctors thought might save her. It was a form of radium that a druggist in the same town had recently discovered. The drug was expensive to make, but the druggist was charging ten times what the drug cost him to make. He paid $200 for the radium and charged $2,000 for a small dose of the drug. The sick woman's husband, Heinz, went to everyone he knew to borrow the money, but he could only get together $1,000, which is half of what it cost. He told the druggist that his wife was dying and asked him to sell it cheaper or let him pay later. But the druggist said, "No, I discovered the drug, and I am going to make money from it." So Heinz got desperate and broke into the man's store to steal the drug for his wife. (Kohlberg, 1969, p. 379)

This story is one of 11 that Kohlberg devised to investigate the nature of moral thought. After reading the story, the interviewee answers a series of questions about the moral dilemma. Should Heinz have stolen the drug? Was stealing it right or wrong? Why? Is it a husband's duty to steal the drug for his wife if he can get it no other way? Would a good husband steal? Did the druggist have the right to charge that much when there was no law setting a limit on the price? Why or why not?

**The Kohlberg Stages**  Based on the answers interviewees gave for this and other moral dilemmas, Kohlberg described three levels of moral thinking, each of which is characterized by two stages (see Figure 13.1). A key concept in understanding progression through the levels and stages is that the person's morality gradually becomes more internal or mature. That is, their reasons for

| LEVEL 1<br><br>Preconventional Level<br><br>**Stage 1**<br>Punishment and Obedience Orientation<br><br>*Children obey because adults tell them to obey. People base their moral decisions on fear of punishment.*<br><br>**Stage 2**<br>Individualism, Instrumental Purpose, and Exchange<br><br>*Individuals pursue their own interests but let others do the same. What is right involves equal exchange.* | LEVEL 2<br><br>Conventional Level<br><br>**Stage 3**<br>Mutual Interpersonal Expectations, Relationships, and Interpersonal Conformity<br><br>*Individuals value trust, caring, and loyalty to others as a basis for moral judgments.*<br><br>**Stage 4**<br>Social System Morality<br><br>*Moral judgments are based on understanding and the social order, law, justice, and duty.* | LEVEL 3<br><br>Postconventional Level<br><br>**Stage 5**<br>Social Contract or Utility and Individual Rights<br><br>*Individuals reason that values, rights, and principles undergird or transcend the law.*<br><br>**Stage 6**<br>Universal Ethical Principles<br><br>*The person has developed moral judgments that are based on universal human rights. When faced with a dilemma between law and conscience, a personal, individualized conscience is followed.* |

FIGURE **13.1**

**KOHLBERG'S THREE LEVELS AND SIX STAGES OF MORAL DEVELOPMENT.**

moral decisions or values begin to go beyond the external or superficial reasons they gave when they were younger. Let's further examine Kohlberg's stages.

*Kohlberg's Level 1: Preconventional Reasoning*  **Preconventional reasoning** is the lowest level of reasoning in Kohlberg's theory and consists of two stages: punishment and obedience orientation (stage 1) and individualism, instrumental purpose, and exchange (stage 2).

- Stage 1. *Punishment and obedience orientation* is the first Kohlberg stage of moral development. At this stage, moral thinking is often tied to punishment. For example, children and adolescents obey adults because adults tell them to obey.
- Stage 2. *Individualism, instrumental purpose, and exchange* is the second stage of Kohlberg's theory. At this stage, individuals pursue their own interests but also let others do the same. Thus, what is right involves an equal exchange. People are nice to others so that others will be nice to them in return.

*Kohlberg's Level 2: Conventional Reasoning*  **Conventional reasoning** is the second, or intermediate, level in Kohlberg's theory of moral development. Individuals abide by certain standards (internal), but they are the standards of others (external), such as parents or the laws of society. The conventional reasoning level consists of two stages: mutual interpersonal expectations, relationships, and interpersonal conformity (stage 3) and social systems morality (stage 4).

- Stage 3. *Mutual interpersonal expectations, relationships, and interpersonal conformity* is Kohlberg's third stage of moral development. At this stage, individuals value trust, caring, and loyalty to others as a basis of moral judgments. Children and adolescents often adopt their parents' moral standards at this stage, seeking to be thought of by their parents as a "good girl" or a "good boy."
- Stage 4. *Social systems morality* is the fourth stage in Kohlberg's theory of moral development. At this stage, moral judgments are based on under-standing the social order, law, justice, and duty. For example, adolescents may say that for a community to work effectively it needs to be protected by laws that are adhered to by its members.

*Kohlberg's Level 3: Postconventional Reasoning*  **Postconventional reasoning** is the third and highest level in Kohlberg's theory. At this level, morality is more

**preconventional reasoning** The lowest level in Kohlberg's theory. At this level, morality is often focused on reward and punishment. The two stages in preconventional reasoning are punishment and obedience orientation (stage 1) and individualism, instrumental purpose, and exchange (stage 2).

**conventional reasoning** The second, or intermediate, level in Kohlberg's theory of moral development. At this level, individuals abide by certain standards (internal), but they are the standards of others such as parents or the laws of society (external). The conventional level consists of two stages: mutual interpersonal expectations, relationships, and interpersonal conformity (stage 3), and social systems morality (stage 4).

**postconventional reasoning** The third and highest level in Kohlberg's theory of moral development. At this level, morality is more internal. The postconventional level consists of two stages: social contract or utility and individual rights (stage 5), and universal ethical principles (stage 6).

internal. The postconventional level of morality consists of two stages: social contract or utility and individual rights (stage 5) and universal ethical principles (stage 6).

- Stage 5. *Social contract or utility and individual rights* is the fifth Kohlberg stage. At this stage, individuals reason that values, rights, and principles undergird or transcend the law. A person evaluates the validity of actual laws and examines social systems in terms of the degree to which they preserve and protect fundamental human rights and values.

- Stage 6. *Universal ethical principles* is the sixth and highest stage in Kohlberg's theory of moral development. At this stage, the person has developed a moral standard based on universal human rights. When faced with a conflict between law and conscience, the person will follow conscience, even though the decision might involve personal risk.

Kohlberg observed that these levels and stages occur in a sequence and are age related: Before age 9, most children use stage 1, preconventional reasoning based on external rewards and punishments, when they consider moral choices. By early adolescence, their moral reasoning is increasingly based on the application of standards set by others. Most adolescents reason at stage 3, with some signs of stages 2 and 4. By early adulthood, a small number of individuals reason in postconventional ways.

What evidence supports this model of moral development? A 20-year longitudinal investigation found that use of stages 1 and 2 decreased with age (Colby & others, 1983) (see Figure 13.2). Stage 4, which did not appear at all in the moral reasoning of 10-year-olds, was reflected in the moral thinking of 62 percent of the 36-year-olds. Stage 5 did not appear until age 20 to 22 and never characterized more than 10 percent of the individuals.

Thus, the moral stages appeared somewhat later than Kohlberg initially envisioned, and reasoning at the higher stages, especially stage 6, was rare. Although stage 6 has been removed from the Kohlberg moral judgment scoring manual, it still is considered to be theoretically important in the Kohlberg scheme of moral development.

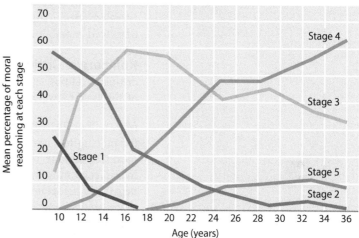

## FIGURE 13.2

**AGE AND THE PERCENTAGE OF INDIVIDUALS AT EACH KOHLBERG STAGE.** In one longitudinal study of males from 10 to 36 years of age, at age 10 most moral reasoning was at stage 2 (Colby & others, 1983). At 16 to 18 years of age, stage 3 became the most frequent type of moral reasoning, and it was not until the mid-twenties that stage 4 became the most frequent. Stage 5 did not appear until 20 to 22 years of age and it never characterized more than 10 percent of the individuals. In this study, the moral stages appeared somewhat later than Kohlberg envisioned, and stage 6 was absent.

**Influences on the Kohlberg Stages** What factors influence movement through Kohlberg's stages? Although moral reasoning at each stage assumes a certain level of cognitive development, Kohlberg argued that advances in children's cognitive development did not ensure development of moral reasoning. Instead, moral reasoning also reflects children's experiences in dealing with moral questions and moral conflict.

Several investigators have tried to advance individuals' levels of moral development by having a person present arguments that reflect moral thinking one stage above the individuals' established levels. This approach

*Why did Piaget and Kohlberg think peer relations are so important in moral development?*

applies the concepts of equilibrium and conflict that Piaget used to explain cognitive development. By presenting arguments slightly beyond the children's level of moral reasoning, the researchers created a disequilibrium that motivated the children to restructure their moral thought. The upshot of studies using this approach is that virtually any plus-stage discussion, for any length of time, seems to promote more advanced moral reasoning (Walker, 1982).

Kohlberg emphasized that peer interaction and perspective taking are crucial aspects of the social stimulation that challenges children to change their moral reasoning. Whereas adults characteristically impose rules and regulations on children, the give-and-take among peers gives children an opportunity to take the perspective of another person and to generate rules democratically. Kohlberg stressed that, in principle, encounters with any peers can produce perspective-taking opportunities that may advance a child's moral reasoning. One research review of cross-cultural studies involving Kohlberg's theory revealed strong support for a link between perspective-taking skills and more advanced moral judgments (Gibbs & others, 2007).

**Kohlberg's Critics** Kohlberg's theory has provoked debate, research, and criticism (Gibbs, 2010; Narvaez & Lapsley, 2009). First, let's examine the extent of the link between moral thought and moral behaviour.

*Moral Thought and Moral Behaviour* Kohlberg's theory has been criticized for placing too much emphasis on moral thought and not enough emphasis on moral behaviour (Walker, 2004). One study found that Canadian adolescents' moral reasoning was positively associated with prosocial behaviour and was negatively associated with antisocial behaviour (Schonert-Reichl, 1999). However, moral reasons can sometimes be a shelter for immoral behaviour. Corrupt CEOs and politicians endorse the loftiest of moral virtues in public until their own behaviour is exposed. Whatever the latest public scandal, you will probably find that the culprits displayed virtuous thoughts but engaged in immoral behaviour.

This 14-year-old boy in Nepal is thought to be the sixth holiest Buddhist in the world. In one study of 20 adolescent male Buddhist monks in Nepal, the issue of justice, a basic theme in Kohlberg's theory, was not a central focus in the monks' moral views (Huebner & Garrard, 1993). Also, the monks' concerns about prevention of suffering and the importance of compassion are not captured in Kohlberg's theory.

No one wants a nation of cheaters and thieves who can reason at the postconventional level. The cheaters and thieves may know what is right yet still do what is wrong. Heinous actions can be cloaked in a mantle of moral virtue.

*Culture and Moral Reasoning* Culture influences moral development more than Kohlberg thought (Tappan, 2013; Wainryb, 2013). Kohlberg emphasized that his stages of moral reasoning are universal, but some critics claim his theory is culturally biased (Miller, 2007, 2013). Both Kohlberg and his critics may be partially correct.

One review of 45 studies in 27 cultures around the world, mostly non-European, provided support for the universality of Kohlberg's first four stages (Snarey, 1987). Individuals in diverse cultures developed through these four stages in sequence as Kohlberg predicted. A more recent research study revealed support for the qualitative shift from stage 2 to stage 3 across cultures (Gibbs & others, 2007).

Stages 5 and 6, however, have not been found in all cultures (Gibbs & others, 2007; Snarey, 1987). Furthermore, Kohlberg's scoring system does not recognize the higher-level moral reasoning of certain cultures—thus, moral reasoning is more culture-specific than Kohlberg envisioned (Snarey, 1987).

In particular, researchers have heard moral judgments based on the principles of communal equity and collective happiness in Israel, the unity and sacredness of all life forms in India, and collective moral responsibility in New Guinea (Snarey, 1987). These examples of moral reasoning would not be scored at the highest level in Kohlberg's system because they are not based on principles of justice. Similar results occurred in a study that assessed the moral development of 20 adolescent male Buddhist monks in Nepal (Huebner & Garrod, 1993). Justice, a basic theme in Kohlberg's theory, was not of paramount importance in the monks' moral views, and their concerns about the prevention of suffering and the role of compassion are not captured by Kohlberg's theory.

In the view of John Gibbs (2010), most young adolescents around the world use the moral judgment of mutuality (stage 3) that makes intimate friendships possible. And by late adolescence, many individuals also are beginning to grasp the importance of agreed-upon standards and institutions for the common good (stage 4). A main exception, though, is the delayed moral judgment of adolescents who regularly engage in delinquency.

One study explored links between culture, mindset, and moral judgment (Narvaez & Hill, 2010). In this study, a higher level of multicultural experience was linked to closed-mindedness (being cognitively inflexible), a growth mindset (perceiving that one's qualities can change and improve through effort), and higher moral judgment.

In sum, although Kohlberg's approach does capture much of the moral reasoning voiced in various cultures around the world, his approach misses or misconstrues some important moral concepts in particular cultures (Gibbs, 2010). To read further about cultural variations in moral reasoning, see *Connecting with Diversity.*

*Families and Moral Development*   Kohlberg argued that family processes are essentially unimportant in children's moral development. As noted earlier, he argued that parent-child relationships usually provide children with little opportunity for

## connecting with diversity

### Moral Reasoning in India

Cultural meaning systems vary around the world, and these systems shape children's morality (Gibbs, 2010; Shiraev & Levy, 2010). Consider Indian Hindu Brahman children (Shweder, Mahapatra, & Miller, 1987). Like people in many other non-Western societies, Indians view moral rules as part of the natural world order. This means that Indians do not distinguish between physical, moral, and social regulation, as North Americans do. For example, in India, violations of food taboos and marital restrictions can be just as serious as acts intended to cause harm to others. In India, social rules are seen as inevitable, much like the law of gravity.

According to William Damon (1988), in places where culturally specific practices take on profound moral and religious significance, as in India, the moral development of children focuses extensively on their adherence to custom and convention. In contrast, Western moral doctrine tends to elevate abstract principles, such as justice and welfare, to a higher moral status than customs or conventions. As in India, socialization practices in many Third World countries actively instill in children a great respect for their culture's traditional codes and practices.

*How would you revise Kohlberg's stages of moral development to better accommodate other cultures? Or can you?*

*How might Asian Indian children and Canadian children reason differently about moral issues?*

Carol Gilligan. *What is Gilligan's view of moral development?*

**developmental connection**

**Gender.** Janet Shibley Hyde concluded that many views and studies of gender exaggerate differences. Chapter 12, LO 3

**justice perspective** A moral perspective that focuses on the rights of the individual; individuals independently make moral decisions.

**care perspective** The moral perspective of Carol Gilligan, in which people are assessed in terms of their connectedness with others and the quality of their interpersonal communication, relationships with others, and concern for others.

give-and-take or perspective taking. Rather, Kohlberg said that such opportunities are more likely to be provided by children's peer relations.

Did Kohlberg underestimate the contribution of family relationships to moral development? A number of developmentalists stress that parents' moral values influence children's developing moral thoughts (Dunn, 2013; Grusec, 2013; Thompson, Meyer, & McGinley, 2013). Nonetheless, most developmentalists agree with Kohlberg, and Piaget, that peers play an important role in the development of moral reasoning.

*Gender and the Care Perspective*   The most publicized criticism of Kohlberg's theory has come from Carol Gilligan (1982, 1992, 1996), who argues that Kohlberg's theory reflects a gender bias. According to Gilligan, Kohlberg's theory is based on a male norm that puts abstract principles above relationships and concern for others and sees the individual as standing alone and independently making moral decisions. It puts justice at the heart of morality. In contrast to Kohlberg's **justice perspective**, which focuses on the rights of the individual, Gilligan argues for a **care perspective**, a moral perspective that views people in terms of their connectedness with others and emphasizes interpersonal communication, relationships with others, and concern for others. According to Gilligan, Kohlberg greatly underplayed the care perspective, perhaps because he was a male, because most of his research was with males rather than females, and because he used male responses as a model for his theory.

A meta-analysis (a statistical analysis that combines the results of many different studies) casts doubt on Gilligan's claim of substantial gender differences in moral judgment (Jaffee & Hyde, 2000). In this study, overall, only a small sex difference in care-based reasoning favoured females, but this sex difference was greater in adolescence than childhood. When differences occurred, they were better explained by the nature of the dilemma than by gender (for example, both males and females tended to use care-based reasoning to deal with interpersonal dilemmas and justice reasoning to handle societal dilemmas). In sum, experts now conclude that there is no evidence to support Gilligan's claim that Kohlberg downplayed females' moral thinking (Hyde, 2007; Walker, 2006, 2013).

## MORAL BEHAVIOUR

What are the basic processes responsible for moral behaviour? What is the nature of self-control and resistance to temptation? How do social cognitive theorists view moral development?

**Basic Processes**   According to Joan Grusec at the University of Toronto, the processes of reinforcement, punishment, and imitation can explain how individuals learn certain responses and why their responses differ from one another (Grusec, 2006). When individuals are reinforced for behaviour that is consistent with laws and social conventions, they are likely to repeat that behaviour. When provided with models who behave morally, individuals are likely to adopt their actions. Finally, when individuals are punished for immoral behaviours, those behaviours can be eliminated, but at the expense of sanctioning punishment by its very use and of causing emotional side effects for the individual.

These general conclusions come with some important qualifiers. The effectiveness of reward and punishment depends on the consistency and timing with which they are administered. For example, it is generally more effective to reward moral behaviour soon after the event occurs than to do so later. The effectiveness of modelling depends on the characteristics of the model and the cognitive skills of the observer. For example, if a parent models giving a donation to a charity, her child must be old enough to understand this behaviour in order for these actions to have an impact on the child's moral development.

Behaviour is situationally dependent. Thus, individuals do not consistently display moral behaviour in different situations. How consistent is moral behaviour? In a classic investigation of moral behaviour, one of the most extensive ever conducted, Hugh Hartshorne and Mark May (1928–1930) observed the moral responses of 11,000 children who were given the opportunity to lie, cheat, and steal in a variety of circumstances—at home, at school, at social events, and in athletics. A completely honest or a completely dishonest child was difficult to find. Situation-specific behaviour was the rule. Children were more likely to cheat when their friends put pressure on them to do so and when the chance of being caught was slim. However, other analyses suggest that although moral behaviour is influenced by situational determinants, some children are more likely than others to cheat, lie, and steal (Burton, 1984).

**Social Cognitive Theory** The **social cognitive theory of morality** emphasizes a distinction between an individual's moral competence (the ability to perform moral behaviours) and moral performance (performing those behaviours in specific situations) (Mischel & Mischel, 1975). *Moral competencies* include what individuals are capable of doing, what they know, their skills, their awareness of moral rules and regulations, and their cognitive ability to construct behaviours. Moral competence is the outgrowth of cognitive-sensory processes. *Moral performance*, or behaviour, however, is determined by motivation and the rewards and incentives to act in a specific moral way.

Canadian-born scholar Albert Bandura (1991, 2002) also stresses that moral development is best understood by considering a combination of social and cognitive factors, especially those involving self-control. He proposes that in developing a moral self, individuals adopt standards of right and wrong that serve as guides and deterrents for conduct. In this self-regulatory process, people monitor their conduct and the conditions under which it occurs, judge it in relation to moral standards, and regulate their actions by the consequences they apply to themselves. They do things that provide them satisfaction and a sense of self-worth. They refrain from behaving in ways that violate their moral standards because such conduct will bring self-condemnation. Self-sanctions keep conduct in line with internal standards (Bandura, 2002). Thus, in Bandura's view, self-regulation rather than abstract reasoning is the key to positive moral development.

**social cognitive theory of morality** The theory that distinguishes between moral competence—the ability to produce moral behaviours—and moral performance—use of those behaviours in specific situations.

*developmental* **connection**

**Social Cognitive Theory.** What are the main themes of Bandura's social cognitive theory? Chapter 1, LO 4

## MORAL FEELING

Think about how you feel when you do something you sense is wrong. Does it affect you emotionally? Maybe you get a twinge of guilt. And when you give someone a gift, you might feel joy. What role do emotions play in moral development, and how do these emotions develop?

**Psychoanalytic Theory** According to Sigmund Freud, guilt and the desire to avoid feeling guilty are the foundation of moral behaviour. In Freud's theory, the *superego* is the moral branch of personality. According to Freud, children fear losing their parents' love and being punished for their unacceptable sexual attraction to the opposite-sex parent. To reduce anxiety, avoid punishment, and maintain parental affection, children identify with the same-sex parent. Through this identification, children *internalize* the parents' standards of right and wrong, which reflect societal prohibitions, and hence develop the superego. In the psychoanalytic account of moral development, children conform to societal standards to avoid guilt. In this way, self-control replaces parental control.

Freud's claims regarding the formation of the ego ideal and conscience cannot be verified. However, researchers can examine the extent to which children feel guilty when they misbehave. Grazyna Kochanska and her colleagues (Kochanska & Askan, 2007; Kochanska & others, 2002, 2005, 2008) have conducted a number of studies that explore children's conscience development.

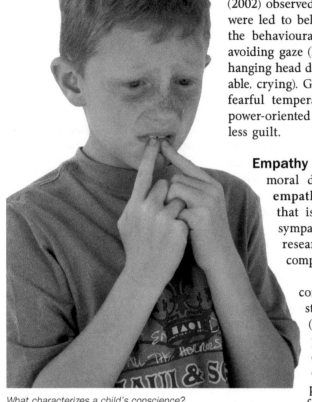

*What characterizes a child's conscience?*

developmental **connection**

**Identity.** In Robert Selman's view, perspective taking is a key aspect of whether children develop prosocial or antisocial attitudes and behaviour. Chapter 11, LO 1

**empathy** Reacting to another's feelings with an emotional response that is similar to the other's feelings.

*What are some developmental changes in empathy?*

In a research review of the subject, she concluded that young children are aware of right and wrong, have the capacity to show empathy toward others, experience guilt, indicate discomfort following a transgression, and are sensitive to violating rules (Kochanska & Aksan, 2007). In one study, Kochanska and her colleagues (2002) observed 106 preschool children in laboratory situations in which they were led to believe that they had damaged valuable objects. In these mishaps, the behavioural indicators of guilt that were coded by observers included avoiding gaze (looking away or down), body tension (squirming, backing away, hanging head down, covering face with hands), and distress (looking uncomfortable, crying). Girls expressed more guilt than boys did. Children with a more fearful temperament expressed more guilt. Children of mothers who used power-oriented discipline (such as spanking, slapping, and yelling) displayed less guilt.

**Empathy**   Positive feelings, such as empathy, contribute to the child's moral development (Eisenberg, Spinrad, & Sadovsky, 2013). Feeling **empathy** means reacting to another's feelings with an emotional response that is similar to the other's feelings. To empathize is not just to sympathize; it is to put oneself in another's place emotionally. Canadian researchers have found that girls demonstrate higher empathy compared to boys (Catherine & Schonert-Reichl, 2011).

Although empathy is an emotional state, it has a cognitive component—the ability to discern another's inner psychological states, or what we have previously called *perspective taking* (Eisenberg & others, 2009). Infants have the capacity for some purely empathic responses, but for effective moral action, children must learn to identify a wide range of emotional states in others and to anticipate what kinds of action will improve another person's emotional state. In a recent Canadian study, researchers found that compared to younger children, empathic older children are able to generate more reasons for an infant's cries and also can generate more strategies to comfort a crying infant (Catherine & Schonert-Reichl, 2011). Thus, empathy develops across childhood.

What are the milestones in children's development of empathy? According to an analysis by child developmentalist William Damon (1988), changes in empathy take place in early infancy, at 1 to 2 years of age, in early childhood, and at 10 to 12 years of age.

*Global empathy* is the young infant's empathic response in which clear boundaries between the feelings and needs of the self and those of another have not yet been established. For example, one 11-month-old infant fought off her own tears, sucked her thumb, and buried her head in her mother's lap after she had seen another child fall and hurt himself. Not all infants cry every time someone else is hurt, though. Many times, an infant will stare at another's pain with curiosity. Although global empathy is observed in some infants, it does not consistently characterize all infants' behaviour.

When they are 1 to 2 years of age, infants may feel genuine concern for the distress of other people, but only when they reach early childhood can they respond appropriately to another person's distress. This ability depends on children's new awareness that people have different reactions to situations. By late childhood, they may begin to feel empathy for the unfortunate.

At about 10 to 12 years of age, individuals develop empathy for people who live in unfortunate circumstances (Damon, 1988). Children's concerns are no longer limited to the feelings of specific persons in situations they directly observe. Instead, 10- to 12-year-olds expand their concerns to the general problems of people in unfortunate circumstances—those who are poor, social outcasts, and so forth. This newfound sensitivity may lead older children to behave altruistically, and later may give a humanitarian flavour to adolescents' development of ideological and political views.

**372**    CHAPTER 13   Moral Development

Although every adolescent may be capable of responding with empathy, not everyone does so. Adolescents' empathic behaviour varies considerably. For example, in older children and adolescents, empathic dysfunctions can contribute to antisocial behaviour. Some delinquents convicted of violent crimes show a lack of feeling for their victims' distress. A 13-year-old boy convicted of violently mugging a number of older adults, when asked about the pain he had caused one blind woman, said, "What do I care? I'm not her" (Damon, 1988). To read further about Damon's description of the developmental changes in empathy from infancy through adolescence, see Figure 13.3.

Efforts to actively teach children to become more empathic are in place in many Canadian schools. For example, the Canadian program, Roots of Empathy, fosters school-aged children's understanding of emotions through lessons with a Roots of Empathy program instructor, in addition to lessons with their regular classroom teacher. Most unique about the program, however, are monthly classroom visits with an infant from their community accompanied by his/her caregiver(s). The classroom "adopts" the infant and the children learn about the baby's growth and development through observation and interaction. A recent study found that children from Vancouver and Toronto in classrooms receiving the Roots of Empathy program better understood the infant's emotions and improved their relationships with peers after experiencing the program (Schonert-Reichl & others, 2012).

**The Contemporary Perspective on the Role of Emotion in Moral Development**   We have seen that classical psychoanalytic theory emphasizes the power of unconscious guilt in moral development but that other theorists, such as Damon, emphasize the role of empathy. Today, many child developmentalists conclude that both positive feelings—such as empathy, sympathy, admiration, and self-esteem—and negative feelings—such as anger, outrage, shame, and guilt—contribute to children's moral development (Damon, 1988; Eisenberg & others, 2009; Thompson, 2013c, d). When strongly experienced, these emotions influence children to act in accord with standards of right and wrong (Prinz, 2009).

## MORAL PERSONALITY

So far we have examined three key dimensions of moral development: thoughts, behaviour, and feelings. Recently, there has been a surge of interest in a fourth dimension: personality (Walker & Frimer, 2009; Walker, 2013). Three aspects of moral personality that have recently been emphasized are (1) moral identity, (2) moral character, and (3) moral exemplars.

**Moral Identity**   A central aspect of the recent interest in the role of personality in moral development focuses on **moral identity**. Individuals have a moral

*developmental* **connection**

**Identity.** According to James Marcia, what are the four statuses of identity development? Chapter 11, LO 3

**moral identity** The aspect of personality that is present when individuals have moral notions and commitments that are central to their lives.

| Age Period | Nature of Empathy |
|---|---|
| Early infancy | Characterized by global empathy, the young infant's empathic response does not distinguish between feelings and needs of self and others. |
| 1 to 2 years of age | Undifferentiated feelings of discomfort at another's distress grow into more genuine feelings of concern, but infants cannot translate realization of other's unhappy feelings into effective action. |
| Early childhood | Children become aware that every person's perspective is unique and that someone else may have a different reaction to a situation. This awareness allows the child to respond more appropriately to another person's distress. |
| 10 to 12 years of age | Children develop an emergent orientation of empathy for people who live in unfortunate circumstances—the poor and the socially outcast. In adolescence, this newfound sensitivity may give a humanitarian flavour to the individual's ideological and political views. |

## FIGURE 13.3
**DAMON'S DESCRIPTION OF DEVELOPMENTAL CHANGES IN EMPATHY.**

The statue commemorating the Famous Five (*left photo*) and Doug Wilson (*right photo*) represent moral exemplars. The Famous Five were five Canadian women who filed a petition in 1928 seeking to have women granted the right to be appointed to the Senate. They posed the following question to the Supreme Court of Canada: "Does the word 'Persons' in Section 24 of the British North America Act, 1867, include female persons?" Although Canada's Supreme Court unanimously decided women are not such persons, this decision was overturned by the British Judicial Committee of the Privy Council in 1929. Doug Wilson (1950–1992) was a graduate student at the University of Saskatchewan in 1975 when he placed an ad in the campus newspaper interested in forming a gay organization at the university. Wilson was immediately suspended from supervising students and began engaging in a legal and political battle to overturn the decision and develop an anti-discrimination policy on campus. Wilson's case is recognized as one of the turning points for attitudes toward homosexuality in Saskatchewan and was an important campaign of the early gay rights movement in Canada.

identity when moral notions and commitments are central to their life (Blasi, 2005). In this view, behaving in a manner that violates this moral commitment places the integrity of the self at risk (Walker, 2013).

Darcia Narvaez (2010b) concluded that a mature moral individual cares about morality and being a moral person. For these individuals, moral responsibility is central to their identity. Mature moral individuals engage in moral metacognition, including moral self-monitoring and moral self-reflection. Moral self-monitoring involves monitoring one's thoughts and actions related to moral situations, and engaging in self-control when it is needed. Moral self-reflection encompasses critical evaluations of one's self-judgments and efforts to minimize bias and self-deception.

**Moral Character** In James Rest's (1995) view, *moral character* involves having the strength of your convictions, persisting, and overcoming distractions and obstacles. If individuals don't have moral character, they may wilt under pressure or fatigue, fail to follow through, or become distracted and discouraged, and fail to behave morally. Moral character presupposes that the person has set moral goals and that achieving those goals involves the commitment to act in accord with those goals.

Lawrence Walker at the University of British Columbia (2002; 2013; Walker & Pitts, 1998) has studied moral character by examining people's conceptions of moral excellence. Among the moral virtues people emphasize are "honesty, truthfulness, and trustworthiness, as well as those of care, compassion, thoughtfulness, and considerateness. Other salient traits revolve around virtues of dependability, loyalty, and conscientiousness" (Walker, 2002, p. 74).

**moral exemplars** People who have lived exemplary lives. Emphasizes the development of personality, identity, character, and virtue to a level that reflects moral excellence and commitment.

**Moral Exemplars** Moral exemplars are people who have lived exemplary lives. Moral exemplars have a moral personality, identity, character, and set of virtues that reflect moral excellence and commitment (Walker, 2013).

In one Canadian study, three different exemplars of morality were examined—brave, caring, and just (Walker & Hennig, 2004). Different personality profiles emerged for the three exemplars. The brave exemplar was characterized by being dominant and extraverted, the caring exemplar by being nurturant and agreeable, and the just exemplar by being conscientious and open to experience. However, a number of traits characterized all three moral exemplars, considered by the researchers to reflect a possible core of moral functioning. This core included being honest and dependable.

## SOCIAL-COGNITIVE DOMAIN THEORY

Judith Smetana (2011a, b; 2013a, b; Smetana & others, 2012) has proposed *social-cognitive domain theory*, which states that there are different domains of social knowledge and reasoning, including moral, social conventional, and personal domains. In social-cognitive domain theory, children's and adolescents' moral, social conventional, and personal knowledge and reasoning emerge from their attempts to understand and deal with different forms of social experience.

**Social conventional reasoning** focuses on conventional rules that have been established by social consensus in order to control behaviour and maintain the social system. The rules themselves are arbitrary, such as raising your hand in class before speaking, using one staircase at school to go up and the other to go down, not cutting in front of someone standing in line to buy movie tickets, and stopping at a stop sign when driving. There are sanctions if we violate these conventions, although the rules can be changed by consensus.

In contrast, moral reasoning focuses on ethical issues and rules of morality. Unlike conventional rules, moral rules are not arbitrary. They are obligatory, widely accepted, and somewhat impersonal (Helwig & Turiel, 2011). Rules pertaining to cheating, stealing, and physically harming another person are moral rules because violation of these rules affronts ethical standards that exist apart from social consensus and convention. Moral judgments involve concepts of justice, whereas social conventional judgments are concepts of social organization. Violating moral rules is usually more serious than violating conventional rules. In a recent study of 2½- to 4-year-olds, children distinguished moral from conventional transgressions on many criteria, but only older preschoolers did so when rating whether others deserved punishment (Smetana & others, 2012). Although rules about lying are often seen as moral rules, rules about certain types of lies are seen as conventional rules. To read more about lying among children, see *Connecting Through Research*.

*How does social conventional reasoning differ from moral reasoning? What are some examples of social conventional reasoning?*

**social conventional reasoning** Focuses on conventional rules established by social consensus, as opposed to moral reasoning that stresses ethical issues.

## connecting through research

### Can Lying Be Viewed Positively?

Kang Lee at the University of Toronto has studied the development of lying among Canadian and Chinese children. In one study (Lee & others, 1997), 7-, 9-, and 11-year old children from Canada and China rated whether a hypothetical character's admission or denial of performing a prosocial or antisocial behaviour was viewed positively or negatively. Both Chinese and Canadian children believed telling the truth about committing a transgression was good and denying one's antisocial behaviour was bad. However, Chinese and Canadian children differed in their evaluation of lying or telling the truth about performing prosocial acts. Lying about performing a good deed was viewed positively for Chinese children but not for Canadian children. In

Chinese culture, modesty is highly valued. Not taking credit for one's prosocial behaviour (known as a modesty lie) is viewed favourably by Chinese children.

Sometimes, "little white lies" are viewed positively because they can help others. Children's willingness to lie to help someone depends on who will benefit from the prosocial act. In another study by Lee and his colleagues, Chinese children were more willing to lie to help a group than to lie to help a friend or themselves, whereas Canadian children showed the opposite pattern (Fu & others, 2007).

*How do children's perceptions of telling "little white lies" differ in Canada and China?*

The social conventional approach is a serious challenge to Kohlberg's approach because Kohlberg argued that social conventions are a stopover on the road to higher moral sophistication. For social conventional reasoning advocates, social conventional reasoning is not lower than postconventional reasoning but rather something that needs to be disentangled from the moral thread (Helwig & Turiel, 2011; Smetana, 2011a, b, 2013a, b; Smetana & others, 2012).

Recently, a distinction also has been made between moral and conventional issues, which are viewed as legitimately subject to adult social regulation, and personal issues, which are more likely subject to the child's or adolescent's independent decision making and personal discretion (Helwig & Turiel, 2011; Smetana, 2011a, b). Personal issues include control over one's body, privacy, and choice of friends and activities. Thus, some actions belong to a *personal* domain not governed by moral strictures or social norms.

## Review *Connect* Reflect

 **LO1** Discuss theory and research on the domains of moral development.

### Review

- What is moral development?
- What are Piaget's and Kohlberg's theories of moral development? What are some criticisms of Kohlberg's theory?
- What processes are involved in moral behaviour? What is the social cognitive theory of moral development?
- How are moral feelings related to moral development?
- What characterizes moral personality?
- What is social conventional reasoning?

### Connect

- In this section, you learned that, according to Piaget, children from 7 to 10 years of age are in a transition period between the heteronomous morality and autonomous morality stages of development. In which stage of cognitive development (as discussed on Chapter 1) would these children be in, according to Piaget?

### Reflect *Your Own Personal Journey of Life*

- Which of the five approaches—cognitive, psychoanalytic, behavioural/ social cognitive, personality, and social-cognitive domain—do you think best describes the way you developed morally? Explain.

## Contexts of Moral Development  **LO2** Explain how parenting and schools influence moral development.

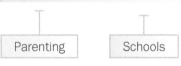

What other contexts play a role in moral development? In particular, what are the roles of parents and schools?

## PARENTING

Both Piaget and Kohlberg held that parents do not provide unique or essential inputs to children's moral development. Parents, in their view, are responsible for providing role-taking opportunities and cognitive conflict, but peers play the primary role in moral development. Canadian research reveals that both parents and peers contribute to children's moral maturity (Hastings & others, 2007; Walker, Hennig, & Krettenauer, 2000). One study found that adolescents' moral motivation was positively linked to the quality of their relationship with their parents (Malti & Buchmann, 2010). Another study revealed that dimensions of authoritative parenting (such as a combination of responsiveness, autonomy-granting, and demandingness) predicted an increase in adolescents' moral identity (Hardy & others, 2010).

In Ross Thompson's (2006, 2010) view, young children are moral apprentices, striving to understand what is moral. They can be assisted in this quest by adult mentors in the home who communicate lessons about morality in everyday experiences (Thompson, Meyer, McGinley, 2013). Among the most important aspects of the relationship between parents and children that contribute to children's moral development are relational quality, parental discipline, and proactive strategies.

**Relational Quality**  Parent-child relationships introduce children to the mutual obligations of close relationships (Laible & Thompson, 2007; Thompson, 2013a, c, d; Thompson, Meyer, & McGinley, 2013). Parents' obligations include engaging in positive caregiving and guiding children to become competent human beings. Children's obligations include responding appropriately to parents' initiatives and maintaining a positive relationship with parents.

In terms of relationship quality, secure attachment may play an important role in children's and adolescents' moral development. A secure attachment can place children on a positive path for internalizing parents' socializing goals and family values. For example, in a recent study, early secure attachment defused a maladaptive trajectory toward antisocial outcomes (Kochanska, Barry, & others, 2010). And in another study, securely attached children's willing, cooperative stance was linked to positive future socialization outcomes such as a lower incidence of externalizing problems (high level of aggression, for example) (Kochanska, Woodard, & others, 2010).

**Parental Discipline**  Discipline techniques used by parents can be classified as love withdrawal, power assertion, and induction (Hoffman, 1970, 1988):

- **Love withdrawal** is a discipline technique in which a parent withholds attention or love from the child, as when the parent refuses to talk to the child or states a dislike for the child. For example, the parent might say, "I'm going to leave you if you do that again" or "I don't like you when you do that."

- **Power assertion** is a discipline technique in which a parent attempts to gain control over the child or the child's resources. Examples include spanking, threatening, or removing privileges.

- **Induction** is a discipline technique in which a parent uses reasoning and explains how the child's actions are likely to affect other people. Examples of induction include, "Don't hit him. He was only trying to help" and "Why are you yelling at her? She didn't mean to trip you."

In contrast to love withdrawal and power assertion, induction is more likely to produce a moderate level of arousal in children, a level that permits them to attend to the cognitive rationale parents offer. Furthermore, induction focuses the child's attention on the action's consequences for others, not on the child's own shortcomings. Thus, child developmentalists recommend induction over power assertion and love withdrawal in disciplining children. A recent study explored the role of inductive discipline in the moral development of adolescents (Patrick & Gibbs, 2012). In this study, adolescents considered parental induction and expression of disappointed expectations as more appropriate than power assertion and love withdrawal and responded with more positive emotion, as well as guilt, to parental induction than to the other parenting techniques. Further, parental induction was linked to a higher moral identity in this study.

**Proactive Strategies**  An important parenting strategy is to proactively avert potential misbehaviour by children before it takes place (Thompson, 2009a; Thompson, McGinley, & Meyer, 2013). With younger children, being proactive means using diversion, such as distracting their attention or moving them to alternative activities. With older children, being proactive may involve talking with them about values that the parents deem important.

> Both theory and empirical data support the conclusion that parents play an important role in children's moral development.
>
> —Nancy Eisenberg
> *Contemporary Psychologist, Arizona State University*

**love withdrawal** A discipline technique in which a parent withholds attention or love from the child in an effort to control the child's behaviour.

**power assertion** A discipline technique in which a parent attempts to gain control over the child or the child's resources.

**induction** A discipline technique in which a parent uses reasoning and explains how the child's actions are likely to affect others.

How are parents' discipline techniques linked to children's moral development? What proactive strategies can parents use to avert potential misbehaviour by children before it happens?

Transmitting these values can help older children and adolescents to resist the temptations that inevitably emerge in contexts such as peer relations and the media that can be outside the scope of direct parental monitoring.

A research review (Eisenberg & Valiente, 2002, p. 134) concluded that, in general, children who behave morally tend to have parents who

- are warm and supportive rather than punitive
- use inductive discipline
- provide opportunities for the children to learn about others' perspectives and feelings
- involve children in family decision making and in the process of thinking about moral decisions
- model moral behaviours and thinking themselves, and provide opportunities for their children to do so
- provide information about what behaviours are expected and why
- foster an internal rather than an external sense of morality

Parents who show this configuration of behaviours likely foster concern and caring about others in their children, and create a positive parent-child relationship.

## SCHOOLS

No matter how parents treat their children at home, they may feel that they have little control over a great deal of their children's moral education. Children spend extensive time away from their parents at school, and the time spent in that environment can influence children's moral development (Berkowitz & others, 2013; Narvaez, 2013; Narvaez & Lapsley, 2009; Nucci, 2013).

**The Hidden Curriculum**   More than 60 years ago, educator John Dewey (1933) recognized that even when schools do not have specific programs in moral education, they provide moral education through a "hidden curriculum." The **hidden curriculum** is conveyed by the moral atmosphere that is a part of every school. The moral atmosphere is created by school and classroom rules, the moral orientation of teachers and school administrators, and text materials. Teachers serve as models of ethical or unethical behaviour. Classroom rules and peer relations at school transmit attitudes about cheating, lying, stealing, and consideration of others. And through its rules and regulations, the school administration infuses the school with a value system.

**hidden curriculum** The pervasive moral atmosphere that characterizes each school.

**Character Education**   Yet another approach to moral education is **character education**, a direct education approach that involves teaching students a basic "moral literacy" to prevent them from engaging in immoral behaviour and doing harm to themselves or others (Narvaez & Lapsley, 2009). The argument is that behaviours such as lying, stealing, and cheating are wrong, and students should be taught this throughout their education (Berkowitz & others, 2013; Berkowitz, Battistich, & Bier, 2008).

Schools adopting character education should have an explicit moral code that is clearly communicated to students. Any violations of the code should be met with sanctions. Instruction in specified moral concepts, such as cheating, can take the form of example and definition, class discussions and role-playing, or rewarding students for proper behaviour. More recently, an emphasis on the importance of encouraging students to develop a care perspective has been accepted as a relevant aspect of character education (Noddings, 2008). Rather than just instructing adolescents to refrain from engaging in morally deviant behaviour, a care perspective advocates educating students in the importance of engaging in prosocial behaviours, such as considering others' feelings, being sensitive to others, and helping others in

**character education** A direct moral education approach that involves teaching students a basic "moral literacy" to prevent them from engaging in immoral behaviour or doing harm to themselves or others.

a semester-long course to discuss a number of moral issues. The hope is that students will develop more advanced notions of concepts such as cooperation, trust, responsibility, and community (Enright & others, 2008).

Although character education is becoming commonplace in Canadian schools, it is not without controversy. For example, Sue Winton at the University of Toronto argues that character education "limits opportunities for students to learn to value diverse perspectives, consider the complexity of morality and decision-making, and develop a disposition towards critical thinking and a view of themselves as social actors" (Winton, 2012, p. 42).

**Values Clarification**   One approach to providing moral education is **values clarification**, which means helping people clarify what their lives are for and what is worth working for. Unlike character education, which tells students what their values should be, values clarification encourages students to define their own values and understand the values of others (Williams & others, 2003).

Advocates of values clarification say it is beneficial to students because it promotes critical thinking and personal reflection in addition to perspective taking skills. However, critics argue that its content offends community standards and that the values-clarification exercises fail to stress right behaviour.

**Cognitive Moral Education**   Another approach to moral education, **cognitive moral education**, is based on the belief that students should learn to value such things as democracy and justice as their moral reasoning develops. Kohlberg's theory has served as the foundation for a number of cognitive moral education programs. In a typical program, high school students meet in a semester-long course to discuss a number of moral issues. The instructor acts as a facilitator rather than as a director of the class. The hope is that students will develop more advanced notions of concepts such as cooperation, trust, responsibility, and community (Power & Higgins-D'Alessandro, 2008).

**Service Learning**   At the beginning of the chapter you read about Craig Kielburger, who is strongly motivated to make a positive difference in the lives of children worldwide. Craig Kielburger has a sense of social responsibility that an increasing number of educational programs seek to promote in students through **service learning**, a form of education that promotes social responsibility through service to the community. In service learning, adolescents engage in activities such as tutoring, helping older adults, working in a hospital, assisting at a child-care centre, or cleaning up a vacant lot to make a play area.

An important goal of service learning is to help adolescents become less self-centred and more strongly motivated to help others (Hart, Adkins, & Donnelly, 2013; Schmidt, Shumow, & Kackar, 2012). Service learning takes education out into the community. Adolescent volunteers tend to be extraverted, be committed to others, and have a high level of self-understanding (Eisenberg & others, 2009). A recent study found that volunteering among Canadian adolescents led to a reduction in cardiovascular risk factors (Schreier, Schonert-Reichl, & Chen, 2013). Also, one study revealed that adolescent girls participated in service learning more than adolescent boys (Webster & Worrell, 2008). A number of studies have found that that adolescents who are involved in religious institutions are more likely to engage in service learning than their counterparts who don't participate in religious institutions (Oser, Scarlett, & Bucher, 2006).

Researchers have found that service learning benefits adolescents in a number of ways (Hart, Adkins, & Donnelly, 2013). Improvements in adolescent development attributed to service learning include higher grades in school, increased goal-setting, higher self-esteem, an improved sense of being able to make a difference for others, and an increased likelihood that they will serve as volunteers in the future. A study of more than 4,000 high school students revealed that those who worked directly with individuals in need were better adjusted academically, while those who worked for organizations had better civic outcomes

More than just about anything else, 12-year-old Katie Bell (*at bottom*) wanted a playground in her town. She knew that other kids also wanted one so she put together a group that generated fund-raising ideas for the playground. They presented their ideas to the town council and helped raise money by selling candy and sandwiches door-to-door. Katie says, "We learned to work as a community. This will be an important place for people to go and have picnics and make new friends." Katie's advice: "You won't get anywhere if you don't try."

**values clarification** Helping people clarify their sense of their purpose in life and what is worth working for. Students are encouraged to define their own values and understand others' values.

**cognitive moral education** Education based on the belief that students should learn to value things like democracy and justice as their moral reasoning develops; Kohlberg's theory has been the basis for many of the cognitive moral education approaches.

**service learning** A form of education that promotes social responsibility and service to the community.

Nina Vasan (*centre*) founded a group of adolescent volunteers who have raised hundreds of thousands of dollars for cancer research. She created a letter-writing campaign to obtain volunteers, established a website and set up an e-mail network, started a newsletter, and arranged monthly phone calls to communicate ideas and plan projects.

In Nina's words.

> . . . I realized that teenagers like myself could make a big difference in the fight against cancer. I knew that the best way to help was to start a teen organization. . . To be a beneficial part of the human race, it is essential and fundamental to give back to the community and others. (Vasan, 2002, p. 1)

Nina Vasan's work on behalf of cancer involved pursuing a purpose. She says that the success of her work involving cancer far outweighs the many honours she has been awarded (Damon, 2008).

(Schmidt, Shumow, & Kackar, 2007). The benefits of service learning, both for the volunteer and the recipient, suggest that more adolescents should be required to participate in such programs (Enfield & Collins, 2008; Nelson & Eckstein, 2008).

**Cheating**   A moral education concern is whether students cheat and how to handle the cheating if teachers discover it (Anderman & Anderman, 2010). Academic cheating can take many forms, including plagiarism, using "cheat sheets" during an exam, copying from a neighbour during a test, purchasing papers, and falsifying lab results. A 2008 survey of almost 30,000 high school students revealed that 64 percent of the students said they had cheated on a test in school during the past year and 36 percent of the students reported that they had plagiarized information from the Internet for an assignment in the past year (Josephson Institute of Ethics, 2008).

Why do students cheat? Among the reasons students give for cheating include pressure to get high grades, compressed schedules, poor teaching, and lack of interest (Stephens, 2008). In terms of poor teaching, "students are more likely to cheat when they perceive their teacher to be incompetent, unfair, and uncaring" (Stephens, 2008, p. 140).

The context affects whether or not students cheat (Vandehey, Diekhoff, & LaBeff, 2007). For example, students are more likely to cheat when they are not being closely monitored during a test, when they know their peers are cheating, when they know whether another student has been caught cheating, and when student scores are made public (Anderman & Anderman, 2010).

Among the strategies for decreasing academic cheating are preventive measures such as making sure students are aware of what constitutes cheating and what the consequences will be if they cheat, closely monitoring students' behaviour while they are taking tests, and emphasizing the importance of being a moral, responsible individual who engages in academic integrity. In promoting academic integrity, many post-secondary institutions have instituted an honour code policy that emphasizes self-responsibility, fairness, trust, and scholarship. However, few secondary schools have developed honour code policies.

**An Integrative Approach**   Darcia Narvaez (2006, 2013) emphasizes an *integrative approach* to moral education that encompasses both the reflective moral thinking and commitment to justice advocated in Kohlberg's approach and the process of developing a particular moral character emphasized in the character education approach. She highlights the Child

*Why do students cheat? What are some strategies teachers can adopt to prevent cheating?*

Development Project as an excellent example of an integrative moral education approach. In the Child Development Project, students are given multiple opportunities to discuss other students' experiences, which encourages empathy and perspective taking, and they participate in exercises that encourage them to reflect on their own behaviours in terms of values such as fairness and social responsibility (Solomon & others, 2002). Adults coach students in ethical decision making and guide them in becoming more caring individuals. Students experience a caring community, not only in the classroom, but also in after-school activities and through parental involvement in the program. Research evaluations of the Child Development Project indicate that it is related to an improved sense of community, an increase in prosocial behaviour, better interpersonal understanding, and enhanced social problem solving (Battistich, 2008).

## Review *Connect* Reflect

 **L02** Explain how parenting and schools influence moral development.

### Review

- How does parental discipline affect moral development? What are some effective parenting strategies for advancing children's moral development?
- What is the hidden curriculum? What are some contemporary approaches to moral education?

### *Connect*

- In this section, you learned that secure attachment in infancy was linked to

early development of conscience. What characterizes secure attachment (discussed in Chapter 10)?

### **Reflect** *Your Own Personal Journey of Life*

- What type of discipline did your parents use with you? What effect do you think this approach has had on your moral development?

## Prosocial and Antisocial Behaviour   **L03**  Describe the development of prosocial and antisocial behaviour.

Prosocial Behaviour

Antisocial Behaviour

Service learning encourages positive moral behaviour. This behaviour is not just moral behaviour but behaviour that is intended to benefit other people, and psychologists call it *prosocial behaviour* (Carlo, 2013; Eisenberg, Spinrad, & Morris, 2013). Craig Kielburger, whose story was introduced at the beginning of the chapter, is an exemplary model of someone committed to prosocial behaviour. Of course, people have always engaged in antisocial behaviour, as well. In this section, we will take a closer look at prosocial and antisocial behaviour, focusing on how each type of behaviour develops.

## PROSOCIAL BEHAVIOUR

Caring about the welfare and rights of others, feeling concern and empathy for them, and acting in a way that benefits others are all components of prosocial behaviour. The purest forms of prosocial behaviour are motivated by **altruism**, an unselfish interest in helping another person (Grusec, Hastings, & Almas, 2011). As we see next, learning to share is an important aspect of prosocial behaviour.

**altruism** An unselfish interest in helping another person.

William Damon (1988) described a developmental sequence by which sharing develops in children. Most sharing during the first three years of life is done for non-empathic reasons, such as for the fun of the social play ritual or out of imitation. Then, at about 4 years of age, a combination of empathic awareness and adult encouragement produces a sense of obligation on the part of the child to share with others. Most 4-year-olds are not selfless saints, however. Children

*How does children's sharing change from the preschool to the elementary school years?*

believe they have an obligation to share but do not necessarily think they should be as generous to others as they are to themselves. Neither do their actions always support their beliefs, especially when they covet an object. What is important developmentally is that the child has developed a belief that sharing is an obligatory part of a social relationship and involves a question of right and wrong. These early ideas about sharing set the stage for giant strides that children make in the years that follow.

By the start of the elementary school years, children begin to express more complicated notions of what is fair. Throughout history, varied definitions of fairness have been used as the basis for distributing goods and resolving conflicts. These definitions involve the principles of equality, merit, and benevolence: *Equality* means that everyone is treated the same; *merit* means giving extra rewards for hard work, a talented performance, or other laudatory behaviour; *benevolence* means giving special consideration to individuals in a disadvantaged condition.

Equality is the first of these principles used regularly by elementary school children. In one Canadian study, 10-year-olds divided the use of a toy more equally among peers than did 6-year-olds (Benenson & others, 2003). Children also believe that equity means special treatment for those who deserve it—a belief that applies the principles of merit and benevolence. Canadian research shows that preschool children consider an actor's intentions when making moral judgments (Chandler, Sokel, & Weinryb, 2000). Other recent research shows that 5- and 9-month-old Canadian infants prefer those who share to those who are selfish (Hamlin & Wynn, 2011).

Parental advice and prodding certainly foster standards of sharing, but the give-and-take of peer requests and arguments provide the most immediate stimulation of sharing. Parents can set examples that children carry into their interactions and communication with peers, but parents are not present during all of their children's peer exchanges. The day-to-day construction of fairness standards is done by children in collaboration and negotiation with each other. A recent study found that authoritative parenting by mothers, but not fathers, contributed to adolescents' subsequent engagement in prosocial behaviour one year later (Padilla-Walker & others, 2012). Other research also has found that mothers are more likely to influence adolescents' prosocial behaviour than are fathers (Carlo & others, 2011).

How does prosocial behaviour change through childhood and adolescence? A recent study of 5- to 13-year-olds found that with increasing age children attributed more positive emotions to people who sacrifice their own desires to help others who are needy and that they become more discriminating about contexts that call for altruistic action (Weller & Lagattuta, 2013). Prosocial behaviour occurs more often in adolescence than in childhood, although examples of caring for others and comforting someone in distress occur even during the preschool years (Eisenberg, Spinrad, & Sadovsky, 2006).

Also, keep in mind the gender differences in prosocial behaviour described in Chapter 12. Recall that females view themselves as more prosocial and empathic, and they also engage in more prosocial behaviour than males (Eisenberg, Spinrad, & Morris, 2013).

Are there different types of prosocial behaviour? In a recent study, Gustavo Carlo and his colleagues (2010, pp. 340–341) explored this topic and confirmed the presence of six types of prosocial behaviour in young adolescents:

- altruism ("One of the best things about doing charity work is that it looks good.")
- public ("Helping others while I'm being watched is when I work best.")
- emotional ("I usually help others when they are very upset.")
- dire ("I tend to help people who are hurt badly.")

- anonymous ("I prefer to donate money without anyone knowing.")
- compliant ("I never wait to help others when they ask for it.")

In this study, adolescent girls reported more emotional, dire, compliant, and altruistic behaviour than did boys, while boys engaged in more public prosocial behaviour. Parental monitoring was positively related to emotional, dire, and compliant behaviour but not to the other types of behaviour. Compliant, anonymous, and altruistic prosocial behaviour were positively related to religiosity.

Most research on prosocial behaviour depicts the concept in a global and unidimensional manner. The study by Carlo & others (2010) illustrates that in thinking about and studying prosocial behaviour, it is important to consider multiple dimensions.

Two other aspects of prosocial behaviour are forgiveness and gratitude. **Forgiveness** is an aspect of prosocial behaviour that occurs when the injured person releases the injurer from possible behavioural retaliation. In one investigation, individuals from the fourth grade through adulthood were asked questions about forgiveness (Enright, Santos, & Al-Mabuk, 1989). The individuals were especially swayed by peer pressure in their willingness to forgive others. Also, a recent study revealed that when adolescents encountered hurtful experiences in school settings if they disliked the transgressor they had more hostile thoughts, feelings of anger, and avoidance/revenge tendencies than when they liked the transgressing peer (Peets, Hodges, & Salmivalli, 2013).

**Gratitude** is a feeling of thankfulness and appreciation, especially in response to someone doing something kind or helpful (Grant & Gino, 2010). Interest in studying adolescents' gratitude or lack thereof is increasing. Consider the following recent studies:

- Gratitude was linked to a number of positive aspects of development in young adolescents, including satisfaction with one's family, optimism, and prosocial behaviour (Froh, Yurkewicz, & Kashdan, 2009).
- Adolescents' expression of gratitude was linked to having fewer depressive symptoms (Lambert, Fincham, & Stillman, 2012).
- Chinese adolescents who had a higher level of gratitude were less likely to engage in suicidal ideation and suicide attempts (Li & others, 2012).
- A longitudinal study assessed the gratitude of adolescents at 10 to 14 years of age (Bono, 2012). Four years later, the most grateful adolescents (top 20 percent) had a stronger sense of the meaning of life, were more satisfied with their life, were happier and more hopeful, and had a lower level of negative emotions and were less depressed than the least grateful students (bottom 20 percent).

Compared with antisocial behaviour such as juvenile delinquency, less attention has been given to prosocial behaviour in adolescence. We still do not have adequate research information about such topics as how youth perceive prosocial norms and how school policies and peers influence prosocial behaviour (Siu, Shek, & Law, 2012).

**forgiveness** An aspect of prosocial behaviour that occurs when an injured person releases the injurer from possible behavioural retaliation.

**gratitude** A feeling of thankfulness and appreciation, especially in response to someone doing something kind or helpful.

## ANTISOCIAL BEHAVIOUR

Most children and adolescents at one time or another act out or do things that are destructive or troublesome for themselves or others. If these behaviours occur often, clinical psychologists or psychiatrists diagnose them as conduct disorders. If these behaviours result in illegal acts by youth, society labels them *delinquents*. Both problems are much more common in males than in females.

**Conduct Disorder**   Conduct disorder refers to age-inappropriate actions and attitudes that violate family expectations, society's norms, and the personal or property rights of others. Children with conduct problems show a wide range

**conduct disorder** Age-inappropriate actions and attitudes that violate family expectations, society's norms, and the personal or property rights of others.

of rule-violating behaviours, from swearing and temper tantrums to severe vandalism, theft, and assault (Burke, 2011; Farrington, 2009). Conduct disorder is much more common among boys than girls (McCabe & others, 2004).

An estimated 5 percent of children show serious conduct problems. Among Canadian adolescents aged 12 to 16 years, the 6-month prevalence of conduct disorder is 10 percent for boys and 4 percent for girls (Murray & Farrington, 2010). These children are often described as showing an *externalizing*, or *undercontrolled*, pattern of behaviour. Children who show this pattern often are impulsive, overactive, and aggressive and engage in delinquent actions.

Conduct problems in children are best explained by a confluence of causes, or risk factors, operating over time (Burke, 2011; Thio, 2010). These include possible genetic inheritance of a difficult temperament, ineffective parenting, living in a neighbourhood where violence is common, and ineffective schools. On the positive side, one study revealed that young adolescents' school connectedness served as a protective factor for early adolescent conduct problems (Loukas, Roalson, & Herrera, 2010).

Despite considerable efforts to help children with conduct problems, there is a lack of consensus on what works (Mash & Wolfe, 2013). Sometimes recommended is a multisystem treatment carried out with all family members, school personnel, juvenile justice staff, and other individuals in the child's life.

*What are some characteristics of conduct disorder?*

### Juvenile Delinquency

What is juvenile delinquency? What are the antecedents of delinquency? What types of interventions have been used to prevent or reduce delinquency?

*What Is Juvenile Delinquency?* The term **juvenile delinquency** refers to a broad range of behaviours, from socially unacceptable behaviour (such as acting out in school) to non-criminal delinquent acts (such as running away and truancy) to criminal acts (such as burglary, rape, and homicide). Males are more likely to engage in delinquency than are females (Thio, 2010). Among Canadians between the ages of 12 to 17, 18.9 percent said they engaged in violent delinquency in the past year, the majority of these youth being males (Fitzgerald & Carrington, 2011).

According to the Criminal Code of Canada, children under the age of twelve years cannot be convicted of a criminal offence. However, under the *Youth Criminal Justice Act*, adolescents between the ages of 12 and 18 who commit criminal acts can be tried in youth justice court. As you will read in *Connecting to Current Controversy*, these laws may not necessarily apply under certain circumstances.

As adolescents reach adulthood, do their rates of delinquency and crime change? Research indicates that theft, property damage, and physical aggression decrease from 18 to 26 years of age (Schulenberg & Zarrett, 2006). The peak for property damage is 16 to 18 years of age for males, and 15 to 17 years of age for females. However, the peak for violence is 18 to 19 years of age for males and 19 to 21 years of age for females (Farrington, 2009).

A distinction is made between early-onset (before age 11) and late-onset (11 and older) antisocial behaviour. Early-onset antisocial behaviour is associated with more negative developmental outcomes than late-onset antisocial behaviour (Schulenberg & Zarrett, 2006). Early-onset antisocial behaviour is more likely to persist into emerging adulthood and is associated with increased problems involving mental health and relationships.

*Antecedents of Juvenile Delinquency* Predictors of delinquency include conflict with authority, minor covert acts that are followed by property damage and other more serious acts, minor aggression followed by fighting and violence, identity (negative identity), self-control (low degree), cognitive distortions (egocentric bias), age (early initiation), sex (male), expectations for education (low expectations, little commitment), school achievement (low achievement in early

**juvenile delinquency** Refers to a great variety of behaviours by an adolescent, ranging from unacceptable behaviour to breaking the law.

## Should Young People Be Tried Based on the Severity of the Crime, Regardless of Age?

Two issues in juvenile justice are whether a child who commits a crime should be tried as a young criminal and whether an adolescent who commits a crime should be tried as an adult. Some psychologists have proposed that individuals 12 and under should not be evaluated under adult criminal laws and that those 17 and older should be (Steinberg & Cauffman, 2001; Steinberg, 2009). They also recommend that individuals 13 to 16 years of age be given some type of individualized assessment in terms of

whether to be tried as an adult. This framework argues strongly against court placement based solely on the nature of an offence and takes into account the offender's developmental maturity.

Canada's *Youth Criminal Justice Act* (YCJA) makes it mandatory that the Crown consider seeking an adult sentence for individuals over the age of 14 who are charged with violent crimes including murder, attempted murder, manslaughter, or aggravated sexual assault. In addition, children between the ages of 10 and 12 who commit criminal acts may be dealt with as young criminals and be sentenced under the YCJA.

*Do you think Canadian youth justice laws appropriately consider children and adolescents' cognitive development?*

grades), peer influence (heavy influence, low resistance), socioeconomic status (low), parental role (lack of monitoring, low support, and ineffective discipline), siblings (having an older sibling who is a delinquent), and neighbourhood quality (urban, high crime, high mobility).

Family support systems are also associated with delinquency (Farrington, 2009; Lansford & others, 2013). Parental monitoring of adolescents is especially important in determining whether an adolescent becomes a delinquent (Laird & others, 2008). For example, among families living in high-risk neighbourhoods, parents' lack of knowledge of their young adolescents' whereabouts has been linked to whether the adolescents engaged in delinquency later in adolescence (Lahey & others, 2008). Indeed, early parental monitoring in adolescence and ongoing parental support have been linked to a lower incidence of criminal behaviour in emerging adulthood (Johnson & others, 2011). One recent study also found that low parental control predicted delinquency, indirectly through its link to deviant peer affiliation (Deutsch & others, 2012). And in another recent study, authoritative parenting increased adolescents' perception of the legitimacy of parental authority, while authoritarian parenting reduced the perception of legitimacy of parental authority (Trinkner & others, 2012). In this study, youths' perception of parental legitimacy was linked to a lower level of future delinquency.

Family discord and inconsistent and inappropriate discipline are also associated with delinquency (Capaldi & Shortt, 2003). Thankfully, recent research indicates that family therapy is often effective in reducing delinquency (Baldwin & others, 2012; Henggeler & Sheidow, 2012). A recent meta-analysis found that of five program types (case management, individual treatment, youth court, restorative justice, and family treatment), family treatment was the only one that was linked to a reduction in recidivism for youth offenders (Schwalbe & others, 2012).

Rare are the studies that actually demonstrate in an experimental design that changing parenting practices in childhood can lead to a lower incidence of juvenile delinquency in adolescence. However, one study by Marion Forgatch and her colleagues (2009) randomly assigned divorced mothers of sons to an experimental group (mothers received extensive parenting training) or a control group (mothers received no parenting training) when their sons were in the first through third grades. The parenting training consisted of 14 parent group meetings that focused primarily on improving parenting practices (skill encouragement, limit setting, monitoring, problem solving, and positive involvement). Best practices for emotion regulation, managing interparental conflict, and talking with children about divorce also were included in the sessions. Improved

*developmental* **connection**

**Parenting.** A neglectful parenting style is linked with a low level of self-control in children. Chapter 14, LO 2

parenting practices and reduced contact with deviant peers were linked with lower rates of delinquency in the experimental group than in the control group at a 9-year follow-up assessment.

An increasing number of studies have found that siblings can have a strong influence on delinquency (Bank, Burraston, & Snyder, 2004). For example, in one study, high levels of hostile sibling relationships and older sibling delinquency were linked with younger sibling delinquency in both brother pairs and sister pairs (Slomkowski & others, 2001).

Having delinquent peers increases the risk of becoming delinquent. In one Canadian study, peer rejection and having deviant friends at 7 to 13 years of age were linked with increased delinquency at 14 to 15 years of age (Vitaro, Pedersen, & Brendgen, 2007). Among Canadian children with delinquent friends, those who also have a problematic family background, low academic achievement, advanced puberty status, high novelty seeking, and low harm avoidance, are at even greater risk for delinquency (Fergusson & others, 2007).

Although delinquency is less exclusively a lower-SES phenomenon than it was in the past, some characteristics of lower-SES culture can promote delinquency. The norms of many low-SES peer groups and gangs are antisocial, or counterproductive, with respect to the goals and norms of society at large. Getting into and staying out of trouble are prominent features of life for some adolescents in low-income neighbourhoods. Adolescents from low-income backgrounds may sense that they can gain attention and status by performing antisocial actions. Being "tough" and "masculine" are high-status traits for low-SES boys, and these traits are often measured by the adolescent's success in performing and getting away with delinquent acts. Families play an important role in delinquency among low-SES youth. For example, one study revealed that engaged parenting and the mothers' social network support were linked to a lower level of delinquency in low-income families (Ghazarian & Roche, 2010). And another study found that youth whose families had experienced repeated poverty were more than twice as likely to be delinquent at 14 and 21 years of age (Najman & others, 2010).

The nature of a community can contribute to delinquency (Loeber, Burke, & Pardini, 2009). A community with a high crime rate allows adolescents to observe many models who engage in criminal activities and might be rewarded for their criminal accomplishments. Such communities often are characterized by poverty, unemployment, and feelings of alienation. Poor-quality schools, lack of funding for education, and the absence of organized neighbourhood activities are other community factors that might be related to delinquency.

Lack of success in school is also associated with delinquency. Indeed, a recent study found that poor academic performance and reduced attachment to school at age 15 predicted a higher level of criminal activity at 17 to 19 years of age (Savolainen & others, 2012).

Cognitive factors such as low self-control, low intelligence, and lack of sustained attention also are implicated in delinquency. For example, researchers found that low-IQ habitual delinquents were characterized by low self-control (Koolhof & others, 2007). Another study found that at age 16 non-delinquents were more likely to have a higher verbal IQ and engage in sustained attention than delinquents (Loeber & others, 2007). And in a longitudinal study, one of the strongest predictors of reduced likelihood of engaging in serious theft was academic achievement in high school (Loeber & others, 2008).

*Intervention and Prevention in Canada*  Can criminal involvement be prevented? In one recent Canadian study by Frank Vitaro and his colleagues (2012), low-SES boys identified as disruptive in kindergarten participated in a preventive intervention at age 7 to 9. Participants were randomly assigned to participate in the intervention or a control group. Those who participated in the intervention showed less criminal involvement in early adulthood compared to those in the control group.

There are several excellent initiatives in place in Canada to prevent violence. Some of these initiatives are described below:

- The Promoting Relationships and Eliminating Violence Network (PREVNet) consists of over 100 Canadian researchers and 59 national youth-serving organizations whose collective aim is to reduce bullying, foster positive relationships, and eliminate violence among Canada's youth.
- Acting Together (AT) is a project funded by the federal government and led by Kwantlen Polytechnic University in Surrey, British Columbia. AT brings together 12 community partner organizations and researchers from 4 post-secondary institutions with the goal of identifying factors that protect youth from gang involvement and support resilience among youth in the community.
- Leave Out Violence Everywhere (LOVE) is Canada's leading charitable not-for-profit organization dedicated to youth violence prevention. LOVE helps youth who have experienced violence in their lives to make positive changes through arts and self-expression and creates a safe space and sense of community. Youth involved in LOVE begin to serve as role models for other youth struggling with violence and eventually become community leaders of violence prevention.

Some Canadian communities including Prince Albert, Saskatchewan, Halifax, Nova Scotia, and New Brunswick have begun implementing a hub approach to prevent criminal acts among adolescents identified as being at risk for delinquency (D'Entremont, 2014). Using the hub approach, a network of police officers and professionals working in the areas of mental health, addictions, housing, school (guidance counsellors), and family and community services work together to intervene and get youth off a pathway toward criminality. In New Brunswick, where the hub model has been implemented since 2012, youth crime has dropped by one third and the severity of youth crime decreased by 30 percent over a two-year period.

## Review Connect Reflect

 **LO3** Describe the development of prosocial and antisocial behaviour.

### Review

- How is altruism defined? How does prosocial behaviour develop?
- What is juvenile delinquency? What is conduct disorder? What are key factors in the development of juvenile delinquency?

### Connect

- In this section, you learned that being "tough" and "masculine" are high-status traits for low-SES boys and that this can lead to delinquent acts. In Chapter 12, what did researcher Joseph Pleck say about boys who adopt a strong masculine role in adolescence?

### Reflect *Your Own Personal Journey of Life*

- Did you commit acts of delinquency as an adolescent? Most adolescents commit one or more acts of juvenile delinquency without becoming habitual juvenile delinquents. Reflect on your experiences of either committing juvenile offences or not committing them, then review the discussion of factors that are likely causes of juvenile delinquency and apply them to your development.

# case study connections

1. In this chapter, you learned about Kohlberg's stages of moral development. In which stage of moral development would Craig Kielburger be, as described in the chapter opening vignette?

2. As described in the chapter opening vignette, Craig Kielburger is strongly motivated to make a positive difference in the world. Based on what you learned in this chapter about the benefits of service learning for adolescents, what positive effects do you expect Craig enjoys as a result of his activism?

3. Based on what you learned in this chapter about altruism, why do you think Craig Kielburger, as described in the chapter opening vignette, was motivated to become a children's rights activist? What role did his peers play in his prosocial behaviour?

# reach your **learning goals**

# Moral Development

## Domains of Moral Development

**LO1** Discuss theory and research on the four domains of moral development.

### What Is Moral Development?

- Moral development involves changes in thoughts, feelings, and behaviours regarding right and wrong. Moral development includes intrapersonal and interpersonal dimensions.

### Moral Thought

- Piaget distinguished between the heteronomous morality of younger children and the autonomous morality of older children. Kohlberg developed a provocative theory of moral reasoning. He argued that development of moral reasoning consists of three levels—preconventional, conventional, and postconventional—and six stages (two at each level). Kohlberg reasoned that these stages were age related. Influences on the Kohlberg stages include cognitive development, dealing with moral questions and moral conflict, peer relations, and perspective taking. Criticisms of Kohlberg's theory have been made, especially by Gilligan, who advocates a stronger care perspective. Other criticisms focus on the inadequacy of moral reasoning to predict moral behaviour, account for the influences of culture and family, and assess moral reasoning.

### Moral Behaviour

- The processes of reinforcement, punishment, and imitation have been used to explain the acquisition of moral behaviour, but they provide only a partial explanation. Situational variability is stressed by behaviourists. Social cognitive theory emphasizes a distinction between moral competence and moral performance.

### Moral Feeling

- In Freud's theory, the superego is the moral branch of personality. According to Freud, guilt is the foundation of children's moral behaviour. Empathy is an important aspect of moral feelings, and it changes developmentally. In the contemporary perspective, both positive and negative feelings contribute to moral development.

### Moral Personality

- Recently, there has been a surge of interest in studying moral personality. This interest has focused on moral identity, moral character, and moral exemplars. Moral character involves having strong convictions, persisting, overcoming distractions and obstacles; and having virtues such as honesty, truthfulness, loyalty, and compassion. Moral exemplars have a moral character, identity, personality, and a set of virtues reflecting excellence and commitment; they are honest and dependable.

### Social-Cognitive Domain Theory

- Social-cognitive domain theory states that there are different domains of social knowledge and reasoning, including moral, social conventional, and personal domains.

## Contexts of Moral Development

 **LO2** Explain how parenting and schools influence moral development.

Parenting

- Warmth and responsibility in mutual obligations of parent-child relationships provide important foundations for the child's positive moral growth. Love withdrawal, power assertion, and induction are discipline techniques. Induction is most likely to be linked with positive moral development. Moral development can be advanced by parenting strategies such as being warm and supportive rather than punitive, using inductive discipline, providing opportunities to learn about others' perspectives and feelings, involving children in family decision making, modelling moral behaviours, and averting misbehaviour before it takes place.

Schools

- The hidden curriculum, initially described by Dewey, is the moral atmosphere of each school. Contemporary approaches to moral education include character education, values clarification, cognitive moral education, service learning, and integrative ethical education. Cheating is a moral education concern that can take many forms. Various aspects of the school situation influence whether students will cheat or not.

## Prosocial and Antisocial Behaviour

 **LO3** Describe the development of prosocial and antisocial behaviour.

Prosocial Behaviour

- An important aspect of prosocial behaviour is altruism, an unselfish interest in helping others. Damon described a sequence by which children develop their understanding of fairness and come to share more consistently. Peers play a key role in this development. Forgiveness and gratitude are two additional aspects of prosocial behaviour.

Antisocial Behaviour

- Conduct disorder is a psychiatric diagnostic category used to describe multiple delinquent-type behaviours occurring over a six-month period. Juvenile delinquency consists of a broad range of behaviours, from socially undesirable behaviour to criminal acts. Predictors of juvenile delinquency include authority conflict, minor covert acts such as lying, overt acts of aggression, a negative identity, cognitive distortions, low self-control, early initiation of delinquency, being a male, low expectations for education and school grades, low parental monitoring, low parental support and ineffective discipline, having an older delinquent sibling, heavy peer influence and low resistance to peers, low socioeconomic status, and living in a high-crime, urban area. Several Canadian initiatives are in place to prevent juvenile delinquency and violence among youth.

# section **five**

*It is not enough for parents to understand children. They must also accord children the privilege of understanding them.*

—**Milton Sapirstein**
*American Psychiatrist and Writer, 20th Century*

# Social Contexts of Development

Parents cradle children's lives, but children's growth is also shaped by successive choirs of siblings, peers, friends, and teachers. Children's small worlds widen as they discover new refuges and new people. In the end, there are but two lasting bequests that parents can leave children, one being roots, the other wings. In this section, we will study three chapters: "Families" (Chapter 14), "Peers" (Chapter 15), and "Schools and Technology" (Chapter 16).

Families | chapter 14

chapter outline

## Family Processes

 **LO1** Discuss family processes.

Interactions in the Family System

Cognition and Emotion in Family Processes

Multiple Developmental Trajectories

Domain-Specific Socialization

Sociocultural and Historical Changes

## Parenting

 **LO2** Explain how parenting is linked to children's and adolescents' development.

Parental Roles and the Timing of Parenthood

Adapting Parenting to Developmental Changes in Children

Parents as Managers of Children's Lives

Parenting Styles and Discipline

Parent-Adolescent Relationships

Intergenerational Relationships

## Siblings

 **LO3** Identify how siblings influence children's development.

Sibling Relationships

Birth Order

## The Changing Family in a Changing Social World

**LO4** Characterize the changing family in a changing social world.

Working Parents

Children in Divorced Families

Stepfamilies

Gay and Lesbian Parents

Cultural, Ethnic, and Socioeconomic Variations in Families

W hen Shelley Peterman Schwarz (2004) and her husband, David, had been married four years, they decided to have children. They had two children, Jamie and Andrew. When the children were 3 and 5 years old, Shelley was diagnosed with multiple sclerosis. Two years later, she had to quit her job as a teacher of hearing-impaired children because of her worsening condition.

By the time the children were 7 and 9 years old, it was more difficult for Shelley to prepare meals for the family by herself, so David began taking over that responsibility. They also enlisted the children's help in preparing meals.

Despite her multiple sclerosis, Shelley participated in parenting classes and workshops at her children's school. She even initiated a Mothers-of-10-Year-Olds support group. But parenting with multiple sclerosis had its frustrations for Shelley. In her words,

Shelley Peterman Schwarz (*left*) with her family.

. . . attending school functions, teacher's conferences, and athletic events often presented problems because the facilities weren't always easily wheelchair accessible. I felt guilty if I didn't at least "try" to attend. I didn't want my children to think I didn't care enough to try. . .

When Jamie was 19 and Andrew was 17, I started to relax a little. I could see how capable and independent they were becoming. My having a disability hadn't ruined their lives. In fact, in some ways, they are better off because of it. They learned to trust themselves and to face personal challenges head-on. When the time came for them to leave the nest and head off to college, I knew they were ready.

As for me, I now understand that having a disability wasn't the worst thing in the world that could happen to a parent. What would be a tragedy is letting your disability cripple your ability to stay in your children's lives. Parenting is so much more than driving car pools, attending gymnastic meets, or baking cookies for an open house. It's loving, caring, listening, guiding, and supporting your child. It's consoling a child crying because her friends thought her haircut was ugly. It's counselling a child worried because his 12-year-old friend is drinking. It's helping a child understand relationships and what it's like to "be in love." (Schwarz, 2004, p. 5)

# preview

This chapter is about the many aspects of children's development in families. We will explore how families work, ways to parent children, relationships among siblings, and the changing family in a changing social world. Along the way, we will examine topics such as child maltreatment, working parents, children in divorced families, stepfamilies, and many others.

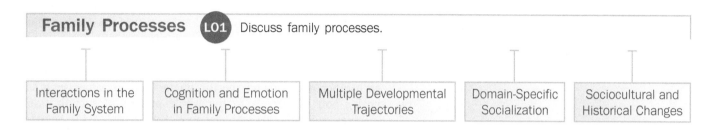

**Family Processes** **LO1** Discuss family processes.

| Interactions in the Family System | Cognition and Emotion in Family Processes | Multiple Developmental Trajectories | Domain-Specific Socialization | Sociocultural and Historical Changes |

As we examine the family and other social contexts of development, it will be helpful to keep in mind Urie Bronfenbrenner's (2000, 2004) ecological theory, which we discussed in Chapter 1. Recall that Bronfenbrenner analyzes the social contexts of development in terms of five environmental systems:

- The microsystem or the setting in which the individual lives, such as a family, the world of peers, schools, work, and so on
- The mesosystem, which consists of links between microsystems, such as the connection between family processes and peer relations
- The exosystem, which consists of influences from another setting that the individual does not experience directly, such as how parents' experiences at work might affect their parenting at home
- The macrosystem or the culture in which the individual lives, such as a nation or an ethnic group
- The chronosystem or sociohistorical circumstances, such as increased numbers of working mothers in Canada in the last 30 to 40 years

Let's begin our examination of the family at the level of the microsystem.

## INTERACTIONS IN THE FAMILY SYSTEM

Every family is a *system*—a complex whole made up of interrelated and interacting parts. The relationships never go in just one direction. For example, the interaction of mothers and their infants is sometimes symbolized as a dance in which successive actions of the partners are closely coordinated. This coordinated dance can assume the form of *mutual synchrony*, which means that each person's behaviour depends on the partner's previous behaviour. Or the interaction can be *reciprocal* in a precise sense, which means that the actions of the partners can be matched, as when one partner imitates the other or when there is mutual smiling (Cohn & Tronick, 1988). An important example of early synchronized interaction is mutual gaze or eye contact.

Another example of synchronization occurs in scaffolding, which means adjusting the level of guidance to fit the child's performance, as we discussed in Chapter 6 (Bibok, Carpendale, & Muller, 2009; Melzi, Schick, & Kennedy, 2011). The parent responds to the child's behaviour with scaffolding, which in turn affects the child's behaviour. For example, in a recent longitudinal study, parental scaffolding at age 3 had a direct effect on the development of executive function among Canadian preschoolers at age 4 (Hammond & others, 2012).

*developmental* **connection**

**Theories.** An important contribution of Bronfenbrenner's ecological theory is its focus on a range of social contexts that influence the child's development. Chapter 1, LO 3

There's no vocabulary for love within a family, love that's lived in but not looked at, love within the light of which all else is seen, the love within which all other love finds speech. That love is silent.

—T. S. ELIOT
*American-Born English Poet, 20th Century*

*developmental* **connection**

**Attention.** Joint attention can play an important role in interchanges between a caregiver and an infant. Chapter 7, LO 2

*How does the game of peek-a-boo reflect the concept of scaffolding?*

**reciprocal socialization** The bidirectional process by which children socialize parents just as parents socialize them.

Children socialize parents just as parents socialize children.

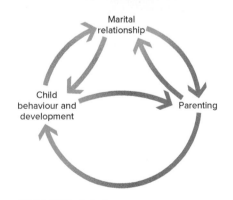

FIGURE **14.1**

**INTERACTION BETWEEN CHILDREN AND THEIR PARENTS: DIRECT AND INDIRECT EFFECTS.**

The game peek-a-boo, in which parents initially cover their babies, then remove the covering and register "surprise" at the babies' reappearance, reflects the concept of scaffolding. As infants become more skilled at peek-a-boo, infants gradually do some of the covering and uncovering. Parents try to time their actions in such a way that the infant takes turns with the parent.

In addition to peek-a-boo, patty-cake and so-big are other caregiver games that exemplify scaffolding and turn-taking sequences. In one investigation, infants who had more extensive scaffolding experiences with their parents, especially in the form of turn taking, were more likely to engage in turn taking as they interacted with their peers (Vandell & Wilson, 1988). Engaging in turn taking and games like peek-a-boo reflect the development of joint attention by the caregiver and infant, which we discussed in Chapter 7, "Information Processing" (Tomasello, 2009).

The mutual influence that parents and children exert on each other goes beyond specific interactions in games such as peek-a-boo; it extends to the whole process of socialization (Crouter & Booth, 2013; Shanahan & Sobolewski, 2013). Socialization between parents and children is not a one-way process. Parents do socialize children, but socialization in families is reciprocal (Capaldi, 2013; McHale & Crouter, 2013). **Reciprocal socialization** is socialization that is bidirectional; children socialize parents just as parents socialize children. These reciprocal interchanges and mutual influence processes are sometimes referred to as *transactional* (Sameroff, 2009).

Of course, while parents are interacting with their children, they are also interacting with each other. To understand these interactions and relationships, it helps to think of the family as a constellation of subsystems defined in terms of generation, gender, and role. Each family member participates in several subsystems—some *dyadic* (involving two people) and some *polyadic* (involving more than two people). The father and child represent one dyadic subsystem, the mother and father another; the mother-father-child represent one polyadic subsystem, the mother and two siblings another (Parke & others, 2008).

These subsystems interact and influence one another (Carlson & others, 2011). Thus, as Figure 14.1 illustrates, marital relations, parenting, and infant/child behaviour can have both direct and indirect effects on one another (Belsky, 1981). The link between marital relationships and parenting has received increased attention. The most consistent findings are that compared with unhappily married parents, happily married parents are more sensitive, responsive, warm, and affectionate toward their children (Grych, 2002).

Researchers have found that promoting marital satisfaction often leads to good parenting. The marital relationship provides an important support for parenting (Cowan & others, 2013; Cummings & others, 2012). When parents report more intimacy and better communication in their marriage, they are more affectionate with their children (Grych, 2002). Thus, marriage-enhancement programs may end up improving parenting and helping children. Programs that focus on parenting skills might also benefit from including attention to the participants' marriages.

## COGNITION AND EMOTION IN FAMILY PROCESSES

Both cognition and emotion are increasingly thought to be central to understanding how family processes work (Crockenberg & Leerkes, 2013; Thompson, 2013c, d). The role of cognition in family socialization takes many forms, including parents' cognitions, beliefs, and values about their parental role, as well as how parents perceive, organize, and understand their children's behaviours and beliefs. For example, one Canadian study found a link between mothers' beliefs and their preschool children's social problem-solving skills (Rubin, Mills, & Rose-Krasnor, 1989). Mothers who placed a higher value on skills such as making friends, sharing with others, and leading or influencing other children had children who were more assertive, prosocial, and competent problem solvers than mothers who valued these skills less.

Children's social competence is also linked to the emotional lives of their parents (Ablow, 2013). For example, one study found that parents who expressed positive emotions had children who were high in competence (Boyum & Parke, 1995). Through positive interaction with parents, children learn to express their emotions in appropriate ways. Likewise, engaging in negative interactions with parents can lead to emotional difficulties in children. For example, according to research from the Canadian National Longitudinal Survey of Children and Youth, parents who exhibited depressive symptoms were more likely to engage in coercive family interactions which contributed to children's emotional problems (Elgar & others, 2007).

Researchers are also finding that parental sensitivity to children's emotions is related to children's ability to manage their emotions in positive ways (Thompson, 2013c, d). Recall from Chapter 10, "Emotional Development," the distinction that was made between emotion-coaching and emotion-dismissing parents (Gottman, 2012). *Emotion-coaching parents* monitor their children's emotions, view their children's negative emotions as opportunities for teaching, assist them in labelling emotions, and coach them in how to deal effectively with emotions. In contrast, *emotion-dismissing parents* view their role as to deny, ignore, or change negative emotions.

*How are cognition and emotion involved in understanding family processes in children's development?*

## MULTIPLE DEVELOPMENTAL TRAJECTORIES

The concept of **multiple developmental trajectories** refers to the fact that adults follow one trajectory and children and adolescents another one (Parke & Buriel, 2006; Parke & Clarke-Stewart, 2011). How adult and child/adolescent developmental trajectories mesh is important for understanding the timing of entry into various family tasks. Adult developmental trajectories include timing of entry into marriage, cohabitation, or parenthood; child developmental trajectories include timing of child care and entry into middle school. The timing of some family tasks and changes are planned, such as reentry into the workforce or delaying parenthood, whereas others are not, such as job loss or divorce (Parke & Buriel, 2006).

Consider the developmental period of adolescence. Most adolescents' parents either are in middle adulthood or are rapidly approaching this period of life. However, parenthood takes place earlier for some, and later for others. In the United States, the adolescent pregnancy rate remains one of the highest in the developed world. By comparison, the adolescent pregnancy rate in Canada is considerably lower, and has decreased from 29.9 per 1,000 adolescent females in 1974 to 12.0 in 2009 (Human Resources and Skills Development Canada, 2013). However, the number of Canadian women over the age of thirty having children has increased from 20 percent in 1974 to 50 percent in 2009 (Human Resources and Skills Development Canada, 2013).

What are some advantages of having children early or late? There are advantages to having children early (in the twenties): (1) the parents are likely to have more physical energy—for example, they can cope better with such matters as getting up in the middle of the night with infants and waiting up until adolescents come home at night; (2) the mother is likely to have fewer medical problems with pregnancy and childbirth; and (3) the parents may be less likely to build up expectations for their children, as do many couples who have waited many years to have children.

There are also advantages to having children later (in the thirties): (1) the parents will have had more time to consider their goals in life, such as what they want from their family and career roles; (2) the parents will be more mature and will be able to benefit from their experiences to engage in more competent parenting; and (3) the parents will be better established in their careers and have more income for child-rearing expenses.

**multiple developmental trajectories** Concept that adults follow one trajectory and children and adolescents another one; understanding how these trajectories mesh is important.

*developmental* **connection**

**Parenting.** Emotion-coaching parents use more scaffolding and praise when interacting with their children than do emotion-dismissing parents. Chapter 10, LO 2

## DOMAIN-SPECIFIC SOCIALIZATION

When discussion turns to how parents socialize children, it has been common to describe the socialization process and child outcomes in general terms, such as *parents who are warm, sensitive, and involved with their children have children who are socially competent.* In such broad descriptions, too often the complexity and specificity of parental socialization and child outcomes become lost.

Recently, interest in the domain-specificity of socializing children has increased. Joan Grusec of the University of Toronto and Marilyn Davidov of The Hebrew University of Jerusalem (2010) proposed a domain-specific view of parenting that emphasizes how parents often operate in different domains characterized by different types of relationships. The five domains are described below:

- *Protection.* Many species, including Homo sapiens, have evolved so that their young maintain proximity to a caregiver, especially when they are in stressful or dangerous circumstances. In this domain, effective parenting involves responding in such a manner that the child develops a sense of security and perceives being comforted. Child outcomes of appropriate parental protection include the ability to respond appropriately to danger and to engage in self-regulation of distress.

- *Reciprocity.* This domain is not involved when the child is distressed but rather when the parent and child are interacting on an equal basis as partners, as in the context of play. Child outcomes in the reciprocity domain include the development of cooperativeness and the desire to comply with parental requests.

- *Control.* In the control domain, interactions between parents and children typically involve conflict because parents want one thing and children another. The control domain is often activated when the children misbehave. In such circumstances, parents can use their power advantage to discourage the misbehaviour through various means such as reasoning, social isolation, and physical punishment. Child outcomes in the control domain include the development of moral and principled behaviour.

- *Guided Learning.* In this domain, parents guide children's learning of skills through the use of effective strategies and feedback. In the guided learning domain, parents function as teachers and their children as students. Children's outcomes in the guided learning domain include acquiring knowledge and skills.

- *Group Participation.* In this domain, socialization involves increasing children's participation in cultural practices. Child outcomes include conformity to cultural group practices and values that provide the child with a sense of social identity.

Grusec and Davidov (2010) acknowledge that real-life interactions in families often involve overlapping across the domains, but the extent of this overlapping has not yet been identified (Dunn, 2010). Also, how the different domains might play out at different points in children's development has not been adequately researched.

## SOCIOCULTURAL AND HISTORICAL CHANGES

Family development does not occur in a social vacuum. Important sociocultural and historical influences affect family processes, which reflect Bronfenbrenner's concepts of the macrosystem and chronosystem (Bronfenbrenner & Morris, 2006). Great, such as war, famine, or massive immigration, as well as subtle transitions in ways of life may stimulate changes in families (Fuligni, 2012). One example is the effect on North American families of the Great Depression of the 1930s. During its height, the Depression produced economic deprivation, adult discontent, and widespread unemployment. It also increased marital conflict, inconsistent child rearing, and unhealthy lifestyles—heavy drinking, demoralized attitudes, and health impairments—especially in fathers (Elder & Shanahan, 2006).

Subtle changes in a culture have significant influences on the family (Mistry, Contreras, & Dutta, 2013). Such changes include increased longevity of older adults, movement to urban and suburban areas, technological advances, and a general dissatisfaction and restlessness (Mead, 1978).

In the first part of the twentieth century, individuals who survived infancy were usually hardy and still closely linked to the family, often helping to maintain the family's existence. Today, individuals live longer, which means that middle-aged children are often pressed into a caregiving role for their parents, or the elderly parents may be placed in a nursing home (Antonucci, Birditt, & Ajrouch, 2013; Fingerman, Secrest, & Birditt, 2013). Older parents may have lost some of their socializing role in the family during the twentieth century as many of their children moved great distances away. However, in the twenty-first century an increasing number of grandparents are raising their grandchildren (Matzek & Cooney, 2009).

Many of the family moves in the last 75 years have been away from farms and small towns to urban and suburban settings. In the small towns and farms, individuals were surrounded by lifelong neighbours, relatives, and friends. Today, neighbourhood and extended-family support systems are not nearly as prevalent. Families now move all over the country, often uprooting children from a school and peer group they have known for a considerable length of time. And it is not unusual for this type of move to occur every several years, as one or both parents are transferred from job to job.

The media and technology also play a major role in the changing family (Jackson & others, 2012; Levinson, 2013; te Velde & others, 2012). Many children who watch television find that parents are too busy working to share this with them. Children increasingly experience a world in which their parents are not participants. Instead of interacting in neighbourhood peer groups, children come home after school and watch television, play video games, or use the Internet for entertainment and social networking.

Another change in families has been an increase in general dissatisfaction and restlessness. The result of such restlessness and the tendency to divorce and remarry has been a hodgepodge of family structures, with far greater numbers of divorced and remarried families than ever before in history (Lansford, 2009).

Many of the changes we have described in this section apply not only to Canadian families but also to families in many countries around the world. Later in this chapter, we discuss aspects of the changing social world of the child and the family in greater detail.

## Review Connect Reflect

 **LO1** Discuss family processes.

### Review

- How can the family be viewed as a system? What is reciprocal socialization?
- How are cognition and emotion involved in family processes?
- What characterizes multiple developmental trajectories?
- What are five domain-specific socialization practices?
- What are some sociocultural and historical changes that have influenced the family?

### Connect

- In this section, scaffolding was mentioned as an example of synchronization. Which concept of Vygotsky's is scaffolding also linked to in Chapter 6?

### Reflect Your Own Personal Journey of Life

- Reflect on your own family as you were growing up for several moments and give some examples of the family processes discussed in this section as you experienced them in your own family.

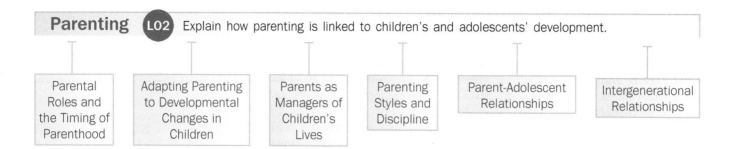

| Parental Roles and the Timing of Parenthood | Adapting Parenting to Developmental Changes in Children | Parents as Managers of Children's Lives | Parenting Styles and Discipline | Parent-Adolescent Relationships | Intergenerational Relationships |

Parenting calls on a number of interpersonal skills and makes intense emotional demands, yet there is little in the way of formal education for this task. Most parents learn parenting practices from their own parents. Some of these practices they accept and others they discard. Couples may bring different views of parenting to the relationship.

Unfortunately, when parents' methods are passed on from one generation to the next, both desirable and undesirable practices are perpetuated. What have developmentalists learned about parenting? How should parents adapt their style of parenting to developmental changes in their children? How important is it for parents to be effective managers of their children's lives? And how do various parenting styles and methods of discipline influence children's development?

## PARENTAL ROLES AND THE TIMING OF PARENTHOOD

Many adults decide when they would like to become parents and consider how parenting will fit with their economic situation. For others, the discovery that they are about to become parents is a surprise. In either event, the prospective parents may have mixed emotions and romantic illusions about having a child (Carl, 2012). The needs and expectations of parents have stimulated many myths about parenting.

Currently, there is a tendency to have fewer children. The number of one-child families is increasing. Is there a best time to have children? What are some of the restrictions individuals face when they become parents? These are some of the questions we now consider.

Like the age when people marry for the first time, the age at which individuals have children has been increasing (Lauer & Lauer, 2012). In 2009, the average age of women who gave birth was 29.4 years of age, up from 26.7 years of age in 1975 (Human Resources and Skills Development Canada, 2013).

As birth control has become common practice, many individuals choose when they will have children and how many children they will raise. They are not only marrying later but also having children later or not at all.

## ADAPTING PARENTING TO DEVELOPMENTAL CHANGES IN CHILDREN

Children change as they grow from infancy to early childhood and on through middle and late childhood and adolescence. The 5-year-old and the 2-year-old have different needs and abilities. A competent parent adapts to the child's developmental changes (Maccoby, 1984). As we see next, though, considerable adaptation also is required in making the transition to parenting.

**The Transition to Parenting**  Whether people become parents through pregnancy, adoption, or stepparenting, they face disequilibrium and must adapt (Dew & Wilcox, 2011). Parents want to develop a strong attachment with their infant, but they still want to maintain strong attachments to their spouse and friends, and possibly continue their careers. Parents ask themselves how this new being will change their lives. A baby places new restrictions on partners; no longer will they be able to rush out to a movie on a moment's notice, and money may not be readily available for vacations and other luxuries. Dual-career parents ask, "Will it harm the baby to place her in child care? Will we be able to find responsible babysitters?"

In a longitudinal investigation of couples from late pregnancy until 3½ years after the baby was born, couples enjoyed more positive marital relations before the baby was born than after (Cowan & Cowan, 2000, 2009; Cowan, Cowan, & Barry, 2011; Cowan & others, 2005). Still, almost one-third showed an increase in marital satisfaction. Some couples said that the baby had both brought them closer together and moved them farther apart; being parents enhanced their sense of themselves and gave them a new, more stable identity as a couple. Babies opened men up to a concern with intimate relationships, and the demands of juggling work and family roles stimulated women to manage family tasks more efficiently and pay attention to their own personal growth.

*What characterizes the transition to parenting?*

Other recent studies have explored the transition to parenthood (Brown, Feinberg, & Kan, 2012). One study found similar negative change in relationship satisfaction for married and cohabiting women during the transition to parenthood (Mortensen & others, 2012). Another study revealed that mothers experienced unmet expectations in the transition to parenting, with fathers doing less than their partners had anticipated (Biehle & Mickelson, 2012). When new mothers have low marital satisfaction, it is often linked to reductions in quality time spent with husbands and perception of unfairness in dividing up household tasks (Dew & Wilcox, 2011).

**Infancy**   During the first year, parent-child interaction moves from a heavy focus on routine caregiving—feeding, changing diapers, bathing, and soothing—to later include more non-caregiving activities, such as play and visual-vocal exchanges (Bornstein, 2002).

**Early Childhood**   Parent-child interactions during early childhood focus on such matters as modesty, bedtime regularities, control of temper, fighting with siblings and peers, eating behaviour and manners, autonomy in dressing, and attention seeking (Edwards & Liu, 2002). Although some of these issues—fighting with siblings, for example—are carried forward into the elementary school years, many new issues appear by the age of 7. These include whether children should be made to perform chores and, if so, whether they should be paid for them, how to help children learn to entertain themselves rather than relying on parents for everything, and how to monitor children's lives outside the family in school and peer settings.

**Middle and Late Childhood**   As children move into the middle and late childhood years, parents spend less time with them. In one study, parents spent less than half as much time with their children aged 5 to 12 in caregiving, instruction, reading, talking, and playing as when the children were younger (Hill & Stafford, 1980). Although parents spend less time with their children in middle and late childhood than in early childhood, parents continue to be extremely important in their children's lives. In an analysis of the contributions of parents during middle and late childhood, the following conclusion was reached: "Parents serve as gatekeepers and provide scaffolding as children assume more responsibility for themselves and . . . regulate their own lives" (Huston & Ripke, 2006, p. 422).

Parents especially play an important role in supporting and stimulating children's academic achievement in middle and late childhood (Cowan & Heming, 2013; Huston & Ripke, 2006). The value parents place on education can determine whether children do well in school. Parents not only influence children's in-school achievement, but they also make decisions about children's out-of-school activities (Eccles & Roeser, 2013). Whether children participate in sports, music, and other activities is heavily influenced by the extent to which parents sign up children for such activities and encourage their participation (Simpkins & others, 2006).

Elementary school children tend to receive less physical discipline than they did as preschoolers. Instead of spanking or coercive holding, their parents are more likely to use deprivation of privileges, appeals to the child's self-esteem, comments designed to increase the child's sense of guilt, and statements that the child is responsible for his or her actions.

During middle and late childhood, some control is transferred from parent to child. The process is gradual, and it produces *coregulation* rather than control by either the child or the parent alone. Parents continue to exercise general supervision and control, and children are allowed to engage in moment-to-moment self-regulation. The major shift to autonomy does not occur until about the age of 12 or later. A key developmental task as children move toward autonomy is learning to relate to adults outside the family on a regular basis—adults such as teachers who interact with the child much differently from parents.

In sum, considerable adaptation in parenting is required as children develop. Later in the chapter, we will further examine adaptations in parenting when discussing family influences on adolescents' development.

## PARENTS AS MANAGERS OF CHILDREN'S LIVES

Parents can play important roles as managers of children's opportunities, as monitors of their lives, and as social initiators and arrangers (Bradley & Corwyn, 2013 Parke & Buriel, 2006; Parke & Clarke-Stewart, 2011). An important developmental task of childhood and adolescence is to develop the ability to make competent decisions in an increasingly independent manner. To help children and adolescents reach their full potential, an important parental role is to be an effective manager, one who finds information, makes contacts, helps structure choices, and provides guidance. Parents who fulfill this important managerial role help children and adolescents to avoid pitfalls and to work their way through a myriad of choices and decisions. Mothers are more likely than fathers to engage in a managerial role in parenting.

From infancy through adolescence, parents can serve important roles in managing their children's experiences and opportunities. In infancy, this might involve taking a child to a doctor and arranging for child care; in early childhood, it might involve a decision about which preschool the child should attend; in middle and late childhood, it might include directing the child to take a bath, to match their clothes and wear clean clothes, and to put away toys; in adolescence, it could involve participating in a parent-teacher conference and subsequently managing the adolescent's homework activity.

**Managing and Guiding the Infant's Behaviour** In addition to sensitive parenting involving warmth and caring that can result in infants being securely attached to their parents, other important aspects of parenting infants involve managing and guiding their behaviour in an attempt to reduce or eliminate undesirable behaviours (Holden, Vittrup, & Rosen, 2011). This management process includes (1) being proactive and childproofing the environment so infants won't encounter potentially dangerous objects or situations, and (2) using corrective methods when infants engage in undesirable behaviours, such as excessive fussing and crying, throwing objects, and so on.

One study assessed results of discipline and corrective methods that parents had used by the time their infants were 12 and 24 months old (Vittrup, Holden, &

Buck, 2006) (see Figure 14.2). Notice in Figure 14.2 that the main corrective method parents had used by the time their infant was 12 months old was diverting the infant's attention, followed by reasoning, ignoring, and negotiating. Also note in Figure 14.2 that more than one-third of parents had yelled at their infant, about one-fifth had slapped the infant's hands or threatened the infant, and approximately one-sixth had spanked the infant by their first birthday.

As infants move into the second year of life and become more mobile and capable of exploring a wider range of environments, parental management of the toddler's behaviour often involves increased corrective feedback and discipline (Holden, Vittrup, & Rosen, 2011). As indicated in Figure 14.2, in the study just described, yelling increased from 36 percent at 1 year of age to 81 percent by 2 years of age, slapping the infant's hands increased from 21 percent at 1 year to 31 percent by age 2, and spanking increased from 14 percent at age 1 to 45 percent by age 2 (Vittrup, Holden, & Buck, 2006).

A special concern is that such corrective discipline tactics not become abusive. Too often what starts out as mild to moderately intense discipline on the part of parents can move into highly intense anger. Later in this chapter, you will read more extensively about the use of punishment with children and child maltreatment.

**Parental Monitoring in Childhood and Adolescence**  A key aspect of the managerial role of parenting is effective monitoring, which becomes especially important as children move into the adolescent years (Bradley & Corwyn, 2013). Monitoring includes supervising an adolescent's choices of social settings, activities, and friends. A recent study of more than 36,000 eighth- and tenth-grade students revealed that a higher level of parental monitoring was associated with lower alcohol and marijuana use, with the strongest effects among girls and adolescents who had the highest risk-taking profile (Dever & others, 2013).

A current interest involving parental monitoring focuses on adolescents' management of their parents' access to information, especially the extent to which adolescents disclose or conceal strategies about their activities (Amsel & Smetana, 2011; Metzger & others, 2013; Rote & others, 2012). Researchers have found that adolescents' disclosure to parents about their whereabouts, activities, and friends is linked to positive adolescent adjustment and achievement (Laird & Marrero, 2011; Smetana, 2011a, b).

Researchers also have found that family management practices are related positively to students' grades and self-responsibility, and negatively to school-related problems (Eccles, 2007; Eccles & Roeser, 2013; Taylor & Lopez, 2005). Among the most important family management practices in this regard are maintaining a structured and organized family environment, such as establishing routines for homework, chores, bedtime, and so on, and effectively monitoring the child's behaviour.

# PARENTING STYLES AND DISCIPLINE

Good parenting takes time and effort. You can't do it in a minute here and a minute there. Of course, as Canadian researcher Joan Grusec (2013; Grusec & others, 2013) notes, it's not just the quantity of time parents spend with children that is important for children's development—the quality of the parenting is clearly important. To understand variations in parenting, let's consider the styles parents use when they interact with their children, how they discipline their children, and coparenting.

| Method | 12 Months | 24 Months |
|---|---|---|
| Spank with hand | 14 | 45 |
| Slap infant's hand | 21 | 31 |
| Yell in anger | 36 | 81 |
| Threaten | 19 | 63 |
| Withdraw privileges | 18 | 52 |
| Time-out | 12 | 60 |
| Reason | 85 | 100 |
| Divert attention | 100 | 100 |
| Negotiate | 50 | 90 |
| Ignore | 64 | 90 |

## FIGURE 14.2

**PARENTS' METHODS FOR MANAGING AND CORRECTING INFANTS' UNDESIRABLE BEHAVIOUR.** Shown here are the percentages of parents who had used various corrective methods by the time their infant was 12 and 24 months old. *Source:* Based on data presented in Table 1 in Vittrup, Holden, & Buck (2006).

> Parenting is a very important profession, but no test of fitness for it is ever imposed in the interest of children.
>
> —GEORGE BERNARD SHAW
> *Irish Playwright, 20th Century*

*How is parental monitoring beneficial for children and adolescents?*

**Baumrind's Parenting Styles** Diana Baumrind (1971, 2012) points out that parents should be neither punitive nor aloof. Rather, they should develop rules for their children and be affectionate with them. She has described four types of parenting styles:

- **Authoritarian parenting** is a restrictive, punitive style in which parents exhort the child to follow their directions and respect their work and effort. The authoritarian parent places firm limits and controls on the child and allows little verbal exchange. For example, an authoritarian parent might say, "You do it my way or else." Authoritarian parents also might spank the child frequently, enforce rules rigidly but not explain them, and show rage toward the child. Children of authoritarian parents are often unhappy, fearful, and anxious about comparing themselves with others, fail to initiate activity, and have weak communication skills. Canadian research has shown children of authoritarian parents may behave aggressively (Ho & others, 2008).

- **Authoritative parenting** encourages children to be independent but still places limits and controls on their actions. Extensive verbal give-and-take is allowed, and parents are warm and nurturant toward the child. An authoritative parent might put his arm around the child in a comforting way and say, "You know you should not have done that. Let's talk about how you can handle the situation better next time." Authoritative parents show pleasure and support in response to children's constructive behaviour. They also expect mature, independent, and age-appropriate behaviour by children. Children whose parents are authoritative are often cheerful, self-controlled and self-reliant, and achievement oriented; they tend to maintain friendly relations with peers, cooperate with adults, and cope well with stress.

- **Neglectful parenting** is a style in which the parent is very uninvolved in the child's life. Children whose parents are neglectful develop the sense that other aspects of the parents' lives are more important than they are. These children tend to be socially incompetent. Many have poor self-control and don't handle independence well. They frequently have low self-esteem, are immature, and may be alienated from the family. In adolescence, they may show patterns of truancy and delinquency.

- **Indulgent parenting** is a style in which parents are highly involved with their children but place few demands or controls on them. Such parents let their children do what they want. The result is that the children never learn to control their own behaviour and always expect to get their way. Some parents deliberately rear their children in this way because they believe the combination of warm involvement and few restraints will produce a creative, confident child. However, children whose parents are indulgent rarely learn respect for others and have difficulty controlling their behaviour. They might be domineering, egocentric, noncompliant, and have difficulties in peer relations.

These four classifications of parenting involve combinations of acceptance and responsiveness on the one hand and demand and control on the other (Maccoby & Martin, 1983). How these dimensions combine to produce authoritarian, authoritative, neglectful, and indulgent parenting is shown in Figure 14.3.

**Parenting Styles in Context** Do the benefits of authoritative parenting transcend the boundaries of ethnicity, socioeconomic status (SES), and household

**authoritarian parenting** A restrictive, punitive style in which the parent exhorts the child to follow the parent's directions and to respect their work and effort. Firm limits and controls are placed on the child, and little verbal exchange is allowed. This style is associated with children's social incompetence, including a lack of initiative and weak communication skills.

**authoritative parenting** This style encourages children to be independent but still places limits and controls on their actions. Extensive verbal give-and-take is allowed, and parents are warm and nurturant toward the child. This style is associated with children's social competence, including being achievement-oriented and self-reliant.

**neglectful parenting** A style in which the parent is very uninvolved in the child's life. It is associated with children's social incompetence, especially a lack of self-control and poor self-esteem.

**indulgent parenting** A style in which parents are highly involved with their children but place few demands or controls on them. This is associated with children's social incompetence, especially a lack of self-control and a lack of respect for others.

composition? Although occasional exceptions have been found, evidence linking authoritative parenting with competence on the part of the child occurs in research across a wide range of ethnic groups, social strata, cultures, and family structures (Low, Snyder, & Shortt, 2012; Milevsky, 2012; Morris, Cui & Steinberg, 2012; Steinberg & Silk, 2002). In one study, the parenting behaviours of Aboriginal Canadian parents were found to be similar to the indulgent style, but no negative outcomes were associated for Aboriginal children (Johnson & Cremo, 1995).

Researchers have found that in some ethnic groups, aspects of the authoritarian style may be associated with more positive child outcomes than Baumrind predicts (Parke & Buriel, 2006). For example, more strict and controlling parenting has been associated with positive outcomes for South Asian children (Jambunathan, Burts, & Pierce, 2000; Stewart & others, 2000). Similarly, among Middle Eastern families in Canada, there are no links between authoritarian parenting and low warmth or negative feelings toward the child, unlike among European Canadian families (Rudy & Grusec, 2006).

Even physical punishment, another characteristic of the authoritarian style, may have varying effects in different contexts. African American parents are more likely than Caucasian parents to use physical punishment (Deater-Deckard & Dodge, 1997). The use of physical punishment has been linked with increased externalized child problems (such as acting out and high levels of aggression) in Caucasian families but not in African American families. One explanation of this finding points to the need for African American parents to enforce rules in the dangerous environments in which they are more likely to live (Harrison-Hale, McLoyd, & Smedley, 2004).

In Canada, Caroline Ho and her colleagues at the University of Toronto studied parental harshness, which includes hostile parenting behaviours and punishment. The study showed that parents from a variety of ethnic backgrounds, including Aboriginal, Caribbean, East Asian, and South Asian, did not report higher levels of parental harshness than European Canadian parents (Ho & others, 2008). Parental harshness was associated with emotional problems for children from all ethnic backgrounds. However, the association between parental harshness and aggression was more complex. Specifically, parental harshness was associated with more aggression at school for European Canadian children and less aggression at school for South Asian Canadian children. In addition, parental harshness was associated with more aggression at home for East Asian Canadian children, Caribbean Canadian children, although to a lesser extent than for European Canadian children (Ho & others, 2008).

**Further Thoughts on Parenting Styles**   Several caveats about parenting styles are in order. First, the parenting styles do not capture the important themes of reciprocal socialization and synchrony (Crouter & Booth, 2013). Keep in mind that children socialize parents, just as parents socialize children (Capaldi, 2013; Shanahan & Sobolewski, 2013). Second, many parents use a combination of techniques rather than a single technique, although one technique may be dominant. Although consistent parenting is usually recommended, the wise parent may sense the importance of being more permissive in certain situations, more authoritative in others, and yet more authoritarian in

|  | Accepting, responsive | Rejecting, unresponsive |
|---|---|---|
| **Demanding, controlling** | Authoritative | Authoritarian |
| **Undemanding, uncontrolling** | Indulgent | Neglectful |

## FIGURE 14.3

**CLASSIFICATION OF PARENTING STYLES.** The four types of parenting styles (authoritarian, authoritative, indulgent, and neglectful) involve the dimensions of acceptance and responsiveness, on the one hand, and demand and control on the other. For example, authoritative parenting involves being both accepting/responsive and demanding/controlling.

*Are there cultural differences in parental harshness among Canadians?*

others. Also, some critics argue that the concept of parenting style is too broad and that more research needs to be conducted to "unpack" parenting styles by studying various components of the styles (Grusec, 2011; Maccoby, 2007). For example, is parental monitoring more important than warmth in predicting child and adolescent outcomes?

**Punishment**   For centuries, corporal (physical) punishment, such as spanking, has been considered a necessary and even desirable method of disciplining children. In Canada, spanking with non-excessive force as a form of punishment is allowed, provided the child is between the ages of two and 12. One study showed that 71 percent of Canadian mothers have used physical punishment. Among mothers who have used physical punishment, 33 percent did so once a week or more (Durrant, Rose-Krasnor, & Broberg, 2003). A cross-cultural comparison found that individuals in Canada, the United States and South Korea were among those with the most favourable attitudes toward corporal punishment and were the most likely to remember it being used by their parents. In contrast, Swedes had the least favourable view toward corporal punishment, as it was outlawed in Sweden in 1979 (Curran & others, 2001) (see Figure 14.4).

An increasing number of studies have examined the outcomes of physically punishing children, although those that have been conducted are correlational. Clearly, it would be highly unethical to randomly assign parents to either spank or not spank their children in an experimental study. Recall that cause and effect cannot be determined in a correlational study. In one correlational study, spanking by parents was linked with children's antisocial behaviour, including cheating, telling lies, being mean to others, bullying, getting into fights, and being disobedient (Strauss, Sugarman, & Giles-Sims, 1997).

A research review concluded that corporal punishment by parents is associated with higher levels of immediate compliance and aggression by the children (Gershoff, 2002). The review also found that corporal punishment is linked to lower levels of moral internalization and mental health (Gershoff, 2002). A study in six countries revealed that mothers' use of physical punishment was linked to highest rates of aggression in their children (Gershoff & others, 2010). Another study also discovered that a history of harsh physical discipline was related to adolescent depression and externalized problems, such as juvenile delinquency (Bender & others, 2007). And several longitudinal studies also have found that physical punishment of young children is associated with higher levels of aggression later in childhood and adolescence (Berlin & others, 2009; Gershoff & others,

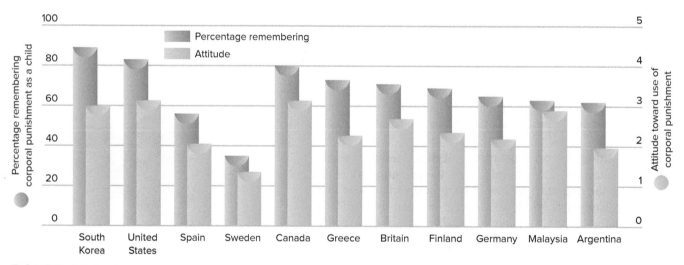

## FIGURE **14.4**

**CORPORAL PUNISHMENT IN DIFFERENT COUNTRIES.** A 5-point scale was used to assess attitudes toward corporal punishment with scores closer to 1 indicating an attitude against its use and scores closer to 5 suggesting an attitude favouring its use. *Why are studies of corporal punishment correlational studies, and how does that affect their interpretation?*

2012; Lansford & others, 2011; Taylor & others, 2010). To read more about the potential effects of physical punishment on children's development, see *Connecting to Current Controversy.*

What are some reasons to avoid spanking or similar punishments? The reasons include:

- When adults punish a child by yelling, screaming, or spanking, they are presenting children with out-of-control models for handling stressful situations. Children may imitate this aggressive, out-of-control behaviour.
- Punishment can instill fear, rage, or avoidance. For example, spanking the child may cause the child to avoid being around the parent and to fear the parent.
- Punishment tells children what not to do rather than what to do. Children should be given feedback, such as "Why don't you try this?"
- Punishment can be abusive. Parents might unintentionally become so emotional when they are punishing the child that they become abusive (Durrant, 2008; Knox, 2010).

Most child psychologists recommend handling misbehaviour by reasoning with the child, especially explaining the consequences of the child's actions for others. *Time out,* in which the child is removed from a setting that offers positive reinforcement, can also be effective. For example, when the child has misbehaved, a parent might take away TV viewing for a specified time.

What predicts the use of physical punishment in parenting? One longitudinal study assessed couples across the transition to parenting to investigate possible links between marital conflict, individual adult hostility, and the use of physical punishment with young children (Kanoy & others, 2003). The researchers found that both hostility and marital conflict were linked with the use of physical punishment.

## connecting to current controversy

### Is the Use of Physical Punishment in Parenting Harmful to Children's Development?

The debate about physical punishment's effects on children's development continues (Gershoff & others, 2012; Grusec, 2011; Lansford & Deater-Deckard, 2012). Some experts, including Diana Baumrind, argue that much of the evidence for the negative effects of physical punishment has been based on studies in which parents acted in an abusive manner (Baumrind, Larzelere, & Cowan, 2002). She concludes from her research that when parents used punishment in a calm, reasoned manner (which she says characterized most of the authoritative parents in her studies), children's development benefitted. Thus, Baumrind emphasizes that physical punishment does not need to present children with an out-of-control adult who is yelling and screaming as well as spanking. A research review of 26 studies concluded that only severe or predominant use of spanking, not mild spanking, compared unfavourably with alternative practices for disciplining children (Larzelere & Kuhn, 2005).

Indeed, there are few longitudinal studies of punishment and few studies that distinguish adequately between moderate and heavy use of punishment. Thus, in the view of some experts, such as Joan Grusec of the University of Toronto, available research evidence makes it difficult to tell whether the effects of physical punishment are harmful to children's development, even though such a view might be distasteful to some individuals (Grusec, 2009).

In addition to considering whether physical punishment is mild or out of control, another factor in evaluating effects on children's development involves cultural contexts. Recent research has indicated that in countries such as Kenya, in which physical punishment is considered normal and necessary for handling children's transgressions, the effects of physical punishment are less harmful than in countries such as Thailand in which physical punishment is perceived as more harmful to children's development (Lansford & others, 2005, 2013).

One thing that is clear regarding research on punishment of children is that if physical punishment is used, it needs to be mild, infrequent, age-appropriate, and used in the context of a positive parent-child relationship (Grusec, 2011). It is also clear that when physical punishment involves abuse, it can be very harmful to children's development (Cicchetti, 2013; Garcia, McKee, & Forehand, 2012).

*How might the use of physical punishment harm a child's development?*

**coparenting** Support parents provide for each other in jointly raising children.

*What characterizes coparenting?*

Child maltreatment involves grossly inadequate and destructive aspects of parenting.

—DANTE CICCHETTI
*Contemporary Developmental Psychologist, University of Minnesota*

**Coparenting** The relationship between marital conflict and the use of punishment highlights the importance of **coparenting**, which is the support that parents provide one another in jointly raising a child. Poor coordination between parents, undermining of the other parent, lack of cooperation and warmth, and disconnection by one parent are conditions that place children at risk for problems (Talbot, Baker, & McHale, 2009). For example, one study revealed that coparenting influenced young children's effortful control above and beyond maternal and paternal parenting by themselves (Karreman & others, 2008). And a recent study found that greater father involvement in young children's play was linked to an increase in supportive coparenting (Jia & Schoppe-Sullivan, 2011).

**Child Maltreatment** Unfortunately, punishment sometimes leads to the abuse of infants and children (Cicchetti, 2011, 2013). There is little available information about the number of Canadian children who are victims of abuse, particularly since most victims do not report abuse. One study by Harriett MacMillan and her colleagues at McMaster University examined adults' recollection of being physically and sexually abused as children (MacMillan & others, 2013). The researchers found that 20 percent of adults recalled severe physical abuse, 15 percent recalled sexual abuse, and 8 percent recalled both physical and sexual abuse. Over three times more females recalled experiencing sexual abuse as children than did males.

Whereas the public and many professionals use the term *child abuse* to refer to both abuse and neglect, developmentalists increasingly use the term *child maltreatment* (Cicchetti, 2011, 2013; Cicchetti & Toth, 2011). This term does not have quite the emotional impact of the term *abuse* and acknowledges that maltreatment includes diverse conditions.

*Types of Child Maltreatment* The four main types of child maltreatment are physical abuse, child neglect, sexual abuse, and emotional abuse (National Clearinghouse on Child Abuse and Neglect, 2004):

- *Physical abuse* is characterized by the infliction of physical injury as result of punching, beating, kicking, biting, burning, shaking, or otherwise harming a child. The parent or other person may not have intended to hurt the child; the injury may have resulted from excessive physical punishment (Milot & others, 2010).

- *Child neglect* is characterized by failure to provide for the child's basic needs (Newton & Vandeven, 2010; Thompson, 2010). Neglect can be physical (abandonment, for example), educational (allowing chronic truancy, for example), or emotional (marked inattention to the child's needs, for example). Child neglect is by far the most common form of child maltreatment. In every country where relevant data have been collected, neglect occurs up to three times as often as abuse (Benoit, Coolbear, & Crawford, 2008).

- *Sexual abuse* includes fondling a child's genitals, intercourse, incest, rape, sodomy, exhibitionism, and commercial exploitation through prostitution or the production of pornographic materials (Bahali & others, 2010; Leventhal, Murphy, & Asnes, 2010).

- *Emotional abuse (psychological/verbal abuse/mental injury)* includes acts or omissions by parents or other caregivers that have caused, or could cause, serious behavioural, cognitive, or emotional problems (van Harmelen & others, 2010).

Although any of these forms of child maltreatment may be found separately, they often occur in combination. Emotional abuse is almost always present when other forms are identified. The Canadian Incidence Study of Reported Child Maltreatment (CIS) revealed that primary reasons for child maltreatment investigations in Canada were physical abuse (31 percent), neglect (40 percent), sexual abuse (11 percent), and emotional abuse (19 percent) (Trocme & others, 2003).

*The Context of Abuse*   No single factor causes child maltreatment (Cicchetti, 2011, 2013). A combination of factors, including the culture, family, and developmental characteristics of the child, likely contribute to child maltreatment (Cicchetti & Toth, 2011).

The family itself is obviously a key part of the context of abuse. Among the family and family-associated characteristics that may contribute to child maltreatment are parenting stress, substance abuse, social isolation, single parenting, and socioeconomic difficulties (especially poverty) (Cicchetti, 2013; Laslett & others, 2012; MacMillan & others, 2013; Turner & others, 2012). The interactions of all family members need to be considered, regardless of who performs the violent acts against the child. For example, even though the father may be the one who physically abuses the child, the behaviour of the mother, the child, and siblings also should be evaluated.

Were abusive parents abused by their own parents? About one-third of parents who were abused themselves when they were young go on to abuse their own children (Cicchetti & Toth, 2006, 2011). Thus, some, but not a majority, of parents are involved in an intergenerational transmission of abuse.

*Developmental Consequences of Abuse*   Among the consequences of child maltreatment in childhood and adolescence are poor emotional regulation, attachment problems, problems in peer relations, difficulty in adapting to school, and other psychological problems such as depression and delinquency. A longitudinal study found that early maltreatment was linked to emotional negativity (age 7) that increased poor emotional regulation (age 8), which in turn predicted an increase in internalized symptoms (from age 8 to 9) (Kim-Spoon, Cicchetti, & Rogosch, 2013). As shown in Figure 14.5, maltreated young children in foster care were more likely to show abnormal stress hormone levels than middle-SES young children living with their birth family (Gunnar & Fisher, 2006). In this study, the abnormal stress hormone levels were mainly present in the foster children who were neglected, best described as "institutional neglect" (Fisher, 2005). Abuse also may have this effect on young children (Gunnar & Fisher, 2006). Adolescents who experienced abuse or neglect as children are more likely than adolescents who were not maltreated as children to engage in violent romantic relationships, delinquency, sexual risk taking, and substance abuse (Shin, Hong, & Hazen, 2010; Wekerle & others, 2009). And a recent study revealed that a significant increase in suicide attempts before age 18 occurred with repeated child maltreatment (Jonson-Reid, Kohl, & Drake, 2012).

Later, during the adult years, individuals who were maltreated as children are more likely to experience problems with physical health, mental health, and sexual function (Lacelle & others, 2012). A 30-year longitudinal study found that middle-aged adults who had experienced child maltreatment had increased risk for diabetes, lung disease, malnutrition, and vision problems (Widom & others, 2012). Another study revealed that child maltreatment was linked to depression (Nanni, Uhr, & Danese, 2012). Further, adults who were maltreated as children often have difficulty establishing and maintaining healthy intimate relationships (Dozier, Stovall-McClough, & Albus, 2009). As adults, maltreated children are also at higher risk for violent behaviour toward other adults—especially dating partners and marital partners—as well as for substance abuse, anxiety, and depression (Miller-Perrin, Perrin, & Kocur, 2009).

An important agenda is to discover how to prevent child maltreatment or intervene in children's lives when they have been maltreated (Cicchetti &

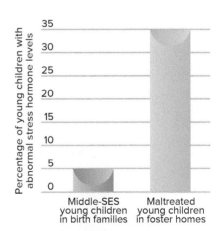

**FIGURE 14.5**

**ABNORMAL STRESS HORMONE LEVELS IN YOUNG CHILDREN IN DIFFERENT TYPES OF REARING CONDITIONS.**

others, 2013; Shapiro, Prinz, & Sanders, 2012). In one study of maltreating mothers and their 1-year-olds, two treatments were effective in reducing child maltreatment: (1) home visitation that emphasized improved parenting, coping with stress, and increasing support for the mother; and (2) parent-infant psychotherapy that focused on improving maternal-infant attachment (Cicchetti, Toth, & Rogosch, 2005).

## PARENT-ADOLESCENT RELATIONSHIPS

Even the best parents may find their relationship with their child strained during adolescence. Important aspects of parent-adolescent relationships include autonomy/attachment and conflict.

**Autonomy and Attachment**  With most adolescents, parents are likely to find themselves engaged in a delicate balancing act, weighing competing needs for autonomy and control, for independence and connection.

*The Push for Autonomy*  The typical adolescent's push for autonomy and responsibility puzzles and angers many parents. Most parents anticipate that their teenager will have some difficulty adjusting to the changes that adolescence brings, but few parents imagine and predict just how strong an adolescent's desires will be to spend time with peers or how intensely adolescents will want to show that it is they—not their parents—who are responsible for their successes and failures. Although both boys and girls desire autonomy, boys are usually given more independence than girls.

Adolescents' ability to attain autonomy and gain control over their behaviour is acquired through appropriate adult reactions to their desire for control (Laursen & Collins, 2009; McElhaney & Allen, 2012). At the onset of adolescence, the average individual does not have the knowledge to make appropriate or mature decisions in all areas of life. As the adolescent pushes for autonomy, the wise adult relinquishes control in those areas where the adolescent can make reasonable decisions, but continues to guide the adolescent to make reasonable decisions in areas in which the adolescent's knowledge is more limited. Gradually, adolescents acquire the ability to make mature decisions on their own.

Autonomy-granting can positively affect adolescents' well-being. For example, in a recent study, young adolescents' perception that their parents promoted more psychological autonomy and less psychological control predicted fewer depressive symptoms two years later (Sher-Censor, Parke, & Coltrane, 2011).

*The Role of Attachment*  Recall from Chapter 10 that one of the most widely discussed aspects of socioemotional development in infancy is secure attachment to caregivers. In the past decade, researchers have explored whether secure attachment also might be an important concept in adolescents' relationships with their parents (Laursen & Collins, 2009). For example, Joseph Allen and his colleagues (2009) found that adolescents who were securely attached at 14 years of age were more likely to report that they were in an exclusive relationship, comfortable with intimacy in relationships, and achieving increased financial independence at 21 years of age. And a recent analysis concluded that the most consistent outcomes of secure attachment in adolescence involve positive peer relations and development of the adolescent's emotion regulation capacities (Allen & Miga, 2010).

*developmental* **connection**

**Attachment.** Securely attached infants use the caregiver as a secure base from which to explore the environment. Chapter 10, LO 4

*What are strategies that parents can use to guide adolescents in effectively handling their increased motivation for autonomy?*

*Balancing Freedom and Control*   We have seen that parents play very important roles in adolescent development (McKinney & Renk, 2011). Although adolescents are moving toward independence, they still need to stay connected with families (McElhaney & Allen, 2012). For example, the National Longitudinal Study on Adolescent Health surveyed more than 12,000 American adolescents and found that those who did not eat dinner with a parent five or more days a week had dramatically higher rates of smoking, drinking, marijuana use, getting into fights, and initiation of sexual activity (Council of Economic Advisors, 2000). To read about the role of having family dinners for Canadian adolescent development, see *Connecting Through Research*.

**Parent-Adolescent Conflict**   Although parent-adolescent conflict increases in early adolescence, it does not reach the tumultuous proportions G. Stanley Hall envisioned at the beginning of the twentieth century (Laursen & Collins, 2009). Rather, much of the conflict involves the everyday events of family life, such as keeping a bedroom clean, dressing neatly, getting home by a certain time, and not talking forever on the phone. The conflicts rarely involve major dilemmas such as drugs or delinquency.

Conflict with parents often escalates during early adolescence, remains somewhat stable during the high school years, and then lessens as the adolescent reaches 17 to 20 years of age. Parent-adolescent relationships become more positive if adolescents go away to university than if they attend university while living at home (Sullivan & Sullivan, 1980).

Conflict with parents increases in early adolescence. *What is the nature of this conflict in a majority of Canadian families?*

# connecting through research

## How Important Are Family Dinners for Canadian Adolescents' Well-Being?

Frank Elgar of McGill University and Wendy Craig and Stephen Trites of Queen's University examined the association between the frequency of family dinners and adolescent mental health (Elgar, Craig, & Trites, 2013). Adolescents completed a survey assessing how often (on average) they eat dinner with their family each week and how easy or difficult it is for them to communicate with their parents. Adolescents also reported on their own mental health.

The researchers found that, on average, adolescents had family dinners 4.7 times per week. Around one-third of adolescents had all seven dinners during the week with their family. Adolescents who never had family dinners reported the poorest mental health. Mental health was better for each additional meal adolescents had with their family during the week. Eating dinner often with family was negatively related to internalizing problems (such as low mood, anxious thoughts and loneliness) and externalizing problems (such as fighting, school truancy, and stealing). In addition, more frequent family dinners were positively related to emotional well-being (such as self-confidence

*Do family dinners affect the well-being of adolescents?*

and energy), prosocial behaviour, and life satisfaction. The results showed that frequent family dinners provided an opportunity for families to socialize, which benefits all adolescents, even those who do not feel that talking to their parents is easy.

Stacey Christensen, age 16: "I am lucky enough to have open communication with my parents. Whenever I am in need or just need to talk, my parents are there for me. My advice to parents is to let your teens grow at their own pace, be open with them so that you can be there for them. We need guidance; our parents need to help but not be too overwhelming."

The everyday conflicts that characterize parent-adolescent relationships may actually serve a positive developmental function. These minor disputes and negotiations facilitate the adolescent's transition from being dependent on parents to becoming an autonomous individual. Recognizing that conflict and negotiation can serve a positive developmental function can tone down parental hostility.

The old model of parent-adolescent relationships suggested that as adolescents mature they detach themselves from parents and move into a world of autonomy apart from parents. The old model also suggested that parent-adolescent conflict is intense and stressful throughout adolescence. The new model emphasizes that parents serve as important attachment figures and support systems while adolescents explore a wider, more complex social world. The new model also emphasizes that, in most families, parent-adolescent conflict is moderate rather than severe and that the everyday negotiations and minor disputes not only are normal but also can serve the positive developmental function of helping the adolescent make the transition from childhood dependency to adult independence (see Figure 14.6).

Still, a high degree of conflict characterizes some parent-adolescent relationships. And this prolonged, intense conflict is associated with various adolescent problems: movement out of the home, juvenile delinquency, school dropout, pregnancy and early marriage, membership in religious cults, and drug abuse (Brook & others, 1990). Further, a recent study revealed that a higher level of parent-adolescent conflict was related to peer-reported aggression and delinquency (Ehrlich, Dykas, & Cassidy, 2012).

## INTERGENERATIONAL RELATIONSHIPS

Connections between generations play important roles in development through the life span (Antonucci, Birditt, & Ajrouch, 2013; Fingerman, Cheng, & others, 2012; Fingerman, Pillemer, & others, 2012). With each new generation, personality characteristics, attitudes, and values are replicated or changed (Pratt & others, 2008). As older family members die, their biological, intellectual, emotional, and personal legacies are carried on in the next generation. Their children become the oldest generation and their grandchildren the second generation. In many families, females' relationships across generations are closer and more intimate than are males' relationships (Etaugh & Bridges, 2010).

The following studies provide evidence of the importance of intergenerational relationships in children's development:

- Supportive family environments and parenting in childhood (assessed when the children were 3 to 15 years of age) were linked with more positive relationships (in terms of contact, closeness, conflict, and reciprocal assistance) between the children and their middle-aged parents when the children were 26 years of age (Belsky & others, 2001).

- Children of divorce were disproportionately likely to end their own marriage than were children from intact, never-divorced families, although the

**Old Model**

Autonomy, detachment from parents; parent and peer worlds are isolated

Intense, stressful conflict throughout adolescence; parent-adolescent relationships are filled with storm and stress on virtually a daily basis

**New Model**

Attachment and autonomy; parents are important support systems and attachment figures; adolescent-parent and adolescent-peer worlds have some important connections

Moderate parent-adolescent conflict is common and can serve a positive developmental function; conflict greater in early adolescence

## FIGURE 14.6

**OLD AND NEW MODELS OF PARENT-ADOLESCENT RELATIONSHIPS.**

transmission of divorce across generations has declined in recent years (Wolfinger, 2011).

- Parents who smoked early and often, and persisted in becoming regular smokers, were more likely to have adolescents who became smokers (Chassin & others, 2008).
- Evidence was found for the intergenerational transmission of conduct disorder (multiple delinquent activities) across three generations, with the connection stronger for males than females (D'Onofrio & others, 2007).

The generations of living things pass in a short time, and like runners hand on the torch of life.

—Lucretius
*Roman Poet, 1st Century BC*

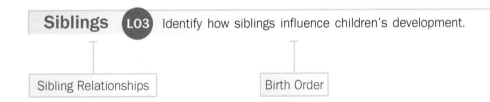

## Review *Connect* **Reflect**

**LO2** Explain how parenting is linked to children's and adolescents' development.

### Review

- What characterizes parental roles and the timing of parenthood?
- In what ways do parents need to adapt their behaviour to developmental changes in their children?
- How can parents be effective managers of children's lives?
- What are the main parenting styles and variations in discipline?
- What are some important aspects of parenting adolescents?
- How do intergenerational relationships influence children's development?

### *Connect*

- In this section, we learned about Baumrind's four parenting styles. In Chapter 13, we learned about three types of discipline techniques. Which techniques are more likely to be used by parents from each parenting style?

### **Reflect** *Your Own Personal Journey of Life*

- What was the nature of your relationship with your parents during middle school and high school? Has your relationship with your parents changed since then? Does it involve less conflict today? What do you think are the most important characteristics of a competent parent of adolescents?

---

## Siblings **LO3** Identify how siblings influence children's development.

Sibling Relationships

Birth Order

What are sibling relationships like? How extensively does birth order influence behaviour?

## SIBLING RELATIONSHIPS

The majority of Canadian children grow up with at least one sibling. If you grew up with siblings, you probably have a rich memory of aggressive, hostile interactions. Siblings in the presence of each other when they are 2 to 4 years of age, on average, have a conflict once every 10 minutes. The conflicts go down somewhat from 5 to 7 years of age (Kramer, 2006). One study revealed that an increase in sibling conflict was linked to an increase in children's depressive symptoms, whereas an increase in sibling intimacy was related to an increase in children's peer competence (Kim & others, 2007). And a research review concluded that sibling relationships in adolescence are not as close, are not as intense, and are more egalitarian than in childhood (East, 2009).

Issues of equality and fairness, as well as invasion of one's personal domain, are common in sibling relationships. For example, a recent study of young adolescents revealed that sibling conflicts involving equality and fairness were associated with an increase in depressed mood one year later, while conflicts associated with invasion of one's personal domain were linked to higher anxiety and lower self-esteem one year later (Campione-Barr, Bassett Greer, & Kruse, 2013).

What do parents do when they encounter siblings in the midst of a verbal or physical confrontation? One study revealed that they do one of three things: (1) intervene and try to help them resolve the conflict, (2) admonish or threaten them, or (3) do nothing at all (Kramer & Perozynski, 1999). Of interest is that in families with two siblings 2 to 5 years of age, the most frequent parental reaction is to do nothing at all.

Laurie Kramer (2006), who has conducted a number of research studies on siblings, says that not intervening and letting sibling conflict escalate is not a good strategy. Indeed, a study of 5- to 10-year-old siblings and their parents found that training parents to mediate sibling disputes increased children's understanding of conflicts and reduced sibling conflict (Smith & Ross, 2007). Children themselves can also be taught to manage conflict with siblings. For example, Laurie Kramer developed a program titled More Fun with Sisters and Brothers that teaches 4- to 8-year-old siblings social skills for developing positive interactions (Kramer & Radey, 1997). Among the social skills taught in the program are how to appropriately initiate play, how to accept and refuse invitations to play, how to understand another person's perspective, how to deal with angry feelings, and how to manage conflict.

As intense as it can be, however, conflict is only one of the many dimensions of sibling relations (Dunn, 2013; McHale, Updegraff, & Whiteman, 2011; Milevsky, 2011; Whiteman, Jensen, & Bernard, 2012). Sibling relations include helping, sharing, teaching, fighting, and playing, and siblings can act as emotional supports, rivals, and communication partners (East, 2009).

Judy Dunn (2007), a leading expert on sibling relationships, described three important characteristics of sibling relationships:

- *Emotional quality of the relationship.* Both intensive positive and negative emotions are often expressed by siblings toward each other. Many children and adolescents have mixed feelings toward their siblings.

  - *Familiarity and intimacy of the relationship.* Siblings typically know each other very well, and this intimacy suggests that they can either provide support or tease and undermine each other, depending on the situation.

  - *Variation in sibling relationships.* Some siblings describe their relationships more positively than others. Thus, there is considerable variation in sibling relationships. We previously indicated that many siblings have mixed feelings about each other, but some children and adolescents mainly describe their sibling in warm, affectionate ways, whereas others primarily talk about how irritating and mean a sibling is.

Negative aspects of sibling relationships, such as high conflict, are linked to negative outcomes for adolescents. The negative outcomes can develop not only through conflict but also through direct modelling of a sibling's behaviour, as when a younger sibling has an older sibling who has poor study habits and engages in delinquent behaviour. By contrast, close and supportive sibling relationships can buffer the negative effects of stressful circumstances in an adolescent's life (East, 2009).

*What are some characteristics of sibling relationships?*

# BIRTH ORDER

Whether a child has older or younger siblings has been linked to development of certain personality characteristics. For example, a recent review concluded that "firstborns are the most intelligent, achieving, and conscientious, while later-borns are the most rebellious, liberal, and agreeable" (Paulhus, 2008, p. 210). Compared with later-born children, firstborn children have also been described as more adult oriented, helpful, conforming, and self-controlled. However, when such birth order differences are reported, they often are small.

What accounts for differences related to birth order? Proposed explanations usually point to variations in interactions with parents and siblings associated with being in a particular position in the family. This is especially true in the case of the firstborn child (Teti, 2001). The oldest child is the only one who does not have to share parental love and affection with other siblings—until another sibling comes along. An infant requires more attention than an older child; this means that the firstborn sibling receives less attention after the newborn arrives. Does this result in conflict between parents and the firstborn? In one research study, mothers became more negative, coercive, and restraining and played less with the firstborn following the birth of a second child (Dunn & Kendrick, 1982).

What is the only child like? The popular conception is that the only child is a "spoiled brat," with such undesirable characteristics as dependency, lack of self-control, and self-centred behaviour. But researchers present a more positive portrayal of the only child. Only children often are achievement oriented and display a desirable personality, especially in comparison with later-borns and children from large families (Falbo & Poston, 1993; Jiao, Ji, & Jing, 1996).

So far, our discussion suggests that birth order might be a strong predictor of behaviour. However, an increasing number of family researchers stress that when all of the factors that influence behaviour are considered, birth order itself shows limited ability to predict behaviour.

Think about some of the other important factors in children's lives that influence their behaviour beyond birth order. They include heredity, models of competency or incompetency that parents present to children on a daily basis, peer influences, school influences, socioeconomic factors, sociohistorical factors, and cultural variations. When someone says firstborns are *always like this* but last-borns are *always like that*, the person is making overly simplistic statements that do not adequately take into account the complexity of influences on a child's development.

The one-child family is becoming much more common in China because of the strong motivation to limit the population growth in the People's Republic of China. The effects of this policy have not been fully examined. *In general, what have researchers found the only child to be like?*

---

## Review Connect Reflect

 **L03** Identify how siblings influence children's development.

### Review

- How can sibling relationships be characterized?
- What role does birth order play in children's development?

### Connect

- In this section, you learned that parents typically respond in one of three ways to sibling conflict. How do these three ways align with Baumrind's parenting styles discussed earlier in this chapter?

### Reflect *Your Own Personal Journey of Life*

- If you grew up with a sibling, you likely showed some jealousy of your sibling and vice versa. If you had one or more siblings, how did your parents handle sibling conflict? If and when you become a parent and have two or more children, what strategies will you use to reduce sibling conflict?

Working Parents | Children in Divorced Families | Stepfamilies | Gay and Lesbian Parents | Cultural, Ethnic, and Socioeconomic Variations in Families

*developmental* **connection**

**Environment.** Research consistently shows that family factors are considerably better at predicting children's developmental outcomes than are child-care experiences. Chapter 10, LO 4

Canadian children are growing up in a greater variety of family contexts than ever before. As we discussed in Chapter 10, "Emotional Development," children are experiencing many sorts of caregiving—not only from stay-at-home mothers but also from stay-at-home fathers, from various types of child-care programs, and from after-school programs. The structure of Canadian families also varies. As shown in Figure 14.7, Canada has a higher percentage of single-parent families than several countries with similar levels of economic and technological development. And some Canadian children are being raised in stepfamilies formed after a divorce and by gay or lesbian parents. How are these and other variations in family life affecting children?

## WORKING PARENTS

The increased number of mothers in the labour force represents one source of change in families and society in Canada (Bushnik, 2006). In 2005, over 70 percent of two-parent Canadian families with children under the age of 16 were dual-income families compared to 36 percent in 1976 (Marshall, 2006). Among single mothers, 51 percent work full time compared to 65 percent of single fathers (La Rochelle-Cote, Gougen, & Pinard, 2009). Many parents spend the greatest part of their day away from their children, even their infants. How have these changes influenced children's development?

Most research on parental work has focused on young children and the mother's employment (Brooks-Gunn, Han, & Waldfogel, 2010). Research on maternal employment and children's development usually reveals few links between a mother's work status and children's cognitive and socioemotional development (Goldberg & Lucas-Thompson, 2008). However, maternal employment may be especially influential in the first several years of the child's life. For example, a recent study of low-income families found that 7-year-old children whose mothers were employed early, especially in the first 8 months, had better socioemotional functioning than their peers whose mothers had remained unemployed (Coley & Lombardi, 2013).

However, it is important to recognize that the effects of working parents in two-parent families involves both parents when such matters as work schedules

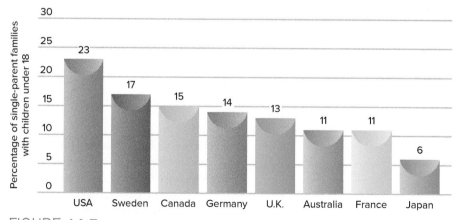

FIGURE **14.7**

**SINGLE-PARENT FAMILIES IN DIFFERENT COUNTRIES.**

and work-family stress are considered (O'Brien & Moss, 2010; Parke & Clarke-Stewart, 2011; Peeters & others, 2013). Recent research indicates that children's development is affected more strongly by the nature of parents' work than by the employment of one or both parents outside the home (Goodman & others, 2011; Han, 2009; Parke & Clarke-Stewart, 2011).

Ann Crouter (2006) described how parents bring their experiences at work into their homes. She concluded that parents who have poor working conditions, such as long hours, overtime work, stressful work, and lack of autonomy on the job, are likely to be more irritable at home and engage in less effective parenting than their counterparts who enjoy better working conditions. A consistent finding is the children (especially girls) of working mothers engage in less gender stereotyping and have more egalitarian views of gender (Goldberg & Lucas-Thompson, 2008).

## CHILDREN IN DIVORCED FAMILIES

Divorce rates changed rather dramatically in many countries around the world during the late twentieth century (Amato & Dorius, 2010). In 1987, Canada's divorce rate was at a high point with 96,200 divorces. This number has since declined, with 71,269 divorces in 2005 (Ambert, 2009). It is estimated that 30 percent of Canadian children born in the early 2000s will experience their parents' divorce before the children are 15 years old (Ambert, 2009). Let's examine some important questions about children in divorced families:

*How does work affect parenting?*

- *Are children better adjusted in intact, never-divorced families than in divorced families?* Most researchers agree that children from divorced families show poorer adjustment than their counterparts in non-divorced families (Amato & Dorius, 2010; Hetherington, 2006; Lansford, 2009; Wallerstein, 2008) (see Figure 14.8). Those who have experienced multiple divorces are at greater risk. Children in divorced families are more likely than children in non-divorced families to have academic problems, to show externalizing problems (such as acting out and delinquency) and internalizing problems (such as anxiety and depression), to be less socially responsible, to have less competent intimate relationships, to drop out of school, to become sexually active at an early age, to take drugs, to associate with antisocial peers, to have low self-esteem, and to be less securely attached as young adults (Lansford, 2009). Indeed, one study revealed that adolescent girls with divorced parents were especially vulnerable to developing depressive symptoms (Oldehinkel & others, 2008). Another study found that experiencing a divorce in childhood was associated with insecure attachment in early adulthood (Brockmeyer, Treboux, & Crowell, 2005). And a recent study found that adolescent girls from divorced families displayed lower levels of romantic competence (Shulman & others, 2012). However, mothers' ability to provide their daughters with a coherent account of their own adolescent romantic experiences alleviated the negative link of divorce to daughters romantic behaviour. Nonetheless, it is important to remember that most of the children in divorced families do *not* have significant adjustment problems.

- *Should parents stay together for the sake of the children?* Whether parents should stay in an unhappy or conflicted marriage for the sake of their children is one of the most commonly asked questions about divorce (Deutsch & Pruett, 2009; Hetherington, 2006; Ziol-Guest, 2009). If the stresses and disruptions in family relationships associated with an unhappy, conflictual marriage that erode the well-being of children are

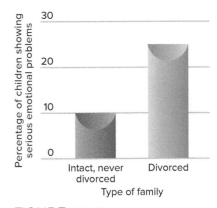

## FIGURE **14.8**

**DIVORCE AND CHILDREN'S EMOTIONAL**
**PROBLEMS.** In Hetherington's research, 25 percent of children from divorced families showed serious emotional problems compared with only 10 percent of children from intact, never-divorced families. However, keep in mind that a substantial majority (75 percent) of the children from divorced families did not show serious emotional problems.

reduced by the move to a divorced, single-parent family, divorce can be advantageous. However, if the diminished resources and increased risks associated with divorce also are accompanied by inept parenting and sustained or increased conflict, not only between the divorced couple but also among the parents, children, and siblings, the best choice for the children would be for an unhappy marriage to be retained (Hetherington & Stanley-Hagan, 2002). It is difficult to determine how these "ifs" will play out when parents either remain together in an acrimonious marriage or become divorced.

Note that marital conflict may have negative consequences for children in the context of marriage or divorce (Cummings & Davies, 2010; Kleinsorge & Covitz, 2012). A longitudinal study revealed that conflict in non-divorced families was associated with emotional problems in children (Amato, 2006). Indeed, many of the problems children from divorced homes experience begin during the pre-divorce period, a time when parents are often in active conflict with each other. Thus, when children from divorced homes show problems, the problems may be due not only to the divorce, but also to the marital conflict that led to it (Thompson, 2008).

E. Mark Cummings and his colleagues (Cummings & Davies, 2010; Cummings, El-Sheikh, & Kouros, 2009; Cummings & Kouros, 2008; Cummings & others, 2012) have proposed *emotion security theory,* which has its roots in attachment theory and states that children appraise marital conflict in terms of their sense of security and safety in the family. These researchers make a distinction between marital conflict that is negative for children (such as hostile emotional displays and destructive conflict tactics) and marital conflict that can be positive for children (such as marital disagreement that involves a calm discussion of each person's perspective and working together to reach a solution). In a recent study, Cummings and his colleagues (2012) found that parental conflict during the kindergarten year was linked to children's emotional insecurity later in childhood, which in turn was associated with adolescent adjustment, including higher levels of depression and anxiety.

- *How much do family processes matter in divorced families?* In divorced families, family processes matter a great deal (Hetherington, 2006; Lansford, 2009, 2012; Parke & Clarke-Stewart, 2011). When divorced parents have a harmonious relationship and use authoritative parenting, the adjustment of adolescents is improved (Hetherington, 2006). When divorced parents can agree on child-rearing strategies and can maintain a cordial relationship with each other, frequent visits by the non-custodial parent usually benefit the child (Fabricius & others, 2010). Following a divorce, father involvement with children drops off more than mother involvement, especially for fathers of girls. Also, a recent study in divorced families revealed that an intervention focused on improving the mother-child relationship was linked to improvements in relationship quality that increased children's coping skills over the short term (6 months) and long term (6 years) (Velez & others, 2011).

- *What factors influence an individual child's vulnerability to suffering negative consequences as a result of living in a divorced family?* Among the factors influencing the child's risk and vulnerability are the child's adjustment prior to the divorce, as well as the child's personality and temperament, gender, and custody situation (Hetherington, 2005, 2006). Children whose parents later divorce show poorer adjustment before the breakup (Amato & Booth, 1996; Lansford, 2009). Children who are socially mature and responsible, who show few behavioural problems, and who have an easy temperament are better able to cope with their parents' divorce. Moreover, children with a difficult temperament often have problems in coping with their parents' divorce (Hetherington, 2005).

*What concerns are involved in whether parents should stay together for the sake of their children or become divorced?*

Earlier studies reported gender differences in response to divorce, with divorce being more negative for girls than boys in mother-custody families. However, more recent studies have shown that gender differences are less pronounced and consistent than was previously believed. Some of the inconsistency may be due to the increase in father custody, joint custody, and increased involvement of non-custodial fathers, especially in their sons' lives (Ziol-Guest, 2009). One analysis of studies found that children in joint-custody families were better adjusted than children in sole-custody families (Bauserman, 2002). Joint custody works best for children when the parents can get along with each other (Parke & Clark-Stewart, 2011). Some studies have shown that boys adjust better in father-custody families, girls in mother-custody families, whereas other studies have not (Maccoby & Mnookin, 1992; Santrock & Warshak, 1979).

- *What role does socioeconomic status play in the lives of children in divorced families?* Custodial mothers experience the loss of about one-fourth to one-half of their predivorce income, in comparison with a loss of only one-tenth by custodial fathers (Emery, 1994). This income loss for divorced mothers is accompanied by increased workloads, high rates of job instability, and residential moves to less desirable neighbourhoods with inferior schools (Lansford, 2009).

## STEPFAMILIES

In 2011, nearly half a million Canadian families were stepfamilies (Statistics Canada, 2013). It takes time for parents to marry, have children, get divorced, and then remarry. Consequently, there are far more elementary and secondary school children than infant or preschool children living in stepfamilies.

Remarried parents face some unique tasks. The couple must define and strengthen their marriage and at the same time renegotiate the biological parent-child relationships and establish stepparent-stepchild and stepsibling relationships (Ganong, Coleman, & Jamison, 2011). The complex histories and multiple relationships make adjustment difficult in a stepfamily (Goldscheider & Sassler, 2006). Only one-third of stepfamily couples stay remarried. And some remarried individuals are more adult-focused, responding more to the concerns of their partner, while others are more child-focused, responding more to the concerns of the children (Anderson & Greene, 2011).

In some cases, the stepfamily may have been preceded by the death of a spouse. However, by far the largest number of stepfamilies are preceded by divorce rather than death (Pasley & Moorefield, 2004). Three common types of stepfamily structure are (1) stepfather, (2) stepmother, and (3) blended or complex. In stepfather families, the mother typically had custody of the children and remarried, introducing a stepfather into her children's lives. In stepmother families, the father usually had custody and remarried, introducing a stepmother into his children's lives. In a blended or complex stepfamily, both parents bring children from previous marriages to live in the newly formed stepfamily.

In E. Mavis Hetherington's (2006) longitudinal analyses, children and adolescents who had been in a simple stepfamily (stepfather or stepmother) for a number of years were adjusting better than in the early years of the remarried family and were functioning well in comparison with children and adolescents in conflicted non-divorced families and children and adolescents in complex (blended) stepfamilies. More than 75 percent of the adolescents in long-established

*How does living in a stepfamily influence a child's development?*

simple stepfamilies described their relationships with their stepparents as "close" or "very close." Hetherington (2006) concluded that in long-established simple stepfamilies adolescents seem to eventually benefit from the presence of a stepparent and the resources provided by the stepparent.

Children often have better relationships with their custodial parents (mothers in stepfather families, fathers in stepmother families) than with stepparents (Santrock, Sitterle, & Warshak, 1988). Also, children in simple families (stepmother, stepfather) often show better adjustment than their counterparts in complex (blended) families (Anderson & others, 1999; Hetherington & Kelly, 2002).

As in divorced families, children in stepfamilies show more adjustment problems than children in non-divorced families (Hetherington, 2006). The adjustment problems are similar to those found among children of divorced parents—academic problems and lower self-esteem, for example (Anderson & others, 1999). However, it is important to recognize that a majority of children in stepfamilies do not have problems. In one analysis, 25 percent of children from stepfamilies showed adjustment problems compared with 10 percent in intact, never-divorced families (Hetherington & Kelly, 2002).

Adolescence is an especially difficult time for the formation of a stepfamily (Anderson & others, 1999). Becoming part of a stepfamily may exacerbate normal adolescent concerns about identity, sexuality, and autonomy.

## GAY AND LESBIAN PARENTS

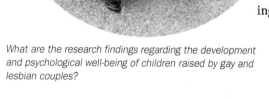

What are the research findings regarding the development and psychological well-being of children raised by gay and lesbian couples?

Increasingly, gay and lesbian couples are creating families that include children (Patterson & D'Augelli, 2013; Patterson & Farr, 2012). In 2011, approximately 10 percent of same-sex couples in Canada were parents, and of these same-sex parents, 80 percent were lesbian couples (Statistics Canada, 2013).

Like heterosexual couples, gay and lesbian parents vary greatly. They may be single or they may have same-gender partners. Many lesbian mothers and gay fathers are non-custodial parents because they lost custody of their children to heterosexual spouses after a divorce. In addition, gay and lesbian adults are increasingly choosing parenthood through donor insemination or adoption. Researchers have found that the children conceived through new reproductive technologies—such as in vitro fertilization—are as well adjusted as their counterparts conceived by natural means (Golombok, 2011a, b; Golombok & Tasker, 2010).

Researchers have found few differences in children growing up with lesbian mothers or gay fathers in comparison with adolescents growing up with heterosexual parents (Patterson, 2013). For example, children growing up in gay or lesbian families are just as popular with their peers, and there are no differences in the adjustment and mental health of children living in these families as compared with children in heterosexual families (Hyde & DeLamater, 2011). Also, the overwhelming majority of children growing up in a family with gay or lesbian parents have a heterosexual orientation (Golombok & Tasker, 2010).

## CULTURAL, ETHNIC, AND SOCIOECONOMIC VARIATIONS IN FAMILIES

Parenting can be influenced by culture, ethnicity, and socioeconomic status. In Bronfenbrenner's theory (introduced in Chapter 1), these influences are described as part of the macrosystem.

**Cross-Cultural Studies** Different cultures often give different answers to such basic questions as what a father's role in the family should be, what support systems are available to families, and how children should be disciplined (Conger & others, 2012; Hewlett & McFarlen, 2010; Mistry, Contreras, & Dutta, 2013).

There are important cross-cultural variations in parenting (Bornstein & Lansford, 2010). In some countries, authoritarian parenting is widespread. For example, in the Arab world, many families today are very authoritarian, dominated by the father's rule, and children are taught strict codes of conduct and family loyalty (Booth, 2002). Chinese parents also often appear more authoritarian, but there are differences between the North American and Chinese understanding of *authoritarian* (Chao, 2001). Chinese parents exert considerable control over their children's lives. However, Ruth Chao (2001, 2005, 2007; Chao & Tseng, 2002) argues that the style of parenting used by many Chinese parents is distinct from the domineering control of the authoritarian style. The predominant Chinese parenting style involves the concepts of *chiao sun* (training) and *guan* (to govern), which require a great amount of parental involvement and control with focus on educating their children, but also caring for them (Chao, 2001). The high academic achievement of Asian children may be a consequence of their "training" parents (Stevenson & Zusho, 2002).

What type of parenting is most frequent? In one study of parenting behaviour in 186 cultures around the world, the most common pattern was a warm and controlling style, one that was neither permissive nor restrictive (Rohner & Rohner, 1981). The investigators commented that the majority of cultures have discovered, over many centuries, that children's healthy social development is most effectively promoted by love and at least moderate parental control.

Cultural change is coming to families in many countries around the world. There are trends toward greater family mobility, migration to urban areas, separation as some family members work in cities or countries far from their homes, smaller families, fewer extended-family households, and increases in maternal employment (Brown & Larson, 2002). These trends can change the resources that are available to children. For example, when several generations no longer live near each other, children may lose support and guidance from grandparents, aunts, and uncles. Also, smaller families may produce more openness and communication between parents and children.

**Ethnicity**  Families within different ethnic groups differ in their typical size, structure, composition, reliance on kinships networks, and levels of income and education (Fuligni, Hughes, & Way, 2009; Galindo & Durham, 2009; Livas-Dlott & others, 2010). Large and extended families are common among minority groups and can serve as an important source of support for children. The family can filter out destructive racist messages, and parents can present alternative frames of reference to counter those presented by the majority. For example, TV shows may tell a 10-year-old boy that he will grow up to be either a star athlete or a chronic underachiever; his parents can show him that his life holds many possibilities other than these. The extended family also can serve as an important buffer to stress (McAdoo, 2006).

Of course, individual families vary, and how ethnic minority families deal with stress depends on many factors (Nieto & Bode, 2012; Schaefer, 2013; Urdan, 2012). Whether the parents are native-born or immigrants, how long the family has been in the country, their socioeoncomic status, and their national origin all make a difference (Cooper, 2011). The characteristics of the family's social context also influence its adaptation. What are the attitudes toward the family's ethnic group within its neighbourhood or city? Can the family's children attend good schools? Are there community groups that welcome people from the family's ethnic group? Do members of the family's ethnic group form community groups of their own? To read further about ethnic minority parenting, see *Connecting with Diversity*.

*What are some characteristics of ethnic minority families?*

## Acculturation and Ethnic Minority Parenting

As immigrants to Canada, ethnic minority children and their parents undergo varying degrees of **acculturation,** which refers to cultural changes that occur when one culture comes in contact with another. John Berry and his colleagues have theorized that, through the process of acculturation, ethnic minority groups in multicultural societies like Canada face the task of successfully integrating within the dominant culture while maintaining their own cultural traditions and values (Berry, 2005). According to Sabatier and Berry (2008), children's well-being is nurtured in immigrant families that openly discuss cultural differences and values. When immigrant parents accept the values of the majority culture and children accept the cultural values of their parents, immigrant families are most likely to thrive.

The level of family acculturation can affect parenting style by influencing expectations for children's development and parent-child interactions (Fuligni, Hughes, & Way, 2009). Maintaining cultural traditions and values among immigrant families may be most successfully accomplished through an authoritative parenting style. Ethnic pride is fostered by controlling yet warm parents who promote autonomy (Chiu, Feldman, & Rosenthal, 1992; Rosenthal & Feldman, 1992). Similarly, family values are most easily passed on to children by parents who are more empathic and less authoritarian (Schonpflug, 2001).

The family's level of acculturation also influences important decisions about child care and early childhood education. For example, an ethnic minority mother may prefer to have her children cared for by extended family while she is at work given that the kinship network is a natural source of support when a mother is absent. Although this is a well-intentioned, culturally appropriate decision, the child could potentially be placed at an educational and social disadvantage, as other children of similar age may have the benefit of preschool experiences that may ease the transition into elementary school (Garcia Coll & Pachter, 2002). Less acculturated and more acculturated family members may disagree about the appropriateness of various caregiving practices, possibly creating conflict or confusion.

The opportunities for acculturation that children experience depend mainly on their parents and extended family. If parents send their children to a child-care centre, school, church, or other community setting, the children are likely to learn about the values and behaviours of the dominant culture, and they may be expected to adapt to that culture's norms. For example, Chinese Canadian children, whose traditional parents value behavioural inhibition (as discussed in Chapter 10), may be rewarded outside the home for being active and emotionally expressive (Chen, 2011). Over time, the differences in the level of acculturation experienced by children and by their parents and extended family may grow.

*Minority children's experiences outside their homes may encourage behaviour that is at odds with some ethnic groups' parenting styles. Is this common worldwide? Which type of parenting is most frequently found worldwide?*

*How is acculturation involved in ethnic minority parenting?*

---

**acculturation** Cultural changes that occur when one culture comes in contact with another culture.

**Socioeconomic Status**   Low-income families have less access to resources than higher-income families (Duncan, 2012). The differential in access to resources includes nutrition, health care, protection from danger, and enriching educational and socialization opportunities, such as tutoring and lessons in various activities. These differences are compounded in low-income families characterized by long-term poverty (Santiago & others, 2012).

In most Western cultures, differences also have been found in child rearing among different socioeconomic-status (SES) groups (Hoff, Laursen, & Tardif, 2002, p. 246):

- "Lower-SES parents (1) are more concerned that their children conform to society's expectations, (2) create a home atmosphere in which it is clear that parents have authority over children," (3) use physical punishment more in disciplining their children, and (4) are more directive and less conversational with their children.

- "Higher-SES parents (1) are more concerned with developing children's initiative" and delay of gratification, "(2) create a home atmosphere in which children are more nearly equal participants and in which rules are discussed as opposed to being laid down" in an authoritarian manner, (3) are less likely to use physical punishment, and (4) "are less directive and more conversational" with their children.

Parents in different socioeconomic groups also tend to think differently about education (Huston & Ripke, 2006). Middle- and upper-income parents more often think of education as something that should be mutually encouraged by parents and teachers. By contrast, low-income parents are more likely to view education as the teacher's job. Thus, increased school-family linkages especially can benefit students from low-income families.

## Review Connect Reflect

**LO4** Characterize the changing family in a changing social world.

### Review

- How are children influenced by working parents?
- What characterizes the effects of divorce on children's development?
- How does living in a stepfamily influence children's development?
- How does growing up in a family with same-sex parents influence children's development?
- In what ways is children's development affected by their family's culture, ethnicity, and socioeconomic status?

### Connect

- In this section, you learned that low-income families have less access to nutrition, health care, protection from danger, and enriching educational and socialization opportunities. In Chapter 4, what did you learn regarding the specific health outcomes for children living in poverty?

### Reflect Your Own Personal Journey of Life

- Now that you have studied many aspects of families in this chapter, imagine that you have decided to write a book on some aspect of your own family. What aspect of your family would you focus on? What would be the title of your book? What would be the major theme of the book?

# case study connections

1. In this chapter, you learned about family susbsystems. What family subsystems can you identify within Shelley Peterman Schwartz's family as described in the chapter opening vignette?

2. What characterizes Shelley Peterman Schwartz's parenting style as described in the chapter opening vignette?

3. In this chapter, you learned about cultural, ethnic, and socioeconomic variations in families. How do you think these factors affected Shelley Peterman Schwartz's family as described in the chapter opening vignette?

# reach your learning goals

# Families

## Family Processes

 **LO1** Discuss family processes.

Interactions in the Family System

- The family is a system of interrelated and interacting individuals with different subsystems—some dyadic, some polyadic. The subsystems have both direct and indirect effects on one another. Positive marital relations can have a positive influence on parenting. Reciprocal socialization is the bidirectional process by which children socialize parents just as parents socialize them.

Cognition and Emotion in Family Processes

- Cognition and emotion are central to understanding how family processes work. The role of cognition includes parents' cognitions, beliefs, and values about their parental role, as well as the way they perceive, organize, and understand their children's behaviours and beliefs. The role of emotion includes the regulation of emotion in children, understanding emotion in children, and emotion in carrying out the parenting role. Children learn to express and manage emotions appropriately through interaction with emotion-coaching parents and have fewer behaviour problems than children of emotion-dismissing parents.

Multiple Developmental Trajectories

- Adults follow one developmental trajectory and children and adolescents another one. How these trajectories mesh is important for understanding the effects of timing of entry into various family tasks.

Domain-Specific Socialization

- Increasingly a domain-specific approach to socialization is being emphasized. One recent proposal focuses on five domains, each linked to specific child outcomes. The five domains are: protection, reciprocity, control, guided learning, and group participation.

Sociocultural and Historical Changes

- Changes in families may be due to great upheavals, such as war, or more subtle changes, such as technological advances and greater mobility of families. Increased restlessness and dissatisfaction in families has resulted in more divorced and remarried families than at any other point in history.

## Parenting

 **LO2** Explain how parenting is linked to children's and adolescents' development.

Parental Roles and the Timing of Parenthood

- Currently, there is a trend toward having fewer children and choosing when to have children. Many adults are waiting longer to have children or not having children at all.

Adapting Parenting to Developmental Changes in Children

- The transition to parenthood requires considerable adaptation and adjustment on the part of parents. As children grow older, parents increasingly turn to reasoning or withholding privileges in disciplining children. Parents spend less time with children in middle and late childhood, a time when parents play an especially important role in their children's academic achievement. Control is more coregulatory in middle and late childhood.

Parents as Managers of Children's Lives

- A recent trend is to conceptualize parents as managers of children's lives. Parents play important roles as managers of children's opportunities, effectively monitoring children's relationships and acting as social initiators and arrangers. Parental monitoring is linked to lower levels of juvenile delinquency, and effective parental management is related to children's higher academic achievement.

| Parenting Styles and Discipline | • Authoritarian, authoritative, neglectful, and indulgent are the four main categories of parenting styles. Authoritative parenting is associated with socially competent child behaviour more than the other styles. There are a number of reasons not to use physical punishment in disciplining children. Intense punishment presents the child with an out-of-control model. Punishment can instill fear, rage, or avoidance in children. Punishment tells children what not to do rather than what to do. Punishment can be abusive. Coparenting has positive outcomes for children. Child maltreatment is a multifaceted problem that involves the cultural context and family influences. Child maltreatment places the child at risk for a number of developmental problems. |

| Parent-Adolescent Relationships | • Many parents have a difficult time handling the adolescent's push for autonomy. Secure attachment to parents increases the likelihood that the adolescent will be socially competent. Conflict with parents often increases in early adolescence, but this conflict is generally moderate rather than severe. The increase in conflict probably serves the positive developmental functions of facilitating adolescent autonomy and identity. A subset of adolescents experience high parent-adolescent conflict, and this is linked with negative outcomes for adolescents. |

| Intergenerational Relationships | • Connections between parents play important roles in development through the life span. An increasing number of studies indicate that intergenerational relationships influence children's development. Marital interaction, a supportive family environment, divorce, and conduct disorder in the child's family of origin are among the factors that are linked to the child's development. |

## Siblings

 Identify how siblings influence children's development.

| Sibling Relationships | • Three important aspects of sibling relationships involve (1) emotional quality of the relationship, (2) familiarity and intimacy of the relationship, and (3) variation in sibling relationships. Sibling relationships include not only conflict and fighting but also helping, teaching, sharing, and playing—and siblings can function as rivals, emotional supports, and communication partners. |

| Birth Order | • Birth order is related in certain ways to child characteristics. Firstborn children are more self-controlled, conforming, have more guilt and anxiety, argue and excel academically and professionally compared with later-born children. However, some critics argue that the influence of birth order has been overestimated as a predictor of child behaviour. |

## The Changing Family in a Changing Social World

 Characterize the changing family in a changing social world.

| Working Parents | • In general, having both parents employed full-time outside the home has not been shown to have negative effects on children. However, depending on the circumstances, work can produce positive or negative effects on parenting. If parents experience poor work conditions, they frequently become inattentive to their children, who show more behavioural problems and do more poorly at school. There is a positive link between participation in extracurricular activities and academic achievement, psychological adjustment, and positive interaction with parents. |

| Children in Divorced Families | • Children in divorced families show more adjustment problems than their counterparts in non-divorced families. Whether parents should stay in an unhappy or conflicted marriage for the sake of the children is difficult to determine. Children show better adjustment in divorced families when parents' relationships with each other are harmonious and authoritative parenting is used. Factors to |

| | be considered in the adjustment of children in divorced families are adjustment prior to the divorce, personality and temperament, developmental status, gender, and custody. Income loss for divorced mothers may be linked with a number of stresses that can affect the child's adjustment. |
|---|---|

Stepfamilies

- As in divorced families, children in stepfamilies have more problems than their counterparts in non-divorced families. Restabilization often takes longer in step-families than in divorced families. Children often have better relationships with their biological parents than with their stepparents and show more problems in complex, blended families than simple ones. Adolescence is an especially difficult time to experience the remarriage of parents.

Gay and Lesbian Parents

- Approximately 10 percent of same-sex couples in Canada are parents. There is considerable diversity among lesbian mothers, gay fathers, and their children. Researchers have found few differences between children growing up with gay or lesbian parents and children growing up with heterosexual parents.

Cultural, Ethnic, and Socioeconomic Variations in Families

- Cultures vary on a number of issues regarding families. Ethnic minority children are most likely to live in larger families, and families with extended connections. Higher-SES families tend to avoid using physical discipline, strive to create a home atmosphere in which rules are discussed, and are concerned with developing children's initiative and delay of gratification. Lower-SES families are more likely to use physical punishment in disciplining their children, are more directive and less conversational, and want their children to conform to society's expectations.

**connect** **LEARNSMART** **SMARTBOOK**

For more information on the resources available from McGraw-Hill Ryerson, go to www.mheducation.ca/he/solutions

Peers | chapter 15

Lynn Brown and Carol Gilligan (1992) conducted in-depth interviews of one hundred 10- to 13-year-old girls who were making the transition to adolescence. They listened to what these girls were saying.

A number of the girls talked about how many girls say nice things to be polite but often don't really mean them. The girls know the benefits of being perceived as the perfect, happy girl. Judy spoke about her interest in romantic relationships. Although she and her girlfriends were only 13, they wanted to be romantic, and she talked about her lengthy private conversations with her girlfriends about boys. Noura said that she learned how very painful it is to be the person everyone doesn't like.

Cliques figured largely in these girls' lives. They provided emotional support for girls who were striving to be perfect but knew they were not. Victoria commented that sometimes girls like her, who weren't very popular, nonetheless were accepted into a "club" with three other girls. Now when she was sad or depressed she could count on the club for support. Though they were "leftovers" and did not get into the most popular cliques, these four girls knew they were liked.

Through these interviews, we see the girls' curiosity about the social world they lived in. They kept track of what was happening to their peers and friends. The girls spoke at length about the pleasure they derived from the intimacy and fun of human connection, about the potential for hurt in relationships, and about the importance of friends.

# preview

This chapter is about peers, who clearly are very important in the lives of the adolescent girls just described. They also are very important in the lives of children. We begin this chapter by examining a number of ideas about children's peer relations, including their functions and variations. Then we turn to children's play and the roles of friends in children's development. We conclude by discussing peer relationships in adolescence.

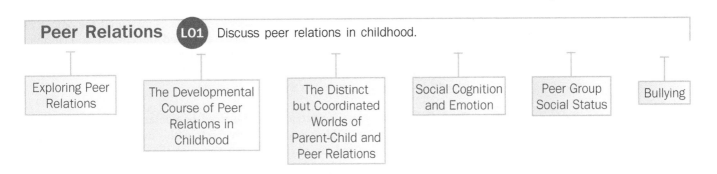

Peer Relations | **LO1** Discuss peer relations in childhood.

Exploring Peer Relations

The Developmental Course of Peer Relations in Childhood

The Distinct but Coordinated Worlds of Parent-Child and Peer Relations

Social Cognition and Emotion

Peer Group Social Status

Bullying

As children grow up, they spend increasing amounts of time with their peers. What are some key aspects of peer relations?

## EXPLORING PEER RELATIONS

**Peers** are children who share the same age or maturity level. They fill a unique role in the child's development. One of their most important functions is to provide a source of information and comparison about the world outside the family. Children receive feedback about their abilities from their peer group. They evaluate what they do in terms of whether it is better than, as good as, or worse than what other children do. It is hard to do this at home because siblings are usually older or younger.

**Are Peers Necessary for Development?** Good peer relations may be necessary for normal social development (Bowker, Rubin & Coplan, 2012; Brown & Larson, 2009; Rubin & others, 2013). Social isolation, or the inability to "plug in" to a social network, is linked with different problems and disorders ranging from delinquency and problem drinking to depression (Benner, 2011; Bornstein, Jager, & Steinberg, 2013; Dishion & Tispsord, 2011; Gorrese & Ruggieri, 2012).

**Positive and Negative Peer Relations** Peer influences can be both positive and negative (Bukowski, Motzoi, & Meyer, 2009; Cillessen & Bellmore, 2011; Rubin & others, 2013; Wentzel, 2013). A recent study found that children who associated with peers who engaged in prosocial behaviour at age 9 had a higher level of self-control at age 10 and that those whose peers engaged in deviant behaviour at age 9 had a lower level of self-control at age 10 (Meldrum & Hay, 2012). Children and adolescents also explore the principles of fairness and justice by working through disagreements with peers. They also learn to be keen observers of peers' interests and perspectives in order to smoothly integrate themselves into ongoing peer activities. And children and adolescents learn to be skilled and sensitive partners in relationships by forging close friendships with selected peers. They carry these intimacy skills forward to help form the foundation of later dating and marital relationships.

**peers** Children who share the same age or maturity level.

You are troubled at seeing him spend his early years in doing nothing. What! Is it nothing to be happy? Is it nothing to skip, to play, to run about all day long? Never in his life will he be so busy as now.

—JEAN-JACQUES ROUSSEAU
*Swiss-Born French Philosopher, 18th Century*

*In what ways can peer relations be positive and negative?*

In contrast, some theorists and researchers have emphasized the negative influences of peers on children's and adolescents' development (Dishion & Tipsord, 2011). According to Shelley Hymel at the University of British Columbia and her colleagues, being rejected or overlooked by peers leads some children and adolescents to feel lonely or hostile. Further, such rejection and neglect by peers are related to an individual's subsequent mental health (Hymel & others, 2011). For some adolescents, the peer culture is a corrupt influence that undermines parental values and control. Further, peer relations are linked to adolescents' patterns of drug use, delinquency, and depression. For example, a recent study found that low parental control was linked to higher delinquency in adolescence through its association with deviant peer affiliation (Deutsch & others, 2012).

As you read further about peers, keep in mind that findings about the influence of peers vary according to the way peer experience is measured, the outcomes specified, and the developmental trajectories traversed (Brechwald & Prinstein, 2011; Brown & Larson, 2009; Hartup, 2005). *Peers* and *peer group* are global concepts. A child's peer group might refer to neighbourhood playmates, a sports team, a friendship group, classmates, or even a best friend.

**Peer Contexts**   Peer interaction is influenced by contexts, which can include the type of peer the child or adolescent interacts with—such an acquaintance, a crowd, a clique, a friend, or a romantic partner—and the situation or location—such as a school, neighbourhood, community centre, dance, religious setting, sporting event, and so on, as well as the culture in which when the child or adolescent lives (Brown & Larson, 2009; Dishion & Tipsord, 2011; Rubin & others, 2013). As they interact with peers in these various contexts, children and adolescents likely encounter different messages and different opportunities to engage in adaptive and maladaptive behaviour that can influence their development (Brechwald & Prinstein, 2011).

In terms of contexts, peers play an important role in the development of individuals in all cultures. However, as indicated in *Connecting with Diversity,* cultures vary in the significance of the socializing role of peers (Way & Silverman, 2012).

**Individual Difference Factors**   Individual differences among peers are also important to consider in understanding peer relations (Brechwald & Prinstein, 2011). Among the wide range of individual differences that can affect peer relations are personality traits such as how shy or outgoing children are. For example, as noted by Robert Coplan at Carleton University and his colleagues, a very shy child is more likely than a gregarious child to be neglected by peers and have anxiety about introducing himself or herself to new peers (Coplan & others, 2013). One individual difference factor that impairs peer relations is the trait of negative emotionality, which involves a relatively low threshold for experiencing anger, fear, anxiety, and irritation. For example, one study revealed that adolescents characterized by negative emotionality tended to engage in negative interpersonal behaviour when interacting with a friend or a romantic partner (Hatton & others, 2008).

## THE DEVELOPMENTAL COURSE OF PEER RELATIONS IN CHILDHOOD

Some researchers argue that the quality of peer interaction in infancy provides valuable information about socioemotional development (Hughes & Dunn, 2007; Williams, Ontai, & Mastergeorge, 2010). For example, in one investigation, positive affect in infant peer relations was related to easy access to peer play groups and to peer likeability in early childhood (Howes, 1985). As increasing numbers of children attend child care, peer interaction in infancy takes on a more important developmental role.

## Cross-Cultural Comparisons of Peer Relations

In some countries, adults restrict adolescents' access to peers. For example, in many areas of rural India and in Arab countries, opportunities for peer relations in adolescence are severely restricted, especially for girls (Brown & Larson, 2002). If girls attend school in these regions of the world, it is usually in sex-segregated schools. In these countries, interaction with the other sex or opportunities for romantic relationships are restricted (Booth, 2002).

According to cross-cultural analyses, the peer group is more important to North American adolescents than to Japanese adolescents (Rothbaum & others, 2000). Japanese adolescents spend less time outside the home, have less recreational leisure time, and engage in fewer extracurricular activities with peers than North American adolescents (White, 1993). Also, North American adolescents are more likely to put pressure on their peers

Street youth in Rio de Janeiro

to resist parental influence than Japanese adolescents are (Rothbaum & others, 2000).

In some cultures, children are placed in peer groups for much greater lengths of time at an earlier age than they are in Canada. For example, in the Murian culture of eastern India, both male and female children live in a dormitory from the age of 6 until they get married (Barnouw, 1975). The dormitory is a religious haven where members are devoted to work and spiritual harmony. Children work for their parents, and the parents arrange the children's marriages.

In some cultural settings, peers even assume responsibilities usually handled by parents. For example, street youth in South America rely on networks of peers to help them negotiate survival in urban environments (Welti, 2002).

*In Chapter 1, you learned that cross-cultural studies compare aspects of two or more cultures, and the comparison provides information about the degree to which development is similar—or universal—across cultures or is culture-specific. From the results of this cross-cultural study, what can you say about peer pressure?*

Around the age of 3, children already prefer to spend time with same-sex rather than opposite-sex playmates, and this preference increases in early childhood. A recent study of 4-year-olds found that gender was a strong influence on who children selected as playmates (Martin & others, 2013). In this study, young children selected playmates of the same sex with similar levels of gender-typed activities, with the child's sex being a more powerful influence than the child's activities.

During the preschool years the frequency of peer interaction, both positive and negative, picks up considerably (Hartup, 1983; Rubin & others, 2013). Although aggressive interaction and rough-and-tumble play increase, the proportion of physically aggressive exchanges, compared with friendly exchanges, decreases. Many preschool children spend considerable time in peer interaction just conversing with playmates about such matters as "negotiating roles and rules in play, arguing, and agreeing" (Rubin, Bukowski, & Parker, 2006).

In early childhood, children distinguish between friends and non-friends (Howes, 2009a). For most young children, a friend is someone to play with. Young preschool children are more likely than older children to have friends who are of a different gender or ethnicity (Howes, 2009a).

As children enter the elementary school years, reciprocity becomes especially important in peer interchanges. Children play games, function in groups, and cultivate friendships. The amount of time children spend in peer interaction also rises during middle and late childhood and adolescence. Researchers estimate that the percentage of time spent in social interaction with peers increases from approximately 10 percent at 2 years of age to more than 30 percent in middle and late childhood (Rubin, Bukowski, & Parker, 2006). Other changes in peer relations as children move through middle and late childhood involve an increase in the size of their peer group and peer interaction that is supervised less closely by adults (Rubin, Bukowski, & Parker, 2006).

*What are some developmental changes in peer relations?*

Peer interactions take varied forms—cooperative and competitive, boisterous and quiet, joyous and humiliating. According to William Bukowski at Concordia University and his colleagues, there is increasing evidence that gender plays an important role in these interactions (Bukowski, Buhrmester, & Underwood, 2011). Gender influences not only the composition of children's groups but also their size and the types of interactions within them (Maccoby, 2002). From about 5 years of age onward, boys tend to associate in large clusters more than girls do; girls are more likely than boys to play in groups of two or three. As discussed in Chapter 12, "Gender," boys' groups and girls' groups also tend to favour different types of activities. Boys' groups are more likely to engage in rough-and-tumble play, competition, conflict, ego displays, risk taking, and dominance seeking. By contrast, girls' groups are more likely to engage in collaborative discourse (Leman, Ahmed, & Ozarow, 2005).

## THE DISTINCT BUT COORDINATED WORLDS OF PARENT-CHILD AND PEER RELATIONS

Parents may influence their children's peer relations in many ways, both direct and indirect (Booth-LaForce & Kerns, 2009; Ross & Howe, 2009; Updegraff & others, 2010). Parents affect their children's peer relations through their interactions with their children, how they manage their children's lives, and the opportunities they provide their children (Brown & Bakken, 2011). For example, one study revealed that warmth, advice giving, and provision of opportunities by mothers and fathers were linked to children's social competence (high prosocial behaviour, low aggression), and subsequently to social acceptance (being well-liked by peers and teachers) one year later (McDowell & Parke, 2009).

Basic lifestyle decisions by parents—their choices of neighbourhoods, churches, schools, and their own friends—largely determine the pool from which their children select possible friends. These choices in turn affect which children their children meet, their purpose in interacting, and eventually which children become their friends.

Do these results indicate that children's peer relations always are linked to parent-child relationships? Although parent-child relationships influence children's subsequent peer relations, children also learn other modes of relating through their relationships with peers. For example, rough-and-tumble play occurs mainly with other children, not in parent-child interaction. In times of stress, children often turn to parents rather than peers for support. In parent-child relationships, children learn how to relate to authority figures. With their peers, children are likely to interact on a much more equal basis and to learn a mode of relating based on mutual influence.

*What are some ways that parents influence their children's peer relations?*

**developmental connection**

**Attachment.** Securely attached infants use the caregiver as a secure base from which to explore their environment. Chapter 10, LO 4

Also remember from Chapter 8 that one of the most consistent findings of attachment research involving adolescents is that secure attachment to parents is linked to positive peer relations (Allen & Miga, 2010). A recent meta-analysis found that the link between mother and peer attachment was much stronger than the relation between father and peer attachment (Gorrese & Ruggieri, 2012).

However, whereas adolescent-parent attachments are correlated with adolescent outcomes, the correlations are moderate, an indication that the success or failure of parent-adolescent attachments does not guarantee success or failure in peer relationships. Clearly, secure attachment with parents can be an asset for the adolescent, fostering the trust to engage in close relationships with others and lay down the foundation for close relationship skills. Nonetheless, a significant minority of adolescents from strong, supportive families struggle in peer relations for a variety of reasons, such as being physically unattractive, maturing late, and experiencing cultural and socioeconomic-status (SES) discrepancies. On the other hand, some adolescents from troubled families find a positive, fresh start with peer relations that can compensate for their problematic family backgrounds.

## SOCIAL COGNITION AND EMOTION

Mariana expects all her playmates to let her play with their toys whenever she asks. When Josh isn't picked for a team on the playground, he thinks his friends have turned against him. These are examples of social cognitions, which involve thoughts about social matters (Dodge, 2011a, b; Lewis & Carpendale, 2011; Peets, Hodges, & Salmivalli, 2011). How might children's social cognitions contribute to their peer relations? Possibilities include their perspective-taking ability, social information-processing skills, and emotional regulation.

**Perspective Taking** As children enter the elementary school years, both their peer interaction and their perspective-taking ability increase. As we discussed in Chapter 13, "Moral Development," perspective taking involves perceiving another's point of view. Research by Lucy LeMare at Simon Fraser University has documented a link between perspective-taking skills and the quality of peer relations, especially in the elementary school years (LeMare & Rubin, 1987).

Perspective taking is important in part because it helps children communicate effectively. In one investigation, the communication exchanges among peers at kindergarten, first-, third-, and fifth-grade levels were evaluated (Krauss & Glucksberg, 1969). Children were asked to instruct a peer in how to stack a set of blocks. The peer sat behind a screen with blocks similar to those the other child was stacking (see Figure 15.1). The kindergarten children made numerous errors in telling the peer how to duplicate the novel block stack. The older children, especially the fifth-graders, were much more efficient in communicating to a peer how to stack the blocks. They were far superior at perspective taking and figuring out how to talk to a peer so that the peer could understand them.

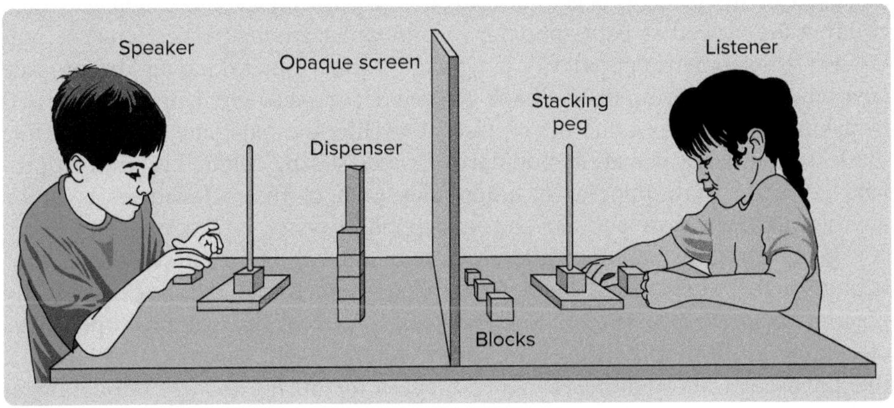

developmental **connection**

**Social Cognitive Theory.** Social cognition refers to the processes involved in understanding the world around us, especially how we think and reason about others. Chapter 11, LO 1

FIGURE **15.1**

**THE DEVELOPMENT OF COMMUNICATION SKILLS.** This is an experimental arrangement of speaker and listener in the investigation of the development of communication skills.

During the elementary school years, children also become more efficient at understanding complex messages, so the listening skills of the peer in this experiment probably helped the communicating peer as well.

### Social Information-Processing Skills

How children process information about peer relationships also influences those relationships (Dodge, 2011a, b; Peets, Hodges, & Salmivalli, 2011). For example, suppose Andrew accidentally trips and knocks Alex's soft drink out of his hand. Alex misinterprets the encounter as hostile, which leads him to retaliate aggressively against Andrew. Through repeated encounters of this kind, other peers come to perceive Alex as habitually acting inappropriately. A child such as Alex may develop a **hostile attribution bias**, where peers' motives and behaviours during ambiguous social interactions are perceived as deliberately hostile.

Peer relations researcher Kenneth Dodge (1993) argues that children go through five steps in processing information about their social world: decoding social cues, interpreting, searching for a response, selecting an optimal response, and enacting it. Dodge has found that overtly aggressive boys are more likely to perceive another child's actions as hostile when the child's intention is ambiguous—and when overtly aggressive boys search for clues to determine a peer's intention, they respond more rapidly, less efficiently, and less reflectively than non-aggressive children.

### Social Intelligence

As children and adolescents develop, they become more socially intelligent, and there is considerable individual variation in how much one child or adolescent knows about what it takes to make friends, to get peers to like him or her, and so forth. One study of 14- and 15-year-olds examined links between social intelligence and popularity (Meijs & others, 2010). In this study, social intelligence was related to popularity but not to academic achievement.

### Emotional Regulation

Not only does cognition play an important role in peer relations, so does emotion (Calkins, 2012). The ability to regulate emotion is linked to successful peer relations (Rubin, Bukowski, & Parker, 2006). For example, in a recent study, preschool children who showed high levels of aggressive peer interactions also displayed low levels of self-regulation (Olson & others, 2011). Moody and emotionally negative individuals experience greater rejection by peers, whereas emotionally positive individuals are more accepted (Saarni & others, 2006). Children who have effective self-regulatory skills can modulate their emotional expressiveness in contexts that evoke intense emotions, as when a peer says something negative (Denham & others, 2011).

## PEER GROUP SOCIAL STATUS

Which types of children are likely to be well liked by peers or popular, and which ones tend to be disliked or unpopular? Developmentalists address these questions by examining **sociometric popularity**, the extent to which children are liked or disliked by peers and **perceived popularity**, the extent to which children are viewed as being popular or unpopular among peers (Hymel & others, 2011). Sociometric popularity is typically assessed by asking children to rate how much they like or dislike each of their classmates. Or it may be assessed by asking children to name the children they like the most and those they like the least. Similarly, perceived popularity is assessed by asking children to provide ratings of how popular or unpopular each of their classmates is or by nominating their most popular and least popular peers.

Sociometrically popular children have a number of social skills that contribute to their being well liked. Researchers have found that sociometrically popular children give out reinforcements, listen carefully, maintain open lines of communication with peers, are happy, control their negative emotions, act like themselves, show enthusiasm and concern for others, and are self-confident without being conceited (Hartup, 1983; Rubin, Bukowski, & Parker, 2006).

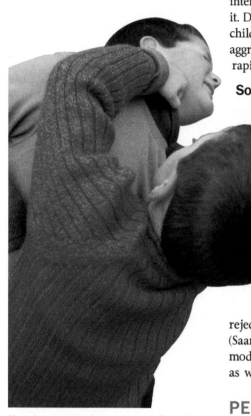

**hostile attribution bias** The tendency to perceive a peer's motives and behaviours during ambiguous social interactions as deliberately hostile.

*How do aggressive boys process information about their social world?*

**sociometric popularity** The extent to which children are liked or disliked by peers.

**perceived popularity** The extent to which children are viewed as being popular or unpopular among peers.

In comparison, perceived popular children and adolescents often are described as having a mix of both positive and negative characteristics (Hymel & others, 2011). Canadian research indicates that adolescents perceived as popular are described by peers as being cool, physically attractive, athletic, socially connected, nice, and funny, yet they are also seen as being mean, snobby, conceited, and rude (Closson, 2009a; Vaillancourt & Hymel, 2006). Perceived popularity is also linked to all forms of aggression, including relational aggression (Hymel & others, 2011). **Relational aggression** involves behaviours that are intended to harm a peer by manipulating his or her relationships with others, such as spreading rumours or exclusion.

**relational aggression** Behaviours that are intended to harm a peer by manipulating his or her relationships with others, such as spreading rumours or exclusion.

Longitudinal studies have found that relational aggression enables adolescents to maintain their level of status in the peer group and also to increase their perceived popularity over time, especially for girls (Cillessen & Mayeux, 2004; Prinstein & Cillessen, 2003; Rose, Swenson, & Waller, 2004).

How is it that perceived popular adolescents are aggressive yet still are able to maintain their position of status within the peer group? One reason is that adolescents who are perceived as popular engage in prosocial behaviour (Closson, 2009b; Dijkstra & others, 2009; Puckett & others, 2008). According to a study by Tracy Vaillancourt at the University of Ottawa and Shelley Hymel at the University of British Columbia, another reason is that perceived popular adolescents embody peer-valued characteristics, such as dressing well, being good-looking, being good at sports, and making people laugh (Vaillancourt & Hymel, 2006). Being nice toward peers and possessing characteristics that peers admire may offset negative repercussions often associated with aggressive behaviour.

One study revealed that the importance of being popular in comparison with other priorities (such as friendship, achievement, and romantic interests) peaked in early adolescence (LaFontana & Cillessen, 2010). Given that perceived popularity is associated with aggressive behaviour, is striving for popularity something parents and teachers should discourage? To read more about this controversial question, see *Connecting to Current Controversy.*

*How is relational aggression linked with popularity?*

**Peer Rejection** **Rejected children** are those who are actively disliked by their peers. The combination of being rejected by peers and being aggressive especially forecasts problems (Bukowski, 2012). For example, one study found that when third-grade boys were highly aggressive and rejected by their peers, they showed markedly higher levels of delinquency as adolescents and young adults than other boys did (Miller-Johnson, Coie, & Malone, 2003).

**rejected children** Children who are actively disliked by their peers.

An analysis by John Coie (2004, pp. 252–253) provided three reasons why aggressive peer-rejected boys have problems in social relationships:

- First, the rejected, aggressive boys are more impulsive and have problems sustaining attention. As a result, they are more likely to be disruptive of ongoing activities in the classroom and in focused group play.
- Second, rejected, aggressive boys are more emotionally reactive. They are aroused to anger more easily and probably have more difficulty calming down once aroused. Because of this they are more prone to become angry at peers and to attack them verbally and physically.
- Third, rejected children have fewer social skills for making friends and maintaining positive relationships with peers.

Not all rejected children are aggressive (Hymel & others, 2011; Rubin, Cheah, & Menzer, 2010; Vaillancourt & Hymel, 2006). Although aggression,

## Is Striving for Popularity Something Parents and Teachers Should Discourage?

In early adolescence, many young teens' social priorities shift to a focus on being popular (LaFontana & Cillessen, 2010). Some adolescents are even willing to betray their friends in order to impress popular peers and gain entry into their social circle (Adler & Adler, 1998; Merten, 2004). Adolescents who are seen by peers as putting *too* much effort into becoming popular actually tend to be less respected by their peers (Dijkstra & others, 2010; Neal, 2010; Witvliet & others, 2010). And isolation from the popular crowd can lead to feelings of depression (Buck & Dix, 2012; Witvliet & others, 2010).

Those who are successful at becoming popular face several risks. For example, being in a rebellious, popular crowd in early adolescence leads to increased aggression over time (Sijtsema & others, 2010). And being perceived as popular is associated with low academic achievement and failing in school (Troop-Gordon, Visconti, & Kuntz, 2011; Wilson, Karimpour, & Rodkin, 2011). Adolescents perceived as popular also are likely to engage in risk behaviours such as drinking alcohol, smoking, having sex, and carrying a weapon (Dijkstra & others, 2010; Mayeux, Sandstrom, & Cillessen, 2008).

Perhaps, rather than discouraging children from striving to become more popular, adults should encourage young adolescents to focus on strengthening their relationships with peers. Although they are perceived to be of average popularity, early adolescents who wish to improve their peer relationships enjoy more positive qualities within their friendships compared to those who aim to improve their status (Adler & Adler, 1998; Closson, 2009b; Ryan & Shim, 2008).

*As a parent, would you discourage your child from striving for popularity? Why or why not?*

---

*Peer rejection contributes to subsequent problems of adaptation, including antisocial behaviour.*

—John Coie
*Contemporary Psychologist, Duke University*

impulsiveness, and disruptiveness underlie rejection about half the time, approximately 10 to 20 percent of rejected children are shy.

What are the origins of peer rejection? One Canadian study found that rejected adolescents also were rejected during middle childhood and that this rejection resulted from emotional and behavioural problems during early elementary school (Pedersen & others, 2007).

How can rejected children be taught to interact more effectively with their peers? Rejected children may be taught to more accurately assess whether the intentions of their peers are negative. They may be asked to engage in role playing or to discuss hypothetical situations involving negative encounters with peers, such as times when a peer cuts into a line ahead of them. In some programs, children are shown videotapes of appropriate peer interaction and asked to draw lessons from what they have seen (Ladd, Buhs, & Troop, 2004).

Despite the positive outcomes of some programs that attempt to improve the social skills of adolescents, researchers have often found it difficult to improve the social skills of adolescents who are actively disliked and rejected. Many of these adolescents are rejected because they are aggressive or impulsive and lack the self-control to keep these behaviours in check. Still, some intervention programs have been successful in reducing the aggressive and impulsive behaviours of these adolescents (Ladd, Kochenderfer-Ladd, & Rydell, 2011).

Social-skills training programs have generally been more successful with children 10 years of age or younger than with adolescents (Malik & Furman, 1993). Peer reputations become more fixed as cliques and peer groups become more salient in adolescence. Once an adolescent gains a negative reputation among peers as being "weird" or a "loner," the peer group's attitude is often slow to change, even after the adolescent's problem behaviour has been corrected. Thus, researchers have found that skill interventions may need to be supplemented by efforts to change the minds of peers.

## BULLYING

**bullying** Repeated acts of physical, verbal, relational, or cyber aggression intended to harm a less powerful peer.

**Bullying** involves repeated acts of physical, verbal, relational, or cyber aggression intended to harm a less powerful peer (Dittrick & others, 2011; Vaillancourt & others, 2008). Significant numbers of students are victimized by bullies (Espelage & Holt, 2012). One Canadian study by Wendy Craig at Queen's University and Debra

Pepler at York University (2003) found that around 10 percent of boys and 7 percent of girls report having bullied others, and 17 percent of boys and 18 percent of girls report having been the victims of bullying at least twice in the previous week. Another study revealed that bullying decreased as students went from the beginning of sixth grade (20 percent were bullied extensively) through the end of eighth grade (6 percent were bullied extensively) (Nylund & others, 2007).

A recent Canadian study examined what adolescents are bullied about (Dittrick & others, 2011) (see Figure 15.2). These researchers found that greater victimization among girls was associated with being bullied about personality or school performance, whereas greater victimization in boys was predicted by being bullied about popularity or physical strength/weakness.

Who is likely to be bullied? Researchers have found that anxious, socially withdrawn, and aggressive children are often the victims of bullying (Hanish & Guerra, 2004). Anxious and socially withdrawn children may be victimized because they are non-threatening and unlikely to retaliate if bullied, whereas aggressive children may be the targets of bullying because their behaviour is irritating to bullies (Rubin, Bukowski, & Parker, 2006). In one study, children who said they were bullied reported more loneliness and difficulty in making friends, while those who did the bullying were more likely to have low grades and to smoke and drink alcohol (Nansel & others, 2001).

Social contexts also influence bullying (Schwartz & others, 2010; Veenstra & others, 2010). Research indicates that 70 to 80 percent of victims and their bullies are in the same school classroom (Salmivalli & Peets, 2009). Classmates are often aware of bullying incidents and in many cases witness bullying. The larger social context of the peer group plays an important role in bullying (Salmivalli & Peets, 2009). In many cases, bullies torment victims to gain higher status in the peer group, and bullies need others to witness their power displays. Many bullies are not rejected by the peer group, but are often powerful and perceived to be popular by peers (Vaillancourt, Hymel, & McDougall, 2003; Witvliet & others, 2010). In one study, bullies were only disliked by peers for whom they were a potential threat (Veenstra & others, 2010).

Another concern is peer bullying and harassment on the Internet (called *cyberbullying*) (Bonnano & Hymel, 2013). One survey found that peer bullying offline and online were the most frequent threats that children and adolescents encountered (Palfrey & others, 2009). Another study of third- to sixth-graders revealed that engaging in cyber aggression was related to increased loneliness, lower self-esteem, fewer mutual friendships, and lower peer popularity (Schoffstall & Cohen, 2011). And a recent meta-analysis showed that normative beliefs about aggression and moral disengagement are strongly associated with cyberbullying perpetration, whereas stress and suicidal ideation are strongly associated with cyberbullying victimization (Kowalski & others, 2014). Currently, Nova Scotia is the only province in Canada with legislation in place to address and prevent cyberbullying. Under Nova Scotia's *Cyber-safety Act*, victims of cyberbullying are protected and perpetrators of cyberbullying are accountable under the law.

What are the outcomes of bullying? Recent studies indicate that bullies and their victims in adolescence

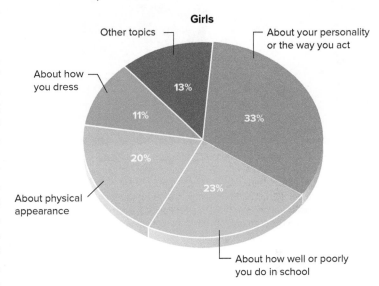

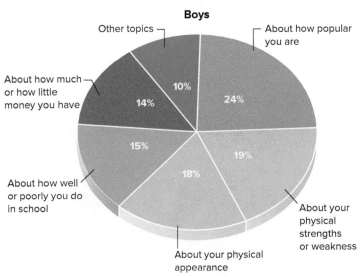

FIGURE **15.2**

**BULLYING BEHAVIOURS AMONG CANADIAN YOUTH.** This graph shows what Canadian youth report being bullied about (Dittrick & others, 2011). The percentages reflect the extent to which bullied students said that they had experienced being bullied about a certain topic.

Seventeen-year old Rehtaeh Parsons of Dartmouth, Nova Scotia (top) committed suicide on April 4, 2013, and 15-year-old Amanda Todd of Port Coquitlam, British Columbia (bottom), committed suicide on October 10, 2012. Their deaths have been attributed to cyberbullying victimization. Four months after Parsons' death, Nova Scotia enacted the Cyber-safety Act, providing protection for victims and accountability for perpetrators.

were more likely to experience depression, engage in suicide ideation, and attempt suicide than their counterparts who were not involved in bullying (Bonanno & Hymel, 2013; Brunstein Klomek & others, 2007). Another study revealed that bullies, victims, or those who were both bullies and victims had more health problems (such as headaches, dizziness, sleep problems, and anxiety) than their counterparts who were not involved in bullying (Srabstein & others, 2006). And a meta-analysis of 33 studies revealed that peer victimization had a small but significant link with lower academic achievement (Nakamoto & Schwartz, 2010).

Extensive interest is developing in preventing and treating bullying and victimization (Biggs & Vernberg, 2010; Guerra & Williams, 2010; Singh, Orpinas, & Horne, 2010). Two reviews of research studies indicated mixed results for school-based intervention (Merrell & others, 2008; Vreeman & Carroll, 2007). School-based interventions vary greatly, ranging from involving the whole school in an anti-bullying campaign to providing individualized social skills training. Three of the most promising bullying intervention programs are described below.

- *Olweus Bullying Prevention.* Created by Dan Olweus, this program focuses on 6- to 15-year-olds, with the goal of decreasing opportunities and rewards for bullying. School staff are instructed in ways to improve peer relations and make schools safer. When properly implemented, the program reduces bullying by 30 to 70 percent (Ericson, 2001; Olweus, 2003). Information on how to implement the program can be obtained from the Center for the Prevention of Violence at the University of Colorado (www.colorado.edu/espv/blueprints).

- *Steps to Respect.* This anti-bullying program consists of three steps: (1) establishing a school-wide approach, such as creating anti-bullying policies and specifying consequences for bullying, (2) training staff and parents to deal with bullying, and (3) teaching students to recognize—not tolerate—and handle bullying. In this third step, teachers provide skills training, such as how to be assertive, and information about bullying to students in grades 3 through 6. The skills training by teachers occurs over a 12- to 14-week period. A recent assessment found that Steps to Respect was successful in reducing bullying and argumentativeness in third- through fifth-grade students (Frey & others, 2005, 2009). In this study, two-year declines in playground bullying and victimization occurred. For more information about Steps to Respect, visit www.cfchildren.org.

- *WITS.* The WITS program is a Canadian anti-bullying program designed to reduce peer victimization among elementary school children. The WITS acronym stands for Walk Away, Ignore, Talk it out, and Seek help. By involving families, school, and community, children are taught to "use their WITS" to respond to bullying. The WITS program includes lesson plans for home use or the classroom that are easily integrated into the school curriculum. A recent evaluation demonstrated the WITS program reduced peer victimization among children in grades 1 through 3 (Leadbeater & Sukhawathanakul, 2011). For more information about WITS, visit www.witsprogram.ca.

What role do peer bystanders play in bullying? To find out, see *Connecting Through Research.*

*What are some strategies to reduce bullying?*

# connecting through research

## What Role Do Peer Bystanders Play in Bullying?

Peers often witness bullying. One Canadian observational study found that when peer bystanders intervene, bullying stopped immediately over 50 percent of the time (Hawkins, Pepler, & Craig, 2001).

A recent study revealed that within the past 3 weeks, 67 percent of Canadian children report witnessing bullying at least once (Cappadocia & others, 2012). Among those who witnessed bullying, 80 percent chose to intervene. Children who intervened in bullying reported that they did so because they recognized bullying was not deserved or fair, whereas children who chose not to intervene remained passive because they did not want to get involved or were afraid. Girls reporting high social self-efficacy were 32 times more likely than other girls to intervene during the last bullying episode they witnessed. In comparison, boys reporting high empathy were 17 times more likely than other boys to report intervening during the last bullying episode they witnessed.

Another Canadian study examined peer bystander behaviour among grade 4 through 11 students (Trach & others, 2010). The results showed that younger students were more likely than older students to intervene directly in the bullying episode, help the victim, or talk to an adult. Compared to younger students, older students were more likely to report that they "did nothing" when they witnessed bullying.

*What are some characteristics of peer bystanders who are most likely to try to stop bullying?*

---

## Review *Connect* Reflect

 **LO1** Discuss peer relations in childhood.

### Review

- What are some key aspects of peer relations?
- What is the developmental course of peer relations in childhood?
- In what ways are the worlds of parents and peers distinct but coordinated?
- How is social cognition involved in peer relations? How is emotion involved in peer relations?
- What characterizes sociometric popularity, perceived popularity, and peer rejection?
- What is the nature of bullying?

### *Connect*

- In Chapter 13, you learned that most developmentalists agree that peers play an important role in children's development of moral reasoning. Recall what you learned about peer group social status in this section. Do you think children's social status would have an impact on the development of their moral reasoning capacities? Why?

### Reflect *Your Own Personal Journey of Life*

- Think back to your elementary and middle school/junior high school years. What kind of relationship did you have with your peers? How do you think your peer relationships in elementary and middle school/junior high school have affected the relationships you have with your peers today?

---

## Play  **LO2**  Describe children's play.

Play's Functions  Types of Play  Trends in Play

Much of the time when children, especially young children, are interacting with their peers, they are playing. **Play** is a pleasurable activity that is engaged in for its own sake, and social play is just one type of play.

**play** A pleasurable activity that is engaged in for its own sake.

## PLAY'S FUNCTIONS

Play makes important contributions to young children's cognitive and socioemotional development (Bergen & Fromberg, 2009; Coplan & Arbeau, 2009). Theorists have focused on different aspects of play and highlighted a long list of functions.

According to Freud and Erikson, play helps the child master anxieties and conflicts. Because tensions are relieved in play, the child can cope more effectively with life's problems. Play permits the child to work off excess physical energy and to release pent-up tensions. Therapists use **play therapy** both to allow the child to work off frustrations and to analyze the child's conflicts and ways of coping with them (Sanders, 2008). Children may feel less threatened and be more likely to express their true feelings in the context of play.

Play also is an important context for cognitive development (Coplan & Arbeau, 2009). Both Piaget and Vygotsky concluded that play is the child's work. Piaget (1962) maintained that play advances children's cognitive development. At the same time, he said that children's cognitive development *constrains* the way they play. Play permits children to practice their competencies and acquired skills in a relaxed, pleasurable way. Piaget thought that cognitive structures needed to be exercised and that play provided the perfect setting for this exercise.

Vygotsky (1962) also considered play to be an excellent setting for cognitive development. He was especially interested in the symbolic and make-believe aspects of play, as when a child substitutes a stick for a horse and rides the stick as if it were a horse. For young children, the imaginary situation is real. Parents should encourage such imaginary play, because it advances the child's cognitive development, especially creative thought.

Daniel Berlyne (1960) described play as exciting and pleasurable in itself because it satisfies our exploratory drive. This drive involves curiosity and a desire for information about something new or unusual. Play encourages exploratory behaviour by offering children the possibilities of novelty, complexity, uncertainty, surprise, and incongruity.

More recently, Canadian researchers have described play as an important context for the development of language and communication skills (Coplan & Arbeau, 2009) through discussions and negotiations regarding roles and rules in play. These types of social interactions during play can benefit young children's literacy skills (Coplan & Arbeau, 2009). And as we will discuss in Chapter 16, "Schools and Technology," play is a central focus of the child-centred kindergarten and thought to be an essential aspect of early childhood education (Feeney, Moravcik, & Nolte, 2013; Henninger, 2013).

An increasing concern is that the large number of hours children spend with electronic media, such as television and computers, takes time away from play (Bergen & Fromberg, 2009). An important priority for parents should be to include ample time for play in their children's lives.

**play therapy** Therapy that allows the child to work off frustrations and is a medium through which the therapist can analyze the child's conflicts and ways of coping with them. Children may feel less threatened and be more likely to express their true feelings in the context of play.

*developmental* **connection**

**Cognitive Theory.** Vygotsky emphasized that children mainly develop their ways of thinking and understanding through social interaction. Chapter 6, LO 3

*developmental* **connection**

**Social Cognitive Theory.** The child-centred kindergarten emphasizes the education of the whole child, not just his or her cognitive development, because play is extremely important in the child's development. Chapter 16, LO 1

# TYPES OF PLAY

The contemporary perspective on play emphasizes both the cognitive and the social aspects of play (Fung & Cheng, 2012; Vong, 2012). Among the most widely studied types of children's play today are sensorimotor and practice play, pretense/ symbolic play, social play, constructive play, and games (Bergen, 1988).

**Sensorimotor and Practice Play** **Sensorimotor play** is behaviour that allows infants to derive pleasure from exercising their sensorimotor schemes. The development of sensorimotor play follows Piaget's description of sensorimotor thought, which we discussed in Chapter 6. Infants initially engage in exploratory and playful visual and motor transactions during the second quarter of the first year of life. At 9 months of age, infants begin to select novel objects for exploration and play, especially those that are responsive, such as toys that make noise or bounce. At 12 months of age, infants enjoy making things work and exploring cause and effect.

Practice play involves repeating behaviour when new skills are being learned or when physical or mental mastery and coordination of skills are required for games or sports. Sensorimotor play, which often involves practice play, is primarily confined to infancy, whereas practice play can be engaged in throughout life. During the preschool years, children often engage in play that involves practicing various skills. Although practice play declines during the elementary school years, practice play activities such as running, jumping, sliding, twirling, and throwing balls or other objects are frequently observed on the playgrounds at elementary schools.

**Pretense/Symbolic Play** **Pretense/symbolic play** occurs when the child transforms the physical environment into a symbol. Between 9 and 30 months of age, children increase their use of objects in symbolic play (Lillard, 2007). They learn to transform objects, substituting them for other objects and acting toward them as if they were those other objects (Smith, 2007). For example, a preschool child treats a table as if it were a car and says, "I'm fixing the car" as he grabs a leg of the table.

Many experts on play view the preschool years as the golden age of symbolic/pretense play that is dramatic or sociodramatic in nature (Fein, 1986; Rubin, Bukowski, & Parker, 2006). This type of make-believe play often appears at about 18 months of age and reaches a peak at 4 to 5 years of age, then gradually declines. Some child psychologists conclude that pretend play is an important aspect of young children's development and often reflects advances in their cognitive development, especially their capacity for symbolic understanding. For example, Catherine Garvey (2000) and Angeline Lillard (2007) emphasize that hidden in young children's pretend play narratives are remarkable capacities for role-taking, balancing of social roles, metacognition (thinking about thinking), testing of the reality-pretense distinction, and numerous non-egocentric capacities that reveal the remarkable cognitive skills of young children. According to one analysis, a major accomplishment in early childhood is the development of children's ability to share their pretend play with peers (Coplan & Arbeau, 2009).

**Social Play** **Social play** is play that involves interaction with peers. Social play increases dramatically during the preschool years and includes varied interchanges such as turn taking, conversations about numerous topics, social games and routines, and physical play (Sumaroka & Bornstein, 2008). Social play often evokes a high degree of pleasure on the part of the participants (Sumaroka & Bornstein, 2008).

**Constructive Play** **Constructive Play** combines sensorimotor/practice play with symbolic representation of ideas. Constructive play occurs when children engage in the self-regulated creation of a product or a solution. Constructive play increases in the preschool years as symbolic play increases and sensorimotor play decreases. During the preschool years, some practice play is replaced

**sensorimotor play** Behaviour that allows infants to derive pleasure from exercising their existing sensorimotor schemes.

**practice play** Play that involves repetition of behaviour when new skills are being learned or when physical or mental mastery and coordination of skills are required for games or sports. Practice play can be engaged in throughout life.

**pretense/symbolic play** Play that occurs when a child transforms the physical environment into a symbol.

A preschool "soldier" at play

**social play** Play that involves interactions with peers.

**constructive play** Play that combines sensorimotor/practice play with symbolic representation of ideas. Constructive play occurs when children engage in self-regulated creation or construction of a product or a solution.

by constructive play. For example, instead of moving their fingers around and around in finger paint (practice play), children are more likely to draw the outline of a house or a person in the paint (constructive play). Constructive play is also a frequent form of play in the elementary school years, both within and outside the classroom. Constructive play is one of the few play-like activities allowed in work-centred classrooms. For example, if children create a skit about a social studies topic, they are engaging in constructive play.

**Games**   Games are activities that are engaged in for pleasure and are governed by rules. Often they involve competition between two or more individuals. Preschool children may begin to participate in social game play that involves simple rules of reciprocity and turn taking. However, games take on a much more prominent role in the lives of elementary school children. In one study, the highest incidence of game playing occurred between 10 and 12 years of age (Eiferman, 1971). After age 12, games decline in popularity (Bergen, 1988).

In sum, play ranges from an infant's simple exercise of a new sensorimotor talent to a preschool child's riding a tricycle to an older child's participation in organized games. It is also important to note that children's play can involve a combination of the play categories we have described. For example, social play can be sensorimotor (rough-and-tumble), symbolic, and constructive.

## TRENDS IN PLAY

Some researchers are concerned about the decline in the amount of free play time that young children have, reporting that it has declined considerably in recent decades (Hirsh-Pasek & others, 2009; Singer, Golinkoff, & Hirsh-Pasek, 2006). They especially are worried about young children's playtime being restricted at home and school so they can spend more time on academic subjects. They also point out that many schools have eliminated recess. And it is not just the decline in time allotted to free play that bothers them. They underscore that learning in playful contexts captivates children's minds in ways that enhance their cognitive and socio-emotional development—Singer, Golinkoff, and Hirsh-Pasek's (2006) first book on play was titled *Play = Learning*. Among the cognitive benefits of play they described are creativity; abstract thinking; imagination; attention, concentration, and persistence; problem-solving; social cognition, empathy, and perspective taking; language; and mastering new concepts. Among the socioemotional experiences and development they believe play promotes are enjoyment, relaxation, and self-expression; cooperation, sharing, and turn-taking; anxiety reduction; and self-confidence. With so many positive cognitive and socioemotional outcomes of play, clearly it is important that we find more time for play in young children's lives.

**games** Activities engaged in for pleasure that include rules and often competition with one or more individuals.

In the elementary school years, children, such as those playing hopscotch here on a school playground, increasingly play games.

## Review *Connect* Reflect

**L02** Describe children's play.

### Review
- What are the functions of play?
- What are the different types of play?
- What are some trends in play?

### *Connect*
- Pretense/symbolic play takes place during what Piaget called the symbolic function substage of the preoperational stage. According to Piaget, what are two important limitations of children's thought during this substage?

### **Reflect** *Your Own Personal Journey of Life*
- Do you think most young children's lives today are too structured? If and when you become a parent, how will you manage your children's development to provide enough time for play?

## Friendship **L03** Explain friendship.

- Friendship's Functions
- Similarity and Intimacy
- Gender and Friendship
- Mixed-Age Friendships

Children play with varying acquaintances. They interact with some children they barely know, and with others they know well, for hours every day. It is to the latter type—friends—that we now turn.

## FRIENDSHIP'S FUNCTIONS

Friendships serve six functions (Gottman & Parker, 1987):

1. *Companionship.* Friendship provides children with a familiar partner, someone who is willing to spend time with them and join in collaborative activities.
2. *Stimulation.* Friendship provides children with interesting information, excitement, and amusement.
3. *Physical support.* Friendship provides resources and assistance.
4. *Ego support.* Friendship provides the expectation of support, encouragement, and feedback that helps children to maintain an impression of themselves as competent, attractive, and worthwhile individuals.
5. *Social comparison.* Friendship provides information about where children stand compared to others and whether children are doing okay.
6. *Intimacy/affection.* Friendship provides children with a warm, close, trusting relationship with another individual, a relationship that involves self-disclosure.

Although having friends can be a developmental advantage, not all friendships are alike. According to Mara Brendgen at the University of Quebec and her colleagues, the quality of friendship is also important to consider (Brendgen & others, 2010). People differ in the company they keep—that is, who their friends are (Wentzel, 2013). Developmental advantages occur when children have friends who are socially skilled, supportive, and oriented toward academic achievement (Crosnoe & others, 2008). However, it is not developmentally advantageous to have coercive, conflict-ridden, and poor-quality friendships (Laursen & Pursell, 2009; Vitaro, Boivin, & Bukowski, 2009).

Positive friendships in adolescence are associated with a host of positive outcomes, including lower rates of delinquency, substance abuse, risky sexual behaviour, and peer victimization, and a higher level of academic achievement (Kendrick, Jutengren, & Stattin, 2012; Tucker & others, 2012; Way & Silverman, 2012; Wentzel, 2013). Not having a close relationship with a best friend, having less contact with friends, having friends who are depressed, and experiencing peer rejection all increase depressive tendencies in adolescents (Brendgen & others, 2010; Schwartz-Mette & Rose, 2013). Researchers have found that interacting with delinquent peers and friends greatly increases the risk of becoming delinquent (Deutsch & others, 2012).

Harry Stack Sullivan (1953) was the most influential theorist to discuss the importance of friendships. In contrast with other psychoanalytic theorists' narrow emphasis on the importance of

*What are some functions of children's friendships?*

How did Sullivan think friendship changes in adolescence?

parent-child relationships, Sullivan contended that friends also played important roles in shaping children's and adolescents' well-being and development.

According to Sullivan, all people have a number of basic social needs, including tenderness (secure attachment), playful companionship, social acceptance, intimacy, and sexual relations. Whether or not these needs are fulfilled largely determines our emotional well-being. For example, if the need for playful companionship goes unmet, then we become bored and depressed; if the need for social acceptance is not met, we suffer a lowered sense of self-worth. Sullivan stressed that the need for intimacy intensifies during early adolescence, motivating teenagers to seek out close friends.

Research findings support many of Sullivan's ideas. For example, adolescents report disclosing intimate and personal information to their friends more often than do younger children (Buhrmester, 1990; Buhrmester & Furman, 1987) (see Figure 15.3). Adolescents also say they depend more on friends than on parents to satisfy their needs for companionship, reassurance of worth, and intimacy (Furman & Buhrmester, 1992).

Friendships are often important sources of support (Berndt, 1999; Wentzel, 2013). Sullivan described how adolescent friends support one another's sense of personal worth. When close friends disclose their mutual insecurities and fears about themselves, they discover that they are not abnormal and that they have nothing to be ashamed of. Friends also act as important confidants who help children and adolescents work through upsetting problems (such as difficulties with parents or the breakup of romantic relationships) by providing both emotional support and informational advice.

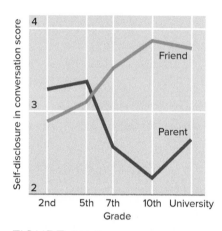

## FIGURE 15.3

**DEVELOPMENTAL CHANGES IN SELF-DISCLOSING CONVERSATIONS.** Self-disclosing conversations with friends increased dramatically in adolescence while declining in an equally dramatic fashion with parents. However, self-disclosing conversations with parents began to pick up somewhat during the college/university years. The measure of self-disclosure involved a 5-point rating scale completed by the children and youth, with a higher score representing greater self-disclosure. The data shown represent the means for each age group.

**intimacy in friendship** Self-disclosure or the sharing of private thoughts.

## SIMILARITY AND INTIMACY

What characteristics do children and adolescents look for in their friends? The answers change somewhat as children grow up, but one characteristic of friends is found throughout the childhood and adolescent years: Friends are generally similar—in terms of age, sex, ethnicity, and many other factors (Giordano, 2009). Similarity is referred to as *homophily*, the tendency to associate with similar others (Brechwald & Prinstein, 2011).

Friends often have similar attitudes toward school, similar educational aspirations, and closely aligned achievement orientations. Friends like the same music, wear the same kinds of clothes, and prefer the same leisure activities (Berndt, 1982). Differences may lead to conflicts that weaken the friendship. For example, if two friends have differing attitudes toward school, one may repeatedly want to play basketball or go to the mall while the other insists on completing homework, and the two may drift apart.

Priorities change as the child reaches adolescence (Brown & Larson, 2009). The most consistent finding in the last two decades of research on adolescent friendships is that intimacy is an important feature of friendship (Berndt & Perry, 1990). In most research studies, **intimacy in friendship** is defined narrowly as self-disclosure or sharing of private thoughts; private or personal knowledge about a friend has been used as an index of intimacy. When young adolescents are asked what they want from a friend or how they can tell someone is their best friend, they frequently say that a best friend will share problems with them, understand them, and listen when they talk about their own thoughts or feelings. When young children talk about their friendships, they rarely comment about intimate self-disclosure or mutual understanding. In one investigation, friendship intimacy was more prominent in 13- to 16-year-olds than in 10- to 13-year-olds (Buhrmester, 1990).

## GENDER AND FRIENDSHIP

Are the friendships of girls different from the friendships of boys? An increasing number of studies indicate that they are different (Coyne, Nelson, & Underwood, 2011; Rose & others, 2012). Are the friendships of adolescent girls more intimate than the friendships of adolescent boys? According to a study led by Patricia McDougall at the University of Saskatchewan, girls reported that intimacy was more important in their friendships, whereas boys indicated that doing things together, such as engaging in common activities like sports or playing computer games, was more important in their friendships (McDougall & Hymel, 2007). A recent meta-analysis concluded that girls' friendships were deeper, more interdependent, showed more empathy, revealed a greater need for nurturance, and involved a greater desire to sustain intimate relationships (Gorrese & Ruggieri, 2012). In contrast, boys gave more importance to having a congenial friend with whom they could share their interests in such activities as hobbies and sports, and boys showed more cooperativeness than girls in their friendships. Also in this meta-analysis, adolescent girls showed higher friend attachment, especially related to trust and communication, than did adolescent boys (Gorrese & Ruggieri, 2012).

Let's further examine gender differences in the intimacy aspect of friendship. When asked to describe their best friends, girls refer to intimate conversations and faithfulness more than boys do (Rose & others, 2012). For example, girls are more likely to describe their best friend as "sensitive just like me" or "trustworthy just like me" (Duck, 1975). When conflict is present, girls place a higher priority on relationship goals such as being patient until the relationship improves, whereas boys are more likely to seek control over a friend (Rose & Asher, 1999; Blakemore, Berenbaum, & Liben, 2009). Although girls' friendships in adolescence are more likely to focus on intimacy, boys' friendships tend to emphasize power and excitement (Rose & Smith, 2009). Boys may discourage one another from openly disclosing their problems because self-disclosure is not viewed as masculine (Maccoby, 1996). Boys make themselves vulnerable to being called "wimps" if they can't handle their own problems and insecurities. These gender differences are generally assumed to reflect a greater orientation toward interpersonal relationships among girls than boys.

*What are some gender differences in friendships in adolescence?*

Friendship often provides social support. Recently, though, researchers have found that some aspects of girls' friendships may be linked to adolescent problems (Tompkins & others, 2011). For example, a study of third- through ninth-graders revealed that girls' co-rumination (as reflected in excessively discussing problems) predicted not only an increase in positive friendship quality but also an increase in further co-rumination as well as an increase in depressive and anxiety symptoms (Rose, Carlson, & Waller, 2007). One implication of the research is that some girls who are vulnerable to developing internalized problems may go undetected because they have supportive friendships (Rose & Smith, 2009).

## MIXED-AGE FRIENDSHIPS

Although most adolescents develop friendships with individuals who are close to their own age, some adolescents become best friends with younger or older individuals. A common fear, especially among parents, is that adolescents who have older friends will be encouraged to engage in delinquent behaviour or early sexual behaviour. Researchers have found that adolescents who interact with older youth do engage in these behaviours more frequently, but it is not known whether the older youth guide younger adolescents toward deviant behaviour or whether the younger adolescents were already prone to deviant behaviour before they developed the friendship with the older youth (Billy, Rodgers, & Udry, 1984). One Canadian study also revealed that over time, from the sixth through tenth grades, girls were more likely to have older male friends, which places some girls on a developmental trajectory for engaging in problem behaviour (Poulin & Pedersen, 2007).

## OTHER-SEX FRIENDSHIPS

Although adolescents are more likely to have same-sex friends, associations with other-sex friends are more common than is often thought (Brown, 2004). The number of other-sex friendships increases in early adolescence, with girls reporting more other-sex friends than boys, and the number of other-sex friendships increases as adolescence proceeds (Poulin & Pedersen, 2007). Other-sex friendships and participation in mixed-sex groups provide a context for adolescents to learn how to communicate with the other sex and reduce anxiety in social and dating heterosexual interactions.

However, researchers have found that other-sex friendships are sometimes linked to negative behaviours such as earlier sexual intercourse, as well as increases in alcohol use and delinquency (Billari & Mencarini, 2003; Dick & others, 2007; Mrug, Borch, & Cillessen, 2011). Parents likely monitor their daughters' other-sex friendships more closely than their sons' because they perceive boys as having a more negative influence, especially in initiating problem behaviour (Poulin & Denault, 2012). A recent Canadian study revealed that a higher level of parental monitoring led to fewer other-sex friendships, which in turn was associated with a lower level of subsequent alcohol use (Poulin & Denault, 2012).

## Review *Connect* Reflect

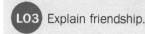 Explain friendship.

### Review

- What are six functions of friendship? What is Sullivan's view of friendship?
- What roles do similarity and intimacy play in friendship?
- How does gender influence friendship?
- What is the developmental outcome of mixed-age friendship?
- What characterizes other-sex friendships in adolescence?

### *Connect*

- In this section you read about how delinquency is related to mixed-age

friendships and other-sex friendships. How does this compliment research on the antecedents of juvenile delinquency described in Chapter 13?

### Reflect *Your Own Personal Journey of Life*

- Examine the list of six functions of friendships at the beginning of this section. Rank the six functions from most (1) to least (6) important to you as you were developing in three different time frames: early childhood, middle and late childhood, and adolescence.

## Peer Relations in Adolescence    LO4    Characterize peer relations in adolescence.

Peer Pressure and Conformity

Cliques and Crowds

Dating and Romantic Relationships

We already have discussed a number of changes in adolescents' peer relations, including the increasing importance of friendships. Peer relations play such a powerful role in the lives of adolescents that we further consider additional aspects in this section.

Peer relations undergo important changes in adolescence (Wentzel, 2013). In childhood, the focus of peer relations is on being liked by classmates and being included in games or lunchroom conversations. Being overlooked or, worse yet, being rejected can have damaging effects on children's development that sometimes are carried forward to adolescence. Beginning in early adolescence, teenagers typically prefer to have a smaller number of friendships that are more intense and intimate than those of young children. Cliques are formed and shape the social lives of adolescents as they begin to "hang out" together. And romantic relationships become a more central aspect of adolescents' lives.

## PEER PRESSURE AND CONFORMITY

Young adolescents conform more to peer standards than children do. Around the eighth and ninth grades, conformity to peers—especially to their antisocial standards—peaks (Berndt, 1979; Brown & Larson, 2009). At this point, adolescents are most likely to go along with a peer to steal hubcaps off a car, draw graffiti on a wall, or steal cosmetics from a store counter. One study revealed that 14 to 18 years of age is an especially important time for developing the ability to stand up for what one believes and resist peer pressure to do otherwise (Steinberg & Monahan, 2007).

Which adolescents are most likely to conform to peers? Mitchell Prinstein and his colleagues (Brechwald & Prinstein, 2011; Cohen & Prinstein, 2006; Prinstein, 2007; Prinstein & Dodge, 2008) have recently conducted research addressing this question. They conclude that adolescents who are uncertain about their social identity, which can appear in the form of low self-esteem and high social anxiety, are most likely to conform to peers. This uncertainty often increases during times of transition, such as school and family transitions. Also, peers are more likely to conform when they are in the presence of someone they perceive to have higher status than they do.

*I didn't belong as a kid, and that always bothered me. If only I'd known that one day my differentness would be an asset, then my early life would have been much easier.*

—Bette Midler
*Contemporary American Actress*

## CLIQUES AND CROWDS

Cliques and crowds assume more important roles in adolescence than in childhood (Brown, 2011; Doornwaard & others, 2012). **Cliques** are small groups that range from 2 to about 12 individuals and average about 5 or 6 individuals. The clique members are usually of the same sex and about the same age. Cliques can form because adolescents engage in similar activities, such as being in a club or on a sports team. Some cliques also form because of friendship. Several adolescents may form a clique because they have spent time with each other and enjoy each other's company. Not necessarily friends, they often develop a friendship if they stay in the clique. What do adolescents do in cliques? They share ideas, hang out together, and may develop an in-group identity in which they believe that their clique is better than other cliques.

*What characterizes adolescent cliques? How are they different from crowds?*

Some cliques also form because of friendship (Closson, 2009b). In the high school years, friendship cliques become more heterosexual with many high school seniors averaging two other-sex and four same-sex friendships (Buhrmester & Chong, 2009). High school seniors average two other-sex and four same-sex friendships compared with sixth graders, who typically have one or no other-sex friendships and five or more same-sex friends. These mixed-sex friendships can provide adolescents with access to potential romantic partners.

**cliques** Small groups that range from 2 to about 12 individuals and average about 5 or 6 individuals. Cliques can form because of friendship or because individuals engage in similar activities, and members usually are of the same sex and about the same age.

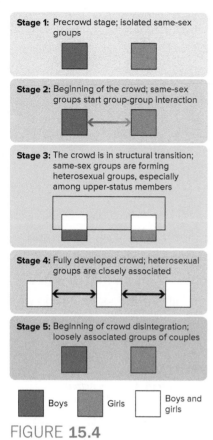

Stage 1: Precrowd stage; isolated same-sex groups

Stage 2: Beginning of the crowd; same-sex groups start group-group interaction

Stage 3: The crowd is in structural transition; same-sex groups are forming heterosexual groups, especially among upper-status members

Stage 4: Fully developed crowd; heterosexual groups are closely associated

Stage 5: Beginning of crowd disintegration; loosely associated groups of couples

Boys    Girls    Boys and girls

FIGURE 15.4

**DUNPHY'S PROGRESSION OF PEER GROUP RELATIONS IN ADOLESCENCE.**

**crowds** The crowd is a larger group structure than a clique. Adolescents usually are members of a crowd based on reputation and may or may not spend much time together. Many crowds are defined by the activities in which adolescents engage.

Dexter Dunphy (1963) documented this increase in mixed-sex groups in a well-known observational study. Figure 15.4 outlines his view of how these mixed-sex groups develop. In late childhood, boys and girls participate in small, same-sex cliques. As they move into the early adolescent years, the same-sex cliques begin to interact with each other. Gradually, the leaders and high-status members form further cliques based on mixed-sex relationships. Eventually, the newly created mixed-sex cliques replace the same-sex cliques. The mixed-sex cliques interact with each other in large crowd activities, too—at dances and athletic events, for example. In late adolescence, the crowd begins to dissolve as couples develop more serious relationships and make long-range plans that may include engagement and marriage.

**Crowds** are a larger group structure than cliques. Adolescents are usually members of a crowd based on reputation and may or may not spend much time together. Crowds are less personal than cliques. Many crowds are defined by the activities adolescents engage in (such as "jocks," who are good at sports, or "druggies," who take drugs) (Brown, 2011).

In one study, crowd membership was associated with adolescent self-esteem (Brown & Lohr, 1987). The crowds included jocks (athletically oriented), populars (well-known students who led social activities), normals (middle-of-the-road students who made up the masses), druggies or toughs (known for illicit drug use or other delinquent activities), and nobodies (low in social skills or intellectual abilities). The self-esteem of the jocks and the populars was highest, whereas that of the nobodies was lowest. One group of adolescents not in a crowd had self-esteem equivalent to that of the jocks and the populars; this group was the independents, who indicated that crowd membership was not important to them. Keep in mind that these data are correlational; self-esteem could increase an adolescent's probability of becoming a crowd member, just as crowd membership could increase the adolescent's self-esteem.

## DATING AND ROMANTIC RELATIONSHIPS

According to Jennifer Connolly at York University, adolescents spend considerable time either dating or thinking about dating (Connolly & McIsaac, 2009). Dating can be a form of recreation, a source of status, or a setting for learning about close relationships, as well as a way of finding a mate.

**Types of Dating and Developmental Changes**    A number of dating variations and developmental changes characterize dating and romantic relationships. First, we examine heterosexual romantic relationships and then we turn to romantic relationships among sexual minority youth (gay and lesbian adolescents).

**Heterosexual Romantic Relationships**    Three stages characterize the development of romantic relationships in adolescence (Connolly & McIsaac, 2009):

1. *Entry into romantic attractions and affiliations at about 11 to 13 years of age.* This initial stage is triggered by puberty. From 11 to 13, adolescents become intensely interested in romance, and the topic dominates many conversations with same-sex friends. Developing a crush on someone is common, and the crush often is shared with a same-sex friend. Young adolescents may or may not interact with the individual who is the object of their infatuation. When dating occurs, it usually takes place in a group setting.

2. *Exploring romantic relationships at approximately 14 to 16 years of age.* At this point in adolescence, two types of romantic involvement occur: (1) *Casual dating* emerges between individuals who are mutually attracted. These dating experiences are often short-lived, last a few months at best,

and usually only endure for a few weeks. (2) *Dating in groups* is common and reflects embeddedness in the peer context. Friends often act as a third-party facilitator of a potential dating relationship by communicating their friend's romantic interest and confirming whether this attraction is reciprocated.

3. *Consolidating dyadic romantic bonds at about 17 to 19 years of age.* At the end of the high school years, more serious romantic relationships develop. This is characterized by strong emotional bonds more closely resembling those in adult romantic relationships. These bonds often are more stable and enduring than earlier bonds, typically lasting one year or more.

Two variations on these stages in the development of romantic relationships in adolescence involve early and late bloomers (Connolly & McIssac, 2009). *Early bloomers* include 15 to 20 percent of 11- to 13-year-olds who say that they currently are in a romantic relationship and 35 percent who indicate that they have had some prior experience in romantic relationships. *Late bloomers* comprise approximately 10 percent of 17- to 19-year-olds who say that they have had no experience with romantic relationships and another 15 percent who report that they have not engaged in any romantic relationships that lasted more than 4 months.

In their early romantic relationships, today's adolescents are not motivated to fulfill attachment or even sexual needs. Rather, early romantic relationships serve as a context for adolescents to explore how attractive they are, how to interact romantically, and how all of these aspects look to the peer group.

*What are some developmental changes in romantic relationships in adolescence?*

Only after adolescents acquire some basic competencies in interacting with romantic partners does the fulfillment of attachment and sexual needs become a central function of these relationships (Furman & Wehner, 1998).

Adolescents often find comfort in numbers during their early exploration of romantic relationships (Connolly & McIsaac, 2009). They may begin hanging out together in heterosexual groups. Sometimes they just hang out at someone's house or get organized enough to ask an adult to drive them to a mall or a movie.

### Romantic Relationships Among Sexual Minority Youth   Most research on romantic relationships in adolescence has focused on heterosexual relationships. Recently, researchers have begun to study romantic relationships among gay, lesbian, and bisexual youth (Diamond, 2013a, b).

The average age of the initial same-sex activity for females ranges from 14 to 18 years of age and for males from 13 to 15 (Diamond, 2013a, b). The most common initial same-sex partner is a close friend. More lesbian adolescent girls have sexual encounters with boys before same-sex activity, whereas gay adolescent boys are more likely to show the opposite sequence (Savin-Williams, 2011, 2013).

Most sexual minority youth have same-sex sexual experience, but relatively few have same-sex romantic relationships because of limited opportunities and the social disapproval such relationships may generate from families or heterosexual peers (Diamond, 2013a, b; Diamond & Savin-Williams, 2013). The importance of romance to sexual

*What characterizes romantic relationships in sexual minority youth?*

minority youth was underscored in a study that found that they rated the breakup of a current romance as their second most stressful problem, second only to disclosure of their sexual orientation to their parents (D'Augelli, 1991).

The romantic possibilities of sexual minority youth are complex (Diamond, 2013a, b; Savin-Williams, 2013). To adequately address the relational interests of sexual minority youth, we can't generalize from heterosexual youth and simply switch the labels. Instead, we need to consider the full range of variation in sexual minority youths' sexual desires and romantic relationships for same- and other-sex partners.

**Romantic Relationships and Adjustment**  Researchers have linked dating and romantic relationships with various measures of how well adjusted adolescents are (Connolly & McIsaac, 2009). Dating and romantic relationships at an early age can be especially problematic. Researchers have found that early dating and "going out with" someone are linked with adolescent pregnancy and problems at home and school (Florsheim, Moore, & Edgington, 2003).

Consider also the following studies that link romantic relationships and adjustment in adolescence:

- The more romantic experiences tenth graders had, the more they reported higher levels of social acceptance, friendship competence, and romantic competence; however, having more romantic experience also was linked to a higher level of substance use, delinquency, and sexual behaviour (Furman, Low, & Ho, 2009).
- Adolescent girls who engaged in co-rumination (excessive discussion of problems with friends) were more likely to be involved in a romantic relationship, and together co-rumination and romantic involvement predicted an increase in depressive symptoms (Starr & Davila, 2009). A recent study also found that romantic activity was linked to depression in early adolescent girls (Starr & others, 2013).
- Among adolescent girls, but not adolescent males, having an older romantic partner was linked to an increase in depressive symptoms, largely influenced by an increase in substance use (Haydon & Halpern, 2010).
- Adolescents with a stronger romantic involvement were more likely to engage in delinquency than their counterparts with a lower level of romantic involvement (Cui & others, 2012).

**Relationships with Parents and Adolescent Romantic Relationships**  Adolescents' relationships with their parents influence their dating and romantic relationships (Ivanova, Veenstra, & Mills, 2012; Nosko & others, 2011; Shulman, Davila, & Shachar-Shapira, 2011; Shulman & others, 2012). Attachment history is linked to couple relationships in adolescence and emerging adulthood (Sroufe & others, 2005; Sroufe, Coffino, & Carlson, 2010). For example, infants who have an anxious attachment with their caregivers in infancy are less likely to develop positive romantic relationships in adolescence than are their securely attached counterparts. It might be that adolescents with a history of secure attachment are better able to control their emotions and more comfortable self-disclosing in romantic relationships. A recent study also found that a positive relationship with parents during adolescence was linked to better-quality romantic relationships in emerging adulthood (Madsen & Collins, 2011). And another recent study revealed that young adolescent girls who had negative relationships with their parents turned to romantic relationships for intimacy and support, which in turn provided the opportunity for early sexual initiation (de Graaf & others, 2012).

Adolescents' observations of their parents' marital relationship also contribute to their own construction of dating relationships. A recent study of 17-year-old Israeli girls and their mothers revealed that mothers who reported a higher level of marital satisfaction had daughters who were more romantically competent (based on multiple dimensions, such as maturity, coherence, and realistic perception of the romantic relationship) (Shulman, Davila, & Shachar-Shapira, 2011).

Marital conflict and divorce also are linked to adolescents' and emerging adults' dating and romantic relationships. One study revealed that parents' marital conflict was linked to increased conflict in an emerging adult's romantic relationships (Cui, Fincham, & Pasley, 2008). Recent research also confirms that parental divorce affects adolescents' romantic relationships. For example, a recent study revealed that an adolescent's first romantic relationship occurred earlier in divorced than non-divorced intact families but only when the divorce occurred in early adolescence (Ivanova, Veenstra, & Mills, 2012).

A longitudinal study examined how youths' personality traits and beliefs about marriage are related to romantic relationships in early adulthood (Masarik & others, 2013). In this study, a higher level of neuroticism in the ninth grade was linked with the belief in late adolescence/early adulthood that marriage is not likely to lead to fulfillment in life and happiness as an adult. And less endorsement of the marriage/fulfillment belief, in turn, predicted fewer observed positive interactions with a romantic partner and lower perceived relationship quality in early adulthood.

---

## Review *Connect* Reflect

 **LO4** Characterize peer relations in adolescence.

### Review

- How are peer pressure and conformity shown in adolescence?
- How are cliques and crowds involved in adolescent development?
- What characterizes adolescents' dating and romantic relationships?

### *Connect*

- In this section you read about adolescents' dating and romantic relationships. What impact might these relationships have on adolescents' sense of identity as discussed in Chapter 11?

### **Reflect** *Your Own Personal Journey of Life*

- What were your peer relationships like during adolescence? What peer groups were you involved in? How did they influence your development? If you could change anything about the way you experienced peer relations in adolescence, what would it be?

---

# case study **connections**

1. In this chapter, you learned about the difference between being well-liked and perceived as popular by peers. How does what you learned about sociometric popularity and perceived popularity relate to the girls' experiences described in the chapter-opening vignette?

2. Are the girls' friendships described in the chapter-opening vignette similar to what you would expect based on what you learned in this chapter about the functions of friendship and the differences between the friendships of boys and girls?

3. How does research by Brown and Gilligan (1992) described in the chapter-opening vignette apply to what you learned in this chapter about cliques and romantic relationships?

# Peers

## Peer Relations

**L01** Discuss peer relations in childhood.

#### Exploring Peer Relations

- Peers are children who share the same age or maturity level. Peers provide a means of social comparison and a source of information about the world outside the family. Good peer relations may be necessary for normal social development. The inability to "plug in" to a social network is associated with a number of problems. Peer relations can be both positive and negative. Piaget and Sullivan stressed that peer relations provide the context for learning important aspects of relationships, such as observing others' interests and perspectives and exploring fairness and justice by working through disagreements. Peer relations vary according to the way peer experience is measured, the outcomes specified, and the developmental trajectories traversed. Contexts and individual differences influence peer relations.

#### The Developmental Course of Peer Relations in Childhood

- Some researchers argue that the quality of social interaction with peers in infancy provides valuable information about socioemotional development. As increasing numbers of infants attend child care, infant peer relations have increased. The frequency of peer interaction, both positive and negative, increases during the preschool years. Children spend even more time with peers in the elementary and secondary school years, and their preference for same-sex groups increases. Boys' groups are larger than girls', and they participate in more organized games than girls. Girls engage in more collaborative discourse in peer groups than boys do.

#### The Distinct but Coordinated Worlds of Parent-Child and Peer Relations

- Healthy family relations usually promote healthy peer relations. Parents can model or coach their children in ways of relating to peers. Parents' choices of neighbourhoods, churches, schools, and their own friends influence the pool from which their children might select possible friends. Rough-and-tumble play occurs mainly in peer relations rather than in parent-child relations. In times of stress, children usually turn to parents rather than peers.

#### Social Cognition and Emotion

- Perspective taking and social information-processing skills are important dimensions of social cognition in peer relations. Perspective taking helps children communicate effectively. Self-regulation of emotion is associated with positive peer relations.

#### Peer Group Social Status

- Sociometrically popular children are well liked by peers and have a number of positive attributes. Perceived popularity is associated with both positive features such as physical attractiveness and prosocial behaviour and negative features such as aggression and risk behaviour. Rejected children are disliked by peers and often experience serious adjustment problems.

#### Bullying

- Bullying is repeated aggressive behaviour meant to disturb a less powerful individual. Significant numbers of students are bullied, and this is linked to adjustment problems for the victim, the bully, or the individual who is both a bully and a victim.

## Play

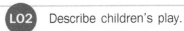 Describe children's play.

- Play's Functions
- Types of Play
- Trends in Play

- The functions of play include affiliation with peers, tension release, advances in cognitive development, and exploration.

- The contemporary perspective emphasizes both social and cognitive aspects of play. The most widely studied types of play include sensorimotor and practice play, pretence/symbolic play, social play, constructive play, and games.

- Children's free play time has declined considerably in recent years. Especially important is that children often learn best when they are in playful contexts. Play promotes numerous aspects of socioemotional development.

## Friendship

**LO3** Explain friendship.

- Friendship's Functions
- Similarity and Intimacy
- Gender and Friendship
- Mixed-Age Friendships
- Mixed-Age Friendships
- Other-Sex Friendships

- The functions of friendship include companionship, stimulation, physical support, ego support, social comparison, and intimacy/affection. Sullivan pointed out that whether or not these functions of friendship are fulfilled largely determines our emotional well-being. Sullivan argued that there is a dramatic increase in the psychological importance and intimacy of close friends in early adolescence. Research findings support his view.

- Similarity and intimacy are two of the most common characteristics of friendships. Friends often have similar attitudes toward school, similar educational aspirations, and so on. Intimacy in friendship is much more common among adolescents than children.

- An increasing number of studies indicate that the friendships of girls differ from the friendships of boys. The influence of friendship, both positive and negative, may be stronger for girls. Intimacy plays a powerful role in girls' friendships, and power, excitement, and control play important roles in boys' friendships.

- Children and adolescents who become friends with older individuals engage in more deviant behaviours than do their counterparts with same-age friends. Girls in grades 6 through 10, who often have older male friends, may be more likely to engage in problem behaviour.

- The number of other-sex friendships increases as adolescence proceeds. Other-sex friendships provide a context for learning how to communicate with the other sex and reduce anxiety in social and dating contexts. However, some aspects of other-sex friendships are linked to negative outcomes, such as earlier intercourse and drug use.

## Peer Relations in Adolescence

 Characterize peer relations in adolescence.

- Peer Pressure and Conformity
- Cliques and Crowds

- The pressure to conform to peers is strong during adolescence, especially in eighth and ninth grade, and can have positive or negative effects.

- Cliques and crowds assume more importance in the lives of adolescents than in the lives of children. Cliques become increasingly mixed-sex in adolescence. Membership in certain crowds—especially jocks and populars—is associated with increased self-esteem.

- Three stages characterize the development of romantic relationships in adolescence: (1) entry into romantic attractions and affiliations at about 11 to 13 years of age, (2) exploring romantic relationships at approximately 14 to 16 years of age, and (3) consolidating dyadid romantic bonds at about 17 to 19 years of age. A special concern is early dating, which is associated with a number of problems. Most sexual minority youth have same-sex sexual experience, but relatively few have same-sex romantic relationships. Many sexual minority youth date other-sex peers, which can help them to clarify their sexual orientation or disguise it from others. Adolescents who date have more problems, such as substance abuse, than those who do not date, but they also have more acceptance with peers.

**connect**  **LEARNSMART**  **SMARTBOOK**

# Schools and Technology | chapter 16

The Reggio Emilia approach is an educational program for young children that was developed in the northern Italian city of Reggio Emilia. Children of single parents and children with disabilities have priority in admission; other children are admitted according to a scale of needs. Parents pay on a sliding scale based on income.

The children are encouraged to learn by investigating and exploring topics that interest them. A wide range of stimulating media and materials is available for children to use as they learn—music, movement, drawing, painting, sculpting, collages, puppets and disguises, and photography, for example (Strong-Wilson & Ellis, 2007).

A Reggio Emilia classroom in which young children explore topics that interest them.

In this program, children often explore topics in a group, which fosters a sense of community, respect for diversity, and a collaborative approach to problem solving (Hyson, Copple, & Jones, 2006). Two co-teachers are present to serve as guides for children. The Reggio Emilia teachers view a project as an adventure, which can start from an adult's suggestion, from a child's idea, or from an event, such as a snowfall or something else unexpected. Every project is based on what the children say and do. The teachers allow children enough time to think and craft a project.

At the core of the Reggio Emilia approach is the image of children who are competent and have rights, especially the right to outstanding care and education. Parent participation is considered essential, and cooperation is a major theme in the schools. Many early childhood education experts believe the Reggio Emilia approach provides a supportive, stimulating context in which children are motivated to explore their world in a competent and confident manner (New, 2005, 2007).

This chapter is about becoming educated and achieving. We will explore topics such as contemporary approaches to student learning, school transitions, the roles that socioeconomic status and ethnicity play in schools, educational issues involving children with disabilities, and motivation to achieve goals. We will also explore the impact of technology on children's lives.

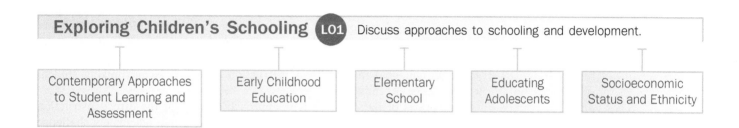

**Exploring Children's Schooling** **L01** Discuss approaches to schooling and development.

| Contemporary Approaches to Student Learning and Assessment | Early Childhood Education | Elementary School | Educating Adolescents | Socioeconomic Status and Ethnicity |

We have discussed many aspects of schools throughout this book, especially in Section 3, "Cognition and Language." Recall our coverage of applications of Piaget's and Vygotsky's theories to education in Chapter 6, strategies for encouraging children's critical thinking in schools in Chapter 7, applications of Gardner's and Sternberg's theories of intelligence to education in Chapter 8, and bilingual education in Chapter 9. Here we take a closer look at contemporary approaches to student learning in schools, variations in schooling from early childhood education through high school, and the influence of socioeconomic status and ethnicity on children's education.

For most children, entering the first grade signals new obligations. They form new relationships and develop new standards by which to judge themselves. School provides children with a rich source of new ideas to shape their sense of self. They will spend many years in schools as members of small societies in which there are tasks to be accomplished, people to be socialized and to be socialized by, and rules that define and limit behaviour, feelings, and attitudes. By the time students graduate from high school, they will have spent 12,000 hours in the classroom.

**developmental connection**

**Cognitive Theory.** Piaget's and Vygotsky's theories can be applied to children's education. Chapter 6, LO 2; Chapter 6, LO 3

The whole art of teaching is the art of awakening the natural curiosity of young minds.

—ANATOLE FRANCE
*French Novelist, 20th Century*

## CONTEMPORARY APPROACHES TO STUDENT LEARNING AND ASSESSMENT

Controversy swirls about the best ways to teach children and how to hold schools and teachers accountable for whether children are learning (McCombs, 2013; Miller & Reynolds, 2013).

**Constructivist and Direct Instruction Approaches** The **constructivist approach** is a learner-centred approach that emphasizes the importance of individuals actively constructing their knowledge and understanding with guidance from the teacher. In the constructivist view, teachers should not attempt to simply pour information into children's minds. Rather, children should be encouraged to explore their world, discover knowledge, reflect, and think critically, with careful monitoring and meaningful guidance from the teacher (Appleton, 2012; O'Donnell, 2012). The constructivists believe that for too long in North American education children have been required to sit still,

*Is the teaching philosophy in this classroom more likely constructivist or direct instruction? Explain.*

**constructivist approach** A learner-centred approach that emphasizes the importance of individuals actively constructing their knowledge and understanding, with guidance from the teacher.

Education is the transmission of civilization.

—Ariel and Will Durant
*American Authors and Philosophers, 20th Century*

*What characterizes direct instruction?*

**direct instruction approach** A teacher-centred approach characterized by teacher direction and control, mastery of academic material, high expectations for students' progress, and maximum time spent on learning tasks.

**child-centred kindergarten** Education that involves the whole child by considering both the child's physical, cognitive, and socioemotional development, and the child's needs, interests, and learning styles.

be passive learners, and rotely memorize irrelevant as well as relevant information (Webb, Mehta, & Jordan, 2013).

Today, constructivism may include an emphasis on collaboration—children working with each other in their efforts to know and understand (Mahn & John-Steiner, 2013). A teacher with a constructivist instructional philosophy would not have children memorize information rotely but would give them opportunities to meaningfully construct the knowledge and understand the material while guiding their learning (Cruikshank, Jenkins, & Metcalf, 2012).

By contrast, the **direct instruction approach** is a structured, teacher-centred approach that is characterized by teacher direction and control, high teacher expectations for students' progress, maximum time spent by students on academic tasks, and efforts by the teacher to keep negative affect to a minimum. An important goal in the direct instruction approach is maximizing student learning time (Arends, 2012).

Advocates of the constructivist approach argue that the direct instruction approach turns children into passive learners and does not adequately challenge them to think in critical and creative ways (McCombs, 2013). The direct instruction enthusiasts say that the constructivist approaches do not give enough attention to the content of a discipline, such as history or science. They also believe that the constructivist approaches are too relativistic and vague.

Some experts in educational psychology believe that many effective teachers use both a constructivist *and* a direct instruction approach rather than relying on either exclusively (Bransford & others, 2006; Parkay, 2013). Further, some circumstances may call more for a constructivist approach and others for a direction instruction approach. For example, experts increasingly recommend an explicit, intellectually engaging direct instruction approach when teaching students with a reading or a writing disability (Berninger & O'Malley, 2011).

Let's now explore what schools are like at different developmental levels of students. We will begin with early childhood education.

## EARLY CHILDHOOD EDUCATION

To the teachers in a Reggio Emilia program (described at the beginning of this chapter), preschool children are active learners, exploring the world with their peers, constructing their knowledge of the world in collaboration with their community, aided but not directed by their teachers. In many ways, the Reggio Emilia approach applies ideas consistent with the views of Piaget and Vygotsky discussed in Chapter 6, "Cognitive Developmental Approaches." Our exploration of early childhood education focuses on variations in programs, educational strategies for young children who are disadvantaged, and some controversies in early childhood education.

**Variations in Early Childhood Education**  Attending preschool is rapidly becoming the norm for Canadian children. There are many variations in the way young children are educated. The foundation of early childhood education has been the child-centred kindergarten.

*The Child-Centred Kindergarten*  Nurturing is a key aspect of the **child-centred kindergarten**, which emphasizes the education of the whole child and concern for his or her physical, cognitive, and socioemotional development (Segal & others,

2012). Instruction is organized around children's needs, interests, and learning styles. Emphasis is placed on the process of learning, rather than what is learned (Jalongo & Isenberg, 2012). The child-centred kindergarten honours three principles: (1) each child follows a unique developmental pattern, (2) young children learn best through firsthand experiences with people and materials, and (3) play is extremely important in the child's total development. Experimenting, exploring, discovering, trying out, restructuring, speaking, and listening are frequent activities in excellent kindergarten programs. Such programs are closely attuned to the developmental status of 4- and 5-year-old children.

**developmental connection**

**Cognitive Theory.** Both Piaget and Vygotsky believed that play is an excellent setting for young children's cognitive development. Chapter 15, LO 2

*The Montessori Approach* Montessori schools are patterned after the educational philosophy of Maria Montessori (1870–1952), an Italian physician-turned-educator who crafted a revolutionary approach to young children's education at the beginning of the twentieth century. The **Montessori approach** is a philosophy of education in which children are given considerable freedom and spontaneity in choosing activities. They are allowed to move from one activity to another as they desire. The teacher acts as a facilitator rather than a director. The teacher shows the child how to perform intellectual activities, demonstrates interesting ways to explore curriculum materials, and offers help when the child requests it (Drake, 2008; Isaacs, 2012; Lillard, 2008). "By encouraging children to make decisions from an early age, Montessori programs seek to develop self-regulated problem solvers who can make choices and manage their time effectively" (Hyson, Copple, & Jones, 2006, p. 14).

**Montessori approach** An educational philosophy in which children are given considerable freedom and spontaneity in choosing activities and are allowed to move from one activity to another as they desire.

Some developmentalists favor the Montessori approach, but others conclude that it neglects children's socioemotional development. For example, although Montessori fosters independence and the development of cognitive skills, it deemphasizes verbal interaction between the teacher and child and between the children themselves. Montessori's critics also argue that it restricts imaginative play and that its heavy reliance on self-corrective materials may not adequately allow for creativity or accommodate a variety of learning styles.

To read about additional controversies in early childhood education, see *Connecting to Current Controversy.*

*Developmentally Appropriate and Inappropriate Education* Many educators and psychologists conclude that preschool and young elementary school children learn best through active, hands-on teaching methods such as games and dramatic play. They know that children develop at varying rates and that schools need to allow for these individual differences. They also argue that schools should focus on facilitating children's socioemotional development as well as their cognitive development. Educators refer to this type of schooling as **developmentally appropriate practice** (DAP), which is based on knowledge of the typical development of children within an age span (age-appropriateness), as well as the uniqueness of the child (individual-appropriateness) (Bredekamp, 2011; Squires & others, 2013). In contrast, developmentally inappropriate practice for young children relies on abstract paper-and-pencil activities presented to large groups. Desired outcomes for DAP include thinking critically, working cooperatively, solving problems, developing self-regulatory skills, and enjoying learning. The emphasis in DAP is on the process of learning rather than its content (Ritchie, Maxwell, & Bredekamp,

Larry Page and Sergey Brin, founders of the highly successful Internet search engine, Google, said that their early years at Montessori schools were a major factor in their success. During an interview with Barbara Walters, they said they learned how to be self-directed and self-starters at Montessori. They commented that Montessori experiences encouraged them to think for themselves and allowed them the freedom to develop their own interests.

**developmentally appropriate practice** Education that focuses on the typical developmental patterns of children (age-appropriateness) and the uniqueness of each child (individual-appropriateness). Such practice contrasts with developmentally inappropriate practice, which relies on abstract paper-and-pencil activities presented to large groups of young children.

## Early Childhood Education: Three Current Controversies

Three current controversies in early childhood education involve (1) what the curriculum for early childhood education should be (Epstein & Barnette, 2012; Moravick, Nolte, & Feeney, 2013), (2) whether preschool education should be universal (Zigler, Gilliam, & Jones, 2006), and (3) whether kindergarten should be an entire school day.

A current curriculum controversy in early childhood involves, on one side, those who advocate a child-centred, constructivist approach along the lines of developmentally appropriate practice. On the other side are those who endorse an academic, direct instruction approach. In reality, many high-quality early childhood education programs include both academic and constructivist approaches.

*What are three controversies in early childhood education?*

Many education experts worry about academic approaches that place too much pressure on young children to achieve and don't provide any opportunities to actively construct knowledge (Katz, 1999). Researchers from the University of British Columbia argue that competent early childhood programs also should focus on both cognitive development and socioemotional development, not exclusively on cognitive development (Hymel, Schonert-Reichl, & Miller, 2006).

Another early childhood education controversy focuses on whether preschool education should be instituted for all 4-year-old children. Edward Zigler and his colleagues (2006) argue that quality preschools prepare children for success in school. Zigler and his colleagues (2006) cite research that shows quality preschool programs increase the likelihood that once children go to elementary and secondary school they will be less likely to be retained in a grade or to drop out of school. They also point to analyses indicating that universal preschool would bring considerable cost savings on the order of billions of dollars because of a diminished need for remedial and justice services (Karoly & Bigelow, 2005). Critics of universal preschool education argue that the gains attributed to preschool and kindergarten education are often overstated. They especially stress that research has not proven that non-disadvantaged children improve as a result of attending a preschool. Thus, the critics say it is more important to improve preschool education for young children who are disadvantaged than to mandate preschool education for all 4-year-old children. Some critics, especially homeschooling advocates, emphasize that young children should be educated by their parents, not by schools.

Thus, controversy continues to surround the issue of universal preschool education.

Most provinces across Canada offer full-day kindergarten, although it is only mandatory in New Brunswick and Prince Edward Island and not all programs receive government funding. Some critics believe having children attend kindergarten for a full school day provides no additional educational impact and serves only as a babysitting service for working parents. Much of the concern comes from research conducted on the impact of full-day kindergarten on American children. In a meta-analysis, researchers concluded that academic gains from full-day kindergarten appear only in the short run for U.S. children, disappearing by Grade 3 (Cooper & others, 2010). We know very little about the impact for Canadian children, yet Ontario spends 1.5 billion dollars each year on full-day kindergarten. Is this money well spent? One study by Claire Maltais and her colleagues at the University of Ottawa found that attending a full-day preschool program at age 4 led to enhanced linguistic, reading, and mathematic skills but had no impact on writing competence or socio-emotional and psychomotor development (Maltais & others, 2011). In fact, a recent report evaluating the effects of full-day kindergarten in Ontario found that children in full-day classrooms showed poorer emotional maturity, communication skills, and general knowledge than those in half-day classrooms (Vanderlee & others, 2012). Evaluations of full-day kindergarten in both the U.S. and Ontario suggest that positive effects are primarily among children attending schools marked by low income and/or poor test scores (Cooper & others, 2010; Vanderlee & others, 2012).

2009). Figure 16.1 provides recommendations for developmentally appropriate education in a number of areas (NAEYC, 2009).

Many but not all studies show significant positive benefits for developmentally appropriate education (Hyson, 2007). Among the reasons it is difficult to

**1 Knowledge to Consider in Making Decisions**

In all aspects of working with children, early childhood practitioners need to consider these three areas of knowledge: 1) What is known about child development and learning, especially age-related characteristics; 2) What is known about each child as an individual; and 3) What is known about the social and cultural contexts in which children live.

**2 Challenging and Achieveable Goals**

Keeping in mind desired goals and what is known about the children as a group and individually, teachers plan experiences to promote children's learning and development.

**Principles of Child Development and Learning that Inform Practice**

**1** All the domains of development and learning—physical, cognitive, emotional, and social—are important, and they are linked.

**2** Many aspects of children's learning and development follow well-documented sequences, with later abilities, skills, and knowledge building on those already acquired.

**3** Development and learning proceed at varying rates from child to child, and at uneven rates across different areas of a child's individual functioning.

**4** Development and learning result from the interaction of biological maturation and experience.

**5** Early experiences have strong effects—both cumulative and delayed—on children's development and learning; optimal periods exist for certain types of development and learning.

**6** Development proceeds toward greater complexity, self-regulation, and symbolic or representational capacities.

**7** Children develop best when they have secure, consistent relationships with responsive adults and opportunities for positive peer relations.

**8** Development and learning occur in and are influenced by multiple social and cultural contexts.

**9** Always mentally active in seeking to understand the world around them, children learn in a variety of ways; a wide range of teaching strategies can be effective in guiding children's learning.

**10** Play is an important context for developing self-regulation and for promoting language, cognition, and social competence.

**11** Development and learning advance when children are challenged to achieve at a level just beyond their current mastery and when they are given opportunities to practice newly acquired skills.

**12** Children's experiences shape their motivation and approaches to learning, such as persistence, initiative, and flexibility; in turn, these characteristics influence their learning and development.

**Selected Guidelines for Developmentally Appropriate Practice**

**1 Creating a Caring Community of Learners**

Each member of the community should be valued by the others; relationships are an important context through which children learn; practitioners ensure that members of the community feel psychologically safe.

**2 Teaching to Enhance Development and Learning**

The teacher takes responsibility for stimulating, directing, and supporting children's learning by providing the experiences that each child needs.

**3 Planning Curriculum to Achieve Important Goals**

The curriculum is planned to help children achieve goals that are developmentally appropriate and educationally significant.

**4 Assessing Children's Development and Learning**

In developmentally appropriate practice, assessments are linked to the program's goals for children.

**5 Establishing Reciprocal Relationships with Families**

A positive partnership between teachers and families benefits children's learning and development.

## FIGURE 16.1

**RECOMMENDATIONS BY NAEYC FOR DEVELOPMENTALLY APPROPRIATE PRACTICE IN EARLY CHILDHOOD PROGRAMS SERVING CHILDREN FROM BIRTH THROUGH AGE 8.** Adapted from: NAEYC (2009).

generalize about research on developmentally appropriate education is that individual programs often vary, and developmentally appropriate education is an evolving concept. Recent changes in the concept have focused more attention on sociocultural factors, the teacher's active involvement and implementation of systematic intentions, as well as the degree to which academic skills should be emphasized and how they should be taught.

In Japan and many developing countries, some of the goals of early childhood education are quite different from those of North American programs. To read about the differences, see *Connecting with Diversity*.

## ELEMENTARY SCHOOL

For many children, entering the first grade signals a change from being a "home child" to being a "school child"—a situation in which new roles and obligations are experienced. Children take up the new role of being a student, interact with peers and teachers, develop new relationships, adopt new reference groups, and discover new standards by which to judge themselves. School provides children with a rich source of new ideas to shape their sense of self.

## Early Childhood Education in Japan and Developing Countries

As in North America, there is diversity in Japanese early childhood education. Some Japanese kindergartens have specific aims, such as early musical training or the practice of Montessori strategies. In large cities, some kindergartens are attached to universities that have elementary and secondary schools. In most Japanese preschools, however, little emphasis is put on academic instruction.

In one study, 300 Japanese preschool teachers, child development specialists, and parents were asked about various aspects of early childhood education (Tobin, Wu, & Davidson, 1989). Only 2 percent of the Japanese respondents listed "to give children a good start academically" as one of their top three reasons for a society to have preschools. Japanese schools do not teach reading, writing, and mathematics but rather skills like persistence, concentration, and the ability to function as a member of a group. The vast majority of young Japanese children are taught to read at home by their parents.

More than 60 percent of the Japanese parents in the study said that the purpose of preschool is to give children experience being a member of the group (Tobin, Wu, & Davidson, 1989). Lessons in living and working together grow naturally out of the Japanese culture. In many Japanese kindergartens,

A kindergarten class in Kingston, Jamaica. *What characterizes kindergarten in many developing countries like Jamaica?*

children wear the same uniforms, including caps in different colours to indicate the classrooms to which they belong. They have identical sets of equipment, kept in identical drawers and shelves. This is not intended to turn the young children into robots, but to impress on them that other people, just like themselves, have needs and desires that are equally important (Hendry, 1995).

Japan is a highly advanced industrialized country. What about developing countries? The wide range of programs and emphasis on the education of the whole child—physically, cognitively, and socioemotionally—that characterize North American early childhood education do not exist in many developing countries (Roopnarine & Metindogan, 2006). Economic pressures and parents' belief that education should be academically rigorous have produced teacher-centred rather than child-centred early childhood education programs in most developing countries. Among the countries in which this type of early childhood education has been observed are Jamaica, rural China, Thailand, Kenya, and Turkey. In these countries, young children are usually given few choices and are educated in highly structured settings. Emphasis is on learning academic skills through rote memorization and recitation (Lin, Johnson, & Johnson, 2003). Programs in Mexico, Singapore, Korea, and Hong Kong have been observed to be closer to those in North America in their emphasis on curriculum flexibility and play-based methods (Cisneros-Cohernour, Moreno, & Cisneros, 2000).

*What characterizes early childhood education in Japan?*

Too often early schooling proceeds mainly on the basis of negative feedback. For example, children's self-esteem in the latter part of elementary school is lower than it is in the earlier part, and older children rate themselves as less smart, less good, and less hard-working than do younger ones (Blumenfeld & others, 1981; Eccles, 2003).

Intervention programs can help make the transition into elementary school easier for children. Various Head Start programs are in place across Canada focusing on school readiness by working with children and their families. For example, ABC Head Start is a preschool and family support program for low-income families available in Alberta. On a national level, the federal government established the Aboriginal Head Start program in 1995, which specifically focuses on aiding the development and school readiness of First Nations, Métis and Inuit children in Canada.

## EDUCATING ADOLESCENTS

What is the transition from elementary to middle or junior high school like? What are the characteristics of effective schools for young adolescents? How can adolescents be encouraged to stay in school?

As children make the transition to elementary school, they interact and develop relationships with new and significant others. School provides them with a rich source of new ideas to shape their sense of self.

**The Transition to Middle or Junior High School**   The first year of middle school or junior high school can be difficult for many students (Anderman, 2012; Anderman, Gray, & Chang, 2013; Eccles & Roeser, 2013). For example, in one study of the transition from sixth grade in an elementary school to seventh grade in a junior high school, adolescents' perceptions of the quality of their school life plunged during the seventh grade (Hirsch & Rapkin, 1987). Compared with their earlier feelings as sixth-graders, the seventh-graders were less satisfied with school, were less committed to school, and liked their teachers less. The drop in school satisfaction occurred regardless of how academically successful the students were. The transition to middle or junior high school is less stressful when students have positive relationships with friends and go through the transition in team-oriented schools in which 20 to 30 students take the same classes together (Hawkins & Berndt, 1985).

The transition to middle or junior high school takes place at a time when many changes—in the individual, in the family, and in school—are occurring simultaneously (Anderman, Gray, & Chang, 2013; Eccles & Roeser, 2013). These changes include puberty and related concerns about body image; the emergence of at least some aspects of formal operational thought, including accompanying changes in social cognition; increased responsibility and decreased dependency on parents; change to a larger, more impersonal school structure; change from one teacher to many teachers and from a small, homogeneous set of peers to a larger, more heterogeneous set of peers; and an increased focus on achievement and performance. Moreover, when students make the transition to middle or junior high school, they experience the **top-dog phenomenon** of moving from being the oldest, biggest, and most powerful students in

The transition from elementary to middle or junior high school occurs at the same time as a number of other developmental changes. *What are some of these other developmental changes?*

**top-dog phenomenon** The circumstance of moving from the top position in elementary school to the lowest position in middle or high school.

elementary school to being the youngest, smallest, and least powerful students in middle or high school.

There can also be positive aspects to the transition to middle or junior high school. Students are more likely to feel grown up, have more subjects from which to select, have more opportunities to spend time with peers and locate compatible friends, and enjoy increased independence from direct parental monitoring. They also may be more challenged intellectually by academic work.

**Early School Leaving**   Students leaving high school early is a major concern, particularly among Aboriginal students in Canada. Among Aboriginal Canadians living off reserve, 28 percent are early school leavers (The Daily, 2013). Overall, Canada's dropout rates have been declining steadily between 1990 to 2012, with the decline most significant in the Atlantic provinces (Statistics Canada, 2012). In the academic year 1990–1991, 16.6 percent of Canadian youth aged 20–24 were not currently attending school and had not

An important educational goal is to increase the high school graduation rate of Aboriginal adolescents.

*How does participation in extracurricular activities influence development in adolescence and emerging adulthood?*

graduated from high school compared to 7.8 percent in 2011–2012 (Statistics Canada, 2012).

Students drop out of school for many reasons (Jimerson, 2009). In one study, almost 50 percent of the early school leavers cited school-related reasons for leaving school, such as not liking school or being expelled or suspended (Rumberger, 1995). Twenty percent of the early school leavers cited economic reasons for leaving school. One-third of the female students dropped out for personal reasons such as pregnancy or marriage.

According to one review, the most effective programs to discourage dropping out of high school provide early reading programs, tutoring, counselling, and mentoring (Lehr & others, 2003). They also emphasize the creation of caring environments and relationships, use block scheduling, and offer community-service opportunities.

**Extracurricular Activities** Adolescents in Canadian schools usually can choose from a wide array of extracurricular activities in addition to their academic courses. These adult-sanctioned activities typically occur in the after-school hours and can be sponsored either by the school or the community. They include such diverse activities as sports, academic clubs, band, drama, and math clubs. Researchers have found that participation in extracurricular activities is linked to higher grades, increased school engagement, reduced likelihood of early school leaving, improved probability of going to college or university, higher self-esteem, and lower rates of depression, delinquency, and substance abuse (Eccles & Roeser, 2013). Adolescents benefit from a breadth of extracurricular activities more than focusing on a single extracurricular activity.

Of course, the quality of the extracurricular activities matters (Eccles & Roeser, 2013). High-quality extracurricular activities that are likely to promote positive adolescent development include competent and supportive adult mentors, opportunities for increasing school connectedness, challenging and meaningful activities, and opportunities for improving skills.

## SOCIOECONOMIC STATUS AND ETHNICITY

Children from low-income, ethnic minority backgrounds have more difficulties in school than do their middle-socioeconomic-status, Caucasian counterparts (Hutson, 2008). Why? Critics argue that schools are not doing a good job of educating low-income or ethnic minority students (Gollnick & Chinn, 2013; Leong & others, 2013; Spring, 2013). Let's further explore the roles of socioeconomic status and ethnicity in schools.

**Educating Students from Low-Income Backgrounds** Many children living in poverty face problems that present barriers to their learning (Chen & Brooks-Gunn, 2012; Duncan, 2012). They might have parents who don't set high educational standards for them, who are incapable of reading to them, or who don't have enough money to pay for educational materials and experiences, such as books and trips to zoos and museums. They might be malnourished or live in areas where crime and violence are a way of life. One study revealed that the longer children experienced poverty, the more detrimental the poverty was to their cognitive development (Najman & others, 2009).

The schools that children from impoverished backgrounds attend often have fewer resources than schools in higher-income neighbourhoods (Nelson, Palonsky,

& McCarthy, 2013). In low-income areas, schools are more likely to be staffed by young teachers with less experience than schools in higher-income neighbourhoods (Liu & Hernandez, 2008). Schools in low-income areas also are more likely to encourage rote learning, whereas schools in higher-income areas are more likely to work with children to improve their thinking skills (Koppelman & Goodhart, 2011). In sum, far too many schools in low-income neighbourhoods provide students with environments that are not conducive to effective learning (McLoyd & others, 2011).

Elementary school children in Gjoa Haven, Nunavut, an Inuit community north of the Arctic Circle.

**Ethnicity in Schools**     The school experiences of students from different ethnic groups vary considerably (Ceballo, Huerta, & Ngo, 2010). Students from African or Latin American ethnic backgrounds are much less likely than students from European or Asian ethnic backgrounds to be enrolled in academic, university preparatory programs and are much more likely to be enrolled in remedial and special education programs. Asian students are far more likely than other ethnic minority groups to take advanced math and science courses in high school.

Following are some strategies for improving interaction among ethnically diverse students:

- *Turn the class into a jigsaw classroom.* When Eliot Aronson was a professor at the University of Texas at Austin, the school system contacted him for ideas on how to reduce the increasing racial tension in classrooms. Aronson (1986) developed the concept of *jigsaw classroom,* in which students from different cultural backgrounds are placed in a cooperative group in which they have to construct different parts of a project to reach a common goal. Aronson used the term *jigsaw* because he saw the technique as much like a group of students cooperating to put different pieces together to complete a jigsaw puzzle. How might this work? Team sports, drama productions, and music performances are examples of contexts in which students participate cooperatively to reach a common goal; however, the jigsaw technique also lends itself to group science projects, history reports, and other learning experiences with a variety of subject matter.

- *Encourage students to have positive personal contact with diverse other students.* Mere contact does not do the job of improving relationships with diverse others. For example, bussing ethnic minority students to predominantly Caucasian schools, or vice versa, has not reduced prejudice or improved interethnic relations. What matters is what happens after children get to school. Especially beneficial in improving interethnic relations is sharing one's worries, successes, failures, coping strategies, interests, and other personal information with people of other ethnicities. When this happens, people tend to look at others as individuals rather than as members of a homogeneous group.

- *Reduce bias.* Teachers can reduce bias by displaying images of children from diverse ethnic and cultural groups, selecting play materials and classroom activities that encourage cultural understanding, helping students resist stereotyping, and working with parents to reduce children's exposure to bias and prejudice at home.

*What are some features of a jigsaw classroom?*

- *View the school and community as a team.* James Comer (1988, 2004, 2006, 2010) advocates a community-wide, team-oriented approach as the best way to educate children. Three important aspects of the Comer Project for Change are (1) a governance and management team that develops a comprehensive school plan, assessment strategy, and staff development plan; (2) a mental health or school support team; and (3) a program for parents. Comer believes that the entire school community should have a cooperative rather than an adversarial attitude.

- Be *a competent cultural mediator.* Teachers can play a powerful role as cultural mediators by being sensitive to biased content in curriculum materials and classroom interactions, learning more about different ethnic groups, being sensitive to children's ethnic attitudes, viewing students of colour positively, and thinking of positive ways to get parents of colour more involved as partners with teachers in educating children (Manning & Baruth, 2009; Taylor & Whittaker, 2009).

## Review *Connect* Reflect

**L01** Discuss approaches to schooling and development.

### Review

- What are some contemporary approaches to student learning?
- What are some variations in early childhood education?
- What are some characteristics of elementary education?
- What are the challenges in educating adolescents?
- How do socioeconomic status and ethnicity affect children's education?

### Connect

- In this section, you learned about socioeconomic status (SES) and education. In Chapter 14, what did you learn about SES and how parents think about education?

### Reflect *Your Own Personal Journey of Life*

- How would you characterize the approach of the schools that you attended as a child and as an adolescent? Do you think your schools were effective? Explain.

## Children with Disabilities **L02** Characterize children with disabilities and their education.

| Learning Disabilities | Attention Deficit Hyperactivity Disorder (ADHD) | Emotional and Behavioural Disorders | Autism Spectrum Disorders |

What are some of the disabilities that children have?

## LEARNING DISABILITIES

**learning disabilities** Disabilities involving understanding or using spoken or written language. The difficulty can appear in listening, thinking, reading, writing, spelling, or mathematics. To be classified as a learning disability, the problem must not be primarily the result of visual, hearing, or motor disabilities; intellectual disability; emotional disorders; or environmental, cultural, or economic disadvantage.

A child with a **learning disability** has difficulty in learning that involves understanding or using spoken or written language, and the difficulty can appear in listening, thinking, reading, writing, and spelling. A learning disability also may involve difficulty in doing mathematics. To be classified as a learning disability, the learning problem is not primarily the result of visual, hearing, or motor disabilities; intellectual disability; emotional disorders; or due to environmental, cultural, or economic disadvantage.

About three times as many boys as girls are classified as having a learning disability. Among the explanations for this gender difference are a greater biological vulnerability among boys and *referral bias*. That is, boys are more likely to be referred by teachers for treatment because of troublesome behaviour.

Approximately 80 percent of children with a learning disability have a reading problem (Shaywitz, Gruen, & Shaywitz, 2007). Three types of learning disabilities are dyslexia, dysgraphia, and discalculia:

- **Dyslexia** is a category reserved for individuals who have a severe impairment in their ability to read and spell (Allor & Al Otaiba, 2013; Kirk & others, 2012).

- **Dysgraphia** is a learning disability that involves difficulty in handwriting (Mason, Harris, & Graham, 2013). Children with dysgraphia may write very slowly, their writing products may be virtually illegible, and they may make numerous spelling errors because of their inability to match up sounds and letters.

- **Dyscalculia**, also known as developmental arithmetic disorder, is a learning disability that involves difficulty in math computation (Fuchs & others, 2013).

The precise causes of learning disabilities have not yet been determined (Hallahan, Kauffman, & Pullen, 2012; Lerner & Johns, 2012; Rosenberg, Westling, & McLeskey, 2011). Researchers have used brain-imaging techniques, such as magnetic resonance imaging, to reveal any regions of the brain that might be involved in learning disabilities (Shaywitz, Lyon, & Shaywitz, 2006) (see Figure 16.2). This research indicates that it is unlikely learning disabilities reside in a single, specific brain location. More likely, learning disabilities are due to problems in integrating information from multiple brain regions or subtle abnormalities in brain structures and functions.

Interventions with children who have a learning disability often focus on improving reading ability (Lovett, Barron, & Frijters, 2013; Schmitt, Justice, & Pentimonti, 2013). Intensive instruction over a period of time by a competent teacher can help many children (Berninger & Swanson, 2013).

# ATTENTION DEFICIT HYPERACTIVITY DISORDER (ADHD)

**Attention deficit hyperactivity disorder (ADHD)** is a disability in which children consistently show one or more of the following characteristics over a period of time: (1) inattention, (2) hyperactivity, and (3) impulsivity. Children who are inattentive have so much difficulty focusing on any one thing that they may get bored with a task after only a few minutes—or even seconds. Children who are hyperactive show high levels of physical activity, seeming to be almost constantly in motion. Children who are impulsive have difficulty curbing their reactions; they do not do a good job of thinking before they act. Depending on the characteristics that children with ADHD display, they can be diagnosed as (1) ADHD with predominantly inattention, (2) ADHD with predominantly hyperactivity/impulsivity, or (3) ADHD with both inattention and hyperactivity/impulsivity.

The number of children diagnosed and treated for ADHD has increased substantially in recent decades. The disorder occurs as much as four to nine times more frequently in boys than in girls. There is controversy, however, about the increased diagnosis of ADHD (Friend, 2011). Some experts attribute the increase mainly to heightened awareness of the disorder; others are concerned that many children are being incorrectly diagnosed (Parens & Johnston, 2009).

**dyslexia** A category of learning disabilities involving a severe impairment in the ability to read and spell.

**dysgraphia** A learning disability that involves difficulty in handwriting.

**dyscalculia** Also known as developmental arithmetic disorder; a learning disability that involves difficulty in math computation.

*developmental* **connection**

**Attention.** Attention, which involves the focusing of mental resources, improves cognitive processing on many tasks. Chapter 7, LO 2

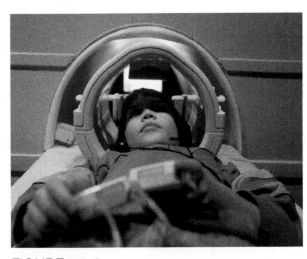

FIGURE **16.2**

**BRAIN SCANS AND LEARNING DISABILITIES.** An increasing number of studies are using MRI brain scans to examine the brain pathways involved in learning disabilities. Shown here is 9-year-old Patrick Price, who has dyslexia. Patrick is going through an MRI scanner. Inside the scanner, children must lie virtually motionless as words and symbols flash on a screen, and they are asked to identify them by clicking different buttons.

**attention deficit hyperactivity disorder (ADHD)** A disability in which children consistently show one or more of the following characteristics: (1) inattention, (2) hyperactivity, and (3) impulsivity.

Many children with ADHD show impulsive behaviour, such as this child who is getting ready to hurl a paper airplane at other children. *How would you handle this situation if you were a teacher and this happened in your classroom?*

A recent study examined the possible misdiagnosis of ADHD (Bruchmiller, Margraf, & Schneider, 2012). In this study, child psychologists, psychiatrists, and social workers were given vignettes of children with ADHD (some vignettes matched the diagnostic criteria for the disorder, while others did not). Whether each child was male or female varied. The researchers assessed whether the mental health professionals gave a diagnosis of ADHD to the child described in the vignette. The professionals overdiagnosed ADHD almost 20 percent of the time, and regardless of the symptoms described, boys were twice as likely as girls to be given a diagnosis of ADHD.

Definitive causes of ADHD have not been found. However, a number of causes have been proposed (Faraone & Mick, 2010; Swanson, Harris, & Graham, 2013). Some children likely inherit a tendency to develop ADHD from their parents (Durston, 2010; Pennington & others, 2009). Other children likely develop ADHD because of damage to their brain during prenatal or postnatal development (Linblad & Hjern, 2010). Among early possible contributors to ADHD are low birth weight and exposure to cigarette smoke and alcohol during prenatal development (Choudry & others, 2012; Knopik, 2009). For example, one study revealed cigarette smoking during pregnancy was linked to ADHD in elementary-school-aged children (Sciberras, Ukoumunne, & Efron, 2011).

As with learning disabilities, the development of brain-imaging techniques is leading to a better understanding of ADHD (Cubillo & others, 2012). One study revealed that peak thickness of the cerebral cortex occurred three years later (10.5 years) in children with ADHD than in children without ADHD (peak at 7.5 years) (Shaw & others, 2007). The delay was more prominent in the prefrontal regions of the brain that are especially important in attention and planning (see Figure 16.3). A recent study also found delayed development of the brain's frontal lobes in children with ADHD, likely due to delayed or decreased myelination (Nagel & others, 2011). Researchers also are exploring the roles that various neurotransmitters, such as serotonin and dopamine might play in ADHD (Dalley & Roiser, 2013; Shen, Liao, & Tseng, 2013).

The delays in brain development just described are in areas linked to executive functioning. An increasing focus of interest in the study of children and adolescents with ADHD is their difficulty with executive functioning tasks, such as inhibiting behaviour when necessary, use of working memory, and effective planning (Jacobson & others, 2011; Rinsky & Hinshaw, 2011; Van De Voorde & others, 2011). Researchers also have found deficits in theory of mind in children with ADHD (Buhler & others, 2011; Shuai, Chan, & Wang, 2011).

Adjustment and optimal development also are difficult for children who have ADHD, so it is important that the diagnosis be accurate. Children diagnosed with ADHD have an increased risk of school dropout, adolescent pregnancy, substance use problems, and antisocial behaviour (Chang, Lichtenstein, & Larsson, 2012; Von Polier, Vioet, & Herpertz-Dahlmann, 2012).

Stimulant medication such as Ritalin or Adderall (which has fewer side effects than Ritalin) is effective in improving the attention of many children with ADHD, but it usually does not improve their attention to the same level as children who do not have ADHD (Sclar & others, 2012). A meta-analysis concluded that behaviour management treatments are effective in reducing the effects of ADHD (Fabiano & others, 2009). Researchers have often found that a combination of medication (such as Ritalin) and behaviour management tends to improve the behaviour of children with ADHD better than medication alone or behaviour management alone, although this is not true in all cases (Parens & Johnston, 2009).

Prefrontal cortex          Prefrontal cortex

■ Greater than 2 years delay
■ 0 to 2 years delay

FIGURE **16.3**

**REGIONS OF THE BRAIN IN WHICH CHILDREN WITH ADHD HAD A DELAYED PEAK IN THE THICKNESS OF THE CEREBRAL CORTEX.** *Note:* The greatest delays occurred in the prefrontal cortex.

Recently, mindfulness training has been given to adolescents with ADHD. In a recent study, 11- to 15-year-old adolescents with ADHD were given 8 weeks of mindfulness training (van de Weijer-Bergsma & others, 2012). Immediately after and 8 weeks following the training the adolescents' attention improved and they engaged in fewer behavioural problems, although at 16 weeks post-training the effects had waned.

## EMOTIONAL AND BEHAVIOURAL DISORDERS

Most children have minor emotional difficulties at some point during their school years. A small percentage have problems so serious and persistent that they are classified as having an emotional or a behavioural disorder (Mash & Wolf, 2013).

**Emotional and behavioural disorders** consist of serious, persistent problems that involve relationships, aggression, depression, and fears associated with personal or school matters, as well as other inappropriate socioemotional characteristics. Approximately 8 percent of children who have a disability and require an individualized education plan fall into this classification. Boys are three times as likely as girls to have these disorders.

**emotional and behavioural disorders** Serious, persistent problems that involve relationships, aggression, depression, fears associated with personal or school matters, as well as other inappropriate socioemotional characteristics.

## AUTISM SPECTRUM DISORDERS

**Autism spectrum disorders** (ASD), also called pervasive developmental disorders, range from the severe disorder labeled *autistic disorder* to the milder disorder called Asperger syndrome. Autism spectrum disorders are characterized by problems in social interaction, problems in verbal and nonverbal communication, and repetitive behaviours (Hall, 2013). Children with these disorders may also show atypical responses to sensory experiences (National Institute of Mental Health, 2011). Autism spectrum disorders often can be detected in children as young as 1 to 3 years of age.

Recent estimates of autism spectrum disorders indicate that they are increasing in occurrence or are increasingly being detected and labelled (Neal, 2009). Once thought to affect only 1 in 2,500 individuals, today's estimates suggest that they occur in about 1 in 150 individuals (Centers for Disease Control and Prevention, 2012).

**Autistic disorder** is a severe developmental autism spectrum disorder that has its onset in the first three years of life and includes deficiencies in social relationships, abnormalities in communication, and restricted, repetitive, and stereotyped patterns of behaviour.

**Asperger syndrome** is a relatively mild autism spectrum disorder in which the child has relatively good verbal ability, milder nonverbal language problems, and a restricted range of interests and relationships (Soares & Patel, 2012). Children with Asperger syndrome often engage in obsessive, repetitive routines and preoccupations with a particular subject. For example, a child may be obsessed with baseball scores or railroad timetables.

What causes the autism spectrum disorders? The current consensus is that autism is a brain dysfunction with abnormalities in brain structure and neurotransmitters (Toma & others, 2012). Recently, interest has focused on a lack of connectivity between brain regions as a key factor in autism (Just & others, 2012; Philip & others, 2012). Genetic factors likely play a role in the development of the autism spectrum disorders (Yates, 2013). One study revealed that mutations—missing or duplicated pieces of DNA—on chromosome 16 can raise a child's risk of developing autism 100-fold (Weiss & others, 2008). There is no evidence that family socialization causes autism. Intellectual disability is present in some children with autism; others show average or above-average intelligence (Hoekstra & others, 2010).

**autism spectrum disorders (ASDs)** Also called pervasive developmental disorders, they range from the severe disorder labelled autistic disorder to the milder disorder called Asperger syndrome. Children with these disorders are characterized by problems in social interaction, verbal and nonverbal communication, and repetitive behaviours.

**autistic disorder** A severe developmental autism spectrum disorder that has its onset in the first three years of life and includes deficiencies in social relationships; abnormalities in communication; and restricted, repetitive, and stereotyped patterns of behaviour.

**Asperger syndrome** A relatively mild autism spectrum disorder in which the child has relatively good verbal skills, milder nonverbal language problems, and a restricted range of interests and relationships.

*What characterizes autism spectrum disorders?*

**FIGURE 16.4**

**A SCENE FROM THE DVD ANIMATIONS USED IN A STUDY BY BARON-COHEN AND OTHERS (2007).** *What did they do to improve autistic children's ability to read facial expressions?* © Crown copyright MMVI, www.thetransporters.com, courtesy of Changing Media Development

It is estimated that boys are five times as likely as girls to have autism spectrum disorders as girls (Centers for Disease Control and Prevention, 2012). Expanding on autism's male linkage, Simon Baron-Cohen (2008) recently argued that autism reflects an extreme male brain, especially indicative of males' lesser ability to show empathy and read facial expressions and gestures. In an attempt to improve these skills in 4- to 8-year-old autistic boys, Baron-Cohen and his colleagues (2007) produced a number of animations on a DVD that place faces with different emotions on toy trains and tractor characters in a boy's bedroom (see Figure 16.4). (See www.thetransporters.com for a look at a number of the facial expression animations in addition to the ones shown in Figure 16.4.) After the autistic children watched the animations 15 minutes every weekday for one month, their ability to recognize real faces in a different context equaled that of children without autism.

Children with autism benefit from a well-structured classroom, individualized instruction, and small-group instruction. Behaviour modification techniques are sometimes effective in helping autistic children learn (Iovannone, 2013). One research review concluded that when these behaviour modifications are intensely provided and used early in the autistic child's life, they are more effective (Howlin, Magiati, & Charman, 2009).

## Review *Connect* Reflect

 **LO2** Characterize children with disabilities and their education.

### Review

- Who are children with disabilities? What characterizes children with learning disabilities? How would you describe children with attention deficit hyperactivity disorder? What are emotional and behavioural disorders? What are autism spectrum disorders, what are they caused by, and how are they characterized?

### *Connect*

- In this section, you learned that exposure to cigarette smoke during prenatal development may be linked to ADHD. In Chapter 3, what were agents that can potentially cause a birth defect or negatively alter cognitive and behavioural outcomes called?

### Reflect *Your Own Personal Journey of Life*

- Think about your own schooling and how children with learning disabilities or ADHD either were or were not diagnosed. Were you aware of such individuals in your classes? Were they helped by specialists? You may know one or more individuals with a learning disability or ADHD. Ask them about their educational experiences and whether they think schools could have done a better job of helping them.

## Achievement  **LO3** Explain the development of achievement in children.

Extrinsic and Intrinsic Motivation

Cognitive Processes

In any classroom, no matter who the teacher is or what approach is used, some children achieve more than others. Why? The reasons for variations in achievement include motivation, expectations, goals, and other characteristics of the child as well as sociocultural contexts.

# EXTRINSIC AND INTRINSIC MOTIVATION

**Extrinsic motivation** involves external incentives such as rewards and punishments. **Intrinsic motivation** is based on internal factors such as self-determination, curiosity, challenge, and effort. Cognitive approaches stress the importance of intrinsic motivation in achievement. Some students study hard because they want to make good grades or avoid parental disapproval (extrinsic motivation). Other students work hard because they are internally motivated to achieve high standards in their work (intrinsic motivation).

Current evidence strongly favours establishing a classroom climate in which students are intrinsically motivated to learn (Eccles & Roeser, 2013; Weinstein, Deci, & Ryan, 2011). For example, a study of third- through eighth-grade students found that intrinsic motivation was positively linked with grades and standardized test scores, whereas extrinsic motivation was negatively related to achievement outcomes (Lepper, Corpus, & Iyengar, 2005). Moreover, a longitudinal study revealed that parental intrinsic/extrinsic motivational practices were linked to children's motivation (Gottfried & others, 2009). In this study, children had higher intrinsic motivation in math and science from 9 to 17 years of age when their parents engaged in task-intrinsic practices (encouraging children's pleasure and engagement in learning) than when their parents engaged in task-extrinsic practices (providing external rewards and consequences contingent on children's performance).

Students are more motivated to learn when they are given choices, become absorbed in challenges that match their skills, and receive rewards that have informational value but are not used for control. Praise also can enhance students' intrinsic motivation. To see why these things are so, let's first explore three perspectives on intrinsic motivation: (1) self-determination and personal choice, (2) interest, and (3) cognitive engagement and self-responsibility. Then we'll discuss how external rewards can either enhance or undermine intrinsic motivation. Finally, we will offer some concluding thoughts about intrinsic and extrinsic motivation.

### Self-Determination, Personal Choice and Self-Responsibility
One view of intrinsic motivation emphasizes self-determination (Deci & Ryan, 2000; Ryan & Deci, 2009; Mclellan & Remedios, 2011; Weinstein, Deci, & Ryan, 2011). In this view, students want to believe that they are doing something because of their own will, not because of external success or rewards (Vansteenkiste & others, 2009). The architects of self-determination theory, Richard Ryan and Edward Deci (2009) refer to teachers who create circumstances for students to engage in self-determination as *autonomy-supportive teachers*. A recent study of 34 high school classrooms found that students who perceived their classrooms as allowing and encouraging autonomy in the first several weeks of the semester increased their engagement throughout the course (Hafen & others, 2012).

Researchers have found that students' internal motivation and intrinsic interest in school tasks increase when students have some choice and are given opportunities to take personal responsibility for their learning (Perry, 2013; Perry & Rahim, 2011). The goal is to get students to become motivated to expend the effort to persist and master ideas rather than simply doing enough work to just get by and make passing grades. Especially important in encouraging students to become cognitively engaged and responsible for their learning is to embed subject matter content and skills learning within meaningful contexts, especially real-world situations that mesh with students' interests (Eccles & Roeser, 2013).

### Some Final Thoughts About Intrinsic and Extrinsic Motivation
It is important for parents and teachers to encourage students to become intrinsically motivated and to create learning environments that promote students' cognitive engagement and self-responsibility for learning (Perry, 2013; Perry & Rahim,

**extrinsic motivation** Response to external incentives such as rewards and punishments.

**intrinsic motivation** Internal motivational factors such as self-determination, curiosity, challenge, and effort.

These students were given an opportunity to write and perform their own play. These kinds of self-determining opportunities can enhance students' motivation to achieve.

# Calvin and Hobbes

**by Bill Watterson**

2011). That said, the real world is not just one of intrinsic motivation, and too often intrinsic and extrinsic motivation have been pitted against each other as polar opposites. In many aspects of students' lives, both intrinsic and extrinsic motivation are at work (Cameron & Pierce, 2008; Schunk, 2012). Keep in mind, though, that many psychologists recommend that extrinsic motivation by itself is not a good strategy.

## COGNITIVE PROCESSES

Our discussion of extrinsic and intrinsic motivation sets the stage for introducing other cognitive processes involved in motivating students to learn. As we explore these additional cognitive processes, notice how intrinsic and extrinsic motivation continue to be important. The processes are (1) sustained attention, effort, and task persistence; (2) mastery motivation and mindset; (3) self-efficacy; (4) expectations; and (5) goal setting, planning, and self-monitoring; and (6) purpose.

**Sustained Attention, Effort, and Task Persistence**    Of course, it is important not only to perceive that effort is an important aspect of achieving, but also to actually engage in sustained attention, effort, and task persistence in school, work, and a career (Padilla-Walker & others, 2013). Recall from Chapter 7 that sustained attention is the ability to maintain attention to a selected stimulus for a prolonged period of time. Sustained attention requires effort and as individuals develop through adolescence, school tasks, projects, and work become more complex and require longer periods of sustained attention, effort, and task persistence than in childhood.

Might the extent to which adolescents persist at tasks be linked to how successful they are in a career as an adult? One study revealed that task persistence at 13 years of age was related to occupational success in middle age (Andersson & Bergman, 2011).

**Mastery Motivation and Mindset**    Becoming cognitively engaged and self-motivated to improve are reflected in adolescents with a mastery motivation. These children also have a growth mindset—a belief that they can produce positive outcomes if they put forth the effort.

*Mastery Motivation*    Developmental psychologists Valanne Henderson and Carol Dweck (1990) have found that children often show two distinct responses to difficult or challenging circumstances. Children who display **mastery motivation**

**mastery motivation** An orientation in which one is task oriented, focusing on learning strategies and the achievement process rather than ability or the outcome.

are task oriented; they concentrate on learning strategies and the process of achievement rather than their ability or the outcome. Those with a **helpless orientation** seem trapped by the experience of difficulty, and they attribute their difficulty to lack of ability. They frequently say such things as "I'm not very good at this," even though they might earlier have demonstrated their ability through many successes. And, once they view their behaviour as failure, they often feel anxious, and their performance worsens even further. Figure 16.5 describes some behaviours that might reflect helplessness (Stipek, 2002).

In contrast, mastery-oriented children often instruct themselves to pay attention, to think carefully, and to remember strategies that have worked for them in previous situations. They frequently report feeling challenged and excited by difficult tasks, rather than being threatened by them (Anderman, 2012; Dweck, 2013).

Another issue in motivation involves whether to adopt a mastery or a performance orientation. Children with a **performance orientation** are focused on winning, rather than on achievement outcome, and believe that happiness results from winning. Does this mean that mastery-oriented children do not like to win and that performance-oriented children are not motivated to experience the self-efficacy that comes from being able to take credit for one's accomplishments? No. A matter of emphasis or degree is involved, though. For mastery-oriented individuals, winning isn't everything; for performance-oriented individuals, skill development and self-efficacy take a back seat to winning. One study of seventh-grade students found that girls were more likely than boys to have mastery rather than performance goals in their approach to math achievement (Kenny-Benson & others, 2006).

A final point needs to be made about mastery and performance goals: They are not always mutually exclusive. Students can be both mastery and performance oriented, and researchers have found that mastery goals combined with performance goals often enhance students' success (Schunk, 2012).

*Mindset*  Carol Dweck's (2006, 2007) analysis of motivation for achievement stresses the importance of children developing a **mindset**, which she defines as the cognitive view individuals develop for themselves. She concludes that individuals have one of two mindsets: (1) *fixed mindset*, in which they believe that their qualities are carved in stone and cannot change; or (2) *growth mindset*, in which they believe their qualities can change and improve through their effort. A fixed mindset is similar to a helpless orientation; a growth mindset is much like having mastery motivation (Dweck, 2007, 2013).

In her book *Mindset*, Dweck (2006) argued that individuals' mindsets influence whether they will be optimistic or pessimistic, shape their goals and how hard they will strive to reach those goals, and affect many aspects of their lives, including achievement and success in school and sports. Dweck says that mindsets begin to be shaped as children interact with parents, teachers, and coaches, who themselves have either a fixed mindset or a growth mindset. She described the growth mindset of Patricia Miranda:

> [She] was a chubby, unathletic school kid who wanted to wrestle. After a bad beating on the mat, she was told, "You're a joke." First she cried, then she felt: "That really set my resolve . . . I had to keep going and had to know if effort and focus and belief and training could somehow legitimize me as a wrestler." Where did she get this resolve?
>
> Miranda was raised in a life devoid of challenge. But when her mother died of an aneurysm at age forty, ten-year-old Miranda . . . [thought] "If you only go through life doing stuff that's easy, shame on you." So when wrestling presented a challenge, she was ready to take it on. Her effort paid off. At twenty-four, Miranda was having the last laugh. She won a spot on the U.S. Olympic team and came home from Athens with a bronze medal. And what was next? Yale Law School. People urged her to stay where she was already on top, but Miranda felt it was more exciting to start at the bottom again and see what she could grow into this time. (Dweck, 2006, pp. 22–23)

**The student:**
- Says "I can't"
- Doesn't pay attention to teacher's instructions
- Doesn't ask for help, even when it is needed
- Does nothing (for example, stares out the window)
- Guesses or answers randomly without really trying
- Doesn't show pride in successes
- Appears bored, uninterested
- Is unresponsive to teacher's exhortations to try
- Is easily discouraged
- Doesn't volunteer answers to teacher's questions
- Maneuvers to get out of or to avoid work (for example, has to go to the nurse's office)

## FIGURE **16.5**
**BEHAVIOURS THAT SUGGEST A HELPLESS ORIENTATION.**

**helpless orientation** An orientation in which one seems trapped by the experience of difficulty and attributes one's difficulty to a lack of ability.

**performance orientation** An orientation in which one focuses on winning rather than achievement outcomes, and happiness is thought to result from winning.

**mindset** Dweck's concept that refers to the cognitive view individuals develop for themselves; individuals have either a fixed or growth mindset.

Patricia Miranda (*in blue*) winning the bronze medal in the 2004 Olympics. *What characterizes her growth mindset and how is it different from someone with a fixed mindset?*

Related to her emphasis on encouraging students to develop a growth mindset, Dweck and her colleagues (Blackwell & Dweck, 2008; Blackwell, Trzesniewski, & Dweck, 2007; Dweck, 2013; Dweck & Master, 2009) have recently incorporated information about the brain's plasticity into their effort to improve students' motivation to achieve and succeed. In one study, they assigned two groups of students to eight sessions of either (1) study skills instruction or (2) study skills instruction plus information about the importance of developing a growth mindset (called incremental theory in the research) (Blackwell & others, 2007). One of the exercises in the growth mindset group was titled You Can Grow Your Brain, which emphasized that the brain is like a muscle that can change and grow as it gets exercise and develops new connections. Students were informed that the more you challenge your brain to learn, the more your brain cells grow. Both groups had a pattern of declining math scores prior to the intervention. Following the intervention, the group who only received the study skills instruction continued to decline, but the group that received the combination of study skills instruction plus the growth mindset information reversed the downward trend and improved their math achievement.

In other work, Dweck has been creating a computer-based workshop, Brainology, to teach students that their intelligence can change (Blackwell & Dweck, 2008; Dweck, 2012). Students experience six modules about how the brain works and how they can make their brains improve. After being tested in 20 New York City schools, students strongly endorsed the value of the computer-based brain modules. Said one student, "I will try harder because I know that the more you try the more your brain knows" (Dweck & Master, 2009, p. 137).

Dweck and her colleagues (Good, Rattan, & Dweck, 2012) also recently have found that a growth mindset can prevent negative stereotypes from undermining achievement. For example, they found that believing math ability can be learned protected women from negative gender stereotyping about math. And other research indicated that willpower is a virtually unlimited mindset that predicts how long people will work and resist temptations during successful circumstances (Dweck, 2012; Job, Dweck, & Walton, 2010; Miller & others, 2012).

**Self-Efficacy**   Like having a growth mindset, **self-efficacy**—the belief that one can master a situation and produce favorable outcomes—is an important cognitive view for children to develop. Canadian-born psychologist Albert Bandura (1997, 2000, 2004, 2008, 2009, 2010, 2012), whose social cognitive theory we described in Chapter 1, argues that self-efficacy is a critical factor in whether or not children achieve. Self-efficacy has much in common with mastery motivation. Self-efficacy is the belief that "I can"; helplessness is the belief that "I cannot" (Stipek, 2002). Children with high self-efficacy agree with statements such as "I know that I will be able to learn the material in this class" and "I expect to be able to do well at this activity."

Dale Schunk (2008, 2012) has applied the concept of self-efficacy to many aspects of students' achievement. In his view, self-efficacy influences a student's choice of activities. Students with low self-efficacy for learning might avoid many learning tasks, especially those that are challenging. In contrast, their high-self-efficacy counterparts eagerly work at learning tasks. High-self-efficacy students are more likely to expend effort and persist longer at a learning task than low-self-efficacy students. High-self-efficacy students are more likely to have confidence in exploring challenging career options (Betz, 2004).

Children's and adolescents' development is influenced by their parents' self-efficacy. For example, one study revealed a number of positive developmental outcomes, including more daily opportunities for optimal functioning, better peer relations, and fewer problems, for children and adolescents whose parents had high self-efficacy (Steca & others, 2011).

**Expectations**   Children's motivation, and likely their performance, are influenced by the expectations that their parents, teachers, and other adults have for

*developmental* **connection**

**Cognitive Theory.** Social cognitive theory holds that behaviour, environment, and person/cognitive factors are the key influences on development. Chapter 1, LO 4

**self-efficacy** The belief that one can master a situation and produce favourable outcomes.

They can because they think they can.

—Virgil
*Roman Poet, 1st Century BC*

their achievement. Children benefit when both parents and teachers have high expectations for them and provide the necessary support for them to meet those expectations. An especially important factor in the lower achievement of students from low-income families is lack of adequate resources, such as an up-to-date computer in the home (or even any computer at all) to support students' learning (Schunk, Pintrich, & Meece, 2008).

Teachers' expectations influence students' motivation and performance (Eccles & Roeser, 2013). "When teachers hold high generalized expectations for student achievement and students perceive these expectations, students achieve more, experience a greater sense of self-esteem and competence as learners, and resist involvement in problem behaviours both during childhood and adolescence" (Wigfield & others, 2006, p. 976). In an observational study of twelve classrooms, teachers with high expectations spent more time providing a framework for students' learning, asked higher-level questions, and were more effective in managing students' behaviour than teachers with average and low expectations (Rubie-Davies, 2007).

*How do teachers' expectations influence students' achievement?*

In thinking about teachers' expectations, it also is important to examine these expectations in concert with parents' expectations. For example, one study revealed that mothers' and teachers' high expectations had a positive effect on youths' achievement outcomes, and further that mothers' high achievement expectations for their youth had a buffering effect in the face of low teacher expectations (Benner & Mistry, 2007). Interestingly, in another study, teachers' positive expectations for students' achievement tended to protect students from the negative influence of low parental expectations (Wood, Kaplan, & McLoyd, 2007).

Teachers often have more positive expectations for high-ability than for low-ability students, and these expectations are likely to influence their behaviour toward them. For example, teachers require high-ability students to work harder, wait longer for them to respond to questions, respond to them with more information and in a more elaborate fashion, criticize them less often, praise them more often, are more friendly to them, call on them more often, seat them closer to the teachers' desks, and are more likely to give them the benefit of the doubt on close calls in grading than they are for students with low ability (Brophy, 2004). An important strategy for teachers is to monitor their expectations and be sure to have positive expectations for students with low abilities. Fortunately, researchers have found that with support teachers can adapt and raise their expectations for students with low abilities (National Research Council, 2004).

**Goal Setting, Planning, and Self-Monitoring** Goal setting, planning, and self-monitoring are important aspects of children's and adolescents' achievement (Eccles & Roeser, 2013; Urdan, 2010). Researchers have found that self-efficacy and achievement improve when individuals set goals that are specific, proximal, and challenging (Bandura, 1997). An example of a nonspecific, fuzzy goal is "I want to be successful." A more concrete, specific goal is "I want to make the honor roll at the end of this semester."

Individuals can set both long-term (distal) and short-term (proximal) goals. It is okay to set some long-term goals, such as "I want to graduate from high school" or "I want to go to university," but it also is important to create short-term goals, which are steps along the way. "Getting an A on the next math test" is an example of a short-term, proximal goal. So is "Doing all of my homework by 4 p.m. Sunday."

Another good strategy is to set challenging goals. A challenging goal is a commitment to self-improvement. Strong interest and involvement in activities is sparked by challenges. Goals that are easy to reach generate little interest or effort. However, goals should be optimally matched to the adolescent's skill level. If goals are unrealistically high, the result will be repeated failures that lower self-efficacy.

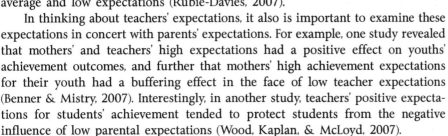

Life is a gift . . . Accept it.
Life is an adventure . . . Dare it.
Life is a mystery . . . Unfold it.
Life is a struggle . . . Face it.
Life is a puzzle . . . Solve it.
Life is an opportunity . . . Take it.
Life is a mission . . . Fulfill it.
Life is a goal . . . Achieve it.

—AUTHOR UNKNOWN

Yet another good strategy is to develop personal goals about desired and undesired future circumstances (Wigfield & Cambria, 2010). Personal goals can be a key aspect of an individual's motivation for coping and dealing with life's challenges and opportunities (Maehr & Zusho, 2009).

It is not enough to simply set goals. It also is important to plan how to reach the goals (Urdan, 2010). Being a good planner means managing time effectively, setting priorities, and being organized.

Researchers have found that high-achieving individuals often are self-regulatory learners (Perry, 2013; Perry & Rahim, 2011). For example, high-achieving students self-monitor their learning more and systematically evaluate their progress toward a goal more than low-achieving students do. When parents and teachers encourage students to self-monitor their learning, they give them the message that they are responsible for their own behaviour and that learning requires their active, dedicated participation (Zimmerman, Bonner, & Kovach, 1996).

One type of self-regulation is *intentional self-regulation*, which involves selecting goals or outcomes, optimizing the means to achieve desired outcomes, and compensating for setbacks along the path to goal achievement (Gestsdottir & others, 2009). A recent study found that intentional self-regulation was especially beneficial to young adolescents from low-income backgrounds (Urban, Lewin-Bizan, & Lerner, 2010). In this study, these high self-regulating adolescents were more likely to seek out extracurricular activities, which resulted in more positive developmental outcomes such as academic achievement. Selecting goals or outcomes was assessed by items such as, "When I decide upon a goal, I stick to it"; optimizing the means to achieve desired outcomes was assessed by items such as, "I think exactly about how I can best realize my plans"; and compensating for setbacks was assessed by items such as, "When things don't work the way they used to, I look for other ways to achieve them."

Barry Zimmerman and his colleagues (Zimmerman, 2002, 2012; Zimmerman & Kitsantas, 1997; Zimmerman & Labuhn, 2012) have developed a model of self-regulation in achievement contexts that has three phrases:

- *Forethought.* Adolescents assess task demands, set goals, and estimate their ability to reach the goals.
- *Performance.* Adolescents create self-regulating strategies such as managing time, attentional focusing, help seeking, and metacognition.
- *Self-Reflection.* Adolescents evaluate their performance, including attributions about factors that affected the outcome and how satisfied they are with their behaviour.

In addition to planning and self-regulation/monitoring, delaying gratification is an important aspect of reaching goals—especially long-term goals (Cheng, Shein, & Chiou, 2012; Schlam & others, 2013). Delayed gratification involves postponing immediate rewards in order to attain a larger, more valuable reward at a later point in time. While adolescents may find it more appealing to hang out with friends today than to work on a project that is due for a class assignment later in the week, their decision not to delay gratification can have negative consequences for their academic achievement.

**Purpose**   In Chapter 11, "The Self and Identity," we discussed William Damon's (2008) ideas on the importance of purpose in identity development. Here we explore how purpose is a missing ingredient in many adolescents' and emerging adults' achievement.

For Damon, *purpose* is an intention to accomplish something meaningful to oneself and to contribute something to the world beyond the self. Finding purpose involves answering questions such as "*Why* am I doing this? *Why* does it matter? *Why* is it important for me and the world beyond me? *Why* do I strive to accomplish this end?" (Damon, 2008, pp. 33–34).

In interviews with 12- to 22-year-olds, Damon found that only about 20 percent had a clear vision of where they wanted to go in life, what they wanted to achieve, and why. The largest percentage—about 60 percent—had engaged in some potentially purposeful activities, such as service learning or fruitful discussions with a career counsellor, but they still did not have a real commitment or any reasonable plans for reaching their goals. And slightly more than 20 percent expressed no aspirations and in some instances said they didn't see any reason to have aspirations.

Damon concludes that most teachers and parents communicate the importance of goals such as studying hard and getting good grades, but rarely discuss what the goals might lead to—the purpose for studying hard and getting good grades. Damon emphasizes that too often students focus only on short-term goals without exploring the big, long-term picture of what they want to do in life. The following interview questions that Damon (2008, p. 135) has used in his research are good springboards for getting students to reflect on their purpose:

What's most important to you in your life?

Why do you care about those things?

Do you have any long-term goals?

Why are these goals important to you?

What does it mean to have a good life?

What does it mean to be a good person?

If you were looking back on your life now, how would you like to be remembered?

Hari Prabhakar (*in rear*) at a screening camp in India that he created as part of his Tribal India Health Foundation. Hari Prabhakar reflects William Damon's concept of finding a path to purpose. Hari's ambition is to become an international health expert. Hari graduated from Johns Hopkins University in 2006 with a double major in public health and writing. A top student (3.9 GPA), he took the initiative to pursue a number of activities outside the classroom, in the health field. As he made the transition from high school to college, Hari created the Tribal India Health Foundation (www.tihf.org), which provides assistance in bringing low-cost health care to rural areas in India. Juggling his roles as a student and as the foundation's director, Hari spent about 15 hours a week leading Tribal India Health throughout his four undergraduate years.

In describing his work, Hari said (Johns Hopkins University, 2006):

I have found it very challenging to coordinate the international operation. . . . It takes a lot of work, and there's not a lot of free time. But it's worth it when I visit our patients and see how they and the community are getting better.

(*Sources:* Johns Hopkins University (2006); Prabhakar (2007)).

## Review *Connect* Reflect

 **LO3** Explain the development of achievement in children.

### Review

- What are intrinsic and extrinsic motivation? How are they related to achievement?
- What role do mastery motivation and mindset play in children's achievement?
- What is self-efficacy, and how is it related to achievement? How are expectations involved in children's achievement? Why are goal setting, planning, and self-monitoring important in achievement? What is purpose and how is it involved in achieving?

### *Connect*

- In this section, you learned about the importance of purpose in adolescents' and emerging adults' achievement. In Chapter 11, what did Damon identify as some of the possible negative outcomes of not having purpose?

### Reflect *Your Own Personal Journey of Life*

- Think about several of your own past schoolmates who showed low motivation in school. Why do you think they behaved that way? What teaching strategies might have helped them?

## Technology  **LO4** Summarize the influence of technology on children's development.

| Media Use and Screen Time | Television and Electronic Media | Computers and the Internet |

Few developments in society over the last 40 years have had a greater impact on adolescents than television and the Internet (Gross, 2013; Roblyer & Doering, 2013). The persuasion capabilities of television and the Internet are staggering.

Many of today's adolescents have spent more time since infancy in front of a television set, and more recently in front of a computer, than with their parents or in the classroom. Canadian youth spend an average of 4.5 hours a day in front of a screen (Baer & others, 2012). Although television continues to have a strong influence on adolescents, their increasing use of other media and information/communication devices has led to the creation of the term *screen time*, which encompasses how much time they spend watching/using television, DVDs, computers, video game systems, and mobile media such as smartphones (De Decker & others, 2012).

## MEDIA USE AND SCREEN TIME

More than likely, the technology revolution is affecting children and adolescents in both positive and negative ways. Technology can provide expansive knowledge and can be used in a constructive way to enhance children's and adolescents' education (Maloy & others, 2014). However, according to Mark Bauerlein (2008), there are possible downsides of technology. Many of today's youth are more interested in information retrieval than information formation, don't read books and aren't motivated to read them, can't spell without spellcheck, and have become encapsulated in a world of cell phones, iPods, text messaging, Facebook, YouTube, and other technology contexts. In terms of retaining general information and historical facts, Bauerlein may be correct. However, in terms of cognitive skills such as thinking and reasoning, Bauerlein likely is wrong given that IQ scores have been rising significantly since the 1930s (Flynn, 2007, 2013). Further, there is no research evidence that being immersed in a technological world of iPods and YouTube impairs thinking skills (Begley & Interlandi, 2008). In fact, a Canadian study found that adolescents' use of text messaging had no association with spelling ability (Varnhagen & others, 2010).

A major trend in the use of technology is the dramatic increase in media multitasking (Brown & Bobkowski, 2011; Levinson, 2013). One study found that when the amount of time spent multitasking was included in total media use, 11- to 14-year-olds spent nearly 12 hours a day (compared with almost 9 hours a day when multitasking was not included) exposed to media (Rideout, Foehr, & Roberts, 2010). In this survey, 39 percent of seventh- to twelfth-graders said "most of the time" they use two or more media concurrently, such as surfing the Web while listening to music. In some cases, media multitasking—such as text messaging, listening to an iPod, and updating a YouTube site—is engaged in at the same time as doing homework. It is hard to imagine that this allows a student to do homework efficiently, although there is little research on media multitasking. Another study that compared heavy and light media multitaskers revealed that heavy media multitaskers were more susceptible to interference from irrelevant information (Ophir, Nass, & Wagner, 2009). Further, a recent study of 8- to 12-year-old girls also found that a higher level of media multitasking was linked to negative social well-being, while a higher level of face-to-face communication was associated with positive social well-being indicators, such as greater social success, feeling more normal, and having fewer friends whom parents thought were a bad influence (Pea & others, 2012). Mobile media, such as cell phones and iPods, are mainly driving the increased media use by adolescents. For example, one study found that in 2004, only 18 percent of youth owned an iPod or MP3 player; in 2009, 76 percent owned them; in 2004, 39 percent owned a cell phone, a figure that jumped to 66 percent in 2009 (Rideout, Foehr, & Roberts, 2010).

## TELEVISION AND ELECTRONIC MEDIA

Few developments during the second half of the twentieth century had a greater impact on children than television (Maloy & others, 2014). And in the last several decades, children increasingly have played video games (De Wall, Anderson, & Bushman, 2013).

**Television** Many children spend more time in front of the television set than they do with their parents. Although it is only one of the many mass media that affect children's behaviour, television may be the most influential. The persuasive capabilities of television are staggering.

Television can have positive or negative effects on children's and adolescents' development. Television can have a positive influence by presenting motivating educational programs, increasing children's and adolescents' information about the world beyond their immediate environment, and providing models of prosocial behaviour (Schmidt & Vandewater, 2008; Wilson, 2008). However, television can have a negative influence on children and adolescents by making them passive learners, distracting them from doing homework, teaching them stereotypes, providing them with violent models of aggression, and presenting them with unrealistic views of the world (Murray & Murray, 2008). Further, researchers have found that a high level of TV viewing is linked to a greater incidence of obesity in children and adolescents (Escobar-Chaves & Anderson, 2008). In one study, sleep problems were more common in 3- to 5-year-old children who (1) watched TV after 7 p.m., and (2) watched TV shows with violence (Garrison, Liekweg, & Christakis, 2011). Next, we will further explore the influence of media violence on children's development.

A research review concluded that children and adolescents who experience a heavy media diet of violence are more likely to perceive the world as a dangerous place and to view aggression as more acceptable than their counterparts who see media violence less frequently (Wilson, 2008). Another research review concluded that there is strong evidence that media violence is a risk factor for aggressive behaviour but less evidence linking it to juvenile delinquency and crime (Escobar-Chaves & Anderson, 2008). Much of the media violence described in these two research reviews comes from television, but as we see next, it also includes violent video games.

**Video Games** Canadian boys play an average of two hours of video games each day compared to an average of one hour for girls (Baer & others, 2012). Violent video games, especially those that are highly realistic, also raise concerns about their effects on children and adolescents (DeWall, Anderson, & Bushman, 2013). Correlational studies indicate that children and adolescents who extensively play violent electronic games are more aggressive and more likely to engage in delinquent acts than are their counterparts who spend less time playing the games or do not play them at all (DeWall, Anderson, & Bushman, 2013; Gentile, 2011). A recent Canadian longitudinal study found that video game use significantly predicted physical violence among youth, even when controlling for time spent watch television or using the computer (Janssen, Boyce, & Pickett, 2012).

Are there any positive outcomes when adolescents play video games? Far more studies of video game use by adolescents have focused on possible negative outcomes, but an increasing number of studies are examining possible positive outcomes (Adachi & Willoughby, 2012). For example, researchers have found that middle-school students who played prosocial video games subsequently behaved in more prosocial ways (Gentile & others, 2009). Research also indicates that playing video games can improve adolescents' visuospatial skills (Schmidt & Vandewater, 2008).

Further, researchers have found that video games requiring exercise (exergames) are linked to weight loss in overweight adolescents (Bond, Richards, & Calvert, 2013; Calvert, Bond, & Staiano, 2013). For example, a recent experimental

How does television viewing affect children's development?

How might playing violent video games be linked to aggression?

*developmental* **connection**

**Moral Development.** Prosocial behaviour is behaviour that is intended to help other people. Chapter 13, LO 3

What have researchers found about TV watching by infants?

study found that overweight adolescents lost more weight when they participated in a 10-week competitive exergame video condition (video games that require gross motor activity—in this study the Nintendo Wii EA Sports Active video game was used) than their overweight counterparts in a cooperative exergame condition or a no video game play control condition (Staiano, Abraham, & Calvert, 2012). The weight loss in the competitive condition also was linked to improved executive functioning in this study.

**Electronic Media, Learning, and Achievement** The effects of electronic media on children depend on the child's age and the type of media. A research review reached the following conclusions about infants and young children (Kirkorian, Wartella, & Anderson, 2008):

- *Infancy:* Learning from electronic media is difficult for infants and toddlers, and they learn much more easily from direct experiences with people.
- *Early childhood:* At about 3 years of age, children can learn from electronic media with educational material if the media use effective strategies, such as repeating concepts a number of times, using images and sounds that capture young children's attention, and speaking with the voices of children rather than adults. However, the vast majority of media young children experience is entertainment rather than education oriented.

The American Academy of Pediatrics (2001) has recommended that children under 2 years of age should not watch television because it likely reduces direct interactions with parents. One study found that the more hours 1- and 3-year-olds watched TV per day, the more likely they were to have attention problems at 7 years of age (Christakis & others, 2004), and another study also revealed that daily TV exposure at 18 months was linked to increased inattention/hyperactivity at 30 months of age (Cheng & others, 2010). A study of 2- to 48-month-olds indicated that each hour of audible TV was linked to a reduction in child vocalizations (Christakis & others, 2009) and another study revealed that 8- to 16-month-olds who viewed baby DVDs/videos had poor language development (Zimmerman, Christakis, & Meltzoff, 2007). A recent recommendation stated that for children 2 to 4 years of age screen time should be limited to no more than 1 hour per day (Tremblay & others, 2012). Many children spend more time with various screen media than they do interacting with their parents and peers.

How does television influence children's attention, creativity, and mental ability? Overall, media use has not been found to cause attention deficit hyperactivity disorder, but a small link has been identified between heavy television viewing and nonclinical reduced attention levels in children (Schmidt & Vandewater, 2008).

Are media use and screen time linked to children's and adolescents' creativity? A research review concluded that there is a negative association between children's and adolescents' TV viewing and their creativity (Calvert & Valkenberg, 2011). An exception, though, occurs when they watch educational TV content that is designed to teach creativity through the use of imaginative characters (Calvert & Valkenberg, 2011).

The more children watch TV, the lower their school achievement (Comstock & Scharrer, 2006). Why might TV watching be negatively linked to children's achievement? Three possibilities involve interference, displacement, and self-defeating tastes/preferences (Comstock & Scharrer, 2006). In terms of interference, having a television on while doing homework can distract children while they are doing cognitive tasks. In terms of displacement, television can take away time and attention from engaging in achievement-related tasks, such as homework, reading, writing, and mathematics. Researchers have found that children's reading achievement is negatively linked with the amount of time they watch TV (Comstock & Scharrer, 2006). In terms of self-defeating tastes and preferences, television attracts children to entertainment, sports, commercials, and other activities that capture their interest more than school achievement. Children who are heavy TV watchers tend to view books as dull and boring (Comstock & Scharrer, 2006).

However, some types of television content—such as educational programming for young children—may enhance achievement. In one longitudinal study, viewing educational programs, such as *Sesame Street* and *Mr. Rogers' Neighborhood*, as preschoolers was related to a number of positive outcomes through high school, including higher grades, reading of more books, and enhanced creativity (Anderson & others, 2001) (see Figure 16.6). Newer technologies, especially interactive television, hold promise for motivating children to learn and become more exploratory in solving problems.

## COMPUTERS AND THE INTERNET

Between 93 to 95 percent of Canadian adolescents use the Internet (Willoughby, 2008). Culture involves change, and nowhere is that change greater than in the technological revolution individuals are experiencing with increased use of computers and the Internet (Jackson & others, 2012; Maloy & others, 2014). Society still relies on some basic nontechnological competencies—for example, good communication skills, positive attitudes, and the ability to solve problems and to think deeply and creatively. But how people pursue these competencies is changing in ways and at a speed that few people had to cope with in previous eras. For youth to be adequately prepared for tomorrow's jobs, technology needs to become an integral part of their lives (Edwards, 2014; Gross, 2013).

The digitally mediated social environment of youth includes email, instant messaging, texting, social networking sites such as Facebook, Tumblr, and Twitter, chat rooms, videosharing and photosharing, multiplayer online computer games, and virtual worlds. The remarkable increase in the popularity of Facebook was reflected in its replacement of Google in 2010 as the most frequently visited Internet site. Most of these digitally mediated social interactions began on computers but more recently have also shifted to cell phones, especially smartphones (Valkenburg & Peter, 2011).

Text messaging has now become the main way that adolescents connect with their friends, surpassing face-to-face contact, email, instant messaging, and voice calling (Lenhart & others, 2010). However, voice mail is the primary way that most adolescents prefer to connect with parents.

Special concerns have emerged about children's and adolescents' access to information on the Internet, which has been largely unregulated. Youth can access adult sexual material, instructions for making bombs, and other information that is inappropriate for them. Lucia O'Sullivan at the University of New Brunswick has recently raised concerns about adolescents' tendency to perceive their online behaviour as private, particularly in the sense that their parents may be unaware of what they are doing online, when in fact online behaviour is typically open to the public (O'Sullivan, 2012).

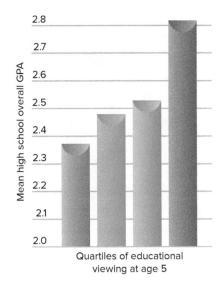

## FIGURE 16.6

**EDUCATIONAL TV VIEWING IN EARLY CHILDHOOD AND HIGH SCHOOL GRADE-POINT AVERAGE FOR BOYS.** When boys watched more educational television (especially *Sesame Street*) as preschoolers, they had higher grade-point averages in high school. The graph displays the boys' early TV viewing patterns in quartiles and the means of their grade-point averages. The bar on the left is for the lowest 25 percent of boys who viewed educational TV programs, the next bar the next 25 percent, and so on, with the bar on the right for the 25 percent of the boys who watched the most educational TV shows as preschoolers. Source: Anderson & others (2009).

## developmental **connection**

**Media Influence.** Significant numbers of children are victimized by bullies, and bullying has a number of negative outcomes for children. Chapter 15, LO 1

*What characterizes the online social environment of adolescents?*

One study of post-secondary students—mean age 20 years old—found that when the Internet was used for shopping, entertainment, and pornography, negative outcomes included higher levels of drinking and drug use, greater numbers of sexual partners, worse relationships with friends and parents, and lower self-worth; however, when students used the Internet for school-work, positive outcomes included a lower level of drug use and higher self-worth (Padilla-Walker & others, 2010). Does computer and Internet use affect the quality of adolescents' friendships? To find out, see *Connecting Through Research*.

Clearly, adolescents' use of the Internet requires parental monitoring and regulation (Jackson & others, 2012; Padilla-Walker & others, 2012). Consider Bonita Williams, who began to worry about how obsessed her 15-year-old daughter, Jade, had become with MySpace (Kornblum, 2006). She became even more concerned when she discovered that Jade was posting suggestive photos of herself and giving her cell phone number to people in different parts of the country. She grounded her daughter, blocked MySpace at home, and moved Jade's computer from her bedroom to the family room.

The following studies explored the role of parents in guiding adolescents' use of the Internet and other media:

- Parents' high estimates of online dangers were not matched by their low rates of setting limits and monitoring their adolescents' online activities (Rosen, Cheever, & Carrier, 2008). Also in this study, adolescents who perceived that their parents had an indulgent parenting style (high warmth and involvement but low levels of strictness and supervision) reported engaging in the most risky online behaviour, such as meeting someone in person whom they had initially contacted on the Internet.

- Both maternal and paternal authoritative parenting predicted proactive monitoring of adolescent media use, including restriction of certain media from adolescent use and parent-adolescent discussion of exposure to questionable media content (Padilla-Walker & Coyne, 2011).

- Problematic mother-adolescent (age 13) relationships (such as insecure attachment and autonomy conflicts) predicted emerging adults' preference for online communication and greater probability of forming a relationship of poor quality with someone they met online (Szwedo, Mikami, & Allen, 2011).

## connecting through research

### Does Computer and Internet Use Affect the Quality of Adolescents' Friendships?

Research by Teena Willoughby (2008) at Brock University has shown that greater Internet use is linked with higher ratings of self-reported friendship quality. In a study by Teena Willoughby and her colleague, the researchers explored whether using a computer with friends and online chatting affected adolescents' friendship quality (Desjarlais & Willoughby, 2010). In this study, adolescent girls who used a computer with friends or chatted online with friends reported more positive friendship quality than those who used the computer or Internet less frequently. For boys, computer use with friends and online chatting did not affect adolescents' friendship quality. However, higher levels of computer use with friends were associated with higher friendship quality among socially anxious boys compared to socially anxious boys who rarely used a computer with friends.

Frequent Internet use may contribute to adolescents' experiences of loneliness (Prezza & others, 2004). Additionally, shy adolescents tend to prefer online communication with friends to offline (Pierce, 2009; Valkenburg & Peter, 2007). A recent study found that both Canadian and Italian adolescents who were shy were more likely than non-shy adolescents to express negative feelings and events to their friends online, contributing to feelings of loneliness (Laghi & others, 2013).

*How does computer and Internet use affect the friendships of shy or socially anxious adolescents compared to their peers?*

## Review Connect Reflect

**LO4** Summarize the influence of technology on children's development.

### Review

- What role do mass media play in the lives of children and adolescents?
- How do television and electronic media influence children's development?
- What roles do computers and the Internet play in children's development?

### Connect

- In this section, you learned about children and adolescents' use of various forms of media. How does this information relate to what you learned about cyberbullying in Chapter 15?

### Reflect *Your Own Personal Journey of Life*

- How much television did you watch as a child? What effect do you believe TV viewing has had on your development?

# case study **connections**

1. Do you think the Reggio Emilia approach described in the chapter-opening vignette would be effective for Canadian children? Why or why not?

2. How might a child who attends an early childhood education setting where educators adopt the Reggio Emilia approach described in the chapter-opening vignette differ from a child attending public school in terms of their motivation to achieve?

3. In the Reggio Emilia approach described in the chapter-opening vignette a wide range of media and materials is available for children to use as they learn. What impact do you think technology may have on young children's learning in such early childhood education settings?

# reach your **learning goals**

# Schools and Technology

## Exploring Children's Schooling

 **LO1** Discuss approaches to schooling and development.

Contemporary Approaches to Student Learning and Assessment

Early Childhood Education

- Contemporary approaches to student learning include direct instruction, which is a teacher-centred approach, and constructivist instruction, which is learner centred. Some experts recommend that both a constructivist and direct instruction approach be used, depending on circumstances.

- The child-centred kindergarten emphasizes the education of the whole child, paying particular attention to individual variation, the process of learning, and the importance of play in development. The Montessori approach is an increasingly popular early childhood education choice. Developmentally appropriate practice focuses on the typical patterns of children (age-appropriateness) and the uniqueness of each child (individual-appropriateness). Such practice contrasts with developmentally inappropriate practice, which relies on pencil-and-paper activities. Controversy surrounds early childhood education curricula. On the one side are the child-centred, constructivist advocates, on the other are those who advocate an instructivist, academic approach. Another controversy focuses on whether universal preschool education should be implemented.

Elementary School

- Children take up the new role of student, interact, develop new relationships, and discover rich sources of new ideas in elementary school. A special concern is that early elementary school education proceeds too much on the basis of negative feedback to children.

Educating Adolescents

- The transition to middle or junior high school coincides with many social, familial, and individual changes in the adolescent's life, and this transition is often stressful. One source of stress is the move from the top dog to the lowest position in school. Early school leaving is of concern, particularly among Aboriginal students. Participation in extracurricular activities is associated with positive academic and psychological outcomes. Adolescents benefit from participating in a variety of high-quality extracurricular activities.

Socioeconomic Status and Ethnicity

- Children living in poverty face problems at home and at school that present barriers to learning. Neighbourhoods are dangerous, and fear may be a way of life. Many schools' buildings are crumbling with age. Teachers are likely to encourage rote learning, and parents often don't set high educational standards. The school experiences of children from different ethnic groups vary considerably. Teachers often have low expectations for ethnic minority children. A number of strategies can be adopted to improve relationships with diverse others.

## Children with Disabilities

 Characterize children with disabilities and their education.

Learning Disabilities

- A child with a learning disability has difficulty in learning that involves understanding or using spoken or written language, and the difficulty can appear in listening, thinking, reading, writing, and spelling. A learning disability also may involve difficulty in doing mathematics. To be classified as a learning disability, the learning problem is not primarily the result of visual, hearing, or motor disabilities; intellectual disability; emotional disorders; or due to environmental, cultural, or economic disadvantage. Dyslexia is a category of learning disabilities that involves a severe impairment in the ability to read and spell. Dysgraphia is a learning disability that involves difficulty in expressing thoughts in writing. Dyscalculia is a learning disability that involves difficulties in math computation.

Attention Deficit Hyperactivity Disorder (ADHD)

- Attention deficit hyperactivity disorder (ADHD) is a disability in which individuals consistently show problems in one or more of these areas: (1) inattention, (2) hyperactivity, and (3) impulsivity. ADHD has been increasingly diagnosed.

Emotional and Behavioural Disorders

- Emotional and behavioural disorders consist of serious, persistent problems that involve relationships, aggression, depression, fears associated with personal or school matters, as well as other inappropriate socioemotional characteristics.

Autism Spectrum Disorders

- Autism spectrum disorders (ASD), also called pervasive developmental disorders, range from autistic disorder, a severe developmental disorder, to Asperger syndrome, a relatively mild autism spectrum disorder. The current consensus is that autism is a brain dysfunction with abnormalities in brain structure and neurotransmitters. Children with autism spectrum disorders are characterized by problems in social interaction, verbal and nonverbal communication, and repetitive behaviours.

## Achievement

 Explain the development of achievement in children.

Extrinsic and Intrinsic Motivation

- Extrinsic motivation involves external incentives such as rewards and punishment. Intrinsic motivation is based on internal factors such as self-determination, curiosity, challenge, and effort. One view is that giving students some choice and providing opportunities for personal responsibility increase intrinsic motivation. It is important for teachers to create learning environments that encourage students to become cognitively engaged and to develop a responsibility for their learning. Overall, the overwhelming conclusion is that it is a wise strategy to create learning environments that encourage students to become intrinsically motivated. In many real-world situations, both intrinsic and extrinsic motivation are involved, although too often intrinsic and extrinsic motivation have been pitted against each other as polar opposites.

- A mastery orientation is preferred over helpless or performance orientations in achievement situations. Mindset is the cognitive view that individuals develop regarding their own potential. Dweck argues that a key aspect of adolescents' development is to guide them in developing a growth mindset. Self-efficacy is the belief that one can master a situation and produce positive outcomes. Bandura points out that self-efficacy is a critical factor in whether students will achieve. Schunk argues that self-efficacy influences a student's choice of tasks, with low-efficacy students avoiding many learning tasks. Students' expectations for success influence their motivation. Children benefit when their parents, teachers, and other adults have high expectations for their achievement. Setting specific, proximal (short-term), and challenging goals benefits students' self-efficacy and achievement. Being a good planner means managing time effectively, setting priorities, and being organized. Self-monitoring is a key aspect of self-regulation and benefits student learning. Recently, Damon has proposed that purpose is an especially important aspect of achievement that has been missing from many adolescents' lives. Purpose is the intention to accomplish something meaningful in one's life and to contribute something to the world beyond oneself. Finding purpose involves answering a number of questions.

## Technology

 **LO4** Summarize the influence of technology on children's development.

- In terms of exposure, a significant increase in media use and screen time has occurred recently, especially among 11- to 14-year-olds. Adolescents are increasing the amount of time they spend in media multitasking. The social environment of adolescents has increasingly become digitally mediated.

- One negative aspect of television is that it involves passive learning. Watching violence on television is linked to higher levels of aggression in children. There also is concern about adolescents playing violent video games. Recently, researchers have found some positive influences of prosocial and exergame videos. Children's cognitive skills and abilities influence their TV viewing experiences. TV viewing is negatively related to children's mental ability and achievement. However, educational TV programming can enhance achievement.

- Today's children and adolescents are experiencing a technology revolution through the use of computers, the Internet, and sophisticated cell phones. The social environment of children and adolescents has increasingly become digitally mediated. The Internet continues to serve as the main focus of digitally mediated social interaction for adolescents but increasingly involves a variety of digital devices, including cell phones (especially smartphones). Adolescents' online time can have positive or negative outcomes. Large numbers of adolescents engage in social networking on Facebook. A special concern is the difficulty parents face in monitoring the information their children are accessing.

For more information on the resources available from McGraw-Hill Ryerson, go to www.mheducation.ca/he/solutions

# glossary

## A

**accommodation**  Piagetian concept of adjusting schemes to fit new information and experiences.

**acculturation**  Cultural changes that occur when one culture comes in contact with another culture.

**active (niche-picking) genotype-environment correlations**  Correlations that exist when children seek out environments they find compatible and stimulating.

**adolescence**  The developmental period of transition from childhood to early adulthood, entered at approximately 10 to 12 years of age and ending at 18 or 19 years of age.

**adolescent egocentrism**  The heightened self-consciousness of adolescents, which is reflected in adolescents' beliefs that others are as interested in them as they are in themselves, and in adolescents' sense of personal uniqueness and invulnerability.

**adoption study**  A study in which investigators seek to discover whether, in behaviour and psychological characteristics, adopted children are more like their adoptive parents, who provided a home environment, or more like their biological parents, who contributed their heredity. Another form of the adoption study is one that compares adoptive and biological siblings.

**affordances**  Opportunities for interaction offered by objects that are necessary to perform activities.

**afterbirth**  The third stage of birth, when the placenta, umbilical cord, and other membranes are detached and expelled.

**altruism**  An unselfish interest in helping another person.

**amnion**  Prenatal life-support system that is a bag or envelope that contains a clear fluid in which the developing embryo floats.

**amygdala**  The seat of emotions in the brain.

**androgens**  The main class of male sex hormones.

**androgyny**  The presence of masculine and feminine characteristics in the same person.

**anger cry**  A cry similar to the basic cry but with more excess air forced through the vocal cords.

**animism**  A facet of preoperational thought: the belief that inanimate objects have lifelike qualities and are capable of action.

**A-not-B error**  Also called A-B, error, this occurs when infants make the mistake of selecting the familiar hiding place (A) rather than the new hiding place (B) as they progress into substage 4 of Piaget's sensorimotor stage.

**Apgar Scale**  A widely used method to assess the health of newborns at one and five minutes after birth. The Apgar Scale evaluates an infant's heart rate, respiratory effort, muscle tone, body colour, and reflex irritability.

**aphasia**  A disorder resulting from brain damage to Broca's area or Wernicke's area that involves a loss or impairment of the ability to use or comprehend words.

**Asperger syndrome**  A relatively mild autism spectrum disorder in which the child has relatively good verbal skills, milder nonverbal language problems, and a restricted range of interests and relationships.

**assimilation**  Piagetian concept of the incorporation of new information into existing knowledge.

**attachment**  A close emotional bond between two people.

**attention**  Concentrating and focusing mental resources.

**attention deficit hyperactivity disorder (ADHD)**  A disability in which children consistently show one or more of the following characteristics: (1) inattention, (2) hyperactivity, and (3) impulsivity.

**authoritarian parenting**  A restrictive, punitive style in which the parent exhorts the child to follow the parent's directions and to respect their work and effort. Firm limits and controls are placed on the child, and little verbal exchange is allowed. This style is associated with children's social incompetence, including a lack of initiative and weak communication skills.

**authoritative parenting**  This style encourages children to be independent but still places limits and controls on their actions. Extensive verbal give-and-take is allowed, and parents are warm and nurturant toward the child. This style is associated with children's social competence, including being achievement oriented and self-reliant.

**autism spectrum disorders (ASDs)**  Also called pervasive developmental disorders, they range from the severe disorder labeled autistic disorder to the milder disorder called Asperger syndrome. Children with these disorders are characterized by problems in social interaction, verbal and nonverbal communication, and repetitive behaviors.

**autistic disorder**  A severe developmental autism spectrum disorder that has its onset in the first three years of life and includes deficiencies in social relationships; abnormalities in communication; and restricted, repetitive, and stereotyped patterns of behavior.

**automaticity**  The ability to process information with little or no effort.

**autonomous morality**  The second stage of moral development in Piaget's theory, displayed by older children (about 10 years of age and older). The child becomes aware that rules and laws are created by people and that, in judging an action, one should consider the actor's intentions as well as the consequences.

## B

**basic cry**  A rhythmic pattern usually consisting of a cry, a briefer silence, a shorter inspiratory whistle that is higher pitched than the main cry, and then a brief rest before the next cry.

**Bayley Scales of Infant Development**  Initially created by Nancy Bayley, these scales are widely used in assessing infant development. The current version has five scales: cognitive, language, motor, socioemotional, and adaptive.

**behaviour genetics**  The field that seeks to discover the influence of heredity and environment on individuals' differences in human traits and development.

**bicultural identity**  Identity formation that occurs when adolescents identify in some ways with their ethnic group and in other ways with the majority culture.

**biological processes**  Changes in an individual's body.

**blastocyst**  The inner layer of cells that develops during the germinal period. These cells later develop into the embryo.

**brainstorming**  A technique in which children are encouraged to come up with creative ideas in a group, play off one another's ideas, and say practically whatever comes to mind.

**Brazelton Neonatal Behavioral Assessment Scale (NBAS)**  A measure that is used in the first month of life to assess the newborn's neurological development, reflexes, and reactions to people and objects.

**breech position**   The baby's position in the uterus that causes the buttocks to be the first part to emerge from the vagina.

**Broca's area**   An area of the brain's left frontal lobe that is involved in speech production and grammatical processing.

**Bronfenbrenner's ecological theory**   An environmental systems theory that focuses on five environmental systems: microsystem, mesosystem, exosystem, macrosystem, and chronosystem.

**bullying**   Repeated acts of physical, verbal, relational, or cyber aggression intended to harm a less powerful peer.

# C

**care perspective**   The moral perspective of Carol Gilligan, in which people are assessed in terms of their connectedness with others and the quality of their interpersonal communication, relationships with others, and concern for others.

**case study**   An in-depth look at a single individual.

**centration**   Focusing attention on one characteristic to the exclusion of all others.

**cephalocaudal pattern**   The sequence in which the fastest growth occurs at the top of the body—the head—with physical growth in size, weight, and feature differentiation gradually working from top to bottom.

**Caesarean delivery**   Removal of the baby from the mother's uterus through an incision made in her abdomen.

**character education**   A direct moral education approach that involves teaching students a basic "moral literacy" to prevent them from engaging in immoral behaviour or doing harm to themselves or others.

**child-centred kindergarten**   Education that involves the whole child by considering both the child's physical, cognitive, and socioemotional development and the child's needs, interests, and learning styles.

**child-directed speech**   Language spoken in a higher pitch than normal, with simple words and sentences.

**chromosomes**   Threadlike structures that come in 23 pairs, with one member of each pair coming from each parent. Chromosomes contain the genetic substance DNA.

**cliques**   Small groups that range from 2 to about 12 individuals and average about 5 or 6 individuals. Cliques can form because of friendship or because

individuals engage in similar activities, and members usually are of the same sex and about the same age.

**cognitive moral education**   Education based on the belief that students should learn to value things like democracy and justice as their moral reasoning develops; Kohlberg's theory has been the basis for many of the cognitive moral education approaches.

**cognitive processes**   Changes in an individual's thinking, intelligence, and language.

**cohort effects**   Effects due to a person's time of birth, era, or generation, but not to actual age.

**commitment**   Personal investment in identity.

**concrete operational stage**   Piaget's third stage, which lasts from approximately 7 to 11 years of age, when children can perform concrete operations, and logical reasoning replaces intuitive reasoning as long as the reasoning can be applied to specific or concrete examples.

**concepts**   Cognitive groupings of similar objects, events, people, or ideas.

**conduct disorder**   Age-inappropriate actions and attitudes that violate family expectations, society's norms, and the personal or property rights of others.

**connectedness**   Consists of two dimensions: mutuality, sensitivity to and respect for others' views, and permeability, openness to others' views.

**conservation**   The idea that altering an object's or substance's appearance does not change its basic properties.

**constructive play**   Play that combines sensorimotor/practice play with symbolic representation of ideas. Constructive play occurs when children engage in self-regulated creation or construction of a product or a solution.

**constructivist approach**   A learner-centred approach that emphasizes the importance of individuals actively constructing their knowledge and understanding, with guidance from the teacher.

**context**   The settings, influenced by historical, economic, social, and cultural factors, in which development occurs.

**continuity-discontinuity issue**   Debate about whether development involves gradual, cumulative change (continuity) or distinct stages (discontinuity).

**conventional reasoning**   The second, or intermediate, level in Kohlberg's theory of moral development. At this level, individuals abide by certain standards (internal), but they are the standards of others such as parents or the laws

of society (external). The conventional level consists of two stages: mutual interpersonal expectations, relationships, and interpersonal conformity (stage 3) and social systems morality (stage 4).

**convergent thinking**   Thinking that produces one correct answer; characteristic of the kind of thinking required on conventional intelligence tests.

**coparenting**   Support parents provide for each other in jointly raising children.

**core knowledge approach**   States that infants are born with domain-specific innate knowledge systems, such as those involving space, number sense, object permanence, and language.

**corpus callosum**   Brain area where fibres connect the brain's left and right hemispheres.

**correlation coefficient**   A number based on statistical analysis that is used to describe the degree of association between two variables.

**correlational research**   Research in which the goal is to describe the strength of the relationship between two or more events or characteristics.

**creativity**   The ability to think in novel and unusual ways and come up with unique solutions to problems.

**crisis**   A period of identity development during which the adolescent is choosing among meaningful alternatives.

**critical thinking**   Thinking reflectively and productively, and evaluating the evidence.

**cross-cultural studies**   Comparisons of one culture with one or more other cultures. These provide information about the degree to which children's development is similar, or universal, across cultures, and to the degree to which it is culture-specific.

**cross-sectional approach**   A research strategy in which individuals of different ages are compared at the same point in time.

**crowds**   The crowd is a larger group structure than a clique. Adolescents usually are members of a crowd based on reputation and may or may not spend much time together. Many crowds are defined by the activities in which adolescents engage.

**culture**   The behaviour patterns, beliefs, and all other products of a particular group of people that are passed on from generation to generation.

**culture-fair tests**   Intelligence tests that aim to avoid cultural bias.

## D

**descriptive research**   Research that involves observing and recording behaviour.

**development**   The pattern of movement or change that begins at conception and continues through the life span.

**developmental cascade model**   Involves connections across domains over time that influence developmental pathways and outcomes.

**developmental quotient (DQ)**   An overall developmental score that combines subscores on motor, language, adaptive, and personal-social domains in the Gesell assessment of infants.

**developmentally appropriate practice**   Education that focuses on the typical developmental patterns of children (age-appropriateness) and the uniqueness of each child (individual-appropriateness). Such practice contrasts with developmentally inappropriate practice, which relies on abstract paper-and-pencil activities presented to large groups of young children.

**dialect**   A variety of language that is distinguished by its vocabulary, grammar, or pronunciation.

**difficult child**   A temperament style in which the child tends to react negatively and cry frequently, engages in irregular daily routines, and is slow to accept new experiences.

**direct instruction approach**   A teacher-centred approach characterized by teacher direction and control, mastery of academic material, high expectations for students' progress, and maximum time spent on learning tasks.

**dishabituation**   The recovery of a habituated response after a change in stimulation.

**divergent thinking**   Thinking that produces many answers to the same question; characteristic of creativity.

**divided attention**   Concentrating on more than one activity at the same time.

**DNA**   A complex molecule that contains genetic information.

**doula**   A caregiver who provides non-clinical physical, emotional, and educational support for the mother before, during, and after childbirth.

**Down syndrome**   A chromosomally transmitted form of intellectual disability, caused by the presence of an extra copy of chromosome 21.

**dual-process model**   States that decision making is influenced by two systems, one analytical and one experiential, that

compete with each other. In this model, it is the experiential system—monitoring and managing actual experiences—that benefits adolescent decision making.

**dynamic systems theory**   A theory, proposed by Esther Thelen, that seeks to explain how motor behaviours are assembled for perceiving and acting.

**dyscalculia**   Also known as developmental arithmetic disorder; a learning disability that involves difficulty in math computation.

**dysgraphia**   A learning disability that involves difficulty in handwriting.

**dyslexia**   A category of learning disabilities involving a severe impairment in the ability to read and spell.

## E

**early childhood**   The developmental period that extends from the end of infancy to about 5 or 6 years of age, sometimes called the preschool years.

**early-later experience issue**   Controversy regarding the degree to which early experiences (especially during infancy) or later experiences are the key determinants of children's development.

**easy child**   A temperament style in which the child is generally in a positive mood, quickly establishes regular routines, and adapts easily to new experiences.

**eclectic theoretical orientation**   An orientation that does not follow any one theoretical approach but rather selects from each theory whatever is considered its best aspects.

**ecological view**   The view, proposed by the Gibsons, that people directly perceive information in the world around them. Perception brings people in contact with the environment in order to interact with it and adapt to it.

**egocentrism**   An important feature of preoperational thought: the inability to distinguish between one's own and someone else's perspective.

**embryonic period**   The period of prenatal development that occurs from two to eight weeks after conception. During the embryonic period, the rate of cell differentiation intensifies, support systems for the cells form, and organs appear.

**emotion**   Feeling, or affect, that occurs when people are engaged in an interaction that is important to them, especially one that influences their well-being.

**emotional and behavioural disorders**   Serious, persistent problems that involve

relationships, aggression, depression, fears associated with personal or school matters, as well as other inappropriate socioemotional characteristics.

**emotional intelligence**   The ability to perceive and express emotion accurately and adaptively, to understand emotion and emotional knowledge, to use feelings to facilitate thought, and to manage emotions in oneself and others.

**empathy**   Reacting to another's feelings with an emotional response that is similar to the other's feelings.

**encoding**   The mechanism by which information gets into memory.

**epigenetic view**   Emphasizes that development is the result of a bidirectional interchange between heredity and environment, in which environmental factors can influence how genes are expressed.

**equilibration**   A mechanism that Piaget proposed to explain how children shift from one stage of thought to the next. The shift occurs as children experience cognitive conflict, or disequilibrium, in trying to understand the world. Eventually, they resolve the conflict and reach a balance, or equilibrium, of thought.

**Erikson's theory**   Description of eight stages of human development. Each stage consists of a unique developmental task that confronts individuals with a crisis that must be resolved.

**estradiol**   An estrogen that is a key hormone in girls' pubertal development.

**estrogens**   The main class of female sex hormones.

**ethnic gloss**   Use of an ethnic label such as *Asian* or *Middle Eastern* in a superficial way that portrays an ethnic group as being more homogeneous than it really is.

**ethnic identity**   An enduring aspect of the self that includes a sense of membership in an ethnic group, along with the attitudes and feelings related to that membership.

**ethnicity**   A characteristic based on cultural heritage, nationality, race, religion, and language.

**ethology**   Stresses that behaviour is strongly influenced by biology, is tied to evolution, and is characterized by critical or sensitive periods.

**evocative genotype-environment correlations**   Correlations that exist when the child's genotype elicits certain types of physical and social environments.

**evolutionary psychology**   Branch of psychology that emphasizes the importance of adaptation, reproduction, and "survival of the fittest" in shaping behaviour.

**executive attention** Involves action planning, allocating attention to goals, error detection and compensation, monitoring progress on tasks, and dealing with novel or difficult circumstances.

**executive function** An umbrella-like concept that consists of a number of higher-level cognitive processes linked to the development of the brain's prefrontal cortex. Executive function involves managing one's thoughts to engage in goal-directed behaviour and to exercise self-control.

**expanding** Restating, in a linguistically sophisticated form, what a child has said.

**experiment** A carefully regulated procedure in which one or more of the factors believed to influence the behaviour being studied are manipulated while all other factors are held constant.

**explicit memory** Conscious memory of facts and experiences.

**extrinsic motivation** Response to external incentives such as rewards and punishments.

## F

**fast mapping** A process that helps to explain how young children learn the connection between a word and its referent so quickly.

**fertilization** A stage in reproduction whereby an egg and a sperm fuse to create a single cell, called a zygote.

**fetal alcohol spectrum disorders (FASD)** An umbrella term that describes a range of neuropsychological and behavioural deficits that appear in the offspring of mothers who drink alcohol heavily during pregnancy.

**fetal period** The period from two months after conception until birth, lasting about seven months in typical pregnancies.

**fine motor skills** Actions that involve more finely tuned movements, such as finger dexterity.

**forgiveness** An aspect of prosocial behaviour that occurs when an injured person releases the injurer from possible behavioural retaliation.

**formal operational stage** Piaget's fourth and final stage, which occurs between the ages of 11 and 15, when individuals move beyond concrete experiences and think in more abstract and logical ways.

**fragile X syndrome** A genetic disorder involving an abnormality in the X chromosome, which becomes constricted and often breaks.

**fuzzy trace theory** States that memory is best understood by considering two types of memory representations: (1) verbatim memory trace, and (2) fuzzy trace, or gist. In this theory, older children's better memory is attributed to the fuzzy traces created by extracting the gist of information.

## G

**games** Activities engaged in for pleasure that include rules and often competition with one or more individuals.

**gender** The characteristics of people as males and females.

**gender identity** The sense of being male or female, which most children acquire by the time they are 2 years old.

**gender dysphoria** The experience of extreme discomfort with one's gender assigned at birth.

**gender role** A set of expectations that prescribes how females or males should think, act, and feel.

**gender schema theory** According to this theory, gender typing emerges as children gradually develop schemas of what is gender-appropriate and gender-inappropriate in their culture.

**gender stereotypes** Broad categories that reflect impressions and widely held beliefs about what behaviour is appropriate for females and males.

**gender typing** Acquisition of a traditional masculine or feminine role.

**gene × environment (G × E) interaction** The interaction of a specific measured variation in the DNA and a specific measured aspect of the environment.

**genes** Units of hereditary information composed of DNA. Genes direct cells to reproduce themselves and manufacture the proteins that maintain life.

**genotype** A person's genetic heritage; the actual genetic material.

**germinal period** The period of prenatal development that takes place in the first two weeks after conception. It includes the creation of the zygote, continued cell division, and the attachment of the zygote to the uterine wall.

**giftedness** Possession of above-average intelligence (an IQ of 130 or higher) and/or superior talent for something.

**goodness of fit** The match between a child's temperament and the environmental demands the child must cope with.

**grasping reflex** A neonatal reflex that occurs when something touches the

infant's palms. The infant responds by grasping tightly.

**gratitude** A feeling of thankfulness and appreciation, especially in response to someone doing something kind or helpful.

**gross motor skills** Actions that involve large-muscle activities, such as arm movements and walking.

## H

**habituation** Decreased responsiveness to a stimulus after repeated presentations of the stimulus.

**helpless orientation** An orientation in which one seems trapped by the experience of difficulty and attributes one's difficulty to a lack of ability.

**heritability** The fraction of the variance in a population that is attributed to genetics.

**heteronomous morality** The first stage of moral development in Piaget's theory, occurring from 4 to 7 years of age. Justice and rules are conceived of as unchangeable properties of the world, removed from the control of people.

**hidden curriculum** The pervasive moral atmosphere that characterizes each school.

**horizontal décalage** Piaget's concept that similar abilities do not appear at the same time within a stage of development.

**hormones** Powerful chemical substances secreted by the endocrine glands and carried through the body by the bloodstream.

**hostile attribution bias** The tendency to perceive a peer's motives and behaviours during ambiguous social interactions as deliberately hostile.

**hypothesis** Specific assumption and prediction that can be tested to determine its accuracy.

**hypothetical-deductive reasoning** Piaget's formal operational concept that adolescents have the cognitive ability to develop hypotheses about ways to solve problems and can systematically deduce which is the best path to follow in solving the problem.

## I

**identity achievement** Marcia's term for the status of individuals who have undergone a crisis and made a commitment.

**identity diffusion** Marcia's term for the status of individuals who have not yet experienced a crisis (that is, they have not yet explored meaningful alternatives) or made any commitments.

**identity foreclosure** Marcia's term for the status of individuals who have made a commitment but have not experienced a crisis.

**identity moratorium** Marcia's term for the status of individuals who are in the midst of a crisis but whose commitments either are absent or are only vaguely defined.

**identity versus identity confusion** Erikson's fifth developmental stage, which individuals experience during the adolescent years. At this time, adolescents examine who they are, what they are all about, and where they are going in life.

**imaginary audience** The aspect of adolescent egocentrism that involves attention-getting behaviour motivated by a desire to be noticed, visible, and "onstage."

**immanent justice** Piaget's concept of the childhood expectation that if a rule is broken, punishment will be meted out immediately.

**implicit memory** Memory without conscious recollection; memory of skills and routine procedures that are performed automatically.

**individuality** Consists of two dimensions: self-assertion—the ability to have and communicate a point of view—and separateness—the use of communication patterns to express how one is different from others.

**induction** A discipline technique in which a parent uses reasoning and explains how the child's actions are likely to affect others.

**indulgent parenting** A style in which parents are highly involved with their children but place few demands or controls on them. This is associated with children's social incompetence, especially a lack of self-control and a lack of respect for others.

**infancy** The developmental period that extends from birth to about 18 to 24 months.

**infinite generativity** The ability to produce an endless number of meaningful sentences using a finite set of words and rules.

**information-processing approach** An approach that focuses on the ways children process information about their world—how they manipulate information, monitor it, and create strategies to deal with it.

**information-processing theory** Emphasizes that individuals manipulate information, monitor it, and strategize about it. Central to this theory are the processes of memory and thinking.

**insecure avoidant babies** Babies who show insecurity by avoiding the caregiver.

**insecure disorganized babies** Babies who show insecurity by being disorganized and disoriented.

**insecure resistant babies** Babies who might cling to the caregiver, then resist her by fighting against the closeness, perhaps by kicking or pushing away.

**intellectual disability** A condition of limited mental ability in which the individual (1) has a low IQ, usually below 70 on a traditional intelligence test, (2) has difficulty adapting to everyday life, and (3) has an onset of these characteristics during the developmental period.

**intelligence** The ability to solve problems and to adapt to and learn from experiences.

**intelligence quotient (IQ)** An individual's mental age divided by chronological age and multiplied by 100; devised in 1912 by William Stern.

**intermodal perception** The ability to relate and integrate information about two or more sensory modalities, such as vision and hearing.

**intimacy in friendship** Self-disclosure or the sharing of private thoughts.

**intrinsic motivation** Internal motivational factors such as self-determination, curiosity, challenge, and effort.

**intuitive thought substage** The second substage of preoperational thought, occurring between approximately 4 and 7 years of age, when children begin to use primitive reasoning.

## J

**joint attention** Individuals focusing on the same object or event; requires the ability to track another's behaviour, one person directing another's attention, and reciprocal interaction.

**justice perspective** A moral perspective that focuses on the rights of the individual; individuals independently make moral decisions.

**juvenile delinquency** Refers to a great variety of behaviours by an adolescent, ranging from unacceptable behaviour to breaking the law.

## K

**kangaroo care** Treatment for preterm infants that involves skin-to-skin contact.

**Klinefelter syndrome** A chromosomal disorder in which males have an extra X chromosome, making them XXY instead of XY.

**kwashiorkor** Severe malnutrition caused by a protein-deficient diet, causing the feet and abdomen to swell with water.

## L

**labelling** Identifying the names of objects.

**laboratory** A controlled setting from which many of the complex factors of the "real world" have been removed.

**language** A form of communication, whether spoken, written, or signed, that is based on a system of symbols.

**language acquisition device (LAD)** Chomsky's term that describes a biological endowment that enables the child to detect the features and rules of language, including phonology, syntax, and semantics.

**lateralization** Specialization of function in one hemisphere of the cerebral cortex or the other.

**learning disabilities** Disabilities involving understanding or using spoken or written language. The difficulty can appear in listening, thinking, reading, writing, spelling, or mathematics. To be classified as a learning disability, the problem must not be primarily the result of visual, hearing, or motor disabilities; intellectual disabilities; emotional disorders; or environmental, cultural, or economic disadvantage.

**longitudinal approach** A research strategy in which the same individuals are studied over a period of time, usually several years.

**long-term memory** A relatively permanent and unlimited type of memory.

**love withdrawal** A discipline technique in which a parent withholds attention or love from the child in an effort to control the child's behaviour.

**low birth weight infant** Infant that weighs less than 2.4 kilograms at birth.

## M

**marasmus** Severe malnutrition caused by an insufficient protein-calorie intake, resulting in a shrunken, elderly appearance.

**mastery motivation** An orientation in which one is task oriented, focusing on learning strategies and the achievement process rather than ability or the outcome.

**meiosis** A specialized form of cell division that forms eggs and sperm (or gametes).

**memory** Retention of information over time.

**menarche** A girl's first menstruation.

**mental age (MA)** An individual's level of mental develop relative to others.

**metacognition** Cognition about cognition, or "knowing about knowing."

**metalinguistic awareness** Knowledge about language.

**metamemory** Knowledge about memory.

**metaphor** An implied comparison between two unlike things.

**middle and late childhood** The developmental period that extends from about 6 to 11 years of age, sometimes called the elementary school years.

**Millennials** The generation born after 1980, the first to come of age and enter emerging adulthood in the new millennium.

**mindfulness** Being alert, mentally present, and cognitively flexible while going through life's everyday activities and tasks.

**mindset** Dweck's concept that refers to the cognitive view individuals develop for themselves; individuals have either a fixed or growth mindset.

**mitosis** Cellular reproduction in which the cell's nucleus duplicates itself with two new cells being formed, each containing the same DNA as the parent cell, arranged in the same 23 pairs of chromosomes.

**Montessori approach** An educational philosophy in which children are given considerable freedom and spontaneity in choosing activities and are allowed to move from one activity to another as they desire.

**moral development** Changes in thoughts, feelings, and behaviours regarding standards of right and wrong.

**moral exemplars** People who have lived extraordinary lives. Emphasizes the development of personality, identity, character, and virtue to a level that reflects moral excellence and commitment.

**moral identity** The aspect of personality that is present when individuals have moral notions and commitments that are central to their lives.

**Moro reflex** A neonatal startle response that occurs in reaction to a sudden, intense noise or movement. When startled, the newborn arches its back, throws its head back, and flings out its arms and legs. Then the newborn rapidly closes its arms and legs to the centre of the body.

**morphology** The rule system that governs how words are formed in a language.

**multiple developmental trajectories** Concept that adults follow one trajectory and children and adolescents another one; understanding how these trajectories mesh is important.

**myelination** The process of encasing axons with a myelin sheath that increases the speed of processing information.

## N

**natural childbirth** This method attempts to reduce the mother's pain by decreasing her fear through education about childbirth and relaxation techniques during delivery.

**naturalistic observation** Behavioural observation that takes place in real-world settings.

**nature-nurture issue** Debate about whether development is primarily influenced by nature or nurture. The nature proponents claim biological inheritance is the most important influence on development; the nurture proponents claim that environmental experiences are the most important.

**neglectful parenting** A style in which the parent is very uninvolved in the child's life. It is associated with children's social incompetence, especially a lack of self-control and poor self-esteem.

**Neonatal Intensive Care Unit Network Neurobehavioural Scale (NNNS)** An offspring of the NBAS, the NNNS provides an assessment of the at-risk newborn's behaviour, neurological and stress responses, and regulatory capacities.

**neo-Piagetians** Developmentalists who have elaborated on Piaget's theory, incorporating aspects of information processing theory to explain cognitive development.

**Neuroconstructivist view** Theory of brain development emphasizing the following points: (a) biological processes and environmental conditions influence brain development, (b) the brain has plasticity and is context dependent, and (c) the development of the brain and the child's cognitive development are closely linked.

**neurons** Nerve cells that handle information processing at the cellular level in the brain.

**non-shared environmental experiences** The child's own unique experiences, both within the family and outside the family, that are not shared by another sibling. Thus, experiences occurring within the family can be part of the non-shared environment.

**normal distribution** A symmetrical distribution with a majority of the cases falling in the middle of the possible range of scores and few scores appearing toward the extremes of the range.

## O

**object permanence** The Piagetian term for one of an infant's most important accomplishments: understanding that objects and events continue to exist even when they cannot directly be seen, heard, or touched.

**operations** Internalized actions that allow children to do mentally what before they had done only physically. Operations also are reversible mental actions.

**organization** Piaget's concept of grouping isolated behaviours into a higher-order, more smoothly functioning cognitive system; the grouping or arranging of items into categories.

**organogenesis** Organ formation that takes place during the first two months of prenatal development.

## P

**pain cry** A sudden appearance of loud crying without preliminary moaning, and a long initial cry followed by an extended period of breath holding.

**passive genotype-environment correlations** Correlations that exist when the natural parents, who are genetically related to the child, provide a rearing environment for the child.

**peers** Children who share the same age or maturity level.

**perceived popularity** The extent to which children are viewed as being popular or unpopular among peers.

**perception** The interpretation of sensation.

**performance orientation** An orientation in which one focuses on winning rather than achievement outcomes, and happiness is thought to result from winning.

**personal fable** The part of adolescent egocentrism that involves an adolescent's sense of uniqueness and invincibility.

**perspective taking** The social cognitive process involved in assuming the perspective of others and understanding their thoughts and feelings.

**phenotype** The way an individual's genotype is expressed in observable and measurable characteristics.

**phenylketonuria (PKU)** A genetic disorder in which an individual cannot properly metabolize an amino acid. PKU is now easily detected but, if left untreated, results in intellectual disability and hyperactivity.

**phonics approach** An approach that emphasizes that reading instruction should focus on phonics and its basic rules for translating written symbols into sounds.

**phonology** The sound system of a language, which includes the sounds used and rules about how they may be combined.

**Piaget's theory** Theory stating that children actively construct their understanding of the world and go through four stages of cognitive development.

**placenta** A life-support system that consists of a disk-shaped group of tissues in which small blood vessels from the mother and offspring intertwine.

**play** A pleasurable activity that is engaged in for its own sake.

**play therapy** Therapy that allows the child to work off frustrations and is a medium through which the therapist can analyze the child's conflicts and ways of coping with them. Children may feel less threatened and be more likely to express their true feelings in the context of play.

**possible self** What an individual might become, would like to become, and is afraid of becoming.

**postconventional reasoning** The third and highest level in Kohlberg's theory of moral development. At this level, morality is more internal. The postconventional level consists of two stages: social contract or utility and individual rights (stage 5) and universal ethical principles (stage 6).

**postpartum depression** Characteristic of women who have such strong feelings of sadness, anxiety, or despair that they have trouble coping with daily tasks during the postpartum period.

**postpartum period** The period after childbirth when the mother adjusts, physically, emotionally and psychologically, to the process of childbirth. This period lasts about six weeks or until her body has completed its adjustment and returned to a near pre-pregnant state.

**power assertion** A discipline technique in which a parent attempts to gain control over the child or the child's resources.

**practice play** Play that involves repetition of behaviour when new skills are being learned or when physical or mental mastery and coordination of skills are required for games or sports. Practice play can be engaged in throughout life.

**pragmatics** The appropriate use of language in different contexts.

**precocious puberty** Very early onset and rapid progression of puberty.

**preconventional reasoning** The lowest level in Kohlberg's theory. At this level, morality is often focused on reward and punishment. The two

stages in preconventional reasoning are punishment and obedience orientation (stage 1) and individualism, instrumental purpose, and exchange (stage 2).

**prefrontal cortex** The highest level of the frontal lobes that is involved in reasoning, decision making, and self-control.

**prenatal period** The time from conception to birth.

**preoperational stage** The second Piagetian developmental stage, which lasts from about 2 to 7 years of age, when children begin to represent the world with words, images, and drawings.

**prepared childbirth** Developed by French obstetrician Ferdinand Lamaze, this childbirth strategy is similar to natural childbirth but includes a special breathing technique to control pushing in the final stages of labour and a more detailed anatomy and physiology course.

**pretense/symbolic play** Play that occurs when a child transforms the physical environment into a symbol.

**preterm infants** Those born before the completion of 37 weeks of gestation (the time between fertilization and birth).

**primary emotions** Emotions that are present in humans and other animals, and emerge early in life; examples are joy, anger, sadness, fear, and disgust.

**proximodistal pattern** The sequence in which growth starts at the centre of the body and moves toward the extremities.

**psychoanalytic theories** Theories that describe development as primarily unconscious and heavily coloured by emotion. Behaviour is merely a surface characteristic, and the symbolic workings of the mind have to be analyzed to understand behaviour. Early experiences with parents are emphasized.

**psychoanalytic theory of gender** A theory that stems from Freud's view that preschool children develop erotic feelings toward the opposite-sex parent. Eventually these feeling cause anxiety, so that at 5 or 6 years of age, children renounce these feelings and identify with the same-sex parent, unconsciously adopting the same-sex parent's characteristics.

**psychosocial moratorium** Erikson's term for the gap between childhood security and adult autonomy that adolescents experience as part of their identity exploration.

**puberty** A period of rapid physical maturation involving hormonal and bodily changes that take place primarily in early adolescence.

## R

**rapport talk** The language of conversation and a way of establishing connections and negotiating relationships; more characteristic of females than of males.

**recasting** Rephrasing a statement that a child has said, perhaps turning it into a question, or restating a child's immature utterance in the form of a fully grammatical utterance.

**reciprocal socialization** The bidirectional process by which children socialize parents just as parents socialize them.

**reflexes** Built-in reactions to stimuli.

**reflexive smile** A smile that does not occur in response to external stimuli. It happens during the month after birth, usually during sleep.

**rejected children** Children who are actively disliked by their peers.

**relational aggression** Behaviours that are intended to harm a peer by manipulating his or her relationships with others, such as spreading rumours or exclusion.

**religion** An organized set of beliefs, practices, rituals, and symbols that increases an individual's connection to a sacred or transcendent other (God, higher power, or higher truth).

**religiousness** The degree of affiliation with an organized religion, participation in prescribed rituals and practices, connection with its beliefs, afnd involvement in a community of believers.

**report talk** Talk that conveys information; more characteristic of males than females.

**rooting reflex** A built-in reaction that occurs when a newborn's cheek is stroked or the side of the mouth is touched. In response, the infant turns its head toward the side that was touched, in an apparent effort to find something to suck.

## S

**satire** The use of irony, derision, or wit to expose folly or wickedness.

**scaffolding** In cognitive development, Vygotsky used this term to describe the practice of changing the level of support provided over the course of a teaching session, with the more-skilled person adjusting guidance to fit the child's current performance level.

**schema theory** States that when people reconstruct information, they fit it into information that already exists in their minds.

**schemas** Mental frameworks that organize concepts and information.

**schemes** In Piaget's theory, actions or mental representations that organize knowledge.

**scientific method** An approach that can be used to obtain accurate information by carrying out four steps: (1) conceptualize the problem, (2) collect data, (3) analyze data and draw conclusions, and (4) revise research conclusions and theory.

**securely attached babies** Babies who use the caregiver as a secure base from which to explore the environment.

**selective attention** Focusing on a specific aspect of experience that is relevant while ignoring others that are irrelevant.

**self** All of the characteristics of a person.

**self-concept** Domain-specific self-evaluations.

**self-conscious emotions** Emotions that require self-awareness, especially consciousness and a sense of "me"; examples include jealousy, empathy, and embarrassment.

**self-efficacy** The belief that one can master a situation and produce favourable outcomes.

**self-esteem** The global evaluative dimension of the self; also called self-worth or self-image.

**self-understanding** A child's cognitive representation of the self—the substance and content of a child's self-conceptions.

**semantics** The meaning of words and sentences.

**sensation** Reaction that occurs when information contacts sensory receptors—the eyes, ears, tongue, nostrils, and skin.

**sensorimotor play** Behaviour that allows infants to derive pleasure from exercising their existing sensorimotor schemes.

**sensorimotor stage** The first of Piaget's stages, which lasts from birth to about 2 years of age; infants construct an understanding of the world by coordinating sensory experiences (such as seeing and hearing) with motoric actions.

**separation protest** Occurs when infants experience a fear of being separated from a caregiver, which results in crying when the caregiver leaves.

**sequential approach** A research strategy in which two or more groups of individuals are studied over a period of time, usually several years, thus combining the cross-sectional and longitudinal approaches.

**seriation** The concrete operation that involves ordering stimuli along a quantitative dimension (such as length).

**service learning** A form of education that promotes social responsibility and service to the community.

**shape constancy** Recognition that an object remains the same even though its orientation to the viewer changes.

**shared environmental experiences** Siblings' common environmental experiences, such as their parents' personalities and intellectual orientation, the family's socioeconomic status, and the neighbourhood in which they live.

**short-term memory** Limited-capacity memory system in which information is usually retained for up to 30 seconds, assuming there is no rehearsal of the information. Using rehearsal, individuals can keep the information in short-term memory longer.

**sickle-cell anemia** A genetic disorder that affects the red blood cells and occurs most often in people of African descent.

**size constancy** Recognition that an object remains the same even though the retinal image of the object changes.

**slow-to-warm-up child** A temperament style in which the child has a low activity level, is somewhat negative, and displays a low intensity of mood.

**small for date infants** Also called small for gestational age infants, these infants have birth weights that are below normal when the length of pregnancy is considered. Small for date infants may be preterm or full term.

**social cognition** The processes involved in understanding the world around us, especially how we think and reason about other people.

**social cognitive theory** The view of psychologists who emphasize behaviour, environment, and cognition as the key factors in development.

**social cognitive theory of gender** This theory emphasizes that children's gender development occurs through observation and imitation of gender behaviour, and through rewards and punishments they experience for gender-appropriate and gender-inappropriate behaviour.

**social cognitive theory of morality** The theory that distinguishes between moral competence—the ability to produce moral behaviours—and moral performance—use of those behaviours in specific situations.

**social constructivist approach** An emphasis on the social contexts of learning and the construction of knowledge through social interaction. Vygotsky's theory reflects this approach.

**social conventional reasoning** Focuses on conventional rules established by social consensus, as opposed to moral reasoning that stresses ethical issues.

**social play** Play that involves interactions with peers.

**social referencing** Reading emotional cues in others to help determine how to act in a particular situation.

**social role theory** A theory stating that gender differences result from the contrasting roles of women and men—social hierarchy and division of labour strongly influence gender differences in power, assertiveness, and nurture.

**social smile** A smile in response to an external stimulus, which, early in development, typically is a face.

**socioeconomic status (SES)** Categorization based on a person's occupational, educational, and economic characteristics.

**socioemotional processes** Changes in an individual's relationships with other people, emotions, and personality.

**sociometric popularity** The extent to which children are liked or disliked by peers.

**standardized test** A test with uniform procedures for administration and scoring. Many standardized tests allow a person's performance to be compared with the performance of other individuals.

**stereotype threat** Anxiety that one's behaviour might confirm a stereotype about one's group.

**Strange Situation** Ainsworth's observational measure of infant attachment to a caregiver, which requires the infant to move through a series of introductions, separations, and reunions with the caregiver and an adult stranger in a prescribed order.

**stranger anxiety** An infant's fear of and wariness toward strangers; it tends to appear in the second half of the first year of life.

**strategy construction** Creation of new procedures for processing information.

**sucking reflex** A newborn's built-in reaction to automatically suck an object placed in its mouth. The sucking reflex enables the infant to get nourishment before it has associated a nipple with food.

**sudden infant death syndrome (SIDS)** A condition that occurs when an infant stops breathing, usually during the night, and suddenly dies without an apparent cause.

**sustained attention** The ability to maintain attention to a selected stimulus for a prolonged period of time. Sustained attention is also called *focused attention* and *vigilance*.

**symbolic function substage**   The first substage of preoperational thought, occurring roughly between the ages of 2 and 4. In this substage, the young child gains the ability to represent mentally an object that is not present.

**syntax**   The ways words are combined to form acceptable phrases and sentences.

## T

**telegraphic speech**   The use of short, precise words without grammatical markers such as articles, auxiliary verbs, and other connectives.

**temperament**   Involves individual differences in behavioural styles, emotions, and characteristic ways of responding.

**teratogen**   From the Greek word *teras*, meaning "monster." Any agent that causes a birth defect. The field of study that investigates the causes of birth defects is called teratology.

**testosterone**   An androgen that is a key hormone in boys' pubertal development.

**theory**   An interrelated, coherent set of ideas that helps to explain and make predictions.

**theory of mind**   Awareness of one's own mental processes and the mental processes of others.

**thinking**   Manipulating and transforming information in memory, usually to form concepts, reason, think critically, and solve problems.

**top-dog phenomenon**   The circumstance of moving from the top position in elementary school to the lowest position in middle or high school.

**transitivity**   Principle that if a relation holds between a first object and a second object, and holds between the second object and a third object, then it holds between the first object and the third object. Piaget argued that an understanding of transitivity is characteristic of concrete operational thought.

**triarchic theory of intelligence**   Sternberg's theory that intelligence comes in three forms: analytical, creative, and practical.

**trophoblast**   The outer layer of cells that develops in the germinal period. These cells provide nutrition and support for the embryo.

**Turner syndrome**   A chromosome disorder in females in which either an X chromosome is missing, making the person XO instead of XX, or the second X chromosome is partially deleted.

**twin study**   A study in which the behavioural similarity of identical twins is compared with the behavioural similarity of fraternal twins.

## U

**umbilical cord**   A life-support system that contains two arteries and one vein, and connects the baby to the placenta.

## V

**values clarification**   Helping people clarify their sense of their purpose in life and what is worth working for. Students are encouraged to define their own values and understand others' values.

**visual preference method**   Developed by Fantz to determine whether infants can distinguish one stimulus from another by measuring the length of time they attend to different stimuli.

**Vygotsky's theory**   A sociocultural cognitive theory that emphasizes how culture and social interaction guide cognitive development.

## W

**Wernicke's area**   An area of the brain's left hemisphere that is involved in language comprehension.

**whole-language approach**   An approach that stresses that reading instruction should parallel children's natural language learning. Reading materials should be whole and meaningful.

**working memory**   A mental "workbench" where individuals manipulate and assemble information when making decisions, solving problems, and comprehending written and spoken language.

## X

**XYY syndrome**   A chromosomal disorder in which males have an extra Y chromosome.

## Z

**zone of proximal development (ZPD)** Vygotsky's term for tasks that are too difficult for children to master alone but can be mastered with assistance from adults or more-skilled children.

**zygote**   A single cell formed through fertilization.

# references

## A

**Abasi, M., & others.** (2009). The effect of hypnosis on pain relief during labor and childbirth in Iranian pregnant women. *International Journal of Clinical and Experimental Hypnosis, 57,* 174–183.

**Abbott, L. C., & Winzer-Serhan, U. H.** (2012). Smoking during pregnancy: Lessons learned from epidemiological studies and experimental studies using animals. *Critical Reviews in Toxicology, 42,* 279–303.

**Ablow, J. C.** (2013). When parents conflict or disengage: Children's perception of parents' marital distress predicts school adaptation. In P. A. Cowan & others (Eds.), *The family context of parenting in children's adaptation to elementary school.* New York: Routledge.

**Accornero, V. H., Anthony, J. C., Morrow, C. E., Xue, L., & Bandstra, E. S.** (2006). Prenatal cocaine exposure: An examination of childhood externalizing and internalizing behavior problems at age 7 years. *Epidemiology, Psychiatry, and Society, 15,* 20–29.

**Achieve, Inc.** (2005). *An action agenda for improving America's high schools.* Washington, DC: Author.

**Ackerman, J. P., Riggins, T., & Black, M. M.** (2010). A review of the effects of prenatal cocaine exposure among school-aged children. *Pediatrics, 125,* 554–565.

**Adachi, P. J. C., & Willoughby, T.** (2012). Do video games promote positive youth development? *Journal of Adolescent Research, 28*(2): 155–165.

**Adams, M. A.** (2012). Mass media. In M. Kosut (Ed.), *Encyclopedia of gender in media.* Thousand Oaks, CA: Sage.

**Adamson, L., & Frick, J.** (2003). The still face: A history of a shared experimental paradigm. *Infancy, 4,* 451–473.

**Adler, P.A., & Adler, P.** (1998). *Peer power: Preadolescent culture and identity.* New Brunswick, NJ: Rutgers University Press.

**Adolph, K. E.** (1997). Learning in the development of infant locomotion. *Monographs of the Society for Research in Child Development, 62* (3, Serial No. 251).

**Adolph, K. E., & Berger, S. E.** (2005). Physical and motor development. In M. H. Bornstein & M. E. Lamb (Eds.), *Developmental psychology* (5th ed.). Mahwah, NJ: Erlbaum.

**Adolph, K. E., & Berger, S. E.** (2011). Development of the motor system. In H. Pashler & others (Eds.), *Encyclopedia of the mind.* Thousand Oaks, CA: Sage.

**Adolph, K. E., & Berger, S. E.** (2013). Development of the motor system. In H. Pashler, T. Crane, M. Kinsbourne, F. Ferreira, & R. Zemel (Eds.), *Encyclopedia of the mind.* Thousand Oaks, CA: Sage.

**Adolph, K. E., Cole, W. G., Komati, M., Garciaguirre, J. S., Badaly, D., Lingeman, J. M., Chan, G. L. Y. , & Sotsky, R. B.** (2012). How do you learn to walk? Thousands of steps and dozens of falls per day. *Psychological Science, 23,* 1387–1394.

**Adolph, K. E., Eppler, M. A., & Joh, A. S.** (2010, in press). Infants' perception of affordances of slopes under low and high friction conditions. *Journal of Experimental Psychology: Human Perception & Performance.*

**Adolph, K. E. & Joh, A. S.** (2009). Multiple learning mechanisms in the development of action. In A. Woodward & A. Needham (Eds.), *Learning and the infant mind.* New York: Oxford University Press.

**Adolph, K. E., Karasik, L. B., & Tamis-LeMonda, C. S.** (2010). Using social information to guide action: Infants' locomotion over slippery slopes. *Neural Networks, 23,* 1033–1042. (Special issue on social cognition).

**Adolph, K. E., & Robinson, S. R. R.** (2013). The road to walking: What learning to walk tells us about development. In P. Zelazo (Ed.) *Oxford handbook of developmental psychology.* New York: Oxford University Press.

**Adolph, K. E., Vereijken, B., & Shrout, P. E.** (2003). What changes in infant walking and why. *Child Development, 74,* 475–497.

**Agency for Healthcare Research and Quality.** (2007). *Evidence report/technology assessment number 153: Breastfeeding and maternal and health outcomes in developed countries.* Rockville, MD: U.S. Department of Health and Human Services.

**Agras, W. S., Hammer, L. D., McNicholas, F., & Kraemer, H. C.** (2004). Risk factors for childhood overweight: A prospective study from birth to 9.5 years. *Journal of Pediatrics, 145,* 20–25.

**Ainsworth, M. D. S.** (1979). Infant-mother attachment. *American Psychologist, 34,* 932–937.

**Akbari, A., & others.** (2010, in press). Parity and breastfeeding are preventive measures against breast cancer in Iranian women. *Breast Cancer.*

**Akhavan, S., & Lundgren, I.** (2012). Midwives' experiences of doula support for immigrant women in Sweden—A qualitative study. *Midwifery, 28,* 80–85.

**Akhtar, N., & Herold, K.** (2008). Pragmatic development. In M. M. Haith & J. B. Benson (Eds.), *Encyclopedia of infant and early childhood development.* Oxford, UK: Elsevier.

**Albert, D., & Steinberg, L.** (2011a). Judgment and decision making in adolescence. *Journal of Research in Adolescence, 21,* 211–224.

**Albert, D., & Steinberg, L.** (2011b). Peer influences on adolescent risk behavior. In M. Bardo, D. Fishbein, & R. Milich (Eds.), *Inhibitory control and drug abuse prevention.* New York: Springer.

**Allen, E. G., Freeman, S. B., Druschel, C., Hobbs, C. A., O'Leary, L. A., Romitti, P. A., Royle, M. H., Torfs, C. P., & Sherman, S. L.** (2009). Maternal age and risk for trisomy 21 assessed by the origin of chromosome nondisjunction: A report from the Atlanta and National Down Syndrome Projects. *Human Genetics, 125,* 41–52.

**Allen, J. P., & Miga, E. M.** (2010). Attachment in adolescence: A move to the level of emotion regulation. *Journal of Social and Personal Relationships, 27,* 181–190.

**Allen, J. P., & others.** (2009, April). *Portrait of the secure teen as an adult.* Paper presented at the meeting of the Society for Research in Child Development, Denver.

**Allen, M.** (2004). Reading achievement of students in French immersion programs. *Educational Quarterly Review, 9,* 25–30.

**Allor, J., & Al Otaiba, S. A.** (2013). In B. G. Cook & M. G. Tankersley (Eds.), *Research-based practices in special education.* Upper Saddle River, NJ: Pearson.

**Alloway, T. P., Gathercole, S. E., & Elliott, J.** (2010). Examining the link between working memory behavior and academic attainment in children with ADHD. *Developmental Medicine and Child Neurology.*

**Allstate Foundation.** (2005). *Teen driving: Chronic—A report on the state of teen driving.* Northbrook, IL: Author.

**Al-Sahab, B., Ardern, C. I., Hamadeh, M. J., & Tamim, H.** (2010). Age at menarche in Canada: Results from the National

Longitudinal Survey of Children & Youth. *BMC Public Health, 10,* www.biomedcentral.com/1471-2458/10/736

**Altarac, M., & Saroha, E.** (2007). Lifetime prevalence of learning disability among U.S. children. *Pediatrics, 119,* Suppl. 1, S77–S83.

**Alvarez, A.** (2009). Racism: "It isn't fair." In N. Tewari & A. Alvarez (Eds.), *Asian American psychology.* Clifton, NJ: Psychology Press.

**Amato, P. R.** (2006). Marital discord, divorce, and children's well-being: Results from a 20-year longitudinal study of two generations. In A. Clarke-Stewart & J. Dunn (Eds.), *Families count.* New York: Cambridge University Press.

**Amato, P. R., & Booth, A.** (1996). A prospective study of divorce and parent-child relationships. *Journal of Marriage and the Family, 58,* 356–365.

**Amato, P. R., & Dorius, C.** (2010). Fathers, children, and divorce. In M. E. Lamb (Ed.), *The role of the father in child development* (5th ed.). New York: Wiley.

**Ambert, A.** (2009). *Divorce: Facts, causes, and consequences* (3rd ed.). Ottawa: Vanier Institute of the Family.

**Amed, S., Daneman, D., Mahmud, F. H., & Hamilton, J.** (2010). Type 2 diabetes in children and adolescents. *Expert Review of Cardiovascular Therapy, 8,* 393–406.

**Amed, S., Dean, H. J., Panagiotopoulos, C. & others.** (2010). Type 2 diabetes, medication-induced diabetes, and monogenic diabetes in Canadian children: A prospective national surveillance study. *Diabetes Care, 33*(4), 786–791.

**American Academy of Pediatrics.** (2001). Committee on Public Education: Children, adolescents, and television. *Pediatrics, 107,* 423–426.

**American Academy of Pediatrics.** (2001). Health care supervision for children with Williams syndrome. *Pediatrics, 107,* 1192–1204.

**American Academy of Pediatrics Work Group on Breastfeeding.** (1997). Breastfeeding and the use of human milk. *Pediatrics, 100,* 1035–1039.

**American Association on Mental Retardation, Ad Hoc Committee on Terminology and Classification.** (1992). *Mental retardation* (9th ed.). Washington, DC: Author.

**Amos, D., & Johnson, S. P.** (2010). Building object knowledge from perceptual input. To appear in B. Hood & L. Santos (Eds.), *The origins of object knowledge.* New York: Oxford University Press.

**Amsel, E., & Smetana, J. G.** (Eds.). (2011). *Adolescent vulnerabilities and opportunities: Constructivist and development perspectives.* New York: Cambridge University Press.

**Amsterdam, B. K.** (1968). *Mirror behavior in children under two years of age.* Unpublished doctoral dissertation, University of North Carolina, Chapel Hill.

**Anastasi, A., & Urbina, S.** (1997). *Psychological testing* (7th ed.). Upper Saddle River, NJ: Prentice Hall.

**Anderman, E. M.** (2012). Adolescence. In K. Harris, S. Graham, & T. Urdan (Eds.), *APA handbook of educational psychology.* Washington, DC: American Psychological Association.

**Anderman, E. M., & Anderman, L. H.** (2010). *Classroom motivation.* Upper Saddle River, NJ: Prentice Hall.

**Anderman, E. M., Gray, D. L., & Chang, Y.** (2013). Motivation and classroom learning. In I. B. Weiner & others (Eds.), *Handbook of psychology* (2nd ed., Vol. 7). New York: Wiley.

**Anderson, C. A., Gentile, D. A., & Buckley, K. E.** (2007). *Violent video game effects on children and adolescents.* New York: Oxford University Press.

**Anderson, D. R., Huston, A. C., Schmitt, K., Linebarger, D. L., & Wright, J. C.** (2001). Early childhood viewing and adolescent behavior: The recontact study. *Monographs of the Society for Research in Child Development, 66*(1), Serial No. 264.

**Anderson, D. R., Lorch, E. P., Field, D. E., Collins, P. A., & Nathan, J. G.** (1985, April). *Television viewing at home: Age trends in visual attention and time with TV.* Paper presented at the biennial meeting of the Society of Research in Child Development, Toronto.

**Anderson, E., Greene, S. M., Hetherington, E. M., & Clingempeel, W. G.** (1999). The dynamics of parental remarriage. In E. M. Hetherington (Ed.), *Coping with divorce, single parenting, and remarriage.* Mahwah, NJ: Erlbaum.

**Anderson, E. R., & Greene, S. M.** (2011). "My child and I are a package deal": Balancing adult and child concerns in repartnering after divorce. *Journal of Family Psychology, 25,* 741–750.

**Anderson, P. J., & others** (2011). Attention problems in a representative sample of extremely preterm/extremely low birth weight children. *Developmental Neuropsychology, 36,* 57–73.

**Anderson, S. E., Gooze, R. A., Lemeshow, S., & Whitaker, R. C.** (2012). Quality of early maternal-child relationship and risk of adolescent obesity. *Pediatrics, 129,* 132–140.

**Andersson, H., & Bergman, L. R.** (2011). The role of task persistence in young adolescence for successful educational and occupational attainment in middle adulthood. *Developmental Psychology, 47,* 950–960.

**Ang, S., Dyne, L. V., & Tan, M. L.** (2011). Cultural intelligence. In R. J. Sternberg & S. B. Kaufman (Eds.), *Cambridge handbook of intelligence.* New York: Cambridge University Press.

**Ang, S. Y., & Lee, K.** (2010). Exploring developmental differences in visual short-term memory and working memory. *Developmental Psychology, 46,* 279–285.

**Ansary, N. S., & Luthar, S. S.** (2009). Distress and academic achievement among adolescents of affluence: A study of externalizing and internalizing problem behaviors and school performance. *Development and Psychopathology, 21,* 319–341.

**Anspaugh, D., & Ezell, G.** (2013). *Teaching today's health* (10th ed.). Upper Saddle River, NJ: Pearson.

**Antonopoulos, C., & others** (2011). Maternal smoking during pregnancy and childhood lymphoma: A meta-analysis. *International Journal of Cancer, 129,* 2694–2703.

**Antonucci, T. C., Birditt, K., & Ajrouch, K.** (2013, in press). Social relationships and aging. In I. B. Weiner & others (Eds.), *Handbook of psychology* (2nd ed., Vol. 6). New York: Wiley.

**Apperly, I. A.** (2012). EPS prize lecture. "What is theory of mind?": Concepts, cognitive processes, and individual differences. *Quarterly Journal of Experimental Psychology, 65,* 825–839.

**Appleton, J. J.** (2012). Student engagement in school. In J. R. Levesque (Ed.), *Encyclopedia of adolescence.* New York: Springer.

**Arends, R. I.** (2012). *Learning to teach* (9th ed.). New York: McGraw-Hill.

**Arim, R. G., Tramonte, L., Shapka, J. D., Dahinten, V. S., & Willms, J. D.** (2011). The family antecedents and the subsequent outcomes of early puberty. *Journal of Youth and Adolescence, 40,* 1423–1435.

**Armstrong, A. R., Galligan, R. F., & Critchley, C. R.** (2011). Emotional intelligence and psychological resilience to negative life events. *Personality and Individual Differences, 51,* 331–336.

**Arnett, J. J.** (2006). Emerging adulthood: Understanding the new way of coming of age. In J. J. Arnett & J. L. Tanner (Eds.), *Emerging adults in America.* Washington, DC: American Psychological Association.

**Aronson, E.** (1986, August). *Teaching students things they think they already know about: The case of prejudice and desegregation.* Paper presented at the meeting of the American Psychological Association, Washington, DC.

**Aronson, J.** (2002). Stereotype threat: Contending and coping with unnerving expectations. In J. Aronson (Ed.), *Improving academic achievement.* San Diego: Academic Press.

**Arseth, A., Kroger, J., Martinussen, M., & Marcia, J. E.** (2009). Meta-analytic studies of identity status and the relational issues of attachment and intimacy. *Identity, 9,* 1–32.

**Arterberry, M. E.** (2008). Perceptual development. In M. E. Haith & J. B. Benson (Eds.), *Encyclopedia of infant and early childhood development.* Oxford, UK: Elsevier.

**Asendorph, J. B.** (2008). Shyness. In M. M. Haith & J. B. Benson (Eds.), *Encyclopedia of infant and early childhood development.* Oxford, UK: Elsevier.

**Ashmead, D. H., Wall, R. S., Ebinger, K. A., Hill, M. M., Yang, X., and Eaton, S.** (1998). Spatial hearing in children with visual disabilities. *Perception, 27,* 105–122.

**Aslin, R. N.** (2009). The role of learning in cognitive development. In A. Woodward & A. Needham (Eds.), *Learning and the infant mind.* New York: Oxford University Press.

**Aslin, R. N.** (2012). Infant eyes: A window on cognitive development. *Infancy, 17,* 126–140.

**Aslin, R. N., Jusczyk, P. W., & Pisoni, D. B.** (1998). Speech and auditory processing during infancy: Constraints on and precursors to language. In W. Damon (Ed.), *Handbook of child psychology* (5th ed., Vol. 2). New York: Wiley.

**Aslin, R. N., & Lathrop, A. L.** (2008). Visual perception. In M. M. Haith & J. B. Benson (Eds.), *Encyclopedia of infant and early childhood development.* Oxford, UK: Elsevier.

**Astington, J. W., & Hughes, C.** (2013). Theory of mind: Self-reflection and social understanding. In P. D. Zelazo (Ed.), *Oxford handbook of developmental psychology.* New York: Oxford University Press.

**Atkinson, J., & Braddick, O.** (2013). Visual development. In P. D. Zelazo (Ed.), *Oxford handbook of developmental psychology.* New York: Oxford University Press.

**Attorp, A., Scott, J. E., Yew, A. C., Rhodes, R. E., Barr, S. I., & Naylor, P.** (2014). Associations between socioeconomic, parental and home environment factors and fruit and vegetable consumption of children in grades five and six in British Columbia, Canada. *BMC Public Health,* 14:150 doi:10.1186/1471-2458-14-150

**Audesirk, G., Audesirk, T., & Byers, B. E.** (2011). *Biology* (9th ed.). Upper Saddle River, NJ: Benjamin Cummings.

**Auyeung, B., Baron-Cohen, S., Ashwin, E., Knickmeyer, R., Taylor, K., Hackett, G., & Hines, M.** (2009). Fetal testosterone predicts sexually differentiated childhood behavior in girls and boys. *Psychological Science, 20,* 144–148.

**Avent, N. D., Plummer, Z. E., Madgett, T. E., Maddocks, D. G., & Soothill, P. W.** (2008). Post-genomic studies and their application to non-invasive prenatal diagnosis. *Seminars in Fetal and Neonatal Medicine, 13,* 91–98.

**Awong, T., Grusec, J. E., & Sorenson, A.** (2008). Respect-based control and anger as determinants of children's socio-emotional development. *Social Development, 17*(4), 941–959.

# B

**Babble, E. R.** (2011). *The basics of social research* (5th ed.). Boston: Cengage.

**Babiss, L. A., & Gangwisch, J. E.** (2009). Sports participation as a protective factor against depression and suicidal ideation in adolescents as mediated by self-esteem and social support. *Journal of Developmental and Behavioral Pediatrics, 30*(5), 376–384.

**Bacchini, D., & Magliulo, F.** (2003). Self-image and perceived self-efficacy during adolescence. *Journal of Youth and Adolescence. 32,* 337–349.

**Badaly, D. & Adolph, K. E.** (2008). Beyond the average: Walking infants take steps longer than their leg length. *Infant Behavior and Development, 31,* 554–558.

**Baddeley, A. D.** (1990). *Human memory: Theory and practice.* Boston: Allyn & Bacon.

**Baddeley, A. D.** (2010). Working memory. *Current Biology, 20,* 136–140.

**Baddeley, A.** (2012). Working memory: Theories, models, and controversies. *Annual Review of Psychology, 63,* 1–29.

**Baer, S., Saran, K., Green, D.A., & Hong, I.** (2012). Electronic media use and addiction among youth in psychiatric clinic versus school populations. *Canadian Journal of Psychiatry, 57*(12), 728–735.

**Bahali, K., Akcan, R., Tahiroglu, A. Y., & Avci, A.** (2010, in press). Child sexual abuse: Seven years into practice. *Journal of Forensic Science.*

**Bahrick, L. E.** (2010). Intermodal perception and selective attention to intersensory redundancy: Implications for social development and autism. In J. G. Bremner & T. D. Wachs (Eds.), *Wiley-Blackwell handbook of infant development* (2nd ed.). New York: Wiley.

**Bahrick, L. E., & Hollich, G.** (2008). Intermodal perception. In M. M. Haith & J. B. Benson (Eds.), *Encyclopedia of infant and early childhood development.* Oxford, UK: Elsevier.

**Baillargeon, R.** (1995). The object concept revisited: New directions in the investigation of infants' physical knowledge. In C. E. Granrud (Ed.), *Visual perception and cognition in infancy.* Hillsdale, NJ: Erlbaum.

**Baillargeon, R.** (2004). The acquisition of physical knowledge in infancy: A summary in eight lessons. In U. Goswami (Ed.), *Blackwell handbook of childhood cognitive development.* Malden, MA: Blackwell.

**Baillargeon, R.** (2008). Innate ideas revisited: For a principle of persistence in infants' physical reasoning. *Perspectives on Psychological Science, 3,* 2–13.

**Baillargeon, R.** (2014). Cognitive development in infancy. *Annual Review of Psychology* (Vol. 65). Palo Alto, CA: Annual Reviews.

**Baillargeon, R., & Devoe, S. J.** (1991). Object permanence in young children: Further evidence. *Child Development, 62,* 1227–1246.

**Baillargeon, R., Li, J., Gernter, Y., & Wu, D.** (2011). How do infants reason about physical events? *Wiley-Blackwell handbook of childhood cognitive development* (2nd ed.). New York: Wiley-Blackwell.

**Baillargeon, R., Li, J., Ng, W., & Yuan, S.** (2009). A new account of infants' physical reasoning. In A. Woodward & A. Needham (Eds.), *Learning and the infant mind* (pp. 66–116). New York: Oxford University Press.

**Baillargeon, R., & others.** (2012). Object individuation and physical reasoning in infancy: An integrative account. *Language, Learning, and Development, 8,* 4–46.

**Baker, J. K., Fenning, R. M., & Crnic, K. A.** (2011). Emotion socialization by mothers and fathers: Coherence among behaviors and associations with parent attitudes and children's competence. *Social Development, 20,* 412–430.

**Bakermans-Kranenburg, M. J., Breddels-Van Bardewijk, F., Juffer, M. K., Velderman, M. H., & van IJzendoorn, M. H.** (2007). Insecure mothers with temperamentally reactive infants. In F. Juffer, M. J. Bakermans-Kranenburg, & M. H. van IJzendoorn (Eds.), *Promoting positive parenting.* Mahwah, NJ: Erlbaum.

**Bala, N., Lee, K., Lindsay, R. C. L., & Talwar, V.** (2010). The competency of children to testify: Psychological research informing Canadian law reform. *International Journal of Children's Rights, 18,* 53–77.

**Baldwin, S. A., Christian, S., Berkeljon, A., & Shadish, W. R.** (2012). The effects of family therapies for adolescent delinquency and substance abuse: A meta-analysis. *Journal of Marital and Family Therapy, 38,* 281–304.

Baldwin, S. A. & Hoffmann, J. P. (2002). The dynamics of self-esteem: A growth-curve analysis. *Journal of Youth and Adolescence, 31,* 101–113.

Balsano, A. B., Theokas, C., & Bobek, D. L. (2009). A shared commitment to youth: The integration of theory, research practice, and social policy. In R. M. Lerner & L. Steinberg (Eds.), *Handbook of adolescent psychology* (3rd ed.). New York: Wiley.

Baltes, P. B., & Smith, J. (2008). The fascination of wisdom: Its nature, ontogeny, and function. *Perspectives in Psychological Sciences, 3,* 56–64.

Bandura, A. (1991). Social cognitive theory of moral thought and action. In W. M. Kurtines & J. L. Gewirtz (Eds.), *Handbook of moral behavior and development* (Vol. 1). Hillsdale, NJ: Erlbaum.

Bandura, A. (1997). *Self-efficacy.* New York: W. H. Freeman.

Bandura, A. (1998, August). *Swimming against the mainstream: Accentuating the positive aspects of humanity.* Paper presented at the meeting of the American Psychological Association, San Francisco.

Bandura, A. (2000). Self-efficacy. In A. Kazdin (Ed.), *Encyclopedia of psychology.* Washington, DC, and New York: American Psychological Association and Oxford University Press.

Bandura, A. (2001). Social cognitive theory. *Annual Review of Psychology* (Vol. 52). Palo Alto, CA: Annual Reviews.

Bandura, A. (2002). Selective moral disengagement in the exercise of moral agency. *Journal of Moral Education, 31,* 101–119.

Bandura, A. (2004, May). *Toward a psychology of human agency.* Paper presented at the meeting of the American Psychological Society, Chicago.

Bandura, A. (2007). Social cognitive theory. In W. Donsbach (Ed.), *International encyclopedia of communication.* Thousand Oaks, CA: Sage.

Bandura, A. (2008). Reconstrual of "free will" from the agentic perspective of social cognitive theory. In J. Baer, J. C. Kaufman, & R. F. Baumeister (Eds.), *Are we free? Psychology and free will.* Oxford, UK: Oxford University Press.

Bandura, A. (2010a). Self-efficacy. In D. Matsumoto (Ed.), *Cambridge dictionary of psychology.* Cambridge, UK: Cambridge University Press.

Bandura, A. (2010b). Vicarious learning. In D. Matsumoto (Ed.), *Cambridge dictionary of psychology.* New York: Cambridge University Press.

Bandura, A. (2012). Social cognitive theory. *Annual Review of Clinical Psychology* (Vol. 8). Palo Alto, CA: Annual Reviews.

Bank, L., Burraston, B., & Snyder, J. (2004). Sibling conflict and ineffective parenting as predictors of adolescent boys' antisocial behavior and peer difficulties: Additive and interactive effects. *Journal of Research on Adolescence, 14,* 99–125.

Banks, J. A. (Ed.) (2010). *The Routledge international companion to multicultural education.* New York: Routledge.

Barabasz, A., & Perez, N. (2007). Salient findings: Hypnotizability as core construct and the clinical utility of hypnosis. *International Journal of Clinical Hypnosis, 55,* 372–379.

Barac, R., & Bialystok, E. (2012). Bilingual effects on cognitive and linguistic development: Role of language, cultural background, and education. *Child Development, 83,* 413–422.

Barakat, R., & others (2011). Exercise during pregnancy improves maternal health perception: A randomized controlled trial. *American Journal of Obstetrics and Gynecology, 204,* 402.

Barbarin, O. A., & Miller, K. M. (2009). Developmental science and early education: An introduction. In O. A. Barbarin & B. H. Wasik (Eds.), *Handbook of child development and early education.* New York: Oxford University.

Barlett, C. P., & Anderson, C. A. (2009). Violent video games and public policy. In T. Bevc & H. Zapf (Eds.), *Wie wir spielen, was wir werden: Computerspiele in unserer Gesellschaft. Konstanz: UVK Verlagsgesellschaft.* (German version)

Barlett, C. P., Anderson, C. A., & Swing, E. L. (2009). Video game effects confirmed, suspected and speculative: A review of the evidence. *Simulation & Gaming, 40,* 377–403.

Barnett, S. M., Rindermann, H., Williams, W. M., & Ceci, S. J. (2011). Society and intelligence. In R. J. Sternberg & S. B. Kaufman (Eds.), *Cambridge handbook of intelligence.* New York: Cambridge University Press.

Barnett, W. S., & others. (2006). *Educational effectiveness of the Tools of the Mind curriculum: A randomized trial.* New Brunswick, NJ: National Institute of Early Education Research, Rutgers University.

Barnouw, V. (1975). *An introduction to anthropology: Vol. 2. Ethnology.* Homewood, IL: Dorsey Press.

Baron-Cohen, S. (2008). Autism, hypersystemizing, and truth. *Quarterly Journal of Experimental Psychology, 61,* 64–75.

Baron-Cohen, S. (2009). Autism: The empathizing-systemizing (E-S) theory. *Annals of the New York Academy of Sciences, 1156,* 68–80.

Baron-Cohen, S. (2011). The empathizing-systematizing (E-S) theory of autism: A cognitive developmental account. In U. Goswami (Ed.), *Wiley-Blackwell handbook of childhood cognitive development* (2nd ed.). New York: Wiley-Blackwell.

Baron-Cohen, S., Golan, O., Chapman, E., & Granader, Y. (2007). Transported to a world of emotions. *The Psychologist, 20,* 76–77.

Barrett, D. E., Radke-Yarrow, M., & Klein, R. E. (1982). Chronic malnutrition and child behavior: Effects of calorie supplementation on social and emotional functioning at school age. *Developmental Psychology, 18,* 541–556.

Bartle, C. (2007). Developing a service for children with iron deficiency anemia. *Nursing Standard, 21,* 44–49.

Bartsch, K., & Wellman, H. M. (1995). *Children talk about the mind.* Oxford, UK: Oxford University Press.

Bascandziev, I., & Harris, P. L. (2011). The role of testimony in young children's solution of a gravity-driven invisible displacement task. *Cognitive Development, 25,* 233–246.

Batanova, M. D., & Loukas, A. (2011). Social anxiety and aggression in early adolescents: Examining the moderating roles of empathic concern and perspective taking. *Journal of Youth and Adolescence, 40,* 1534–1543.

Bates, J. E. (2008). Unpublished review of J. W. Santrock, *Children* (11th ed.). New York: McGraw-Hill.

Bates, J. E. (2012a). Behavioral regulation as a product of temperament and environment. In S. L. Olson & A. J. Sameroff (Eds.), *Biopsychosocial regulatory processes in the development of childhood behavioral problems.* New York: Cambridge University Press.

Bates, J. E. (2012b). Temperament as a tool in promoting early childhood development. In S. L. Odom, E. P. Pungello, & N. Gardner-Neblett (Eds.), *Infants, toddlers, and families in poverty.* New York: Guilford University Press.

Bates, J. E. & Pettit, G. S. (2007). Temperament, parenting, and socialization. In J. E. Grusec & P. D. Hastings (Eds.), *Handbook of socialization.* New York: Guilford.

Battistich, V. A. (2008). The Child Development Project: Creating caring school communities. In L. Nucci & D. Narváez (Eds.), *Handbook of moral and character education.* Clifton, NJ: Psychology Press.

Bauer, P. (2013). Memory. In P. D. Zelazo (Ed.), *Oxford handbook of developmental psychology.* New York: Oxford University Press.

Bauer, P. J. (2009). Learning and memory: Like a horse and carriage. In A. Netdham & A. Woodward (Eds.), *Learning and the infant mind*. New York: Oxford University Press.

Bauer, P. J., & Fivush, R. (Eds.). (2013, in press). *Wiley-Blackwell handbook of children's memory*. New York: Wiley.

Bauer, P. J., Wenner, J. A., Dropik, P. I., & Wewerka, S. S. (2000). Parameters of remembering and forgetting in the transition from infancy to early childhood. *Monographs of the Society for Research in Child Development, 65* (4, Serial No. 263).

Bauerlein. M. (2008). *The dumbest generation: How the digital age stupefies young Americans and jeopardizes our future (Or, don't trust anyone under 30)*. New York: Tarcher.

Baumeister, R. F. (2013, in press). Self-esteem. In E. Anderson (Ed.), *Psychology of classroom learning: An encyclopedia*. Detroit: Macmillan.

Baumeister, R. F., Campbell, J. D., Krueger, J. L., & Vohs, K. D. (2003). Does high self-esteem cause better performance, interpersonal success, happiness, or healthier lifestyles? *Psychological Science in the Public Interest, 4*(1), 1–44.

Baumrind, D. (1971). Current patterns of parental authority. *Developmental Psychology Monographs, 4* (1, Pt. 2).

Baumrind, D. (1999, November). Unpublished review of J. W. Santrock's *Child development* (9th ed.). New York: McGraw-Hill.

Baumrind, D., Larzelere, R. E., & Cowan, P. A. (2002). Ordinary physical punishment: Is it harmful? Comment on Gershoff. *Psychological Bulletin, 128,* 590–595.

Baumrind, D. (2012). Authoritative parenting revisited: History and current status. In R. Larzelere, A. S. Morris, & A. W. Harist (Eds.), *Authoritative parenting*. Washington, DC: American Psychological Association.

Bauserman, R. (2002). Child adjustment in joint-custody versus sole-custody arrangements: A meta-analytic review. *Journal of Family Psychology. 16,* 91–102.

Bayley, N. (1969). *Manual for the Bayley Scales of Infant Development*. New York: Psychological Corporation.

Bayley, N. (2006). *Bayley Scales of Infant and Toddler Development* (3rd ed.). San Antonio: Harcourt Assessment.

Baysinger, C. (2010). Imaging during pregnancy. *Anesthesia & Analgesia, 110,* 863–867.

Beach, J., Bertrand, J., & Cleveland, G. (1998). *Our child care workforce: From recognition to remuneration, a human resource study of child care in Canada*. The Child Care Sector Study Steering Committee, Human Resources Development Canada.

Beach, J., Friendly, M., Ferns, C., Prabhu, N., & Forer, B. (2009). *Early childhood education and care in Canada 2008*. Child Care Canada.

Beatty, J. J., & Pratt, L. (2011). *Early literacy in preschool and kindergarten* (3rd ed.). Boston: Allyn & Bacon.

Beauchamp, G. K., & Mennella, J. A. (2009). Early flavor learning and its impact on later feeding behavior. *Journal of Pediatric Gastroenterology and Nutrition 48*(Suppl 1.):S25–S30.

Bechtold, A. G., Bushnell, E. W., & Salapatck, P. (1979, April.) Infants' visual localization of visual and auditory targets. Paper presented at the meeting of the Society for Research in Child Development, San Francisco.

Becker, A. J., McCulloch, E. A., & Till, J. E. (1963). Cytological demonstrations of the clonal nature of spleen colonies derived from transplanted mouse marrow cells. *Nature, 197,* 452–454.

Bedford, R., & others. (2012). Precursors to social and communication difficulties in infants at-risk for autism: Gaze following and attentional engagement. *Journal of Autism and Developmental Disorders, 42,* 2208–2218.

Beebe, D. W., Rose, D., & Amin, R. (2010). Attention, learning, and arousal of experimentally sleep-restricted adolescents in a simulated classroom. *Journal of Adolescent Health, 47,* 523–525.

Beeghly, M., Martin, B., Rose-Jacobs, R., Cahral, H., Heeren, T., Augustyn, M., Bellinger, D., & Frank, D. A. (2006). Prenatal cocaine exposure and children's language functioning at 6 and 9.5 years: Moderating effects of child age, birthweight, and gender. *Journal of Pediatric Psychology, 31,* 98–115.

Beets, M. W., & Foley, J. T. (2008). Association of father involvement and neighborhood quality with kindergarteners' physical activity: A multilevel structural equation model. *American Journal of Health Promotion, 22,* 195–203.

Beghetto, R. A., & Kaufman, J. C. (Eds.). (2010). *Nurturing creativity in the classroom*. New York: Cambridge University Press.

Begley, S., & Interlandi, J. (2008, June 2). The dumbest generation? Don't be dumb. *Newsweek*. Retrieved on July 22, 2008, from www.newsweek.com/id/138536/

Begus, K., & Southgate, V. (2012). Infant pointing serves an interrogative function. *Developmental Science, 15,* 611–617.

Behrens, H. (2012). Grammatical categories. In E. L. Bavin (Ed.), *Cambridge handbook of child language*. New York: Cambridge University Press.

Beilock, S. L, Rydell, R. J., & McConnell, A. R. (2007). Stereotype threat and working memory: Mechanisms, alleviation, and spillover. *Journal of Experimental Psychology: General, 136,* 256–276.

Bell, M. A., & Cuevas, K. (2012). Using EEG to study cognitive development: Issues and practices. *Journal of Cognition and Development, 13,* 281–294.

Bell, M. A., & Cuevas, K. (2013). Psychobiology of executive function in early development. In J. A. Griffin, L. S. Freund, & P. McCardle (Eds.), *Executive function in preschool children*. Washington, DC: American Psychological Association.

Bell, S. M., & Ainsworth, M. D. S. (1972). Infant crying and maternal responsiveness. *Child Development, 43,* 1171–1190.

Belsky, J. (1981). Early human experience: A family perspective. *Developmental Psychology. 17,* 3–23.

Belsky, J., Jaffe, S., Hsieh, K., & Silva, P. (2001). Child-rearing antecedents of intergenerational relations in young adulthood: A prospective study. *Developmental Psychology, 37,* 801–813.

Belson, W. (1978). *Television violence and the adolescent boy*. London: Saxon House.

Bem, S. L. (1977). On the utility of alternative procedures for assessing psychological androgyny. *Journal of Consulting and Clinical Psychology. 45,* 196–205.

Bender, H. L., Allen, J. P., McElhaney, K. B., Antonishak, J., Moore, C. M., Kello, H. O., & Davis, S. M. (2007). Use of harsh physical discipline and developmental outcomes in adolescence. *Development and Psychopathology. 19,* 227–242.

Bendersky, M., & Sullivan, M. W. (2007). Basic methods in infant research. In A. Slater & M. Lewis (Eds.), *Infant development* (2nd ed.). New York: Oxford University Press.

Benediktsson, I., McDonald, S. W., Vekved, M., McNeil, D. A., Dolan, S. M., & Tough, S. C. (2013). Comparing CenteringPregnancy to standard prenatal care plus prenatal education. *BMC Pregnancy and Childbirth 2013, 13* (Suppl 1):S5 doi:10.1186/1471-2393-13-S1-S5

Benenson, J. F., Markovits, H., Roy, R., & Denko, P. (2003). Behavioural rules underlying learning to share: Effects of development and context. *International Journal of Behavioral Development, 27*(2), 116–121.

Bengtsson, H., & Arvidsson, A. (2011). The impact of developing social perspective-taking skills on emotionality in middle and late childhood. *Social Development, 20,* 353-375.

Benn, P. A., & Chapman, A. R. (2010). Ethical challenges in providing noninvasive prenatal diagnosis. *Current Opinion in Obstetrics and Gynecology, 22,* 128-134.

Benner, A. D. (2011). Latino adolescents' loneliness, academic performance, and the buffering nature of friendships. *Journal of Youth and Adolescence, 5,* 556-567.

Benner, A. D., & Mistry, R. S. (2007). Congruence of mother and teacher educational expectations and low-income youth's academic competence. *Journal of Educational Psychology, 99,* 140-153.

Bennett, S. A., Bagot, C. N., & Arya, R. (2012). Pregnancy loss and thrombophilia: The elusive link. *British Journal of Hematology, 157,* 529-542.

Benoit, D., Coolbear, J., & Crawford, A. (2008). Abuse, neglect, and maltreatment of infants. In M. M. Haith & J. B. Benson (Eds.), *Encyclopedia of infant and early childhood development.* Oxford, UK: Elsevier.

Benowitz-Fredericks, C. A., Garcia, K., Massey, M., Vassagar, B., & Borzekowski, D. L. (2012). Body image, eating disorders, and the relationship to adolescent media use. *Pediatric Clinics of North America, 59,* 693-704.

Benson, J. M., & Therrell, B. L. (2010). History and current status of newborn screening for hemoglobinopathies. *Seminars in Perinatology, 34,* 134-144.

Benveniste, L., Carnoy, M., & Rothstein, R. (2003). *All else equal.* New York: Routledge-Farmer.

Berenbaum, S. A., & Bailey, J. M. (2003). Effects on gender identity of prenatal androgens and genital appearance: Evidence from girls with congenital adrenal hyperplasia. *Journal of Clinical Endocrinology and Metabolism, 88,* 1102-1106.

Bergen, D. (1988). Stages of play development. In D. Bergen (Ed.), *Play as a medium for learning and development.* Portsmouth, NH: Heinemann.

Bergen, D., & Fromberg, D. P. (2009). Play and social interaction in middle childhood. *Phi Delta Kappan, 90,* 426-430.

Berlin, L. J., & others. (2009). Correlates and consequences of spanking and verbal punishment for low-income, White, African American, and Mexican American toddlers. *Child Development, 80,* 1403-1420.

Berman, S. L., You, Y., Schwartz, S., Teo, G., & Mochizuki, K. (2011). Identity exploration, commitment, and distress: A cross national investigation in China, Taiwan, Japan, and the United States. *Child Youth Care Forum, 40,* 65-75.

Berk, L. E. (1994). Why children talk to themselves. *Scientific American, 271*(5), 78-83.

Berk, L. E., & Spuhl, S. T. (1995). Maternal interaction, private speech, and task performance in preschool children. *Early Childhood Research Quarterly, 10,* 145-169.

Berko, J. (1958). The child's learning of English morphology. *Word, 14,* 15-177.

Berko Gleason, J. (2003). Unpublished review of J. W. Santrock's *Life-span development,* 9th ed. (New York: McGraw-Hill).

Berko Gleason, J. (2005). The development of language: An overview and a preview. In J. Berko Gleason (Ed.), *The development of language* (6th ed.). Boston: Allyn & Bacon.

Berko Gleason, J. (2009). The development of language. An overview. In J. Berko Gleason & N. B. Rather (Eds.), *The development of language* (7th ed.). Boston: Allyn & Bacon.

Berko Gleason, J., & Ratner, N. B. (Eds.). (2009). *The development of language* (7th ed.). Boston: Allyn & Bacon.

Berkowitz, M. W., Battistich, V. A., & Bier, M. (2008). What works in character education: What is known and what needs to be known. In L. Nucci & D. Narvaez (Eds.), *Handbook of moral and character education.* New York: Psychology Press.

Berkowitz, M. W., Sherblom, S., Bier, M., & Battistich, V. (2013). Educating for positive youth development. In M. Killen & J. G. Smetana (Eds.), *Handbook of moral development* (2nd ed.). New York: Routledge.

Berlin, C. M., Paul, I. M., & Vesell, E. S. (2009). Safety issues of maternal drug therapy during breastfeeding. *Clinical Pharmacology and Therapeutics, 85,* 20-22.

Berlin, L. J. (2012). Leveraging attachment research to re-vision infant/toddler care for poor families. In S. L. Odom, E. P. Pungello, & N. Gardner-Nesblett (Eds.), *Infants, toddlers, and families in poverty.* New York: Guilford.

Berlyne, D. E. (1960). *Conflict, arousal, and curiosity.* New York: McGraw-Hill.

Berman, R. A. (2010). Developing linguistic knowledge and language use across adolescence. In E. Hoff & M. Shatz (Eds.), *Blackwell handbook of language development.* New York: Wiley.

Bernard, K., & Dozier, M. (2008). Adoption and foster placement. In M. M. Haith & J. B. Benson (Eds.), *Encyclopedia of infant and early childhood development.* Oxford, UK: Elsevier.

Berndt, T. J. (1979). Developmental changes in conformity to peers and parents. *Developmental Psychology, 15,* 608-616.

Berndt, T. J. (1982). The features and effects of friendships in early adolescence. *Child Development, 53,* 1447-1460.

Berndt, T. J. (1999). Friends' influence on children's adjustment. In W. A. Collins & B. Laursen (Eds.), *Relationships as developmental contexts.* Mahwah, NJ: Erlbaum.

Berndt, T. J., & Perry, T. B. (1990). Distinctive features and effects of early adolescent friendships. In R. Montemayor (Ed.), *Advances in adolescent research.* Greenwich, CT: JAI Press.

Berninger, V. W. (2006). Learning disabilities. In W. Damon & R. Lerner (Eds.), *Handbook of child psychology* (6th ed.). New York: Wiley.

Berninger, V. W., & Abbott, R. (2005, April). *Paths leading to reading comprehension in at-risk and normally developing second-grade readers.* Paper presented at the meeting of the Society for Research in Child Development, Atlanta.

Berninger, V. W., & O'Malley, M. M. (2011). Evidence-based diagnosis and treatment for specific learning disabilities involving impairments in written and/ or oral language. *Journal of Learning Disabilities, 44,* 167-183.

Berninger, V., & Swanson, H. L. (2013). Diagnosing and treating specific learning disabilities in reference to the brain's working memory system. In H. L. Swanson & others (Eds.), *Handbook of learning disabilities* (2nd ed.). New York: Guilford.

Berry, J. W. (2005). Acculturation: Living successfully in two cultures. *Journal of Intercultural Relations, 29,* 697-712.

Berry, J. W., Phinney, J. S., Sam, D. L., & Vedder, P. (2006). Immigrant youth: Acculturation, ethnic identity, and adaptation. *Journal of Applied Psychology: An International Review, 55,* 303-332.

Bertenthal, B. I. (2008). Perception and action. In M. M. Haith & J. B. Benson (Eds.), *Infant and early childhood development.* Oxford, UK: Elsevier.

Bertenthal, B. I., Longo, M. R., & Kenny, S. (2007). Phenomenal permanence and the development of predictive tracking in infancy. *Child Development, 78,* 350-363.

Bertoglio, K., & Hendren, R. L. (2009). New developments in autism. *Psychiatric Clinics of North America, 32,* 1-14.

Best, D. L. (2010). Gender. In M. H. Bornstein (Ed.), *Handbook of cultural developmental science.* New York: Psychology Press.

Betz, N. E. (2004). Contributions of self-efficacy theory to career counseling: A personal perspective. *Career Development Quarterly, 52,* 340-353.

Bialystok, E. (1997). Effects of bilingualism and biliteracy on children's emerging concepts of print. *Developmental Psychology, 33,* 429-440.

Bialystok, E. (2001). *Bilingualism in development: Language, literacy, and cognition.* New York: Cambridge University Press.

Bialystok, E. (2007). Acquisition of literacy in preschool children: A framework for research. *Language Learning, 57,* 45-77.

Bialystok, E. (2011). Reshaping the mind: The benefits of bilingualism. *Canadian Journal of Experimental Psychology, 65,* 229-235.

Bialystok, E., & Craik, F.I.M. (2010). Cognitive and linguistic processing in the bilingual mind. *Current Directions in Psychological Science, 19,* 19-23.

Bialystok, E., Craik, F. I. M., & Luk, G. (2012). Bilingualism: Consequences for mind and brain. *Trends in Cognitive Sciences, 16,* 240-250.

Bialystok & DePape, A.-M. (2009). Musical expertise, bilingualism, and executive functioning. *Journal of Experimental Psychology: Human Perception and Performance, 35,* 565-574.

Bibok, M. B., Carpendale, J. I. M., & Muller, U. (2009). Parental scaffolding and the development of executive function. *New Directions in Child and Adolescent Development, 123,* 17-34.

Biehle, S. N., & Mickelson, K. D. (2012). First-time parents' expectations about the division of childcare and play. *Journal of Family Psychology, 26,* 36-45.

Bigelow, A. E., MacLean, K., & Proctor, J. (2004). The role of joint attention in the development of infants' play with objects. *Developmental Science 7:5 (2004),* 518-526

Bigelow, A. E., & others. (2010). Maternal sensitivity throughout infancy: Continuity and relation to attachment security. *Infant Behavior and Development, 33,* 50-60.

Bigelow, A. E., & Power, M. (2012). The effect of mother-infant skin-to-skin contact on infants' response to the Still Face Task from newborn to three months of age. *Infant Behavior and Development, 35,* 240-251.

Bigelow, A. E., Power, M., Gillis, D. E., Maclellan-Peters, J., Alex, M. and McDonald, C. (2014), breastfeeding, skin-to-skin contact, and mother-infant interactions over infants' first three months. *Infant Mental Health Journal, 35,* 51-62. doi: 10.1002/imhj.21424

Biggs, B. K., & Vernberg, E. M. (2010). Preventing and treating bullying and victimization: Best practices and future directions. In E. M. Vernberg & B. K. Biggs (Eds.), *Preventing and treating bullying and victimization.* New York: Oxford University Press.

Bill and Melinda Gates Foundation. (2006). *The silent epidemic: Perspectives on high school dropouts.* Available at https://docs.gatesfoundation.org/Documents/TheSilentEpidemic3-06Final.pdf

Billari, F., & Mencarini, L. (2003). Gender composition of friendship networks and age at first intercourse: A life-course data analysis. *Statistical Methods and Applications, 12,* 377-390.

Billy, J. O. G., Rodgers, J. L., & Udry, J. R. (1984). Adolescent sexual behavior and friendship choice. *Social Forces, 62,* 653-678.

Binder, T., & Vavrinkova, B. (2008). Prospective randomized comparative study of the effect of buprenorphine, methadone, and heroin on the course of pregnancy, birthweight of newborns, early postpartum adaptation, and the course of neonatal abstinence syndrome (NAS). *Neuoroendocrinology Letters, 29,* 80-86.

Bishop, K. M., & Wahlsten, D. (1997). Sex differences in the human corpus callosum: Myth or reality? *Neuroscience and Biobehavioral Reviews, 21,* 581-601.

Bjorklund, D. (2005). *Children's thinking* (4th ed.). Belmont, CA: Wadsworth.

Bjorklund, D. F. (2007). *Why youth is not wasted on the young.* Malden, MA: Blackwell.

Bjorklund, D. F. (2012). *Children's thinking* (5th ed.). Boston: Cengage.

Bjorklund, D. F. (2013). Cognitive development: An overview. In P. D. Zelazo (Ed.), *Oxford handbook of developmental psychology.* New York: Oxford University Press.

Bjorklund, D. F., Dukes, C., & Brown, R. D. (2009). The development of memory strategies in infancy and childhood. In M. Courage & N. Cowan (Eds.) *The development of memory in infancy and childhood.* New York: Psychology Press.

Bjorklund, D. F., & Pellegrini, A. D. (2002). *The origins of human nature.* New York: Oxford University Press.

Black, M. M., & Hurley, K. M. (2007). Helping children develop healthy eating habits. In Tremblay, R. E., Barr, R. G., Peters, R., & Boivin, M. (Eds.), *Encyclopedia on early childhood development* (Rev. Ed.). Available at www.child-encyclopedia.com/pages/PDF/Eating_behaviourANGmcP.pdf

Black, M. M., & Lozoff, B. (2008). Nutrition and diet. In M. M. Haith & J. B. Benson (Eds.), *Encyclopedia of infant and early childhood development.* Oxford, UK: Elsevier.

Blackwell, L. S., & Dweck, C. S. (2008). *The motivational impact of a computer-based program that teaches how the brain changes with learning.* Unpublished manuscript, Department of Psychology, Stanford University, Palo Alto, CA.

Blackwell, L. S., Trzesniewski, K. H., & Dweck, C. S. (2007). Implicit theories of intelligence predict achievement across an adolescent tradition: A longitudinal study and an intervention. *Child Development, 78,* 246-263.

Blaga, O. M., Shaddy, D. J., Anderson, C. J., Kannass, K. N., Little, T. D., & Colombo, J. (2009). Structure and continuity of intellectual development in early childhood. *Intelligence, 37,* 106-113.

Blair, C., & Razza, R. P. (2007). Relating effortful control, executive functioning, and false belief understanding to emerging math and literacy ability in kindergarten. *Child Development, 78,* 647-663.

Blake, J. S. (2011). *Nutrition and you.* Upper Saddle River, NJ: Pearson.

Blakemore, S-J., & Mills, K. (2014, in press). The social brain in adolescence. *Annual Review of Psychology* (Vol. 65). Palo Alto, CA: Annual Reviews.

Blasi, A. (2005). Moral character: A psychological approach. In D. K. Lapsley & F. C. Power (Eds.), *Character psychology and character education.* Notre Dame, IN: University of Notre Dame Press.

Blass, E. (2008). Suckling. In M. M. Haith & J. B. Benson (Eds.), *Encyclopedia of infant and early childhood development.* Oxford, UK: Elsevier.

Blencowe, H., Cousens, S., Oestergaard, M. Z., Chou, D., Moller, A., Narwal, R., Adler, A., Garcia, C. V., Rohde, S., Say, L., & Lawn, J. E. (2012). National, regional, and worldwide estimates of preterm birth rates in the year 2010 with time trends since 1990 for selected countries: A systematic analysis and implications. *Lancet, 379,* 2162-2172.

Block, J. (1993). Studying personality the long way. In D. Funder, R. D. Parke, C. Tomlinson-Keasey, & K. Widaman (Eds.), *Studying lives through time.* Washington, DC: American Psychological Association.

Bloom, B. (1985). *Developing talent in young people.* New York: Ballantine.

Bloom, L. (1998). Language acquisition in its developmental context. In W. Damon (Ed.),

*Handbook of child psychology* (5th ed., Vol. 2). New York: Wiley.

Bloom, L., Lifter, K., & Broughton, J. (1985). The convergence of early cognition and language in the second year of life. Problems in conceptualization and measurement. In M. Barrett (Ed.), *Single word speech*. London: Wiley.

Blumenfeld, P. C., Pintrich, P. R., Wessles, K., & Meece, J. (1981, April). *Age and sex differences in the impact of classroom experiences on self-perceptions.* Paper presented at the biennial meeting of the Society of Research in Child Development, Boston.

Bo, L. (1994). The sociocultural environment as a source of support. In F. Nestmann & K. Hurrelmann (Eds.), *Social networks and social support in childhood and adolescence*. New York: Walter de Gruyter.

Bodrova, E., & Leong, D. J. (2007). *Tools of the mind* (2nd ed.). Geneva, Switzerland: International Bureau of Education, UNESCO.

Bohannon, J. N., & Bonvillian, J. D. (2009). Theoretical approaches to language acquisition. In J. Berko Gleason & N. B. Ratner (Eds.), *The development of language*. Boston: Allyn & Bacon.

Bohlin, G., Eninger, L., Brocki, K. C., & Thorell, L. B. (2012). Disorganized attachment and inhibitory capacity: Predicting externalizing problem behaviors. *Journal of Abnormal Child Psychology, 40*, 449–458.

Bohlin, G., & Hagekull, B. (1993). Stranger wariness and sociability in the early years. *Infant Behavior and Development, 16*, 53–67.

Bohlin, G. & Hagekull, B. (2009). Socio-emotional development: from infancy to young adulthood. *Scandinavian Journal of Psychology, 50(6)*, 592–601.

Boks, M. P., Derks, E. M., Dolan, C. V., Kahn, R. S., & Ophoff, R. A. (2010). "Forward genetics" as a method to maximize power and cost-efficiency in studies of human complex traits. *Behavior Genetics*, published online March 16, 2010.

Bolling, C. F., & Daniels, S. R. (2008). Obesity. In M. M. Haith & J. B. Benson (Eds.), *Encyclopedia of infant and early childhood development*. Oxford UK: Elsevier.

Bonanno, R. A. & Hymel, S. (2013). Cyber bullying and internalizing difficulties: Above and beyond the impact of traditional forms of bullying. *Journal of Youth and Adolescence, 42*, 685–697.

Bond, B. J., Richards, M. N., & Calvert, S. L. (2013). Media and pediatric obesity. In D. Lemish (Ed.), *The handbook of children and the media*. New York: Routledge.

Bono, G. (2012, August 5). *Searching for the developmental role of gratitude: A 4-year longitudinal analysis.* Paper presented at the American Psychological Association, Orlando.

Booth, A. E., & Ware, E. A. (2010). Categories, concepts, and causality: A reply to Samuelson and Perone. *Cognitive Development, 25*, 154–157.

Booth, M. (2002). Arab adolescents facing the future: Enduring ideals and pressures to change. In B. B. Brown, R. W. Larson, & T. S. Saraswathi (Eds.), *The world's youth*. New York: Cambridge University Press.

Booth-LaForce, C., & Kerns, K. A. (2009). Child-parent attachment relationships, peer relationships, and peer-group functioning. In K. H. Rubin, W. M. Bukowksi, & B. Laursen (Eds.), *Handbook of peer interactions, relationships, and groups*. New York: Guilford.

Bornstein, M. H. (1975). Qualities of color vision in infancy. *Journal of Experimental Child Psychology, 19*, 401–409.

Bornstein, M. H. (2002). Parenting infants. In M. H. Bornstein (Ed.), *Handbook of parenting* (2nd ed., Vol. 1). Mahwah, NJ: Erlbaum.

Bornstein, M. H., & Cote, L. R. (2010). Immigration and acculturation. In M. H. Bornstein (Ed.), *Handbook of cultural developmental science*. New York: Routledge.

Bornstein, M. H., Jager, J., & Steinberg, L. (2013). Adolescents, parents/friends/peers: A relationship model. In I. B. Weiner & others (Eds.), *Handbook of psychology* (2nd ed., Vol. 6). New York: Wiley.

Bornstein, M. H., & Lansford, J. E. (2010). Parenting. In M. H. Bornstein (Ed.), *Handbook of cultural developmental science*. New York: Psychology Press.

Bosacki, S. L., Varnish, A., & Akseer, S. (2008). Children's gendered sense of self and play as represented through drawings and written descriptions. *Canadian Journal of School Psychology, 23(2)*, 190–205.

Bosma, H. A., & Kunnen, E. S. (2001). Determinants and mechanisms in ego identity development: A review and synthesis. *Developmental Review, 21*, 39–66.

Bouchard, T. J., Lykken, D. T., McGue, M., Segal, N. L., & Tellegen, A. (1990). Source of human psychological differences: The Minnesota Study of Twins Reared Apart. *Science, 250*, 223–228.

Boucher, J. (2012). Putting theory of mind in its place: Psychological explanations of the socioemotional-communicative impairments in autism spectrum disorder. *Autism, 16*, 603–611.

Boucher, J. (2012). Research review: Structural language in autistic spectrum disorder—characteristics and causes. *Journal of Child Psychology and Psychiatry, 53*, 219–233.

Boucher, J., Mayes, A., & Bigham, S. (2012). Memory in autism spectrum disorder. *Psychological Bulletin, 138*, 458–496.

Boukydis, C. F., & Lester, B. M. (2008). Mother-infant consultation during drug treatment: research and innovative clinical practice. *Harm Reduction Journal, 5*, 6.

Boulware-Gooden, R., Carreker, S., Thornill, A., & Joshi, R. M. (2007). Instruction of metacognitive strategies enhances reading comprehension and vocabulary achievement of third-grade students. *Reading Teacher, 61*, 70–77.

Bower, T. G. R. (1966). Slant perception and shape constancy in infants. *Science, 151*, 832–834.

Bowker, A. (2006). The relationship between sports participation and self-esteem during early adolescence. *Canadian Journal of Behavioural Science, 38(3)*, 214–229.

Bowker, J. C., Rubin, K., & Coplan, R. (2012). Social withdrawal during adolescence. In J. R. Levesque (Ed.), *Encyclopedia of adolescence*. New York: Springer.

Bowlby, J. (1969). *Attachment and loss* (Vol. 1). London: Hogarth Press.

Bowlby, J. (1989). *Secure and insecure attachment*. New York: Basic Books.

Bowles, T. (1999). Focusing on time orientation to explain adolescent self concept and academic achievement: Part II. Testing a model. *Journal of Applied Health Behaviour, I*, 1–8.

Boyer, K., & Diamond, A. (1992). Development of memory for temporal order in infants and young children. In A. Diamond (Ed.), *Development and neural bases of higher cognitive function*. New York Academy of Sciences.

Boyle, J., & Cropley, M. (2004). Children's sleep: Problems and solutions. *Journal of Family Health Care, 14*, 61–63.

Boynton-Jarrett, R., & others. (2013). Childhood abuse and age at menarche. *Journal of Adolescent Health, 52*, 241–247.

Boyum, L., & Parke, R. D. (1995). Family emotional expressiveness and children's social competence. *Journal of Marriage and the Family, 57*, 593–608.

Bradley, R. H., & Corwyn, R. F. (2013 in press). From parent to child to parent. . . Paths in and out of problem behavior. *Journal of Abnormal Child Psychology.*

Bradley, R. H., Corwyn, R. F., McAdoo, H., & Coll, C. (2001). The home environments of children in the United States: Part I. Variations by age, ethnicity, and poverty status. *Child Development, 72,* 1844-1867.

**Brainerd, C. J., & Gordon, L. L.** (1994). Development of verbatim and gist memory for numbers. *Developmental Psychology, 30,* 163-177.

**Brainerd, C. J., & Reyna, V. F.** (2012). Reliability of children's testimony in the era of developmental reversals. *Developmental Review, 32,* 224-267.

**Brans, R. G., & others.** (2010). Brain plasticity and intellectual ability are influenced by shared genes. *Journal of Neuroscience, 30,* 5519-5524.

**Bransford, J., & others.** (2006). Learning theories in education. In P. A. Alexander & P. H. Winne (Eds.), *Handbook of educational psychology* (2nd ed.). Mahwah, NJ: Erlbaum.

**Brant, A. M., Haberstick, B. C., Corley, R. P., Wadsworth, S. J., DeFries, J. C., Hewitt, J. K.** (2009). The developmental etiology of high IQ. *Behavioral Genetics, 39,* 393-405.

**Brazelton, T. B.** (1956). Sucking in infancy. *Pediatrics, 17,* 400-404.

**Brazelton, T. B.** (2004). Preface: The Neonatal Intensive Care Unit Network Neurobehavioral Scale. *Pediatrics, 113,* Suppl. S632-S633.

**Brechwald, W. A., & Prinstein, M. J.** (2011). Beyond homophily: A decade of advances in understanding peer influence processes. *Journal of Research on Adolescence, 21,* 166-179.

**Bredekamp, S.** (2011). *Effective practices in early childhood education.* Upper Saddle River, NJ: Merrill.

**Breedlove, G., & Fryzelka, D.** (2011). Depression screening in pregnancy. *Journal of Midwifery and Women's Health, 56,* 18-25.

**Bremner, G.** (2007). Perception and knowledge of the world. In A. Slater & M. Lewis (Eds.), *Introduction to infant development* (2nd ed.). Malden, MA: Blackwell.

**Bremner, J. G., & others.** (2011). Two- to 8-month-old infants' cross-modal perception of dynamic auditory-visual spatial co-location. *Child Development, 82,* 1210-1223.

**Brendgen, M., Lamarche, V., Wanner, B., & Vitaro, F.** (2010). Links between friendship relations and early adolescents' trajectories of depressed mood. *Developmental Psychology, 46*(2), 491-501.

**Brendgen, R. M.** (2009). Aggression, Childhood and adolescence. In D. Carr (Ed.), *Encyclopedia of the life course and human development.* Boston: Gale Cengage.

**Brent, R.** (2011). The pulmonologist's role in caring for pregnant women with

regard to reproductive risks of diagnostic radiological studies or radiation therapy. *Clinics in Chest Medicine, 32*(1), 33-42.

**Brent, R. L.** (2009). Saving lives and changing family histories: Appropriate counseling of pregnant women and men and women of reproductive age concerning the risk of diagnostic radiation exposure during and before pregnancy. *American Journal of Obstetrics and Gynecology, 200,* 4-24.

**Brent, R. L., Christian, M. S., & Diener, R. M.** (2011). Evaluation of the reproductive and developmental risks of caffeine. *Birth Defects Research, Part B: Developmental and Reproductive Toxicology, 92,* 152-187.

**Bretherton, I.** (2012). Afterword. In K. H. Brisch, *Treating attachment disorders* (2nd ed.). New York: Guilford.

**Bretherton, I., Stolberg, U., & Kreye, M.** (1981). Engaging strangers in proximal interaction: Infants' social initiative. *Developmental Psychology, 17,* 746-755.

**Brewer, M. B., & Campbell, D. T.** (1976). *Ethnocentrism and intergroup attitudes.* New York: Wiley.

**Bridgett, D. J., & others.** (2009). Maternal and contextual influences and the effect of temperament development during infancy on parenting in toddlerhood. *Infant Behavior and Development, 32,* 103-116.

**Brion, M., & others.** (2012, in press). Sarcomeric gene mutations in sudden infant death syndrome (SIDS). *Forensic Science International.*

**Britton, J. R., Britton, H. L., & Gronwaldt, V.** (2006). Breastfeeding, sensitivity, and attachment. *Pediatrics, 118,* e1436-e1443.

**Broadbent, K. G., & others.** (2012). Brainstem deficiency of the 14-3-3 regulator of serotonin synthesis: A proteomics analysis in the sudden infant death syndrome. *Molecular and Cellular Proteomics, 11,* M111.009530

**Brocardo, P. S., Gil-Mohapel, J., & Christie, B. R.** (2011). The role of oxidative stress in fetal alcohol spectrum disorders. *Brain Research Reviews, 67,* 209-225.

**Brock, J.** (2007). Language abilities in Williams syndrome: A critical review. *Developmental Psychopathology, 19,* 97-127.

**Brockmeyer, S., Treboux, D., & Crowell, J. A.** (2005, April). *Parental divorce and adult children's attachment status and marital relationships.* Paper presented at the meeting of the Society for Research in Child Development, Atlanta.

**Brockmeyer, T., & others.** (2012, in press). The thinner the better: Self-esteem and low body weight in anorexia nervosa. *Clinical Psychology and Psychotherapy.*

**Brody, G. H., & others.** (2001). The influence of neighborhood disadvantage, collective socialization, and parenting on African American children's affiliation with deviant peers. *Child Development, 72,* 1231-1246.

**Brody, N.** (2000). Intelligence. In A. Kazdin (Ed.), *Encyclopedia of psychology.* Washington, DC, & New York: American Psychological Association and Oxford University Press.

**Brody, N.** (2007). Does education influence intelligence? In P. C. Kyllonen, R. D. Roberts, & L. Stankov (Eds.), *Extending intelligence.* Mahwah, NJ: Erlbaum.

**Brodzinsky, D. M., & Pinderhughes, E.** (2002). Parenting and child development in adoptive families. In M. H. Bornstein (Ed.), *Handbook of parenting* (Vol. 1). Mahwah, NJ: Erlbaum.

**Bronfenbrenner, U.** (1986). Ecology of the family as a context for human development: Research perspectives. *Developmental Psychology, 22,* 723-742.

**Bronfenbrenner, U.** (2000). Ecological theory. In A. Kazdin (Ed.), *Encyclopedia of psychology.* Washington, DC, & New York: American Psychological Association and Oxford University Press.

**Bronfenbrenner, U.** (2004). *Making human beings human.* Thousand Oaks, CA: Sage.

**Bronfenbrenner, U., & Morris, P.** (1998). The ecology of developmental processes. In W. Damon (Ed.), *Handbook of child psychology* (5th ed., Vol. 1). New York: Wiley.

**Bronfenbrenner, U., & Morris, P. A.** (2006). The ecology of developmental processes. In W. Damon & R. Lerner (Eds.), *Handbook of child psychology* (6th ed.). New York: Wiley.

**Bronstein, P.** (2006). The family environment: Where gender role socialization begins. In J. Worell & C. D. Goodheart (Eds.), *Handbook of girls' and women's psychological health.* New York: Oxford University Press.

**Brook, J. S., Brook, D. W., Gordon, A. S., Whiteman, M., & Cohen, P.** (1990). The psychological etiology of adolescent drug use: A family interactional approach. *Genetic, Social, and General Psychology Monographs, 116,* 110-267.

**Brooker, R.** (2011). *Biology* (2nd ed.). New York: McGraw-Hill.

**Brooks, J. G., & Brooks, M. G.** (1993). *The case for constructivist classrooms.* Alexandria, VA: Association for Supervision and Curriculum.

**Brooks, J. G., & Brooks, M. G.** (2001). *The case for constructivist classrooms.* (2nd ed.). Upper Saddle River, NJ: Erlbaum.

**Brooks. R., & Meltzoff. A. N.** (2005). The development of gaze following and its relation to language. *Developmental Science, 8,* 535-543.

Brooks-Gunn, J. (2003). Do you believe in magic?: What we can expect from early childhood programs. *Social Policy Report, Society for Research in Child Development, XVII* (1), 1–13.

Brooks-Gunn, J., Han, W-J., & Waldfogel, J. (2010). First-year maternal employment and child development in the first seven years. *Monographs of the Society for Research in Child Development, 75*(2), 1–147.

Brooks-Gunn, J., Johnson, A., & Leventhal, T. (2010). Disorder, turbulence, and resources in children's homes and neighborhoods. In G. W. Evans & T. D. Wachs (Eds.), *Chaos and its influence on children's development: An ecological perspective.* Washington, DC: American Psychological Association.

Brooks-Gunn, J., & Warren, M. P. (1989). The psychological significance of secondary sexual characteristics in 9- to 11-year-old girls. *Child Development, 59,* 161–169.

Brookshear, J. G. (2009). *Computer science* (10th ed.). Upper Saddle River, NJ: Addison-Wesley.

Brophy, J. (2004). *Motivating students to learn* (2nd ed.). Mahwah, NJ: Erlbaum.

Broverman, I., Vogel, S., Broverman, D., Clarkson, F., & Rosenkranz, P. (1972). Sex-role stereotypes: A current appraisal. *Journal of Social Issues, 28,* 59–78.

Brown, A. L., & Day, J. D. (1983). Macrorules for summarizing texts: The development of expertise. *Journal of Verbal Learning and Verbal Behavior, 22,* 1–14.

Brown, B. B. (1999). Measuring the peer environment of American adolescents. In S. L. Friedman & T. D. Wachs (Eds.), *Measuring environment across the life span.* Washington, DC: American Psychological Association.

Brown, B. B. (2011). Popularity in peer group perspective: The role of status in adolescent peer systems. In A. H. N. Cillessen, D. Schwartz, & L. Mayeux (Eds.), *Popularity in the peer system.* New York: Guilford.

Brown, B. B., & Bakken, J. P. (2011). Parenting and peer relationships: Reinvigorating research on family-peer linkages in adolescence. *Journal of Research on Adolescence, 21,* 153–165.

Brown, B. B., & Larson, J. (2009). Peer relationships in adolescence. In R. L. Lerner & L. Steinberg (Eds.), *Handbook of adolescent psychology* (3rd ed.). New York: Wiley.

Brown, B. B., & Larson, R. W. (2002). The kaleidoscope of adolescence: Experiences of the world's youth at the beginning of the 21st century. In B. B. Brown, R. W. Larson, & T. S. Saraswathi (Eds.), *The world's youth.* New York: Cambridge University Press.

Brown, B. B., & Lohr, M. J. (1987). Peer-group affiliation and adolescent self-esteem: An integration of ego-identity and symbolic-interaction theories. *Journal of Personality and Social Psychology, 52,* 47–55.

Brown, D. (2013). Morphological typology. In J. J. Song (Ed.), *Oxford handbook of linguistic typology.* New York: Oxford University Press.

Brown, H. L., & Graves, C. R. (2013). Smoking and marijuana in pregnancy. *Clincial Obstetrics and Gynecology, 56,* 107–113.

Brown, J. D., & Bobkowski, P. S. (2011). Older and newer media: Patterns of use and effects on adolescents' health and well-being. *Journal of Research on Adolescence, 21,* 95–113.

Brown, L. D., Feinberg, M., & Kan, M. L. (2012). Predicting engagement in a transition to parenthood program for couples. *Evaluation and Program Planning, 35,* 1–8.

Brown, L. M., & Gilligan, C. (1992). *Meeting at the crossroads: Women's and girls' development.* Cambridge, MA: Harvard University Press.

Brown, R. (1958). *Words and things.* Glencoe, IL: Free Press.

Brown, R. (1973). *A first language: The early stage.* Cambridge, MA: Harvard University Press.

Brown, W. H., Pfeiffer, K. A., McIver, K. L., Dowda, M., Addy, C. L., & Pate, R. R. (2009). Social and environmental factors associated with preschoolers' nonsedentary physical activity. *Child Development, 80,* 45–58.

Brownell, C. (2009). *Brownell—Early social development lab.* Retrieved on November 9, 2009, from www.pitt.edu/?toddlers/ESDL/brownell.html

Brownell, C. A., Ramani, G. B., & Zerwas, S. (2006). Becoming a social partner with peers: Cooperation and social understanding in one-and two-year-olds. *Child Development, 77,* 803–821.

Brownell, C. A., Svetlova, M., Anderson, R., Nichols, S. R., & Drummond, J. (2012, in press). Socialization of early prosocial behavior: Parents' talk about emotions is associated with sharing and helping in toddlers. *Infancy.*

Bruce, S. G., Riediger, N. D., Zacharias, J. M., Young, T. K. (2011). Obesity and obesity-related comorbidities in a Canadian First Nation population. *Preventing Chronic Disease: Public Health Research, Practice, and Policy, 8,* 1–8.

Bruchmiller, K., Margraf, J., & Schneider, S. (2012). Is ADHD diagnosed in accord with diagnostic criteria? Overdiagnosis and influence of client gender on diagnosis. *Journal of Consulting and Clinical Psychology, 80,* 128–138.

Bruck, M., & Ceci, S. J. (2012). Forensic developmental psychology in the courtroom. In D. Faust & M. Ziskin (Eds.), *Coping with psychiatric and psychological testimony.* New York: Cambridge University Press.

Brumarui, L. E., & Kerns, K. A. (2010). Mother-child attachment patterns and different types of anxiety symptoms: Is there specificity of relations? *Child Psychiatry and Human Development, 41,* 663–674.

Brumariu, L. E., Kerns, K. A., & Siebert, A. C. (2012, in press). Mother-child attachment, emotion regulation, and anxiety symptoms in middle childhood. *Personal Relationships.*

Brune, C. W., & Woodward, A. L. (2007). Social cognition and social responsiveness in 10-month-old infants. *Journal of Cognition and Development, 2,* 3–27.

Bruner, J. S. (1983). *Child talk.* New York: W. W. Norton.

Bruner, J. S. (1996). *The culture of education.* Cambridge, MA: Harvard University Press.

Brunstein Klomek, A., Marrocco, F., Kleinman, M., Schofeld, I. S., & Gould, M. S. (2007). Bullying, depression, and suicidality in adolescents. *Journal of the American Academy of Child and Adolescent Psychiatry, 46,* 40–49.

Bryant, J. (Ed.). (2007). *The children's television community.* Mahwah, NJ: Erlbaum.

Bryant, J. B. (2012). Pragmatic development. In E. L. Bavin (Ed.), *Cambridge handbook of child language.* New York: Cambridge University Press.

Brynes, J. P. (2012). How neuroscience contributes to our understanding of learning and development in typically developing and special needs students. In K. R. Harris, S. Graham, & T. Urdan (Eds.), *APA educational psychology handbook.* Washington, DC: American Psychological Association.

Buck, K. A. & Dix, T. (2012). Can developmental changes in inhibition and peer relationships explain why depressive symptoms increase in early adolescence? *Journal of Youth and Adolescence, 41,* 403–413.

Buhler, E., & others. (2011). Differential diagnosis of autism spectrum disorder and attention deficit hyperactivity disorder by means of inhibitory control and 'theory of mind.' *Journal of Autism and Developmental Disorders, 41,* 718–726.

Buhrmester, D. (1990). Friendship, interpersonal competence, and adjustment in preadolescence and adolescence. *Child Development, 61*, 1101–1111.

**Buhrmester, D., & Chong, C. M.** (2009). Friendship in adolescence. In H. Reis & S. Sprecher (Eds.), *Encyclopedia of human relationships*. Thousand Oaks, CA: Sage.

**Buhrmester, D., & Furman, W.** (1987). The development of companionship and intimacy. *Child Development, 58*, 1101–1113.

**Bukowski, R., & others.** (2008, January). *Folic acid and preterm birth*. Paper presented at the meeting of the Society for Maternal-Fetal Medicine, Dallas.

**Bukowski, W. M.** (2012, April). *Gender, culture, and positive and negative experiences with peers*. Paper presented at the Gender Development Research Conference, San Francisco.

**Bukowski, W. M., Buhrmester, D., & Underwood, M. K.** (2011). Peer relations as a developmental context. In M. K. Underwood & L. H. Rosen (Eds.), *Social development*. New York: Guilford.

**Bukowski, W. M., Motzoi, C., & Meyer, F.** (2009). Friendship as process, function, and outcome. In K. H. Rubin, W. M. Bukowski, & B. Laursen (Eds.), *Handbook of peer interactions, relationships, and groups*. New York: Guilford.

**Bullock, M., & Lutkenhaus, P.** (1990). Who am I? Self-understanding in toddlers. *Merrill-Palmer Quarterly, 36*, 217–238.

**Burke, J. D.** (2011). The relationship between conduct disorder and oppositional defiant disorder and their continuity with antisocial behaviors. In D. Shaffer, E. Leibenluft, & L. A. Rohde (Eds.), *Externalizing disorders of childhood: Refining the research agenda for DSM-V*. Arlington, VA: American Psychiatric Association.

**Burke, M. G., & Miller, M. D.** (2011). Practical guidelines for evaluating lead exposure in children with mental health conditions: Molecular effects and clinical implications. *Postgraduate Medicine, 123*, 160–168.

**Burnham, D., & Mattock, K.** (2010). Auditory development. In J. G. Bremner & T. D. Wachs (Eds.), *Wiley-Blackwell handbook of infant development* (2nd ed.). New York: Wiley.

**Burstyn, I., Kuhle, S., Allen, A. C., & Veugelers, P.** (2012). The role of maternal smoking in effect of fetal growth restriction on poor scholastic achievement in elementary school. *International Journal of Environmental Research and Public Health, 9*, 408–420.

**Burt, S. A., McGue, M., & Iacono, W. G.** (2010). Environmental contributions to the stability of antisocial behavior over time:

Are they shared or non-shared? *Journal of Abnormal Child Psychology, 38*, 327–337.

**Burton, R. V.** (1984). A paradox in theories and research in moral development. In W. M. Kurtines & J. L. Gewirtz (Eds.), *Morality, moral behavior, and moral development*. New York: Wiley.

**Bushman, B. J., Baumeister, R., Thomaes, S., Ryu, E., Begeer, S., & West, S.** (2009). Looking again, and harder, for a link between low self-esteem and aggression. *Journal of Personality, 77*, 427–446.

**Bushnell, I. W. R.** (2003). Newborn face recognition. In O. Pascalis & A. Slater (Eds.), *The development of face processing in infancy and early childhood*. New York: NOVA Science.

**Bushnik, T.** (2006). *Child care in Canada*. Ottawa: Statistics Canada Cat. No. 89-599-MIE-No. 003.

**Bushnik T., Cook J. L., Yuzpe, A. A., Tough, S., & Collins, J.** (2012). Estimating the prevalence of infertility in Canada. *Human Reproduction, 27*, 738–746.

**Buss, D. M.** (1995). Psychological sex differences: Origins through sexual selection. *American Psychologist, 50*, 164–168.

**Buss, D. M.** (2004). *Evolutionary psychology* (2nd ed.). Boston: Allyn & Bacon.

**Buss, D. M.** (2008). *Evolutionary psychology* (3rd ed.). Boston: Allyn & Bacon.

**Buss, D. M.** (2012). *Evolutionary psychology* (4th ed.). Boston: Allyn & Bacon.

**Buss, K. A.** (2011). Which fearful toddlers should we worry about? Context, fear regulation, and anxiety risk. *Developmental Psychology, 47*, 804–819.

**Bussey, K., & Bandura A.** (1999). Social cognitive theory of gender development and differentiation. *Psychological Review, 106*, 676–713.

**Bussiere, P., Knighton, T., & Pennock, D.** (2007). Measuring up: Canadian results of the OECD PISA study: The performance of Canada's youth in mathematics, reading, and problem-solving: 2003 first findings for Canadians aged 15. Statistics Canada, Catalogue no. 81-590-XPE-No. 3.

**Butler, B. E., & Trainor, L. J.** (2013). Brief pitch-priming facilitates infants' discrimination of pitch-evoking noise: Evidence from event-related potentials. *Brain and Cognition, 83*, 271–278.

**Byrnes, James P.** (2008). Piaget's theory. In M. M. Haith & J. B. Benson (Eds.), *Encyclopedia of infant and early childhood development* (Vol. 2., pp. 543–552). New York, NY: Elsevier.

**Byard, R. W.** (2012a). Should infants and adults sleep in the same bed together? *Medical Journal of Australia, 196*, 10–11.

**Byard, R. W.** (2012b). The triple risk model for shared sleeping. *Journal of Pediatric Child Health, 48*, 947–948.

**Byars, K. C., Yolton, K., Rausch, J., Lanphear, B., & Beebe, D. W.** (2012). Prevalence, patterns, and persistence of sleep problems in the first 3 years of life. *Pediatrics, 129*, doi: 10.1542/peds.2011-0372

## C

**Cabrera, N., Hutchens, R., & Peters, H. E.** (Eds.) (2006). *From welfare to childcare*. Mahwah, NJ: Erlbaum.

**Cabrera, N. J., Hofferth, S. L., & Chae, S.** (2011). Patterns and predictors of father-infant engagement across race/ethnic groups. *Early Childhood Research Quarterly, 26*, 365–375.

**Cain, M. A., Bornick, P., & Whiteman, V.** (2013). The maternal, fetal, and neonatal effects of cocaine exposure in pregnancy. *Clinical Obstetrics and Gynecology, 56*, 124–132.

**Calkins, S. D.** (2012). Regulatory competence and early disruptive behavior problems: Role of physiological regulation. In S. L. Olson & A. J. Sameroff (Eds.), *Biopsychosocial regulatory processes in the development of childhood behavioral problems*. New York: Cambridge University Press.

**Calkins, S. D., & Bell, M. A.** (Eds.) (2010). *Child development at the intersection of emotion and cognition*. Washington, DC: American Psychological Association.

**Callaghan, T. Moll, H., Rakoczy, H., Warneken, F., Liszkowski, U., Behne, T., Tomasello, M.** Early social cognition in three cultural contexts: III. Individual studies. *Monographs of the Society for Research in Child Development, 76*(2), 34–104.

**Callan, J. E.** (2001). Gender development: Psychoanalytic perspectives. In J. Worrel (Ed.), *Encyclopedia of women and gender*. San Diego: Academic Press.

**Calvert, S. L., Bond, B. J., & Staiano, A. E.** (2013). Electronic game changers for the obesity crisis. In F. Blumberg (Ed.), *Learning by playing: Frontiers of video gaming in education*. New York: Oxford University Press.

**Calvert, S. L., & Valkenburg, P. M.** (2011). The influence of television, video games, and the Internet on children's creativity. In M. Taylor (Ed.), *Handbook of the development of imagination*. New York: Oxford University Press.

**Cameron, J., & Pierce, D.** (2008). Intrinsic versus extrinsic motivation. In N. J. Salkind (Ed.), *Encyclopedia of educational psychology*. Thousand Oaks, CA: Sage.

CAMH (2012). Gender identity service. Retrieved May 15, 2014 from: www.camh.ca/en/hospital/care_program_and_services/child_youth_and_family_program/Pages/guide_gender_identitycyf.aspx

Campbell, F. A. (2007). The malleability of the cognitive development of children of low-income African American families: Intellectual test performance over twenty-one years. In P. C. Kyllonen, R. D. Roberts, & L. Stankov (Eds.), *Extending intelligence*. Mahwah, NJ: Erlbaum.

Campbell, F. A., Pungello, E. P., Miller-Johnson, S., Burchinal, M., & Ramey, C. T. (2001). The development of cognitive and academic abilities: Growth curves from an early childhood educational experiment. *Developmental Psychology, 37,* 231–243.

Campbell, F. A., & others. (2012). Adult outcomes as a function of an early childhood educational program: An Abcedarian Project follow-up. *Developmental Psychology, 48,* 1033–1043.

Campbell, J. (2012). Self-esteem and the clarity of self-concept. In K. Vohs & R. F. Baumeister (Eds.), *Self and identity*. Thousand Oaks, CA: Sage.

Campbell, L., Campbell, B., & Dickinson, D. (2004). *Teaching and learning through multiple intelligences* (3rd ed.), Boston: Allyn & Bacon.

Campione-Barr, N., Bassett-Greer, K., & Kruse, A. (2013, in press). Differential associations domain of sibling conflict and adolescent emotional development. *Child Development*.

Campos, J. J. (2005). Unpublished review of J. W. Santrock's *Life-span development* (11th ed.). New York: McGraw-Hill.

Campos, J. J. (2009). Unpublished review of J. W. Santrock's *Life-span development,* (13th ed.). New York: McGraw-Hill.

Campos, J. J., Langer, A., & Krowitz, A. (1970). Cardiac responses on the visual cliff in prelocomotor human infants. *Science, 170,* 196–197.

Camras, L. A., & others. (1998). Production of emotional facial expressions in European American, Japanese, and Chinese infants. *Developmental Psychology, 34,* 616–628.

Canadian Child Care Federation. (2013). *Child care: A Canadian snapshot*. Retrieved May 6, 2014 from www.cccf-fcsge.ca/wp-content/uploads/RS_102-e.pdf

Canadian Heritage (2013). Sports participation 2010. Catalogue No. CH24-1/2012E-PDF. Ottawa: Statistics Canada.

Canadian Institute for Health Information. Health indicators 2012: Caesarean section. Available at: www.cihi.ca/hirpt/search.jspa

Canadian Institutes of Health Research, Natural Sciences and Engineering Research Council of Canada, and Social Sciences and Humanities Research Council of Canada. *Tri-council policy statement: Ethical conduct for research involving humans,* December 2010.

Capaldi, D. M. (2013). Parental monitoring: A person-environment interaction perspective on this key parenting skill. In A. C. Crouter & A. Booth (Eds.), *Children's influence on family dynamics*. New York: Routledge.

Capaldi, D. M., & Shortt, J. W. (2003). Understanding conduct problems in adolescence from a lifespan perspective. In G. R. Adams & M. D. Berzonsky (Eds.), *Blackwell handbook of adolescence*. Malden, MA: Blackwell.

Cappadocia, M.C., Pepler, D., Cummings, J.G., & Craig, W. (2012). Individual motivations and characteristics associated with bystander intervention during bullying episodes. *Canadian Journal of School Psychology, 27*(3), 201–216.

Carbonell, O. A., Alzte, G., Bustamante, M. R., & Quiceno, J. (2002). Maternal caregiving and infant security in two cultures. *Developmental Psychology, 38,* 67–78.

Cardelle-Elawar, M. (1992). Effects of teaching metacognitive skills to students with low mathematics ability. *Teaching and Teacher Education, 8*(2), 109–121.

Carey, D. P. (2007). Is bigger really better? The search for brain size and intelligence in the twenty-first century. In S. Della Sala (Ed.), *Tall tales about the mind and brain: Separating fact from fiction*. Oxford: Oxford University Press.

Carey, S. (1977). The child as word learner. In M. Halle, J. Bresman, & G. Miller (Eds.), *Linguistic theory and psychological reality*. Cambridge, MA: MIT Press.

Carl, J. D. (2012). *Short introduction to the U.S. Census*. Upper Saddle River, NJ: Pearson.

Carlo, G. (2013). Care-based and altruistically based morality. In M. Killen & J. G. Smetana (Eds.), *Handbook of moral development* (2nd ed.). New York: Routledge.

Carlo, G., Knight, G. P., McGinley, M., Zamboanga, B. L., & Jarvis, L. H. (2010). The multidimensionality of prosocial behaviors and evidence of measurement equivalence in Mexican American and European American early adolescents. *Journal of Research on Adolescence, 20,* 334–358.

Carlo, G., Mestre, M. V., Samper, P., Tur, A., & Armenta, B. E. (2011). The longitudinal relations among dimensions of parenting styles, sympathy, prosocial moral reasoning, and prosocial behaviors. *International Journal of Behavioral Development, 35,* 116–124.

Carlson, M. J., Pilkauskas, N. V., McLanahan, S. S., & Brooks-Gunn, J. (2011). Couples as partners and parents over children's early years. *Journal of Marriage and the Family, 73,* 317–334.

Carlson, S. M., & White, R. (2013). Executive function and imagination. In M. Taylor (Ed.), *Handbook of imagination*. New York: Oxford University Press.

Carlson, S. M., & Zelazo, P. D. (2008). Symbolic thought. In M. M. Maith, & J. B. Benson (Eds.), *Encyclopedia of infant and early childhood development,* Vol. 3. London: Elsevier.

Carlson, S. M., Zelazo, P. D., & Faja, S. (2013). Executive function. In P. D. Zelazo (Ed.), *Oxford handbook of developmental psychology*. New York: Oxford University Press.

Carnegie Council on Adolescent Development. (1995). *Great transitions*. New York: Carnegie Foundation.

Carney, D. P., Brown, J. H., & Henry, L. A. (2013). Executive function in Williams and Down syndromes. *Research in Developmental Disabilities, 34,* 46–55.

Carpendale, J. I., & Chandler, M. J. (1996). On the distinction between false belief understanding and subscribing to an interpretive theory of mind. *Child Development, 67,* 1686–1706.

Carpendale, J. I. M. & Carpendale, A. B. (2010). The development of pointing: From personal directedness to interpersonal direction. *Human Development, 53,* 110–126.

Carpendale, J. I. M., & Lewis, C. (2010). The development of social understanding: A relational perspective. In R. M. Lerner, W. F. Overton, A. M. Freund, & M. E. Lamb (Eds.), *Handbook of life-span development,* New York: Wiley.

Carpenter, M. (2011). Social cognition and social motivations in infancy. In U. Goswami (Ed.), *Wiley-Blackwell handbook of childhood cognitive development* (2nd ed.). New York: Wiley-Blackwell.

Carpenter, R., & others (2013). Bed sharing when parents do not smoke: Is there a risk of SIDS? An individual level analysis of five major case–control studies. BMJ Open: doi:10.1136/bmjopen-2012-002299

Carroll, D. J., & others. (2012, in press). How do alternative ways of responding influence 3- and 4-year-olds' performance on tests of executive function and theory of mind? *Journal of Experimental Child Psychology*.

Carroll, J. (1993). *Human cognitive abilities*. Cambridge: Cambridge University Press.

Carskadson, M. A. (Ed.). (2002). *Adolescent sleep patterns*. New York: Cambridge University Press.

Carskadon, M. A. (2004). Sleep difficulties in young people. *Adolescent Medicine, 158*, 597-598.

Carskadon, M. A. (2005). Sleep and circadian rhythms in children and adolescents: Relevance for athletic performance of young people. *Clinical Sports Medicine, 24*, 319-328.

Carskadon, M. A. (2006, March). *Too little, too late: Sleep bioregulatory across adolescence*. Paper presented at the meeting of the Society for Research on Adolescence, San Francisco.

Carskadon, M. A. (2011). Sleep in adolescents: The perfect storm. *Pediatric Clinics of North America, 58*, 637-647.

Cartwright, R., Agargun, M. Y., Kirkby, J., & Friedman, J. K. (2006). Relation of dreams to waking concerns. *Psychiatry Research, 141*, 261-270.

Case, R. (1987). Neo-Piagetian theory: Retrospect and prospect. *International Journal of Psychology, 22*, 773-791.

Case, R. (1999). Conceptual development in the child and the field: A personal view of the Piagetian legacy. In E. K. Skolnick, K. Nelson, S. A. Gelman, & P. H. Miller (Eds.), *Conceptual development*. Mahwah, NJ: Erlbaum.

Case, R., Kurland, D. M., & Goldberg, J. (1982). Operational efficiency and the growth of short-term memory span. *Journal of Experimental Child Psychology, 33*, 386-404.

Casey, P. H. (2008). Growth of low birth weight preterm children. *Seminars in Perinatology, 32*, 20-27.

Caspers, K. M., Paraiso, S., Yucuis, R., Troutman, B., Arndt, S., & Philibert, R. (2009). Association between the serotonin transporter polymorphism (5-HTTLPR) and adult unresolved attachment. *Developmental Psychology, 45*, 64-76.

Caspi, A. (1998). Personality development across the life course. In W. Damon (Ed.), *Handbook of child psychology* (Vol. 3). New York: Wiley.

Caspi, A., (2003). Influence of life stress on depression: Moderation by a polymorphism in the 5-HTT gene. *Science, 301*, 386-389.

Caspi, A., Hariri, A. R., Holmes, A., Uher, R., & Moffitt, T. E. (2010). Genetic sensitivity to the environment: The case of serotonin transporter gene and its implications for studying complex diseases and traits. *American Journal of Psychiatry, 167*(5), 509-527.

Castle, J., & others. (2010). Parents' evaluation of adoption success: A follow-up study of intercountry and domestic adoptions. *American Journal of Orthopsychiatry, 79*, 522-531.

Catani, C., & others. (2010). Tsunami, war, and cumulative risk in the lives of Sri Lankan school children. *Child Development, 81*, 1176-1191.

Catherine, N. L. A., & Schonert-Reichl, K. A. (2011). Children's perceptions and comforting strategies to infant crying: Relations to age, sex, and empathy-related responding. *British Journal of Developmental Psychology, 29*, 524-551.

Caughey, A. B., Hopkins, L. M., & Norton, M. E. (2006). Chorionic villus sampling compared with amniocentesis and the difference in the rate of pregnancy loss. *Obstetrics and Gynecology, 108*, 612-616.

Cavanagh, S. E. (2009). Puberty. In D. Carr (Ed.), *Encyclopedia of the life course and human development*. Boston: Gale Cengage.

Cave, R. K. (2002, August). *Early adolescent language: A content analysis of child development and educational psychology textbooks*. Unpublished doctoral dissertation. University of Nevada-Reno, Reno, NV.

Ceballo, R., Huerta, M., & Ngo, Q. E. (2010). Schooling experience of Latino students. In J. Meece & J. Eccles (Eds.), *Handbook of research on schools, schooling, and human development*. New York: Routledge.

Center for Science in the Public Interest. (2008, August). *Kids' meals: Obesity on the menu*. Washington, DC: Author.

Centers for Disease Control and Prevention. (2009). *Autism and developmental disabilities monitoring (ADDM) network*. Atlanta: Author.

Centers for Disease Control and Prevention. (2012). CDC estimates 1 in 88 children in the United States has been identified as having an autism spectrum disorder. *CDC Division of News & Electronic Media*. Retrieved January 21, 2013, from www.cdc.gov/media/releases/2012/p0329_autism_disorder.html

Ceci, S. J., & Gilstrap, L. L. (2000). Determinants of intelligence: Schooling and intelligence. In A. Kazdin (Ed.), *Encyclopedia of psychology*. Washington, DC, & New York: American Psychological Association and Oxford University Press.

Ceci, S. J., Papierno, P. B., & Kulkovsky, S. (2007). Representational constraints on children's suggestibility. *Psychological Science, 18*, 503-509.

Cerda, M., Sagdeo, A., Johnson, J., & Galea, S. (2010). Genetic and environmental influences on psychiatric comorbidity: A systematic review. *Journal of Affective Disorders*. (Available online December 11, 2009.)

Chabris, C. F. (1999). Prelude or requiem for the Mozart effect? *Nature, 400*, 826-827.

Chall, J. S. (1979). The great debate: Ten years later with a modest proposal for reading stages. In L. B. Resnick & P. A. Weaver (Eds.), *Theory and practice of early reading*. Hillsdale. NJ: Erlbaum.

Chan, C. (2008). Childhood obesity and adverse health effects in Hong Kong. *Obesity Reviews, 9*, Suppl. 1, S87-S90.

Chance, P. (2009). *Learning and behavior* (6th ed.). Boston: Cengage.

Chandler, M. (1973). Egocentrism and antisocial behavior: The assessment and training of social perspective-taking skills. *Developmental Psychology, 9*, 326-332.

Chandler, M. J., Sokol, B. W., & Wainryb, C. (2000). Beliefs about truth and beliefs about rightness. *Child Development, 71* (1), 91-97.

Chang, H. H., Larson, J., Blencowe, H., Spong, C. Y., Howson, C. P., Cairns-Smith, S., Lackritz, E. M., Lee, S. K., Mason, E., Serazin, A. C., Walani, S., Simpson, J. L., & Lawn, J. E. (2013). Preventing preterm births: Analysis of trends and potential reductions with interventions in 39 countries with very high human development index. *Lancet, 381*, 223-234.

Chang, J. J., Pien, G. W., Duntley, S. P., & Macones, G. A. (2010). Sleep deprivation during pregnancy and maternal and fetal outcomes: Is there a relationship? *Sleep Medicine Review, 14*, 107-114.

Chang, J. S. (2009). Parental smoking and childhood leukemia. *Methods in Molecular Biology, 472*, 103-137.

Chang, M. Y., Chen, C. H., & Huang, K. F. (2006). A comparison of massage effects on labor pain using the McGill Pain Questionnaire. *Journal of Nursing Research, 14*, 190-197.

Chang, Z., Lichtenstein, P., & Larsson, H. (2012). The effects of childhood ADHD symptoms on early-onset substance use: A Swedish twin study. *Journal of Abnormal Child Psychology, 40*, 425-435.

Chao, R. (2001). Extending research on the consequences of parenting style for Chinese Americans and European Americans. *Child Development, 72*, 1832-1843.

Chao, R., & Tseng, V. (2002). Parenting of Asians. In M. H. Bornstein (Ed.), *Handbook of parenting*. Mahwah, NJ: Erlbaum.

Chao, R. K. (2005, April). *The importance of Guan in describing control of immigrant Chinese*. Paper pesented at a meeting of the Society for Research in Child Development, Atlanta.

Chao, R. K. (2007, March). *Research with Asian Americans: Looking back and moving forward*. Paper presented at a meeting of the Society for Research in Child Development, Boston.

Charpak, N., Ruiz-Pelaez, J. G., Figueroa de Calume, Z., & Charpak, Y. A. (2001). Randomized controlled trial of kangaroo mother care: Results of follow-up at 1 year of corrected age. *Pediatrics: 108*, 1072–1079.

Chaplin, T. M., & Aldao, A. (2013, in press). Gender differences in emotion in children: A meta-analytic review. *Psychological Bulletin.*

Charlet, J., Schnekenburger, M., Brown, K. W., & Diederich, M. (2012). DNA demethylation increases sensitivity of neuroblastoma cells to chemotherapeutic drugs. *Biochemical Pharmacology, 83*, 858–865.

Chassin, L., & others. (2008). Multiple trajectories of cigarette smoking and the intergenerational transmission of smoking: A multigenerational, longitudinal study of a midwestern community sample. *Health Psychology, 27*, 819–828.

Chemtob, C. M., & others. (2010). Impact of maternal posttraumatic stress disorder and depression following exposure to the September 11 attacks on preschool children's behavior. *Child Development, 81*, 1129–1141.

Chen, J. J., & Brooks-Gunn, J. (2012). Neighborhoods, schools, and achievement. In K. R. Harris, S. Graham, & T. Urdan (Eds.), *APA handbook of educational psychology.* Washington, DC: American Psychological Association.

Chen, X. (2011). Culture, peer relationships, and human development. In L.A. Jensen (Ed.), *Bridging cultural and developmental approaches to psychology* (pp. 92–111). New York, NY: Oxford University Press.

Chen, X., & others. (2009). Interactions of IL-12A and IL-12B polymorphisms on the risk of cervical cancer in Chinese women. *Clinical Cancer Research, 15*, 400–405.

Chen, X., Chung, J., Lechccier-Kimel, R., & French, D. (2011). Culture and social development. In P. K. Smith & C. H. Hart (Eds.), *Wiley-Blackwell perspectives on childhood social development* (2nd ed.). New York: Wiley.

Chen, X., Hastings, P. D., Rubin, K. H., Chen, H., Cen, G., & Stewart, S. L. (1998). Childrearing attitudes and behavioral inhibition in Chinese and Canadian toddlers: A cross-cultural study. *Developmental Psychology, 34*, 677–686.

Chen, X. & Tse, H. C. (2008). Social functioning and adjustment in Canadian-born children with Chinese and European backgrounds. *Developmental Psychology, 44*, 1184–1189.

Chen, X., & Wang, L. (2010). China. In M. H. Bornstein (Ed.), *Handbook of cultural developmental science.* New York: Psychology Press.

Chen, Y., Keen, R., Rosancer, K., & von Hosten, C. (2010). Movement planning reflects skill level and age change in toddlers. *Child Development, 81*, 1846–1858.

Cheng, M., & Berman, S. L. (2013, in press). Globalization and identity development: A Chinese perspective. In S. J. Schwartz (Ed.), *Identity around the world: New directions for child and adolescent development.* San Francisco: Jossey-Bass.

Cheng, S., Maeda, T., Yoichi, S., Yamagata, Z., Tomiwa, K., & Japan Children's Study Group. (2010). Early television exposure and children's behavioral and social outcomes at age 30 months. *Journal of Epidemiology,* Suppl. 2, S482–S489.

Cheng, Y. Y., Shein, P. P., & Chiou, W. B. (2012). Escaping the impulse to immediate gratification: The prospect concept promotes a future-oriented mindset, prompting an inclination towards delayed gratification. *British Journal of Psychology, 103*, 129–141.

Cheok, M. H., Pottier, N., Kager, L., & Evans, W. E. (2009). Pharmacokinetics in acute lymphoblastic leukemia. *Seminars in Hematology, 46*, 39–51.

Chess, S., & Thomas, A. (1977). Temperamental individuality from childhood to adolescence. *Journal of Child Psychiatry, 16*, 218–226.

Chi, M. T. (1978). Knowledge structures and memory development. In R. S. Siegler (Ed.), *Children's thinking: What develops?* Hillsdale, NJ: Erlbaum.

Chick, C. F., & Reyna, V. F. (2012). A fuzzy trace theory of adolescent risk taking: Beyond self-control and sensation seeking. In V. F. Reyna & others (Eds.), *The adolescent brain.* Washington, DC: American Psychological Association.

Childers, J. B., & Tomasello, M. (2002). Two-year-olds learn novel nouns, verbs and conventional actions from massed or distributed exposures. *Developmental Psychology, 38*, 967–978.

Children's Defense Fund. (1992). *The state of America's children, 1992.* Washington, DC: Author.

Children's Defense Fund. (2009). *Children's welfare and mental health.* Retrieved July 2, 2009, from www.childrensdefense.org

Children's Defense Fund. (2010). *Children's health.* Retrieved January 5, 2010, from www.childrensdefense.org/helping-americas-children/

Chiu, L. M., Feldman, S. S., & Rosenthal, D. A. (1992). The influence of immigration on parental behavior and adolescent distress in Chinese families residing in two western nations. *Journal of Research on Adolescence, 2*, 205–240.

Choi, N. (2004). Sex role group differences in specific, academic, and general self-efficacy. *Journal of Psychology, 138*, 149–159.

Chomsky, N. (1957). *Syntactic structures.* The Hague: Mouton.

Choudhry, Z., & others. (2012). LPHN3 and attention deficit/hyperactivity disorder: Interaction with maternal stress during pregnancy. *Journal of Child Psychology and Psychiatry, 53*, 892–902.

Christakis, D. A., & others. (2009). Audible television and decreased adult words, infant vocalizations, and conversational turns. *Archives of Pediatrics & Adolescent Medicine, 163*, 554–558.

Christakis, D. A., & Zimmerman, F. J. (2007). Violent television viewing during preschool is associated with antisocial behavior during school age. *Pediatrics, 120*, 993–999.

Christakis, D. A., Zimmerman, F. J., DiGiuseppe, D. L., & McCarty, C. A. (2004). Early television exposure and subsequent attentional problems in children *Pediatrics, 113*, 708–713.

Christenfeld, N. J. S., & Mandler, G. (2013). Emotion. In I. B. Weiner & others (Eds.), *Handbook of psychology* (2nd ed., Vol. 1). New York: Wiley.

Christensen, L. B., Johnson, R. B., & Turner, L. A. (2011). *Research methods, design, & analysis* (11th ed.). Upper Saddle River, NJ: Pearson.

Cicchetti, D. (2011). Developmental psychopathology. In R. M. Lerner, W. F. Overton, A. M. Freund, & M. E. Lamb (Eds.), *Handbook of life-span development.* New York: Wiley.

Cicchetti, D. (2013). Developmental psychopathology. In P. Zelazo (Ed.), *Oxford handbook of developmental psychology.* New York: Oxford University Press.

Cicchetti, D., & Toth, S. L. (2006). Developmental psychopathology and preventive intervention. In W. Damon & R. Lerner (Eds.), *Handbook of child psychology.* (6th ed.). New York: Wiley.

Cicchetti, D., & Toth, S. L. (2011). Child maltreatment: The research imperative and the exploration of results to clinical contexts. In B. Lester & J. D. Sparrow (Eds.), *Nurturing children and families.* New York: Wiley.

Cicchetti, D., Toth, S. L., Nilsen, W. J., & Manly, J. T. (2013, in press). What do we know and why does it matter? The dissemination of evidence-based interventions for maltreatment. In H. R. Schaffer & K. Durkin (Eds.), *Blackwell handbook of developmental psychology.* Oxford, UK: Blackwell.

Cicchetti, D., Toth, S. L., & Rogosch, F. A. (2005). *A prevention program for child maltreatment*. Unpublished manuscript, University of Rochester, Rochester, NY.

Cillessen, A. H. N., & Bellmore, A. D. (2011). Social skills and social competence in interactions with peers. In P. K. Smith & C. H. Hart (Eds.), *Wiley-Blackwell handbook of childhood social development* (2nd ed.). New York: Wiley.

Cillessen, A. H. N. & Mayeux, L. (2004). From censure to reinforcement: Developmental changes in the association between aggression and social status. *Child Development, 75*(1), 147–163.

Cisneros-Cohernour, E. J., Moreno, R. P., & Cisneros, A. A. (2000). Curriculum reform in Mexico: Kindergarten teachers' challenges and dilemmas. Proceedings of the Lilian Katz Symposium. In D. Rothenberg (Ed.), *Issues in early childhood education: Curriculum reform, teacher education, and dissemination of information.* Urbana-Champaign: University of Illinois.

Clark, E. (1993). *The lexicon in acquisition.* New York: Cambridge University Press.

Clark, E. V. (2009). What shapes children's language? Child-directed speech and the process of acquisition. In V. C. M. Gathercole (Ed.), *Routes to language: Essays in honor of Melissa Bowerman.* New York: Psychology Press.

Clark, E. V. (2012). Lexical meaning. In E. L. Bavin (Ed.), *Cambridge handbook of child language.* New York: Cambridge University Press.

Clarke-Stewart, K. A., & Miner, J. L. (2008). Effects of child and day care. In M. M. Haith & J. B. Benson (Eds.), *Encyclopedia of infant and early childhood development.* Oxford, UK: Elsevier.

Class, Q. A., Lichtenstein, P., Langstrom, N., & D'Onofrio, B. M. (2011). Timing of prenatal maternal exposure to severe life events and adverse pregnancy outcomes: A population study of 2.6 million pregnancies. *Psychosomatic Medicine, 73*, 234–241.

Clauss, J. A., & Blackford, J. U. (2012). Behavioral inhibition and risk for developing social anxiety disorder: A meta-analytic study. *Journal of the American Academy of Child and Adolescent Psychiatry, 51*, 1066–1075.

Clay, R. (2001, February). Fulfilling an unmet need. *Monitor on Psychology,* No. 2.

Clearfield, M. W., Diedrich, F. J., Smith, L. B., & Thelen, E. (2006). Young infants reach correctly in A-not-B tasks: On the development of stability and perseveration. *Infant Behavior and Development, 29,* 435–444.

Clearfield, M. W., Dineva, E., Smith, L. B., Diedrich, F. J., & Thelen, E. (2009). Cue salience and infant perseverative reaching: Tests of the dynamic field theory. *Developmental Science, 12,* 26–40.

Clifton, R. K., Morrongiello, B. A., Kulig, J. W., & Dowd, J. M. (1981). Developmental changes in auditory localization in infancy. In R. N. Aslin, J. R. Alberts, & M. R. Petersen (Eds.), *Development of perception* (Vol. 1). Orlando, FL: Academic Press.

Clifton, R. K., Muir, D. W., Ashmead, D. H., & Clarkson, M. G. (1993). Is visually guided reaching in early infancy a myth? *Child Development, 64,* 1099–1110.

Clinkinbeard, S. S., Simi, P., Evans, M. K., & Anderson, A. L. (2011). Sleep and delinquency: Does amount of sleep matter? *Journal of Youth and Adolescence, 40,* 916–930.

Cloninger, S. C. (2013). *Theories of personality* (6th ed.). Upper Saddle River, NJ: Pearson.

Closson, L. M. (2009a). Status and gender differences in early adolescents' descriptions of popularity. *Social Development, 18*(2), 412–426.

Closson, L. M. (2009b). Aggressive and prosocial behaviors within early adolescent friendship cliques: What's status got to do with it? *Merrill-Palmer Quarterly, 55*(4), 406–435.

Closson, L. M., Darwich, L., Hymel, S., & Waterhouse, T. (2014). Ethnic discrimination among recent immigrant adolescents: Variations as a function of ethnicity and school context. *Journal of Research on Adolescence.*

Cluett, E. R., & Burns, E. (2009). Immersion in water in labour and birth. *Cochrane Database of Systematic Reviews,* CD000111.

Coatsworth, J. D., & Conroy, D. E. (2009). The effects of autonomy-supportive coaching, need satisfaction, and self-perceptions on initiative and identity in youth swimmers. *Developmental Psychology, 45,* 320–328.

Cohen, G. L., & Prinstein, M. J. (2006). Peer contagion of aggression and health-risk behavior among adolescent males: An experimental investigation of effects on public conduct and private attitudes. *Child Development, 77,* 967–983.

Cohen, L. B. (2002, April). *Can infants really add and subtract?* Paper presented at the meeting of the International Conference on Infant Studies, Toronto.

Cohen, N. J., Lojkasek, M., Zadch, Z. Y., Pugliese, M., & Kiefer. H. (2008). Children adopted from China: A prospective study of their growth and development. *Journal of Child Psychology and Psychiatry, 49,* 458–468.

Cohn, J. F., & Tronick, E. Z. (1988). Mother-infant face-to-face interaction. Influence is bidirectional and unrelated to periodic cycles in either partner's behavior. *Developmental Psychology, 24,* 396–397.

Coie, J. (2004). The impact of negative social experiences on the development of antisocial behavior. In J. B. Kupersmidt & K. A. Dodge (Eds.), *Children's peer relations: From development to intervention.* Washington, DC: American Psychological Association.

Colapinto, J. (2000). *As nature made him.* New York: Simon & Schuster.

Colby, A., Kohlberg, L., Gibbs, J., & Lieberman, M. (1983). A longitudinal study of moral judgment. *Monographs of the Society for Research in Child Development, 48* (21, Serial No. 201).

Cole, M., & Cagigas, X. E. (2010). Cognition. In M. Bornstein (Ed.), *Handbook of cultural developmental science.* New York: Psychology Press.

Cole, M. W., Yarkoni, T., Repovs, G., Anticevic, A., & Braver, T. S. (2012). Global connectivity of prefrontal cortex predicts cognitive control and intelligence. *Journal of Neuroscience, 32,* 8988–8999.

Cole, P. M., Dennis, T. A., Smith-Simon, K. E., & Cohen, L. H. (2009). Preschoolers' emotion regulation strategy understanding: Relations with emotion socialization and child self-regulation. *Social Development, 18*(2), 324–352.

Cole, P. M., & Tan, P. Z. (2007). Emotion socialization from a cultural perspective. In J. E. Grusec & P. D. Hastings (Eds.), *Handbook of socialization.* New York: Guilford.

Coleman-Phox, Odouli, R., & Li, D. K. (2008). Use of a fan during sleep and the risk of sudden infant death syndrome. *Archives of Pediatric and Adolescent Medicine, 162,* 963–968.

Coley, R. L., & Lombardi, C. M. (2013, in press). Does maternal employment following childbirth support or inhibit low-income children's long-term development? *Child Development.*

Collins, J. S., Atkinson, K. K., Dean, J. H., Best, R. G., & Stevenson, R. E. (2011). Long-term maintenance of neural tube defects prevention in a high prevalence state. *Journal of Pediatrics, 159,* 143–149.

Collins, S., A., Surmala, P., Osborne, G., Greenberg, C., Bathory, L. W., Edmunds-Potvin, S., & Arbour, L. (2012). Causes and risk factors for infant mortality in Nunavut, Canada 1999–2011. BMC Pediatrics 2012, 12:190  doi:10.1186/1471-2431-12-190

Colom, R., & others. (2009). Gray matter correlates of fluid, crystallized, and spatial intelligence. *Intelligence, 37,* 124-135.

Colom, R., Jung, R. E., & Haier, R. J. (2007). General intelligence and memory span: Evidence for a common neuro-anatomic framework. *Cognitive Neuropsychology, 24*(8), 867-878.

Colombo, J., Brez, C., & Curtindale, L. (2013, in press). Infant perception and cognition. In I. B. Weiner & others (Eds.), *Handbook of psychology* (2nd ed., Vol. 6). New York: Wiley.

Colombo, J., McCardle, P., & Freund, L. (Eds.). (2009). *Infant pathways to language.* New York: Psychology Press.

Colombo, J., Shaddy, D. J., Blaga, O. M., Anderson, C. J., Kannass, K. N., & Richman, W. A. (2009a). Attentional predictors of vocabulary from infancy. In J. Colombo, P. McCardle, & L. Freund (Eds.), *Infant pathways to language.* New York: Psychology Press.

Colombo, J., Shaddy, D. J., Blaga, O. M., Anderson, C. J., Kannass, K. N., & Richman, W. A. (2009b). Early attentional predictors of vocabulary in childhood. In J. Colombo, P. McCardle, & L. Freund (Eds.), *Infant pathways to language.* New York: Psychology Press.

Colombo, J., Shaddy, D. J., Anderson, C. J., Gibson, L. J., Blaga, O. M., & Kannass, K. N. (2010). What habituates in infant visual habituation? A psychophysiological analysis. *Infancy, 15,* 107-124.

Colombo, J., Shaddy, D. J., Blaga, O. M., Anderson, C. J., & Kannass, K. N. (2009). High cognitive ability in infancy and early childhood. In F. D. Horowitz, R. F. Subotnik, & D. J. Matthews (Eds.), *The development of giftedness and talent across the life span.* Washington, DC: American Psychological Association.

Colombo, J., Shaddy, D. J., Richman, W. A., Maikranz, J. M., & Blaga, O. M. (2004). The developmental course of attention in infancy and preschool cognitive outcome. *Infancy, 4,* 1-38.

Colonnesi, C., Stams, G. J., Koster, I., & Noom, M. J. (2010). The relation between pointing and language development: A meta-analysis. *Developmental Review, 30,* 352-366.

Comer, J. (1988). Educating poor minority children. *Scientific American, 259,* 42-48.

Comer, J. (2004). *Leave no child behind.* New Haven, CT: Yale University Press.

Comer, J. (2006). Child development: The under-weighted aspect of intelligence. In P. C. Kyllonen, R. D. Roberts, & L. Stankov (Eds.), *Extending intelligence.* Mahwah, NJ: Erlbaum.

Comer, J. (2010). Comer School Development Program. In J. Meece & J. Eccles (Eds.), *Handbook of research on schools, schooling, and human development.* New York: Routledge.

Commoner, B. (2002). Unraveling the DNA myth: The spurious foundation of genetic engineering. *Harper's Magazine, 304,* 39-47.

Compas, B. E. (2004). Processes of risk and resilience during adolescence: Linking contexts and individuals. In R. Lerner & L. Steinberg (Eds.), *Handbook of adolescent psychology.* New York: Wiley.

Comstock, G., & Scharrer, E. (2006). Media and popular culture. In W. Damon & R. Lerner (Eds.), *Handbook of child psychology* (6th ed.). New York: Wiley.

Conde, C. (2012). Preventing injury. *Texas Medicine,* 108, 35-39.

Conde-Aguedelo, A., Belizan, J. M., & Diaz-Rossello, J. (2011, March 16). Kangaroo care to reduce morbidity and mortality in low birthweight infants. *Cochrane Database of Systematic Reviews,* (3) CD002771.

Confer, J. C., & others. (2010). Evolutionary psychology. *American Psychologist, 65,* 110-126.

Cong, X., Ludington-Hoe, S. M., & Walsh, S. (2011). Randomized crossover trial of kangaroo care to reduce biobehavioral pain responses in preterm infants: A pilot study. *Biological Research for Nursing, 13,* 204-216.

Conger, R., & Conger, K. J. (2008). Understanding the processes through which economic hardship influences rural families and children. In D. R. Crane & T. B. Heaton (Eds.), *Handbook of families and poverty.* Thousand Oaks, CA: Sage.

Conger, R. D., & others. (2012). Resilience and vulnerability of Mexican origin youth and their families: A test of a culturally-informed model of family economic stress. In P. K. Kerig, M. S. Schulz, & S. T. Hauser (Eds.), *Adolescence and beyond.* New York: Oxford University Press.

Conley, M. W. (2008). *Content area literacy: Learners in context.* Boston: Allyn & Bacon.

Connolly, J. A., & McIsaac, C. (2009). Romantic relationships in adolescence. In R. M. Lerner & L. Steinberg (Eds.), *Handbook of adolescent psychology* (3rd ed.). New York: Wiley.

Conry-Murray, C., Kim, J. M., & Turiel, E. (2012, April). *U.S. and Korean children's judgments of gender norm violations.* Paper presented at the Gender Development Research conference, San Francisco.

Constanzo, M., & others. (2010). The genetic landscape of a cell. *Science, 327,* 425-431.

Cook, M., & Birch, R. (1984). Infant perception of the shapes of tilted plane forms. *Infant Behavior and Development, 7,* 389-402.

Cooper, C. R. (2011). *Bridging multiple worlds.* New York: Oxford University Press.

Cooper, C. R., & Grotevant, H. D. (1989, April). *Individuality and connectedness in the family and adolescent's self and relational competence.* Paper presented at the meeting of the Society for Research in Child Development, Kansas City.

Cooper, H., Allen, A. B., Patall, E. A., & Dent, A. L. (2010). Effects of full-day kindergarten on academic achievement and social development. *Review of Educational Research, 80*(1), 34-70.

Coopersmith, S. (1967). *The antecedents of self-esteem.* San Francisco: W. H. Freeman.

Coplan, R. J., & Arbeau, K. A. (2009). Peer interactions and play in early childhood. In K. H. Rubin, W. M. Bukowski, & B. Laursen (Eds.), *Handbook of peer interactions, relationships, and groups.* New York: Guilford.

Coplan, R. J., Closson, L. M., & Arbeau, K. A. (2007). Gender differences in the behavioral associates of loneliness and social dissatisfaction in kindergarten. *Journal of Child Psychology and Psychiatry, 48*(10), 988-995.

Coplan, R. J., Rose-Krasnor, L., Weeks, M., Kingsbury, A., Kingsbury, M., & Bullock, A. (2013). Alone is a crowd: Social motivations, social withdrawal, and socioemotional functioning in later childhood. *Developmental Psychology, 49*(5), 861-875.

Coplan, R. J., Schneider, B. H., Matheson, A., & Graham, A. (2010). 'Play skills' for shy children: Development of a social skills facilitated play early intervention program for extremely inhibited preschoolers. *Infant and Child Development, 19,* 223-237.

Copple, C., & Bredekamp, S. (2009). Developmentally appropriate practice in early childhood programs serving children from birth through age 8. Washington, DC: National Association for the Education of Young Children.

Corbetta, D., & Snapp-Childs, W. (2009). Seeing and touching: The role of sensory-motor experience on the development of reaching. *Infant Behavior and Development, 32,* 44-58.

Cordier, S. (2008). Evidence for a role of paternal exposure in developmental toxicity. *Basic and Clinical Pharmacology and Toxicology, 102,* 176-181.

Corenblum, B. & Armstrong, H. D. (2012). Racial-ethnic identity development in children in a racial-ethnic minority group. *Canadian Journal of Behavioural Science, 44*(2), 124–137.

Cornew, L., & others. (2012, in press). Atypical social referencing in infant siblings of children with autism spectrum disorders. *Journal of Autism and Developmental Disorders.*

Cosmides, L. (2011). Evolutionary psychology. *Annual Review of Psychology* (Vol. 62). Palo Alto, CA: Annual Reviews.

Costa, R., & Figueiredo, B. (2011). Infants' psychophysiological profile and temperament at 3 and 12 months. *Infant Behavior and Development, 34,* 270–279.

Costanzo, M., & others, (2010). The genetic landscape of a cell. *Science, 327,* 425–431.

Costigan, C. L., & Su, T. F. (2004). Orthogonal versus linear models of acculturation among immigrant Chinese Canadians: A comparison of mothers, fathers, and children. *International Journal of Behavioral Development, 28,* 518–527.

Costigan, C., Su, T. F., & Hua, J. M. (2009). Ethnic identity among Chinese Canadian youth: A review of the Canadian literature. *Canadian Psychology, 50*(4), 261–272.

Costigan, S. A., Barnett, L., Plotnikoff, R. C., & Lubans, D. R. (2013). The health indicators associated with screen-based sedentary behavior among adolescent girls: A systematic review. *Journal of Adolescent Health, 52,* 382–392.

Costley, K. C. (2012). An overview of the life, central concepts, including classroom applications for Lev Vygotsky. *ERIC,* ED529565.

Cote, J. E. (2009). Identity formation and self development in adolescence. In R. M. Lerner & L. Steinberg (Eds.), *Handbook of adolescent psychology* (3rd ed.). New York: Wiley.

Council of Economic Advisors. (2000). *Teens and their parents in the 21st century: An examination of trends in teen behavior and the role of parent involvement.* Washington, DC: Author.

Courage, M. L., Edison, S. C., & Howe, M. L. (2004). Variability in the early development of visual self-recognition. *Infant Behavior and Development, 27,* 509–532.

Courage, M. L., Howe, M. L., & Squires, S. E. (2004). Individual differences in 3.5-month-olds' visual attention: What do they predict at 1 year? *Infant Behavior and Development, 127,* 19–30.

Courage, M. L., & Richards, J. E. (2008). Attention. In M. M. Haith & J. B. Benson (Eds.), *Encyclopedia of infant and early childhood development.* Oxford, UK: Elsevier.

Courage, M. L., & Setliff, A. E. (2010). When babies watch television: Attention-getting, attention-holding, and the implications for learning from video material. *Developmental Review, 30,* 220–238.

Cowan, C. P., Cowan, P. A., & Barry, J. (2011). Couples' groups for parents of preschoolers: Ten-year outcomes of a randomized trial. *Journal of Family Psychology, 25,* 240–250.

Cowan, P. & Cowan, C. (2000) *When partners become parents: The big life change for couples.* Mahwah, NJ: Erlbaum.

Cowan, P., Cowan, C., Ablow, J., Johnson, V. K., & Measelle, J. (2005). *The family context of parenting in children's adaptation to elementary school.* Mahwah, NJ: Erlbaum.

Cowan, P. A., & Cowan, C. P. (2009). How working with couples fosters children's development. In M. S. Schulz, P. K., Kerig, M. K. Pruett, & R. D. Parke (Eds.), *Feathering the nest.* Washington, DC: American Psychological Association.

Cowan, P. A., & Heming, G. (2013). How children and parents fare during transition to school. In P. A. Cowan & others (Eds.), *The family context of parenting in children's adaptation to elementary school.* New York: Routledge.

Cowan, P. A., & others. (2013). Family factors in children's adaptation to elementary school: A discussion and integration. In P. A. Cowan & others (Eds.), *The family context of parenting in children's adaptation to elementary school.* New York: Routledge.

Cox, M. J., Burchinal, M., Taylor, L. C., Frosch, B., Goldman, B., & Kanoy, K. (2004). The transition to parenting: Continuity and change in early parenting behavior and attitudes. In R. D. Conger, F. O. Lorenz, & K. A. S. Wickrama (Eds.), *Continuity and change in family relations.* Mahwah, NJ: Erlbaum.

Coyne, S. M., Nelson, D. A., & Underwood, M. (2011). Aggression in children. In P. K. Smith & C. H. Hart (Eds.), *Wiley-Blackwell handbook of childhood social development* (2nd ed.). New York: Wiley.

Cozzi, B., & others. (2010). Ontogenesis and migration of metallothionein I/II-containing glial cells in the human telencephalon during the second trimester. *Brain Research, 1327,* 16–23.

Craig, W. & Pepler, D. (2003). Identifying and targeting risk for involvement in bullying and victimization. *Canadian Journal of Psychiatry, 48,* 577–582.

Crain, S. (2012). Sentence scope. In E. L. Bavin (Ed.), *Cambridge handbook of child language.* New York: Cambridge University Press.

Crain, S., & Zhou, P. (2012). Semantics and pragmatics: Acquisition of logical connectives and focus. In C. T. J. Huang & R. Sybesma (Eds.), *Encyclopedia of Chinese language and linguistics.* The Netherlands: Brill.

Crespi, B. (2011). The evolutionary biology of child health. *Proceedings of the Royal Society, Biological Sciences, 278,* 1441–1449.

Creswell, J. W. (2008). *Educational research* (3rd ed.). Upper Saddle River, NJ: Prentice Hall.

Crick, N. R., Murray-Close, D., Marks, P. E. L., & Mohajeri-Nelson, N. (2009). Aggression and peer relationships in school-age children: Relational and physical aggression in group and dyadic contexts. In K. H. Rubin, W. M. Bukowski, & B. Laursen (Eds.), *Handbook of peer interactions, relationships, and groups.* New York: Guilford.

Cristino, L., & Di Marzo, V. (2014). Fetal cannabinoid receptors and the "disjoint-ed" brain. *The EMBO Journal, 33,* 665–667.

Crockenberg, S. B. (1986). Are temperamental differences in babies associated with predictable differences in caregiving? In J. V. Lerner & R. M. Lerner (Eds.), *Temperament and social interaction during infancy and childhood.* San Francisco: Jossey-Bass.

Crockenberg, S., & Leerkes, E. (2013). Infant negative emotionality, caregiving, and family relationships. In A. C. Crouter & A. Booth (Eds.), *Children's influence on family dynamics.* New York: Routledge.

Cromer, R. (1987). Receptive language in the mentally retarded: Processes and diagnostic distinctions. In R. Schielebusch & L. Lloyd (Eds.), *Language perspectives: Acquisition, retardation, and intervention.* Baltimore: University Park Press.

Crosnoe, R., Riegle-Crumb, C., Field, S., Frank, K., & Muller, C. (2008). Peer group contexts of girls' and boys' academic experiences. *Child Development, 79,* 139–155.

Crouter, A. C. (2006). Mothers and fathers at work. In A. Clarke-Stewart & J. Dunn (Eds.), *Families count.* New York: Cambridge University Press.

Crouter, A. C., & Booth, A. (Eds.). (2013). *Children's influence on family dynamics.* New York: Routledge.

Crowley, K., Callahan, M. A., Tenenbaum, H. R., & Allen, E. (2001). Parents explain more to boys than to girls during shared scientific thinking. *Psychological Science, 12,* 258–261.

Crugnola, C. R., & others. (2013, in press). Maternal attachment influences mother-infant styles of regulation and play with objects at nine months. *Attachment and Human Development*.

Cruikshank, D. R., Jenkins, D. B., & Metcalf, K. K. (2012). *The act of teaching* (6th ed.). New York: McGraw-Hill.

Cubillo, A., Halari, R., Smith, A., Taylor, E., & Rubia, K. (2012). A review of fronto-spatial brain abnormalities in children and adults with Attention Deficit Hyperactivity Disorder (ADHD) and new evidence for dysfunction in adults with ADHD during motivation and attention. *Cortex, 48,* 194-215.

Cuevas, K., Swingler, M. M., Bell, M. A., Maracovitch, S., & Calkins, S. D. (2012). Measures of frontal functioning and the emergence of inhibitory control processes at 10 months of age. *Developmental Cognitive Neuroscience, 2,* 235-243.

Cui, M., Fincham, F. D., & Pasley, B. K. (2008). Young adult romantic relationships: The role of parents' marital problems and relationship efficiency. *Personality and Social Psychology Bulletin, 34,* 1226-1235.

Cui, M., Ueno, K., Fincham, F. D., Donnellan, M. B., & Wickrama, K. A. (2012). The association between romantic relationships and delinquency in adolescence and young adulthood. *Personal Relationships, 19,* 354-366.

Culicover, P. W. (2013). Simpler syntax. In B. Heine & H. Narrog (Eds.), *Oxford handbook of linguistic analysis*. New York: Oxford University Press.

Cummings, C. (2012). Melatonin for the management of sleep disorders in children and adolescents. *Paediatric and Child Health, 17,* 331-333.

Cummings, E. M., & Davies, P. T. (2010). *Marital conflict and children: An emotional security perspective*. New York: Guilford.

Cummings, E. M., El-Sheikh, M., & Kouros, C. D. (2009). Children and violence: The role of children's regulation in the marital aggression-child adjustment link. *Clinical Child and Family Psychology Review, 12*(1), 3-15.

Cummings, E. M., George, M. R. W., McCoy, K. P., & Davies, P. T. (2012). Interparental conflict in kindergarten and adolescent adjustment: Prospective investigation of emotion security as an explanatory mechanism. *Child Development, 83,* 1703-1715.

Cummings, E. M., & Kouros, C. D. (2008). Stress and coping. In M. M. Haith & J. B. Benson (Eds.), *Encyclopedia of infant and early childhood development, Vol. 3* (pp. 267-281). San Diego: Academic Press.

Cunningham, J. N., Kliewer, W., & Garner, P. W. (2009). Emotion socialization, child emotion understanding and regulation, and adjustment in urban African American families: Differential associations across child gender. *Development and Psychopathology, 21,* 261-283.

Cunningham, P. M. (2009). *What really matters in vocabulary*. Boston: Allyn & Bacon.

Cunningham, P. M. (2013). *Phonics they use: Words for reading and writing* (6th ed.). Boston: Allyn & Bacon.

Cunningham, P. M., & Hall, D. P. (2009). *Making words first grade*. Boston: Allyn & Bacon.

Curran, K., DuCette, J., Eisenstein, J., & Hyman, I. A. (2001, August). *Statistical analysis of the cross-cultural data: The third year*. Paper presented at the meeting of the American Psychological Association, San Francisco, CA.

Curtin, S., & Werker, J. F. (2007). The perceptual foundations of phonological development. In G. Gaskell (Ed.), *The Oxford handbook of psycholinguistics* (pp. 579-599). Oxford, England: Oxford University Press.

Cushner, K. H., McClelland, A., & Safford, P. (2009). *Human diversity in education* (6th ed.). New York: McGraw-Hill.

# D

da Fonseca, E. B., Bittar, R. E., Damiao, R., & Zugiab, M. (2009). Prematurity prevention: The role of progesterone. *Current Opinion in Obstetrics and Gynecology, 21,* 142-147.

Dahl, R. E. (2004). Adolescent brain development: A period of vulnerabilities and opportunities. *Annals of the New York Academy of Sciences, 1021,* 1-22.

Daley, A. J., Macarthur, C., & Winter, H. (2007). The role of exercise in treating postpartum depression: A review of the literature. *Journal of Midwifery & Women's Health, 52,* 56-62.

Dalley, J. W., & Roiser, J. P. (2013, in press). Dopamine, serotonin, and impulsivity. *Neuroscience*.

Dalton, T. C., & Bergenn, V. W. (2007). *Early experience, the brain, and consciousness*. Mahwah, NJ: Erlbaum.

Daltro, P., & others. (2010). Congenital chest malformations: A multimodality approach with emphasis on fetal MRI imaging. *Radiographics, 30,* 385-395.

Damon, W. (1988). *The moral child*. New York: Free Press.

Damon, W. (2008). *The path to purpose*. New York: The Free Press.

Daniels, H. (2011). Vygotsky and psychology. In U. Goswami (Ed.), *Wiley-Blackwell handbook of childhood cognitive development* (2nd ed.). New York: Wiley-Blackwell.

D'Ardenne, K., & others. (2012). Feature article: Role of the prefrontal cortex and the midbrain dopamine system in working memory updating. *Proceedings of the National Academy of Sciences U.S.A., 109,* 19900-19909.

Darrah. J., & Bartlett, D. J. (2013, in press). Infant rolling abilities—the same or different 20 years after the back to sleep campaign? *Early Human Development*.

Darrah, J., Bartlett, D., Maguire, T. O., Avison, W. R. and Lacaze-Masmonteil, T. (2014). Have infant gross motor abilities changed in 20 years? A re-evaluation of the Alberta Infant Motor Scale normative values. *Developmental Medicine & Child Neurology.* doi: 10.1111/dmcn.12452

Darwich, L. (2013). Growing up in Canada: Youth ethnic identity and Canadian identity (Unpublished doctoral dissertation). The University of British Columbia, Vancouver.

Darwin, C. (1859). *On the origin of species*. London: John Murray.

Dasen, P. R. (1984). The cross-cultural study of intelligence: Piaget and the Baoulé. *International Journal of Psychology, 19*(4-5), 407-434.

D'Augelli, A. R. (1991). Gay men in college: Identity processes and adaptations. *Journal of College Student Development, 32,* 140-146.

Davalos, D. B., Yadon, C. A., & Tregellas, H. C. (2012). Untreated prenatal maternal depression and the potential risks to offspring: A review. *Archives of Women's Mental Health, 15,* 1-14.

Davidson, J. (2000). Giftedness. In A. Kazdin (Ed.), *Encyclopedia of psychology*. Washington, DC, & New York: American Psychological Association and Oxford University Press.

Davidson, M. R., Davidson, M., London, M. L., & Ladewig, P. W. (2012). *Olds' maternal-newborn nursing & women's health across the lifespan: International Edition* (9th ed.). Upper Saddle River, NJ: Pearson.

Davies, G., & others. (2011). Genome-wide association studies establish that human intelligence is highly heritable and polygenic. *Molecular Psychiatry, 16,* 996-1005.

Davies, J., & Brember, I. (1999). Reading and mathematics attainments and self-esteem in years 2 and 6: An eight-year cross-sectional study. *Educational Studies, 25,* 145-157.

Davis, B. E., Moon, R. Y., Sachs, H. C., & Ottolini, M. C. (1998). Effects of sleep position on infant motor development. *Pediatrics, 102,* 1135-1140.

**Davis, C. L., & others.** (2007). Effects of aerobic exercise on overweight children's cognitive functioning: A randomized controlled trial. *Research Quarterly for Exercise and Sport, 78,* 510-519.

**Davis, C. L., & others.** (2011). Exercise improves executive function and alters neural activation in overweight children. *Health Psychology, 30,* 91-98.

**Davis, E. L., & Buss, K. A.** (2012). Moderators of the relation between shyness and behavior with peers: Cortisol dysregulation and maternal emotional socialization. *Social Development, 21,* 801-820.

**Davis, K., Christodoulou, J., Seider, S., & Gardner, H.** (2011). The theory of multiple intelligences. In R. J. Sternberg & S. B. Kaufman (Eds.), *Cambridge handbook of intelligence.* New York: Cambridge University Press.

**Davis, K., Desrocher, M., & Moore, T. E.** (2011). Fetal Alcohol Spectrum Disorder: A review of neuropsychological findings and interventions. *Journal of Developmental & Physical Disabilities, 23*(2), 143-167.

**Davis, L., & Keyser, J.** (1997). *Becoming the parent you want to be.* New York: Broadway Books.

**Davis, O. S. P., Arden, R., & Plomin, R.** (2008). *g* in middle childhood: Moderate genetic and shared environmental influence diverse measures of general cognitive ability at 7, 9, and 10 years in large population sample of twins. *Intelligence, 36,* 68-80.

**Davis, S. M., & others.** (2013). CHILE: An evidence-based preschool intervention for obesity prevention in Head Start. *Journal of School Health, 83,* 223-229.

**Day, R. H., & McKenzie, B. E.** (1973). Perceptual shape constancy in early infancy. *Perception, 2,* 315-320.

**Deamen, S., & others.** (2012). Identity and perceived peer relationship quality in emerging adulthood: The mediating role of attachment-related emotions. *Journal of Adolescence, 35,* 1417-1425.

**Deardorff, J., & others.** (2011). Father absence, body mass index, and pubertal timing in girls: Differential effects by family income and ethnicity. *Journal of Adolescent Health, 48,* 441-447.

**Deary, I. J.** (2012). Intelligence. *Annual Review of Psychology* (Vol. 63). Palo Alto, CA: Annual Reviews.

**Deary, I. J., & Batty, G. D.** (2011). Intelligence as a predictor of health, illness, and death. In R. J. Sternberg & S. B. Kaufman (Eds.), *Cambridge handbook of intelligence.* New York: Cambridge University Press.

**Deary, I. J., Penke, L., & Johnson, W.** (2010). The neuroscience of human intelligence differences. *Nature Review: Neuroscience, 11,* 201-211.

**Deary, I. J., Strand, S., Smith, P., & Fernandes, C.** (2007). Intelligence and educational achievement. *Intelligence, 35,* 13-21.

**Deater-Deckard, K.** (2013). The social environment and the development of psychopathology. In P. D. Zelazo (Ed.), *Oxford handbook of developmental psychology.* New York: Oxford University Press.

**Deater-Deckard, K., & Dodge K.** (1997). Externalizing behavior problems and discipline revisited: Non-linear effects and variation by culture, context and gender. *Psychological Inquiry, 8,* 161-175.

**DeBoer, T., Scott, L. S., & Nelson, C. A.** (2007). Methods for acquiring and analyzing infant event-related potentials. In M. de Haan (Ed.) *Infant EEG and event-related potentials.* (pp. 5-38). New York: Psychology Press.

**de Brigard, F., Szpunar, K. K., & Schacter, D. L.** (2013). Coming to grips with the past: Effect of repeated stimulation on the perceived plausibility of episodic counterfactual thoughts. *Psychological Science.*

**DeCasper, A. J., & Spence, M. J.** (1986). Prenatal maternal speech influences newborn's perception of speech sounds. *Infant Behavior and Development, 9,* 133-150.

**De Castro Ribas, R.** (2010). Central and South America. In M. H. Bornstein (Ed.), *Handbook of cultural developmental science.* New York: Psychology Press.

**Deci, E. L., & Ryan, R. M.** (2000). The "what" and "why" of goal pursuits: Human needs and the self-determination of behavior. *Psychological Inquiry, 11,* 227-268.

**De Decker, E., & others.** (2012). Influencing factors of screen time in preschool children: An exploration of parents' perceptions through focus groups in six European countries. *Obesity Reviews, 13*(Suppl. 1), S75-S84.

**Deeley, Q., & Murphy, D.** (2009). Pathophysiology of autism: Evidence from brain imaging. *British Journal of Hospital Medicine, 70,* 138-142.

**DeGarmo, D. S., & Martinez, C. R.** (2006). A culturally informed model of academic well-being for Latino youth: The importance of discriminatory experiences and social support. *Family Relations, 55,* 267-278.

**De Giovanni, N., & Marchetti, D.** (2012). Cocaine and its metabolites in the placenta: A systematic review of the literature. *Reproductive Toxicology, 33,* 1-14.

**Degnan, K. A., & Fox, N. A.** (2007). Behavioral inhibition and anxiety disorders: Multiple levels of a resilience process. *Development and Psychopathology, 19,* 729-746.

**de Graaf, H., van de Schoot, R., Woertman, L., Hawk, S. T., & Meeus, W.** (2012). Family cohesion and romantic and sexual initiation: A three wave longitudinal study. *Journal of Youth and Adolescence, 41,* 583-592.

**de Haan, M., & Matheson, A.** (2009). The development and neural bases of processing emotion in faces and voices. In M. De Haan & M. R. Gunnar (Eds.), *Handbook of developmental social neuroscience.* New York: Guilford.

**de Hevia, M. D. & Spelke, E. S.** (2010). Number-space mapping in human infants. *Psychological Science.*

**DeLoache, J. S.** (1989). The development of representation in young children. In H. W. Reese (Ed.), *Advances in child development and behavior.* New York: Academic Press.

**DeLoache, J. S.** (2011). Early development and use of symbolic artifacts. In U. Goswami (Ed.), *Wiley-Blackwell handbook of childhood cognitive development* (2nd ed.). New York: Wiley-Blackwell.

**DeLoache, J. S., Simcock, G., & Macari, S.** (2007). Planes, trains, and automobiles—and tea sets: Extremely intense interests in very young children. *Developmental Psychology, 43,* 1579-1586.

**Demetriou, A.** (2006). Neo-Piagetian theories of cognitive development. English translation. Published under the title "Neo-Piagetische Ansatze" in W. Schneider & F. Wilkening (Eds.), (2006). *Theorien, modelle, und methoden der Endwicklungspsychologie.* Volume of *Enzyklopadie der Psychologie* (191-263). Gotingen: Hogrefe-Verlag.

**Dempster, F. N.** (1981). Memory span: Sources of individual and developmental differences. *Psychological Bulletin, 80,* 63-100.

**Denham, S., & others.** (2012). Preschoolers' emotion knowledge: Self-regulatory foundations and predictors of school success. *Cognition and Emotion, 26,* 667-679.

**Denham, S. A., Bassett, H. H., & Wyatt, T.** (2007). The socialization of emotional competence. In J. E. Grusec & P. D. Hastings (Eds.), *Handbook of socialization.* New York: Guilford.

Denham, S., Warren, H., von Salisch, M., Benga, O., Chin, J-C., & Geangu, E. (2011). Emotions and social development in childhood. In P. K. Smith & C. H. Hart (Eds.), *Wiley-Blackwell handbook of childhood social development* (2nd ed.). New York: Wiley.

D'Entremont, Y. (2014, June 4). A proactive approach. *Halifax Herald*, 6.

de Onis, M., de Onis, M., Onyango, A. W., Borghi, E., Garza, C., & Yang, H. (2006). Comparison of the World Health Organization (WHO) child growth standards and the National Center for Health Statistics/WHO international growth reference: Implications for child health programs. *Public Health Nutrition, 9,* 942-947.

Denmark, F. L., Russo, N. F., Frieze, I. H., & Eschuzur, J. (1988). Guidelines for avoiding sexism in psychological research: A report of the ad hoc committee on nonsexist research. *American Psychologist, 43,* 582-585.

Depp, C., Vahia, I. V., & Jeste, D. (2010). Successful aging: Focusing on cognitive and emotional health. *Annual Review of Clinical Psychology,* Vol. 6. Palo Alto, CA: Annual Reviews.

de Rose, L. M., Shiyko, M. P., Foster, H., & Brooks-Gunn, J. (2011). Associations between menarcheal timing and behavioral developmental trajectories for girls from age 6 to age 15. *Journal of Youth and Adolescence, 40,* 1329-1342.

Desai, M., Beall, M., & Ross, M. G. (2013, in press). Developmental origins of obesity: Programmed adipogenesis. *Current Diabetes Reports.*

Desjarlais, M. & Willoughby, T. (2010). A longitudinal study of the relation between adolescent boys and girls' computer use with friends and friendship quality: Support for the social compensation or the rich-get-richer hypothesis? *Computers in Human Behavior, 26,* 896-905.

Deutsch, A. R., Crockett, L. J., Wolf, J. M., & Russell, S. T. (2012). Parent and peer pathways to adolescent delinquency: Variations by ethnicity and neighborhood context. *Journal of Youth and Adolescence, 41,* 1078-1094.

Deutsch, R. & Pruett, M. K. (2009). Child adjustment and high conflict divorce. In R. M. Galatzer-Levy and L. Kraus (Eds.), *The scientific basis of custody decisions* (2nd ed.). New York: Wiley.

Dever, B. V., & others. (2013, in press). Predicting risk-taking with and without substance use: The effects of parental monitoring, school bonding, and sports participation. *Prevention Science.*

de Villiers, J., & de Villiers, P. (2013). Syntax acquisition. In P. D. Zelazo (Ed.), *Oxford handbook of developmental psychology.* New York: Oxford University Press.

Dew, J., & Wilcox, W. B. (2011). "If momma ain't happy": Explaining declines in marital satisfaction among new mothers. *Journal of Marriage and the Family, 73,* 1-12.

DeWall, C. N., Anderson, C. A., & Bushman, B. J. (2013). Aggression. In I. B. Weiner & others (Eds.), *Handbook of psychology* (2nd ed., Vol. 5). New York: Wiley.

Dewey, J. (1933). *How we think.* Lexington, MA: D. C. Heath.

DeZolt, D. M., & Hull, S. H. (2001). Classroom and school climate. In J. Worell (Ed.), *Encyclopedia of women and gender.* San Diego: Academic Press.

Diamond, A. (2009). The interplay of biology and the environment broadly defined. *Developmental Psychology, 45,* 1-8.

Diamond, A. (2011). Biological and social influences on cognitive control processes dependent on prefrontal cortex. *Progress in Brain Research, 89,* 317-337.

Diamond, A. (2012). Activities and programs that improve children's executive function. *Current Directions in Psychological Science, 21,* 335-341.

Diamond, A. (2013). Executive functioning. *Annual Review of Psychology* (Vol. 64). Palo Alto, CA: Annual Reviews.

Diamond, A. D. (1985). Development of the ability to use recall to guide action as indicated by infants' performance on AB. *Child Development, 56,* 868-883.

Diamond, A., Barnett, W. S., Thomas, J., & Munro, S. (2007). Preschool program improves cognitive control. *Science, 318,* 1387-1388.

Diamond, A., Casey, B. J., & Munakata, Y. (2011). *Developmental cognitive neuroscience.* New York: Oxford University Press.

Diamond, A., & Lee, K. (2011). Interventions shown to aid executive function development in children 4 to 12 years old. *Science, 333,* 959-964.

Diamond, L. M. (2013a). Gender and same-sex sexuality. In D. T. Tolman & L. M. Diamond (Eds.), *APA handbook on sexuality and psychology.* Washington, DC: American Psychological Association.

Diamond, L. M. (2013b). Sexuality and same-sex sexuality in relationships. In J. Simpson & J. Davidio (Eds.), *Handbook of personality and social psychology.* Washington, DC: American Psychological Association.

Diamond, L. M., & Savin-Williams, R. C. (2013). Same-sex activity in adolescence: Multiple meanings and implications. In R. F. Fassinger & S. L. Morrow (Eds.), *Sex in the margins.* Washington, DC: American Psychological Association.

Diamond, M., & Sigmundson, H. K. (1997). Sex reassignment at birth: Long-term review and clinical implications. *Archives of Pediatric and Adolescent Medicine, 151,* 298-304.

Diaz, A., & Bell, M. A. (2012). Frontal EEG asymmetry and fear reactivity in different contexts at 10 months. *Developmental Psychobiology, 54,* 536-545.

Dick, D. M., & others. (2007). Gender differences in friends' influences on adolescent drinking: A genetic epidemiological study. *Alcoholism: Clinical and Experimental Research, 31,* 2012-2019.

Diener, E., & Diener, M. (1995). Cross-cultural correlates of life satisfaction and self-esteem. *Journal of Personality and Social Psychology, 68,* 653-663.

Dietz, L. J., Jennings, K. D., Kelley, S. A., & Marshal, M. (2009). Maternal depression, paternal psychopathology, and toddlers' behavior problems. *Journal of Clinical Child and Adolescent Psychology, 38,* 48-61.

Dietz, P. M., & others. (2010). Infant morbidity and mortality attributable to prenatal smoking in the U.S. American *Journal of Preventive Medicine, 39,* 45-62.

Dijkstra, J. K., Cillessen A. H. N., Lindenberg, S. & Veenstra, R. (2010). Basking in reflected glory and its limits: Why adolescents hang out with popular peers. *Journal of Research on Adolescence, 20,* 942-958.

Dijkstra, J. K., Lindenberg, S., Verhulst, F. C., Ormel, J., & Veenstra, R. (2009). The relation between popularity and antisocial behaviors: Moderating effects of athletic abilities, physical attractiveness, and prosociality. *Journal of Research on Adolescence, 19,* 401-413.

Dimmitt, C., & McCormick, C. B. (2012). Metacognition in education. In K. R. Harris, S. Graham, & T. Urdan (Eds.), *Handbook of educational psychology.* Washington, DC: American Psychological Association.

Dishion, T. J., & Tipsord, J. M. (2011). Peer contagion in child and adolescent social and emotional development. *Annual Review of Psychology* (Vol. 62). Palo Alto, CA: Annual Reviews.

Dittrick, C. J., Closson, L. M., Shumka, E., & Hymel, S. (2011, June). *Middle school students' perceptions of their victimization experiences.* Poster presented at the 2011 Canadian Psychological Association 72nd Annual Convention, Toronto, ON.

Diwadkar, V. A., & others (2012). Differences in cortico-striatal-cerebellar activation during working memory in syndromal and nonsyndromal children with prenatal exposure to alcohol. *Human Brain Mapping, 69,* 231-242.

Dodge, K. A. (1993). Social cognitive mechanisms in the development of conduct disorder and depression. *Annual Review of Psychology, 44,* 559-584.

Dodge, K. A. (2011a). Context matters in child and family policy. *Child Development, 82,* 433-442.

Dodge, K. A. (2011b). Social information processing models of aggressive behavior. In M. Mikulincer & P. R. Shaver (Eds.), *Understanding and reducing aggression, violence, and their consequences.* Washington, DC: American Psychological Association.

Doherty, M. (2009). *Theory of mind.* Philadelphia: Psychology Press.

Don, B. P., & Michelson, K. D. (2012). Paternal postpartum depression: The role of maternal postpartum depression, spousal support, and relationship satisfaction. *Couple and Family Psychology: Research and Practice, 1,* 323-334.

Donatelle, R. J. (2011). *Health* (9th ed.). Upper Saddle River, NJ: Pearson.

Dondi, M., Simion, F., & Caltran, G. (1999). Can newborns discriminate between their own cry and the cry of another newborn infant? *Developmental Psychology, 35*(2), 418-426.

Donegan, S., Maluccio, J. A., Myers, C. K., Menon, P., Ruel, M. T., & Habicht, J. P. (2010, in press). Two food-assisted maternal and child health nutrition programs help mitigate the impact of economic hardship on child stunting in Haiti. *Journal of Nutrition.*

Donnerstein, E. (2002). The Internet. In V. C. Strasburger & B. J. Wilson (Eds.), *Children, adolescents, and the media.* Newbury Park, CA: Sage.

D'Onofrio, B. M., & others. (2007). Intergenerational transmission of childhood conduct problems: A children of twins study. *Archives of General Psychiatry, 64,* 820-829.

Doornwaard, S. M., Branje, S., Meeus, W. H. J., & ter Bogt, T. F. M. (2012). Development of adolescents' peer crowd identification in relation to changes in problem behaviors. *Developmental Psychology, 48,* 1366-1380.

Dopp, P. R., Mooney, A. J., Armitage, R., & King, C. (2012). Exercise for adolescents with depressive disorders: A feasibility study. *Depression Research and Treatment.* Article ID: 257472.

Doty, R. L., & Shah, M. (2008). Taste and smell. In M. M. Haith & J. B. Benson (Eds.),

*Encyclopedia of infant and early childhood development.* Oxford, UK: Elsevier.

Dow, R. S., & Baer, G. T. (2013). *Self-paced phonics* (5th ed.). Boston: Allyn & Bacon.

Dozier, M., Stovall-McClough, K. C., & Albus, K. E. (2009). Attachment and psychopathogy in adulthood. In J. Cassidy & P. R. Shaver (Eds.), *Handbook of attachment* (2nd ed.). New York: Guilford.

Draghi-Lorenz, Reddy, V., & Costall, A. (2001). Rethinking the development of "nonbasic" emotions: A critical review of existing theories. *Developmental Review, 21,* 263-304.

Drake, K. M., & others. (2012). Influence of sports, physical education, and active commuting to school on adolescent weight status. *Pediatrics, 130,* e296-e304.

Drake, M. (2008). Developing resilient children after 100 years of Montessori education. *Montessori Life, 20*(2), 28-31.

Dregan, A., & Armstrong, D. (2010). Adolescent sleep disturbances as predictors of adult sleep disturbances—A cohort study. *Journal of Adolescent Health, 46,* 482-487.

Driesen, N. R., & Raz, N. (1995). The influence of sex, age, and handedness on corpus callosum morphology: A meta-analysis. *Psychobiology, 23,* 240-247.

Drummond, R. J., & Jones, K. D. (2010). *Assessment procedures* (7th ed.). Upper Saddle River, NJ: Pearson.

Duck, S. W. (1975). Personality similarity and friendship choices by adolescents. *European Journal of Social Psychology, 5,* 351-365.

Duczkowska, A., & others. (2010). Magnetic resonance imaging in the evaluation of fetal spinal canal contents. *Brain Development.* (Available online February 24, 2010.)

Dufour-Rainfray, D., & others. (2011). Fetal exposure to teratogens: Evidence of genes involved in autism. *Neuroscience and Biobehavioral Reviews, 35,* 1254-1265.

Duggan, P. M., Lapsley, D. K., & Norman, K. (2000, April). Adolescent invulnerability and personal uniqueness: Scale development and initial contact validation. Paper presented at the biennial meeting of the Society for Research in Child Development, Chicago.

Duncan, G., & Magnuson, K. (2008). Can society profit from investing in early education programs? In A. Tarlov (Ed.), *Nurturing the national treasure: Childhood education and development before kindergarten.* New York: Palgrave Macmillan.

Duncan, G. J. (2012). Give us this day our daily breadth. *Child Development, 83,* 6-15.

Duncan, G. J., & Brooks-Gunn, J. (2000). Family poverty, welfare reform and child development. *Child Development, 71*(1), 188-196.

Duncan, G. J., Ziol-Guest, K. M., & Kalil, A. (2010). Early-childhood poverty and adult attainment, behavior, and health. *Child Development, 81,* 306-325.

Duncan, J. R., & others. (2010). Brainstem serotonergic deficiency in sudden infant death syndrome. *Journal of the American Medical Association, 303,* 430-437.

Duncombe, M. E., Havighurst, S. S., Holland, K. A., & Frankling, E. J. (2012). The contribution of parenting practice and parent emotion factors in children at risk for disruptive behavior disorders. *Child Psychiatry and Human Development, 43,* 715-733.

Dunkel Schetter, C. (2011). Psychological science in the study of pregnancy and birth. *Annual Review of Psychology* (Vol. 62). Palo Alto, CA: Annual Reviews.

Dunn, J. (2007). Siblings and socialization. In J. E. Grusec & P. D. Hastings (Eds.), *Handbook of socialization.* New York: Guilford.

Dunn, J. (2010). Commentary and challenges to Grusec and Davidov's domain-specific approach. *Child Development, 81,* 710-714.

Dunn, J. (2013). Moral development in early childhood and social interaction in the family. In M. Killen & J. G. Smetana (Eds.), *Handbook of moral development* (2nd ed.). New York: Routledge.

Dunn, J., & Kendrick, C. (1982). *Siblings.* Cambridge, MA: Harvard University Press.

Dunphy, D. C. (1963). The social structure of urban adolescent peer groups. *Society, 26,* 230-246.

Dunst, C. J., Simkus, A., & Hamby, D. W. (2012). Relationship between age of onset and frequency of reading and infants' and toddlers' early language and literacy development. *CELLreviews, 5*(3), 1-10.

Durik, A. M., Hyde, J. S., Marks, A. C., Roy, A. L., Anaya, D., & Schultz, G. (2006). Ethnicity and stereotypes of emotions. *Sex Roles, 54*(7-8), 429-445.

Durrant, J. E. (2008). Physical punishment, culture, and rights: Current issues for professionals. *Journal of Developmental and Behavioral Pediatrics, 29,* 55-66.

Durrant, J. E., Rose-Krasnor, L., & Broberg, A. G. (2003). Physical punishment and maternal beliefs in Sweden and Canada. *Journal of Comparative Family Studies, 34,* 586-604.

Durston, S. (2010, in press). Imaging genetics in ADHD. *Neuroimage.*

Dusek, J. B., & McIntyre, J. G. (2003). Self-concept and self-esteem development. In G. Adams & M. Berzonsky (Eds.), *Blackwell handbook of adolescence*. Malden, MA: Blackwell.

Dvornyk, V., & Waqar-ul-Haq, H. (2012). Genetics of age at menarche: A systematic review. *Human Reproduction Update*, 18, 198-210.

Dweck, C. S. (2006). *Mindset*. New York: Random House.

Dweck, C. S. (2007). Boosting achievement with messages that motivate. *Education Canada*, 47, 6-10.

Dweck, C. S. (2012). Mindsets and human nature: Promoting change in the Middle East, the school yard, the racial divide, and willpower. *American Psychologist*, 67, 614-622.

Dweck, C. S. (2013). Social development. In P. Zelazo (Ed.), *Oxford handbook of developmental psychology*. New York: Oxford University Press.

Dweck, C. S., & Master, A. (2009). Self-theories and motivation: Students' beliefs about intelligence. In K. R. Wentzel & A. Wigfield (Eds.), *Handbook of motivation at school*. New York: Routledge.

Dyck, M., & Piek, J. (2010). How to distinguish normal from disordered children with poor language or motor skills. *International Journal of Language and Communication Disorders*, 45, 336-344.

## E

Eagly, A. H. (2001). Social role theory of sex differences and similarities. In J. Worrell (Ed.), *Encyclopedia of women and gender*. San Diego: Academic Press.

Eagly, A. H. (2009). Gender roles. In J. Levine & M. Hogg (Eds.), *Encyclopedia of group processes and intergroup relations*. Thousand Oaks, CA: Sage.

Eagly, A. H. (2010). Gender roles. In J. Levine & M. Hogg (Eds.), *Encyclopedia of group process and intergroup relations*. Thousand Oaks, CA: Sage.

Eagly, A. H. (2013). Women as leaders: Paths through the labyrinth. In M. C. Bligh & R. Riggio (Eds.), *When near is far and far is near: Exploring distance in leader-follower relationships*. New York: Wiley Blackwell.

Eagly, A. H., & Crowley, M. (1986). Gender and helping behavior: A meta-analytic review of the social psychological literature. *Psychological Bulletin*, 100, 283-308.

Eagly, A. H., & Steffen, V. J. (1986). Gender and aggressive behavior: A meta-analytic review of the social psychological literature. *Psychological Bulletin*, 100, 309-330.

East, P. (2009). Adolescent relationships with siblings. In R. M. Lerner & L. Steinberg (Eds.), *Handbook of adolescent psychology* (3rd ed.). New York: Wiley.

Easterbrooks, M. A., Bartlett, J. D., Beeghly, M., & Thompson, R. A. (2013). Social and emotional development in infancy. In R. M. Lerner, M. A. Easterbrooks, & J. Mistry (Eds.), *Handbook of psychology* (2nd ed., Vol. 6). New York: Wiley.

Eaton, W. O. (2008). Milestones: Physical. In M. M. Haith & J. B. Benson (Eds.), *Encyclopedia of infant and early childhood development*. Oxford, UK: Elsevier.

Ebstein, R. P., Knafo, A., Mankuta, D., Chew, S. H., & Lai, P. S. (2012). The contributions of oxytocin and vasopressin pathway genes to human behavior. *Hormones and Behavior*, 61, 359-379.

Eccles, J. (2003). Education: Junior and high school. In G. Adams & M. Berzonsky (Eds.), *Blackwell handbook of adolescence*. Malden, MA: Blackwell.

Eccles, J. S., & Roeser, R. W. (2013). Schools as developmental contexts during adolescence. In I. B. Weiner & others (Eds.), *Handbook of psychology* (2nd ed., Vol. 6). New York: Wiley.

Eccles, J. S. (2007). Families, schools, and developing achievement-related motivations and engagement. In J. E. Grusec & P. D. Hastings (Eds.), *Handbook of socialization*. New York: Guilford.

Eckerman, C. & Whitehead, H. (1999). How toddler peers generate coordinated action: A cross-cultural exploration. *Early Education & Development*, 10, 241-266.

Edwards, C. P., & Liu, W. (2002). Parenting toddlers. In M. H. Bornstein (Ed.), *Handbook of parenting* (2nd ed., Vol. 1). Mahwah, NJ: Erlbaum.

Edwards, M. (2014, in press). *Every child, every day: A digital conversion model for student achievement*. Upper Saddle River, NJ: Pearson.

Edwards, R., & Hamilton, M. A. (2004). You need to understand my gender role: An empirical test of Tannen's model of gender and communication. *Sex Roles*, 50, 491-504.

Egbert, J. L. (2009). *Supporting learning with technology*. Boston: Allyn & Bacon.

Ehrhardt, A. A., & Baker, S. W. (1974). Fetal androgens, human central nervous system differentiation, and behavior sex differences. In R. C. Friedman, R. M. Richart, & R. L. Vande Wiele (Eds.), *Sex differences in behavior*. New York: Wiley.

Ehrlich, K. B., Dykas, M. J., & Cassidy, J. (2012). Tipping points in adolescent adjustment: Predicting social functioning from adolescents' conflict with parents

and friends. *Journal of Family Psychology*, 26, 776-783.

Eiferman, R. R. (1971). Social play in childhood. In R. Herron & B. Sutton-Smith (Eds.), *Child's play*. New York: Wiley.

Eisenberg, N. (2010). Emotion regulation in children. *Annual Review of Clinical Psychology* (Vol. 6). Palo Alto, CA: Annual Reviews.

Eisenberg, N., Fabes, R. A., & Spinrad, T. L. (2006). Prosocial development. In W. Damon & R. Lerner (Eds.), *Handbook of child psychology* (6th ed.). New York: Wiley.

Eisenberg, N., Spinrad, T. L., & Morris, A. S. (2013). Prosocial development. In P. D. Zelazo (Ed.), *Oxford handbook of developmental psychology*. New York: Oxford University Press.

Eisenberg, N., Spinrad, T., & Sadovsky, A. (2006). Empathy-related responding in children. In M. Killen & J. Smetana (Eds.), *Handbook of moral development*. Mahwah, NJ: Erlbaum.

Eisenberg, N., Spinrad, T., & Sadovsky, A. (2013). Empathy-related responding in children. In M. Killen & J. G. Smetana (Eds.), *Handbook of moral development* (2nd ed.). New York: Routledge.

Eisenberg, N., & Valiente, C. (2002). Parenting and children's prosocial and moral development. In M. H. Bornstein (Ed.), *Handbook of parenting* (2nd ed.). Mahwah, NJ: Erlbaum.

Eisenhower Foundation. (2010). *Quantum Opportunities Program*. Available at www.eisenhowerfoundation.org/docs/Quantum_Evaluation.pdf

Ekeblad, S. (2010). Islet cell tumors. *Advances in Experimental Medicine and Biology*, 654, 771-789.

Elder, G. H., & Shanahan, M. J. (2006). The life course and human development. In W. Damon & R. Lerner (Eds.), *Handbook of child psychology* (6th ed.). New York: Wiley.

Elgar, F. J., Craig, W., & Trites, S. J. (2013). Family dinners, communication, and mental in Canadian adolescents. *Journal of Adolescent Health*, 52, 433-438.

Elgar, F. J., Mills, R. S. L., McGrath, P. J., Waschbusch, D. A., & Brownridge, D. A. (2007). Maternal and paternal depressive symptoms and child maladjustment: The mediating role of parental behavior. *Journal of Abnormal Child Psychology*, 35, 943-955.

Elkind, D. (1976). *Child development and education. A Piagetian perspective*. New York: Oxford University Press.

Elkind, D. (1978). Understanding the young adolescent. *Adolescence*, 13, 127-134.

Elkind, D. (2007). The power of play: Learning what comes naturally. New York: Da Capo.

Ellis, B. J., Shirtcliff, E. A., Boyce, W. T., Deardorff, J., & Essex, M. J. (2011). Quality of early family relationships and the timing and tempo of puberty: Effects depend on biological sensitivity to context. *Development and Psychopathology, 23,* 85–99.

El-Sheikh, M. (Ed.). (2011). *Sleep and development.* New York: Oxford University Press.

El-Sheikh, M. (2013). *Auburn University Child Sleep, Health, and Development Center.* Auburn, AL: Auburn University.

Emery, R. E. (1994). *Renegotiating family relationships.* New York: Guilford Press.

Emery, R. E., & Laumann-Billings, L. (1998). An overview of the nature, causes, and consequences of abusive family relationships. *American Psychologist, 53,* 121–135.

Enfield, A., & Collins, D. (2008). The relationship of service-learning social justice multicultural competence, and civic engagement. *Journal of College Student Development, 49,* 95–109.

Enright, M. S., Schaefer, L. V., Schaefer, P., & Schaefer, K. A. (2008). Building a just adolescent community. *Montessori Life, 20,* 36–42.

Enright, R. D., Santos, M. J. D., & Al-Mabuk, R. (1989). The adolescent as forgiver. *Journal of Adolescence, 12,* 95–110.

Ensor, R., Spencer, D., & Hughes, C. (2010, in press). "You feel sad?" Emotional understanding mediates effects of verbal ability and mother-child mutuality on prosocial behaviors: Findings from 2 to 4 years. *Social Development.*

Epstein, D., & Barnett, W. S. (2012). Early education in the United States: Programs and access. In R. C. Pianta (Ed.), *Handbook of early childhood education.* New York: Guilford.

Erath, S. A., Flanagan, K. S., Bierman, K. L., & Tu, K. M. (2010). Friendships moderate psychosocial maladjustment in socially anxious early adolescents. *Journal of Applied Developmental Psychology, 31,* 15–26.

Ericson, N. (2001, June). *Addressing the problem of juvenile bullying.* Washington, DC: Office of Juvenile Justice and Delinquency Prevention, Office of Justice Programs, U.S. Department of Justice.

Ericsson, K. A., N. Charness, P. J. Feltovich, & R. R. Hoffman. (Eds.). (2006). *The Cambridge handbook of expertise and expert performance.* New York: Cambridge University Press.

Ericsson, K. A., Krampe, R., & Tesch-Romer, C. (1993). The role of deliberate practice in the acquisition of expert performance. *Psychological Review, 100,* 363–406.

Erikson, E. H. (1950). *Childhood and society.* New York: W. W. Norton.

Erikson, E. H. (1968). *Identity: Youth and crisis.* New York: W. W. Norton.

Escobar-Chaves, S. L., & Anderson, C. A. (2008). Media and risky behavior. *Future of Children, 18*(1), 147–180.

Espelage, D. L., & Holt, M. K. (2012). Understanding and preventing bullying and sexual harassment in school. In K. R. Harris & others (Eds.), *APA handbook of educational psychology.* Washington, DC: American Psychological Association.

Etaugh, C. A., & Bridges, J. S. (2010). *Women's lives* (2nd ed.). Boston: Allyn & Bacon.

Evans, B. J., & Whitfield, J. R. (Eds.). (1988). *Black males in the United States: An annotated bibliography from 1967 to 1987.* Washington, DC: American Psychological Association.

Evans, G. W. (2004). The environment of childhood poverty. *American Psychologist, 59,* 77–92.

Evans, G. W., & English, K. (2002). The environment of poverty: Multiple stressor exposure, psychophysiological stress, and socioemotional adjustment. *Child Development, 73,* 1238–1248.

Evans, G. W., & Kim, P. (2007). Childhood poverty and health: Cumulative risk exposure and stress dysregulation. *Psychological Science, 18,* 953–957.

## F

Fabiano, G. A., Pelham, W. E., Coles, E. K., Gnagy, E. M., Chronis-Tuscano, A., & O'Connor, B. C. (2009). A meta-analysis of behavioral treatments for attention deficit/hyperactivity disorder. *Clinical Psychology Review, 29*(2), 129–140.

Fabricius, W. V., Braver, S. L., Diaz, P., & Schenck, C. (2010). Custody and parenting time: Links to family relationships and well-being after divorce. In M. E. Lamb (Ed.), *The role of the father in child development* (5th ed.). New York: Wiley.

Fagan, J. F. (1992). Intelligence: A theoretical viewpoint. *Current Directions in Psychological Science, 1,* 82–86.

Fagan, J. F. (2011). Intelligence in infancy. In R. J. Sternberg & S. B. Kaufman (Eds.), *Handbook of intelligence.* New York: Cambridge University Press.

Fagan, J. F., Holland, C. R., & Wheeler, K. (2007). The prediction, from infancy, of adult IQ and achievement. *Intelligence, 35,* 225–231.

Fair, D., & Schlaggar, B. L. (2008). Brain development. In M. M. Haith & J. B. Benson (Eds.), *Encyclopedia of infant and early childhood development.* London, UK: Elsevier.

Faissner, A., & others. (2010). Contributions of astrocytes to synapse formation and maturation—potential functions of the perisynaptic extracellular matrix. *Brain Research Reviews.* (Available online January 21, 2010.)

Falbo, T., & Poston, D. L. (1993). The academic, personality, and physical outcomes of only children in China. *Child Development, 64,* 18–35.

Falck-Ytter, T., & others. (2012, in press). Gaze performance in children with autism spectrum disorder when observing communicative actions. *Journal of Autism and Developmental Disorders.*

Fantz, R. L. (1963). Pattern vision in newborn infants. *Science, 140,* 296–297.

Faraone, S. V., & Mick, E. (2010). Molecular genetics of attention deficit hyperactivity disorder. *Psychiatric Clinics of North America, 33,* 159–180.

Faria, L. (2001). Harter's self-perception profile for children adapted for use with young Portuguese students. *Perceptual and Motor Skills, 92,* 711–720.

Farrington, D. P. (2009). Conduct disorder, aggression, and delinquency. In R. M. Lerner & L. Steinberg (Eds.), *Handbook of adolescent psychology* (3rd ed.). New York: Wiley.

Fasig, L. (2000). Toddlers' understanding of ownership: Implications for self-concept development. *Social Development, 9,* 370–382.

Fauth, R. S., Roth, J. L., & Brooks-Gunn, J. (2007). Does the neighborhood context alter the link between youths' after-school time activities and developmental outcomes? A multilevel analysis. *Developmental Psychology, 43,* 760–777.

Fearon, R. P., & others. (2010). The significance of insecure attachment and disorganization in the development of children's externalizing behavior: A meta-analytic study. *Child Development, 81,* 435–456.

Federal Interagency Forum on Child and Family Statistics. (2008). *America's children in brief: Key national indicators of well-being, 2008.* Retrieved July 31, 2008, from www.childstats.gov/

Feeney, S., Moravcik, E., & Nolte, S. (2013). *Who am I in the lives of children?* (9th ed.). Upper Saddle River, NJ: Pearson.

Fein, G. G. (1987). Pretend play. In D. Görlitz & J. E. Wohlwill (Eds.), *Curiosity, imagination, and play.* Hillsdale, NJ: Erlbaum.

Feldman, H. D. (2001, April). *Contemporary developmental theories and the concept of talent.* Paper presented at the meeting of the Society for Research in Child Development, Minneapolis.

Feldman, H. D., & Morelock, M. J. (Eds.). (2011). Prodigies and savants. In R. J. Sternberg & S. B. Kaufman (Eds.), *Handbook of intelligence.* New York: Cambridge University Press.

Feldman, R. (2012). Oxytocin and social affiliation in humans. *Hormones and Behavior, 61,* 380–391.

Feldman, R., & Eidelman, A. (2003). Mother-infant skin-to-skin contact (kangaroo care) accelerates autonomic and neurobehavioral maturation in preterm infants. Developmental Medicine and Child. *Neurology, 4,* 274–281.

Ferguson, D. M., Harwood, L. J., & Shannon, F. T. (1987). Breastfeeding and subsequent social adjustment in 6- to 8-year-old children. *Journal of Child Psychology and Psychiatry, 28,* 378–386.

Fergusson, D.M., Vitaro, F., Wanner, B., & Brendgen, M. (2007). Protective and compensatory factors mitigating the influence of deviant friends on delinquent behaviors during early adolescence. *Journal of Adolescence, 30,* 33–50.

Fidler, D. J. (2008). Down syndrome. In M. M. Haith & J. B. Benson (Eds.), *Encyclopedia of infancy and early childhood development.* Oxford, UK: Elsevier.

Field, A., Cartwright-Hatton, S., Reynolds, S., & Creswell, C. (Eds.). (2008). *Child anxiety theory and treatment.* New York: Psychology Press.

Field, T. (2010). Postpartum depression effects on early interactions, parenting, and safety practices: A review. *Infant Behavior and Development, 33,* 1–6.

Field, T., Diego, M., & Hernandez-Reif, M. (2010). Preterm infant massage therapy research: A review. *Infant Behavior and Development, 33,* 115–124.

Field, T. M. (2012). Prenatal exercise research. *Infant Behavior and Development, 35,* 397–407.

Field, T. M., & others. (1997). Brief report: Autistic children's attentiveness and responsivity improve after touch therapy. *Journal of Autism and Developmental Disorders, 27,* 333–338.

Field, T. M., & others. (1998). Children with asthma have improved pulmonary functions after massage therapy. *Journal of Pediatrics, 132,* 854–858.

Field, T. M., Delgado, J., Diego, M., & Medina, L. (2013). Tai chi/yoga reduces prenatal depression, anxiety, and sleep disturbances. *Complementary Therapies in Clinical Practice, 19,* 6–10.

Field, T. M., Grizzle, N., Scafidi, F., & Schanberg, S. (1996). Massage and relaxation therapies' effects on depressed adolescent mothers. *Adolescence, 31,* 903–911.

Field, T. M., Hernandez-Reif, M., Diego, M., Feijo, L., Vera, Y., & Gil, K. (2004). Massage therapy by parents improves early growth and development. *Infant Behavior & Development, 27,* 435–442.

Fein, G. G. (1987). Pretend play: Creativity and consciousness. In P. Gorlitz & J. Wohlwill (Eds.), *Curiosity, imagination and play* (pp. 281–304). Hillsdale, NJ: Lawrence Erlbaum Associates.

Findlay, L. C., & Bowker, A. (2009). The link between competitive sport participation and self-concept in early adolescence: A consideration of gender and sport orientation. *Journal of Youth and Adolescence, 38,* 29–40.

Findlay, L. C., Coplan, R. J., & Bowker, A. (2009). Keeping it all inside: Shyness, internalizing coping strategies and socio-emotional adjustment in middle childhood. *International Journal of Behavioural Development, 33*(1), 47–54.

Finger, B., Hans, S. L., Bernstein, V. J., & Cox, S. M. (2009). Parent relationship quality and infant-mother attachment. *Attachment and Human Development, 11,* 285–306.

Fingerman, K. L., Cheng, Y. P., & others. (2012, in press). Helicopter parents and landing pad kids: Intense parental support of grown children. *Journal of Marriage and the Family.*

Fingerman, K. L., Pillemer, K. A., Silverstein, M., & Suitor, J. J. (2012). The Baby Boomers' intergenerational relationships. *Gerontologist, 52,* 199–209.

Fingerman, K. L., Sechrest, J., & Birditt, K. S. (2013, in press). Intergenerational relationships in a changing world. *Gerontology.*

Fischhoff, B., Bruine de Bruin, W., Parker, A. M., Millstein, S. G., & Halpern-Felsher, B. L. (2010). Adolescents' perceived risk of dying. *Journal of Adolescent Health, 46,* 265–269.

Fisher, A., Thiessen, E., Godwin, K., Kloos, H., & Dickerson, J. (2013). Assessing selective sustained attention in 3- to 5-year-old children: Evidence for a new paradigm. *Journal of Experimental Child Psychology, 114,* 275–294.

Fisher, C. B. (2009). *Decoding the ethics code: A practical guide for psychologists* (2nd ed.). Thousand Oaks, CA: SagePublications.

Fisher, P. A. (2005, April). *Translational research on underlying mechanisms of risk among foster children: Implications for prevention science.* Paper presented at the meeting of the Society for Research in Child Development, Washington, DC.

Fitzgerald, A., Fitzgerald, N., & Aherne, C. (2012). Do peers matter? A review of peer and/or friends' influence on physical activity among American adolescents. *Journal of Adolescence, 35,* 941–958.

Fitzgerald, R. T., & Carrington, P. J. (2011). Disproportionate minority contact in Canada: Police and visible minority youth. *Canadian Journal of Criminology and Criminal Justice, 53*(4), 449–486.

Fitzpatrick, C., Barnett, T., & Pagani, L. S. Early exposure to media violence and later child adjustment. *Journal of Developmental and Behavioral Pediatrics, 33*(4), 291–297.

Fitzpatrick, C., & Pagani, L. S. Toddler working memory skills predict kindergarten school readiness. Intelligence, 40(2), 205–212.

Fivush, R., Haden, C., & Reese, E. (2006). Elaborating on elaborations: Role of maternal reminiscing style in cognitive and socioemotional development. *Child Development, 77,* 1568–1588.

Fivush, R., & Wang, Q. (2005). Emotion talk in mother–child conversations of the shared past: The effects of culture, gender, and event valence. *Journal of Cognition and Development, 6,* 489–506.

Flanagan, T., Iarocci, G., D'Arrisso, A., Mandour, T., Tootoosis, C., Robinson, S., & Burack, J. A. (2011). Reduced ratings of physical and relational aggression for youths with a strong cultural identity: Evidence from the Naskapi people. *Journal of Adolescent Health, 49,* 155–159.

Flavell, J. H. (1979). Metacognition and cognitive monitoring. A new area of psychological inquiry. *American Psychologist, 34,* 906–911.

Flavell, J. H. (2004). Theory-of-mind development: Retrospect and prospect. *Merrill-Palmer Quarterly, 50,* 274–290.

Flavell, J. H., Friedrichs, A., & Hoyt, J. (1970). Developmental changes in memorization processes. *Cognitive Psychology, 1,* 324–340.

Flavell, J. H., Green, F. L., & Flavell, E. R. (1993). Children's understanding of the stream of consciousness. *Child Development, 64,* 95–120.

Flavell, J. H., Green, F. L., and Flavell, E. R. (1998). The mind has a mind of its own developing knowledge about mental uncontrollability. *Cognitive Development, 13,* 127–138.

Flavell, J. H., & Miller, P. H. (1998). Social cognition. In W. Damon (Ed.), *Handbook of child psychology* (5th ed.). New York: Wiley.

Flavell, J. H., Miller, P. H., & Miller, S. (2002). *Cognitive development* (4th ed.). Upper Saddle River, NJ: Prentice Hall.

Flavell, J., Mumme, D., Green, F., and Flavell E. (1992). Young children's understanding of different types of beliefs. *Child Development, 63,* 960-977.

Flegal, W. A. (2007). Blood group genotyping in Germany. *Transfusion, 47* (Suppl. I), S47-S53.

Flint, M. S., Baum, A., Chambers, W. H., & Jenkins, F. J. (2007). Induction of DNA damage, alteration of DNA repair, and transcriptional activation by stress hormones. *Psychoneuroendocrinology, 32,* 470-479.

Flom, R., & Pick, A. D. (2003). Verbal encouragement and joint attention in 18-month-old infants. *Infant Behavior and Development, 26,* 121-134.

Florence, N. (2010). *Multiculturalism 101.* New York: McGraw-Hill.

Florin, T., & Ludwig, S. (2011). *Netter's Pediatrics.* New York: Elsevier.

Florsheim, P., Moore, D., & Edgington, C. (2003). Romantic relationships among adolescent parents. In P. C. Florsheim (Ed.), *Adolescent romantic relations and sexual behavior.* Oxford, UK: Routledge.

Flouri, E., & Buchanan, A. (2004). Early father's and mother's involvement and child's later educational outcomes. *British Journal of Educational Psychology, 74,* 141-153.

Flynn, J. R. (1999). Searching for justice: The discovery of IQ gains over time. *American Psychologist, 54,* 5-20.

Flynn, J. R. (2007a). The history of the American mind in the 20th century: A scenario to explain gains over time and a case for the irrelevance of *g.* In P. C. Kyllonen, R. D. Roberts, & L. Stankov (Eds.), *Extending intelligence.* Mahwah, NJ: Erlbaum.

Flynn, J. R. (2007b). *What is intelligence? Beyond the Flynn effect.* New York: Cambridge University Press.

Flynn, J. R. (2013). *Are we getting smarter?* New York: Cambridge University Press.

Flynn, J. R., & Rossi-Case, L. (2012). IQ gains in Argentina between 1964 and 1998. *Intelligence, 40,* 145-150.

Fonseca, E. B., Celik, E., Parra, M., Singh, M., Nicolaides, K. H., & Fetal Medicine Foundation Second Trimester Screening Group. (2007). Progesterone and the risk of preterm birth among women with a short cervix. *New England Journal of Medicine, 357,* 462-469.

Forcier, R. C., & Descy, D. E. (2008). *Computer as an educational tool* (5th ed.). Boston: Allyn & Bacon.

Ford, D. Y. (2012). Gifted and talented education: History, issues, and recommendations. In K. R. Harris, S. Graham, & T. Urdan (Eds.), *APA handbook of educational psychology.* Washington, DC: American Psychological Association.

Forgatch, M. S., Patterson, G. R., Degarmo, D. S., & Beldavs, Z. G. (2009). Testing the Oregon delinquency model with 9-year follow-up of the Oregon Divorce Study. *Development and Psychopathology, 21,* 637-660.

Fox, B. J. (2012). *Word identification strategies* (5th ed.). Boston: Allyn & Bacon.

Fox, C. L. & Farrow, C. V. (2009). Global and physical self-esteem and body dissatisfaction as mediators of the relationship between weight status and being a victim of bullying. *Journal of Adolescence, 32*(5), 1287-1301.

Fox, N. A., Henderson, H. A., Marshall, P. J., Nichols, K. E., & Ghera, M. M. (2005). Behavioral inhibition: Linking biology and behaviour within a developmental framework. *Annual Review of Psychology, 56,* 235-262.

Fox, S. E., Levitt, P., & Nelson, C. A. (2010). How the timing and quality of early experiences influence the development of brain architecture. *Child Development, 81,* 28-40.

Fraley, R. C., Roisman, G. I., & Haltigan, J. D. (2013, in press). The legacy of early experiences in development: Formalizing alternative models of how early experiences are carried forward over time. *Developmental Psychology.*

Franchak, J. M., Kretch, K. S., Soska, K. C., & Adolph, K. E. (2011). Head-mounted eye-tracking: A new method to describe the visual ecology of infants. *Child Development, 82,* 1738-1750.

Francis, D. D., Szegda, K., Campbell, G., Martin, W. D., & Insel, T. R. (2003). Epigenetic sources of behavioural differences in mice. *Nature Neuroscience, 6,* 445-446.

Frank, M. C., Vul, E., & Johnson, S. P. (2009). Development of infants' attention to faces during the first year. *Cognition, 110,* 160-170.

Franklin, A., Bevis, L., Ling, Y., & Hulbert, A. (2010). Biological components of color preference in infancy. *Developmental Science, 13,* 346-354.

Franz, C. E. (1996). The implications of preschool tempo and motoric activity level for personality decades later. Reported in A. Caspi (1998), Personality development across the life course. In W. Damon (Ed.), *Handbook of child psychology* (Vol. 3, p. 337). New York: Wiley.

Fraser, A. M., Padilla-Walker, L. M., Coyne, S. M., Nelson, L. J., & Stockdale, L. A. (2012). Association between violent video gaming, empathic concern, and prosocial behavior toward strangers, friends, and family members. *Journal of Youth and Adolescence, 41,* 636-649.

Frechette, J. (2012). Beauty and body image: Beauty myths. In M. Kosut (Ed.), *Encyclopedia of gender in media.* Thousand Oaks, CA: Sage.

Frederickson, N., Petrides, K. V., & Simmonds, E. (2012). Trait emotional intelligence as a predictor of socioemotional outcomes in early adolescence. *Personality and Individual Differences, 52,* 323-328.

Frederikse, M., Lu, A., Aylward, E., Barta, P., Sharma, T., & Pearlson, G. (2000). Sex differences in inferior lobule volume in schizophrenia. *American Journal of Psychiatry, 157,* 422-427.

Freedman, J. L. (1984). Effects of television violence on aggressiveness. *Psychological Bulletin, 96,* 227-246.

Freeman, S. (2011). *Biological Science with Mastering Biology* (4th ed.). Upper Saddle River, NJ: Benjamin Cummings.

Frey, K., Hirschstein, M. K., Edstrom, L. V., & Snell, J. (2009). Observed reductions in school bullying, nonbullying aggression, and destructive bystander behavior: A longitudinal evaluation. *Journal of Educational Psychology, 101,* 466-481.

Frey, K. S., Hirschstein, M. K., Snell, J. L., Edstrom, L. V. S., & Broderick, C. J. (2005). Reducing playground bullying and supporting beliefs: An experimental trial of the Steps to Respect program. *Developmental Psychology, 41,* 479-790.

Fried, P. A. (2011). Cannabis use during pregnancy: its effects on offspring from birth to young adulthood. In P. M. Preece, & E. P. Riley (Eds.), *Alcohol, drugs and medication in pregnancy: the long-term outcome for the child* (pp. 153-168). London, UK: MacKeith Press.

Friedman, S. L., Melhuish, E. & Hill, C. (2009). Childcare research at the dawn of a new millennium: An update. In G. Bremner & T. Wachs (Eds.), *Wiley-Blackwell handbook of infant development* (2nd ed.). Oxford, UK: Wiley-Blackwell.

Friend, M. (2011). *Special education* (3rd ed.). Upper Saddle River, NJ: Merrill.

Freud, S. (1917). *A general introduction to psychoanalysis.* New York: Washington Square Press.

Frisbie, W. P., Hummer, R. A., & McKinnon, S. (2009). Infant and child mortality. In D. Carr (Ed.), *Encyclopedia of the life course and human development*. Boston: Gale Cengage.

Frisco, M. L. (2009). Obesity, childhood and adolescence. In D. Carr (Ed.), *Encyclopedia of the life course and human development*. Boston: Gale Cengage.

Froh, J. J., Yurkewicz, C., & Kashdan, T. B. (2009). Gratitude and subjective well-being in early adolescence: Examining gender differences. *Journal of Adolescence, 32*(3), 633–650.

Frost, E. A., Gist, R. S., & Adriano, E. (2011). Drugs, alcohol, pregnancy, and fetal alcohol syndrome. *International Anesthesiology Clinics, 49*, 119–133.

Fry, B. G. (2009). Mining genomes to identify toxins. *Annual Review of Genomics and Human Genetics* (Vol. 10). Palo Alto, CA: Annual Reviews.

Fryberg, S. A. & others. (2013). Cultural mismatch and the education of Aboriginal youths: The interplay of cultural identities and teacher ratings. *Developmental Psychology, 49*(1), 72–79.

Frye, D. (1999). Development of intention: The relation of executive function to theory of mind. In P. D. Zelazo, J. W. Astington, & D. R. Olson (Eds.), *Developing theories of intention: Social understanding and self-control*. Mahwah, NJ: Erlbaum.

Frye, D. (2004). Unpublished review of Santrock, J. W., *Child development* (11th ed.). New York: McGraw-Hill.

Fu, G., Xu, F., Cameron, C.A., Heyman, G., & Lee, K. (2007). Cross-cultural differences in children's choices, categorizations, and evaluations of truths and lies. *Developmental Psychology, 43*, 278–293.

Fuchs, L. S., & others. (2013). Instructional intervention for students with mathematical learning disabilities. In H. L. Swanson & others (Eds.), *Handbook of learning disabilities* (2nd ed.). New York: Guilford.

Fujioka, T., Mourad, N., & Trainor, L. J. (2011). Development of auditory-specific brain rhythm in infants. *European Journal of Neuroscience, 33*, 521–529.

Fuligni, A. J. (2012). Gaps, conflicts, and arguments between adolescents and their parents. *New Directions for Child and Adolescent Development, 135*, 105–110.

Fuligni, A. J., Hughes, D. L., & Way, N. (2009). Ethnicity and immigration. In R. M. Lerner & L. Steinberg (Eds.), *Handbook of adolescent psychology* (3rd ed.). New York: Wiley.

Fung, C. K. H., & Cheng, D. P. W. (2012). Consensus or disconsensus? Stakeholders' view on the role of play in learning. *Early years: An International Journal of Research and Development, 32*, 17–33.

Fung, H. (2011). Cultural psychological perspectives on social development. In P. K. Smith & C. H. Hart (Eds.), *Wiley-Blackwell handbook of childhood social development* (2nd ed.). New York: Wiley.

Furman, W., & Buhrmester, D. (1992). Age and sex differences in perceptions of networks of personal relationships. *Child Development, 63*, 103–115.

Furman, W., Low, S., & Ho, M. J. (2009). Romantic experience and psychosocial adjustment in middle adolescence. *Journal of Clinical Child and Adolescent Psychology, 38*, 75–90.

Furman, W., & Wehner, E. A. (1998). Adolescent romantic relationships: A developmental perspective. In S. Shulman & W. A. Collins (Eds.), *New directions for child development: Adolescent romantic relationships*. San Francisco: Jossey-Bass.

Furth, H. G. (1973). *Deafness and learning: A psychosocial approach*. Belmont, CA: Wadsworth.

Furth, H. G., & Wachs, H. (1975). *Thinking goes to school*. New York: Oxford University Press.

Fussell, E., & Greene, M. E. (2002). Demographic trends affecting youth around the world. In B. B. Brown, R. W. Larson, & T. S. Saraswathi (Eds.), *The world's youth*. New York: Cambridge University Press.

## G

Gabbe, S., & others. (Eds.). (2012). *Obstetrics* (6th ed.). New York: Elsevier.

Gaias, L. M., & others. (2012). Cross-cultural temperamental differences in infants, children, and adults in the United States of America and Finland, *53*, 119–128.

Galambos, N. L., Barker, E. T., & Krahn, H. J. (2006). Depression, self-esteem, and anger in emerging adulthood: Seven-year trajectories. *Developmental Psychology, 42*, 350–365.

Galambos, N. L., Berenbaum, S. A., & McHale, S. M. (2009). Gender development in adolescence. In R. M. Lerner & L. Steinberg (Eds.), *Handbook of adolescent psychology*. New York: Wiley.

Galbally, M., Lewis, A. J., IJzendoorn, M., & Permezel, M. (2011). The role of oxytocin in mother-infant relations: A systematic review of human studies. *Harvard Review of Psychiatry, 19*, 1–14.

Galindo, C., & Durham, R. E. (2009). Immigration, childhood, and adolescence. In D. Carr (Ed.), *Encyclopedia of the life course and human development*. Boston: Gale Cengage.

Galinsky, E. (2010). *Mind in the making*. New York: Harper Collins.

Gall, B. M., & Wood, J. J. (2012). Emotional self-efficacy modulates anxiety-related impairments in math performance in elementary school-aged youth. *Personality and Individual Differences, 52*, 118–122.

Galla, B. M. & Wood, J. J. (2012). Emotional self-efficacy moderates anxiety-related impairments in math performance in elementary school-age youth. *Personality and Individual Differences, 52*, 118–122.

Galland, B. C., Taylor, B. J., Edler, D. E., & Herbison, P. (2012). Normal sleep patterns in infants and children: A systematic review of observational studies. *Sleep Medicine Review, 16*, 213–222.

Galliher, R. V., & Kerpelman, J. L. (2012). The intersection of identity development and peer relationship processes in adolescence and young adulthood: Contributions of the special issue. *Journal of Adolescence, 35*, 1409–1415.

Ganong, L., Coleman, M., & Jamison, T. (2011). Patterns of stepchild-stepparent relationship development. *Journal of Marriage and the Family, 73*, 396–413.

Garcia, E. P., McKee, L. G., & Forehand, R. (2012). Discipline. In J. R. Levesque (Ed.), *Encyclopedia of adolescence*. New York: Springer.

Garcia Coll, C., & Pachter, L. M. (2002). Ethnic and minority parenting. In M. H. Bornstein (Ed.), *Handbook of parenting* (2nd ed., Vol. 4). Mahwah, NJ: Erlbaum.

Gardner, D. S., Hosking, J., Metcalf, B. S., An, J., Voss, L. D., & Wilkin, T. J. (2009). Contribution of early weight gain to childhood overweight and metabolic health: A longitudinal study (EarlyBird 36). *Pediatrics, 123*, e67–e73.

Gardner, H. (1983). *Frames of mind*. New York: Basic Books.

Gardner, H. (1993). *Multiple intelligences*. New York: Basic Books.

Gardner, H. (2002). Learning from extraordinary minds. In M. Ferrari (Ed.), *The pursuit of excellence through education*. Mahwah, NJ: Erlbaum.

Gardner, M., & Steinberg, L . (2005). Peer influence on risk taking, risk preference, and risky decision making in adolescence and adulthood: An experimental study. *Developmental Psychology, 41*, 625–635.

Garofalo, R. (2010). Cytokines in human milk. *Journal of Pediatrics, 156*, Suppl. 2, S36–S40.

Garriguet, D. (2004). Overview of Canadians' eating habits. Nutrition: Findings from the Canadian Community Health Survey. Statistics Canada,

Health Statistics Division. Catalogue no. 82-620-MIE

Garrison, M. M., Liekweg, K., & Christakis, D. A. (2011). Media use and child sleep: The impact of content, timing, and environment. *Pediatrics, 128*, 29–35.

Garvey, C. (2000). *Play* (Enlarged Ed.). Cambridge, MA: Harvard University Press.

Gates, W. (1998, July 20). Charity begins when I'm ready (interview). *Fortune.*

Gathwala, G., Singh, B., & Balhara, B. (2008). KMC facilitates baby attachment in low birth weight infants. *Indian Journal of Pediatrics, 75*, 43–47.

Gaudernack, L. C., Forbord, S., & Hole, E. (2006). Acupuncture administered after spontaneous rupture of membranes at term significantly reduces the length of birth and use of oxytocin. *Acta Obstetricia et Gynecologica Scandinavica, 85*, 1348–1353.

Gaudineau, A., & others. (2010). Factors associated with early menarche: Results from the French Health Behavior in School-Aged Children (HBSC) Study. *BMC Public Health, 10*, 175.

Gauvain, M. (2008). Vygotsky's sociocultural theory. In M. M. Haith & J. B. Benson (Eds.). *Encyclopedia of infant and early childhood development.* Oxford, UK: Elsevier.

Gauvain, M. (2013). Sociocultural contexts of development. In P. D. Zelazo (Ed.), *Oxford handbook of developmental psychology.* New York: Oxford University Press.

Gauvain, M., & Parke, R. D. (2010). Socialization. In M. Bornstein (Ed.), *Handbook of cross-cultural developmental science* (pp. 239–258). Mahwah, N.J.: Erlbaum.

Gee, C. L., & Heyman, G. D. (2007). Children's evaluations of other people's self-descriptions. *Social Development, 16*(4), 800–818.

Gelman, R. (1969). Conservation acquisition: A problem of learning to attend to relevant attributes. *Journal of Experimental Child Psychology, 7*, 67–87.

Gelman, S. A. (2009). Generics as a window onto young children's concepts. In F. J. Pelletier (Ed.). *Kinds, things, and stuff: The cognitive side of generics and mass terms. (New Directions in Cognitive Science v. 12.)* New York: Oxford University Press.

Gelman, S. A. (2013). Concepts in development. In P. D. Zelazo (Ed.), *Oxford handbook of developmental psychology.* New York: Oxford University Press.

Gelman, R., & Williams, E. M. (1998). Enabling constraints for cognitive development and learning. In W. Damon (Ed.), *Handbook of child psychology* (5th ed., Vol. 4). New York: Wiley.

Gelman, S. A., & Kalish, C. W. (2006). Conceptual development. In W. Damon & R. Lerner (Eds.), *Handbook of child psychology* (6th ed.). New York: Wiley.

Gelman, S. A., & Opfer, J. E. (2004). Development of the animate-inanimate distinction. In U. Goswami (Ed.), *Blackwell handbook of childhood cognitive development.* Malden, MA: Blackwell.

Gelman, S. A., Taylor, M. G., & Nguyen, S. P. (2004). Mother-child conversations about gender. *Monographs of the Society for Research in Child Development, 69* (1, Serial No. 275).

Genesee, F. (1978). A longitudinal evaluation of an early immersion program. *Canadian Journal of Education. 3*, 31–50.

Genesee, F. (2007). French immersion and at-risk students: A review of research findings. *Canadian Modern Language Review, 63*, 655–688.

Genesee, F. (2012a). The suitability of immersion for all learners: What does the research say? The State of French-Second-Language Education in Canada 2012, Executive Summary. Canadian Parents for French.

Genesee, F., & Jared, D. (2008). Literacy development in early French immersion programs. *Canadian Psychologist, 49*(2), 140–147.

Genesee, F., & Lindholm-Leary, K. (2007). Dual language education in Canada and the United States. In J. Cummins & N. Hornberger (Eds), *Encyclopedia of Language and Education* (2nd ed., pp. 253–266). New York: Springer.

Gennetian, L. A., & Miller, C. (2002). Children and welfare reform: A view from an experimental welfare reform program in Minnesota. *Child Development, 73*, 601–620.

Gentile, D. A. (2011). The multiple dimensions of video game effects. *Child Development Perspectives, 5*, 75–81.

Gentile, D. A., & others. (2009). The effects of prosocial video games on prosocial behaviors: International evidence from correlational, experimental, and longitudinal studies. *Personality and Social Psychology Bulletin, 35*(6), 752–763.

Gentile, D. A., Mathieson, L. C., & Crick, N. R. (2010, in press). Media violence associations with the form and function of aggression among elementary school children. *Social Development.*

Gentle, M., Milne, R. Powell, M. B., & Sharman, S. J. (2013). Does the cognitive interview promote the coherence of narrative accounts in children with and without an intellectual disability? *International Journal of Disability, Development and Education, 60*, 30–43.

Geoffroy, M., Cote, S.M., Parent, S., & Seguin, J. R. (2006). Daycare attendance, stress, and mental health. *Canadian Journal of Psychiatry, 51*(9), 607–615.

Georgiou, G. K., Torppa, M., Manolitsis, G., Lyytinen, H., & Parrila, R. (2012). Longitudinal predictors of reading and spelling across languages varying in orthographic consistency. *Reading and Writing, 25*, 321–346.

Gerards, F. A., Twisk, J. W., Fetter, W. P., Wijnaendts, L. C., & van Vugt, J. M. (2008). Predicting pulmonary hypoplasia with 2- or 3-dimensional ultrasonography in complicated pregnancies. *American Journal of Gynecology and Obstetrics, 198*, e1–e6.

Gershkoff-Stowe, L., & Hahn, E. R. (2007). Fast mapping skills in the developing lexicon. *Journal of Speech, Language, and Hearing, 50*, 682–697.

Gershoff, E. T. (2002). Corporal punishment by parents and associated child behaviors and experiences: A meta-analysis and theoretical review. *Psychological Bulletin, 128*, 539–579.

Gershoff, E. T., & others. (2010). Parent discipline practices in an international sample: Associations with child behaviors and moderation by perceived normativeness. *Child Development, 81*, 487–502.

Gershoff, E. T., Lansford, J. E., Sexton, H. R., Davis-Kean, P., & Sameroff, A. (2012). Longitudinal links between spanking and children's externalizing behaviors in a national sample of White, Black, Hispanic, and Asian American families. *Child Development, 83*, 838–843.

Gertner, Y., & Fisher, C. (2012, in press). Predicted errors in children's early sentence comprehension. *Cognition.*

Gesell, A. L. (1934). *Infancy and human growth.* New York: MacMillan.

Gestsdottir, S., Lewin-Bizan, S., von Eye, A., Lerner, J. V., & Lerner, R. M. (2009). The structure and function of selection, optimization, and compensation in adolescence: Theoretical and applied implications. *Journal of Applied Developmental Psychology, 30*(5), 585–600.

Gewirtz, J. (1977). Maternal responding and the conditioning of infant crying: Directions of influence within the attachment-acquisition process. In B. C. Etzel, J. M. LeBlanc, & D. M. Baer (Eds.), *New developments in behavioral research.* Hillsdale, NJ: Erlbaum.

Gfellner, B. M. & Armstrong, H. D. (2011). Ego development, ego strengths, and ethnic identity among First Nation adolescents. *Journal of Research on Adolescence, 22*(2), 225–234.

Ghazarian, S. R., & Roche, K. M. (2010). Social support and low-income, urban mothers: Longitudinal associations with delinquency. *Journal of Youth and Adolescence, 39,* 1097-1108.

Ghetti, S., & Alexander, K. W. (2004). "If it happened, I would remember it": Strategic use of event memorability in the rejection of false autobiographical events. *Child Development, 75,* 542-561.

Ghetti, S., & Bauer, P. J. (Eds.). (2012). *Origins and development of recollection.* New York: Oxford University Press.

Ghosh, S., Feingold, E., Chakaborty, S., & Dey, S. K. (2010). Telomere length is associated with types of chromosome 21 nondisjunction: A new insight into the maternal age effect on Down syndrome birth. *Human Genetics.* (Available online January 10, 2010.)

Gibbons, J., & Ng, S. H. (2004). Acting bilingual and thinking bilingual. *Journal of Language and Social Psychology, 23,* 4-6.

Gibbons, L., & others (2013). Inequities in the use of cesarean section deliveries in the world. *American Journal of Obstetrics and Gynecology, 206.*

Gibbons, R. D., Hedeker, D., & DuToit, S. (2010). Advances in analysis of longitudinal data. *Annual Review of Clinical Psychology* (Vol. 6). Palo Alto, CA: Annual Reviews.

Gibbs, J. C. (2010). *Moral development and reality.* (2nd ed.). Boston: Allyn & Bacon.

Gibbs, J. C., Basinger, K. S., Grime, R. L., & Snarey, J. R. (2007). Moral judgment development across cultures: Revisiting Kohlberg's universality claims. *Developmental Review, 27,* 443-500.

Gibbs, J. T., & Huang, L. N. (1989). A conceptual framework for assessing and treating minority youth. In J. T. Gibbs & L. N. Huang (Eds.), *Children of color.* San Francisco: Jossey-Bass.

Gibson, E. J. (1969). *Principles of perceptual learning and development.* New York: Appleton-Century-Crofts.

Gibson, E. J. (1989). Exploratory behavior in the development of perceiving, acting, and the acquiring of knowledge. *Annual Review of Psychology, 39.* Palo Alto, CA: Annual Reviews.

Gibson, E. J. (2001). *Perceiving the affordances.* Mahwah, NJ: Erlbaum.

Gibson, E. J., & Walk, R. D. (1960). The "visual cliff." *Scientific American, 202,* 64-71.

Gibson, J. J. (1966). *The senses considered as perceptual systems.* Boston: Houghton Mifflin.

Gibson, J. J. (1979). *The ecological approach to visual perception.* Boston: Houghton Mifflin.

Gibson, L. Y., Byrne, S. M., Blair, E., Davis, E. A., Jacoby, P., & Zubrick, S. R. (2008). Clustering of psychological symptoms in overweight children. *Australian and New Zealand Journal of Psychiatry, 42,* 118-125.

Giedd, J. N. (2012). The digital revolution and the adolescent brain. *Journal of Adolescent Health, 51,* 101-105.

Giedd, J. N., & others. (2012). Anatomic magnetic resonance imaging of the developing child and adolescent brain. In V. F. Reyna & others (Eds.), *The adolescent brain.* Washington, DC: American Psychological Association.

Gill, S. V., Adolph, K. E., & Vereijken, B. (2009). Change in action: how infants learn to walk down slopes. *Developmental Science, 12,* 888-902.

Gillen-O'Neel, C., Huynh, V. W., & Fuligni, A. J. (2013). To study or to sleep? The academic costs of extra studying at the expense of sleep. *Child Development, 84,* 133-42.

Gillig, P. M., & Sanders, R. D. (2011). Higher cortical functions: Attention and vigilance. *Innovations in Clinical Science, 8,* 43-46.

Gilligan, C. (1982). *In a different voice.* Cambridge, MA: Harvard University Press.

Gilligan, C. (1992, May). *Joining the resistance: Girls' development in adolescence.* Paper presented at the symposium on development and vulnerability in close relationships, Montreal, Quebec.

Gilligan, C. (1996). The centrality of relationships in psychological development: A puzzle, some evidence, and a theory. In G. G. Noam & K. W. Fischer (Eds.), *Development and vulnerability in close relationships.* Hillsdale, NJ: Erlbaum.

Giordano, P. C. (2009). Friendship, childhood and adolescence. In D. Carr (Ed.), *Encyclopedia of the life course and human development.* Boston: Gale Cengage.

Giorgis, C., & Glazer, J. (2013). *Literature for young children: Supporting emergent literacy, ages 0-8* (7th ed.). Upper Saddle River, NJ: Pearson.

Glascher, J., & others. (2009). Lesion mapping of cognitive abilities linked to intelligence. *Neuron, 61,* 681-691.

Glascher, J., & others. (2010). Distributed neural system for general intelligence revealed by lesion mapping. *Proceedings of the National Academy of Sciences USA, 107,* 4705-4709.

Glessner, J. T., & others. (2009). Autism genome-wide copy number variation reveals ubiquitin and neuronal genes. *Nature, 459,* 569-573.

Glover, M. B., Mullineaux, P. Y., Deater-Deckard, K., & Petrill, S. A. (2010). Parents' feelings toward their adoptive and non-adoptive children. *Infant and Child Development, 19*(3), 238-251.

Gluck, M. E., Venti, C. A., Lindsay, R. S., Knowler, W. C., Salbe, A. D., & Krakoff, J. (2009). Maternal influence, not diabetic intraturine environment, predicts children's energy intake. *Obesity, 17,* 772-777.

Gobet, F., & Charness, N. (2006). Chess. In K. A. Ericsson, N. Charness, P. J. Feltovich, & R. R. Hoffman (Eds.), *The Cambridge handbook of expertise and expert performance.* New York: Cambridge University Press.

Goga, A. E., & others. (2012, in press). Infant feeding practices at routine PMTCT site, South Africa: Results of a prospective observational study amongst HIV exposed and unexposed infants—birth to 9 months. *International Breastfeeding Journal.*

Gogtay, N., & Thompson, P. M. (2010). Mapping gray matter development: Implications for typical development and vulnerability to psychopathology. *Brain and Cognition, 72,* 6-15.

Goldbeck, L., Gagsteiger, F., Minderman, I., Strobele, S., & Izat, Y. (2008). Cognitive development of singletons conceived by intracytoplasmic sperm injection or in vitro fertilization at age 5 and 10 years. *Journal of Pediatric Psychology, 34,* 774-781.

Goldberg, W. A., & Lucas-Thompson, R. (2008). Maternal and paternal employment, effects of. In M. M. Haith & J. B. Benson (Eds.), *Encyclopedia of infant and early childhood development.* Oxford, UK: Elsevier.

Goldenberg, R. L., & Culhane, J. F. (2007). Low birth weight in the United States. *American Journal of Clinical Nutrition, 85,* Suppl. S584-S590.

Goldenberg R. L., & Nagahawatte, N. T. (2008). Poverty, mental health, and adverse pregnancy outcomes. *Annals of the New York Academy of Sciences, 1136,* 80-85.

Goldfield. B. A., & Snow, C. A. (2009). Individual differences in language development. In J. Berko Gleason & N. Ratner (Eds.), *The development of language* (7th ed.). Boston: Allyn & Bacon.

Goldfield, G. S. (2011). Making access to TV contingent on physical activity: Effects on liking and relative reinforcing value of TV and physical activity in overweight and obese children. *Journal of Behavioral Medicine, 35,* 1-7.

Goldfield, G. S., Adamo, K. B., Rutherford, J., & Murray, M. (2012). The effects of aerobic exercise on psychosocial functioning of adolescents who are overweight or obese. *Journal of Pediatric and Adolescent Psychology, 37,* 1136–1147.

**Goldin-Meadow, S., & Alibali, M. W. A.** (2013, in press). Gesture's role in learning and development. In P. Zelazo (Ed.), *Oxford University handbook of developmental psychology.* New York: Oxford University Press.

**Goldman, N. Giel, D. A., Lin, Y. H., & Weinstein, M.** (2010). The serotonin transporter polymorphism (5-HTTLPR): Allelic variation and links with depressive symptoms. *Depression and Anxiety, 27,* 260–269.

**Goldscheider, F., & Sassler, S.** (2006). Creating stepfamilies: Integrating children into the study of union formation. *Journal of Marriage and the Family, 68,* 275–291.

**Goldsmith, H. H.** (2011). Human development: Biological and genetic processes. *Annual Review of Psychology, 62.* Palo Alto, CA: Annual Reviews.

**Goldstein, E. B.** (2011). *Cognitive psychology.* Boston: Cengage.

**Goldstein, M. H., King, A. P., & West, M. J.** (2003). Social interaction shapes babbling: Testing parallels between birdsong and speech. Proceedings of the National Academy of Sciences, *100*(13), 8030–8035.

**Goldstein, T. R., & Winner, E.** (2012). Enhancing empathy and theory of mind. *Journal of Cognition and Development, 13,* 19–37.

**Goleman, D.** (1995). *Emotional intelligence.* New York: Basic Books.

**Gollnick, D. M., & Chinn, P. C.** (2013). *Multicultural education in a pluralistic society* (9th ed.). Boston: Allyn & Bacon.

**Golombok, S.** (2011a). Children in new family forms. In R. Gross (Ed.), *Psychology* (6th ed.). London: Hodder Education.

**Golombok, S.** (2011b). Why I study lesbian families. In S. Ellis & others (Eds.), *LGBTQ psychologies.* New York: Cambridge University Press.

**Golombok, S., MacCallum, F., & Goodman, E.** (2001). The "test-tube" generation: Parent-child relationships and the psychological well-being of in vitro fertilization children at adolescence. *Child Development, 72,* 599–608.

**Golombok, S., Rust, J., Zervoulis, K., Croudace, T., Golding, J., & Hines, M.** (2008). Developmental trajectories of sex-typed behavior in boys and girls: A longitudinal general population study of children aged 2.5–8 years. *Child Development, 79,* 1583–1593.

**Golombok, S., & Tasker, F.** (2010). Gay fathers. In M. E. Lamb (Ed.), *The role of the father in child development* (5th ed.). New York: Wiley.

**Gomez-Raposo, C., & others.** (2010). Male breast cancer. *Cancer Treatment Reviews.* (in press.)

**Goncu, A., & Gauvain, M.** (2012). Sociocultural approaches in educational psychology. In K. H. Harris, S. Graham, & T. Urdan (Eds.), *APA educational psychology handbook.* Washington, DC: American Psychological Association.

**Gonzalez, A., Atkinson, L., & Fleming, A. S.** (2009). Attachment and the comparative psychobiology of mothering. In M. De Haan & M. R. Gunnar (Eds.), *Handbook of developmental social neuroscience.* New York: Guilford.

**González, J. M.** (Ed.). (2009). *Encyclopedia of bilingual education.* Thousand Oaks, CA: Sage.

**Gonzales, N. A., Dumka, L. E., Muaricio, A. M., & German, M.** (2007). Building bridges: Strategies to promote academic and psychological resilience for adolescents of Mexican origin. In J. E. Lansford, K. Deater Deckhard, & M. H. Bornstein (Eds.), *Immigrant families in contemporary society.* New York: Guilford.

**Gonzales, N. A., & others.** (2008). Mexican American adolescents' cultural orientation, externalizing behavior and academic engagement: The role of traditional cultural values. *American Journal of Community Psychology, 41,* 151–164.

**Gonazalez, V., Yawkey, T. D., & Minaya-Rowe, L.** (2006). *English-as-a-second-language (ESL) teaching and learning.* Boston: Allyn & Bacon.

**Good, C., Rattan, A., & Dweck, C. S.** (2012). Why do women opt out? Sense of belonging and women's representation in mathematics. *Journal of Personality and Social Psychology, 102,* 700–717.

**Goodman, W. B., & others.** (2011). Parental work stress and latent profiles of father-infant parenting quality. *Journal of Marriage and the Family, 73,* 588–604.

**Goodnow, J.** (2010). Culture. In M. H. Bornstein (Ed.), *Handbook of cultural developmental science.* New York: Psychology Press.

**Goodvin, R., Meyer, S., Thompson, R. A., & Hayes, R.** (2008). Self-understanding in early childhood: Associations with child attachment security and maternal negative affect. *Attachment and Human Development, 10,* 433–450.

**Gopnik, A., & Meltzoff, A.** (1997). *Words, thoughts, and theories.* Cambridge, MA: MIT Press.

**Gorgens-Eckermans, G., & Brand, T.** (2012). Emotional intelligence as a moderator in the stress-burnout relationship: A questionnaire study on nurses. *Journal of Clinical Nursing, 21,* 2275–2285.

**Gorrese, A., & Ruggieri, R.** (2012). Peer attachment: A meta-analytic review of gender and age differences and associations with parent attachment. *Journal of Youth and Adolescence, 41,* 650–672.

**Gottfried, A. E., Marcoulides, G. A., Gottfried, A. W., & Oliver, P. H.** (2009). A latent curve model of motivational practices and developmental decline in math and science academic intrinsic motivation. *Journal of Educational Psychology, 101,* 729–739.

**Gottlieb, G.** (2007). Probabilistic epigenesis. *Developmental Science, 10,* 1–11.

**Gottleib, G., Wahlsten, D., & Lickliter, R.** (2006). The significance of biology for human development: A developmental psychobiological systems view. In W. Damon & R. Lerner (Eds.), *Handbook of child psychology* (6th ed.). New York: Wiley.

**Gottman, J. M.** (2012). *Emotion coaching.* Retrieved from www.gottman.com/parenting/

**Gottman, J. M.** (2013). *Research on parenting.* Available at www.gottman.com /research/published-research-abstracts-articles/parenting-research/

**Gottman, J. M., & DeClaire, J.** (1997). *The heart of parenting: Raising an emotionally intelligent child.* New York: Simon & Schuster.

**Gottman, J. M., & Parker, J. G.** (Eds.). (1987). *Conversations of friends.* New York: Cambridge University Press.

**Gouin, K., & others** (2011). Effects of cocaine use during pregnancy on low birthweight and preterm birth: Systematic and metanalyses. *American Journal of Obstetrics and Gynecology, 201,* e1–e12.

**Gould, S. J.** (1981). *The mismeasure of man.* New York: W. W. Norton.

**Graber, J. A.** (2008). Pubertal and neuroendocrine development and risk for depressive disorders. In N. B. Allen, & L. Sheeber (Eds.), *Adolescent emotional development and the emergence of depressive disorders.* New York: Cambridge University Press.

**Grafenhain, M., Behne, T., Carpenter, M., & Tomasello, M.** (2009). Young children's understanding of joint commitments. *Developmental Psychology, 45* (5), 1430–1443.

**Graham, S.** (2005, February 16). Commentary in *USA TODAY,* p. 2D.

Graham, S., & Perin. D. (2007). A meta-analysis of writing instruction for adolescent students. *Journal of Educational Psychology, 99,* 445–476.

Grant, A. M., & Gino, F. (2010). A little thanks goes a long way: Explaining why gratitude expressions motivate prosocial behavior. *Journal of Personality and Social Psychology, 98,* 946–955.

Grant, J. P. (1997). *The state of the world's children.* New York: UNICEF and Oxford University Press.

Graven, S. (2006). Sleep and brain development. *Clinical Perinatology, 33,* 693–706.

Gray, J. (1992). *Men are from Mars, women are from Venus.* New York: HarperCollins.

Gray, L., Watt, L., & Blass, E. M. (2000). Skin-to-skin contact is analgesic in healthy newborns. *Pediatrics: 105,* e14.

Graziano, A. M., & Raulin, M. L. (2010). *Research methods* (7th ed.). Boston: Allyn & Bacon.

Greenfield, P. M. (2003, February). Commentary. *Monitor on Psychology, 3*(2), 58.

Greenfield, P. M. (2009). Linking social change and developmental change: Shifting pathways of human development. *Developmental Psychology, 43,* 401–418.

Greer, F. R., Sicherer, S. H., Burks, A. W., & Committee on Nutrition and Section on Allergy and Immunology. (2008). Effects of early nutritional interventions on the development of atopic disease in infants and children: The role of maternal dietary restriction, breast feeding, timing of introduction of complementary foods, and hydrolyzed formulas. *Pediatrics, 121,* 183–191.

Gregorson, M., Kaufman, J. C., & Snyder, H. (Eds.). (2013). *Teaching creatively and teaching creativity.* New York: Springer.

Gregory, A. M., & Sadeh, A. (2012). Sleep, emotional and behavioral difficulties in children and adolescents. *Sleep Medicine Reviews,* 16, 129–136.

Greif, M. L., & Needham, A. (2012). The development of tool use early in life. In T. McCormack, C. Hoerl, & S. Butterfill (Eds.), *Tool use and causal cognition.* New York: Oxford University Press.

Greve, W., & Bjorklund, D. F. (2009). The nestor effect: Extending evolutionary developmental psychology to a lifespan perspective. *Developmental Review, 29,* 163–179.

Griffiths, J. D., Marslen-Wilson, W. D., Stamatakis, E. A., & Tyler, L. K. (2013, in press). Functional organization of the neural language system: Dorsal and ventral pathways are critical for syntax. *Cerebral Cortex.*

Grigorenko, E., Kornilov, S. A., Tan, M., Elliott, J., & Sternberg, R. J. (2012). Gifted identification with Aurora: Widening the spotlight. *Journal of Psychoeducational Assessment, 30,* 117–133.

Grigorenko, E. L., & Takanishi, R. (2010). *Immigration, diversity, and education.* New York: Routledge.

Grolnick, W. S., Bridges, L. J., & Connell, J. P. (1996). Emotion regulation in two-year-olds: Strategies and emotional expression in four contexts. *Child Development, 67,* 928–941.

Gross, L. S. (2013). *Electronic media.* (11th ed.). New York: McGraw-Hill.

Grosse, S. D. (2010). Late-treated phenylketonuria and partial reversibility of intellectual impairment. *Child Development, 81,* 200–211.

Grossmann, K., Grossmann, K. E., Spangler, G., Suess, G., & Unzner, L. (1985). Maternal sensitivity and newborns' orientation responses as related to quality of attachment in northern Germany. In I. Bretherton & E. Waters (Eds.), Growing points of attachment theory and research. *Monographs of the Society for Research in Child Development, 50* (1–2, Serial No. 209).

Grotevant, H. D., & Cooper, C. R. (1985). Patterns of interaction in family relationships and the deyelopment of identity exploration in adolescence. *Child Development, 56,* 415–428.

Grotevant, H. D., & Cooper, C. R. (1998). Individuality and connectedness in adolescent development: Review and prospects for research on identity, relationship, and context. In E. Skoe & A. von der Lippe (Eds.), *Personality development in adolescence: A cross-national and life-span perspective.* London: Routledge.

Grusec, J. E. (2006). Development of moral behavior and a conscience from a socialization perspective. In M. Killen & J. G. Smetana (Eds.), *Handbook of moral development.* Mahwah, NJ: Erlbaum.

Grusec, J. E. (2009). Unpublished review of J. W. Santrock's *Child Development,* (13th ed.). New York: McGraw-Hill.

Grusec, J. E. (2011). Human development: Development in the family. *Annual Review of Psychology* (Vol. 62). Palo Alto, CA: Annual Reviews.

Grusec, J. E. (2011). Socialization processes in the family: Social and emotional development. *Annual Review of Psychology* (Vol. 62). Palo Alto, CA: Annual Reviews.

Grusec, J. E. (2013). The development of moral behavior and conscience from a socialization perspective. In M. Killen & J. G. Smetana (Eds.), *Handbook of moral*

*development* (2nd ed.). New York: Routledge.

Grusec, J. E., Chaparro, M. P., Johnston, M., & Sherman, A. (2013). Social development and social relationships in middle childhood. In I. B. Weiner & others (Eds.), *Handbook of psychology* (2nd ed., Vol. 6). New York: Wiley.

Grusec, J. E., & Davidov, M. (2010). Integrating different perspectives on socialization theory and research: A domain-specific approach. *Child Development, 81,* 687–709.

Grusec, J. E., Hastings, P., & Almas, A. (2011). Prosocial behavior. In P. K. Smith & C. H. Hart (Eds.), *Wiley-Blackwell handbook of childhood social development* (2nd ed.). New York: Wiley.

Grych, J. H. (2002). Marital relationships and parenting. In M. H. Bornstein (Ed.), *Handbook of parenting.* Mahwah, NJ: Erlbaum.

Guerra, N. G., & Williams, K. R. (2010). Implementing bullying prevention in diverse settings: Geographic, economic, and cultural influences. In E. M. Vernberg & B. K. Biggs (Eds.), *Preventing and treating bullying and victimization.* New York: Oxford University Press.

Guevremont, A. & Kohen, D. (2012). Knowledge of an Aboriginal language and school outcomes for children and adults. *International Journal of Bilingual Education and Bilingualism, 15,* 1–27.

Guilford, J. P. (1967). *The structure of intellect.* New York: McGraw-Hill.

Gunby, J., Bissonnette, F., Librach, C., & Cowan L. (2010). Assisted reproductive technologies (ART) in Canada: 2006 results from the Canadian ART Register. *Fertility and Sterility, 93,* 2189–2201.

Gunderson, E. P., & others. (2008). Association of fewer hours of sleep at 6 months postpartum with substantial weight retention at 1 year postpartum. *American Journal of Epidemiology, 167,* 178–187.

Gunnar, M. R., Fisher, P. A., & Early Experience, Stress, and Prevention Network. (2006). Bringing basic research on early experience and stress neurobiology to bear on preventive interventions for neglected and maltreated children. *Development and Psychopathology, 18,* 651–677.

Gunnar, M. R., Malone, S., & Fisch, R. O. (1987). The psychobiology of stress and coping in the human neonate: Studies of the adrenocortical activity in response to stress in the first week of life. In T. Field, P. McCabe, & N. Scheiderman (Eds.). *Stress and coping.* Hillsdale, NJ: Erlbaum.

Gunnar, M. R., & Quevado, K. (2007). The neurobiology of stress and development.

*Annual Review of Psychology* (Vol. 58). Palo Alto, CA: Annual Reviews.

**Gunning, T. G.** (2013). *Creating literature instruction for all children in grades pre-K to 4* (2nd ed.). Boston: Allyn & Bacon.

**Guo, G., & Tillman, K. H.** (2009). Trajectories of depressive symptoms, dopamine D2 and D4 receptors, family socioeconomic status, and social support in adolescence and young adulthood. *Psychiatric Genetics, 19,* 14–26.

**Gupta, A., Thornton, J. W., & Huston, A. C.** (2007). Working families should not be poor—the New Hope project. In D. R. Crane & T. B. Heaton (Eds.), *Handbook of families and poverty.* Thousand Oaks, CA: Sage.

**Gur, R. C., & others.** (1995). Sex differences in regional cerebral glucose metabolism during a resting state. *Science, 267,* 528–531.

**Gurwitch, R. H., Silovksy, J. F., Schultz, S., Kees, M., & Burlingame, S.** (2001). *Reactions and guidelines for children following trauma/disaster.* Norman, OK: Department of Pediatrics, University of Oklahoma Health Sciences Center.

**Gustafsson, J-E.** (2007). Schooling and intelligence: Effects of track of study on level and profile of cognitive abilities. In P. C. Kyllonen, R. D. Roberts, & L. Stankov (Eds.), *Extending intelligence.* Mahwah, NJ: Erlbaum.

**Gutman, L. M.** (2008). Risk and resilience. In M. M. Haith & J. B. Benson (Eds.), *Encyclopedia of infancy and early childhood.*

**Guzzetta, A., & others.** (2008). Language organization in left perinatal stroke. *Neuropediatrics, 39,* 157–163.

# H

**Haas, B. W., Mills, D., Yam, A., Hoeft, F., Bellugi, U., & Reiss, A.** (2009). Genetic influences on sociability: Heightened amygdala reactivity and event-related responses to positive stimuli in Williams syndrome. *Journal of Neuroscience, 29,* 1132–1139.

**Habib, C.** (2012). Paternal perinatal depression: An overview and suggestions towards an intervention model. *Journal of Family Studies, 18,* 4–16.

**Hafen, C. A., & others.** (2012). The pivotal role of adolescent autonomy in secondary school classrooms. *Journal of Youth and Adolescence, 41,* 245–255.

**Haga, M.** (2008). The relationship between physical fitness and motor competence in children. *Child: Child Care and Health Development, 34,* 329–334.

**Hahn, D. B., Payne, W. A., & Lucas, E. B.** (2011). *Focus on health* (10th ed.). New York: McGraw-Hill.

**Haier, R. J.** (2011). Biological basis of intelligence. In R. J. Sternberg & S. B. Kaufman (Eds.), *Cambridge handbook of intelligence.* New York: Cambridge University Press.

**Halford, G. S., & Andrews, G. S.** (2011). Information processing models of cognitive development. In U. Goswami (Ed.), *Wiley-Blackwell handbook of childhood cognitive development* (2nd ed.). New York: Wiley-Blackwell.

**Hall, C. M., & others.** (2004). Behavioral and physical masculinization are related to genotype in girls with congenital adrenal hyperplasia. *Journal of Clinical Endocrinology and Metabolism, 89,* 419–424.

**Hall, G. N.** (2010). *Multicultural psychology* (2nd ed.). Upper Saddle River, NJ: Prentice Hall.

**Hall, L. J.** (2013). *Autism spectrum disorders* (2nd ed.). Upper Saddle River, NJ: Pearson.

**Hall, W. A., & Long, B. C.** (2007). Relations among prenatal role quality, life satisfaction, and dual-earner parents' postnatal depression. *Journal of Prenatal & Perinatal Psychology & Health. 2007; 21(3):231–248.*

**Hallahan, D. P., Kauffman, J. M., & Pullen, P. C.** (2012). *Exceptional learners* (12th ed.). Boston: Allyn & Bacon.

**Hallgrimsdottir, H. K., Benoit, C., & Phillips, R.** (2013). The mother-citizen and the working girl: First-wave feminist citizenship claims in Canada and discursive opportunities for twenty-first century childcare policy. *Canadian Review of Sociology, 50(1),* 27–51.

**Halpern, D. F.** (2012). *Sex differences in cognitive abilities* (4th ed.). New York: Psychology Press.

**Halpern, D. F., Benbow, C. P., Geary, D. C., Gur, R. C. & Hyde, J. S.** (2007). The science of sex differences in science and mathematics. *Psychological Science in the Public Interest, 8,* 1–51.

**Hamadani, J. D., & others.** (2011). Critical windows of exposure for arsenic-associated impairment of cognitive function in pre-school girls and boys: A population-based cohort study. *International Journal of Epidemiology, 40* (6): 1593-1604 doi: 10.1093/ije/dyr176

**Hamlin, J. K., & Wynn, K.** (2011). Five- and 9-month-old infants prefer prosocial to antisocial others. *Cognitive Development, 26,* 30–39.

**Hammond, S. I., Muller, U., Carpendale, J. I. M., Bibok, M. B., & Liebermann-Finestone, D. P.** (2012). The effects of parental scaffolding on preschoolers' executive function. *Developmental Psychology, 48(1),* 271–281.

**Han, W-J.** (2009). Maternal employment. In D. Carr (Ed.). *Encyclopedia of the life course and human development.* Boston: Gale Cengage.

**Hanish, L., D., & Guerra, N. G.** (2004). Aggressive victims, passive victims, and bullies: Developmental continuity or developmental change? *Merrill-Palmer Quarterly, 50,* 17–38.

**Hannon, E. E., & Trainor, L. J.** (2007). Music acquisition: Effects of enculturation and formal training on development. *Trends in Cognitive Sciences, 11,* 466–472.

**Hansen, M. L., Gunn, P. W., & Kaelber, D. C.** (2007). Underdiagnosis of hypertension in children and adolescents. *Journal of the American Medical Association, 298,* 874–879.

**Hansen, M., Janssen, I., Schiff, A., Zee, P. C., & Dubocovich, M. L.** (2005). The impact of school daily schedule on adolescent sleep. *Pediatrics, 115,* 1555–1561.

**Hardy, S. A., Bhattacharjee, A., Reed, A., & Aquino, K.** (2010). Moral identity and psychological distance: The case of adolescent socialization. *Journal of Adolescence, 33,* 111–123.

**Hare, B. R., & Castenell, L. A.** (1985). No place to run, no place to hide: Comparative status and future prospects of Black boys. In M. B. Spencer, G. K. Brookins, & W. R. Allen (Eds.), *Beginnings: The social and affective development of Black children.* Hillsdale, NJ: Erlbaum.

**Harkness, S., & Super, B. M.** (1995). Culture and parenting. In M. H. Bornstein (Ed.), *Handbook of parenting* (Vol. 3). Hillsdale, NJ: Erlbaum.

**Harlow, H. F.** (1958). The nature of love. *American Psychologist, 13,* 673–685.

**Harris, G., Thomas, A., & Booth, D. A.** (1990). Development of salt taste in infancy. *Developmental Psychology, 26,* 534–538.

**Harris, J., Golinkoff, R. M., & Hirsh-Pasek, K.** (2012). Lessons from the crib for the classroom: How children really learn vocabulary. In S. B. Neuman & D. K. Dickinson (Eds.), *Handbook of early literacy research.* New York: Guilford.

**Harris, J. J., & Attwell, D.** (2012). The energetics of CNS white matter. *Journal of Neuroscience, 32,* 356–371.

**Harris, J. R.** (1998). *The nurture assumption: Why children turn out the way they do: Parents matter less than you think and peers matter more.* New York: Free Press.

**Harris, J. R.** (2009). *The nurture assumption* (Rev. ed.). New York: The Free Press.

**Harris, P. L.** (2000). *The work of the imagination.* Oxford University Press.

Harris, P. L. (2006). Social cognition. In W. Damon & R. Lerner (Eds.), *Handbook of child psychology* (6th ed.). New York: Wiley.

Harrison-Hale, A. O., McLoyd, V. C., & Smedley, B. (2004). Racial and ethnic status: Risk and protective processes among African-American families. In K. L. Maton, C. J. Schellenbach, B. J. Leadbetter, & A. L. Solarz (Eds.), *Investing in children, families, and communities.* Washington, DC: American Psychological Association.

Hart, B., & Risley, T. R. (1995). *Meaningful differences.* Baltimore, MD: Paul Brookes.

Hart, D., Atkins, R., & Donnelly, T. M. (2013). Community service and moral development. In M. Killen & J. G. Smetana (Eds.), *Handbook of moral development* (2nd ed.). New York: Routledge.

Hart, D., & Karmel, M. P. (1996). Self-awareness and self-knowledge in humans, great apes, and monkeys. In A. Russon, K. Bard, & S. Parker (Eds.), *Reaching into thought.* New York: Cambridge University Press.

Hart, S., & Carrington, H. (2002). Jealousy in 6-month-old infants. *Infancy, 3,* 395–402.

Harter, S. (1985). *Self-perception profile for children.* Denver: University of Denver. Department of Psychology.

Harter, S. (1986). Processes underlying the construction, maintenance, and enhancement of the self-concept of children. In. J. Suls & A. Greenwald (Eds.), *Psychological perspectives on the self* (Vol. 3). Hillsdale, NJ: Erlbaum.

Harter, S. (1989). *Self-Perception Profile for Adolescents.* Denver: University of Denver. Department of Psychology.

Harter, S. (1998). The development of self-representations. In W. Damon (Ed.), *Handbook of child psychology* (5th ed., Vol. 3). New York: Wiley.

Harter, S. (1999). *The construction of the self.* New York: Guilford.

Harter, S. (2002). Unpublished review of J. W. Santrock's *Child development* (10th ed.). (New York: McGraw-Hill).

Harter, S. (2006). The self. In W. Damon & R. Lerner (Eds.), *Handbook of child psychology* (6th ed.), New York: Wiley.

Harter, S. (2012). *The construction of the self, second edition: Developmental and sociocultural foundations.* New York: Guilford Press.

Hartshorne, H., & May, M. S. (1928–1930). *Moral studies in the nature of character: Studies in deceit* (Vol. 1); *Studies in self-control* (Vol. 2). *Studies in the organization of character* (Vol. 3). New York: Macmillan.

Hartup, W. W. (1983). The peer system. In P. H. Mussen (Ed.), *Handbook of child psychology* (4th ed., Vol. 4). New York: Wiley.

Hartup, W. W. (2005). Peer interaction: What causes what? *Journal of Abnormal Child Psychology, 33,* 387–394.

Hartup, W. W. (2009). Critical issues and theoretical viewpoints. In K. H. Rubin, W. M. Bukowski, & B. Laursen (Eds.). *Handbook of peer interactions, relationships, and groups.* New York: Guilford Press.

Hartwig, S., & others. (2010). Genomic characterization of Wilms' tumor suppressor 1 targets in nephron progenitor cells during kidney development. *Development, 137,* 1189–1203.

Harwood, R., Leyendecker, B., Carlson, V., Asencio, M., & Miller, A. (2002). Parenting among Latino families in the U.S. In M. H. Bornstein (Ed.), *Handbook of parenting* (2nd ed.). Mahwah, NJ: Erlbaum.

Hashim, H. A., Freddy, G., & Rosmatunisah, A. (2012). Relationships between negative affect and academic achievement among secondary school students: The mediating effects of habituated exercise. *Journal of Physical Activity and Health, 9,* 1012–1019.

Hastings, P. D., Utendale, W. T., & Sullivan, C. (2007). The socialization of prosocial development. In J. E. Grusec & P. D. Hastings (Eds.), *Handbook of socialization.* New York: Guilford.

Hatton, H., Donnellan, M. B., Maysn, K., Feldman, B. J., Larsen-Riffe, D., & Conger, R. D. (2008). Family and individual difference predictors of trait aspects of negative interpersonal behaviors during emerging adulthood. *Journal of Family Psychology, 22,* 448–455.

Hauck, F. R., & others. (2011). Breastfeeding and reduced risk of sudden infant death syndrome : A meta-analysis. *Pediatrics, 128,* 103–110.

Hawkins, D. L., Pepler, D. J., & Craig, W. M. (2001). Naturalistic observations of peer interventions in bullying. *Social Development, 10,* 512–527.

Hawkins, J. A., & Berndt, T. J. (1985, April). *Adjustment following the transition to junior high school.* Paper presented at the biennial meeting of the Society for Research in Child Development, Toronto.

Haydon, A., & Halpern, G. T. (2010). Older romantic partners and depressive symptoms during adolescence. *Journal of Youth and Adolescence, 39,* 1240–1251.

Health Canada. (2006). Melatonin product monograph.

Health Canada. (2000). Certain circumstances: Issues in equity and responsiveness in access to health care

in Canada. Available at www.hc-sc .gc.ca/hcs-sss/alt_formats/hpb-dgps/pdf/pubs/2001-certain-equit-acces/2001-certain-equit-acces_e.pdf

Health Canada. (2001). Family-centred and newborn care: National guidelines (4th ed., Chapter 5). Retrieved November 27, 2013 from: www.phac-aspc.gc.ca/hp-ps/dca-dea/publications/fcm-smp/

Health Canada. (2006). Melatonin product monograph.

Health Canada. (2014). Nutrition for Healthy Term Infants: Recommendations from Birth to Six Months: www.hc-sc.gc.ca/fn-an/nutrition/infant-nourisson/recom/index-eng.php

Hegaard, H. K., Hedegaard, M., Damm, P., Ottesen, B., Petersson, K., & Henriksen, T. B. (2008). Leisure time physical activity is associated with a reduced risk of preterm delivery. *American Journal of Obstetrics and Gynecology, 198,* e1–e5.

Heiman, G. W. (2011). *Basic statistics for the behavioral sciences* (6th ed.). Boston: Cengage.

Heimann, M., Strid, K., Smith, L., Tjus, T., Ulvund, S. E., & Melzoff, A. N. (2006). Exploring the relation between memory, gestural communication, and the emergence of language in infancy: A longitudinal study. *Infant and Child Development, 15,* 233–249.

Helgeson, V. (2009) *Psychology of gender* (3rd ed.). Upper Saddle River, NJ: Prentice Hall.

Helwig, C. C., & Turiel, E. (2011). Children's social and moral reasoning. In P. K. Smith & C. H. Hart (Eds.), *Wiley-Blackwell handbook of childhood social development* (2nd ed.). New York: Wiley.

Henderson, J., McCandlish, R., Kumiega, L., & Petrou, S. (2001). Systematic review of economic aspects of alternative modes of delivery. *British Journal of Obstetrics and Gynecology, 108,* 149–157.

Henderson, V. L., & Dweck, C. S. (1990). Motivation and achievement. In S. S. Feldman & G. R. Elliott (Eds.), *At the threshold: The developing adolescent.* Cambridge, MA: Harvard University Press.

Hendry, J. (1995). *Understanding Japanese society.* London: Routledge.

Henggeler, S. W., & Sheidow, L. J. (2012). Empirically supported family-based treatments for conduct disorder and delinquency in adolescents. *Journal of Marital and Family Therapy, 38,* 30–58.

Hennessey, B. (2011). Intrinsic motivation and creativity: Have we come full circle? In R. A. Beghetto & J. C. Kaufman (Eds.), *Nurturing creativity in the classroom.* New York: Cambridge University Press.

Hennessey, B. A. (2010). Intrinsic motivation and creativity: Have we come full circle? In R. A. Beghetto & J. C. Kaufman (Eds.), *Nurturing creativity in the classroom*. New York: Cambridge University Press.

Hennessey, B. A., & Amabile, T. M. (2010). Creativity. *Annual Review of Psychology* (Vol. 61). Palo Alto, CA: Annual Reviews.

Henninger, M. L. (2013). *Teaching young children* (5th ed.). Upper Saddle River, NJ: Pearson.

Henriksen, T. B., & others. (2004). Alcohol consumption at the time of conception and spontaneous abortion. *American Journal of Epidemiology, 160,* 661-667.

Herman-Giddens, M. E. (2007). The decline in the age of menarche in the United States: Should we be concerned? *Journal of Adolescent Health, 40,* 201-203.

Herman-Giddens, M. E., & others. (2012). Secondary sex characteristics in boys: Data from the pediatric research in office settings network. *Pediatrics, 130,* e1058-e1068.

Herrell, A. L., Jordan, M. L., & Eby, J. W. (2013). *Teaching in elementary school* (6th ed.). Upper Saddle River, NJ: Pearson.

Hernandez-Martinez, C., & others. (2011). Effects of iron deficiency on neonatal behavior at different stages of pregnancy. *Early Human Development, 87,* 165-169.

Hernandez-Reif, M., Diego, M., & Field, T. (2007). Preterm infants show reduced stress behaviors and activity after 5 days of massage therapy. *Infant Behavior and Development, 30,* 557-561.

Hertzman, C. (2009). The state of child development in Canada: Are we moving toward, or away from, equity from the start? *Paediatric Child Health, 14*(10), 673-676.

Hertzman, C., A. A. Siddiqi, A. A., Hertzman, E., Irwin, L. G., Vaghri, Z., Houweling, T. A. J., Bell, R., Tinajero, A., & Marmot, M. (2010). Tackling inequality: Get them while they're young. *British Medical Journal, 340*(7742), 346-348.

Hetherington, E. M. (1993). An overview of the Virginia Longitudinal Study of Divorce and Remarriage with a focus on early adolescence. *Journal of Family Psychology, 7,* 39-56.

Hetherington, E. M. (2005). Divorce and the adjustment of children. *Pediatrics in Review, 26,* 163-169.

Hetherington, E. M. (2006). The influence of conflict, marital problem solving, and parenting on children's adjustment in nondivorced, divorced, and remarried families. In A. Clarke-Stewart & J. Dunn (eds.), *Families count.* New York: Oxford University Press.

Hetherington, E. M., & Kelly, J. (2002). *For better or for worse: Divorce reconsidered.* New York: Norton.

Hetherington, E. M., & Stanley-Hagan, M. (2002). Parenting in divorced and remarried families. In M. H. Bornstein (Ed.), *Handbook of parenting* (2nd ed., Vol. 3). Mahwah, NJ: Erlbaum.

Heuwinkel, M. K. (1996). New ways of learning: Five new ways of teaching. *Childhood Education, 72,* 27-31.

Hewlett, B. S. (1991). *Intimate fathers: The nature and context of Aka Pygmy.* Ann Arbor: University of Michigan Press.

Hewlett, B. S. (2000). Culture, history and sex: Anthropological perspectives on father involvement. *Marriage and Family Review, 29,* 324-340.

Hewlett, B. S., & MacFarlan, S. J. (2010). Fathers' roles in hunter-gatherer and other small-scale cultures. In M. E. Lamb (Ed.), *The role of the father in child development* (5th ed.). New York: Wiley.

Heyman, G. D., & Legare, C. H. (2005). Children's evaluation of source of information about traits. *Developmental Psychology, 41,* 636-647.

Highfield, R. (2008, April 30). *Harvard's baby brain research lab.* Retrieved on January 24, 2009, from www.telegraph .co.uk/scienceandtechnology/science/sciencenews/3341166/

Hill, C. R., & Stafford, E. P. (1980). Parental care of children: Time diary estimate of quantity, predictability, and variety. *Journal of Human Resources, 15,* 219-239.

Hill, P. L., Duggan, P. M., & Lapsley, D. K. (2012). Subjective invulnerability, risk behavior, and adjustment in early adolescence. *Journal of Early Adolescence, 31,* 489-501.

Hilliard, L. & Liben, L. (2012, April). *No boys in ballet: Response to gender bias in mother-child conversations.* Paper presented at the Gender Development Research conference, San Francisco.

Hillman, C. H., Buck, S. M., Themanson, J. R., Pontifex, M. B., & Castelli, D. M. (2009). Aerobic fitness and cognitive development: Event-related brain potential and task performance indices of executive control in preadolescent children. *Developmental Psychology, 45,* 114-129.

Hines, M. (2013). Sex and sex differences. In P. D. Zelazo (Ed.), *Oxford handbook of developmental psychology,* New York: Oxford University Press.

Hirsch, B. J., & Rapkin, B. D. (1987). The transition to junior high school: A longitudinal study of self-esteem, psychological symptomatology, school life, and social support. *Child Development, 58,* 1235-1243.

Hirsh-Pasek, K., Golinkoff, R., Berk, L., & Singer, D. (2009). *A mandate for playful learning.* Oxford, NY: Oxford University Press.

Hirsh-Pasek, K., & Golinkoff, R. M. (2013). Early language and literacy: Six principles. In S. Gilford (Ed.), *Head Start teacher's guide.* New York: Teacher's College Press.

Ho, C., Bluestein, D. N., & Jenkins, J. M. (2008). Cultural differences in the relationship between parenting and children's behavior. *Developmental Psychology, 44*(2), 507-522.

Ho, J., & Birman, D. (2010). Acculturation gaps in Vietnamese immigrant families: Impact on family relationships. *International Journal of Intercultural Relations, 34,* 22-23.

Hockenberry, M., & Wilson, D. (2009). *Wong's essentials of pediatric nursing.* Oxford, UK: Elsevier.

Hoekstra, R. A., Happe, F., Baron-Cohen, S, & Ronald, A. (2010, in press). Limited genetic covariance between autistic traits and intelligence: Findings from a longitudinal twin study. *American Journal of Medical Genetics, B. Neuropsychiatric Genetics.*

Hoff, E., Laursen, B., & Tardif, T. (2002). Socioeconomic status and parenting. In M. H. Bornstein (Ed.), *Handbook of parenting* (2nd ed.). Mahwah, NJ: Erlbaum.

Hofferth S. L., Sandberg J. F. (2010, pp. 193-229). Changes in American children's time, 1981-1997. In: Hofferth S, Owens T. (Eds.). *Children at the millennium—Where did we come from, where are we going?* Elsevier Science; New York.

Hoffman, M. L. (1970). Moral development. In P. H. Mussen (Ed.), *Manual of child psychology* (3rd ed., Vol. 2). New York: Wiley.

Hoffman, M. L. (1988). Moral development. In M. H. Bornstein & E. Lamb (Eds.), *Developmental psychology: An advanced textbook* (2nd ed.). Hillsdale, NJ: Erlbaum.

Hogan, M. J., Parker, J. D. A., Wiener, J., Watters, C. Wood, L. M., & Oke, A. (2010). Academic success in adolescence: Relationships among verbal IQ, social support and emotional intelligence. *Australian Journal of Psychology, 62,* 30-41.

Holden, G. W., Vittrup, B., & Rosen, L. H. (2011). Families, parenting, and discipline. In M. K. Underwood & L. H. Rosen (Eds.), *Social Development.* New York: Guilford.

Hollich, G. J., Newman, R. S., & Jusczyk, P. W. (2005). Infants' use of synchronized visual information to separate streams of speech. *Child Development, 76*, 598–613.

**Holliday, R. E., Brainerd, C. J., & Reyna, V. F.** (2011). Developmental reversals in false memory: Now you see them, now you don't! *Developmental Psychology, 47*, 442–449.

**Hollier, L., & Wendel, G.** (2008). Third trimester antiviral prophylaxis for preventing maternal genital herpes simplex virus (HSV) recurrences and neonatal infection. *Cochrane Database of Systematic Reviews, 1*, CD004946.

**Hollis-Sawyer, L. A., & Sawyer, T. P.** (2008). Potential stereotype threat and face validity effects on cognitive-based test performance in the classroom. *Educational Psychology, 28*, 291–304.

**Holmes, L. B.** (2011). Human teratogens: Update 2010. *Birth Defects Research Part A: Clinical and Molecular Teratology, 91*, 1–7.

**Holzman, L.** (2009). *Vygotsky at work and play*. Oxford, UK: Routledge.

**Homae, F., Watanabe, H., Nakano, T., & Taga, G.** (2011). Large-scale brain networks underlying language acquisition in early infancy. *Frontiers of Psychology, 2*, 93.

**Holsen, I., Carlson Jones, D., & Skogbrott Birkeland, M.** (2012). Body image satisfaction among Norwegian adolescents and young adults: A longitudinal study of interpersonal relationships and BMI. *Body Image, 9*, 201–208.

**Hommel, B., Li, K. Z. H., & Li, S-C** (2004). Visual search across the life span. *Developmental Psychology, 40*, 545–558.

**Honzik, M. P., MacFarlane, I. W., & Allen, L.** (1948). The stability of mental test performance between two and eighteen years. *Journal of Experimental Education, 17*, 309–324.

**Hood, B. M.** (1995). Gravity rules for 2- to-4 year-olds? *Cognitive Development, 10*, 577–598.

**Hooper, S. R., & others.** (2008). Executive functions in young males with fragile X syndrome in comparison to mental age-matched controls: baseline findings from a longitudinal study. *Neuropsychology, 22*, 36–47.

**Hopkins, B.** (1991). Facilitating early motor development: An intracultural study of West Indian mothers and their infants living in Britain. In J. K. Nugent, B. M. Lester, & T. B. Brazelton (Eds.), *The cultural context of infancy. Vol. 2: Multicultural and interdisciplinary approaches to parent-infant relations*. Norwood, NJ: Ablex.

**Hopkins, B., & Westra, T.** (1988). Maternal handling and motor development: An intracultural study. *Genetic Psychology Monographs, 14*, 377–420.

**Hopkins, B., & Westra, T.** (1990). Motor development, maternal expectations, and the role of handling. *Infant Behavior and Development, 13*, 117–122.

**Horn, J.** (2007). Spearman, *g*, expertise, and the nature of human cognitive capacity. In P. C. Kyllonen, R. D. Roberts, & L. Stankov (Eds.), *Extending intelligence*. Mahwah, NJ: Erlbaum.

**Horne, R. S., Franco, P., Adamson, T. M., Groswasser, J., & Kahn, A.** (2002). Effects of body position on sleep and arousal characteristics in infants. *Early Human Development, 69*, 25–33.

**Hospital for Sick Children, Dipchard, A., Friedman, J., Gupta, S., Bismilla, Z., & Lam, C.** (2010). *The Hospital for Sick Children's handbook of pediatrics* (11th ed.). London: Elsevier.

**Houde, O., & others.** (2011). Functional magnetic resonance imaging study of Piaget's conservation-of-number task in preschool and school-age children: A neo-Piagetian approach. *Journal of Experimental Child Psychology, 110*, 332–346.

**Howe, M. J. A., Davidson, J. W., Moore, D. G., & Sloboda, J. A.** (1995). Are there early childhood signs of musical ability? *Psychology of Music, 23*, 162–176.

**Howe, M. L.** (2011). *The nature of early memory: An adaptive theory of the genesis and development of memory*. New York: Oxford University Press.

**Howe, M. L., Courage, M. L., & Rooksby, M.** (2009). The genesis and development of autobiographical memory. In M. Courage & N. Cowan (Eds.), *The development of memory in infancy and childhood*. New York: Psychology Press.

**Howell, D. C.** (2010). *Statistical methods for psychology* (7th ed.). Boston: Cengage.

**Howes, C.** (1985, April). *Predicting preschool sociometric status from toddler peer interaction*. Paper presented at the meeting of the Society for Research in Child Development, Toronto.

**Howes, C.** (2009). Friendship in early childhood. In K. H. Rubin, W. M., Bukowski, & B. Laursen (Eds.), *Handbook of peer interactions, relationships, and groups*. New York: Guilford.

**Howes, C.** (2009). The impact of child care on young children (0–2). In R. E. Tremblay, R. deV. Peters, M. Boivan, & R. G. Barr (Eds.), *Encyclopedia on early childhood development*. Montreal: Centre of Excellence for Early Childhood Development.

**Howlin, P., Magiati, I., & Charman, T.** (2009). Systematic review of early intensive behavioral interventions with autism. *American Journal on Intellectual and Developmental Disabilities, 114*, 23–41.

**Huang, L. N., and Ying, Y.** (1989). Chinese American children and adolescents. In J. T. Gibbs and L. N. Huang (Eds.), *Children of color*. San Francisco: Jossey-Bass.

**Hudon, T. M., Fennell, C. T., & Hoftyzer, M.,** (2013). Quality not quantity of television viewing is associated with bilingual toddlers' vocabulary scores. *Infant Behavior & Development*, Vol. 36(2), April, 2013, 245–254.

**Hudson, J. L., & Rapee, R. M.** (2000). The origins of social phobia. *Behavior Modification, 24*, 102–129.

**Huebner, A. M., & Garrod, A. C.** (1993). Moral reasoning among Tibetan monks: A study of Buddhist adolescents and young adults in Nepal. *Journal of Cross-Cultural Psychology, 24*, 167–185.

**Huesmann, L. R., Moise-Titus, J., Podolski, C., & Eron, L. D.** (2003). Longitudinal relations between children's exposure to TV violence and their aggressive and violent behavior in young adulthood, 1977–1992. *Developmental Psychology, 39*, 201–221.

**Hughes, C., & Dunn, J.** (2007). Children's relationships with other children. In C. A. Brownell & C. B. Kopp (Eds.), *Socioemotional development in the toddler years*. New York: Guilford.

**Human Resources and Skills Development Canada** (2013). Family life–age of mother at childbirth. Retrieved from: www4.hrsdc. gc.ca/.3ndic.1t.4r@-eng.jsp?iid=75

**Hunter, L. P., Rychnovsky, J. D., & Yount, S. M.** (2009). A selective review of maternal sleep characteristics in the postpartum period. *Journal of Obstetric, Gynecologic, and Neonatal Nursing, 38*, 60–68.

**Hurt, H., Brodsky, N. L., Roth, H., Malmud, F., & Glannetta, J. M.** (2005). School performance of children with gestational cocaine exposure. *Neurotoxicology and Teratology, 27*, 203–211.

**Huston, A. C., & Bentley, A. C.** (2010). Human development in societal context. *Annual Review of Psychology* (Vol. 61). Palo Alto, CA: Annual Reviews.

**Huston, A. C., Epps, S. R., Shim, M. S., Duncan, G. J., Crosby, D. A., & Ripke, M. N.** (2006). Effects of a family poverty intervention program last from middle childhood to adolescence. In A. C. Huston, & M. N. Ripke (Eds.). *Developmental contexts of middle childhood*. New York: Cambridge University Press.

**Huston, A. C., & Ripke, M. N.** (2006). Experiences in middle childhood and children's development: A summary and integration of research. In A. C. Huston & M. N. Ripke (Eds.), *Developmental contexts in middle childhood*. New York: Cambridge University Press.

**Hutson, J. R., & others.** (2013, in press). Adverse placental effect of formic acid on hCG secretion is mitigated by folic acid. *Alcohol and Alcoholism, Vol. 38*(3), 283-287.

**Hutson, R. A.** (2008). Poverty. In N. J. Salkind (Ed.), *Encyclopedia of educational psychology*. Thousand Oaks, CA: Sage.

**Huttenlocher, J., Haight, W., Bruk, A., Seltzer, M., & Lyons, T.** (1991). Early vocabulary growth: Relation to language input and gender. *Developmental Psychology, 27*, 236-248.

**Huttenlocher, P. R., & Dabholkar, A. S.** (1997). Regional differences in synaptogenesis in human cerebral cortex. *Journal of Comparative Neurology, 37*(2), 167-178.

**Hyde, D. C. & Spelke, E. S.** (2009). All numbers are not equal: An electrophysiological investigation of small and large number representations. *Journal of Cognitive Neuroscience, 21*, 1039-1053.

**Hyde, D. C., & Spelke, E. S.** (2011). Neural signatures of number processing in human infants: Evidence for two core systems underlying numerical cognition. *Developmental Science, 14*, 360-371.

**Hyde, D. C., & Spelke, E. S.** (2012, in press). Spatio-temporal dynamics of numerical processing: An ERP source localization study. *Human Brain Mapping*.

**Hyde, J. S.** (2005). The gender similarities hypothesis. *American Psychologist, 60*, 581-592.

**Hyde, J. S.** (2007a). *Half the human experience* (7th ed.). Boston: Houghton Mifflin.

**Hyde, J. S.** (2007b). New directions in the study of gender similarities and differences. *Current Directions in Psychological Science, 16*, 259-263.

**Hyde, J. S.** (2014). Gender similarities and differences. *Annual Review of Psychology, 65*, 373-398.

**Hyde, J. S., & DeLamater, J. D.** (2011). *Understanding human sexuality* (11th ed.). New York: McGraw-Hill.

**Hyde, J. S. & Else-Quest, N.** (2013). *Half the human experience* (8th ed.). Boston: Cengage.

**Hymel, S., Closson, L. M., Caravita, C. S., & Vaillancourt, T.** (2011). Social status among peers: From sociometric attraction to peer acceptance to perceived popularity. In P. K. Smith & C. H. Hart (Eds.), *Wiley-Blackwell handbook of childhood social development* (2nd ed.). New York: Wiley.

**Hymel, S., LeMare, L., Ditner, E. & Woody, E.** (1999). Assessing self-concept in children: Variations across self concept domains. *Merrill Palmer Quarterly, 45*, 602-623.

**Hymel, S., Schonert-Reichl, K. A., & Miller, L. D.** (2006). Reading, 'riting, 'rithmetic and relationships: Considering the social side of education. *Exceptionality Education Canada, 16*(3), 1-44.

**Hyson, M.** (2007). Curriculum. In R. New & M. Cochran (Eds.), *Early childhood education: An international encyclopedia of early childhood education*. New York: Greenwood.

**Hyson, M., Copple, C., & Jones, J.** (2006). Early childhood development and education. In K. A. Renninger & I. Sigel (Eds.), Handbook of child psychology: Volume 4. Child psychology in practice. New York: Wiley.

## I

**Ibrahim, R., & Eviatar, Z.** (2013, in press). The contribution of two hemispheres to lexical decision in different languages. *Behavioral and Brain Functions*.

**"I Have a Dream" Foundation.** (2010). *About us*. Retrieved June 6, 2010, from www.ihad.org

**Imada, T., Zhang, Y., Cheour, M., Taulu, S., Ahonen, A., & Kuhl, P. K.** (2007). Infant speech perception activates Boca's area: A developmental magnetoencephalography study. *Neuroreport, 17*, 957-962.

**Impett, E. A., Schoolder, D., Tolman, L., Sorsoli, L., & Henson, J. M.** (2008). Girls' relationship authenticity and self-esteem across adolescence. *Developmental Psychology, 44*, 722-733.

**Iovannone, R.** (2013). Teaching students with autism spectrum disorders. In B. G. Cook & M. G. Tankerslee (Ed.), *Research-based practices in special education*. Upper Saddle River, NJ: Pearson.

**Ip, S., Chung, M., Raman, G., Trikalinos, T. A., & Lau, J.** (2009). A summary of the Agency for Healthcare Research and Quality's evidence report on breastfeeding in developed countries. *Breastfeeding Medicine, 4, Suppl 1*, S17-S30.

**Iqbal, M., & others.** (2012). Placental drug transporters and their role in fetal protection. *Placenta, 33*, 137-142.

**Irvin, J. L., Buehl, D. R., & Klemp, R. M.** (2007). *Reading and the high school student* (2nd ed.). Boston: Allyn & Bacon.

**Irvine, S. H., & Berry, J. W.** (Eds.). (2010). *Human abilities in cultural contexts*. New York: Cambridge University Press.

**Isaacs, B.** (2012). *Understanding the Montessori approach: Early years education practice*. New York: Routledge.

**Isen, J., & Baker, L. A.** (2008). Genetic disorders: Sex-linked. In M. M. Haith & J. B. Benson (Eds.), *Encyclopedia of infancy and early childhood development*. Oxford, UK: Elsevier.

**Isen, J. D., Baker, L. A., Raine, A., & Bezdjian, S.** (2009). Genetic and environmental influences on the Junior Temperament and Character Inventory in a preadolescent twin sample. *Behavior Genetics, 39*, 36-47.

**Ivanova, K., Veenstra, R., & Mills, M.** (2012). Who dates? The effects of temperament, puberty, and parenting on early adolescent experiences with dating. *Journal of Early Adolescence, 42*, 340-363.

**Izard, C. E.** (2009). Emotion theory and research: Highlights, unanswered questions, and emerging issues. *Annual Review of Psychology* (Vol. 60). Palo Alto, CA: Annual Reviews.

**Izard, V., & Spelke, E. S.** (2010, in press). Development of sensitivity of geometry in visual forms. *Human Evolution*.

## J

**Jackson, L. A., & others.** (2012). The digital divide. In J. R. Levesque (Ed.), *Encyclopedia of adolescence*. New York: Springer.

**Jacobson, L. A., & others.** (2011). Working memory influences processing speed and reading fluency in ADHD. *Child Neuropsychology, 17*(3), 209-224.

**Jaffee, S., & Hyde, J. S.** (2000). Gender differences in moral orientation: A meta-analysis. *Psychological Bulletin, 126*, 703-726.

**Jago, R., Froberg, K., Cooper, A. R., Eiberg, S., & Andersen, L. B.** (2010). Three-year changes in fitness and adiposity are independently associated with cardiovascular risk factors among Danish children. *Journal of Physical Activity and Health, 7*, 37-44.

**Jalongo, M. R.** (2011). *Early childhood language arts* (5th ed.). Boston: Allyn & Bacon.

**Jalongo, M. R., & Isenberg, J.** (2012). *Exploring your role in early childhood education* (4th ed.). Upper Saddle River, NJ: Pearson.

**Jambunathan, S., Burts, D. C., & Pierce, S.** (2000). Comparisons of parenting attitudes among five ethnic groups in the United States. *Journal of Comparative Family Studies, 31*, 395-406.

**Jan, J. E., & others.** (2010). Long-term sleep disturbances in children: A cause of neuronal loss. *European Journal of Pediatric Neurology, 14*(5), 380-390.

**Jansen, J., de Weerth, C., & Riksen-Walraven, J. M.** (2008). Breastfeeding and the mother-infant relationship—A review. *Developmental Review, 28,* 503–521.

**Janssen, I., Boyce, W. F., & Pickett, W.** (2012). Screen time and physical violence in 10 to 16-year-old Canadian youth. *International Journal of Public Health, 57*(2), 325–331.

**Janssen, P., A., Saxell, L., Page, L. A., Klein, M. C., Liston, R. M., & Lee, S. K.** (2009). Outcomes of planned home birth with registered midwife versus planned hospital birth with midwife or physician. *Canadian Medical Association Journal, 181,* 377–383.

**Jardri, R., & others.** (2012). Assessing fetal response to maternal speech using a noninvasive functional brain imaging technique. *International Journal of Developmental Neuroscience, 30,* 159–161.

**Jared, D., Cormier, P., Levy, B. A., & Wade-Woolley, L.** (2011). Early predictors of biliteracy development in Children in French Immersion: A 4-year longitudinal study. *Journal of Educational Psychology, 103,* 119–139.

**Jarrett, R. L.** (1995). Growing up poor: The family experiences of socially mobile youth in low-income African-American neighborhoods. *Journal of Adolescent Research, 10,* 111–135.

**Jarvin, L., Newman, T., Randi, J., Sternberg, R. J., & Grigorenko, E. L.** (2008). Matching instruction and assessment. In J. A. Plucker & C. M. Callahan (Eds.), *Critical issues and practices in gifted education* (pp. 345–365). Waco, TX: Prufrock.

**Jaswal, V. K., & Fernald, A.** (2007). Learning to communicate. In A. Slater & M. Lewis (Eds.), *Introduction to infant development* (2nd ed.). New York: Oxford University Press.

**Jayson, S.** (2006, June 29). The 'millenials' come of age. *USA TODAY,* pp. 1–2D.

**Jencks, C.** (1979). *Who gets ahead? The determinants of economic success in America.* New York: Basic Books.

**Jenik, A. G., & Vain, N.** (2010). The pacifier debate. *Early Human Development, 85* (Suppl. 10), S89–S91.

**Jenkins, J. M., & Astington, J. W.** (1996). Cognitive factors and family structure associated with theory of mind development in young children. *Developmental Psychology, 32,* 70–78.

**Jenni, O. G., Chaouch, A., Caflisch, J., Rousson, V.** (2012). Infant motor milestones: Poor predictive value for outcome of healthy children. *Acta Paediatrica,* December 13, 2012: doi 10.1111/apa.12129

**Jensen, A. R.** (1998). *The g factor.* Westport, CT: Praeger.

**Jensen, A. R.** (2008). Book review. *Intelligence, 36,* 96–97.

**Jesse, D. E., & Kirkpatrick, M. K.** (2013). Catching the spirit in cultural care: A midwifery exemplar. *Journal of Midwifery and Women's Health, 58,* 49–56.

**Ji, B. T., & others.** (1997). Paternal cigarette smoking and the risk of childhood cancer among offspring of nonsmoking mothers. *Journal of the National Cancer Institute, 89,* 238–244.

**Jia, R., & Schoppe-Sullivan, S. J. (2011).** Relations between coparenting and father involvement in families with preschool-age children. *Developmental Psychology, 47,* 106–118.

**Jiao, S., Ji, G., & Jing, Q.** (1996). Cognitive development of Chinese urban only children and children with siblings. *Child Development, 67,* 387–395.

**Jimerson, S. R.** (2009). High school dropout. In D. Carr (Ed.), *Encyclopedia of the life course and human development.* Boston: Gale Cengage.

**Jin, M. K., Jacobvitz, D., Hagen, N., & Jung, S. H.** (2012). Maternal sensitivity and infant attachment security in Korea: Cross-cultural validation of the Strange Situation. *Attachment and Human Development, 14,* 33–44.

**Job, V., Dweck, C. S., & Walton, G. M.** (2010). Ego-depletion—Is it all in your head? Implicit theories about willpower affect self-regulation. *Psychological Science, 21,* 1686–1693.

**Joh, A. S., Jaswal, V. K., & Keen, R.** (2011). Imaging a way out of the gravity bias: Preschoolers can visualize the solution to a spatial problem. *Child Development, 82,* 744–750.

**Johns Hopkins University.** (2006). *Research: Tribal connections.* Retrieved on January 31, 2008 from www.krieger.jhu.edu/research/spotlight/prabhakar.html

**Johnson, G. B., & Losos, J.** (2010). *The living world* (6th ed.). New York: McGraw-Hill.

**Johnson, J. L., & Cameron, M C.** (2001). Barriers to providing effect mental health services to American Indians. *Mental Health Services Research, 3,* 215–223.

**Johnson, J. S., & Newport, E. L.** (1991). Critical period effects on universal properties of language: The status of subjacency in the acquisition of a second language. *Cognition, 39,* 215–258.

**Johnson, L., Giordano, P. C., Manning, W. D., & Longmore, M. A.** (2011). Parent-child relations and offending in young adulthood. *Journal of Youth and Adolescence, 40,* 786–799.

**Johnson, M. H., Grossmann, T. and Cohen-Kadosh, K.** (2009). Mapping functional brain development: Building a social brain through Interactive Specialization. *Developmental Psychology, 45,* 151–159.

**Johnson, N. & Cremo, E.** (1995). Socialization and the native family. In K. Covell (Ed.), *Readings in child development.* Toronto, ON: Nelson.

**Johnson, S. B., Dariotis, J. K., & Wang, C.** (2012). Adolescent risk taking under stressed and nonstressed conditions: Conservative, calculating, and impulsive types. *Journal of Adolescent Health, 51*(Suppl. 2), S34–S40.

**Johnson, S. P.** (2004). Development of perceptual completion in infancy. *Psychological Science, 15,* 769–775.

**Johnson, S. P.** (2010a, in press). Perceptual completion in infancy. In S. P. Johnson (Ed.), *Neoconstructivism: The new science of cognitive development.* New York: Oxford University Press.

**Johnson, S. P.** (2010b, in press). A constructivist view of object perception in infancy. infancy. To appear in L. M. Oakes, C. H. Cashon, M. Casasola, & D. H. Rakison (Eds.), *Early perceptual and cognitive development.* New York: Oxford University Press.

**Johnson, S. P.** (2012). Development of the visual system. In P. Rakic & J. Rubenstein (Eds.), *Developmental neuroscience—Basic and clinical mechanisms.* New York: Oxford University Press.

**Johnson, S. P.** (2013). Object perception. In P. D. Zelazo (Ed.), *Handbook of developmental psychology.* New York: Oxford University Press.

**Johnson, S. P., Bremner, J. G., Slater, A., & Mason, U.** (2000). The role of good form in young infants' perception of partly occluded objects. *Journal of Experimental Child Psychology, 76,* 1–25.

**Johnson, W., & Bouchard, T. J., Jr.** (2007). Sex differences in mental abilities: g masks the dimensions on which they lie. *Intelligence, 35,* 23–39.

**Johnson, W., te Nijenhuis, J., & Bouchard, T. J.** (2008). Still just 1 g: Consistent results from five test batteries. *Intelligence, 36,* 81–95.

**John-Steiner, V.** (2007). Vygotsky on thinking and speaking. In H. Daniels, J. Wertsch, & M. Cole (Eds.), *The Cambridge companion to Vygotsky.* New York: Cambridge University Press.

**Johnston, M.** (2008, April 30). Commentary in R. Highfield *Harvard's baby brain research lab.* Retrieved on January 24, 2008, from www.telegraph.co.uk/scienceandtechnology/science/sciencenews/3341166/

**Jones, H. W.** (2007). Iatrogenic multiple births: A 2003 checkup. *Fertility and Sterility, 87,* 453–455.

Jones, M. C. (1965). Psychological correlates of somatic development. *Child Development, 36,* 899–911.

Jones, N. A. (2012). Delayed reactive cries demonstrate emotional and physiological dysregulation in newborns of depressed mothers. *Biological Psychiatry, 89,* 374–381.

Jonson-Reid, M., Kohl, P. L., & Drake, B. (2012). Child and adolescent outcomes of chronic child maltreatment. *Pediatrics, 129,* 839–845.

Jordan, S. J., & others. (2008). Serious ovarian, fallopian tube, and primary peritoneal cancers: A comprehensive epidemiological analysis. *International Journal of Cancer, 122,* 1598–1603.

Joseph, J. (2006). *The missing gene.* New York: Algora.

Josephson Institute of Ethics. (2008). *The ethics of American youth 2008.* Los Angeles: Josephson Institute.

Josselyn, S. A., & Frankland, P. W. (2012). Infantile amnesia: A neurogenic hypothesis. *Learning and Memory, 19,* 423–433

Juffer, F., & van IJzendoorn, M. H. (2005). Behavior problems and mental health referrals of international adoptees: A meta-analysis. *Journal of the American Medical Association, 293,* 2501–2513.

Juffer, F., & van IJzendoorn, M. H. (2007). Adoptees do not lack self-esteem: A meta-analysis of studies on self-esteem of transracial, international, and domestic adoptees, *Psychological Bulletin, 133,* 1067–1083.

Just, M. A., Keller, T. A., Malave, V. L., Kana, R. K., & Varma, S. (2012). Autism as a neural systems disorder: A theory of frontal-posterior underconnectivity. *Neuroscience and Biobehavioral Reviews, 36,* 1292–1313.

Jusczyk, P. W., & Hohne, E. A. (1997). Infants' memory for spoken words. *Science, 277,* 1984–1986.

Jylhava, J., & others. (2009). Genetics of C-reactive protein and complement factor H have an epistatic effect on carotid artery compliance: The Cardiovascular Risk in Young Finns Study. *Clinical and Experimental Immunology, 155,* 53–58.

## K

Kaffashi, F., Scher, M. S., Ludington-Hoe, S. M., & Loparo, K. A. (2013). An analysis of kangaroo care intervention using neonatal EEG complexity: A preliminary study. *Clinical Neurophysiology, 124,* 238–246.

Kagan, J. (1987). Perspectives on infancy. In J. D. Osofsky (Ed.), *Handbook on infant development* (2nd ed.). New York: Wiley.

Kagan, J. (1992). Yesterday's promises, tomorrow's promises. *Developmental Psychology, 28,* 990–997.

Kagan, J. (2000). Temperament. In A. Kazdin (Ed.), *Encyclopedia of psychology.*

Kagan, J. (2002). Behavioral inhibition as a temperamental category. In R. J. Davidson, K. R. Scherer, & H. H. Goldsmith (Eds.), *Handbook of affective sciences.* New York: Oxford University Press.

Kagan, J. (2003). Biology, context, and development. *Annual Review of Psychology* (Vol. 54). Palo Alto, CA: Annual Reviews.

Kagan, J. (2008). Fear and wariness. In M. M. Haith & J. B. Benson (Eds.), *Encyclopedia of infant and early childhood development.* Oxford, UK: Elsevier.

Kagan, J. (2013). Temperamental contributions to inhibited and uninhibited profiles. In P. D. Zelazo (Ed.), *Oxford handbook of developmental psychology.* New York: Oxford University Press.

Kagan, J. (2010). Emotions and temperament. In M. H. Bornstein (Ed.), *Handbook of cultural developmental science.* New York: Psychology Press.

Kagan, J., Kearsley, R. B., & Zelazo, P. R. (1978). *Infancy: Its place in human development.* Cambridge, MA: Harvard University Press.

Kagan, J., & Snidman, N. (1991). Infant predictors of inhibited and uninhibited behavioral profiles. *Psychological Science, 2,* 40–44.

Kagan, J., Snidman, N., Kahn, V., & Towsley, S. (2007). The preservation of two infant temperaments into adolescence. *Monographs of the Society for Research in Child Development, 72*(2), 1–75.

Kalak, N., & others. (2012). Daily morning running for 3 weeks improved sleep and psychological functioning in health of adolescents compared to controls. *Journal of Adolescent Health, 51,* 615–622.

Kail, R. V. (2007). Longitudinal evidence that increases in processing speed and working memory enhance children's reasoning. *Psychological Science, 18,* 312–313.

Kalder, M., Knoblauch, K., Hrgovic, I., & Munstedt, K. (2010). Use of complementary and alternative medicine during pregnancy and delivery. *Archives of Gynecology and Obstetrics.* (Available online February 23, 2010.)

Kale, R. (2012). "It's a girl" – could be a death sentence. *Canadian Medical Association Journal, 184,* 387–388.

Kamii, C. (1985). *Young children reinvent arithmetic: Implications of Piaget's theory.* New York: Teachers College Press.

Kamii, C. (1989). *Young children continue to reinvent arithmetic.* New York: Teachers College Press.

Kamil, M. L. (2012). Current and historical perspectives on reading research and instruction. In K. R. Harris, S. Graham, & T. Urdan (Eds.), *APA handbook of educational psychology.* Washington, DC: American Psychological Association.

Kandler, C., Riemann, R., & Kampfe, N. (2009). Genetic and personality mediation between measures of personality and family environment in twins reared together. *Behavior Genetics, 39,* 24–35.

Kanoy, K., Ulku-Steiner, B., Cox, M., & Burchinal, M. (2003). Marital relationship and individual psychological characteristics that predict physical punishment of children. *Journal of Family Psychology, 17,* 20–28.

Kao, G., & Turney, K. (2010). Adolescents and schooling: Differences by race, ethnicity, and immigrant status. In D. P. Swanson, M. C. Edwards, & M. B. Spencer (Eds.), *Adolescence: Development in a global era.* San Diego: Academic Press.

Kar, B. R., Rao, S. L, & Chandramouli, B. A. (2008). Cognitive development in children with chronic energy malnutrition. *Behavioral and Brain Functions, 4,* 31.

Karama, S., & others. (2009). Positive association between cognitive ability and cortical thickness in a representative sample of healthy 6- to 18-year-olds. *Intelligence, 37,* 145–155.

Karevold, E., Ystrom, E., Coplan, R. J., Sanson, A. V., & Mathiesen, K. S. (2012). A prospective longitudinal study of shyness from infancy to adolescence: Stability, age-related changes, and prediction of socio-emotional functioning. *Journal of Abnormal Child Psychology, 40,* 1167–177.

Karoly, L. A. & Bigelow, J. A. (2005). *The economics of investing in universal preschool education in California.* Santa Monica, CA: The RAND Corporation.

Karpov, Y. V. (2006). *The neo-Vygotskian approach to child development.* New York: Cambridge University Press.

Karreman, A., van Tuijl, C., van Aken, M. A. G., & Dekovic, M. (2008). Parenting, coparenting, and effortful control in preschoolers. *Journal of Family Psychology, 22,* 30–40.

Katz, L. (1999). Curriculum disputes in early childhood education. *ERIC Clearinghouse on Elementary and Early Childhood Education,* Document EDO-PS-99-13.

Kaufman, J. C., & Sternberg, R. J. (Eds.) (2010). *Cambridge handbook of creativity.* New York: Cambridge University Press.

Kavsek, M. (2009). The perception of subjective contours and neon color spreading figures in young infants. *Attention, Perception, and Psychophysics, 71,* 412–420.

Kavsek, M. (2013, in press). The comparator model of infant visual habituation and dishabituation: Recent insights. *Developmental Psychobiology.*

Keating, D. P. (1990). Adolescent thinking. In S. S. Feldman & G. R. Elliott (Eds.), *At the threshold: The developing adolescent.* Cambridge, MA: Harvard University Press.

Keating, D. P. (2007). Understanding adolescent development: Implications for driving safety. *Journal of Safety Research, 38,* 147–157.

Keating, D. P. (2009). Developmental science and giftedness: An integrated life-span framework. In F. D. Horowitz, R. F. Subotnik, & D. J. Matthews (Eds.), *The development of giftedness and talent across the life span.* Washington, DC: American Psychological Association.

Keen, R. (2005). Unpublished review of Santrock, *Topical Life-Span Development,* 3rd ed. New York: McGraw-Hill

Keen, R. (2011). The development of problem solving in young children: A critical cognitive skill. *Annual Review of Psychology (Vol. 62).* Palo Alto, CA: Annual Reviews.

Keers, R., & others. (2010). Interaction between serotonin transporter gene variants and life events predicts response to antidepressants in the GENDEP project. *Pharmacogenomics.* (Available online March 9, 2010.)

Keller, P., & El-Sheikh, M. (2010). Children's emotional security and sleep: Longitudinal relations and directions of effects. *Journal of Child Psychology and Psychiatry, 52*(1), 64–71.

Kellman, P. J., & Arterberry, M. E. (2006). Infant visual perception. In W. Damon & R. Lerner (Eds.), *Handbook of child psychology* (6th ed.). New York: Wiley.

Kellman, P. J., & Banks, M. S. (1998). Infant visual perception. In W. Damon (Ed.), *Handbook of child psychology* (5th ed., Vol. 2). New York: Wiley.

Kellogg, R. T. (2007). *Fundamentals of cognitive psychology.* Thousand Oaks, CA: Sage.

Kellow, J. T., & Jones, B. D. (2008). The effects of stereotypes on the achievement gap: Reexamining the academic performance of African American high school students. *Journal of Black Psychology, 34,* 94–120.

Kelly, D. J., & others. (2007). Cross-race preferences for same-race faces extend beyond the African versus Caucasian contrast in 3-month-old infants. *Infancy, 11,* 87–95.

Kelly, D. J., Liu, S., Lee, K., Quinn, P. C., Pascalls, O., Slater, A. M., & Ge, L. (2009). Development of the other-race effect in infancy: Evidence toward universality? *Journal of Experimental Child Psychology, 104*(1), 105–114.

Kelly, J. P., Borchert., J., & Teller, D. Y. (1997). The development of chromatic and achromatic sensitivity in infancy as tested with the sweep VEP. *Vision Research, 37,* 2057–2072.

Kelly, K. M., & others. (2013, in press). Children's Oncology Group's 2013 blueprint for research on Hodgkin's lymphoma. *Pediatric and Blood Cancer.*

Kelly, R., Hammond, S., Dissanayake, C., & Ihsen, E. (2011). The relationship between symbolic play and executive function in young children. *Australasian Journal of Early Childhood, 36,* 21–28.

Kelmanson, I. A. (2010). Sleep disturbances in two-month-old infants sharing the bed with parent(s). *Minerva Pediatrica, 62,* 162–169.

Kempe, C., Eriksson-Gustavsson, A., & Samuelsson, S. (2011). Are there any Matthew effects in literacy and cognitive development? *Scandinavian Journal of Educational Research, 55,* 181–196.

Kendrick, K., Jutengren, G., & Stattin, H. (2012). The protective role of supportive friends against bullying perpetration and victimization. *Journal of Adolescence, 35,* 1069–1080.

Kenney-Benson, G. A., Pomerantz, E. M., Ryan, A. M., & Patrick, H. (2006). Sex differences in math performance: The role of children's approach to schoolwork. *Developmental Psychology, 42,* 11–26.

Keon, W. J. (2009). Early childhood education and care: Canada's challenges and next steps. *Paediatric Child Health, 14*(10), 660–661.

Kerns, K. A., & Siebert, A. C. (2012). Finding your way through the thicket: Promising approaches to assessing attachment in middle childhood. In E. Waters & B. Vaughn (Eds.), *Measuring attachment.* New York: Guilford.

Kerns, K. A., Siener, S., & Brumariu, L. E. (2011). Mother-child relationships, family context, and child characteristics as predictors of anxiety symptoms in middle childhood. *Development and Psychopathology, 23,* 593–604.

Kessen, W., Haith, M. M., & Salapatek, P. (1970). Human infancy. In P. H. Mussen (Ed.), *Manual of child psychology* (3rd ed., Vol. 1). New York: Wiley.

Keyes, M. A., Sharma, A., Elkins, I. J., Iacono, W. G., & McGue, M. (2008). The mental health of U.S. adolescents adopted in infancy. *Archives of Pediatric and Adolescent Medicine, 162,* 419–425.

Khuc, K., & others. (2013, in press). Adolescent metabolic syndrome risk is increased with higher infancy weight gain and decreased with longer breast feeding. *Indian Journal of Pediatrics.*

Kiess, H. O., & Green, B. A. (2010). *Statistical concepts for the behavioral sciences* (4th ed.). Boston: Allyn & Bacon.

Kilic, S., & others. (2012, in press). Environmental tobacco smoke exposure during intrauterine period promotes granulosa cell apoptosis: A prospective, randomized study. *Journal Maternal-Fetal and Neonatal Medicine.*

Kim, J-K., McHale, S. M., Crouter, A. C., & Osgood, D. W. (2007). Longitudinal linkages between sibling relationships and adjustment from middle childhood through adolescence. *Developmental Psychology, 43,* 960–973.

Kim, K. H. (2010, July 10). Interview. *Newsweek,* pp. 42–48.

Kim, S. Y., Su, J., Yancura, L., & Yee, B. (2009). Asian American and Pacific Islander families. In N. Tewari & A. Aluarez (Eds.), *Asian American Psychology.* New York Psychology Press.

Kimber, L., McNabb, M., McCourt, C., Haines, A., & Brocklehurst, P. (2008). Massage or music for pain relief in labor: A pilot randomized placebo controlled trial. *European Journal of Pain, 12,* 961–969.

Kim-Spoon, J., Cicchetti, D., & Rogosch, F. A. (2013, in press). A longitudinal study of emotion regulation, emotion lability-negativity, and internalizing symptomatology in maltreated and nonmaltreated children. *Child Development.*

Kini, S., Morrell, D., Thong, K. J., Kopakaki, A., Hillier, S., & Irvine, D. S. (2010). Lack of impact of semen quality on fertilization in assisted conception. *Scottish Medicine, 55,* 20–23.

Kirk, S. A., Gallagher, J. J., Coleman, M. R., & Anastaslow, N. J. (2012). *Educating exceptional children* (13th ed.). Boston: Cengage.

Kirkorian, H. L., Anderson, D. R., & Keen, R. (2012). Age differences in online processing of video: An eye movement study. *Child Development, 83,* 497–507.

Kirkorian, H. L., Wartella, E. A., & Anderson, D. A. (2008). Media and young children's learning. *Future of Children, 18*(1), 39–61.

Kisilevsky, B. S., & others (2009). Fetal sensitivity to properties of maternal speech and language. *Infant Behavior and Development, 32,* 59-71.

Kisilevsky, B. S., & Hains, S. M. J. (2011). Onset and maturation of fetal heart rate response to the mother's voice over late gestation. *Developmental Science, 14,* 214-223.

Kisilevsky, S., Hains, S. M., Jacquet, A. Y., Granier-Deferre, C., & Lecanuet, J. P. (2004). Maturation of fetal responses to music. *Developmental Science, 7,* 550-559.

Kitayama, S. (2011). Psychology and culture: Cross-country or regional comparisons. *Annual Review of Psychology* (Vol. 62). Palo Alto, CA: Annual Reviews.

Kleiman, E. M., & Riskand, J. H. (2013, in press) Utilized social support and self-esteem mediate the relationship between perceived social support and suicide ideation. *Crisis.*

Kleinsorge, C., & Covitz, L. M. (2012). Impact of divorce on children: Developmental considerations. *Pediatrics in Review, 33,* 147-154.

Klimstra, T. A., Hale, W. W., Raaijmakers, Q. A., Branje, S. J. T., & Meeus, W. H. (2010). Identity formation in adolescence: Change or stability? *Journal of Youth and Adolescence, 39,* 150-162.

Klingenberg, C. P., & others. (2010). Prenatal alcohol exposure alters the patterns of facial asymmetry. *Alcohol.* (Available online January 7, 2010.)

Klug, W. S., Cummings, M. R., Spencer, C., & Palladino, M. A. (2010). *Essentials of genetics* (7th ed. ). Upper Saddle River, NJ: Benjamin Cummings.

Knopik, V. S. (2009). Maternal smoking during pregnancy and child outcomes: Real or spurious? *Developmental Neuropsychology, 34,* 1-36.

Knox, M. (2010). On hitting children: A review of corporal punishment in the United States. *Journal of Pediatric Health Care, 24,* 103-107.

Kochanska, G., & Aksan, N. (2007). Conscience in childhood: Past, present, and future. *Merrill-Palmer Quarterly, 50,* 299-310.

Kochanska, G., Aksan, N., Prisco, T. R., & Adams, E. E. (2008). Mother-child and father-child mutually responsive orientation in the first two years and children's outcomes at preschool age: Mechanisms of influence. *Child Development, 79,* 30-44.

Kochanska, G., Barry, R. A., Stellern, S. A., & O'Bleness, J. J. (2010). Early attachment organization moderates the parent-child mutually coercive pathway to children's antisocial conduct. *Child Development, 80,* 1288-1300.

Kochanska, G., Forman, D. R., Aksan, N., & Dunbar, S. B. (2005). Pathways to conscience: Early mother-child mutually responsive orientation and children's moral emotion, conduct, and cognition. *Journal of Child Psychology and Psychiatry, 46,* 19-34.

Kochanska, G., Gross, J. N., Lin, M., & Nichols, K. E. (2002). Guilt in young children: Development, determinants, and relations with a broader set of standards. *Child Development, 73,* 461-482.

Kochanska, G., & Kim, S. (2013, in press). Early attachment organization with both parents and future behavior problems: From infancy to middle childhood. *Child Development.*

Kochanska, G., & others. (2010). Positive socialization mechanisms in secure and insecure parent-child dyads: Two longitudinal studies. *Journal of Child Psychology and Psychiatry, 51,* 998-1009.

Kohen, D. E., Leventhal, T., Dahinten, V. S., & McIntosh, C. N. (2008). Neighborhood disadvantage: Pathways of effects for young children. *Child Development, 79,* 156-169.

Kopp, F., & Lindenberger, U. (2012). Effects of joint attention on long-term memory in 9-month-old infants: An event-related potentials study. *Developmental Science, 15,* 540-556.

Kopp, C. B., & Neufeld, S. J. (2002). Emotional development in infancy. In R. Davidson & K. Scherer (Eds.), *Handbook of affective sciences.* New York: Oxford University Press.

Koppelman, K., & Goodhart, L. (2011). *Understanding human differences* (3rd ed.). Boston: Allyn & Bacon.

Kornblum, J. (2006, March 9). How to monitor the kids? *USA TODAY, 1D,* p. 1.

Koerner, M. V., & Barlow, D. P. (2010). Genomic imprinting—an epigenetic regulatory model. *Current Opinion in Genetics & Development, 202*(2), 164-170.

Kohlberg, L. (1958). *The development of modes of moral thinking and choice in the years 10 to 16.* Unpublished doctoral dissertation, University of Chicago.

Kohlberg, L. (1969). Stage and sequence: The cognitive-developmental approach to socialization. In D. A. Goslin (Ed.), *Handbook of socialization theory and research.* Chicago: Rand McNally.

Kohlberg, L. (1986). A current statement on some theoretical issues. In S. Modgil & C. Modgil (Eds.), *Lawrence Kohlberg.* Philadelphia: Falmer.

Kolb, B., & Gibb, R. (2011). Brain plasticity and behaviour in the developing brain. *Journal of the Canadian Academy of Child Adolescent Psychiatry, 20:4,* November, 2011.

Kong, A., & others. (2012). Rate of *de novo* mutations and the importance of father's age to disease risk. *Nature, 488,* 471-475.

Koo, Y. J., & others. (2012). Pregnancy outcomes according to increasing maternal age. *Taiwan Journal of Obstetrics and Gynecology, 51,* 60-65.

Koolhof, R. Loeber, R., Wei, E. H., Pardini, D., & D'Escury, A. C. (2007). Inhibition deficits of serious delinquent boys of low intelligence. *Criminal Behavior and Mental Health, 17,* 274-292.

Kopp, C. P. (2011). Socio-emotional development in the early years: Socialization and consciousness. *Annual Review of Psychology* (Vol. 62). Palo Alto, CA: Annual Reviews.

Kopp, C. B., & Neufeld, S. J. (2002). Emotional development in infancy. In R. Davidson & K. Scherer (Eds.), *Handbook of affective sciences.* New York: Oxford University Press.

Kopp F., Lindenberger U. (2011). Effects of joint attention on long-term memory in 9-month-old infants: An event-related potentials study. *Developmental Science,* 14, 660-672.

Koren, G., & Nordeng, H. (2012). Antidepressant use during pregnancy: The benefit-risk ratio. *American Journal of Obstetrics and Gynecology, 207,* 157-163.

Kostovic, I., Judas, M., & Sedmak, G. (2011). Developmental history of the subplate zone, subplate neurons, and interstitial white matter neurons: Relevance for schizophrenia. *International Journal of Developmental Neuroscience, 29*(3), 193-205.

Kotovsky, L., & Baillargeon, R. Calibration-based reasoning about collision events in 11-month-old infants. *Cognition, 51,* 107-129.

Kowalski, R. M., Giumetti, G. W., Schroeder, A. N., & Lattanner, M. R. (2014). Bullying in the digital age: A critical review and meta-analysis of cyberbullying research among youth. *Psychological Bulletin.* Advance Online Publication. http://dx.doi.org/10.1037/a0035618

Kramer, L. (2006, July 10). Commentary in "How your siblings make you who you are" by J. Kluger. *Time,* pp. 46-55.

Kramer, L., & Perozynski, L. (1999). Parental beliefs about managing sibling conflict. *Developmental Psychology, 35,* 489-499.

Kramer, L., & Radey, C. (1997). Improving sibling relationships among young children: A social skills training model. *Family Relations, 46,* 237-246.

Kramer, M. (2003). Commentary: Breastfeeding and child health, growth, and survival. *International Journal of Epidemiology, 32,* 96-98.

Krauss, R. A., & Glucksberg, S. (1969). The development of communication: Competence as a function of age. *Child Development, 40,* 255-266.

Kreutzer, L. C., & Flavell, J. H. (1975). An interview study of children's knowledge about memory. *Monographs of the Society for Research in Child Development, 40*(1), Serial No. 159.

Krimer, L. S., & Goldman-Rakic, P. S. (2001). Prefrontal microcircuits. *Journal of Neuroscience, 21,* 3788-3796.

Kroger, J., Martinussen, M., & Marcia, J. E. (2010, in press). Identity change during adolescence and young adulthood: A meta-analysis. *Journal of Adolescence.*

Kronenberg, G., & others. (2010). Impact of actin filament stabilization on adult hippocampal and olfactory bulb neurogenesis. *Journal of Neuroscience, 30,* 3419-3431.

Kruk, R. S., & Reynolds, K. A. A. (2012). French immersion experience and reading skill development in at-risk readers. Journal of Child Language, 39(3), 580-610.

Kuebli, J. (1994, March). Young children's understanding of everyday emotions. *Young Children,* pp. 36-48.

Kuehnle, K., & Connell, M. (2013). Child sexual abuse evaluations. In I. B. Weiner & others (Eds.), *Handbook of psychology* (2nd ed., Vol. 11). New York: Wiley.

Kuhl, P. K., & Damasio, A. (2012). Language. In E. R. Kandel & others (Eds.), *Principles of neural science* (5th ed.). New York: McGraw-Hill.

Kuhn, D. (1998). Afterword to Volume 2: Cognition, perception, and language. In W. Damon (Ed.), *Handbook of child psychology* (5th ed., Vol. 2). New York: Wiley.

Kuhn, D. (2008). Formal operations from a twenty-first century perspective. *Human Development, 51,* 48-55.

Kuhn, D. (2009). Adolescent thinking. In R. M. Lerner & L. Steinberg (Eds.), *Handbook of adolescent psychology* (3rd ed.). New York: Wiley.

Kuhn, D. (2011). What is scientific thinking and how does it develop? In U. Goswami (Ed.), *Wiley-Blackwell handbook of childhood cognitive development* (2nd ed.). New York: Wiley-Blackwell.

Kuhn, D. (2013). Reasoning. In P. D. Zelazo (Ed.), *Oxford handbook of developmental psychology.* New York: Oxford University Press.

Kuhn, D., Cheney, R., & Weinstock, M. (2000). The development of epistemological understanding. *Cognitive Development, 15,* 309-328.

Kuhn, D., & Franklin, S. (2006). The second decade: What develops (and how)? In W. Damon & R. Lerner (Eds.), *Handbook of child psychology* (6th ed.). New York: Wiley.

Kuhn, D., Schauble, L., & Garcia-Mila, M. (1992). Cross-domain development of scientific reasoning. *Cognition and Instruction, 9,* 285-327.

Kwak, H. K., Kim, M., Cho, B. H., & Ham, Y. M. (1999, April). *The relationship between children's temperament, maternal control strategies, and children's compliance.* Paper presented at the meeting of the Society for Research in Child Development, Albuquerque.

## L

Lacelle, C., Hebert, M., Lavoie, F., Vitaro, F., & Tremblay, R. E. (2012). Sexual health in women reporting a history of child sexual abuse. *Child Abuse and Neglect, 36,* 247-259.

Ladd, G., Buhs, E., & Troop, W. (2004). School adjustment and social skills training. In P. K. Smith & C. H. Hart (Eds.), *Blackwell handbook of childhood social development.* Malden, MA: Blackwell.

Ladd, G. W., Kochenderfer-Ladd, B., & Rydell, A-M. (2011). Children's interpersonal skills and school-based relationships. In P. K. Smith & C. H. Hart (Eds.), *Wiley-Blackwell handbook of social development* (2nd ed.). New York: Wiley.

LaFontana, K. M., & Cillessen, A. H. N. (2010). Developmental changes in the priority of perceived status in childhood and adolescence. *Social Development, 19,* 130-147.

Laghi, F. & others. (2013). Knowing when not to use the Internet: Shyness and adolescents' on-line and off-line interactions with friends. *Computers in Human Behavior, 29,* 51-57.

Lahey, B. B., Van Hulle, C. A., D'Onofrio, B. M., Roders, J. L., & Waldman, I. D. (2008). Is parental knowledge of their offspring's whereabouts and peer associations spuriously associated with offspring delinquency? *Journal of Abnormal Child Psychology, 36,* 807-823.

Laible, D., & Thompson, R. A. (2007). Early socialization: A relationship perspective. In J. E. Grusec & P. D. Hastings (eds.), *Handbook of socialization.* New York: Guilford.

Laird, R. D. Criss, M. M., Pettit, G. S., Dodge, K. A., & Bates, J. E. (2008). Parents' monitoring knowledge attenuates the link between antisocial friends and adolescent delinquent behavior. *Journal of Abnormal Child Psychology, 36,* 299-310.

Laird, R. D., & Marrero, M. D. (2011). Mothers' knowledge of early adolescents' activities following the middle school transition and pubertal maturation. *Journal of Early Adolescence, 31,* 209-233.

Lam, S., Jimerson, S., Kikas, E., Cefai, C., Veiga, F. H., & others. (2012). Do girls and boys perceive themselves as equally engaged in school? The results of an international study from 12 countries. *Journal of School Psychology, 50,* 77-94.

Lamb, M. E. (2010). How do fathers influence children's development? In M. E. Lamb (Ed.), *The role of the father in child development* (5th ed.). New York: Wiley.

Lamb, M. E. (2013a). Commentary: Early experience, neurobiology, plasticity, vulnerability, and resilience. In D. Narvaez & others (Eds.), *Evolution, early experience, and human development.* New York: Oxford University Press.

Lamb, M. E., Bornstein, M. H., & Teti, D. M. (2002). *Development in infancy* (4th ed.). Mahwah, NJ: Erlbaum.

Lamb, M. E., & Lewis, C. (2013). Father-child relationships. In C. S. Tamis-LeMonda & N. Cabrera (Eds.), *Handbook of father involvement* (2nd ed.). New York: Psychology Press.

Lamb, M. E., & Malloy, L. C. (2013). Child development and the law. In I. B. Weiner & others (Eds.), *Handbook of psychology* (2nd ed., Vol. 6). New York: Wiley.

Lamb, M. E., & Sternberg, K. J. (1992). Sociocultural perspectives in nonparental childcare. In M. E. Lamb, K. J. Sternberg, C. Hwang, & A. G. Broberg (Eds.), *Child care in context.* Hillsdale, NJ: Erlbaum.

Lambert, N. M., Fincham, F. D., & Stillman, T. F. (2012). Gratitude and depressive symptoms: The role of positive reframing and positive emotion. *Cognition and Emotion, 26,* 615-633.

Lampl, M. (2008). Physical growth. In M. M. Hath & J. B. Benson (Eds.), *Encyclopedia of infant and early childhood development.* Oxford, UK: Elsevier.

Landa, S. (2000, Fall). If you can't make waves, make ripples. *Intelligence Connections Newsletter of the ASCD. X*(1), 6-8.

Landau, B., Smith, L., & Jones, S. (1998). Object perception and object naming in early development. *Trends in Cognitive Science, 2,* 19-24.

Lane, H. (1976). *The wild boy of Aveyron.* Cambridge, MA: Harvard University Press.

Langer, E. J. (2005). *On becoming an artist.* New York: Ballantine.

Langlois, K. A., Samokhvalov, A. V., Rehm, J., Spence, S. T., Connor Gorber, S. (2011). Health state descriptions for Canadians: Mental illnesses. Statistics Canada, catalogue no. 82-619-MIE2005002. Ottawa: Statistics Canada.

Lansford, J. E. (2009). Parental divorce and children's adjustment. *Perspectives on Psychological Science, 4,* 140-152.

Lansford, J. E. (2012). Divorce. In R. J. R. Levesque (Ed.), *Encyclopedia of adolescence.* New York: Springer.

Lansford, J. E., & Deater-Deckard, K. (2012, in press). Childrearing discipline and violence in developing countries. *Child Development.*

Lansford, J. E., & others. (2005). Cultural normativeness as a moderator of the link between physical discipline and children's adjustment: A comparison of China, India, Italy, Kenya, Philippines, and Thailand. *Child Development, 76,* 1234-1246.

Lansford, J. E., & others. (2011). Reciprocal relations between parents' physical discipline and children's externalizing behavior during middle childhood and adolescence. *Development and Psychopathology, 23,* 225-238.

Lansford, J. E., Wager, L. B., Bates, J. E., Pettit, G. S., & Dodge, K. A. (2013 in press). Forms of spanking and children's externalizing problems. *Family Relations.*

Laopaiboon, M., & others. (2009). Music during caesarean section under regional anaesthesia for improving maternal and infant outcomes. *Cochrane Database of Systematic Reviews,* CD006914.

Laplante, D. P., Barr, R. G., Brunet, A., & others. (2004). Stress during pregnancy affects general intellectual and language functioning in human toddlers, *Pediatric Research,* Vol. 56, no. 3, 400-410.

Laplante, D. P., Brunet, A., Schmitz, N., Ciampi, A., and King, S. (2008). Project ice storm: Prenatal maternal stress affects cognitive and linguistic functioning in 5 ½-year-old children, *Journal of the American Academy of Child and Adolescent Psychiatry,* Vol. 47, no. 9, 1063-1072.

Lapsley, D. K., & Hill, P. L. (2010). Subjective invulnerability, optimism bias, and adjustment in emerging adulthood. *Journal of Youth and Adolescence, 39,* 847-857.

Lapsley, D. K., & Stey, P. (2012). Adolescent narcissism. In R. Levesque (Ed.), *Encyclopedia of adolescence.* New York: Springer.

La Rochelle-Cote, S., Gougeon, S., & Pinard, D. (2009). Changes in parental work time and earnings. *Perspectives on Labour and Income, 10,* 5-16.

La Rooy, D. J., Brown, D., & Lamb, M. E. (2013). Suggestibility and witness interviewing. In A. Ridley, F. Gabber, & D. J. La Rooy (Eds.), *Investigative suggestibility.* New York: Wiley.

Larson, R. W., Wilson, Z., & Rickman, A. (2009). Globalization, societal change, and adolescence across the world. In R. M. Lerner & L. Steinberg (Eds.), *Handbook of adolescent psychology* (3rd ed.). New York: Wiley.

Larzelere, R. E., & Kuhn, B. R. (2005). Comparing child outcomes of physical punishment and alternative disciplinary tactics: a meta-analysis. *Clinical Child and Family Psychology Review, 8,* 1-37.

Laslett, A. M., Room, R., Dietze, P., & Ferris, J. (2012, in press). Alcohol's involvement in recurrent child abuse and neglect cases. *Addiction.*

Lauer, R. H., & Lauer, J. C. (2012). *Marriage and family* (8th ed.). New York: McGraw-Hill.

Laursen, B., & Collins, W. A. (2009). Parent-child relationships during adolescence. In R. M. Lerner & L. Steinberg (Eds.), *Handbook of adolescent psychology* (3rd ed.). New York: Wiley.

Laursen, B., & Pursell, G. (2009). Conflict in peer relationships. In K. H. Rubin, W. M. Bukowski, & B. Laursen (Eds.), *Handbook of peer interaction, relationships, and groups.* New York: Guilford.

Lawrence, J. M., Contreras, R., Chen, W., & Sacks, D. A. (2008). Trends in the prevalence of preexisting diabetes and gestational diabetes mellitus among a racially/ethnically diverse population of pregnant women, 1999-2005. *Diabetes Care, 31,* 899-904.

Leadbeater, B. & Sukhawathanakul, P. (2011). Multicomponent programs for reducing peer victimization in early elementary school: A longitudinal evaluation of the WITS primary program. *Journal of Community Psychology, 39*(5), 606-620.

Leach, P. (1990). *Your baby and child: From birth to age five.* New York: Knopf.

Leaper, C. (2013). Gender development during childhood. In P. D. Zelazo (Ed.), *Oxford handbook of developmental psychology.* New York: Oxford University Press.

Leaper, C., & Bigler, R. S (2004). Commentary. Gender language and sexist thought. *Monographs of the Society for Research in Child Development, 69* (1, Serial No. 275), 128-142.

Leaper, C., & Friedman, C. K. (2007). The socialization of gender. In J. E. Grusec & P. D. Hastings (Eds.), *Handbook of socialization.* New York: Guilford.

Lee, H. C., El-Sayed, Y. Y., & Gould, J. B. (2008). Population trends in cesarean delivery for breech presentation in the United States, 1997-2003. *American Journal of Obstetrics and Gynecology, 199,* e1-e8.

Lee, J. W., & Hebert, Y. M. (2006). The meaning of being Canadian: A comparison between youth of immigrant and non-immigrant origins. *Canadian Journal of Education, 29,* 497-520.

Lee, K., Bull, R., & Ringo, M. H. (2013). Developmental Changes in Executive Functioning. *Child Development,* November/December 2013, Volume 84, Number 6, 1933-1953

Lee, K., Cameron, C. A., Doucette, J., & Talwar, V. (2002). Phantoms and fabrications: Young children's detection of implausible lies. *Child Development, 73,* 1688-1702.

Lee, K., Cameron, C.A., Xu, F., Fu, G., & Board, J. (1997). Chinese and Canadian children's evaluations of lying and truth telling: Similarities and differences in the context of pro- and antisocial behaviors. *Child Development, 68,* 924-934.

Lee, K., Quinn, P. C., Pascalis, O., & Slater, A. (2013). Development of face processing ability in childhood. In P. D. Zelazo (Ed.), *Oxford handbook of developmental psychology.* Oxford, UK: Oxford University Press.

Lee, K. C., Shults, R. A., Greenspan, A. I., Haileyesus, T., & Dellinger, A. M. (2008). Child passenger restraint use and emergency department-reported injuries: A special study using the National Electronic Injury Surveillance System—All Injury Program, 2004. *Journal of Safety Research, 39,* 25-31.

Lee, S. J., & Wong, A. N. (2009). The model minority and the perceptual foreigner: Stereotypes of Asian Americans. In N. Tewari & A. Alvaraez (Eds.), *Asian American psychology.* Clifton, NJ: Psychology Press.

Lee, T.-W., Wu, Y-T., Yu, Y., Wu, H-C., & Chen, T-J. (2012). A smarter brain is associated with stronger neural interaction in healthy young females: A resting EEG coherence study. *Intelligence, 40,* 38-48.

Lee, Y. S., Turkeltaub, P., Granger, R., & Raizada, R. D. (2012). Categorical speech processing in Broca's area: An fMRI study using multivariate pattern-based analysis. *Journal of Neuroscience, 32,* 3942-3948.

Leedy, P. D., & Ormrod, J. E. (2010). *Practical research* (9th ed.). Upper Saddle River, NJ: Prentice Hall.

Leerkes, E. M., Parade, S. H., & Gudmundson, J. A. (2011). Mothers' emotional reactions to crying pose risk for subsequent attachment insecurity. *Journal of Family Psychology, 25,* 635-643.

LeFevre, J., Berrigana, L., Vendettia, C., Kamawara, D., Bisanz, J., Skwarchukd, S., & Smith-Chante, B. L. (2013). The role of executive attention in the acquisition of mathematical skills for children in grades 2 through 4. *Journal of Experimental Child Psychology, 114,* 243-261.

Leger, D., Beck, F., Richard, J. B., & Godeau, E. (2012). Total sleep time severely drops in adolescence. *PLoS One, 7*(10), e45204.

Legerstee, M. (1997). Contingency effects of people and objects on subsequent cognitive functioning in 3-month-old infants. *Social Development, 6,* 307-321.

Lehr, C. A., Hanson, A., Sinclair, M. F., & Christensen, S. I. (2003). Moving beyond dropout prevention towards school completion. *School Psychology Review, 32,* 342-364.

Lehrer, R., & Schauble, L. (2006). Scientific thinking and scientific literacy. In W. Damon & R. Lerner (Eds.), *Handbook of child psychology* (6th ed.). New York: Wiley.

Leifer, A. D. (1973). *Television and the development of social behavior.* Paper presented at the meeting of the International Society for the Study of Behavioral Development. Ann Arbor, Michigan.

Leman, P. J., Ahmed, S., & Ozarow, L. (2005). Gender, gender relations, and the social dynamics of children's conversations. *Developmental Psychology, 41,* 64-74.

Lemaire, P., & Lecacheur, M. (2011). Age-related changes in children's executive functions and strategy selection: A study in computational estimation. *Cognitive Development, 26,* 282-294.

LeMare, L. J., & Rubin, K. H. (1987). Perspective taking and peer interaction: Structural and developmental analyses. *Child Development, 58,* 306-315.

Lempers, J. D., Flavell, E. R., & Flavell, J. H. (1977). The development in very young children of tacit knowledge concerning visual perception. *Genetic Psychology Monographs, 95,* 3-53.

Lenhart, A., Purcel, K., Smith, A., & Zickuhr, K. (2010, Feb. 3). *Social media and mobile Internet use among teens and young adults.* Washington, DC: Pew Research Center.

Lenneberg, E. (1967). *The biological foundation of language.* New York: Wiley.

Lennon, E. M., Gardner, J. M., Karmel, B. Z., & Flory, M. J. (2008). Bayley Scales of Infant Development. In M. M. Haith & J. B. Benson (Eds.), *Encyclopedia of Infant and early childhood development.* Oxford, UK: Elsevier.

Lenoir, C. P., Mallet, E., & Calenda, E. (2000). Siblings of sudden infant death syndrome and near miss in about 30 families: Is there a genetic link? *Medical Hypotheses, 54,* 408-411.

Lenroot, R. K., & Giedd, J. N. (2011). Annual research review: Developmental considerations of gene by environment interactions. *Journal of Child and Adolescent Psychiatry, 52,* 429-441.

Lenzi, T. A., & Johnson, T. R. B. (2008). Screening. prenatal. In M. M. Haith & J. B. Benson (Eds.), *Encyclopedia of infant and early childhood development.* Oxford, UK: Elsevier.

Leonardi-Bee, J. A., Smyth, A. R., Britton, J., & Coleman. T. (2008). Environmental tobacco smoke on fetal health: Systematic review and analysis. *Archives of Disease in Childhood. Fetal and Neonatal Edition, 93,* F351-F361.

Leong, F. T. L., & others. (2013). Ethnic minority psychology. In I. B. Weiner & others (Eds.), *Handbook of psychology* (2nd ed., Vol. 1). New York: Wiley.

Leon-Guerrero, A. (2009). *Social problems* (2nd ed.). Thousand Oaks, CA: Sage.

Lepage, J. & Corbeil, J. (2013). Insights on Canadian Society: The evolution of English-French bilingualism in Canada from 1961 to 2011. Statistics Canada (catalogue no. 75-006-X). Ottawa: Statistics Canada.

Leppanen, J. M., Moulson, M., Vogel-Farley, V. K., & Nelson, C. A. (2007). An ERP study of emotional face processing in the adult and infant brain. *Child Development, 78,* 232-245.

Lepper, M. R., Corpus, J. H., & Iyengar, S. S. (2005). Intrinsic and extrinsic orientations in the classroom: Age differences and academic correlates. *Journal of Educational Psychology, 97,* 184-196.

Lerch, C., Cordes, M., & Baumeister, J. (2011). Effectiveness of prevention programs in female youth soccer: A systematic review. *British Journal of Sports Medicine, 45,* 359.

Lerner, J. W., & Johns, B. (2012). *Learning disabilities and related mild disabilities* (12th ed.). Boston: Cengage.

Lerner, R. M., Boyd, M., & Du, D. (2009). Adolescent development. In I. B. Weiner & C. B. Craighead (Eds.), *Encyclopedia of psychology* (4th ed.). Hoboken, NJ: Wiley.

Lessow-Hurley, J. (2009). *The foundation of dual language instruction* (5th ed.). Boston: Allyn & Bacon.

Lester, B. M., Tronick, E. Z., & Brazelton, T. B. (2004). The Neonatal Intensive Care Unit Network Neurobehavioral Scale procedures. *Pediatrics, 113,* Suppl, S641-S667.

Lester, B. M., & others. (2002). The maternal lifestyle study: Effects of substance exposure during pregnancy on neurodevelopmental outcome in 1-month-old infants. *Pediatrics, 110,* 1182-1192.

Letourneau, N., & others. (2012). Support intervention needs and preferences for fathers affected by postpartum depression. *Journal of Perinatal and Neonatal Nursing, 26,* 69-80.

Letourneau, N., Duffett-Leger, L., Dennis, C-L., Stewart, M., & Tryphonopoulos, P. D. (2011). Identifying the support needs of fathers affected by post-partum depression: a pilot study. *Journal of Psychiatric and Mental Health Nursing, 2011, 18,* 41-47.

LeVay, S. (1994). The sexual brain. Cambridge, MA: MIT Press.

Levene, M. I., & Chervenak, F. A. (2009). *Fetal and neonatal neurology and neurosurgery* (4th ed.). London: Elsevier.

Leventhal, J., Dupere, V., & Brooks-Gunn, J. (2009). Neighborhood influences on adolescent development. In R. M. Lerner & L. Steinberg (Eds.), *Handbook of adolescent psychology* (3rd ed.). New York: Wiley.

Leventhal, J. M., Murphy, J. L., & Asnes, A. G. (2010). Evaluations of child sexual abuse: Recognition of overt and latent family concerns. *Child Abuse and Neglect, 34*(5), 289-295.

Levine, L. N., & McCloskey, M. L. (2009). *Teaching learners of English in mainstream classrooms (K-8).* Boston: Allyn & Bacon.

Levine, M., & O'Connor, A. D. (2012). Obstetric toxicology: An overview. *Emergency Medicine Clinics of North America, 30,* 977-990.

Levine, T. P., & others. (2008). Effects of prenatal cocaine exposure on special education in school-aged children. *Pediatrics, 122,* e83-e91.

Levinson, P. (2013). *New media* (2nd ed.). Upper Saddle River, NJ: Pearson.

Levy, G. D., Sadovsky, A. L., & Troseth, G. L. (2000). Aspects of young children's perceptions of gender-typed occupations. *Sex Roles, 42,* 993-1006.

Lewald, J. (2012). Exceptional ability of blind humans to hear sound motion: Implications for the emergence of auditory space. *Neuropsychologia, 51,* 181-186.

Lewinsohn, P. M., Olino, T. M., & Klein, D. N. (2005). Psychosocial impairment in offspring of depressed parents. *Psychological Medicine, 35,* 1493-1503.

Lewis, M. (2005). Selfhood. In B. Hopkins (Ed.), *The Cambridge encyclopedia of child development.* Cambridge, UK: Cambridge University Press.

Lewis, M. (2007). Early emotional development. In A. Slater & M. Lewis (Eds.), *Introduction to infant development.* Malden, MA: Blackwell.

Lewis, M. (2008). The emergence of human emotions. In M. Lewis, J. M. Haviland Jones, & L. Feldman Barrett (Eds.), *Handbook of emotions* (3rd ed.). New York: Guilford.

Lewis, M. (2010). The emergence of consciousness and its role in human development. In W. F. Overton & R. M. Lerner (Eds.), *Handbook of life-span development.* New York: Wiley.

Lewis, M., & Brooks-Gunn, J. (1979). *Social cognition and the acquisition of the self.* New York: Plenum.

Lewis, M., Feiring, C. & Rosenthal, S. (2000). Attachment over time. *Child Development, 71,* 707-20.

Lewis, M., Sullivan, M. W., Sanger, C., & Weiss, M. (1989). Self-development and self-conscious emotions. *Child Development, 60,* 146-156.

Lewis, M. D., Todd, R., & Xu, X. (2011). The development of emotion regulation: A neuropsychological perspective. In R. M. Lerner, W. F. Overton, A. M. Freund, & M. E. Lamb (Eds.), *Handbook of life-span development.* New York: Wiley.

Lewis, R. (2010). *Human genetics* (9th ed.). New York: McGraw-Hill.

Lewis, T. L., & Maurer, D. (2005). Multiple sensitive periods in human visual development: Evidence from visually deprived children. *Developmental Psychology, 46,* 163-183.

Lewis, T. L., & Maurer, D. (2009). Effects of early pattern deprivation on visual development. *Optometry and Vision Science, 86,* 640-646.

Li, B. J., Jiang, Y. J., Yuan, F., & Ye, H. X. (2010). Exchange transfusion of least incompatible blood for severe hemolytic disease of the newborn due to anti-Rh17. *Transfusion Medicine, 20,* 66-69.

Li, D., Zhang, W., Li, X., Li, N., & Ye, B. (2012). Gratitude and suicidal ideation and suicide attempts among Chinese adolescents: Direct, mediated, and moderated effects. *Journal of Adolescence, 35,* 55-66.

Li, J. (2009). Forging the future between two different worlds: Recent Chinese immigrant adolescents tell their cross-cultural experiences. *Journal of Adolescent Research, 24,* 477-504.

Li, J. (2010). 'My home and my school': Examining immigrant adolescent narratives from the critical sociocultural perspective. *Race, Ethnicity, and Education, 13,* 119-137.

Li, J., Olsen, J., Vestergaard, M., & Obel, C. (2011). Low Apgar scores and risk of childhood attention deficit hyperactivity disorder. *Journal of Pediatrics, 158,* 775-779.

Li, L., Law, C., Lo Conte, R., & Power, C. (2009). Intergenerational influences on childhood body mass index: The effect of parental body mass index trajectories. *American Journal of Clinical Nutrition, 89,* 551-557.

Li, P. (2009). What's in a lexical system? Discovering meaning through an interactive eye. In V. C. M. Gathercole (Ed.), *Routes to language: Essays in honor of Melissa Bowerman.* New York: Psychology Press.

Libertus, K., & Needham, A. (2011). Teach to reach: The effects of active versus passive reaching experiences on action and perception. *Vision Research, 50,* 2750-2757.

Lie, E., & Newcombe, N. (1999) Elementary school children's explicit and implicit memory for faces of preschool classmates. *Developmental Psychology, 35,* 102-112.

Lieberman, E., Davidson, K., Lee-Parritz, A., & Shearer, E. (2005). Changes in fetal position during labor and their association with epidural analgesia. *Obstetrics and Gynecology, 105,* 974-982.

Liegeois, F., Connelly, A., Baldeweg, T., & Vargha-Khadem, F. (2008). Speaking with a single cerebral hemisphere: IMRI language organization after hemispherectomy in childhood. *Brain and Language, 106,* 195-203.

Likis, F. E., & others. (2012). Progestogens for preterm birth prevention: A systematic review and meta-analysis. *Obestetrics and Gynecology, 120,* 897-907.

Lillard, A. (2007). Pretend play in toddlers. In C. A. Brownell & C. B. Kopp (Eds.), *Socioemotional development in the toddler years.* New York: Guilford.

Lillard, A. (2008). How important are Montessori materials? *Montessori Life, 20*(4), 20-25.

Lillard, A. S., Lerner, M. D., Hopkins, E. J., Dore, R. A., Smith, E. D., & Palmquist, C. M. (2013). The impact of pretend play on children's development: A review of the evidence. *Psychological Bulletin, 139,* 1-34.

Lima, J. J., Blake, K. V., Tantisira K. G., & Weiss, S. T. (2009). Pharmacogenetics of asthma. *Current Opinion in Pulmonary Medicine, 15,* 57-62.

Lin, M., Johnson, J. E., & Johnson, K. M. (2003). Dramatic play in Montessori kindergartens in Taiwan and Mainland China. Unpublished manuscript. Department of Curriculum and Instruction, Pennsylvania State University, University Park, PA.

Lincoln, A. J., Searcy, Y. M., Jones, W., & Lord, C. (2007). Social interaction behaviors discriminate young children with autism and Williams syndrome. *Journal of the American Academy of Child and Adolescent Psychiatry, 46,* 323-331.

Lindblad, F., & Hjern, A. (2010). ADHD after fetal exposure to maternal smoking. *Nicotine and Tobacco Research, 12,* 408-415.

Lindsey, E. W., & Colwell, M. J. (2013). Pretend and physical play: Links to preschoolers' affective social competence. *Merrill-Palmer Quarterly, 59,* 330-360.

Lippa, R. A. (2005). *Gender, nature, and nurture* (2nd ed.). Mahwah, NJ: Erlbaum.

Lipton, J., & Spelke, E. (2004). Discrimination of large and small numerosities by human infants. *Infancy, 5,* 271-290.

Liszkowski, U. (2007, March). *A new look at infant pointing.* Paper presented at the meeting of the Society for Research in Child Development, Boston.

Liu, C. H., Murakami, J., Eap, S., & Nagayama Hall, G. C. (2009). Who are Asian Americans? An overview of history, immigration, and communities. In N. Tewari & A. Alvarez (Eds.), *Asian American psychology.* Clifton, NJ: Psychology Press.

Liu, J., & others. (2010). Neonatal neurobehavior predicts medical and behavioral outcome. *Pediatrics, 125*(1), e90-e98.

Liu, J., Hay, J., Faught, B. E., Wade, T., Cairney, J., Merchant, A. T., Trevisan, M. (2012). Family eating and activity habits, diet quality and preadolescent overweight and obesity. *Public Health, 126,* 532-534.

Liu, S., & others. (2011). Similarity and difference in the processing of same- and other-race faces as revealed by eye-tracking in 4- to 9-month-old infants. *Journal of Experimental Child Psychology, 108,* 180-189.

Liu, T., Shi, I, Zhang, Q., Zhao, D., & Yang, J. (2007). Neural mechanisms of auditory sensory processing in children with high intelligence. *Neuroreport, 18*(15), 1571-1575.

Liu, W. M., & Hernandez, J. (2008). Social class and classism. In N. J. Salkind (Eds.), *Encyclopedia of educational psychology.* Thousand Oaks, CA: Sage.

Livas-Dlott, A. Fuller, B., Stein, G. L., Bridges, M., Figueroa, A. M., & Mireles, L. (2010). Commands, competence, and

*Carino:* Maternal socialization processes in Mexican American families. *Developmental Psychology, 46,* 566–578.

Lively, W., & Bromley, D. (1973). *Person perception in childhood and adolescence.* New York: Wiley.

Locascio, G., Mahone, E. M., Eason, S., & Cutting, L. (2010). Executive dysfunction among children with reading comprehension deficits. *Journal of Learning Disabilities.*

Lockyer, J. E., Robichaud, E., Lowther, L., & Chiasson, P. (2012). Report of the French Second Language Task Force, Government of New Brunswick.

Loeber, R., Burke, J., & Pardini, D. (2009). The etiology and development of antisocial and delinquent behavior. *Annual Review of Psychology* (Vol. 60). Palo Alto, CA: Annual Reviews.

Loeber, R., Farrington, D. P., Stouthamer-Loeber, M., & White, H. R. (2008). *Violence and serious theft: Development and predictions from childhood to adulthood.* New York: Routledge.

Loeber, R., Pardini, D. A., Stouthamer-Loeber, M., & Raine, A. (2007). Do cognitive, physiological, and psychosocial risk and promotive factors predict desistance from delinquency in males? *Development and Psychopathology, 19,* 867–887.

Loehlin, J. C. (2010). Is there an active gene-environment correlation in adolescent drinking behavior? *Behavior Genetics.* (Available online March 9, 2010.)

Loehlin, J. C., Horn, J. M., & Ernst, J. L. (2007). Genetic and environmental influences on adult life outcomes: Evidence from the Texas adoption project. *Behavior Genetics, 37,* 463–476.

Logsdon, M. C., Wisner, K., & Hanusa, B. H. (2009). Does maternal role functioning improve with antidepressant treatment in women with postpartum depression? *Journal of Women's Health, 18,* 85–90.

London, M. L., & others. (2011). *Maternal and child nursing care* (3rd ed.). Upper Saddle River, NJ: Pearson.

Loosli, S. V., Buschkuehl, M., Perrig, W. J., & Jaeggi, S. M. (2012). Working memory training improves reading processes in typically developing children. *Child Neuropsychology, 18,* 62–78.

Loprinzi, P. D., Cardinal, B. J., Loprinzi, K. L., & Lee, H. (2012). Parenting practices as mediators of child physical activity and weight status. *Obesity Facts, 5,* 420–430.

Lorenz, K. Z. (1965). *Evolution and the modification of behavior.* Chicago: University of Chicago Press.

Loukas, A., Roalson, L. A., & Herrera, D. E. (2010). School connectedness buffers the effects of negative family relations and poor effortful control on early adolescent conduct problems. *Journal of Research on Adolescence, 20,* 13–22.

Lovett, M. R., Barron, R. W., & Frijters, J. C. (2013). Word identification difficulties in children and adolescents with learning disabilities: Intervention research findings. In H. L. Swanson & others (Eds.), *Handbook of learning disabilities* (2nd ed.). New York: Guilford.

Low, J., & Simpson, S. (2012). Effects of labeling on preschoolers' explicit false belief performance: Outcomes of cognitive flexibility or inhibitory control? *Child Development, 83,* 1072–1084.

Low, S., Snyder, J., & Shortt, J. W. (2012). The drift toward problem behavior during the transition to adolescence: The contributions of youth disclosure, parenting, and older siblings. *Journal of Research on Adolescence, 22,* 65–79.

Lowdermilk, D. L., Perry, S. E., & Cashion, M. C. (2010). *Maternity and women's health care.* (10th ed.). Philadelphia, PA: F. A. Davis Company.

Lowe, J. R., & others. (2012). Association of maternal interaction with emotional regulation in 4- and 9-month-old infants during the Still Face Paradigm. *Infant Behavior and Development, 35,* 295–302.

Lozoff, B., & others. (2007). Preschool-aged children with iron deficiency anemia show altered affect and behavior. *Journal of Nutrition, 137,* 683–689.

Lubinski, D. (2000). Measures of intelligence: Intelligence tests. In A. Kazdin (Ed.), *Encyclopedia of psychology.* Washington, DC, & New York: American Psychological Association and Oxford University Press.

Lucas, P. J., McIntosh, K., Petticrew, M., Roberts, H., & Shiell, A. (2008). Financial benefits for child health and well-being in low income or socially disadvantaged families in developed world countries. *Cochrane Database of Systematic Reviews, 16.* CD006358.

Luders, E., & others. (2004). Gender differences in cortical complexity. *Nature Neuroscience, 7,* 799–800.

Luders, E., Narr, K. L., Thompson, P. M., & Toga, A. W. (2009). Neuroanatomical correlates of intelligence. *Intelligence, 37,* 156–163.

Luijk, M. P., & others. (2011). Dopaminergic, serotonergic, and oxytonegic candidate genes associated with infant attachment security and disorganization? In search of main and interaction effects. *Journal of Child Psychology and Psychiatry, 52,* 1295–1307.

Lumeng, J. C., & others. (2012). Observed assertive and intrusive maternal feeding behaviors increase child adiposity. *American Journal of Clinical Nutrition, 95,* 640–647.

Lumpkin, A. (2011). *Introduction to physical education, exercise science, and sports studies* (8th ed.). New York: McGraw-Hill.

Lunkenheimer, E. S., Shields, A. M., & Cortina, K. S. (2007). Parental coaching and dismissing of children's emotions in family interaction. *Social Development, 16,* 232–248.

Luo, Y., & Baillargeon, R. (2010). Toward a mentalistic account of early psychological reasoning. *Current Directions in Psychological Science, 19,* 301–307.

Luo, Y., Kaufman, L., & Baillargeon, R. (2009). Young infants' reasoning about events involving inert and self-propelled objects. *Cognitive Psychology, 58,* 441–486.

Lupart, J. L., Cannon, E., & Telfer, J. (2004). Gender differences in adolescent academic achievement, interests, values and life-role expectations. *High Ability Studies, 15*(1), 25–42.

Luria, A., & Herzog, E. (1985, April). *Gender segregation across and within settings.* Paper presented at the biennial meeting of the Society for Research in Child Development, Toronto.

Luszcz, M. (2013). Executive functioning and cognitive aging. In K. W. Schaie & S. L. Willis (Eds.), *Handbook of the psychology of aging* (8th ed.). New York: Elsevier.

Luthar, S. S. (2006). Resilience in development: A synthesis of research across five decades. In D. Cicchetti & D. J. Cohen (Eds.), *Developmental psychopathology: Vol 3. Risk, disorder, and adaptation* (2nd ed.). Hoboken, NJ: Wiley.

Luthar. S. S., & Goldstein. A. S. (2008). Substance use and related behaviors among suburban late adolescents: The importance of perceived parent containment. *Development and Psychopathology, 20,* 591–614.

Lyberg, A., Viken, B., Haruna, M., & Severinsson, E. (2012). Diversity and challenges in the management of maternity care for immigrant women. *Journal of Nursing Management, 20,* 287–295.

Lykken, D. (2001). *Happiness: What studies on twins show us about nature, nurture, and the happiness set point.* New York: Golden Books.

Lynch, J. (2002). Parents' self-efficacy beliefs, parents' gender, children's reader self-perceptions, reading achievement and gender. *Journal of Research in Reading, 25*(1), 54–67.

Lynn, R. (1996). Racial and ethnic differences in intelligence in the U.S. on the Differential Ability Scale. *Personality and Individual Differences. 26,* 271-273.

Lynn, R. (2009). What caused the Flynn effect? Secular increases in the development quotients of infants. *Intelligence, 37,* 16-24.

Lyon, T. D., & Flavell, J. H. (1993). Young children's understanding of forgetting over time. *Child Development, 64,* 789-800.

# M

MacArthur, C. A. (2012). Strategies instruction. In K. R. Harris, S. Graham, & T. Urdan (Eds.), *Handbook of educational psychology.* Washington, DC: American Psychological Association.

Maccoby, E. E. (1984). Middle childhood in the context of the family. In W. A. Collins (Ed.), *Development during middle childhood.* Washington, DC: National Academy Press.

Maccoby, E. E. (1996). Peer conflict and intra-family conflict: Are there conceptual bridges? *Merrill-Palmer Quarterly, 42,* 165-176.

Maccoby, E. E. (2002). Gender and group process: A developmental perspective. *Current Directions in Psychological Science, 11,* 54-57.

Maccoby, E. E. (2007). Historical overview of socialization research and theory. In J. E. Grusec & P. D. Hastings (Eds.), *Handbook of socialization.* New York: Guilford.

Maccoby, E. E., & Martin, J. A. (1983). Socialization in the context of the family: Parent-child interaction. In P. H. Mussen (Ed.), *Handbook of child psychology* (4th ed., Vol. 4). New York: Wiley.

Maccoby, E. E., & Mnookin, R. H. (1992). *Dividing the child: Social and legal dilemmas of custody.* Cambridge, MA: Harvard University Press.

MacFarlane, J. A. (1975). Olfaction in the development of social preferences in the human neonate. In *Parent-infant interaction.* Ciba Foundation Symposium No. 33. Amsterdam: Elsevier.

MacGeorge, E. L. (2004). The myth of gender cultures: Similarities outweigh differences in men's and women's provisions of and responses to supportive communication. *Sex Roles, 50,* 143-175.

MacMillan, H. L., Tanaka, M., Duku, E., Vaillancourt, T., & Boyle, M. H. (2013). Child physical and sexual abuse in a community sample of young adults: Results from the Ontario Child Health Study. *Child Abuse & Neglect, 37,* 14-21.

MacMillan, K.M., & Violato, C. (2008). Pathways to competence: Parental adversity and the roles of parenting quality and social support. *The Journal of Psychology, 142*(4), 427-443.

Mader, S. S. (2012). *Inquiry into life* (13th ed.). New York: McGraw-Hill.

Madsen, S. D., & Collins, W. A. (2011). The salience of romantic experiences for romantic relationship qualities in young adulthood. *Journal of Research on Adolescence, 21*(4), 789-801.

Maehr, M. L., & Zusho, A. (2009). Goal-directed behavior in the classroom. In K. Wentzel & A. Wigfield (Eds.), *Handbook of motivation at school.* New York: Routledge.

Mael, F. A. (1998). Single-sex and coeducational schooling: Relationships to socioemotional and academic development. *Review of Educational Research, 68*(2), 101-129.

Magno, C. (2010). The role of metacognitive skills in developing critical thinking. *Metacognition and Learning, 5,* 137-156.

Mahn, H., & John-Steiner, V. (2013). Vygotsky and sociocultural approaches to teaching and learning. In I. B. Weiner & others (Eds.), *Handbook of psychology* (2nd ed., Vol. 7). New York: Wiley.

Malamitsi-Puchner, A., & Boutsikou, T. (2006). Adolescent pregnancy and perinatal outcome. *Pediatric Endocrinology Reviews, 3,* Suppl. 1, 170-171.

Malatesta-Muncher, R., & Mitsnefes, M. M. (2012). Management of blood pressure in children. *Current Opinion in Nephrology and Hypertension, 21,* 318-322.

Malik, N. M., & Furman, W. (1993). Practitioner review: Problems in children's peer relations: What can the clinician do? *Journal of Child Psychology and Psychiatry, 34,* 1303-1326.

Malizia, B. A., Hacker, M. R., & Penzias, A. S. (2009). Cumulative live-birth rates after in vitro fertilization. *New England Journal of Medicine, 360,* 236-243.

Malloy, L. C., La Rooy, D. J., Lamb, M. A., & Katz, C. (2012). Developmentally sensitive interviewing for legal purposes. In M. E. Lamb, D. J. La Rooy, L. C. Malloy, & C. Katz (Eds.), *Children's testimony* (2nd ed.). New York: Wiley.

Maloy, R. W., & others. (2014). *Transforming learning with new technologies* (2nd ed.). Upper Saddle River, NJ: Pearson.

Maltais, C., Herry, Y., Emond, I., & Mougeot, C. (2011). Synthese D'une etude longitudinale portant sur les effets d'un programme de maternelle 4 ans a temps plein. *International Journal of Early Childhood, 43*(1), 67-85.

Malti, T., & Buchmann, M. (2010). Socialization and individual antecedents of adolescents' and young adults' moral motivation. *Journal of Youth and Adolescence, 39,* 138-149.

Mandler, J. (2000). Unpublished review of J. W. Santrock's *Life-Span Development,* (8th ed.). New York: McGraw-Hill.

Mandler, J. M. (2004). *The foundations of mind.* New York: Oxford University Press.

Mandler, J. M. (2009). Conceptual categorization. In D. H. Rakison & L. M. Oakes (Eds.), *Early category and concept development.* New York: Oxford University Press.

Mandler, J. M. (2010). Jean Mandler. Retrieved May 26, 2010 from www.cogsci.ucsd.edu/~jean/

Mandler, J. M., & McDonough, L. (1993). Concept formation in infancy. *Cognitive Development, 8,* 291-318.

Manning, M. L., & Baruth, L. G. (2009). *Multicultural education of children and adolescents* (5th ed.). Boston: Allyn & Bacon.

Mak, K. K., Lee, S. L., Ho, S. Y., Lo, W. S., & Lam, T. H. (2012). Sleep and academic performance in Hong Kong adolescents. *Journal of School Health, 82,* 522-527.

Marcdante, K., Kliegman, R. M., & Behrman, R. E. (2011). *Nelson's essentials of pediatrics* (6th ed.). Philadelphia: W. B. Saunders.

Marcia, J. E. (1980). Ego identity development. In J. Adelson (Ed.), *Handbook of adolescent psychology.* New York: Wiley.

Marcia, J. E. (1987). The identity status approach to the study of ego identity development. In T. Honess & K. Yardley (Eds.), *Self and identity: Perspectives across the lifespan.* London: Routledge & Kegan Paul.

Marcia, J. E. (1994). The empirical study of ego identity. In H. A. Bosma, T. L. G. Graafsma, H. D. Grotevant, & D. J. DeLevita (Eds.), *Identity and development.* Newbury Park, CA: Sage.

Marcia, J. E. (1996). Unpublished review of J. W. Santrock's *Adolescence,* (7th ed.). Dubuque, IA: Brown & Benchmark.

Marcia, J. E. (2002). Identity and psychosocial development in adulthood. *Identity, 2,* 7-28.

Marengo, L., Farag, N. H., & Canfield, M. (2013, in press). Body mass index and birth defects: Texas, 2005-2008. *Maternal and Child Health Journal.*

Markant, J. C., & Thomas, K. M. (2013). Postnatal brain development. In P. D. Zelazo (Ed.), *Handbook of developmental psychology.* New York: Wiley.

Marks, A. K., Patton, F., & Garcia Coll, C. (2011). Being bicultural: A mixed-methods study of adolescents' implicitly and explicitly measured ethnic identities. *Developmental Psychology, 47,* 270-288.

Markus, H. R., & Kitayama, S. (2010). Cultures and selves: A cycle of multiple constitution. *Perspectives on Psychological Science, 5,* 420–430.

Markus, H. R., & Kitayama, S. (2012). Culture and the self. In K. Vohs & R. F. Baumeister (Eds.), *Self and identity.* Thousand Oaks, CA: Sage.

Marshall, K. (2003). Benefiting from extended parental leave. *Perspectives on Labour and Income,* Statistics Canada. Catalogue No. 75-001-XIE. Retrieved from www.statcan.gc.ca/pub/75-001-x/00303/6490-eng.html

Marshall, K. (2006). *Converging gender roles.* Statistics Canada catalogue no. 11-010.

Marshall, K. (2008). Father's use of paid parental leave. *Perspectives on Labour and Income,* Statistics Canada. Catalogue No. 75-001-X. Retrieved from www.statcan.gc.ca/pub/75- 001-x/2008106/pdf/10639-eng.pdf

Marshall, K. (2010). Employer top-ups. *Perspectives on Labour and Income.* Statistics Canada. Catalogue no. 75- 001-X. Retrieved from www.statcan.gc.ca/pub/75-001-x/2010102/ pdf/11120-eng.pdf

Martens, M. A., Wilson, S. J., Dudgeon, P., & Reutens, D. C. (2009). Approachability and the amygdala: Insights from Williams syndrome. *Neuropsychologia, 47*(12), 2446–2453.

Martin, A., Razza, R., & Brooks-Gunn, J. (2012). Sustained attention at age 5 predicts attention-related problems at age 9. *International Journal of Behavioral Development, 36,* 413–419.

Martin, C., & Ruble, D. N. (2010). Gender-role development. *Annual Review of Psychology* (Vol. 61). Palo Alto, CA: Annual Reviews.

Martin, C. L., & Fabes, R. A. (2001). The stability and consequences of young children's same-sex peer interactions. *Development Psychology, 37,* 431–446.

Martin, C. L., & others. (2013). The role of sex of peers and gender-typed activities in young children's peer affiliative networks: A longitudinal analysis of selection and influence. *Child Development(84)* 3, 921–937.

Martin, C. L., & Ruble, D. N., & Szkrybalo, J. (2002). Cognitive theories of early gender development. *Psychological Bulletin, 128,* 903–933.

Martin, R., Sexton, C., Franklin, T., & Gerlovich, J. (2005). *Teaching science for all children* (4th ed.). Boston: Allyn & Bacon.

Masarik, A. S., & others. (2013). Romantic relationships in early adulthood: Influences of family, personality, and relationship cognitions. *Personal Relationships(20)* 2, 356–373.

Mash, E. J., & Wolfe, D. A. (2013). Disorders of childhood and adolescence. In I. B. Weiner & others (Eds.), *Handbook of psychology* (2nd ed., Vol. 8). New York: Wiley.

Mascolo, M. F., & Fischer, K. (2007). The co-development of self and socio-moral emotions during the toddler years. In C. A. Brownell & C. B. Kopp (Eds.), *Transitions in early development,* New York: Guilford.

Mash, E. J., & Wolfe, D. A. (2013). Disorders of childhood and adolescence. In I. B. Weiner & others (Eds.), *Handbook of psychology* (2nd ed., Vol. 8). New York: Wiley.

Mashburn, A. J., Justice, L. M., Downer, J. T., & Pianta, R. C. (2009). Peer effects on children's language achievement during pre-kindergarten. *Child Development, 80,* 686–702.

Mason, L., Harris, K. L., & Graham, S. (2013). Strategies for improving student outcomes in written expression. In B. G. Cook & M. G. Tankersley (Eds.), *Research-based practices in special education.* Upper Saddle River, NJ: Pearson.

Masten, A. S. (2006). Developmental psychopathology: Pathways to the future. *International Journal of Behavioral Development, 31,* 46–53.

Masten, A. S. (2009a). Ordinary Magic: Lessons from research on resilience in human development. *Education Canada,* 49(3): 28–32.

Masten, A. S. (2009b). Resilience in children and youth: A practical guide. *Schools for All Encyclopedia.* Vancouver: Health Canada and the Health and Learning Knowledge Centre of the Canadian Council on Learning.

Masten, A. S. (2013). Risk and resilience in development. In P. D. Zelazo (Ed.), *Oxford handbook of developmental psychology.* New York: Oxford University Press.

Masten, A. S., Burt, K., & Coatsworth, J. D. (2006). Competence and psychopathology in development. In D. Cicchetti & D. Cohen (Eds.), *Developmental psychopathology (Vol. 3): Risk, disorder and psychopathology* (2nd ed.) New York: Wiley.

Masten, A. S., Cutuli, J. J., Herbers, J. E., & Gabrielle-Reed, M. J. (2009b). Resilience in development. In Snyder, C. R., & Lopez, S. J. (Eds.), *The handbook of positive psychology* (2nd ed.) (pp. 117–131). New York: Oxford University Press.

Masten, A. S., Long, J. D., Kuo, S. I-C., McCormick, C. M., & Desjardins, C. D. (2009a). Developmental models of strategic intervention. *European Journal of Developmental Science, 3,* 282–291.

Mateus, V., Martins, C., Osorio, A., Martins, E. C., & Soares, I. (2013, in press). Attention at 10 months of age in infant-mother dyads: Contrasting free-toy play with semi-structured toy-play. *Infant Behavior and Development.*

Matheson, H., Moore, C., & Akhtar, N. (2013). The development of social learning in interactive and observational contexts. *Journal of Experimental Child Psychology, 114,* 161–172.

Matlin, M. W. (2012). *The psychology of women* (7th ed.). Boston: Cengage.

Matlow, J. N., Jubetsky, A., Alesksa, K., Berger, H., & Koren, G. (2013, in press). The transfer of ethyl glucuronide across the dually perfused human placenta. *Placenta.*

Matsumoto, D., & Juang, L. (2008). *Culture and psychology* (4th ed.). Belmont, CA: Wadsworth.

Mattson, S., & Smith, J. E. (2011). *Core curriculum for maternal-newborn nursing* (4th ed.). New York: Elsevier.

Matzek, A. E., & Cooney, T. M. (2009). Spousal perceptions of marital stress and support among grandparent caregivers: Variations by life stage. *International Journal of Aging and Human Development, 68,* 109–126.

Maurer, D., & Lewis, T. L. (2013). Sensitive periods in visual development. In P. D. Zelazo (Ed.), New York: Oxford University Press.

Maurer, D., Lewis, T. L., Brent, H. P., & Levin, A. V. (1999). Rapid improvement in the acuity of infants after visual input. *Science, 286,* 108–110.

Maurer, D., Mondloch, C. J., & Leis, T. L. (2007). Effects of early visual deprivation on perceptual and cognitive development. In C. von Hofsten & K. Rosander (Eds.), *Progress in Brain Research, 164,* 87–104.

Mayer, K. D., & Zhang, L. (2009). Short- and long-term effects of cocaine abuse during pregnancy on heart development. *Therapeutic Advances in Cardiovascular Disease, 3,* 7–16.

Mayeux, L., Sandstrom, M., & Cillessen, A. H .N. (2008). Is being popular a risky proposition? *Journal of Research on Adolescence, 18(1),* 49–74.

Mayo Clinic. (2009). *Pregnancy week by week.* Retrieved October 1, 2009, from www.mayoclinic.com/health/pregnancy-nutrition/PR00109

Mayo Clinic. (2013). Pregnancy and fish: What's safe to eat? Retrieved January 2, 2013, from www.mayoclinic.com/health/pregnancy-and-fish/PR00158

McAdams, D. P. (2012). Personality, modernity, and the storied self. In K. Vohs

& R. F. Baumeister (Eds.), *Self and identity*. Thousand Oaks, CA: Sage.

**McAdoo, H. P.** (2006). *Black families* (4th ed.). Thousand Oaks, CA: Sage.

**McBride-Chang, C.** (2004). *Children's literacy development* (Texts in Developmental Psychology Series). London: Edward Arnold/Oxford Press.

**McBride-Chang, C., & others.** (2005). Changing models across cultures: Associations of phonological and morphological awareness to reading in Beijing, Hong Kong, Korea, and America. *Journal of Experimental Child Psychology, 92,* 140–160.

**McBride-Chang, C., Lam, F., Lam, C., Doo, S., Wong, S. W., L., & Chow, Y. Y. Y.** (2008). Word recognition and cognitive profiles of Chinese preschool children at-risk for dyslexia through language delay or familial history of dyslexia. *Journal of Child Psychology and Psychiatry, 49,* 211–218.

**McCabe, K. M., Rodgers, C., Yeh, M., & Hough, R.** (2004). Gender differences in childhood onset conduct disorder. *Development and Psychopathology, 16,* 179–192.

**McCall, R. B., Appelbaum, M. I., & Hogarty, P. S.** (1973). Developmental changes in mental performance. *Monographs of the Society for Research in Child Development, 38* (Serial No. 150).

**McCambridge, T. M., & Stricker, P. R.** (2008). Strength training in children and adolescents. *Pediatrics, 121,* 835–840.

**McCartney, K., Dearing, E., Taylor, B. A., & Bub, K. L.** (2007). Quality child care supports the achievement of low-income children: Direct and indirect pathways through caregiving and the home environment. *Journal of Applied Developmental Psychology, 28,* 411–426.

**McCombs, B.** (2010). Learner-centered practices: Providing the context for positive learner development, motivation, and achievement. In J. Meece & J. Eccles (Eds.), *Handbook of schools, schooling, and human development*. New York: Routledge.

**McCombs, B. L.** (2013). Educational psychology and educational transformation. In I. B. Weiner & others (Eds.), *Handbook of psychology* (2nd ed., Vol. 7). New York: Wiley.

**McCormack, L. A., & others.** (2011). Weight-related teasing in a racially diverse sample of sixth-grade children. *Journal of the American Dietetic Association, 111,* 431–436.

**McCormick, C. B., Dimmitt, C., & Sullivan, F. R.** (2013). Metacognition, learning, and instruction. In I. B. Weiner & others (Eds.),

*Handbook of psychology* (2nd ed., Vol. 7). New York: Wiley.

**McCoy, D. C., & Raver, C. C.** (2011). Caregiver emotional expressiveness, child emotion regulation, and child behavior problems among Head Start families. *Social Development, 20,* 741–761.

**McDermott, B. M., & Cobham, V. E.** (2012, in press). Family functioning in the aftermath of a disaster. *BMC Psychiatry, 12,* 55.

**McDonald, S., & others.** (2009). Preterm birth and low birth weight among in vitro fertilization singletons: A systematic review and meta-analyses. *European Journal of Obstetrics, Gynecology, and Reproductive Biology, 146,* 138–148.

**McDonald, S. D., & others.** (2010). Preterm birth and low birth weight among in vitro fertilization twins: A systematic review and meta-analyses. *European Journal of Obstetrics, Gynecology, and Reproductive Biology, 148,* 105–113.

**McDougall, P., & Hymel, S.** (2007). Same-gender versus cross-gender friendship conceptions. *Merrill-Palmer Quarterly, 53,* 347–380.

**McDowell, D. J., & Parke, R. D.** (2009). Parental correlates of children's peer relations: An empirical test of a tripartite model. *Developmental Psychology, 45,* 224–235.

**McElhaney, K. B., & Allen, J. P.** (2012). Sociocultural perspectives on adolescent autonomy. In P. K. Kerig, M. S. Schulz, & S. T. Hauser (Eds.), *Adolescence and beyond*. New York: Oxford University Press.

**McElwain, N. L.** (2009). Attachment theory. In D. Carr (Ed.), *Encyclopedia of the life course and human development*. Boston: Gale Cengage.

**McGarry, J., Kim, H., Sheng, X., Egger, M., & Baksh, L.** (2009). Postpartum depression and help-seeking behavior. *Journal of Midwifery and Women's Health, 54,* 50–56.

**McGettigan, C., & others.** (2012). An application of univariate and multivariate approaches to fMRI to quantifying the hemispheric lateralization of acoustic and linguistic processes. *Journal of Cognitive Neuroscience, 24,* 636–652.

**McGuire, W., Dyson, L., & Renfrew, M.** (2010). Maternal obesity: Consequences for children, challenges for clinicians and carers. *Seminars in Fetal and Neonatal Medicine, 15,* 108–112.

**McHale, S. M., & Crouter, A. C.** (2013). How do children exert an impact on family life? In A. C. Crouter & A. Booth (Eds.), *Children's influence on family dynamics*. New York: Routledge.

**McHale, S. M., Updegraff, K. A., & Whiteman, S. D.** (2011). Sibling

relationships. In G. W. Peterson & K. R. Bush (Eds.), *Handbook of marriage and family* (3rd ed.). New York: Springer.

**McKinney, C., & Renk, K.** (2011). A multivariate model of parent-adolescent relationship variables in early adolescence. *Child Psychiatry and Human Development, 42*(4), 442–462.

**McLean, K. C., Breen, A. V., & Fournier, M. A.** (2010). Constructing the self in early, middle, and late adolescent boys: Narrative identity, individuation, and well-being. *Journal of Research on Adolescence, 20,* 166–187.

**McLean, K. C., & Jennings, L. E.** (2012). Teens telling tales: How maternal and peer audiences support narrative identity development. *Journal of Adolescence, 35,* 1455–1469.

**McLean, K. C., & Syed, M.** (Eds.). (2013, in press). *Oxford handbook of identity development*. New York: Oxford University Press.

**McLellan, R., & Remedios, R.** (2011). *Psychology for the classroom: Motivation*. New York: Routledge.

**McLoyd, V. C.** (1998). Children in poverty. In I. E. Siegel & K. A. Renninger (Eds.), *Handbook of child psychology* (5th ed., Vol. 4). New York: Wiley.

**McLoyd, V. C., Aikens, N. L., & Burton, L. M.** (2006). Childhood poverty, policy, and practice. In W. Damon & R. Lerner (Eds.), *Handbook of child psychology* (6th ed.). New York: Wiley.

**McLoyd, V. C., Kaplan, R., Purtell, K. M., Bagley, E., Hardaway, C. R., & Smalls, C.** (2009). Poverty and socioeconomic disadvantage in adolescence. In R. M. Lerner & L. Steinberg (Eds.), *Handbook of adolescent psychology* (3rd ed.). New York: Wiley.

**McLoyd, V. C., Kaplan, R., Purtell, K. M., & Huston, A. C.** (2011). Assessing the effects of a work-based antipoverty program for parents on youth's future orientation and employment experiences. *Child Development, 82,* 113–132.

**McMahon, M., & Stryjewski, G.** (2011). *Pediatrics*. New York: Elsevier.

**McMillan, J. H., & Wergin, J. F.** (2010). *Understanding and evaluating educational research* (4th ed.). Upper Saddle River, NJ: Pearson.

**McNamara, F, & Sullivan, C. E.** (2000). Obstructive sleep apnea in infants. *Journal of Pediatrics, 136,* 318–323.

**McNeil, D. A., & others.** (2012). Getting more than they realized they needed: A qualitative study of women's experience of group prenatal care. *BMC Pregnancy and Childbirth, 12,* 17.

McNeill, K. L., & Krajcik, J. S. (2013). *Supporting grade 5-8 students in constructing explanations in science.* Upper Saddle River, NJ: Pearson.

Mead, M. (1978, Dec. 30–Jan. 5). The American family: An endangered species. *TV Guide,* pp. 21–24.

Meaney, M. J. (2010). Epigenetics and the biological definition of gene X environment interactions. *Child Development, 81,* 41–79.

Meece, J. L., & Schaefer, V. A. (2010). Introduction. In J. Meece & J. Eccles (Eds.), *Handbook of research on schools, schooling, and human development.* New York: Routledge.

Meerlo, P., Sgoifo, A., & Suchecki, D. (2008). Restricted and disrupted sleep: Effects on autonomic function, neuroendocrine stress systems, and stress responsivity. *Sleep Medicine Review, 12,* 197–210.

Meeus, W. (2011). The study of adolescent identity formation 2000–2010: A review of longitudinal research. *Journal of Research in Adolescence, 21,* 75–84.

Mehta, C. M., & Strough, J. (2010). Gender segregation and gender-typing in adolescence. *Sex Roles, 63,* 251–263.

Meijs, N., Cillessen, A. H. N., Scholte, R. H. J., Segers, E., & Spikjkerman, R. (2010). Social intelligence and academic achievement as predictors of adolescent popularity. *Journal of Youth and Adolescence, 39,* 62–72.

Mejia-Arauz, R., Rogoff, B., Dexter, A., & Najafi, B. (2007). Cultural variation in children's social organization. *Child Development, 78,* 1001–1014.

Melby-Lervag, M., Lyster, S. H., & Hulme, C. (2012). Phonological skills and their role in learning to read: A meta-analytic review. *Psychological Bulletin, 138,* 3223–52.

Meldrum, R. C., & Hay, C. (2012). Do peers matter in the development of self-control? Evidence from a longitudinal study of youth. *Journal of Youth and Adolescence, 41,* 691–703.

Mello, Z. R. (2009). Racial/ethnic group and socioeconomic status variation in educational and occupational expectations from adolescence to adulthood. *Journal of Applied Developmental Psychology, 30,* 494–504.

Melzi, G., Schick, A. R., & Kennedy, J. L. (2011). Narrative elaboration and participation: Two dimensions of maternal elicitation style. *Child Development, 82*(4), 1282–1296.

Meltzoff, A. N. (2008). Unpublished review of Santrock, J. W., *Life-span development* (12th ed.). New York: McGraw-Hill.

Meltzoff, A. N. (2009). Roots of social cognition: The like-me framework. In D.

Cicchetti & M. R. Gunnar (Eds.), *Minnesota symposia on child psychology: Meeting the challenge of translational research in child psychology.* Hoboken, NJ: Wiley.

Meltzoff, A. N. (2011). Social cognition and the origins of imitation, empathy, and theory of mind. In U. Goswami (Ed.), *Wiley-Blackwell handbook of childhood cognitive development* (2nd ed.). New York: Wiley-Blackwell.

Meltzoff, A. N., & Williamson, R. A. (2013). Imitation: Social, cognitive, and theoretical perspectives. In P. D. Zelazo (Ed.), *Oxford handbook of developmental psychology.* New York: Oxford University Press.

Memon, A., Meissner, C. A., & Fraser, J. (2010). The cognitive interview: A meta-analytic review and study space analysis of the past 25 years. *Psychology, Public Policy, and Law, 16*(4), 340–372.

Menn, L., & Stoel-Gammon, C. (2009). Phonological development: Learning sounds and sound patterns. In J. B. Gleason and N. B. Ratner (Eds.), *The development of language.* Pearson: New York.

Mennella, J. A. (2009). Taste and smell. In R. A. Shweder & others (Eds.), *The child: An encyclopedic companion.* Chicago: University of Chicago Press.

Menon, R., & others. (2011). Cigarette smoking induces oxidative stress and atopsis in normal fetal membranes. *Placenta, 32,* 317–322.

Menyuk, P., Liebergott, J., & Schultz, M. (1995). *Early language development in full-term and premature infants.* Hillsdale, NJ: Erlbaum.

Meredith, N. V. (1978). Research between 1960 and 1970 on the standing height of young children in different parts of the world. In H. W. Reece & L. P. Lipsitt (Eds.), *Advances in child development and behavior* (Vol. 12). New York: Academic Press.

Merrell, K. W., Gueldner, B. A., Ross, S. W., & Isava, D. M. (2008). How effective are school bullying intervention program? A meta-analysis of intervention research. *School Psychology Quarterly, 23,* 26–42.

Merten, D. E. (2004). Securing her experience: Friendship versus popularity. *Feminism & Psychology, 14*(3), 361–365.

Mervis, C. B., & Becerra, A. M. (2007). Language and communicative development in Williams syndrome. *Mental Retardation and Developmental Disabilities Research Review, 13,* 3–15.

Mervis, C. B., & John, A. E. (2010). Cognitive and behavioral characteristics of children with Williams syndrome: Implications for intervention approaches. *American Journal of Medical Genetics. Part C, Seminars in Medical Genetics, 154C,* 229–248.

Mesman, J., van IJzendoorn, M. H., & Bakersman-Kranenburg, M. J. (2009). The many faces of the still-face paradigm: A review and meta-analysis. *Developmental Review, 29,* 120–162.

Messiah, S. E., Miller, T. L., Lipshultz, S. E., & Bandstra, E. S. (2011). Potential latent effects of prenatal cocaine exposure on growth and the risk of cardiovascular and metabolic disease in childhood. *Progress in Pediatric Cardiology, 31,* 59–65.

Messinger, D. (2008). Smiling. In M. M. Haith & J. B. Benson (Eds.), *Encyclopedia of infant and early childhood development.* Oxford, UK: Elsevier.

Metzger, A., & others. (2013, in press). Information management strategies with conversations about cigarette smoking: Parenting correlates and longitudinal associations with teen smoking. *Developmental Psychology.*

Meyer, S. L., Weible, C. M., & Woeber, K. (2010). Perceptions and practice of waterbirth: A survey of Georgia midwives. *Journal of Midwifery and Women's Health, 55,* 55–59.

Mihov, K. M., Denzler, M., & Forster, J. (2010). Hemispheric specialization and creative thinking: A meta-analytic review of lateralization of creativity. *Brain and Cognition, 72,* 442–448.

Mikami, A. Y., Szwedo, D. E., Allen, J. P., Evans, M. A., & Hare, A. L. (2010). Adolescent peer relationships and behavior problems predict young adults' communication on social networking websites. *Developmental Psychology, 46,* 46–56.

Milevsky, A. (2011). *Sibling relations in childhood and adolescence.* New York: Columbia University Press.

Milevsky, A. (2012). Parenting styles in adolescence. In J. R. Levesque (Ed.), *Encyclopedia of adolescence.* New York: Springer.

Millar, K., & Dean, H. J. (2012). Developmental origins of type 2 diabetes in aboriginal youth in canada: It is more than diet and exercise. *Journal of Nutrition and Metabolism,* Volume 2012, Article ID 127452, 7 pages.

Miller, C., Martin, C. L., Fabes, R. & Hanish, D. (2013) Bringing the cognitive and social together: How gender detectives and gender enforcers shape children's gender development. In M. Banaji & S. Gelman (Eds.), *Navigating the social world: A developmental perspective.* New York: Oxford University Press.

Miller, C. F., Lurye, L. E., Zusuls, K. M., & Ruble, D. N. (2009). Accessibility of gender stereotype domains: Developmental and gender differences in children. *Sex Roles, 60,* 870-881.

**Miller, C. F., & Ruble, D. N.** (2005). *Developmental changes in the accessibility of gender stereotypes.* Unpublished manuscript. Department of Psychology, New York University.

**Miller, E. M., & others.** (2012). Theories of willpower affect sustained learning. *PLoS One, 7*(6), e38680.

**Miller, G. E., & Reynolds, W. M.** (2013). Future perspectives in developmental psychology. In I. B. Weiner & others (Eds.), *Handbook of psychology* (2nd ed., Vol. 7). New York: Wiley.

**Miller, J.** (2007). Cultural psychology of moral development. In S. Kitayama & D. Cohen (Eds.), *Handbook of cultural psychology.* New York: Guilford.

**Miller, J.** (2013). Insights into moral development from cultural psychology. In M. Killen & J. G. Smetana (Eds.), *Handbook of moral development* (2nd ed.). New York: Routledge.

**Miller, K., E., & Hoffman, J. H.** (2009). Mental well-being and sport-related identities in college students. *Sociology of Sport Journal, 26,* 335-356.

**Miller, L. J., & Larusso, E. M.** (2011). Preventing postpartum depression. *Psychiatric Clinics of North America, 34,* 53-65.

**Miller, P. H.** (2011). Piaget's theory: Past, present, and future. In U. Goswami (Ed.), *Wiley-Blackwell handbook of childhood cognitive development* (2nd ed.). New York: Wiley-Blackwell.

**Miller-Johnson, S., Coie, J., & Malone, P. S.** (2003, April). *Do aggression and peer rejection in childhood predict early adult outcomes?* Paper presented at the biennial meeting of the Society for Research in Child Development, Tampa, FL.

**Miller-Jones, D.** (1989). Culture and testing. *American Psychologist. 44,* 360-366.

**Miller-Perrin, C. L., Perrin, R. D., & Kocur, J. L.** (2009). Parental physical and psychological aggression: Psychological symptoms in young adults. *Child Abuse and Neglect, 33,* 1-11.

**Mills, C. M.** (2013, in press). Knowing when to doubt: Developing a critical stance when learning from others. *Developmental Psychology, 49,* 404-418.

**Mills, C. M., Elashi, F. B., & Archacki, M. A.** (2011, March). *Evaluating sources of information and misinformation: Developmental and individual differences in the elementary school years.* Paper presented at the biennial meeting

of the Society for Research in Child Development, Montreal.

**Mills, C. M., & Keil. F. C.** (2005). The development of cynicism. *Psychological Science. 16,* 385-390.

**Mills-Koonce, W. R., Propper, C. B., & Barnett, M.** (2012). Poor infant soothability and later insecure-ambivalent attachment: Developmental change in phenotypic markers of risk or two measures of the same construct? *Infant Behavior and Development, 35,* 215-235.

**Milne, E., & others.** (2012). Parental prenatal smoking and risk of childhood acute lymphoblastic leukemia. *American Journal of Epidemiology, 175,* 43-5.

**Milot, T., Ethier, L. S., St-Laurent, D., & Provost, M. A.** (2010). The role of trauma symptoms in the development of behavioral problems in maltreated preschoolers. *Child Abuse and Neglect, 34*(4), 225-234.

**Milunsky, J. M.** (2010). Prenatal diagnosis of sex chromosome abnormalities. In A. Milunsky & J. M. Milunsky (Eds.), *Genetic Disorders and the Fetus: Diagnosis, Prevention, and Treatment* (6th ed., pp. 273-312). Oxford: Wiley-Blackwell.

**Minde, K., & Zelkowitz, P.** (2008). Premature babies. In M. M. Haith & J. B. Benson (Eds.), *Encyclopedia of infancy and early childhood development.* Oxford, UK: Elsevier.

**Mindell, J. A., Sadeh, A., Wiegand, B., How, T. H., & Goh, D. Y.** (2010b). Cross-cultural differences in infant and toddler sleep. *Sleep Medicine, 11,* 274-280.

**Minnes, S., & others.** (2010). The effects of prenatal cocaine exposure on problem behavior in children 4-10 years. *Neurotoxicology and Teratology, 32,* 443-451.

**Minnesota Family Investment Program** (2009). *Longitudinal study of early MFIP recipients.* Available at www.dhs.state.mn.us/main/groups/publications/documents/pub/dhs16_143190~1.pdf

**Mischel, W., & Mischel, H.** (1975, April). *A cognitive social-learning analysis of moral development.* Paper presented at the meeting of the Society for Research in Child Development, Denver.

**Mistry, J., Contreras, M., & Dutta, R.** (2013, in press). Culture and development. In I. B. Weiner & others (Eds.), *Handbook of psychology* (2nd ed., Vol. 6). New York: Wiley.

**Mitchell, E. A., Stewart, A. W., Crampton, P., & Salarnod, C.** (2000). Deprivation and sudden infant death syndrome. *Social Science and Medicine, 51,* 147-150.

**Mitchell, G. L., Farrow, C., Haycraft, E., & Meyer, C.** (2013). Parental influences

on children's eating behavior and characteristics of successful parent-focused interventions. *Appetite, 60,* 85-94.

**Mitchell, J. A., Pate, R. R., & Blair, S. N.** (2012). Screen-based sedentary behavior and cardiorespiratory fitness from age 11 to 13. *Medical Science and Sports Exercise, 44,* 1302-1309.

**Mitchell, M. L., & Jolley, J. M.** (2010). *Research design explained* (7th ed.). Boston: Cengage.

**Miyake, K, Chen, S., & Campos, J.** (1985). Infants' temperament, mothers' mode of interaction and attachment in Japan: An interim report. H. I. Bretherton & F. Waters (Eds.), Growing points of attachment theory and research, *Monographs of the Society for Research in Child Development, 50*(1-2, Serial No. 109), 276-297.

**Miyakoshi, K., & others.** (2013, in press). Perinatal outcomes: Intravenous patient-controlled fentanyl versus no analgesia in labor. *Journal of Obstetrics and Gynecology Research.*

**Mize, K. D., & Jones, N. A.** (2012). Infant physiological and behavioral responses to loss of maternal attention to a social-rival. *International Journal of Psychophysiology, 83,* 16-23.

**Moffitt, A. R.** (1971). Consonant cue perception by twenty- to twenty-four-week-old infants. *Children Development, 42,* 717-731.

**Moffitt, T. E.** (2012). Childhood self-control predicts adult health, wealth, and crime. Paper presented at the Symposium on Symptom Improvement in well-being, Copenhagen.

**Moffitt, T. E., & others.** (2011). A gradient of childhood self-control predicts health, wealth, and public safety. *Proceedings of the National Academy of Sciences U.S.A., 108,* 2693-2698.

**Monette, S., Bigras, M., & Guay, M. C.** (2011). The role of executive functions in school achievement at the end of grade 1. *Journal of Experimental Child Psychology, 109,* 158-173.

**Money, J.** (1975). Ablato penis: Normal male infant sex-reassigned as a girl. *Archives of Sexual Behavior, 4,* 65-71.

**Montemayor, R., & Eisen, M.** (1977). The development of self-conceptions from childhood to adolescence. *Developmental Psychology, 13*(4).

**Montoya Arizabaleta, A. V., & others.** (2010). Aerobic exercise during pregnancy improves health-related quality of life: A randomized trial. *Journal of Physiotherapy, 56,* 253-258.

Moon, R. Y., & Fu, L. (2012). Sudden infant death syndrome: An update. *Pediatric Reviews, 33*, 314–320.

Moore, C. (2007). Understanding self and others in the second year. In C. A. Brownell & C. B. Kopp (Eds.), *Socioemotional development in the toddler years: Transitions and transformations* (pp. 43–65). New York: Guilford.

Moore, C., Mealiea, J., Garon, N., & Povinelli, D. J. (2007). The development of body self-awareness. *Infancy, 11(2)*, 157–174.

Moore, D. (2001). *The dependent gene.* New York: W. H. Freeman.

Moore, D. R. (2002). Auditory development and the role of experience. *The British Medical Bulletin, 63*, 171–181.

Moore E. R., Anderson G. C., Bergman N., Dowswell T. Early skin-to-skin contact for mothers and their healthy newborn infants. Cochrane Database of Systematic Reviews. No.: CD003519. doi: 10.1002/14651858.CD003519.pub3

Moore, M. (2012). Behavioral sleep problems in children and adolescents. *Journal of Clinical Psychology in Medical Settings, 19*, 77–83.

Moore, M. K., & Meltzoff, A. N. (2008). Factors affecting infants' manual search for occluded objects and the genesis of object permanence. *Infant Behavior and Development, 31*, 168–180.

Morales, J., Calvo, A., & Bialystok, E. (2013). Working memory development in monolingual and bilingual children. *Journal of Experimental Child Psychology 114*, 187–202

Moran, G., Forbes, L., Evans, E., Tarabulsy, G.M., & Madigan, M. (2008). Both maternal sensitivity and atypical maternal behavior independently predict attachment security and disorganization in adolescent mother-infant relationships. *Infant Behavior and Development, 31*, 321–325.

Moran, S., & Gardner, H. (2006). Extraordinary achievements. In W. Damon & R. Lerner (Eds.), *Handbook of child psychology* (6th ed.), New York: Wiley.

Morandi, A., & others. (2012). Estimation of newborn risk for child or adolescent obesity: Lessons from longitudinal birth cohorts. *PLoS One, 7(11).* E49919.

Morano, M., Colella, D., & Capranica, L. (2011). Body image, perceived and actual physical abilities in normal-weight and overweight boys involved in individual and team sports. *Journal of Sports Sciences, 29(4)*, 355–362.

Morasch, K. C., Raj, V. R., & Bell, M. A. (2013). The development of cognitive control from infancy through childhood. In D. Reisberg (Ed.), *Oxford handbook of cognitive psychology.* New York: Oxford University Press.

Moravcik, E., Nolte, S., & Feeney, S. (2013). *Meaningful curriculum for young children.* Upper Saddle River, NJ: Pearson.

Morgante, J. C., Zolfaghari, R., & Johnson, S. P. (2012). A critical test of temporal and spatial accuracy of the Tobii T60XL eye tracker. *Infancy, 17,* 9–32.

Mori, R., Khanna, R., Pledge, D. and Nakayama, T. (2010). Meta-analysis of physiological effects of skin-to-skin contact for newborns and mothers. *Pediatrics International, 52*, 161–170.

Morris, A. S., Cui, L., & Steinberg, L. (2012). Parenting research and themes: What we have learned and where to go next. In R. E. Larzelere, A. S. Morris, & A. W. Harrist (Eds.), *Authoritative parenting.* Washington, DC: American Psychological Association.

Morris, C. A. (2010). Introduction: Williams syndrome. *American Journal of Medical Genetics. Part C, Seminars in Medical Genetics, 154C,* 203–208.

Morris, R. J., Thompson, K. C., & Morris, Y. P. (2013). Child psychotherapy. In I. B. Weiner & others (Eds.), *Handbook of psychology* (2nd ed., Vol. 8). New York: Wiley.

Morrissey, T. W. (2009). Multiple child-care arrangements and young children's behavioral outcomes. *Child Development, 80,* 59–76.

Morrison, G., Doumas, L. A. A., & Richland, L. E. (2011). A computational account of children's analogical reasoning: Balancing inhibitory control in working memory and relational representation. *Developmental Science, 14,* 516–529.

Morrow, C. E., & others. (2006). Learning disabilities and intellectual functioning in school-aged children with prenatal cocaine exposure. *Developmental Neuropsychology, 30,* 905–931.

Mortensen, O., Torsheim, T., Melkevik, O., & Thuen, F. (2012). Adding a baby to the equation. Married and cohabiting women's relationship satisfaction in the transition to parenthood. *Family Process, 51,* 122–139.

Moshman, D. (2011). *Adolescent rationality and development: Cognition, morality, and identity* (3rd ed.). New York: Psychology Press.

Moss, E., Cyr, C., Bureau, J.F., Tarabulsy, G.M., & Dubois-Comtois, K. (2005). Stability of attachment during the preschool period. *Developmental Psychology, 41,* 773–783.

Moulson, M. C., & Nelson, C. A. (2008). Neurological development. In M. M. Haith & J. B. Benson (Eds.), *Encyclopedia of infancy and early childhood.* Oxford. UK: Elsevier.

Mrug, S., Borch, C., & Cillessen, A. H. N. (2011). Other-sex friendships in late adolescence: Risky associations for substance abuse and sexual debut? *Journal of Youth and Adolescence, 40,* 875–888.

Mrug, S., & McCay, R. (2013, in press). Parental and peer disapproval of alcohol use and its relationship to adolescent drinking: Age, gender, and racial differences. *Psychology of Addictive Behaviors.*

Muckle, G. & others. (2011). Alcohol, smoking, and drug use among Inuit women of childbearing age during pregnancy and the risk to children. *Alcohol Clinical and Experimental Research, 35*: 1081–1091: doi: 10.1111/j.1530-0277.2011.01441.x

Mueller, V. C., & Hoff, E. (2010). Input and the acquisition of language: Three questions. In E. Hoff & M. Shatz (Eds.), *Blackwell handbook of language development* (2nd ed.). New York: Wiley.

Muller, U., & others. (2012). Knowing minds, controlling actions: The developmental relations between theory of mind and executive function from 2 to 4 years of age. *Journal of Experimental Child Psychology, 111,* 331–348.

Mullola, S., & others. (2012). Gender differences in teachers' perceptions of students' temperament, educational competence, and teachability. *British Journal of Educational Psychology, 82(2),* 185–206.

Murphy, M. M., & Mazzocco, M. M. (2008). Mathematics learning disabilities in girls with fragile X or Turner syndrome during late elementary school. *Journal of Learning Disabilities, 41,* 29–46.

Murray, J. & Farrington, D. P. (2010). Risk factors for conduct disorder and delinquency: Key findings from longitudinal studies. *Canadian Journal of Psychiatry, 55(10),* 633–642.

Murray, J. P. (2007). TV violence: Research and controversy. In N. Pecora, J. P. Murray, & E. A. Wartella (Eds.), *Children and television.* Mahwah, NJ: Erlbaum.

Murray, J. P., & Murray, A. D. (2008). Television: Uses and effects. In M. M. Haith & J. B. Benson (Eds.), *Encyclopedia of infant and early childhood development.* Oxford, UK: Elsevier.

Mustelin, L., Silventoinen, K., Pietilainen, K., Rissanen, A., & Kaprio, J. (2009). Physical activity reduces the influence of genetic effects on BMI and waist circumference: A study of young adult twins. *International Journal of Obesity, 33,* 29–36.

Miyake, A. & Friedman, N. P. (2012). The nature and organization of individual differences in executive functions: Four general conclusions. *Current Directions in Psychological Science, 21*(1), 8–14.

Myer, G. D., & others. (2011). Integrative training for children and adolescents: Techniques and practices for reducing sports-related injuries and enhancing athletic performance. *The Physician and Sports Medicine, 39,* 74–84.

Myers, D. (2008, June 2). Commentary in S. Begley & J. Interlandi, The dumbest generation? Don't be dumb. Retrieved on July 22, 2008, from www.newsweek.com/id/138536/

Myers, D., Baer, W., & Choi, S. (1996). The changing problem of overcrowded housing. *Journal of the American Planning Association, 62,* 66–84.

Myers, D. G. (2010). *Psychology* (9th ed.). New York: Worth.

Myerson, J., Rank, M. R., Raines, F. Q., & Schnitzler, M. A. (1998). Race and general cognitive ability: The myth of diminishing returns in education. *Psychological Science, 9,* 139–142.

# N

NAEYC (National Association for the Education of Young Children). (2009). Developmentally appropriate practice in early childhood programs serving children from birth through age 8. Washington, DC: Author.

Nagata, D. K. (1989). Japanese American children and adolescents. In J. T. Gibbs & L. N. Huang (Eds.), *Children of color.* San Francisco: Jossey-Bass.

Nagel, B. J., & others. (2011). Altered white matter microstructure in children with attention-deficit/hyperactivity disorder. *Journal of the American Academy of Child and Adolescent Psychiatry, 50,* 283–292.

Nagel, H. T., Kneght, A. C, Kloosterman, M. D., Wildschut, H. I., Leschot, N. J., & Vandenbussche, F. P. (2007). Prenatal diagnosis in the Netherlands, 1991–2000: Number of invasive procedures, indications, abnormal results, and terminations of pregnancies. *Prenatal Diagnosis, 27,* 251–257.

Najman, J. M., & others. (2010). Timing and chronicity of family poverty and development of unhealthy behaviors in children: A longitudinal study. *Journal of Adolescent Health, 46,* 538–544.

Najman, J. M., Hayatbakhsh, M. R., Heron, M. A., Bor, W., O'Callaghan, M. J., & Williams, G. M. (2009). The impact of episodic and chronic poverty on

child cognitive development. *Journal of Pediatrics, 154,* 284–289.

Nakamoto, J., & Schwartz, D. (2010). Is peer victimization associated with academic achievement? A meta-analytic review. *Social Development, 19,* 221–242.

Nanni, V., Uher, R., & Danese, A. (2012). Childhood maltreatment predicts unfavorable course of illness and treatment outcome in depression: A meta-analysis. *American Journal of Psychiatry, 169,* 141–151.

Nansel, T. Overpeck, M., Pilla, R.S., Ruan, W.J., Simmons-Morton, B. Schmidt, P. (2001). Bullying behaviors among US youth. *Journal of American Medical Association, 285,* 2094–2100.

Nardi, P. M. (2006). *Doing survey research* (2nd ed.). Boston: Allyn & Bacon.

Narendran, S., Nagarathna, R., Narendran, V., Gunasheela, S., & Nagendra, H. R. (2005). Efficacy of yoga on pregnancy outcomes. *Journal of Alternative and Complementary Medicine, 11,* 234–244.

Narvaez, D. (2006). Integrative moral education. In M. Killen & J. Smetana (Eds.), *Handbook of moral development.* Mahwah, NJ: Erlbaum.

Narvaez, D. (2010b). Moral complexity: Th e fatal attraction of truthiness and the importance of mature moral functioning. *Perspectives on Psychological Science, 5* (2), 163–181.

Narvaez, D. (2013). Integrative moral education. In M. Killen & J. G. Smetana (Eds.), *Handbook of moral development* (2nd ed.). New York: Routledge.

Narvaez, D., & Hill, P. L. (2010). The relation of multicultural experiences to moral judgment and mindsets. *Journal of Diversity in Higher Education, 3,* 43–55.

Narvaez, D., & Lapsley, D. (Eds.). (2009). *Moral personality, identity, and character: An interdisciplinary future.* New York: Cambridge University Press.

National Assessment of Educational Progress. (2000). *Reading achievement.* Washington, DC: National Center for Education Statistics.

National Association for Gifted Children. (2009). State of the states in gifted education: 2008–2009. Washington, DC: Author.

National Center for Health Statistics. (2000). *Health United States, 1999.* Atlanta: Centers for Disease Control and Prevention.

National Center on Shaken Baby Syndrome. (2010). *Shaken baby syndrome.* Retrieved April 22, 2010, from www.dontshake.org/

National Clearinghouse on Child Abuse and Neglect. (2004). *What is child*

*abuse and neglect?* Washington, DC: U.S. Department of Health and Human Services.

National Institute of Mental Health. (2011). *Autism spectrum disorders (pervasive developmental disorders).* Available at www.nimh.nih.gov/health/topics/autism-spectrum-disorders-asd/index.shtml

National Institute of Neurological Disorders and Stroke. (2009). *Brain basics: Understanding sleep.* Retrieved May 5, 2009 from www.ninds.nih.gov/disorders/brain_basics/understanding_sleep.htm

National Research Council. (1999). *Starting out right: A guide to promoting children's reading success.* Washington, DC: National Academy Press.

National Research Council. (2004). *Engaging schools: Fostering high school students' motivation to learn.* Washington, DC: National Academic Press.

National Sleep Foundation (2006). *Sleep in America poll: Children and sleep.* Washington, DC: National Sleep Foundation.

National Sleep Foundation. (2013). *Children's sleep habits.* Retrieved January 3, 2013, from www.sleepfoundation.org

National Vital Statistics Report (2004 March 7). Deaths: Leading causes for 2002. Atlantic: Centers for Disease Control and Prevention.

Navab, A., Gillespie-Lynch, K., Johnson, S. P., Sigman, M., & Hutman, T. (2012). Eye tracking as a measure of responsiveness to joint attention in infants at risk for autism. *Infancy, 17,* 416–431.

Neal, A. R. (2009). Autism. In D. Carr (Ed.), *Encyclopedia of the life course and human development.* Boston: Gale Cengage.

Neal, J. W. (2010). Social aggression and social position in middle childhood and early adolescence: Burning bridges or building them? *Journal of Early Adolescence, 30*(1), 122–137.

Near, C. E. (2013, in press). Selling gender: Associations of box art representation of female characters with sales for teen- and mature-rated video games. *Sex Roles.*

Needham, A. (2011). Perceptual development: Object perception. In B. Goldstein (Ed.), *Encyclopedia of perception.* Thousand Oaks, CA: Sage.

Needham, A., Barrett, T., & Peterman, K. (2002) A pick-me-up for infants' exploratory skills: Early simulated experiences reaching for objects using "sticky mittens" enhances young infants' object exploration skills. *Infant Behavior and Development, 25,* 279–295.

Needham, A., & Libertus, K. (2011). Neonativism. In M. M. Haith & J. Benson

(Eds.), *Encyclopedia of infant and early childhood development* (2nd ed.). New York: Elsevier.

**Negriff, S., Susman, E. J., & Trickett, P. K.** (2011). The development pathway from pubertal timing to delinquency and sexual activity from early to late adolescence. *Journal of Youth and Adolescence, 40,* 1343-1356.

**Neisser, U., & others.** (1996). Intelligence: Knowns and unknowns. *American Psychologist, 51,* 77-101.

**Nelson, C. A.** (2003). Neural development and lifelong plasticity. In R. M. Lerner, F. Jacobs, & D. Wertlieb (Eds.), *Handbook of applied developmental science.* Thousand Oaks, CA: Sage.

**Nelson, C. A.** (2011). Brain development and behavior. In A. M. Rudolph, C. Rudolph, L. First, G. Lister, & A. A. Gersohon (Eds.), *Rudolph's pediatrics* (22nd ed.). New York: McGraw-Hill.

**Nelson, J. A., & Eckstein, D.** (2008). A service-learning model for at-risk adolescents. *Education and Treatment of Children, 31,* 223-237.

**Nelson, J. L., Palonsky, S. B., & McCarthy, M. R.** (2013). *Critical issues in education* (8th ed.). New York: McGraw-Hill.

**Nelson K.** (1993). The psychological and social origins of autobiographical memory. *Psychological Science, 4,* 7-14.

**Nelson, K.** (1999). Levels and modes of representation: Issues for the theory of conceptual change and development. In E. K. Skolnick, K. Nelson, S. A. Gelman, & P. H. Miller (Eds.), *Conceptual development.* Mahwah, NJ: Erlbaum.

**Nelson, K., & Fivush, R.** (2004). The emergence of autobiographical memory: A social cultural developmental theory. *Psychological Review, 111,* 486-511.

**Neubauer, A. C., & Fink, A.** (2009). Intelligence and neural efficiency: Measures of brain activation versus measures of functional connectivity in the brain. *Intelligence, 37,* 223-229.

**Neville, H. J.** (2006). Different profiles of plasticity within human cognition. In Y. Munakata & M. H. Johnson (Eds.), *Attention and Performance XXI: Processes of change in brain and cognitive development.* Oxford, UK: Oxford University Press.

**Nevo, E., & Breznitz, Z.** (2013). The development of working memory from kindergarten to first grade in children with different decoding skills. *Journal of Experimental Child Psychology, 114,* 217-228.

**New, R.** (2005). The Reggio Emilia approach: Provocations and partnerships with U. S. early childhood educators. In J. I. Roopnarine & J. E. Johnson (Eds.), *Approaches to early childhood education* (4th ed.). Columbus, OH: Merrill/Prentice Hall.

**New, R.** (2007). Reggio Emilia as cultural activity. *Theory into Practice, 46*(1), 5-13.

**Newcombe, N.** (2007). The development of implicit and explicit memory. In N. Cowan & M. Courage (Eds.), *The development of memory in childhood.* Philadelphia: Psychology Press.

**Newcombe, N. S.** (2007). Developmental psychology meets the mommy wars. *Journal of Applied Developmental Psychology, 28,* 553-555.

**Newell, K., Scully, D. M., McDonald, P. V., & Baillargeon, R.** (1989). Task constraints and infant grip configurations. *Developmental Psychobiology, 22,* 817-832.

**Newton, A. W., & Vandeven, A. M.** (2010). Child abuse and neglect: A worldwide concern. *Current Opinion in Pediatrics, 22,* 226-233.

**NICHD Early Child Care Research Network.** (2000). Factors associated with fathers' caregiving activities and sensitivity with young children. *Developmental Psychology, 14,* 200-219.

**NICHD Early Child Care Research Network.** (2001). Nonmaternal care and family factors in early development: An overview of the NICHD study of Early Child Care. *Journal of Applied Developmental Psychology, 22,* 457-492.

**NICHD Early Child Care Research Network.** (2002). Structure→Process→Outcome: Direct and indirect effects of child care quality on young children's development. *Psychological Science, 13,* 199-206.

**NICHD Early Child Care Research Network.** (2003). Does amount of time spent in child care predict socioemotional adjustment during the transition to kindergarten? *Child Development, 74,* 976-1005.

**NICHD Early Child Care Research Network.** (2004). Type of child care and children's development at 54 months. *Early Childhood Research Quarterly, 19,* 203-230.

**NICHD Early Child Care Research Network.** (2005). *Child care and development.* New York: Guilford.

**NICHD Early Child Care Research Network.** (2005). Duration and developmental timing of poverty and children's cognitive and social development from birth through third grade. *Child Development, 76,* 795-810.

**NICHD Early Child Care Research Network.** (2006). Infant-mother attachment classification: Risk and protection in relation to changing maternal caregiving quality. *Developmental Psychology, 42,* 38-58.

**NICHD Early Child Care Research Network.** (2010). Testing a series of causal propositions relating time spent in child care to children's externalizing behavior. *Developmental Psychology, 46*(1), 1-17.

**Nickerson, R. S.** (2011). Developing intelligence through instruction. In R. J. Sternberg & S. B. Kaufman (Eds.), *Handbook of intelligence.* New York: Cambridge University Press.

**Nieto, S.** (2010). Multicultural education in the United States: Historical realities, ongoing challenges, and transformative possibilities. In J. A. Banks (Ed.), *The Routledge international companion to multicultural education.* New York: Routledge.

**Nieto, S., & Bode, P.** (2012). *Affirming diversity* (6th ed.). Boston: Allyn & Bacon.

**Nisbett, R.** (2003). *The geography of thought.* New York: Free Press.

**Nisbett, R. E., Aronson, J., Blair, C., Dickens, W., Flynn, J., Halpern, D. F., & Turkheimer, E.** (2012). Intelligence: New findings and theoretical developments. *American Psychologist, 67,* 130-159.

**Noddings, S. N.** (2008). Caring and moral education. In L. Nucci & D. Narvaez (Eds.), *Handbook of moral and character education.* Clifton, NJ: Psychology Press.

**Nodine, P. M., & Hastings-Tolsma, M.** (2012). Maternal obesity: Improving pregnancy outcomes. *MCN American Journal of Maternal Child Nursing, 37,* 110-115.

**Nolen-Hoeksema, S.** (2011). *Abnormal psychology* (5th ed.). New York: McGraw-Hill.

**Norgard, B., Puho, E., Czeilel, A. E., Skriver, M. V., & Sorensen, H. T.** (2006). Aspirin use during early pregnancy and the risk of congenital abnormalities. *American Journal of Obstetrics & Gynecology, 192,* 922-923.

**Norman, J. E., & others.** (2009). Progesterone for the prevention of preterm birth in twin pregnancy (STOPPIT): A randomized, double-blind, placebo-controlled study and meta-analysis. *Lancet, 373,* 2034-2040.

**Nosko, A., Tieu, T. T., Lawford, H., & Pratt, M. W.** (2011). How do I love thee? Let me count the ways: Parenting during adolescence, attachment styles, and romantic narratives in emerging adulthood. *Developmental Psychology, 47,* 645-657.

**Nottleman, E. D., & others.** (1987). Gonadal and adrenal hormone correlates of adjustment in early adolescence. In R. M. Lerner & T. T. Foch (Eds.), *Biological-psychological interactions in early adolescence.* Hillsdale, NJ: Erlbaum.

Nova Scotia Government (2013, April). *Families, children benefit from expansion of newborn screening program.* Media release. Retrieved May 7, 2013 from http://novascotia.ca/news/release/?id=20130422004

Nucci, L. (2013). Education for moral development. In M. Killen & J. G. Smetana (Eds.), *Handbook of moral development* (2nd ed.). New York: Routledge.

Nylund, K., Bellmore, A., Nishina, A., & Graham, S. (2007). Subtypes, severity, and structural stability of peer victimization: What does latent class analysis say? *Child Development, 78,* 1706–1722.

## O

Oakes, L. M. (2012). Advances in eye-tracking in infancy research. *Infancy, 17,* 1–8.

Oates, J., & Abraham, S. (2010). *Llewellyn-Jones fundamentals of obstetrics and gynecology* (9th ed.). New York: Elsevier.

Oates, J., & Grayson, A. (2004). *Cognitive and language development in children.* Malden, MA: Blackwell.

Obenauer, S., & Maestre, L. A. (2008). Fetal MRI of lung hypoplasia: Imaging findings. *Clinical Imaging, 32,* 48–50.

Oberlander, T. F. (2012). Fetal serotonin signaling: Setting pathways for early childhood development and behavior. *Journal of Adolescent Health.*

O'Brien, J. M., & Lewis, D. F. (2009). Progestins for the prevention of spontaneous preterm birth: Review and implications of recent studies. *Journal of Reproductive Medicine, 54,* 73–87.

O'Brien, M., & Moss, P. (2010). Fathers, work, and family policies in Europe. In M. E. Lamb (Ed.), *The role of the father in child development* (5th ed.). New York: Wiley.

O'Callaghan, F. V., & others. (2010). The link between sleep problems in infancy and early childhood and attention problems at 5 and 14 years: Evidence from a birth cohort study. *Early Human Development 86,* 419–424.

Ochs, E., & Schieffelin, B. (2008). Language socialization and language acquisition. In P. A. Duff & N. H. Hornberger (Eds.), *Encyclopedia of language and education.* New York: Springer.

O'Donnell, A. M. (2012). Constructivism. In K. R. Harris, S. Graham, & T. Urdan (Eds.), *APA educational psychology handbook.* Washington, DC: American Psychological Association.

OECD (2005). Starting strong: Early education and care. Available at www.oecd.org/edu/school/earlychildhoodeducationandcare.htm

Ogbu, J., & Stern, P. (2001). Caste status and intellectual ability. In R. J. Sternberg & E. L. Grigorento (Eds.), *Environmental effects on cognitive abilities.* Mahwah, NJ: Erlbaum.

Ogden, C. L., Carroll, M. D., & Flegal, K. M. (2008). High body mass index for age among U.S. children and adolescents, 2003–2006. *Journal of the American Medical Association, 299,* 2401–2405.

O'Hearn, K., & Luna, B. (2009). Mathematical skills in Williams syndrome: Insight into the importance of underlying representations. *Developmental Disabilities Research Reviews, 15,* 11–20.

Okuma, K., & Tanimura, M. (2009). A preliminary study on the relationship between characteristics of TV content and delayed speech development in young children. *Infant Behavior and Development, 32,* 312–321.

Oldehinkel, A. J., Ormel, J., Veenstra, R., De Winter, A., & Verhulst, F. C. (2008). Parental divorce and offspring depressive symptoms: Dutch developmental trends during early adolescence. *Journal of Marriage and the Family, 70,* 284–293.

Oller, D. K., & Jarmulowicz, L. (2010). Language and literacy in bilingual children in the early school years. In E. Hoff & M. Shatz (Eds.), *Blackwell handbook of language development.* New York: J Wiley.

Olson, D., & others. (2009). Exercise in pregnancy. *Current Sports Medicine Reports, 8,* 147–153.

Olson, S. L., Lopez-Duran, N., Lunkenheimer, E. S., Chang, H., & Sameroff, A. J. (2011). Individual differences in the development of early peer aggression: Integration contributions of self-regulation, theory of mind, and parenting. *Development and Psychopathology, 23,* 253–266.

Olweus, D. (2003). Prevalence estimation of school bullying with the Olweus bully/victim questionnaire. *Aggressive Behavior, 29(3),* 239–269.

O'Neill, S., & others. (2013, in press). Cesarean section and subsequent ectopic pregnancy: A systematic review and meta-analysis. *BJOG.*

Opfer, J. E., & Gelman, S. A. (2011). Development of the animate-inanimate distinction. In U. Goswami (Ed.), *Wiley-Blackwell handbook of childhood cognitive development* (2nd ed.). New York: Wiley-Blackwell.

Ophir, E., Nass, C., & Wagner, A. D. (2009). Cognitive control in media multitaskers. *Proceedings of the National Academy of Sciences USA, 106,* 15583–15587.

Ornstein, M. & Stalker, G. J. (2013). Canadian families' strategies for employment and care for preschool children. *Journal of Family Issues, 34(1),* 53–84.

Ornstein, P., Coffman, J. L., & Grammer, J. K., (2007, April). *Teachers' memory-relevant conversations and children's memory performance.* Paper presented at the biennial meeting of the Society for Research in Child Development, Boston.

Ornstein, P. A., Coffman, J. L., & Grammer, J. K. (2009). Learning to remember. In O. A. Barbarin & B. H. Wasik (Eds.), *Handbook of child development and early education.* New York: Guilford.

Ornstein, P. A., Coffman, J. L., Grammer, J. K., San Souci, P. P., & McCall, L. E. (2010, in press). Linking the classroom context and the development of children's memory skills. In J. Meece & J. Eccles (Eds.), *The handbook of research on schools, schooling, and human development.* New York: Routledge.

Orth, U., Robins, R. W., & Roberts. B. W. (2008). Low self-esteem prospectively predicts depression in adolescence and young adulthood. *Journal of Personality and Social Psychology, 95,* 695–708.

Orth, U., Robins, R. W., Trzesniewski, K. H., Maes, J., & Schmitt, M. (2009). Low self-esteem is a risk factor for depressive symptoms from young adulthood to old age. *Journal of Abnormal Psychology, 118(3),* 472–478

Osborne, J. (2010). Arguing to learn in science: The role of collaborative, critical discourse. *Science, 328,* 463–468.

Oser, F. K., Scarlett, W. G., & Bucher, A. (2006). Religious and spiritual development throughout the life span. In W. Damon & R. Lerner (Eds.), *Handbook of child psychology* (4th ed.). New York: Wiley.

Ostchega, Y., Carroll, M., Prineas, R. J., McDowell, M. A., Louis, T., & Tilert, T. (2009). Trends of elevated blood pressure among children and adolescents: Data from the National Health and Nutrition Examination Survey 1988–2006. *American Journal of Hypertension, 22,* 59–67.

O'Sullivan, L. F. (2012). Open to the public: How adolescents blur the boundaries online between the private and public spheres of their lives. *Journal of Adolescent Health, 50,* 429–430.

Otto, B. W. (2010). *Language development in early childhood* (3rd ed.). Upper Saddle River, NJ: Prentice Hall.

Ouellette-Kuntz, H., & others. (2012). National Epidemiologic Database for the Study of Autism in Canada (NEDSAC). *Chronic Diseases and Injuries in Canada, 32.*

Owens, J. A., Belon, K., & Moss, P. (2010). Impact of delaying school start time on adolescent sleep, mood, and behavior. *Archives of Pediatric and Adolescent Medicine, 164,* 608-614.

## P

Padilla-Walker, L. M., Carlo, G., Christensen, K. J., & Yorgason, J. B. (2012). Bidirectional relations between authoritative parenting and adolescents' prosocial behaviors. *Journal of Research on Adolescence, 22,* 400-408.

Padilla-Walker, L. M., & Coyne, S. M. (2011). "Turn that thing off!" Parent and adolescent predictors of proactive media monitoring. *Journal of Youth and Adolescence, 34*(4), 705-715.

Padilla-Walker, L. M., Coyne, S. M., Fraser, A. M., Dyer, W. J., & Yorgason, J. B. (2012). Parents and adolescents growing up in the digital age: Latent growth curve analysis of proactive media monitoring. *Journal of Adolescence, 35*(5), 1153-1165.

Padilla-Walker, L. M., Day, R. D., Dyer, W. J., & Black, B. (2013). *"Keep on keeping on even when it's hard!"* Predictors and outcomes of adolescence persistence. Unpublished manuscript, Brigham Young University, Provo, Utah.

Padilla-Walker, L. M., Nelson, L. J., Carroll, J. S., & Jensen, A. C. (2010). More than just a game: Video game and Internet use during emerging adulthood. *Journal of Youth and Adolescence, 39,* 103-113.

Pagani, L., Fitzpatrick, C., Archambault, I., & Janosz, M. (2010). School readiness and later achievement: A French Canadian replication and extension. *Developmental Psychology,* Vol. 46, No. 5, 984-994.

Paintner, A., Williams, A. D., & Burd, L. (2012). Fetal alcohol spectrum disorders—implications for child neurology, part 1: Prenatal exposure and dosimetry. *Journal of Child Neurology, 27,* 258-263.

Pakzad-Vaezi, K., & Singhal, A. (2012). Trends in pediatric sport- and recreation-related injuries: An injury surveillance study at the British Columbia Children's Hospital (Vancouver, British Columbia) from 1992 to 2005. *Pediatrics & Child Health, 16,* 217-221.

Palfrey, J., Sacco, D., Boyd, D., & DeBonis, L. (2009). *Enhancing child safety and online technologies.* Cambridge, MA: Berkman Center for Internet & Society.

Palomares, M., Landau, B., & Egeth, H. (2009). Orientation perception in Williams syndrome: Discrimination and integration. *Brain and Cognition, 70,* 21-30.

Paluck, E. L., & Green, D. P. (2009). Prejudice reduction: What works? A review and assessment of research and practice. *Annual Review of Psychology* (Vol. 60). Palo Alto, CA: Annual Reviews.

Pan, B. A., Rowe, M. L., Singer, J. D., & Snow, C. E. (2005). Maternal correlates of growth in toddler vocabulary production in low-income families. *Child Development, 76,* 763-782.

Pan, B. A., & Uccelli, P. (2009). Semantic development. In J. Berko Gleason & N. Ratner (Eds.), *The development of language* (7th ed.). Boston: Allyn & Bacon.

Panigrahy, A., Borzaga, M., & Blumi, S. (2010). Basic principles and concepts underlying recent advances in magnetic resonance imaging of the developing brain. *Seminars in Perinatology, 34,* 3-19.

Paradis, J. (2010). Second-language acquisition in childhood. In E. Hoff & M. Shatz (Eds.), *Blackwell handbook of language development.* New York: Wiley.

Parens, E., & Johnston, J. (2009). Facts, values, and attention-deficit hyperactivity disorder (ADHD): An update on the controversies. *Child and Adolescent Psychiatry and Mentol Health, 3,* 1.

Parish-Morris, J., Golinkoff, R. M., & Hirsh-Pasek, K. (2013). From coo to code: A brief story of language development. In P. D. Zelazo (Ed.), *Oxford handbook of developmental psychology.* New York: Oxford University Press.

Park, C. L. (2012a). Meaning, spirituality, and growth: Protective and resilience factors in health and illness. In A. S. Baum, T. A. Revenson, & J. E. Singer (Eds.), *Handbook of health psychology* (2nd ed.). New York: Sage.

Park, C. L. (2012b). Meaning making in cancer survivorship. In P. T. P. Wong (Ed.), *Handbook of meaning* (2nd ed.). Thousand Oaks, CA: Sage.

Park, C. J., Yelland, G. W., Taffe, J. R., & Gray, K. M. (2012). Morphological and syntactic skills in language samples of pre-school aged children with autism: Atypical development? *International Journal of Speech and Language Pathology, 14,* 95-108.

Park, W., & Epstein, N. B. (2013, in press). The longitudinal causal directionality between body image distress and self-esteem among Korean adolescents: The moderating effect of relationships with parents. *Journal of Adolescence.*

Parkay, F. W. (2013). *Becoming a teacher* (9th ed.). Upper Saddle River, NJ: Pearson.

Parke, R. D., & Buriel, R. (2006). Socialization in the family: Ethnic and ecological perspectives. In W. Damon & R. Lerner (Eds.), *Handbook of child psychology* (6th ed.). New York: Wiley.

Parke, R. D., & Clarke-Stewart, A. K. (2011). *Social development.* New York: Wiley.

Parke, R. D., Leidy, M. S., Schofield, T. J., Miller, M. A., & Morris, K. L. (2008). Socialization. In M. M. Haith & J. B. Benson (Eds.), *Encyclopedia of infant and early childhood development.* Oxford, UK: Elsevier.

Parker, J. D. A., Saklofske, D. H., Shaughnessy ,P. A., Huang, S. H. S., Wood, L. M., & Eastabrook, J. M. (2005). Generalizability of the emotional intelligence construct: A cross-cultural study of North American aboriginal youth. *Personality and Individual Differences, 39,* 215-227.

Parlade, M. V., Messinger, D. S., Delgado, C. D., Kaiser, M. Y., Van Hecke, A. V., & Mundy, P. C. (2009). Anticipatory smiling: Linking early affective communication and social outcome. *Infant Behavior and Development, 32,* 33-43.

Partanen, M., & Siegel, L. S., (2014). Long-term outcome of the early identification and intervention of reading disabilities. *Reading and Writing,* Vol. 27(4), 665-684.

Pascual, A., Extebarria, I., Ortega, I., & Ripalda, A. (2012). Gender differences in adolescence in emotional variables relevant to eating disorders. *International Journal of Psychology and Psychological Therapy, 12,* 59-68.

Pasley, K., & Moorefield, B. S. (2004). Stepfamilies. In M. Coleman & L. Ganong (Eds.), *Handbook of contemporary families.* Thousand Oaks, CA: Sage.

Pasterski, V., Golombok, S., & Hines, M. (2011). Sex differences in social behavior. In P. K. Smith & C. H. Hart (Eds.), *Wiley-Blackwell handbook of childhood social development* (2nd ed.). New York: Wiley.

Patrick, R. B., & Gibbs, J. C. (2012). Inductive discipline, parental expression of disappointed expectations, and moral identity in adolescence. *Journal of Youth and Adolescence, 41,* 973-983.

Patterson, C., & D'Augelli, A. R. (Eds.). (2013, in press). *The psychology of sexual orientation.* New York: Cambridge University Press.

Patterson, C. J. (2009). Lesbian and gay parents and their children: A social science perspective. *Nebraska Symposium on Motivation, 54,*

Patterson, C. J. (2013, in press). Sexual minority youth with sexual minority parents. In A. Ben-Arieh & others (Eds.), *Handbook of child research.* Thousand Oaks, CA: Sage.

Patterson, C. J., & Farr, R. H. (2012). Children of lesbian and gay parents: Reflections on the research-policy interface. In H. R. Schaeffer & K. Durkin (Eds.), *Wiley-Blackwell handbook of developmental psychology in action*. New York: Wiley.

Paulhus, D. L. (2008). Birth order. In M. M. Haith & J. B. Benson (Eds.), *Encyclopedia of infant and early childhood development*. Oxford, UK: Elsevier.

Pauli-Pott, U., Friedl, S., Hinney, A., & Hebebrand, J. (2009). Serotonin transporter gene polymorphism (5-HTTLPR), environmental conditions, and developing negative emotionality and fear in early childhood. *Journal of Neural Transmission 116*(4), 503–512.

Paulson, F., & Bazemore, S. D. (2010). Prenatal and postpartum depression in fathers and its association with maternal depression. *Journal of the American Medical Association, 303,* 1961–1969.

Paus, T., & others. (2007). Morphological properties of the action-observation cortical network in adolescents with low and high resistance to peer influence. *Social Neuroscience, 3,* 303–316.

Pavlov, I. P. (1927). In G. V. Anrep (Trans.), *Conditioned reflexes*. London: Oxford University Press.

Pea, R., & others. (2012). Media use, face-to-face communication, media multitasking, and social well-being among 8- to 12-year-old girls. *Developmental Psychology, 48,* 327–336.

Pearson, B. Z., Fernandez, S. C., & Oller, D. K. (1993). Lexical development in bilingual infants and toddlers: Comparison to monolingual norms. *Language Learning, 43,* 93–120.

Pecot-Hebert, L. (2012). Beauty & body-image: Anorexia/eating disorders. In M. Kosut (Ed.), *Encyclopedia of gender in media*. Thousand Oaks, CA: Sage.

Pedersen, S., Vitaro, F., Barker, E. D., & Borge, A. I. H. (2007). The timing of middle childhood peer rejection and friendship: Linking early behavior to early-adolescent adjustment. *Child Development, 78,* 1037–1051.

Pederson, D. R., & Moran, G. (1996). Expressions of the attachment relationship outside of the Strange Situation. *Child Development, 67,* 915–927.

Pedroso, F. S. (2008). Reflexes. In M. H. Haith & J. B. Benson (Eds.), *Infant and early childhood development*. Oxford, UK: Elsevier.

Peek, L., & Stough, L. M. (2010). Children with disabilities in the context of disaster: A social vulnerability perspective. *Child Development, 81,* 1260–1270.

Peeters, M. C. W., & others. (2013). Consequences of combining work and family roles: A closer look at cross-domain versus within-domain relations. In J. Grzywacz & E. Demerouti (Eds.), *New frontiers in work and family research*. New York: Routledge.

Peets, K., Hodges, E. V., & Salmivalli, C. (2013). Forgiveness and its determinants depending on the interpersonal context of hurt. *Journal of Experimental Child Psychology*.

Pelaez, M., Virues-Ortega, J., & Gewirtz, J. L. (2012). Acquisition of social referencing via discrimination training in infants. *Journal of Applied Behavior Analysis, 45,* 23–36.

Pelayo, R., Owens, J., Mindell, J., & Sheldon, S. (2006). Bed sharing with unimpaired parents is not an important risk for sudden infant death syndrome: Letter to the editor, *Pediatrics, 117,* 993–994.

Peltzer-Karpf, A. (2012). The dynamic matching of neural and cognitive growth cycles. *Nonlinear Dynamics, Psychology, and Life Sciences, 16,* 61–78.

Pena, E., & Bedore, J. A. (2009). Bilingualism. In R. G. Schwartz (Ed.), *Handbook of child language disorders*. Clifton, NJ: Psychology Press.

Penagarikano, O., Mulle, J. G., & Warren, S. T. (2007). The pathophysiology of fragile X syndrome. *Annual Review of Genomics and Human Genetics* (Vol. 8). Palo Alto, CA: Annual Reviews.

Penela, E. C., & others. (2012). Maternal caregiving moderates the relation between temperamental fear and social behavior with peers. *Infancy, 17,* 715–730.

Pennington, B. F., & others. (2009). Gene × environment interactions in reading disability and attentions deficit/hyperactivity disorder. *Developmental Psychology, 45,* 77–89.

Perin, D. (2007). Best practices in teaching writing to adolescents. In S. Graham, C. A. MacArthur, & J. Fitzgerald (Eds.), *Best practices in writing instruction*. New York: Guilford.

Perner, J., & Ruffman, T. (1995). Episodic memory and autonoetic consciousness: Developmental evidence and a theory of childhood amnesia. *Journal of Experimental Child Psychology, 59,* 516–548.

Perner, J., Stummer, S., Sprung, M., & Doherty, M. (2002). Theory of mind finds its Piagetian perspective: Why alternative naming comes with understanding belief. *Cognitive Development, 17,* 1451–1472.

Perron, A., Brendgen, M., Vitaro, F., Cote, S. M., Tremblay, R. E., Boivin, M. (2012). Moderating effects of team sports participation on the link between peer victimization and mental health problems. *Mental Health and Physical Activity, 5*(2), 107–115.

Perron, M. & Gosselin, P. (2004). Le developpement de l'evocation des emotions, *Enfance, 56,* 133–147.

Perry, D. G. (2012, April). *The intrapsychics of gender*. Paper presented at the Gender Development Research conference. San Francisco.

Perry, D. G. & Pauletti, R. E. (2011). Gender and adolescent development. *Journal of Research on Adolescence, 21,* 61–74.

Perry, N. B., & others. (2013). The relation between maternal emotional support and child physiological regulation across the preschool years. *Developmental Psychobiology, 55,* 382–394.

Perry, N. E. (2013, in press). Classroom processes that support self-regulation in young children (Monograph). *British Journal of Educational Psychology*.

Perry, N. E. & Rahim, A. (2011). Studying self-regulated learning in classrooms. In B. J. Zimmerman & D. H. Schunk (Eds.), *Handbook of self-regulation of learning and performance* (pp. 122–136). New York: Routledge.

Persky, H. R., Dane, M. C., & Jin, Y. (2003). *The nation's report card: Writing 2002*. U.S. Department of Education.

Persson, K. E., Fridlund, B., Kvist, L. J., & Dykes, A. K. (2011). Mothers' sense of security in the first postnatal week: Interview study. *Journal of Advanced Nursing, 67,* 105–116.

Peskin, H. (1967). Pubertal onset and ego functioning. *Journal of Abnormal Psychology, 72,* 1–15.

Peters, H., Whincup, P. H., Cook, D. G., Law, C., & Li, L. (2012). Trends in blood pressure in 9- to 11-year-old children in the United Kingdom, 1980–2008: The impact of obesity. *Journal of Hypertension, 30,* 1708–1717.

Peters, Ray DeV., & others. (2010a). The Better Beginnings, Better Futures projects: Findings from grade 3 to grade 9. *Monographs of the Society for Research in Child Development. 75*(3), 1–174.

Peters, R. DeV., & others. (2010b). *Investing in our future: Highlights of Better Beginnings, Better Futures research findings at grade 12*. Kingston, ON: Better Beginnings, Better Futures Research Coordination Unit, Queen's University.

Petersen, A. C. (1979, January). Can puberty come any faster? *Psychology Today,* pp. 45–56.

Petersen, M. B., Wang, Q., & Willems, P. J. (2008). Sex-linked deafness. *Clinical Genetics, 73,* 14–23.

Peterson, C. (2012). Children's autobiographical memories across the years: Forensic implications of childhood amnesia and eyewitness memory for stressful events. *Developmental Review, 32,* 287–306.

Peterson, C., & Grant, M. (2001). Forced-choice: Are forensic interviewers asking the right questions? *Canadian Journal of Behavioural Science, 33,* 118–127.

Peterson, C., & McCabe, A. (2004). Echoing our parents: Parental influences on children's narration. In M. W. Pratt & B. H. Fiese (Eds.), *Family stories and the life course: Across time and generations* (pp. 27–54). Mahwah, NJ: Erlbaum.

Peterson, C., Wang, Q., & Hou, Y. (2009). "When I was little": Childhood recollections in Chinese and European Canadian grade school children. *Child Development, 80,* 506–518.

Peterson, C. C. (2005). Mind and body: Concepts of human cognition, physiology and false belief in children with autism or typical development. *Journal of Autism and Developmental Disorders, 35,* 487–497.

Peterson, C. C., Garnett, M., Kelly, A., & Attwood, T. (2009). Everyday social and conversation applications of theory-of-mind understanding by children with autism-spectrum disorders or typical development. *European Child and Adolescent Psychiatry, 18,* 105–115.

Petrick-Steward, E. (2012). *Beginning writers in the zone of proximal development.* New York: Psychology Press.

Petrill, S. A., & Deater-Deckard, K. (2004). The heritability of general cognitive ability: A within-family adoption design. *Intelligence, 32,* 403–409.

Pew Research Center (2010). Millenials: confident, connected, open to change. Washington, DC: Pew Research Center.

Pfeifer, M., Goldsmith, H. H., Davidson, R. J., & Rickman, M. (2002). Continuity and change in inhibited and uninhibited children. *Child Development, 73,* 1474–1485.

Philip, R. C., & others. (2012). A systematic review and meta-analysis of the fMRI investigation of autism spectrum disorders. *Neuroscience and Biobehavioral Reviews, 36,* 901–942.

Phillips, L. M., Norris, S. P., Osmond, W. C., & Maynard, A. M. (2002). Relative reading achievement: A longitudinal study of 187 children from first through sixth grades. *Journal of Educational Psychology, 94*(1), 3–13.

Phillips, S., & Edwards, S. (2013). Adolescent health. In I. B. Weiner & others (Eds.), *Wiley handbook of psychology,* (2nd ed., Vol. 9). New York: Wiley.

Phinney, J. S. (2003). Identity and acculturation. In K. M. Chun, P. B. Organista, & G. Marin (Eds.), *Acculturation.* Washington. DC: American Psychological Association.

Phinney, J. S. (2006). Ethnic identity exploration in emerging adulthood. In J. J. Arnett & J. L. Tanner (Eds.), *Emerging adults in America.* Washington, DC: American Psychological Association.

Phinney, J. S. (2008). Bridging identities and disciplines: Advances and challenges in understanding multiple identities. In M. Azmitia, M. Syed, & K. Radmacher (Eds.), *The intersections of personal and social identities. New Directions for Child and Adolescent Development, 120,* 81–95.

Phinney, J. S., & Alipuria, L. L. (1990). Ethnic identity in college students from four ethnic groups. *Journal of Adolescence, 13,* 171–183.

Phinney, J. S., & Baldelomar, O. A. (2011). Identity development in multiple developmental contexts. In L. Jensen (Ed.), *Bridging cultural and developmental approaches to psychology.* New York: Oxford University Press.

Phinney, J. S., & Ong, A. D. (2007). Conceptualization and measurement of ethnic identity: Current status and future directions. *Journal of Counseling Psychology, 54,* 271–281.

Piaget, J. (1932). *The moral judgment of the child.* New York: Harcourt Brace Jovanovich.

Piaget, J. (1952). *The origins of intelligence in children.* (M. Cook, Trans.). New York: International Universities Press.

Piaget, J. (1954). *The construction of reality in the child.* New York: Basic Books.

Piaget, J. (1962). *Play, dreams, and imitation in childhood* (G. Gattegno & F. M. Hodgson, Trans.). New York, NY: Norton.

Piaget, J., & Inhelder, B. (1969). *The child's conception of space* (F. J. Langdon & J. L. Lunger, Trans.). New York: W. W. Norton.

Pickrell, J., & Loftus, E. F. (2001). *Creating false memories.* Paper presented at the American Psychological Society, Toronto.

Pierce, T. (2009). Social anxiety and technology: Face-to-face communication versus technological communication among teens. *Computers in Human Behavior, 25,* 1367–1372.

Pinette, M., Wax, J. & Wilson, E. (2004). The risks of underwater birth. *American Journal of Obstetrics & Gynecology, 190,* 1211–1215.

Ping, H., & Hagopian, W. (2006). Environmental factors in the development of type 1 diabetes. *Review in Endocrine and Metabolic Disorders, 7,* 149–162.

Pinker, S. (1994). *The language instinct.* New York: HarperCollins.

Piper, B. J., & others. (2011). Abnormalities in parentally rated executive function in methamphetamine/ polysubstance exposed children. *Pharmacology, Biochemistry, and Behavior, 98,* 432–439.

Pipp, S. L., Fischer, K. W., & Jennings, S. L. (1987). The acquisition of self and mother knowledge in infancy. *Developmental Psychology, 23,* 86–96.

Pittman, J. F., Kerpleman, J. L., Soto, J. B., & Adler-Baeder, F. M. (2012). Identity exploration in the dating domain: The role of attachment dimensions and parenting practices. *Journal of Adolescence, 35,* 1485–1499.

Pleck, J. H. (1983). The theory of male sex role identity: Its rise and fall, 1936–present. In M. Levin (Ed.), *In the shadow of the past: Psychology portrays the sexes.* New York: Columbia University Press.

Pleck, J. H. (1995). The gender-role strain paradigm. In R. F. Levant & W. S. Pollack (Eds.), *A new psychology of men.* New York: Basic Books.

Plomin, R. (2004). Genetics and developmental psychology. *Merrill-Palmer Quarterly, 50,* 341–352.

Plomin, R., DeFries, J. C., & Fulker, D. W. (2007). *Nature and nurture during infancy and early childhood* (2nd ed.). New York: Cambridge University Press.

Plomin, R., DeFries, J. C., McClearn, G. E., & McGuffin, P. (2009). *Behavioral genetics* (5th ed.). New York: W. H. Freeman.

Plucker, J. (2010, July 10). Interview. In P. Bronson & A. Merryman. The creativity crisis. *Newsweek,* pp. 42–48.

Pluess, M., & Belsky, J. (2009). Differential susceptibility to rearing experience: the case of child care. *Journal of Child Psychology and Psychiatry, 50*(4), 396–404.

Poirel, N., & others. (2012). Number conservation is related to children's prefrontal inhibitory control: An fMRI study of a Piagetian task. *PLoS One, 7*(7), e40802.

Polce-Lynch, M., Myers, B. J., Kliewer, W., & Kilmartin, C. (2001). Adolescent self-esteem and gender: Exploring relations to sexual harassment, body image, media influence, and emotional expression. *Journal of Youth and Adolescence, 30,* 225–244.

Pollack, W. (1999). *Real boys.* New York: Owl Books.

Pomerleau, A., Malcuit, G., Chicoine, J., Sequin, R., Belhumeur, C., Germain, P., Amyot, I., & Jeliu, G. (2005). Health status, cognitive and motor development of young children adopted from China, East Asia, and Russia across the first 6 months after adoption. *International Journal of Behavioral Development, 29,* 445–457.

Pon, J., Davies, L., Macintyre, G., & Cox, D. (2011). Functional testing of Wilson disease patient variants in the ATP binding domain and C-terminus of ATP7B. *UBC Medical Journal.* April 2011, Vol. 2, Issue 2, 40.

Poole, D. A., & Lindsay, D. S. (1996). *Effects of parents' suggestions, interviewing techniques, and age on young children's event reports.* Presented at the NATO Advanced Study Institute, Port de Bourgenay, France.

Posada, G., & Kaloustian, G. (2010). Parent-infant interaction. In J. G. Bremner & T. D. Wachs (Eds.), *Wiley-Blackwell handbook of infant development* (2nd ed.). New York: Wiley.

Posner, M. I., & Rothbart, M. K. (2007). *Educating the human brain.* Washington, DC: American Psychological Association.

Poulin, F., & Denault, A-S. (2012). Other-sex friendship as a mediator between parental monitoring and substance use in boys and girls. *Journal of Youth and Adolescence, 41,* 1488–1501.

Poulin, F., & Pedersen, S. (2007). Developmental changes in gender composition of friendship networks in adolescent girls and boys. *Developmental Psychology, 43,* 1484–1496.

Poulin-Dubois, D. & Serbin, L. A. (2006). La connaissance des categories de genre et des stereotypes sexues chez le jeune enfant. *Enfance, 58,* 283–310.

Poulin-Dubois, D., Serbin, L. A., Eichstedt, J., Sen, M. G., & Beissel, C. F. (2002). Men don't put on makeup: Toddlers' knowledge of the gender stereotyping of household activities. *Social Development, 11,* 166–181.

Power, F. C., & Higgins-D'Alessandro, A. (2008). The just community approach to moral education and moral atmosphere of the school. In L. Nucci & D. Narvaez (Eds.), *Handbook of moral and character education.* Clifton, NJ: Psychology Press.

Prabhakar, H. (2007). Hopkins Interactive Guest Blog: *The public health experience at Johns Hopkins.* Available at http://hopkins.typepad.com/guest/2007/03/the_public_heal.html

Prakash, A., Powell, A. J., & Geva, T. (2010). Multimodality noninvasive imaging for assessment of congenital heart disease. *Circulation and Cardiovascular Imaging, 3,* 112–125.

Prameela, K. K. (2011). Breastfeeding—anti-viral potential and relevance to the influenza virus pandemic. *Medical Journal of Malaysia, 66,* 166–169.

Pratt, C., & Bryant, P. E. (1990). Young children understand that looking leads to knowing (so long as they are looking in a single barrel). *Child Development, 61,* 973–982.

Pratt, M. W., Norris, J. E., Hebblethwaite, S., & Arnold, M. L. (2008). Intergenerational transmission of values: Family generativity and adolescents' narratives of parent and grandparent value teaching. *Journal of Personality, 76,* 171–198.

Pressley, M. (2003). Psychology of literacy and literacy instruction. In I. B. Weiner (Ed.). *Handbook of psychology* (Vol. 7). New York: Wiley.

Pressley, M., Allington, R., Wharton-McDonald, R., Block, C. C., & Morrow, L. M. (2001). *Learning to read: Lessons from exemplary first grades.* New York: Guilford.

Pressley, M., Cariliga-Bull, T., Deane, S., & Schneider, W. (1987). Short-term memory, verbal competence, and age as predictors of imagery instructional effectiveness. *Journal of Experimental Child Psychology, 43,* 194–211.

Pressley, M., Dolezal, S. E., Raphael, L. M., Welsh, L. M. Bogner, K., & Roehrig, A. D. (2003). *Motivating primary-grades teachers.* New York: Guilford.

Pressley, M., & Harris, K. (2006). Cognitive strategies instruction. In P. A. Alexander & P. H. Winne (Eds.), *Handbook of educational psychology* (2nd ed.). Mahwah, NJ: Erlbaum.

Pressley, M., & Hilden, K. (2006). Cognitive strategies. In W. Damon & R. Lerner (Eds.), *Handbook of child psychology* (6th ed.). New York: Wiley.

Pressley, M., Mohan, L., Fingeret, L., Reffitt, K., & Raphael Bogaert, L. R. (2007). Writing instruction in engaging and effective elementary settings. In S. Graham, C. A. MacArthur, & J. Fitzgerald (Eds.), *Best practices in writing instruction.* New York: Guilford.

Pressley, M., Mohan, L., Raphael, L. M., & Fingeret, L. (2007). How does Bennett Woods Elementary School produce such high reading and writing achievement? *Journal of Educational Psychology, 99,* 221–240.

Pressley, M., Raphael, L. Gallagher, D., & Dibella, J. (2004). Providence-St. Mel School: How a school that works for African-American students works. *Journal of Educational Psychology, 96,* 216–235.

Presson, J. C., & Jenner, J. V. (2008). *Biology.* New York: McGraw-Hill.

Prezza, M., Pacilli, M. G., & Dinelli, S. (2004). Loneliness and new technologies in a group of Roman adolescents. *Computers in Human Behavior, 20,* 691–709.

Priess, H. A., & Hyde, J. S. (2010). Gender and academic abilities and preferences. In J. Chrisler & D. R. McCreary (Eds.), *Handbook of gender research in psychology: Vol. 1: Gender research in general and experimental psychology* (pp. 297–316). New York, NY: Springer.

Prinstein, M. J. (2007). Moderators of peer contagion: A longitudinal examination of depression socialization between adolescents and their best friends. *Journal of Clinical Child and Adolescent Psychology, 36,* 159–170.

Prinstein, M. J., & Cillessen, A. H. N. (2003). Forms and functions of adolescent peer aggression associated with high levels of peer status. *Merrill-Palmer Quarterly, 49*(3), 310–342.

Prinstein, M. J., & Dodge, K. A. (2008). Current issues in peer influence. In M. J. Prinstein & K. A. Dodge (Eds.), *Understanding peer influence in children and adolescents.* New York: Guilford.

Prinz, J. (2009). *The emotional construction of morals.* New York: Oxford University Press.

Prinz, R. J., Sanders, M. R., Shapiro, C. J., Witaker, D. J., Lutzker, J. R. (2009). Population-based prevention of child maltreatment: The U.S. Triple P System Population Trial. *Prevention Science, 10*(1), 1–12.

Proulx, M. J., Brown, D. J., Pasqualotto, A., & Meijer, P. (2013, in press). Multisensory perceptual learning and sensory substitution. *Neuroscience and Behavioral Reviews.*

Provenzo, E. F. (2002). *Teaching, learning, and schooling in American culture: A critical perspective.* Boston: Allyn & Bacon.

Public Health Agency of Canada. (2004). Results-based management and accountability framework and risk assessment for the Aboriginal Head Start in Urban and Northern Communities program, annex to the promotion of population health grants and contributions. (Ottawa: Public Health Agency of Canada).

Public Health Agency of Canada (2008). Canadian Perinatal Health Report. 2008 Edition. Ottawa: Public Health Agency of Canada; 2008. www.phac-aspc.gc.ca/publicat/2008/cphr-rspc/pdf/cphr-rspc08-eng.pdf

Public Health Agency of Canada. Diabetes in Canada: Facts and figures from a public health perspective. Ottawa, 2011. Available at www.nichd.nih.gov/sts/Pages/default.aspx

Public Health Agency of Canada (2011). Joint statement on safe sleep: Preventing sudden infant deaths in Canada. Public Health Agency of Canada. www.phac-aspc.gc.ca/hp-ps/dca-dea/stages-etapes/childhood-enfance_0-2/sids/pdf/jsss-ecss2011-eng.pdf

Public Health Agency of Canada. (2011). The AHSUNC program's impact on school readiness and other program outcomes (internal study). Ottawa: Public Health Agency of Canada.

Public Health Agency of Canada (2012). HIV and AIDS in Canada: Surveillance Report to December 31, 2012. www.phac-aspc.gc.ca/aids-sida/publication/survreport/2012/dec/index-eng.php

Puckett, M. B., Aikins, J. W., & Cillessen, A. H. N. (2008). Moderators of the association between relational aggression and perceived popularity. *Aggressive Behavior, 34,* 1–14.

Pujol, J., & others. (2004). Delayed myelination in children with developmental delay detected by volumetric MRI. *Neuroimage, 22,* 897–903.

Pulgaron, E. R. (2013). Childhood obesity: A review of increased risk for physical and psychological morbidities. *Clinical Therapeutics, 35,* A18–A32.

Pungello, E. P., Iruka, I. U., Dotterer, A. M., Mills-Koonce, R., & Reznick, J. S. (2009). The effects of socioeconomic status, race, and parenting on language development in early childhood. *Developmental Psychology, 45,* 544–557.

Putallaz, M., Grimes, C. L., Foster, K. J., Kupersmidt, J. B., Coie, J. D., & Dearing, K. (2007). Overt and relational aggression and victimization: Multiple perspectives within the school setting. *Journal of School Psychology, 45,* 523–547.

Putnam, S. P., Sanson, A. V., & Rothbart, M. K. (2002). Child temperament and parenting. In M. H. Bornstein (Ed.), *Handbook of parenting* (2nd ed.). Mahwah, NJ: Erlbaum.

## Q

Quadrelli, R., Quadrelli, A., Mechoso, B., Laufer, M., Jaumandreu, C., & Vaglio, A. (2007). Parental decisions to abort or continue a pregnancy following prenatal diagnosis of chromosomal abnormalities in a setting where termination of pregnancy is not legally available. *Prenatal Diagnosis, 27,* 228–232.

Quinn, P. C. (2011). Born to categorize. In U. Goswami (Ed.), *Wiley-Blackwell handbook of childhood cognitive development* (2nd ed.). New York: Wiley-Blackwell.

Quinn, P. C., & others. (2013, in press). On the developmental origins of differential responding to social category information.

In M. R. Banaji & S. A. Gelman (Eds.), *Navigating the social world.* New York: Oxford University Press.

## R

Raikes, H., & others. (2006). Mother-child bookreading in low-income families: Correlates and outcomes during the first three years of life. *Child Development, 77,* 924–953.

Raikes, H. A., & Thompson, R. A. (2009). Attachment security and parenting quality predict children's problem-solving, attributions, and loneliness with peers. *Attachment and Human Development, 10,* 319–344.

Rajaraman, P., & others. (2011). Early life exposure to diagnostic radiation and ultrasound scans and risk of childhood cancer: Case-control study. *British Medical Journal, 342.*

Rajendran, G., & Mitchell, P. (2007). Cognitive theories of autism. *Developmental Review, 27,* 224–260.

Rakison, D. H., & Lawson, C. A. (2013). Categorization. In P. D. Zelazo (Ed.), *Oxford handbook of developmental psychology.* New York: Oxford University Press.

Rakoczy, H. (2012). Do infants have a theory of mind? *British Journal of Developmental Psychology, 30,* 59–74.

Ram, K. T., & others. (2008). Duration of lactation is associated with lower prevalence of the metabolic syndrome in midlife—SWAN, the study of women's health across the nation. *American Journal of Obstetrics and Gynecology, 198,* e1–e6.

Ramchandani, P. G., & others. (2011). Paternal depression: An examination of its links with father, child, and family functioning in the postnatal period. *Depression and Anxiety, 28,* 471–477.

Ramchandani, P. G., & others. (2013). Do early father-infant interactions predict the onset of externalizing behaviors in young children? Findings from a longitudinal cohort study. *Journal of Child Psychology and Psychiatry, 54,* 56–64.

Ramchandani, P. G., O'Connor, T. G., Evans, J., Heron, J., Murray, L., & Stein, A. (2008). The effects of pre- and postnatal depression in fathers: A natural experiment comparing the effects of exposure to depression on offspring. *Journal of Child Psychology and Psychiatry, 49*(10), 1069–1078.

Ramey, C. T., Ramey, S. L., & Lanzi, R. G. (2001). Intelligence and experience. In R. J. Sternberg & E. L. Grigorenko (Eds.), *Environmental effects on cognitive abilities.* Mahwah, NJ: Erlbaum.

Ramey, S. L. (2005). Human developmental science serving children and families: Contributions of the NICHD study of early child care. In NICHD Early Child Care Network (Eds.), *Child care and development.* New York: Guilford.

Ramirez, T. L., & Malloy, M. H. (2013). Sudden infant death syndrome: are we any closer to identifying which infants will be affected? *Pediatric Health, Medicine and Therapeutics* 2013:4 13–21.

Ramphal, C. (1962). *A study of three current problems in education.* Unpublished doctoral dissertation, University of Natal, India.

Rasmussen, C., Horne, K. A, & Witol, A. (2006). Neurobehavioral functioning in children with Fetal Alcohol Spectrum Disorder. *Child Neuropsychology, 12,* 453–468.

Rasmussen, S. A. (2012). Human teratogens update 2011: Can we ensure safety during pregnancy? *Birth Defects Research A: Clinical and Molecular Teratology, 94,* 123–128.

Rauscher, F., H., Shaw, G. L., & Ky, C. N. (1993). Music and spatial task performance. *Nature, 365,* 611.

Raven, P. H. (2011). *Biology* (9th ed.). New York: McGraw-Hill.

Raver, C. C., & others. (2011). CSRP's impact on low-income preschoolers preacademic skills: Self-regulation as a mediating mechanism. *Child Development, 82,* 362–378.

Raver, C. C., & others. (2012). Testing models of children's self-regulation within educational contexts: Implications for measurement. *Advances in Child Development and Behavior, 42,* 245–270.

Reed, D. (2009). *Balanced introduction to computer science* (2nd ed.). Upper Saddle River, NJ: Prentice Hall.

Reed, S. K. (2010). *Cognition* (8th ed.). Boston: Cengage.

Regev, R. H., & others. (2003). Excess mortality and morbidity among small-for-gestational-age premature infants: A population based study. *Journal of Pediatrics, 143,* 186–191.

Reiner, W. G., & Gearhart, J. P. (2004). Discordant sexual identity in some genetic males with cloacal exstrophy assigned to female sex at birth. *New England Journal of Medicine, 350,* 333–341.

Reis, S. M., & Renzulli, J. S. (2011). Intellectual giftedness. In R. J. Sternberg & S. B. Kaufman (Eds.), *Cambridge handbook of intelligence.* New York: Cambridge.

Repacholi, B. M., & Gopnik, A. (1997). Early reasoning about desires: Evidence from 14- and 18-month-olds. *Developmental Psychology, 33,* 12–21.

Reproductive Endocrinology and Infertility Committee & others. (2012). Advanced reproductive age and fertility. *Journal of Obstetrics and Gynecology Canada.*

Rest, J. R. (1995). *Concern for the social-psychological development of youth and educational strategies: Report for the Kaufmann Foundation.* Minneapolis: University of Minnesota, Department of Educational Psychology.

Reyna, V. F., & Brainerd, C. J. (1995). Fuzzy-trace theory: An interim synthesis. *Learning and Individual Differences, 7,* 1–75.

Reyna, V. F., & Brainerd, C. J. (2011). Dual processes in decision making and developmental neuroscience: A fuzzy-trace model. *Developmental Review, 31,* 180–206.

Reyna, V. F., & Farley, F. (2006). Risk and rationality in adolescent decision-making: Implications for theory, practice, and public policy. *Psychological Science in the Public Interest, 7,* 1–44.

Reyna, V. F., & others. (2010). Gist-based conceptions of risk in adolescent alcohol consumption: A fuzzy trace theory approach. *Annals of Behavioral Medicine, 39,* s196.

Reyna, V. F., & others. (2011). Neurobiological and memory models of risky decision making in adolescents versus young adults. *Journal of Experimental Psychology: Learning, Memory, and Cognition, 37,* 1125–1142.

Reyna, V. F., & Rivers, S. E. (2008). Current theories of risk and rational decision making. *Developmental Review, 28,* 1–11.

Reynolds, C. R., & Livingston, R. B. (2012). *Mastering modern psychological testing.* Upper Saddle River, NJ: Pearson.

Reynolds, F. (2010). The effects of maternal labour analgesia on the fetus. *Best Practices & Research. Clinical Obstetrics & Gynaecology.* (Available online December 11, 2009.)

Richards, J. E. (2011). Infant attention, arousal, and the brain. In L. Oakes & others (Eds.), *Infant perception and cognition.* New York: Oxford University Press.

Richardson, G. A., Goldschmidt, L., & Willford, J. (2008). The effects of prenatal cocaine use on infant development. *Neurotoxicology and Teratology, 30,* 96–106.

Richardson, G. A., Goldschmidt, L., Leech, S., & Willford, J. (2011). Prenatal cocaine exposure: Effects on mother- and teacher-rated behavior problems and growth in school-aged children. *Neurotoxicology and Teratology, 33,* 69–77.

Richter, L. (2004). Poverty, underdevelopment, and infant mental health. *Journal of Pediatric and Child Health, 39,* 243–248.

Rickards, T., Moger, S., & Runco, M. (2009). *The Routledge companion to creativity.* Oxford, UK: Routledge.

Rideout, V. J. (2007). Parents, children and media (Report). Menlo Park, CA: The Henry J. Kaiser Family Foundation, Children's Digital Media Centers.

Rideout, V. J., Foehr, U. G., & Roberts, D. F. (2010). *Generation M2: Media in the lives of 8- to 18- year-olds.* Menlo Park, CA: Kaiser Family Foundation.

Rideout, V., Roberts, D. F., & Foehr, U. G. (2005). *Generation M: Media in the lives of 8- to 18-year-olds.* San Francisco: Kaiser Family Foundation.

Riggins, T. (2012). Building blocks of recollection. In S. Ghetti & P. J. Bauer (Eds.), *Origins of recollection.* New York: Oxford University Press.

Rijlaarsdam, G., & others. (2012). Writing. In K. R. Harris, S. Graham, & T. Urdan (Eds.), *APA handbook of educational psychology.* Washington, DC: American Psychological Association.

Riley, M., & Bluhm, B. (2012). High blood pressure in children and adolescents. *American Family Physician, 85,* 693–700.

Rinsky, J. R., & Hinshaw, S. P. (2011). Linkages between childhood executive functioning and adolescent social functioning and psychopathology in girls with ADHD. *Child Neuropsychology, 17*(4), 368–390.

Risch, N., & others. (2009). Interaction between the serotonin transporter gene (5-HTTLPR), stressful life events, and risk of depression: A meta-analysis. *Journal of the American Medical Association, 301,* 2462–2471.

Ritchie, S., Maxwell, K. L., & Bredekamp, S. (2009). Rethinking early schooling: Using developmental science to transform young children's early school experiences. In O. A. Barbarin & B. H. Wasik (Eds.), *Handbook of child development and early education.* New York: Oxford University Press.

Roberts, D. F., Henriksen, L., & Foehr, U. G. (2004). Adolescents and the media. In R. Lerner & L. Steinberg (Eds.), *Handbook of adolescent psychology* (2nd ed.). New York: Wiley.

Roberts, D. F., Henriksen, L., & Foehr, U. G. (2009). Adolescence, adolescents, and the media. In R. M. Lerner & L. Steinberg (Eds.), *Handbook of adolescent psychology* (3rd ed.). New York: Wiley.

Roberts, K. C., Shields, M., de Groh, M., Aziz, A., & Gilbert, J. (2012). Overweight and obesity in children and adolescents: Results from the 2009 to 2011 Canadian Health Measures Survey. Statistics Canada,

Catalogue no. 82-003-XPE. *Health Reports,* Vol. 23, no. 3.

Robins, R. W., Trzesniewski, K. H., Tracy, J. L., Gosling, S. D., & Potter, J. (2002). Global self-esteem across the life span. *Psychology and Aging, 17,* 423–434.

Robinson G. C., Conry J. L., Conry R. F. (1987). Clinical profile and prevalence of fetal alcohol syndrome in an isolated community in British Columbia. CMAJ 137: 203–207.

Robinson-Riegler, B., & Robinson-Riegler, G. L. (2012). *Cognitive psychology* (3rd ed.). Upper Saddle River, NJ: Pearson.

Robledo-Colonia, A. F., & others. (2012). Aerobic exercise training during pregnancy reduces symptoms in nulliparous women: A randomized trial. *Journal of Physiotherapy, 58,* 9–15.

Roblin, L. (2007). Childhood obesity: food, nutrient, and eating-habit trends and influences. *Applied Physiology, Nutrition and Metabolism,* Aug;32(4):635–45.

Roblyer, M. D., & Doering, A. H. (2013). Integrating educational technology into teaching. (6th ed.). Upper Saddler River, NJ: Pearson.

Rocha, E. M., Marche, T. A., & Briere, J. L. (2013). The effect of forced-choice questions on children's suggestibility: A comparison of multiple-choice and yes/no questions. *Canadian Journal of Behavioural Science, 45,* 1–11.

Rochat, P. (2013). Self-conceptualizing in development. In P. D. Zelazo (Ed.), *Oxford handbook of developmental psychology.* New York: Oxford University Press.

Rode, J. C., & others. (2008). An examination of the structural, discriminant, nomological, incremental predictive validity of the MSCEIT. *Intelligence, 36,* 350–366.

Rode, L., & others. (2009). Systematic review of progesterone for the prevention of preterm birth in singleton pregnancies. *Acta Obstetrica et Gynecologica Scandinavica, 88,* 1180–1189.

Rodenburg, G., Kremers, S. P., Oenema, A., & van de Mheen, D. (2012). Associations of children's appetitive traits with weight and dietary behaviors in the context of general parenting. *PLoS One, 7*(12), 50642.

Rodriguez, E. T., & others. (2009). The formative role of home literacy experiences across the first three years of life in children from low-income families. *Journal of Applied Developmental Psychology, 30*(6), 677–694.

Roemmich, J. N., & Lambiase, M., Slavy, S. J., & Horvath, P. J. (2009).

Protective effect of interval exercise on psychophysical stress reactivity in children. *Psychophysiology, 46,* 852-861.

Roeser, R. W., & Zelazo, P. D. (2012). Contemplative science, education and child development. *Child Development Perspectives, 6,* 143-145.

Rogaev, E. L., Grigorenko, A. P., Faskhutdinova, G., Kittler, E. L., & Moliaka, Y. K. (2009). *Genotype analysis identifies the cause of the* "royal disease" *Science, 326,* 817.

Rogoff, B. (1990). *Apprenticeship in thinking.* New York: Oxford University Press.

Rogoff, B. (2003). *The cultural nature of human development.* New York: Oxford University Press.

Rogoff, B., Correa-Chavez, M. & Silva, K. G. (2011). Cultural variation in children's learning and attention. In M. A. Gernsbacher & others (Eds.), *Psychology and the real world.* New York: Worth.

Rogoff, B., Moore, L., Najafi, B., Dexter, A., Correa-Chavez, M., & Solis, J. (2007). Children's development of cultural repertoires through participation in everyday routines and practices. In J. E. Grusec & P. D. Hastings (Eds.), *Handbook of socialization.* New York: Guilford.

Rogoff, B., Morelli, G. A., & Chavajay, P. (2010). Children's integration in communities and segregation of people of differing ages. *Perspectives on Psychological Science, 5,* 431-440.

Rohner, R. P., & Rohner, E. C. (1981). Parental acceptance-rejection and parental control: Cross-cultural codes. *Ethnology, 20,* 245-260.

Roisman, G. I., & Fraley, R. C. (2012). The legacy of early interpersonal experience. *Advances in Child Development and Behavior, 42,* 79-112.

Roisman, G. I., & Groh, A. M. (2011). Attachment theory and research in developmental psychology: An overview and appreciative critique. In M. K. Underwood & L. H. Rosen (Eds.), *Social development.* New York: Guilford.

Romano, E., Babchishin, L., Pagani, L. S., & Kohen, D. (2010). School readiness and later achievement: Replication and extension using a nationwide Canadian survey. *Developmental Psychology, 46,* 995-1007.

Roopnarine, J. L., & Metindogan, A., (2006). Early childhood education research in cross-national perspective. In B. Spodek & O. N. Saracho (Eds.). *Handbook of research on the education of young children.* Mahwah, NJ: Erlbaum.

Rose, A. J., & Asher, S. R. (1999). Children's goals and strategies in response to conflicts within a friendship. *Developmental Psychology, 35,* 69-79.

Rose, A. J., Carlson, W., & Waller, E. M. (2007). Prospective associations of co-rumination with friendship and emotional adjustment: Considering the socioemotional trade-offs of co-rumination. *Developmental Psychology, 43,* 1019-1031.

Rose, A. J., & Smith, R. L. (2009). Sex differences in peer relationships. In K. H. Rubin, W. M. Bukowski, & B. Laursen (Eds.), *Handbook of peer interactions, relationships, and groups.* New York: Guilford.

Rose, A. J., Swenson, L. P., & Waller, E. M. (2004). Overt and relational aggression and perceived popularity: Developmental differences in concurrent and prospective relations. *Developmental Psychology, 40*(3), 378-387.

Rose, S., Feldman, J. F., Jankowski, J. J., & Van Rossem, R. (2012). Information processing from infancy to 11 years: Continuities and prediction of IQ. *Intelligence, 40,* 445-457.

Rose, S. A., Feldman, J. F., & Jankowski, J. J. (2009). A cognitive approach to the development of early language. *Child Development, 80,* 134-150.

Rosen, L. D., Cheever, N. A., & Carrier, L. M. (2008). The association of parenting style and child age with parental limit setting and adolescent MySpace behavior. *Journal of Applied Developmental Psychology, 29,* 459-471.

Rosenberg, M. S., Westling, D. L., & McLeskey, J. (2011). *Special education for today's teachers* (2nd ed.). Upper Saddle River, NJ: Merrill.

Rosenblith, J. F. (1992). *In the beginning* (2nd ed.). Newbury Park, CA: Sage.

Rosenheck, R. (2008). Fast food consumption and increased caloric intake: A systematic review of a trajectory towards weight gain and obesity risk. *Obesity Reviews, 9*(6), 535-547.

Rosenkoetter, L. I., Rosenkoetter, S. E., & Acock, A. C. (2009). Television violence: An intervention to reduce its impact on children. *Journal of Applied Developmental Psychology, 30,* 381-397.

Rosenstein, D., & Oster, H. (1988). Differential facial responses to four basic tastes in newborns. *Child Development, 59,* 1555-1568.

Rosenthal, D. A., & Feldman, S. S. (1992). The relationship between parenting behaviour and ethnic identity in Chinese-American and Chinese-Australian adolescents. *International Journal of Psychology, 27,* 19-31.

Rosnow, R. L., & Rosenthal, R. (1996). *Beginning behavioral research* (2nd ed.). Upper Saddle River, NJ: Prentice Hall.

Ross, H., & Howe, N. (2009). Family influences on children's peer relationships. In K. H. Rubin, W. M. Bukowksi, & B. Laursen (Eds.), *Handbook of peer interactions, relationships, and groups.* New York: Guilford.

Ross, J. L., & others. (2008). Cognitive and motor development during childhood in boys with Klinefelter syndrome. *American Journal of Medical Genetics A, 146A,* 708-719.

Rossano, F., Carpenter, M., & Tomasello, M. (2012). One-year-old infants follow others' voice direction. *Psychological Science, 23,* 1298-1302.

Rote, W. M., Smetana, J. G., Campione-Barr, N., Villalobos, M., & Tasopouos-Chan, M. (2012). Associations between observed mother-adolescent interactions and adolescent information management. *Journal of Research on Adolescence, 22,* 206-214.

Rothbart, M. K. (2004). Temperament and the pursuit of an integrated developmental psychology. *Merrill-Palmer Quarterly, 50,* 492-505.

Rothbart, M. K. (2011). *Becoming who we are.* New York: Guilford.

Rothbart, M. K., & Bates, J. E. (2006). Temperament. In W. Damon & R. Lerner (Eds.), *Handbook of child psychology* (6th ed.). New York: Wiley.

Rothbart, M. K., & Gartstein, M. A. (2008). Temperament. In M. M. Haith & J. B. Benson (Eds.), *Encyclopedia of infant and early childhood development.* Oxford, UK: Elsevier.

Rothbart, M. K., & Sheese, B. E. (2007). Temperament and emotion regulation. In J. J. Gross (Ed.), *Handbook of emotion regulation.* New York: Guilford Press.

Rothbaum, F., Poll, M., Azuma, H., Miyake, K., & Weisz, J. (2000). The development of close relationships in Japan and the United States: Paths of symbiotic harmony and generative tension. *Child Development, 71,* 1121-1142.

Rothbaum, F., & Trommsdorff, G. (2007). Do roots and wings complement or oppose one another?: The socialization of relatedness and autonomy in cultural context. In J. E. Grusec & P. D. Hastings (Eds.), *Handbook of Socialization.* New York: Guilford.

Roussotte, F. F. (2011). Abnormal brain activation during working memory in children with prenatal exposure to drugs of abuse: The effects of methamphetamine, alcohol, and polydrug exposure. *NeuroImage, 54,* 3067–3075.

Rovee-Collier, C. (1987). Learning and memory in children. In J. D. Osofsky (Ed.), *Handbook of infant development* (2nd ed.). New York: Wiley.

Rovee-Collier, C. (2004). Infant learning and memory. In U. Goswami (Ed.), *Blackwell handbook of childhood cognitive development.* Malden, MA: Blackwell.

Rovee-Collier, C. (2007). The development of infant memory. In N. Cowan & M. Courage (eds.), *The development of memory in childhood.* Philadelphia: Psychology Press.

Rovee-Collier, C., & Barr, R. (2010). Infant learning and memory. In J. G. Bremner & T. D. Wachs (Ed.), *Wiley-Blackwell handbook of infant development* (2nd ed.). New York: Wiley.

Rovers, M. M., de Kok, I. M., & Schilder, A. G. (2006). Risk factors for otitis media: An international perspective. *International Journal of Otorhinolaryngology, 70,* 1251–1256.

Row, C., Burns, S., & Griffin, P. (Eds.). (1998). *Preventing reading difficulties in young children.* Washington, DC: National Academy Press.

Rowe, M. L., & Goldin-Meadow, S. (2009). Differences in early gesture explain SES disparities in child vocabulary size at school entry. *Science, 323,* 951–953.

Rowley, S., Kurtz-Costes, B., & Cooper, S. M. (2010). The role of schooling in ethnic minority achievement and attainment. In J. Meece & J. Eccles (Eds.), *Handbook of research on schools, schooling, and human development.* New York: Routledge.

Roza, S. J., & others. (2010). Maternal folic acid supplement use in early pregnancy and child behavioural problems: The Generation R study. *British Journal of Nutrition, 103,* 445–452.

Ruano, D., & others. (2010). Functional gene group analysis reveals a role of synaptic heterotrimeric G proteins in cognitive ability. *American Journal of Human Genetics, 86,* 113–125.

Rubenstein, R. S. (2012). *Adolescent social perspective taking in contexts of social justice: Examining perceptions of social group differences.* Master of Arts Thesis, Department of Human Development and Applied Psychology, Ontario Institute for Studies of Education, University of Toronto, Toronto, CA.

Rubie-Davies, C. M. (2007). Classroom interactions: exploring the practices of high- and low-expectation teachers. *British Journal of Educational Psychology, 77,* 289–306.

Rubin, K. H., Bowker, J. C., McDonald, K. L., & Menzer, M. (2013). Peer relationships in childhood. In P. D. Zelazo (Ed.), *Oxford handbook of developmental psychology.* New York: Oxford University Press.

Rubin, K. H., Bukowski, W., & Parker, J. (2006). Peer interactions, relationships, and groups. In W. Damon & R. Lerner (Eds.), *Handbook of child psychology* (6th ed.). New York: Wiley.

Rubin, K. H., Cheah, C., & Menzer, M. M. (2010). Peers. In M. H. Bornstein (Ed.), *Handbook of cultural developmental science.* New York: Psychology Press.

Rubin, K. H., Coplan, R., Bowker, J. C., & Menzer, M. (2011). Social inhibition and withdrawal in childhood. In P. K. Smith & C. Hart (Eds.), *Handbook of Childhood Social Development* (2nd Edition, pp. 434–452). New York, NY: Wiley-Blackwell.

Rubin, K. H., Hemphill, S. A., Chen, X., Hastings, P., Sanson, A., Lo Coco, A., & others. (2006). A cross-cultural study of behavioral inhibition in toddlers: East-west-north-south. *International Journal of Behavioral Development, 30,* 219–226.

Rubin, K. H., Mills, R. S. L., & Rose-Krasnor, L. (1989). Maternal beliefs and children's competence. In B. Schneider, G. Attili, J. Nadel, & R. Weissberg (Eds.), *Social competence in developmental perspective.* Amsterdam: Kluwer Academic.

Ruchat, S. M., & others. (2012). Nutrition and exercise reduce excessive weight gain in normal-weight pregnant women. *Medicine and Science in Sports and Exercise, 44,* 1419–1426.

Rudang, R., Mellstrom, D., Clark, E., Ohlsson, C., & Lorentzon, M. (2012). Advancing maternal age is associated with lower bone mineral density in young adult male offspring. *Osteoporosis International, 23,* 475–482.

Rudy, D. & Grusec, J. E. (2006). Authoritarian parenting in individualistic and collectivistic groups: Associations with maternal emotion and cognition and children's self-esteem. *Journal of Family Psychology, 20,* 68–78.

Rueda, M. R., & Posner, M. I. (2013). Development of attentional networks. In P. D. Zelazo (Ed.), *Oxford handbook of developmental psychology.* New York: Oxford University Press.

Ruel, M. T., & others. (2008). Age-based preventive targeting of food assistance and behavior change and communication for reduction of childhood undernutrition in Haiti: A cluster randomized trial. *Lancet, 371,* 588–595.

Ruffman, T., Slade, L., & Crowe, E. (2002). The relation between children's and mothers' mental state language and theory-of-mind understanding. *Child Development, 73,* 734–751.

Rumberger, R. W. (1995). Dropping out of middle school: The influence of race, sex, and family background. *American Educational Research Journal, 3,* 583–625.

Runquist, J. (2007). Persevering through postpartum fatigue. *Journal of Obstetric, Gynecologic, and Neonatal Nursing, 36,* 28–37.

Rusen, L., Liu, S., Sauve, R., Joseph, K. S., Kramer, M. S. (2004). Sudden infant death syndrome in Canada: Trends in rates and risk factors, 1985–1998. *Chronic Diseases in Canada,* 2004 Winter; 25(1):1-6.

Russ, S. W., & Dillon, J. A. (2011). Changes in children's pretend play over two decades. *Creativity Research Journal, 23,* 330–338.

Ryan, A. M. & Shim, S. S. (2008). An exploration of young adolescents' social achievement goals and social adjustment in middle school. *Journal of Educational Psychology, 100*(3), 672–687.

Ryan, R. M., & Deci, E. L. (2009). Promoting self-determined school engagement: Motivation, learning, and well-being. In K. Wentzel, & A. Wigfield (Eds.), *Handbook of motivation at school.* New York: Routledge.

## S

Saarni, C. (1999). *The development of emotional competence.* New York: Guilford.

Saarni, C., Campos, J., Camras, L. A., & Witherington, D. (2006). Emotional development. In W. Damon & R. Lerner (Eds.), *Handbook of child psychology* (6th ed.). New York: Wiley.

Sabatier, C. & Berry, J. W. (2008). The role of family acculturation, parental style, and perceived discrimination in the adaptation of second-generation immigrant youth in France and Canada. *European Journal of Developmental Psychology, 5*(2), 159–185.

Sachs, J. (2009). Communication development in infancy. In J. Berko Gleason & N. B. Ratner (Eds.), *The development of language* (7th ed.). Boston: Allyn & Bacon.

Sackett, P. R., Hardison, C. M., & Cullen, M. J. (2005). On interpreting research on stereotype threat and test performance. *American Psychologist, 60,* 271–272.

Sadker, M. P., & Sadker, D. M. (2005). *Teachers, schools, and society* (7th ed.). New York: McGraw-Hill.

Saffran, J. R. (2009). Acquiring grammatical patterns: Constraints on learning. In J. Colombo, P. McCardle, & L. Freund (Eds.), *Infant pathways to language.* Clifton, NJ: Psychology Press.

Sagiv, S. K., Epstein, J. N., Bellinger, D. C., & Korrick, S. A. (2013, in press). Pre- and postnatal risk factors for ADHD in a nonclinical pediatric population. *Journal of Attention Disorders.*

Saifer, S. (2007, August 29). *Tools of the Mind—A Vygotskian-inspired early childhood curriculum.* Paper presented at the 17th Annual Conference of the European Early Childhood Education Research Association, Prague.

Salem, S. S., Lim, K., & Van den Hof, M. C. (2014). Joint SOGC/CAR policy statement on non-medical use of fetal ultrasound. *Journal of Obstetrics and Gynaecology Canada, 36,* 184–185.

Salloum, A., & Overstreet, S. (2012). Grief and trauma intervention for children after disaster: Exploring coping skills versus trauma narration. *Behavior Research and Therapy, 50,* 169–179.

Salley, B., Miller, A., & Bell, M.A. (2013, in press). Associations between temperament and social responsiveness in young children. *Infant and Child Development.*

Salmivalli, C., & Peets, K. (2009). Bullies, victims, and bully-victim relationships in middle childhood and adolescence. In K. H. Rubin, W. M. Bukowski, & B. Laursen (Eds.), *Handbook of peer interactions, relationships, and groups.* New York: Guilford.

Salovey, P., & Mayer, J. D. (1990). Emotional intelligence. *Imagination, Cognition, and Personality, 9,* 185–211.

Salthouse, T. A. (2005). Relations between cognitive abilities and measures of executive functioning. *Neuropsychology, 19,* 532–545.

Salthouse, T. A., Atkinson, T. M., & Berish, D. E. (2003). Executive functioning as a potential mediator of age-related cognitive decline in normal adults. *Journal of Experimental Psychology: General, 132,* 566–594.

Sameroff, A. (2010). A unified theory of development: A dialectic integration of nature and nurture. *Child Development, 81,* 6–22.

Sameroff, A. J. (2009). The transactional model. In A. J. Sameroff (Ed.), *The transactional model of development: How children and contexts shape each other.* Washington, DC: American Psychological Association.

Samhan, Y. M., El-Sabae, H. H., Khafagy, H. F., & Masher, M. A. (2013). A pilot study to compare epidural identification and catheterization using a saline-filled syringe versus a continuous hydrostatic pressure system. *Journal of Anesthesia, 27*(4).

Sanders, E. (2008). Medical art and play therapy with accident survivors. In C. A. Malchiodi (Ed.), *Creative interventions with traumatized children.* New York: Guilford.

Sandler, I., Wolchik, S., & Schoenfelder, E. (2011). Evidence-based family-focused prevention programs for children. *Annual Review of Psychology* (Vol. 62). Palo Alto, CA: Annual Reviews.

Santiago, C. D., Etter, E. M., Wadsworth, M. E., & Raviv, T. (2012). Predictors of responses to stress among families coping with poverty-related stress. *Anxiety, Stress, and Coping, 25*(3), 239–258.

Santrock, J. W., Sitterle, K. A., & Warshak, R. A. (1988). Parent-child relationships in stepfather families. In P. Bronstein & C. P. Cowan (Eds.), *Fatherhood today: Men's changing roles in the family.* New York: Wiley.

Santrock, J. W., & Warshak, R. A. (1979). Father custody and social development in boys and girls. *Journal of Social Issues, 35,* 112–125.

Sas, L. (2002). The interaction between children's developmental capabilities and the courtroom environment: The impact on testimonial competency. Department of Justice Canada: Policy Centre for Victims Issues. Retrieved from http://publications.gc.ca/collections/Collection/J3-2-2002-6-1-1E.pdf

Sasson, N. J., & Elison, J. T. (2013, in press). Eye tracking in young children with autism. *Journal of Visualized Experiments.*

Saunders, N. R., Liddelow, S. A., & Dziegielewska, K. M. (2012). Barrier mechanisms in the developing brain. *Frontiers in Pharmacology, 3,* 46.

Savage, R. S., Abrami, P., Hipps, G., & Dealut, L. (2009). A randomized controlled trial study of the ABRACADABRA reading intervention program in grade 1. *Journal of Educational Psychology, 101,* 590–604.

Savelsbergh, G., van der Kamp, J., & van Wersmerskerken, M. (2013). The development of reaching actions. In P. D. Zelazo (Ed.), *Oxford handbook of developmental psychology.* New York: Oxford University Press.

Savin-Williams, R. (2011). Identity development in sexual-minority youth. In S. Schwartz, K. Luyckx, & V. Vignoles (Eds.), *Handbook of identity theory and research.* New York: Springer.

Savin-Williams, R. C. (2013). The new sexual-minority teenager. In J. S. Kaufman & D. A. Powell (Eds.), *Sexual identities.* Thousand Oaks, CA: Sage.

Savolainen, J., & others. (2012). Antisocial personality, adolescent school outcomes, and the risk of criminal conviction. *Journal of Research on Adolescence, 22,* 54–64.

Scarr, S. (1984, May). Interview. *Psychology Today.* pp. 59–63.

Scarr, S. (1993). Biological and cultural diversity: The legacy of Darwin for development. *Child Development, 64,* 1333–1353.

Scarr, S., & Weinberg, R. A. (1983). The Minnesota adoption studies: Genetic differences and malleability. *Child Development, 54,* 182–259.

Schaefer, R. T. (2013). *Race and ethnicity in the United States* (7th ed.). Upper Saddle River, NJ: Pearson.

Schaffer, H. R. (1996). *Social development.* Cambridge, MA: Blackwell.

Schaie, K. W. (2009). "When does age-related cognitive decline begin?" Salthouse again reifies the "cross-sectional fallacy." *Neurobiology of Aging, 30*(4), 528–529.

Schaie, K. W. (2010, in press). Adult intellectual abilities. *Corsini encyclopedia of psychology.* New York: Wiley.

Schaie, K. W. (2011). *Developmental influences on adult intellectual development.* New York: Oxford University Press.

Schaie, K. W. (2012). *Developmental influences on adult intellectual development: The Seattle longitudinal study.* New York: Oxford University Press.

Scheibe, S., & Carstensen, L. L. (2010). Emotional aging: Recent findings and future trends. *Journal of Gerontology: Psychological Sciences, 65B,* 135–144.

Schellenberg, E. G. (2004). Music lessons enhance IQ. *Psychological Science, 15,* 511–514.

Schellenberg, E. G. (2006b). Long-term positive associations between music lessons and IQ. *Journal of Educational Psychology, 98,* 457–468.

Schellenberg, E. G. (2011). Examining the association between music lessons and intelligence. *British Journal of Psychology, 102,* 283–302.

Schellenberg, E. G. (2012). Cognitive performance after music listening: A review of the Mozart effect. In R.A.R. MacDonald, G. Kreutz, & L. Mitchell (Eds.), *Music, health and wellbeing* (pp. 324–338). Oxford, UK: Oxford University Press.

Schellenberg, E. G., & Peretz, I. (2008). Music, language, and cognition: Unresolved issues. *Trends in Cognitive Sciences, 12,* 45–46.

Scher, A., & Harel, J. (2008). Separation and stranger anxiety. In M. M. Haith & J. B. Benson (Eds.), *Encyclopedia of infant and early childhood development.* Oxford, UK: Elsevier.

Schieffelin, B. (2005). *The give and take of everyday life.* Tucson, AZ: Fenestra.

Schiff, W. J. (2013). *Nutrition for healthy living* (2nd ed.). New York: McGraw-Hill.

Schlam, T. R., Wilson, N. L., Shoda, Y., Mischel, W., & Ayduk, O. (2013). Preschoolers' delay of gratification predicts their body mass 30 years later. *Journal of Pediatrics.*

Schlegal, A. (2009). Cross-cultural issues in the study of adolescent development. In R. M. Lerner & L. Steinberg (Eds.), *Handbook of adolescent psychology* (3rd ed.). New York: Wiley.

Schlegel, M. (2000). All work and play. *Monitor on Psychology, 31*(11), 50–51.

Schmidt, J., Shumow, L., & Kacker, H. (2007). Adolescents' participation in service activities and its impact on academic, behavioral, and civic outcomes. *Journal of Youth and Adolescence. 36,* 127–140.

Schmidt, J. A., Shumow, L., & Kackar, H. Z. (2012). Associations of participation in service activities with academic, behavioral, and civic outcomes of adolescents at varying risk levels. *Journal of Youth and Adolescence, 41,* 932–947.

Schmitt, M. B., Justice, L. M., & Pentimonti, J. M. (2013). Language processes: Characterization and prevention of learning disabilities. In H. L. Swanson & others (Eds.), *Handbook of learning disabilities* (2nd ed.). New York: Guilford.

Schmidt, M. E., & Anderson, D. R. (2007). The impact of television on cognitive development and educational achievement. In N. Pecora, J. P. Murray, E. E. A. Wartella (Eds). *Children and television: Fifty years of research.* (pp. 65–84). Mahwah, NJ: Erlbaum.

Schmidt, M. E., & Vandewater, E. A. (2008). Media and attention, cognition, and school achievement. *Future of Children, 18*(1), 64–85.

Schmuckler, M. A. (2013). Perceptual-motor relations in obvious and non-obvious domains: A history and review. In P. D. Zelazo (Ed.), *Oxford handbook of developmental psychology.* New York: Oxford University Press.

Schneider, B. H., & others. (2011). Cooperation and competition. In P. K. Smith & C. H. Hart (Eds.), *Wiley-Blackwell handbook of childhood social development* (2nd ed.). New York: Wiley.

Schneider, W. (2004). Memory development in childhood. In P. Smith & C. Han (Eds.), *Blackwell handbook of childhood cognitive development.* Malden, MA: Blackwell.

Schneider, W. (2011). Memory development in childhood. In U. Goswami (Ed.), *Wiley-Blackwell handbook of childhood cognitive development* (2nd ed.). New York: Wiley-Blackwell.

Schneider, W., & Pressley, M. (1997). *Memory development between two and twenty.* Mahwah, NJ: Erlbaum.

Schoffstall, C. L., & Cohen, R. (2011). Cyber aggression: The relation between online offenders and offline social competence. *Social Development, 20*(3), 587–604.

Schonert-Reichl, K. A. (1999). Relations of peer acceptance, friendship adjustment, and social behavior to moral reasoning during early adolescence. *Journal of Early Adolescence, 19,* 249–279.

Schonert-Reichl, K. A., Smith, V., Zaidman-Zait, A., & Hertzman, C. (2012). Promoting children's prosocial behaviors in school: Impact of the "Roots of Empathy" program on the social and emotional competence of school-aged children. *School Mental Health 4,* 1–21.

Schonert-Reichl, K. A., & Stewart-Lawlor, M. (2010). The effects of a mindfulness-based education program on pre- and early adolescents' well-being and social and emotional competence. *Mindfulness 1,* 137–151.

Schonpflug, U. (2001). Intergenerational transmission of values: The role of transmission belts. *Journal of Cross-Cultural Psychology, 32*(2), 174–185.

Schoon, I., Parsons, S., & Sacker, A. (2004). Socioeconomic adversity, educational resilience, and subsequent levels of adult adaptation. *Journal of Adolescent Research, 19,* 383–404.

Schouten, A. P., Valkenburg, P. M., & Peter, J. (2007). Precursors and underlying processes of adolescents' online self-disclosure: Developing and testing an "Internet-attribute-perception" model. *Media Psychology, 10,* 292–314.

Schreier, H.M.C., Schonert-Reichl, K.A., & Chen, E. (2013). Effect of volunteering on risk factors for cardiovascular disease in adolescents: A randomized controlled trial. *JAMA Pediatrics.*

Schulenberg, J. E., & Zarrett, N. R. (2006). Mental health during emerging adulthood: Continuities and discontinuities in course, content, and meaning. In J. J. Arnett & J. Tanner (Eds.), *Advances in emerging adulthood.* Washington, DC: American Psychological Association.

Schultz, M. S., Kerig, P. K., Pruett, M. K., & Parke, R. D. (Eds.). (2009) *Feathering the nest.* Washington, DC: American Psychological Association.

Schunk, D. H. (2012). *Learning theories: An educational perspective* (6th ed.). Upper Saddle River, NJ: Prentice Hall.

Schunk, D. H., Pintrich, P. R., & Meece, J. L. (2008). *Motivation in education: Theory,* research, and applications (3rd ed.). Upper Saddle River, NJ: Prentice Hall.

Schwalbe, C. S., Gearing, R. E., MacKenzie, M. J., Brewer, K. B., & Ibrahim, R. (2012). A meta-analysis of experimental studies of diversion programs for juvenile defenders. *Clinical Psychology Review, 32,* 26–33.

Schwartz, D., Kelly, B. M., Duong, M., & Badaly, D. (2010). Contextual perspective on intervention and prevention efforts for bully/victim problems. In E. M. Vernberg & B. K. Biggs (Eds.), *Preventing and treating bullying and victimization.* New York: Oxford University Press.

Schwartz, S. J., Donnellan, M. B., Ravert, R. D., Luyckx, K., & Zamboanga, B. L. (2013). Identity development, personality, and well-being in adolescence and emerging adulthood: Theory, research, and recent advances. In I. B. Weiner & others (Eds.), *Handbook of psychology* (2nd ed., Vol. 6). New York: Wiley.

Schwarz, S. P. (2004). A mother's story. Available at www.makinglifeeasier.com/StrategiesforLiving/StrategiesforLiving DetailPage/tabid/573/ArticleId/72/A-Mothers-Story.aspx

Schwartz-Mette, R. A., & Rose, A. J. (2013). Co-rumination mediates contagion of internalizing symptoms within youths' friendships. *Developmental Psychology.*

Sciberras, E., Ukoumunne, O. C., & Efron, D. (2011). Predictors of parent-reported attention-deficit/hyperactivity disorder in children aged 6–7 years: A national longitudinal study *Journal of Abnormal Child Psychology, 39*(7), 1025–1034.

Science Daily. (2008, January 15). Human gene count tumbles again (p. 1).

Sclar, D. A., & others. (2012). Attention deficit/hyperactivity disorder among children and adolescents in the United States: Trend in diagnosis and use of pharmacotherapy by gender. *Clinical Pediatrics, 51,* 584–589.

Scott, R. M., & Baillargeon, R. (2013). Do infants really expect others to act efficiently? A critical test of the rationality principle. *Psychological Science, 24,* 466–474.

Scott-Jones, D. (1995, March). *Incorporating ethnicity and socioeconomic status in research with children.* Paper presented at the meeting of the Society for Research in Child Development, Indianapolis.

Scourfield, J., Van den Bree, M., Martin, N., & McGuffin, P. (2004). Conduct problems in children and adolescents: A twin study. *Archives of General Psychiatry, 61,* 489–496.

Seabrook, J. A., & Avison, W. R. (2010). Genotype-environment interaction and sociology: Contributions and complexities. *Social Science & Medicine, 70*(9), 1277–1284.

Seaton, E. K., Yip, T., & Sellers, R. M. (2009). A longitudinal examination of racial identity and racial discrimination among African American adolescents. *Child Development, 80,* 406–417.

Segal, M., & others. (2012). *All about child care and early education* (2nd ed.). Upper Saddle River, NJ: Pearson.

Sellers, E. A., Moore, K., & Dean, H. J. (2009). Clinical management of type 2 diabetes in indigenous youth, *Pediatric Clinics of North America,* Vol. 56, no. 6, 1441–1459.

Sellers, R. M., Linder, N. C., Martin., P. P., & Lewis, R. L. (2006). Racial identity matters: The relationship between racial discrimination and psychological functioning in African American adolescents. *Journal of Research on Adolescence, 16*(2), 187–216.

Sellner, J., & others. (2009). A case of maternal herpes simplex virus encephalitis during pregnancy. *Nature Clinical Practice: Neurology, 5,* 51–56.

Selman, R. L. (1980). *The growth of interpersonal understanding.* New York: Academic Press.

Sénéchal, M. (2006). Testing the home literacy model: Parent involvement in kindergarten is differentially related to grade 4 reading comprehension, fluency, spelling, and reading for pleasure. *Scientific Studies of Reading, 10,* 59–87.

Sénéchal, M., & Ouellette, G., Pagan, S., & Lever, R. (2012). The role of invented spelling on learning to read in low-phoneme awareness kindergartners: A randomized-control-trial study. *Reading and Writing, 25,* 917–934.

Sénéchal, M., & Young, L. (2008). The effect of family literacy interventions on children's acquisition of reading from kindergarten to grade 3: A meta-analytic review. *Review of Educational Research, 78*(4), 880–907.

Senter, L., Sackoff, J., Landi, K., & Boyd, L. (2010). Studying sudden and unexpected deaths in a time of changing death certification and investigation practices: Evaluating sleep-related risk factors for infant death in New York City. *Maternal and Child Health, 15*(2), 242–248.

Serbin, L. A., Poulin-Dubois, D., Colburne, K. A., Sen, M. G., & Eichstedt, J. A. (2001). Gender stereotyping in infancy: Visual preferences for and knowledge of gender-stereotyped toys in the second year. *International Journal of Behavioral Development, 25*(1), 7–15.

Serbin, L. A., Poulin-Dubois, D., & Eichstedt, J. (2002). Infants' responses to gender-inconsistent events. *Infancy, 3,* 531–542.

Serpell, R. (1974). Aspects of intelligence in a developing country. *African Social Research, 17,* 576–596.

Serpell, R. (1982). Measures of perception, skills, and intelligence. In W. W. Hartup (Ed.), *Review of child development research* (Vol. 6). Chicago: University of Chicago Press.

Serpell, R. (2000). Culture and intelligence. In A. Kazdin (Ed.), *Encyclopedia of psychology.* Washington, DC, & New York: American Psychological Association and Oxford University Press.

Sethna, V., Murray, L., & Ramchandani, P. G. (2012, in press). Depressed fathers' speech to their 3-month-old infants: A study of cognitive and mentalizing features in paternal speech. *Psychological Medicine.*

Setliff, A. E., & Courage, M. L. (2011). Background television and infants' allocation of their attention during toy play. *Infancy,* Vol. 16(6), Nov-Dec, 2011, 611–639.

Shafer, V. L., & Garrido-Nag, K. (2010). The neurodevelopmental bases of language. In E. Hoff & M. Shatz (Eds.), *Blackwell handbook of language development* (2nd ed.). New York: Wiley.

Shah, R., & others. (2012). Prenatal methamphetamine exposure and short-term maternal and infant medical outcomes. *American Journal of Perinatology, 29,* 391–400.

Shamah, T., & Villalpando, S. (2006). The role of enriched foods in infant and child nutrition. *British Journal of Nutrition, 96,* Suppl, S73–S77.

Shanahan, L., & Sobolewski, J. M. (2013). Child effects on family processes. In A. C. Crouter & A. Booth (Eds.), *Children's influence on family dynamics.* New York: Routledge.

Shankaran, S., & others. (2010). Prenatal cocaine exposure and BMI and blood pressure at 9 years of age. *Journal of Hypertension, 28,* 1166–1175.

Shankaran, S., & others. (2011). Risk for obesity in adolescence starts in childhood. *Journal of Perinatology, 31,* 711–716.

Shapira, N. (2008). Prenatal nutrition: A critical window of opportunity for mother and child. *Women's Health, 4,* 639–656.

Shapiro, C. J., Prinz, R. J., & Sanders, M. R. (2012). Facilitators and barriers to implementation of an evidence-based parenting intervention to prevent child maltreatment: The Triple P—Positive Parenting Program. *Child Maltreatment, 17,* 86–95.

Sharma, A. R., McGue, M. K., & Benson, P. L. (1996). The emotional and behavioral adjustment of adopted adolescents: Part I: Age at adoption. *Children and Youth Services Review, 18,* 101–114.

Shatz, M., & Gelman, R. (1973). The development of communication skills: Modifications in the speech of young children as a function of the listener. *Monographs of the Society for Research in Child Development, 38* (152).

Shaw, D. S. (2013). Commentary: Early father-infant interaction and externalizing behaviors—a response to Ramchandani et al. (2013). *Journal of Child Psychology and Psychiatry, 54,* 65–66.

Shaw, P., & others. (2007). Attention-deficit/hyperactivity disorder is characterized by a delay in cortical maturation. *Proceedings of the National Academy of Sciences, 104*(49), 19649–19654.

Shayer, M., & Adhami, M. (2010, in press). Realizing the cognitive potential of children 5-7 with a mathematics focus: Post-test and long-term effects of a 2-year intervention. *British Journal of Educational Psychology.*

Shaywitz, B. A., Lyon, G. R., & Shaywitz, S. E. (2006). The role of functional magnetic resonance imaging in understanding reading and dyslexia. *Developmental Neuropsychology, 30,* 613–632.

Shaywitz, S. E., Gruen, J. R., & Shaywitz, B. A. (2007). Management of dyslexia, its rationale, and underlying neurobiology. *Pediatric Clinics of North America, 54,* 609–623.

Shehata, F., & others. (2011). Placenta/birthweight ratio and perinatal outcome: A retrospective cohort analysis. *British Journal of Obstetrics and Gynecology, 118,* 741–747.

Shema, L., Ore, L., Ben-Shachar, M., Haj, M., & Linn, S. (2007). The association between breastfeeding and breast cancer occurrence among Jewish women: A case control study. *Journal of Cancer Research and Clinical Oncology, 133,* 903.

Shen, J. (2009). Evaluation of environmental and personal susceptibility characteristics that modify genetic risks. *Methods in Molecular Biology, 471,* 163–177.

Shen, L. H., Liao, M. H., & Tseng, Y. C. (2013, in press). Recent advances in imaging of dopaminergic neurons for evaluation of neuropsychiatric disorders. *Journal of Biomedicine and Biotechnology.*

Sher-Censor, E., Parke, R. D., & Coltrane, S. (2011). Parents' promotion of psychological autonomy, psychological control, and Mexican-American adolescents' adjustment. *Journal of Youth and Adolescence, 40,* 620-632.

**Sherrie, K., & others.** (2013). Examining caesarean section rates in Canada using the Robson classification system. *Journal of Obstetrics and Gynecology, 35,* 206-214.

**Shields, S. A.** (1998, August). What Jerry Maguire can tell us about gender and emotion. Paper presented at the meeting of the International Society for Research on Emotions, Wurzburg, Germany.

**Shin, S. H., Hong, H. G., & Hazen, A. L.** (2010, in press). Childhood sexual abuse and Sadolescence substance use: A latent class analysis. *Drug and Alcohol Dependence, 109*(1), 226-235.

**Shiner, R. L., & DeYoung, C. G.** (2013). The structure of temperament and personality: A developmental approach. In P. D. Zelazo (Ed.), *Oxford handbook of developmental psychology.* New York: Oxford University Press.

**Shiraev, E., & Levy, D.** (2010). *Cross-cultural psychology: Critical thinking and critical applications* (4th ed.). Boston: Allen & Bacon.

**Short, M. A., Gradisar, M., Lack, L. C., Wright, H. R., & Dohnt, H.** (2012, in press). The sleep patterns and well-being of Australian adolescents. *Journal of Adolescence.*

**Short, S. J., & others.** (2013). Associations between white matter microstructure and infants' working memory. *NeuroImage, 64,* 156-166.

**Shuai, L., Chan, R. C., & Wang, Y.** (2011). Executive function profile of Chinese boys with attention-deficit hyperactivity disorder: Different subtypes and comorbidity. *Archives of Clinical Neuropsychology, 26,* 120-132.

**Shulman, S., Davila, J., & Shachar-Shapira, L.** (2011). Assessing romantic competence among older adolescents. *Journal of Adolescence, 34,* 397-406.

**Shulman, S., Scharf, M., & Shachar-Shapira, S.** (2012). The intergenerational transmission of romantic relationships. In P. K. Kerig, M. S. Schulz, & S. T. Hauser (Eds.), *Adolescence and beyond.* New York: Oxford University Press.

**Shulman, S., Zlotnik, A., Shachar-Shapira, L., Connolly, J., & Bohr, Y.** (2012). Adolescent daughters' romantic competence: The role of divorce, quality of parenting, and maternal romantic history. *Journal of Youth and Adolescence, 41,* 593-606.

**Shwalb, D. W., & others.** (2010). East and Southeast Asia: Japan, South Korea, Vietnam, and Indonesia. In M. H.

Bornstein (Ed.), *Handbook of cultural developmental science.* New York: Psychology Press.

**Shweder, R., Mahapatra, M., & Miller, J.** (1987). Culture and moral development. In J. Kagan & S. Lamb (Eds.), *The emergence of morality in young children.* Chicago: University of Chicago Press.

**Siegal, M., & Surian, L.** (2010). Conversational understanding in young children. In E. Hoff & M. Shatz (Eds.), *Blackwell handbook of language development.* New York: Wiley.

**Siegel, L. S., & Wiener, J.** (1993, Spring). Canadian special education policies: Children with disabilities in a bilingual and multicultural society. *Social Policy Report, Society for Research in Child Development, 7,* 1-16.

**Siegler, R.** (1996). *Emerging minds: The process of change in children's thinking.* New York: Oxford University Press.

**Siegler, R.** (2005). Children's learning. *American Psychologist, 60,* 769-778.

**Siegler, R. S.** (1976). Three aspects of cognitive development. *Cognitive Psychology, 8,* 481-520.

**Siegler, R. S.** (1998). *Children's thinking* (3rd ed.). Upper Saddle River, NJ: Prentice Hall.

**Siegler, R. S.** (2006). Microgenetic analysis of learning. In W. Damon & R. Lerner (Eds.), *Handbook of child psychology* (6th ed.). New York: Wiley.

**Siegler, R. S.** (2012). From theory to application and back: Following in the giant footsteps of David Klahr. In S. M. Carver & J. Shrager (Eds.), *The journey from child to scientist: Integrating cognitive development and the education sciences.* Thousand Oaks, CA: Sage.

**Siegler, R. S.** (2013, in press). How do people become experts? In J. Staszewski (Ed.), *Experience and skill acquisition.* New York: Taylor & Francis.

**Siener, S., & Kerns, K. A.** (2012). Emotion regulation and depressive symptoms in preadolescence. *Child Psychiatry and Human Development, 43,* 414-430.

**Sijtsema, J. J., Ojanen, T., Veenstra, R., Lindenberg, S., Hawley, P. H., & Little, T. D.** (2010). Forms and functions of aggression in adolescent friendship selection and influence: A longitudinal social network analysis. *Social Development, 19*(3), 515-534.

**Silberg, J. L., Maes, H., & Eaves, L. J.** (2010). Genetic and environmental influences on the transmission of parental depression to children's depression and conduct disturbance: an extended

Children of Twins study. *Journal of Child Psychology and Psychiatry.* (Available online February 16, 2010.)

**Silverman, R.** (2012). Stereotypes. In M. Kohut (Ed.), *Encyclopedia of gender in media.* Thousand Oaks, CA: Sage.

**Simkin, P., & Bolding, A.** (2004). Update on nonpharmacological approaches to relieve labor pain and prevent suffering. *Journal of Midwifery and Women's Health, 49,* 489-504.

**Simonetti, G. D., & others.** (2011). Determinants of blood pressure in preschool children: The role of parental smoking. *Circulation, 123,* 292-298.

**Simpkins, S. D., Fredricks, J. A., Davis-Kean, P. E., & Eccles, J. S.** (2006). Healthy mind, healthy habits: The influence of activity involvement in middle childhood. In A. C. Huston & M. N. Ripke (Eds.), *Developmental contexts in middle childhood.* Mahwah, NJ: Erlbaum.

**Singer, D., Golinkoff, R. M., & Hirsh-Pasek, K.** (Eds.). (2006). *Play 5 learning: How play motivates and enhances children's cognitive and social-emotional growth.* New York: Oxford University Press.

**Singer, T.** (2012, in press). The past, present, and future of social neuroscience: A European perspective. *Neuroimage.*

**Singh, A. A., Orpinas, P., & Horne, A. M.** (2010). Empowering schools to prevent bullying: A holistic approach. In E. M. Vernberg & B. K. Biggs (Eds.), *Preventing and treating bullying and victimization.* New York: Oxford University Press.

**Sisson, S. B., Broyles, S. T., Baker, B. L., & Katzmarzyk, P. T.** (2010). Screen time, physical activity, and overweight in U.S. youth: National Survey of Children's Health 2003. *Journal of Adolescent Health, 47,* 309-311.

**Siu, A. M., Shek, D. T., & Law, B.** (2012). Prosocial norms as a positive youth development construct: A conceptual review. *Scientific World Journal, 489-156.*

**Sivell, S. & others.** (2008). How risk is perceived, constructed, and interpreted by clients in clinical genetics, and the effects on decision making: A review. *Journal of Genetic Counseling, 17,* 30-63.

**Skiba, T., Tan, M., Sternberg, R. J., & Grigorenko, E. L.** (2010, in press). Roads not taken, new roads to take: Looking for creativity in the classroom. In J. Kaufman & R. Beghetto (Eds.), *Creativity in classrooms.* New York: Springer.

**Skinner, B. F.** (1938). *The behavior of organisms: An experimental analysis.* New York: Appleton-Century-Crofts.

Skinner, B. F. (1957). *Verbal behavior.* New York: Appleton-Century-Crofts.

Skoog, T., Stattin, H., & Kerr, M. (2009). The role of pubertal timing in what adolescent boys do online. *Journal of Research on Adolescence, 19,* 1–7.

Slater, A. M., & others. (2010). Visual perception. In G. Bremner & T. Wachs (Eds.), *Blackwell handbook of infant development,* (2nd ed.). Oxford, UK: Blackwell.

Slater, A. M., Bremner, J. G., Johnson, S. P., & Hayes, R. (2011). The role of perceptual processes in infant addition/subtraction events. In L. M. Oakes, C. H. Cashon, M. Casasola, & D. H. Rakison (Eds.), *Early perceptual and cognitive development.* New York: Oxford University Press.

Slater, A., Field, T., & Hernandez-Reif, M. (2007). The development of the senses. In A. Slater and M. Lewis (Eds.), *Introduction to infant development.* New York, NY: Oxford University Press.

Slater, A., Morison, V., & Somers, M. (1988). Orientation discrimination and cortical function in the human newborn. *Perception, 17,* 597–602.

Slobin, D. (1972, July). Children and language: They learn the same way around the world. *Psychology Today,* 71–76.

Slomkowski, C., Rende, R., Conger, K. J., Simmons, R. L., & Conger, R. D. (2001). Sisters, brothers, and delinquency: Social influence during early and middle adolescence. *Child Development, 72,* 271–283.

Smetana, J. G. (2011a). *Adolescents, families, and social development: How adolescents construct their worlds.* New York: Wiley-Blackwell.

Smetana, J. G. (2011b). Adolescents' social reasoning and relationships with parents: Conflicts and coordinations within and across domains. In E. Amsel & J. Smetana (Eds.), *Adolescent vulnerabilities and opportunities: Constructivist and developmental perspectives.* New York: Cambridge University Press.

Smetana, J. G. (2013a). Moral development: The social domain theory view. In P. D. Zelazo (Ed.), *Oxford handbook of developmental psychology.* New York: Oxford University Press.

Smetana, J. G. (2013b). Social-cognitive domain theory: Consistencies and variations in children's moral and social judgments. In M. Killen & J. Smetana (Eds.), *Handbook of moral development* (2nd ed.). New York: Routledge.

Smetana, J. G., & others. (2012). Developmental changes and individual differences in young children's moral judgments. *Child Development, 83,* 683–696.

Smith, J., & Ross, H. (2007). Training parents to mediate sibling disputes affects children's negotiation and conflict understanding. *Child Development, 78,* 790–805.

Smith, L. E., & Howard, K. S. (2008). Continuity of paternal social support and depressive symptoms among new mothers. *Journal of Family Psychology, 22,* 763–773.

Smith, J. B. (2009). High school organization. In D. Carr (Ed.), *Encyclopedia of the life course and human development.* Boston: Gale Cengage.

Smith, P. K. (2007). Pretend play and children's cognitive and literacy development: Sources of evidence and some lessons from the past. In K. A. Roskos & J. F. Christie (Eds.), *Play and literacy in early childhood.* Mahway, NJ: Erlbaum.

Smith, P. K. (2010). *Children and play.* West Sussex, England: Wiley-Blackwell.

Smith, R. A., & Davis, S. F. (2010). *The psychologist as detective* (5th ed.). Upper Saddle River, NJ: Prentice Hall.

Smith, R. L., & Rose, A. J. (2011). The "cost of caring" in youths' friendships: Considering associations among social perspective taking, co-rumination, and empathetic distress. *Developmental Psychology, 47,* 1792–1803.

Smith, R. L., Rose, A.. J., & Schwartz-Mette, R. A. (2010). Relational andovert aggression in childhood and adolescence: Clarifying mean-level gender differences and associations with peer acceptance. *Social Development, 19,* 243–269.

Snarey, J. (1987, June). A question of morality. *Psychology Today,* pp. 6–8.

Snijders, B. E., & others. (2007). Breast-feeding duration and infant atopic manifestations, by maternal allergic status, in the first two years of life (KOALA study). *Journal of Pediatrics, 151,* 347–351.

Snowdon, A. W., Hussein, A., High, L., Millar-Polgar, J., Patriack, L., & Ahmed, E. (2008). The effectiveness of a multimedia intervention on parents' knowledge and use of vehicle safety systems for children. *Journal of Pediatric Nursing, 23,* 126–139.

So, H. K., Li, A. M., Choi, K. C., Sung, R. Y., & Nelson, E. A. (2013, in press). Regular exercise and a healthy dietary pattern are associated with lower resting blood pressure in non-obese adolescents: A population-based study. *Journal of Human Hypertension.*

Soares, N. S., & Patel, D. R. (2012). Office screening and early identification of children with autism. *Pediatric Clinics of North America, 59,* 89–102.

Sokol, B. W., Snjezana, H., & Muller, U. (2010). Social understanding and self-regulation: From perspective-taking to theory of mind. In B. Sokol, U. Muller, J. Carpendale, A. Young, & G. Larocci (Eds.), *Self-and social cognition.* New York: Oxford University Press.

Solomon, D., Watson, M. S., & Battistich, V. A. (2002). Teaching and school effects on moral/prosocial development. In V. Richardson (Ed.), *Handbook for research on teaching.* Washington, DC: American Educational Research Association.

Sood, B., Delaney-Black, V., Covington, C., Nordstrom-Klee, B., Ager, J., Templin, T., & others. (2001). Prenatal alcohol exposure and childhood behavior at age 6 to 7 years: I. dose-response effect. *Pediatrics, 108*(2), e34–e34.

Sophian, C. (1985). Perseveration and infants' search: A comparison of two- and three-location tasks. *Developmental Psychology, 21,* 187–194.

Sorte, J., Daeschel, I., & Amador, C. (2011). Nutrition, health, and wellness. Upper Saddle River, NJ: Merrill.

Spangler, G., Johann, M., Ronai, Z., & Zimmermann, P. (2009). Genetic and environmental influence on attachment disorganization. *Journal of Child Psychology and Psychiatry, 50,* 952–961.

Sparling, P., & Redican, K. (2011). *MP iHealth.* New York: McGraw-Hill.

Spector, L. G., & others. (2013, in press). Children's Oncology Group's 2013 blueprint for research: Epidemiology. *Pediatric and Blood Cancer.*

Spelke, E. S. (1979). Perceiving bimodally specified events in infancy. *Developmental Psychology, 5,* 626–636.

Spelke, E. S. (1991). Physical knowledge in infancy: Reflections on Piaget's theory. In S. Carey & R. Gelman (Eds.), *The epigenesis of mind: Essays on biology and cognition.* Hillsdale, NJ: Erlbaum.

Spelke, E. S. (2000). Core knowledge. *American Psychologist, 55,* 1233–1243.

Spelke, E. S. (2011). Natural number and natural geometry. In E. Brannon & S. Dehaene (Eds.), *Space, time, and number in the brain.* New York: Oxford University Press.

Spelke, E. S., Bernier, E. P., & Snedeker, J. (2013, in press). Core social cognition. In M. R. Banaji & S.A. Gelman (Eds.), *Navigating the social world: What infants, children, and other species can teach us.* New York: Oxford University Press.

Spelke, E. S., Breinlinger, K., Macomber, J., & Jacobson, K. (1992). Origins of knowledge. *Psychological Review, 99,* 605–632.

Spelke, E. S., & Hespos. S. J. (2001). Continuity, competence, and the object concept. In E. Dupoux (Ed.), *Language, brain, and behavior.* Cambridge, MA: Bradford/MIT Press.

Spelke, E. S., & Kinzler, K. D. (2007). Core knowledge. *Development Science, 10,* 89–96.

Spelke, E. S., & Owsley, C. J. (1979). Intermodal exploration and knowledge in infancy. *Infant Behavior and Development, 2,* 13–28.

Spence, J. T., & Buckner, C. E. (2000). Instrumental and expressive traits, trait stereotypes, and sexist attitudes: What do they signify? *Psychology of Women Quarterly, 24,* 44–62.

Spence, J. T., & Helmreich, R. (1978). *Masculinity and femininity: Their psychological dimensions.* Austin: University of Texas Press.

Spencer, J. R., & Lamb, M. E. (Eds.). (2013, in press). *Children and cross-examination: Time to change the rules.* Oxford, UK: Hart.

Spencer, J. P., Blumberg, M. S., McMurray, B., Robinson, S. R., Samuelson, L. K., & Tomlin, J. B. (2009). Short arms and talking eggs: Why we should no longer abide the nativist-empiricist debate. *Child Development Perspectives, 3,* 79–87.

Spinney, J., & Millward, H. (2010). Time and money: A new look at poverty and the barriers to physical activity in Canada. *Social Indicators Research, 99*(2), 341–356.

Spring, J. (2013). *Deculturalization and the struggle for equality* (6th ed.). New York: McGraw-Hill.

Squires, J., Pribble, L., Chen, C-I., & Pomes, M. (2013, in press). Early childhood education: Improving outcomes for young children and families. In I. B. Weiner & others (Eds.), *Handbook of psychology* (2nd ed., Vol. 7). New York: Wiley.

Srabstein, J. C., McCarter, R. J., Shao, C., & Huang, Z. J. (2006). Morbidities associated with bullying behaviors in adolescents: School-based study of American adolescents. *International Journal of Adolescent Medicine and Health, 18,* 587–596.

Sroufe, L. A., Coffino, B., & Carlson, E. A. (2010). Conceptualizing the role of early experience: Lessons from the Minnesota longitudinal study. *Developmental Review, 30,* 36–51.

Sroufe, L. A., Egeland, B., Carlson, E., & Collins, W. A. (2005b). The place of early attachment in developmental context. In K. E. Grossman, K. Grossman, & E. Waters (Eds.), *The power of longitudinal attachment research: From infancy and childhood to adulthood.* New York: Guilford.

Sroufe, L. A., Waters, E., & Matas, L. (1974). Contextual determinants of infant affectional response. In M. Lewis & L. Rosenblum (Eds.), *Origins of fear.* New York: Wiley.

St. Pierre, R., Layzer, J., & Barnes, H. (1996). *Regenerating two-generation programs.* Cambridge, MA: Abt Associates.

Stack, D. M., Serbin, L. A., Enns, L. N., Ruttle, P. L., & Barrieau, L. (2010). Parental effects on children's emotional development over time and across generations. *Infants & Young Children, 23*(1), 52–69.

Stager, L. (2009–2010). Supporting women during labor and birth. *Midwifery Today with International Midwife, 23,* 12–15.

Staiano, A. E., Abraham, A. A., & Calvert, S. L. (2012). Competitive versus cooperative exergame play for African American adolescents' executive functioning skills. *Developmental Psychology, 48,* 337–342.

Stangor, C. (2011). *Research methods for the behavioral sciences* (4th ed.). Boston: Cengage.

Stanovich, K. E. (1986). Matthew effects in reading: Some consequences of individual differences in the acquisition of literacy. *Reading Research Quarterly, 21,* 360–406.

Stanovich, K. E., West, R. F., & Toplak, M. E. (2012). Judgment and decision making in adolescence: Separating intelligence from rationality. In V. F. Reyna (Ed.), *The adolescent brain.* Washington, DC: American Psychological Association.

Starr, C. (2011). *Biology* (8th ed.). Boston: Cengage.

Starr, L. R., & Davila, J. (2009). Clarifying co-rumination: Associations with internalizing symptoms and romantic involvement among adolescent girls. *Journal of Adolescence, 32,* 19–37.

Starr, L. R., & others. (2013). Love hurts (in more ways than one): Specificity of psychological symptoms as predictors and consequences of romantic activity among early adolescent girls. *Journal of Clinical Psychology.*

Staszewski, J. (Ed.). (2013, in press). *Expertise and skill acquisition: The impact of William C. Chase.* New York: Taylor & Francis.

Statistics Canada. (2011). Aboriginal peoples and language (catalogue no. 99-011-X2011003). National Household Survey. Ottawa: Statistics Canada.

Statistics Canada (2012). Labour Force Survey 2012. Ottawa: Statistics Canada.

Statistics Canada. (2012a). Leading causes of death in Canada. Catalogue no.: 84-215-XWE

Statistics Canada. (2012b). Income in Canada 2010. Catalogue no. 75-202-XWE

Statistics Canada. (2013). Public postsecondary enrolments by institution type, sex, and field of study. Retrieved from: www.statcan.gc.ca/tables-tableaux/sum-som/l01/cst01/educ72c-eng.htm

Statistics Canada (2013). Census family structure including intact families and stepfamilies for couple families with children in private households. Available at www12.statcan.gc.ca/census-recensement/2011/dp-pd/hlt-fst/fam/Pages/highlight.cfm?TabID=1&Lang=E&Asc=1&OrderBy=4&View=1&tableID=303&Couples=1&queryID=3&PRCode=48

Staudinger, U. M., & Gluck, J. (2011). Psychological wisdom research. *Annual Review of Psychology* (Vol. 62). Palo Alto, CA: Annual Reviews.

Steca, P., Bassi, M., Caprara, G. V., & Fave, A. D. (2011). Parents' self-efficacy beliefs and their children's psychosocial adaptation during adolescence. *Journal of Youth and Adolescence, 40*(3), 320–331.

Steel, A. J., & Sutcliffe, A. (2010). Long-term health implications for children conceived by IVF/ ICSI. *Human Fertility, 12,* 21–27.

Steele, C. M., & Aronson, J. A. (2004). Stereotype threat does not live by Steele and Aronson (1995) alone. *American Psychologist, 59,* 47–48.

Steensma & others. (2014). Behavioral and emotional problems on the teacher's report form: A cross-national, cross-clinic comparative analysis of gender dysphoric children and adolescents. *Journal of Abnormal Child Psychology, 42,* 635–647.

Steinberg, L. (2009). Adolescent development and juvenile justice. *Annual Review of Clinical Psychology* (Vol. 5). Palo Alto, CA: Annual Reviews.

Steinberg, L. (2012). Adolescent risk-taking: A social neuroscience perspective. In E. Amsel & J. Smetana (Eds.), Adolescent vulnerabilities and opportunities: *Constructivist developmental perspectives.* New York: Cambridge University Press.

Steinberg, L. (2013, in press). How should the science of adolescent brain development inform legal policy? In J. Bhabha (Ed.), *Coming of age: A new framework for adolescent rights.* Philadelphia: University of Pennsylvania Press.

Steinberg, L. D., & Cauffman, E. (2001). Adolescents as adults in court. *SRCD Social Policy Report, 15*(4), 1–13.

Steinberg, L. D., & Monahan, K. (2007). Age differences in resistance to peer influence. *Developmental Psychology, 43,* 1531-1543.

Steinberg, L. D., & Silk, J. S. (2002). Parenting adolescents. In M. Bornstein (Ed.), *Handbook of parenting* (2nd ed., Vol. 1). Mahwah, NJ: Erlbaum.

Steiner, J. E. (1979). Human facial expressions in response to taste and smell stimulation. In H. Reese & L. Lipsitt (Eds.), *Advances in child development and behavior* (Vol. 13). New York: Academic Press.

Steiner, N. J., Sheldrick, R. C., Gotthelf, D., & Perrin, E. C. (2011). Computer-based attention training in schools for children with attention deficit hyperactivity disorder: A preliminary trial. *Clinical Pediatrics, 50,* 615-622.

Steinhausen, H. C., & Blattmann, B., & Pfund, F. (2007). Developmental outcome in children with intrauterine exposure to substances. *European Addiction Research, 13,* 94-100.

Steming, C. (2008). CenteringPregnancy: Group prenatal care. *Creative Nursing, 14,* 182-183.

Stephens, J. M. (2008). Cheating. In N. J. Salkind (Ed.), *Encyclopedia of educational psychology.* Thousand Oaks, CA: Sage.

Stern, S. J., Matok, I., Kapur, B., & Koren, G. (2011). A comparison of folic acid pharmacokinetics in obese and nonobese women of childbearing age. *Therapeutic Drug Monitoring, 33,* 336-340.

Sternberg, R. J. (1986). *Intelligence applied.* Fort Worth, TX: Harcourt Brace.

Sternberg, R. J. (Ed.). (1998). *Wisdom.* New York: Cambridge University Press.

Sternberg, R. J. (2004). Individual differences in cognitive development. In P. Smith & C. Hart (Eds.), *Blackwell handbook of cognitive development.* Malden, MA: Blackwell.

Sternberg, R. J. (2008). The triarchic theory of successful intelligence. In N. Salkind (Ed.), *Encyclopedia of educational psychology.* Thousand Oaks, CA: Sage.

Sternberg, R. J. (2009a). *Cognitive psychology* (5th ed.). Belmont, CA: Wadsworth.

Sternberg, R. J. (2009b). Intelligence. In *The Chicago companion to the child.* Chicago: University of Chicago Press.

Sternberg, R. J. (2009c). Leadership and giftedness. In B. MacFarlane & T. Stambaugh (Eds.), *Leading change in gifted education* (pp. 513-526). Waco, TX: Prufrock.

Sternberg, R. J. (2009d). The triarchic theory of successful intelligence. In B. Kerr (Ed.), *Encyclopedia of giftedness, creativity, and talent.* Thousand Oaks, CA: Sage.

Sternberg, R. J. (2009e). Wisdom. In S. J. Lopez (Ed.), *Encyclopedia of positive psychology* (Vol. 2). New York: Wiley-Blackwell.

Sternberg, R. J. (2009f). Wisdom, intelligence, and creativity synthesized. *The School Administrator, 66*(2), 10-14.

Sternberg, R. J. (2010a, in press). Human intelligence. In V. S. Ramachandran (Ed.), *Encyclopedia of human behavior* (2nd ed.). New York: Elsevier.

Sternberg, R. J. (2010c, in press). Componential models of creativity. In M. Runco & S. Spritzker (Eds.), *Encyclopedia of creativity.* New York: Elsevier.

Sternberg, R. J. (2010d). Intelligence. In B. McGaw, P. Peterson, & E. Baker (Eds.), *International encyclopedia of education* (3rd ed.). New York: Elsevier.

Sternberg, R. J. (2010e, in press). Teaching for creativity. In R. A. Beghetto & J. C. Kaufman (Eds.), *Nurturing creativity in the classroom.* New York: Cambridge University Press.

Sternberg, R. J., & Grigorenko, E. L. (2008). Ability testing across cultures. In L. A. Suzuki & J. G. Ponterotto (Eds.), *Handbook of multicultural assessment* (3rd ed.). San Francisco: Jossey-Bass.

Sternberg, R. J., Jarvin, L., & Rezmtskaya, A. (2009). Teaching for wisdom through history: Infusing wise thinking skills in the school curriculum. In M. Ferrari (Ed.), *Teaching for wisdom.* Amsterdam: Springer.

Sternberg, R. J., & others. (2001). The relationship between academic and practical intelligence: A case study in Kenya. *Intelligence. 29,* 401-418.

Sternberg, R. J., & Sternberg, K. (2013). Teaching cognitive science. In D. Dunn (Ed.), *Teaching psychology education.* New York: Oxford University Press.

Steur, F. B., Applefield, J. M., & Smith, R. (1971). Televised aggression and the interpersonal aggression of preschool children. *Journal of Experimental Child Psychology, 11,* 442-447.

Stevens, C., & Bavelier, D. (2012). The role of selective attention on academic foundations: A cognitive neuroscience perspective. *Developmental Cognitive Neuroscience, 15*(Suppl. 1), S30-S48.

Stevenson, H. W., & Zusho, A. (2002). Adolescence in China and Japan: Adapting to a changing environment. In B. B. Brown, R. W. Larson, & T. S. Saraswathi (Eds.), *The world's youth.* New York: Cambridge University Press.

Stewart, S. M., Bond, M. H., Ho, L. M., Zaman, R. M., Dar, R., & Anwar, M. (2000). Perceptions of parents and adolescent outcomes in Pakistan. *British Journal of Developmental Psychology, 18,* 335-352.

Stipek, D. (2005, February 16). Commentary in *USA TODAY,* p.1D.

Stipek, D. J. (2002). *Motivation to learn* (4th ed.). Boston: Allyn & Bacon.

Stocker, C., & Dunn, J. (1990). Sibling relationships in childhood: Links with friendships and peer relationships. *British Journal of Developmental Psychology, 8,* 227-244.

Strasberger, V. C. (2009). Why do adolescent health researchers ignore the impact of the media? *Journal of Adolescent Health, 44,* 203-205.

Strathearn, L. (2007). Exploring the neurobiology of attachment. In L. C. Mayes, P. Fonagy, & M. Target (Eds.), *Developmental science and psychoanalysis.* London: Karnac Press.

Strathearn, L. (2011). Maternal neglect: Oxytocin, dopamine, and the neurobiology of attachment. *Journal of Neuroendocrinology, 23,* 1054-1065.

Strathearn, L., Iyenger, U., Fonagy, P., Kim, S. (2012). Maternal oxytocin response during mother-infant interaction: Associations with adult temperament. *Hormones and Behavior, 61,* 429-435.

Strauss, M. A., Sugarman, D. B., & Giles-Sims, J. (1997). Spanking by parents and subsequent anti-social behavior in children. *Archives of Pediatrics and Adolescent Medicine, 151,* 761-767.

Strenze, T. (2007). Intelligence and socioeconomic success: A meta-analytic review of longitudinal research. *Intelligence, 35,* 401-426.

Streri, A. (1993). *Seeing, reaching, touching: The relations between vision and touch in infancy.* London: Harvester Wheatshaft.

Strong-Wilson, T., & Ellis, J. (2007). Children and place: Reggio Emilia's environment as a third teacher. *Theory Into Practice, 46,* 5-13.

Stuebe, A. M., & Schwartz, E. G. (2010). The risks and benefits of infant feeding practices for women and their children. *Journal of Perinatology, 30,* 155-162.

Su, R., Rounds, J., & Armstrong, P. I. (2009). Men and things, women and people: A meta-analysis of sex differences in interests. *Psychological Bulletin, 135,* 859-884.

Suarez-Orozco, C. (2007, March). *Immigrant family educational advantages and challenges.* Paper presented at the meeting of the Society for Research in Child Development, Boston.

Suarez-Orosco, M., & Suarez-Orozco, C. (2010). Globalization, immigration, and schooling. In J. A. Banks (Ed.), *The Routledge international companion to multicultural education.* New York: Routledge.

Subrahmanyam, K., & Greenfield, P. (2008). Online communication and adolescent relationships. *Future of Children, 18*(1), 119–146.

Subrahmanyam, K., Smahel, D., & Greenfield, P. (2006). Connecting developmental constructions on the Internet: Identity presentation and sexual exploration in online chat rooms. *Developmental Psychology, 42,* 395–406.

Sue, S. (1990, August). *Ethnicity and culture in psychological research and practice.* Paper presented at the meeting of the American Psychological Association, Boston.

Sue, S., & Morishima, J. K. (1982). *The mental health of Asian Americans: Contemporary issues in identifying and treating mental problems.* San Francisco: Jossey-Bass.

Sugita, Y. (2004). Experience in early infancy is indispensable for color perception. *Current Biology, 14,* 1267–1271.

Sullivan, H. S. (1953). *The interpersonal theory of psychiatry.* New York: W. W. Norton.

Sullivan, K., & Sullivan, A. (1980). Adolescent-parent separation. *Developmental Psychology, 16,* 93–99.

Sumaroka, M., & Bornstein, M. H. (2008). Play. In M. M. Haith & J. B. Benson (Eds.), *Enyclopedia of infant and early childhood development.* Oxford, UK: Elsevier.

Super, C. M., & Harkness, S. (2010). Culture and infancy. In J. G. Bremner & T. D. Wachs (Eds.), *Wiley-Blackwell handbook of infant development* (2nd ed.). New York: Wiley.

Susman, E. J., & others. (2010). Longitudinal development of secondary sexual characteristics in girls and boys between 9½ and 15½ years. *Archives of Pediatric and Adolescent Medicine, 164,* 166–173.

Susman, E. J., & Dorn, L. D. (2013). Puberty: Its role in development. In I. B. Weiner & others (Eds.), *Handbook of psychology* (2nd ed., Vol. 6). New York: Wiley.

Susman, M. R., Amor, D. J., Muggli, E., Jaques, A. M., & Halliday, J. (2010). Using population-based data to predict the impact of introducing noninvasive prenatal diagnosis for Down syndrome. *Genetics in Medicine, 12*(5), 298–303.

Sutcliffe, K., & others. (2012). Comparing midwife-led and doctor-led maternity care: A systematic review of reviews. *Journal of Advanced Nursing, 68,* 2376–2386.

Suyemoto. K. L. (2009). Multiracial Asian Americans. In N. Tewari & A. Alvarez (Eds.), *Asian American psychology.* New York: Psychology Press.

Swaab, D. F., Chung, W. C., Kruijver, F. P., Hofman, M. A., & Ishunina, T. A. (2001). Structural and functional sex differences in the human hypothalamus. *Hormones and Behavior, 40,* 93–98.

Swamy, G. K., Ostbye, T., & Skjaerven, R. (2008). Association of preterm birth with long-term survival, reproduction, and next generation preterm birth. *Journal of the American Medical Association, 299,* 1429–1436.

Swanson, H. L. (1999). What develops in working memory? A life-span perspective. *Developmental Psychology, 35,* 986–1000.

Swanson, H. L., Harris, K. R., & Graham, S. (2013). Overview of foundations, causes, instruction, and methodology in the field of learning disabilities. In H. L. Swanson, K. R. Harris, & S. Graham (Eds.), *Handbook of learning disabilities* (2nd ed.). New York: Guilford.

Swing, E. L., Gentile, D. A., Anderson, C.A., & Walsh, D. A. (2010). Television and video game exposure and the development of attention problems. *Pediatrics, 126,* 214–221.

Syed, M. (2010). Memorable everyday events in college: Narratives of the intersection of ethnicity and academia. *Journal of Diversity in Higher Education, 3,* 56–69.

Syed, M. (2011). Developing an integrated self: Academic and ethnic identities among ethnically-diverse college students. *Developmental Psychology, 46,* 1590–1604.

Syed, M. (2013, in press). Assessment of ethnic identity and acculturation. In K. Geisinger (Ed.), *APA handbook of testing and assessment in psychology.* Washington, DC: American Psychological Association.

Syed, M., & Azmitia, M. (2010). Narrative and ethnic identity exploration: A longitudinal account of emerging adults' ethnicity-related experiences. *Developmental Psychology, 46,* 208–219.

Szwedo, D. E., Mikami, A. Y., & Allen, J. P. (2011). Qualities of peer relations on social networking websites: Predictions from negative mother-teen interactions. *Journal of Research on Adolescence, 21,* 595–607.


## T

Taddio, A. (2008). Circumcision. In M. M. Haith & J. B. Benson (Eds.), *Encyclopedia of infant and early childhood development.* Oxford, UK: Elsevier.

Talbot, J., Baker, J. K., & McHalo, J. P. (2009). Sharing the love: Prebirth adult attachment status and coparenting adjustment during infancy. The transition to parenthood. *Parenting: Science & Practice, 9,* 56–77.

Tamis-Lemonda, C. S., & McFadden, K. E. (2010). The United States of America. In M. H. Bornstein (Ed.), *Handbook of cultural developmental science.* New York: Psychology Press.

Tamis-LeMonda, C. S., & Song, L. (2013, in press). Parent-infant communicative interactions in cultural context. In R. M. Lerner (Ed.), *Handbook of psychology* (Vol. 6). New York: Wiley.

Tamis-LeMonda, C. S., Way, N., Hughes, D., Yoshikawa, H., Kallman, R. K., & Niwa, E. Y. (2008). Parents' goals for children: The dynamic coexistence of individualism and collectivism in cultures and individuals. *Social Development, 17,* 183–209.

Tamis-LeMonda, C. S., & Song, L. (2013). Parent-infant communicative interactions in cultural context. In R. M. Lerner (Ed.), *Handbook of psychology* (Vol. 6). New York: Wiley.

Tannen, D. (1990). *You just don't understand!* New York: Ballantine.

Tappan, M. B. (1998). Sociocultural psychology and caring psychology: Exploring Vygotsky's "hidden curriculum." *Educational Psychologist, 33,* 23–33.

Tappan, M. B. (2013). Mediated moralities: Sociocultural approaches to moral development. In M. Killen & J. G. Smetana (Eds.), *Handbook of moral development* (2nd ed.). New York: Routledge.

Taylor, C. A., Manganello, J. A., Lee, S. J., & Rice, J. C. (2010). Mothers' spanking of 3-year-old children and subsequent risk of children's aggressive behavior. *Pediatrics, 125,* e1057–e1065.

Taylor, L. S., & Whittaker, C. R. (2009). *Bridging multiple worlds* (2nd ed.). Boston: Allyn & Bacon.

Taylor, R. D., & Lopez, E. I. (2005). Family management practice, school achievement, and problem behavior in African American adolescents: Mediating processes. *Applied Developmental Psychology, 26,* 39–49.

Taylor, S. E. (2002). *The tending instinct.* New York: Times Books.

Teenage Research Unlimited (2004). Diversity in word and deed: Most teens claim multicultural friends. Northbrook, IL: Teenage Research Unlimited.

Temple, C. A., Nathan, R., & Temple, C. (2013). *Beginnings of writing* (4th ed.). Boston: Allyn & Bacon.

Temple, C., Nathan, R., Temple, F., & Burris, N. A. (1993). *The beginnings of writing* (3rd ed.). Boston: Allyn & Bacon.

Tenenbaum, H. R., Callahan, M., Alba-Speyer, C., & Sandoval, L. (2002). Parent-child science conversations in Mexican-descent families: Educational background, activity, and past experience as moderators. *Hispanic Journal of Behavioral Sciences, 24,* 225–248.

Terman, L. (1925). *Genetic studies of genius. Vol. 1: Mental and physical traits of a thousand gifted children.* Stanford, CA: Stanford University Press.

Teti, D. (2001). Retrospect and prospect in the psychological study of sibling relationships. In J. P. McHale & W. S. Grolnick (Eds.), *Retrospect and prospect in the psychological study of families.* Mahwah, NJ: Erlbaum.

te Velde, S. J., & others. (2012). Energy balance-related behaviors associated with overweight and obesity in preschool children: A systematic review of prospective studies. *Obesity Reviews, 13*(Suppl. 1), S56–S74.

Teti, D. M., Kim, B. R., Mayer G., & Countermine, M. (2010). Maternal emotional availability at bedtime predicts infant sleep quality. *Journal of Family Psychology, 24,* 307–315.

Thabet, A. A., Ibraheem, A. N., Shivram, R., Winter, E. A., & Vostanis, P. (2009). Parenting support and PTSD in children of a war zone. *International Journal of Social Psychiatry, 55,* 225–227.

Tharp, R. G. (1994). Intergroup differences among Native Americans in socialization and child cognition: An erthogenetic analysis. In P. M. Greenfield & R. Cocking (Eds.), *Cross-cultural roots of minority child development.* Mahwah, NJ: Erlbaum.

Tharp, R. G., & Gallimore, R. (1988). *Rousing minds to life: Teaching, learning, and schooling in social context.* New York: Cambridge University Press.

The Daily (2013, November 25). The education and employment experiences of First Nations people living off reserve, Inuit and Metis: Selected findings from the 2012 Aboriginal Peoples Survey. *Statistics Canada catalogue no. 11-001-X.*

Thelen, E. (2000). Perception and motor development. In A. Kazdin (Ed.), *Encyclopedia of psychology.* Washington, DC, & New York: American Psychological Association and Oxford University Press.

Thelen, E., Corbetta, D., Kamm, K., Spencer, J. P., Schneider, K., & Zernicke, R. F. (1993). The transition to reaching: Mapping intention and intrinsic dynamics. *Child Development. 64,* 1058–1098.

Thelen, E., & Smith, L. B. (1998). Dynamic systems theory. In W. Damon (Ed.), *Handbook of child psychology* (5th ed., Vol. 1.). New York: Wiley.

Thelen, E., & Smith, L. B. (2006). Dynamic development of action and thought. In W. Damon & R. Lerner (Eds.), *Handbook of child psychology* (6th ed.). New York: Wiley.

Theokas, C. (2009). Youth sports participation—A view of the issues: Introduction to the special section. *Developmental Psychology, 45,* 303–306.

Therrell, B. L., & others. (2010). Newborn Screening System Performance Evaluation Assessment (PEAS). *Seminars in Perinatology, 34,* 105–120.

Thio, A. (2010). *Deviant behavior* (10th ed.). Boston: Allyn & Bacon.

Thomas, A., & Chess, S. (1991). Temperament in adolescence and its functional significance. In R. M. Lerner, A. C. Petersen, & J. Brooks-Gunn (Eds.), *Encyclopedia of adolescence* (Vol. 2). New York: Garland.

Thomas, M. S. C., & Johnson, M. H. (2008). New advances in understanding sensitive periods in brain development. *Current Directions in Psychological Science, 17,* 1–5.

Thompson, D. R., & others. (2007). Childhood overweight and cardiovascular disease risk factors: The National Heart, Lung, and Blood Institute Growth and Health Study. *Journal of Pediatrics, 150,* 18–25.

Thompson, J., Manore, M., & Vaughan, L. (2011). *Science of nutrition* (2nd ed.). Upper Saddle River, NJ: Pearson.

Thompson, P. M., Giedd, J. N., Woods, R. P., MacDonald, D., Evans, A. C., & Toga, A. W. (2000). Growth patterns in the developing brain detected by using continuum mechanical tensor maps. *Nature, 404,* 190–193.

Thompson, R. (2010). Maltreatment and mental health care: Focusing on child neglect. *Psychiatric Services, 61,* 96.

Thompson, R. A. (1994). Emotion regulation: A theme in search of a definition. *Monographs of the Society for Research in Child Development, 59* (Serial No. 240), 2–3.

Thompson, R. A. (2006). The development of the person. In W. Damon & R. Lerner (Eds.), *Handbook of child psychology* (6th ed.). New York: Wiley.

Thompson, R. A. (2007). Unpublished review of J. W. Santrock's *Children* (10th ed.). (New York: McGraw-Hill).

Thompson, R. A. (2011). The emotionate child. In D. Cicchetti & G. I. Roisman (Eds.), *The origins and organization of adaptation and maladaptation. Minnesota Symposium on Child Psychology* (Vol. 36). New York: Wiley.

Thompson, R. A. (2012). Whither the preoperational child? Toward a life-span moral development theory. *Child Development Perspectives, 6,* 423–429.

Thompson, R. A. (2013a, in press). Attachment development: Precis and prospect. In P. Zelazo (Ed.), *Oxford*

*handbook of developmental psychology.* New York: Oxford University Press.

Thompson, R. A. (2013b, in press). Interpersonal relations. In A. Ben-Arieh, I. Frones, F. Cases, & J. Korbin (Eds.), *Handbook of child well-being.* New York: Springer.

Thompson, R. A. (2013c, in press). Relationships, regulation, and development. In R. M. Lerner (Ed.), *Handbook of child psychology* (7th ed.). New York: Wiley.

Thompson, R. A. (2013d, in press). Socialization of emotion regulation in the family. In J. Gross (Ed.), *Handbook of emotion regulation* (2nd ed.). New York: Guilford.

Thompson, R. A., & Goodvin, R. (2005). The individual child: Temperament, emotion, self and personality. In M. J. Bornstein & M. E. Lamb (Eds.) *Developmental psychology* (5th ed.). Mahwah, NJ: Erlbaum.

Thompson, R. A., McGinley, M., & Meyer, S. (2006). Understanding values in relationships. In M. Killen & J. G. Smetana (Eds.), *Handbook of moral development.* Mahwah, NJ: Erlbaum.

Thompson, R. A., Meyer, M., & McGinley, M. (2013). Understanding values in relationships: The development of conscience. In M. Killen & J. G. Smetana (Eds.), *Handbook of moral development* (2nd ed.). New York: Routledge.

Thompson, R. A., Meyer, S., Virmani, E., Waters, S., Raikes, H. A., & Jochem, R. (2009, April). *Parent-child relationships, conversation, and developing emotion regulation.* Paper presented at the meeting of the Society for Research in Child Development, Denver.

Thompson, R. A., & Virmani, E. A. (2010). Creating persons: Culture, self, and personality development. In M. H. Bornstein (Ed.), *Handbook of cultural developmental science.* New York: Psychology Press.

Tikotzky, L., Sadeh, A., & Glickman-Gavrieli, T. (2010). Infant sleep and paternal involvement in infant caregiving during the first 6 months of life. *Journal of Pediatric Psychology, 36*(1), 36–46.

Tikotzky, L., & Shaashua, L. (2012). Infant sleep and early parental sleep-related cognitions predict sleep in pre-school children. *Sleep Medicine, 13,* 185–192.

Tincoff, R., & Jusczyk, P. W. (2012, in press). Six-month-olds comprehend words that refer to parts of the body. Infancy.

Tobin, J. J., Wu, D. Y. H., & Davidson, D. H. (1989). *Preschool in three cultures.* New Haven, CT: Yale University Press.

Tolani, N., & Brooks-Gunn, J. (2008). Family support, international trends. In

M. M. Haith & J. B. Benson (Eds.), *Encyclopedia of infant and early childhood development*. Oxford, UK: Elsevier.

**Toma, C., & others.** (2012). Neurotransmitter systems and neurotrophic factors in autism: Association study of 37 genes suggests involvement of DDC. *World Journal of Biology*.

**Tomasello, M.** (2008). *Origins of human communication*. Cambridge, MA: MIT Press.

**Tomasello, M.** (2009). *Why we cooperate*. Cambridge, MA: MIT Press.

**Tomasello, M.** (2011b). Language development. In U. Goswami (Ed.), *Wiley-Blackwell handbook of childhood cognitive development* (2nd ed.). New York: Wiley.

**Tomasello, M., Carpenter, M., & Liszkowski, U.** (2007). A new look at infant pointing. *Child Development, 78*, 705–722.

**Tomasello, M., & Hamann, K.** (2012). Collaboration in young children. *Quarterly Journal of Experimental Psychology, 65*, 1–12.

**Tomasello, M., & Vaish, A.** (2013). Origins of human cooperation and morality. *Annual Review of Psychology*. Palo Alto, CA: Annual Reviews.

**Tompkins, G. E.** (2011). *Literacy in the early grades*. (3rd ed.). Boston: Allyn & Bacon.

**Tompkins, G. E.** (2013). *Language arts* (8th ed.). Boston: Allyn & Bacon.

**Tompkins, T. L., Hockett, A. R., Abraibes, N., & Witt, J. L.** (2011). A closer look at co-rumination: Gender, coping, peer functioning, and internalizing/externalizing problems. *Journal of Adolescence, 34*(5), 801–811.

**Torres, J. M.** (2013, in press). Breast milk and labor support: Lactation consultants' and doulas' strategies for navigating the medical context of maternity care. *Sociology of Health and Illness*.

**Tortoriello, G., Morris, C. V., Alpar, A., Fuzik, J., Shirran, S. L., Calvigioni, D., Keimpema, E., Botting, C. H., Reinecke, K., Herdegen, T., Courtney, M., Hurd, Y. L., & Harkany, T.** (2014). Miswiring the brain: Δ9-tetrahydrocannabinol disrupts cortical development by inducing an SCG10/stathmin-2 degradation pathway. *The EMBO Journal, 33*, 668–685.

**Trach, J., Hymel, S., Waterhouse, T., & Neale, K.** (2010). Bystander responses to school bullying: A cross-sectional investigation of grade and sex differences. *Canadian Journal of School Psychology, 25*(1), 114–130.

**Trafimow, D., Triandis, H. C., & Goto, S. G.** (1991). Some tests of the distinction between the private and collective self. *Journal of Personality and Social Psychology, 60*, 649–655.

**Trainor, L. J., Lee, K., & Bosnyak, D. J.** (2011). Cortical plasticity in 4-month-old infants: Specific effects of experience with musical timbres. *Brain Topography, 24*, 192–203.

**Trainor, L. J., Marie, C., Gerry, D., Whiskin, E., & Unrau, A.** (2012). Becoming musically enculturated: Effects of music classes for infants on brain and behaviour. *Annals of the New York Academy of Sciences, 1252*, 129–138.

**Trautner, H. M., Ruble, D. N., Cyphers, L., Kirsten, B., Behrendt, R., & Hartmann, P.** (2005). Rigidity and flexibility of gender stereotypes in children: Developmental or differential? *Infant and Child Development, 14*, 365–381.

**Trehub, S. E., Schneider, B. A., Thorpe, L. A., & Judge, P.** (1991). Observational measures of auditory sensitivity in early infancy. *Developmental Psychology, 27*, 40–49.

**Tremblay, M. S., & others.** (2012). Canadian sedentary behavior guidelines for the early years (0–4 years). *Applied Physiology, Nutrition, and Metabolism, 37*, 370–380.

**Tremblay, R. E.** (2009). Development of aggression from early childhood to adulthood. In R. E. Tremblay, R. deV. Peters, M. Boivin, & R. G. Barr (Eds.), *Encyclopedia on early childhood development*. Montreal: Center of Excellence for Early Childhood Development.

**Trentacosta, C. J., & Fine, S. E.** (2009). Emotion knowledge, social competence, and behavior problems in childhood and adolescence: A meta-analytic review. *Social Development, 19*(1), 1–29.

**Triandis, H. C.** (2007). Culture and psychology: A history of their relationship. In S. Kitayama & D. Cohen (Eds.), *Handbook of cultural psychology*. New York: Guilford.

**Triche, E. W., & Hossain, N.** (2007). Environmental factors implicated in the causation of adverse pregnancy outcome. *Seminars in Perinatology, 31*, 240–242.

**Tri-Council Policy Statement: Ethical Conduct for Research Involving Humans:** See Canadian Institutes of Health Research, Natural Sciences and Engineering Research Council of Canada, and Social Sciences and Humanities Research Council of Canada.

**Trimble, J. E.** (1988, August). *The enculturation of contemporary psychology*. Paper presented at the meeting of the American Psychological Association. New Orleans.

**Trinkner, R., Cohn, E. S., Rebellon, C. J., & Van Gundy, K.** (2012). Don't trust anyone over 30: Parental legitimacy as a mediator between parenting style and changes in delinquent behavior over time. *Journal of Adolescence, 35*, 119–132.

**Trocme, N. M., Tourigny, M., MacLaurin, B., & Fallon, B.** (2003). Major findings from the Canadian incidence study of reported child abuse and neglect. *Child Abuse and Neglect, 27*, 1427–1439.

**Tronick, E., Als, H., Adamson, L., Wise, S., & Brazelton, T. B.** (1978). The infant's response to entrapment between contradictory messages in face-to-face interaction. *Journal of American Academy of Child Psychiatry: 17*, 1–13.

**Troop-Gordon, W., Visconti, K. J., & Kuntz, K. J.** (2011). Perceived popularity during early adolescence: Links to declining school adjustment among aggressive youth. *The Journal of Early Adolescence, 31*(1), 125–151.

**Trost, S. G., Fees, B., & Dzewaltowski, D.** (2008). Feasibility and efficacy of "move and learn" physical activity curriculum in preschool children. *Journal of Physical Activity and Health, 5*, 88–103.

**Tsang, C. D., & Conrad, N. J.** (2010). Does the message matter? The effect of song type on infants' pitch preference for lullabies and playsongs. *Infant Behavior and Development, 33*, 96–100.

**Tseng, V.** (2004). Family interdependence and academic adjustment in college: Youth from immigrant and U.S.-born families. *Child Development, 75*, 966–983.

**Tucker, J. S., & others.** (2012). Resisting smoking when a best friend smokes: Do intrapersonal and contextual factors matter? *Journal of Research on Adolescence, 22*, 113–122.

**Turcotte-Tremblay, A., Lim, R., Laplante, D. P., Kobzik, L., Brunet, A., King, S.** (2014). Prenatal maternal stress predicts childhood asthma in girls: Project ice storm. Hindawi Publishing Corporation. *BioMed Research International Volume 2014*, Article ID 201717, 10 pages http://dx.doi.org/10.1155/2014/201717.

**Turnbull, M., Hart, D., & Lapkin, S.** (2003). Grade 6 French immersion students' performance on large-scale reading, writing, and mathematics tests: Building explanations. *Journal of Educational Research, 49*, 6–23.

**Turner, H. A., & others.** (2012). Family context, victimization, and child trauma symptoms: Variations in safe, stable, and nurturing relationships during early and middle childhood. *American Journal of Orthopsychiatry, 82*, 209–219.

**Turrigiano, G.** (2010). Synaptic homeostasis. *Annual Review of Neuroscience* (Vol. 33). Palo Alto, CA: Annual Reviews.

# U

Udry, J. R., & others. (1985). Serum androgenic hormones motivate sexual behavior in adolescent boys. *Fertility and Sterility, 43,* 90–94.

Ueno, K., & McWilliams, S. (2010). Gender-typed behaviors and school adjustment. *Sex Roles, 63,* 580–591.

Uhls, Y. T., & Greenfield, P. M. (2009). Adolescents and electronic communication. Retrieved June 25, 2010, from www.education.com/reference/article/adolescents-online-social-networking/

Umana-Taylor, A. J. (2009). Research with Latino early adolescents. *Journal of Early Adolescence, 29,* 5–15.

UNICEF. (2003). *The state of the world's children: 2003.* Geneva, Switzerland: Author.

UNICEF (2004). The s*tate of the worlds' children 2004.* Geneva: SWIT: UNICEF.

UNICEF (2006). *The state of the world's children 2006.* Geneva, SWIT: UNICEF.

UNICEF (2007). *The state of the world's children 2007.* Geneva, SWIT: UNICEF.

UNICEF. (2009. *The state of the world's children:* 2009. Geneva, Switzerland: Author.

UNICEF. (2010). *The state of the world's children:* 2010. Geneva, Switzerland: Author.

UNICEF. (2011). *The state of the world's children:* 2011. Geneva, Switzerland: Author.

UNICEF. (2012). *The state of the world's children:* 2012. Geneva, Switzerland: Author.

United Nations. (2002). *Improving the quality of life of girls.* Geneva: UNICEF.

Updegraff, K. A., Kim, J-Y., Killoren, S. E., & Thayer, S. M. (2010). Mexican American parents' involvement in adolescents' peer relationships: Exploring the role of culture and adolescents' peer experiences. *Journal of Research on Adolescence, 20,* 65–87.

Urban, J. B., Lewin-Bizan, S., & Lerner, R. M. (2010). The role of intentional self-regulation, lower neighborhood ecological assets, and activity involvement in youth developmental outcomes. *Journal of Youth and Adolescence, 39,* 783–800.

Urbano, M. T., & Tait, D. M. (2004). Can the irradiated uterus sustain a pregnancy? *Clinical Oncology, 16,* 24–28.

Urdan, T. (2010). Classroom goal structures, motivation, and learning. In J. Meece & J. Eccles (Eds.), *Handbook of research on schools, schooling, and motivation.* New York: Routledge.

Urdan, T. (2012). Factors affecting the motivation and achievement of immigrant students. In K. R. Harris, S. Graham, & T. Urdan (Eds.), *APA educational psychology handbook.* Washington, DC: American Psychological Association.

Ursache, A., Blair, C., & Raver, C. C. (2012). The promotion of self-regulation as a means of enhancing school readiness and early achievement in children at risk for school failure. *Child Development Perspectives, 6,* 122–128.

Ursache, A., Blair, C., Stifter, C., & Voegtline, K. (2013, in press). Emotional reactivity and regulation in infancy interact to predict executive functioning in early childhood. *Developmental Psychology.*

Usborne, E., Peck, J., Smith, D., & Taylor, D. M. (2011). Learning through an Aboriginal language: The impact on students' English and Aboriginal language skills. *Canadian Journal of Education, 34,* 200–215.

U.S. Department of Energy. (2001). *The human genome project.* Washington, DC: U.S. Department of Energy.

U.S. Department of Health and Human Services. (2009). *Folic acid.* Retrieved January 19, 2009, from www.cdc.gov/ncbddd/folicacid/

# V

Vacca, J. A., Vacca, R. T., Gove, M. K., Burkey, L. C., Lenhart, L. A., & McKeon, C. A. (2009). *Reading and learning to read* (7th ed.). Boston: Allyn & Bacon.

Vaillancourt, T. & Hymel, S. (2006). Aggression and social status: The moderating roles of sex and peer-valued characteristics. *Aggressive Behavior, 32*(4), 396–408.

Vaillancourt, T., Hymel, S., & McDougall, P. (2003). Bullying is power: Implications for school-based intervention strategies. *Journal of Applied School Psychology, 19,* 157–176.

Vaillancourt, T., McDougall, P., Krygsman, A., Hymel, S., Miller, J., Stiver, K., & Davis, C. (2008). Bullying: Are researchers and children/youth talking about the same thing? *International Journal of Behavioral Development, 32,* 486–495.

Vaish, A., Carpenter, M., & Tomasello, M. (2010). Young children selectively avoid helping people with harmful intentions. *Child Development, 81,* 1661–1669.

Valenzuela, C. F., Morton, R. A., Diaz, M. R., & Topper, L. (2012, in press). Does moderate drinking harm the fetal brain? Insights from animal models. *Trends in Neuroscience.*

Valkenburg, P. M., & Peter, J. (2007). Preadolescents' and adolescents' online communication and their closeness to friends. *Developmental Psychology, 43,* 267–277.

Valkenburg, P. M., & Peter, J. (2009). Social consequences of the Internet for adolescents. *Current Directions in Psychological Science, 18,* 1–5.

Valkenburg, P. M., & Peter, J. (2011). Online communication among adolescents: An integrated model of its attraction, opportunities, and risks. *Journal of Adolescent Health, 48,* 121–127.

Vandehey, M., Diekhoff, G., & LaBeff, E. (2007). College cheating: A 20-year follow-up and the addition of an honor code. *Journal of College Development, 48,* 468–480.

Vandell, D. L., & Wilson, K. S. (1988). Infants' interactions with mother, sibling, and peer: Contrasts and relations between interaction systems. *Child Development, 48,* 176–186.

van den Boom, D. C. (1989). Neonatal irritability and the development of attachment. In G. A. Kohnstamm, J. E. Bates, & M. K. Rothbart (Eds.), *Temperament in childhood.* New York: Wiley.

Vanderlee, M., Youmans, S., Peters, R., & Eastabrook, J. (2012). *Final report: Evaluation of the implementation of the Ontario full-day early learning-kindergarten program.* Retrieved on June 6, 2014 from: www.edu.gov.on.ca/kindergarten/FDELK_ReportFall2012.pdf

van der Stel, M., & Veenman, M. V. J. (2010). Development of metacognitive skillfulness: A longitudinal study. *Learning and Individual Differences, 20,* 220–224.

Van De Voorde, S., Roeyers, H., Verte, S., & Wiersema, J. R. (2011). The influence of working memory load on response inhibition in children with attention-deficit/hyperactivity disorder or reading disorder. *Journal of Clinical Neuropsychology, 33*(7), 753–764.

van de Weijer-Bergsma, E., Formsma, A. R., de Bruin, E. I., & Bogels, S. M. (2012). The effectiveness of mindfulness training on behavioral problems and attentional functioning in adolescents with ADHD. *Journal of Child and Family Studies, 21,* 775–787.

Van Dyck, P. C. (2007). Final commentary on the special volume of articles from the National Survey of Children's Health. *Pediatrics, 119,* Suppl. S122–S123.

van Harmelen, A. L., & others. (2010). Child abuse and negative explicit and automatic self-associations: The cognitive scars of emotional maltreatment. *Behavior Research and Therapy, 48*(6), 486–494.

Van Hecke, V., & others. (2012). Infant responding to joint attention, executive processes, and self-regulation in preschool children. *Infant Development and Behavior, 35,* 303–311.

van IJzendoorn, M. H., & Kroonenberg, P. M. (1988). Cross-cultural patterns of attachment: A meta-analysis of the Strange Situation. *Child Development, 59,* 147–156.

Van Norstrand, D. W., & others. (2012). Connexin43 mutation causes heterogeneous gap junction loss and sudden infant death. *Circulation, 125,* 474–481.

Van Ryzin, M. J., Carlson, E. A., & Sroufe, L. A. (2011). Attachment discontinuity in a high-risk sample. *Attachment and Human Development, 13,* 381–401.

van Spronsen, F. J., & Enns, G. M. (2010). Future treatment strategies in phenylketonuria. *Molecular Genetics and Metabolism, 99, Suppl 1,* S90–S95.

Vansteenkiste, M., Sierens, E., Soenens, B., Luyckx, K., & Lens, W. (2009). Motivational profiles from a self-determination perspective: The quality of motivation matters. *Journal of Educational Psychology, 101*(3), 671–688.

Varnhagen, C. K., & others. (2010). lol: New language and spelling in instant messaging. *Reading and Writing, 23,* 719–733.

Vasdev, G. (2008). *Obstetric anesthesia.* Oxford, UK: Elsevier.

Veenstra, R., Lindenberg, S., Munniksma, A., & Dijkstra, J. K. (2010). The complex relationship between bullying, victimization, acceptance, and rejection: Giving special attention to status, affection, and sex differences. *Child Development, 81*(2), 480–486.

Velagaleti, R. S., & O'Donnell, C. J. (2010). Genomics of heart failure. *Heart Failure Clinics, 6,* 115–124.

Velez, C. E., Wolchik, S. A., Tein, J. Y., & Sandler, I. (2011). Protecting children from the consequences of divorce: A longitudinal study of the effects of parenting on children's coping responses. *Child Development, 82,* 244–257.

Venners, S. A., & others. (2005). Paternal smoking and pregnancy loss: A prospective study using a biomarker of pregnancy. *American Journal of Epidemiology, 159,* 993–1001.

Verhaak, C. M., Linsten, A. M., Evers, A. W., & Braat, D. D. (2010). Who is at risk of emotional problems and how do you know? Screening of women going for IVF treatment. *Human Reproduction.* (Available online March 13, 2010.)

Verkampt, F., & Ginet, M. (2010). Variations of the cognitive interview: Which one is the most effective in enhancing children's testimonies? *Applied Cognitive Psychology, 24,* 1279–1296.

Verma, S., & Saraswathi, T. S. (2002). Adolescence in India: Street urchins or Silicon Valley millionaires? In B. B. Brown, R. W. Larson, & T. S. Saraswathi (Eds.), *The world's youth.* New York: Cambridge University Press.

Vermeersch, H., T'Sjoen, G., Kaufman, J. M., & Vincke, J. (2008). The role of testosterone in aggressive and non-aggressive risk-taking in boys. *Hormones and Behavior, 53,* 463–471.

Vesco, K. K., & others. (2012). Healthy Moms, a randomized trial to promote and evaluate weight maintenance among obese pregnant women: Study design and rationale. *Contemporary Clinical Trials, 33,* 777–785.

Vida, M., & Maurer, D. (2012). The development of fine-grained sensitivity to eye contact after 6 years of age. *Journal of Experimental Child Psychology, 112,* 243–256.

Viet, C. T., & Schmidt, B. L. (2010). Understanding oral cancer in the genome era. *Head and Neck.* (Available online February 24, 2010.)

Vigod, S. N., Tarasoff, L. A., Bryja, B., Dennis, C., Yudin, M. H., & Ross, L. E. (2013). Relation between place of residence and postpartum depression. *Canadian Medical Association Journal,* doi:10.1503/cmaj.122028.

Villar, J., Carroli, G., Zavaleta, N., Donner, A., Wojdyla, D., Faundes, A., & others. (2007). Maternal and neonatal individual risks and benefits associated with caesarean delivery: Multicenter prospective study. *British Medical Journal, 335,* 1025.

Villegas, R., & others. (2008). Duration of breast-feeding and the incidence of type 2 diabetes mellitus in the Shanghai Women's Health Study. *Diabetologia, 51,* 258–266.

Vimaleswaran, K. S., & Loos, R. J. (2010). Progress in the genetics of common obesity and type 2 diabetes. *Expert Reviews in Molecular Medicine, 12,* e7.

Vinik, J., Almas, A., & Grusec, J. (2011). Mothers' knowledge of what distresses and comforts their children predicts children's coping, empathy, and prosocial behavior. *Parenting: Science and Practice, 11,* 56–71.

Vitaro, F., Barker, E.D., Brendgen, M., & Tremblay, R.E. (2012). Pathways explaining the reduction of adult criminal behavior by a randomized preventive intervention for disruptive kindergarten children. *Journal of Child Psychology and Psychiatry, 53*(7), 748–756.

Vitaro, F., Boivin, M., & Bukowski, W. M. (2009). The role of friendship in child and adolescent psychosocial development.

In K. H. Rubin, W. M. Bukowski, & B. Laursen (Eds.), *Handbook of peer interaction, relationships, and groups.* New York: Guilford.

Vitaro, F., Pedersen, S., & Brendgen, M. (2007). Children's disruptiveness, peer rejection, friends' deviancy, and delinquent behaviors: A process-oriented approach. *Development and Psychopathology, 19,* 433–453.

Vittrup, B., Holden, G. W., & Buck, M. (2006). Attitudes predict the use of physical punishment: A prospective study of the emergence of disciplinary practices. *Pediatrics, 117,* 2055–2064.

Vladutiu, C. J., Evenson, K. R., & Marshall, S. W. (2010). Physical activity and injuries during pregnancy. *Journal of Physical Activity and Health, 7,* 761–769.

Vohs, K., & Baumeister, R. F. (Eds.). (2012). *Self and identity.* Thousand Oaks, CA: Sage.

Volbrecht, M. M., & Goldsmith, H. H. (2010). Early temperamental and family predictors of shyness and anxiety. *Developmental Psychology, 46,* 1192–1205.

Vong, K-I. (2012). Play—A multimodal manifestation in kindergarten education in China. *Early Years: An International Journal of Research and Development, 32, 1,* 35–48.

Von Hofsten, C. (2008). Motor and physical development manual. In M. M Haith & J. B. Benson (Eds.), *Encyclopedia of infant and early childhood development.* Oxford, UK: Elsevier.

Von Polier, G. G., Vioet, T. D., & Herpertz-Dahlmann, B. (2012). ADHD and delinquency—A developmental perspective. *Behavioral Sciences and the Law, 30,* 121–139.

Votavova, H., & others. (2012). Deregulation of gene expression induced by environmental tobacco smoke exposure in pregnancy. *Nicotine and Tobacco Research, 14,* 1073–1082.

Votruba-Drzal, E., Coley, R. L., & Chase-Lansdale, P. L. (2004). Child care and low-income children's development: Direct and moderated effects. *Child Development, 75,* 296–312.

Voyer, D., Voyer, S., & Bryden, M. P. (1995). Magnitude of sex differences in spatial abilities: A meta-analysis and consideration of critical variables. *Psychological Bulletin, 117,* 250–270.

Vreeman, R. C., & Carroll, A. E. (2007). A systematic review of school-based interventions to prevent bullying. *Archives of Pediatric and Adolescent Medicine, 161,* 78–88.

Vriend, J. L., Davidson, F. D., Corium, P. V., Rusak, B., McLaughlin, E. N., Chambers, C. T. (2013). Sleep quantity and quality in relation to daytime functioning in children. *Child Health Care—Special Issue: Pediatric Behavioral Sleep Medicine.*

Vukelich, C., Christie, J., & Enz, B. J. (2008). *Helping children learn language and literacy.* Boston: Allyn & Bacon.

Vygotsky, L. S. (1962). *Thought and language.* Cambridge, MA: MIT Press.

# W

Wachs, T. D. (1994). Fit, context and the transition between temperament and personality. In C. Halverson, G. Kohnstamm, & R. Martin (Eds.), *The developing structure of personality from infancy to adulthood.* Hillsdale, NJ: Erlbaum.

Wachs, T. D. (2000). *Necessary but not sufficient.* Washington, DC: American Psychological Association.

Wachs, T. D., & Bates, J. E. (2010). Temperament. In J. G. Bremner & T. D. Wachs (Eds.), *Wiley-Blackwell handbook of infant development* (2nd ed.). New York: Wiley.

Waddell, L. (2012). The power of vitamins. *Journal of Family Health Care, 22,* 16-20, 22-25.

Wadsworth, S. J., Olson, R. K., & Defries, J. C. (2010). Differential genetic etiology of reading difficulties as a function of IQ: An update. *Behavior Genetics.*

Wagner, D. A. (2010). Literacy. In M. H. Bornstein (Ed.), *Handbook of cultural developmental science.* New York: Psychology Press.

Wagner, L., & Hoff, E. (2013). Language development. In I. B. Weiner & others (Eds.), *Handbook of psychology* (2nd ed.). New York: Wiley.

Wagner, R. K., & Sternberg, R. J. (1986). Tacit knowledge and intelligent functioning in the everyday world. In R. J. Sternberg & R. K. Wagner (Eds.), *Practical intelligence.* New York: Cambridge University Press.

Wainryb, C. (2013). Moral development in culture: Diversity, tolerance, and justice. In M. Killen & J. G. Smetana (Eds.), *Handbook of moral development* (2nd ed.). New York: Routledge.

Waiter, G. D., & others. (2009). Exploring possible neural mechanisms of intelligence differences using processing speed and working memory tasks. *Intelligence, 37,* 199-206.

Walden, T. (1991). Infant social referencing. In J. Garber & K. Dodge (Eds.), *The development of emotional regulation and dysregulation.* New York: Cambridge University Press.

Walker, C. M., & Gopnik, A. (2013). Pretense and possibility—A theoretical proposal about the effects of pretend play on development: Comment on Lillard et al. (2013). *Psychological Bulletin, 139,* 40-44.

Walker, L. (1982). The sequentiality of Kohlberg's stages of moral development. *Child Development, 53,* 1130-1136.

Walker, L. (2006). Gender and morality. In M. Killen & J. G. Smetana (Eds.), *Handbook of moral development.* Mahwah, NJ: Erlbaum.

Walker, L. J. (2002). Moral exemplarity. In W. Damon (Ed.), *Bringing in a new era of character education.* Stanford, CA: Hoover Press.

Walker, L. J. (2004). Progress and prospects in the psychology of moral development. *Merrill-Palmer Quarterly, 50,* 546-557.

Walker, L. J. (2013). Moral personality, motivation, and identity. In M. Killen & J. G. Smetana (Eds.), *Handbook of moral development* (2nd ed.). New York: Routledge.

Walker, L. J., & Frimer, J. A. (2009). Moral personality exemplified. In D. Narváez & D. K. Lapsley (Eds.), *Moral personality, identity, and character: Prospects for a new field of study.* New York: Cambridge University Press.

Walker, L. J., & Hennig, K. H. (2004). Differing conceptions of moral exemplars: Just, brave, and caring. *Journal of Personality and Social Psychology, 86,* 629-647.

Walker, L.J. & Hennig, K.H. (1999). Parenting style and the development of moral reasoning. *Journal of Moral Education, 28,* 359-374.

Walker, L. J., Hennig, K. H., & Krettenauer, T. (2000). Parent and peer contexts for children's moral development. *Child Development, 71,* 1033-1048.

Walker, L. J., & Pitts, R. C. (1998). Naturalistic conceptions of moral maturity. *Developmental Psychology, 34,* 403-419.

Walker, L. J. & Taylor, J. H. (1991). Family interactions and the development of moral reasoning. *Child Development, 62,* 264-283.

Wallerstein, J. S. (2008). Divorce. In M. M. Haith & J. B. Benson (Eds.), *Encyclopedia of infant and early childhood development.* Oxford, UK: Elsevier.

Wallis, C. (2011). Performing gender: A content analysis of gender display in music videos. *Sex Roles, 64,* 160-172.

Walsh, R. (2011). Lifestyle and mental health. *American Psychologist, 66,* 579-592.

Walsh, T. J., Pera, R. R., & Turek, P. J. (2010). The genetics of male infertility. *Seminars in Reproductive Medicine, 27,* 124-136.

Wang, M. L., & others. (2013). Dietary and physical activity factors related to eating disorder symptoms among middle school youth. *Journal of School Health, 83,* 14-20.

Wang, Q. (2001). Culture effects on adults' earliest childhood recollection and self-description: Implications for the relation between memory and the self. *Journal of Personality and Social Psychology, 81,* 220-233.

Wang, Q., & Conway, M. A. (2004). The stories we keep: Autobiographical memory in American and Chinese middle-aged adults. *Journal of Personality, 72,* 911-938.

Wang, Q., Conway, M. A., & Hou, Y. (2004). Infantile amnesia: A cross-cultural investigation. *Cognitive Sciences, 1,* 123-135.

Wang, Q., & Pomerantz, E. M. (2009). The motivational landscape of early adolescence in the United States and China: A longitudinal study. *Child Development, 80*(4), 1272-1287.

Ward, L. M. (2004). Wading through stereotypes: Positive and negative associations between media use and black adolescents' conceptions of self. *Developmental Psychology, 40,* 284-294.

Warrington, M., & Younger, M. (2003). "We decided to give it a twirl": Single-sex teaching in English comprehensive schools. *Gender and Education, 15,* 339-350.

Watamura, S. E., Phillips, D. A., Morrissey, D. A., McCartney, T. W., & Bub, K. (2011). Double jeopardy: Poorer social-emotional outcomes for children in the NICHD SECCYD who experience home and child-care environments that convey risk. *Child Development, 82,* 48-65.

Waterman, A. S. (1985). Identity in the context of adolescent psychology. In A. S. Waterman (Ed.), *Identity in adolescence: Processes and contents* San Francisco: Jossey-Bass.

Waterman, A. S. (1992). Identity as an aspect of optimal psychological functioning. In G. R. Adams, T. P. Gullotta, & R. Montemayor (Eds.), *Adolescent identity formation.* Newbury Park, CA: Sage.

Watson, J. B. (1928). *Psychological care of infant and child.* New York: W. W. Norton.

Watson, J. B., & Rayner, R. (1920). Conditioned emotional reactions. *Journal of Experimental Psychology, 3,* 1-14.

Watt, H. M. G., Shapka, J. D., Morris, Z. A., Durik, A. M., Keating, D. P., & Eccles, J. S. (2012). Gendered motivational processes affecting high school mathematics participation, educational aspirations, and career plans: A comparison of samples from Australia, Canada, and the United States. *Developmental Psychology, 48*(6), 1594-1611.

Waxman, S. (2009) How infants discover distinct word types and map them to distinct meanings. In J. Colombo, P. McCardle, & L. Freund (Eds.), *Infant pathways to language: Methods, models, and research disorders* (pp. 99–118). New York: Taylor and Francis.

Way, N., & Silverman, L. R. (2012). The quality of friendships during adolescence: Patterns across context, culture, and age. In P. K. Kerig, M. S. Shulz, & S. T. Hauser (Eds.), *Adolescence and beyond*. New York: Oxford University Press.

Wayne, A. (2011). Commentary in interview: Childhood cancers in transition. Retrieved April 12, 2011, from http://home.ccr.cancer.gov/connections/2010/Vol4_No2/clinic2.asp

Webb, J. T., Gore, J. L., Mend, E. R., & DeVries, A. R. (2007). *A parent's guide to gifted children*. Scottsdale, AZ: Great Potential Press.

Webb, L. D., Metha, A., & Jordan, K. F. (2013). *Foundations of American education* (7th ed.). Upper Saddle River, NJ: Pearson.

Weber, M. A., Risdon, R. S., Ashworth, M. T., Malone, M. T., & Sebire, N. J. (2012). Autopsy findings of co-sleeping-associated sudden unexpected death in infancy: Relationship between pathological features and asphyxial mode of death. *Journal of Pediatric and Child Health, 48,* 335–341.

Webster, N. S., & Worrell, F. C. (2008). Academically-talented adolescents' attitudes toward service in the community. *Gifted Child Quarterly, 52,* 170–179.

Wei, R., & others. (2013, in press). Dynamic expression of microRNAs during the differentiation of human embryonic stem cells into insulin-producing cells. *Gene.*

Weikum W. , Mayes L. , Grunau R. , Brain U. , & Oberlander T. F. (2013). The impact of prenatal serotonin reuptake inhibitor (SRI) antidepressant exposure and maternal mood on mother–infant interactions at 3 months of age. *Infant Behavior and Development.*

Weiner, C. P., & Buhimschi, C. (2009). *Drugs for pregnant and lactating women* (2nd ed.). London: Elsevier.

Weinraub, M., & others. (2012, in press). Patterns of developmental change in infants' nighttime sleep awakenings from 6 through 36 months of age. *Developmental Psychology.*

Weinstein, N., Deci, E. L., & Ryan, R. M. (2011). Motivational determinants of integrating positive and negative past identities. *Journal of Personality and Social Psychology, 100,* 527–544.

Weinstein, R. S. (2004). *Reaching higher: The power of expectations in schooling* (paperback ed.). Cambridge, MA: Harvard University Press.

Weiss, L. A., & others. (2008). Association between microdeletion and microduplication at 16p 11.2 and autism. *New England Journal of Medicine, 358,* 667–675.

Weiss, S. K., & Corium, P. (20120). Pediatric behavioural insomnia—"good night, sleep tight" for child and parent. *Insomnia Rounds, 1*(5), publication of the Canadian Sleep Society.

Wekerle, C., & others. (2009). The contribution of childhood emotional abuse to teen dating violence among child protective services-involved youth. *Child Abuse and Neglect, 33*(1), 45–58.

Weller, D., & Lagattuta, K. H. (2013). Helping the in-group feels better: Children's judgments and emotion attributions in response to prosocial dilemmas. *Child Development.*

Wellman, H. M. (2011). Developing a theory of mind. In U. Goswami (Ed.), *The Blackwell handbook of childhood cognitive development* (2nd Ed.). New York: Wiley.

Wellman, H. M., Cross, D., & Watson, J. (2001). Meta-analysis of theory-of-mind development: The truth about false belief. *Child Development, 72,* 655–684.

Wellman, H. M. & Woolley, J. D. (1990). From simple desires to ordinary beliefs: The early development of everyday psychology. *Cognition, 35,* 245–275.

Wells, E. M., & others. (2011). Body burdens of mercury, lead, selenium, and copper among Baltimore newborns. *Environmental Research, 111,* 411–417.

Welti, C. (2002). Adolescents in Latin America: Facing the future with skepticism. In B. B. Brown, R. W. Larson, & T. S. Saraswathi (Eds.), *The world's youth.* New York: Cambridge University Press.

Wentzel, K. R. (2013). School adjustment. In I. B. Weiner & others (Eds.), *Handbook of psychology* (2nd ed., Vol. 7). New York: Wiley.

Werker, J. F. (1989). Becoming a native listener. *American Scientist, 77,* 54–59.

Werker, J. F., Gilbert, J. H. V., Humphrey, K., & Tees, R. C. (1981). Developmental aspects of cross-language speech perception. *Child Development, 52,* 349–355.

Werker, J. F., & Tees, R. C. (1983). Developmental changes across childhood in the perception of non-native speech sounds. *Canadian Journal of Psychology, 37,* 287–286.

Werker, J. F., & Tees, R. C. (1984). Cross-language speech perception: Evidence for perceptual reorganization during the first year of life. *Infant Behavior & Development, 7,* 49–63.

Wermter, A. K., & others. (2010). From nature versus nurture, via nature and nurture, to gene X environment interaction in mental disorders. *European Journal of Child and Adolescent Psychiatry, 19,* 199–210.

Wertsch, J. V. (2007). Mediation. In H. Daniels, J. Wertsch, & M. Cole (Eds.), *The Cambridge companion to Vygotsky.* New York: Cambridge University Press.

Westerman, G., Thomas, M. S. C., & Karmiloff-Smith, A. (2011). Neuroconstructivism. In U. Goswami (Ed.), *Wiley-Blackwell handbook of childhood cognitive development* (2nd ed.). New York: Wiley.

Weston, M. J. (2010). Magnetic resonance imaging in fetal medicine: A pictorial review of current and developing indications. *Postgraduate Medicine Journal, 86,* 42–51.

Whaley, L. (2013, in press). Syntactic typology. In J. J. Song (Ed.), *Oxford handbook of linguistic typology.* New York: Oxford University Press.

Wheeden, A., Scafidi, F. A., Field, T., Ironson, G., Valdeon, C. & Bandstra, E. (1993). Massage effects on cocaine-exposed preterm neonates. *Journal of Developmental and Behavioral Pediatrics, 14,* 318–322.

Whitehurst, G., & Lonigan, C. (1998). Child development and emergent literacy. *Child Development, 69*(3), 848–872.

Whittle, S., & others. (2008). Prefrontal and amygdala volumes are related to adolescents' affective behaviors during parent-adolescent interactions. *Proceedings of the National Academy of Sciences USA, 105,* 3652–3657.

White, M. (1993). *The material child: Coming of age in Japan and America.* New York: Free Press.

Whiteman, S. D., Jensen, A., & Bernard, J. M. (2012). Sibling influences. In J. R. Levesque (Ed.), *Encyclopedia of adolescence.* New York: Springer.

Wider, C., Foroud, T., & Wszolek, Z. K. (2010). Clinical implications of gene discovery in Parkinson's disease and parkinsonism. *Movement Disorders, 25,* Suppl. 1, S15–S20.

Widom, C. S., Czaja, S. J., Bentley, T., & Johnson, M. S. (2012). A prospective investigation of physical health outcomes in abused and neglected children: New findings from a 30-year follow-up. *American Journal of Public Health, 102,* 1135–1144.

Wiesel, A., Spix, C., Mergenthaler, A., & Queisser-Luft, A. (2011). Maternal occupational exposure to ionizing radiation and birth defects. *Radiation and Environmental Biophysics, 50,* 325-328.

Wigfield, A., & Cambria, J. (2010). Students' achievement values, goal orientations, and interest: Definitions, development, and relations to achievement outcomes. *Developmental Review, 30,* 1-35.

Wigfield, A., Eccles, J. S., Schiefele, U., Roeser, R., & Davis-Kean, P. (2006). Development of achievement motivation. In W. Damon & R. Lerner (Eds.), *Handbook of child psychology* (6th ed.). New York: Wiley.

Williams, C. R. (1986). *The impact of television: A natural experiment in three communities.* New York: Academic Press.

Williams, E. P., Wyatt, S. B., & Winters, K. (2013, in press). Framing body size among African American women and girls. *Journal of Child Health Care.*

Williams, S. T., Ontai, L. L., & Mastergeorge, A. M. (2010). The development of peer interaction in infancy: Exploring the dyadic process. *Social Development, 19,* 348-368.

Willoughby, T. (2008). A short-term longitudinal study of Internet and computer game use by adolescent boys and girls: Prevalence frequency of use, and psychosocial predictors. *Developmental Psychology, 44,* 195-204.

Wilson, B. J. (2008). Media and children's aggression, fear, and altruism. *Future of Children, 18*(1), 87-118.

Wilson, S., & Durbin, E. C. (2010). Effects of paternal depression on fathers' parenting behaviors: A meta-analytic review. *Clinical Psychology Review, 30,* 167-180.

Wilson, T., Karimpour, R., & Rodkin, P. C. (2011). African American and European American students' peer groups during early adolescence: Structure, status, and academic achievement. *The Journal of Early Adolescence, 31*(1), 74-98.

Willey, J., Sherwood, L., & Woolverton, C. (2011). *Prescott's microbiology* (8th ed.). New York: McGraw-Hill.

Williams, D. D., Yancher, S. C., Jensen, L. C., & Lewis, C. (2003). Character education in a public high school: A multi-year inquiry into unified studies. *Journal of Moral Education, 32,* 3-33.

Williams, J. E., & Best, D. L. (1982). *Measuring sex stereotypes: A thirty-nation study.* Newbury Park, CA: Sage.

Williams, J. E., & Best, D. L. (1989). *Sex and psyche: Self-concept viewed cross-culturally.* Newbury Park, CA: Sage.

Williamson, R. A., Jaswal, V. K., & Meltzoff, A. N. (2010). Learning the rules: Observation and imitation as a sorting strategy by 36-month-old children. *Developmental Psychology, 46,* 57-65.

Wiltshire, K. M., Hegeleb, R. A., Innesc, A, M., & Brownella, A. K. W. (2013). Homozygous Lamin A/C familial lipodystrophy R482Q mutation in autosomal recessive Emery Dreifuss muscular dystrophy. *Neuromuscular Disorders, 23,* 265-268.

Windingstad, S., McCallum, R. S., Bell, S. M., & Dunn, P. (2011). Measures of emotional intelligence and social acceptability in children: A concurrent validity study. *Canadian Journal of School Psychology, 26,* 107-126.

Windle, W. F. (1940). *Physiology of the human fetus.* Philadelphia: W. B. Saunders.

Winn, I. J. (2004). The high cost of uncritical teaching. *Phi Delta Kappan, 85,* 496-497.

Winner, E. (1986, August). Where pelicans kiss seals. *Psychology Today,* pp. 24-35.

Winner, E. (1996). *Gifted children: Myths and realities.* New York: Basic Books.

Winner, E. (2000). The origins and ends of giftedness. *American Psychologist, 55,* 159-169.

Winner, E. (2006). Development in the arts: Drawing and music. In W. Damon & R. Lerner (Eds.), *Handbook of child psychology* (6th ed.), New York: Wiley.

Winsler, A., Carlton, M. P., & Barry, M. J. (2000). Age-related changes in preschool children's systematic use of private speech in a natural setting. *Journal of Child Language, 27,* 665-687.

Winton, S. (2012). Character education: Implications for critical democracy. *International Critical Childhood Policy Studies, 1*(1), 42-63.

Wisborg, K., Ingerslev, H. J., & Henriksen, T. B. (2010). In vitro fertilization and preterm delivery, low birth weight, and admission to the neonatal intensive care unit: A prospective follow-up study. *Fertility and Sterility.* (Available online February 24, 2010.)

Wise, N. (2012). Access to special education for exceptional pupils in French immersion programs: An equity issue. The State of French-Second-Language Education in Canada 2012, Executive Summary. Canadian Parents for French.

Wit, J. M., Kiess, W., & Mullis, P. (2011). Genetic evaluation of short stature. *Best Practices & Research: Clinical Endocrinology and Metabolism, 25,* 1-17.

Witelson, S. F., Kigar, D. L., & Harvey, T. (1999). The exceptional brain of Albert Einstein. *The Lancet, 353,* 2149-2153.

Witherington, D. C., Campos, J. J., Harriger, J. A., Bryan, C., & Margett, T. E. (2010). Emotion and its development in infancy. In J. G. Bremner & T. D. Wachs

(Eds.), *Wiley-Blackwell handbook of infant development* (2nd ed.). New York: Wiley.

Witkin, H. A., & others. (1976). Criminality in XYY and XXY men. *Science, 193,* 547-555.

Wittig, S. L., & Spatz, D. L. (2008). Induced lactation: Gaining a better understanding. *MCN. The Journal of Maternal Child Nursing, 33,* 76-81.

Witvliet, M., & others. (2010). Peer group affiliation in children: The role of perceived popularity, likeability, and behavioral similarity in bullying. *Social Development, 19,* 285-303.

Wolfinger, N. H. (2011). More evidence for trends in the intergenerational transmission of divorce: A completed cohort approach using data from the general social survey. *Demography, 48,* 581-592.

Wolten, K., Michael, I. P., Mohseni, P., Desai, R., Mileikovsky, M., Hamalainen, R., Cowling, R., Wang, W., Liu, P., Gertsenstein, M., Kaji, K., Sung, H., & Nagy, A. (2009). piggyBac transposition reprograms fibroblasts to inducted pluripotent stem cells. *Nature, 458,* 766-770.

Women's Sports Foundation. (2001). *The 10 commandments for parents and coaches in youth sports.* Eisenhower Park, NY: Women's Sports Foundation.

Wong, M. M., Brower, K. J., Nigg, J. T., & Zucker, R. A. (2010). Childhood sleep problems, response inhibition, and alcohol and drug outcomes in adolescence and young adulthood. *Alcoholism, Clinical and Experimental Research, 34,* 10033-10044.

Wood, D., Kaplan, R., & McLoyd, V. C. (2007). Gender differences in educational expectations of urban, low-income African American youth: The role of parents and school. *Journal of Youth and Adolescence, 36,* 417-427.

Woodard, E. (2000). *Media in the home 2000: The Fifth Annual Survey of Parents and Children.* Philadelphia: Annenberg Public Policy Center.

Woodhill, B. M., & Samuels, C. A. (2004). Desirable and undesirable androgyny: A prescription for the twenty-first century. *Journal of Gender Studies, 13,* 15-28.

Woodward, A., Markman, E., & Fitzsimmons, C. (1994). Rapid word learning in 13- and 18-month-olds. *Developmental Psychology, 30,* 553-566.

Woodward, A., & Needham, A. (Eds.). (2009). *Learning and the infant mind.* New York: Oxford University Press.

Woodward, A. L., & Markman, E. M. (1998). Early word learning. In D. Kuhn &

R. S. Siegler (Eds.), *Handbook of child psychology* (5th ed., Vol. 2). New York: Wiley.

**Woolett, L. A.** (2011). Review: Transport of maternal cholesterol to the fetal circulation. *Placenta, 32* (Suppl. 2), S18–S21.

**Wright, R. O., & Christiani, D.** (2010). Gene-environment interaction and children's health and development. *Current Opinion in Pediatrics, 22*(2), 197–201.

**Wright, S. C., & Taylor, D. M.** (1995). Identity and the language of the classroom: Investigating the impact of heritage versus second language instruction on personal and collective self-esteem. *Journal of Educational Psychology, 87,* 241–252.

**Wu, Y. & Smith, D. E.** (1997). Self-esteem of Taiwanese children. *Child Study Journal, 27*(1), 1–19.

**Wuest, D. A., & Fisette, J. L.** (2012). *Foundations of physical education, exercise science, and sport* (17th ed.). New York: McGraw-Hill.

**Wyatt, P.** (2000). New Down syndrome statistics: Cytogenetic specimens with trisomy 21 and translocation 21—Canada. *Canadian Down Syndrome Society Quarterly, 13,* 8.

**Wynn, K.** (1992). Addition and subtraction by human infants. *Nature, 358,* 749–750.

# X

**Xia, Q., & Grant, S. F.** (2013, in press). The genetics of human aging. *Annals of the New York Academy of Sciences.*

**Xie, Q., & Young, M. E.** (1999). Integrated child development in rural China. *Education: The World Bank.* Washington, DC: The World Bank.

**Xu, F., Spelke, E., & Goddard, S.** (2005). Number sense in human infants. *Developmental Science, 8,* 88–101.

**Xue, F., Holzman, C., Rahbar, M. H., Trosko, K., & Fischer, L.** (2007). Maternal fish consumption, mercury levels, and risk of preterm delivery. *Environmental Health Perspectives, 115,* 42–47.

# Y

**Yang, C., & Brown, B.** (2009, April). *From Facebook to cell calls: Layers of electronic intimacy in college students' peer relations.* Paper presented at the meeting of the Society for Research in Child Development, Denver.

**Yang, S., & Sternberg, R. J.** (1997). Taiwanese Chinese people's conceptions of intelligence. *Intelligence, 25,* 21–36.

**Yates, D.** (2013). Neurogenetics: Unraveling the genetics of autism. *Nature Reviews: Neuroscience.*

**Yi, O., & others.** (2012). Association between environmental tobacco smoke exposure of children and parental socioeconomic status: A cross-sectional study in Korea. *Nicotine and Tobacco Research, 14,* 607–615.

**Yolton, K., & others** (2010). Associations between secondhand smoke exposure and sleep patterns in children. *Pediatrics, 125,* e261–e268.

**Young, K. T.** (1990). American conceptions of infant development from 1955 to 1984: What the experts are telling parents. *Child Development, 61,* 17–28.

**Yuen, R., Chen, B., Blair, J. D., Robinson, W. P., & Nelson, D. M.** (2013). Hypoxia alters the epigenetic profile in cultured human placental trophoblasts, *Epigenetics.*

# Z

**Zaghloul, N. A., & Katsanis, N.** (2010). Functional modules, mutational load, and human genetic disease. *Trends in Genetics, 26*(4), 168–176.

**Zaitoun, I., Downs, K. M., Rosa, G. J., & Khatib, H.** (2010). Upregulation of imprinted genes in mice: An insight into the intensity of gene expression and the evolution of genomic imprinting. *Epigenetics, 5,* 149–158.

**Zeanah, C. H., Fox, N. A., & Nelson, C. A.** (2012). Case study in ethical issues in research: The Bucharest Early Intervention Project. *Journal of Nervous and Mental Disease, 200,* 243–247.

**Zelazo, P. D.** (2013). Developmental psychology: A new synthesis. In P. D. Zelazo (Ed.), *Oxford handbook of developmental psychology.* New York: Oxford University Press.

**Zelazo, P. D., Carlson, S. M., & Kesek, A.** (2008). Development of executive function in childhood. In C. A. Nelson, & M. Luciana (Eds.), *Handbook of developmental cognitive neuroscience,* (2nd ed., pp. 553–574). Cambridge, MA: MIT.

**Zelazo, P. D., & Muller, U.** (2011). Executive function in typical and atypical development. In U. Goswami (Ed.), *Wiley-Blackwell handbook of childhood cognitive development.* New York: Wiley.

**Zelazo, P. D., & Lyons, K. E.** (2012). The potential benefits of mindfulness training in early childhood: A developmental social cognitive perspective. *Child Development Perspectives, 6,* 154–160.

**Zeller, M. H., Reiter-Purtell, J., & Ramey, C.** (2008). Negative peer perceptions of obese children in the classroom environment. *Obesity, 16,* 755–762.

**Zembal-Saul, C. L., McNeill, K. L., & Hershberger, K.** (2013). *What's your evidence?* Upper Saddle River, NJ: Pearson.

**Zeskind, P. S., Klein, L., & Marshall, T. R.** (1992). Adults' perceptions of experimental modifications of durations of pauses and expiratory sounds in infant crying. *Developmental Psychology, 28,* 1153–1162.

**Zhai, F., Raver, C. C., & Jones, S.** (2012). Quality of subsequent schools and impacts of early interventions: Evidence from a randomized controlled trial in Head Start settings. *Children and Youth Services Review, 34,* 946–954.

**Zhang, L., Zhang, X. H., Liang, M. Y., & Ren, M. H.** (2010). Prenatal cytogenetic diagnosis study of 2782 cases of high-risk pregnant women. *China Medicine (English), 123,* 423–430.

**Zhang, L-F., & Sternberg, R. J.** (2011). Learning in a cross-cultural perspective. In T. Husén & T. N. Postlethwaite (Eds.) *International Encyclopedia of Education* (3rd ed., Learning and Cognition). Oxford: Elsevier.

**Zhang, L-F., & Sternberg, R. J.** (2013, in press). Learning in cross-cultural perspective. In T. Husen & T. N. Postlethwaite (Eds.), *International encyclopedia of education* (3rd ed.). New York: Elsevier

**Zhou, Q., Lengua, L. J., & Wang, Y.** (2009). The relations of temperament reactivity and effortful control to children's adjustment problems in the United States and China. *Developmental Psychology, 45,* 724–739.

**Ziemer, C. J., Plumert, J. M., & Pick, A. D.** (2012). To grasp or not to grasp: Infants' actions toward objects and pictures. *Infancy, 17,* 479–497.

**Zigler, E., Gilliam, W. S., & Jones, S. M.** (2006). *A vision for universal preschool education.* New York: Cambridge University Press.

**Zigler, E. F., & Styfco, S. J.** (1994). Head Start: Criticisms in a constructive context. *American Psychologist, 49,* 127–132.

**Zimmerman, B. J.** (2002). Becoming a self-regulated learner: An overview. *Theory into Practice, 41,* 64–70.

**Zimmerman, B. J.** (2012). Motivational sources and outcomes of self-regulated learning and performance. In B. J. Zimmerman & D. H. Schunk (Eds.), *Handbook of self-regulation of learning and performance.* New York: Routledge.

**Zimmerman, B. J., Bonner, S., & Kovach, R.** (1996). *Developing self-regulated learners.*

Washington, DC: American Psychological Association.

**Zimmerman, B. J., & Kitsantas, A.** (1997). Developmental phases in self-regulation: Shifting from process goals to outcome goals. *Journal of Educational Psychology, 89,* 29–36.

**Zimmerman, B. J., & Labuhn, A. S.** (2012). Self-regulation of learning: Process approaches to personal development. In K. R. Harris & others (Eds.), *APA handbook of educational psychology.* Washington, DC: American Psychological Association.

**Zimmerman, F. J., & Christakis, D. A.** (2007). Association between content types of early media exposure and subsequent attention problems. *Pediatrics, 120,* 986–992.

**Zimmerman, F. J., Christakis, D. A., & Meltzoff, A. N.** (2007). Association between media viewing and language development in children under age 2 years. *Journal of Pediatrics, 151,* 364–368.

**Zimmerman, F. J., Christakis, D. A., & Meltzoff, A. N.** (2007). Television and DVD/video viewing by children 2 years and younger. Archives of *Pediatric and Adolescent Medicine, 161,* 437–479.

**Ziol-Guest, K. M.** (2009). Child custody and support. In D. Carr (Ed.), *Encyclopedia of the life course and human development.* Boston: Cengage.

**Zitzer-Comfort, C., Doyle, T. F., Masataka, N., Korenberg, J., & Bellugi, U.** (2007). Nature and nurture: Williams syndrome across cultures. *Developmental Science, 10,* 755–762.

**Zosuls, K. M., Ruble, D. N., Tamis-LeMonda, C. S., Shrout, P. E., Bornstein, M. H., & Greulich, F. K.** (2009). The acquisition of gender labels in infancy: Implications for gender-typed play. *Developmental Psychology, 45,* 688–701.

**Zotter, H., & Pichler, G.** (2012). Breast feeding is associated with decreased risk of sudden infant death syndrome. *Evidence Based Medicine, 17,* 126–127.

**Zucker, K. J., & Bradley, S. J.** (1995). *Gender identity disorder and psychosexual problems in children and adolescents.* New York: Guilford.

# credits

Dr. Carolyn Rovee-Collier; **205:** © Pacific Press Service/Alamy; **208 (top):** © Travel Pictures/Alamy; **208 (bottom):** © Joe Sohm/Visions of America, LLC/Alamy; **209:** © 2013 www.polychromemedia.com/; **210:** From Jean Mandler, University of California, San Diego. Reprinted by permission of Oxford University Press, Inc.; **211:** Courtesy of Dr. John Santrock; **212:** Anthony Harvel/Getty Images RF; **215:** Courtesy of Judy DeLoache; **217:** © Scott Houston/Corbis; **219:** © John Flavell; **221:** © Robin Nelson/PhotoEdit

## Chapter 8

**Page 227:** © Dimitri Vervitsiotis/Getty Images; **230:** © Bettmann/Corbis; **232:** Courtesy of Robert Sternberg; **235:** © ER Productions/Getty Images RF; **237:** © Owen Franken/Corbis **239 (top):** © David Austin/Stock Boston, Inc.; **239 (bottom):** © Ben Simmons Photography; **240:** © Image Source/Alamy RF; **242:** © Inspirestock/Punchstock; **243:** *Bayley Scales of Infant and Toddler Development*, Third Edition (Bayley-III). © 2006 by NCS Pearson, Inc. Reproduced with permission. All rights reserved.; **245 (top):** © Stockbyte/Veer RF; **245 (bottom):** © Koichi Kamoshida/Newsmakers/Getty Images

## Chapter 9

**Page 250:** © Yarinca/iStock.com; **251:** Library of Congress, Prints and Photographs Division, LC-USZ61-326; **253:** © Vanessa Davies/Dorling Kindersley/Getty Images; **255:** © Don Hammond/Design Pics/Corbis RF; **256:** © Niki Mareschal/Photographer's Choice/Getty Images; **257 (top, both):** © Peter McLeod; **257 (bottom):** © Yang Liu/Corbis; **258:** © ABPL Image Library/Animals Animals/Earth Scenes; **260:** © Image Source/Getty Images; **262 (top):** © Aflo Foto Agency/Alamy; **262 (bottom):** © Jose Luis Pelaez Inc/Blend Images/Jupiterimages; **264 (top):** © Gideon Mendel/Corbis; **264 (bottom):** © Comstock/PunchStock RF; **266:** Berko Gleason, Jean, The Development of Language, 3rd ed., © 1993. Printed and Electronically reproduced by permission of Pearson Education, Inc., Upper Saddle River, New Jersey. TA 9.16; **267:** © Digital Vision/PunchStock RF; **270:** © Digital Vision/PunchStock RF; **271:** © AFP/Getty Images; **272 (top):** © Michael Goldstein, Cornell University; **272 (bottom):** © KidStock/Getty Images RF; **273:** © Elyse Lewin/Brand X Pictures/Getty Images RF

## Chapter 10

**Page 278:** © Ariel Skelley/Blend Images LLC RF; **279:** © Tim Gainey/Alamy; **280:** © Rick Gomez/Corbis; **282:** © Jose Luis Pelaez Inc/Getty Images RF; **284 (clockwise from top left):** © BananaSTock/PictureQuest RF; © The McGraw-Hill Companies, Inc./Jill Braaten, photographer; © Getty Images RF; © David Sacks/Getty Images; **285 (top):** Photo by Kenny Barun and courtesy of Dr. Sybil L. Hart, Texas Tech University; **285 (bottom):** © Andy Cox/Stone/Getty Images; **286:** © Dr. Daniel Messinger, University of Miami, FL; **287:** © Photodisc/Getty Images RF; **288:** © James Woodson/Digital Vision/Getty Images RF; **289:** © MacGregor & Gordon/Getty Images RF; **290:** KYODO/Reuters/Landov; **292–293:** © Tom Merton/Getty Images; **295:** © Jack Sullivan/Alamy; **297:** © MIXA/Getty Images RF; **299 (top):** © Britt Erlanson/Getty Images; **299 (bottom):** Courtesy of Celia A. Brownell,

University of Pittsburgh; **301 (top):** © Martin Rogers/Stock Boston; **301 (bottom):** © George Doyle/Stockbyte/Getty Images RF; **305:** © Penny Tweedie/Stone/Getty Images; **306:** © ER Productions/Getty Images RF; **307:** Courtesy of Dr. Barry Hewlett; **308:** © Lawrence Schwartzwald; **310:** © BananaStock/PunchStock RF

## Chapter 11

**Page 315:** © Image Source/Alamy; **316 (top):** © joSon/Iconica/Getty Images; **316 (bottom):** © Steve Coleman/OJO Images/Getty Images; **318:** © Digital Vision/Getty Images RF; **320:** © Kevin Dodge/Corbis; **321 (top):** © RF/Corbis; **321 (bottom):** © Stockbyte/PictureQuest RF; **323 (top):** © RF/Corbis; **323 (bottom):** © Image Source/PunchStock RF; **327:** © Inti St. Clair/Getty Images RF; **329:** Carl Stewart/Shutterstock; **330:** © Bettmann/Corbis; **333:** © BananaStock/Jupiterimages RF; **334:** © Robert Llewellyn/Workbook Stock/Getty Images; **335:** © Masterfile RF

## Chapter 12

**Page 339:** © Bubbles Photolibrary/Alamy; **340:** © Thomas Dallal/SIPA PRESS; **341:** © RubberBall Productions/Getty Images RF; **344:** © Getty Images RF; **345:** © Digital Vision RF; **347 (top):** © Carson Ganci/Design Pics/Corbis RF; **347 (bottom):** © Cindy Charles/PhotoEdit; **349:** © Peter Dazeley/Getty Images; **350:** © Turbo/zefa/Corbis; **352:** © RF/Corbis; **353:** © Rob Melnychuk/Brand X Pictures/Corbis RF; **354:** © Somos Images/Corbis RF; **358:** © Owen Franken/Corbis

## Chapter 13

**Page 361:** © Datacraft Co Ltd./Getty Images; **362:** MARK BLINCH/Reuters/Landov; **364:** © Tom Grill/Corbis RF; **365:** © Harvard University Archives, UAV 605.295.8, Box 7, Kohlberg; **367:** © Randy Faris/Corbis; **368:** © Raghu-Rai/Magnum Photos; **369:** © David Fraser Photo Library; **370:** Courtesy of Dr. Carol Gilligan; **372 (top):** © Martin Harvey/Corbis; **372 (bottom):** © Thinkstock/Corbis RF; **374 (left):** © Michael Wheatley/Alamy; **374 (right):** © Saskatchewan Archives Board, Neil Richards Collections (#S_B13391); **375:** © Jim Craigmyle/Corbis; **377:** © RubberBall Productions/Getty Images RF; **379:** © Ronald Cortes; **380 (top):** © Newscom Images; **380 (bottom):** © PhotoAlto; **382:** © Photodisc/Getty Images RF; **384 (top):** © Stockdisc/PunchStock RF; **384 (bottom):** © Comstock Images/Alamy RF

## Chapter 14

**Page 390:** © Monkey Business Images/Getty Images RF; **391:** © Science Photo Library/Alamy; **392:** Courtesy of Shelley Peterman Schwarz; **394 (top):** © Tom Grill/Getty Images; **394 (bottom):** © Photodisc/Getty Images RF; **395:** © Image Source/PunchStock; **399:** © BananaStock/PictureQuest RF; **401:** © Ryan McVay/Getty Images RF; **402:** © JGI/Blend Images/Getty Images; **403 (top):** © Plush Studios/Bill Reitzel/Blend Images LLC; **403 (bottom):** © Digital Archive Japan/PunchStock; **406:** © BananaStock/PunchStock RF; **408:** © BananaStock/PunchStock RF; **409 (top):** © BananaStock/PunchStock RF; **409 (bottom):** © Mark Bowden/iStock.com; **410 (top):** © Pat Vasquez-Cunningham; **410 (bottom):** © BananaStock/PunchStock RF; **412 (both):** © RubberBall Productions/Getty Images RF; **413:** © Image Source/Getty Images RF; **415:**

© Eric Audras/PhotoAlto/PictureQuest RF; **416:** © Image Source/PunchStock RF; **417:** © Todd Wright/Blend Images/Getty Images RF; **418:** © 2009 Jupiterimages RF; **419:** © Big Cheese Photo/PunchStock RF; **420:** © Ocean/Corbis RF

## Chapter 15

**Page 425:** © Squaredpixels/iStock.com; **428 (top):** © Randy Faris/Corbis; **428 (bottom):** © Creasource/Corbis; **429:** © Tom Stoddard/Getty Images; **430 (top):** © Image Source/PunchStock RF; **430 (bottom):** © BananaStock/PunchStock RF; **432:** © Pixland/PunchStock RF; **433:** © BananaStock RF; **436 (from top):** Andrew Vaughan/THE CANADIAN PRESS; Darryl Dyck/THE CANADIAN PRESS; © MachineHeadz/iStock.com; **438:** © The McGraw-Hill Companies, Inc./Ken Karp, photographer; **439:** © Jean-Pierre Pieuchot/Getty Images; **440:** © Laurence Moulton/PhotoAlto/PictureQuest RF; **441:** © Purestock/PunchStock RF; **442:** © Ocean/Corbis RF; **443 (top):** © Kevin Dodge/Corbis; **443 (bottom):** © Michael A. Keller/zefa/Corbis; **445:** © Rolf Bruderer/Corbis; **447 (top):** © Digital Vision/Getty Images RF; **447 (bottom):** Jim Mone/AP Photo/The Canadian Press

## Chapter 16

**Page 453:** © Gallery Stock; **454:** From 'Open Window' 1994 Municipality of Reggio Emila Infant-Toddler Centers and Preschools. Published by Reggio Children; **455:** © Elizabeth Crews; **456 (top):** © Martin Poole/Getty Images; **456 (bottom):** © Image Source/Alamy RF; **457:** © James Leynse/Corbis; **458:** © Ronnie Kaufman/The Stock Market/Corbis; **460 (top):** © SOS Children's Village (www.sos-usa.org); **460 (bottom):** © Andreas Meichsner/liaf/Redux; **461 (top):** © Ghislain & Marie David de Lossy/The Image Bank/Getty Images; **461 (bottom):** © Maskot/Corbis; **462 (top):** © Ed Kashi/Corbis; **462 (bottom):** © Patrick Giardino/Corbis; **463 (top):** © Horizons WWP/Alamy; **463 (bottom):** © Jose Luis Pelaez Inc./Corbis; **465:** © AP Wide World Photos; **466:** © Photos.com/Thinkstock; **467:** © Robin Nelson/PhotoEdit; **468:** © Crown copyright MMVI, www.thetransporters.com, courtesy of Changing Media Development; **469:** © Elizabeth Crews/The Image Works; **471:** © AP Wide World Photos; **473:** © Ralf-Finn Hestoft/Corbis; **475:** Courtesy of Hari Prabahakar; **477 (top):** © Newscom Images; **477 (bottom):** © BananaStock/PunchStock RF; **478:** © Davo Blair/Alamy; **480:** © Digital Vision/Alamy RF

## TEXT/LINE ART CREDITS

### Chapter 1

**Page 7:** From *The State of the World's Children*, 2004, Geneva, Switzerland: UNICEF. Fig.5, p. 27. Reprinted by permission of UNICEF.; **9:** PEANUTS © United Features Syndicate, Inc.; **10:** © The New Yorker Collection, 2001. Robert Weber. www.cartoonbank.com. All rights reserved.; **23:** From "Bronfenbrenner's Ecological Theory of Development," C.B. Kopp & J.B. Krakow, 1982, *Child Development in the Social Context*, p. 648. Reprinted by permission of Pearson Education, Inc.; **26:** Crowley et al., *Psychological Science*, Vol. 12, Issue 3, 2001 by Sage. Reproduced with permission of Sage

Publications.; **28:** From Santrock, *Adolescence*, 12th ed. © 2008. Reprinted by permission of The McGraw-Hill Companies, Inc.; **29:** From Santrock, *Children*, 7th ed., Fig. 2.11. © 2003. Reprinted by permission of The McGraw-Hill Companies, Inc.; **31:** David Shaffer and Katherine Kipp (2014) *Developmental Psychology: Childhood and Adolescence*, 9th Edition. Figure 1.6, p. 31. Cengage

## Chapter 2

**Page 43:** From John T. Bonner, *The Evolution of Culture in Animals* © 1980 Princeton University Press. Reprinted by permission of Princeton University Press; **45:** From Santrock, *Life-Span Development* 13th Ed. "Cells, Chromosomes, DNA, and Genes" from p. 58. Reprinted by permission of The McGraw-Hill Companies, Inc.; **47 (top):** From *Child Psychology: A Contemporary Viewpoint*, 3rd Canadian edition by Ross Parke Mary Gauvain Mark Schmuckler. Figure 2.2, p. 46. © 2010; **47 (bottom):** From *Child Psychology: A Contemporary Viewpoint*, 3rd Canadian edition by Ross Parke Mary Gauvain Mark Schmuckler. Figure 2.1, p. 45. © 2010; **49 (bottom):** © Alila Medical Media/Shutterstock; **50:** From Santrock, *Life-Span Development* 11th ed., Fig. 3.7. © 2008. Reprinted by permission of The McGraw-Hill Companies, Inc.; **56:** Gunby & others, 2010; **57:** From Golombok et al., 2001, "The 'Test-Tube' Generation," *Child Development*, 72, 599–608. Reprinted with permission of the Society for Research in Child Development; **60:** From Santrock, *Children*, 7th ed., Fig. 3.14. © 2003. Reprinted by permission of The McGraw-Hill Companies, Inc.

## Chapter 3

**Page 74:** From K.L. Moore, *The Developing Human: Clinically Oriented Embryology*, 4th ed., Reprinted with permission from Elsevier; **85:** Virginia Apgar, "The Apgar Scale" from "A Proposal for a New Method of Evaluation of a Newborn Infant," *Anesthesia and Analgesia* (32), pp. 260–267. © 1975. Reprinted by permission.; **86:** Chang & others, 2013; **87 (top):** Swamy, Ostbye, & Skjaerven, 2008; **87 (bottom):** Hernandez-Reif, Diego, & Field, 2007

## Chapter 4

**Page 97:** From Santrock, *Children*, 7th ed., Fig. 3.14. © 2003. Reprinted by permission of The McGraw-Hill Companies, Inc.; **99:** From Penguin *Dreams and Stranger Things*, by Berkeley Breathed. © 1985 by The Washington Post company. By permission of Little, Brown & Company, Inc. and International Creative Management; **101 (top):** From Santrock, *Adolescence*, 8th ed. Fig. 3.4. © 2001. Reprinted by permission of The McGraw-Hill Companies, Inc.; **101 (bottom):** From J.M. Tanner, R.H. Whitehouse, "Standards from Birth to Maturity for Height, Weight, Height Velocity: British Children" in *Archives of Diseases in Childhood*, Vol. 4, Issue 220. © 1966 with permission from BMJ Publishing Group Ltd.; **102:** © ZITS Partnership. King Features Syndicate; **105:** From Santrock, *Children*, 9th ed., Fig. 6.6. © 2003. Reprinted by permission of The McGraw-Hill Companies, Inc.; **106:** From Santrock, *Child Development*, 9th ed. © 2001. Reprinted by permission of The McGraw-Hill Companies, Inc.; **109:** Reprinted by permission of the publisher from *The Postnatal Development of the Human Cerebral Cortex*, Volumes I-VIII by Jesse LeRoy Conel, Cambridge, MA.: Harvard

University Press, © 1939, 1941, 1947, 1951, 1955, 1959, 1963, 1967 by the President and Fellows of Harvard College. © renewed 1967, 1969, 1975, 1983, and 1991; **110 (top):** From Santrock, *Child Psychology*, 7th ed., p. 128. © 2003. Reprinted by permission of The McGraw-Hill Companies, Inc.; **111:** From Santrock, *Essentials of Life-Span Development*, Fig. 9.3. © 2008. Reprinted by permission of The McGraw-Hill Companies, Inc.; **113:** From Santrock, *Children* 10th ed., Fig 5.10. © 2008, reprinted by permission of The McGraw-Hill Companies, Inc.; **118:** Statistics Canada. (2012a). "Leading causes of death in Canada." Cat. No.: 84-215-XWE. Reproduced and distributed on an "as is" basis with the permission of Statistics Canada.

## Chapter 5

**Page 146 (both):** From Slater, et al., 1988, "Orientation Discrimination and Cortical Function in the Human Newborn," *Perception*, 17, pp. 597–602. (Figure 1 and Table 1). Reprinted with permission of Pion Limited, London.; **150 (top):** From Bennet I. Bertenthal, Matthew R. Longo, and Sarah Kenny, "Phenomenal Permanence and the Development of Predictive Tracking in Infancy" *from Child Development*, 78, p. 354. © 2007 by John Wiley & Sons. Reprinted with permission.

## Chapter 6

**Page 164:** From Santrock, *Topical Life-Span*, 2nd ed., Fig. 6.1. © 2005. Reprinted by permission of The McGraw-Hill Companies, Inc.; **165:** From Santrock, *Life-Span Development*, 11th ed., Fig. 6.1. © 2008. Reprinted by permission of The McGraw-Hill Companies, Inc.; **167:** Adapted from Piaget, J. (1970). Piaget's Theory. In P. H. Mussen (ed). Carmichael's *Manual of Child Development*, (3rd edition, Volume 1, pp. 703–732. New York: Wiley.); **168:** From R. Baillargeon & J. Devoe, "Object Permanence in Young Children: Further Evidence," *Child Development*, 62, pp. 1227–1246. Reprinted with permission of the Society for Research in Child Development; **170:** Reprinted by permission from Macmillan Publishers Ltd: *NATURE*, 358, pp. 749–750, "Addition and Subtraction by Human Infants" by Karen Wynn. © 1992; **172 (top):** From Santrock, *Children*, 7th ed., Fig. 10.1. © 2003. Reprinted by permission of The McGraw-Hill Companies, Inc.; **172 (left, both):** Reprinted courtesy of D. Wolf and J. Nove; **173 (top):** © New Yorker Collection, 1989. Lee Lorenz from cartoonbank.com. All rights reserved. Reprinted with permission; **173 (bottom):** From Santrock, *Children*, 7th ed., Fig. 10.4. © 2003. Reprinted by permission of The McGraw-Hill Companies, Inc.; **175:** From Santrock, *Children*, 7th ed., Fig. 10.5. © 2003. Reprinted by permission of The McGraw-Hill Companies, Inc.; **176:** From Santrock, *Children*, 7th ed., Fig. 13.1. © 2003. Reprinted by permission of The McGraw-Hill Companies, Inc.

## Chapter 7

**Page 201:** © Wm Hoest Enterprises, Inc. Reprinted courtesy of Bunny Hoest; **202:** Adapted from Baddeley, "Working Memory: Looking Back and Looking Forward." *Nature Reviews Neuroscience* 4(10), October 2003, 829–839. doi:10.1038/nrn1201; **203:** Chi (1978); **204 (top):** *Learning and the Infant Mind* edited by A. Woodward & A. Needham (2009), Ch. 1 "Learning and Memory: Like a Horse and

Carriage" by Patricia J. Bauer pp. 3–28, Table 1 from p. 12. By permission of Oxford University Press, USA; **204 (bottom):** From Santrock, *Psychology*, 7th ed. Fig. 8.15. © 2003. Reprinted by permission of The McGraw-Hill Companies, Inc.; **206 (top):** Dempster, 1981; **206 (bottom):** Adapted from Siegler, R. (2005). Children's learning. *American Psychologist*, 60(8) Nov 2005, pp. 769–778. Adapted with permission by American Psychologist Association; **207 (top):** Pressley & others, 1987; **207 (bottom):** Frank & Ernest © Thaves/Dist. By United Features Syndicate, Inc.; **209:** After data from Dempster, F.N. (1981). "Memory and developmental differences." *Psychological Bulletin*, (89) 63–100. Published by the American Psychological Association; **210:** © The New Yorker Collection, 1998. Sam Gross from cartoonbank.com. All rights reserved; **215:** From Robert S. Siegler, *Four Rules for Solving the Balance Scale Task*. © Robert S. Siegler. Reprinted by permission; **220 (top):** Wellman, Cross, & Watson, 2001; **220 (bottom):** From U. Frith, "The Sally and Anne False-Belief Task" from *Autism: Explaining the Enigma*, p. 83. © 1989 by Wiley-Blackwell; **221:** No credit

## Chapter 8

**Page 230:** From Santrock, *Psychology*, 7th ed., Fig. 10.1. © 2003. Reprinted by permission of The McGraw-Hill Companies, Inc.; **231:** © 2003 by NCS Pearson, Inc. Reproduced with permission. All rights reserved. "Weshcler Intelligence Scale for Children" and "WISC" are trademarks, in the U.S. and/or other countries, of Pearson Education, Inc. or its affiliates.; **232:** © Edward Koren/The New York Collection, www.cartoonbank.com; **237:** From Santrock, *Life-Span Development*, 14th ed. © 2012. Reprinted by permission of The McGraw-Hill Companies, Inc.; **239:** © 1998 by NCS Pearson, Inc. reproduced by permission. All rights reserved. "Raven's Progressive Matrices" is a trademark, in the U.S. and/or other countries, of Pearson Education, Inc. or its affiliates.; **244:** From Santrock, *Psychology*, 7th ed., Fig. 10.6. © 2003. Reprinted by permission of The McGraw-Hill Companies, Inc.

## Chapter 9

**Page 254 (top):** Frank & Ernest © Thaves/Dist. By United Features Syndicate, Inc.; **254 (bottom):** From S.L. Haight, "The Rule Systems of Language," *Language Overview*. Reprinted by permission.; **257:** From Santrock, *Children*, 7th ed., Fig. 7.6. © 2003. Reprinted by permission of The McGraw-Hill Companies, Inc.; **258:** From Santrock, *Children*, 7th ed., Fig. 7.7. © 2003. Reprinted by permission of The McGraw-Hill Companies, Inc.; **259:** From Jean Berko, 1958, "The Child's Learning of English Morphology," in *Word*, Vol. 14, p. 154; **261:** From B. Hart and T.R. Risley, *Meaningful Differences in the Everyday Experiences of Young American Children*. Figures 2 and 3, pp. 47 and 60. © 1995. Baltimore: Paul H. Brookes Publishing Co., Inc. Reprinted by permission.; **264:** From J.S. Chall, *Theory and Practice of Early Reading*. © 1980 by TAYLOR & FRANCIS GROUP LLC - BOOKS. Reproduced with permission of Taylor & Francis Group LLC - Books via Copyright Clearance Center; **266:** PEANUTS © United Features Syndicate, Inc.; **271:** From Santrock, *Life-Span Development*, 14th ed. © 2012. Reprinted by permission of The McGraw-Hill Companies, Inc.; **274:** © Dr. Ursula Bellugi, The Salk Institute for Biological Studies, La Jolla, CA.

## Chapter 10

**Page 283:** From C. Saarni, *The Development of Emotional Competence*, p. 5. © 1999 by Guilford Publications, Inc. Reprinted by permission.; **287:** From Jerome Kagan, R.B. Kearsley, and P.R. Zelazo, *Infancy: Its Place in Human Development*, p. 107, Cambridge, MA. Harvard University Press. © 1978 by the President and Fellows of Harvard College. Reprinted by permission of the publisher.; **297:** From Santrock, *Topical Life-Span*, Fig. 10.3. © 2002. Reprinted by permission of The McGraw-Hill Companies, Inc.; **301:** Harlow, 1958; **303:** From M.H. van Ijzendoorn and P.M. Kroonenberg, "Cross-Cultural Patterns of Attachment: A Meta-Analysis of the Strange Situation" from *Child Development*, 59, pp. 147–156. © 1988 by Blackwell Publishing Ltd. Reprinted with permission of Blackwell Publishing Ltd.; **306:** From Santrock, *Topical Life-Span Development*, 5th ed., Fig. 6.1. © 2010. Reprinted by permission of The McGraw-Hill Companies, Inc.

## Chapter 11

**Page 318:** From M. Lewis and J. Brooks-Gunn, "The Development of Self-Recognition in Infancy" from *Social Cognition and the Acquisition of the Self*, p. 64. Reprinted with kind permission from Springer Science and Business Media; **326:** Canada (Hymel & others, 1999), the United States (Harter, 2012), England (Fox & others, 2009), Portugal (Faria, 2001), and Taiwan (Wu & Smith, 1997); **328:** From Santrock, *Children*, 8th ed., Fig. 17.2. © 2005. Reprinted by permission of The McGraw-Hill Companies, Inc.; **331:** From Santrock, *Children*, 8th ed., Fig. 17.3. © 2005. Reprinted by permission of The McGraw-Hill Companies, Inc.; **332:** From Santrock, *Children*, 7th ed., p. 542. © 2003. Reprinted by permission of The McGraw-Hill Companies, Inc.

## Chapter 12

**Page 345:** Maccoby, 2002; **348:** Levy, Sadovsky, & Troseth, 2000; **351:** © 1994 Joel Pett. All rights reserved.; **352:** From Santrock, *Topical Life-Span Development*, 3rd ed., Fig. 12.4. © 2007. Reprinted by permission of The McGraw-Hill Companies, Inc.; **356:** From Sandra Bem, *The BEM Sex Role Inventory*. © 1978, 1981 by Consulting Psychologists Press, Inc. Reproduced by special permission of the Publisher, MIND GARDEN, Inc., www.mindgarden.com. Further reproduction is prohibited without the Publisher's written consent.

## Chapter 13

**Page 366:** From R.S. Selman, "Social-Cognitive Understanding," in Thomas Lickona (Ed.) *Moral Development and Behavior*, 1976. Reprinted by permission of Thomas Lickona.; **367:** From Colby, et al., 1983, "A Longitudinal Study of Moral Judgment," *Monographs for the Society for Research in Child Development*, Serial #201. Reprinted with permission for the Society for Research in Child Development.; **373:** Damon, 1988

## Chapter 14

**Page 401:** Based on data presented in Table 1 in Wittrup, Holden, & Buck (2006); **403:** From Santrock, *Adolescence*, 13th ed. © 2010. Reprinted by permission of The McGraw-Hill Companies, Inc.; **404:** Curran & others, 2001. From M.R. Gunnar and P.A. Fisher, and the Early Experience, Stress, and Prevention Network (2006), "Bringing basic research on early experience and stress neurobiology to bear on preventative interventions for neglected and maltreated children," p. 666, from *Development and Psychopathology*, 18, pp. 651–677. Reprinted

with permission of Cambridge University Press; **407:** From Santrock, *Child Development*, 9th ed. © 2001. Reprinted by permission of The McGraw-Hill Companies, Inc.; **415:** From Santrock, *Life-Span Development*, 11th ed., Fig. 15.9. © 2008. Reprinted by permission of The McGraw-Hill Companies, Inc.

## Chapter 15

**Page 431:** Krauss & Glucksberg, 1969; **435 (both):** Dittrick & others, 2011; **442:** Buhrmester, 1990; Buhrmester & Furman, 1987; **446:** From Dexter C. Dunphy, "The Social Structure of Urban Adolescent Peer Groups," *Sociometry*, Vol. 26, 1963. American Sociological Association, Washington, DC.

## Chapter 16

**Page 459:** Adapted from NAEYC (2009). "Developmentally appropriate practice in early childhood programs serving children from birth through age 8." Position statement. Washington, DC: Author. Www.naeyc.org/files/naeyc/file/positions/PSDAP.pdf; **466:** From Shaw et al. (2007). "Attention deficit/hyperactivity disorder is characterized by a delay in cortical maturation." PNAS, Dec. 4, 2007. National Acadamy of Sciences, USA. Reprinted by permission.; **470:** CALVIN & HOBBES, © 1991, 1993 Watterson. Dist. By Universal Uclick. Reprinted with permission. All rights reserved.; **471:** From Santrock, *Adolescence*, 12th ed. Fig. 16.6. © 2008. Reprinted by permission of The McGraw-Hill Companies, Inc.; **479 (top):** Anderson & others (2009); **479 (bottom):** © Tribune Media Services, Inc. All rights reserved. Reprinted with permission.

# name index

Needham, A., 141, 142, 142*f*, 170
Negriff, C.A., 103
Neisser, U., 236
Nelson, C.A., 27, 72, 204
Nelson, D.A., 443
Nelson, J.A., 380
Nelson, J.L., 462–463
Nelson, K., 170, 205
Neubauer, A.C., 235
Neufeld, S.J., 287
Neville, H.J., 266
Nevo, E., 201
New, R., 454
Newcombe, N., 204
Newell, K., 142
Newman, R.S., 154
Newport, E.L., 266
Newton, A.W., 406
Ng, S.H., 267
Ngo, Q.E., 34, 463
Nguyen, S.P., 350
Nieto, S., 419
Nisbett, R.E., 236, 238, 239
Noddings, N., 378
Nodine, P.M., 78
Nolen-Hoeksema, S., 91
Nolte, S., 438, 458
Nordeng, H., 73
Norgard, B., 73
Norman, J.E., 86
Norton, M.E., 55
Nosko, A., 448
Nottleman, E.D., 101
Nova Scotia Government, 52
Nucci, L., 378
Nylund, K., 435

O

O'Brien, J.M., 308
O'Brien, M., 415
O'Connor, A.D., 73
O'Donnell, A.M., 455
O'Donnell, C.J., 52
O'Hearn, K., 274
O'Malley, M.M., 456
O'Brien, J.M., 86
O'Neill, S., 84
O'Sullivan, L., 479
Oakes, L.M., 147
Oates, J., 83, 275
Obenauer, S., 55
Oberlander, T.F., 62
Ochs, E., 273
Ogbu, J., 240
Oldehinkel, A.J., 415
Olino, T.M., 90
Oller, D.K., 268
Olson, D., 81
Olson, R.K., 238
Olson, S.L., 432
Olweus, D., 436
Ong, A.D., 335, 336
Ontai, L.L., 428
Opfer, J.E., 172
Ophir, 476
Ormrod, J.E., 28
Ornstein, M., 307
Ornstein, P., 207–208
Orpinas, P., 436

Orth, U., 327
Osborne, J., 213
Oser, F.K., 379
Ostbye, T., 86
Oster, H., 153
Otto, B.W., 262
Ouellette-Kuntz, H., 221
Overstreet, S., 290
Owens, J.A., 117
Owsley, C.J., 154, 167
Ozarow, L., 430

P

Pachter, L.M., 420
Padilla-Walker, L.M., 382, 470, 480
Pagani, L., 199
Pagani, L.S., 202
Paintner, A., 74
Pakzad-Vaezi, K., 140
Palfrey, J., 435
Palomares, M., 274
Palonsky, S.B., 462–463
Pan, B.A., 257, 260, 261, 263
Panigrahy, A., 55
Papierno, P.B., 208
Paradis, J., 267
Pardini, D., 386
Parens, E., 465, 466
Parish-Morris, J., 255, 257
Park, C.J., 102, 259
Parkay, F.W., 456
Parke, R.D., 12, 18, 23, 63, 307, 394, 395, 400, 403, 408, 415, 416, 417, 430
Parker, J., 429, 432, 435, 439
Parker, J.D.A., 234
Parker, J.G., 441
Parlade, M.V., 286
Partanen, M., 202
Pascual, A., 354
Pascual-Leone, J., 181, 182
Pasley, B.K., 449
Pasley, K., 417
Pasterski, V., 345
Patel, D.R., 467
Patrick, R.B., 377
Patterson, C., 5
Patterson, C.J., 5, 418
Patton, F., 335
Paul, I.M., 62
Pauletti, R.E., 354, 355
Paulhus, D.L., 413
Pauli-Pott, U., 62, 295
Paulson, F., 90
Paus, T., 112
Pavlov, I.P., 19, 37
Payne, W.A., 4
Pea, R., 476
Pearson, B.Z., 268
Peck, J., 269
Pecot-Hebert, L., 346
Pedersen, S., 386, 434, 444
Pederson, D.R., 303
Pedroso, F.S., 135
Peek, L., 291
Peeters, M.C.W., 415
Peets, K., 353, 383, 430, 432, 435
Pelaez, M., 300
Pellegrini, A.D., 43
Pena, E., 267

Penagarikano, O., 51
Penela, E.C., 298
Penke, L., 235, 238
Pentimonti, J.M., 465
Penzias, A.S., 79
Pepler, D., 434–435
Pepler, D.J., 437
Pera, R.R., 56
Peretz, I., 242
Perin, D., 266
Perner, J., 204, 214
Perozynski, L., 412
Perrin, R.D., 407
Perron, A., 140
Perron, M., 354
Perry, D.G., 341, 354, 355, 474
Perry, N.B., 288
Perry, N.E., 469–470
Perry, S.E., 83
Perry, T.B., 442
Persson, K.E., 92
Peter, J., 479, 480
Peterman, K., 142
Peters, H.E., 311
Peters, R., 238
Petersen, A.C., 100
Petersen, M.B., 49
Peterson, C., 205, 208, 221
Peterson, C.C., 221
Petrick-Steward, E., 182
Petrides, K.V., 234
Petrill, S.A., 236
Pettit, G.S., 293
Pew Research Center, 11
Pfeifer, M., 293
Pfund, F., 76
Philip, R.C., 467
Phillips, L.M., 351
Phinney, J.S., 333, 335, 336
Piaget, J., 17–19, 18*f*, 24, 24*f*, 30*f*, 37, 154, 160, 161, 162, 162*v*, 163, 164, 164*v*, 165, 165*f*, 166, 166*f*, 167, 167*f*, 168, 169*f*, 170, 170*f*, 171, 173, 174, 175, 176, 176*v*, 177, 178, 179, 180, 180*f*, 181, 181*f*, 182, 183, 184, 185, 186, 186*f*, 187, 188, 189, 190, 192, 194, 195, 203, 209, 211, 224, 267, 275, 320, 322, 364, 364*f*, 365, 367*f*, 368, 376, 438, 439, 450, 455, 456, 457
Pick, A.D., 144, 197
Pickett, W., 477
Pickrell, J., 208
Piek, J., 201
Pierce, D., 469–470
Pierce, S., 403
Pierce, T., 480
Pillemer, K.A., 410
Pinard, D., 414
Pinderhughes, E., 58
Pinker, S., 270
Pintrich, P.R., 473
Piper, B.J., 76
Pipp, S.L., 317
Pisoni, D.B., 152
Pittman, J.F., 334
Pitts, R.C., 374
Pleck, J.H., 356, 357
Plomin, R., 61, 235, 236, 295
Plucker, J., 247
Pluess, M., 293
Plumert, J.M., 144

Salovey, P., 233, 234, 234f
Salthouse, T.A., 242
Sameroff, A., 63, 394
Samhan, Y.M., 83
Samuels, C.A., 356
Sandberg, J.F., 174
Sanders, E., 438
Sanders, M.R., 408
Sanders, R.D., 200
Sandstrom, M., 434
Sanson, A.V., 296
Santiago, C.D., 420
Santos, M.J.D., 383
Santrock, J.W., 417, 418
Saraswathi, T.S., 358
Saroha, E., 58
Sassler, S., 417
Sasson, N.J., 147
Saunders, N.R., 69
Savage, R.S., 265
Savelsbergh, G., 141
Savin-Williams, R., 447, 448
Savolainen, J., 386
Sawyer, T.P., 240
Scarlett, W.G., 379
Scarr, S., 60, 65, 236, 239, 240
Schacter, D.L., 202
Schaefer, R.T., 419
Schaffer, H.R., 301
Schaie, K.W., 11, 13, 23
Scharrer, E., 478, 479
Schauble, L., 213, 214
Scheibe, S., 13
Schellenberg, E.G., 242
Scher, A., 286
Schick, A.R., 393
Schieffelin, B., 273
Schlam, T.R., 474
Schmidt, B.L., 52, 478
Schmidt, J.A., 379, 380
Schmidt, M.E., 198, 477
Schmitt, M.B., 465
Schmuckler, M.A, 148
Schneider, B.H., 322
Schneider, S., 466
Schneider, W., 206, 207, 222
Schoffstall, C.L., 435
Schonert-Reichl, K.A., 213, 283, 368, 372, 373,
    379, 458
Schonpflug, U., 420
Schoppe-Sullivan, S.J., 406
Schreier, H.M.C., 379
Schulenberg, J.E., 384
Schultz, M., 257
Schultz, M.S., 61
Schunk, D.H., 470, 471, 472, 473, 483
Schwalbe, C.S., 385
Schwartz, D., 435, 436
Schwartz, S.J., 330, 332, 334
Schwartz-Mette, R.A., 353, 441
Schwarz, S.P., 392, 392f, 421
Sciberras, E., 466
Sclar, D.A., 466
Scott, R.M., 167
Scourfield, J., 59
Seabrook, J.A., 62
Sechrest, J., 397
Sedmak, G., 72
Segal, M., 456–457
Sellner, J., 77

Selman, R.L., 323, 372
Sénéchal, M., 262, 265
Senter, L., 115
Serbin, L.A., 341, 349, 350
Sethna, V., 307
Setliff, A.E., 198, 199
Sgoifo, A., 90
Shachar-Shapira, L., 448, 449
Shafer, V.L., 270, 273
Shah, M., 153
Shah, R., 76
Shanahan, L., 394, 403
Shanahan, M.J., 397
Shankaran, S., 76
Shapira, N., 78
Shapiro, C.J., 408
Sharma, A.R., 57, 58
Shatz, M., 262
Shaw, D.S., 307
Shaw, G.L., 242
Shaw, P., 466
Shayer, M., 184
Shaywitz, B.A., 465
Shaywitz, S.E., 465
Sheese, B.E., 294
Shehata, F., 84
Sheidow, L.J., 385
Shein, P.P., 474
Shek, D.T., 383
Shen, J., 62
Shen, L.H., 466
Sher-Censor, E., 408
Sherrie, K., 84
Sherwood, L., 45
Shields, A.M., 289
Shields, S.A., 357
Shim, S.S., 434
Shin, S.H., 407
Shiner, R.L., 297
Shiraev, E., 5, 23, 369
Shortt, J.W., 385, 403
Shuai, L., 466
Shulman, S., 415, 448, 449
Shumow, L., 379, 380
Shweder, R., 369
Siebert, A.C., 306
Siegal, M., 254
Siegel, L.S., 202
Siegler, R.S., 19, 192, 193, 194, 206, 206f, 214,
    215, 216, 224
Siener, S., 306
Sigmundson, H.K., 340
Sijtsema, J.J., 434
Silberg, J.L., 59
Silk, J.S., 403
Silva, K.G., 183, 184
Silverman, L.R., 428, 441
Silverman, R., 346
Simcock, G., 210
Simion, F., 285
Simkus, A., 272
Simmonds, E., 234
Simon, T., 230
Simpkins, S.D., 400
Simpson, S., 220
Singer, D., 174, 440
Singer, T., 306
Singh, A.A., 436
Singh, B., 87
Singhal, A., 140

Sitterle, K.A., 418
Siu, A.M., 383
Sivell, S., 53
Skinner, B.F., 20, 20f, 21, 37, 192, 271
Skjaerven, R., 86
Slade, L., 221
Slater, A., 146, 146f, 149, 154, 169, 196
Slater, A.M., 149
Slobin, D., 258
Slomkowski, C., 386
Smedley, B., 403
Smetana, J.G., 375, 376, 401
Smith, D., 269
Smith, D.E., 326
Smith, J., 13, 412
Smith, J.B., 83
Smith, J.E., 90
Smith, L., 210
Smith, L.B., 133, 134, 136, 155, 156
Smith, L.E., 92
Smith, P.K., 174, 439
Smith, R.A., 14
Smith, R.L., 324, 353, 443
Snapp-Childs, W., 154
Snarey, J., 368
Snedeker, J., 169
Snidman, N., 13
Snjezana, H., 322
Snow, C.A., 271, 273
Snyder, H., 247
Snyder, J., 386, 403
Soares, N.S., 467
Sobolewski, J.M., 394, 403
Sokol, B.W., 322, 382
Solomon, D., 381
Somers, M., 146, 146f
Song, L., 271, 282
Sood, B., 75
Sophian, C., 168f
Sorenson, A., 327
Southgate, V., 256
Spangler, G., 304
Sparling, P., 4
Spelke, E.S., 154, 166, 167, 169, 169f
Spence, J.T., 356
Spence, M.J., 151
Spencer, D., 288
Spencer, J.P., 134
Spencer, J.R., 209
Spinney, J., 140
Spinrad, T.L., 323, 354, 372, 381, 382
Spring, J., 6, 462
Spuhl, S.T., 184
Squires, J., 457
Squires, S.E., 203
Srabstein, J.C., 436
Sroufe, L.A., 286, 303, 304, 305, 448
Stack, D.M., 283
Stafford, E.P., 399
Staiano, A.E., 477, 478
Stalker, G.J., 307
Stangor, C., 14
Stanley-Hagan, M., 416
Stanovich, K.E., 216, 265
Starr, C., 48
Starr, L.R., 448
Statistics Canada, 118, 118f, 119, 269, 352, 417,
    418, 461, 462
Stattin, H., 441
Staudinger, U.M., 13

Vandehey, M., 380
Vandell, D.L., 394
Vanderlee, M., 458
Vandeven, A.M., 406
Vandewater, E.A., 477, 478
Vansteenkiste, M., 469
Varnhagen, C.K., 476
Varnish, A., 345
Vasdev, G., 83
Vavrinkova, B., 76
Veenman, M.V.J., 222
Veenstra, R., 435, 448, 449
Velagaleti, R.S., 52
Velez, C.E., 416
Venners, S.A., 80
Vereijken, B., 136
Verhaak, C.M., 56
Verkampt, F., 209
Verma, S., 358
Vermeersch, H., 101
Vernberg, E.M., 436
Vesco, K.K., 78
Vesell, E.S., 62
Vida, M., 150
Viet, C.T., 52
Vigod, S.N., 91
Villar, J., 84
Villegas, R., 121
Vimaleswaran, K.S., 49
Vinik, J., 289
Vioet, T.D., 466
Violato, C., 283
Virmani, E., 318
Virues-Ortega, J., 300
Visconti, K.J., 434
Vitaro, F., 386, 441
Vittrup, B., 400–401, 401*f*
Vohs, K.D., 326
Volbrecht, M.M., 296
Vong, K-I., 439
von Hofsten, C., 133
Von Polier, G.G., 466
Votavova, H., 75
Votruba-Drzal, E., 311
Voyer, D., 352
Voyer, S., 352
Vreeman, R.C., 436
Vriend, J.L., 116
Vukelich, C., 263
Vul, E., 148
Vygotsky, L.S., 17, 18, 18*f*, 19, 24, 24*f*, 30*f*, 37,
    160, 162, 182, 183, 183*f*, 184, 185, 185*f*,
    186, 186*f*, 187, 189, 192, 229, 269, 438,
    455, 456, 457

## W

Wachs, H., 176
Wachs, T.D., 296, 297
Waddell, L., 78
Wadsworth, S.J., 238
Wagner, A.D., 476
Wagner, D.A., 262
Wagner, L., 257, 273
Wagner, R.K., 234
Wahlsten, D., 46, 52, 351
Wainryb, C., 382
Waiter, G.D., 235
Walden, T., 300
Waldfogel, J., 414

Walk, R.D., 150, 150*f*, 158
Walker, C.M., 174
Walker, L., 121, 363, 370
Walker, L.J., 365, 368, 373, 374, 376
Waller, E.M., 433, 443
Wallerstein, J.S., 415
Wallis, C., 346
Walsh, R., 200
Walsh, S., 87
Walsh, T.J., 56
Walton, G.M., 472
Wang, C., 217
Wang, Q., 49, 205
Wang, Y., 294, 466
Waqar-ul-Haq, 100
Ward, L.M., 326
Ware, E.A., 210
Warren, M.P., 101
Warren, S.T., 51
Warrington, M., 352
Warshak, R.A., 417, 418
Wartella, E.A., 478
Watamura, S.E., 311
Waterman, A.S., 332
Waters, E., 286
Watson, J., 220, 220*f*
Watson, J.B., 19, 20, 20*f*
Watt, H.M.G., 352
Waxman, S., 257
Way, N., 419, 420, 428, 441
Webb, J.T., 246
Webb, L.D., 456
Weber, M.A., 114
Webster, N.S., 379
Wechsler, D., 231, 248
Wehner, E.A., 447
Wei, R., 70
Weikum, W., 62
Weinberg, R.A., 236, 240
Weiner, C.P., 73
Weinstein, N., 469
Weinstein, R.S., 232
Weinstock, M., 221
Weiss, L.A., 467
Wekerle, C., 407
Weller, D., 382
Wellman, H.M., 219, 220,
    220*f*, 322
Wells, E.M., 79
Welti, C., 429
Wendel, G., 77
Wentzel, K.R., 427, 441, 442, 445
Wergin, J.F., 27, 28
Werker, J.F., 256, 257*f*
Wermter, A.K., 63
Wertsch, J.V., 183
West, M.J., 271, 272*f*
West, R.F., 216
Westling, D.L., 465
Weston, M.J., 55
Westra, T., 139
Whaley, L., 253
Wheeler, K., 243
White, M., 429
White, R., 288
Whitehead, H., 299
Whitehurst, G., 272
Whiteman, S.D., 412
Whiteman, V., 76
Whittaker, C.R., 464

Wider, C., 53
Widom, C.S., 407
Wiesel, A., 77
Wigfield, A., 473, 474
Wilcox, W.B., 398, 399
Willems, P.J., 49
Willey, J., 45
Willford, J., 76
Williams, A.D., 74
Williams, D.D., 379
Williams, E.M., 181
Williams, E.P., 102
Williams, J.E., 349
Williams, K.R., 436
Williams, S.T., 428
Williamson, R.A., 166, 211, 214
Willoughby, T., 477, 479, 480
Wilson, B.J., 477
Wilson, D., 99
Wilson, K.S., 394
Wilson, S., 5, 90
Wilson, T., 434
Wiltshire, K.M., 52
Windingstad, S., 234
Winn, I.J., 213
Winner, E., 172, 174, 234, 245, 246
Winsler, A., 183
Winter, H., 91
Winters, K., 102
Winton, S., 379
Winzer-Serhan, U.H., 75
Wisborg, K., 57
Wise, N., 268
Wise, S., 88
Wisner, K., 91
Wit, J.M., 98
Witelson, S.F., 235
Witherington, D.C., 281, 286
Witkin, H.A., 51
Wittig, S.L., 122
Witvliet, M., 434, 435
Wolfe, D.A., 290, 384, 467
Wolfinger, N.H., 411
Wolten, K., 53
Wong, J.M., 115
Wood, D., 473
Wood, J.J., 234
Woodard, E., 377
Woodhill, B.M., 356
Woodward, A., 170, 259
Woodward, A.L., 257, 300
Woolett, L.A., 69
Woolley, J.D., 219
Woolverton, C., 45
Worrell, F.C., 379
Wright, R.O., 62
Wright, S.C., 269
Wszolek, Z.K., 53
Wu, D.Y.H., 460
Wu, Y., 326
Wuest, D.A., 141
Wyatt, P., 50
Wyatt, S.B., 102
Wyatt, T., 290
Wynn, K., 169, 170*f*, 382

## X

Xia, Q., 125
Xie, Q., 139

Xu, F., 169
Xu, X., 288
Xue, F., 79

## Y

Yang, S., 239
Yates, D., 467
Young, L., 262
Young, M.E., 139
Younger, M., 352
Yount, S.M., 90
Yuen, R., 69
Yurkewicz, C., 383

## Z

Zaghloul, N.A., 53
Zaitoun, I., 49
Zarrett, N.R., 384
Zeanah, C.H., 106
Zelazo, P.D., 171, 193, 194, 211, 213, 214, 242
Zelazo, P.R., 286, 287f
Zelkowitz, P., 86
Zembal-Saul, C.L., 214
Zerwas, S., 299, 299f
Zeskind, P.S., 285
Zhai, F., 289
Zhang, L., 55, 76, 239
Zhang, L.-F., 236, 240

Zhou, M., 294
Zhou, P., 259
Zhou, Q., 294
Ziemer, C.J., 144
Zigler, E., 458
Zimmerman, B.J., 474, 478
Zimmerman, F.J., 198, 199
Ziol-Guest, K.M., 63, 415, 417
Zitzer-Comfort, C., 274
Zolfaghari, R., 146
Zosuls, K.M., 341
Zotter, H., 115, 121
Zucker, K.J., 341
Zusho, A., 358, 419, 474

# subject index

attachment—*Cont.*
 insecure resistant babies, 302
 internal working model, 302
 interpretation of differences in, 303–304
 physical comfort, 301
 securely attached babies, 302
 Strange Situation, 302, 303
 theories of attachment, 301–302
attention, 195–200, 224
 adolescence, 199–200
 childhood, 197–199
 dishabituation, 196
 divided attention, 195
 executive attention, 196
 focused attention, 196
 habituation, 196
 infancy, 196–197
 joint attention, 196–197, 300
 meaning of, 195–196
 orienting/investigative process, 196
 selective attention, 195
 sustained attention, 196
 vigilance, 196
attention deficit hyperactivity disorder
  (ADHD), 198, 465–467, 466*f*
auditory myelination, 108
Australia, 125
authoritarian parenting, 402, 403
authoritative parenting, 402, 403
autism, 221
autism spectrum disorders (ASDs), 467–468
autistic disorder, 467
autobiographical memory, 205
automaticity, 194
autonomous morality, 364
autonomy, 408
autonomy-supportive teachers, 469
autonomy *versus* shame and doubt, 16, 16*f*
axon, 105

## B

babbling, 255–256, 272*f*
Babinski reflex, 135*f*
balance scale, 215*f*
Bandura, Albert, 20–21, 20*f*
Bangladesh, 7
basic cry, 285
Bayley Scales of Infant Development, 241
Beckwith-Wiedemann syndrome, 49
behaviour genetics, 59
behavioural disorders, 467
behavioural inhibition, 293, 296
behavioural teratology, 73
behavioural theories, 19–20, 21, 24*f*
 classical conditioning, 19–20
 evaluation of, 21
 operant conditioning, 20
behaviourism, 19
Bell, Alexander Graham, 251
Bell, Katie, 379*f*
Bem Sex-Role Inventory, 356*f*
benevolence, 382
Bernardo, Paul, 3, 3*f*
Better Beginnings, Better Futures, 238
Better Nights, Better Days program, 116
bias
 cultural bias, 34–35
 cultural bias in testing, 239–240

ethnic bias, 34–35
 gender bias, 34, 346, 370
 minimization of, in research, 34–35
 reducing bias at school, 463
 referral bias, 465
bicultural identity, 335
bilingualism, 266–267, 268
Bill C-6, 53
Binet, Alfred, 230
Binet tests, 230–231
biological influences
 emotions, 281
 gender development, 342–343
 on language, 270–271, 277
 temperament, 295
biological processes, 8, 9
birth, 81–89, 94
 afterbirth, 82
 assessment of the newborn, 84–85
 birth process, 82–84
 breech position, 84
 Caesarean delivery, 83, 84
 childbirth setting and attendants, 82–83
 doula, 83
 extremely preterm infants, 86
 low birth weight infants, 85–88
 medication, 83
 methods of childbirth, 83–84
 midwives, 82
 natural childbirth, 83–84
 prepared childbirth, 84
 preterm infants, 85–88, 87*f*
 small for date infants, 85–88
 small for gestational age infants, 86
 stages of birth, 82
 very preterm infants, 86
birth defects, 72
 *see also* teratogen
birth order, 413
birth process, 82–84
Blackstock, Cindy, 5*f*
blastocyst, 68
blinking reflex, 135*f*
Bocelli, Andrea, 132
bodily-kinesthetic skills, 233
body growth and change, 97–103, 97*f*, 128–129
 adolescence, 99–103
 cephalocaudal pattern, 97
 early childhood, 98
 infancy, 98
 middle and late childhood, 99
 patterns of growth, 97–98
 proximodistal pattern, 98
body image, 102
bottle feeding, 121–122, 123
Bowlby, John, 301, 302
the brain, 129
 adolescence, 111–112, 111*f*
 amygdala, 105, 111
 and attachment, 306, 306*f*
 attention deficit hyperactivity disorder
  (ADHD), 466*f*
 axon, 105
 "blooming and pruning," 109
 brain scans and learning disabilities, 465*f*
 Broca's area, 270, 271*f*
 cerebral cortex, 104
 childhood, 109–111
 corpus callosum, 111, 351

dendrites, 105, 108
dendritic spreading, 109*f*
development of, 104–112
and early deprivation, 107*f*
and early experience, 106–108
electroencephalogram (EEG), 106–107, 106*f*
forebrain, 104
frontal lobes, 104, 234
function of, 104–105
growth curves, 110*f*
hemispheres, 104*f*, 351
hippocampus, 105
hypothalamus, 351
infancy, 105–109
intelligence, 235, 235*f*
language, role in, 270
lateralization, 105
left-brained, 105
lobes, 104, 105*f*
myelination, 108
neural circuits, 105
neuroconstructivist view, 104
neurons, 105, 106, 108–109
neurotransmitters, 105
occipital lobes, 104
parietal lobes, 104, 351
physiology of, 104–105
plasticity, 108*f*
prefrontal cortex, 109, 110, 111, 212
during prenatal period, 72
right-brained, 105
sizes, humans and primates, 43*f*
structure, 104–105, 109
synapses, 105, 108
synaptic density, 110*f*
temporal lobes, 104
weight at birth, 72
Wernicke's area, 270, 271*f*
brain imaging, 27, 27*f*
brainstorming, 247
Brazelton, T. Berry, 85
Brazelton Neonatal Behavioral Assessment
  Scale (NBAS), 84–85
breast cancer, 122
breastfeeding, 121–122, 123
breech position, 84
Broca's area, 270, 271*f*
Bronfenbrenner, Urie, 22–23, 23*f*
Bronfenbrenner's ecological theory,
  22–23, 23*f*
bullying, 434–436, 435*f*, 437
bullying intervention programs, 436

## C

Caesarean delivery, 83, 84
caffeine, 74
Canada
 Canadian identity, 336
 child care, 309
 educated women, 7
 official languages, 263
 sleep, and infants, 114
Canadian Diabetes Association, 119
Canadian Fertility and Andrology Society, 56
Canadian Foundation for the Study of Infant
  Deaths, 114
Canadian Incidence Study of Reported Child
  Maltreatment (CIS), 407

Canadian Institute of Health Research, 33
Canadian National Longitudinal Survey of
    Children and Youth, 103, 395
Canadian Prenatal Nutrition Program
    (CPNP), 80
Canadian Society for Exercise Physiology, 126
cancer, 119
capacity of processing, 192-193
cardiovascular disease, 119
care perspective, 370
caregiving styles, and attachment, 305-306
caring for children, 4-8, 36
    diversity, 5-6
    education, 5
    health and well-being, 4
    improving the lives of children, 4-7
    parenting, 5
    resilience, 6, 6f
    sociocultural contexts, 5-6
carriers, 49
case study, 26-27
casual dating, 446
categorization, 210, 210f, 263
causality, 168
causation, 28
CenteringPregnancy, 80
central executive, 201
central nervous system, 143
central processing structures, 181-182
centration, 173-174
cephalocaudal pattern, 97
cerebral cortex, 104
change, mechanisms of, 193-194
character education, 378-379
cheating, 380
Chess and Thomas's classification of
    temperament, 292-293
child abuse, 406
    see also child maltreatment
child care, 309-311, 314
    in Canada, 309
    effects of, 309-311
    nation-wide child care system, 310
    quality, 311
child-centred kindergarten, 456-457
Child Development, 32
child development journals, 32
Child Development Project, 381
child development research. See research
child development theories. See theories of
    child development
child-directed speech, 272
child maltreatment, 406-408
    context of abuse, 407
    developmental consequences, 407-408
    types of, 406-407
child neglect, 406
child protective services, 76
childbirth. See birth
childhood
    see also early childhood; middle and late
        childhood
    attention, 197-199
    brain development, 109-111
    critical thinking, 212-213
    death, main causes of, 118, 118f
    executive function, 211-212
    exercise, 128-129
    fine motor skills, 142-143

gross motor skills, 139-141
intelligence, stability and change, 243
masculinity in, 356
memory, 205-209
memory span, 205-206, 206f
memory strategies, 206-208
metacognition, 222
motor development, 139-141, 142-143
nutrition and eating behaviour, 124-126
overweight children, 124-126
parental feeding styles, 124
parental monitoring, 401
peer relations, developmental course of,
    428-430
problem solving, 214-216
reconstructive memory, 208-209
scientific thinking, 213-214
sleep, 115
sleep disturbances, 116
temperament, 297f
thinking, 211-216
visual perception, 150-151
childhood amnesia, 204
childhood cancers, 119
children as eyewitnesses, 208-209
children with disabilities, 291,
    464-468, 482
    attention deficit hyperactivity disorder
        (ADHD), 465-467, 466f
    autism spectrum disorders, 467-468
    emotional and behavioural disorders, 467
    learning disability, 464-465, 465f
child's theory of mind, 219-221
Chile, 122
China, 58, 114, 125, 296, 334, 375, 413, 419
cholesterol levels, 125
Chomsky, Noam, 270-271, 271f
Chomsky's language acquisition device (LAD),
    270-271
chorionic villus sampling (CVS), 55
Christensen, Stacey, 410f
chromosomal abnormalities, 50-51, 50f
    Down syndrome, 50, 50f
    fragile X syndrome, 50f, 51
    sex-linked chromosomal abnormalities,
        50-51
    Turner syndrome, 50f, 51
    XYY syndrome, 50f, 51
chromosomes, 45, 45f, 46-48
chronosystem, 23, 393
circular reaction, 165
classical conditioning, 19-20
classification, 176, 176f
cliques, 426, 445-446
cocaine, 75-76
cognition, 163
    see also thinking
    in family processes, 394-395
    guided participation, 184
    and language, 183-184, 274-275, 277
cognitive activities, 21
cognitive control, 111
cognitive coping strategies, 290
cognitive development, 142
cognitive developmental approaches
    Piaget's theory of cognitive development,
        162-178, 187-189
    Vygotsky's theory of cognitive
        development, 182-186, 189

cognitive developmental theory (Piaget's),
    17-18
cognitive influences on gender
    development, 347
cognitive moral education, 379
cognitive processes, 8, 9, 470-475
    effort, 470
    expectations, 472-473
    goal setting, 473-474
    mastery motivation, 470-471
    mindset, 471-472
    planning, 473-474
    purpose, 474-475
    self-efficacy, 472
    self-monitoring, 473-474
    sustained attention, 470
    task persistence, 470
cognitive resources, 192-193
cognitive similarities and differences,
    351-352
cognitive theories, 17-19, 24f
    evaluation of, 19
    information-processing theory, 19
    Piaget's cognitive development theory,
        17-18, 17f
    Vygotsky's sociocultural cognitive theory,
        18-19
cohort, 11
cohort effects, 11
collaborative knowledge, 18-19
colour vision, 148-149
commitment, 331
communication skills, 431f
companionship, 441
computers, 479-480
concepts, 210
concrete descriptions, 318-319
concrete operational stage, 17f, 18, 175-176
concrete operations, 175
conduct disorder, 383-384
confidentiality, 33
conflict
    marital conflict, 416, 449
    with parents, 409-410
conformity, 445
confusion of self, mind, and body, 318
congenital adrenal hyperplasia (CAH), 343
connectedness, 334
conscience, 371
conservation, 173, 175, 175f
conservation task, 173-174, 173f
constructive play, 439-440
constructivist approach, 179, 455-456, 458
content knowledge, 203
context, 4, 5
continuity, 11
    see also continuity-discontinuity issue
continuity-discontinuity issue, 11, 11f, 19, 163
control, 396
control groups, 29
conventional reasoning, 366
convergent thinking, 247
convolutions, 351
cooing, 255
cooperation, 300
cooperation task, 299f
coordination of secondary circular reactions,
    165-166
coparenting, 406

coping, 287
coping with stress, 290–291
core knowledge approach, 169
coregulation, 400
corporal punishment, 404–405, 404*f*
corpus callosum, 111, 351
correlation, 28
    active (niche-picking) genotype-
       environment correlations, 60
    evocative genotype-environment
       correlations, 60
    heredity-environment correlations, 59–60
correlation coefficient, 28
correlational research, 28, 28*f*
crawling, 137*f*
creative intelligence, 232
creative thinking, 245
creativity, 247, 249
crib death, 75
crisis, 331
critical period, 22, 73
critical thinking, 212–213, 216
cross-cultural studies, 5
cross-sectional approach, 29–30
crowds, 446
crying, 255, 285
cultural bias, 34–35
cultural bias in testing, 239–240
cultural-familial intellectual disability, 245
cultural mediator, 464
cultural variations
    attachment, 303*f*, 305
    emotion, 282
    families, 418–419
    gender roles, 357–358
    guided participation, 184
    intelligence, view of, 239
    language milestones, 257, 257*f*
    low birth weight, 87
    motor development, 139
    peer relations, 429
culture, 4, 5, 204
    and children's memory, 205
    cross-cultural studies, 5
    display rules, 282
    and identity, 334–336
    and moral reasoning, 368–369
    and stereotyping, 349
    temperament, 296
culture-fair tests, 239–240
curiosity, 166
*Cyber-safety Act*, 436*f*
cyberbullying, 435
cystic fibrosis, 52, 52*f*, 55

**D**

danger invulnerability, 178
Darwin, Charles, 42, 45
data collection methods, 24–27
    case study, 26–27
    interview, 26
    observation, 24–26
    physiological measures, 27
    standardized test, 2
    survey, 26
dating, 446
deaf children, 275
death, main causes of, 118, 118*f*

debriefing, 33
deception, 33–34
decision making, 216–218
delinquency. *See* juvenile delinquency
dendrites, 105, 108
dendritic spreading, 109*f*
Denmark, 308
*The Dependent Gene* (Moore), 46
dependent variables, 29
depth perception, 150, 150*f*
descriptive research, 28
designer babies, 58
desires, 219
developing countries, 460
development, 4
    epigenetic view, 104
    stages of development, 163
development periods, 9–10, 10*f*, 36–37
developmental cascade model, 304
developmental cognitive neuroscience, 9
developmental issues, 11–13, 36–37
    continuity-discontinuity issue, 11, 11*f*
    early-later experience issue, 12–13
    evaluation of, 13
    nature-nurture issue, 11–12
developmental processes, 10*f*, 36–37
    biological processes, 8
    cognitive processes, 8
    connecting the processes, 9
    socioemotional processes, 8–9
*Developmental Psychology*, 32
developmental quotient (DQ), 241
*Developmental Review*, 32
*Developmental Science*, 32
developmental social neuroscience,
    9, 111, 306
developmentally appropriate practice (DAP),
    457–459, 459*f*
Dhaka, Bangladesh, 7
diabetes, 52, 52*f*, 53, 121, 125
    *see also* type 2 diabetes
*Diagnostic and Statistical Manual of Mental*
    *Disorders*, 244
dialect, 269
dialogue, 183
difficult child, 292
digitally mediated social environment, 479
direct instruction approach, 456, 458
disabilities. *See* children with disabilities
disasters, 290–291
discontinuity, 11, 11*f*
    *see also* continuity-discontinuity issue
discovery, 179–180
dishabituation, 145–146, 145*f*, 147, 196, 243
displacement, 478
display rules, 282
distortion, 208
divergent thinking, 247
diversity, 5–6
    of adopted children and adoptive parents,
      58
    ethnic diversity, 11
    positive personal contact, 463
divided attention, 195
divorce, 449
divorced families, 415–417, 415*f*
dizygotic twins, 48, 236
    *see also* fraternal twins
DNA, 44, 45, 45*f*, 48

domain-specific giftedness, 246
domain-specific socialization, 396
dominant gene, 48–49
dominant-recessive genes principle, 48–49
dose, 73
dose-response effects, 291
doula, 83
Down syndrome, 50, 50*f*, 55, 56, 79, 245, 274
driver training, 217
dual-process model, 218
dyadic subsystem, 394
dynamic systems theory, 133–134, 299
dyscalculia, 465
dysgraphia, 263, 465
dyslexia, 263, 465

**E**

early bloomers, 447
early childhood, 9–10
    *see also* childhood
    body growth and change, 98
    brain development, 109–110
    early literacy, 262–263
    educational TV viewing, 479*f*
    electronic media, learning from, 478
    emotional development, 287–289
    emotional expression, 288
    emotional regulation, 288–289
    fast mapping, 259
    gender stereotypes, 349–350
    illnesses and injuries, 118
    intelligence, stability and change, 243
    language development, 258–263
    metacognition, 222
    morphology, 259
    parent-child interactions, 399
    peers, 429
    perspective taking, 323
    phonology, 259
    pragmatics, 260–262
    self-understanding, 318–320
    semantics, 259–260
    syntax, 259–260
    understanding others, 322–323
early childhood education, 456–459
    child-centred kindergarten, 456–457
    constructivist approach, 458
    current controversies, 458
    in developing countries, 460
    developmentally appropriate practice
      (DAP), 457–459, 459*f*
    developmentally inappropriate
      practice, 457
    direct instruction approach, 458
    full-day kindergarten, 458
    in Japan, 460
    Montessori approach, 457
    preschool education, 458
    variations in, 456–459
early-later experience issue, 12–13
early literacy, 262–263
early maturation, 103
early school leaving, 461–462
East Asia, 58, 296, 334
easy child, 292
eating behaviour, 120–126
    childhood, 124–126
    infancy, 120–124

eclectic theoretical orientation, 23-24
ecological theory, 22-23, 24f
ecological view, 144, 154
ectoderm, 69
education, 5, 7
  see also schools and schooling
educational programs, 479, 479f
the Efe culture, 44
effort, 470
effortful control, 293-294
ego ideal, 371
ego support, 441
egocentrism, 171, 177-178, 322
elaboration, 206-207
electroencephalogram (EEG), 27,
  106-107, 106f
electronic media, 476-479
elementary school, 459-461
embryo, 68
embryonic period, 68-70
emerging adulthood, 332-333
Emerson, Ralph Waldo, 252
emotion, 281, 312-313
  biological influences, 281
  cultural variations, 282
  development of. See emotional
    development
  early emotions, 284-285
  emotional competence, 282-283, 283f
  and experience, 281, 282
  exploring emotions, 281-283
  in family processes, 394-395
  functionalist view, 282
  meaning of, 281-282
  and moral development, 373
  negative emotions, 281
  other-conscious emotions, 284
  peer relations, 431-432
  positive emotions, 281
  primary emotions, 284
  self-conscious emotions, 284, 288
  social relationships, 281-282
  understanding emotions, 288
emotion coaching, 288-289
emotion-coaching parents, 289, 395
emotion-dismissing approach,
  288-289, 395
emotion-dismissing parents, 289
emotional abuse, 406
emotional and behavioural disorders, 467
emotional competence, 282-283, 283f
emotional development, 284-291, 313
  coping with stress, 290-291
  developmental changes, 219, 289-290
  early childhood, 287-289
  infancy, 284-287, 284f
  middle and late childhood, 289-291
emotional expression, 285-286, 288, 351
emotional intelligence, 233-234, 282
Emotional Intelligence (Goleman), 233
emotional regulation, 287, 288-289,
  354, 432
emotional state, in prenatal period, 79
empathy, 290, 372-373, 373f
empiricists, 154
Employment Insurance Act, 308
encoding, 193
endoderm, 68
environmental hazards, 77

environmental influences
  intelligence, 236-238, 240
  language, 271-273, 277
environmental pollutants, 77
epidural block, 83
epigenetic view, 61-62, 134
episodic buffer, 201
equality, 382
equilibration, 163
Erikson, Erik, 15-17, 16f, 26f, 301,
  329-330, 330f
Erikson's theory, 15-17, 16f, 24
estradiol, 101, 101f
estrogens, 101, 342
ethical research, 33-34
Ethiopia, 58
ethnic bias, 34-35
ethnic diversity, 11
ethnic gloss, 34-35
ethnic groups, 6
ethnic identity, 335, 336
ethnic label, 34
ethnicity, 6
  and families, 419
  and identity, 334-336
  intelligence, and environmental
    influences, 240
  in schools, 463-464
ethological research, 22
ethological theory, 21-22, 24f
ethology, 21
European Union, 308
event-related potential (ERP), 107
evocative genotype-environment
  correlations, 60
evolution, and language, 270
evolutionary developmental psychology, 43
evolutionary perspective, 42-44, 64
  adaptive behaviour, 42
  evolutionary developmental
    psychology, 43
  evolutionary psychology, 42-44
  natural selection, 42
evolutionary psychology, 42-44, 343
Exceptional Children, 32
exchange, 366
executive attention, 196
executive function, 211-212
exercise, 126-127
  adolescence, 127
  childhood, 128-129
  media, 127
  parents, 127
  peers, 127
  schools, 127
  and thinking skills, 213
exosystem, 23, 393
expanding, 272, 273
expectations, 472-473
experiment, 29, 29f
experimental groups, 29
expertise, 203
explicit memory, 204
exploration, 179-180, 331
expressive traits, 349
externalizing, 384
extracurricular activities, 462
extraversion/surgency, 293
extremely preterm infants, 86

extrinsic motivation, 469-470
eye-tracking, 146-147
eyewitnesses, 208-209

## F

face perception, 148
face-to-face play, 299
Facebook, 479
facial expressions, 354
facilitation of learning, 179
Fagan Test of Infant Intelligence, 243
false beliefs, 220, 220f
families
  acculturation, 420
  changes, 414-421, 423-424
  and child care, 310
  and children's development, 7
  cultural variations, 418-419
  and delinquency, 385
  divorced families, 415-417, 415f
  and ethnicity, 419
  family processes, 393-397
  fathers as caregivers, 307-308
  gay and lesbian parents, 418
  and identity, 333-334
  and language development, 261
  marital conflict, 416
  and moral development, 369-370
  mothers as caregivers, 307-308
  never-divorced families, 415
  parenting. See parenting
  siblings, 411-413
  socioeconomic status, 420-421
  stepfamilies, 417-418
  as systems, 393
  working parents, 414-415
family dinners, 409
family processes, 393-397, 422
  cognition in, 394-395
  in divorced families, 416
  domain-specific socialization, 396
  emotion in, 394-395
  historical changes, 396-397
  interactions in the family system,
    393-394, 394f
  multiple developmental trajectories, 395
  sociocultural changes, 396-397
Famous Five, 374f
fast mapping, 259
fathers
  as caregivers, 307-308
  socialization strategies, 345
fear, 286
fertilization, 46-48
fetal alcohol spectrum disorder (FASD),
  74-75, 74f
fetal MRI, 55, 55f
fetal period, 70-72
fine motor skills, 141-143
  central nervous system, 143
  childhood, 142-143
  infancy, 141-142
first habits, 164-165
first memories, 203-204
First Nations and Family Caring Society, 5f
first trimester, 71f
first words, 257-258
fish, 79

5-HTTLPR, 62
flexibility, 212
fluctuating self, 321
fluent reading, 265
Flynn effect, 237
focused attention, 196
folic acid, 78
forebrain, 104
forethought, 474
forgiveness, 383
formal operational stage, 17f, 18, 176–178, 267
fragile X syndrome, 50f, 51, 245
fraternal twins, 48, 59
    *see also* dizygotic twins
Frederick II, Emperor of Germany, 255
Free the Children, 362
French immersion programs, 268
Freud, Sigmund, 15, 15f
Freudian stages, 15f
friendship, 451
    cliques, 445
    and computer and Internet use, 480
    functions of, 441–442
    and gender, 443
    intimacy in friendship, 442
    mixed-age friendships, 443–444
    other-sex friendships, 444
    positive friendships, 441
    similarity, 442
frontal lobes, 104, 234
full-day kindergarten, 458
functional magnetic resonance imaging
    (fMRI), 27, 110, 111
functionalist view of emotions, 282
fuzzy trace, or gist, 202
fuzzy trace theory, 202

## G

games, 440
Gandhi, Mahatma, 26f
Gardner's eight frames of mind, 233
gastrointestinal infections, 121
Gates, Bill, 247
gay parents, 418
gaze following in infancy, 197f
gender, 6, 341–342, 359
    and children's development, 7
    in context, 357
    and friendship, 443
    gender-role classification, 355–357
    temperament, 295–296
gender bias, 34, 346, 370
gender development, 359
    biological influences, 342–343
    cognitive influences, 347
    evolutionary psychology view, 343
    hormones, 342–344
    influences on, 342–347
    media influences, 346–347
    parental influences, 344–345, 344f
    peers, 345
    schools, 346
    social influences, 344–347
    teachers, 346
gender differences, 350–354, 359–360
    aggression, 352–353
    body image, 102
    cognitive differences, 351–352

debate about extent of, 354–355
divorce, response to, 417
emotional expression, 354
emotional regulation, 354
in intimacy aspect of friendship, 443
math aptitude, 352
physical differences, 351
prosocial behaviour, 354
relationship communication, 353–354
social role theory, 344
socioemotional differences, 352–354
gender dysphoria, 341
gender identity, 341
gender identity clinics, 342
gender role, 341, 357–358
gender-role classification, 355–357, 360
gender-role transcendence, 356–357
gender schema, 347–348
gender schema theory, 347
"gender school," 345
gender similarities, 350–354, 359–360
    cognitive similarities, 351–352
    physical similarities, 351
    socioemotional similarities, 352–354
gender stereotypes, 349–350, 359–360
gender typing, 341
gene-gene interaction, 49
gene-linked abnormalities, 51–52
    phenylketonuria (PKU), 51
    sickle-cell anemia, 51–52
gene × environment (G × E) interaction, 62
generativity versus stagnation, 16, 16f
genes, 45
    the collaborative gene, 45–46
    dominant gene, 48–49
    fertilization, 46–48
    gene-gene interaction, 49
    meiosis, 46–48, 47f
    mitosis, 46–48, 47f
    recessive gene, 49f
    sex-linked genes, 49
    sources of variability, 48
    zygote, 46, 47
genetic abnormalities
    chromosomal abnormalities, 50–51, 50f
    dealing with, 52–53
    gene-linked abnormalities, 51–52
genetic foundations of development, 44–53,
    64–65
    chromosomal abnormalities, 50–51, 50f
    chromosomes, 45, 45f
    the collaborative gene, 45–46, 45f
    DNA, 44, 45, 45f, 48
    gene-linked abnormalities, 51–52
    genes and chromosomes, 46–48
    genetic influences on behaviour, 44
    genetic principles, 48–49
genetic imprinting, 49
genetic influences
    on behaviour, 44
    intelligence, 236
genetic plan, 133
genetic principles, 48–49
    dominant-recessive genes principle, 48–49
    genetic imprinting, 49
    polygenic inheritance, 49
    sex-linked genes, 49
genetic susceptibility, 73
genetic transmission, 49

Genie, 252, 273
genital herpes, 77
genotype, 48
German measles, 77
Germany, 255, 305, 308
germinal period, 68, 69f
Gesell test, 241
gestational diabetes, 78
Ghana, 122, 123
giftedness, 245–247
global empathy, 372
global perspective
    health, illness and poverty, 119–120
    malnutrition in infancy, 122–124
    parental leave policies, 308
global self-esteem, 326, 326f
Go Fuel Bingo, 96
goal-directed behaviour, 300
goal setting, 473–474
gonads, 100
goodness of fit, 297–298
grammar, 263–264
grasping reflex, 135, 135f
grasps, 141
gratitude, 383
Great Britain, 114
Great Depression, 11, 396
gross motor skills, 136–141
    childhood, 139–141
    in the first year, 137–138
    infancy, 137–139
    learning to walk, 136–137, 137f
    milestones, 137–138, 138f
    posture, development of, 136
    in the second year, 138–139
group comparisons of intelligence, 238–240
group participation, 396
growth patterns, 97–98
growth spurt, 101, 101f
Guatemala, 114, 124
guided learning, 396
guided participation, 184

## H

habit, 164–165
habituation, 145–146, 145f, 147, 196, 243
Haiti, 58, 122
Hausa culture, 305f
Head Start programs, 460–461
health, 118–127, 130
    cancer, 119
    cardiovascular disease, 119
    exercise, 126–127
    global perspective, 119–120
    illnesses and injuries among children,
        118–120
    nutrition and eating behaviour, 120–126
    role of, 4
    type 2 diabetes, 119
Health Canada, 96, 121
hearing, 151–152, 151f
helpless orientation, 471, 471f
hemispheres of the brain, 104f
hemophilia, 52, 52f
heredity
    intelligence, influence on, 235–236
    and temperament, 295
heredity-environment correlations, 59–60, 65

heredity-environment interaction, 59–63
    active (niche-picking) genotype-environment correlations, 60
    behaviour genetics, 59
    conclusions, 62–63
    epigenetic view, 61–62
    evocative genotype-environment correlations, 60
    gene × environment (G × E) interaction, 62
    heredity-environment correlations, 59–60
    non-shared environmental experiences, 60–61
    passive genotype-environment correlations, 60
    shared environmental experiences, 60–61
heritability, 236
heritability index, 236
heroin, 76
heteronomous morality, 364
heterosexual romantic relationships, 446–447
hidden curriculum, 378
high-amplitude sucking, 146
high blood pressure. *See* hypertension
hippocampus, 105
historical changes, 396–397
HIV/AIDS, 77–78
Homolka, Karla, 3, 3*f*, 6, 11
homophily, 442
Hong Kong, 125
horizontal décalage, 175
hormones, 100–101
    androgens, 101, 342
    and attachment, 306
    estradiol, 101, 101*f*
    estrogens, 101, 342
    and gender development, 342–344
    testosterone, 101, 101*f*
hostile attribution bias, 432
Hubbard, Jerry, 52*f*
Human Early Learning Partnership (HELP), 310
human genome, 45–46
Human Genome Project, 45, 46*f*
human life span, 22
Huntington disease, 52, 52*f*, 55
hypertension, 119, 125
hypothalamus, 100, 351
hypotheses, 14
hypothetical-deductive reasoning, 177

**I**

ideal self, 320, 321
idealistic thinking, 176–177, 320–321
identical twins, 41, 48, 59
    *see also* monozygotic twins
identity, 329–336, 338
    bicultural identity, 335
    developmental changes, 330–331
    emerging adulthood and beyond, 332–333
    Erikson's view, 329–330
    ethnic identity, 335, 336
    meaning of, 329
    moral identity, 373–374
    psychosocial moratorium, 330
    social contexts, 333–336
    statuses, 331–332, 331*f*
identity achievement, 331
identity confusion, 330

identity diffusion, 331
identity foreclosure, 331
identity moratorium, 331
identity versus identity confusion, 16, 16*f*, 329
illnesses, 118–120
imagery, 207, 207*f*
imaginary audience, 177
imitation, 21
immanent justice, 364
implantation, 68
implicit memory, 203–204
imprinting, 21, 49
improving the lives of children, 4–7
in vitro fertilization (IVF), 56, 57*f*, 58*f*, 59
incompatible blood types, 76–77
independent variables, 29
India, 7, 369, 429
individual differences
    among peers, 428
    attachment, 302–305
    intelligence, 229
    social understanding, 322–323
individual rights, 367
individualism, 366
individuality, 333
induction, 377
indulgent parenting, 402
industry *versus* inferiority, 16, 16*f*
infancy, 9
    *see also* newborns
    attention, 196–197
    babbling, 255–256, 272*f*
    body growth and change, 98
    brain development, 105–109
    breast *vs.* bottle feeding, 121–122
    changing brain structures, 109
    changing neurons, 108–109
    childhood amnesia, 204
    colour vision, 148–149
    cooing, 255
    crying, 255, 285
    depth perception, 150, 150*f*
    developmental quotient (DQ), 241
    dishabituation, 196
    early emotions, 284–285
    early experience and the brain, 106–108
    electronic media, learning from, 478
    emotional development, 284–287, 284*f*
    emotional expression, 285–286
    emotional regulation and coping, 287
    face perception, 148
    fear, 286
    fine motor skills, 141–142
    first memories, 203–204
    first words, 257–258
    gaze following, 197*f*
    gestures, 256
    grasps, 141
    gross motor skills, 137–139
    habituation, 196
    hearing, 152
    intelligence, tests of, 241–243
    joint attention, 196–197
    language development, 255–258, 258*f*
    learning to walk, 136–137, 137*f*
    malnutrition, 122–124
    managing and guiding infant's behaviour, 400–401
    memory, 203–204

motor development, 137–139, 141–142
movement restrictions, 139
number sense, 170*f*
nutritional and eating behaviour, 120–124
nutritional needs, 120–121
object permanence, 168
orienting/investigative process, 196
other-awareness, 319
palmer grasp, 141
parent-child interactions, 399
pattern perception, 148
perception of occluded objects, 149–150, 150*f*
perceptual constancy, 149
pincer grip, 141
recognition of language sounds, 256
reflexes, 134–136, 135*f*
REM sleep, 113, 113*f*
self-awareness, 319
self-recognition, 317–318, 318*f*
self-understanding, 317–318
separation protest, 286
shaken baby syndrome, 106
shared sleeping, 113–114
sleep, 112–115
sleep disturbances, 116
smiling, 286
social sophistication and insight, 300
specificity of learning, 137
stranger anxiety, 286
sudden infant death syndrome (SIDS), 75, 114
television, exposure to, 198–199
thinking, 210–211
two-word utterances, 258
visual acuity, 147–148
visual perception, 147–150, 147*f*
*Infant Behavior and Development*, 32
infantile amnesia, 204
infertility, 56–57
infinite generativity, 252
information processing
    attention, 195–200, 224
    information-processing approach, 192–194, 223–224
    memory, 200–209, 201*f*, 224–225
    metacognition, 218–222, 226, 263
    thinking, 210–218, 225–226
information-processing approach, 192–194, 223–224
    automaticity, 194
    capacity of processing, 192–193
    cognitive resources, 192–193
    encoding, 193
    mechanisms of change, 193–194
    vs. Piaget's theory, 194
    speed of processing, 192–193
    strategy construction, 194
information-processing theory, 19, 24
informed consent, 33
inhibited temperament, 295
inhibition, 211–212
inhibition to the unfamiliar, 293
initiative versus guilt, 16, 16*f*
injuries, 118–120
inner speech, 183
insecure avoidant babies, 302
insecure disorganized babies, 303
insecure resistant babies, 302

insight, 300
instrumental purpose, 366
instrumental traits, 349
integrity versus despair, 16, 16*f*
intellectual disability, 244-245, 244*f*
intellectual health, 179
intelligence, 229, 232
    analytical intelligence, 232
    and the brain, 235, 235*f*
    concept of intelligence, 229-240, 248-249
    creative intelligence, 232
    vs. creativity, 247
    cross-cultural comparisons, 239
    development of, 241-243, 249
    emotional intelligence, 233-234
    environmental influences, 236-238, 240
    ethnic comparisons, 240
    extremes of intelligence, 244-247, 249
    Gardner's eight frames of mind, 233
    genetic influences, 236
    giftedness, 245-247
    group comparisons, 238-240
    heredity, influence of, 235-236
    infant intelligence, tests of, 241-243
    intellectual disability, 244-245, 244*f*
    intelligence tests, 229-232
    male-female comparisons, 238-239
    meaning of intelligence, 229
    multiple intelligences, 232-234
    and music, 242
    nature-nurture issue, 238
    neuroscience of intelligence, 235
    practical intelligence, 232
    social intelligence, 432
    stability and change through
      adolescence, 243
    triarchic theory of intelligence, 232
intelligence quotient (IQ), 230
intelligence tests, 229-232
    Binet tests, 230-231
    cultural bias, 239-240
    culture-fair tests, 239-240
    Flynn effect, 237
    infant-testing movement, 241-243
    normal distribution, 230, 230*f*
    Stanford-Binet test, 230, 230*f*
    use and misuse of, 231-232
    Wechsler Scales, 231
intention, 300
intentional self-regulation, 474
interactionist view of language, 273
interference, 478
intergenerational relationships, 410-411
intermodal perception, 153-154
internal working model, 302
internalization of schemes, 166
International Association of Infant Formula
    Manufacturers, 123
Internet
    access to information on, 479
    adolescents and, 479-480
    and cyberbullying, 435
    use of, 479-480
interpersonal conformity, 366
interpersonal skills, 233
intervention programs, 460
interview, 26
intimacy, 441
intimacy in friendship, 442

intimacy versus isolation, 16, 16*f*
intra-psychic phenomena, 282
intrapersonal skills, 233
intrinsic motivation, 469-470
intuitive thought substage, 172-173
involution, 90
IQ tests. *See* intelligence tests

## J

James, William, 147
Japan, 305, 429, 460
jealousy, 284-285
jigsaw classroom, 463
joint attention, 300
*Journal of Abnormal Child Psychology,* 32
*Journal of Cross-Cultural Research,* 32
*Journal of Educational Psychology,* 32
*Journal of Experimental Child Psychology,* 32
*Journal of Marriage and the Family,* 32
*Journal of Research on Adolescence,* 32
journals in child development, 32
junior high school, 461
justice perspective, 370
juvenile delinquency, 383, 384-387

## K

Kagan's behavioural inhibition, 293
Kamehameha Elementary Education
    Program, 185
kangaroo care, 86-88
Keller, Helen, 251, 252
Kielburger, Craig, 362, 381
kilogram kid, 85*f*
Klinefelter syndrome, 50-51, 50*f*
knowledge, 18-19
Kohlberg, Lawrence, 365, 365*f*
Kohlberg's theory of moral development,
    365-370
    age, 367*f*
    conventional reasoning, 366
    critics of, 368-370
    culture and moral reasoning, 368-369
    families, and moral development, 369-370
    gender and the care perspective, 370
    influences on the Kohlberg stages,
      367-368
    the Kohlberg stages, 365-367
    moral thought and moral behaviour, 368
    postconventional reasoning, 366-367
    preconventional reasoning, 366
    and social conventional approach, 376
Kwantlen Polytechnic University, 387
kwashiorkor, 123-124

## L

labelling, 272, 273
laboratory, 25
Lamaze, Ferdinand, 84
language, 183-184, 252, 276
    biological influences, 270-271, 277
    brain, role of, 270
    child-directed speech, 272
    and cognition, 183-184, 274-275, 277
    defining language, 252
    development. *See* language development
    dialect, 269

    environmental influences, 271-273, 277
    and evolution, 270
    interactionist view of language, 273
    language acquisition device (LAD),
      270-271
    memory-relevant language, 207
    morphology, 253, 254*f,* 259
    phonology, 252-253, 254*f,* 259
    pragmatics, 254, 254*f,* 260-262
    private speech, 183, 185
    rule systems, 252-254, 254*f*
    for self-regulation, 183
    semantics, 253-254, 254*f,* 259-260
    syntax, 253, 254*f,* 259-260
language acquisition device (LAD), 270-271
language development, 255-269, 276-277
    Aboriginal language learning, 269
    adolescence, 267-269
    babbling, 255-256, 272*f*
    bilingualism, 266-267, 268
    cultural variation in milestones, 257, 257*f*
    early childhood, 258-263
    early literacy, 262-263
    expanding, 272
    family environment and, 261
    fast mapping, 259
    first words, 257-258
    gestures, 256
    grammar, 263-264
    infancy, 255-258, 258*f*
    labelling, 272
    metalinguistic awareness, 263-264
    middle and late childhood, 263-267
    reading, 264-265, 264*f*
    recasting, 272
    recognition of language sounds, 256
    second-language learning, 266-267
    telegraphic speech, 258
    two-word utterances, 258
    vocabulary, 263-264
    writing, 265-266
late bloomers, 447
late childhood. *See* middle and late
    childhood
late maturation, 103
lateralization, 105
Latin America, 7
learn by doing, 179
learning, and electronic media, 478
learning disability, 464-465, 465*f*
learning to walk, 136-137, 137*f*
Leave Out Violence Everywhere (LOVE), 387
left-brained, 105
lesbian parents, 418
Lester, Barry, 85
letter knowledge, 262
leukemia, 119
Lewis, Jim, 41
literacy activities, 262
Little Albert, 20, 20*f*
"little white lies," 375
lobes, 104, 105*f*
localization, 152
locomotion, 136-137, 299-300
logical thinking, 176-177
long-term memory, 201
longitudinal approach, 30
looking glass self, 321
Lorenz, Konrad, 21

loudness, 152
love withdrawal, 377
low birth weight infants, 85–88
low-income backgrounds, 462–463
lower respiratory tract infections, 121
lying, 375

# M

macrosystem, 23, 393
magnetic resonance imaging (MRI), 55, 106
male-female comparisons, 238–239
MAMA cycles, 333
marasmus, 123
marijuana, 76
marital conflict, 416, 449
Martinez, Hector, 86
masculinity, 356
massage therapy, 88
mastery motivation, 470–471
maternal age, 79
maternal diet and nutrition, 78–80
maternal diseases, 77–78
mathematical skills, 233, 352
maturation, 133
mechanisms of change, 193–194
media
    educational programs, 479, 479f
    electronic media, 476–479
    and exercise, 127
    gender development, influences on,
        346–347
    media multi-tasking, 200
    media use, 476
    and Millennials, 11
    television, 476–477, 479f
    video games, 477–478
meiosis, 46–48
melatonin, 117
memory, 200–209, 224–225
    adolescence, 209
    age-related changes, 204f
    autobiographical memory, 205
    childhood, 205–209
    childhood amnesia, 204
    construction of memories, 202–203
    content knowledge and expertise, 203
    and culture, 205
    elaboration, 206–207
    explicit memory, 204
    first memories, 203–204
    fuzzy trace theory, 202
    imagery, 207, 207f
    implicit memory, 203–204
    infancy, 203–204
    information processing, 201f
    long-term memory, 201
    meaning of, 200
    memory span, 205–206
    for numbers and chess pieces, 203f
    organization, 206
    processes, 201–202
    reconstructive memory, 208–209
    schema theory, 202
    short-term memory, 201
    strategies, 206–208
    teaching strategies, 207–208
    types of, 201–202
    working memory, 201, 202f, 209f, 212

memory-relevant language, 207
memory span, 205–206, 206f
memory-span task, 205
*Men Are from Mars, Women Are from Venus*
    (Gray), 355
menarche, 100, 102
mental age (MA), 230
mental injury, 406
mercury, 79
mesoderm, 69
mesosystem, 22, 393
meta-analysis, 59, 370
metacognition, 194, 218–222, 226, 263, 324
    in adolescence, 222
    in childhood, 222
    child's theory of mind, 219–221
metalinguistic awareness, 263–264
metamemory, 219
metaphor, 267
methamphetamine, 76
method section, 32
microsystem, 22, 393
middle and late childhood, 10
    *see also* childhood
    academic achievement, 399–400
    bilingualism, 266–267
    body growth and change, 99
    brain development, 110–111
    coping with stress, 290–291
    emotional development, 289–291
    gender stereotypes, 350
    grammar, 263–264
    illness and injuries, 118–119
    language development, 263–267
    metalinguistic awareness, 263–264
    parenting, 399–400
    peers, 429
    perspective taking, 323
    reading, 264–265, 264f
    second-language learning, 266–267
    self-understanding, 320
    understanding others, 323
    vocabulary, 263–264
    writing, 265–266
Middle East, 7, 357
middle school, 461
midwives, 82
Millennials, 11
mindfulness, 213
mindset, 471–472
*Mindset* (Dweck), 471
Miranda, Patricia, 471, 471f
mis-match negativity (MMN), 107
mitosis, 46–48, 47f, 68
mixed-age friendships, 443–444
modeling, 21
Money, John, 340
monozygotic twins, 41, 48, 236
    *see also* identical twins
Montessori approach, 457
moral behaviour, 370–371
moral character, 374
moral competencies, 371
moral decisions, 363
moral development, 363
    contexts of, 376–381
    domains of, 363–376
    emotion, role of, 373
    and families, 369–370

interpersonal dimension, 363
intrapersonal dimension, 363
meaning of, 363–364
moral behaviour, 370–371
moral feeling, 371–373
moral personality, 373–374
moral thought, 364–370
parenting, 376–378
schools, 378–381
social-cognitive domain theory, 375
social cognitive theory of morality, 371
moral dilemmas, 365
moral education
    character education, 378–379
    cheating, 380
    cognitive moral education, 379
    hidden curriculum, 378
    integrative approach, 380–381
    service learning, 379–380
    values clarification, 379
moral exemplars, 374, 374f
moral feeling, 371–373
moral identity, 373–374
moral performance, 371
moral personality, 373–374
moral reasoning, 368–369, 369
moral thought, 364–370
    Kohlberg's theory, 365–370
    Piaget's theory, 364–365
Moro reflex, 134f, 135, 135f
morpheme, 253
morphology, 253, 254f, 259
Morris, Steveland, 132
mothers
    as caregivers, 307–308
    socialization strategies, 345
motivation
    extrinsic motivation, 469–470
    intrinsic motivation, 469–470
    mastery motivation, 470–471
motor development, 133–143, 157
    childhood, 139–141, 142–143
    cultural variations, 139
    delays in, 139
    dynamic systems theory, 133–134
    fine motor skills, 141–143
    gross motor skills, 136–141
    infancy, 137–139, 141–142
    organized sports, 140
    reflexes, 134–136, 135f
motor skills
    fine motor skills, 141–143
    gross motor skills, 136–141
    infants and, 133, 134
    mastering, 134
    organized sports, 140
movement restrictions, 139
Mozart Effect, 242
*Mr. Rogers' Neighborhood,* 479
Mudd, Anna, 266
multiple developmental trajectories, 395
multiple intelligences, 232–234
    advocates of, 234
    comparison of theories of, 234f
    critics of, 234
    emotional intelligence, 233–234
    Gardner's eight frames of mind, 233
    triarchic theory of intelligence, 232
the Murian culture of India, 429

exploration of, 427–428
negative peer relations, 427–428
parent-child and peer relations, 430–431
peer group social status, 432–434
peer pressure, 445
peer rejection, 433–434
perspective taking, 431–432
positive peer relations, 427–428
romantic relationships, 446–449
social cognition, 431–432
social information-processing skills, 432
peers, 6, 427
*see also* peer relations
in adolescence, 345
development, necessity for, 427
and emotional regulation, 289
and exercise, 127
gender development, 345
and identity, 334
individual differences, 428
more-skilled peers, as teachers, 185
peer contexts, 428
pelvic field defect, 343
perceived popularity, 432
perception, 143–144, 219
perception of occluded objects, 149–150, 150*f*
perceptual categorization, 210
perceptual constancy, 149
perceptual development. *See* sensory and perceptual development
perceptual expectations, 169
perceptual-motor coupling, 141–142, 155–156, 158
performance, 474
performance orientation, 471
periods of development, 9–10, 10*f*
Perkins Institution, 251
Perry, Nora, 162
personal choice, 469
personal fable, 178
personality in adulthood, 297*f*
perspective taking, 323–324, 372–373, 431–432
pharmacogenetics, 62
phenotype, 48
phenylketonuria (PKU), 51
phonics approach, 264–265
phonological awareness, 262, 263
phonology, 252–253, 254*f* 259
physical abuse, 406
physical descriptions, 319
physical development
body growth and change, 97–103, 128–129
the brain, 104–112
the brain, 129
sleep, 112–117, 130
physical punishment, 403, 404–405, 404*f*
physical self-recognition, 318
physical similarities and differences, 351
physical support, 441
physiological measures, 27
Piaget, Jean, 161, 203
*see also* Piaget's theory of cognitive development
Piaget's theory of cognitive development, 17–18, 17*f* 24, 154, 162–178, 187–189
application of, 179–180

concrete operational stage, 175–176
conservation, 173, 175, 175*f*
contributions, 180
criticisms, 180–182
culture and education, 181
and education, 179–180
effects of training, 181
estimates of children's competence, 180
evaluation of, 180–181
formal operational stage, 176–178
vs. information-processing approach, 194
neo-Piagetian approach, 181–182
object permanence, 166, 168
preoperational stage, 171–174
processes of development, 162–163
sensorimotor stage, 17, 17*f* 164–171, 165*f*
stages of cognitive development, 164*f*, 180
vs. Vygotsky's theory, 186*f*
Piaget's theory of moral development, 364–365
pincer grip, 141
pitch, 152
pituitary gland, 100
placenta, 69, 70*f*
planning, 473–474
play, 174, 437, 451
constructive play, 439–440
face-to-face play, 299
free play time, 440
functions of, 438
games, 440
gender-stereotypical play preferences, 341
helping inhibited children, 295
practice play, 439
pretense/symbolic play, 439
sensorimotor play, 439
social play, 439
trends in play, 440
types of play, 439–440
play therapy, 438
polyadic subsystem, 394
polygenic inheritance, 49
popularity, 432
positive emotions, 281
positive friendships, 441
positive peer relations, 427–428
positron-emission tomography (PET) scans, 106
possible self, 321
post-traumatic stress disorder (PTSD), 291
postconventional reasoning, 366–367
postpartum blues, 90
postpartum depression, 91–92
postpartum period, 89–92, 94
emotional adjustments, 90–92
paternal postpartum depression, 90–91
physical adjustments, 90
postpartum blues, 90
postpartum depression, 91–92
psychological adjustments, 90–92
posture, 136
poverty, in global perspective, 119–120
power assertion, 377
practical intelligence, 232
practice play, 439
pragmatics, 254, 254*f* 260–262
precocious puberty, 100

precocity, 245
preconventional reasoning, 366
prefrontal cortex, 109, 110, 111, 212
prenatal development, 68–81, 93
the brain, 72
course of prenatal development, 68–72
embryonic period, 68–70
fetal period, 70–72
germinal period, 68, 69*f*
hearing, 151–152
nervous system, 72*f*
normal prenatal development, 81
prenatal care, 80–81
teratology and hazards, 72–80
three trimesters of, 71*f*
prenatal diagnostic tests, 54–56
prenatal hazards
emotional states and stress, 79
maternal age, 79
maternal diet and nutrition, 78–80
other parental factors, 78–80
paternal factors, 79–80
teratogens. *See* teratogen
prenatal period, 9
preoperational, 171
preoperational stage, 17, 17*f* 171–174
animism, 172
centration, 173–174
conservation, lack of, 173
conservation task, 173–174
egocentrism, 171
intuitive thought substage, 172–173
limitations of preoperational thought, 173–174
operations, 171
preoperational thought, 171
symbolic function substage, 171–172
preoperational thought, 171, 173–174
prepared childbirth, 84
preschool years, 10
*see also* early childhood
prescription drugs, as teratogens, 73
pretend play, 174
pretense/symbolic play, 439
preterm infants, 85–88, 87, 87*f*
primary circular reactions, 165
primary emotions, 284
private speech, 183, 185
problem solving, 214–216
processes of development, 162–163
accommodation, 162–163
assimilation, 162–163
equilibration, 163
organization, 163
schemes, 162
stages of development, 163
processing capacity, 192–193
processing speed, 192–193
Promoting Relationships and Eliminating Violence Network (PREVNet), 387
prosocial behaviour, 354, 381–383
protection, 396
proximodistal pattern, 98
psychoactive drugs
alcohol, 74–75
caffeine, 74
cocaine, 75–76
heroin, 76
marijuana, 76

self-concept, 320, 325–326, 337–338
self-conscious emotions, 284, 288
self-consciousness, 321
self-control, 211–212
self-defeating tastes/preferences, 478
self-determination, 469
self-efficacy, 472
self-esteem, 325–326, 337–338
    across the lifespan, 328, 328*f*
    assessment, 326
    evaluation of, 325*f*
    global self-esteem, 326, 326*f*
    and happiness, 327
    variations in, 326–328
self-evaluation, 319, 320
self-integration, 321
self-modification, 194
Self-Perception Profile for Children, 326
self-recognition, 317–318, 318*f*
self-reflection, 474
self-regulation, 183, 293–294, 474
self-responsibility, 469
self-understanding, 317–321, 337
    adolescence, 320–321
    developmental changes, 317–320
    early childhood, 318–320
    infancy, 317–318
    middle and late childhood, 320
semantics, 253–254, 254*f* 259–260
sensation, 143–144
sensitive period, 22
sensorimotor play, 439
sensorimotor stage, 17, 17*f* 164–171, 165*f*
    A-not-B error, 167
    coordination of secondary circular
        reactions, 165–166
    evaluation of, 166–171
    habit, 164–165
    nature-nurture issue, 169–170
    object permanence, 166, 166*f* 167*f* 168
    primary circular reactions, 165
    schemes, 166
    secondary circular reactions, 165–166
    simple reflexes, 164
    substages, 164–166, 165*f*
    tertiary circulation reactions, 166
sensory and perceptual development,
        143–155, 157–158
    ecological view, 144
    expectations, and perceptual development,
        167–168
    hearing, 151–152, 151*f*
    intermodal perception, 153–154
    nature, nurture, and perceptual
        development, 154–155
    newborns, 145–147
    pain, 152–153
    perception, 143–144
    sensation, 143–144
    smell, 153, 153*f*
    taste, 153, 153*f*
    touch, 152–153
    visual perception, 147–151
sensory receptors, 144
separation protest, 286, 287*f*
sequential approach, 31, 31*f*
seriation, 176
service learning, 379–380
*Sesame Street*, 479

sex glands, 100
sex-linked chromosomal abnormalities,
        50–51
sex-linked genes, 49
*Sex Roles*, 32
sexual abuse, 406
sexual maturation, 101–102, 102*f*
sexual minority youth, 447–448
shaken baby syndrome, 106
shape constancy, 149
shared environmental experiences,
        60–61
shared experiences, 11
shared sleeping, 113–114
short-term memory, 201
sibling relationships, 411–412
siblings, 411–413, 423
    birth order, 413
    sibling relationships, 411–412
sickle-cell anemia, 51–52, 52*f*
SIDS. *See* sudden infant death syndrome
Siegler's adaptive strategy choice
        model, 206*f*
Siegler's balance scale, 215*f*
sign language, 251
similarity, 442
simple reflexes, 164
situated knowledge, 18–19
size constancy, 149
skin-to-skin contact. *See* kangaroo care
Skinner, B.F., 20
sleep, 112–117, 130
    adolescence, 115–117
    childhood, 115, 116
    infancy, 112–115, 116
    REM sleep, 113, 113*f*
    shared sleeping, 113–114
    sleep disturbances, 116
slow-to-warm-up child, 292
small for date infants, 85–88
small for gestational age infants, 86
smell, 153, 153*f*
smiling, 286
smoking, 75, 118
Social Adjustment Inventory for Children
        and Adolescents, 57
social cognition, 321, 431–432
social-cognitive domain theory, 375
social cognitive monitoring, 324
social cognitive theory, 20–21, 21*f* 24*f*
social cognitive theory of gender, 344
social cognitive theory of morality, 371
social comparison, 319, 320, 321, 441
social constructivist approach, 186
social context, 217, 435
social contract or utility, 367
social conventional reasoning, 375–376
social descriptions, 320
social influences on gender development,
        344–347
social information-processing skills, 432
social intelligence, 432
social orientation/understanding,
        298–300, 314
social play, 439
social referencing, 300
social relationships, and emotion, 281–282,
        285–286
social role theory, 344

Social Sciences and Humanities Research
        Council of Canada, 33
social smile, 286
social sophistication, 300
social systems morality, 366
social understanding. *See* understanding
        others
Society of Obstetricians and
        Gynaecologists, 54
sociocultural changes, 396–397
sociocultural contexts, 5–6
sociocultural theory (Vygotsky), 18–19
socioeconomic status, 6, 256, 417, 420–421,
        462–463
socioemotional development, 57
socioemotional processes, 8–9
socioemotional similarities and differences,
        352–354
    aggression, 352–353
    emotional regulation, 354
    prosocial behaviour, 354
    relationship communication, 353–354
sociometric popularity, 432
Southeast Asia, 7
spanking, 404–405
spatial skills, 233
specificity of learning, 137
speed of processing, 192–193
spina bifida, 72
spinal cord injury, 53
spoken vocabulary, 257
sports, participation in, 140
Springer, Jim, 41
Sri Lanka, 291
standardized test, 2
Stanford-Binet intelligence test, 26,
        236–237, 237*f*
Stanford-Binet test, 230, 230*f*
startle reflex, 135, 135*f*
*The State of the World's Children*, 120
stem cell research, 53
stepfamilies, 417–418
stepping reflex, 135*f*
Steps to Respect, 436
stereotype threat, 240
stereotypes, gender. *See* gender stereotypes
Stern, William, 230
Sternberg, Robert J., 232, 232*f*
Sternberg's triarchic theory of
        intelligence, 232
sticky mittens, 142
Still Face Effect, 88, 148
still-face paradigm, 299
Still Face Task, 88, 89
stimulation, 441
Strange Situation, 302, 303
stranger anxiety, 286
strategies
    memory strategies, 206–208
    memory teaching strategies, 207–208
    problem solving, 215
strategy construction, 194
stress
    coping with stress, 290–291
    in prenatal period, 79
structural defect, 73
substages of sensorimotor development,
        164–166, 165*f*
sucking reflex, 134, 135, 135*f* 136